MW01148582

BIOLOGY

Exploring the Science of Life

Gustavo Loret de Mola

The McGraw·Hill Companies

Author

Dr. Gustavo Loret de Mola is a science educator with more than 35 years of teaching and administrative experience at the middle school, high school, and college level. He holds a B.S. degree in education from the University of Miami, an M.S. degree in science from Nova University, and an Ed.D. in Educational Leadership from Nova University. Dr. Loret de Mola taught high school science for 11 years before serving as a project manager in science and a middle school assistant principal for Dade County Public Schools. Dr. Loret de Mola then served 20 years as District Science Supervisor for Dade County Public Schools. As a committee member, Dr. Loret de Mola helped develop the Teacher Certification Tests in Science for the State of Florida. He also served as State Chairperson for the State of Florida Life Sciences Instructional Materials Council. Currently, Dr. Loret de Mola continues to work in the sciences as adjunct professor at the University of Miami, where he teaches science and science methodology courses for graduate students in education.

Series Consultants

Richard Audet, EdD
Roger Williams University

Matthew Marino, PhD
Washington State University

Barbara Scott, MD
Los Angeles Unified School District

Lisa Soll, BS
San Antonio Independent School District

Content Reviewers

Tamara Kirshtein, MAT, Charleston, South Carolina
Sonja Oliveri, MA, Chicago, Illinois
Surey Rios, BS, Miami, Florida
Ann Shioji, MA, Long Beach, California
Gary Yoham, EdD, Miami, Florida

ELL Consultants

Mary Smith, MA, Merced, California
Brian Silva, Long Beach, California

Laboratory Reviewer

Garrett Hall, Pleasant Hill, Iowa

Laboratory Safety Consultant

Jeff Vogt, MED, West Virginia University at Parkersburg

About the Cover

Photo credits are on pages 497–498.

---

www.WrightGroup.com

Copyright © 2009 by Wright Group/McGraw-Hill.

All rights reserved. Except as permitted under the United States Copyright Act, no part of this publication may be reproduced or distributed in any form or by any means, or stored in a database or retrieval system, without the prior written permission from the publisher, unless otherwise indicated.

Printed in the United States of America.

Send all inquiries to:
Wright Group/McGraw-Hill
P.O. Box 812960
Chicago, IL 60681

ISBN 978-0-07-704130-4
MHID 0-07-704130-5

1 2 3 4 5 6 7 8 9 YAK 13 12 11 10 09 08 07

The McGraw·Hill Companies

Contents

Biology: Exploring the Science of Life invites students to enter a wonderfully exciting and important world: the world of living things. The Student Edition is a valuable tool for students as they gain knowledge about the nature of life, appreciate the scientific process, and become scientifically literate citizens. To achieve those ends, students should become familiar with the organization and features of the textbook and use the textbook effectively. The following pages illustrate the features that were designed with student and teacher success in mind.

CHAPTER OPENER

This **introduction to the chapter** puts the content in context and reflects the relevance of biology in today's world. The introductory story captures interest and motivates continued reading.

UNIT OPENER

The **Unit Opener** provides a preview of the material students will learn in upcoming chapters. Through striking visuals and thought-provoking questions representative of each chapter in the unit, students are encouraged to begin thinking about the content of the unit and making connections among its chapters.

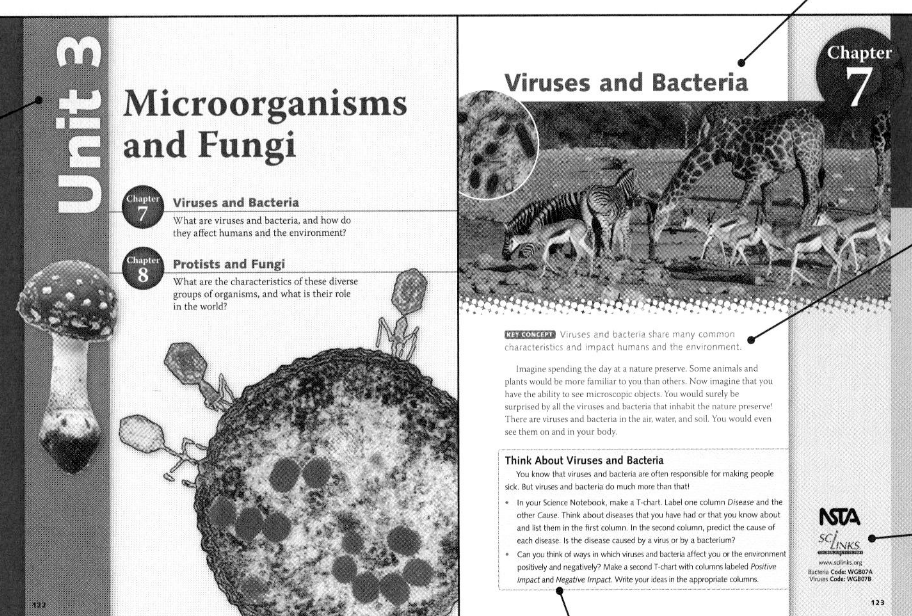

KEY CONCEPT

The standards-based **Key Concept** identifies the "big idea" of the chapter and connects the various concepts within the chapter and represents the basic principles of biology.

SciLinks CODES

SciLinks codes direct students to NSTA approved web sites.

BEFORE YOU READ

One of a trio of literacy activities, **Before You Read** is a prereading exercise that incorporates appropriate reading comprehension and literacy skills strategies. Each Before You Read activity is closely integrated with the As You Read and After You Read activities within a lesson, providing introduction, reinforcement, and assessment of essential literacy skills.

THINK ABOUT . . .

A strategy for activating prior knowledge, the **Think About . . .** feature relates directly to the Chapter Opener story and to the chapter content. Encouraging students to identify previously acquired information and/or skills, the feature presents a brief set of questions or activities for students to complete using that information or skill. Students can practice expressing their knowledge, experiences, and ideas by recording their answers in their **Science Notebooks**.

LEARNING GOALS

Each chapter is divided into lessons of manageable length. Each lesson begins with standards-based **Learning Goals**, which help students focus on the cognitive outcomes they should achieve as a result of reading the lesson. The Learning Goals are further used at the end of the chapter to help students prepare for the Chapter Test.

NEW VOCABULARY

New Vocabulary is a list of the important terms in the lesson that appear in boldface type upon initial reference. The list serves as a preview for students, identifying both familiar and unfamiliar terms.

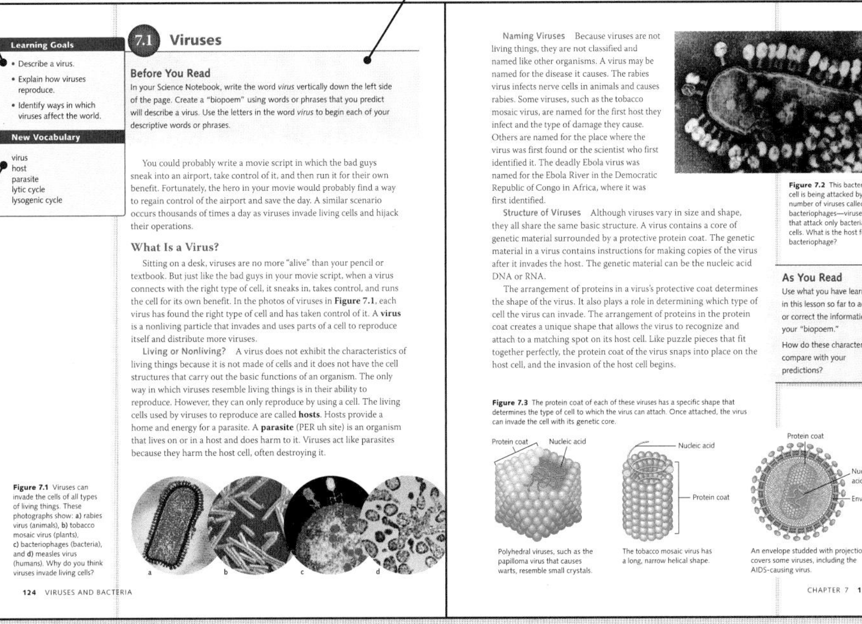

AS YOU READ

This during-reading literacy activity focuses on both the science content that has been presented in the lesson and the literacy activity introduced in Before You Read. **As You Read** poses a content-related question that incorporates the literacy skill and encourages students to work collaboratively.

NARRATIVE AND VISUALS

Most important to students' understanding of the nature of life and their appreciation of the scientific process is content presentation that makes learning easier and more accessible. Great care has been taken to write and present the concepts of biology in a way that motivates students and guarantees their success. Both the **narrative** and the **visuals** support all students, particularly English-language learners and struggling readers. Visuals are functional, interesting, and understandable. Narrative is clear, concise, logically sequenced, and is presented in an outline-style format. Consideration of a range of reading levels and learning styles is evident in the friendly, engaging, and appropriate prose.

DID YOU KNOW?

Information about the role of biology in students' lives is presented in a lively, engaging manner in the **Did You Know?** feature. These intriguing and often humorous stories address common misconceptions, provide additional content, and present fun factoids—all for the purpose of stimulating student thinking and class discussion.

EXPLAIN IT!

Students can practice expressing their knowledge, ideas, and experiences by completing the activities contained in **Explain It!** These writing activities assess students' understanding of the content by providing practice in analyzing and applying concepts.

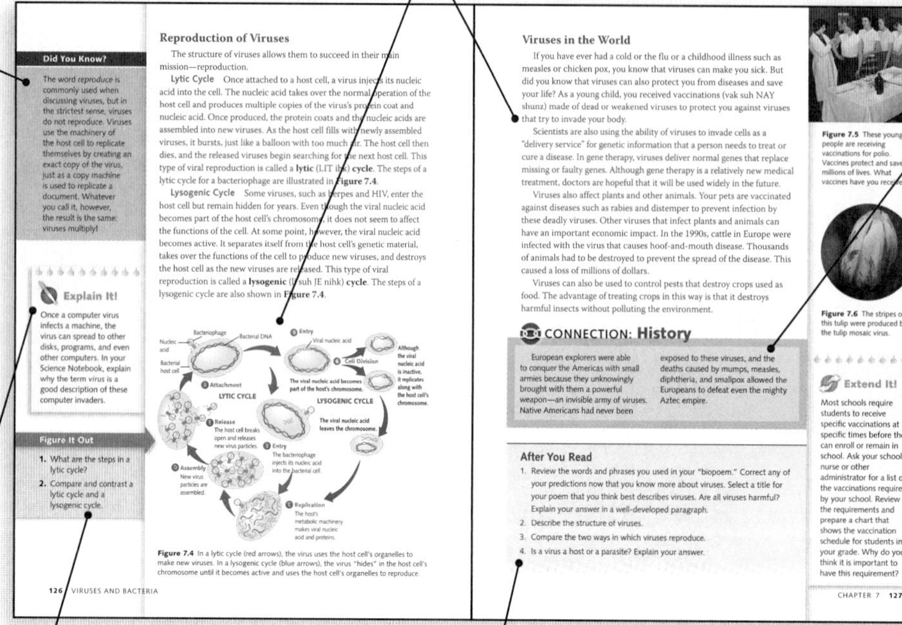

Did You Know?

The word *reproduce* is commonly used when discussing viruses, but in the strictest sense, viruses do not reproduce. Viruses use the machinery of the host cell to replicate themselves by creating an exact copy of the virus, just as a copy machine is used to replicate a document. Whatever you call it, however, the result is the same: viruses multiply!

Explain It!

Once a computer virus infects a machine, the virus can spread to other disks, programs, and even other computers. In your Science Notebook, explain why the term *virus* is a good description of these computer invaders.

Figure It Out

1. What are the steps in a lytic cycle?
2. Compare and contrast a lytic cycle and a lysogenic cycle.

Reproduction of Viruses

The structure of viruses allows them to succeed in their main mission—reproduction.

Lytic Cycle Once attached to a host cell, a virus injects its nucleic acid into the cell. The nucleic acid takes over the normal operation of the host cell and produces multiple copies of the virus's protein coat and nucleic acid. Once produced, the protein coats and the nucleic acids are assembled into new viruses. As the host cell fills with newly assembled viruses, it bursts, just like a balloon with too much air. The host cell then dies, and the released viruses begin searching for the next host cell. This type of viral reproduction is called a **lytic** (LIT ihk) **cycle**. The steps of a lytic cycle for a bacteriophage are illustrated in **Figure 7.4**.

Lysogenic Cycle Some viruses, such as herpes and HIV, enter the host cell but remain hidden for years. Even though the viral nucleic acid becomes part of the host cell's chromosome, it does not seem to affect the functions of the cell. At some point, however, the viral nucleic acid becomes active. It separates itself from the host cell's genetic material, takes over the functions of the cell to produce new viruses, and destroys the host cell as the new viruses are released. This type of viral reproduction is called a **lysogenic** (li suh JE nihk) **cycle**. The steps of a lysogenic cycle are also shown in **Figure 7.4**.

Figure 7.4 In a lytic cycle (red arrows), the virus uses the host cell's organelles to make new viruses. In a lysogenic cycle (blue arrows), the virus "hides" in the host cell's chromosome until it becomes active and uses the host cell's organelles to reproduce.

126 VIRUSES AND BACTERIA

Viruses in the World

If you have ever had a cold or the flu or a childhood illness such as measles or chicken pox, you know that viruses can make you sick. But did you know that viruses can also protect you from diseases and save your life? As a young child, you received vaccinations (vak suh NAY shunz) made of dead or weakened viruses to protect you against viruses that try to invade your body.

Scientists are also using the ability of viruses to invade cells as a "delivery service" for genetic information that a person needs to treat or cure a disease. In gene therapy, viruses deliver normal genes that replace missing or faulty genes. Although gene therapy is a relatively new medical treatment, doctors are hopeful that it will be used widely in the future.

Viruses also affect plants and other animals. Your pets are vaccinated against diseases such as rabies and distemper to prevent infection by these deadly viruses. Other viruses that infect plants and animals can have an important economic impact. In the 1990s, cattle in Europe were infected with the virus that causes hoof-and-mouth disease. Thousands of animals had to be destroyed to prevent the spread of the disease. This caused a loss of millions of dollars.

Viruses can also be used to control pests that destroy crops used as food. The advantage of treating crops in this way is that it destroys harmful insects without polluting the environment.

CONNECTION: History

European explorers were able to conquer the Americas with small armies because they unknowingly brought with them a powerful weapon—an invisible army of viruses. Native Americans had never been exposed to these viruses, and the deaths caused by mumps, measles, diphtheria, and smallpox allowed the Europeans to defeat even the mighty Aztec empire.

After You Read

1. Review the words and phrases you used in your "biopoem." Correct any of your predictions now that you know more about viruses. Select a title for your poem that you think best describes viruses. Are all viruses harmful? Explain your answer in a well-developed paragraph.
2. Describe the structure of viruses.
3. Compare the two ways in which viruses reproduce.
4. Is a virus a host or a parasite? Explain your answer.

Figure 7.5 These young people are receiving vaccinations for polio. Vaccines protect and save millions of lives. What vaccines have you received?

Figure 7.6 The stripes on this tulip were produced by the tulip mosaic virus.

Extend It!

Most schools require students to receive specific vaccinations at specific times before they can enroll or remain in school. Ask your school nurse or other administrator for a list of the vaccinations required by your school. Review the requirements and prepare a chart that shows the vaccination schedule for students in your grade. Why do you think it is important to have this requirement?

CHAPTER 7 127

CONNECTION

The relevance of biology to other areas of science and to other disciplines is emphasized by the **Connection** feature. Students are made aware of the ways in which biology concepts and thinking skills can be applied to other areas of learning. Although they are studying biology, students will become more scientifically literate as they understand the interconnections presented in this feature.

FIGURE IT OUT

An essential skill for student success, reading and interpreting visuals is practiced and reinforced by the **Figure It Out** feature. Important tables, graphs, diagrams, and photos are highlighted in the lessons and accompanied by questions that assess student comprehension of the visuals.

AFTER YOU READ

The final part of the literacy skill strategy and an assessment tool, **After You Read** poses content-related questions that correspond to the lesson's Learning Goals. The questions range from recall to higher-level thinking skills, and one question utilizes the literacy activity introduced in Before You Read and supplemented in As You Read.

EXTEND IT!

Providing an opportunity to go beyond the content of the textbook, **Extend It!** activities encourage students to research related topics and report their findings in an appropriate way.

EXPLORE IT!

The quick and effective hands-on activities that comprise **Explore It!** can be done by students in class with partners or in groups, or at home as a homework assignment. Requiring easily obtained materials, the activities support content by providing students with an active-learning experience. They also help students experience biology as a process as well as a body of knowledge, and they reinforce the scientific approach to problem-solving.

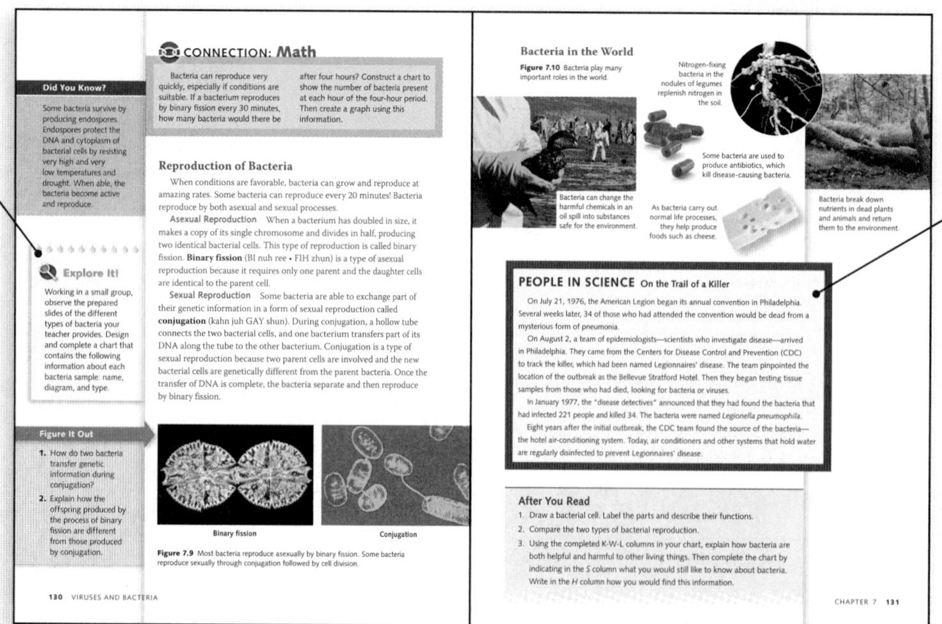

Did You Know?

Some bacteria survive by producing endospores. Endospores protect the DNA and cytoplasm of bacterial cells by resisting very high and very low temperatures and drought. When able, the bacteria become active and reproduce.

Explore It!

Working in a small group, observe the prepared slides of the different types of bacteria your teacher provides. Design and complete a chart that contains the following information about each bacteria sample: name, diagram, and type.

Figure It Out

1. How do two bacteria transfer genetic information during conjugation?
2. Explain how the offspring produced by the process of binary fission are different from those produced by conjugation.

CONNECTION: Math

Bacteria can reproduce very quickly, especially if conditions are suitable. If a bacterium reproduces by binary fission every 30 minutes, how many bacteria would there be after four hours? Construct a chart to show the number of bacteria present at each hour of the four-hour period. Then create a graph using this information.

Reproduction of Bacteria

When conditions are favorable, bacteria can grow and reproduce at amazing rates. Some bacteria can reproduce every 20 minutes! Bacteria reproduce by both asexual and sexual processes.

Asexual Reproduction When a bacterium has doubled in size, it makes a copy of its single chromosome and divides in half, producing two identical bacterial cells. This type of reproduction is called binary fission. **Binary fission** (BI nuh ree • FIH zhun) is a type of asexual reproduction because it requires only one parent and the daughter cells are identical to the parent cell.

Sexual Reproduction Some bacteria are able to exchange part of their genetic information in a form of sexual reproduction called **conjugation** (kahn juh GAY shun). During conjugation, a hollow tube connects the two bacterial cells, and one bacterium transfers part of its DNA along the tube to the other bacterium. Conjugation is a type of sexual reproduction because two parent cells are involved and the new bacterial cells are genetically different from the parent bacteria. Once the transfer of DNA is complete, the bacteria separate and then reproduce by binary fission.

Figure 7.9 Most bacteria reproduce asexually by binary fission. Some bacteria reproduce sexually through conjugation followed by cell division.

130 VIRUSES AND BACTERIA

Bacteria in the World

Figure 7.10 Bacteria play many important roles in the world.

PEOPLE IN SCIENCE On the Trail of a Killer

On July 21, 1976, the American Legion began its annual convention in Philadelphia. Several weeks later, 34 of those who had attended the convention would be dead from a mysterious form of pneumonia.

On August 2, a team of epidemiologists—scientists who investigate disease—arrived in Philadelphia. They came from the Centers for Disease Control and Prevention (CDC) to track the killer, which had been named Legionnaires' disease. The team pinpointed the location of the outbreak as the Bellevue Stratford Hotel. Then they began testing tissue samples from those who had died, looking for bacteria or viruses.

In January 1977, the "disease detectives" announced that they had found the bacteria that had infected 221 people and killed 34. The bacteria were named *Legionella pneumophila*.

Eight years after the initial outbreak, the CDC team found the source of the bacteria—the hotel air-conditioning system. Today, air conditioners and other systems that hold water are regularly disinfected to prevent Legionnaires' disease.

After You Read

1. Draw a bacterial cell. Label the parts and describe their functions.
2. Compare the two types of bacterial reproduction.
3. Using the completed K-W-L columns in your chart, explain how bacteria are both helpful and harmful to other living things. Then complete the chart by indicating in the *S* column what you would still like to know about bacteria. Write in the *H* column how you would find this information.

CHAPTER 7 131

PEOPLE IN SCIENCE

The study of biology is essentially the story of individual and group contributions to the understanding of living things and their interactions. The **People in Science** feature highlights a figure or figures of historical or current importance in biology by providing biographical information and emphasizing the contribution to scientific knowledge and/or research.

CHAPTER SUMMARY

The **Chapter Summary** provides concept review, vocabulary review and assessment, and content and concept evaluation.

VOCABULARY REVIEW

Vocabulary terms are essential to students' understanding of biology. The key terms listed in **Vocabulary Review** are those students should be especially familiar with. Students are encouraged to demonstrate their understanding of the terms by defining them in complete, well-developed sentences or paragraphs.

KEY CONCEPTS

Key scientific principles in each lesson are listed in **Key Concepts** to help students review the chapter content. Students should be encouraged to make sure they understand each concept and its relationship to other concepts in the chapter, to the main idea of the chapter, and to the basic principles of biology.

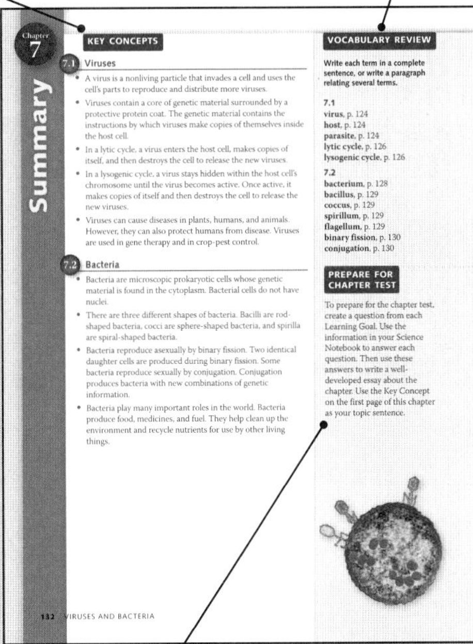

MASTERING CONCEPTS

Students can test their knowledge of the facts, evaluate their understanding of the concepts, and apply their factual knowledge and conceptual understanding by answering the various types of assessments contained in **Mastering Concepts**. Assessment forms include modified true or false, short answer, and critical thinking. Also included is a standardized test question, which helps familiarize students with this test format, and a **Test-Taking Tip**.

PREPARE FOR CHAPTER TEST

To help students prepare for the chapter test, this self-assessment activity integrates the lesson Learning Goals with the chapter Key Concept. As students convert the Learning Goals into questions that they answer, they evaluate their understanding of the chapter's main ideas. As students then use those answers to write a well-developed essay summarizing the chapter content, they demonstrate their ability to support the Key Concept with pertinent facts and vocabulary.

RESEARCH AND REPORT

Research and Report provides students a research topic related to the unit content.

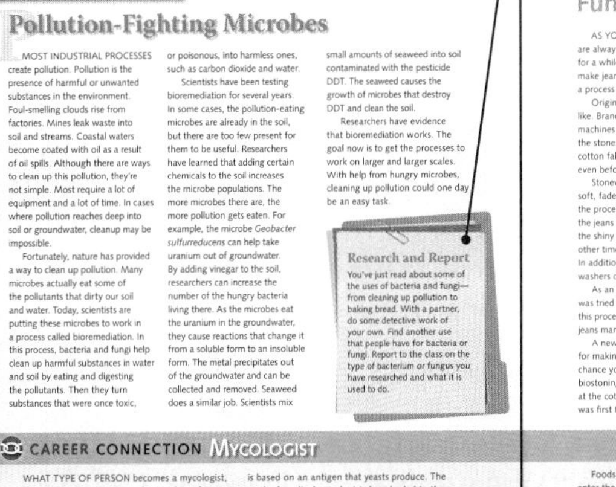

SCIENCE JOURNAL

This end-of-unit enrichment feature is designed to extend chapter content with motivating articles that address connections, breakthroughs, and issues in biology. All of the concepts of a unit are integrated in articles that demonstrate the relevance and role of biology in students' lives and the lives of others. **Science Journal** contains several case studies and a career connection, which highlights how the study of biology can be applied to a variety of interesting and important vocations.

The **Teacher's Edition** is designed to support and supplement teaching efforts and knowledge of biology as well as maximize the opportunities for both student and teacher success. Organization tools, teaching strategies, background information, and suggestions for reaching all students are provided within a user-friendly and visually concise wraparound format.

UNIT AND CHAPTER FEATURES

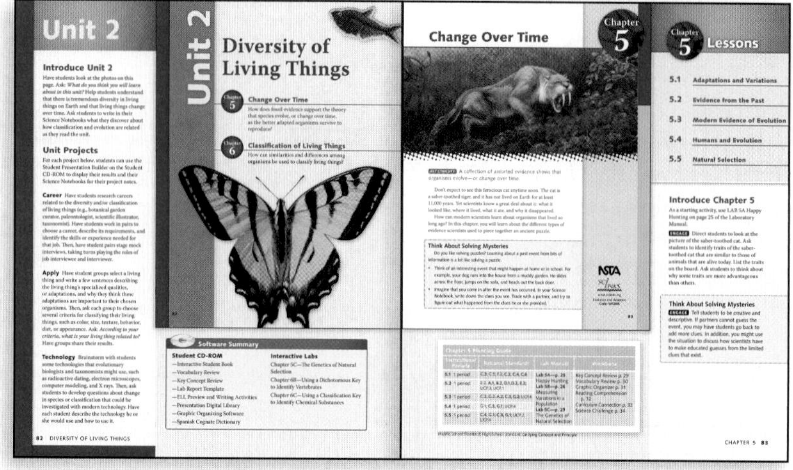

The **Unit Opener** copy offers strategies for introducing the unit content and suggestions for Unit Projects in the areas of career research, hands-on research, and technology research. Each project is intended to address the main ideas of the unit and to extend over the duration of the unit coverage. For each Unit Project, students are encouraged to use the Student Presentation Builder on the Student CD-ROM to display their results.

The **End-of-Unit** copy addresses each of the unit case studies by suggesting research activities and providing background information. It also connects the Unit Opener career research activity with the selected unit career.

The **Chapter Opener** and **Chapter Planning Guide** provide an overview of the chapter's organization. The Chapter Opener also includes a reference to the Getting Started! activity in the Lab Manual, a strategy for introducing the chapter content, and suggestions for the Think About . . . feature. The Chapter Planning Guide identifies the various print and computer ancillaries designed to be used with each lesson, as well as the National Standards covered by the lesson content. The Chapter Planning Guide also includes suggested numbers of instructional periods needed for the lessons.

LESSON CYCLE

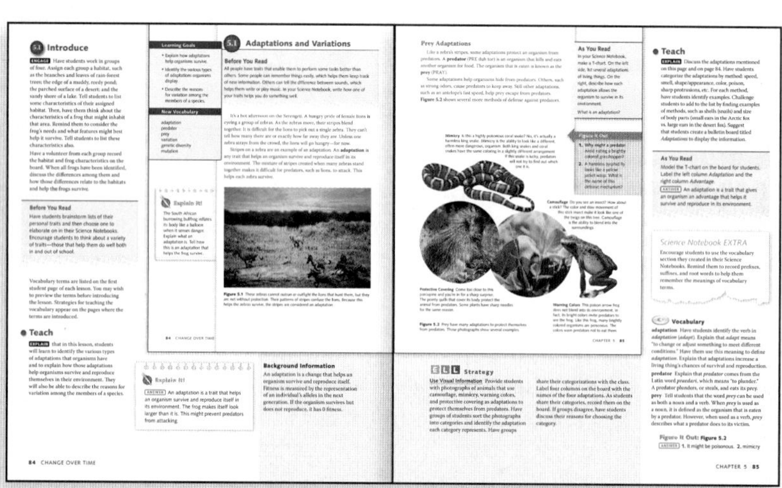

A **three-step lesson cycle** based on current educational methodology—INTRODUCE, TEACH, ASSESS—incorporates the **five *Es*** of effective science teaching: Engage, Explore, Explain, Evaluate, and Extend.

Point-of-use support for text and margin features, including answers to lesson and chapter assessment questions, is found in the side columns. This support is designed to enhance the teacher's ability to maximize student learning. Also included in the side columns are features that extend vocabulary, reinforce visual learning, encourage student writing, and assess understanding: **Vocabulary**, **Use the Visual**, **Science Notebook**, and **Alternative Assessment**.

The bottom margins of wraparound copy contain information to support, supplement, and extend teacher resources. Included here are **Background Information**, **Differentiate Instruction**, **ELL Strategy**, **Teacher Alert**, **Field Study**, and **Reading Links**.

LABORATORY MANUAL TEACHER'S EDITION

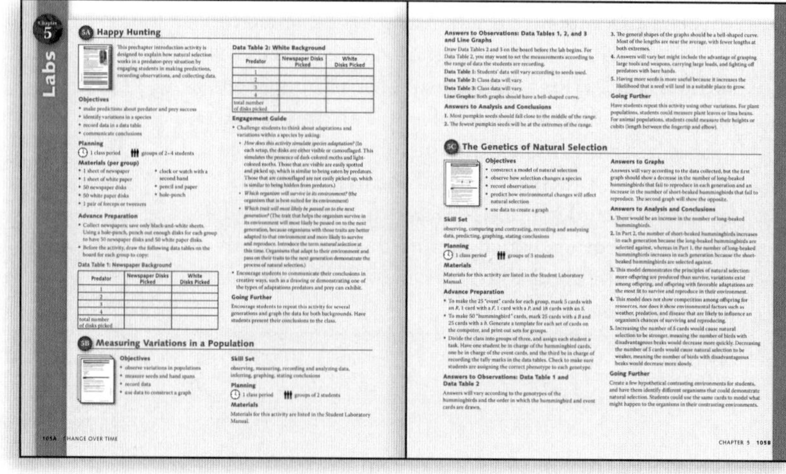

This two-page spread found at the end of a chapter provides important information and guidance for each of the three chapter laboratory activities found in the Laboratory Manual. Activity teaching notes include **Objectives**, **Skill Set**, **Planning**, **Materials**, **Advance Preparation**, **Answers to Observations**, **Answers to Analysis and Conclusions**, and **Going Further**.

A complete **Equipment and Materials List** is found on pages 508A–508B of the Teacher's Edition. The easily accessible materials are referenced by lab activity and reported in total for the program to help the teacher in ordering yearly supplies. It is assumed that safety goggles, laboratory aprons, tap water, laboratory manuals, paper, pencils, and pens are available for all activities. The Equipment and Materials List is followed by a list of **Equipment Suppliers**.

The Student Edition and Teacher's Edition of *Biology: Exploring the Science of Life* are supplemented by the **Workbook**, **Laboratory Manual**, **Blackline Master Assessment Packet**, and **Electronic Material**.

Chapter content is reviewed, reinforced, and extended by **Workbook** activities of the following kind: **Key Concept Review**, **Vocabulary Review**, **Interpreting Diagrams**, **Graphic Organizer**, **Reading Comprehension**, **Curriculum Connection**, and **Science Challenge**. Answers to all Workbook activities are found in the Teacher's Edition. The **Laboratory Manual** provides three opportunities for students to engage in hands-on learning for each chapter.

Lab A is a one-page, 15- to 20-minute activity that activates prior knowledge and introduces the chapter concepts in an innovative, motivating, and fun-to-do way. It uses limited materials and can be done as a classroom demonstration or homework assignment. **Lab B** and **Lab C** are scaffolded according to difficulty level. Both are two- to three-page activities designed to be completed in a class period of 45 to 50 minutes.

Information about preparation and implementation of all Laboratory Manual activities, as well as answers to all Observations and Analysis and Conclusions questions, are found in the Teacher's Edition.

ABOUT THE STUDENT SOFTWARE

The Student Software contains several instructional tools:

Student Electronic Material (CD-ROM)

The entire Student Edition is available in e-book PDF format with links to audio, animation, searches, glossary, laboratory activities, Spanish introductions and activities, and instructional interactivities.

Student Presentation Builder

The Student Presentation Builder utilizes PowerPoint technology with graphics from the Student Edition.

Interactive Laboratory Activities

The interactive laboratory activities will provide students with: 1) activities that are a higher level in difficulty and more complicated to conduct in a school setting; 2) activities that are lower in difficulty but more efficient to conduct on the computer; and 3) activities that will trigger and build prior knowledge.

Spanish Introductions and Activities

Research has shown that English Language Learners benefit from first generating prior knowledge verbally about a given topic in their first language. Also, by writing about a concept in their first language, students increase comprehension and are better prepared for content acquisition in English.

Graphic Organizer Software

This component will provide printable PDF graphic organizers, electronic graphic organizer templates that can export to and from an outline format, and a template for students to complete lab reports with nonprintable prompts.

TEACHER'S RESOURCES

Teacher's Electronic Manual (CD-ROM)

The entire teacher's edition is available via e-book, along with links to all related ancillaries. This CD-ROM also includes instructional interactivities, a Teacher Presentation Builder, interactive library activities, electronic graphic organizer software, Spanish introductions and activities, and links to PDFs of ELL Blackline Masters, Overhead Transparencies, the Student Workbook Answer Key, and the Laboratory Manual.

Blackline Masters

The Blackline Masters are designed to enhance the curriculum.

Test Question Generator (CD-ROM)

Question-bank development can be used to create various book assessments. The questions are cross-correlated to National Science Standards.

Overhead Transparencies

This 48-page component provides teachers with key graphics related to the curriculum.

Correlation to the National Science Education Standards

Content Standard	Chapters
(UCP) Unifying Concepts and Processes (Grades 5–8, 9–12)	
1. Systems, order, and organization	1, 2, 3, 4, 5, 6, 7, 8, 9, 10, 11, 12, 13, 14, 15, 16, 17, 18, 19, 20, 21, 22, 23, 24, 25
2. Evidence, models, and explanation	1, 2, 3, 4, 5, 6, 7, 8, 9, 10, 11, 12, 13, 14, 15, 16, 17, 18, 19, 20, 21, 22, 23, 24, 25
3. Constancy, change, and measurement	1, 2, 3, 4, 5, 6, 7, 8, 9, 10, 11, 12, 13, 14, 15, 16, 17, 18, 19, 20, 21, 22, 23, 24, 25
4. Evolution and equilibrium	5, 6
5. Form and function	6 ,7, 8, 10, 11, 12, 13, 14, 15, 19, 20, 21, 22, 23, 24
(A) Science as Inquiry (Grades 5–8, 9–12)	
1. Abilities necessary to do scientific inquiry	1, 2, 3, 4, 5, 6, 7, 8, 9, 10, 11, 12, 13, 14, 15, 16, 17, 18, 19, 20, 21, 22, 23, 24, 25
2. Understandings about scientific inquiry	1, 2, 3, 4, 5, 6, 7, 8, 9, 10, 11, 12, 13, 14, 15, 16, 17, 18, 19, 20, 21, 22, 23, 24, 25
(B) Physical Science (Grades 5–8)	
2. Motions and forces	12
3. Transfer of energy	2, 7, 9, 10, 14, 15, 16
(B) Physical Science (Grades 9–12)	
2. Structure and properties of matter	2, 9, 20, 21
3. Chemical Reactions	2, 3, 5, 9, 11, 21
4. Motions and forces	8, 10, 13, 14, 15, 19, 20
6. Interactions of energy and matter	2, 3, 7, 9, 10, 16, 17, 18, 21
(C) Life Science (Grades 5–8)	
1. Structure and function in living systems	2, 3, 4, 6, 7, 8, 9, 10, 11, 12, 13, 14, 15, 19, 20, 21, 22, 23, 24
2. Reproduction and heredity	2, 4, 5, 7, 8, 10, 11, 12, 14, 15, 20, 22, 23
3. Regulation and behavior	2, 5, 9, 13, 14, 15, 19, 20, 21, 22, 23, 24, 25
4. Populations and ecosystems	4, 5, 7, 8, 14, 16, 17, 18, 22
5. Diversity and adaptations of organisms	2, 3, 4, 5, 8, 10, 11, 12, 13, 14, 15, 17, 18, 20
(C) Life Science (Grades 9–12)	
1. The Cell	2, 3, 4, 6, 7, 8, 9, 10, 11, 12, 14, 19, 20, 21, 22, 23
2. Molecular basis of heredity	2, 3, 4, 5, 6, 19, 23
3. Biological evolution	2, 3, 5, 6, 7, 8, 9, 10, 11, 12, 14, 15, 24
4. Interdependence of organisms	2, 5, 7, 8, 10, 11, 12, 16, 17, 18, 21
5. Matter, energy, and organization in living systems	2, 3, 7, 8, 9, 10, 11, 14, 15, 16, 17, 18, 21, 22, 23
6. Behavior of organisms	2, 5, 8, 9, 11, 13, 15, 22

Correlation to the National Science Education Standards (continued)

Content Standard	Chapters
(D) Earth and Space Science (Grades 9–12)	
1. Energy in the earth system	5, 11, 17
2. Geochemical cycles	5, 8, 16
(E) Science and Technology (Grades 5–8, 9–12)	
1. Abilities of technological design	7, 22, 24
2. Understandings about science and technology	4, 5, 18
(F) Science in Personal and Social Perspectives (Grades 5–8)	
1. Personal Health	2, 7, 8, 13, 18, 19, 20, 21, 24, 25
2. Populations, resources, and environments	5, 9, 16, 17, 18
4. Risks and benefits	4, 24
5. Science and technology in society	4, 18, 21, 22, 24
(F) Science in Personal and Social Perspectives (Grades 9–12)	
1. Personal and community health	2, 7, 8, 13, 18, 19, 20, 21, 24, 25
2. Population growth	16, 18
3. Natural resources	10, 17, 18, 25
4. Environmental quality	9, 11, 14
5. Natural and human-induced hazards	7, 8, 17, 25
6. Science and technology in local, national, and global challenges	4, 6, 8, 9, 10, 11, 12, 14, 16, 17, 18, 20, 21, 24, 25
(G) History and Nature of Science (Grades 5–8)	
1. Science as a human endeavor	1, 3, 4, 5, 6, 7, 8, 9, 13, 15, 18, 19, 20, 23, 25
2. Nature of science	1, 3, 4, 5, 6, 8, 17, 21, 23
3. History of science	1, 3, 4, 7, 13, 15, 19, 24
(G) History and Nature of Science (Grades 9–12)	
1. Science as a human endeavor	1, 3, 4, 5, 6, 7, 8, 9, 13, 15, 18, 19, 20, 23, 25
2. Nature of scientific knowledge	1, 3, 4, 5, 6, 8, 17, 21, 23
3. Historical perspectives	1, 3, 4, 7, 12, 13, 15, 19, 24

Unit 1

Introduce Unit 1

Have students look at the Unit Opener photos. Ask: *What do the photos show you about living things?* Help students write questions in their Science Notebooks about living things: their characteristics, needs, composition, organization, diversity, and heredity. Encourage students to make predictions, look for answers, and develop new questions as they read each chapter.

Unit Projects

For each project below, students can use the Student Presentation Builder on the Student CD-ROM to display their results and their Science Notebooks for their project notes.

Career Have each student research a career related to the life sciences (e.g., medical researcher, biology teacher, zookeeper, florist). Ask students to define the job, describe what it entails, and identify the skills or experience needed for the job in a special section of their Science Notebooks. Then, have students prepare brochures that include graphics and specific examples of work in the chosen fields to inform their classmates about their career choices.

Apply Have each student choose a living thing he or she can observe (e.g., classroom animals or plants, pets, garden plantings, urban wildlife). Tell students to be prepared to present information about the physical characteristics, basic needs, and habitat of the living thing to the class. Afterward, have students compare and contrast the needs, characteristics, and functions of the living things presented.

Technology Have students work in groups to select a characteristic of living things that would require technology to investigate. Cell structure and heredity are two examples. Then, have each group write a question its members would like to answer, choose a technology or technologies they would use, and explain the reasons for their choice.

Unit 1

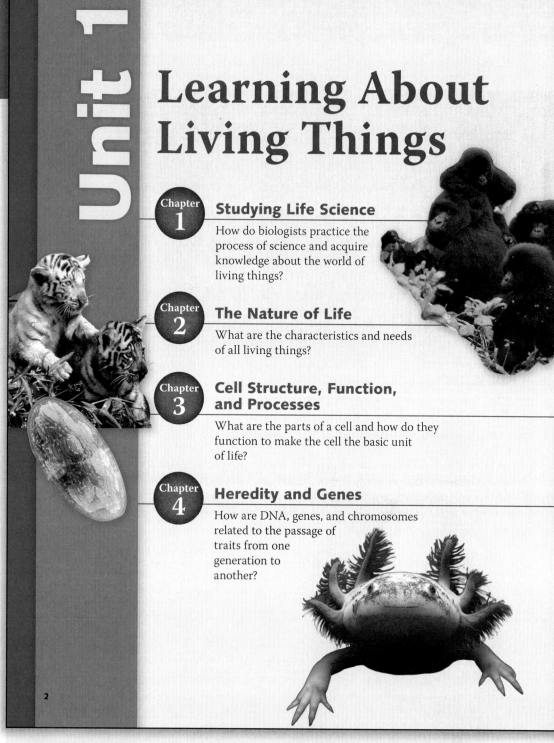

Learning About Living Things

Chapter 1 **Studying Life Science**

How do biologists practice the process of science and acquire knowledge about the world of living things?

Chapter 2 **The Nature of Life**

What are the characteristics and needs of all living things?

Chapter 3 **Cell Structure, Function, and Processes**

What are the parts of a cell and how do they function to make the cell the basic unit of life?

Chapter 4 **Heredity and Genes**

How are DNA, genes, and chromosomes related to the passage of traits from one generation to another?

2

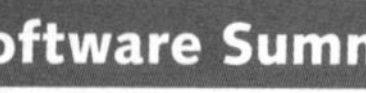

Software Summary

Student CD-ROM

—Interactive Student Book
—Vocabulary Review
—Key Concept Review
—Lab Report Template
—ELL Preview and Writing Activities
—Presentation Digital Library
—Graphic Organizing Software
—Spanish Cognate Dictionary

Interactive Labs

Chapter 1B—Identifying Peapods

Studying Life Science

Chapter 1

KEY CONCEPT Science is a process of observation and investigation through which information about the natural world is learned.

Did you know that communities teeming with living things can be found in warm, shallow waters around the world? This home to many creatures is known as a coral reef. Do you wonder what a coral reef is? Are you interested in knowing if a reef is alive, if it can grow, or what living things can be found in it? If you want to ask any of these questions, you are acting like a scientist. In other words, scientists ask questions about the world and try to find answers to those questions.

Think About Acting Like a Scientist

You probably ask many questions in the course of a day. Each time you learn the answer to a question, you acquire new information. Some answers may even lead you to ask more questions. Think about an animal or plant you find interesting.

- In your Science Notebook, draw a picture of the animal or plant. Then write three questions you have about it.
- Write one or two sentences explaining how you can find answers to each of your questions.

www.scilinks.org
Scientific Method
Code: WGB01

3

Chapter 1 Planning Guide

Instructional Periods	National Standards	Lab Manual	Workbook
1.1 1 period	A.2, G.2; G.2; UCP.1	**Lab 1A—p. 1** Can You Explain This? **Lab 1B—p. 2** Measuring Peapods **Lab 1C—p. 5** Design an Experiment	Key Concept Review p. 1 Vocabulary Review p. 2 Interpreting Diagrams p. 3 Reading Comprehension p. 4 Curriculum Connection p. 5 Science Challenge p. 7
1.2 1 period	A.2, G.1, G.3; G.1, G.3; UCP.2		
1.3 2 periods	A.1, G.3; A.1, G.3; UCP.3		

Middle School Standard; High School Standard; Unifying Concept and Principle

Chapter 1 Lessons

Introduce Chapter 1

As a starting activity, use LAB 1A Can You Explain This? on page 1 of the Laboratory Manual.

ENGAGE Ask students to describe what they know about coral reefs. Then, review the five senses with students. Suggest that students describe what they know through observations using the five senses. Make a list of the questions that students have about coral reefs. Ask students how they might find answers to these questions. Point out that scientists engage in the same process of activating prior knowledge, developing questions, and searching for answers.

Think About Acting Like a Scientist

ENGAGE Ask students to give examples of some of the questions they ask themselves or others in a day. Encourage students to think about both complex and simple questions. Discuss the different ways in which students might find answers to their questions. Give an example of a scientific question, such as "Is the world round?" Remind students that when they first asked this question, scientists didn't have many tools to find the answer. Ask students to suggest ways in which scientists may have tried to answer that question when it was first asked and how scientists might answer the question now.

Direct students to complete each bulleted activity. As a class, discuss student results. On the board, record student ideas about how they might find answers to their questions.

1.1 Introduce

ENGAGE students by having them close their eyes and picture a scientist. Ask: *What does the scientist look like? What is he or she wearing? What is he or she doing?* As a class, brainstorm a list of verbs that describe the actions of a scientist. Record the verbs on the board. Try to elicit verbs such as *observe, question, measure, predict, test,* and *study.* Tell students that all scientists perform these actions regardless of the type of science they practice.

Before You Read

Remind students that descriptive words are adjectives that give more information about a noun. Start by recording students' predictions on the board if they need help.

Vocabulary terms are listed on the first student page of each lesson. You may wish to preview the terms before introducing each lesson. Strategies for teaching the vocabulary appear throughout the lesson on the pages where the terms are introduced.

Teach

EXPLAIN that in this lesson, students will learn how to define science and identify its many branches. Suggest that students visualize a tree with many branches.

Science Notebook EXTRA

Encourage students to set up a section in their Science Notebooks large enough for recording prefixes, root words, and suffixes of the science vocabulary words and terms that appear in each lesson throughout the student text. A two-column format will allow students to include definitions and to look for patterns among the words and terms.

Vocabulary

science Tell students that *science* comes from the Latin *scire,* which means "to know." Ask students to suggest reasons why this Latin word is a good term for the process of science.

1.1 What Is Science?

Learning Goals

- Define science.
- Differentiate among the branches of science.
- Examine the topics of life science.

New Vocabulary

science

Before You Read

Make predictions about what you think is the definition of science. Preview the Learning Goals and the headings in this lesson. Write at least five descriptive words and examples in your Science Notebook to describe your predictions.

There is a sunflower plant growing in your garden. Unfortunately, the plant does not look healthy. You try giving it more water. Then you try giving it less water. Perhaps you place it in direct sunlight, or you move it into the shade. After each action, you study the plant's condition and decide whether your action has helped. It may surprise you to know that when you follow this type of organized process of learning about the plant, you are acting like a scientist.

The Nature of Science

What comes to mind when you think about science? Perhaps you imagine a set of books packed with information. Maybe you think of a laboratory filled with colored liquids in a variety of containers. Although these images are related to science, they do not completely describe the true nature of science. **Science** is an organized method of using evidence to propose explanations for events in the natural world. Science is both the process of gaining knowledge and the resulting body of knowledge.

Explain It!

Scientists from many different fields usually work together. Choose an example of a scientific task, such as sending astronauts into space or forming images of structures inside the body. In your Science Notebook, explain how the input of different scientists would be needed to complete the task.

Figure 1.1 Trying to learn more about living things, such as these sunflowers, is one goal of science.

Background Information

While science has three distinct branches, there are many cases of overlap among the branches. Scientists who study the chemical processes that occur in our bodies are engaged in both life and physical science, or biochemistry. The study of the physics of stars, or astrophysics, combines Earth and space science and physical science. The work of paleontologists, scientists who study the fossils of extinct organisms, fits into both Earth and space science and life science. The sunflowers in Figure 1.1 might be investigated by biologists who study the nutritional value of parts of sunflowers (such as the seeds), chemists who are interested in the dyes that can be obtained from sunflowers, and geologists who evaluate the soil in which sunflowers grow. Thus, the three branches of science often overlap when looked at through the eyes of a practicing scientist.

Branches of Science

Imagine being a scientist. Are you wearing a lab coat and mixing substances together? Are you looking at images of the newest spot on Jupiter? Perhaps you are scuba diving to see animals that live in the ocean. Scientists do all of these things and many more. The specific description of a scientist's work depends on the topics that scientist investigates. The topics of scientific study are divided into three main branches: life science, Earth and space science, and physical science.

Life Science Scientists who study life science work with living things. This might include the more obvious life forms, such as animals and plants, or the living things that are so small they cannot be seen with the unaided eye. In addition, life scientists investigate how living things interact with one another and obtain the things they need from their environments.

Earth and Space Science Scientists who study Earth and space science examine the characteristics of planet Earth. They study Earth's water, land, and air, as well as weather events and natural disasters. Earth and space scientists also consider the process through which Earth developed, how it changes, and where it fits into the universe.

Physical Science Scientists who study physical science investigate topics such as motion, forces, matter, energy, sound, light, electricity, and magnetism. Physical scientists also study the interactions that occur between different types of particles and different types of matter. Even roller coaster designers need to know a lot about physical science to do their job well.

Figure 1.2 Jane Goodall, who studies chimpanzees, is a life scientist.

As You Read

In your Science Notebook, make a chart with three columns. Label the columns *Life Science, Earth and Space Science*, and *Physical Science*. What are the general topics studied in each branch? What are two specific topics that are studied in each branch? Write your answers in the chart.

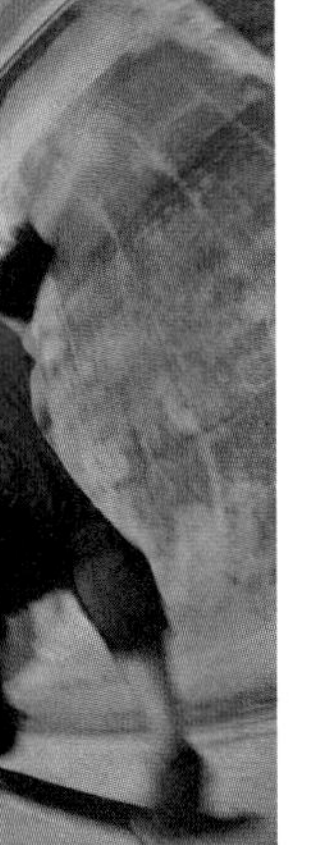

Figure 1.4 The way in which objects move and the properties of light are two of the many topics studied by physical scientists.

Figure 1.3 The weather on Earth and the flow of water over a mountain are some of the topics studied by Earth and space scientists.

Teach

EXPLAIN to students that science is divided into three branches: life science, Earth and space science, and physical science. All science as we know it fits into at least one of these three branches.

As You Read

English-language learners may benefit from working with a partner to brainstorm answers or to check the accuracy of their response.

ANSWER The main topics of life science are living things. Earth and space science is devoted to the study of Earth and its role in the universe. Physical science studies how and why things move; the characteristics of light; sound, electricity, and magnetism; and the nature and interactions of matter. Answers will vary.

Explain It!

Have students make a list of scientific tasks in their Science Notebooks. Allow students to use the library and the Internet to help them develop their lists. Have pairs of students discuss their lists and add to them as they compare.

Provide each student with a graphic organizer that includes a place to record a scientific task at the top and space below to list the different types of scientists needed to complete the task.

Have pairs share the information from their organizers with the class. Create an organizer on the board to record the answers.

Students should recognize that the work of scientists in different fields often overlaps. Explain that most natural phenomena lend themselves to study in a variety of ways, so one science cannot explore everything about a phenomenon.

ELL Strategy

Model As they read the lesson, have each student draw a diagram of the different branches of science. For struggling English-language learners, one strategy might be to have them translate the word for each branch of science into their own language and create a bulleted list of related concepts. They can also add words in their native language that are related to each branch of science. Another strategy might be to have students discuss with a partner what they already know about each branch.

Practice Using Vocabulary Remind students that *science* is defined as an organized method of using evidence to propose explanations for events in the natural world. Ask students to discuss what it means to organize information. Have them give examples of times when they had to organize something that they learned in order to better understand it.

Teach

EXPLAIN Emphasize the fact that almost every job requires the use or knowledge of science. Ask students to brainstorm a list of professions. Record that list. Then, have students look at the jobs on the list and discuss the role of science in each one.

Figure It Out: Figure 1.5

ANSWER **1.** A botanist, who studies plants, or a geneticist, who studies how traits are passed down from one generation to another, might do this work. **2.** An ecologist, who studies how living things interact with one another and their environment, might need to know the scientific names and general characteristics of the plants in an ecosystem being studied. A plant taxonomist studies how plants are organized into groups and named.

Assess

EVALUATE Use the After You Read questions and the Alternative Assessment to help you assess students' understanding of this lesson.

After You Read

1. *Science* is the action of asking questions and learning about the world. It is also the body of knowledge learned, which is a thing.
2. Earth and space scientist, specifically a meteorologist
3. A botanist studies plants. Many of the foods people eat, such as fruits, vegetables, and grains, are plant products.
4. A microbiologist studies very tiny living things, whereas a zoologist studies animals. In many cases, tiny living things can affect larger animals, so the two sciences may overlap. For example, bacteria are microorganisms that can both help and harm animals.

Alternative Assessment

EVALUATE Have students look at and refine their lists of scientific tasks. Lists should include the scientific process skills: observe, classify, compare, organize, evaluate, predict, experiment, and apply. To help them understand these tasks, have students draw pictures to illustrate each term's meaning.

Figure It Out

1. Which type of life scientist would most likely conduct an experiment to find out how to produce tomato plants that yield a greater number of tomatoes?
2. How might the work of a plant taxonomist and an ecologist be related?

Major Fields of Life Science

Branch of Life Science	The Study of	Branch of Life Science	The Study of
botany	plants	taxonomy	how living things can be organized
zoology	animals	ecology	how living things interact with one another and with their environments
genetics	how traits are passed from one generation to the next	microbiology	living things too small to be seen with the unaided eye
anatomy	the structures of living things	medicine	diagnosing, treating, and preventing disease

Figure 1.5 Life scientists specialize in certain fields.

Branches of Life Science

Each branch of science is further divided into more specific groups. This textbook explores the world of life science. Not all life scientists study the same things. **Figure 1.5** describes some of the major fields of life science. These fields are discussed throughout this textbook.

Did You Know?

The names of many fields of science end with the suffix *-ology*. When this suffix is added to a word, it means "the study of." The name *zoology* means "the study of animals."

Who Studies Science?

Perhaps you are thinking that science is only for scientists in laboratories. How wrong you are! Many people working in other fields study science or use the work of scientists.

For example, people who work in government need an understanding of many science topics in order to make useful decisions. They must have knowledge of how hurricanes and tornadoes behave in order to prepare safety and response plans. They should understand how living things interact with their environments in order to make decisions about water conservation. Almost every job imaginable requires some understanding of scientific topics.

After You Read

1. Using the notes in your Science Notebook, describe how science can be both an action and a thing.
2. Explain which type of scientist is most likely to study weather patterns.
3. How might the work of a botanist be related to some of the foods you eat?
4. The work of a microbiologist differs from that of a zoologist. Predict how the two scientists might work on different research that is somehow related.

6 STUDYING LIFE SCIENCE

English-language learners may benefit from checking their answers with a peer. Students can also check each other's answers in another color of ink or pencil lead. This allows the students to work on understanding and consolidating the concepts, while affording teachers the ability to recognize the gaps in specific students' understanding.

Differentiated Instruction

Interpersonal Have students reach out to scientists in their community. As a class, brainstorm a list of questions that students might ask a local scientist. Students might visit a hospital, lab, water-treatment plant, or local zoo to discover what the daily life of a scientist is like.

1.2 How Is Science Studied?

Before You Read

Create a sequence chart in your Science Notebook. Imagine your teacher giving you a topic to research. You are not familiar with the topic, but your teacher would like you to prepare a report on it. In your sequence chart, write the steps that you might follow to learn about the topic.

Learning Goals

- Describe the steps of the scientific method.
- Identify safe practices in the science laboratory.
- Distinguish between a hypothesis and a theory.

New Vocabulary

scientific method
observation
hypothesis
experiment
variable
controlled experiment
independent variable
dependent variable
control group
experimental group
safety symbol
data
conclusion
theory
prediction

The process scientists use to attempt to answer questions about the natural world is generally known as the **scientific method**. Although there is no single series of steps that is always followed in the scientific method, all scientific investigations use an orderly approach.

Making Observations

The process of science often begins with an observation. An **observation** is information you gather by using your senses. Your senses involve seeing, hearing, smelling, tasting, and touching. Maybe you *see* that the leaves of a tree have turned orange. It could be that you *hear* a frog in a swampy forest. Perhaps you *smell* the fragrance of a flower. Can you think of other examples of observations that use your senses?

Asking Questions

Suppose you step outside one morning and smell smoke in the air. The first thing you might do is ask yourself what is burning. The scientific process happens in a similar way. A scientist asks a question about an observation. A scientific question is one that can be studied through observation, testing, and analysis.

Figure 1.6 A scientist studying whales can make observations by looking at the size, shape, and color of whales. The scientist might also listen to the sounds whales make to communicate.

1.2 Introduce

ENGAGE students by having them draw upon prior knowledge about things that they do in a particular sequence. Ask: *What are some activities that you have to do in a particular order?*

As a class, brainstorm examples. Encourage students to think about baking a cake or getting ready to go to school. Choose one example, and have students describe the steps involved in completing that task. Help students recognize that scientists go about finding answers to their questions in an organized and orderly way. Tell students that the way scientists organize this process is known as the scientific method.

Before You Read

Draw a blank sequence chart on the board. If students need help, fill out the first few steps of the chart with the whole class. Check students' sequence charts throughout the lesson.

Teach

EXPLAIN to students that scientists carefully record their observations. They take careful notes about all of the information they gather, and they will usually observe something on more than one occasion to compare their findings.

Use the Visual: Figure 1.6

EXTEND Ask students to make observations about the whale in Figure 1.6. Have students share their observations with the class.

Vocabulary

scientific method Explain that *scientific method* encompasses all other vocabulary words in this lesson. It describes the process scientists use to answer questions about the natural world.

observation Tell students that scientific *observation* uses all five senses. Scientists attempt to be as detailed as possible when recording observations.

ELL Strategy

Relate to Personal Experience As they read the lesson, encourage students to think about their own experiences of observing and questioning their observations. Encourage struggling learners to discuss their experiences in their native language and then translate their comments into English.

Practice Using Vocabulary Have students create crossword puzzles using the vocabulary words. Photocopy the puzzles and distribute them. Allow students to fill in each other's puzzles. Word lists may be beneficial for some students.

Field Study

Take students outside to practice their observation skills. Have students find something outside to observe and record their observations in their Science Notebooks. Encourage students to use all five senses to describe their observations.

Teach

EXPLAIN the difference between guessing and hypothesizing. A hypothesis must be based on observations, previous knowledge, and research, while a guess does not need to be based on such strict criteria.

As You Read

ANSWER A hypothesis is a statement that describes how a scientist thinks the dependent variable will respond to the independent variable.

Vocabulary

hypothesis Explain that *hypothesis* is derived from the ancient Greek word *hypotithenai*, in which *hypo* means "under" and *tithenai* means "to place."

experiment Explain that an experiment consists of a repeatable set of steps used to test a hypothesis.

variable Tell students that variables are factors that change or can be changed during an experiment. Have students list variables that can be changed to grow the tallest bean plant.

controlled experiment Explain that in a controlled experiment, only one possible variable at a time is changed or allowed to change to determine whether it has an effect. The other possible variables are held constant by the scientist.

independent variable Tell students that this is a variable in an experiment that can be controlled by the scientist. The quality of soil, amount of sunlight, and amount of water are all independent variables that can be changed one at a time.

dependent variable The dependent variable is the one observed and measured as an independent variable changes. Tell students that they can distinguish independent and dependent variables by remembering that changes in a dependent variable *depend* on other factors.

control group Tell students that a control group in an experiment is a standard of comparison for the group being tested. Control groups often represent normal conditions, or no deliberate changes. If there is no difference between a control group and an experimental group, the independent variable had no effect.

experimental group Explain that variables are changed for the experimental group in an experiment. The experimental group is measured and compared with the control group.

Use the Visual: Figure 1.7

ANSWER temperature

Did You Know?

When a person attempts to explain an observation based on what he or she already knows, that person is inferring. This explanation is called an inference. An inference is not a fact and can, therefore, be wrong.

Developing a Hypothesis

When wondering about the source of the smoke, you guess that it might be a brush fire in a nearby forest. This is your hypothesis. A **hypothesis** (hi PAH thuh sus, plural: hypotheses) is a proposed explanation for an observation. A hypothesis is not a random guess. It must be based on observations, previous knowledge, and research.

A good hypothesis is proposed in a way that it can be tested to find out if it is true. Some hypotheses are tested by making more observations. Others are tested with experiments. An **experiment** is an investigation in which information is collected under controlled conditions.

As You Read

Review the sequence chart you created in your Science Notebook. Make changes or additions so that your chart describes the steps of the scientific method.

How does the hypothesis relate the dependent variable to the independent variable?

Designing an Experiment

All experiments involve **variables**, which are factors that can vary, or change. For example, suppose you want to conduct an experiment to find out if the temperature of turtle eggs affects whether the hatching turtles are male or female. Variables include the amount of moisture in the eggs' environment and the temperature of the eggs. If you allow both of the variables to change throughout the experiment, you will not be able to determine which variable affected the resulting turtles.

Instead, you must do a **controlled experiment**, or an experiment in which only one variable at a time is allowed to change. The variable that changes during the experiment is called the **independent variable**. In the turtle experiment, temperature is the independent variable. Something that is independent does not rely on other factors in order to vary.

The variable that is observed to find out if it also changes as a result of a changing independent variable is called the **dependent variable**. Something that is dependent relies on another factor. The gender of the hatching turtles is the dependent variable. All other variables must remain unchanged.

Turtle Eggs Exposed to Different Temperatures

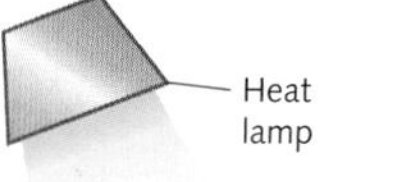

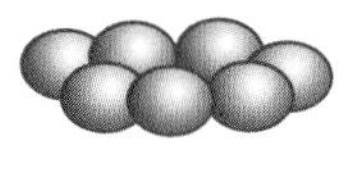

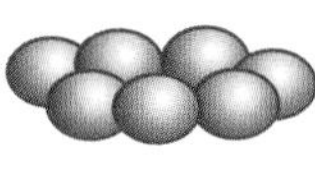

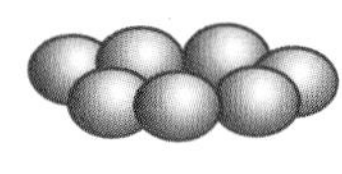

Figure 1.7 Every variable must remain unchanged, or constant, except for the independent variable. What is the independent variable in this experiment?

8 STUDYING LIFE SCIENCE

ELL Strategy

Model Have students work in small groups to make a diagram that represents the scientific method. For struggling English-language learners, be sure to clarify all vocabulary words that have multiple meanings. When introducing and explaining new concepts and terms, direct students' attention to vocabulary, syntax, grammar, and context clues. Identifying cognates may also help English-language learners master new concepts and terms.

Teacher Alert

Students often confuse the definition of the word *hypothesis* with the definition of the word *theory*. Emphasize that a scientist's hypothesis is only a specific assumption that can be made based on a theory. Many testable hypotheses can be made by applying the principle described by a theory.

Control Group Some experiments have two groups. In the **control group**, all the variables are kept the same. In the **experimental group**, the independent variable is allowed to change or made to change. The control group is used for comparison. The control group shows what would have happened if nothing were to change.

Not every experiment can be controlled, however. Imagine a scientist trying to find out how changes to wetlands affect a population of local birds. The scientist would need to observe the birds in their natural habitat without disturbing them. Although this type of research must be conducted in the field, it still requires the same methods of questioning and observation as an experiment conducted in a laboratory.

Explore It!

Design an experiment to find out how the amount of water a plant receives affects the number of tomatoes it produces. Propose a hypothesis. Identify the independent and dependent variables. Describe the control and experimental groups. Share your experiment with a partner.

PEOPLE IN SCIENCE Ignaz Philipp Semmelweis 1818–1865

It may seem obvious to you that washing your hands is a good way to get rid of germs, but that wasn't always obvious. Long before people knew that germs existed, a doctor named Ignaz Philipp Semmelweis, working at Vienna General Hospital in Austria, made an important observation. He noticed that a large number of women were dying of a condition known as puerperal (pyhew ER pe ral) fever shortly after delivering their babies. Doctors of the time thought the illness could not be prevented. However, Semmelweis noticed something very interesting. The hospital had two identical clinics for delivering babies. In one clinic, roughly 13 percent of new mothers died from puerperal fever. In the other clinic, the number of deaths was only about 2 percent.

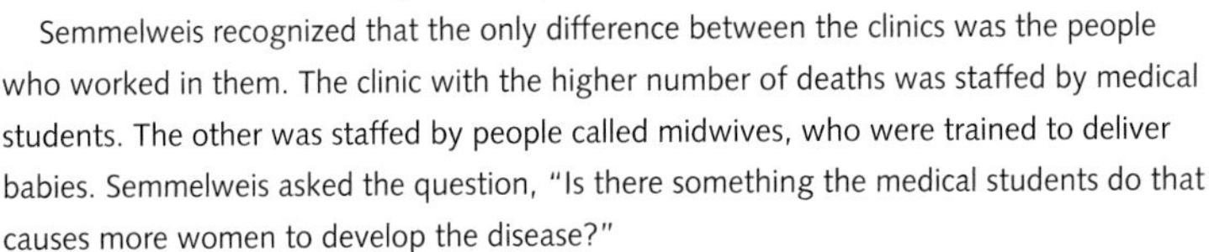

Semmelweis recognized that the only difference between the clinics was the people who worked in them. The clinic with the higher number of deaths was staffed by medical students. The other was staffed by people called midwives, who were trained to deliver babies. Semmelweis asked the question, "Is there something the medical students do that causes more women to develop the disease?"

At about the same time, a friend of Semmelweis's performed an examination of the body of a person who had died. During the procedure, the friend accidentally cut his finger. Shortly after, he died of symptoms similar to those of women who died of puerperal fever. Semmelweis hypothesized that the medical students were carrying some type of particles from the dead bodies they were studying to the women in the hospital.

To test his hypothesis, Semmelweis began requiring doctors to wash their hands in a cleaning solution before delivering babies. The death rate in the medical students' clinic immediately dropped. Semmelweis concluded that some agent was indeed causing disease.

It took a while for Semmelweis's conclusions to be accepted by other doctors. His work, however, not only saved many lives, it also laid the groundwork for later scientists to discover the microscopic germs that cause disease.

Teach

EXPLORE Discuss with students examples of experiments that can and cannot be controlled. Make two lists on the board, and record students' examples.

Explore It!

Suggest that students list all of the steps in the scientific method in their Science Notebooks and fill in their plans for each step. Provide an example of an experiment to the whole class. Have students design a similar experiment. Be sure students understand that the independent variable is the amount of sunlight the plant receives and that the dependent variable is the height of the plant.

PEOPLE IN SCIENCE

Direct students to discuss the larger benefits of Semmelweis's work. Point out that Semmelweis's discovery of the importance of hygiene not only helped women in labor but also helped save many more lives as doctors in all fields of medicine began, and continue, to wash their hands before treating patients.

Today, we accept the importance of hand washing without question. Semmelweis, however, had a very difficult time convincing others of his discovery's significance. It wasn't until after his death that the medical community embraced his discovery.

EXTEND Have students apply the steps of the scientific method to Semmelweis's work. Ask them to identify his hypothesis, the independent and dependent variables, the data he might have collected, and the conclusion that he reached.

Background Information

Scientists adhere to the strict guidelines of the scientific method to eliminate bias and prejudice in their conclusions. Before a scientist's conclusions are accepted, the experiment must be replicated by other scientists with the same results. Scientists keep careful records of their procedures so that their experiments can be precisely repeated and confirmed by others.

Reading Comprehension Workbook, p. 4

Science Notebook EXTRA

Ask students to write a paragraph in their Science Notebooks describing how Semmelweis must have felt when his conclusions were attacked by other scientists. Then, ask students to describe what he might have done to try to convince those scientists that he was right.

Teach

EXPLAIN Emphasize the importance of safety in a lab setting. Remind students that when they are working with dangerous substances, it is essential that they follow all safety instructions. Point out to students the safety features of the lab, such as the eye wash station and shower, if available.

Vocabulary

safety symbol Tell students that scientists use easily recognizable symbols to provide information about the hazards associated with an experiment. Emphasize that it is extremely important to heed these warnings, as not doing so could result in a serious injury.

data Explain to students that the word *data* is the plural of the Latin word *datum*, which means "something given." In a scientific experiment, the data are the information "given" to scientists by their observations.

conclusion Explain that the word *conclusion* has many common usages. It is often used to describe the ending of a book or a piece of music. Have students compare these meanings with the scientific meaning of *conclusion* as a statement that uses evidence from an experiment to indicate whether a *hypothesis* is supported.

Figure It Out: Figure 1.9

ANSWER **1.** The two variables are the temperature of the eggs and gender of the hatching turtles. **2.** As the temperature increases, the percentage of males decreases and the percentage of females increases.

Safety An important aspect of every scientific experiment is working safely. Scientists and students alike must take precautions to protect themselves from possible dangers. In the experiments you will be doing as you study life science, you will see **safety symbols** that warn you about possible dangers. The chart in **Figure 1.8** describes what you should do when you see some of the major safety symbols. Appendix A contains more information about laboratory safety.

Most important, always read the instructions for every experiment in advance. Make sure you understand what you need to do. Tell your teacher if you have questions or if there is an accident in the laboratory.

Lab Safety Symbols

	This symbol appears when a danger exists for cuts or punctures caused by the use of sharp objects.
	This symbol appears when substances used could stain or burn clothing.
	This symbol appears when a danger to the eyes exists. Safety goggles should be worn when this symbol appears.
	This symbol appears when chemicals used can cause burns or are poisonous if absorbed through the skin.

Figure 1.8 These and other safety symbols alert you to follow safety procedures when doing a laboratory experiment.

Collecting and Analyzing Data

The information obtained through observation is called **data** (singular: datum). Some experiments produce huge amounts of data. To make sense of all the information, scientists organize data into forms that are easier to read and analyze. One way to organize data is in a table. **Figure 1.9** shows a possible data table resulting from the turtle experiment.

Figure It Out

1. What are the two variables represented in this table?
2. What trend do the data show?

Turtle Egg Data

Temperature of Eggs	Percentage of Males	Percentage of Females
27.0°C	68.4	31.6
29.5°C	47.8	52.2
32.0°C	29.3	70.7

Figure 1.9 The data for this experiment consist of numbers that can be organized in a table. A table has rows and columns with headings that describe the information.

ELL Strategy

Illustrate Invite students to use the chart in Figure 1.8 to make posters for the lab that illustrate each safety symbol and its meaning. For struggling English-language learners, translate the meaning of each safety symbol into the student's native language. Students might choose to include multiple languages on their posters.

Another way to organize data is to create a graph. Line graphs, such as the one in **Figure 1.10a**, are best for data that change continuously, such as the size of a population of bacteria. Bar graphs, such as the one in **Figure 1.10b**, are useful for comparing data, such as the data from the turtle experiment. Circle graphs, such as the one in **Figure 1.10c**, are best for analyzing data that are divided into parts of a whole, such as the elements in the human body.

Drawing Conclusions

Once the experiment has been conducted and the data have been collected, a scientist tries to determine if the hypothesis is supported. A **conclusion** is a statement that uses evidence from an experiment to indicate whether or not the hypothesis is supported.

A conclusion is not necessarily the end of the investigation. If the hypothesis is not supported, the scientist might develop a new hypothesis and design a new experiment to test it. If the hypothesis is supported, the scientist needs to repeat the experiment many times to make sure that the conclusion is valid.

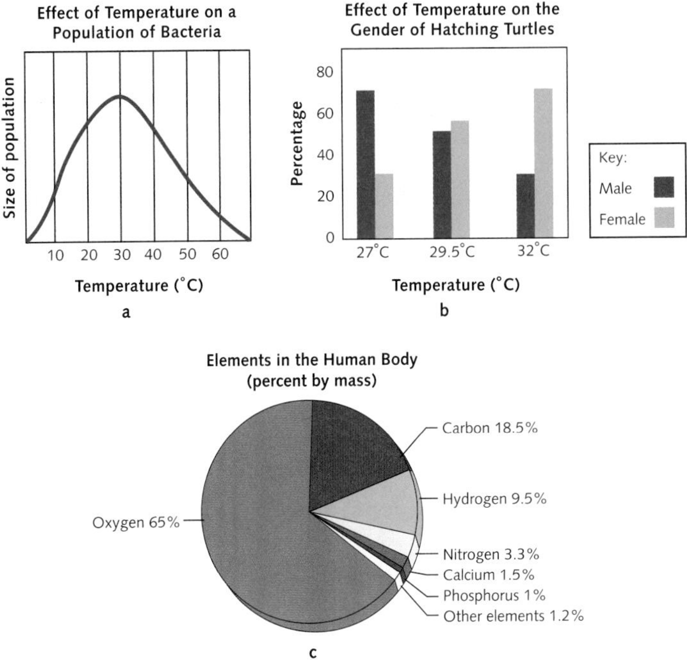

Figure 1.10 Data can be presented in a variety of formats, including **a)** a line graph, **b)** a bar graph, and **c)** a circle graph.

Teach

EXPLAIN to students that in addition to using tables to organize data, scientists also use many types of graphs. Ask students to list the different kinds of graphs that they have used to organize data.

Use the Visual: Figure 1.10

EXTEND Discuss with students the types of data that lend themselves to each type of graph. For example, line graphs are used to show data that change continuously. Discrete observations are best represented with a bar graph or a scatter plot. Circle graphs, or pie charts, are best for comparing the magnitudes of the parts of a whole.

Differentiated Instruction

Kinesthetic Have students collect data on the heights of the students in the class. Then, have them create a bar graph to represent the data. Finally, have students assemble themselves into a "human bar graph" for a hands-on experience of the way that data can be organized.

Teach

EXPLAIN to students that a hypothesis is a statement that can be tested in an investigation. Hypotheses are generated by applying explanations for natural events described in scientific theories. Ask students to think about scientific theories that they have heard about, such as the Big Bang theory or the theory of relativity.

Vocabulary

theory Tell students that the word *theory* is derived from the Greek word *theōríā*, meaning "a looking at." A theory is an explanation for a broad range of observations, or "things looked at." Explain that a theory is an explanation supported by a large body of scientific evidence while a hypothesis is a tentative explanation for one observation.

prediction Explain to students that the prefix *pre-* in the word *prediction* means "before." A prediction is a statement, based on a theory, that suggests what a person thinks will happen "before" completing an experiment.

Assess

EVALUATE Use the After You Read questions and the Alternative Assessment to help you assess students' understanding of this lesson.

After You Read

1. A hypothesis is a possible explanation for an observation.
2. A hypothesis might become part of a theory if repeated experiments to test the hypothesis provide evidence that the hypothesis and the theory are supported.
3. The independent variable is changed during the experiment. The dependent variable is observed to find out if and how it changes in response to the independent variable.
4. The experiment might involve substances that could stain or burn clothing.
5. The conclusion might cause a scientist to propose a new hypothesis and design a new experiment.

Alternative Assessment

EVALUATE Have students create sequence charts to describe the steps they would follow when designing an experiment.

Communicating the Results

A scientist also must share his or her experimental procedures and results with the scientific community. In this way, other scientists can repeat the experiment to confirm the results. Throughout an experiment, the scientist must keep careful records that describe everything about the research. These records should include not only the data but also information about the experimental design, possible sources of error, unexpected results, and any remaining questions.

Scientists share their results with one another by communicating through written reports and journal articles, as well as through oral presentations. Sharing information in this way not only adds to the body of scientific knowledge, it also gives other scientists an opportunity to repeat the experiment and confirm its results. The results of an investigation can only be considered valid if they are continually achieved during repeated trials of the same procedure.

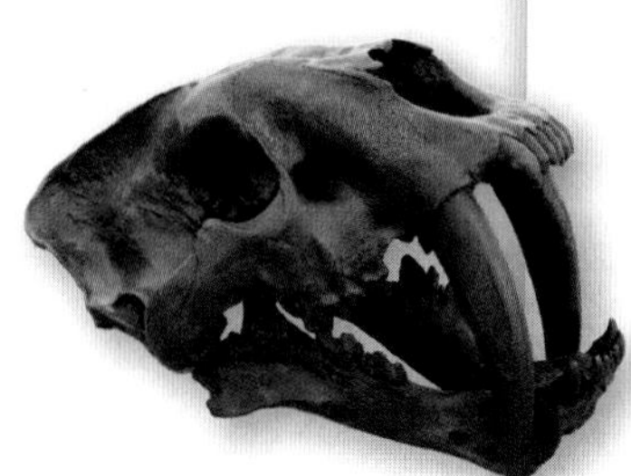

Figure 1.11 One theory you will learn about later in this textbook suggests how some living things change over time and how others, such as saber-toothed cats, disappear completely. The skull of a saber-toothed cat is shown above.

Scientific Theories

If a hypothesis is supported by many separate investigations over a long period of time, it may lead to the development of, or become part of, a theory. A **theory** is an explanation for a broad range of observations that is supported by a body of scientific evidence. A theory is not the same as a scientific law. A scientific law is a rule that describes an observed pattern in nature.

Scientists use theories to make predictions about new situations. A **prediction** is a statement that suggests what a person thinks will happen in the future based on past experience and evidence.

A theory is not considered to be absolute truth, but it is supported by a vast amount of scientific evidence. Scientists continually analyze the strengths and weaknesses of a theory. If new evidence is discovered, a theory can be revised or replaced.

After You Read

1. How is a hypothesis related to an observation?
2. How might a hypothesis become part of a theory?
3. What is the difference between the independent and dependent variables in a controlled experiment?
4. You see a symbol of an apron in a laboratory procedure. What does this symbol tell you about the experiment you will be conducting?
5. Look at the sequence chart you completed. In a well-developed paragraph, explain how the last step might lead back to the first step.

Background Information

The Big Bang theory is the most widely accepted scientific theory of the origin of our universe. According to the Big Bang theory, the universe was created between 10 and 20 billion years ago as a result of a cosmic explosion that spread matter in all directions.

1.3 Measurements in Science

Before You Read

Look at the headings in the lesson to find the measurements discussed. In your Science Notebook, create a chart with three columns. Label one column *Quantity,* the next column *Units,* and the third column *Examples.* Include a row for each measurement you find.

Learning Goals

- Identify the SI units of several scientific measurements.
- Recognize how prefixes indicate the magnitude of a unit.
- Describe how common tools of measurement are used.

New Vocabulary

measurement
International System of Units (SI)
mass
volume
meniscus
derived unit
density

It's a fly ball to center field. You run to catch the baseball. You've got it! Now all you have to do is throw it to home plate to catch the runner. Can you throw the ball that far? Can you get it there in time? How far and how fast you throw the ball are examples of measurements. A **measurement** is a quantity, dimension, or amount. Scientists rely on measurements to gather and analyze data.

Units of Measurement

Would you say that it takes you 15 to get to school? Probably not. You would probably say that it takes you 15 minutes to get to school. That description would help another person know how long it takes for you to get from your home to school. Minutes are an example of units. A unit is a precise quantity that does not change. All measurements must be described with the appropriate unit.

During the 1700s, people used all sorts of different units to describe measurements. To describe the length of an object, a person could use any one of more than ten different units. In addition, because many of the units were based on body parts such as feet and hands, the size of a unit could vary from one person to another. The variety of units not only made it confusing to talk about measurements, it also made it difficult to buy and sell goods.

To put an end to the confusion, the French government asked the Academy of Sciences to develop a standard system of measurement. The Academy produced a system, known as the metric system, based on the number 10. This makes it very simple to change a unit of one magnitude to a unit of a different magnitude by dividing or multiplying by 10. You can learn more about the metric system in Appendix B.

In 1960, some elements of the metric system became part of the **International System of Units (SI)**. This system of measurement is used by most countries throughout the world and in almost all scientific activities.

Figure 1.12 The distance from the outfield to home plate is one measurement on a baseball field. What are some other measurements related to a baseball game?

1.3 Introduce

ENGAGE Provide pairs of students with measuring tapes, and have them measure each other's heights and arm spans from middle finger to middle finger with arms outstretched. These measurements should be close to equal for each person. Ask: *How does the length of your arm span compare with your height?*

Have each student divide his or her height by his or her arm span. As a class, collect height-to-arm span ratio data. Ask: *Could you come up with a theory about height-to-arm span ratio from the data?* Help students recognize that this ratio is close to one.

EXPLORE As a class, brainstorm other ways you could measure your height and arm span without a tape measure. Ask students if measuring by hand span would change the ratios. Help students see that if the units change, the ratio will remain the same as long as the measuring tool remains constant.

Before You Read

As a class, have students look at the headings in the lesson. Write each measurement on the board. Have students practice making each of the measurements listed in his or her chart. Check students' charts throughout the lesson.

Teach

EXPLORE Have students work in pairs to measure the length and width of the classroom using the length of their feet, span of their hands, or length of their strides. Have students compare their results and discuss the benefits and drawbacks of using body parts as measuring tools.

Use the Visual: Figure 1.12

EXTEND Have students work in groups of three or four to brainstorm a list of measurements. (Answer: distance from one base to another, distance from home plate to the pitcher's mound, size of the ball, speed at which the ball is hit, the length of the baseball bat, or size of each base)

ELL Strategy

Act Out Have students pretend to play baseball. As they are playing, ask them to call out possible measurements. For struggling English-language learners, pair students with peer tutors who can explain the game of baseball if it is unfamiliar.

Practice Using Vocabulary If time permits, have students create posters for each unit of measurement that includes a picture of something being measured.

Vocabulary

measurement Explain to students that the word *measurement* indicates a description of dimension, quantity, or amount and applies to length, mass, and volume.

International System of Units (SI) Explain that a common system of measurement allows scientists around the world to communicate about data in the same language.

Teach

EXPLAIN Point out that all SI measurements use the same prefixes, *milli-*, *centi-*, and *kilo-*. Remind students that *milli-* and *centi-* indicate measurements less than one and that *kilo-* indicates a measurement greater than one.

Extend It!

Resistance to the metric system has left the United States as a minority in the world of measurement. The majority of the world has been metric since 1975, when the United States adopted a voluntary approach to the change. This has kept the U.S. system of measurement the same as it always has been.

In 1991, President George H. W. Bush issued Executive Order 12770 mandating the use of metric measurement for all federal agencies. All scientific and engineering work has used metric measurements since the early 2000s. Discuss with students the advantages and disadvantages of mandating the use of the metric system nationwide.

Vocabulary

mass Emphasize that the mass of an object is the amount of matter in the object. An object's mass will remain constant no matter where the object is. It is important to distinguish mass from weight, which measures the pull of gravity on an object and changes based on where the object is.

volume Explain that volume can be a measure of either a solid or a liquid. Solids are measured using cubic meters, and liquids are measured using liters.

meniscus Tell students that the word *meniscus* is derived from the Greek word *mēniskos*, which means "moon." The curve at the top surface of a liquid resembles the shape of a waxing or waning moon.

derived unit Tell students that a derived unit is obtained by combining other units.

Use the Visual: Figure 1.13

ANSWER one million

Use the Visual: Figure 1.14

EXTEND Have students examine rulers in class. Have them practice measuring the length of various objects using millimeters and centimeters.

Metric Prefixes

Prefix	Meaning
kilo-	1,000
hecto-	100
deka-	10
base unit	1
deci-	0.1 (one-tenth)
centi-	0.01 (one-hundredth)
milli-	0.001 (one-thousandth)

Figure 1.13 You can use the prefix of an SI unit to figure out how large or small a measurement is. How many millimeters are in one kilometer?

Extend It!

The United States is the only major industrialized nation in the world that does not use the metric system. Work in a small group to research the history of the metric system. Prepare a poster or time line showing the major developments in the system and the laws governing it. Then separate into teams and debate the topic of whether the United States should adopt this system.

Length

When you describe how far you throw a ball, how long a table is, or how tall a building is, you are describing length. The base SI unit of length is the meter (m). A baseball bat is about one meter long. An average doorknob is about one meter above the floor.

A meter is divided into smaller units called centimeters (cm) and millimeters (mm). The prefix *centi-* means "one-hundredth." There are 100 centimeters in a meter. The prefix *milli-* means "one-thousandth." There are 1,000 millimeters in a meter. A millimeter is about the thickness of one dime.

For longer lengths, scientists use a unit called a kilometer (km). The prefix *kilo-* means "one thousand." There are 1,000 meters in a kilometer. The distance from San Diego, California, to New York, New York, is 3,909 km. The tallest mountain in the world, Mt. Everest, has a height of almost 9 km.

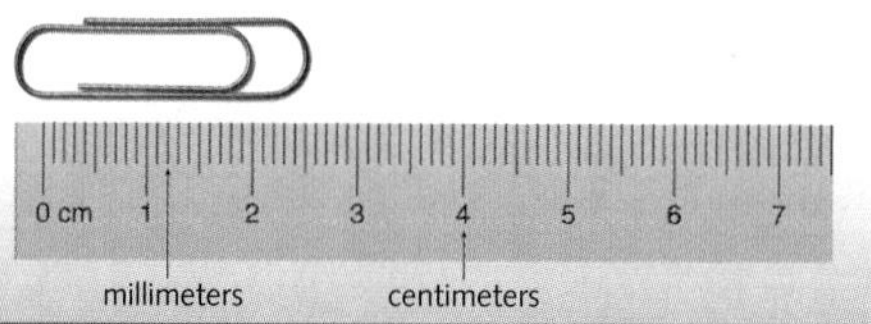

Figure 1.14 Length can be measured with a metric ruler. Line up one end of an object with the first mark on the ruler. Find the line closest to the other end of the object. The longer lines show centimeters, and the shorter lines show millimeters.

Mass

The amount of matter in an object is that object's **mass.** The base unit of mass in the SI system is the kilogram (kg). Recall that the prefix *kilo-* means "one thousand." A kilogram consists of one thousand smaller units called grams (g). The mass of a paper clip is about one gram. Even smaller masses are measured in milligrams (mg). There are 1,000 milligrams in one gram. A tool called a balance is used to measure mass.

CONNECTION: Math

All number systems have a base number. The number system you use every day has a base of 10. This makes it convenient to multiply or divide by multiples of 10. To multiply a number by a multiple of 10, move the decimal point to the right the same number of places as there are zeroes. For example, to multiply a number by 100, move the decimal point two places to the right. You can follow a similar process to divide by multiples of 10. However, move the decimal point to the left instead.

CONNECTION: Math

Have students practice using this shortcut for dividing by multiples of ten. Ask them to use their Science Notebooks to record the answers to 145 ÷ 10; 145 ÷ 100; 145 × 10; and 145 × 100. (Answers: 145 ÷ 10 = 14.5; 145 ÷ 100 = 1.45; 145 × 10 = 1,450; 145 × 100 = 14,500.)

Background Information

France began using the metric system in 1795 but allowed its citizens to continue using other systems of measurement. In 1837, France passed a law requiring all of its citizens to use the metric system. Since the 1890s, the U.S. Congress has attempted to change the American system of measurement to the metric system. It has never been successful in doing so. The average American is not yet comfortable with the metric system.

Volume

Have you ever tried to pour all the liquid from a large container into a smaller container? If so, you probably made a mess! That's because the liquid takes up a certain amount of space. If the smaller container does not have enough space, the liquid spills over the sides.

The amount of space an object takes up is its **volume**. How volume is measured depends on the sample being measured. The sample being measured also determines the units used for the measurement. The three basic types of samples are liquids, regular solids, and irregular solids.

Finding the Volume of a Liquid The volume of a liquid, such as water, is measured in a unit called a liter (L). A liter is not an SI unit, but because it is important and widely used, it is accepted for use with the SI. You may have seen one-liter and two-liter bottles of drinks at the grocery store. Smaller volumes can be measured in milliliters. Recall that the prefix *milli-* means "one-thousandth." There are 1,000 milliliters in a liter.

One way to measure the volume of a liquid is by pouring the liquid into a container that has measured markings on it. Perhaps you have poured milk into a measuring cup to find a specific amount for a recipe. Scientists often use a graduated cylinder to measure liquid volumes.

Figure 1.15 shows a liquid being measured in a graduated cylinder marked in one-milliliter intervals. You can see that the top surface of the liquid is slightly curved. The curve is known as the **meniscus** (meh NIHS cus). To find the volume of the liquid, you must read the measurement of the marking at the bottom of the meniscus.

Finding the Volume of a Regular Solid A regular solid is an object that has matching shapes for sides. A number cube and a shoebox are examples of regular solids. You can find the volume of a regular solid by multiplying its length by its width by its height.

volume = length × width × height

If the measurements are made in centimeters, the unit of volume is cm^3 (cubic centimeters: cm × cm × cm). If the measurements are made in meters, the unit of volume is m^3 (cubic meters: m × m × m). A unit that consists of more than one base unit is called a **derived unit**. Volume is a derived unit.

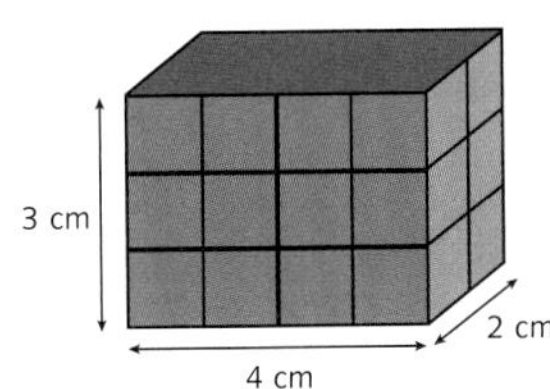

Figure 1.16 The volume of this solid is 4 cm × 2 cm × 3 cm = 24 cm^3.

As You Read

In your chart of measurements, fill in the second column with the units in which each measurement can be described. Provide at least two examples of each measurement in the third column.

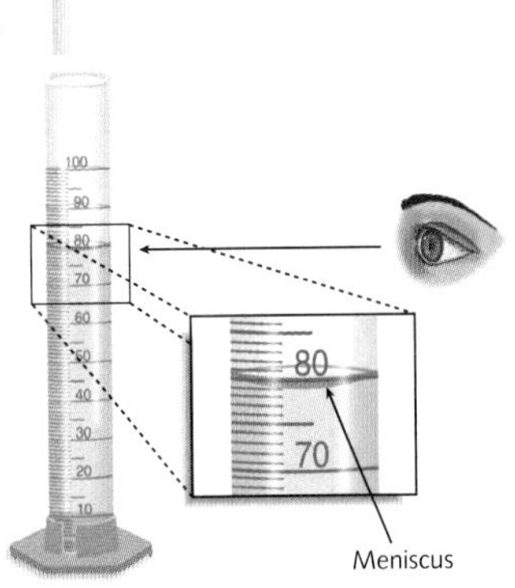

Figure 1.15 According to the graduated cylinder, what is the volume of this liquid?

Explore It!

Find three regular solids in your home or classroom. Examples include a book, an eraser, and a tissue box. Work with a partner to find the volume of each solid.

Teach

ENGAGE Ask students to give some examples of liquids, regular solids, and irregular solids. Make three columns on the board, and write each example in the proper column. Discuss with students the challenges of measuring the amount of space taken up by each substance.

EXPLAIN that there are different methods for measuring the volume of each type of substance.

As You Read

Remind students that the units for measuring volume depend upon the type of substance being measured.

Use the Visual: Figure 1.15

ANSWER 79 milliliters

Explore It!

Collect a variety of regular solids, and place them at different stations around the room. Give pairs of students a ruler or measuring tape. Have students find the volume of the objects at each station. Allow them to use calculators to compute volume.

Have students create charts in their Science Notebooks to record the length, width, and height of each object. Remind them to describe each object and include the units they are using.

After pairs have finished their measurements, ask them to share one volume measurement with the class. Record each measurement on the board. Then, have students compare their results to those of the class.

English-language learners could be paired with peer tutors to assure that vocabulary will be reinforced. Additionally, students could take turns measuring and recording the findings, providing English-language learners a greater opportunity to listen for and use terminology as well as gain confidence in working with numbers.

ELL Strategy

Relate to Personal Experience and Discuss Students born in other countries may have personal experience with using the metric system. Have students in small groups discuss these experiences. Encourage students from other countries to share their experiences of using inches and feet in the United States instead of centimeters and meters.

Teacher Alert

Remind students that in order to properly measure the volume of a liquid, they will need to look at the bottom of the meniscus from eye level. It might be necessary to bend down to do this.

Teach

EXPLAIN Ask students to give examples of some irregular solids. Have students suggest ways to find the volume of these objects. Discuss with students the difficulties of finding the volume of solids that are not easily measured.

Science Notebook EXTRA

Provide students with some of the common substances listed in the chart in Figure 1.18. **DO NOT** provide any samples of mercury for students to handle. Have students place these objects in water to see if they will sink or float. Students should create tables in their Science Notebooks to record whether each object sinks or floats, as well as the object's density. Challenge students to find a connection between the density of an object and its buoyancy in water.

Vocabulary

density Explain that density is a derived unit, made up of the ratio of mass to volume. Every substance has a unique density; this number can help scientists identify unknown materials.

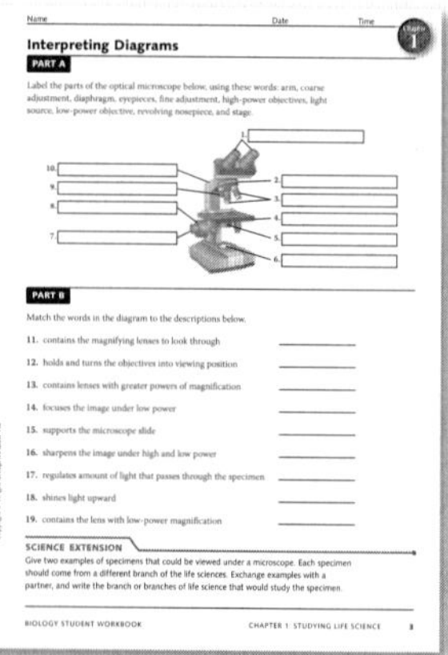

Interpreting Diagrams

Workbook, p. 3

Did You Know?

A microscope is a device that makes objects appear larger than they actually are. A compound light microscope bends light through curved pieces of glass called lenses. To view objects too small to be seen even with a compound light microscope, scientists can use an electron microscope. Rather than using light, this type of microscope uses a stream of tiny particles called electrons. You can learn more about microscopes in Appendix C.

Finding the Volume of an Irregular Solid Not all solids have regular shapes. A stone or a shell, for example, has an irregular shape. One method for finding the volume of an irregular solid is to place the object in water. Once you place the object in water, the level of the water will rise. If you subtract the original water level from the new water level, you will find the volume of the solid.

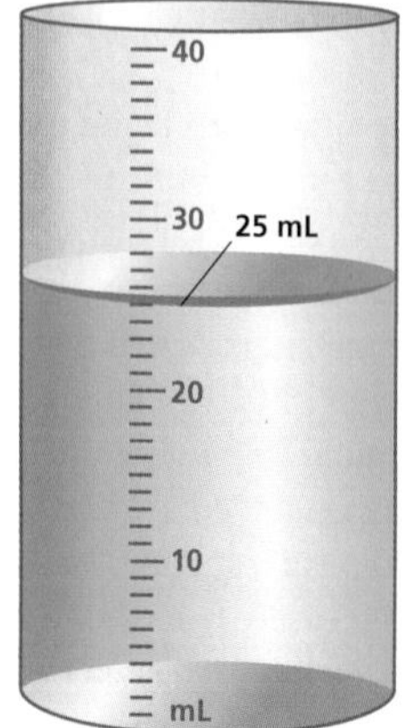

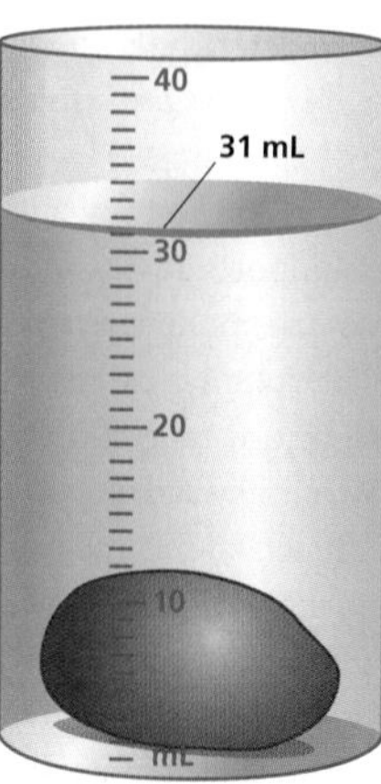

Figure 1.17 The water rises from the 25-mL mark to the 31-mL mark after the stone is placed in it. Therefore, the volume of the stone is 6 mL.

Density

If you place a table tennis ball in water, it will float. If you place a golf ball in water, it will sink. Even though the balls have about the same volume, they have different masses. The amount of mass in a given volume is an object's **density**. Density can be affected by temperature. For example, the density of water is different at room temperature than at 32°F. This is because the particles are farther apart at higher temperatures and closer together at lower temperatures. As a result, the same amount of mass can take up more or less space depending on its temperature.

You can find the density of an object by dividing its mass by its volume.

density = mass/volume

Density is a derived unit. The units of density are made up of a unit of mass and a unit of volume. If mass is measured in grams and volume is measured in cubic centimeters, the unit of density is grams per cubic centimeter (g/cm^3). If volume is measured in milliliters, the unit of density is grams per milliliter (g/mL).

Sample Densities

Substance	Density (g/cm^3)
air	0.001293
aluminum	2.7
gold	19.3
mercury	13.6
water	1.00

Figure 1.18 This table lists the densities of several common substances at room temperature.

Background Information

A substance that has a density greater than the density of water (1g/mL) will sink. A substance that has a density less than the density of water will float. Finding the buoyancy of an unknown substance can help scientists identify the substance.

The Greek mathematician Archimedes discovered the water displacement method for finding the volume of an irregular solid while he was in the bathtub. According to legend, when he realized that the water displaced by his body in the tub was equal to his volume, he ran naked through the streets shouting "Eureka," which means "I have found it" in Greek.

Temperature

Before going outside, many people check the air temperature so they know what to wear. Most people think temperature is a measure of heat. To a scientist, temperature is the measure of the average kinetic energy of the particles in an object.

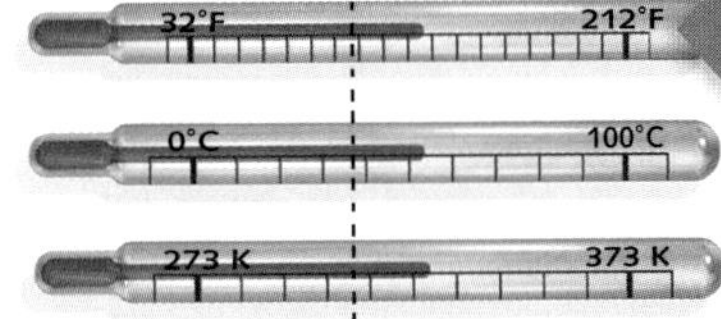

Figure 1.19 This diagram compares the Fahrenheit, Celsius, and Kelvin scales.

Temperature can be measured on different scales. One temperature scale commonly used in science is the Celsius scale. On this scale, temperature is measured in degrees Celsius. Water freezes at 0°C and boils at 100°C.

The SI base unit of temperature is the kelvin. Units on the Kelvin scale are the same size as those on the Celsius scale. However, each value on the Kelvin scale is 273 degrees more than on the Celsius scale.

The scale with which you may be most familiar is the Fahrenheit scale. On this scale, water freezes at 32°F and boils at 212°F. Fahrenheit measurements are generally not used in science.

A thermometer is used to measure temperature. To use a thermometer, place the device in the substance being measured. Allow time for the liquid in the thermometer to move up or down. Then read the number next to the top of the liquid. Some thermometers are digital and display a number once the temperature of the substance is recorded. Scientists often use probes that automatically make temperature measurements and create a table or graph of the data when attached to a computer.

Figure It Out

1. Normal human body temperature is about 98°F. What is this temperature on the Celsius scale?
2. Is the range of whole-number temperatures between the freezing point of water and the boiling point of water the same on both the Celsius and the Fahrenheit scales? Explain your answer.

Time

Time describes how long an event takes to occur. The second (s) is the SI base unit of time. Short periods of time are measured in parts of one second, such as milliseconds (ms). There are 1,000 milliseconds in a second. Longer periods of time are measured in multiples of a second, such as minutes and hours. There are 60 seconds in one minute and 60 minutes in one hour. Time is measured using such instruments as clocks, watches, and stopwatches.

CONNECTION: Social Studies

Before clocks and watches were invented, people used the Sun to tell time. A sundial is a device that forms a shadow of a stick. As Earth rotates on its axis, the shadow moves and changes in length. By designing a sundial so that adjustments can be made for the location on Earth and the time of year, a person can keep an accurate record of time.

After You Read

1. Which type of measurement can be made using a graduated cylinder? Describe how to use this tool.
2. How many milliseconds are in five seconds?
3. Review your chart of measurements. Which units are base units in the SI system? Which units are derived units? Explain your answers.

Teach

EXPLAIN that temperature is a measure of the amount of movement of the molecules in a substance. The faster the molecules move, the higher the temperature. Absolute zero on the Kelvin scale corresponds to the theoretical state of an object in which molecules are completely motionless. While scientists have come close, they have not yet been able to cool a substance to a state in which all molecular movement ceases.

Figure It Out: Figure 1.19

ANSWER **1.** 37°C **2.** No. On the Celsius scale, the range is 100 degrees (100–0). On the Fahrenheit scale, the range is 180 degrees (212–32).

CONNECTION: Social Studies

Have students create their own sundials using paper plates or cardboard circles. On a sunny day, students can use them to tell the time. Have them write in their Science Notebooks about the advantages and disadvantages of using a sundial to tell time.

Assess

EVALUATE Use the After You Read questions and the Alternative Assessment to help you assess students' understanding of this lesson.

After You Read

1. Measurements of liquid volume and the volume of irregular solids are made with a graduated cylinder. A liquid is added to the cylinder, and then the level of the bottom of the meniscus is read at eye level.
2. 5,000 ms
3. The meter, kilogram, Kelvin, and second are base units. Volume and density are derived units because they consist of more than one base unit.

Background Information

The sundial is the oldest-known device for telling the time. Its first recorded use was in Babylon in the year 2000 B.C. Clocks as we know them were not invented until A.D. 1400. A sundial is made up of two parts: the plane (or dial face) and the gnomon (or style). The gnomon is a flat piece of metal that points toward the north or south pole, depending on the hemisphere in which it is used. The gnomon is shaped such that the upper edge slants away from the dial face at an angle equal to the latitude of the sundial's location.

Alternative Assessment

EVALUATE Provide students with several different items, including regular and irregular solids and liquids. Have students find the volume, mass, and density of each item.

Chapter 1 Summary

VOCABULARY REVIEW

Check students' sentences or paragraphs to make sure they understand the meaning of each vocabulary term.

PREPARE FOR CHAPTER TEST

Before students begin their essays, review the process for writing explanatory or descriptive paragraphs. Go over the elements of paragraph structure, including main idea/topic sentence, supporting sentences, and concluding sentence.

Evaluate students' essays using the following criteria:

1. The topic sentence, or main idea, should restate the Key Concept.
2. The supporting paragraphs should incorporate the answers to the Learning Goal questions students have written and include details, facts, and examples they have recorded in their Science Notebooks.
3. The concluding sentence should summarize the main idea of the chapter and restate the Key Concept.

MASTERING CONCEPTS

True or False

1. True
2. False, hypothesis
3. False, independent
4. False, data
5. False, volume
6. True

Short Answer

7. Alike: all three branches study the natural world; different: focus on different aspects of the natural world
8. A hypothesis must be testable in order to find out whether it is false. If it is proved false, the hypothesis can be discarded and a new one written. If it is not proved false, the test is repeated to confirm the result, or additional tests are designed to test it in different ways.
9. Controlled experiments involve an independent variable, which is purposely changed during the experiment, and a dependent variable, which is observed to find out if and how it changes as a result of changes in the independent variable.

Chapter 1

Summary

KEY CONCEPTS

1.1 What Is Science?

- Science is a process of observation and investigation through which information about the natural world is learned.
- The branches of science are life science, Earth and space science, and physical science.
- Life scientists focus on different fields such as botany, zoology, ecology, and microbiology.

1.2 How Is Science Studied?

- The scientific method is an organized process of obtaining evidence to learn about the natural world.
- Scientists make observations, ask questions, develop hypotheses, conduct experiments, analyze data, and draw conclusions.
- The steps of the scientific method are not always followed in the same order or in the same way.
- A hypothesis is a proposed answer to a scientific question.

1.3 Measurements in Science

- SI base units include the meter for length, the kilogram for mass, the kelvin for temperature, and the second for time. The liter, for volume, is a non-SI unit.
- Derived units are made up of two or more base units. Volume is a derived unit. Density is a derived unit made up of a unit of mass divided by a unit of volume.

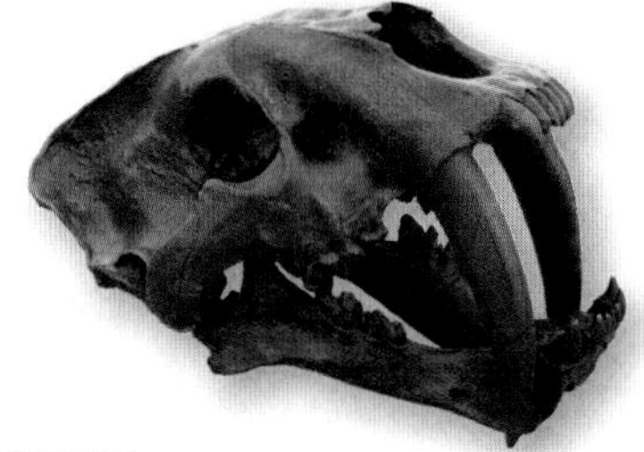

VOCABULARY REVIEW

Write each term in a complete sentence, or write a paragraph relating several terms.

1.1
science, p. 4

1.2
scientific method, p. 7
observation, p. 7
hypothesis, p. 8
experiment, p. 8
variable, p. 8
controlled experiment, p. 8
independent variable, p. 8
dependent variable, p. 8
control group, p. 9
experimental group, p. 9
safety symbol, p. 10
data, p. 10
conclusion, p. 11
theory, p. 12
prediction, p. 12

1.3
measurement, p. 13
International System of Units (SI), p. 13
mass, p. 14
volume, p. 15
meniscus, p. 15
derived unit, p. 15
density, p. 16

PREPARE FOR CHAPTER TEST

To prepare for the chapter test, create a question from each Learning Goal. Use the information in your Science Notebook to answer each question. Then use these answers to write a well-developed essay about the chapter. Use the Key Concept on the first page of this chapter as your topic sentence.

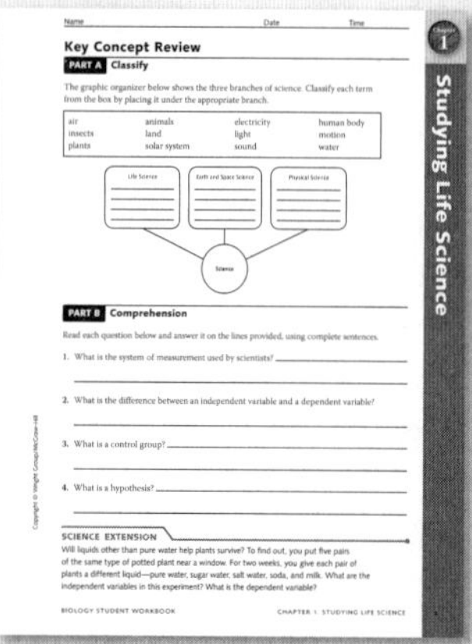

Key Concept Review Workbook, p. 1

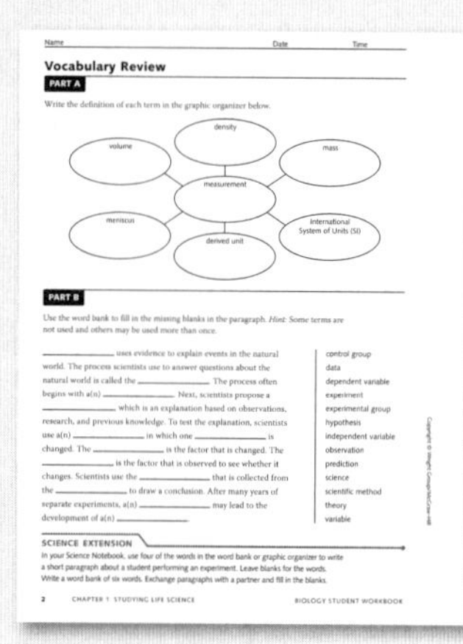

Vocabulary Review Workbook, p. 2

MASTERING CONCEPTS

True or False

If the statement is true, write "true." If it is false, change the underlined word or words to make the statement true.

1. The amount of salt in ocean water is a topic of study in <u>Earth and space</u> science.
2. A <u>conclusion</u> is an educated guess that attempts to explain an observation.
3. The variable that a scientist changes during an experiment is called the <u>dependent</u> variable.
4. The facts, figures, and other evidence obtained during an experiment make up the <u>hypothesis</u>.
5. A graduated cylinder is used to measure the <u>length</u> of an object.
6. The <u>mass</u> of an object is measured with a balance.

Short Answer

Answer each of the following in a sentence or brief paragraph.

7. Describe how the three branches of science are alike. Describe how they are different.
8. Explain why a hypothesis needs to be testable.
9. What are the two types of variables in a controlled experiment? Distinguish between them.
10. Discuss why using a common system of measurement is useful to scientists.
11. A student pours 14.2 mL of water into a graduated cylinder. She then places a stone in the cylinder. The meniscus of the water rises to 18.8 mL. Calculate the volume of the stone.

Critical Thinking

Use what you have learned in this chapter to answer each of the following.

12. **Infer** Plants take in carbon dioxide and release oxygen during photosynthesis. A researcher places ten plants in separate containers. Nine of the plants receive different levels of carbon dioxide. After a period of time, the researcher measures the amount of oxygen produced by each plant. Propose a possible hypothesis for this experiment.

13. **Compare and Contrast** Compare the figures. Which object has a greater volume?

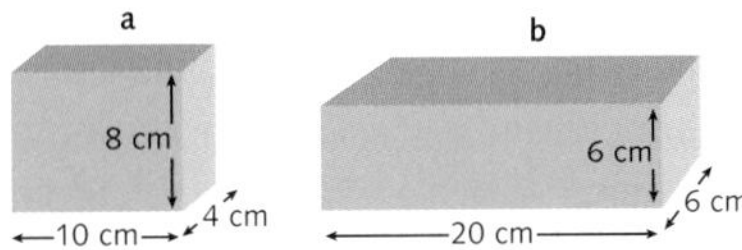

14. **Sequence** List and describe the steps you could follow to find the density of a marble.

Standardized Test Question

Choose the letter of the response that correctly answers the question.

The Effect of Temperature on Germination

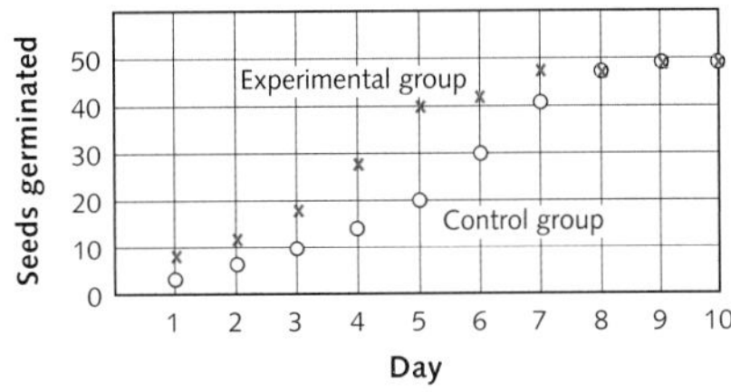

15. A team of scientists measured the number of seeds that germinated (grew into plants). A control group was kept at 18°C and an experimental group at 25°C. The graph shows their data. According to the data, what is the independent variable in the experiment?
    - A. the number of seeds they studied
    - B. the number of seeds that germinated
    - C. the temperature of the seeds
    - D. the type of seeds they used

Test-Taking Tip

Quickly look over the entire test so you know how to use your time wisely. Allow more time for sections of the test that look the most difficult.

10. Using a common system of measurement enables scientists all over the world to use the same values when describing quantities. This helps them communicate effectively and enables them to repeat each other's experiments using the same design.
11. 18.8 mL – 14.2 mL = 4.6 mL

Critical Thinking

12. A possible hypothesis would be that the amount of oxygen a plant gives off as a result of photosynthesis depends on the amount of carbon dioxide it takes in. (Note: If tested, this hypothesis would be found to be false.)
13. The volume of Object a is 320 cm^3, and the volume of Object b is 720 cm^3. Object b has the greater volume.
14. First, use a balance to find the marble's mass. Then, place it in a graduated cylinder partially filled with water to find its volume. Dividing the mass by the volume will give its density.

Standardized Test Question

15. C

Reading Links

Science at the Extreme: Scientists on the Cutting Edge of Discovery

Photojournalist Taylor follows nine scientists to harsh and exotic frontiers, from glacial cores to active volcanoes, where they risk their lives to collect data. Through engaging narrative and startling photography, this insider's look at the scientific discovery process transports readers far away from the laboratory.

Taylor, Peter Lane. McGraw-Hill. Illustrated with over 100 original photographs. 256 pp. Trade ISBN 978-0-07-140029-9.

Letters from Yellowstone

This fictional account of a Smithsonian-sponsored field study in the spring of 1898 is told entirely through letters and other correspondence. Its protagonist, a spirited young botanist who conceals the fact that she is a woman, broadens her view of science and current controversial issues as she explores the American wilderness with a quirky team of specialists.

Smith, Diane. Penguin Books. 256 pp. Trade ISBN 978-0-14-029181-0.

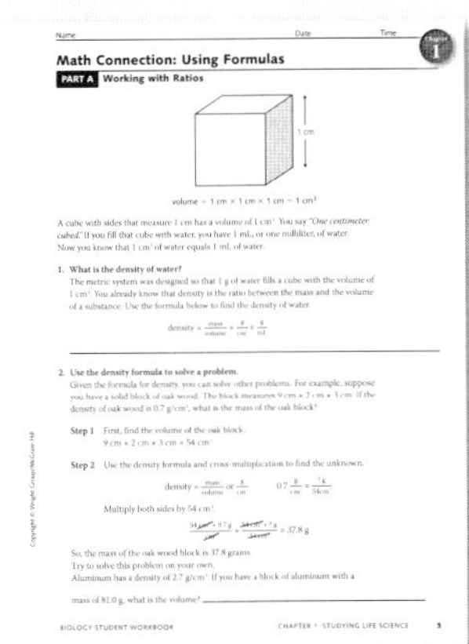

Curriculum Connection Workbook, pp. 5–6

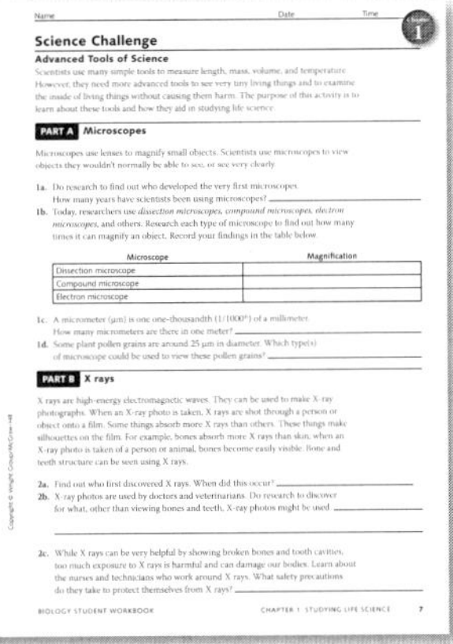

Science Challenge Workbook, pp. 7–8

CHAPTER 1 19

Chapter 1

Labs

1A Can You Explain This?

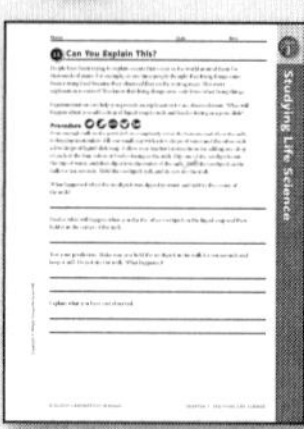

This prechapter introduction activity is designed to determine what students already know about conducting an experiment and managing variables by engaging them in making observations, predictions, and inferences; conducting an experiment; and identifying variables.

Objectives

- conduct a controlled experiment
- make predictions
- identify independent and dependent variables
- make inferences

Planning

 1 class period  groups of 2–4 students

Materials (per group)

- petri dish
- 2 toothpicks
- food coloring (4 colors)
- whole milk
- water
- liquid dish soap
- 2 small cups (one for water and one for soap)
- pencil and paper

Lab Tip

Avoid using liquid soap that has a strong perfume additive.

Advance Preparation

- Direct students as they place drops of food coloring in the milk. Each drop must be placed halfway between the center and the edge of the petri dish. If the petri dish were a clock, red should be at twelve o'clock, blue at three o'clock, green at six o'clock, and yellow at nine o'clock. Spreading out the colors this way creates a swirling rainbow effect.
- The fat and protein molecules in whole milk bend and twist when the soap is added. As the molecules in the food coloring collide, they create the swirling activity of the milk and soap.

Engagement Guide

- Challenge students to think about how to conduct a controlled experiment. Introduce the differences between an independent variable and a dependent variable by asking:
  - *Which substance changed the outcome of your experiment?* (Introduce and discuss independent and dependent variables. Soap caused the swirling of colors in the milk. Therefore, the soap is the independent variable. The swirling of the milk is the dependent variable because it was the result of the change.)
  - *How many variables should be tested at one time during a controlled experiment?* (Testing one variable at a time allows a researcher to determine which variable affected the results. For example, changing the soap brand and the type of milk at one time would not allow for determination of the variable that affected the results.
- After the discussion, have students write their own definitions of the terms *variable, independent variable, dependent variable,* and *controlled experiment.* Having students create their own meanings for concepts will help them better understand what the concept or word means in science.

Going Further

Encourage students to repeat this activity using different types of milk (skim, 1%, and 2%) or different brands of liquid soap. Have students present their conclusions to the class.

1B Identifying Peapods

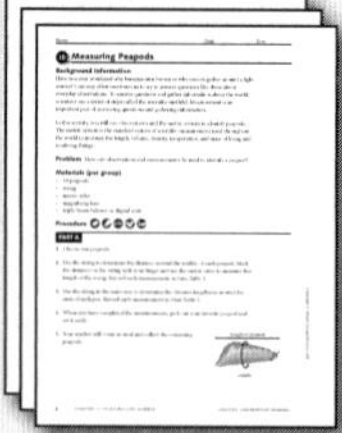

Objectives

- make observations
- record observations
- measure irregular objects

Skill Set

observing, comparing and contrasting, recording and analyzing data, measuring

Planning

 1 class period  groups of 2 students

Materials

Materials for this activity are listed in the Student Laboratory Manual.

Advanced Preparation

Use only washed peapods. Have students wash their hands with soap after working with the peapods. Place all the peapods for Part A in one large container. Have each group take ten peapods from this container.

Answers to Observations: Data Table 1

Students' measurements will vary. Be sure the students measure in mm, not cm.

Answers to Observations: Data Table 2

Students' answers will vary. Encourage students to use their senses as they observe the peapods and record their descriptions. Descriptions should include size, shape, color, and unusual markings.

Answers to Analysis and Conclusions

1. The end measurements are approximately twice as long as the middle measurements.
2. Answers will vary.
3. Answers will be based on the drawing and the written description of distinct characteristics.
4. The metric system and SI units are used by all scientists to communicate observations without confusion.

Going Further

- Repeat the procedure using other objects in place of peapods, such as plant leaves, shells, or rocks.
- Instead of using the book's data table, use the data collected by students to create a class-specific data group. Students can use this to compare their data with their own classmates' and with data from other classes in the school.
- Many students think the scientific method is a step-by-step process that all scientists follow. In a lab, scientists do follow protocols and have certain methods for doing experiments. However, scientists do not follow a written guide to research. Creative processes influence the scientific method for any given scientist. It is important to push for students to think creatively when designing their own experiments.
- Have students list measurements/units that they use in their daily lives. Then, have them list measurements used in science class. Compare these lists. Ask students to point out similarities and differences between these lists. Next, make a third list labeled *SI Units*. Explain to students that because science is a worldwide endeavor, scientists need to use the same units when doing experiments. List and describe the SI units that are used in your class. This will help students better understand the answer to question 4.

1C Design an Experiment

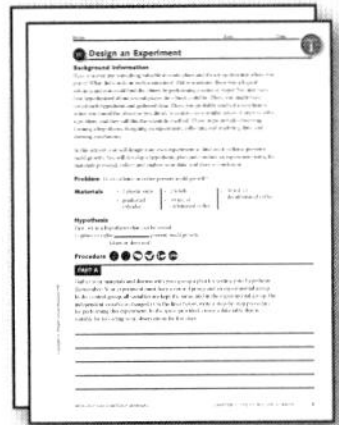

Objectives

- apply the scientific method
- measure using a graduated cylinder
- record observations
- make predictions
- draw conclusions

Skill Set

measuring, observing, comparing and contrasting, recording and analyzing data, stating conclusions

Planning

1 class period (plus one week for observations during class)

groups of 2–4 students

Materials

Materials for this activity are listed in the Student Laboratory Manual.

Lab Tip

Cover the cups with plastic wrap to control spills and contain mold spores. Poke several holes in the wrap.

Advance Preparation

Prepare 12 cups of caffeinated coffee and 12 cups of decaffeinated coffee (instant or brewed). You can set a limit of 30 mL of coffee per cup. Pour the coffee into pots, and label each pot for students. **CAUTION:** *Let the coffee cool. Do not give students hot coffee.* **CAUTION:** *Some students may be allergic to mold spores or have an asthmatic reaction. Have students wash their hands with soap after working with mold.*

Answers to Procedure A

Students' procedures will vary but should include the following:

1. Put on your lab apron and safety goggles.
2. Use the labels to identify each cup. Write your group name and *Caffeinated Coffee* on one label and your group name and *Decaffeinated Coffee* on the second label.
3. Add 30 mL of caffeinated coffee to the first cup and 30 mL of decaffeinated coffee to the second cup.
4. Place both cups, uncovered, in the same location.
5. Make daily observations of your cups for five days. Check for the presence of mold. Record the observations in your data table.

Answers to Observations: Data Table 1

Students' data tables will vary but should include columns titled *Day, Caffeinated Coffee,* and *Decaffeinated Coffee* and rows indicating each day of the experiment.

Observation answers will vary depending on how fast the mold grows. Students should begin to see growth within a few days and should record their observations in the data table.

Answers to Analysis and Conclusions

1. Both types of coffee allow mold to grow.
2. Answers will vary according to the hypotheses. Caffeine does not prevent mold growth.
3. Control: decaffeinated coffee; independent variable: caffeinated coffee; dependent variable: mold growth
4. Experimenting provides evidence and data that can be used to solve a problem.
5. solving a problem by making observations, asking questions, developing a hypothesis, designing an experiment, collecting and analyzing data, and drawing conclusions

Going Further

Have each student write a different question he or she would like to investigate and then, with your approval, design and perform an experiment to explore that question.

Chapter 2 Lessons

Introduce Chapter 2

As a starting activity, use LAB 2A Is It Alive? on page 7 of the Laboratory Manual.

ENGAGE students by asking them to sketch a picture of a mountain with streams flowing downhill. Students should connect the streams to form a brook and then a river or small lake. Have them include a few fish, other animals, and plants that might inhabit the area. Students can share their drawings with a partner.

Think About Living and Nonliving Things

ENGAGE students by asking them to close their eyes and picture what they see when they leave their homes to come to school in the morning. Ask: *Do you see other people? Plants? Cars driving down the street?* Encourage students to really see and hear their surroundings in their minds.

During the next class, ask students if they noticed anything different as they left their homes in the morning.

Direct students to make a T-chart in their Science Notebooks. As a class, brainstorm a list of ten things from everyday life for students to record in their T-charts. Record students' ideas in a T-chart on the board, and help them classify each thing as living or nonliving. Ask students to explain their reasoning as they identify the objects as living or nonliving.

Chapter 2 The Nature of Life

KEY CONCEPT Living things share the same characteristics and have similar needs.

High on a mountaintop, water collects and begins to flow downhill. Animals from all around come to drink from the brook and find food. Along the brook, a variety of trees and other plants grow.

Although the water flows from one place to another, grows in size, and changes shape, it is not alive. What is the difference between living and nonliving things? Scientists use specific characteristics to define the exact nature of life.

www.scilinks.org
Characteristics of Living Things
Code: WGB02

Think About Living and Nonliving Things

You may take for granted that you know the difference between living and nonliving things. Think about the characteristics you use when deciding if something is living or nonliving.

- In your Science Notebook, make a T-chart. Label one column *Living* and the other *Nonliving*. List at least ten things from your daily life in each column.
- At the bottom of each column, write some of the characteristics of the items in the column. For example, do all of the living things breathe or eat? Review your choices as you read the chapter.

20

Chapter 2 Planning Guide

Instructional Periods	National Standards	Lab Manual	Workbook
2.1 2 periods	A.1, C.1, C.2, C.3, C.5, F.1; C.1, C.6; UCP.1	**Lab 2A—p. 7** Is It Alive? **Lab 2B—p. 8** Organic Molecules for Lunch? **Lab 2C— p. 10** Enzyme Summary	Key Concept Review p. 9 Vocabulary Review p. 10 Interpreting Diagrams p. 11 Reading Comprehension p. 12 Curriculum Connection p. 13 Science Challenge p. 14
2.2 2 periods	B.3, C.3; A.2, B.3, B.6, C.3, C4, C.5; UCP.2		
2.3 2 periods	B.2, B.3, C.2, C.5, F.1; UCP.3		

Middle School Standard; High School Standard; Unifying Concept and Principle

2.1 Characteristics of Living Things

Before You Read

Create a concept map in your Science Notebook. Write and circle the title *Living Things*. Draw five circles surrounding the title. Draw lines connecting each circle to the title. Without writing in the circles, predict some of the characteristics that you will use to fill them in as you read the lesson.

Learning Goals

- Identify the characteristics of living things.
- Classify items as living or nonliving.

New Vocabulary

organism
cell
stimulus
response
homeostasis
adaptation
reproduction
species

Polar bears search for food in the icy waters near the North Pole. Toucans fly among the branches of the rain forests of Brazil. Outside your window, a grasshopper might munch on a leaf. Wherever you look, you will find that Earth's environments are filled with living things. Another name for a living thing is an **organism**.

Many organisms, such as those in **Figure 2.1**, are easy to recognize as living. But often, deciding whether something is living or nonliving is not that simple. For example, the Spanish moss hanging from the tree in **Figure 2.2** does not do many of the things an animal does. The moss, however, is very much alive.

Scientists use several characteristics to describe something as living. Many nonliving things can display *some* of these characteristics. However, living things display *all* of these characteristics.

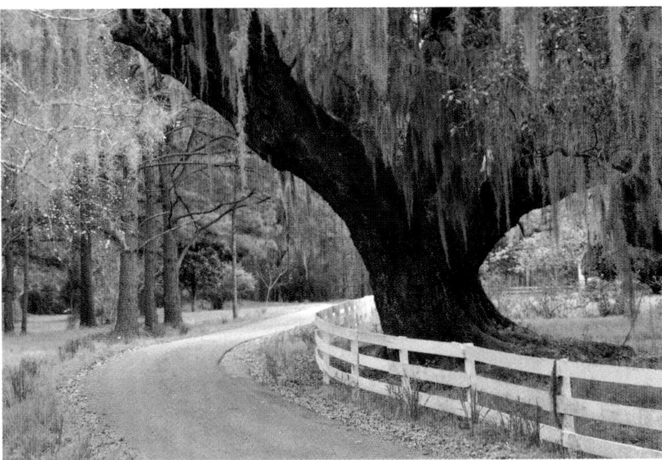

Figure 2.2 Spanish moss is an air plant that grows from tree branches in warm, humid climates. It does not have roots like other plants. Instead, it absorbs what it needs from the air.

Figure 2.1 Bears, birds, and insects are examples of living things. What are some of the characteristics of these organisms?

2.1 Introduce

EXPLAIN Tell students that they will be learning the differences between living and nonliving things. Living things have specific characteristics that scientists use to distinguish them from nonliving things.

EXPLORE what students already know about the idea of living v. nonliving by arranging the following objects on a table: stuffed animal, small fishbowl with fish, toy car, live plant, artificial plant, closed container of live insects or worms, bowl of gelatin. Have students observe the objects, noting their characteristics. Then, have students label each object *living* or *nonliving*.

Before You Read

Review concept maps with the class. If needed, complete a map with the whole class based on an accessible example, such as "Favorite Hobbies." Elicit responses from students to fill the circles. Responses might include playing music, sports, or computer games.

Vocabulary terms are listed on the first student page of each lesson. You may wish to preview the terms before introducing each lesson. Strategies for teaching the vocabulary appear on the pages where the terms are introduced.

Teach

EXPLAIN that students will be learning about characteristics that scientists use to classify items as living or nonliving. Discuss the idea that items can be classified as living only if they display all of the characteristics of living things. Refer back to the objects students classified previously, and talk about the characteristics they identified. Start a list on the board of characteristics of living things.

ELL Strategy

Illustrate Ask students to illustrate vocabulary words in their Science Notebooks by drawing, sketching, or using symbols to represent the words. For additional learning and practice, students could work with partners to paraphrase the meaning of each vocabulary word next to their illustrations.

Vocabulary

organism Point out that the root of *organism* is *organ*, which is a part of a plant or animal that has a specific function. The suffix *-ism* means "a characteristic behavior or quality." Tell students that most organisms are made up of organs and organ systems.

Use the Visual: Figure 2.1

ANSWER They all eat, breathe, and move.

Science Notebook EXTRA

Encourage students to use the vocabulary section they created in their Science Notebooks. Remind them to record prefixes, suffixes, and root words to help them remember the meanings of vocabulary terms.

Teach

EXPLAIN to students that they will be learning about the cell, which is the basic unit of life. Some living things are made up of only one cell and are called unicellular organisms. Multicellular organisms are made up of more than one cell. Discuss with students the definitions of the prefixes *uni-* (one) and *multi-* (many), and encourage them to write these prefixes in their Science Notebooks.

As You Read

Ask students to return to their concept maps and predictions about characteristics of living things. Explain that the headings on pages 22–24 are the five characteristics of living things and that students should replace any characteristics on their maps that do not correspond to these characteristics. Model writing the first heading in the map drawn on the board.

Vocabulary

cell Explain that a cell is the smallest part of an organism. Cells are considered the "building blocks" of organisms. Encourage students to think about common uses of the word *cell*, and discuss them with the class. Students might mention a prison cell, a matrix cell, or a cell phone.

stimulus Ask students what happens when they encounter a bright light suddenly, such as when they go outside on a sunny day after being in a movie theater or turn on a light when they just wake up. Explain that their reaction is called a response and that the bright light is considered a stimulus (a condition or event in the surroundings).

response Tell students that the Latin word *respondēre* is composed of *re-*, meaning "back," and *spondēre,* meaning "to promise." Ask what their response would be if they touched something very hot. (They would move their hand away.)

homeostasis Tell students that *homeo-* means "similar" or "same" and that *-stasis* means "standing" or "stopping." Ask students to relate these meanings to the idea that homeostasis is a stable state of internal conditions an organism is able to maintain in order to survive.

Figure It Out: Figure 2.4

ANSWER **1.** a microscope
2. 100,000,000,000,000

As You Read

Read the headings listing the characteristics of living things. Write the headings in the circles of your concept map.

How do these characteristics compare with your predictions?

Living Things Are Made Up of Cells

What does a giant elephant have in common with a tiny mouse? They are both made up of smaller units called cells. A **cell** is a structure that contains all of the materials needed for life. Each cell is separated from its surroundings by a barrier called a cell membrane. A cell is the smallest unit of an organism that can be considered alive. All living things are made up of cells.

Figure 2.3 All living things, large and small, are made up of cells. Larger organisms, such as elephants, have more cells than do smaller organisms, such as field mice.

Some organisms are made up of only one cell. These organisms, called unicellular organisms, carry out all of their functions in just one cell. Multicellular organisms are made up of more than one cell. Most of the organisms with which you are familiar are multicellular. Some of these organisms are made up of millions or even trillions of cells. In many of these organisms, different types of cells perform specific functions. Groups of cells work together to keep an organism alive.

Figure It Out

1. What tool do scientists use to see cells?
2. An adult human is estimated to have one hundred trillion cells. How is this number expressed?

Figure 2.4 This bird is made up of many cells. Some of these cells are blood cells. Together, the bird's cells carry out all the processes needed for the bird to survive.

Background Information

All cells—whether they are specialized cells or one-celled organisms—"breathe," take in nutrients, rid themselves of wastes, grow, reproduce, and die. In multicellular organisms, cells are specialized and work together to form tissues, such as muscle tissue. Different kinds of tissues form organs, such as the heart, the kidneys, and the lungs. Related organs form organ systems, such as the circulatory system and the digestive system. All of these specialized cells, tissues, organs, and organ systems together form a complete organism, such as a human or a fish.

A cell has a membrane that serves as its "skin" and envelopes the cell's contents. Collectively, the contents are called protoplasm. The cell's nucleus is the brain or operating center of the cell. It contains the genetic material that tells the cell how to function. The cytoplasm is all the protoplasm outside the nucleus, including the other cell organelles and structures.

Living Things Respond to Their Environment

Has a doctor ever shined a light into your eyes during a checkup? The doctor was checking to see if the dark center of each eye, the pupil, would change in size as a result of the light. A condition or event in your surroundings, such as the doctor's light, is called a **stimulus** (STIHM yuh lus, plural: stimuli). A change that happens because of a stimulus, such as a change in the size of your pupils, is known as a **response**. All living things can sense stimuli and respond to them.

Light is just one type of stimulus. Other stimuli include darkness, chemicals, sounds, tastes, and touch. You might think that only animals can respond to stimuli. This is not the case. Although plants cannot get up and move, they can change the way in which they grow in response to stimuli. Many plants can grow toward sunlight and water, for example. Others, such as the plant in **Figure 2.5**, bend to curl around objects that they touch.

Not all stimuli are external, or outside living things. Living things also respond to stimuli that occur inside them. They do so in order to regulate their internal surroundings and maintain conditions necessary for survival. The process by which living things respond to stimuli in ways that allow them to maintain and balance internal conditions necessary for life is called **homeostasis** (hoh mee oh STAY sus). Through homeostasis, living things maintain characteristic internal temperature ranges and the correct amounts of water and minerals in their cells. Homeostasis is a characteristic of all living things.

Figure 2.5 This climbing plant has parts called tendrils that coil when they touch solid objects.

 **Explore It!**

Your body responds to physical activity by changing your heart rate. This is the number of times your heart beats each minute. Design and conduct an activity that compares the heart rate before and after an action such as jumping rope or climbing stairs.

Living Things Can Adapt

Organisms depend on certain traits to help them survive. The hedgehog in **Figure 2.6** has stiff spines that protect it from predators, or animals that might eat it. Any trait that helps an organism survive in its environment is called an **adaptation**. Other adaptations help organisms attract mates, obtain food, build homes, and survive in harsh weather conditions.

An adaptation such as the hedgehog's stiff spines does not develop during an organism's life. Instead, adaptations develop over many generations as conditions in the environment change. In order to survive, living things must be able to adapt.

Living Things Reproduce

Living things make more organisms like themselves in a process called **reproduction**. A group of organisms that has similar physical characteristics and can mate to produce offspring capable of reproducing their own offspring is called a **species** (SPEE sheez). Lions, tigers, and panthers are different species of cats.

Figure 2.6 When this hedgehog feels threatened, it rolls into a ball. This causes the spines to point outward. How does this adaptation help the hedgehog survive?

Teach

EXPLAIN to students that they will be thinking about two more ways to identify whether or not things are living. The ability to respond and adapt allows organisms to survive in adverse and changing environments.

Science Notebook EXTRA

Ask students to think of examples of stimuli that affect humans and other animals and then to write a few examples in their Science Notebooks. Pairs of students can share their lists of stimuli.

 **Explore It!**

Students should select a safe activity such as walking for one minute. They should then measure their own or another student's heart rate before and after the activity. The heart rate can be measured by locating the pulse in the neck or wrist, counting the pulse for 15 seconds, and then multiplying that number by four.

Explain that the heart pumps blood filled with oxygen through the body. When the body performs physical exercise, it needs more oxygen. As a result, the heart beats faster to meet the demand for oxygen. The exercise is the stimulus, and the increase in heart rate is the response.

Differentiated Instruction

Kinesthetic To check student understanding and to reinforce the concepts of adaptation and response to environment, ask student pairs to explore one of the two concepts using movement. Make available some materials to use in skits or pantomimes, such as markers and large paper. Invite pairs to demonstrate their concepts to the class, and ask the other students which concept is being shown.

Use the Visual: Figure 2.6

EXTEND Use a soft-backed hairbrush to demonstrate the hedgehog's response to threat. Roll it so that the bristles stand out. Pass the hairbrush around so that students can bend and feel the difference between the bristles in the two configurations.

ANSWER It helps the hedgehog avoid being eaten.

 **Vocabulary**

adaptation Tell students that adaptations are changes in structure, form, or habits that fit different conditions. For example, birds' wings are adaptations of the front limbs for flight. Explain to students that the verb form of the word, *adapt*, can be found in the noun.

reproduction Ask students what the root word *produce* means. Tell them that the answer is "to bring forth or bear." Explain that the prefix *re-* is Latin and means "again."

species Tell students that the origin of *species* is a Latin word meaning "kind" or "sort."

Teach

EXPLAIN to students that there are two basic types of reproduction. In sexual reproduction, cells from two different parents join together to produce the first cell of the offspring. In asexual reproduction, only one parent produces offspring.

Figure It Out: Figure 2.6

ANSWER **1.** tadpole **2.** A tadpole lives exclusively in the water. When the tadpole metamorphoses into a frog, the frog lives both on land and in water.

Assess

EVALUATE Use the After You Read questions and the Alternative Assessment to help you assess students' understanding of the lesson.

After You Read

1. All living things are made up of cells, respond to their environment, can adapt, reproduce, and grow and develop.
2. Smelling food or an empty stomach might be a stimulus. A response might be to eat or to check the time in order to know when the next meal is due.
3. Reproduction is essential to the continuation of the species but not the organism. As a species, organisms must reproduce in order to be considered living even if not every individual reproduces.
4. A raindrop is made up of water. Water is not made of cells and cannot adapt to its environment. A leaf, however, is made up of cells and is part of a tree that is alive.

Alternative Assessment

EVALUATE Have students make a T-chart, labeling one column *Living* and the other *Nonliving*. Ask students who have difficulty reading and English-language learners to draw pictures of things that are living and nonliving and place them on their T-charts.

Figure 2.7 A female sea turtle lays eggs in a hole she digs on the beach. When the young turtles hatch, they dig their way out and then use clues from the environment to find their way back to the ocean. When they grow up, they will produce another generation of turtles so the species can survive.

Figure It Out

1. What is the first stage in a frog's life?
2. Describe how a frog's place in its environment changes as the frog grows and develops.

Reproduction is essential to the continuation of a species. This means that while not every single organism has to reproduce, members of a species must be able to reproduce so that the species continues to exist on Earth. For example, not every single sea turtle will produce offspring. However, many sea turtles must reproduce or the species will eventually become extinct, or die out.

Living Things Grow and Develop

All living things grow and develop at some point in their lives. For unicellular organisms, growth usually means that the cell becomes larger. Multicellular organisms go through a more complex process of development. They each begin as a single cell that divides into two cells. Each new cell then divides again. This process continues over and over again to produce the many cells of the organism.

In addition, some organisms go through periods of dramatic change. **Figure 2.8** shows the development of a frog. Even humans experience periods of rapid growth at different points in their lives.

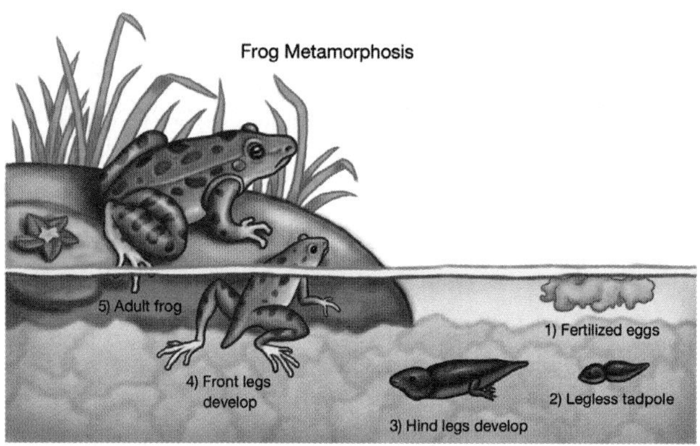

Figure 2.8 An adult frog looks and acts very different from the way it does in its younger form.

After You Read

1. Review your concept map. Use it to list five characteristics of all living things.
2. What type of stimulus might make you feel hungry? What might your response be?
3. Why can an organism be considered living even if it never reproduces?
4. A raindrop grows and becomes larger. It is made up of smaller units, and it moves from a cloud to the ground. Why isn't a raindrop considered living, while a leaf that it falls on is?

Background Information

Responses can be conditioned (learned) or reflexive. Ivan Pavlov was a physiologist who did a famous experiment with dogs to induce conditioned responses. Every time he fed the animals (a natural stimulus that caused the dogs to salivate), he would ring a bell to create an artificial stimulus. Eventually, the dogs would salivate when they heard the bell ring even if they were not being fed. Pavlov was born on September 26, 1849, in Ryazan, Russia, and was educated in Russia and Germany. He won the 1904 Nobel Prize in Physiology or Medicine for his research on digestion. He died on February 27, 1936.

2.2 The Needs of Living Things

Before You Read

In your Science Notebook, make a list of things you would like to have. Classify the items on your list as things you want and things you truly need. Label each item in the list accordingly. Write a few sentences describing the difference between a want and a need.

Learning Goals

- Examine the needs of living things.
- Recognize the importance of water to life on Earth.

New Vocabulary

energy
photosynthesis
autotroph
heterotroph
solvent
endotherm
ectotherm

You have decided to grow a tomato plant. Do you pour the seeds into an empty pot and put the pot in a closet? Not if you ever hope to see tomatoes. Instead, you must add soil to the pot, give the seeds water, and place the pot in sunlight.

Like the tomato plant, all living things have certain needs that must be met in order for them to survive. While the needs of every organism are not exactly the same, they fall into several general categories.

Energy

Living cells need energy for their life processes. **Energy** is the ability to cause change or do work. Many organisms obtain the energy they need from sunlight. Plants, some bacteria, and most algae get energy in this way. In a process called **photosynthesis** (foh toh SIHN thuh sus), these organisms change the energy of sunlight into energy that can be stored. At the same time, they take nonliving matter from the air, soil, and water. Plants store matter and energy in the substances that form their bodies. Organisms that capture matter and energy from their surroundings are called **autotrophs** (AW tuh trohfs). Autotrophs are also called producers.

Figure 2.9 Tomato plants have needs that must be met in order for them to grow and produce tomatoes. What are some of the needs of tomato plants?

When organisms that conduct photosynthesis need energy, they break down certain substances in their bodies to supply energy to their cells. If organisms that conduct photosynthesis, such as plants, are eaten as food, the stored energy is passed on. The animals in **Figure 2.10** obtain stored matter and energy, or food, when they eat grasses. Like plants, these animals use some of the energy and store the rest. Organisms that do not feed on plants get matter and energy by eating organisms that do eat plants. Organisms that get matter and energy by eating plants or other organisms are called **heterotrophs** (HE tuh roh trohfs). Heterotrophs are also called consumers.

Figure 2.10 Grazing animals, such as this gazelle and zebra, get energy by eating plants. This energy is passed along to animals that eat them, such as lions. What are organisms such as gazelles, zebras, and lions called? Why?

2.2 Introduce

ENGAGE students by asking them to think about a living thing for which they have been responsible. Ask: *How did you care for this living thing? What types of things did it need daily?* Ask students to tell a partner about the living thing and the care necessary to sustain its life. Together, they should list the care they provided for the living things.

EXPLAIN Tell students that they will learn more about the needs of living things as they read and discuss this lesson.

Before You Read

Emphasize the difference between what students may want and what they need in order to survive. Discuss examples.

Teach

EXPLAIN that students will learn what living things need to live, grow and develop, and reproduce. Emphasize that plants and animals have similar needs. Have students relate these needs to the characteristics of all living things.

Vocabulary

energy Explain that the word *energy* is derived from the Greek language. The prefix *en-* means "in," and the root *ergon* means "to work."

photosynthesis Ask students what the prefix *photo-* means. Provide some examples, such as *photograph*. Tell them the answer is "light." Explain that *photosynthesis* contains two more parts: *syn-*, meaning "together," and *tithénai*, meaning "to put or place."

autotroph Explain that *auto-* means "self" or "same one" and that the root *troph* means "nutritive." Ask students to use these meanings to define the word *autotroph*.

heterotroph Tell students that the meaning of the prefix *hetero-* is "other" or "different." Have them explain the meaning of *heterotroph* using the meanings of the prefix and root.

ELL Strategy

Sequencing Have students work in pairs to draw a sequence chart in their Science Notebooks demonstrating their understanding of the concept of energy. The first item in the chart should be sunlight. Students should then add the next item to the chart, a plant, using words or pictures. Have them continue until the chart is complete.

Use the Visual: Figure 2.9

ANSWER soil, water, sunlight, air, a place to grow, and fertilizer

Use the Visual: Figure 2.10

ANSWER These organisms are called heterotrophs because they get energy by eating other organisms.

Teach

EXPLAIN to students that in this lesson, they will learn about the importance of water to all living things. They will also learn about the role of water within those living things. Help students understand the idea that about 60 percent of the human body is water. Create a pie chart to show how much 60 percent is.

EXPLORE Discuss the role water plays as a solvent. To help students understand this concept, demonstrate the dissolving of several substances in water. You might use sugar, salt, vegetable coloring, lemon juice, or carbon dioxide (exhale through a straw into the water). Have students identify each substance as solid, liquid, or gas.

Vocabulary

solvent Ask students if they have ever made a beverage by combining a dry mix with water. Tell students that in this example, water is the *solvent*, the substance in which the drink mix dissolves.

endotherm Explain to students that the prefix *endo-* means "within" and that the root *therm* means "heat." Animals that are endothermic are capable of producing their own heat from within their bodies.

ectotherm Tell students that the prefix *ecto-* means "outside." *Ectotherm* is the opposite of *endotherm*; that is, ectotherms are organisms that take on the temperature of their environment.

Use the Visual: Figure 2.11

EXTEND Provide students with a map of the world with continents and oceans. Have students color land with one color and the oceans with a different color. Ask students to estimate the percentage of Earth that land covers and the percentage that water covers. Then, read the figure caption aloud, and ask students to write the correct percentages.

Figure 2.11 Roughly three-quarters of Earth's surface is covered by water. Life on Earth depends on liquid water.

Water

Did you know that humans can survive for weeks without food but only days without water? The reason is that water makes up about 60 percent of the human body. Water is just as important to most other living things.

Water is involved in almost all of the chemical reactions and other processes that take place in living things. Water is important because it acts as a solvent. A **solvent** (SAHL vunt) is a substance in which other substances dissolve, or break apart. Water is known as the universal solvent because it can dissolve so many substances.

Because water can dissolve other substances, it can carry gases, nutrients that come from food, and waste products throughout an organism. For example, water is part of the digestive fluids. These fluids help break down food into nutrients the body can use. As part of blood, water helps carry the nutrients to cells where they are needed. The cells release waste products into the blood. In this way, water helps carry away waste products so they can be removed from the body.

Water is also important in maintaining human body temperature. When a body becomes warm, it releases a fluid called perspiration. As perspiration evaporates from the skin, liquid water changes into a gas. In the process, heat is released from the skin. The result is that the body cools off.

Figure 2.12 The human body needs to remain within a certain temperature range. When the body becomes too warm, it perspires. This causes the body's temperature to fall back within the proper range. This is an example of homeostasis.

Background Information

Only three percent of Earth's water is freshwater; the other 97 percent is contained in oceans and is salty. Most of the freshwater is unavailable for humans to use as a resource, since it is in ice that covers Antarctica, Greenland, and the waters near the north pole. Water is reused over and over again through the water cycle. For more information about the water cycle, visit http://ga.water.usgs.gov/edu/watercycle.html.

Interpreting Diagrams
Workbook, p. 11

CONNECTION: Astronomy

Earth is home to millions of different types of living things. Astrobiologists and exobiologists, or scientists who search for signs of life beyond Earth, subscribe to a basic principle: follow the water. This means that if liquid water is necessary for living things to exist, the only way to find life is to find water.

Astrobiologists describe a habitable zone as the region of space in which a planet could support life because it can have liquid water. Earth is within this habitable zone. So is Mars. To date, scientists have not found liquid water on Mars, but they have found evidence that liquid water existed in the recent past or still exists underground. Such evidence includes the presence of dry riverbeds, flood plains, and gullies.

Scientists are also searching for water in other places, such as the moons of planets. One of Jupiter's moons, Europa, shows signs that it may have a deep ocean of liquid water covered by ice.

Does the presence of liquid water prove that life exists elsewhere in the universe? No one knows for sure, but astrobiologists hope to find out in time.

Temperature

Organisms need to live within a certain temperature range. Some organisms, such as birds and kangaroos, maintain a constant internal temperature. When the environment is too cold for these organisms, they can change the Sun's energy stored in food into thermal energy. This type of energy keeps them warm. An organism that produces thermal energy to maintain its temperature is called an **endotherm**.

If these organisms become too warm, they can remove thermal energy from their bodies. Recall that water in perspiration helps maintain temperature in this way.

Perhaps you have seen a lizard basking on a rock. Lizards do this because they are ectotherms. An **ectotherm** does not maintain a constant temperature. Instead, it takes on the temperature of the environment. When ectotherms become cool, they might bask in the sunlight to absorb energy from it. If they become too warm, they move to a shady area, open their mouths, or even burrow into the soil to stay cool.

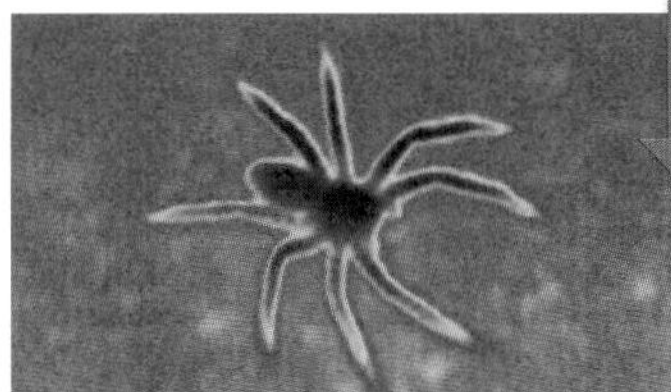

Figure 2.13 The red and orange colors of the bird show that it can stay warmer than its environment. The spider cannot.

As You Read

In your Science Notebook, choose an organism and draw its outline. You might include a picture of the organism, if possible. Around the picture, draw and label the things the organism needs to obtain from its environment in order to survive.

Is this organism an autotroph or a heterotroph? Is it an endotherm or an ectotherm? How do you know?

Figure It Out

1. How can you tell that the spider takes on the temperature of its environment?
2. Which of the organisms would be classified as an ectotherm and which as an endotherm?

Teach

EXPLAIN that another need of living things is to function within a certain temperature range. Some organisms have the capacity to maintain a consistent internal temperature, while other organisms are dependent on the environment for temperature regulation.

CONNECTION: Astronomy

ENGAGE Have students reflect on how popular culture portrays life on other planets. Ask: *What does this life look like? How does it act (in movies and books)?*

Ask students in small groups to review the characteristics of living things. Tell them to sketch in their Science Notebooks what they think life on Mars might really look like. Ask volunteers to share their sketches and explain why they drew what they did.

EXTEND Ask each group to sketch a picture of the solar system and to identify the planets where water has been located. Discuss the location of planets in the solar system, and have students correctly label the pictures in their Science Notebooks.

As You Read

ANSWER Answers will vary with student selections. Students should correctly identify their choices as autotrophs or heterotrophs and as endotherms or ectotherms.

Figure It Out: Figure 2.13

ANSWER **1.** The outside of the spider is the same color as the background, and the inside is dark. **2.** The spider is an ectotherm, and the bird is an endotherm.

Background Information

Mars is the fourth planet from the Sun. It is a "neighbor" of Earth. In June 2000, the *Mars Global Surveyor* spacecraft found evidence that water may have existed on Mars. Astrobiologists still need to answer the following questions: Where was the water? When in the past did it flow, and where could it be today? In what form did it exist? In what quantities?

Endothermic and ectothermic organisms each have suitabilities for surviving in different environments. Endothermic organisms can live in places that are very hot or very cold. These animals can continue to be active, seek food, and defend themselves in those environments. However, endothermic animals' bodies provide an environment conducive for viruses, bacteria, and parasites to live. Ectothermic animals can only be active, seek food, and defend themselves when they are sufficiently warm. However, ectothermic animals require much less energy (food) than endothermic animals do.

Teacher Alert

Warm-blooded and *cold-blooded* are sometimes used in place of *endothermic* and *exothermic* to describe organisms. This can be confusing because endothermic organisms produce their own energy; their internal temperature is not blood-related. Furthermore, ectotherms that bask in sunlight on hot days are not cold inside because they take on the termperature of their surroundings.

Teach

EXPLAIN that all living things require both air and a place to live. The components of air, which include oxygen and carbon dioxide, provide energy to all organisms. A place to live must provide all of an organism's needs and protect it from adverse conditions.

Explain It!

Remind students to write their responses in their Science Notebooks. Ask:

- *What organisms use carbon dioxide?* (plants)
- *What do plants do in the environment?* (Possible answers: They give off oxygen and act as a source of food for most organisms.)

Assess

EVALUATE Use the After You Read questions and the Alternative Assessment to help assess students' understanding of the lesson.

After You Read

1. energy from sunlight
2. Water transports materials in organisms, helps organisms regulate body temperature, and makes chemical reactions in the body possible.
3. A snake, which is a reptile, is an ectotherm. Its body temperature varies with the temperature of its environment. An ostrich, which is a bird, is an endotherm that has a constant body temperature.
4. Answers will vary. Students should recognize the difference between wants and needs and the fact that they share the same needs with other living things.

Alternative Assessment

EVALUATE Have students draw two pictures: one of an ectotherm and one of an endotherm. Ask students to list or draw things that each organism needs in order to survive. Students might include the same number of needs as taught in the chapter and indicate how these needs change depending on the environment of the specific animal selected.

Did You Know?

Many people think that air is made up only of oxygen. Air is actually a mixture of several different gases. Most of the volume of air, almost 80 percent, is made up of nitrogen.

Major Components of Air

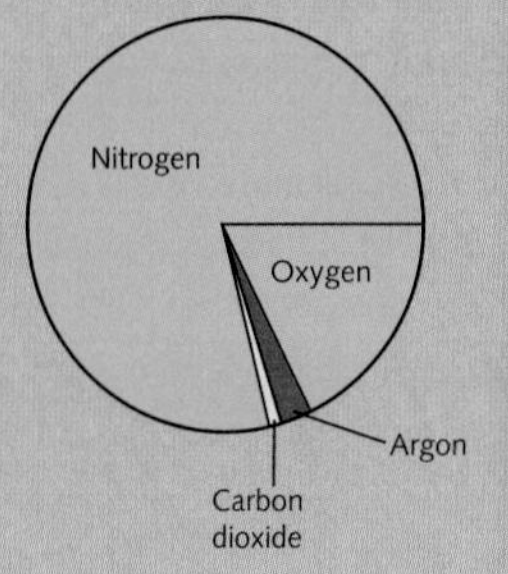

Explain It!

Humans and other animals use the oxygen they take in from the air. In your Science Notebook, explain why carbon dioxide in the air is also important to these organisms.

Air

You need to breathe in order to survive. Each time you breathe in, or inhale, you take in oxygen from the air. Your cells use oxygen to release the energy they need. When you breathe out, or exhale, you release carbon dioxide. Plants use carbon dioxide from the air to conduct photosynthesis. Recall that photosynthesis is the process through which plants store matter and the Sun's energy in their bodies. Because so many organisms depend on plants for food, it is important to all organisms that plants obtain the carbon dioxide they need for photosynthesis.

Even organisms that live in water use gases from the air. Fish, for example, absorb oxygen and release carbon dioxide. Unlike animals on land, however, they exchange gases directly with the water.

Space

All organisms need a place to live. The place must provide all of the things the organism needs to survive. In addition, it should provide the organism with protection from natural events, such as storms, and from other organisms.

For some organisms, such as the Florida panther in **Figure 2.14**, the place must be quite large. A male panther's place will cover an area of about 500 square kilometers. Meanwhile, the dust mite in **Figure 2.14** can fulfill all its needs on the tip of an eyelash.

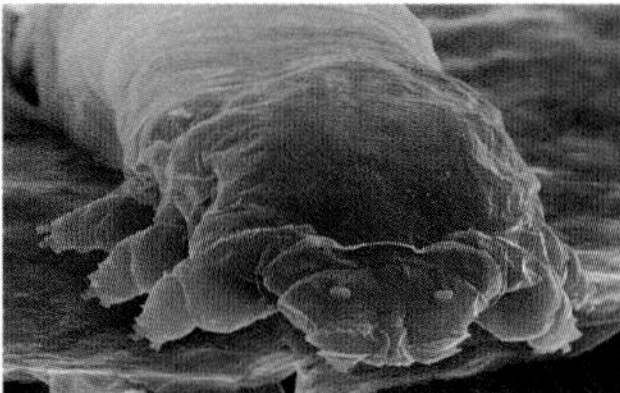

Figure 2.14 All living things need a place to live. This Florida panther *(left)* travels across a large space, whereas this mite *(right)* might never leave an eyelash.

After You Read

1. What is the original source of energy in a salad you eat?
2. What are three ways in which water is essential to living things?
3. How is a snake different from an ostrich in terms of body temperature?
4. Review your list of wants and needs. Based on what you learned about the needs of living things, would you still classify the same items as needs? How are your true needs basically the same as those of the tomato plant described at the beginning of the lesson?

Field Study

Take students outside to observe all organisms on a square foot of land. In their Science Notebooks, students should record the names (or short descriptions if they don't know the names) of all animals and plants they see. Provide magnifying glasses, and encourage students to quietly and carefully observe all organisms for 10 to 15 min. Discuss with students the type and number of organisms.

Differentiated Instruction

Visual and Naturalistic Encourage students to draw all organisms they see in their square foot during the Field Study. Provide reference books, and suggest that students label their pictures as they are able.

2.3 Chemistry of Living Things

Before You Read

Look at the four main headings within this lesson. Create a chart in your Science Notebook with four columns. Write one heading in each column. Then write a sentence summarizing what you know about each one.

Learning Goals

- Compare the structure and function of four types of organic molecules.
- Identify the building blocks of carbohydrates, lipids, proteins, and nucleic acids.

New Vocabulary

matter
atom
organic
carbohydrate
lipid
insoluble
protein
amino acid
nucleic acid
DNA

Everything around you is made up of matter, including living things. **Matter** is defined as anything that has mass and takes up space. Every type of matter is made up of smaller units called **atoms**. The atoms of each element, such as carbon, oxygen, and hydrogen, are different from every other type of atom.

Atoms bond, or join together, to form molecules. The chemical processes in living things involve organic molecules. Scientifically, the term **organic** refers to molecules that contain bonds between carbon and hydrogen atoms. There are four main classes of organic molecules: carbohydrates, proteins, lipids, and nucleic acids.

Carbohydrates

You may have heard that breads, pasta, and fruits contain carbohydrates. A **carbohydrate** (kar boh HI drayt) is a molecule made up of carbon, oxygen, and hydrogen. Carbohydrates provide energy to the cells of an organism.

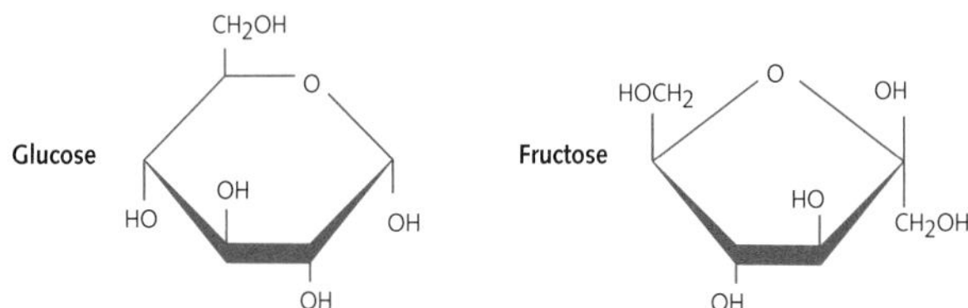

Figure 2.15 Two carbohydrates are glucose and fructose. They are made up of the same atoms arranged in different ways.

The simplest type of carbohydrate is called a monosaccharide (mah nuh SA kuh ride), or simple sugar. Glucose, fructose, and galactose are all simple sugars. Two monosaccharide molecules bonded together form a disaccharide. You may have sprinkled the disaccharide known as sucrose on your oatmeal. Sucrose, or table sugar, is formed when glucose and fructose link together.

CONNECTION: Health

The human body needs to obtain six kinds of nutrients from food: carbohydrates, fats, proteins, minerals, vitamins, and water. These nutrients are required in different amounts for proper health. The Food and Drug Administration has created a Food Pyramid to compare these amounts.

2.3 Introduce

ENGAGE students by asking everyone to observe the back of his or her hand and make a list of observations. Ask: *What is the smallest thing you can see on your hand?* Tell students that the smallest components of all their answers are atoms, which cannot be observed by the unaided eye. Explain that in this lesson, students will learn what atoms and molecules make up all living things.

Before You Read

Model how to identify the main headings, pointing out the importance of bold type and larger words in texts. Write the first main heading for Lesson 2.3 together. Tell students to summarize the main idea of each section after it is read.

Teach

EXPLAIN that students will learn about the chemistry of all living things. Discuss the fact that carbon is found in all organic molecules and that organic molecules make up the carbohydrates, proteins, lipids, and nucleic acids essential to living things.

Vocabulary

matter Tell students that *matter* has many common uses. Elicit several examples of the everyday use of the word. Emphasize that the scientific meaning is "anything that has mass and takes up space."

atom Explain that *atom* comes from the Greek word *atomos*, meaning "indivisible." The prefix *a-* means "without," and *tómos* comes from a verb that means "to cut." One hundred million atoms laid side by side would be one inch long.

organic Explain that molecules that are *organic* contain carbon-to-carbon bonds that hold two to many carbon atoms together and that organic molecules in living things also include hydrogen, oxygen, nitrogen, and other elements.

carbohydrate Explain that molecules of carbohydrates contain carbon, as well as hydrogen and oxygen atoms in a 2:1 ratio, which is the same as the ratio in water. Thus, the name is derived from carbon (*carbo-*) and water (*hydrate*).

ELL Strategy

Activate Background Knowledge Place students in pairs, and ask them to record in their Science Notebooks what they already know about chemistry. If students are not familiar with chemistry, they could brainstorm what they know about the vocabulary terms, headings, or Learning Goal topics. Then, ask them to highlight and discuss the ideas that are specific to living things.

CONNECTION: Health

Explain that the six categories in the Food Guide Pyramid are not identical to the nutrients in this feature because the Pyramid classifies foods by groups not by nutrients.

Pair students and ask them to match the nutrients listed here with the categories in the USDA Food Guide Pyramid. Encourage students to identify the nutrients found in each food category. Discuss the classifications as a class.

Teach

EXPLAIN that many lipids are made up of a glycerol molecule and two or three fatty acid chains. Like carbohydrates, lipids contain carbon, hydrogen, and oxygen.

EXPLORE Provide students with different types of lipids, such as lard, butter, canola oil, corn oil, or olive oil. Also provide students with water and glass beakers. Challenge students to determine if any of the lipids will dissolve in the water. Ask: *Why do you think oil and water mix when washing dishes?* (Soap acts as an emulsifier, a chemical agent that allows an insoluble substance to form an emulsion with water.)

As You Read

Model writing the first summary by drawing a chart on the board.

ANSWER carbohydrates

EXTEND Have students list the foods that they eat for one day. Instruct them to identify the foods according to the USDA Food Guide Pyramid classifications and note which nutrients the foods are rich in.

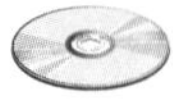

Vocabulary

lipid Explain that lipids are characterized by an oily feeling and insolubility in water. A common term for a lipid is a *fat*.

insoluble Tell students that the prefix *in-* is used to indicate a negative or the absence of something. Explain also that the root *soluble* is derived from the Latin *solvere,* which means "to dissolve."

protein Explain that proteins are organic molecules composed of carbon, hydrogen, oxygen, and nitrogen. Foods that provide protein include meat, poultry, dairy products, fish, and beans.

amino acid Tell students that amino acids combine to form proteins. Amino acids join in different patterns to determine the specific type of protein being formed.

nucleic acid Tell students that there are two types of nucleic acids: DNA and RNA. Nucleic acids are complex molecules.

DNA Explain that DNA contains genetic information that is transmitted from one generation to the next (for example, hair and eye color).

Figure It Out: Figure 2.18

ANSWER **1.** butter, meats, and peanut butter
2. 3 carbon, 5 hydrogen, and 3 oxygen atoms

Figure 2.16 Starch, found in structures such as potatoes, stores energy for plant cells. Glycogen stores energy in the livers of mammals, such as humans. Cellulose makes up the cell walls of plant cells and fibers such as cotton.

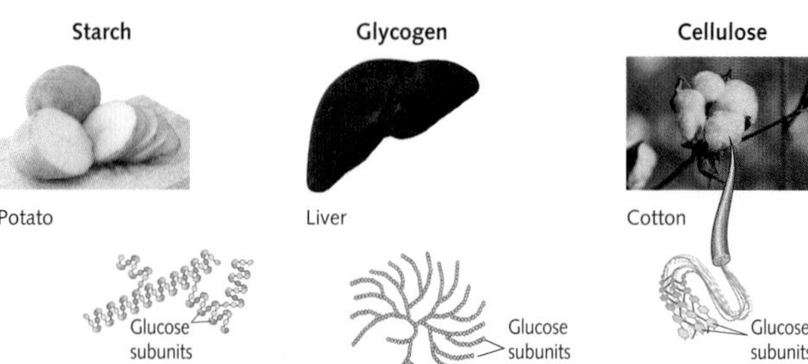

As You Read

In the chart you made in your Science Notebook, summarize the information you learn about each type of organic molecule. Correct any errors you might have included in the information you wrote before reading the lesson.

Which type of organic molecule serves as an energy source for cells?

Chains of monosaccharides form polysaccharides (pah lee SA kuh ridez). Starch, cellulose, and glycogen are polysaccharides made up of chains of glucose. Examples of where these carbohydrates can be found are shown in **Figure 2.16**.

Lipids

Many foods contain fats and oils. These are examples of **lipids**, which are molecules made up mostly of carbon and hydrogen. Lipids also contain small amounts of oxygen. Many lipids are made up of a glycerol molecule and fatty acids. A fatty acid is a long chain of carbon and hydrogen. Examples of food that contain lipids are shown in **Figure 2.17**.

Lipids are said to be **insoluble** (ihn SAHL yuh bul), which means that they do not dissolve, or break apart, in water. This is one reason why lipids are the main component of the membranes that surround living cells. Lipids are also important to cells because they store energy and provide insulation.

Figure It Out

1. What are three foods that contain large amounts of lipids?
2. Determine how many carbon, hydrogen, and oxygen atoms are in a glycerol molecule.

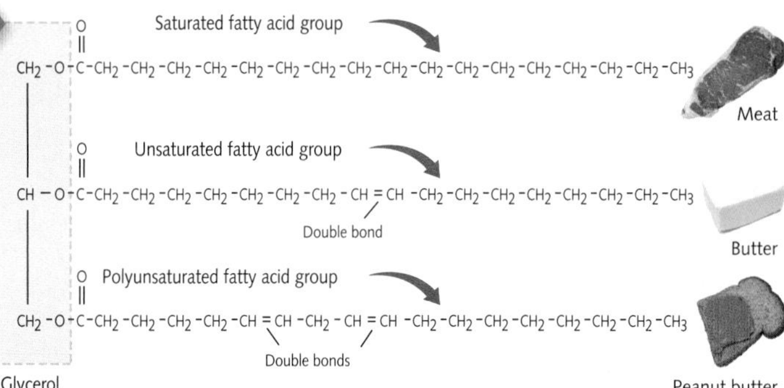

Figure 2.17 A lipid is saturated if each carbon atom in its fatty acid chains is joined to the adjoining carbon atoms by single bonds. A lipid is unsaturated if there is at least one double bond between two carbon atoms. What is a polyunsaturated lipid?

Differentiated Instruction

Kinesthetic Have students in small groups make models of the organic molecules they have learned about. Each person can represent an atom; different-colored labels worn by each person can represent different atoms; arms can represent bonds (two arms for a double bond, one arm for a single bond). Groups can then work to identify the organic molecules created by other groups based on the colors of each component.

Background Information

The prefix *mono-* comes from the Greek word *monos,* which means "single." The prefix *poly-* comes from the Greek word *polus,* which means "many parts." The word *saccharide* comes from the Latin word *saccharum,* which means "sugar." A monosaccharide is a single sugar, and a polysaccharide is made up of many single sugars.

Proteins

A **protein** is an organic molecule made up of carbon, hydrogen, oxygen, and nitrogen. Proteins occasionally contain sulfur, as well. They are made up of building blocks called **amino acids**. Amino acids, such as the one in **Figure 2.18**, join together to form chains.

There are about 20 different amino acids that can join together in a huge number of combinations. The order and arrangement of the amino acids determine the nature of the protein. Some proteins act as the building and binding materials of living things. Collagen, for example, forms tendons, ligaments, and cartilage. Other proteins take part in chemical reactions and transport materials throughout an organism. Others cause actions, such as contraction of muscles, to occur.

H Hydrogen atom

NH_2 — C — COOH

R Variable group

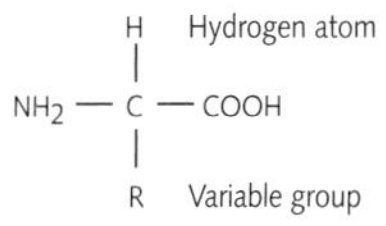

Figure 2.18 An amino acid has an amino group ($-NH_2$) and a carboxyl (organic acid) group (–COOH) attached to the same carbon atom. The rest of the amino acid, or R-group, makes each kind different from the others.

Figure 2.19 Proteins make up structures such as hair, nails, horns, and hoofs.

Nucleic Acids

Living things tend to resemble their parents because of information passed from one generation of cells to the next. This information, known as genetic information, is stored in nucleic acids. A **nucleic** (new KLAY ihk) **acid** is a large molecule made up of smaller units called nucleotides.

One important nucleic acid is deoxyribonucleic (dee AHK sih rib oh noo klay ihk) acid, or **DNA**. Genetic information is stored in DNA. This information makes up the instructions used to form all of a cell's proteins. Another nucleic acid is ribonucleic acid (RNA). The information stored in DNA is translated by RNA and used to direct the production of proteins.

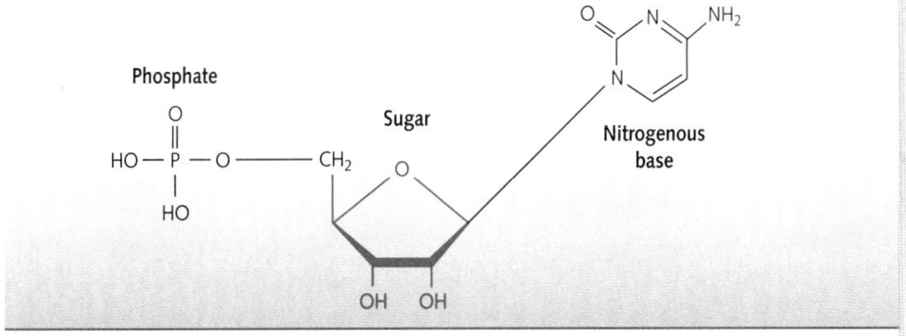

Phosphate

Sugar

Nitrogenous base

HO — P — O — CH_2

OH OH

Figure 2.20 Each nucleotide consists of a phosphate group, a simple sugar, and a nitrogenous base.

Extend It!

Nutrition labels on food products list the amounts of fats, carbohydrates, and proteins in each serving of the food. Compare the nutrition labels for several food products. Identify the types of foods that are sources of each organic molecule. Record your findings in your Science Notebook.

After You Read

1. Why might a runner eat carbohydrates before a race?
2. What are three functions of lipids in living things? Of proteins?
3. Use the information in your Science Notebook to write a well-developed paragraph about the subunits of each type of organic molecule.

Teach

EXPLAIN Tell students that the last two types of organic molecules are proteins and nucleic acids. Both types contain carbon, hydrogen, oxygen, and nitrogen. Proteins also sometimes have sulfur. Nucleic acids also contain phosphorus.

Extend It!

Explain that the ability to interpret food labels enables students to make informed choices about food selection.

Have students gather a variety of labels from foods in boxes, bags, cans, and frozen sources. Have students adhere the labels to a page in their Science Notebooks and highlight the nutrient information about carbohydrates, proteins, and fats. Model this process with a label from a healthful cereal and a label from a sugary cereal. Discuss the differences in the nutritional value of each food.

Assess

EVALUATE Use the After You Read questions and the Alternative Assessment to help you assess students' understanding of the lesson.

After You Read

1. Carbohydrates provide cells with a source of energy that will be needed during a race.
2. Lipids protect cells, store energy, and provide insulation. Proteins provide structure, take part in chemical reactions, transport materials, and control activities.
3. Carbohydrates are chains of simple sugars. Lipids are made up of glycerol molecules and fatty acid chains. Proteins are chains of amino acids. Nucleic acids are chains of nucleotides.

Background Information

The bond that holds two amino acids together is called a peptide bond. When two amino acids bond together, they form a dipeptide. Additional amino acids may join with a dipeptide to form a polypeptide.

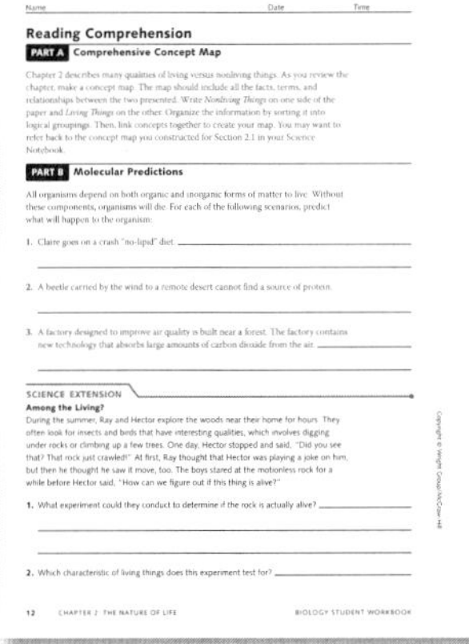
Reading Comprehension

PART A Comprehensive Concept Map

PART B Molecular Predictions

SCIENCE EXTENSION

Reading Comprehension Workbook, p. 12

Alternative Assessment

EVALUATE Have each student list or draw different foods that are necessary to sustain life and then identify the organic molecule that is the dominant part of each food. Students could draw and label the components of the molecule.

CHAPTER 2 31

Chapter 2 Summary

VOCABULARY REVIEW

Check students' sentences or paragraphs to make sure they understand the meaning of each vocabulary term.

PREPARE FOR CHAPTER TEST

Evaluate students' essays using the following criteria:

1. The topic sentence, or main idea, should restate the Key Concept.
2. The supporting paragraphs should incorporate the answers to the Learning Goal questions students have written and include details, facts, and examples they have recorded in their Science Notebooks.
3. The concluding sentence should sum up the main idea of the chapter and restate the Key Concept.

MASTERING CONCEPTS

True or False

1. False, cell
2. True
3. False, reproduction
4. False, ectotherm
5. False, protein
6. True

Short Answer

7. Living things gather information from their external surroundings. Events known as stimuli cause living things to respond by changing their behavior or structure in some way. Any changes in internal conditions are internal stimuli that living things respond to as well.
8. A chameleon can change to a color that blends in with its surrounding environment, thus making it difficult for predators to see the chameleon.
9. More substances dissolve in water than in any other substance, which means that water often takes part in chemical reactions and that many substances can be transported by water.
10. Autotrophs are organisms that can capture energy and matter from their surroundings, usually through photosynthesis. Heterotrophs are organisms that must eat autotrophs or other heterotrophs as food.

Chapter 2

Summary

KEY CONCEPTS

2.1 Characteristics of Living Things

- All living things are made up of cells, respond to stimuli, adapt over time, are capable of reproduction, and grow and develop.
- The process by which living things respond to stimuli in ways that allow them to maintain internal conditions necessary for life is called homeostasis.
- The characteristics of living things can be used to classify objects as living or nonliving.

2.2 The Needs of Living Things

- All living things need to obtain energy, take in water, maintain a proper temperature, exchange gases in air, and have a space in which to live.
- Organisms that capture energy from their surroundings are called autotrophs. Organisms that eat other organisms to get energy to survive are called heterotrophs.
- Water, the universal solvent, is essential to living things because it dissolves substances involved in chemical reactions, carries materials, and helps maintain body temperature.

2.3 Chemistry of Living Things

- Carbohydrates provide energy to all cells and support to plant cells. They can be simple sugars or combinations of simple sugars.
- Lipids store energy, provide insulation, and are the main component of cell membranes. They are often made up of glycerol molecules and fatty acids.
- Proteins play important roles in an organism, such as providing structure, taking part in chemical reactions, and transporting materials. They are made up of chains of amino acids.
- Nucleic acids carry genetic information from one generation to the next. They are made up of nucleotides.

VOCABULARY REVIEW

Write each term in a complete sentence, or write a paragraph relating several terms.

2.1
organism, p. 21
cell, p. 22
stimulus, p. 23
response, p. 23
homeostasis, p. 23
adaptation, p. 23
reproduction, p. 23
species, p. 23

2.2
energy, p. 25
photosynthesis, p. 25
autotroph, p. 25
heterotroph, p. 25
solvent, p. 26
endotherm, p. 27
ectotherm, p. 27

2.3
matter, p. 29
atom, p. 29
organic, p. 29
carbohydrate, p. 29
lipid, p. 30
insoluble, p. 30
protein, p. 31
amino acid, p. 31
nucleic acid, p. 31
DNA, p. 31

PREPARE FOR CHAPTER TEST

To prepare for the chapter test, create a question from each Learning Goal. Use the information in your Science Notebook to answer each question. Then use these answers to write a well-developed essay about the chapter. Use the Key Concept on the first page of this chapter as your topic sentence.

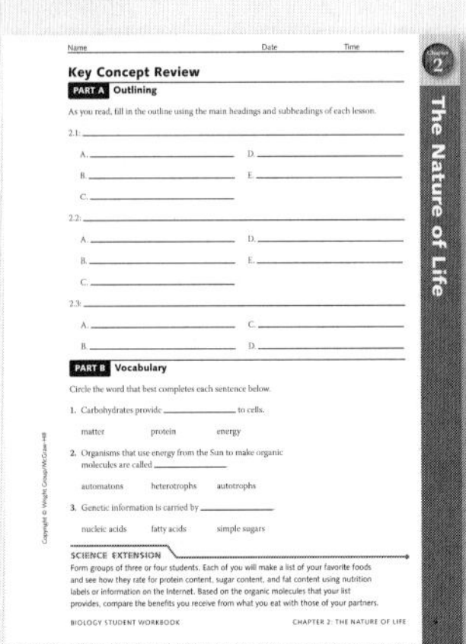

Key Concept Review

Key Concept Review Workbook, p. 9

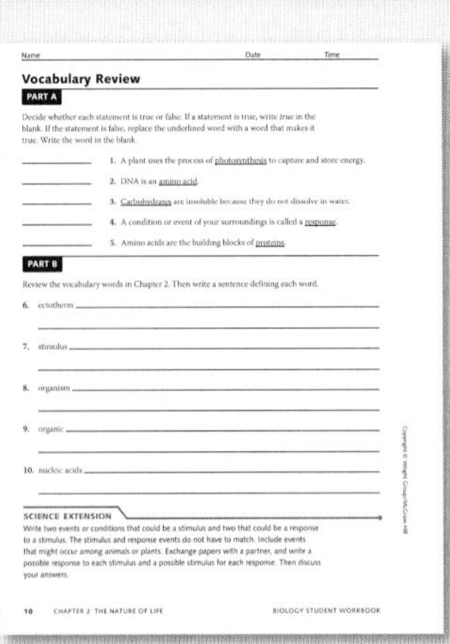

Vocabulary Review

Vocabulary Review Workbook, p. 10

MASTERING CONCEPTS

True or False

If the statement is true, write "true." If it is false, change the underlined word or words to make the statement true.

1. A <u>molecule</u> is the smallest unit that can be considered alive.
2. A living thing can respond to a <u>stimulus</u> in its environment.
3. During the process of <u>adaptation</u>, living things make more organisms like themselves.
4. A rattlesnake is an <u>endotherm</u> because its temperature depends on its environment.
5. <u>Lipid</u> molecules are made up of chains of amino acids.
6. A molecule of <u>DNA</u> carries instructions a cell can use to make proteins.

Short Answer

Answer each of the following in a sentence or brief paragraph.

7. What does it mean to say that living things respond to both their external and internal environments?
8. The ability to change color is an adaptation that helps a chameleon survive in its environment. Analyze how this adaptation increases the chameleon's ability to survive.
9. Water is known as the universal solvent. Summarize why this makes water essential to life on Earth.
10. Explain the relationship between autotrophs and heterotrophs. Include definitions of the terms in your answer.
11. Describe proteins and DNA in your own words. Then relate DNA to proteins.

Critical Thinking

Use what you have learned in this chapter to answer each of the following.

12. **Compare and Contrast** Identify ways in which unicellular organisms are similar to and different from multicellular organisms.
13. **Give Examples** The fire alarm at school is an example of a stimulus. Tell how you and your classmates respond to this stimulus. Then give another example of a stimulus in your environment and your response to it.
14. **Relate** How are carbohydrates and lipids related to the need for energy in the body?

Standardized Test Question

Choose the letter of the response that correctly answers the question.

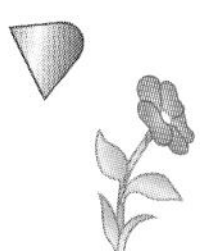
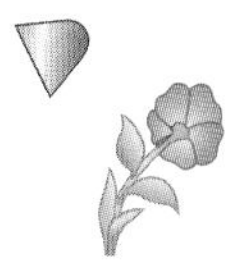
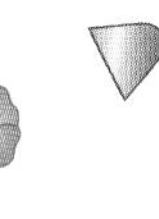

15. The diagrams show the same plant over the course of ten days. What is the plant doing?
    A. changing into a different species
    B. obtaining more space in which to live
    C. passing along its traits
    D. responding to the stimulus of light

Test-Taking Tip

Read each question carefully. Think about what is asked. If you are not sure, read the question again. If you are still not sure, go on to the next question. Sometimes, a later question will help you remember information you need to answer a question you skipped. Remember to check all of your answers before turning in the test.

11. Proteins are organic molecules that have many functions in organisms. DNA is a nucleic acid that stores information used to form proteins.

Critical Thinking

12. Both types of organisms are made up of cells. However, unicellular organisms are made up of one cell, whereas multicellular organisms are made up of more than one cell. In unicellular organisms, all of the functions necessary for life are performed within one cell. In multicellular organisms, cells work together to perform all life functions.
13. When the fire alarm sounds, students respond by performing certain safety procedures. This might include forming a line and walking to a designated location outside the building. Examples of everyday stimuli will vary but may include other alarms, such as the sound of an alarm clock or a kitchen timer.
14. Both store energy and can be broken down to provide energy to cells.
15. D

Reading Links

Hatchet

This memorable story of survival, a favorite among young adult readers, follows 13-year-old Brian as he struggles to stay alive following a plane crash that leaves him stranded in the Canadian wilderness. In the process, the book explores the basic needs of living things, adaptations that aid in survival, environmental challenges and resources, and the taken-for-granted.

Paulsen, Gary. Macmillan, 1986. Fiction, 289 pp. Trade ISBN 978-0-02-527403-7.

Exploding Ants: Amazing Facts About How Animals Adapt

In a style that will hook readers or listeners, this book presents unusual examples of adaptations, behaviors, habits, and specializations that allow animals to survive and thrive in a competitive world. Included are frogs that swallow food with help from their eyeballs, wasps that lay their eggs under a caterpillar's skin, parasites that brainwash their host, and ants that explode.

Settel, Joanne. Simon & Schuster (Atheneum), 1999. Trade ISBN 978-0-02-68981739-7.

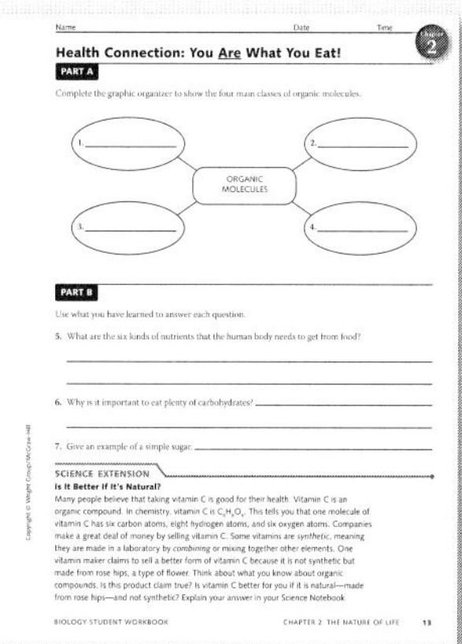
Health Connection: You Are What You Eat!

Curriculum Connection Workbook, p. 13

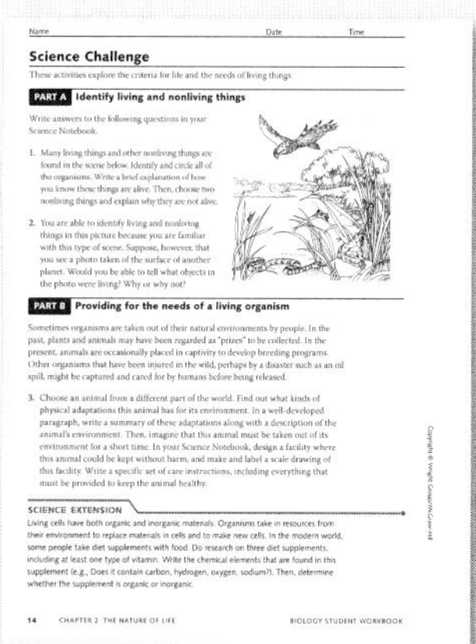
Science Challenge

Science Challenge Workbook, p. 14

CHAPTER 2 33

Chapter 2

Labs

2A Is It Alive?

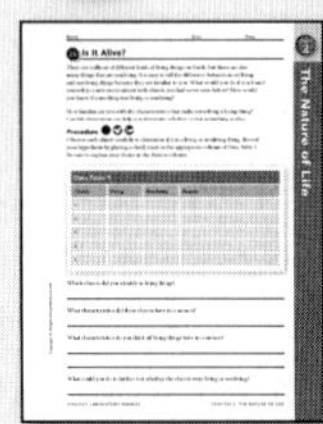

This prechapter introduction activity is designed to determine what students already know about the characteristics of living things by engaging them in observing, examining, comparing, contrasting, and determining if an object is a living or a nonliving thing.

Objectives

- make observations
- identify objects as living or nonliving
- compare and contrast living and nonliving things
- infer the characteristics shared by all living things

Planning

 20 minutes  Class demonstration or groups of 2 students

Materials

- assorted pictures or samples of living and nonliving things
- clear, multipurpose household cement in tube
- water
- petri dish
- overhead projector
- pencil shavings
- pencil and paper

Advance Preparation

- Gather a collection of samples or pictures of unusual living and nonliving things. The first object should be familiar to students. For objects 2 through 4, select three living things that illustrate one of the characteristics of life (made of cells, respond to the environment, able to adapt, and able to reproduce), but try not to use organisms that are familiar to students. You might also include a simple wind-up toy that will move and change direction or a lit match. Many students have the misconception that fire is alive.
- You may prefer to set up this activity at lab stations and allow groups to rotate to each station to make closer observations of each object.

Engagement Guide

- Challenge students to think about the characteristics that all living things share by asking:
  - *How did you decide if an object was living or nonliving?* (Answers will vary depending on which characteristics of life are illustrated by the organisms or pictures.)
  - *Do you think this object is living or nonliving? Explain your answer.* (Perform the following demonstration for the class as object 5: place a petri dish half-filled with water on the overhead projector. Add two to three drops of the clear, multipurpose household cement, but do not let students see what you are adding. Add two to three small pieces of pencil shavings. The glue will react with the water and take on an amoeba-like appearance. It will appear to move, respond to the pencil shavings added to its environment, and ingest the pencil shavings. Most students will identify this object as a living thing.)
- Have groups tally the results in a class data table and discuss their responses. Have students explain why a nonliving object appears to be living. Ask: *What traits made you believe that it is living?* Encourage students to debate their ideas, and explain that scientists debate each other in the same fashion. Reveal to students the correct classification of each of the objects you used, and unveil the household cement as a nonliving object that looks alive.

Going Further

Encourage students to identify other objects that may be difficult to classify as living or nonliving, and have them present these objects to the class to test their classmates' abilities to distinguish between living and nonliving things.

2B Organic Molecules for Lunch?

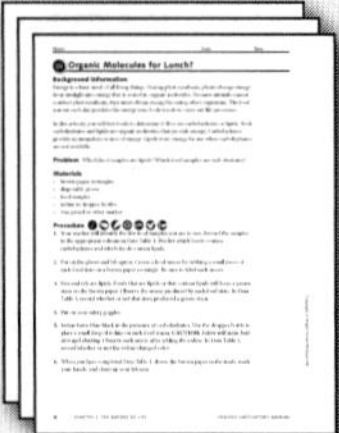

Objectives

- make predictions
- classify foods as carbohydrates or lipids
- conclude from tests which predictions are correct
- compare and contrast carbohydrates and lipids

Skill Set

observing, comparing and contrasting, recording and analyzing data, classifying, stating conclusions

Planning

 1 class period  groups of 2–4 students

Materials

Materials for this activity are listed in the Student Laboratory Manual.

Lab Tips

- There are a variety of iodine test solutions available with different percentages of elemental iodine. **CAUTION:** Do not use tincture of iodine. It is flammable.
- It is recommended that you test samples using the brown paper in advance. The color change with carbohydrates may be difficult to observe against brown paper.

Advance Preparation

- Cut paper grocery bags into 10-cm × 20-cm rectangles for student use. You will need at least five rectangles for each group of students.
- Prepare paper plates with the food samples for each group of students. You may want to mash up the solid foods for better test results.
- You might want to prepare a typical sack lunch to introduce the activity and to engage the students by asking, *Are you eating organic molecules for lunch?* Have students make a list of what they typically eat for lunch and what those foods are made from.

Answers to Observations: Data Table 1

Sample answers for a sack lunch: American cheese: stained paper, no change in iodine, lipid; bread: no stain, iodine turned blue-black, carbohydrate; butter: stained paper, no change in iodine, lipid; lunch meat: stained paper, no change in iodine, lipid; rice: no stain, iodine turned blue-black, carbohydrate.

Answers to Analysis and Conclusions

1. Iodine placed on samples that were carbohydrates turned blue-black; there was no effect with lipids. Samples that were lipids left a grease stain on the brown paper; carbohydrates did not.
2. bun: carbohydrate; cheese, mayonnaise, and meat: lipid
3. The substance tested contains both carbohydrates and lipids.
4. At the end of a race, a marathon runner would be relying on energy stored in lipids because energy in the form of carbohydrates would already have been used.

Going Further

- Provide students with an unknown substance, and have them determine if it is a carbohydrate, a lipid, or both using the tests from this lab activity.
- Have students bring parts of their lunch that have nutrition labels to class and investigate what the nutritional labels identify as products included in the food. Have them figure out what may be the starch or the lipid in the product.

2C Enzyme Action

Objectives

- investigate the activity of an enzyme
- record observations
- draw conclusions
- recognize cause and effect

Skill Set

measuring, observing, comparing and contrasting, recording and analyzing data, stating conclusions

Planning

1 class period for lab procedure and setup, 30 minutes the next day for completing data table and answering Analysis and Conclusions questions

 groups of 4 students

Materials

Materials for this activity are listed in the Student Laboratory Manual.

Advance Preparation

Each group will use a package of gelatin (any flavor will work), a cube of fresh pineapple (cut approximately the same size as a cube of canned pineapple), a cube of canned pineapple, and a cube of another type of fruit (grapes cut in half or canned orange slices work well). One fresh pineapple should supply approximately 25 groups of four when cut into 1- to 2-cm cubes. Have a fruit-supply station with containers of the different types of fruit and plastic spoons. Have hot water ready at the beginning of each class period, and have only one student from each group bring the bowl of gelatin to you for the addition of the hot water.

Answers to Observations: Data Table 1

Cup 1: liquid, liquid, solid; Cup 2: liquid, liquid, liquid; Cup 3: liquid, liquid, solid; Cup 4: liquid, liquid, solid.

Answers to Analysis and Conclusions

1. Answers will vary.
2. Cup 1 was the experimental control. The independent variable is the type of fruit placed in the gelatin.
3. The cup with the fresh pineapple did not solidify; it remained a liquid because of the action of the enzyme. The cup with the canned pineapple did solidify.
4. Gelatin with fresh pineapple did not solidify, while gelatin with canned pineapple did. This indicates that the bromelin in fresh pineapple digests the protein in gelatin. (You might want to explain that when fresh pineapple is processed for canning, it is heated to high temperatures for a very short time in order to kill bacteria. These high temperatures also destroy the enzyme bromelin.)
5. Skin contain proteins. Gloves protect the skin from the protein-digesting enzyme bromelin.

Going Further

Meat tenderizers contain enzymes such as bromelin or papin. Have students design an experiment to test the effect of meat tenderizer on a piece of steak. Upon approval of procedures, allow students to carry out their experiments.

Chapter 3 Lessons

Introduce Chapter 3

As a starting activity, use LAB 3A How Does It Get There? on page 13 of the Laboratory Manual.

ENGAGE students by asking them to look at the photograph of soccer players. Ask students to identify teams to which they belong or have belonged. Write responses on the board. Point out that each team is a small part of a larger organization. Ask students to describe the organizational structure of the teams that you have listed on the board. Explain to students that the structure of a cell is similar to the structures of these teams.

Think About Identifying Groups

ENGAGE students by explaining that a family tree is a diagram that shows the relationships that exist in an extended family. Draw a family tree on the board. Ask students to supply names for the tree. Fill in the tree, and discuss the different groups that exist within a family. Ask students to make a list of groups in their Science Notebooks. Have pairs of students share their lists with each other.

Direct students to complete each bulleted activity. As a class, discuss student results. Point out that dividing larger groups into subgroups often enables the group to function more efficiently.

Chapter 3 Cell Structure, Function, and Processes

KEY CONCEPT Cells are the basic units of structure and function in living things.

The players on your soccer team work to kick the ball into the other team's goal and keep the ball out of your goal. When each player performs his or her job correctly, the team functions efficiently. Your team is part of a league, and your league is part of state and national organizations.

The cells that make up living things are organized in a similar way. Each cell is made up of individual parts that work together. For many organisms, cells are then organized into different levels and groups.

Think About Identifying Groups

Without realizing it, you are part of a group that is part of a larger group.

- Think about a group to which you belong. Consider how the group is part of a larger group.
- In your Science Notebook, draw a diagram showing how the groups are related. Write a few sentences describing your role in the group and why it is important for the largest group to be divided into smaller groups.

www.scilinks.org
Cell Features **Code: WGB03**

34

Chapter 3 Planning Guide

Instructional Periods	National Standards	Lab Manual	Workbook
3.1 1 period	G.1, G.2, G.3; A.1, C.1, G.1, G.2, G.3; UCP.2	**Lab 3A—p. 13** How Does It Get There? **Lab 3B—p. 14** Using a Microscope to Compare Plant and Animal Cells **Lab 3C—p. 17** An "Eggsample" of Osmosis	Key Concept Review p. 15 Vocabulary Review p. 16 Graphic Organizer p. 17 Reading Comprehension p. 18 Curriculum Connection p. 19 Science Challenge p. 20
3.2 2 periods	C.1, C.1; C.2, UCP.2		
3.3 2 periods	A.2, C.3; B.2, B.6, C.5, UCP.3		
3.4 1 period	A.2, B.3; C.1, C.5; B.3, B.6, C.5		
3.5 1 period	A.1, C.1, C.5; UCP.1		

Middle School Standard; High School Standard; Unifying Concept and Principle

3.1 Cells: Basic Units of Life

Before You Read

It is often helpful to summarize information about people and events. In your Science Notebook, draw a horizontal time line. Label the left end of the line *1600* and the right end of the line *1900*. Make marks to show each interval of 50 years on the time line. Skim through the lesson to look for any important years that are mentioned. Write these years in the appropriate places on the time line.

Learning Goals

- Identify the roles played by different scientists in the development of the cell theory.
- Recognize how spontaneous generation came to be disproved over time.

New Vocabulary

microorganism
spontaneous generation
cell theory

Recall Vocabulary

cell (p. 22)

Biologists now know that cells are the basic units of life. As you may recall from Chapter 2, a cell is a structure that contains all of the materials needed for life. Recognizing the importance of cells, however, was not an easy task. After all, most cells are so small that they cannot be seen with the unaided eye. Discovering the structure and function of cells involved the work of many scientists as well as the development of the right scientific tools.

Robert Hooke

In the 1600s, a scientist named Robert Hooke designed one of the first compound microscopes. A microscope is a tool that a scientist can use to look at very small objects. In 1665, Hooke used his microscope to study a slice of cork. He observed that the cork was made up of tiny, empty chambers. These chambers reminded Hooke of rooms in a monastery called cells. He therefore gave this name to the chambers he observed in the cork. **Figure 3.1** shows what Hooke may have seen when observing cells. It also shows the microscope he used to see them.

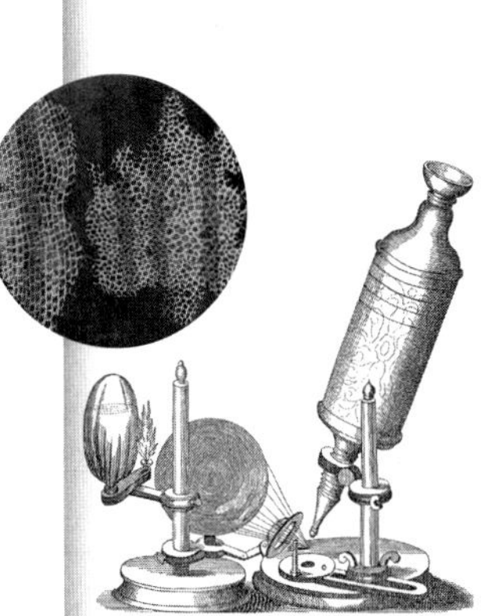

Figure 3.1 Robert Hooke used a compound microscope similar to the one shown here. It uses two lenses to magnify an object. Among the many things Hooke observed through his microscope was a slice of cork. He made drawings to represent the chambers he saw. What did he name these boxlike chambers?

Anton van Leeuwenhoek

The cork that Hooke observed was no longer living. Because of this, the chambers that Hooke saw were not living cells. They were only parts of cells left behind. The first person to observe living cells was Anton van Leeuwenhoek (LAY vun hook). At about the same time that Hooke made his observations, Leeuwenhoek designed and used a simple microscope to study pond water. In 1678, he described how the water was filled with tiny living organisms. He named them *animacules*, which means "tiny animals." Tiny living things that can be seen only through a microscope are now known as **microorganisms** (mi kroh OR guh nih zumz).

3.1 Introduce

ENGAGE Draw a time line on the board. Label the left end of the line with a year not long before the year your students were born. Label the right end with the current year. Ask: *What are some significant events that have occurred in your lifetime?* Discuss both world and personal events, and place them on the time line. Use approximate dates for personal events, such as learning to walk or learning to ride a bike. Discuss with students the ways in which these events have affected their lives.

EXPLAIN Tell students that scientific discoveries over time have changed our lives in many ways. Encourage students to think about the personal impact of the discoveries they will read about in this lesson.

Before You Read

Draw a portion of the time line on the board as an example. Suggest that students turn their Science Notebooks sideways so that they will have enough space for their time lines. Check that the six intervals drawn are of equal length and labeled correctly.

Vocabulary terms are listed on the first student page of each lesson. You may wish to preview the terms before introducing each lesson. Strategies for teaching the vocabulary appear on the pages where the terms are introduced.

Teach

EXPLAIN that in this lesson, students will learn about the different scientists who have contributed to the development of the cell theory.

Background Information

Hooke made many important discoveries, not only in microscopy, but also in astronomy and physics. He discovered a red spot on Jupiter and was the first to recognize the wave properties of light. He is also responsible for numerous inventions. Hooke invented or made improvements to the designs of air pumps, spring-driven watches, barometers, an air gun, carriages, windmills, surveying equipment, and several types of scales.

Use the Visual: Figure 3.1

ANSWER He named them *cells*.

EXTEND Explain that a microscope makes a small object appear much larger than it is. Ask students to examine the drawing in Figure 3.1. The drawing shows the magnified image of what Hooke saw under his microscope.

Science Notebook EXTRA

Encourage students to use the vocabulary section they created in their Science Notebooks. Remind them to record prefixes, suffixes, and root words to help them remember the meanings of vocabulary terms.

Teach

EXPLAIN that students will discover how spontaneous generation was disproved over time. Emphasize that the discoveries made by each scientist built on the discoveries made by the scientist who had come before him or her. Ask students to think about ways in which each discovery laid the foundation for the discoveries to come.

Discuss with students the difference between causation and correlation. Explain that when two outcomes consistently appear together, that indicates a correlation. However, it does not prove that one outcome caused the other. More investigation is required to prove causation.

Science Notebook EXTRA

Provide students with a list of causal statements, such as *The greater the length of study time, the better the grade on the test.* Have students design experiments that might prove or disprove the causal relationships presented in these statements. Students should record their experiments in their Science Notebooks.

As You Read

ANSWER The discoveries of Schleiden and Schwann built on the discoveries made by Hooke and Leeuwenhoek. Schleiden and Schwann had the advantage of more powerful microscopes that enabled them to learn more about cells.

Vocabulary

microorganisms Tell students that the prefix *micro-* comes from the Greek word *mikros,* which means "small." Have students think of other words with this prefix, such as *microchip* or *microphone.*

spontaneous generation Have students brainstorm common meanings of the words *spontaneous* and *generation.* Ask students to describe times when they were spontaneous. Explain that a spontaneous action takes place without premeditation or the involvement of outside forces. The root word of *generation* is *generate,* which means "to bring into being."

Figure 3.2 Matthias Schleiden and Theodor Schwann used observations made using microscopes to conclude that all plants and animals are made up of cells.

Schleiden and Schwann

In 1838, almost 200 years after Robert Hooke first observed microscopic cells, a German botanist named Matthias Schleiden (SHLI dun) studied a variety of plants. By this time, the microscope had been improved. It could be used to see even smaller objects in greater detail. Schleiden used the microscope to study the composition of plants.

After many careful observations, Schleiden concluded that all plants are made of cells. He went on to suggest that plants grow because new cells are produced. Schleiden's friend, German biologist Theodor Schwann, reached the same conclusion about animals the next year.

As You Read

On the time line you drew in your Science Notebook, record the name of each scientist mentioned near the year when that person made an important discovery. Then write a sentence summarizing what that person discovered.

How did the discoveries of Schleiden and Schwann relate to the observations of Hooke and Leeuwenhoek?

Spontaneous Generation

By the mid-1800s, scientists had learned a great deal about cells. They knew that cells were the basic units of plants and animals, and they knew about some structures inside cells. What they did not know was where cells came from. That was part of a much larger question that had been debated for centuries: Can living things arise from nonliving matter?

The belief that living things come from nonliving matter is known as **spontaneous generation**. As early as the fifth century B.C., philosophers concluded that living things developed from nonliving elements in nature. Today, this idea may seem unrealistic based on what you know. Yet these conclusions were based on people's observations. Some of them are summarized in **Figure 3.3**.

a

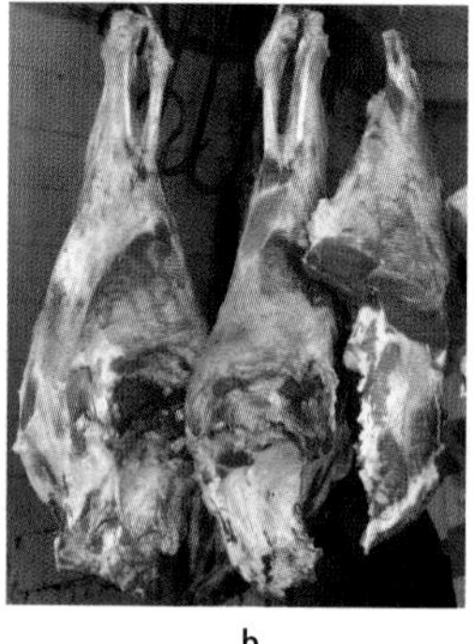

b

c

Figure 3.3 **a)** Farmers of medieval Europe stored grain in barns with thatched roofs. In time, the grain became moldy and overrun with mice. People concluded that mice came from moldy grain. **b)** Before refrigerators were invented, butchers hung meat from hooks. In warm weather, maggots would appear on the meat. People concluded that rotting meat produced maggots. **c)** After the Nile River floods its banks each spring, frogs appear in the mud left behind. Years ago, people observed this and concluded that mud gave rise to frogs.

36 CELL STRUCTURE, FUNCTION, AND PROCESSES

Background Information

Most scientists "believe in" one case of spontaneous generation. More than three billion years ago, the first living organism was spontaneously generated from nonliving chemicals. Scientists have not been able to generate a living organism from nonliving matter. In the mid-1900s, scientists discovered a way to synthesize some of the molecules found in living organisms. Building on that work, scientists hope eventually to find a way to generate simple forms of life in the laboratory.

Redi Critics first questioned the idea of spontaneous generation in 1668. The Italian physician Francesco Redi believed that maggots did not suddenly appear on rotting meat. He proposed, instead, that maggots come from eggs laid by flies that land on the meat.

To test his hypothesis, Redi set out jars similar to those shown in **Figure 3.4**. Some of the jars were open to air, some were completely sealed, and some were covered with cheesecloth. Air can pass through cheesecloth, but flies cannot. After a period of time, Redi observed that maggots appeared only in the jars that could be reached by flies.

Needham Despite Redi's conclusions, most people continued to believe in spontaneous generation. In fact, even Redi believed it could occur under certain conditions. It was around this time that Leeuwenhoek first observed living cells. People used his discovery to support the idea of spontaneous generation. After all, the microscopic world of living things that seemed to suddenly appear had to come from somewhere.

In 1745, an English clergyman named John Needham designed an experiment to test the idea. He boiled chicken broth to kill any microorganisms in it. He then put the broth into a flask, sealed it, and waited. In time, tiny organisms appeared in the broth. Needham concluded that spontaneous generation did occur.

Spallanzani An Italian priest named Lazzaro Spallanzani (spah lahn ZAH nee) was not convinced by Needham's experiment. He suggested that the microorganisms came from the air after the broth was boiled but before the flask was sealed. To test his hypothesis, he placed the chicken broth in a flask, sealed the flask, and then removed the air. Then he boiled the broth. This time, no microorganisms grew in the broth. He concluded that spontaneous generation did not occur. Many critics, however, argued that Spallanzani only proved that spontaneous generation does not occur without air.

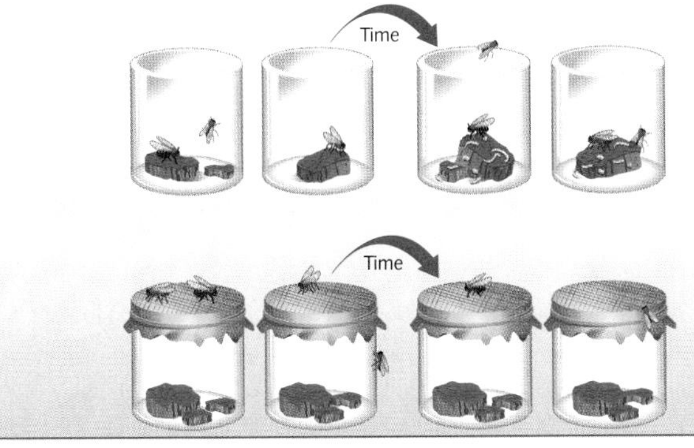

Figure 3.4 In this experiment conducted by Francesco Redi, the spontaneous generation of maggots from rotting meat was tested.

Explain It!

"No scientist works in isolation." In your Science Notebook, write a paragraph explaining this statement. As examples, use the overlapping work of scientists studying cells and others studying spontaneous generation.

Figure It Out

1. What was the control group in Redi's experiment?
2. Did Redi's observation support his hypothesis? Explain.

Teach

ENGAGE Ask students to describe a situation in which they were skeptical about something they learned. Discuss with students the reasons that people are sometimes unwilling to change their minds about a theory that they have believed to be true for a long time. Explain that one purpose of a scientific investigation is to find evidence to support a new theory that refutes a widely held conclusion.

EXTEND Ask students to choose one of the inventions described in the lesson. Have them write a paragraph in their Science Notebooks describing what life would be like without that invention.

Explain It!

Encourage students to think about all of the scientists whom they have heard about and how the work of these scientists has built upon that of those who came before them. If students need help, allow them to work in groups to answer this question.

Check that students' explanations are clear, logical, and correct. Explanations might include that when scientists work together, they can learn from each other and help to prove or disprove each other's theories. The understanding that cells are the basic units of plants and animals led to the question of where organisms come from. This question led to investigations that finally disproved the theory of spontaneous generation.

Figure It Out: Figure 3.4

ANSWER **1.** The jars set out without lids made up the control group. **2.** Maggots appeared only when the flies were able to land on the meat, so the observations supported the hypothesis.

ELL Strategy

Prepare Presentations Organize students into small groups. Assign each group a different scientist mentioned in this lesson. Have students prepare presentations for the class summarizing the work of their assigned scientist. Students may want to add pictures or other visuals to their presentation to capitalize on skills other than language.

Differentiated Instruction

Visual Have students illustrate the paragraphs they wrote in their Science Notebooks by drawing a picture of how they imagine life would be without one of the inventions mentioned in the lesson.

Teach

EXPLAIN Discuss with students the difference between disproving and proving a theory. Explain that it is often necessary to disprove a commonly accepted theory before coming up with an alternate explanation.

Vocabulary

cell theory Explain that the word *cell* has many common uses. People might refer to a small room in a prison as a cell. The word *cell* is also used to describe small hollow places, such as the cells of a honeycomb. Have students compare and contrast these meanings with the scientific meaning of *cell* as the basic unit of living matter.

CONNECTION: History

Discuss with students the benefits of the inventions made by scientists between 1709 and 1837.

Provide students with resources for adding inventions to the time period, such as books and Internet sites. Discuss the inventions students come up with.

Assess

EVALUATE Use the After You Read questions and the Alternative Assessment to help you assess students' understanding of this lesson.

After You Read

1. Leeuwenhoek observed living cells using a single-lens microscope. Hooke observed remnants of cells using a compound microscope.
2. Schleiden and Schwann concluded that all plants and animals are made up of cells. Redi showed that maggots came from eggs laid by flies, but his results were not completely conclusive. Needham concluded that microorganisms arose spontaneously. Spallanzani repeated Needham's work and proved that microorganisms did not appear spontaneously, but might if air were present. Pasteur redesigned the experiment to prove that spontaneous generation does not occur even when air is present.
3. Efforts to disprove spontaneous generation helped Virchow conclude that cells arise only from other cells.

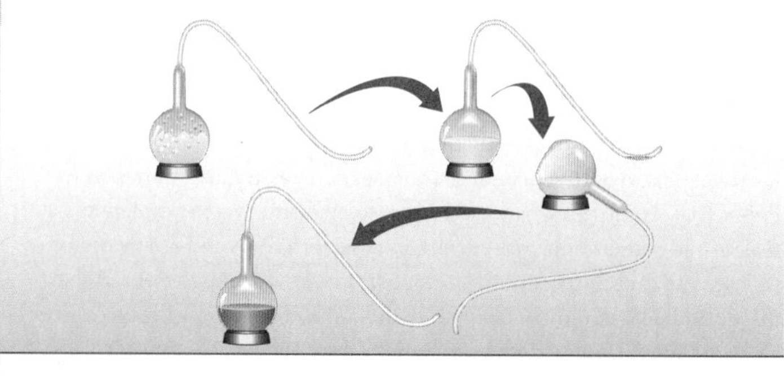

Figure 3.5 Louis Pasteur designed an experiment to settle the issue of spontaneous generation. He used flasks that would allow air to pass through but not microorganisms.

Pasteur In 1859, a French chemist named Louis Pasteur (pas TUHR) designed a variation of the experiments done by Needham and Spallanzani. As shown in **Figure 3.5**, he bent the neck of a flask into an S-shape. This made it possible for air to reach the broth inside. However, any microorganisms in the air would get stuck in the neck of the flask and be unable to reach the broth. As in Spallanzani's experiment, no microorganisms grew in the broth. This time, however, Pasteur knew that spontaneous generation did not occur even in the presence of air. To confirm that microorganisms came from the air, he then tilted the flasks. Microorganisms suddenly appeared in the broth. In this way, Pasteur proved that microorganisms exist in the air and do not arise from nonliving matter.

CONNECTION: History

Inventors were very busy during the years that these scientists were studying cells. For example, the thermometer was invented in 1724, the lightning rod in 1752, and a better steam engine in 1769. The battery was introduced in 1799, the steam locomotive in 1814, and the telegraph in 1837.

The Cell Theory

Around the same time that Pasteur was conducting his experiments, a German physician named Rudolf Virchow was studying cells. Like Pasteur, he did not support the idea of spontaneous generation. In 1855, Virchow presented a theory that cells are produced only by other cells.

This last piece of information on cells helped complete what is now known as the cell theory. The **cell theory** states:

- All living things are made up of cells.
- Cells are the basic units of structure and function in living things.
- New cells are produced from existing cells.

After You Read

1. How were Leeuwenhoek's observations different from those of Hooke?
2. What contribution to the cell theory was made by each scientist studied here.
3. According to the summaries on your time line, how did research into spontaneous generation affect the development of the cell theory?

Alternative Assessment

EVALUATE Have students share their completed time lines with a partner. Encourage students to add any missing events to their time lines. Have each pair create a time line to be displayed in the classroom.

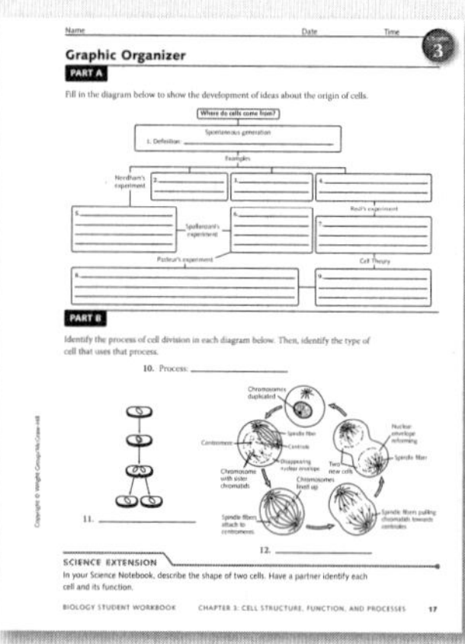

Graphic Organizer

Graphic Organizer
Workbook, p. 17

3.2 The Parts of a Cell

Before You Read

Review the Learning Goals and the vocabulary for this lesson. Many of these terms describe parts of a cell. In your Science Notebook, create a concept map with the word *Cell* in the center. Draw several smaller circles around the word *Cell*. Think about the functions that a cell needs to carry out.

Learning Goals

- Identify the parts of animal cells and plant cells.
- Differentiate between prokaryotic cells and eukaryotic cells.

New Vocabulary

organelle
nucleus
cytoplasm
ribosome
endoplasmic reticulum
Golgi apparatus
mitochondrion
lysosome
vacuole
chloroplast
cell membrane
cell wall
eukaryotic cell
prokaryotic cell

Recall Vocabulary

DNA (p. 31)
photosynthesis (p. 25)

You pull a box of cereal from the kitchen cabinet and head to the table. As your stomach rumbles, you pour some cereal into a bowl. The cereal you're about to eat was processed in a factory. In a factory, many different people and machines work together to manufacture a product. In a cereal factory, ingredients such as grains, sugar, and flour are taken into the factory. They are mixed together and processed to produce cereal. The finished cereal is then placed into packages that are sent out to stores.

In many ways, living cells are like factories that produce goods. They take in raw materials, use them to build products such as proteins, package the products, and transport them to different parts of the cell or to other cells. The different jobs are performed by structures within the cell called **organelles**. The cells of animals and plants share most of the same kinds of organelles and other cell parts. **Figure 3.6** on page 40 shows the structure of a cell from an animal and a cell from a plant.

Nucleus

The **nucleus** (NEW klee us) can be described as the control center of the cell. Almost all of the DNA in a cell is contained in the nucleus. Recall from Chapter 2 that DNA is an organic molecule that stores the instructions for making proteins and other molecules needed by the cell.

The nucleus is surrounded by two thin membranes that make up the nuclear envelope. Pores, or small openings, in the nuclear envelope allow specific materials to move between the nucleus and the rest of the cell.

Cytoplasm

The cell is generally divided into two parts. One part is the nucleus. The part of the cell outside the nucleus is the **cytoplasm**. The cytoplasm contains the organelles as well as chemicals needed by the cell. It also contains the cytoskeleton, which is a network of fibers that gives the cell its shape and anchors organelles in place.

3.2 Introduce

ENGAGE students by having them discuss what they already know about cells. Ask: *Can you name some of the parts of a cell?* Record students' responses on the board. Ask students to name the functions of these parts of the cell. Record their answers on the board. Tell students that in this lesson, they will learn about all of the parts of a cell and how those parts function together.

Before You Read

Tell students that they are creating a concept map showing how the important concepts in the lesson relate to the word *cell*. Tell students that they will be placing the names of parts of the cell in the smaller circles and using the connecting lines to describe the function the parts serve for the entire cell. Check students' drawings throughout the lesson.

Teach

EXPLAIN that in this lesson, students will learn to identify the parts of animal and plant cells. Emphasize that while plant and animal cells have some differences, both types are eukaryotic cells, which are larger and more complex than prokaryotic cells. Tell students that they will learn more about these differences in this lesson.

Vocabulary

organelle Tell students that an organelle is a membrane-bound structure within a cell that does a particular job. Compare an organelle in a cell with an organ, such as the heart, in the body. Both play a specialized role in helping the cell or body to function.

nucleus Explain that a nucleus is the center of something. Ask students to think about other common uses of the word *nucleus*, such as the nucleus of an atom or of a group of people.

cytoplasm Explain that *cytoplasm* comes from the Greek words *kytos,* meaning "anything hollow," and *plasma,* meaning "to form or mold." Ask students to relate this origin to the word's use in science.

ELL Strategy

Illustrate As they read through the lesson, have students draw and label the parts of the cell as they learn them. Suggest that students use a different color for each part of the cell.

Practice Using Vocabulary If time permits, provide students with unlabeled cell drawings and have them practice filling in the labels for each part of a cell.

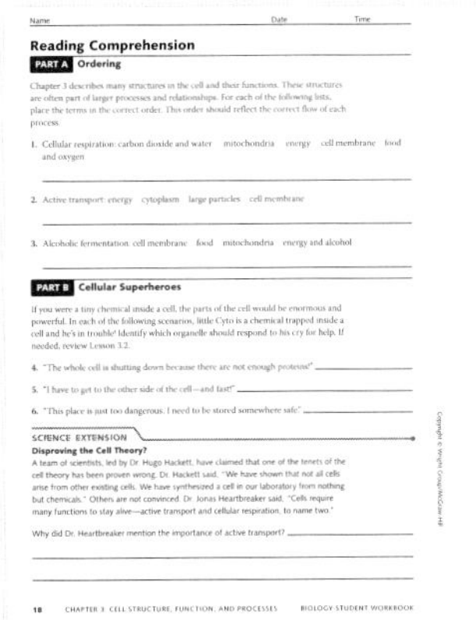
Reading Comprehension
PART A Ordering
PART B Cellular Superheroes
SCIENCE EXTENSION
Disproving the Cell Theory?

Reading Comprehension Workbook, p. 18

Teach

EXPLAIN Discuss with students the similarities and differences between plants and animals. Draw a Venn diagram on the board, and label the similarities and differences. Encourage students to see that the similarities and differences in function between plants and animals have a basis in the similarities and differences between plant cells and animal cells.

Figure It Out: Figure 3.6

ANSWER **1.** The largest and most obvious structure in most cells is the nucleus. However, in the plant cell, the vacuole is even larger. **2.** The plant cell has a cell wall, chloroplasts, and a large vacuole. It also has a boxlike shape, as opposed to the spherical shape of the animal cell.

Figure It Out

1. What is the largest and most obvious structure in each cell?
2. Identify some differences between these two cells.

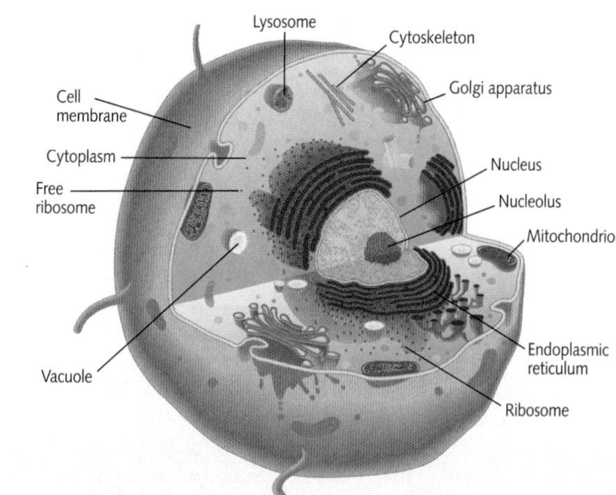

Plant Cell

Mitochondrion
Cytoplasm
Endoplasmic reticulum
Chloroplast
Free ribosome
Ribosome
Golgi apparatus
Cytoskeleton
Cell wall
Cell membrane
Nucleus
Nucleolus
Large vacuole

Figure 3.6 Despite the many differences that might exist among organisms, they are all made up of cells that share many common features. This figure shows the structures of a typical animal cell and a typical plant cell.

Field Study

Take students to a local pond or other body of water. Have them collect water samples and bring these back to the classroom. **CAUTION:** Require students to wear sunscreen and insect repellent, as well as protective gloves for collecting water samples. Students who cannot swim should not be allowed to go near the water. Set up a microscope so that students can examine the samples and look for single-celled organisms. Encourage students to identify the cell parts in the organisms. Alternatively, if enough microscopes are available, have students work in small groups to prepare slides of their water samples and to observe and record what they see.

Ribosomes

The proteins that are made according to instructions in DNA are assembled on **ribosomes** (RI buh sohmz). A ribosome is made up of the nucleic acid RNA and protein. Ribosomes are formed within a structure known as the nucleolus, which is in the nucleus of the cell. Unlike most other organelles, ribosomes are not surrounded by membranes.

Endoplasmic Reticulum

The cell contains a system of membranes and sacs known as the **endoplasmic reticulum** (en duh PLAZ mihk • rih TIHK yuh lum), or ER. The endoplasmic reticulum acts like a highway along which molecules can move from one part of the cell to another.

The part of the ER that is involved in the production of proteins has ribosomes along its surface. As a result, this type of ER is known as rough ER. It is common in cells that make large amounts of proteins. The other part of the ER is known as smooth ER because it does not have ribosomes. This type of ER is involved in regulating processes in cells.

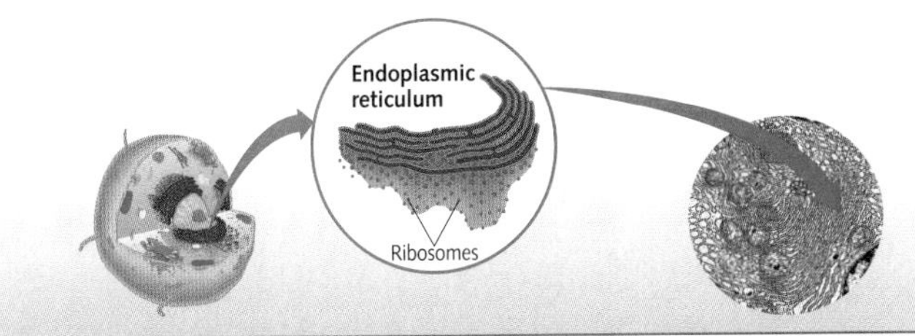

Figure 3.7 The endoplasmic reticulum (ER) is a series of folded membranes. Chemical processes necessary to the cell occur in and on the ER.

Golgi Apparatus

Proteins produced in rough ER are passed along to an organelle known as the **Golgi apparatus**. The Golgi apparatus consists of a stack of membranes. Its job is to modify and package proteins and other molecules so they can either be stored in the cell or sent outside the cell.

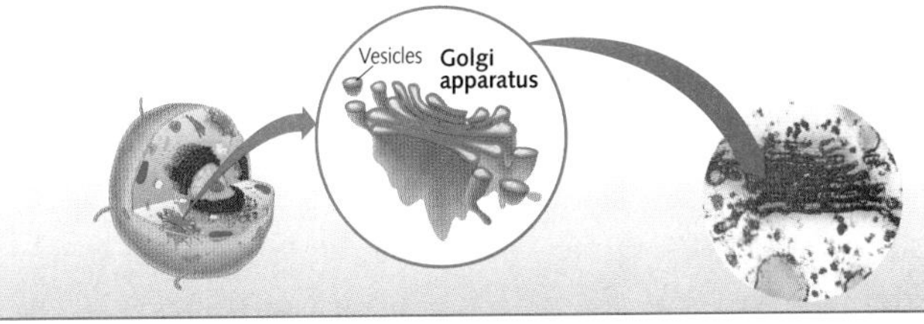

Figure 3.8 The Golgi apparatus looks like a flattened stack of pancakes. What is the role of this organelle?

As You Read

Write the name of one cell part in each smaller circle of your concept map. Add circles as needed. Connect each smaller circle to the circle labeled *Cell* with a line. On each line, write a few words describing the function of that cell part.

Which part of the cell is like the power supply of a factory?

Teach

EXPLAIN to students that despite its small size, a cell has many parts. Each part plays an important role in the functioning of that cell. Encourage students to pay attention to the particular function of each cell part.

As You Read

ANSWER The mitochondrion is the part of the cell that functions like the power supply of a factory.

Vocabulary

ribosomes Tell students that the word *ribose,* which refers to a five-carbon sugar, is part of the word *ribosome.* This sugar, which is part of the structure of RNA molecules, is present in all plant and animal cells.

endoplasmic reticulum Explain to students that the prefix *endo-* means "within." The cytoplasm is the material that fills a cell. Thus, *endoplasmic* refers to something within the cytoplasm. The word *reticulum* contains the root *reticule,* which refers to a "network of fine lines." Thus, the endoplasmic reticulum exists within the cytoplasm, looks like a group of fine parallel lines, and acts as a network along which molecules can move.

Golgi apparatus Tell students that the Golgi apparatus is named for the Nobel Prize-winning scientist Camillo Golgi. Golgi discovered this organelle and identified its function.

Use the Visual: Figure 3.8

EXTEND The Golgi apparatus changes and packages proteins so that they can be sent to other parts of the cell or outside the cell.

Background Information

Camillo Golgi was born in 1843 in a part of Italy that now bears his name. He was an anatomist and pathologist who won the 1906 Nobel Prize in Physiology or Medicine for his work in identifying the structure of the nervous system.

• Teach

EXPLAIN Draw a model of a cell on the board. Label the parts that have been discussed so far in the lesson. Continue to label the diagram as each new part is defined.

Extend It!

The factory analogy can help students better understand the function of a cell. Relating the parts and functions of a cell to a larger and more common experience will help students remember the vocabulary in this lesson.

Suggest that students first sketch their drawings on scrap paper before beginning the final product.

Vocabulary

mitochondrion Tell students that *mitochondrion* comes from the Greek words *mitos*, meaning "a thread," and *chondros*, meaning "lump." Discuss how the word's Greek roots relates to the shape and structure of the cell part it names.

lysosome Explain that the prefix *lyso-* is derived from the Greek word *lysis*, which describes "a loosening." Relate the concept of loosening to the function of the lysosome, which breaks down or loosens the bonds within larger organic molecules.

vacuole Compare and contrast the function of vacuoles in plant cells and in animal cells. In both types of cells, the vacuole serves as storage space. Most plant cells contain one large vacuole, while animal cells contain many smaller vacuoles.

chloroplast Explain to students that the prefix *chloro-* is derived from the Greek word *chlōris*, which means "pale green." Tell students that chloroplasts give the stems and leaves of plants their green color.

cell membrane Tell students that the word *membrane* comes from the Latin word *membrana*, which refers to "a covering." Explain that the membrane of a cell acts as its covering.

cell wall Discuss the common uses of the word *wall*. Ask students to describe the purpose and function of the wall of a house. Compare that purpose and function with that of a cell wall. Explain that both serve as support structures, protecting the house or cell (and those within it) from harm.

eukaryotic cell Explain that the root of *eukaryotic* comes from the Greek word *karyon*, meaning "kernel." Tell students that in biology, this root is used to represent the nucleus of a cell, which resembles a kernel of grain. The prefix *eu-* means "true," so *eukaryotic* means "having a true nucleus."

prokaryotic cell Remind students that the word *prokaryotic* also contains the Greek root *karyon*, meaning "kernel." The prefix *pro-* means "before," so *prokaryotic* means "before a nucleus." Explain that prokaryotic cells, which are less complex, are thought to have appeared before eukaryotic cells.

Differentiated Instruction

Kinesthetic Represent a cell by making a large circle on the floor of the classroom with string or masking tape. Assign students different parts of the cell and have them act out the functions of these parts within the outlined circle.

Extend It!

Think about the ways in which a cell is like a factory. Work with a partner to create a poster that relates each organelle in a cell to a job in a factory. Use both illustrations and descriptions. Then present your poster to the class.

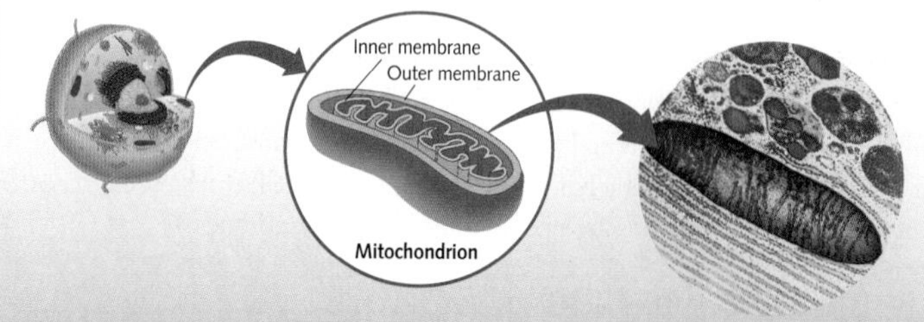

Figure 3.9 Each mitochondrion resembles a seed with a folded inner membrane. The folded shape of the membrane allows a large membrane to fit in a smaller space.

Mitochondria

All cells need energy. Organelles called **mitochondria** (mi tuh KAHN dree uh, singular: mitochondrion) convert energy stored in organic molecules into compounds the cell can use. The greater the energy needs of a cell, the more mitochondria that cell will have.

Lysosomes

The cleanup crew of a cell consists of **lysosomes** (LI suh sohmz). These are small organelles filled with enzymes. An enzyme is a protein that speeds up the rate of a chemical reaction. The enzymes enable the lysosomes to digest, or break down, organic molecules such as carbohydrates, lipids, and proteins. The larger molecules are broken down into small molecules that can be used by the cell. Lysosomes also digest old organelles that are no longer useful to the cell.

Vacuoles

A saclike organelle that stores materials for the cell is known as a **vacuole** (VAK yuh wohl). In some cells, vacuoles store water, salts, carbohydrates, and proteins. Most plant cells have one large central vacuole. The pressure of the liquid in this vacuole helps to structurally support the plant.

Not every cell contains vacuoles. For example, they are found in only some animal cells. For some unicellular organisms, the vacuole plays an important role in motion. The organism pumps water out of the cell in order to move forward.

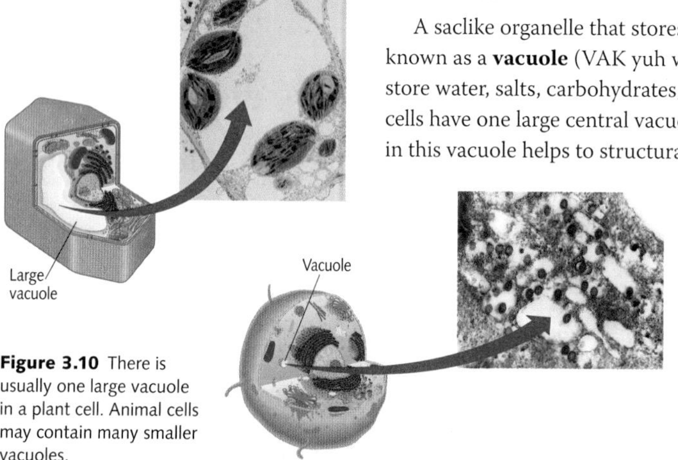

Figure 3.10 There is usually one large vacuole in a plant cell. Animal cells may contain many smaller vacuoles.

Chloroplasts

Plants and some other organisms contain **chloroplasts** (KLOR uh plasts). These organelles are the sites of photosynthesis. Recall from Chapter 2 that during photosynthesis, an organism captures the energy of sunlight and converts it into energy that is stored in organic molecules.

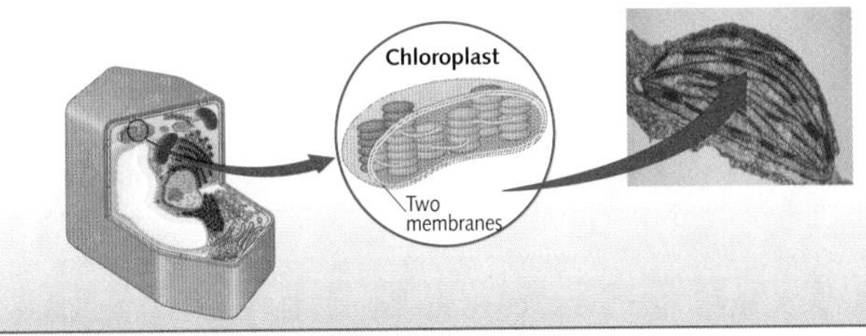

Figure 3.11 Structures within chloroplasts resemble stacks of coins. Chloroplasts trap sunlight and use it to produce organic molecules.

Cell Membrane

At the outer edge of a cell is a thin barrier called the **cell membrane**. A cell must be able to take in nutrients and dispose of wastes. The cell membrane controls how these substances pass into and out of a cell.

Cell Wall

In some cells, such as plant cells, an additional barrier is located outside the cell membrane. The **cell wall** is a rigid outer layer that supports the cell and protects it from harm. Pores in the cell wall allow materials to pass into and out of the cell.

Types of Cells

The animal cells and plant cells you just read about are eukaryotic (yew KAR ee ah tik) cells. Some other organisms, such as bacteria, are prokaryotic (proh KAR ree oht ik) cells. What makes the cells different?

A **eukaryotic cell** is larger and more complex than a **prokaryotic cell**. A eukaryotic cell has a nucleus, and a prokaryotic cell does not. In addition, many of the organelles in a eukaryotic cell are enclosed in their own membranes. A prokaryotic cell does not contain membrane-bound organelles. **Figure 3.12** shows both types of cells.

After You Read

1. What is the role of ribosomes in a cell?
2. List three ways in which a eukaryotic cell is different from a prokaryotic cell.
3. Identify which parts in the diagram you drew in your Science Notebook are found in plant cells but not in animal cells.

CONNECTION: Art

Many of the photographs you may see of cells appear in color. The colors do not represent the actual colors of the cell and cell parts. Instead, they are used to make the cells easier to study and to highlight different parts of the cells. Draw and label your own version of an animal cell. Use different colors to identify the various organelles.

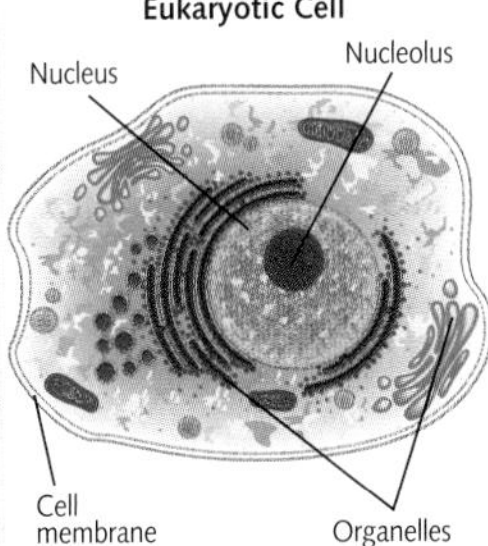

Figure 3.12 Some parts of prokaryotic cells and eukaryotic cells are shown here.

Teacher Alert

Because they share the same root, *karyotic*, the vocabulary words *eukaryotic* and *prokaryotic* are very easy for students to mix up. Understanding the meaning of the prefixes *pro-* (before) and *eu-* (true) will help students remember the difference between the two words.

Teach

EXPLAIN Review with students the process of converting the energy of sunlight into energy that is stored in organic molecules. Remind students that this process, called photosynthesis, occurs in plants, algae, and some bacteria, but it does not occur in animals.

CONNECTION: Art

Encourage students to think about the colors that they are choosing for each part of the cell. For example, in a plant cell, they might color the chloroplasts green. Suggest that students first make rough drafts of their cells on scrap paper and decide upon their colors before starting their final color copies.

Assess

EVALUATE Use the After You Read questions and the Alternative Assessment to help you assess students' understanding of this lesson.

After You Read

1. Ribosomes are the structures on which proteins are made.
2. A eukaryotic cell is larger and more complex, has a nucleus, and has membrane-bound organelles.
3. Plant cells have chloroplasts and cell walls, as well as a large vacuole, which animal cells lack.

Alternative Assessment

EVALUATE Encourage students who have difficulty writing to draw diagrams of a plant cell and an animal cell and label the parts. Ask students to highlight the cell structures that exist only in plant cells.

3.3 Introduce

ENGAGE students by asking if they have ever experienced the wrinkling of their fingers after being in a bath or swimming pool for a long time. Ask: *Does anyone have a name for what their fingers look like when they get all wrinkled?*

Students should suggest that their wrinkled fingers remind them of raisins. Remind students that raisins are dried grapes. Emphasize that while raisins are made by taking the water *out* of grapes, "raisin fingers" are the result of skin cells at the surface *absorbing* water.

Before You Read

Model the T-chart on the board. Discuss with students times when they have used or heard the words *passive* and *active*. Tell them that these words are antonyms, which means that they have opposite meanings.

Teach

EXPLAIN to students that in this lesson, they will learn how diffusion occurs. They will also be able to identify the nature of osmosis and facilitated diffusion. Tell them that they will examine the means by which active transport occurs.

Vocabulary

solution Explain that the word *solution* is commonly used in relation to the act of solving a problem. Have students contrast this meaning with the scientific meaning of *solution* as a liquid containing dissolved materials.

concentration Tell students that the greater the amount of a substance dissolved in a liquid, the greater the concentration of the solution. To enable students to act this out, place a circle on the floor and ask more and more students to stand inside the circle. Explain that the concentration increases as more students enter the circle.

Learning Goals

- Explain how diffusion occurs.
- Identify the nature of osmosis and facilitated diffusion.
- Examine the means by which active transport occurs.

New Vocabulary

solution
concentration
diffusion
equilibrium
passive transport
selectively permeable membrane
osmosis
facilitated diffusion
active transport

3.3 Cellular Transport

Before You Read

In your Science Notebook, draw a T-chart. Label one side *Passive Transport* and the other side *Active Transport*. In your own words, define the terms *passive* and *active*.

Have you ever noticed that after being in a bathtub or swimming pool for a long time, your fingers and toes become wrinkled? Fingers and toes become wrinkled because skin cells at the surface absorb water. The outer skin cells are tightly attached to the layers below. Having nowhere to go, the skin wrinkles to make up for the swelling.

Just as water can pass through the outer membrane of a skin cell, so too can other materials. This enables the cell to obtain materials it needs from its environment and to get rid of wastes.

Concentration of Solutions

The materials that enter and leave a cell are dissolved in the liquids on either side of the cell membrane. A liquid containing dissolved materials is known as a **solution**. A solution is a mixture of two or more substances. The substance in a solution that does the dissolving is known as the solvent. The substance that is dissolved is known as the solute. As discussed in Chapter 2, water is known as the universal solvent because it can dissolve so many substances.

The **concentration** of a solution compares the amount of substance dissolved to the amount of substance doing the dissolving. For example, suppose you add a pinch of powdered drink mix to a glass of water. The drink will not be very flavorful because the concentration of drink mix is low. However, if you add a large spoonful of drink mix to the water, the drink will taste much sweeter. This is because the concentration is high.

Figure 3.13 The concentration of a solution depends on how much of one substance is dissolved in another. The more drink mix that is dissolved in water, the sweeter and more flavorful the drink will taste.

ELL Strategy

Act Out Have students create a solution of sugar and water. Explain that as they continue to add more sugar, the solution becomes more concentrated.

Background Information

Solutions cannot be separated by filtration. Solutions occur when solids, liquids, or gases dissolve in liquids and when gases dissolve in liquids or other gases. When a liquid solution is frozen, it becomes a solid solution. The substance that is dissolved is known as the solute, and the substance that does the dissolving is known as the solvent.

44 CELL STRUCTURE, FUNCTION, AND PROCESSES

Diffusion

As with all particles, the particles in a solution are in constant motion. As they move, they collide with each other. This causes them to spread out. They tend to move from an area where they are more crowded to an area where they are less crowded. The movement of particles from an area of higher concentration to an area of lower concentration is known as **diffusion** (dih FYEW zhun).

Diffusion is one way that particles enter and leave a cell. Suppose, for example, that the concentration of a substance is different on either side of the cell membrane, as in **Figure 3.14**. If the substance can cross the cell membrane, its particles will move toward the area where it is less concentrated.

Particles will continue to diffuse until their concentration is the same on both sides of the cell membrane. The system is then said to be at **equilibrium** (ee kwuh LIH bree um). Once equilibrium is reached, particles continue to move across the cell membrane in both directions. However, the same number of particles moves in each direction, so there is no additional change in concentration.

The difference in concentration between two regions is known as the concentration gradient. Diffusion does not require the cell to use energy because it depends on the random movements of particles to move substances along the concentration gradient. The movement of materials into or out of the cell without the cell's use of energy is called **passive transport**.

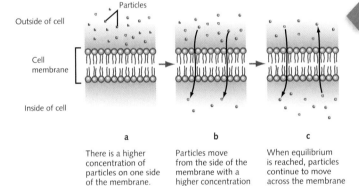

Diffusion Across a Cell Membrane

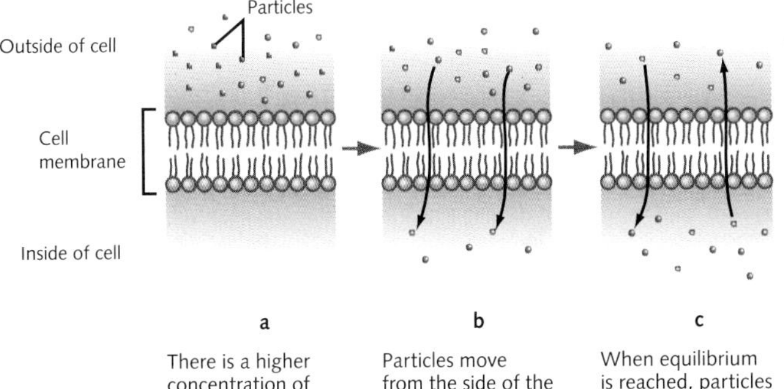

a — There is a higher concentration of particles on one side of the membrane.

b — Particles move from the side of the membrane with a higher concentration to the side of the membrane with a lower concentration.

c — When equilibrium is reached, particles continue to move across the membrane in both directions.

Figure 3.14 During diffusion, particles move from areas of higher concentration to areas of lower concentration.

Explain It!

In your Science Notebook, write a paragraph in which you describe a time that you moved from an area of higher concentration to an area of lower concentration. For example, maybe you have moved to a less crowded area in a store, at a party, or on a beach. Explain how your action was similar to that of particles during diffusion.

Figure It Out

1. In Part a, on which side of the cell membrane are the particles more concentrated?
2. Describe what occurs when the system reaches equilibrium.

Teach

EXPLAIN Point out to students that particles in a cell seek equilibrium. Explain that the particles will move until they have reached this state. Discuss with students why particles seek this state.

Vocabulary

diffusion Tell students that the prefix *dif-* means the "opposite of" and that the definition of *fusion* is "the act of bringing or melting together." Thus, *diffusion* is the opposite of bringing together. Instead, it is the movement of particles away from one another to less crowded areas.

equilibrium Explain to students that the word *equilibrium* is a combination of the Latin words *aequus*, which means "equal," and *libra*, meaning "balance." Tell students that the state of equilibrium exists when the system is equally balanced (i.e., when the concentration on both sides of a cell membrane is the same).

passive transport Remind students that the word *passive* is an antonym for the word *active*. Tell students that the movement of materials into or out of the cell without the cell's use of energy is known as passive transport. The opposite of this would involve use of the cell's energy and is therefore known as active transport.

Background Information

When there is a difference in the concentration of the solution outside the cell compared with the cytoplasm inside the cell, the outside solution is either hypertonic or hypotonic. In a hypertonic solution, the concentration of particles outside the cell is higher than that inside the cell. When a cell is placed in a hypertonic solution, water diffuses out of the cell, causing the cell to shrivel.

In a hypotonic solution, the concentration of particles inside the cytoplasm is higher than the concentration outside the cell. When a cell is placed into a hypotonic solution, the water diffuses into the cell. This causes the cell to swell. Solutions with equal concentrations are called isotonic solutions.

Explain It!

Have students share their stories with the class. Check that students' stories all describe movement from higher to lower concentrations. Invite students to describe why they chose to move to a less concentrated area (students might suggest that it is more comfortable there) and what it would look like once equilibrium was reached (the concentrations of both areas would be the same).

Figure It Out: Figure 3.14

ANSWER **1.** The particles are more concentrated outside the cell membrane.
2. At equilibrium, the concentration is the same on both sides of the cell membrane. It does not mean that particles no longer move.

Teach

EXPLAIN Create two columns on the board. Label one column *permeable* and the other *impermeable.* Give examples of common permeable substances, such as paper towels, and impermeable substances, such as plastic bags. Ask students for additional examples, and record them in the appropriate columns.

As You Read

ANSWER Active transport requires the cell to use energy, while passive transport does not.

Use the Visual: Figure 3.15

ANSWER The number of sugar molecules on each side stays the same, but the number of water molecules decreases on the left side of the membrane and increases on the right side.

Vocabulary

selectively permeable membrane Tell students that the word *permeable* contains the Latin prefix *per-*, meaning "through," and the root *meare,* meaning "to pass." If a membrane is permeable, it allows substances to pass through. Explain that a selectively permeable membrane allows only certain particles to pass through. Other particles cannot. Thus, the membrane is seen as "selecting" what can and cannot pass through.

osmosis Explain to students that the word *osmosis* is commonly used to mean "to learn without trying," as in, "I learned Spanish through osmosis; it just came to me." Compare this to the word's scientific meaning: the diffusion of water molecules across a selectively permeable membrane.

facilitated diffusion Explain to students that the word *facilitate* means "to make easy." In facilitated diffusion, structures in the cell membrane make it easy for certain molecules to pass through.

active transport Tell students that the movement of materials against the concentration gradient is known as active transport and requires energy. Compare this with the idea of transporting a football by running across a field, which also requires energy.

As You Read

List examples of passive and active transport described in the lesson in the T-chart you created in your Science Notebook.

Which form of transport requires the cell to use energy?

Osmosis

Not all particles can diffuse across a cell membrane. Most membranes are **selectively permeable membranes,** which means that some particles can pass across them while others cannot. A membrane is said to be permeable to substances that can pass across it and impermeable to those that cannot.

Perhaps the most important substance that passes through the cell membrane is water. Water molecules pass through a selectively permeable membrane by a type of diffusion known as **osmosis** (ahs MOH sus). During osmosis, water molecules move from a place of higher concentration of water to a place of lower concentration of water—either into or out of the cell.

When there is a difference in the concentration of a solution outside a cell compared with the cytoplasm inside the cell, osmosis will occur. If the concentration of solute particles outside the cell is higher than the concentration inside the cytoplasm, water diffuses out of the cell, causing the cell to shrivel. If the concentration of solute particles inside the cytoplasm is higher than the concentration outside the cell, water diffuses into the cell. This causes the cell to swell.

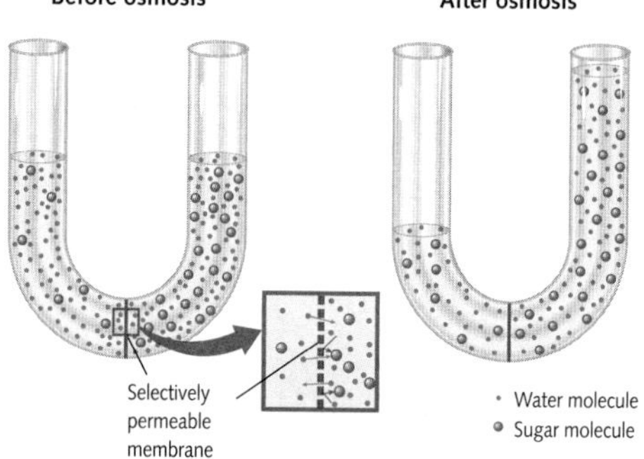

Figure 3.15 The barrier at the bottom of this U-tube is a selectively permeable membrane. It allows water molecules to pass through it, but not sugar molecules. How do the numbers of water and sugar molecules on each side of the membrane change after osmosis?

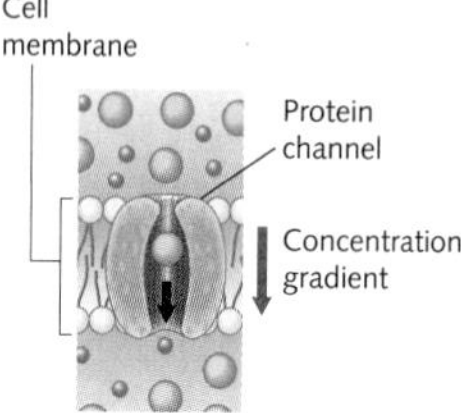

Figure 3.16 Protein channels help certain particles move across the cell membrane. The process is still diffusion and occurs only if there is a difference in concentration.

Facilitated Diffusion

Another type of diffusion is known as **facilitated diffusion.** During this process, a few molecules pass through the cell membrane more easily than might be expected. The reason is that cell membranes have pathways in them known as protein channels. The channels allow specific types of molecules to pass into or out of the cell. Protein channels in red blood cells, for example, allow only glucose to pass through.

Differentiated Instruction

Kinesthetic, Visual Divide the class into thirds. Place a line on the floor. Have two-thirds of the class stand on one side of the line and one-third stand on the other side. Students should simulate osmosis by acting like water molecules and passing from the more populated, or "concentrated," side of the line to the less populated side.

ELL Strategy

Model Have students work in small groups to make posters or diagrams for each of the processes discussed in the lesson. Allow students who have difficulty with English to first describe the process in their native language and then translate their descriptions into English.

Active Transport

Some materials must be moved against the concentration gradient by **active transport**. This type of movement requires the cell to use energy.

Molecule Transport Like facilitated transport, active transport can use proteins in the membrane to move substances across the membrane. For example, sodium ions (Na^+) are pumped out of the cell and potassium ions (K^+) are pumped into the cell by specific carrier proteins. The cell must use energy to pump these ions across the membrane.

Endocytosis and Exocytosis Some large molecules are transported by movements of the cell membrane itself. During endocytosis (en duh sy TOH sus), the cell membrane surrounds a substance and brings it into the cell. In an opposite process known as exocytosis (ek soh si TOH sus), the cell membrane releases substances from the cell.

Cell membrane
Carrier proteins
+
Cellular energy
Step 1
Step 2
Concentration gradient

Figure 3.17 In active transport, carrier proteins can pick up and transport ions and molecules across the cell membrane. Why does this process require energy?

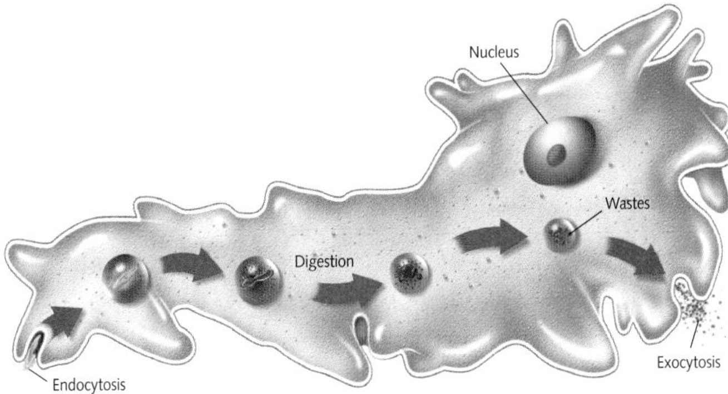

Figure 3.18 Some cells take in or release materials through movements of the cell membrane that use energy. Endocytosis and exocytosis are forms of active transport.

 **Explore It!**

Obtain four raisins. Soak two in water overnight. Set the other two aside. Blot the water-soaked raisins dry. Be careful not to break the skins. Examine both sets of raisins. Carefully poke the ends of each raisin with a toothpick. Squeeze each raisin over a paper towel. How can you account for any differences in the raisins?

After You Read

1. How is diffusion related to the concentration of solutions inside and outside the cell?
2. Compare and contrast osmosis and facilitated diffusion.
3. What is active transport? Give two examples of how it occurs.
4. In a well-developed paragraph, compare active transport and passive transport in terms of the cell's use of energy. Use examples from the T-chart in your Science Notebook in your answer.

Teach

EXPLAIN Tell students that active learning takes place when they do something, such as take notes. Passive learning takes place when they listen to information without doing anything with it. Point out that *active* and *passive* have opposite meanings.

Use the Visual: Figure 3.17

ANSWER because materials are being moved against the concentration gradient

 **Explore It!**

Provide raisins that are approximately the same size to start. Have students measure the beginning and final mass of the raisins and the beginning and final volume of water. (Note: 1 mL of water has a mass of 1 g.) Then, students can calculate the volume (or mass) of water the raisins absorbed by subtracting the final mass of raisins from the original mass or the final volume of the water from its initial volume. Ask students to explain the difference in the raisins before and after soaking (they absorbed water), as well as the difference in volume of the water used for soaking (decreased because the raisins absorbed some of it).

Assess

EVALUATE Use the After You Read questions and the Alternative Assessment to help you assess students' understanding of this lesson.

After You Read

1. Diffusion occurs when there is a difference in concentration.
2. Both are forms of passive transport. In osmosis, water diffuses across a selectively permeable membrane. In facilitated diffusion, particles move through specific protein channels.
3. Active transport is the movement of materials across the cell membrane with the use of energy. Exocytosis and endocytosis are two examples.
4. During both processes, materials move across the cell membrane. However, passive transport does not require the use of energy, whereas active transport does.

Alternative Assessment

EVALUATE For students who have difficulty answering the After You Read questions, refer to their T-charts. Check that they have accurately distinguished between active and passive transport.

3.4 Introduce

ENGAGE Discuss with students the differences between plants and animals. Ask: *How are plants and animals similar and how are they different?*

Allowing students to work in pairs, have half the class brainstorm the differences and the other half brainstorm the similarities between plants and animals.

Draw a Venn diagram on the board, and record students' answers. Point out to students that one of the key differences between plants and animals is the way they obtain energy and nutrients.

Before You Read

Suggest that students use a Venn diagram to record their comparisons. Check students' diagrams throughout the lesson.

Teach

EXPLAIN to students that in this lesson, they will learn to trace the flow of energy that occurs during photosynthesis. They will also examine the process that occurs during cellular respiration and identify the circumstances under which fermentation occurs.

Vocabulary

producers Tell students that the word *producers* comes from the Latin *pro-* meaning "forth," and *ducere*, meaning "to bring" or "to lead." Discuss with students why a word that means "to bring or lead forth" is used to describe organisms that make, or "bring forth," organic molecules for themselves and food for other organisms.

cellular respiration Explain to students that the process of cellular respiration is necessary for life. Just as we need to breathe in oxygen to survive, cells need to use oxygen to break down and release energy. If it is unable to do this, a cell will die.

Learning Goals

- Trace the flow of energy that occurs during photosynthesis.
- Examine the process that occurs during cellular respiration.
- Identify the circumstances under which fermentation occurs.

New Vocabulary

producer
cellular respiration
aerobic
fermentation
anaerobic

Recall Vocabulary

energy (p. 25)
autotroph (p. 25)
heterotroph (p. 25)

Did You Know?

Most environments on land depend on organisms that conduct photosynthesis. However, some organisms rely on another method of capturing matter and energy. Deep beneath the surface of the ocean, near hot vents in the ocean floor, some organisms produce organic molecules from chemicals released into the ocean water. This process is known as chemosynthesis.

3.4 Energy and Cells

Before You Read

Think about what you do when you compare and contrast. Then select a plant and an animal. In your Science Notebook, create a chart to compare and contrast the two organisms. Write words or draw pictures in your chart.

Have you ever felt as if you were filled with energy? Or maybe you have felt drained of energy after a long day. Recall from Chapter 2 that energy is the ability to cause change or do work. Cells need energy to perform their functions. Where does that energy come from? Almost all of the energy used by living things comes from the Sun.

Photosynthesis

Light, such as sunlight, is one type of energy. There are other types of energy as well. A different type of energy known as chemical energy is stored in organic substances such as foods and fuels. Each form of energy can be changed into another form.

The process by which some organisms capture light energy and change it into chemical energy is called photosynthesis. Organisms that conduct photosynthesis are called **producers** because they make, or produce, food for other organisms. All autotrophs, or organisms that capture matter and energy from their surroundings, are producers.

Recall from Lesson 2 that plant cells contain chloroplasts. Within chloroplasts is a pigment known as chlorophyll. It is this pigment that gives plants their green color and allows plants to capture the energy of sunlight. As shown in **Figure 3.19**, this energy is required for a process that uses carbon dioxide gas from the air and water to produce organic molecules, such as carbohydrates, and oxygen gas.

Some of the energy stored in organic molecules is used by the plant's cells. Any remaining energy can be stored in the form of carbohydrates, such as starch and sugar, and lipids.

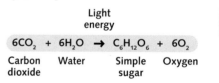

$$6CO_2 + 6H_2O \xrightarrow{\text{Light energy}} C_6H_{12}O_6 + 6O_2$$

Carbon dioxide | Water | Simple sugar | Oxygen

Figure 3.19 The process of photosynthesis can be summarized by this equation. It shows that six molecules of carbon dioxide and six molecules of water are needed to form one simple sugar molecule and six molecules of oxygen.

ELL Strategy

Sequencing, Illustrate Have students illustrate in their Science Notebooks the process of photosynthesis. Encourage students to include all of the steps and allow them to add to their illustrations throughout the lesson.

Teacher Alert

Summary equations for photosynthesis often show glucose as a product. But, glucose is not a product of fixing carbon dioxide. Leaves store excess chemical energy as starch molecules, made of long chains of glucose units. Sucrose, a double sugar with a glucose unit and a fructose unit, transports chemical energy to stems or roots for storage. In fact, all of a plant's organic molecules are made, directly or indirectly, as a result of photosynthesis.

Cellular Respiration

Plants get energy from sunlight. Where do you get energy? You, along with other organisms that do not conduct photosynthesis, get energy from the foods you eat. Such organisms are called heterotrophs.

Organisms must release the energy stored in organic molecules. One way they do this is through a process known as cellular respiration. During **cellular respiration**, glucose and other organic molecules are broken down to release energy in the presence of oxygen. Cellular respiration occurs in the mitochondria of eukaryotic cells.

The process of cellular respiration is summarized in **Figure 3.20**. Despite the simple equation, cellular respiration does not take place in one simple step. Instead, the process occurs in a series of steps. In each step, cells can trap bits of energy and change that energy into a form the cell can use.

Figure 3.20 The complete process of cellular respiration is summarized by this equation. It shows that during cellular respiration, organisms use organic compounds, such as glucose, and oxygen to produce carbon dioxide, water, and energy.

CONNECTION: Physics

Everything you do involves energy. Whether you are riding a skateboard, getting dressed, or reading a book, you are using energy. Energy is all around you in different forms. For example, nuclear energy powers the Sun and other stars. Light, also known as electromagnetic energy, is then given off by the Sun. That energy is captured by plants and changed into chemical energy.

Perhaps you are recognizing the fact that each form of energy can be converted into another form. What you may not know, however, is that no energy is destroyed or created in the process. The total amount of energy in a system remains the same. This fundamental concept of physics is known as the law of conservation of energy. According to this law, energy is neither created nor destroyed by ordinary processes.

Does that mean that the amount of energy in the universe is always exactly the same? Well, not exactly. In 1905, Albert Einstein proposed the idea that in some situations, matter can change into energy and energy can change into matter. Therefore, the total amount of matter *and* energy in the universe remains constant.

As You Read

Extend the chart you made for comparing and contrasting plants and animals so that you can now compare and contrast photosynthesis and cellular respiration.

How are the two processes similar? How are they different?

Figure It Out

1. How many molecules of oxygen are produced for each molecule of glucose that is broken down?
2. Explain where the energy released during cellular respiration came from.

Background Information

The law of conservation of mass and energy is also known as the first law of thermodynamics, which states that energy in a system cannot be gained or lost. Scientists arrived at this understanding after the British physicist James Prescott Joule showed how mechanical energy is changed into heat energy in 1847.

Teach

EXPLAIN to students that the word *energy* comes from the Greek *en-*, meaning "in," and *ergon*, meaning "work." Discuss with students their interpretation of "work," and how that might apply to the idea of energy.

As You Read

ANSWER The processes are similar in that they involve the same materials and they are conducted by living things. However, only producers conduct photosynthesis. In addition, the materials that go into photosynthesis are produced during cellular respiration, and vice versa.

Figure It Out: Figure 3.20

ANSWER **1.** Six molecules of oxygen are released. **2.** The energy released during cellular respiration was captured from sunlight during photosynthesis.

CONNECTION: Physics

Explain to students that there are two types of energy, kinetic energy and potential energy. Kinetic energy describes the energy of motion. Potential energy describes the energy of position.

Have students explore the difference between potential and kinetic energy by allowing them to roll a marble down an inclined plane. Explain that at the top of the incline, the marble has a certain amount of potential energy and that, as it rolls down the plane, the potential energy is converted to a certain (and changing) amount of kinetic energy.

EXTEND Have students describe the difference between the potential and the kinetic energy of the marble as it rolled down the plane. Have them identify where they think the marble has maximum and minimum kinetic energy and potential energy. Ask them to think about how the angle of the plane (thus the height from which the marble is launched) might affect the potential and kinetic energies.

Teach

EXPLAIN Compare the cycles of photosynthesis and cellular respiration to other cycles, such as the water cycle.

Vocabulary

aerobic Explain to students that the word *aerobic* comes from the Greek words *aeros,* meaning "air," and *bios,* meaning "life." An aerobic process requires oxygen, or air, in order to take place.

fermentation Students may be familiar with the process of fermentation that produces alcohol. Explain that there are different types of fermentation and that alcoholic fermentation is one type.

anaerobic Tell students that the prefix *an-* in *anaerobic* means "not." Explain that since *aerobic* means "air" for "life," *anaerobic* means "not air" for "life." Anaerobic processes do not require oxygen.

Use the Visual: Figure 3.22

ANSWER because it doesn't require oxygen

CONNECTION: Nutrition

Fermentation is one of the oldest known processes of food preservation. Fermentation increases the longevity of foods and decreases the need for refrigeration. Pickles and olives are examples of fermented foods.

Bring in some examples of fermented foods. Have students observe, taste, and smell the different foods and describe their observations in their Science Notebooks.

Assess

EVALUATE Use the After You Read questions and the Alternative Assessment to help you assess students' understanding of this lesson.

After You Read

1. Light energy is converted into the chemical energy in organic molecules.
2. to release energy for use by cells.
3. The raw materials of photosynthesis are the products of cellular respiration.
4. Both cellular respiration and fermentation are methods by which organisms release stored energy from organic compounds. However, cellular respiration requires oxygen and fermentation does not.

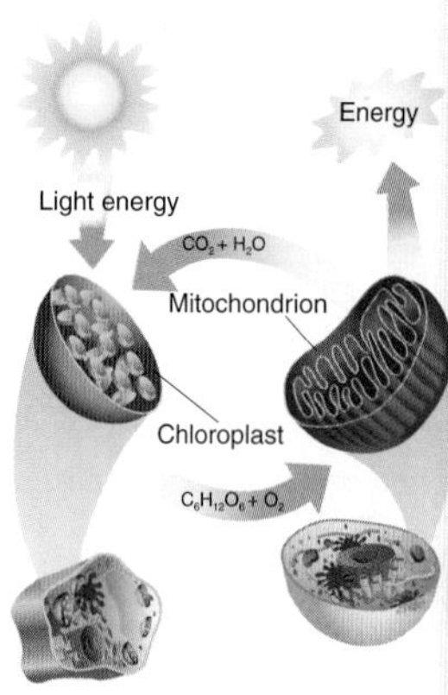

Figure 3.21 Photosynthesis and cellular respiration are related in a continuous process. Both plants and animals conduct cellular respiration, but only plants conduct photosynthesis.

Figure 3.22 Many foods, such as these loaves of bread, are produced using a type of fermentation. Why is fermentation an anaerobic process?

A Continuous Cycle

Did you notice anything familiar about the equation for cellular respiration? It is the opposite of the equation describing photosynthesis. In other words, the materials needed for cellular respiration are the materials produced during photosynthesis. The materials produced during cellular respiration are the materials needed for photosynthesis.

Fermentation

Cellular respiration is said to be an **aerobic** (er ROH bihk) process because it requires oxygen. When cells cannot get the oxygen they need, they use a process called **fermentation** (fur mun TAY shun) to release energy stored in organic molecules. This process is said to be **anaerobic** (an uh ROH bihk) because it does not require oxygen. Fermentation does not provide cells with as much energy as cellular respiration does.

There are two types of fermentation: lactic acid fermentation and alcoholic fermentation.

Lactic Acid Fermentation During this type of fermentation, cells produce a compound called lactic acid. This type of fermentation is used to manufacture certain foods, such as yogurt and cheese. It also occurs in your muscles during strenuous exercise.

Alcoholic Fermentation During alcoholic fermentation, some single-celled organisms produce ethyl alcohol. This type of fermentation is used to produce bread and beverages such as wine and beer.

CONNECTION: Nutrition

Fermentation has been used to preserve foods throughout history. One advantage of fermented foods is that they are partially broken down already, which makes them easier to digest. In addition, important enzymes, vitamins, and other nutrients are preserved because they are not broken down by heat.

After You Read

1. What changes in energy occur during photosynthesis?
2. Why do organisms conduct cellular respiration?
3. How are the raw materials and products of photosynthesis related to those of cellular respiration?
4. Extend the chart in your Science Notebook once more. This time, compare and contrast cellular respiration and fermentation. How are these processes alike? How are they different?

Alternative Assessment

EVALUATE Direct students who have difficulty answering the After You Read questions to share their compare and contrast diagrams with a partner. Have students add to their diagrams. Encourage them to discuss the differences between plants and animals and between cellular respiration and fermentation.

Background Information

Until the late 1970s, many scientists believed that the buildup of lactic acid in muscles caused the muscles to burn and hurt after strenuous exercise. Dr. George Brooks, a biology professor at the University of California, found that lactic acid is, in fact, a source of energy and does not cause muscle soreness or fatigue.

 Cell Growth and Development

Learning Goals

- Examine the relationship between cell shape and function.
- Identify factors that limit cell size.
- Describe the process of cell division.

New Vocabulary

tissue
organ
organ system
cell division
binary fission
cell cycle

Recall Vocabulary

volume (p. 15)

Before You Read

Preview the lesson by looking at the pictures and reading the headings and the Learning Goals. In your Science Notebook, write a paragraph describing what you think the lesson is about based on your preview.

In Chapter 2, you learned that some organisms are made up of one cell and others are made up of more than one cell. Cells of multicellular organisms vary in their structure and function.

Cell Shape

The shape of a cell is often related to its function. Nerve cells, for example, are long and thin, which enables them to send information from one part of the body to another. Another type of cell, a red blood cell, carries oxygen throughout the body. This type of cell is in the form of a flattened disk that can flow through thin blood vessels. A sperm cell is a cell that travels to an egg cell. Each sperm cell has a strong tail that enables it to travel quickly.

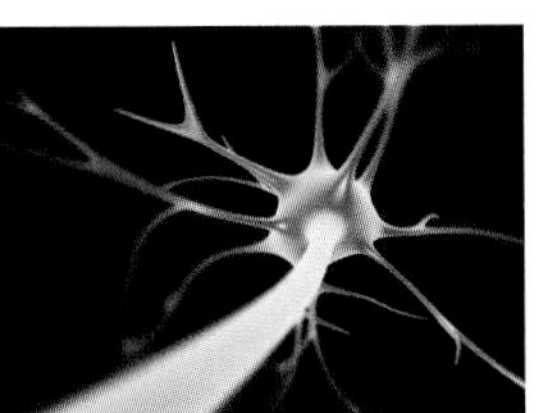

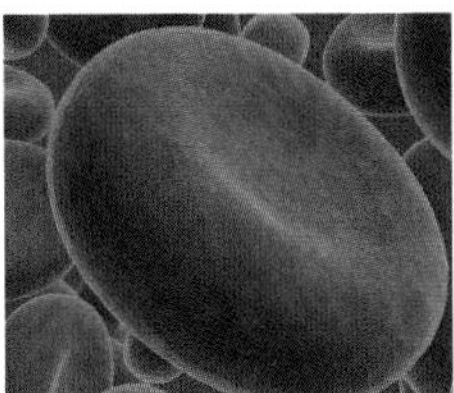

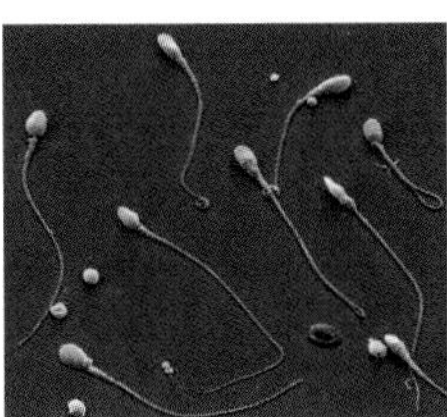

Figure 3.23 The shape of a cell is related to its function. A nerve cell (left) is long and thin. Red blood cells (center) are flattened and have a large area through which oxygen can pass. Sperm cells (right) have tails that propel them through fluids.

Levels of Organization

Your community could not function if many different people did not perform many necessary jobs. For example, letter carriers deliver the mail, trash collectors take away the garbage, and police officers help make sure that everyone is safe. Each person has a specific job to do to make life in the community possible. Groups of people with similar jobs often work together. Just as people perform different jobs within a community, cells perform specific tasks within an organism. Similarly, just as people can work together, so too can cells.

Tissues The cell is the most basic unit of organization. In most multicellular organisms, groups of similar cells are organized into **tissues**. Each tissue has specific functions. Muscle tissues, for example, make the heart beat, the stomach digest food, and the body move.

3.5 Introduce

ENGAGE Discuss with students the relationship between form and function. Ask: *How does the shape of your hand help it function?*

As a class, consider other body parts, such as feet, legs, ears, and the nose. Discuss how the shape and form of each part helps it perform its function effectively.

Tell students that cells come in different shapes and that the shape of each cell is often related to its function.

Before You Read

Have students take turns reading the headings and captions aloud to the class. After they have written their paragraphs, ask a few students to share with the class.

Teach

EXPLAIN to students that in this lesson, they will examine the relationship between cell shape and function. They will also identify factors that limit cell size and describe the process of cell division.

 Vocabulary

tissues Explain that the word *tissue* comes from the French word *tistre*, which means "to weave." Discuss with students the connection between *weaving* and the scientific meaning of *tissue* as a group of similar cells.

Science Notebook EXTRA

Provide students with several different tools, such as a hammer, scissors, and a pencil. Have students sketch each tool in their Science Notebooks and write about how the shape of the tool helps it function.

Differentiated Instruction

Visual Throughout the lesson, have students sketch each type of cell in their Science Notebooks. Students should label each cell and describe its function. Have students who have difficulty with English describe the function of the cell in their native language and then translate their descriptions into English.

Teach

EXPLORE Discuss with students the ways they work together as a class. Have students describe the functions of the different members of the class, including the teacher, and how the members work together. Explain that like the class, cells work together to perform tasks.

Use the Visual: Figure 3.24

ANSWER The cell is the most basic level of organization.

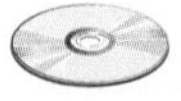

Vocabulary

organ Explain to students that a common use of the word *organ* is to describe a musical instrument with pipes of different lengths that is played by pushing air through the pipes. In a musical organ, the pipes work together to produce music, just as the tissues work together to perform the function of an organ such as the heart or brain.

organ system Tell students that the prefix *syn-* in the Greek origin of the word *system* means "together." In an organ system, the organs work together to perform a set of related tasks.

cell division Tell students that just as in math, the word *division* means "to separate into parts." When cells divide, they separate into two parts.

binary fission Tell students that the prefix *bi-* in *binary* comes from the Latin *bini,* which means "two at a time," and that *fission* comes from the Latin root *findere,* which means "to cleave or split." Explain that binary fission is the process of cells splitting into two parts.

cell cycle Discuss the root word *cycle,* as in *bicycle, tricycle,* and *motorcycle.* Tell students that the word *cycle* comes from the Greek *kyklos,* meaning "wheel or circle." Explain that a cell cycle is a circular sequence of events in cell growth and division.

As You Read

Check student paragraphs. Students should see that in the other lessons, they learned about the parts of the cell and cell functions. In this lesson, they can see how the organization of cells into tissues, tissues into organs, and organs into organ systems keeps an organism alive and functioning.

Figure It Out: Figure 3.25

ANSWER **1.** Divide the surface area by the volume. **2.** The volume is multiplied by 8, whereas the surface area is multiplied by 4.

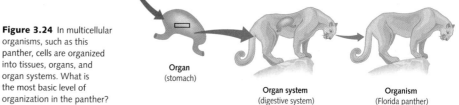

Organs A group of related tissues is an **organ**. An organ performs a more complex function than do individual cells and tissues. The heart, brain, and stomach are examples of organs.

Organ Systems Organs that work together to perform a set of related tasks form an **organ system**. The stomach is one of several organs of the digestive system. Other organs of the digestive system include the esophagus and the intestines. Together, all of the organ systems in a multicellular organism carry out the processes needed to keep the entire organism alive.

Cell (muscle cell)

Tissue (muscle tissue)

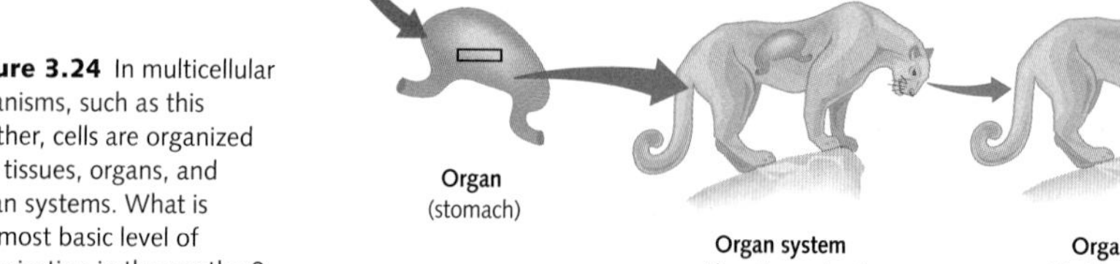

Figure 3.24 In multicellular organisms, such as this panther, cells are organized into tissues, organs, and organ systems. What is the most basic level of organization in the panther?

As You Read

Write a well-developed paragraph in your Science Notebook telling what this lesson is about. Describe how this lesson relates to the other lessons in the chapter.

Was your prediction about the content of the lesson correct, based on your preview? Explain.

Limits on Cell Size

You may be wondering why many small cells group together in an organism instead of simply growing larger. The small size of most cells is for a reason. As a cell grows larger, both its volume and its surface area increase. Recall that volume is the amount of space an object takes up. The surface area is a measure of the size of the outer surface of an object. For example, when you wrap a gift box, you cover the surface area of the box. The surface area of a cell determines the amount of material that can enter and leave the cell.

As shown in **Figure 3.25**, as a cell grows, the volume increases at a faster rate than does the surface area. If the cell grows too large, it will require more materials than can pass through its surface area. Therefore, there is a limit to how large a cell can grow.

Figure It Out

1. How do you find the surface area-to-volume ratio?
2. Calculate how doubling the length of the sides changes the volume of the cube. Then calculate the surface area.

1 mm 1 mm 1 mm

Surface area = 6 mm^2
Volume = 1 mm^3
Ratio = 6:1

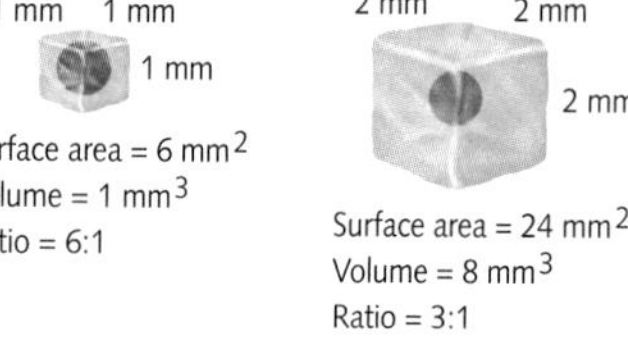

Surface area = 24 mm^2
Volume = 8 mm^3
Ratio = 3:1

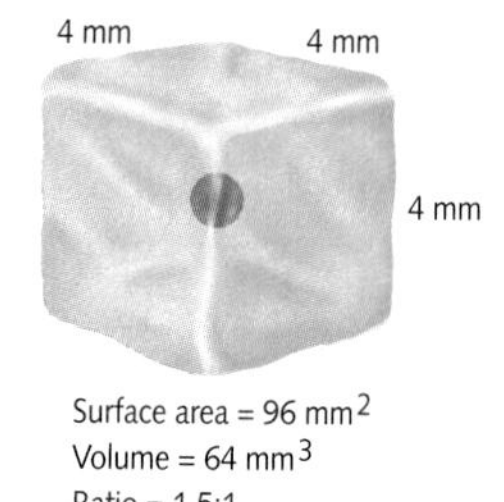

Surface area = 96 mm^2
Volume = 64 mm^3
Ratio = 1.5:1

Figure 3.25 The ratio of a cell's surface area to its volume is one factor that limits cell size. When the sides of the cube double in length from 1 mm to 2 mm, the surface area-to-volume ratio changes from 6:1 to 3:1.

ELL Strategy

Model, Think, Pair, Share Have students diagram different organizations, such as their school, their families, or the government. Assign students a partner and have them share their diagrams and discuss the different types of organizations and how the parts of each organization work together.

Cell Division

Instead of continuing to grow larger, cells form new cells that enable an organism to grow and develop tissues, organs, and organ systems. The process by which one cell (known as the parent cell) divides into two cells (called daughter cells) is known as **cell division**, or cell reproduction. The actual process of cell division depends on the type of cell involved.

Cell division is relatively simple in prokaryotic cells such as bacteria. Prokaryotes reproduce through **binary fission**. During this process, a cell's DNA is copied. The cell then splits into two parts. Each part receives one copy of the DNA.

Eukaryotic cells undergo a more complex process of cell division that is part of the cell cycle. The **cell cycle** is a sequence of events that lead to cell growth and division. The cell cycle is summarized in **Figure 3.26**.

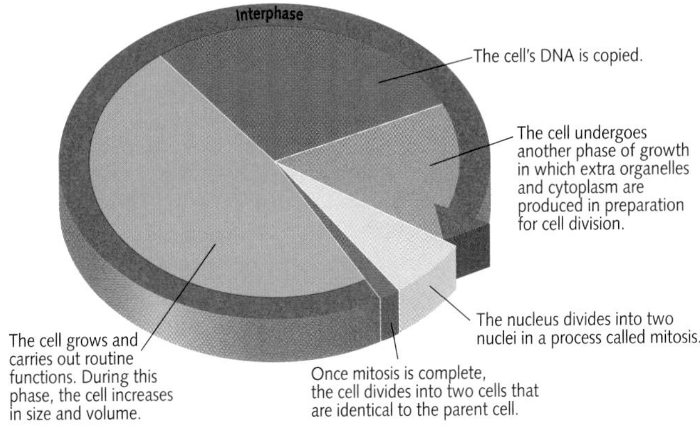

Interphase
The cell's DNA is copied.
The cell undergoes another phase of growth in which extra organelles and cytoplasm are produced in preparation for cell division.
The nucleus divides into two nuclei in a process called mitosis.
Once mitosis is complete, the cell divides into two cells that are identical to the parent cell.
The cell grows and carries out routine functions. During this phase, the cell increases in size and volume.

Figure 3.26 Existing cells divide as part of the cell cycle to produce new cells for growth or to replace old or damaged cells.

CONNECTION: Math

For a regular object, such as a cube, you can find the surface area by first finding the area of each face and then adding the areas together. What is the surface area of a box that is 10 cm long, 6 cm wide, and 5 cm high?

After You Read

1. How is cell shape related to cell function? Give an example.
2. What prevents most cells from becoming very large?
3. What is the purpose of cell division in multicellular organisms?
4. According to the preview and summary you wrote in your Science Notebook, how are cell organization and cell division related to each other?

Teach

EXPLORE Slowly blow up a balloon for the class. As the balloon gets larger, discuss with students the relationship between the surface area of the balloon and its volume. Tell students that, like a balloon, as a cell grows larger, both its surface area and its volume grow larger.

CONNECTION: Math

Suggest that students sketch the box and label the sides as described. Tell students to use their drawings to help them calculate the surface area of the box. Students should discover that the box has two sides that are 50 cm^2 (5 cm × 10 cm), two sides that are 30 cm^2 (6 cm × 5 cm), and two sides that are 60 cm^2 (6 cm × 10 cm). Thus, the total surface area is (2 × 50) + (2 × 30) + (2 × 60) = 280 cm^2.

Assess

EVALUATE Use the After You Read questions and the Alternative Assessment to help you assess students' understanding of this lesson.

After You Read

1. Sample answer: Nerve cells are long, which enables them to carry messages over long distances in the body.
2. The surface area must be large enough to allow the necessary materials to enter and leave the cell. If the volume grows so large that the surface area cannot supply it adequately, the cell cannot survive.
3. Cell division replaces old cells and forms new cells so that the organism can grow and repair damaged tissue.
4. As new cells are produced by cell division, the cells become organized into tissues, organs, and organ systems.

Teacher Alert

Students will often confuse the units for volume (cm^3) with the units for surface area (cm^2). Help students to see that volume is a three-dimensional measurement and that surface area is two-dimensional.

Background Information

The formula for finding the surface area of a rectangular solid is $2(lw + wh + lh)$.

Alternative Assessment

EVALUATE Have students look at their predictions and circle or highlight the parts of their predictions that were correct. Have students share these with the class.

Chapter 3 Summary

VOCABULARY REVIEW

Check students' sentences or paragraphs to make sure they understand the meaning of each vocabulary term.

PREPARE FOR CHAPTER TEST

Evaluate students' essays using the following criteria:

1. The topic sentence, or main idea, should restate the Key Concept.
2. The supporting paragraphs should incorporate the answers to the Learning Goal questions students have written and include details, facts, and examples they have recorded in their Science Notebooks.
3. The concluding sentence should sum up the main idea of the chapter and restate the Key Concept.

MASTERING CONCEPTS

True or False

1. False, Robert Hooke
2. True
3. False, ribosome
4. False, lysosomes
5. False, osmosis
6. True
7. False, photosynthesis
8. False, tissues

Short Answer

9. The cell theory states that the cell is the basic unit of life, all organisms are made up of cells, and cells are produced by existing cells. Hooke observed parts of cells and gave them their names. Leeuwenhoek observed the first living cells. Schleiden and Schwann discovered that all plants and animals are made up of cells. Virchow concluded that cells arise from other cells.
10. cell wall, chloroplast, large vacuole
11. An amoeba might ingest large food particles using endocytosis. Its cell membrane would surround the particle and pull the particle into its cytoplasm.
12. Producers store energy in organic molecules that other organisms eat as food. All organisms need energy to survive and so depend on producers.

Chapter 3 Summary

KEY CONCEPTS

3.1 Cells: Basic Units of Life

- Robert Hooke and Anton van Leeuwenhoek were among the first to observe cells or cell parts under a microscope.
- Francesco Redi, John Needham, and Lazzaro Spallanzani conducted experiments to investigate spontaneous generation. It was Louis Pasteur who finally proved that living things do not arise spontaneously from nonliving matter.
- The cell theory states that all living things are made up of cells, cells are the basic units of life, and cells arise only from existing cells.

3.2 The Parts of a Cell

- Eukaryotic cells contain smaller parts and membrane bound organelles that carry out specific functions.
- Organelles include the nucleus, ribosomes, endoplasmic reticulum, Golgi apparatus, mitochondria, and lysosomes. All cells are bound by a cell membrane. Plant cells also contain chloroplasts, a cell wall, and a large vacuole.
- Prokaryotic cells are smaller than eukaryotic cells and lack a nucleus and membrane-bound organelles.

3.3 Cellular Transport

- Diffusion is the process by which particles move from an area of higher concentration to an area of lower concentration without the use of energy.
- Osmosis is the diffusion of water through a selectively permeable membrane.
- During active transport, the cell uses energy to move particles against a concentration gradient.

3.4 Energy and Cells

- During photosynthesis, energy from the Sun is converted into chemical energy stored in organic molecules.
- The energy stored in organic molecules is released in a form that cells can use during cellular respiration.
- When oxygen is not available, cells release energy using fermentation.

3.5 Cell Growth and Development

- The shape of a cell is often related to its function.
- The surface area-to-volume ratio of a cell limits how large the cell can grow and still obtain the materials it needs to survive.
- During cell division, a parent cell divides into two identical daughter cells.

VOCABULARY REVIEW

Write each term in a complete sentence, or write a paragraph relating several terms.

3.1
microorganism, p. 35
spontaneous generation, p. 36
cell theory, p. 38

3.2
organelle, p. 39
nucleus, p. 39
cytoplasm, p. 39
ribosome, p. 41
endoplasmic reticulum, p. 41
Golgi apparatus, p. 41
mitochondrion, p. 42
lysosome, p. 42
vacuole, p. 42
chloroplast, p. 43
cell membrane, p. 43
cell wall, p. 43
eukaryotic cell, p. 43
prokaryotic cell, p. 43

3.3
solution, p. 44
concentration, p. 44
diffusion, p. 45
equilibrium, p. 45
passive transport, p. 45
selectively permeable membrane, p. 46
osmosis, p. 46
facilitated diffusion, p. 46
active transport, p. 47

3.4
producer, p. 48
cellular respiration, p. 49
aerobic, p. 50
fermentation, p. 50
anaerobic, p. 50

3.5
tissue, p. 51
organ, p. 52
organ system, p. 52
cell division, p. 53
binary fission, p. 53
cell cycle, p. 53

54 CELL STRUCTURE, FUNCTION, AND PROCESSES

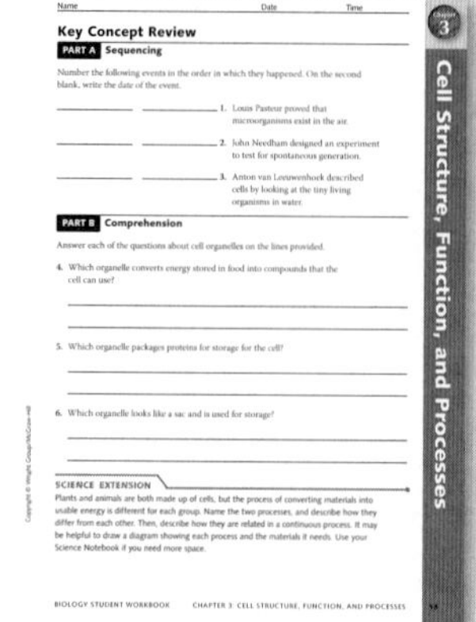

Key Concept Review Workbook, p. 15

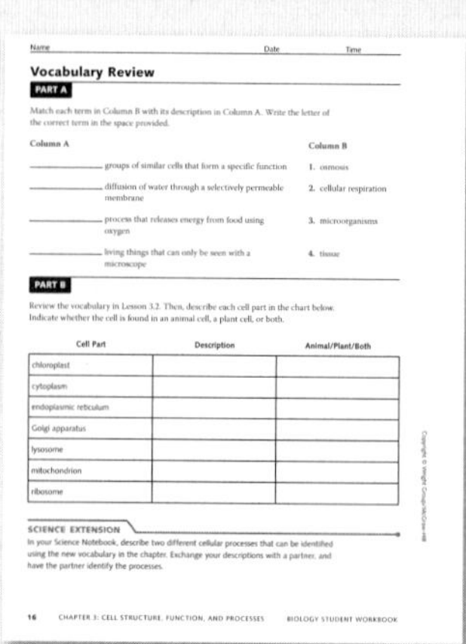

Vocabulary Review Workbook, p. 16

MASTERING CONCEPTS

True or False

If the statement is true, write "true." If it is false, change the underlined word or words to make the statement true.

1. Using a microscope, <u>Theodor Schwann</u> saw "chambers" and called them cells.
2. Louis Pasteur conducted an experiment that disproved the theory of <u>spontaneous generation</u>.
3. An <u>endoplasmic reticulum</u> is an organelle on which proteins are assembled.
4. Worn-out organelles are digested in the <u>vacuoles</u> of a cell.
5. Water moves by <u>facilitated transport</u> across a selectively permeable membrane.
6. Endocytosis is a form of <u>active</u> transport.
7. During <u>cellular respiration</u>, organisms store energy in organic molecules.
8. Groups of similar cells are arranged into <u>organ systems</u> in multicellular organisms.

Short Answer

Answer each of the following in a sentence or brief paragraph.

9. Restate the cell theory in your own words. Be sure to identify scientists who made major contributions to its development.
10. You see a cell under a microscope. List features that indicate the cell came from a plant.
11. Describe the process by which an amoeba would ingest large food particles.
12. Discuss how producers are important to the survival of other organisms.
13. Through what process do multicellular organisms grow?

Critical Thinking

Use what you have learned in this chapter to answer each of the following.

14. **Infer** A liver cell requires a great deal of energy. Which organelle would you expect to find in large numbers in a liver cell? Explain your reasoning.
15. **Compare and Contrast** How are eukaryotic cells similar to and different from prokaryotic cells?
16. **Illustrate** Using diagrams, identify the conditions under which (a) water flows into a cell by osmosis and (b) water flows out of a cell by osmosis. In each diagram, indicate what the appearance of the cell will be as a result.

Standardized Test Question

Choose the letter of the response that correctly answers the question.

17. Which is the only structure responsible for conducting photosynthesis in plant cells?

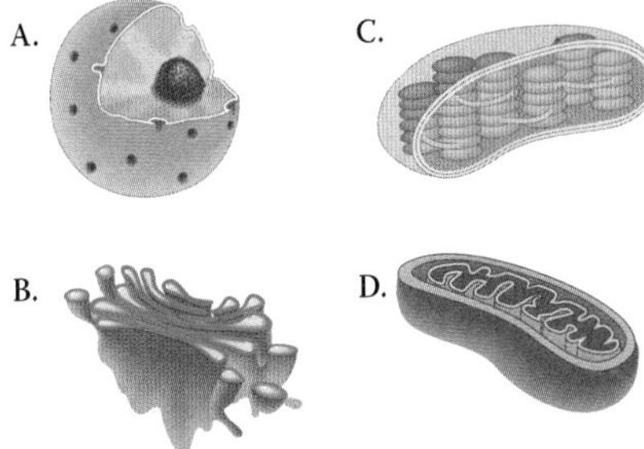

Test-Taking Tip

Remember that qualifying words such as *only, always, all,* and *never* mean that the statement has **no** exceptions.

13. cell division

Critical Thinking

14. A liver cell should have a large number of mitochondria because they supply energy to the cell.
15. Both types of cells have a cell membrane, cytoplasm, and go through cell division. Eukaryotic cells are larger and more complex. They also have nuclei and membrane-bound organelles, which prokaryotic cells lack.
16. (a) Student diagrams should show the concentration of particles inside the cytoplasm as higher than the concentration outside the cell. The cell will become swollen. (b) Student diagrams should show the concentration of particles outside the cell as higher than the concentration inside the cytoplasm. The cell will become shriveled.

Standardized Test Question

17. C

Reading Links

Organ and Tissue Transplants: Medical Miracles and Challenges

After drawing readers into the topic with a sensitive anecdotal approach, this book examines the reality of transplants from a variety of angles. The discussion also underscores the critical role that organs and tissues play in the body systems to which they belong.

McClellan, Marilyn. Enslow Publishers. 128 pp. Illustrated with photos and diagrams. Library ISBN: 978-0-7660-1943-0.

The Cell: Evolution of the First Organism

This study of the cell, from its speculated origins to its role in recent technological advances, offers a useful orientation and resource for students who are new to the topic or looking for enrichment. Panno touches on various aspects of cell biology and explores the ways in which our understanding of the cell has developed and is applied.

Panno, Joseph. Facts on File, Inc. 208 pp. Illustrated. Trade ISBN: 978-0-8160-4946-2.

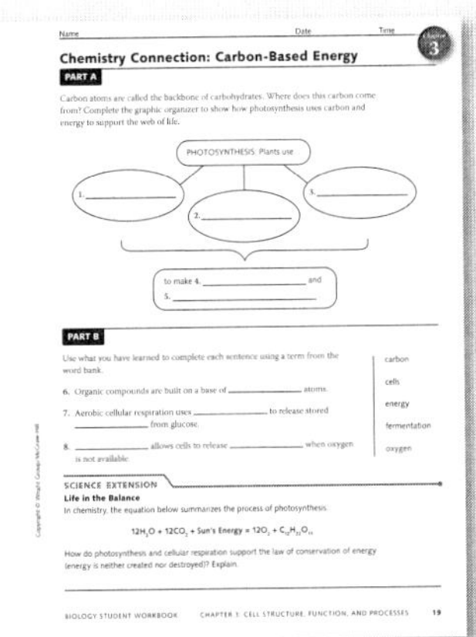
Chemistry Connection: Carbon-Based Energy

Curriculum Connection Workbook, p. 19

Science Challenge Workbook, pp. 20–21

Chapter 3 Labs

3A How Does It Get There?

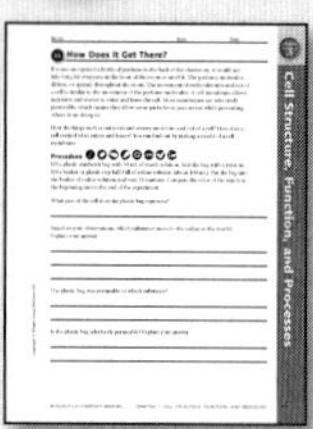

This prechapter introduction activity is designed for students to see how a cell membrane works by observing the diffusion of a substance across a selectively permeable membrane.

Objectives

- compare and contrast permeable and selectively permeable membranes
- construct a model to observe movement of molecules
- communicate conclusions

Planning

 15–20 minutes  groups of 3–4 students

Materials (per group)

- plastic sandwich bags
- cornstarch solution
- twist tie
- iodine solution
- 100-mL graduated cylinder
- 250-mL beaker or small plastic cup

Advance Preparation

- **CAUTION:** *The iodine is toxic, so caution students to rinse with water if iodine gets on their skin.*
- Purchase inexpensive sandwich bags.
- The iodine and starch solutions should be prepared ahead of time. To prepare the iodine solution, use 10 drops of Lugol's iodine for every 100 mL of water. To prepare the starch solution, use 1 teaspoon of cornstarch for every 50 mL of water.
- Have students throw away used bags for easy cleanup.

Engagement Guide

- Explain to students that iodine is an indicator for starch, and it will turn blue-black in the presence of starch.
- Challenge students to think about what they observed and the process of diffusion by asking:
  - *Where is the concentration of iodine molecules the greatest at the beginning of the experiment?* (The concentration is greatest on the outside of the bag. The molecules will go from an area of greater concentration to one of lesser concentration to reach equilibrium.)
  - *Why do you think the iodine molecules could move into the bag but the starch molecules could not move out of the bag?* (The iodine molecules are small enough to move into the bag, but the starch molecules are too large to move out.)
- Encourage students to communicate their conclusions by sketching the beaker and bag to illustrate how diffusion occurred.

Going Further

- Encourage students to repeat the experiment to see what would happen if they placed the iodine solution in the bag and the starch solution in the beaker.
- Have students sketch their results beside the sketch from the first experiment. Have students share their drawings with the rest of the class.

3B Using a Microscope to Compare Plant and Animal Cells

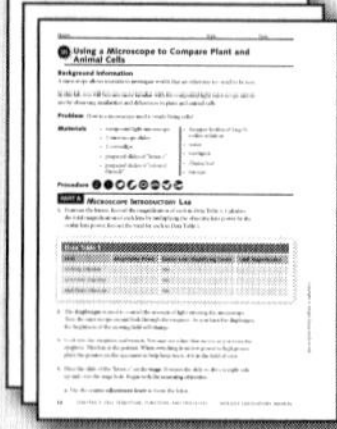

Objectives

- acquire skill in the use of the microscope
- carefully follow directions
- observe the components, organization, and structure of cells
- compare and contrast the structures of plant and animal cells

Skill Set

observing, recording data, comparing and contrasting, analyzing, applying, summarizing, interpreting

Planning

 1 class period 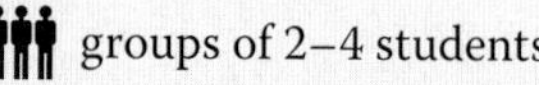 groups of 2–4 students

Materials

Materials for this activity are listed in the Student Laboratory Manual.

Lab Tip

It may be necessary for students to remove goggles while observing with the microscope.

Advance Preparation

- **CAUTION:** Lugol's iodine is toxic. Caution students to rinse with water if iodine gets on their skin.
- The "letter *e*" and "colored threads" slides can be purchased through a biology supply store or made ahead of time. To make the "letter *e*" slide, cut a lowercase letter *e* from a newspaper. To make the "colored threads" slide, use two threads of different colors and cross the strands to form an X. Add a drop of water and a coverslip to both.
- Provide proper waste-disposal for toothpicks used to collect cheek cells. **CAUTION:** Do not allow students to share toothpicks. Monitor them closely for proper use and disposal of toothpicks.
- *Elodea* and other suitable water plants can be purchased at an aquarium supply store.

Answers to Observations: Data Table 2

Cheek Cell: Parts Present: cytoplasm, nucleus, cell membrane.
Elodea Cell: Parts Present: cytoplasm, nucleus, chloroplast, cell wall, cell membrane

Answers to Analysis and Conclusions

1. Present in both cells: cytoplasm, nucleus, cell membrane; Only in plant cells: cell wall and chloroplasts
2. Specimens need to be thin so that the light can pass through, allowing only one layer of cells to be seen.
3. cell wall; cell membrane
4. No; animals obtain their energy by eating other organisms and do not need chloroplasts.
5. Microscopes enable scientists to see and study objects that are not otherwise visible.

Going Further

Bring in a selection of prepared slides to give students additional practice using microscopes. Prepared slides can be made from common objects such as dust, chalk, insect legs, or different kinds of plant and animal tissue. Students can make additional wet mounts of plant and animal cells using materials such as onions, potatoes, or protozoans found in pond or lake water.

Have students make drawings of two or three specimens from the prepared slides they viewed and any wet mounts they prepared.

3C An "Eggsample" of Osmosis

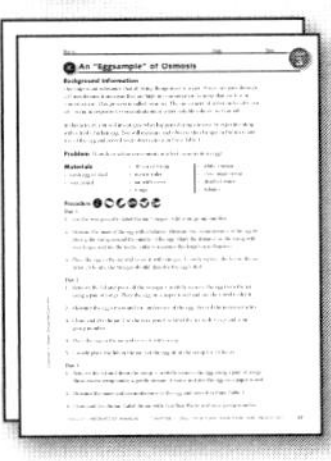

Objectives

- compare the effects of different solute concentrations on the process of osmosis
- use correct measuring techniques to obtain data
- observe and record data in a suitable way
- interpret and analyze data to draw conclusions
- communicate conclusions

Skill Set

measuring, observing, comparing and contrasting, recording and analyzing data, stating conclusions

Planning

4 class periods, 20–30 minutes each period

groups of 2–4 students

Materials

Materials for this activity are listed in the Student Laboratory Manual.

Advance Preparation

- Have an electronic balance or a triple-beam balance available to students for measuring the mass of the egg.
- Remind students to handle and measure the eggs carefully.
- Collect jars (such as clean plastic peanut butter or mayonnaise jars).
- Use light corn syrup for the clear sugar syrup.
- Provide a waste container for all groups to discard eggs on the last day.
- Eggs need to soak in vinegar no less than 24 hours to remove the shell.

Answers to Observations: Data Table 1

(Student data may vary.) Approximate size of egg: Day 1: mass of egg = 70.8 g, circumference = 155 mm, appearance = egg has shell. Day 2: mass of egg in vinegar = 98 g, circumference = 180 mm, appearance = larger, hard, and shell was gone. Day 3: mass of egg in syrup = 65 g, circumference = 150 mm, appearance = egg had shrunk and was softer. Day 4: mass of egg in water = 105.3 g, circumference = 200 mm, appearance = egg color was pale yellow, and egg was larger.

Answers to Analysis and Conclusions

1. The egg's shell was removed to expose the membrane lining the egg and let water pass through.
2. The vinegar and the distilled water made the egg circumference increase because water passed through the membrane into the egg to equalize the water concentrations.
3. The water moved out of the egg. The water moved across a membrane from an area of high water concentration (low sugar concentration) on the inside to an area of low water concentration (high sugar concentration) on the outside of the egg.
4. Passive transport; no energy was needed for the water to diffuse across the membrane.
5. The water will leave the inside of the strawberries by osmosis as it moves from an area of high water concentration (low sugar concentration) to an area of low water concentration (high sugar concentration). It will combine with the sugar to make a juice.

Going Further

Have students investigate the effects of a hypertonic salt solution on plant cells such as those from a red onion or *Elodea* plant.

Chapter 4 Lessons

Introduce Chapter 4

As a starting activity, use LAB 4A DNA in a Banana? on page 19 of the Laboratory Manual.

ENGAGE Direct students to look at the photograph of the scarlet macaws. Pair students and ask them to identify similar traits among the birds. Have students share their observations with the class. Record similar traits on the board. Discuss with students the benefits of these traits to the birds.

Think About Making Observations

ENGAGE Suggest that students observe conveniently located plants, such as a group of nearby trees or shrubs, or plants in a flowerbed or garden. If these are not available, help students obtain photos from magazines, journals, or Web sites. Students should note the characteristics of different plants. Help them understand that the same types of plants have similar characteristics.

Direct students to complete each bulleted activity. As a class, discuss students' results. Point out that different traits give a plant certain advantages. For example, bright colors might attract bees for pollination. Thorns might keep predators away.

Chapter 4 Heredity and Genes

KEY CONCEPT Traits are passed along from one generation to the next through genes that are part of the DNA of chromosomes.

One of the most beautiful birds in the world is the Scarlet macaw. Living mostly in the rain forests of South America, the bird is known for its bright colors, loud calls, and powerful beak.

Macaws are often known to gather in large groups. The matching colors of the many birds make for a spectacular sight. What causes so many birds to share the same colors, sounds, and habits? Why does each generation of birds have the same traits? This chapter is about the traits of organisms and how they are passed down from parents to offspring.

Think About Making Observations

You can often tell that certain students in your school are related because they look alike. The same is true for other organisms, as well.

- Find a group of plants near your home or school. In your Science Notebook, draw the plants that you find and make a list of the features of the plants. For example, write whether they have large leaves or small leaves.
- Based on your observations, decide which plants are the same type and which are different.

NSTA SCiLINKS THE WORLD'S A CLICK AWAY
www.scilinks.org
Genes **Code: WGB04A**
Heredity **Code: WGB04B**

56

Chapter 4 Planning Guide

Instructional Periods	National Standards	Lab Manual	Workbook
4.1 1 period	A.1, C.2 , C.4, G.1, G.2, G.3; G.1, G.2, G.3; UCP.2	**Lab 4A—p. 19** DNA in a Banana? **Lab 4B—p. 20** Looking at Your Traits **Lab 4C—p. 22** Protein Synthesis	Key Concept Review p. 22 Vocabulary Review p. 23 Interpreting Diagrams p. 24 Reading Comprehension p. 25 Curriculum Connection p. 26 Science Challenge p. 27
4.2 1 period	A.2, C.2, C.5 G.1; G.1; UCP.1, UCP.3		
4.3 3 periods	C.1, C.2; C.1		
4.4 3 periods	A.2, C.2; UCP.2		
4.5 2 periods	E.2, F.4, F.5; F.6		

Middle School Standard; High School Standard; Unifying Concept and Principle

4.1 Basic Principles of Heredity

Before You Read

Preview the lesson by reading the headings and the Learning Goals. In your Science Notebook, write each heading as it appears here. Then turn each heading into a question. Leave at least five lines of space after each question. Use one or two of those lines to answer each question based on what you already know.

Learning Goals

- Examine the law of dominance and the experiments that led to it.
- Compare the genotype of an individual with its phenotype.
- Recognize that some traits can be understood as incomplete dominance or codominance.

New Vocabulary

trait
heredity
genetics
gamete
pollination
fertilization
hybrid
dominant
recessive
gene
allele
law of dominance
law of segregation
genotype
homozygous
heterozygous
phenotype
incomplete dominance
codominance

Have you ever heard people say that a certain person looks like her mother, her father, or maybe even her Aunt Inez? People tend to look like other members of their family because they share similar traits. The **traits** of an organism are its characteristics. The color of your eyes, the shape of your nose, and the texture of your hair are just some of your many traits.

Some traits are passed from parents to offspring. The passing of traits from one generation to the next is known as **heredity** (huh REH duh tee). The field of biology devoted to studying heredity is called **genetics** (juh NE tihks).

Gregor Mendel

In the mid-nineteenth century, an Austrian monk named Gregor Mendel became one of the first people to carefully study genetics. For his studies, Mendel observed pea plants from his garden. Pea plants reproduce when sex cells called **gametes** (GA meets) join together. Male gametes, or sperm, are produced in pollen grains formed in a male reproductive organ. Female gametes, or eggs, are produced in a separate female reproductive organ.

During **pollination** (pah luh NAY shun), pollen grains from a male reproductive organ are transferred to a female reproductive organ. There, the male gamete unites with the female gamete in a process called **fertilization** (fur tuh luh ZAY shun). The zygote, or the cell that results, then develops into a seed.

Figure 4.1 These students have many different traits. How would you describe your traits?

4.1 Introduce

ENGAGE Draw a face on the board. Include some or all of the following: eyes, hair, nose, mouth, and ears. Ask: *What are some of the traits that humans share?*

Record students' answers on the board. As students add traits, add to the face drawing.

EXPLAIN Tell students that the genetic makeup of each student's biological parents determines the shape of that student's face, ears, and nose and the color of his or her hair and eyes. It also determines other characteristics of that student, such as height and body shape.

Before You Read

Have students work in pairs to identify the headings in the chapter. Record headings on the board. Suggest that students add any headings that they have missed to their Science Notebooks.

Vocabulary terms are listed on the first student page of each lesson. You may wish to preview the terms before introducing each lesson. Strategies for teaching the vocabulary appear on the pages where the terms are introduced.

Teach

EXPLAIN that in this lesson, students will examine the law of dominance and the experiments that led to it. Tell students that all of the lessons in this chapter will help them understand how their own traits were passed down to them from their parents.

Use the Visual: Figure 4.1

ANSWER Accept all reasonable responses.

Vocabulary

trait Tell students that *trait* does not only apply to physical features but also to personality, intelligence, and character.

heredity Explain that *heredity* comes from the Latin *hereditas,* which means "heirship." Tell students that an *heir* inherits property from a person, usually from a family member, after that person's death.

genetics Explain that the root of *genetics, gene,* is from the Greek *genea,* meaning "breed" or "to produce offspring."

gamete Explain that *gamete* comes from the Latin *gamein,* meaning "to marry."

pollination Tell students that *pollination* can be *self-pollination,* in which pollen is transferred between flowers on the same plant, or *cross-pollination,* in which pollen is transferred between flowers on two different plants.

fertilization Explain that the root *fertile* comes from the Latin *fertilis,* meaning "to bear." If *fertilization* is successful, the parents will "bear" offspring.

Science Notebook EXTRA

Encourage students to use the vocabulary section they created in their Science Notebooks. Remind them to record prefixes, suffixes, and root words to help them remember the meanings of vocabulary terms.

Teach

EXPLAIN to students that Mendel was careful to control for the independent and dependent variables when crossing different types of plants. Encourage students to refer to their Science Notebooks to remember the distinction between these two types of variables. Discuss and review the distinction as a class.

Vocabulary

hybrid Tell students that the word *hybrid* can be used figuratively to refer to anything of mixed origin. Have students give examples of the figurative use of the word *hybrid* in a sentence. Ask students if they know what a hybrid vehicle is.

dominant Explain to students that the word *dominant* comes from the Latin *dominus*, which means "master." Discuss with students the nonscientific definition of the word *dominant*, which is used to describe a person who rules by strength or power. Tell students that this common usage also describes a trait that "rules" over another trait.

recessive Tell students that the word *recessive* comes from the Latin *recessus*, which describes "a retreat." If a gene is recessive, it "retreats" and allows the dominant gene to take the lead.

Figure 4.2 The Austrian monk Gregor Mendel is sometimes known as the father of genetics. He made careful observations of pea plants over many generations to draw conclusions about how traits are inherited.

Monohybrid Cross

In pea plants, both male and female reproductive organs are located in the same flower. They are tightly protected by the flower petals. Pollen from other flowers is therefore unable to enter a flower on a different plant. Pollination that occurs within a single flower is known as self-pollination.

If Mendel wanted two different plants to reproduce, he could open the petals of a flower to remove the male reproductive organs. He could then brush pollen from a different plant onto the female reproductive organ. This process is known as cross-pollination and is illustrated in **Figure 4.3**.

What was so important about being able to cross different plants? By choosing which plants reproduced, Mendel could study how specific traits are inherited, or passed along. For example, he could observe the flower color in the plants produced when a plant with white flowers was crossed with a plant with purple flowers.

Mendel selected plants that were true-breeding for different versions of the same trait. A true-breeding plant is one that, when self-pollinated, always produces offspring with the same version of a trait. He then cross-pollinated them and observed their offspring.

The offspring of parents that have different forms of a trait are called **hybrids** (HI brudz). A cross between two parents that differ only in one trait is called a monohybrid cross. The prefix *mono-* means "one." An example of a monohybrid cross is one between two plants that are identical in every way except height.

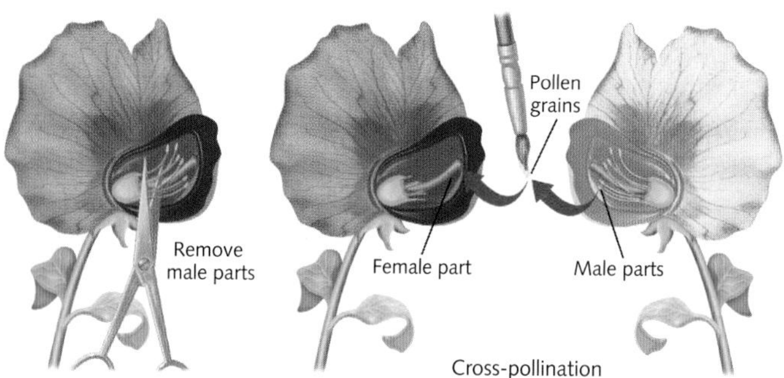

Figure 4.3 Mendel would transfer pollen from one plant to another plant with different traits. This is known as crossing the plants, or making a cross.

Background Information

Gregor Mendel became a priest in 1847. When Mendel was 29, the monastery paid for him to attend university and study math and science. When he returned to the monastery, he taught biology and physics at a local high school for 14 years. His scientific discoveries came from his work in the monastery garden. In 1868, Mendel became abbot of the monastery, which limited further research.

ELL Strategy

Practice Using Vocabulary Have students create flash cards for all of the lesson's vocabulary words. Suggest that students use diagrams to help define each word. Students can write the word on one side and the definition and diagram on the reverse side. For struggling English-language learners, one strategy might be to have them write definitions in their native language and translate these into English.

Dominant and Recessive Traits

For one of his earliest experiments, Mendel crossed a tall pea plant with a short pea plant. The parent plants that are first crossed are known as the P_1 generation.

Mendel planted the seeds that resulted from the cross. The offspring plants are called the F_1 generation. Mendel discovered that all of the offspring in the F_1 generation grew to be tall. It was as if the shortness trait had disappeared.

Mendel then allowed the plants of the F_1 generation to self-pollinate. Again, he planted the seeds that were produced and observed the plants that grew. In this generation, known as the F_2 generation, some plants were tall and some were short. The shortness trait had reappeared.

Mendel conducted similar monohybrid crosses to test for other traits. He tested for such traits as seed shape, seed color, flower color, and flower position. In every case, Mendel discovered that one trait seemed to disappear in the F_1 generation and reappear in the F_2 generation.

Mendel concluded that each trait is controlled by two factors. He called the form of a trait that appeared in the F_1 generation the **dominant** (DAH muh nunt) trait. He named the form of the trait that disappeared until the F_2 generation the **recessive** (rih SEH sihv) trait.

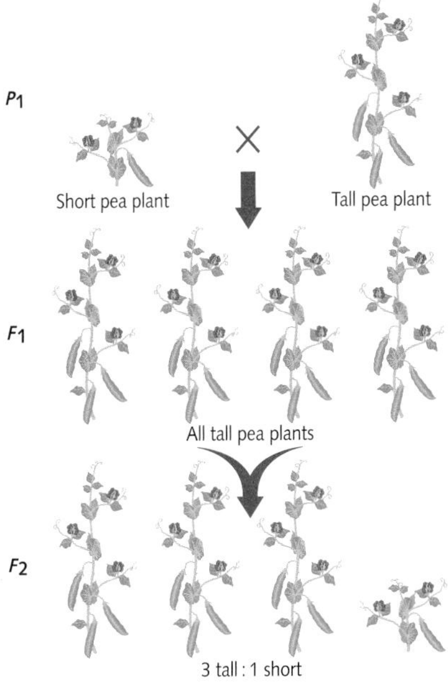

Figure 4.4 Mendel crossed true-breeding tall pea plants with true-breeding short pea plants.

As You Read

As you read the text under each heading, write a summary of the information in your Science Notebook. Then answer the questions you wrote about each heading.

What is a dominant trait? What is a recessive trait?

Figure It Out

1. Which trait for height did the F_1 generation show?
2. What fraction of the plants of the F_2 generation was tall? What fraction was short?

Teach

EXPLAIN Draw a diagram on the board that describes the process Mendel used in his experiment with pea plants. Use markers or chalk of different colors to depict the different traits.

Figure It Out: Figure 4.4

ANSWER **1.** All of the F_1 generation plants were tall. **2.** ¾ of the plants of the F_2 generation were tall; ¼ of the plants of the F_2 generation were short.

As You Read

ANSWER A dominant trait is one that is expressed whenever at least one factor for that form of a characteristic is present. A recessive trait is one that is not seen if a factor for the dominant trait is present.

ELL Strategy

Model Have each student make a diagram that represents the process of cross-pollination that Mendel used. Suggest that students draw two types of plants and then diagram the different combinations of those plants and what the offspring might look like.

Field Study

Discuss with students the different traits that plants have. Make a list of these traits on the board. Take students for a walk around the school. Have them record the number of plants they see that exhibit each trait. Tell students to make bar graphs of their results. Discuss with students the most common traits of the plants found around the school.

Teach

EXPLORE Ask students to list all of the different eye colors and hair colors that they have seen. Have students predict which colors are dominant and which are recessive. Ask students to explain their predictions.

Vocabulary

gene Remind students that the word *gene* comes from the Greek *geneā*, meaning "breed" or "to produce offspring." Explain that a gene is the very small part of a chromosome that determines a trait that we see in an individual organism.

allele Explain that the word *allele* is short for the word *allelomorph*. Tell students that the suffix *-morph* comes from the Greek word *morphē*, which means "form." An allele determines each "form" of a trait expressed in an individual organism.

law of dominance Explain that Mendel discovered the law of dominance by observing that a dominant trait will appear even if an individual has just one dominant allele for that trait.

law of segregation Explain that *segregate* means "to separate." The law of segregation states that only one allele of the pair for a trait is passed from each parent to the next generation. Thus, the two alleles in each parent separate from each other.

genotype Tell students that the word *genotype* combines the word *gene* with the word *type*. A genotype tells the types of genes in an organism.

homozygous Explain that the prefix *homo-* comes from the Greek word meaning "same." An organism is said to be homozygous for a trait if its two alleles for that trait are the same. Tell students that the word *homogeneous*, which describes a mixture made up of the same elements, also uses the prefix *homo-*.

Explore It!

Help students draw their diagrams by modeling the activity on the board. Allow students to work in pairs or groups to complete this activity. Students should find that the F_1 generation of rabbits would all be black. If two such rabbits were then crossed, three out of four of the offspring would be expected to be black and one out of four would be expected to be white.

Use the Visual: Figure 4.6

ANSWER The allele for tall height is dominant.

Explore It!

In domestic rabbits, black fur is dominant over white fur. A breeder crossed a true-breeding black rabbit with a true-breeding white rabbit. Draw a diagram predicting the color of the F_1 offspring. Then predict what would happen if a rabbit from the F_1 generation were crossed with an offspring from an identical cross.

	Seed Shape	Seed Color	Flower Color	Flower Position	Pod Color	Pod Shape	Plant Height
Dominant Trait	round	yellow	purple	axial (side)	green	inflated	tall
Recessive Trait	wrinkled	green	white	terminal (tips)	yellow	constricted	short

Figure 4.5 Mendel studied seven different traits in pea plants. Each trait had a dominant allele and a recessive allele.

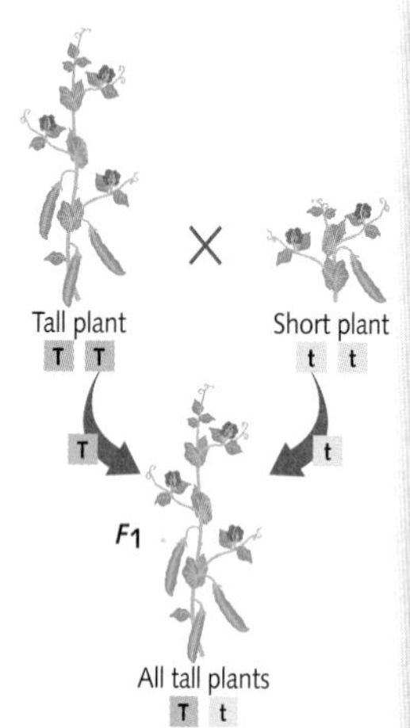

Figure 4.6 A plant receives one allele from each parent. The tall parent can give only the allele for tall height (*T*). The short parent can give only the allele for short height (*t*). Why is the offspring tall?

Alleles

Scientists now call the factors Mendel described **genes**. Different forms of a gene are called **alleles** (uh LEELZ). Pea plants, for example, have one allele for tall height and one allele for short height. In pea plants, tall height is dominant over short height.

Each plant receives two alleles for a trait—one from each parent. The dominant trait will appear if the plant has at least one dominant allele for it. The recessive trait will appear only if the plant does not have a dominant allele and has two recessive alleles. This is known as the **law of dominance**.

To describe alleles, scientists use an uppercase letter for the dominant allele. The lowercase version of the same letter is used for the recessive allele. The allele for tall height, therefore, is written as *T*, and the allele for short height is written as *t*. If an individual has a dominant allele and a recessive allele, the dominant allele is usually written before the recessive allele (*Tt*).

The law of dominance explains what Mendel observed in his pea-plant crosses. Recall that he selected true-breeding plants. These plants had two copies of the same allele for a trait. The tall plants had two alleles for tall height (*TT*), and the short plants had two alleles for short height (*tt*).

The plants in the F_1 generation received one allele from each parent. Therefore, they received an allele for tall height from the tall parent and an allele for short height from the short parent. As a result, every plant in the F_1 generation had both types of alleles (*Tt*). Because tall height is dominant over short height, all of the plants were tall.

Differentiated Instruction

Visual and Kinesthetic Have students cut out white and black paper "rabbits." Allow students to manipulate their "rabbits" to model the crossing of a black rabbit and a white rabbit and their resulting offspring.

Law of Segregation

Each of the plants of the F_1 generation had both types of alleles—T and t. The gametes of these plants randomly receive only one allele. It can be either an allele for tall height (T) or an allele for short height (t). Mendel described this as the **law of segregation**. When two gametes combine, their alleles combine as well. **Figure 4.7** shows the possible combinations of alleles.

Three of the combinations include the dominant allele for tall height. As long as at least one of these alleles is present, the plant will be tall. If only the recessive alleles are present, as in the fourth combination, the plant will be short. This explains why three out of four of the offspring in the F_2 generation are tall and one out of four is short.

Genotypes and Phenotypes

Can you tell which alleles a pea plant has just by looking at it? Not necessarily. After all, a tall pea plant might have two alleles for tall height (TT) or one allele for tall height and one allele for short height (Tt). The combination of alleles is called an organism's **genotype** (JEE no tipe). An organism is said to be **homozygous** (hoe moe ZI gus) for a trait if its two alleles for a trait are the same. It is **heterozygous** (he tuh roe ZI gus) if it has two different alleles for a trait.

The trait that an organism displays is called its **phenotype** (FEE no type). When you see that a plant is tall or short, you observe its phenotype.

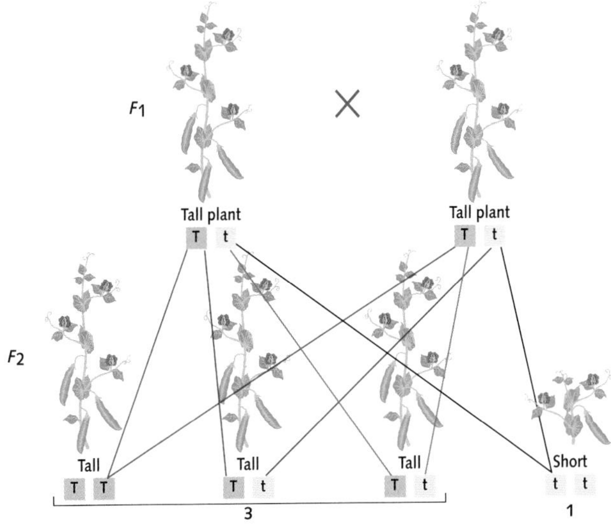

Figure 4.7 According to the law of segregation, a parent passes on at random only one allele for each trait to each offspring.

Did You Know?

You might think that Mendel was thrilled with what he had accomplished. Unfortunately, he never knew. His research, which he published in the 1860s, was largely ignored until about 1900. It was then that the scientist Hugo de Vries rediscovered Mendel's work and made his contributions to genetics known.

Figure It Out

1. How many different genotypes does the F_2 generation have?
2. How many different phenotypes does the F_2 generation have?

Teach

EXPLAIN that an allele is a form of a gene. If there are two alleles for a gene, each allele determines a different form of the trait. For example, one allele for height causes a plant to be tall. A different allele for height causes a plant to be short but only if the allele for tall height is not present.

Draw a diagram on the board illustrating the possible combinations of two alleles for height and the outcome. For each offspring, distinguish between the genotype, or the combination of alleles in the organism, and the phenotype, or the trait that is observed when the alleles are combined.

Vocabulary

heterozygous Explain that the prefix *hetero-* comes from the Greek word meaning "different." An organism is said to be heterozygous for a trait if its two alleles for that trait are different. Tell students that the word *heterogeneous*, which describes a mixture made up of different elements, also uses the prefix *hetero-*. Ask students what the relationship between the words *homozygous* and *heterozygous* is. (They are antonyms.)

phenotype Tell students that the prefix *phen-* comes from the Greek *phainein*, which means "to show forth." The trait that "shows forth," or is displayed, is called a phenotype.

Figure It Out: Figure 4.7

ANSWER **1.** There are three different genotypes. **2.** There are only two phenotypes, tall and short. One phenotype is produced by two different combinations of alleles.

Science Notebook EXTRA

Have students create a vocabulary map in their Science Notebooks to show how all the vocabulary terms in this lesson are related. Remind students that their maps can have smaller maps within in order to show the relationship among terms. Encourage students to share their maps with the class.

Background Information

There are three parts to Mendel's law of segregation. First, each parent contributes only one allele to each offspring. Second, alleles occur in pairs. Third, alleles from each parent separate during the cell division process that produces sex cells. Each sperm or egg receives only one of the alleles that a parent can transmit.

Teach

EXPLAIN that there are situations in which neither allele is dominant, called incomplete dominance, and that in these cases, the offspring will show a blend of the traits of each parent. Ask students to think of some human traits that might be the result of incomplete dominance.

Vocabulary

incomplete dominance Explain that the prefix *in-* means "not," so *incomplete* means "not complete" or "lacking a part." Discuss how the meaning of *incomplete* relates to the idea of incomplete dominance.

codominance Tell students that the prefix *co-* means "with." When alleles are codominant, both forms of a trait appear *with* each other.

Use the Visual: Figure 4.8

ANSWER Plants with red flowers must be homozygous for the color red. Plants with white flowers must be homozygous for white color. Plants with pink flowers must be heterozygous, with one allele for red color and one allele for white color.

Use the Visual: Figure 4.9

ANSWER probably gray

Assess

EVALUATE Use the After You Read questions and the Alternative Assessment to help you assess students' understanding of this lesson.

After You Read

1. two recessive alleles for wrinkled seeds
2. A homozygous organism has two identical alleles for a trait; a heterozygous organism has two different alleles for a trait.
3. In both types of heredity, no one trait is dominant over another. However, in codominance, both traits are displayed. In incomplete dominance, both traits blend together to produce a different trait.

Incomplete Dominance

The traits that Mendel studied were either dominant or recessive. For some traits, however, no trait is completely dominant over another as shown in **Figure 4.8**. Had Mendel chosen a plant known as a snapdragon, he would have observed a very different result. The reason is that snapdragons display **incomplete dominance**, in which the offspring show a blend of the traits of each parent.

Snapdragon plants have alleles for red flowers and alleles for white flowers. Neither allele is dominant over the other. If a homozygous plant with red flowers is crossed with a homozygous plant with white flowers, all of the offspring will have pink flowers.

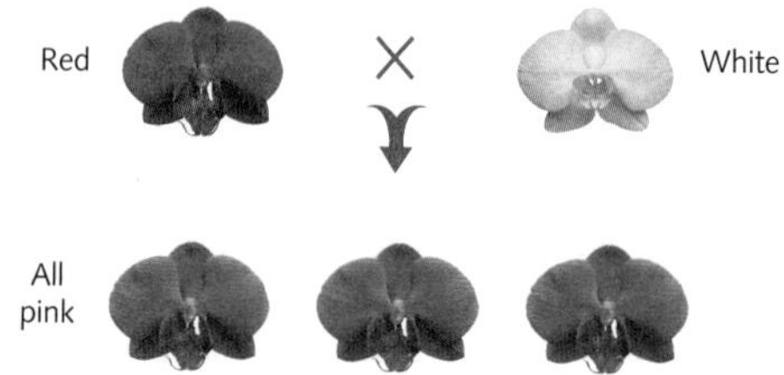

Figure 4.8 Some organisms display incomplete dominance, for example, if neither allele for flower color is dominant over the other. How can you tell the genotype of the plant by looking at the phenotype of the flowers?

Codominance

When a certain variety of black chicken is crossed with a white chicken, the feathers of the offspring are black and white. In this type of inheritance, known as **codominance**, both traits are displayed in the offspring. As in incomplete dominance, neither allele is dominant over the other. However, in codominance, the alleles do not blend together.

Figure 4.9 This chicken is the offspring of a black chicken and a white chicken. What color would the chicken have been if its feather color were determined by incomplete dominance?

After You Read

1. In pea plants, round seeds are dominant over wrinkled seeds. What combination of alleles must a plant have to produce wrinkled seeds?
2. According to the summaries you wrote in your Science Notebook, how is the genotype of a homozygous organism different from the genotype of a heterozygous organism?
3. How is codominance similar to incomplete dominance? How are the two types of inheritance different?

Alternative Assessment

EVALUATE Have students look back at the headings and questions they wrote and read their initial answers. Ask students to write a paragraph for each heading explaining what they learned in that section.

Background Information

To describe two alleles with incomplete dominance, scientists use two uppercase letters but give one a symbol called a prime (') to make it different from the other. To describe codominant alleles, scientists use different uppercase letters.

The body cells of animals and most plants contain chromosomes that exist in pairs. One chromosome in each pair came from the female parent, and the other came from the male parent. A cell that has two of each kind of chromosome is described as a diploid cell. It has a diploid, or $2n$, number of chromosomes. Gametes produced by organisms have one of each kind of chromosome. A cell that has one of each kind of chromosome is described as a haploid cell. It has a haploid, or n, number of chromosomes. A diploid cell of a pea plant has 14 chromosomes. A pea plant gamete has 7 chromosomes, or the haploid number.

62 HEREDITY AND GENES

Punnett Squares

Before You Read

Create a K-W-L-S-H chart in your Science Notebook. In the *K* column, write a few notes describing what you already know about percents and probability. Include examples of events that are described using these two terms.

Learning Goals

- Demonstrate the use of a Punnett square.
- Calculate the percent values that describe the offspring of a cross.
- Recognize the difference between probability and actual outcomes.

New Vocabulary

Punnett square
percent
probability

To learn about heredity, Mendel studied and recorded the details of his crosses over the course of many years. Is it possible, however, to predict the results of a cross in advance? In 1905, an English biologist named Reginald Punnett developed a chart that can be used to predict the possible genotypes of the offspring of a cross between two organisms. The chart he developed is called a **Punnett square**.

To use a Punnett square, a box with four squares in it is drawn. The genotype of one parent is written across the top, and the genotype of the other parent is written down the side of the chart. It does not matter which parent is written in which place. For example, look at the Punnett square in **Figure 4.10**. It shows the cross between two heterozygous pea plants. Remember that a heterozygous organism has two different alleles for a trait. In the box at the top left, the first allele from each parent is written. For this cross, the first allele from each parent is *T*, so *TT* is written in this box. In the box at the bottom left, the first allele from the parent shown at the top (*T*) and the second allele from the parent along the side (*t*) are written. The remaining two boxes are completed using the appropriate combinations.

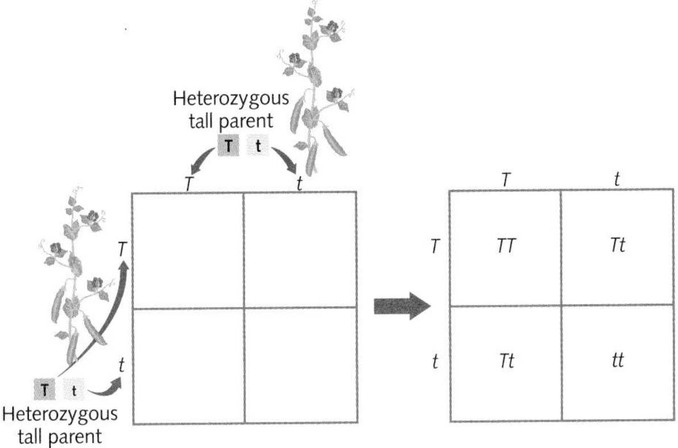

Figure 4.10 A Punnett square shows the alleles of the parents. It also shows the possible combinations of alleles of the offspring.

Figure It Out

1. How many possible combinations are homozygous?
2. How would the results change if one of the parents were homozygous tall?

Introduce

ENGAGE students by discussing the probability of a coin landing on heads when it is flipped. Ask: *What is the chance that a coin will land on heads when I flip it? If I flip a coin 100 times, how many heads will I get?* Explain that when a coin is flipped, there are two possible outcomes: heads or tails. The probability that a coin will land on heads is one out of two, or 50 percent. If a coin is flipped 100 times, it is likely that it will land on heads 50 times and tails 50 times. However, it is important to stress that, while the probability is 50 percent, the actual results do not always match the probable results.

Before You Read

Model a K-W-L-S-H chart on the board. Have students brainstorm in groups of four facts about probability and percents. Record the groups' ideas on the board. Have students include the class ideas in their Science Notebooks.

Teach

EXPLAIN that in this lesson, students will learn to use a Punnett square. They will also learn to calculate the percent values that describe the offspring of a cross, and they will learn to recognize the difference between probability and actual outcomes.

Vocabulary

Punnett square Explain that the Punnett square helps scientists visualize and predict the possible genotypes of offspring. Emphasize that while a Punnett square predicts the genotypes of offspring, the actual outcomes may not match the predictions.

Figure It Out: Figure 4.10

ANSWER **1.** two, one homozygous tall and the other homozygous short **2.** Half would be homozygous tall, and half would be heterozygous tall.

Differentiated Instruction

Visual and Kinesthetic Have students cut out squares with different allele types. Tell students to arrange the alleles into different Punnett squares and physically manipulate the squares to determine different possible outcomes from different combinations of alleles.

ELL Strategy

Compare and Contrast Have students use a compare-and-contrast chart to differentiate between probable outcomes and actual outcomes. Have students brainstorm examples of each type of outcome. Ask students to write a paragraph explaining the difference between the two.

Teach

Have students give examples of ways they use probability in everyday life. Encourage students to think about weather and sports. Record students' ideas on the board.

Vocabulary

percent Explain that the prefix *per-* means "for every" and the root *cent* means "one hundredth." So *percent* means "for every hundredth."

probability Tell students that *probability* comes from the Latin *probare,* meaning "to try or test."

As You Read

ANSWER Explanations should point out that a Punnett square shows the probability of each possible genotype of offspring. These probabilities can be expressed as percents. A percent is a part of 100.

Explore It!

Have students work in pairs. Provide each pair with a coin. Have students take turns flipping the coin. Model the chart for students on the board. Have each pair record its results on the board. Calculate the percents for the class. Students should discover that the actual observations approach the predicted probability as the number of trials increases. If the entire class combines its results, the observed results should be close to 50% for heads and 50% for tails.

Assess

EVALUATE Use the After You Read questions and the Alternative Assessment to help you assess students' understanding of this lesson.

After You Read

1. All four boxes would have that genotype.
2. 100%
3. Each box in a Punnett square represents a percent or a probability. If a Punnett square has four boxes, each one represents 25 percent, or 0.25, or one chance out of four.

Genotypes	Phenotypes
TT = 25%	tall = 75%
Tt = 50%	short = 25%
tt = 25%	

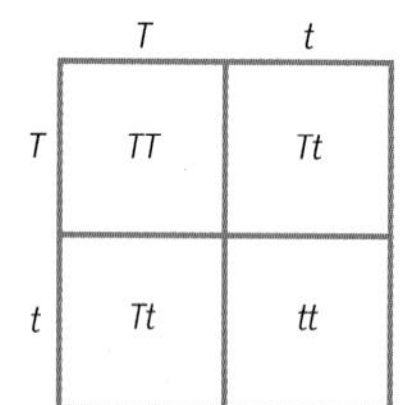

Figure 4.11 Each possible outcome of a cross can be described by a percent (%).

As You Read

Complete the second column in your K-W-L-S-H chart. Fill in three things you want to know about percents and probability, and explain how they relate to heredity.

Explore It!

Flip a coin ten times, and record whether it lands heads-up or tails-up after each flip.

Flip the coin 20 more times, and again record your observations.

How do the actual results compare with the predicted probability of 50 percent? How does the comparison change as the number of flips increases?

Percents

Once the Punnett square is completed, you know the possible genotypes of the offspring. You can then describe them using percents. A **percent** describes a part of one hundred. Fifty percent, for example, means 50 out of 100.

In the Punnett square in **Figure 4.11**, one out of four boxes has the *TT* genotype. Another way to say "one out of four" is one-fourth, or $\frac{1}{4}$. A fraction can be written as a percent. The fraction $\frac{1}{4}$ is equal to 25 percent. So you can predict that 25 percent of the offspring will have the *TT* genotype. The same is true for the *tt* genotype. Half of the boxes, or two out of four, have the *Tt* genotype. The fraction $\frac{2}{4}$ is the same as the fraction $\frac{1}{2}$. This fraction is equal to 50 percent.

Now think about the phenotypes of the offspring. A plant will be tall as long as it inherits one dominant allele. Three of the four boxes, or $\frac{3}{4}$, include a dominant allele. This fraction is equal to 75 percent. Therefore, the Punnett square predicts that 75 percent of the offspring will be tall and that one out of four offspring, or 25 percent, will be short.

Probability

Do the percents you found mean that if two plants produce 100 offspring, exactly 25 will be short? No, they don't. Punnett squares help you predict the likelihood that combinations of alleles will be produced. The likelihood that a certain event will occur is known as **probability**. The actual outcome may be higher or lower than the predicted number.

As an example, think about flipping a coin. When you flip a coin, it might land heads-up or tails-up. There are two possible outcomes. The probability that the coin will land heads-up is one out of two, which is 50 percent. You can predict that if you flip a coin ten times, it will land heads-up 50 percent of the time, or five times. If you then go ahead and flip a coin ten times, it may land heads-up one time, four times, eight times, or even ten times. The result is a matter of chance.

It is the same way with living organisms. The Punnett square helps you make predictions about the offspring of a cross. Only careful observations tell the actual results of the cross.

After You Read

1. In some guinea pigs, black hair (*B*) is dominant over brown hair (*b*). A black guinea pig (*BB*) is crossed with a brown one (*bb*). In a Punnett square for this cross, how many boxes would have the genotype *Bb*?
2. What percent of the offspring of the cross in Question 1 might be black?
3. Complete the last three columns of your K-W-L-S-H chart. Based on your chart, explain how percents and probability are related to Punnett squares.

Alternative Assessment

EVALUATE Have students complete the K-W-L-S-H charts in their Science Notebooks. Ask them to correct any mistakes in the *K* column and to fill in the remaining columns. Check students' responses.

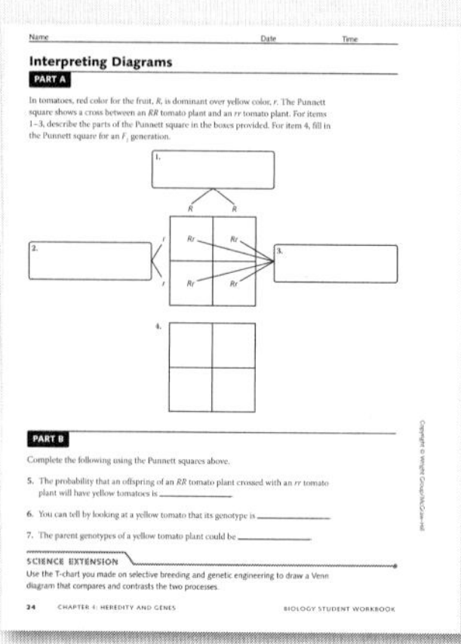
Interpreting Diagrams

PART A

PART B

SCIENCE EXTENSION

Interpreting Diagrams
Workbook, p. 24

4.3 Chromosomes

Before You Read

You can usually trace back every effect you observe to something that caused it. In your Science Notebook, describe an example of a cause and its effect from your everyday life. Then look for examples of cause and effect as you read this lesson.

Learning Goals

- Describe the structure and function of chromosomes.
- Contrast mitosis and meiosis.
- Explain how chromosomes determine gender and sex-linked traits.

New Vocabulary

chromosome
centromere
homologous chromosome
mitosis
cytokinesis
meiosis
sex chromosome
autosome
sex-linked trait

Height in pea plants, color in snapdragons, and feather color in chickens are just a few of the many traits determined by genes. A single organism can have tens of thousands of different genes. Genes are not located randomly in cells. Instead, genes are lined up on structures called **chromosomes** (KROH muh sohmz). Each chromosome can contain more than one thousand genes.

Chromosomes are located within the nucleus of eukaryotic cells. Each chromosome is made up of a combination of DNA wrapped with proteins. Recall from Chapter 2 that DNA is an organic molecule that carries the information of heredity.

Much of the time, a chromosome is a structure that looks like a thin thread. Just before a cell divides, a chromosome shortens and takes on an X shape. Each side of an X-shaped chromosome is called a chromatid. The two chromatids, called sister chromatids, are held together at a point called the **centromere** (SEN truh mihr). Sister chromatids are exact copies of each other. Chromosomes can be seen clearly only when the cell is about to divide.

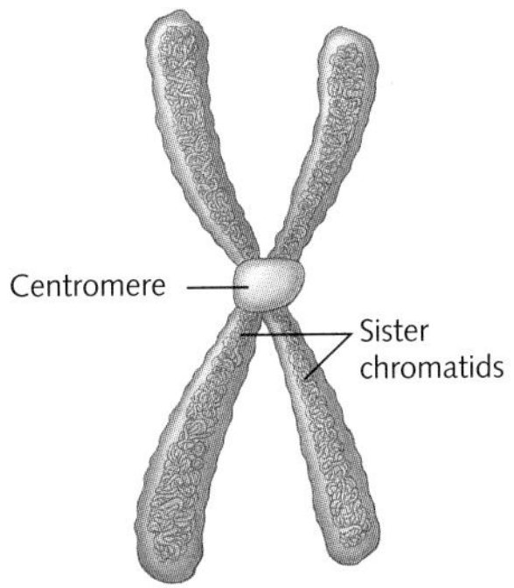

Figure 4.12 A chromosome is shaped like an X just before a cell divides. The sister chromatids are held together by a centromere.

4.3 Introduce

ENGAGE students by asking: *What are some effects of not doing your homework?*

EXPLAIN that a cause makes things happen and that an effect is what happens. Sometimes, a cause has multiple effects.

Before You Read

Model a cause-and-effect diagram on the board. Point out to students that an arrow is often used to show the relationship between a cause and an effect.

Record students' examples of causes and effects on the board. Note cases when there are multiple effects and cases when it is difficult to know what effect some cause will have.

Teach

EXPLAIN to students that in this lesson, they will learn to describe the structure and function of chromosomes. They will also learn to contrast mitosis and meiosis and to explain how chromosomes determine gender and sex-linked traits.

Vocabulary

chromosome Explain that *chromosome* is a combination of two Greek words, *chrōma*, meaning color, and *soma*, meaning body. So, a chromosome is a "colored body." Explain that stains used to make microscopic objects more visible are absorbed by chromosomes and that early researchers who studied cells with microscopes gave these once unknown bodies that take up color their name.

centromere Tell students that the prefix *centro-* means "center." The centromere is at the "center" of a chromosome.

ELL Strategy

Model Have students work in pairs to create a series of cause-and-effect diagrams. Then, have pairs work with other pairs to add to their diagrams. Pairs can first explain their cause-and-effect diagram to other pairs. This will give them an opportunity to explain the validity of their assumptions and to clarify uncertainties. They can then switch diagrams with another pair to see if they can fully understand the drawing and add to the diagram from that point, if necessary. These steps would provide a bit of language and concept assessment. Ask students to use different symbols to indicate when they are fairly certain of an effect and when they are not sure.

Teach

EXPLAIN to students that human chromosomes come in pairs. Each parent contributes one chromosome of each pair of chromosomes, or half of the total number of chromosomes, to an offspring. Tell students that it is not uncommon for complex animals to have fewer chromosomes than less complex animals.

Use the Visual: Figure 4.13

EXTEND Point out that chimpanzees, dogs, and Adder's tongue ferns all have more chromosomes than humans do.

Vocabulary

homologous Tell students that *homologous* comes from the Greek word *homologos*, which means "agreeing." Point out to students that two homologous chromosomes are the same size and have genes for the same characteristics arranged in the same order. The chromosomes "agree." Also remind students that the prefix *homo-* means "same" and was also used in the vocabulary word *homozygous*.

mitosis Explain that the word *mitosis* comes from the Greek word *mitos*, which means "a thread." Point out that chromosomes are said to resemble a string or thread.

Extend It!

Provide students with books and resources such as the official Web site of the Nobel Foundation, which offers information specific to McClintock at **nobelprize.org/nobel_prizes/medicine/laureates/1983/mcclintock-autobio.html**. Suggest that students create posters to show what they have learned. Researching Barbara McClintock allows students to learn more about a prominent female scientist. It also shows students that long-held beliefs in science can be proven wrong.

Homologous Chromosomes

Chromosomes occur in pairs in the cells of organisms that have two parents. This type of reproduction is known as sexual reproduction. One chromosome in each pair came from the male parent. The other came from the female parent. The number of chromosomes is different from one organism to another. **Figure 4.13** lists the chromosome number of several species.

Chromosome Numbers of Common Organisms

Organism	Body Cell (2*n*)	Gamete (*n*)
fruit fly	8	4
garden pea	14	7
corn	20	10
tomato	24	12
leopard frog	26	13
apple	34	17
human	46	23
chimpanzee	48	24
dog	78	39
adder's tongue fern	1,260	630

Figure 4.13 The body cells of each species have a characteristic number of chromosomes. This number is the diploid number, or $2n$. The gametes of each species have a characteristic haploid number, or n.

The chromosomes in each pair are known as **homologous** (huh MAH luh gus) **chromosomes**. Both chromosomes have genes for the same trait arranged in the same order. However, the genes may be different alleles. Recall that alleles are genes that control different versions of the same trait. Therefore, the two chromosomes in a homologous pair are not necessarily genetically identical.

Extend It!

Sometimes, a new discovery disagrees with what scientists already believe. This can make it hard to accept the new finding. This is exactly what happened when a scientist named Barbara McClintock discovered jumping genes in 1950. Find out who she was and what jumping genes are.

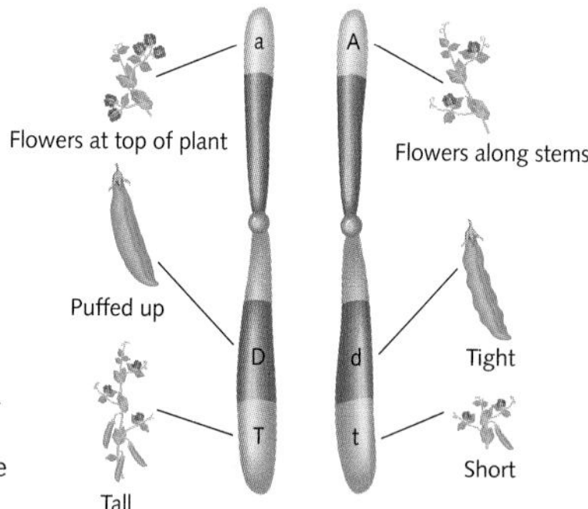

Figure 4.14 This diagram shows two homologous chromosomes from garden pea plants. These particular chromosomes contain genes that determine the position of the flowers, the shape of the pea pod, and the height of the plant. Each chromosome has a different allele for each trait.

Background Information

Barbara McClintock was born in Connecticut. She won the 1983 Nobel Prize for Physiology or Medicine. She was the first woman to singly win a Nobel Prize in this category. Her research helped scientists better understand resistance to antibiotics, viral infections, cancer, immunology, and genetic engineering.

Mitosis

Recall from Chapter 3 that organisms grow when cells divide. Before they divide, cells make a complete copy of their chromosomes. The nucleus of the cell then divides in a process called **mitosis** (mi TOH sis).

Scientists often describe mitosis as having the four stages shown in **Figure 4.15**. During prophase, the first stage, the chromosomes group together and the nuclear envelope disappears. In metaphase, the second stage, the chromosomes line up across the center of the cell. During anaphase, the third stage, the centromeres split and the sister chromatids move to opposite ends of the cell.

In telophase, the final stage, the cell membrane pinches in at the center of the cell. A nuclear envelope reappears around each group of now single chromosomes. Afterwards, in a process called **cytokinesis** (si tuh kih NEE sus), the cell splits into two identical cells called daughter cells. Each cell has a complete set of chromosomes.

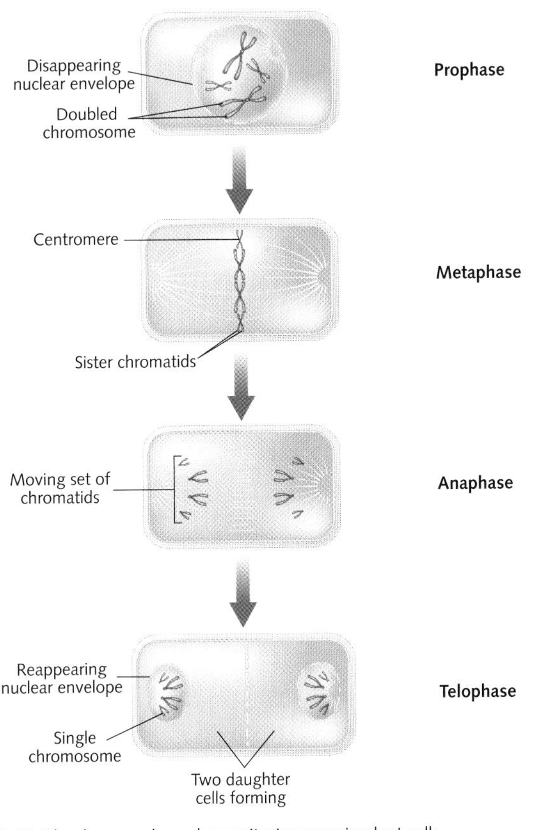

Figure 4.15 The diagram shows how mitosis occurs in plant cells.

As You Read

In your Science Notebook, identify at least three of the cause-and-effect relationships described in this lesson.

What results are caused by mitosis and meiosis?

Teach

EXPLAIN Discuss with students events that happen in phases. For example, before a baby learns to walk, it first learns to sit up, crawl, stand, and "cruise." Explain to students that the events of mitosis must happen in a particular sequence in order for a cell to divide properly. Also explain that the image that represents each stage is a snapshot of a continuous series of events.

Use the Visual: Figure 4.15

EXPLORE Encourage students to describe the continuous series of events that must occur during mitosis, without focusing on the names of the phases.

EXTEND Challenge students to predict the meaning of the name of each phase of mitosis. You may want students to use a dictionary to check their predictions. Or, you may want to give them the following hints: *pro* is the Greek word that means "before"; *meta* is Greek for "along with"; *ana* is Greek for "a piece of each"; and *telo* comes from the Greek word *telos*, meaning "an end."

As You Read

ANSWER Mitosis causes cells to be produced with complete sets of chromosomes. Meiosis causes cells to be produced with half-sets of chromosomes.

Differentiated Instruction

Musical and Kinesthetic To help students remember the stages of mitosis, organize them into groups and have each group make up a song that describes each phase. Have the groups perform their songs for the class.

Teacher Alert

Students often confuse the concepts of correlation and causation. Sometimes, it is hard to know exactly what caused an event. Scientists can sometimes mistake two events that cause each other for two events that just happen together coincidentally. The latter indicates correlation rather than causation.

Teach

EXPLAIN that when an egg cell and a sperm cell combine in sexual reproduction, they each have only half the normal number of chromosomes. (They are haploid cells.) After fertilization, the zygote has a set of chromosomes from each parent. It has the normal (diploid) number of chromosomes. Tell students that this is why offspring display traits from each parent.

Vocabulary

meiosis Explain that the word *meiosis* comes from the Greek word *meioun*, meaning "to make smaller." Tell students that the chromosome number is halved, or "made smaller," by the process of meiosis.

sex chromosome Tell students that the word *sex* indicates gender. *Sex chromosomes* determine the gender of the offspring.

autosome Explain that the prefix *auto-* comes from the Greek word *autos,* meaning "self." Tell students that *autosomes* are the chromosomes that do not determine gender. Ask students to think about the meaning of the prefix *auto-* and its relationship to the word *autosome.*

Figure It Out: Figure 4.17

ANSWER **1.** After telophase II, new gametes are formed. **2.** Prophase I, Metaphase I, Anaphase I, and Telophase I are most like mitosis.

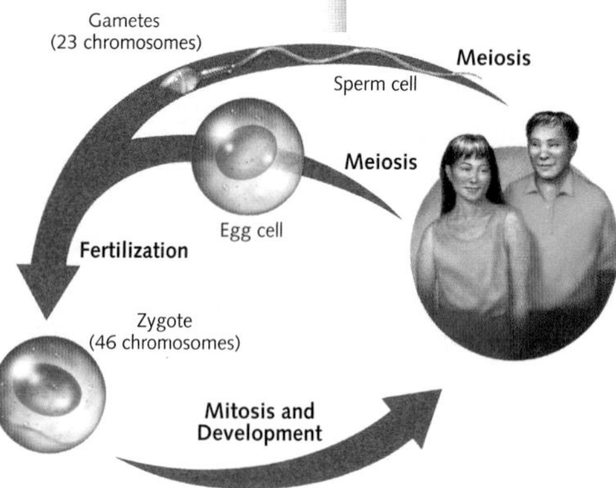

Figure 4.16 Gamete cells contain half the number of chromosomes that are in the body cells of an organism. When two gametes combine, their chromosomes join together in a nucleus. In this way, the zygote receives DNA from both parents.

Meiosis

During sexual reproduction, a male gamete combines with a female gamete. If two normal body cells combined, the resulting cell would have twice the number of chromosomes for an organism. A cell cannot function properly if it has too few or too many chromosomes. Sexual reproduction, then, must involve a form of cell division in which the nucleus divides in a way that is different from mitosis. The number of chromosomes must be reduced by half.

Gametes are produced during a type of cell division that involves **meiosis** (mi OH sus). Unlike mitosis, meiosis leads to cells with half as many chromosomes as there are in a body cell of an organism. Cell division that involves meiosis occurs only in the production of male gametes (sperm) and female gametes (eggs). When a sperm cell then combines with an egg cell, the zygote formed will have a nucleus with the correct number of chromosomes. The zygote then divides mitoticly to form the many cells of a multicellular organism.

Figure It Out

1. After which phase are gametes formed?
2. Which four stages most closely resemble mitosis?

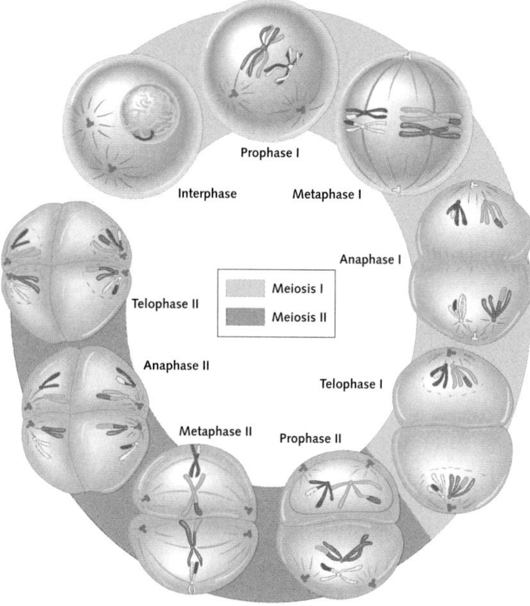

Figure 4.17 The diagram shows the phases of meiosis. Compare this diagram with the phases of mitosis shown in **Figure 4.15**.

ELL Strategy

Use a Venn Diagram Organize students into small groups. Draw an example of a Venn diagram on the board. Have students compare and contrast the stages of meiosis and mitosis using the diagram.

Figure 4.17 shows that meiosis occurs in two parts. The first part, known as meiosis I, is similar to mitosis. Then in meiosis II, the nucleus splits again. In other words, the chromosomes are copied once, but the nucleus splits twice. The result is four cells, each with half the number of chromosomes that are in a body cell of an organism.

Determining Gender

Human body cells have 23 pairs of homologous chromosomes, for a total of 46 chromosomes. One pair is made up of **sex chromosomes** that determine the gender, or sex, of an individual. The other 22 pairs of chromosomes are called **autosomes**. They determine traits other than gender.

In females, sex chromosomes are described by the letters XX. Females have two X chromosomes and can pass only X chromosomes on to any gametes they produce. In males, sex chromosomes are described by the letters XY. Males have only one X chromosome and one Y chromosome. They can pass on either an X chromosome or a Y chromosome to their gametes.

It is the male gamete that determines the sex of the offspring. Look at the Punnett square in **Figure 4.18**. Every egg cell carries an X chromosome. If a sperm cell carrying an X chromosome fertilizes an egg cell, the resulting zygote will have two X chromosomes (XX). It will therefore develop into a female.

If a sperm cell carrying a Y chromosome fertilizes an egg cell, the resulting zygote will have an X chromosome and a Y chromosome (XY). It will develop into a male. The probability of producing a male is the same as that of producing a female—50 percent.

Explain It!

A couple has six children. Use probability to predict how many children should be girls and how many should be boys.

It turns out that all six children are boys. Explain how this can be possible. Write your answers in your Science Notebook.

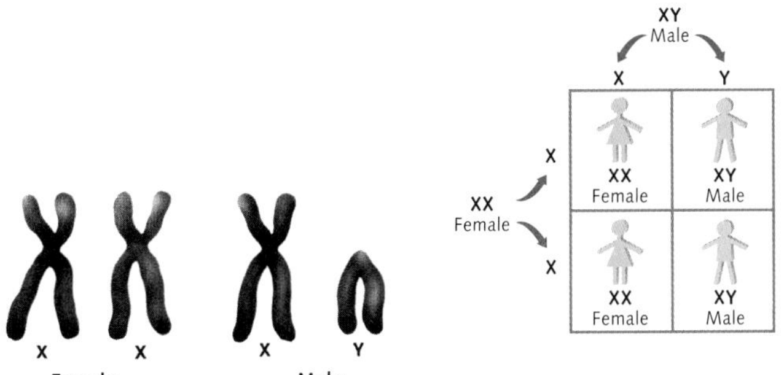

Figure 4.18 Human sex chromosomes are known as X and Y chromosomes. They are named for the letters they look like. If a couple has a child, what is the probability that it will be a girl?

Teach

ENGAGE Ask volunteers to share the number of children in their family and how many of each gender there are. Tell students that the probability of having a child of a particular gender is 50 percent. Ask students to explain why many of the families in the class are not 50 percent female and 50 percent male. Remind students that the probability of an event can be different from the actual outcome. The larger the sample, the more likely it is that the actual outcome will match the predicted outcome.

Use the Visual: Figure 4.18

ANSWER The probability that a couple will have a girl is 50 percent.

The probability is that they will have three boys and three girls. However, remind students of the discussion about gender in their families and the distinction between probable outcomes and actual outcomes. In addition, tell students that chromosomes are passed to gametes at random. Therefore, there is nothing to prevent all six children from having the same gender.

ELL Strategy

Relate to Personal Experience and Analyze Have students collect data about the number of children of each gender in their school. Provide students with access to census data on gender ratios in different countries. Suggest that students research these gender ratios in their native countries. Have students share their data with the class.

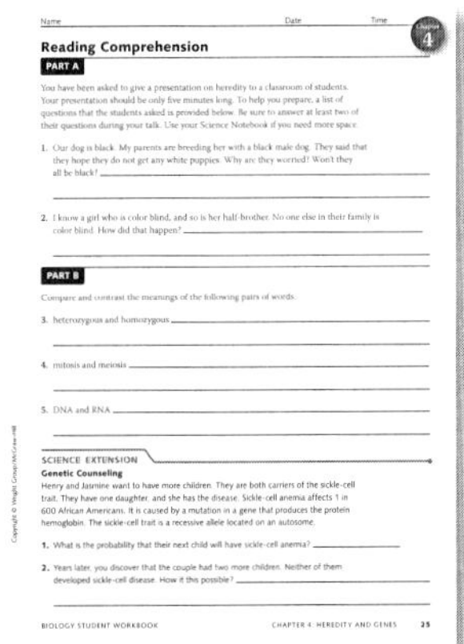

Reading Comprehension Workbook, p. 25

Teach

ENGAGE Ask students if anyone in their family is color blind. Ask students if anyone in their family is bald.

EXPLAIN that these are both sex-linked traits and are determined by genes on the X chromosome.

Vocabulary

sex-linked trait Remind students that *sex* refers to gender. Sex-linked traits are carried by, or "linked" to, the chromosomes that determine gender.

Use the Visual: Figure 4.19

EXTEND 1/4, or 25 percent

CONNECTION: History

Scientists use a chart called a **pedigree** to trace genetic traits over several generations of the same family. One well-known pedigree traces a disorder called hemophilia through a royal European family in the 1800s. Hemophilia is a sex-linked trait caused by a recessive allele carried on the X chromosome. The blood of people with hemophilia does not clot properly.

Queen Victoria did not suffer from hemophilia. However, one of her X chromosomes carried the allele for the trait. Queen Victoria had nine children with Prince Albert, who did not have hemophilia. Three children inherited the allele for hemophilia. Two of those were females who, like Queen Victoria, were carriers. The third was a male who had hemophilia. These three children passed the allele to some of their children and other European royal familes.

Sex-Linked Traits

Like other chromosomes, sex chromosomes carry genes. The X chromosome carries many more genes than the Y chromosome does. Traits determined by genes on sex chromosomes are known as **sex-linked traits**.

One sex-linked trait is color blindness. People who are color blind cannot see the difference between certain colors, such as red and green. Red-green color blindness is caused by a recessive allele that is carried on the X chromosome. If a female inherits the allele for color blindness on one of her X chromosomes, she may have a normal allele on the other chromosome. If this is the case, the female will not be color blind. Because it is a recessive trait, a female will be color blind only if she receives the allele for color blindness from both parents. A female who carries an allele for a disorder but does not exhibit the disorder is considered to be a carrier.

	X	X^C
X	Normal XX	Carrier XX^C
Y	Normal XY	Colorblind X^CY

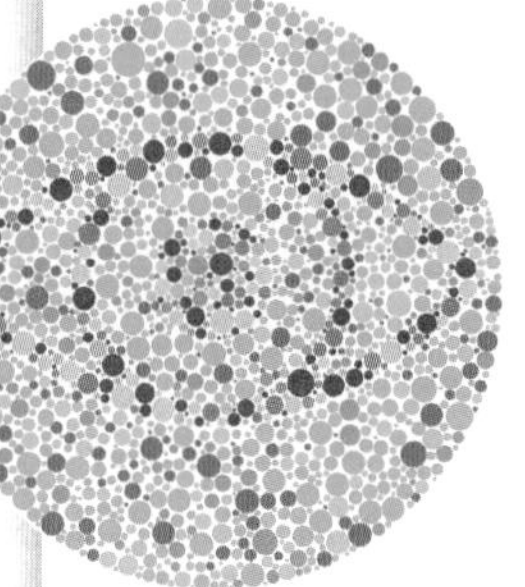

Figure 4.19 In this Punnett square, the normal X chromosome is represented by X. The X chromosome carrying the gene for color blindness is represented by X^C. What is the probability that an offspring of these parents will be color blind?

If a male inherits the allele for color blindness on the X chromosome he receives from his mother, he will be color blind. The reason is that a male has only one X chromosome. He does not have another X chromosome on which the dominant normal allele might appear. Like color blindness, many sex-linked traits are caused by recessive alleles on the X chromosome. As a result, sex-linked traits appear more often in males than they do in females.

CONNECTION: History

An inherited disease called hemophilia was once known as the Royal Disease. Research the disease and the royal families of Europe to find out why. Write a summary of your findings to present to the class. If possible, include photos or diagrams in your presentation.

After You Read

1. How are DNA and genes related to chromosomes?
2. Give an example of a cell produced by mitosis and an example of a cell produced by meiosis. How are the cells different?
3. According to the notes in your Science Notebook, what causes a zygote to develop into a male?

Assess

EVALUATE Use the After You Read questions and the Alternative Assessment to help you assess students' understanding of this lesson.

After You Read

1. DNA is housed in chromosomes, and in turn, divided into segments called genes.
2. Any body cell results from cell division that involves mitosis. Only gametes, sperm and egg cells, result from cell division that involves meiosis. Body cells are diploid, whereas gametes are haploid.
3. The sperm cell must have received a Y chromosome instead of an X chromosome.

Alternative Assessment

EVALUATE Struggling readers can refer to their cause-and-effect charts. Have students add to their charts information from the chapter on cause and effect. Check students' answers.

Background Information

A majority of the approximately 1,000 human X-linked genes determine traits unrelated to the female anatomy. Some of these genes are responsible for hereditary problems such as congenital night blindness, high blood pressure, hemophilia, color blindness, muscular dystrophy, and fragile-X syndrome.

4.4 The Role of DNA

Before You Read

Many events occur in specific orders. In your Science Notebook, describe something you do every day that takes place in a series of steps. Think about how the order of events is important. Imagine doing one of the steps out of order.

Learning Goals

- Identify the structure and function of DNA.
- Recognize the role of RNA.
- Describe the significance of protein synthesis.

New Vocabulary

nucleotide
DNA replication
RNA
protein synthesis
mutation

Recall Vocabulary

amino acid (p. 31)

You have learned that chromosomes and the genes they carry are responsible for passing traits from parents to offspring. Now it is time to find out how they do this. As you read in Chapter 2, genes are made up of molecules of deoxyribonucleic acid, or DNA.

Structure of DNA

DNA is made up of smaller units known as nucleotides. A **nucleotide** (NEW klee uh tide) consists of a phosphate, a sugar, and a nitrogenous base. Each nucleotide contains one of four different nitrogenous bases—adenine (A), thymine (T), guanine (G), and cytosine (C). The nucleotides are arranged in a shape known as a double helix, which looks like a twisted ladder. The sugar and phosphate molecules of the nucleotides make up the sides of the ladder. Pairs of bases make up the steps and hold the two sides together. Only certain bases can pair together. Adenine pairs with thymine, and cytosine pairs with guanine.

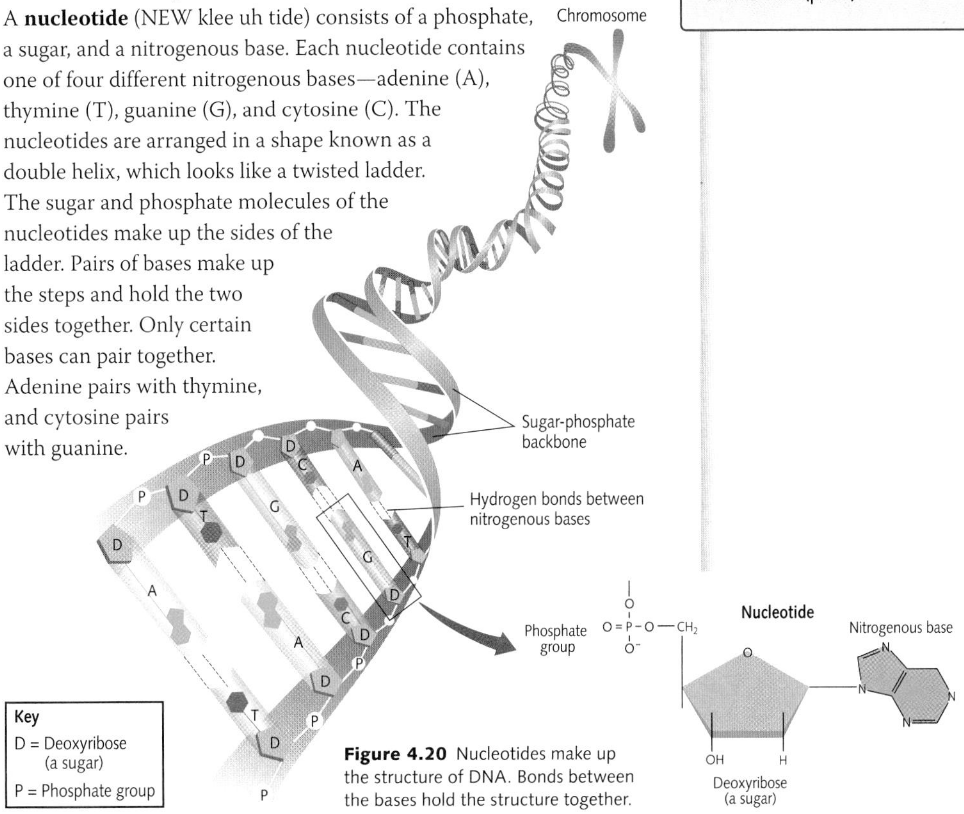

Figure 4.20 Nucleotides make up the structure of DNA. Bonds between the bases hold the structure together.

4.4 Introduce

ENGAGE Discuss with students things they do in a specific order. Ask: *What are the steps required to bake cookies?*

Record students' answers on the board. Encourage students to be as detailed as possible. When you have listed all of the steps, erase one of them. Ask: *What will happen if I miss one of these steps?*

Tell students that, like baking cookies, DNA replication must occur in a particular order.

Before You Read

Give students a few minutes to write their own example of something they do every day that occurs in steps. Then, have them predict what would happen if one step were to be done out of order.

Teach

EXPLAIN that in this lesson, students will learn to identify the structure and function of DNA and recognize the role of RNA. They will also learn about the significance of protein synthesis.

Vocabulary

nucleotide Explain to students that the prefix *nucleo-* refers to the nucleus. It comes from the Latin word *nucleus* and means "kernel." Remind students that the nucleus of a cell is a smaller unit within the cell, just as a nucleotide is a smaller unit, or "kernel," within a DNA molecule.

Differentiated Instruction

Visual and Kinesthetic Cut up four different-colored sheets of paper into small strips. Have students label each strip with a different nitrogen base (adenine, thymine, guanine, and cytosine). From two other sheets of paper, cut long strips. Have students build a model of a DNA double helix using the materials provided. Remind students that only certain bases can pair together. Suggest that students use Figure 4.20 as a guide. Check that students have paired bases correctly. For struggling students, providing a zipper can be a useful technique in explaining how the double helix looks.

Teach

EXPLAIN to students that when the strands of a DNA molecule separate, it is like unzipping a zipper. Tell students that both halves of the zipper then find the nucleotides needed to assemble another half just like the original half that was once there. In the end, there are two identical DNA strands where previously there was one.

PEOPLE IN SCIENCE

Tell students that Watson and Crick are a great example of how scientists work together and build on the work of other scientists. Without the work of Rosalind Franklin, Watson and Crick would not have made their discovery.

Explain to students that the discovery of the structure and function of DNA led to the field of genetic engineering. Through genetic engineering, scientists have been able to manufacture drugs to treat diabetes and heart attacks. Genetic engineering has also made possible the field of gene therapy.

EXTEND Have students do research on genetically engineered drugs or on gene therapy. Direct students to record their findings in their Science Notebooks and share their learning with the class.

Vocabulary

DNA replication Explain that the root of *replication* comes from the Latin word *replicare,* which means to "unroll" or to "fold back." Tell students that in the first stage of DNA replication, the strands of DNA separate or "unroll" from each other.

RNA Explain that the last two letters of *RNA* are the same as in *DNA* and stand for *nucleic acid.* The *R* in *RNA* stands for *ribose,* a sugar. RNA carries information from DNA to the ribosomes in the cytoplasm of a cell and then carries out the process by which proteins are made.

protein synthesis Tell students that the prefix *syn-* in the word *synthesis* means "together." The root of the word *synthesis* comes from the Greek word *tithenai,* which means "put" or "place." The process of protein synthesis involves the putting together of amino acids to synthesize proteins.

Figure It Out: Figure 4.21

ANSWER **1.** They are identical. **2.** Each has one original strand and one new strand.

PEOPLE IN SCIENCE James Watson and Francis Crick

Details about the structure and function of DNA were not learned overnight. Nor were they discovered through the work of a single person. Instead, several scientists contributed to the development of a useful model of DNA. Among them were American biologist James Watson (top) and British physicist Francis Crick (bottom).

In the early 1950s, the pair was working toward making a three-dimensional model of DNA. No matter what they tried, nothing seemed to explain all of the observations other scientists had made about DNA. Then they learned about the research of a British scientist named Rosalind Franklin. She studied DNA by aiming a powerful X-ray beam at it. The X rays were spread out, or scattered, by the DNA. Franklin recorded the pattern of scattered X rays on a film. She found that the pattern was in the shape of an X.

Once they saw the X shape, Watson and Crick suddenly knew what they had been trying to figure out for so long. They developed a model in which the strands of DNA were twisted around each other. Their model immediately explained what was known about DNA and could be used to make predictions about it. On February 28, 1953, Watson and Crick celebrated because they knew that they had discovered the "secret of life." In 1962, they shared the Nobel Prize for their work.

DNA Replication

A copy of all of a cell's genetic material is passed along when cells divide. The process of copying a cell's DNA before cell division is called **DNA replication.** During DNA replication, the two strands of a DNA molecule separate from one another in a process that is similar to the unzipping of a zipper. New bases attach to each separated strand of DNA. As they do, the bases form pairs according to the same rule as in the original strand of DNA. For example, if the base on the old strand was adenine, the base thymine will attach to it. The process, shown in **Figure 4.21,** results in two exact copies of the original DNA molecule.

Figure It Out

1. How do the new DNA molecules compare with each other?
2. Describe the composition of each new molecule.

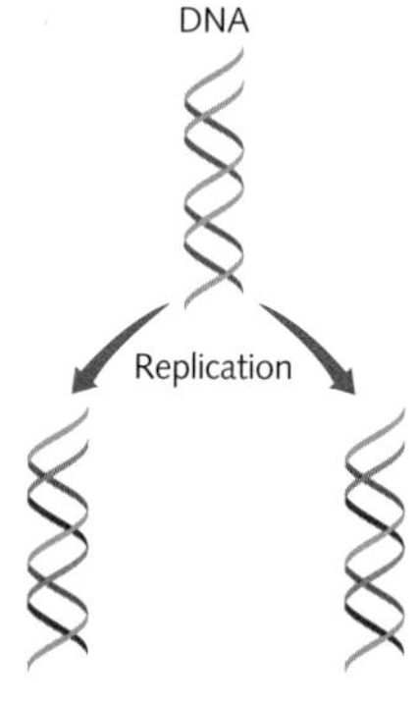

Figure 4.21 During DNA replication, two molecules of DNA are made from one. Each new molecule has one original strand and one new strand. In the diagram, the original strands are blue. The new strands are red.

72 HEREDITY AND GENES

ELL Strategy

Act Out Have students act out DNA replication. Label pieces of paper with the names of the four bases. Give each student a piece of paper with a base. Use a piece of string or tape to affix the paper to each student's shirt. Arrange half the students into a double helix of DNA. Then have the students split. The rest of the students should then combine with their matching bases to make two new strands of DNA.

Genetic Code

The order of the bases on a DNA molecule acts like a genetic code. This code directs how proteins will be put together. It is the proteins that then regulate the cell's activities. More specifically, proteins determine the traits of an organism. In this way, DNA is responsible for determining which traits are inherited from one generation to the next.

The Role of RNA

Proteins are assembled on ribosomes. Recall from Chapter 3 that ribosomes are organelles in the cytoplasm of a cell. DNA does not leave the nucleus of a cell. The cell therefore needs a way to get the information from the DNA in the nucleus to the ribosomes in the cytoplasm. This is where the nucleic acid RNA comes in. **RNA**, or ribonucleic acid, carries information from DNA to the ribosomes and then carries out the process by which proteins are made.

RNA is similar to DNA but has a few important differences. RNA is made up of a single strand of nucleotides rather than a double strand. In addition, RNA has a nitrogenous base called uracil (U) in place of thymine. The sugar in the nucleotides of RNA is ribose rather than deoxyribose, as is found in DNA nucleotides.

Protein Synthesis

The process by which proteins are made is known as **protein synthesis**. It begins when two strands of DNA separate. Bases then attach to the strands, much like they do during DNA replication. Now, however, the new strand is made of RNA instead of DNA. The RNA then leaves the nucleus and carries information into the cytoplasm. The genetic code is translated into a chain of amino acids. Recall from Chapter 2 that amino acids are the building blocks of proteins.

Although organisms have evolved many ways to protect their DNA from changes, changes in DNA sometimes occur. Any change in the DNA sequence is called a **mutation** (myew TAY shun). Mutations can be caused by errors in DNA replication or cell division, or by external agents such as nuclear radiation. Mutations can be harmful or have little or no effect.

As You Read

In your Science Notebook, create a sequence chart to describe the events that must occur for proteins to form.

How does information encoded in DNA get to ribosomes?

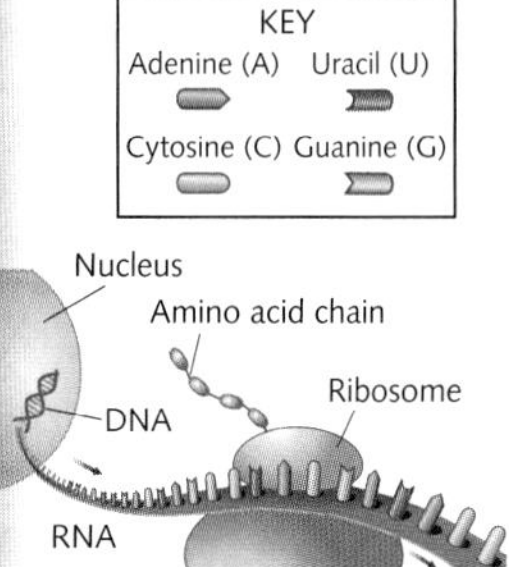

Figure 4.22 The information in RNA is used to direct the arrangement of amino acids to form proteins. On what organelle are proteins formed?

After You Read

1. Builders use blueprints that provide instructions about how to construct a building. How does DNA act as a blueprint for living things?
2. Why is RNA essential to living things?
3. Proteins determine the traits of organisms. Use the information from your chart to write a well-developed paragraph describing the sequence that explains how DNA is related to proteins.

Teacher Alert

Students may mix up the steps in DNA replication with the steps of protein synthesis. To help students remember the difference, stress that in DNA replication, the DNA does not leave the nucleus. Also remind students that RNA is made up of only a single strand of nucleotides and contains the base uracil in place of thymine. Also, the sugar in RNA is ribose rather than deoxyribose.

Teach

EXPLAIN to students that a code is a system of words, symbols, or letters that represent information. Ask students for examples of codes that they may have heard about. Encourage students to suggest codes such as Morse code or computer code. Tell students that, like these codes, the order of the bases on a DNA molecule acts as a *genetic code*, directing the synthesis of proteins.

As You Read

Model a sequence chart on the board. Use DNA replication as an example. Tell students that they should use a similar sequence chart to describe the events that must occur for proteins to form.

ANSWER The information encoded in DNA must be carried by RNA to the ribosomes.

Use the Visual: Figure 4.22

ANSWER Proteins are formed on ribosomes.

Assess

EVALUATE Use the After You Read questions and the Alternative Assessment to help you assess students' understanding of this lesson.

After You Read

1. DNA provides the instructions for how proteins are to be made, much like blueprints provide instructions for how to make a building.
2. DNA does not leave the nucleus; yet, proteins are assembled on ribosomes in the cytoplasm. RNA carries information from DNA to the ribosomes and then acts as the instructions for arranging amino acids into proteins.
3. The genetic code in DNA is carried by RNA to ribosomes and used to arrange amino acids into proteins. Therefore, DNA determines which proteins are made in a cell.

Alternative Assessment

EVALUATE Struggling readers can refer to their Science Notebooks and create two sequence charts, one for DNA replication and one for protein synthesis. Check students' sequence charts for any missing steps.

4.5 Introduce

ENGAGE Discuss with students the difference between a purebred dog and a mutt. Ask: *Does anyone in class have a dog that is a mutt? Does anyone have a purebred dog? What are the differences between these two types of dogs?*

Draw a T-chart on the board. In one column write *Mutt*, and in the other column write *Purebred*. Record students' answers in the chart.

Tell students that purebred dogs are bred through a process called *inbreeding*. A purebred Labrador retriever has dogs of only that breed as parents. A dog that is a mutt has parents that are different types of dogs, and a mutt's parents' parents might also be two different types of dogs. Thus, a mutt may be a mixture of many breeds of dogs, while a purebred is not.

Before You Read

Have students draw the T-charts in their Science Notebooks. Check that students have drawn their charts correctly. Tell students that they will be using these charts to compare two methods of changing heredity.

Teach

EXPLAIN to students that in this lesson, they will compare different types of selective breeding. They will also come to understand methods of genetic engineering and analyze the possible benefits and risks of changing heredity.

Learning Goals

- Compare different types of selective breeding.
- Understand methods of genetic engineering.
- Analyze the possible benefits and risks of changing heredity.

New Vocabulary

selective breeding
hybridization
inbreeding
genetic engineering
recombinant DNA
cloning

4.5 Changing Heredity

Before You Read

Draw a T-chart in your Science Notebook. This chart can be used to compare and contrast processes. Label one side *Selective Breeding* and the other side *Genetic Engineering*. As you read the lesson, describe how the processes are alike and different.

Detailed knowledge of DNA, genes, and chromosomes is relatively new because of the complex technology scientists needed to study such small structures. That does not mean that the study of genetics is new, however. For thousands of years, people have been using their observations to breed plants and animals with specific traits.

Selective Breeding

In a process known as **selective breeding**, people choose plants and animals with preferred traits and allow them to reproduce. A farmer practicing selective breeding might allow only cows that give large quantities of milk or hens that lay large numbers of eggs to reproduce. In a similar way, a plant breeder might cross only plants that produce the largest vegetables or the sweetest fruits.

Increasing the frequency of a desired allele in a population is the goal of selective breeding. However, this often requires time and patience. For animals, it takes several generations of offspring before the desired trait becomes common within the population of the species.

Figure 4.23 Corn is one of many crops grown from seeds that are produced through selective breeding techniques. In the 1930s, midwestern farmers discovered that crossing different plants could result in a plant that was stronger and produced more corn than either plant alone.

ELL Strategy

Practice Using Vocabulary Have students create crossword puzzles using the vocabulary words in this chapter. Students can try to solve each other's puzzles. Students who have difficulty with English might first write definitions in their native language and then translate them into English.

Hybridization One selective breeding technique known as hybridization is used to take advantage of the most desirable traits of different organisms. In **hybridization**, breeders mate or cross organisms with different traits. A wheat plant that produces a large amount of wheat, for example, might be crossed with a wheat plant that is resistant to disease. The goal would be to create plants that produce a large amount of wheat and are resistant to disease.

Occasionally, organisms from different species are bred together. Female horses have been bred with male donkeys to produce mules, such as the one shown in **Figure 4.24**.

Figure 4.24 Although mules cannot reproduce, they are extremely useful. Mules are stronger, healthier, and can stand greater differences in temperature than either the donkeys or horses from which they are produced.

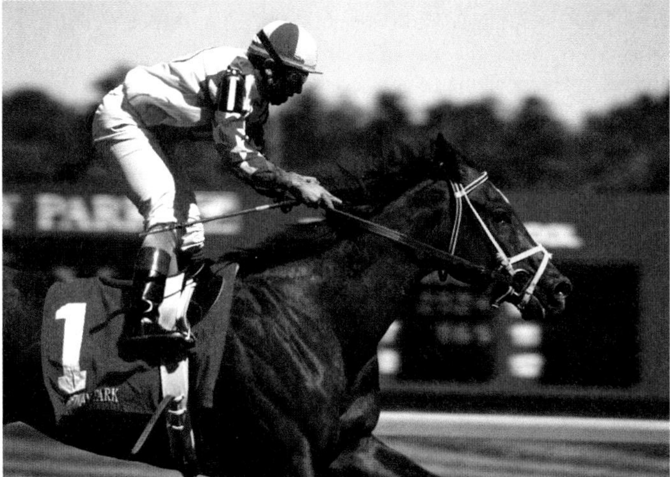

Figure 4.25 This thoroughbred racehorse comes from a line of horses that have been bred to run fast over long distances.

Inbreeding Another type of selective breeding known as **inbreeding** involves mating or crossing organisms with similar traits. The goal of this practice is to keep the traits in an organism the same over time and to eliminate undesired traits. A group of organisms within a species that has been bred to have specific traits is known as a breed. Breeders of dogs and horses often take advantage of inbreeding.

As You Read

On the correct side of the T-chart in your Science Notebook, add the terms *hybridization* and *inbreeding*. Make a list of the characteristics of each.

What is hybridization? What is inbreeding?

Teach

EXPLAIN to students that there are many different ways in which plants and animals are bred. Scientists use these different methods to produce plants and animals that better meet the needs of people.

Vocabulary

selective breeding Explain that the word *selective* comes from the Latin *seligere,* which means "to choose apart." When something is selected, it is "chosen" or "set apart." In selective breeding, people choose the traits they want to see in offspring.

hybridization Tell students that a common usage of the word *hybrid* refers to cars that use a cross of different energy sources, gasoline and electricity, for power. *Hybridization* refers to a cross of organisms with different traits, like a hybrid car.

inbreeding Ask students to think about other words that start with the prefix *in-*, such as *inside, inner,* and *indoors*. Explain to students that the word *inbreeding* shares this prefix. When animals are inbred, they are bred close relatives.

As You Read

Students should fill in their charts as they read through the lesson. Check students' Science Notebooks throughout the lesson.

ANSWER Hybridization is selective breeding involving individuals with different traits. Inbreeding is selective breeding involving individuals with the same traits.

ELL Strategy

Prepare Presentations *Eugenics* is a movement that aims to use selective breeding on humans to improve the human race. Have students learn more about this controversial issue. Divide the class into two groups. Have the class debate the pros and cons of eugenics. Students can also create visual aids to help them in their presentations and encourage proper use of vocabulary terms.

Background Information

Sir Francis Galton came up with the idea of *eugenics* in the 1880s. His ideas were controversial at the time and continue to be so. Not only do eugenists wish to improve the traits of humans through selective breeding, they also want to reduce the number of "inferior" humans born by limiting the reproduction of those "less desirable" parents. Thus far, eugenists have not been successful in their quest to "improve" the human race.

Teach

EXPLAIN Ask students if they have heard of the term *genetic engineering*. Have students share what they know with the class. Explain to students that genetic engineering is a faster and more complex method of controlling an organism's genetic makeup. Today, scientists are using genetic engineering to develop new drugs and foods.

Vocabulary

genetic engineering Tell students that *engine*, the root of the word *engineering*, comes from the Latin word *ingenium*, which means "skill" or "cleverness." The word *engineering* shares this root with the word *genius*. Ask students to think about how the idea of "cleverness" is part of genetic engineering.

recombinant DNA Explain to students that the prefix *re-* in *recombinant* means "again." Point out that the root of *recombinant* is *combine*. *Recombinant* means to "combine again." Then, explain that the last two letters of *DNA* stand for the same words that they stand for in *RNA*, *nucleic acid*. The *D* in *DNA* stands for *deoxyribose*, which, like ribose, is a sugar. DNA that is made by mixing or combining the DNA of two different kinds of organisms is recombinant DNA.

cloning Tell students that the word *clone* in science fiction brings to mind images of people who think, look, and act alike. Point out that cloning replicates the genetics of an individual but not the personality.

Figure It Out: Figure 4.26

ANSWER **1.** It is copied along with the bacterial cell's original DNA. **2.** The gene directs the bacterial cell to produce human insulin.

Did You Know?

Over a period of 11 years, scientists from around the world completed a map of the human genome. The human genome consists of the almost 40,000 genes on the 46 human chromosomes. Scientists hope to use this map to find ways to identify and treat diseases through genetic engineering techniques.

Genetic Engineering

Selective breeding is not a technique that occurs quickly. Changes occur over several generations and only after years of careful observation. A faster and more complex method of controlling the genetic makeup of an organism is **genetic engineering**. This term covers a variety of techniques that directly change the hereditary material of an organism.

Recombinant DNA One method of genetic engineering involves cutting a portion of the DNA from one organism and inserting it into another organism. DNA formed by combining pieces from different sources is described as **recombinant** (ree KAHM buh nunt) **DNA**.

Scientists generally transfer DNA from a more complex organism to a simpler one. For example, they might transfer DNA from a human to a bacterial cell, as **Figure 4.26** shows. In a bacterial cell, some of the DNA is in a circle called a plasmid. Scientists take out the plasmid, cut it open, and insert the human DNA. The plasmid containing the human DNA is then returned to the bacterial cell.

The organism into which the recombinant DNA is inserted is known as the host organism. The host organism uses the foreign DNA as if it were its own. Recall that bacteria reproduce by binary fission. In this process, a copy of all the DNA in a cell is made. The cell then divides into two cells that are identical to the original cell. When a bacterial cell containing human DNA reproduces, the cells produced also contain human DNA.

Figure It Out

1. What happens to the human insulin gene when an engineered bacterial cell reproduces?
2. What does the human insulin gene do in the bacterial plasmid?

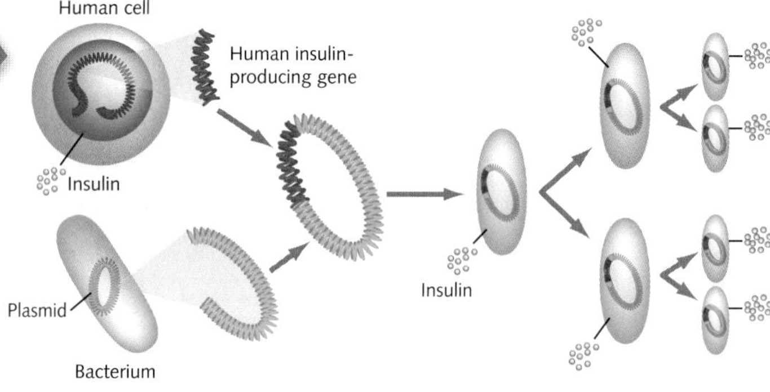

Figure 4.26 An enzyme is used to remove the human gene for insulin. The same enzyme is also used to cut open bacterial plasmids. The human gene is then inserted into the plasmid and returned to the bacterial cell.

Background Information

The scientist who led the effort to map the human genome, J. Craig Venter, did so with his own genetic code. The information he learned about himself led him to discover a gene variant that indicates a propensity for heart disease. He is now taking drugs to lower his cholesterol based on what he learned about himself.

Cloning Another technique in which scientists alter the natural processes of heredity is cloning. **Cloning** involves using a single parent to produce genetically identical offspring.

To produce a clone of a mammal, scientists obtain an egg cell from a donor organism. They then remove the nucleus, and therefore the DNA, from the cell. The next step is to take a cell from the adult being cloned. The nucleus from this cell is fused into the egg cell. The result is a complete cell that can be made to divide. Once the single cell divides into a ball of cells, it is placed inside a host mother. There it develops normally into an offspring that is genetically identical to the original.

Figure 4.27 In 2005, this Afghan hound puppy, named Snuppy, became the first cloned dog. He was formed from an ear cell of an adult dog and developed in a yellow Labrador retriever.

Benefits and Risks

Why would scientists want to insert human DNA into bacteria or clone animals? One reason is to produce substances that humans need. Insulin is a protein humans need to control the level of sugar in the blood. People with a condition known as diabetes must take injections of insulin every day. Genetically engineering bacterial cells that produce human insulin creates a plentiful supply of needed insulin. Researchers hope to use cloning to produce tissues and organs that people need.

Another benefit is the ability to alter the traits of organisms in a way similar to selective breeding. A number of crop plants, such as wheat, have been genetically engineered to grow larger, faster, and more resistant to disease. Cloning is widely used to produce large numbers of identical ornamental plants and fruit and nut trees.

Another goal is to use cloning to produce organisms that are on the verge of extinction.

Unfortunately, changing natural processes raises its own concerns. Fields of genetically identical wheat plants may be wiped out by a single disease. In addition, the risks that altered organisms pose to the environment may not be known for many years. When it comes to cloning animals, many individuals may be hurt or destroyed in the process of creating a single clone. Even when a mammal is cloned, it is often born with disorders that the original animal did not have. Scientists continue to learn more about these processes and their results so that people can make informed decisions about these technologies.

CONNECTION: Economics

Genetic engineering can have economic consequences. For example, plants that produce larger yields might bring greater profits to farmers. The hopes of higher profits, however, might lead people to ignore ethical concerns. Cloned pets are being sold for large sums of money. Although they are purchased by people hoping to replace a beloved pet, the cloned pets merely look like their originals. They may have different personalities or health problems.

After You Read

1. How is the goal of hybridization different from that of inbreeding?
2. How can bacteria be made to produce human insulin?
3. Examine the information in your T-chart. What is a benefit of genetic engineering? What is a possible risk, or problem, caused by genetic engineering?

Teach

EXPLORE Discuss with students the concepts of benefit and risk. Ask them to think of situations in which they had to weigh the benefits and risks of a situation before making a decision. Explain that cloning has a number of benefits as well as many risks. Scientists have had to think about both before conducting their research.

CONNECTION: Economics

In 1997, the first vertebrate animal—a sheep—was cloned in Scotland by a scientist named Ian Wilmut. Success with the cloned sheep, Dolly, led scientists to believe that it will one day be possible to clone a human being. Have students discuss and debate the benefits, risks, and ethical concerns associated with the possibility of human cloning.

Assess

EVALUATE Use the After You Read questions and the Alternative Assessment to help you assess students' understanding of this lesson.

After You Read

1. The goal of hybridization is to obtain the best traits of different individuals. The goal of inbreeding is to maintain the same traits and avoid the introduction of new traits.
2. The gene responsible for producing insulin can be removed from a human cell. That bit of DNA can then be inserted into bacterial DNA. A bacterial cell with the human DNA makes human insulin.
3. Answers will vary but may include the benefits of producing needed medicines. Risks include diseases related to changes in cell makeup.

Differentiated Instruction

Interpersonal Have students choose a bioethical issue to research, such as human cloning, stem cell research, gene testing, or gene therapy. Ask students to write an essay outlining both sides of the ethical issues surrounding their topic and, based on their research, defend what they believe is right and ethical.

Alternative Assessment

EVALUATE Struggling readers can check that the T-charts in their Science Notebooks include the characteristics of hybridization and inbreeding, in addition to comparing the benefits and risks of genetic engineering.

Chapter 4 Summary

VOCABULARY REVIEW

Check students' sentences or paragraphs to make sure that they understand the meaning of each vocabulary term.

PREPARE FOR CHAPTER TEST

Evaluate students' essays using the following criteria:

1. The topic sentence, or main idea, should restate the Key Concept.
2. The supporting paragraphs should incorporate the answers to the Learning Goal questions students have written and include details, facts, and examples they have recorded in their Science Notebooks.
3. The concluding sentence should sum up the main idea of the chapter and restate the Key Concept.

MASTERING CONCEPTS

True or False

1. False, recessive
2. False, heterozygous
3. True
4. False, centromere
5. False, meiosis
6. False, double
7. True

Short Answer

8. *Gg* is the genotype, which is heterozygous, and the phenotype is green. *GG* is a homozygous genotype, and the phenotype is green. *gg* is a homozygous genotype, and the phenotype is yellow.
9. 0 percent
10. Homologous chromosomes are pairs of chromosomes that carry the same genes for the same traits in the same order. One chromosome in the pair comes from the female parent, and the other comes from the male parent.
11. Mitosis enables an organism to grow through cell division. Meiosis enables the organism to produce gametes that combine during sexual reproduction.
12. During DNA replication, the two strands of DNA separate. Bases attach to each strand in the same arrangement as in the original strand.

Chapter 4

Summary

KEY CONCEPTS

4.1 Basic Principles of Heredity

- A dominant allele is expressed over a recessive allele in an organism.
- The genotype of an individual is the alleles it has for a trait. Its phenotype is the form of the trait displayed.
- In incomplete dominance, two traits blend together. In codominance, two different traits are displayed in an offspring.

4.2 Punnett Squares

- A Punnett square can be used to predict the possible genotypes of the offspring of a cross between two individuals.
- The probability, or likelihood, of the outcome of a cross can be predicted. However, the actual outcome of a cross is a matter of chance.

4.3 Chromosomes

- A chromosome is a structure that contains genes.
- Mitosis occurs during cell division that results in two genetically identical cells.
- Meiosis occurs during cell division that results in four gametes with half the normal number of chromosomes.
- Sex chromosomes determine the gender of an individual. Autosomes determine traits other than gender.

4.4 The Role of DNA

- DNA carries the instructions that direct the formation of proteins through its arrangement of nucleotides.
- RNA carries the instructions from DNA to ribosomes and then organizes amino acids into proteins.
- During protein synthesis, the proteins that determine the traits of an organism are made.
- A mutation, or change in the DNA sequence, can result from an error in DNA replication or cell division, as well as from external agents.

4.5 Changing Heredity

- Hybridization involves crossing individuals with different traits, whereas inbreeding involves crossing individuals with similar traits.
- Recombinant DNA is formed when DNA from one organism is combined with DNA from another organism. Cloning occurs when a single parent is used to produce genetically identical offspring.
- Genetic engineering has both possible benefits and risks.

VOCABULARY REVIEW

Write each term in a complete sentence.

4.1
trait, p. 57
heredity, p. 57
genetics, p. 57
gamete, p. 57
pollination, p. 57
fertilization, p. 57
hybrid, p. 58
dominant, p. 59
recessive, p. 59
gene, p. 60
allele, p. 60
law of dominance, p. 60
law of segregation, p. 61
genotype, p. 61
homozygous, p. 61
heterozygous, p. 61
phenotype, p. 61
incomplete dominance, p. 62
codominance, p. 62

4.2
Punnett square, p. 63
percent, p. 64
probability, p. 64

4.3
chromosome, p. 65
centromere, p. 65
homologous chromosome, p. 66
mitosis, p. 67
cytokinesis, p. 67
meiosis, p. 68
sex chromosome, p. 69
autosome, p. 69
sex-linked trait, p. 70

4.4
nucleotide, p. 71
DNA replication, p. 72
RNA, p. 73
protein synthesis, p. 73
mutation, p. 73

4.5
selective breeding, p. 74
hybridization, p. 75
inbreeding, p. 75
genetic engineering, p. 76
recombinant DNA, p. 76
cloning, p. 77

78 HEREDITY AND GENES

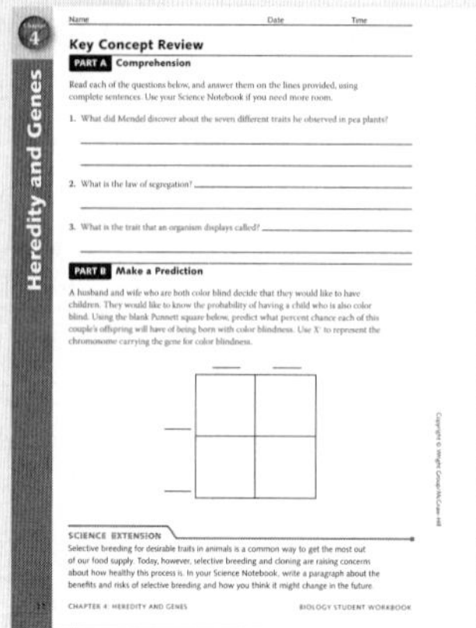

Key Concept Review Workbook, p. 22

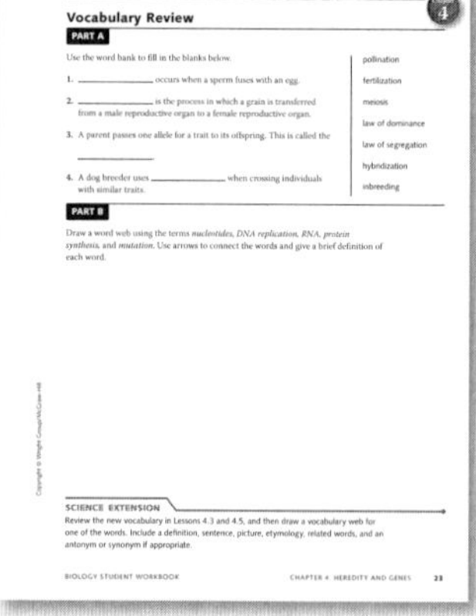

Vocabulary Review Workbook, p. 23

MASTERING CONCEPTS

True or False

If the statement is true, write "true." If it is false, change the underlined word or words to make the statement true.

1. A dominant trait will be expressed only if the organism has two alleles for the trait.
2. A fruit fly is homozygous if it has two different alleles for wing length.
3. A Punnett square is used to predict the genotypes of the offspring of a cross.
4. The sister chromatids of a chromosome are held together at the clone.
5. Gametes are formed through the process of mitosis.
6. DNA is in the form of a single helix.
7. The goal of inbreeding is to maintain the same traits in a line of individuals.

Short Answer

Answer each of the following in a sentence or brief paragraph.

8. In pea plants, green pods (*G*) are dominant over yellow pods (*g*). Compare the genotype and phenotype of a plant that is *Gg* for this trait with plants that are *GG* and *gg*.
9. In pea plants, yellow seeds are dominant over green seeds. Two homozygous parents, one with yellow seeds and one with green seeds, are crossed. What percent of the offspring will display the recessive trait? Use a Punnett square to find the answer.
10. Describe homologous chromosomes, and relate them to the parents of an organism.
11. Discuss how mitosis and meiosis are both essential to multicellular organisms that carry out sexual reproduction.
12. Explain how a single DNA molecule can form two identical copies.
13. Why is the nucleus removed from an egg cell at the start of the mammal cloning process?

Critical Thinking

Use what you have learned in this chapter to answer each of the following.

14. **Cause and Effect** Why is it difficult to determine the genotype of an organism in which one form of a trait is dominant over the other?
15. **Infer** Why are sex-linked traits observed more often in males than in females?
16. **Relate** How has selective breeding been used in farming?

Standardized Test Question

Choose the letter of the response that correctly answers the question.

	T	*t*
T	1	2
t	3	4

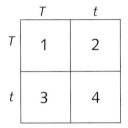

17. The diagram shows a cross between two organisms. Which of the following statements is true?
    A. Individual 1 is heterozygous.
    B. Individuals 1 and 4 are homozygous.
    C. Individuals 2 and 3 are homozygous.
    D. Individual 4 is heterozygous.

Test-Taking Tip

Make sure you understand what kind of answer you are being asked to provide. Pay attention to words such as *illustrate, list, define, compare, explain,* and *predict.* A graphic organizer might help you organize your thoughts if you see a word such as *list* or *compare.*

13. It is removed in order to remove the genetic material from the donor cell so it can be replaced with the genetic material of the organism being cloned.

Critical Thinking

14. Two different genotypes can produce the same phenotype.
15. Sex-linked traits are ususally caused by recessive alleles on the X chromosome. Females can carry the allele without having the trait because they have a second X chromosome that may carry the normal allele. Males have only one X chromosome and therefore display the trait if they receive the allele from their mothers.
16. Selective breeding has been used to cross breed animals and crops with the best traits and produce offspring that have a combination of the best traits of their parents.

Standardized Test Question

17. B

Reading Links

Mutants, Clones, and Killer Corn: Unlocking the Secrets of Biotechnology

This readable overview of past, current, and future issues in biotechnology, with its interesting studies of scientific successes and failures, provides valuable insight into a controversial topic. It also includes a basic introduction to genetics, practical graphics, a time line, a glossary, and other supplementary resources.

Seiple, Samantha, and Todd Seiple. Lerner Publishing Group. 112 pp. Illustrated. Library ISBN: 978-0-8225-4860-7.

Orphan Diseases: New Hope for Rare Medical Conditions

The personal stories told in this book—of rare, serious human diseases, their genetic origins, and the people and treatments associated with them—offer an enrichment opportunity for students studying genetics. Autism, dwarfism, cystic fibrosis, sickle-cell anemia, and other conditions are covered in a lively and sensitive way, often with the involvement of a celebrity associated with a particular condition.

Murphy, Wendy B. Lerner Publishing Group. 144 pp. Illustrated. Library ISBN: 978-0-7613-1919-1.

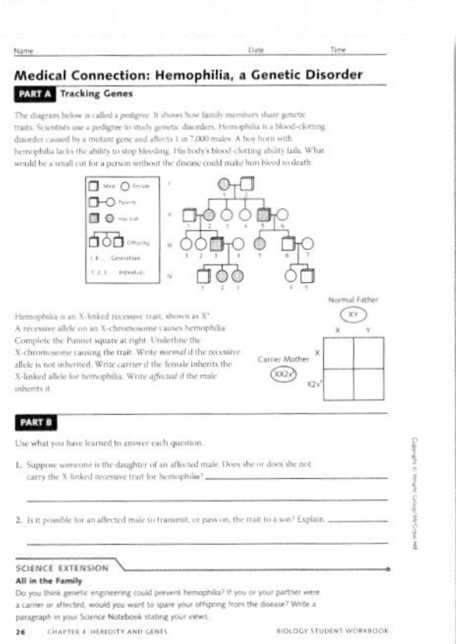

Medical Connection: Hemophilia, a Genetic Disorder

PART A Tracking Genes

Curriculum Connection Workbook, p. 26

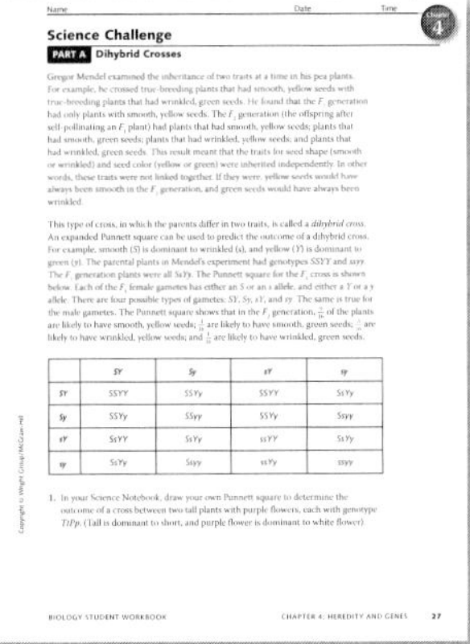

Science Challenge

PART A Dihybrid Crosses

Science Challenge Workbook, pp. 27–28

Chapter 4

Labs

4A DNA in a Banana?

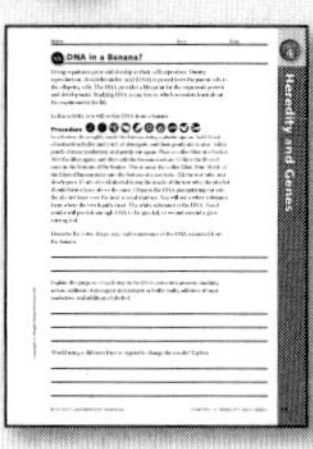

This prechapter introduction activity is designed to introduce students to the concept that DNA is present in all living and once-living cells by having students extract DNA from a fruit and engaging them in examining, comparing, contrasting, inferring, and predicting.

Objectives

- use laboratory procedures to extract DNA from a banana
- compare and contrast the characteristics of the extracted sample and the structural characteristics of DNA
- infer how DNA is released from cells
- predict the results of using different fruits or vegetables

Planning

30 minutes

groups of 2–3 students

Materials (per group)

- 2 small beakers
- 50-mL graduated cylinder
- banana (2-cm piece)
- extraction buffer
- liquid detergent
- unseasoned meat tenderizer
- plastic spoon
- coffee filter
- cold alcohol
- test tube
- 1 glass stirring rod

Advance Preparation

- To prepare the extraction buffer, combine 250 mL of distilled water with 1 teaspoon of salt.
- Use clear, colorless shampoo or liquid detergent containing SDS (sodium dodecyl sulfate). Instruct students to stir the banana mixture gently so as to not make it froth or foam up.
- Use cold ethanol or 70–90% isopropyl alcohol. Cold alcohol makes the DNA precipitate out better, and ethanol is very flammable and must be kept cold.

Engagement Guide

- Challenge students to think about the characteristics of DNA by asking:
- *Where is DNA found in a cell?* (in the nucleus)
- *What characteristics of DNA does your sample have?* (long strands that appear to be coiled)
- *What steps did you perform that caused the cell to break open, releasing the DNA?* (Mashing the banana breaks open the cells, exposing them to the soap, salt, and meat tenderizer. The soap breaks down, or emulsifies, the phospholipids in the cell membranes and releases DNA. The salt in the buffer brings the DNA together, and the meat tenderizer contains enzymes that cut the protein away from the DNA. The alcohol helps the DNA precipitate so it can be collected.)
- Encourage students to communicate their conclusions by writing descriptions of the DNA they collect.

Going Further

Encourage students to choose another fruit, vegetable, or meat. Have students compare their extracted DNA with samples from the rest of the class and determine if there are differences in the appearance or amount.

4B Looking at Your Traits

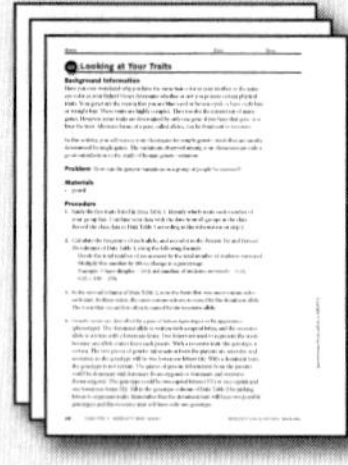

Objectives

- recognize simple inherited traits
- organize data visually
- categorize traits as dominant or recessive
- determine gene frequencies by calculating percentages

Skill Set

observing, differentiating, recording and analyzing data, interpreting, summarizing

Planning

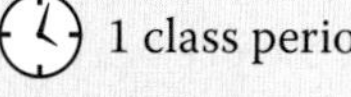

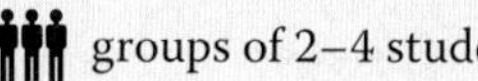

1 class period — groups of 2–4 students

Materials

Materials for this activity are listed in the Student Laboratory Manual.

Lab Tip

If PTC paper strips are used, caution students that PTC is highly toxic when eaten, and remind them to wash their hands at the conclusion of the activity.

Answers to Observations: Data Table 1

Answers will depend on students' surveys.

Answers to Observations: Data Table 2

Attached earlobes: recessive, *ll* genotype; unattached earlobes: dominant, *LL* or *Ll* genotype; hitchhiker's thumb: recessive, *tt* genotype; no hitchhiker's thumb: dominant, *TT* or *Tt* genotype; widow's peak: dominant, *PP* or *Pp* genotype; no widow's peak: recessive, *pp* genotype; cleft chin: dominant, *YY* or *Yy* genotype; no cleft chin: recessive, *yy* genotype; dimples: dominant, *DD* or *Dd* genotype; no dimples: recessive, *dd* genotype

Answers to Analysis and Conclusions

1. A trait is an inherited characteristic determined by genes, and an allele is one of the different forms a gene may have.
2. *Homozygous* means two of the same alleles (*TT*, *tt*), and *heterozygous* means two different alleles (*Tt*).
3. A trait that is more common is usually dominant; one that is less common is usually recessive. Answers may include any of the traits in Data Table 2.
4. A person would have two lowercase letters (such as *ll*). The child would be recessive for earlobes, as are the parents.

Going Further

Have students choose one of the five traits used in this lab and survey at least 30 different people, including family members, for the trait. Instruct students to use their data to make bar graphs, which they should be prepared to present and explain to the class.

4C Protein Synthesis: Like Building Sentences

Objectives

- interpret the genetic code chart to transcribe DNA
- use simulation to observe the relationships among DNA, mRNA, and tRNA
- record and analyze data
- relate the sentence simulation to the way proteins are made

Skill Set

interpreting, observing, recording and analyzing data, comparing and contrasting

Planning

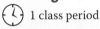

 1 class period 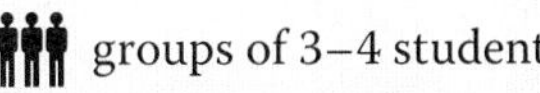

groups of 3–4 students

Materials

- 10 DNA template cards
- 46 anticodon/word cards

Advance Preparation

- Review how to use the genetic code chart. Review base pairings for DNA, and note that in RNA, uracil replaces thymine.
- Have students copy the Data Table 2 format for each DNA template card they transcribe.
- Use 4- × 6-in. index cards for the DNA template cards, using Key A below. Write the number and sequence on each card.

Key A: DNA fragments

Example: CARD **1.** TACAAAAACAGCGTACAAGTCATC

2. TACAATGCCACCTCCACGCTCATC
3. TACGATTTTCGGCTAACTATC
4. TACGAGTTTCTGCGGATC
5. TACCGACCTGGGATC
6. TACAAAGTGTGGCCCACGCCGGCAATC
7. TACCGAGCAGCCGCGCAGATC
8. TACGATTTTACGCGTCGCCTTATGATC
9. TACACGTTGATAGCCACCAGAATC
10. TACACCGCTGCCTTACACATC

- Use 4- × 6-in. index cards for tRNA anticodon/word cards, using Key B. Write the anticodon on one side of the card and the word on the other. Display cards on the wall, anticodon side showing.

Key B: tRNA anticodon/word cards:

UAC (START), AAA (my), AAC (teacher), AAG (fixes), GUA (a), CAC (bright), GUC (car), CAA (new), CAG (cool), GUG (Mom), CAU (clean), AAU (DNA), ACG (to), ACC (the), AGA (best), ACU (we), AGC (has), UUA (very), UCC (key), UCG (for), UGG (wants), UUG (be), UUU (like), AUG (day), GGG (rocks), CCG (study), CCA (day), CCU (science), CCC (me), CGA (learning), CGC (juice), CGG (music), CGU (drink), ACU (exercise), CUA (and), CUC (life), AUA (happy), GAU (I), CUG (piano), CUU (every), GCU (future), GAG (goldfish), GCA (Biology), GCC (is), GCG (pretty), AUC-END (period)

Answers to Observations: Data Table 1

DNA–GTG, CTC; mRNA–GGG; AMINO ACID–histidine, proline

Answers to Observations: Data Table 2

1. My teacher has a new car. AAA, AAC, AGC, GUA, CAA, GUC
2. DNA is the key to life. AAU, GCC, ACC, UCC, ACG, CUC
3. I like music and exercise. GAU, UUU, CGG, CUA, ACU
4. Goldfish like piano music. GAG, UUU, CUG, CGG
5. Learning science rocks. CGA, CCU, GGG
6. My mom wants me to study science. AAA, GUG, UGG, CCC, ACG, CCG, GCA
7. Learning biology is pretty cool. CGA, GCA, GCC, GCG, CAG
8. I like to drink juice. GAU, UUU, ACG, CGU, CGC
9. To be happy is the best. ACG, UUG, AUA, GCC, ACC, AGA
10. The future is very bright. ACC, GCU, GCC, UUA, CAC

Answers to Analysis and Conclusions

1. The completed sentence represented the protein made during protein synthesis.
2. words
3. ribosome
4. adenine–thymine; guanine–cytosine; thymine is replaced by uracil in RNA
5. The steps in protein synthesis are transcription and translation.
6. It would change the meaning of the sentence or make it unreadable. This is similar to mutations that happen in our cells.

Going Further

Students may see how mutations (mistakes) occur if any of their sentences were not correct. Have students research genetic disorders that result from mutations.

Unit 1

Case Study 1: Creatures of the Dark

Gather More Information

Encourage students to use the library or the NSTA SciLinks Web site noted at the start of each chapter to learn more about these case study topics and to conduct further research.

Have students use the following keywords to aid their searches:

- adaptation
- cave life
- cave exploration
- Kings Canyon National Park caves
- Sequoia National Park caves
- troglobite

Research the Big Picture

- Have students form groups to discuss what kinds of skills, equipment, and technologies scientists need to research life-forms in caves. Then, have each group make an expedition "packing list" that details these requirements. Remind students to consider issues such as access to the caves, the environmental conditions in caves, and equipment needed for gathering and documenting samples.
- Have students work in pairs to research and prepare a poster on a species of troglobite. Students should gather information about the troglobite's physical characteristics; method of reproduction; and food, water, and energy requirements. Each poster should highlight the troglobite's unique adaptations to the cave environment and compare it with any closely related species that do not live in caves.
- As a class, discuss the significance of discovering new species. List on the board some reasons biologists might want to explore new environments in the search for living things.

SCIENCE JOURNAL

Creatures of the Dark

DEEP BENEATH the jagged mountains and towering trees of Sequoia National Park is a place unlike any other. It is a world of deep, marble caves full of strange creatures that live in total darkness. Recently, the caves gave up an amazing secret—the existence of at least 27 animal species never before seen on Earth.

You might wonder how it's possible to discover any new forms of life on Earth. Haven't we already found everything there is to find? Not at all! There are still places on Earth so hard to reach that they have yet to be thoroughly explored. These places include the ocean floor and the deepest parts of some caves.

Scientists have been exploring the caves in California's Sequoia and Kings Canyon national parks for years. Finding one or two new species of small invertebrates, or animals without backbones, wouldn't have been startling. But finding 27 new species shocked even the most experienced cave-exploring scientists.

The scientists collected several species of millipedes, centipedes, spiders, animals related to scorpions, and insects. Many of them are very strange-looking. One spider is bright orange and glows in the dark. Another is transparent, eyeless, and has extra-long legs. One spiderlike creature has jaws bigger than the rest of its body. What makes these creatures even more amazing is that they are found *only* in these caves—nowhere else. In fact, some are found only in one room of the caves!

Many of the animals are troglobites, or species adapted to spending their entire lives in caves. In fact, they cannot survive outside of this dark, moist environment. Each cave species is likely related to a species that lives on the surface. However, as a result of evolution, the cave dwellers are better adapted to life underground. Their adaptations are what make some of them so strange-looking. For

CAREER CONNECTION Zookeeper

GIVE AN ELEPHANT A BATH. Make dinner for a rhino. Train a panda to stand still while getting a shot. It's all in a day's work for a zookeeper—someone who feeds, cares for, and sometimes trains zoo animals.

A zookeeper's most important job is daily animal care. First on the list is making sure the animals are fed. That might mean anything from chopping vegetables for rabbits to feeding meat to hungry lions. A keeper also cleans the animal enclosures. That may not be the best part of the job, but a zookeeper is glad to do it because it keeps the animals comfortable. Each zookeeper knows a lot about the animals he or she cares for. So if you're at the zoo and have a question about an animal, a zookeeper is a good person to ask.

Another important duty for a zookeeper is helping to keep the animals healthy. The keeper observes the animals constantly. If there is a change in the way an animal looks, acts, or even smells, it could mean an illness. So the keeper tells the zoo veterinarian right away. The keeper might also assist the veterinarian in examining the animal or giving it medicine.

Most people who become zookeepers like animals and are comfortable around them. They usually have a bachelor's degree in biology or animal science. Some have a two-year degree in zookeeping. Getting a job as a zookeeper can be difficult because there are few jobs available and many people who want them. So a good combination of education and experience working with animals is the best way to start.

80

Case Study 2: Baking with Fungus

Gather More Information

Encourage students to use the library or the NSTA SciLinks Web site noted at the start of each chapter to learn more about these case study topics and to conduct further research.

Have students use the following keywords to aid their searches:

- baking
- enzyme
- fungus
- leavening agent
- microorganism
- *Saccharomyces cerevisiae*
- yeast

Research the Big Picture

- Have students work in pairs to research and draw diagrams showing where fungus, yeast, and *Saccharomyces cerevisiae* appear on the evolutionary tree of life.
- Have each student prepare one or two cards about different types of fungi. The cards should provide information about the fungal species' structure, reproduction, and function in the environment.
- Have students work in groups to investigate the chemical reactions involving the use of common leavening agents. Provide stations for students to try separate recipes that use baker's yeast, baking powder, or baking soda to

example, pigment isn't needed in the sunless world of a cave. Many animals are white or have clear bodies. Absence of eyes is also common. After all, if an animal lives where it's always black as night, there's no need for it to see. The sense of touch would be much more important. That's why cave species often have features such as elongated legs. The extra-long legs help the animals feel their way around and catch prey in the dark.

There isn't much food to eat deep in caves, either, so it's no surprise that many of the species also have small bodies that don't require a lot of food. Some of the newly discovered creatures are so tiny that even a small pair of tweezers was too big to pick them up. Scientists brushed the animals onto the tip of a paintbrush to carry them.

The scientists were eager to share their new discoveries with the world. So they preserved samples and shipped them to taxonomists, or scientists who classify living things. The taxonomists will determine exactly what these creatures are and give them names.

In the meantime, exploration of the caves will continue. There are more than 200 caves under the two national parks. Some are several kilometers long. Who knows what creatures hide in the dark, awaiting the light of curious scientists!

Research and Report

You have just learned about unusual cave creatures. Now do some research to find an animal or plant specially adapted to some other type of extreme environment. With a partner, report on that environment. Also report on the adaptations that allow the plant or animal to survive there. Share what you find with the rest of the class.

Baking with **Fungus**

EVEN IF you're more interested in eating bread than in baking it, you probably know that yeast makes bread rise. What you may *not* know is that yeast isn't a chemical. It's a microorganism—a one-celled organism so tiny that billions can fit in a small packet.

There are about 160 species of yeast, a type of fungus. But *Saccharomyces cerevisiae* (baker's yeast) is the one used to make bread and pizza dough. Mixed in with the dough, the yeast can produce enzymes that break down flour into sugars. Some of these sugars serve as a food supply for the yeast. As the hungry yeast feed on the sugar, two things are produced: ethanol, an alcohol that evaporates during baking, and carbon dioxide gas. The carbon dioxide gas forms little bubbles in the dough. This makes the dough rise. You see these bubbles as the little holes in baked bread or pizza crust.

Today, chemicals such as baking powder and baking soda do the same thing live yeast do. They produce bubbles of carbon dioxide gas that cause baked goods to rise. Baking powder is a mixture of baking soda and a dry acid. When added to a moist batter, the acid and baking soda react to produce carbon dioxide gas. Baking soda, or sodium bicarbonate, does not contain a dry acid. So the batter needs an acidic ingredient such as lemon juice, sour cream, buttermilk, or molasses to produce carbon dioxide gas. Baking powder and baking soda have one big advantage over yeast: they work almost instantly. Yeast takes several hours.

Even though there are other leavening agents, or substances that make dough rise, yeast remains an important one. So the next time you taste a piece of freshly baked bread, you can thank the baker . . . and the fungi that helped him or her make it!

CONNECTION: Career

Before students read the Career Connection feature, have them complete the Career Research project. As students read the feature, ask them to take notes on anything they learn about the career or how to prepare for the career.

Have students imagine they are the zookeeper at a small zoo, and ask them to write out a sample daily schedule for themselves. Encourage them to be creative in imagining the animals at their zoo, but remind them to base the schedule on a zookeeper's actual tasks.

As a class, brainstorm how students might begin preparing for a career as a zookeeper, even before getting an advanced degree. Suggestions might include taking science classes and volunteering at local zoos, animal shelters, veterinarians' offices, farms, or wildlife sanctuaries.

make breads. Examples include yeast rolls, baking powder biscuits, and soda bread. Have groups write separate lab reports for each baking activity, describing materials, procedures, and results.

- As a wrap-up, compare and contrast the effects of the three different leavening agents in the baking process.

Unit 2

Introduce Unit 2

Have students look at the photos on this page. Ask: *What do you think you will learn about in this unit?* Help students understand that there is tremendous diversity in living things on Earth and that living things change over time. Ask students to write in their Science Notebooks what they discover about how classification and evolution are related as they read the unit.

Unit Projects

For each project below, students can use the Student Presentation Builder on the Student CD-ROM to display their results and their Science Notebooks for their project notes.

Career Have students research careers related to the diversity and/or classification of living things (e.g., botanical garden curator, paleontologist, scientific illustrator, taxonomist). Have students work in pairs to choose a career, describe its requirements, and identify the skills or experience needed for that job. Then, have student pairs stage mock interviews, taking turns playing the roles of job interviewee and interviewer.

Apply Have student groups select a living thing and write a few sentences describing the living thing's specialized qualities, or adaptations, and why they think these adaptations are important to their chosen organisms. Then, ask each group to choose several criteria for classifying their living things, such as color, size, texture, behavior, diet, or appearance. Ask: *According to your criteria, what is your living thing related to?* Have groups share their results.

Technology Brainstorm with students some technologies that evolutionary biologists and taxonomists might use, such as radioactive dating, electron microscopes, computer modeling, and X rays. Then, ask students to develop questions about change in species or classification that could be investigated with modern technology. Have each student describe the technology he or she would use and how to use it.

Unit 2

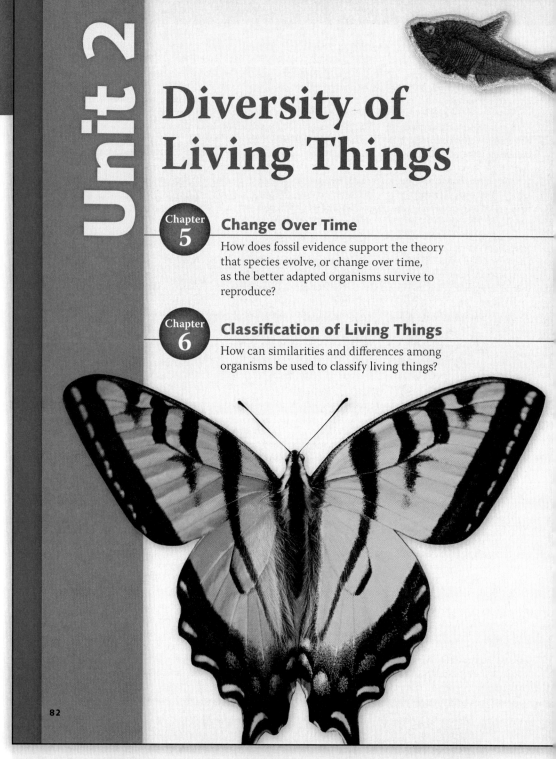

Diversity of Living Things

Software Summary

Student CD-ROM
—Interactive Student Book
—Vocabulary Review
—Key Concept Review
—Lab Report Template
—ELL Preview and Writing Activities
—Presentation Digital Library
—Graphic Organizing Software
—Spanish Cognate Dictionary

Interactive Labs
Chapter 5C—The Genetics of Natural Selection
Chapter 6B—Using a Dichotomous Key to Identify Vertebrates
Chapter 6C—Using a Classification Key to Identify Chemical Substances

Change Over Time

KEY CONCEPT A collection of assorted evidence shows that organisms evolve—or change over time.

Don't expect to see this ferocious cat anytime soon. The cat is a saber-toothed tiger, and it has not lived on Earth for at least 11,000 years. Yet scientists know a great deal about it: what it looked like, where it lived, what it ate, and why it disappeared.

How can modern scientists learn about organisms that lived so long ago? In this chapter, you will learn about the different types of evidence scientists used to piece together an ancient puzzle.

Think About Solving Mysteries

Do you like solving puzzles? Learning about a past event from bits of information is a lot like solving a puzzle.

- Think of an interesting event that might happen at home or in school. For example, your dog runs into the house from a muddy garden. He slides across the floor, jumps on the sofa, and heads out the back door.
- Imagine that you come in after the event has occurred. In your Science Notebook, write down the clues you see. Trade with a partner, and try to figure out what happened from the clues he or she provided.

www.scilinks.org
Evolution and Adaption
Code: WGB05

Chapter 5 Planning Guide			
Instructional Periods	**National Standards**	**Lab Manual**	**Workbook**
5.1 1 period	C.3; C.5; F.2, C.2, C.4, C.6	**Lab 5A—p. 25** Happy Hunting **Lab 5B—p. 26** Measuring Variations in a Population **Lab 5C—p. 29** The Genetics of Natural Selection	Key Concept Review p. 29 Vocabulary Review p. 30 Graphic Organizer p. 31 Reading Comprehension p. 32 Curriculum Connection p. 33 Science Challenge p. 34
5.2 1 period	E.2, A.1, B.2, D.1,D.2, E.2; UCP.3, UCP.1		
5.3 1 period	C.2, G.2, A.2, C.3, G.2; UCP.4		
5.4 1 period	G.1; C.3, G.1; UCP.4		
5.5 1 period	C.4, G.1; C.3, G.1; UCP.2, UCP.4		

Middle School Standard; High School Standard; Unifying Concept and Principle

Chapter 5 Lessons

5.1 Adaptations and Variations

5.2 Evidence from the Past

5.3 Modern Evidence of Evolution

5.4 Humans and Evolution

5.5 Natural Selection

Introduce Chapter 5

As a starting activity, use LAB 5A Happy Hunting on page 25 of the Laboratory Manual.

ENGAGE Direct students to look at the picture of the saber-toothed cat. Ask students to identify traits of the saber-toothed cat that are similar to those of animals that are alive today. List the traits on the board. Ask students to think about why some traits are more advantageous than others.

Think About Solving Mysteries

ENGAGE Tell students to be creative and descriptive. If partners cannot guess the event, you may have students go back to add more clues. In addition, you might use the situation to discuss how scientists have to make educated guesses from the limited clues that exist.

5.1 Introduce

ENGAGE Have students work in groups of four. Assign each group a habitat, such as the branches and leaves of rain-forest trees; the edge of a muddy, reedy pond; the parched surface of a desert; and the sandy shore of a lake. Tell students to list some characteristics of their assigned habitat. Then, have them think about the characteristics of a frog that might inhabit that area. Remind them to consider the frog's needs and what features might best help it survive. Tell students to list these characteristics also.

Have a volunteer from each group record the habitat and frog characteristics on the board. When all frogs have been identified, discuss the differences among them and how those differences relate to the habitats and help the frogs survive.

Before You Read

Have students brainstorm lists of their personal traits and then choose one to elaborate on in their Science Notebooks. Encourage students to think about a variety of traits—those that help them do well both in and out of school.

Vocabulary terms are listed on the first student page of each lesson. You may wish to preview the terms before introducing the lesson. Strategies for teaching the vocabulary appear on the pages where the terms are introduced.

Teach

EXPLAIN that in this lesson, students will learn to identify the various types of adaptations that organisms have and to explain how those adaptations help organisms survive and reproduce themselves in their environment. They will also be able to describe the reasons for variation among the members of a species.

Learning Goals

- Explain how adaptations help organisms survive.
- Identify the various types of adaptations organisms display.
- Describe the reasons for variation among the members of a species.

New Vocabulary

adaptation
predator
prey
variation
genetic diversity
mutation

5.1 Adaptations and Variations

Before You Read

All people have traits that enable them to perform some tasks better than others. Some people can remember things easily, which helps them keep track of new information. Others can tell the difference between sounds, which helps them write or play music. In your Science Notebook, write how one of your traits helps you do something well.

It's a hot afternoon on the Serengeti. A hungry pride of female lions is eyeing a group of zebras. As the zebras move, their stripes blend together. It is difficult for the lions to pick out a single zebra. They can't tell how many there are or exactly how far away they are. Unless one zebra strays from the crowd, the lions will go hungry—for now.

Stripes on a zebra are an example of an adaptation. An **adaptation** is any trait that helps an organism survive and reproduce itself in its environment. The mixture of stripes created when many zebras stand together makes it difficult for predators, such as lions, to attack. This helps each zebra survive.

Explain It!

The South African burrowing bullfrog inflates its body like a balloon when it senses danger. Explain what an adaptation is. Tell how this is an adaptation that helps the frog survive.

Figure 5.1 These zebras cannot outrun or outfight the lions that hunt them, but they are not without protection. Their patterns of stripes confuse the lions. Because this helps the zebras survive, the stripes are considered an adaptation.

Explain It!

ANSWER An adaptation is a trait that helps an organism survive and reproduce itself in its environment. The frog makes itself look larger than it is. This might prevent predators from attacking.

Background Information

An adaptation is a change that helps an organism survive and reproduce itself. Fitness is measured by the representation of an individual's alleles in the next generation. If the organism survives but does not reproduce, it has 0 fitness.

Prey Adaptations

Like a zebra's stripes, some adaptations protect an organism from predators. A **predator** (PRE duh tor) is an organism that kills and eats another organism for food. The organism that is eaten is known as the **prey** (PRAY).

Some adaptations help organisms hide from predators. Others, such as strong odors, cause predators to keep away. Still other adaptations, such as an antelope's fast speed, help prey escape from predators. **Figure 5.2** shows several more methods of defense against predators.

As You Read

In your Science Notebook, make a T-chart. On the left side, list several adaptations of living things. On the right, describe how each adaptation allows the organism to survive in its environment.

What is an adaptation?

Figure It Out

1. Why might a predator avoid eating a brightly colored grasshopper?
2. A harmless syrphid fly looks like a yellow jacket wasp. What is the name of this defense mechanism?

Mimicry Is this a highly poisonous coral snake? No, it's actually a harmless king snake. Mimicry is the ability to look like a different, often more dangerous, organism. Both king snakes and coral snakes have the same coloring in a slightly different arrangement. If this snake is lucky, predators will not try to find out which one it is.

Camouflage Do you see an insect? How about a stick? The color and slow movement of this stick insect make it look like one of the twigs on this tree. Camouflage is the ability to blend into the surroundings.

Protective Covering Come too close to this porcupine and you're in for a sharp surprise. The pointy quills that cover its body protect the animal from predators. Some plants have sharp needles for the same reason.

Warning Colors This poison arrow frog does not blend into its environment. In fact, its bright colors invite predators to see the frog. Like this frog, many brightly colored organisms are poisonous. The colors warn predators not to eat them.

Figure 5.2 Prey have many adaptations to protect themselves from predators. These photographs show several examples.

ELL Strategy

Use Visual Information Provide students with photographs of animals that use camouflage, mimicry, warning colors, and protective covering as adaptations to protect themselves from predators. Have groups of students sort the photographs into categories and identify the adaptation each category represents. Have groups share their categorizations with the class. Label four columns on the board with the names of the four adaptations. As students share their categories, record them on the board. If groups disagree, have students discuss their reasons for choosing the category.

Teach

EXPLAIN Discuss the adaptations mentioned on this page and on page 84. Have students categorize the adaptations by method: speed, smell, shape/appearance, color, poison, sharp protrusions, etc. For each method, have students identify examples. Challenge students to add to the list by finding examples of methods, such as shells (snails) and size of body parts (small ears in the Arctic fox vs. large ears in the desert fox). Suggest that students create a bulletin board titled *Adaptations* to display the information.

As You Read

Model the T-chart on the board for students. Label the left column *Adaptation* and the right column *Advantage.*

ANSWER An adaptation is a trait that gives an organism an advantage that helps it survive and reproduce in its environment.

Science Notebook EXTRA

Encourage students to use the vocabulary section they created in their Science Notebooks. Remind them to record prefixes, suffixes, and root words to help them remember the meanings of vocabulary terms.

Vocabulary

adaptation Have students identify the verb in *adaptation* (*adapt*). Explain that *adapt* means "to change or adjust something to meet different conditions." Have them use this meaning to define *adaptation*. Explain that adaptations increase a living thing's chances of survival and reproduction.

predator Explain that *predator* comes from the Latin word *praedari*, which means "to plunder." A predator plunders, or steals, and eats its prey.

prey Tell students that the word *prey* can be used as both a noun and a verb. When *prey* is used as a noun, it is defined as the organism that is eaten by a predator. However, when used as a verb, *prey* describes what a predator does to its victim.

Figure It Out: **Figure 5.2**

ANSWER **1.** It might be poisonous. **2.** mimicry

Teach

EXPLAIN Tell students that humans have traits that help them hunt, catch, and eat prey. Humans also have other traits that help them survive in their environments. Ask students to describe these human traits. Encourage students to think about our opposable thumbs, which help humans handle tools and weapons, and our sharp teeth, which allow us to chew meat. Students should also identify the hair on our bodies and heads, which keeps us warm.

Science Notebook EXTRA

Have students answer the following questions in their Science Notebooks and then discuss their answers with a partner.

1. In a very mountainous area, which goats would be more successful at surviving, the ones that could climb easily or the ones that could not? Explain your answer. (Answer: The ones that could climb easily would be more successful at obtaining food and escaping predators.)
2. What would happen to the unsuccessful goats in the short term and in the long term? (Answer: They would probably starve. They would be less likely to reproduce. If they did reproduce, their offspring would probably be unable to climb easily, and they would starve. In the long term, the goats that could not climb easily would die out.)

Figure 5.3 Predators have adaptations that help them catch prey. The python *(top)* uses heat and smell to find its prey. The owl *(bottom)* can see and hear its prey well.

Did You Know?

Polar bear fur looks white, but it really isn't. Each hair is a clear, hollow tube. It only looks white because it reflects much of the visible light that strikes it. In fact, the skin underneath a polar bear's hair is black.

Predator Adaptations

Like prey, predators have adaptations that help them survive. These include any traits that help them see and catch their prey. Female lions are very fast. This helps them catch their prey. Once they do, they have large, sharp teeth to hold and kill the prey.

Some other predators, such as owls, have excellent vision. This helps them spot a tiny mouse among the leaves on the forest floor. Most species of owls have outstanding night vision as well. In addition, their feathers direct sound toward their highly sensitive ears. This helps them find prey that might otherwise stay hidden.

Other animals, such as Burmese pythons, have heat sensors in their top lips. Along with a keen sense of smell, the sensors help them find prey. They also have jaws with a loose hinge. Once a snake has captured its prey, this loose hinge makes it possible for the snake to open its mouth wide enough to fit the prey inside.

Environmental Adaptations

Many adaptations help organisms survive in their environment. A polar bear, for example, has thick fur and a layer of fat to keep it warm in its cold surroundings. The only heat that a polar bear gives off comes from its breath. Another adaptation of the polar bear is its large feet. They help the bear paddle through water, and they spread out the bear's weight so that it can walk safely on ice.

The Saguaro cactus lives in the very dry environment of the desert. This plant can reach heights of up to 12 meters and can live to be 200 years old. The cactus has a thick, waxy stem with ribs that can expand to store water. The roots of the cactus do not grow deep into the soil. This makes it possible for the cactus to take in as much water as it can when it rains. The plant then saves some water for periods when there is no rain.

Figure 5.4 Organisms survive in the environments to which they are best adapted. A polar bear *(left)* would not survive in a hot climate because it is adapted to cold conditions. The Saguaro cactus *(right)* is adapted to a dry environment.

Background Information

Polar bears live in cold, icy climates. A polar bear's fur serves to insulate and keep it warm. The fur also helps camouflage the bear against the white snow. Polar bears have a keen sense of smell to help them find food. They can climb, swim, and run fast for short distances. All of these traits help the polar bear survive in its environment.

Differentiated Instruction

Kinesthetic, Naturalistic Have students play a game of "tag" in which some students are prey and other students are predators. Assign some students advantages, such as speed, and assign other students disadvantages, such as limited vision. After one round, have students change roles. Discuss with students how their advantages and disadvantages affected their ability to catch prey and avoid capture.

Variation

Remember the zebras you read about at the beginning of this lesson? As you may already know, all zebras have stripes. What you may not know is that no two zebras have the same pattern of stripes. A zebra's pattern of stripes is like a human fingerprint.

Any difference among individuals of the same species is known as a **variation** (ve ree AY shun). You can look around your classroom to see some of the variation among humans. Your classmates probably have a variety of heights, hair colors, eye colors, and skin colors.

Sources of Variation

Variation among members of the same species depends on genetics. Recall from Chapter 4 that genes are passed on to the offspring of sexual reproduction in a random way. This means that, with the exception of identical twins, individual offspring have a unique set of genes. Although the overall traits they have may be similar, there will be variation among them. This is known as **genetic diversity**. The word *genetic* refers to genes, and the word *diversity* means "difference" or "variety."

Another way that variation is introduced into a population is through mutation. A **mutation** (myew TAY shun) results when an error occurs during DNA replication, which is the process by which a copy of DNA is made. The error changes some of the proteins that are produced in an organism. If the mutation is in a sex cell, it can be passed on to offspring.

Some mutations are harmful and prevent an organism from surviving. Other mutations have little effect on an organism. Occasionally, a mutation is helpful and allows an organism to better survive in its environment.

Figure 5.6 A white tiger is a Bengal tiger that has a recessive mutation in the gene for color. The several hundred white tigers that exist today can all be traced back to the same tiger caught years ago in India.

Papilio ajax ajax

Papilio ajax ampliata

Papilio ajax curvitascia

Papilio ajax ehrmanni

Figure 5.5 These swallowtail butterflies all belong to the same species. However, they live in different parts of North America and have slight variations.

After You Read

1. Using the information you have recorded in your T-chart, hypothesize about how a wide, flat tail is an adaptation for a beaver, which lives mainly in water.
2. What does it mean to say that variation exists among the puppies in a litter?
3. How might a mutation that produces a white tiger affect the tiger's survival?

Teach

EXPLORE Have students look around the room to identify the visible variations among their classmates. List the different traits on the board. Remind students that in addition to visible traits, they also possess a wide variety of nonvisible traits such as musical, athletic, and academic abilities.

Vocabulary

variation Explain to students that the word *variation* has the same root as the verb *vary* and the noun *variable*. Tell students that when you vary something, you change it. A variable in mathematics is a symbol for a value that changes.

genetic diversity Tell students that in common usage, *diversity* means "the quality of being diverse," such as a group whose members come from different backgrounds. Discuss with students how this common usage relates to the scientific meaning of variation, or differences in the genetic makeups of the individuals of a species.

mutation Explain to students that the word *mutation* comes from the Latin *mutare*, which means "to change." A mutation results when an error occurs during DNA replication and changes some of the proteins produced in an organism. Make sure students understand that mutations can be positive, negative, or neutral.

Assess

EVALUATE Use the After You Read questions and the Alternative Assessment to help you assess students' understanding of this lesson.

After You Read

1. The tail would help the beaver move through the water.
2. It means that the puppies are not identical.
3. A white tiger is not able to camouflage itself as an orange or brown tiger does. It will therefore be less successful at hunting and may not get enough food to survive.

Background Information

The white tiger is not an endangered breed that needs to be preserved or protected. White tigers cannot survive in nature; people inbreed tigers to produce them in captivity. Many tigers are harmed in the process.

Alternative Assessment

EVALUATE Refer struggling readers to the T-charts in their Science Notebooks. Have students add to their lists of adaptations and advantages. Check students' T-charts.

5.2 Introduce

ENGAGE Ask students to indicate whether they have visited a museum of natural history. Invite those who have visited to share what they saw there. Have them focus on exhibits of extinct animals such as saber-toothed cats and woolly mammoths, describing as best they can how these animals are represented.

Ask students if they know what a fossil is and if they can name some fossils they have seen in books or displays. Relate the existence of fossils to exhibits of extinct animals in museums. Point out that in many museum exhibits of entire animals, fossil bones are not used. Instead, replicas of the bones are made and used.

Before You Read

Ask students to share their birthdays with the class. Record students' birthdays on the board. Model a time line on the board. Label the left end with the youngest student's birthday, and label the right end with the oldest student's birthday. Have students duplicate the time line in their Science Notebooks and record the remaining birthdays on their time lines.

Teach

EXPLAIN Tell students that in this lesson, they will learn to describe fossils and understand how they are formed. Students will compare relative dating and radioactive dating and learn to recognize what can be inferred from the fossil record.

Vocabulary

fossil Explain to students that the word *fossil* comes from the Latin *fodere*, which means "to dig." Tell students that fossils are often discovered by archaeologists who dig in the ground to find them.

paleontologist Tell students that the prefix *paleo-* refers to something ancient. Explain that *-ologist* refers to someone who studies. Thus, a paleontologist is someone who studies something ancient.

Learning Goals

- Describe fossils and how they are formed.
- Compare relative dating and radioactive dating.
- Recognize what can be inferred from the fossil record.

New Vocabulary

fossil
paleontologist
relative dating
radioactive dating
fossil record
extinct
geologic time scale

5.2 Evidence from the Past

Before You Read

It is often important to place items in order of age. In your Science Notebook, write the names of the students in your class. Work together to arrange the list in order of age from oldest to youngest. You will need to compare the months and days of all students' birthdays.

Scientists can learn a lot about plants and animals that live today just by looking at them. How can they find out about organisms that lived long ago? One way is to discover and study fossils. A **fossil** (FAH sul) is the preserved remains of an organism that was once living.

A fossil can be part of the organism itself, such as bones, teeth, or shells. It can also be a trace of an organism, such as an imprint of a leaf or a footprint. A fossil can even be something left behind by an organism, such as animal droppings.

After many years, a change in Earth's surface might cause a fossil to get near the surface. A scientist digging for fossils might find it. A scientist who uses fossils to study forms of life that existed in prehistoric times is known as a **paleontologist** (pay lee ahn TAH luh just).

Figure 5.7 Fossils, the preserved remains of once-living organisms, include marine animal shells (top), wasps preserved in amber (center), and shrimp imprints (bottom).

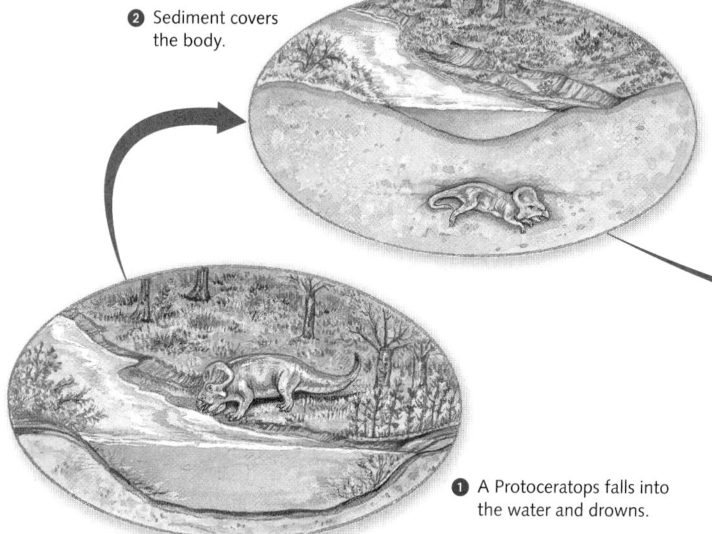

❷ Sediment covers the body.
❶ A Protoceratops falls into the water and drowns.

Figure 5.8 Few organisms become fossils. Sometimes, however, the conditions are just right for a fossil to form.

88 CHANGE OVER TIME

ELL Strategy

Act Out Have students create a human time line of their birthdays in order from youngest to oldest. To make this more challenging, have students wear labels displaying their birthdays and instruct them to remain silent while arranging themselves. For a more difficult activity, students can be instructed to use only their fingers to indicate the numbers of their month, day, and year. This reinforces negotiation and reasoning. Additionally, when the next session proceeds about guessing the age, this activity can be used to elicit student responses about how they tried to determine the age with limited information.

How Fossils Are Formed

When an organism dies, other organisms such as bacteria and fungi feed on it, breaking down its body. Sometimes, however, an organism is buried in mud, clay, or soil soon after it dies. Over many years, layers of sediment build up over the organism. The soft parts of the organism decay, but the harder parts are left behind.

As sediment builds up, the upper layers push down on lower layers. This pressure, along with chemical changes, causes the sediment to harden into rock. The type of rock formed in this way is known as sedimentary rock. The parts of organisms captured in the rock are fossils.

In some cases, the rock particles around an organism retain the shape of the organism even after the soft parts have decayed. This results in an imprint. In other cases, an organism is buried in ash from a volcano or in fine clay before it begins to decay. If this happens, the organism might be perfectly preserved.

Relative Dating

To understand the significance of a fossil and to recognize the conditions in which the organism lived, a scientist needs to know the age of the fossil. If layers of sedimentary rock are not disturbed, the oldest layers are at the bottom. The younger layers are at the top.

Figure 5.9 Sedimentary rocks usually form in horizontal layers. Which layer contains the oldest fossils?

Figure It Out

1. What might cause a fossil to become exposed?
2. What might be the source of the layers of sediment that cover the body?

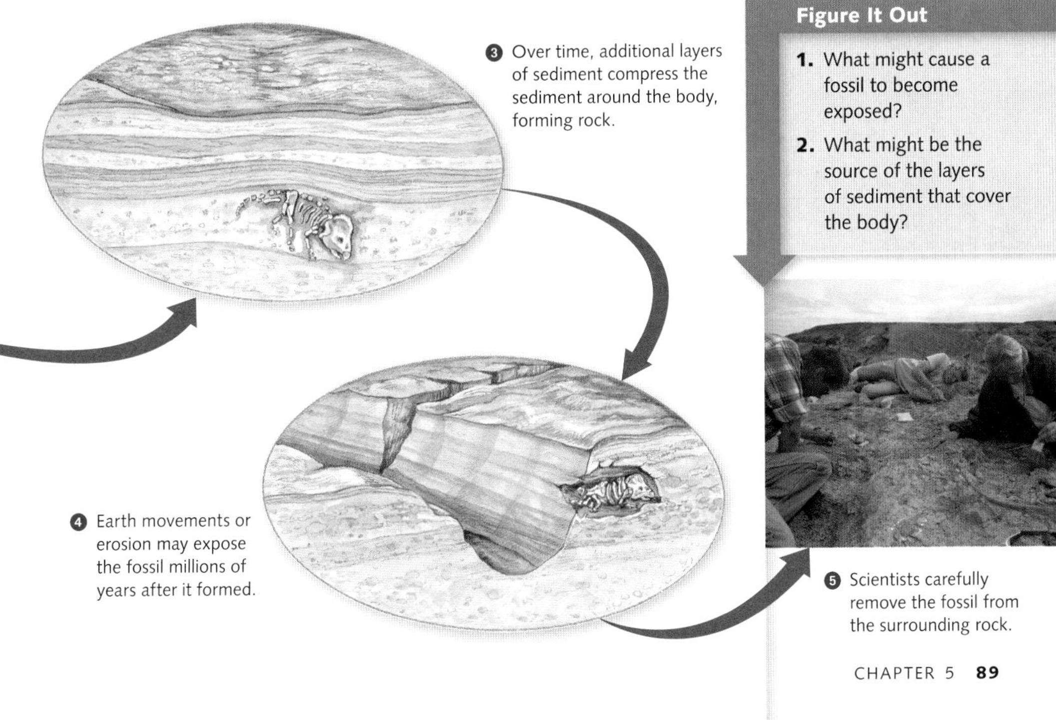

❸ Over time, additional layers of sediment compress the sediment around the body, forming rock.
❹ Earth movements or erosion may expose the fossil millions of years after it formed.
❺ Scientists carefully remove the fossil from the surrounding rock.

Teach

ENGAGE Ask students to describe fossils they have seen. Explain that fossils come in all shapes and sizes. Sometimes, a fossil shows an imprint of a small part of a much larger animal, such as a dinosaur. A fossil might also show an imprint of an entire insect.

EXPLAIN that fossils form in sedimentary rock because of the way in which this type of rock forms. Ask students to identify two other types of rock (igneous and metamorphic). Have them hypothesize why fossils would not be found in these types of rock. (These rocks are formed from extreme heat or from chemical and physical changes in other rock. Fossils would not survive these conditions.) Impress upon students the idea that fossils represent remains "captured" in rock as it forms.

Figure It Out: Figure 5.8

ANSWER **1.** An earthquake or erosion might cause the rock above the fossil to be moved away. **2.** The sediment might have been carried downstream by the water.

Use the Visual: Figure 5.9

ANSWER The lowest layer, or the layer at the bottom, contains the oldest fossils.

Field Study

Bury some objects outside. Organize students into groups, and have them act as paleontologists to carefully uncover the objects that have been buried. Emphasize to students that scientists are very careful not to break or destroy objects when digging. They are also very careful to record where each object was found.

Teach

ENGAGE Ask students whether they could determine the age of each child if a family of four children were standing in front of the class. Point out that while students might be able to estimate each child's age based on his or her height or behavior, they wouldn't be able to determine that child's exact age. Tell students that they could also probably guess the relative ages of the children (who is oldest and who is youngest) based on the children's heights in relation to each other.

EXPLAIN that identifying a characteristic of one object in relation to the same characteristic in another object is also applied to brightness and distance of stars from Earth.

EXTEND Provide students with the fraction of carbon-14 remaining in several objects (1, 1/2, 1/4, 1/8, 1/16). Have students use radioactive dating to estimate the age of each object.

As You Read

Check students' drawings for accuracy.

ANSWER The relative age compares the age of an object with the age of another fossil or rock layer. It does not tell a fossil's specific age.

Vocabulary

relative dating Explain that *relative* means "as compared to." When scientists use relative dating, they compare objects to see which are older and which are younger.

radioactive dating Tell students that the prefix *radio-* comes from the Latin word *radius*, which means "ray" or "beam." When radioactive elements decay, they give off rays of energy. As they do, they turn into different elements. Scientists use the rate of decay to find the age of the rock around a fossil.

fossil record Explain that the fossil record is the total amount of information about past life-forms and environments on Earth that has been inferred from all the fossils that have been found so far.

extinct Explain that the word *extinct* contains the prefix *ex-*, which means "out," and the root *stinguere*, which means "quench." The word *extinct* refers to dying out, or being "quenched," as a species.

geologic time scale Tell students that the geologic time scale shows the order of events in Earth's life as a planet and the amount of time between major events as inferred from the fossil record.

As You Read

In your Science Notebook, draw a sedimentary rock with four layers. Label the layers in order of age.

How is the relative age of a fossil different from its exact age?

Scientists can use the order of the layers of sedimentary rock to estimate the age of any fossils in the rock. Because lower layers of rock are older than upper layers, a fossil in a lower layer must be older than a fossil in an upper layer. This method of dating fossils, called **relative dating**, is used to determine which fossils are older or younger than others without giving an exact age.

Radioactive Dating

Sometimes scientists can find the exact age of a fossil. Organisms are made up of elements. Some elements are unstable. This means that they decay, or break down, into a different form. As they do so, they give off particles and energy called radiation.

An element that decays is called radioactive. Every radioactive element decays at a specific rate. By comparing the original form of the element to the form after decay, scientists can calculate the exact age of a fossil. The method of using radioactive elements to find a fossil's real age is known as **radioactive dating**.

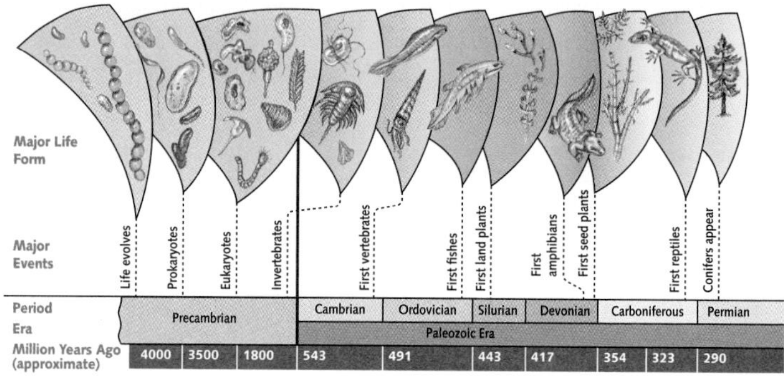

The Fossil Record

As paleontologists study fossils, they organize them into groups. They place similar organisms together and arrange them according to when the organisms lived. All of this information is combined to form the fossil record. The **fossil record** provides a snapshot of life on Earth over time.

The fossil record reveals that life on Earth has changed over time. In addition, certain fossils that appear in older rocks no longer appear in more recent rocks. This shows that some organisms have become **extinct** (ihk STINGT), which means the species died out. In fact, more than 99 percent of all the species that have ever lived on Earth are extinct. New species have also appeared at different points in time.

CONNECTION: Chemistry

An element often used in radioactive dating is carbon-14. This element is present in all living things. Even after an organism dies, carbon-14 continues to decay into nitrogen-14. Carbon-14 has a half-life of 5,730 years. By comparing the amounts of carbon-14 and nitrogen-14 in a fossil, scientists can determine the fossil's age.

CONNECTION: Chemistry

Radioactive dating using carbon-14 was developed by Willard F. Libby in the late 1940s. Radioactive carbon-14 is produced when nitrogen-14 is bombarded by cosmic rays in the atmosphere. The carbon-14 drifts down to Earth and is absorbed from the air by plants. Animals eat the plants or other animals that have eaten the plants and thus take carbon-14 into their bodies.

When an organism dies, it no longer takes in carbon-14. The carbon-14 in the dead organism decays at a slow, steady rate known as its half-life and reverts to nitrogen-14. The half-life of carbon-14 is 5,730 years. After about 50,000 years, the amount of carbon-14 left is too small for the fossil to be reliably dated. That is why carbon-14 dating is useful only for fossils less than 50,000 years old.

Despite the tremendous number of fossils that have been found, the fossil record is far from complete. Only a small fraction of all the species that ever lived are preserved in fossils. One reason is that organisms with soft bodies or thin shells rarely form fossils. Another reason is that rocks containing fossils can be worn away or changed into other types of rocks over time. As rocks are altered, the fossils in them are usually destroyed.

The Geologic Time Scale

Scientists used the fossil record to develop the **geologic time scale**. A version of the scale is shown in **Figure 5.10**. The scale was originally developed by studying fossils and rock layers. Scientists then realized that major changes in the fossils had occurred in specific rock layers. Some of these major changes were mass extinctions. When a mass extinction occurs, many organisms disappear from the fossil record at the same time. These changes were used to divide the time scale into sections. The geologic time scale is divided into four large sections called eras. Each era is further divided into periods, and then into epochs.

Did You Know?

Earth's past is sometimes presented as a clock. On this clock, life first appeared at the 0 hour, 600 million years ago. Of all the organisms that have appeared since that time, only humans appeared in the very last minute!

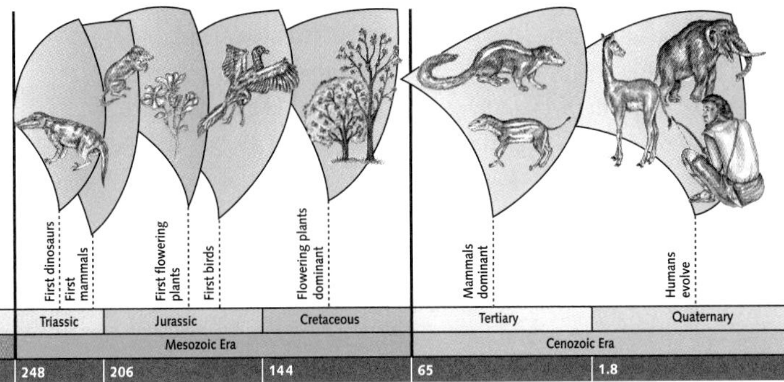

Figure 5.10 The geologic time scale is like a calendar of Earth's past. What evidence did scientists use to develop this scale?

Later on, when scientists were able to use radioactive dating, they identified the ages of specific rock layers. In doing so, they found that the divisions of the geologic time scale were not equal periods of time. The sections of the scale vary in length by millions of years.

After You Read

1. Why are fossils found in sedimentary rocks?
2. How is relative dating different from radioactive dating?
3. Review the sequences of ages you described in your Science Notebook. Consider how these ages are separated. What occurrences are used to separate the divisions of the geologic time scale?

Teach

EXPLAIN to students that Earth is billions of years old. If each year in Earth's life as a planet were a page in a book, the book would be 4,600,000,000 pages long. Tell students that scientists used the fossil record to construct the geologic time scale.

Use the Visual: Figure 5.10

ANSWER Scientists used evidence from rock layers and the fossils within them.

EXTEND Have students create a scale model of a geologic time scale. Students will need a large space outdoors or in a hallway for this activity.

Assess

EVALUATE Use the After You Read questions and the Alternative Assessment to help you assess students' understanding of this lesson.

After You Read

1. Fossils are formed when an organism becomes trapped in sediment soon after it dies. Layers of sediment eventually become sedimentary rock, with the fossil of the organism trapped inside.
2. Relative dating involves inferring whether a fossil is older or younger than another fossil or a rock by comparing it with other fossils or rock layers. This places events in order rather than giving a specific age. Radioactive dating uses amounts of radioactive elements to find the exact age of a fossil.
3. Major changes in the types of plant and animal fossils that were discovered mark divisions in the scale.

Differentiated Instruction

Visual, Logical, and Mathematical

Students often have a difficult time understanding the meaning and size of "a billion." To convey the relative size, tell students that a sheet of paper is about 0.025 mm thick. Ask: *How tall would a pile of one billion pieces of paper be?* (25 km) Have students work in groups to calculate the answers.

Alternative Assessment

EVALUATE If students have difficulty answering the After You Read questions, have them draw a sedimentary rock and label it according to the relative ages of the layers.

5.3 Introduce

ENGAGE Explain to students that many kinds of evidence support the theory that living things have evolved over time. Tell them that humans today are different from early humans. Ask: *Have you ever seen a picture of an early human, such as a Neandertal or Cro-Magnon? What did it look like?*

Record students' responses on the board. Create a Venn diagram comparing and contrasting the traits of early humans and the traits of humans today. Point out that many of the ways in which humans have changed have helped them better survive.

Before You Read

Have students make predictions about what each section will be about, based on the section heading. Students should record headings and predictions in their Science Notebooks.

Teach

EXPLAIN that in this lesson, students will learn to relate body structures to evolutionary change. They will also learn to identify evolutionary relationships and to analyze the ways in which genetic material can serve as evidence of evolution.

Figure It Out: Figure 5.11

ANSWER 1. The skull has become larger. 2. The size of the skull might indicate the size of the brain. The larger the skull is, the larger the brain is.

Learning Goals

- Relate body structures to evolutionary change.
- Compare embryos to identify evolutionary relationships.
- Analyze how genetic material can serve as evidence of evolution.

New Vocabulary

evolution
homologous structure
analogous structure
vestigial structure
embryo

5.3 Modern Evidence of Evolution

Before You Read

Preview the lesson. Read the headings and Learning Goals, and look at the pictures. Think about what you expect the lesson to be about. Write the headings in your Science Notebook.

The fossil record shows that organisms and environments have changed over time. The change in living things over time is **evolution** (eh vuh LEW shun). As an example, consider the modern camel. The camels that inhabit today's deserts look very different from the camels of long ago. **Figure 5.11** shows how scientists think camels have changed over millions of years.

Body Structure

The fossil record is not the only evidence that supports evolution. Scientists also consider the structures of the bodies of living things. For example, most animals with backbones have two pairs of limbs. Each kind of limb, such as forelimbs, has a different function. A whale uses its forelimbs to swim through the water. A crocodile uses them to swim and also to move on land. A bird uses its forelimbs to fly. Despite the different functions, the basic arrangement of bones is similar in each of these animals' forelimbs.

Figure It Out

1. How has the skull of a camel changed over time?
2. How might the size of the skull be related to the size of the camel's brain?

Camel Evolution

Age	Paleocene (65 million years ago)	Eocene (54 million years ago)	Oligocene (33 million years ago)	Miocene (23 million years ago)	Present
Organism					
Skull, teeth, and limb bones					

Figure 5.11 Scientists use fossils to try to determine how camels evolved.

Background Information

The theory that living things had evolved did not begin with Charles Darwin. In fact, Darwin's grandfather, Erasmus Darwin, was among the first to suggest that living things had evolved in writings that date back to 1794. In 1809, French scientist Chevalier de Lamarck suggested that all forms of life could be arranged into one huge "family tree" based on the evidence of homologous structures. Despite his insight, Lamarck proved to be quite incorrect about how the process occurs. He believed that organisms change because they have a wish or a need to and that organisms could change their body structure by using parts in a different way. Using similar reasoning, Lamarck believed that a body part would grow smaller or disappear from lack of use. The scientific community had to wait until Charles Darwin presented his theory of evolution in the late 1850s to correctly understand the nature of evolution.

Homologous Structures The bones in the forelimbs of three vertebrates (animals with backbones) are shown in **Figure 5.12**. Many scientists suggest that it would be unlikely for different species to have such similar structures if each species arose separately. Instead, scientists conclude that these organisms evolved from a common ancestor. Structures that have the same evolutionary origin are called **homologous** (huh MAH luh gus) **structures**. These structures can have the same arrangement or function, or both.

As You Read

In your Science Notebook, paraphrase the information under each heading.

What are homologous structures?

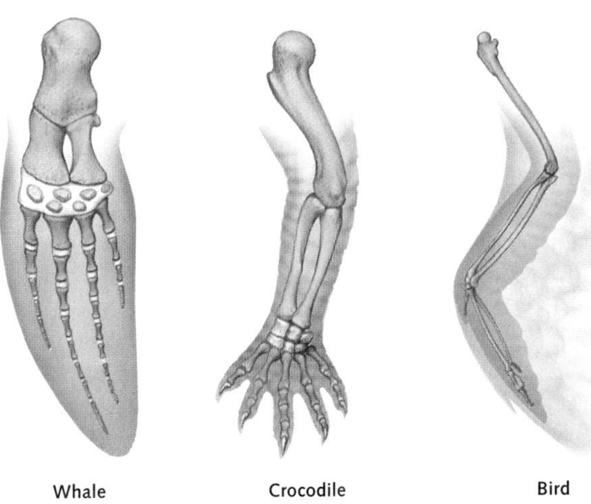

Figure 5.12 The forelimbs of a whale, crocodile, and bird are homologous structures. The similar bones are used to perform different functions. What are the functions?

Analogous Structures Just because two organisms have a similar body feature does not necessarily mean they are related. Birds and butterflies, for example, both have wings. Both organisms use their wings to fly. However, the structure of a bird wing is quite different from that of a butterfly wing. These two types of wings evolved in different ancestors. Body parts that have similar functions but do not have a common evolutionary ancestor are called **analogous** (uh NAL uh gus) **structures**.

Vestigial Structures Another type of body structure that provides evidence for evolution is a vestigial structure. An organism has a **vestigial** (veh STIH jee ul) **structure** if it has a body part that no longer serves its original purpose. The structure was probably useful to an ancestor.

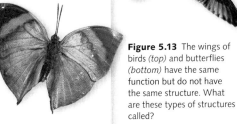

Figure 5.13 The wings of birds *(top)* and butterflies *(bottom)* have the same function but do not have the same structure. What are these types of structures called?

ELL Strategy

Compare and Contrast, Use a Venn Diagram, Use Visual Information Provide students with photographs of different animals, some of which have homologous structures and some of which have analogous structures. Have students compare and contrast the structures of the animals and use Venn diagrams to record their observations.

Teach

EXPLAIN to students that scientists compare the structures of organisms to find relationships. While humans and chimpanzees have similar body structures, humans and dogs are much less similar. Scientists use these observations to learn how humans and other animals have evolved.

As You Read

ANSWER Homologous structures are structures that have the same evolutionary origin.

Vocabulary

evolution Explain that the word *evolution* comes from the Latin *ēvolvere*, which means "to roll out" or "to unfold." Tell students that evolution is change that "unfolds" over time.

homologous structure Remind students that the word *homologous* comes from the Greek word *homologos*, which means "agreeing." Point out that homologous structures have the same arrangement, functions, or both. The structures "agree."

analogous structure Explain to students that the word *analogous* comes from the Greek word *analogos*, which means "proportionate." Analogous structures are related in function but not in ancestry. They are similar but not equal.

vestigial structure Tell students that the word *vestigial* comes from the Latin word *vestigium*, which means "footprint." A vestigial structure is something left behind from an earlier time, much like a footprint is left behind. It marks something that was once useful but no longer is.

Use the Visual: Figure 5.12

ANSWER The whale swims, the crocodile walks, and the bird flies.

Use the Visual: Figure 5.13

ANSWER These are called analogous structures.

Teach

EXPLAIN Ask students if any of them have had their wisdom teeth removed. Tell students that wisdom teeth are vestigial structures, which means they are parts of our body that no longer serve their original purpose.

EXTEND Have students research examples of vestigial structures in humans, such as the appendix, the coccyx, external ear muscles, and goose bumps as a response to stress instead of cold.

Vocabulary

embryo Explain to students that the word *embryo* can be used figuratively to refer to something in its early stages. For example, one might say that when a painter is just beginning a work of art, the artwork is in its embryonic stage.

Use the Visual: Figure 5.15

ANSWER They all have tails and pharyngeal pouches.

Assess

EVALUATE Use the After You Read questions and the Alternative Assessment to help you assess students' understanding of this lesson.

After You Read

1. Evolution means that living things change over time, and the fossil record indicates this.
2. Students should include fossils, body structure, embryos, and genetic information in their paragraphs.
3. They probably share a common ancestor.

Alternative Assessment

EVALUATE If students are having difficulty with the After You Read questions, provide them with the list of section headings from this lesson. Have students write a summary under each heading. Allow students to refer to their Science Notebooks for help.

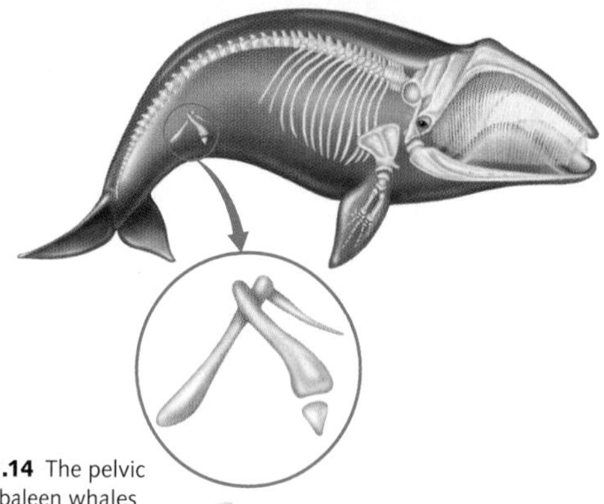

Figure 5.14 The pelvic bones of baleen whales are vestigal structures. The bones suggest that the whales arose from organisms that walked on land.

Human wisdom teeth, or third molars, are an example of a vestigial structure. At one time, humans had larger jaws with more teeth. They ate more plants and needed the teeth to grind the thick cellulose of plant tissues. As the human diet changed and included fewer plants, the size of the jaw decreased. Wisdom teeth still grow in, but they are often removed at some point because they are not needed.

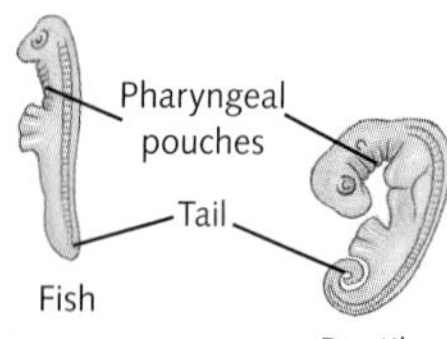

Pharyngeal pouches
Tail
Bird
Mammal

Figure 5.15 The embryos of these organisms reveal an evolutionary relationship. What structures do they have in common?

Embryos

You would probably agree that an adult eagle looks very different from a rhinoceros. As embryos, however, they look very much alike. An **embryo** (EM bree oh) is the earliest stage of growth and development for plants and animals. If two embryos had the same features, scientists would conclude that they evolved from a common ancestor.

Figure 5.15 compares four embryos. The first is for a fish, such as a tuna. The second is for a reptile, such as a crocodile. The third is for a bird, such as an eagle. The last is for a mammal, such as a rhinoceros. If you look at the bottom of each embryo, you will see that it has a tail. Toward the top, each embryo has structures called pharyngeal (fuh RIN jee ul) pouches. In the fish, the pouches are related to gills. In the other organisms, they become parts of the ears, jaws, and throat.

Genetic Material

Scientists can compare the DNA of organisms to find out how they are related. Recall from Chapter 4 that DNA carries information that determines the traits of an organism. The code of bases on a DNA molecule is used to determine the order of amino acids in the proteins of an organism. The more similar the sequence of amino acids is between two organisms, the more closely the organisms are related.

After You Read

1. What does it mean to say that the fossil record suggests that evolution occurs among living things?
2. According to the notes you wrote in your Science Notebook, what are four types of evidence used to support the theory of evolution? Write a well-developed paragraph to answer this question.
3. What might a scientist conclude about the evolutionary relationship between two organisms with very similar DNA?

94 CHANGE OVER TIME

Differentiated Instruction

Visual Provide students with pictures of different animals with vestigial structures. Highlight each structure. Have students make predictions about what each structure might have been used for and why it is no longer needed.

5.4 Humans and Evolution

Learning Goals

- Identify the traits of primates.
- Recognize the importance of hominid fossils.
- Compare Neandertals and Cro-Magnons.

New Vocabulary

primate
opposable thumb
hominoid
hominid
anthropologist

Before You Read

Scientists often use time lines to place events in the sequence in which they occurred. In your Science Notebook, draw a time line as a horizontal line. Preview the lesson to look for important dates that are mentioned. Write any years you find in the correct order on your time line.

Monkeys, chimpanzees, and gorillas all have something in common. They are mammals known as **primates**. A primate can be as small as a mouse lemur with a mass of just 30 grams. It can be as large as the Eastern lowland gorilla, which has a mass of up to 250 kilograms. There are 235 different kinds of primates.

Primates

Despite how different they look, all primates share certain traits. For one thing, primates have rounded heads with faces that are generally flat. Compared with other mammals that live on land, primates have larger, more complex brains.

Most primates live in trees. Several adaptations help them survive there. These adaptations include shoulder and hip joints that have a wide range of motion. Primate hands and feet have fingers and toes with nails instead of claws. Most important, primates have a hand with an **opposable thumb**, which is a thumb that can bend across the palm of the hand. Together, these traits allow primates to grab and hold onto objects such as fruits and tree branches.

Have you ever looked through binoculars? These devices have two eyepieces to look through. Primates have binocular vision. Binocular vision enables primates to see an object through two eyes at the same time. Using two eyes at the same time, primates can figure out how far away objects are. In addition, primates are able to see in color.

Figure 5.16 These animals, the ring-tailed lemur *(left)* and the mountain gorilla *(right)*, are primates. There are several traits that describe a primate. What are some of these traits?

Differentiated Instruction

Kinesthetic Tape students' thumbs across their hands. Ask them to perform a number of tasks, such as writing their names, tying their shoes, and buttoning their shirts. Discuss with students the difficulties they had with these tasks and how important their thumbs are to their everyday activities.

5.4 Introduce

ENGAGE Explain to students that an important trait that humans share with primates, such as gorillas and monkeys, is an opposable thumb. Ask: *How is your thumb useful to you? What would it be like if you didn't have a thumb?*

Record student responses on the board. Discuss with students the things that humans and apes can do that animals without thumbs, such as dogs and cats, cannot do.

Before You Read

As students are creating their time lines, remind them to think about the size of their intervals. Encourage students to try to scale their time lines to accurately represent the amount of time between events.

Teach

EXPLAIN to students that in this lesson, they will learn to identify the traits of primates. They will also learn to recognize the importance of hominid fossils and to compare Neandertals and Cro-Magnons.

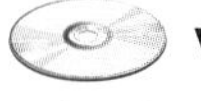

Vocabulary

primate Explain to students that the word *primate* shares a root with the word *primary* and that both come from the Latin word *primus*, which means "first." Primates are thought of as the highest order of mammals. Humans are primates.

opposable thumb Tell students that the word *opposable* comes from the Latin word *opponere*, which means "to place against." An opposable thumb can be "placed against," or bent across, the palm of the hand.

Use the Visual: Figure 5.16

ANSWER Primates have an opposable thumb, hands and feet that have fingers and toes with nails instead of claws, and binocular vision.

Teach

EXPLAIN Tell students that scientists think humans developed from early primates. Other primates share a number of homologous structures with humans. Ask students to think about primates such as monkeys and gorillas. Discuss with students the structures that these primates share with humans. Record student answers on the board.

Figure It Out: Figure 5.17

ANSWER **1.** hominoids or anthropoids **2.** Old World monkeys and New World monkeys

Vocabulary

hominoid Explain to students that the base *homo* means "human being" and that the suffix *-oid* means "like that of." A hominoid is an animal "like a human being."

hominid Tell students that, like *hominoid,* the word *hominid* uses the base *homo.* The suffix *-id* means "structure." Hominids are the evolutionary line that led to the "structure of human beings" today.

Extend It!

It is important for students to realize that scientists sometimes fabricate evidence to further their own agenda. Provide students with books and Web resources such as the Public Broadcasting Service/Nova site at **www.pbs.org/wgbh/nova**.

Have groups of students discuss the reasons why a scientist might choose to mislead people this way.

Extend It!

Like many other things in life, science can be affected by dishonest people. In 1912, Charles Dawson announced the discovery of a skull that "proved" that humans evolved from apes. In 1953, however, the skull was found to be a fake. Research this event, which came to be known as the Piltdown hoax. Find out what happened and how it affected people's views of evolution and science. If possible, find out who is believed to have been responsible for the hoax.

Evolution of Primates

Although scientists do not know for certain how humans developed from early primates, several theories exist. One leading theory suggests that ancient primates split into different evolutionary lines. One line evolved into modern lemurs, aye-ayes, and similar animals. Another line evolved into monkeys and hominoids. Apes and humans are known as **hominoids**. The evolutionary line that led to humans is known as the **hominid** line.

In 1924, a South African named Raymond Dart discovered the skull of an early hominoid child. It was dated to be between 2.5 million and 2.8 million years old. The shapes of the face and the region around the brain were similar to the shapes of those parts on an ape. However, the structure of the brain suggested that it belonged to an organism that walked upright.

Dart concluded that it must be a species of primate that had not been discovered before. He named it *Australopithecus africanus*, which means "southern ape from Africa." When the name of a species is written, the first word is often shown as a single letter (*A. africanus*). Specimens such as these are described as australopithecines. They are hominids that have some features of apes and some of humans.

Figure It Out

1. What are two ways to describe the groups into which gibbons are placed?
2. Which two groups of organisms are anthropoids but not hominoids?

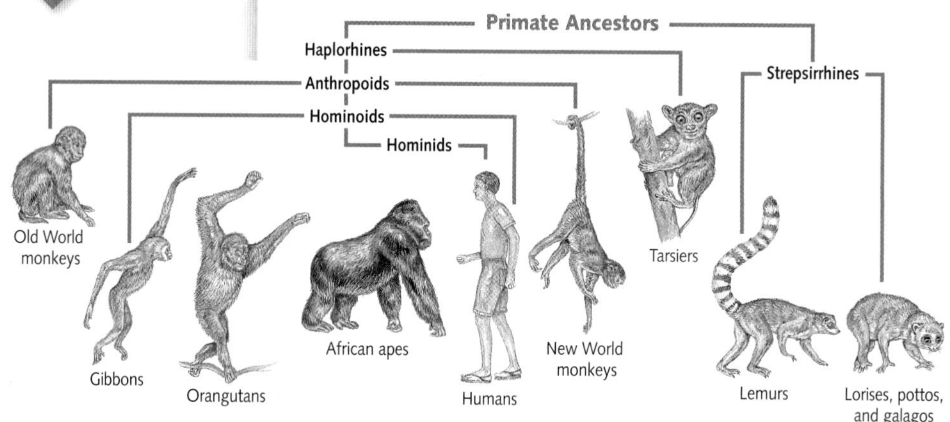

Figure 5.17 This diagram shows how ancient primates split into different groups. Follow the lines to see the organisms that evolved.

Background Information

The skull Charles Dawson used in his attempt to prove that humans evolved from apes turned out to be the jaw of a modern ape and a human skull carbon-dated to A.D. 1230. An unknown person buried an orangutan jaw with a medieval skull, which had been stained to make it look old. The scientific community was fooled by this discovery for many years.

Lucy

After Dart's discovery, many similar sets of fossils were found. An American named Donald Johanson discovered one of the most complete skeletons in 1974. The skeleton, which he called "Lucy," was determined to be about 3.2 million years old. Johanson concluded that Lucy was a new species, which he named *Australopithecus afarensis.*

Individuals described as *A. afarensis* are more like humans, but their brains are still much smaller. **Figure 5.18** shows the skulls and pelvic bones of a chimpanzee, *A. afarensis,* and a modern human.

As You Read

Write a note summarizing the events described in the lesson under the related years on the time line you drew in your Science Notebook.

Why was Raymond Dart's discovery significant?

Chimpanzee
Pan troglodytes

Ancient Hominid
Australopithecus afarensis

Human
Homo sapiens

Ilium

Ischial tuberosity

Acetabulum

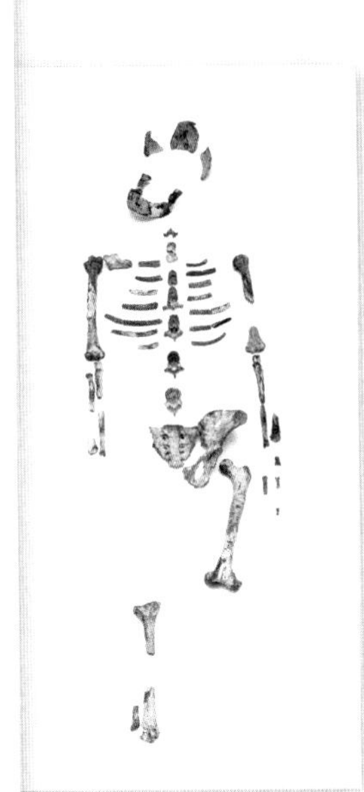

Figure 5.18 Some of the features of an australopithecine, such as Lucy, are intermediate between modern apes and humans. The reconstructed skeleton of Lucy is shown at the far right.

CONNECTION: Music

Donald Johanson named the australopithecine skeleton he found after a song, "Lucy in the Sky with Diamonds." This song was written by John Lennon and recorded by the Beatles in 1967.

Teach

ENGAGE Tell students that scientists make discoveries all of the time, but only some scientists become famous for their discoveries. Ask students if they know of any famous scientists.

EXPLAIN that in this lesson, students will be learning about a few scientists who are famous for their contributions to the understanding of human evolution.

As You Read

Check student time lines for accuracy.

ANSWER Raymond Dart's discovery was significant because it identified a primate that was not quite an ape but not quite a human.

CONNECTION: Music

Tell students that there was much celebrating among the scientists on the night that Johanson discovered *A. afarensis*. During the celebration, a song by the Beatles called "Lucy in the Sky with Diamonds" was playing in the background. Someone in the group started calling the skeleton Lucy, and the name just stuck.

Play the song for the class. Ask students if any of them were named for a song or if they know anyone who was. Discuss the reasons why someone might name someone for a song.

Background Information

Dr. Johanson is still active in the search for fossils today. He has written several books, including *Lucy: The Beginnings of Mankind* (1981), *Lucy's Child: The Search for Our Origins* (1989), and *From Lucy to Language* (1996). He founded the Institute of Human Origins, an evolutionary think tank, in 1981 and serves as its director.

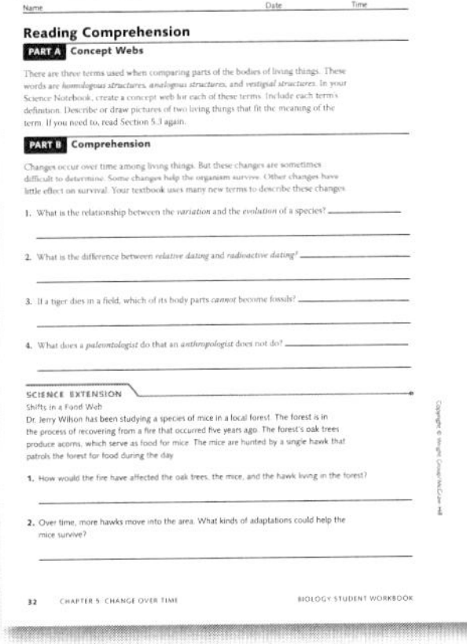

Reading Comprehension

PART A Concept Webs

PART B Comprehension

SCIENCE EXTENSION

Reading Comprehension Workbook, p. 32

Teach

ENGAGE Ask students if they know of any families whose members all work together in the same field. Discuss with students some famous families, such as the von Trapp singers or the Jackson Five.

EXPLAIN Tell students that the Leakey family was a family of anthropologists who all made significant discoveries in the field of anthropology.

Vocabulary

anthropologist Tell students that the word part *anthropo-* comes from the Greek word *anthrōpos,* which means "human being." An *anthropologist* is a scientist who studies the development of humans. Use this opportunity to revisit the meanings of two related terms, *archaeologist* and *paleontologist,* and identify the distinctions. (An archaeologist studies the remains of past human life and activities; a paleontologist studies life from past geological periods as known from fossil remains.) Tell students that scientists often combine their efforts, studying both anthropology and paleontology, for example. Donald Johanson is sometimes described as an anthropaleontologist.

PEOPLE IN SCIENCE

Tell students that Louis Leakey was one of the first scientists to focus on Africa as an important source of early human remains. Leakey discovered fossils of one of the earliest types of humans when he led an expedition to the Olduvai Gorge in Tanzania in the 1960s.

Richard Leakey, in addition to working with his father as an anthropologist, worked to prevent the killing of elephants for ivory from their tusks in Africa. Mary Leakey's important discoveries include footprints that suggest that humans have been walking upright for more than 3,600,000 years.

EXTEND Have students choose an anthropologist and learn more about that person's accomplishments. Tell students to record their research in their Science Notebooks and be prepared to share what they have learned with the class.

More Humanlike Primates

Scientists wondered when hominids developed the large brain that humans have today. The first clue came in 1964, when anthropologists Louis and Mary Leakey discovered a different kind of skull. An **anthropologist** (an thruh PAH luh just) is a scientist who studies the development of humans. This skull, found in Tanzania, Africa, was more like a human's than any other skull that had been discovered. The region that surrounded the brain was larger and the jaw was smaller.

The Leakeys placed this skull into a new grouping known as *Homo.* They named it *Homo habilis,* which means "handy human," because stone tools were found near the skull. The skull was found to be between 1.5 million and 2.5 million years old.

Modern Humans

No one knows for certain exactly how modern humans, *Homo sapiens,* evolved. The fossil record indicates that *H. sapiens* appeared about 100,000 to 500,000 years ago.

PEOPLE IN SCIENCE The Leakey Family

It's not often that an entire family can be credited with making important scientific discoveries. This is exactly the case, however, with the Leakey family. The main members of this family are Louis and Mary (top) and their son, Richard (bottom).

Louis Leakey was born in 1903 in Kenya. Growing up in Africa, he came to learn about the land and the culture. As a child, he eagerly collected and studied stone tools and other materials he found. Louis left Africa to attend college, but he returned to search for fossils in order to learn about the evolution of humans.

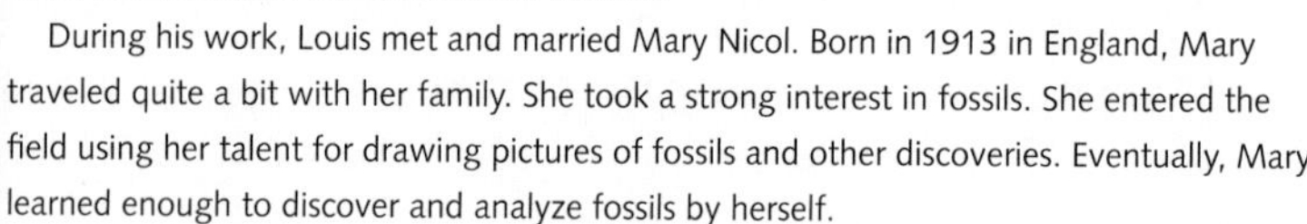

During his work, Louis met and married Mary Nicol. Born in 1913 in England, Mary traveled quite a bit with her family. She took a strong interest in fossils. She entered the field using her talent for drawing pictures of fossils and other discoveries. Eventually, Mary learned enough to discover and analyze fossils by herself.

One of Louis and Mary's three sons, Richard, took up his parents' interest in studying fossils. Born in 1944, Richard originally had planned to pursue a different career, but he eventually found himself studying fossils, just as his parents had.

Together, the Leakeys made many discoveries of fossils. They found that the human evolutionary line went farther back than anyone had imagined. They forced other scientists to rethink their understanding of human development, and they provided insight into early cultures and peoples.

ELL Strategy

Act Out, Model Digging for fossils is tedious and painstaking work. Scientists have to be very careful not to destroy anything in the process of digging. To help students experience and appreciate this process, provide each student with a chocolate-chip cookie and a toothpick. Have students attempt to use the toothpicks to excavate the chocolate chips without damaging them. Discuss with students the process and its challenges.

In the process of investigating, anthropologists gathered information about other *Homo* species. One well-known species is the Neandertals (nee AN dur tawlz). Fossils show that Neandertals had thick bones. They had large faces with large noses. Their brains were about the same size as those of modern humans.

The discovery of Neandertal bones in the 1820s raised many questions. Scientists wondered if they were the ancestors of modern humans. However, studies of DNA taken from a Neandertal bone showed that Neandertals did not evolve into modern humans. Instead, Neandertals eventually became extinct.

Fossil evidence also shows that another group lived at the same time as Neandertals. This group, sometimes known as Cro-Magnons (kroh MAG nunz), was an early form of humans. They were about the same height as modern humans. They also had the same skull structure, tooth structure, and brain size. Cro-Magnons were most likely the earliest humans.

Did You Know?

Many hominids were named according to where their fossils were first discovered. Cro-Magnon bones, for example, were found in a cave of the same name in France.

Figure 5.19 Neandertals *(left)* and Cro-Magnons *(right)* showed many traits of modern humans.

After You Read

1. Describe how an opposable thumb helped primates survive.
2. According to your time line, were fossils of human ancestors discovered in the order in which they were formed? Explain.
3. How are Neandertals and Cro-Magnons believed to be related to modern humans?

Teach

EXPLAIN Tell students that anthropologists have discovered two different humanlike species, Neandertals and Cro-Magnons. One evolved into modern humans, and the other became extinct. Ask students to think about why only one species survived.

Assess

EVALUATE Use the After You Read questions and the Alternative Assessment to help you assess students' understanding of this lesson.

After You Read

1. It enabled them to grab and hold objects, such as branches and food.
2. No. Fossils are found randomly and not in order of age. As each one is found, it adds to the body of scientific knowledge.
3. Neandertals and Cro-Magnons are believed to have lived around the same time. Neandertals are generally described as a different species that eventually became extinct. Cro-Magnons are described as ancestors of modern humans.

Alternative Assessment

EVALUATE Provide students who have difficulty answering the After You Read questions with a blank time line, and ask them to fill in the major events from the chapter. Allow students to refer to their Science Notebooks. Check that student time lines are accurate.

Background Information

The first Neandertal fossil was found in the Neander Valley near Düsseldorf, Germany, in 1856. Neandertals lived approximately 150,000 to 35,000 years ago in Europe and Asia. They made tools and shelters, which helped them survive during the Ice Age. Some scientists believe that Neandertals are part of the ancestry of humans. Since the discovery of the first Cro-Magnon fossil in 1868, more than 100 Cro-Magnon fossils have been found.

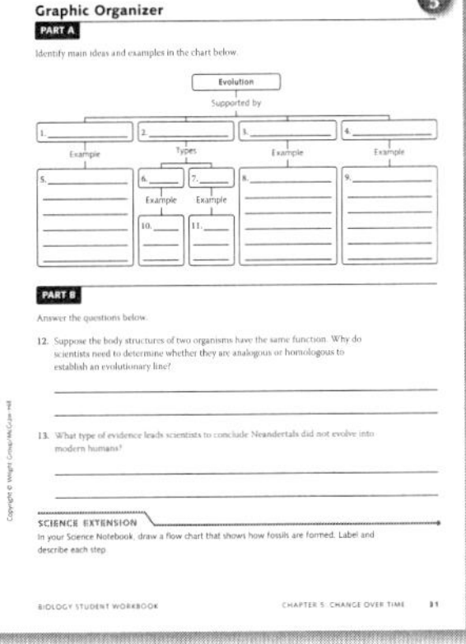
Graphic Organizer
PART A
Evolution
PART B
SCIENCE EXTENSION

Graphic Organizer Workbook, p. 31

5.5 Introduce

ENGAGE Discuss with students the ways in which examples help people explain or understand new ideas. Ask: *Can you think of some examples that would help people understand the idea that 1 kilometer is greater than 500 meters?*

Record students' examples on the board. Remind students that this concept can be hard to understand because the coefficient 1 has a smaller absolute value than the coefficient 500.

EXPLAIN Tell students that scientists also use examples to help people understand complex ideas.

Before You Read

Model a box on the board using the example "1 km > 500 m." Fill in the box with the examples students shared with the class.

Teach

EXPLAIN that in this lesson, students will learn about Darwin's observations on the Galápagos Islands. They will also learn to relate Darwin's theory of natural selection to evolution.

Learning Goals

- Describe Darwin's observations on the Galápagos Islands.
- Relate Darwin's theory of natural selection to evolution.

New Vocabulary

natural selection
survival of the fittest

5.5 Natural Selection

Before You Read

An important way to explain or understand a new idea is through examples. In your Science Notebook, draw three boxes in which you can write a few sentences. As you read the lesson, look for examples that are presented.

Paleontologists and archaeologists had discovered a tremendous amount of evidence suggesting that living things evolve. The big question that had yet to be answered, however, was "Why?" What causes the adaptations of organisms to change over time?

The basis of the modern theory of why things evolved was established by the naturalist Charles Darwin. In 1831, Darwin set sail on an English ship called the HMS *Beagle*. The ship sailed around the world on a five-year voyage. During that time, Darwin's job was to collect and study fossils and other specimens along the way.

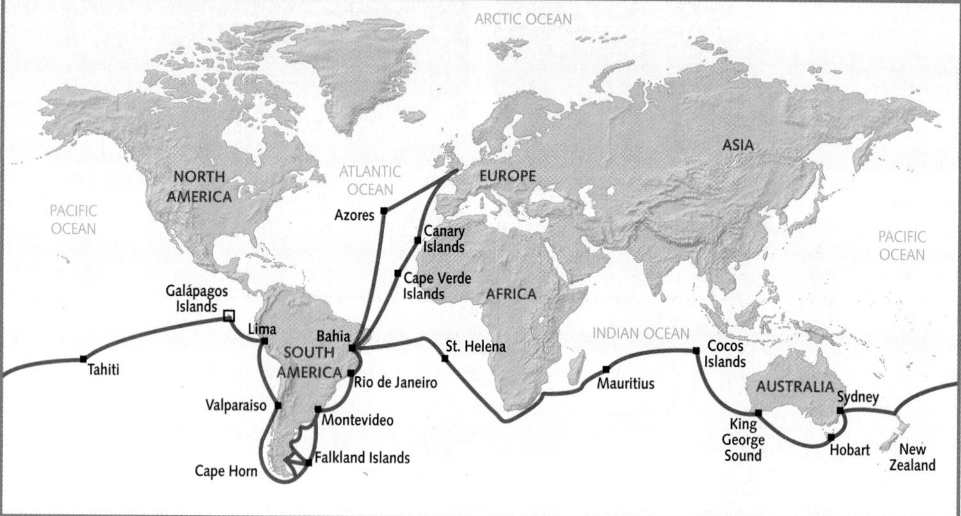

Figure 5.20 Darwin's five-year voyage took him around the world. Along the way, he collected fossils and made detailed notes about his observations.

ELL Strategy

Think, Pair, Share Have students work individually and write in their Science Notebooks their ideas about what causes an organism's adaptations to change over time. Have students share what they wrote with a partner. As students continue with the lesson, have them refer to their ideas to see whether they were correct.

The Galápagos Islands

Darwin's travels took him to a group of small islands off the west coast of South America known as the Galápagos Islands. The islands were close to one another, yet they had different climates and plants. Some islands were hot and dry with few plants. Others received more rainfall and had a larger variety of plants.

Darwin collected information about many species of organisms. In particular, he made extensive observations of giant tortoises that lived on the islands. Darwin noticed that the shells of the tortoises were different on each island. For example, one type of tortoise, the saddleback tortoise, had a long neck and a curved shell. A tortoise on a different island, the domed tortoise, had a shorter neck and a shell that looked like a dome.

In addition, Darwin observed 13 different species of a bird called a finch. Each type of finch had a beak with a different shape. The shape of the beak was adapted to the type of food present on the island where the bird lived.

As You Read

Fill in the boxes in your Science Notebook with examples of natural selection. Include information about the conditions that caused an organism to evolve.

What caused the finches on the Galápagos Islands to evolve with different beaks?

Figure 5.21 The domed tortoise *(left)* and saddleback tortoise *(right)* are two of the types of tortoises Darwin observed on the Galápagos Islands. Which tortoise has a longer neck?

1 2 3 4

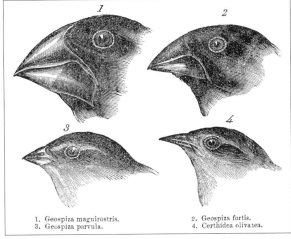

1. Geospiza magnirostris. 2. Geospiza fortis.
3. Geospiza parvula. 4. Certhidea olivacea.

Figure 5.22 These are some of the finches Darwin observed on the Galápagos Islands. Notice how their beaks are different. The shape of the beak is related to the food available where each finch lives.

Teach

EXPLAIN to students that the Galápagos Islands were particularly suited to Darwin's research. Since they were close to each other and contained many of the same species, he was able to compare how those same species adapted to different environments. The species provided the dependent variable and the climate provided the independent variable for his experiments.

As You Read

There were many conditions that caused different organisms to evolve, including climate, plant life, food preferences, and types of predators.

ANSWER The finches on the Galápagos Islands evolved with different beaks because of the type of food available to them on the islands where they lived. Different islands had different environments, which caused different types of food to be present.

Use the Visual: Figure 5.21

ANSWER The saddleback tortoise has a longer neck.

Differentiated Instruction

Naturalistic, Visual Have students draw three different habitats: one that is cold and snowy, one that is warm and dry, and one that is warm and wet. Have students invent an imaginary species and draw pictures of how that species might have evolved in each of the different habitats. Ask students to share their drawings with the class and explain the reasoning behind the adaptations that they invented.

Teach

EXPLAIN to students that competition for survival is the key to natural selection. Organisms fight for the resources available in order to survive. The organisms with traits that allow them to avoid predators, find food, and find shelter will be more likely to survive and reproduce, and those traits will then be passed on to their offspring. Ask students to think of traits that allow them to survive in a competitive world.

Vocabulary

natural selection Explain to students that the term *natural selection* can be understood by thinking of each word separately. *Natural selection* implies that *nature selects* who will survive. Those organisms that are best suited and most fit for the natural environment they are in will be selected to survive.

survival of the fittest Tell students that survival of the fittest can be understood by thinking of the word *survival*, which means outliving others, and *fittest*, which means having the best qualities for a purpose. Those that have the best qualities will be more likely to outlast and outlive those that do not.

Explore It!

Obtain two sheets of brown construction paper and one sheet of green paper. Use a hole-punch or scissors to cut circles out of one sheet of each color. The circles represent beetles.

Sprinkle an even number of green and brown beetles on the other sheet of brown paper. This paper represents a tree. Have a partner pick up as many beetles as he or she can in five seconds.

Collect the remaining beetles and repeat. After several trials, compare the number of green and brown beetles remaining. Explain your results in terms of natural selection.

Darwin's Theory

After returning to his home in England, Darwin spent many years trying to explain the observations he had made. Then, in 1859, Darwin presented his theory in a book titled *On the Origin of Species by Means of Natural Selection.* Darwin's theory is known as **natural selection**.

Darwin's theory was based on the idea that most organisms produce more offspring than are able to survive. The offspring must compete with each other for the things they need, such as food, water, and space. Some offspring have variations that will make them better able to survive. These are known as favorable variations. The organisms are said to be more "fit" than others.

Those organisms that are fit are more likely to live to reproduce. This is sometimes known as **survival of the fittest**. When organisms survive to reproduce, they pass the favorable variations on to their offspring. Over time, the favorable variations are found in more and more members of the species. In this way, the traits of a species evolve. Sometimes, the changes are so great that a new species is formed.

Natural selection can be used to explain changes in most species over time. **Figure 5.23** shows how natural selection might change a species of fish over time.

Figure It Out

1. Why is fast speed a useful variation for a fish?
2. How might a fish with a bold color be less fit than a fish that blends into the ocean floor?

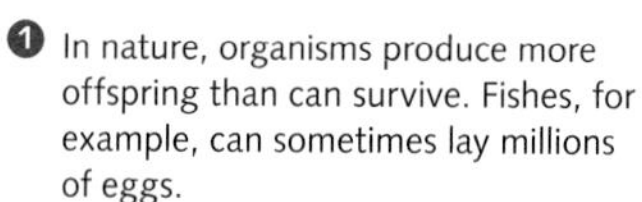

❶ In nature, organisms produce more offspring than can survive. Fishes, for example, can sometimes lay millions of eggs.

❷ In any population, individuals have variations. Fishes, for example, may differ in color, size, and speed.

❸ Individuals with certain useful variations, such as speed, survive in their environment, passing those variations to the next generation.

❹ Over time, offspring with certain variations make up most of the population and may look entirely different from their ancestors.

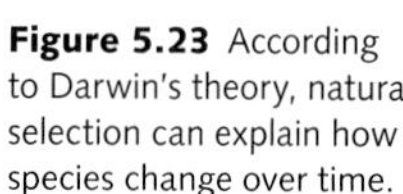

Figure 5.23 According to Darwin's theory, natural selection can explain how species change over time.

Explore It!

You may have the students punch out the "beetles," or you can prepare these in advance and hand them out to students. It is not necessary to have circles represent the beetles. Any shapes and colors will do, as long as one set of beetles is the same color as the paper and one set is not.

Students should find that the number of green beetles decreases. Because they are easier to spot against the brown background, they are more likely to be removed (eaten).

Figure It Out: Figure 5.23

ANSWER **1.** It enables a fish to escape from a predator. **2.** The bold color will make the fish more obvious to predators and, therefore, more likely to be eaten than a fish that blends in. The fish that blends in is more likely to survive and reproduce.

Teacher Alert

Students often think that animals evolve "on purpose." It is important to stress that the evolution of species occurs when a mutation or new combination of genes turns out to be advantageous to the species. This is a "happy accident" that allows more members of the species with certain traits to survive and reproduce, thus passing the traits on.

Understanding Darwin's Tortoises and Finches

The theory of natural selection explains what Darwin observed about tortoises and finches. Darwin suggested, for example, that all of the tortoises evolved from a common ancestor. The domed tortoise, which generally has a short neck and a shell that does not allow it to stretch its neck easily, was found on an island with plenty of plants. It didn't need to stretch its neck to reach food, so it thrived on this island.

The saddleback tortoise lived in a dry habitat with fewer plants. It needed to stretch to reach higher plants. Tortoises with long necks and shells that were open around the legs and neck were favored by natural selection. As a result, they were more likely to survive and reproduce. Over many generations, the adaptations—a saddleback shell and a long neck—increased within this species. Eventually, only saddleback tortoises could be found on the dry, sparsely vegetated islands.

The finches could be explained in a similar way. A single species of finch, which came from nearby South America, originally inhabited the islands. Each island provided a different source of food. Some birds needed a strong beak to crack open seeds. Others needed a narrow beak to reach into plants for food. Natural selection favored those birds with the variation that made them better able to obtain food on their island. Over many generations, the populations of birds on each island became different from one another.

Did You Know?

Darwin was not the only scientist to recognize the significance of natural selection. Another British naturalist named Alfred Russel Wallace reached a similar conclusion. In fact, the two scientists discussed their ideas and presented them to the scientific community together. Darwin continues to be better known because of his extensive research and well-defined theory.

CONNECTION: Economics

Sometimes people apply Darwin's theory of natural selection to business. Though the process is not exactly the same as that which occurs in nature, the idea is related. Often, too many businesses of the same kind compete for customers. For example, there might be more computer companies than available customers in a particular area. As a result, those companies that best serve the customer are more likely to stay in business. Those that do not serve the customer as well usually do not survive.

After You Read

1. How does Darwin's theory of natural selection relate to variations among the individuals of a species?
2. How does producing a large number of offspring affect natural selection?
3. According to the notes you wrote in your Science Notebook, how could the giant tortoises of the Galápagos Islands be explained through natural selection?

Teach

EXPLAIN to students that variations in the tortoises and finches that Darwin found on the Galápagos Islands were an important piece of evidence that supported his survival of the fittest theory. The same species in different environments changed in different ways in order to survive. The fittest species survived, and the traits that were most beneficial were passed on.

CONNECTION: Economics

Social Darwinism applies Darwin's theory of natural selection to society. People compete for survival in the economic marketplace, and those companies that are most "fit" survive, while those that are less fit do not. This theory was first introduced in the late 1800s by Herbert Spencer, a British philosopher. William Graham Sumner, an American sociologist, helped popularize the theory in the United States.

Have students meet in groups to brainstorm businesses in a given field that have been successful and those that have not. Ask students to make a list of traits that likely allowed the successful businesses to thrive and a list of traits that may have caused the unsuccessful businesses to fail. Have groups share their ideas with the class. Record group answers on the board. Ask students if there are any common traits among the different businesses that led to success or failure.

Assess

EVALUATE Use the After You Read questions and the Alternative Assessment to help you assess students' understanding of this lesson.

After You Read

1. Some will have favorable variations that make them fitter than others.
2. A large number of offspring means that individuals must compete for resources. The fittest are most likely to survive.
3. Genetic variation in the ancestral tortoises enabled the tortoises to adapt to different environments. The variations that were most sucessful in each environment became the characteristics that distinguish the different species.

Background Information

Darwin's theories have been controversial since he first introduced them in the late 1800s. Biologists, religious leaders, and the general public have all tried to find fault with his ideas. Over time, however, as the scientific community arrived at a better understanding of genetics and inheritance, scientists have found more and more evidence to support Darwin's theories. Today, the scientific community nearly unanimously accepts his ideas.

Alternative Assessment

EVALUATE Provide students who have difficulty with the After You Read questions with additional examples that support Darwin's theories of survival of the fittest and natural selection. Allow students to refer to their Science Notebooks and to consult books and the Internet to help them find examples.

Chapter 5 Summary

VOCABULARY REVIEW

Check students' sentences or paragraphs to make sure that they understand the meaning of each vocabulary term.

PREPARE FOR CHAPTER TEST

Evaluate students' essays using the following criteria:

1. The topic sentence, or main idea, should restate the Key Concept.
2. The supporting paragraphs should incorporate the answers to the Learning Goal questions students have written and include details, facts, and examples they have recorded in their Science Notebooks.
3. The concluding sentence should sum up the main idea of the chapter and restate the Key Concept.

MASTERING CONCEPTS

True or False

1. False, adaptation
2. False, mutation
3. True
4. False, extinct
5. False, analogous
6. False, Cro-Magnons
7. True

Short Answer

8. It might help the organism stay warm, catch more food, or avoid predators.
9. Sexual reproduction and mutations result in variation.
10. A vestigial structure is homologous to a functional structure of an ancestor.
11. The theories are based on people's interpretations of fossils. As each new fossil is uncovered, another piece of the puzzle is provided. A new fossil may not support current theories. At that point, scientists will revise their theories to include the new finding.
12. Variations among bacterial cells allow some not to be killed by an antibiotic. Those cells survive and reproduce. In time, most cells in a bacterial colony are not killed by the antibiotic.

Chapter 5 Summary

KEY CONCEPTS

5.1 Adaptations and Variations

- An adaptation is a trait that helps an organism survive and reproduce itself in its environment.
- Some adaptations help predators or prey. Others help organisms survive in a particular habitat.
- Although the members of a species are similar, there are variations among them. Variations are the result of sexual reproduction and mutations.

5.2 Evidence from the Past

- Fossils are the remains of organisms that once lived.
- Relative dating compares the age of a fossil with other fossils and rock layers. Radioactive dating gives an exact age of a fossil according to amounts of radioactive elements.
- The fossil record indicates that living things change over time.

5.3 Modern Evidence of Evolution

- Homologous structures have the same evolutionary origin, whereas analogous structures do not.
- Organisms that are related have similar embryos even though they look different as adults.
- Organisms with similar genetic material are likely to share a common ancestor.

5.4 Humans and Evolution

- Primates have feet and hands with toes and fingers that have nails. They have flexible joints and opposable thumbs.
- Hominid fossils show that there were several types of pre-human primates.
- Neandertals were a humanlike species that became extinct. Cro-Magnons were ancestors of modern humans.

5.5 Natural Selection

- Darwin observed many plants and animals on the Galápagos Islands and elsewhere. He noticed that related species had different adaptations on different islands.
- Darwin's theory of natural selection suggests that when more offspring are produced than can survive, they must compete for resources. Only the fittest organisms survive to reproduce. Over time, this changes the traits of a species.

VOCABULARY REVIEW

Write each term in a complete sentence, or write a paragraph relating several terms.

5.1
adaptation, p. 84
predator, p. 85
prey, p. 85
variation, p. 87
genetic diversity, p. 87
mutation, p. 87

5.2
fossil, p. 88
paleontologist, p. 88
relative dating, p. 90
radioactive dating, p. 90
fossil record, p. 90
extinct, p. 90
geologic time scale, p. 91

5.3
evolution, p. 92
homologous structure, p. 93
analogous structure, p. 93
vestigial structure, p. 93
embryo, p. 94

5.4
primate, p. 95
opposable thumb, p. 95
hominoid, p. 96
hominid, p. 96
anthropologist, p. 98

5.5
natural selection, p. 102
survival of the fittest, p. 102

PREPARE FOR CHAPTER TEST

To prepare for the chapter test, create a question from each Learning Goal. Use the information in your Science Notebook to answer each question. Then use these answers to write a well-developed essay about the chapter. Use the Key Concept on the first page of this chapter as your topic sentence.

Key Concept Review
Workbook, p. 29

Name Date Time

Vocabulary Review

PART A

Complete the table below.

Word	Definition	Adaptation Example
adaptation		
genetic diversity		
mutation		
predator		
prey		

PART B

Decide whether each statement is true or false. If the statement is true, write *true*. If the statement is false, replace the underlined word with a word that makes it true.

_____ 1. A paleontologist studies the development of humans.
_____ 2. All primates have an opposable thumb.
_____ 3. A homologous body structure is no longer useful.
_____ 4. Carbon-14 is used in relative dating.
_____ 5. Cro-Magnons had the same skull shape and teeth as modern humans.

SCIENCE EXTENSION

Write two sets of short descriptions of organisms that could be identified using one of the vocabulary words in this chapter. Exchange descriptions with a partner, and then identify the organisms.

30 CHAPTER 5: CHANGE OVER TIME BIOLOGY STUDENT WORKBOOK

Vocabulary Review
Workbook, p. 30

MASTERING CONCEPTS

True or False

If the statement is true, write "true." If it is false, change the underlined word or words to make the statement true.

1. A <u>predator</u> is a trait that helps an organism survive and reproduce itself in its environment.
2. A <u>variation</u> is an error that occurs when DNA is copied.
3. A <u>fossil</u> is the preserved remains of a once-living organism.
4. A species becomes <u>preserved</u> when it no longer lives on Earth.
5. Two structures are <u>homologous</u> if they have the same function but did not evolve in the same way.
6. The <u>Neandertals</u> were an early form of modern humans that had the same height, size, and tooth structure.
7. <u>Natural selection</u> is sometimes described as survival of the fittest.

Short Answer

Answer each of the following in a sentence or brief paragraph.

8. How might an adaptation help an organism survive in a cold environment?
9. Identify the cause(s) of variations within a population of organisms.
10. Explain how a vestigial structure can be used to support evolution.
11. Many scientific theories attempt to explain human evolution. Explain why some of these theories may need to be revised at a later point in time.
12. An antibiotic is a drug that is used to kill bacterial cells. Construct an argument to explain why some bacterial diseases are no longer controlled by an antibiotic.

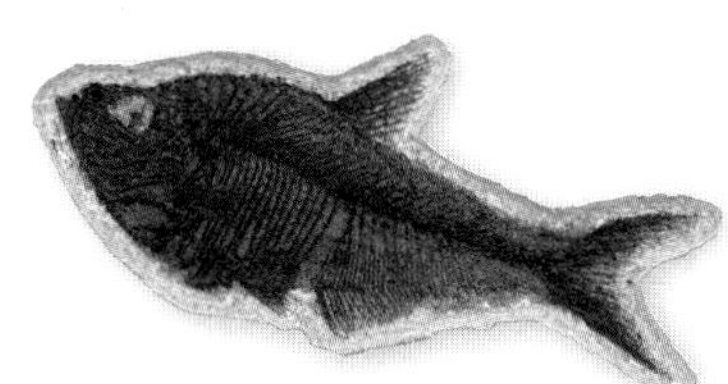

Critical Thinking

Use what you have learned in this chapter to answer each of the following.

13. **Apply** Plants that grow on the floor of a rain forest often have large, flat leaves. How is this structure an adaptation that helps them survive?
14. **Compare** How do the skull and brain sizes of modern humans compare to the skulls of early primates, such as australopithecines?
15. **Relate** What natural selection process might have led to a smaller jaw with fewer teeth in humans?
16. **Infer** About the time of the Industrial Revolution in England, light gray trees turned black from soot. Peppered moths that are white or black lived on these trees. Birds preyed upon the moths. Suggest how the change in tree color affected the population of these moths.

Standardized Test Question

Choose the letter of the response that correctly answers the question.

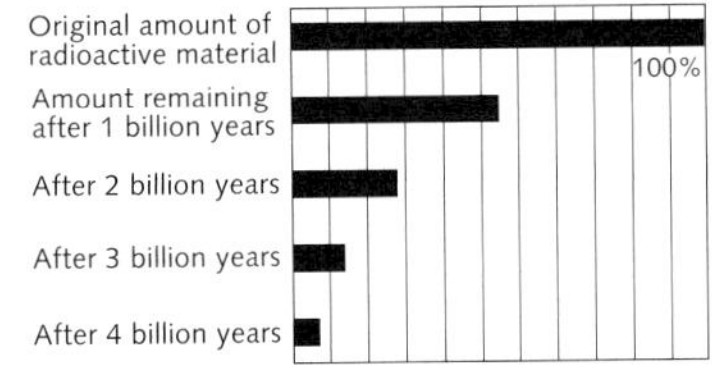

17. The bar graph shows how much of a radioactive element remains after different periods of time. What is the most likely half-life (how long it takes for half of the element to decay) of this element?
    A. 1 billion years
    B. 2 billion years
    C. 3 billion years
    D. 4 billion years

Test-Taking Tip

Remember that words such as *most likely* and *not* may change the meaning of a question. Be sure to read the question carefully before examining all the answer choices.

Critical Thinking

13. Not much sunlight gets to the forest floor. The wide leaves help the plants capture as much sunlight as possible in order to conduct photosynthesis.
14. Modern humans have larger skulls, which hold larger and more complex brains.
15. A change in the diet would have led to this change. Perhaps as humans began to walk on two feet and use tools to find and prepare foods, the individuals with smaller jaws and fewer teeth were more successful.
16. When the trees were gray, natural selection favored the light moths because they were harder for birds to spot. When the trees turned black, natural selection favored the dark moths.

Standardized Test Question

17. A

Reading Links

The Human Story: Our Evolution from Prehistoric Ancestors to Today

Excellent photographs and drawings complement current and informative text in this comprehensive exploration of human evolution and our understanding of it. Along with details about transitional fossils and dating methods, this book includes information about classification systems and the human genome that can serve as a useful introduction to topics that students will encounter as they continue their studies.

Sloan, Christopher. National Geographic Society. 80 pp. Illustrated. Trade ISBN: 978-0-7922-6325-8.

Fossil Fish Found Alive: Discovering the Coelacanth

In 1938, a museum director noticed a strange blue fish in a South African fisherman's net. Scientists scrambled to determine if it was a member of a 360-million-year-old species thought to be extinct. This book tells the dramatic story of that scientific detective work while explaining more about the species and the importance of finding a key evolutionary link between land life and sea life.

Walker, Sally M. Lerner Publishing Group. 64 pp. Illustrated. Trade ISBN: 978-1-57505-536-7.

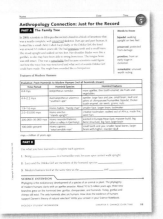

Name Date Time

Anthropology Connection: Just for the Record 5

PART A The Family Tree

In 2000, scientists in Ethiopia discovered a fossil in a block of limestone that was a nearly complete, well-<u>preserved</u> skeleton. Part-ape and part-human, it looked like a small child. Called *Lucy's baby*, or the *Dikika Girl*, the fossil was around 3.3 million years old. She had <u>primitive</u> teeth and a small brain. She stood upright and walked on two feet. Her shoulder blades were like a gorilla's, so she may have been able to swing from trees. The tongue bone was still intact. This was a <u>remarkable</u> find because scientists could figure out how the voice box was structured and what sort of sounds *Dikika Girl* could have made. She might have sounded like a chimpanzee.

Words to Know
bipedal: walking upright on two feet
preserved: protected from damage
primitive: from an early stage in evolution
remarkable: unusual, worth noting

Features of Modern Humans

Evolution: From Hominids to Modern Humans (not all hominids shown)		
Time Period	**Hominid Species**	**Hominid Features**
4.4 mya	*Ardipithecus ramidus*	more apelike; thin tooth enamel; ate fruits and vegetables
4.4–2.2 mya	*Australopithecus afarensis* "southern ape"	apelike: large face and jaw; small brain; skull and pelvis of chimpanzee/humanlike: bipedal; thicker tooth enamel; ate seeds, grains, nuts
1.9–1.6 mya	*Homo habilis* "handy man"	smaller face; larger brain; toolmaker
2.0–53,000 mya	*Homo erectus* "stands upright"	creative toolmaker; walked out of Africa; made fire; wore furs
200,000–30,000 mya	*Homo neanderthalensis* (after a valley in Germany)	existed in Europe/Near East; massive build; big bone structure; big face; large brain
100,000–present	*Homo sapiens* "wise/sensible man"	small teeth and jaw; smaller facial bones; larger brain with higher, rounder skull

mya = million of years ago

PART B

Use what you have learned to complete each question.

1. Being ________ is a humanlike trait, because apes cannot walk upright.
2. Lucy and the Dikika Girl are members of the hominid species ________
3. Modern humans lived at the same time as the ________ and ________

SCIENCE EXTENSION

Phylogeny is the evolutionary development of a species of an animal or plant. The phylogeny of modern humans starts with an apelike ancestor. About 10 to 5 million years ago, three new branches grew on the hominoid tree: gorillas, chimpanzees, and hominids. Today, gorillas and chimps still exist. The only hominids alive are humans. How does the existence of humans support Darwin's theory of natural selection? Write your answer in your Science Notebook.

Copyright © Wright Group/McGraw-Hill

BIOLOGY STUDENT WORKBOOK CHAPTER 5 CHANGE OVER TIME 33

Curriculum Connection Workbook, p. 33

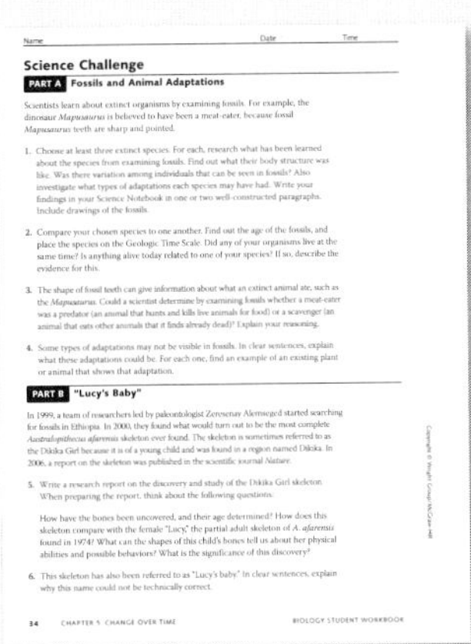

Name Date Time

Science Challenge

PART A Fossils and Animal Adaptations

Scientists learn about extinct organisms by examining fossils. For example, the dinosaur *Mapusaurus* is believed to have been a meat-eater, because fossil *Mapusaurus* teeth are sharp and pointed.

1. Choose at least three extinct species. For each, research what has been learned about the species from examining fossils. Find out what their body structure was like. Was there variation among individuals that can be seen in fossils? Also investigate what types of adaptations each species may have had. Write your findings in your Science Notebook in one or two well-constructed paragraphs. Include drawings of the fossils.
2. Compare your chosen species to one another. Find out the age of the fossils, and place the species on the Geologic Time Scale. Did any of your organisms live at the same time? Is anything alive today related to one of your species? If so, describe the evidence for this.
3. The shape of fossil teeth can give information about what an extinct animal ate, such as the *Mapusaurus*. Could a scientist determine by examining fossils whether a meat-eater was a predator (an animal that hunts and kills live animals for food) or a scavenger (an animal that eats other animals that it finds already dead)? Explain your reasoning.
4. Some types of adaptations may not be visible in fossils. In clear sentences, explain what these adaptations could be. For each one, find an example of an existing plant or animal that shows that adaptation.

PART B "Lucy's Baby"

In 1999, a team of researchers led by paleontologist Zeresenay Alemseged started searching for fossils in Ethiopia. In 2000, they found what would turn out to be the most complete *Australopithecus afarensis* skeleton ever found. The skeleton is sometimes referred to as the Dikika Girl because it is of a young child and was found in a region named Dikika. In 2006, a report on the skeleton was published in the scientific journal *Nature*.

5. Write a research report on the discovery and study of the Dikika Girl skeleton. When preparing the report, think about the following questions:

   How have the bones been uncovered, and their age determined? How does this skeleton compare with the female "Lucy," the partial adult skeleton of *A. afarensis* found in 1974? What can the shapes of this child's bones tell us about her physical abilities and possible behaviors? What is the significance of this discovery?

6. This skeleton has also been referred to as "Lucy's baby." In clear sentences, explain why this name could not be technically correct.

Copyright © Wright Group/McGraw-Hill

34 CHAPTER 5 CHANGE OVER TIME BIOLOGY STUDENT WORKBOOK

Science Challenge Workbook, p. 34

5A Happy Hunting

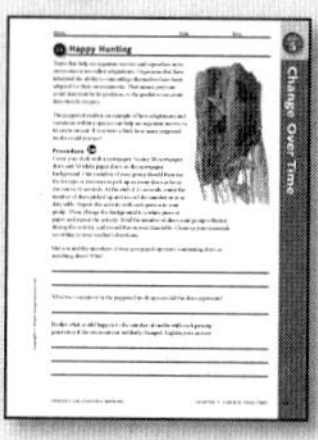

This prechapter introduction activity is designed to explain how natural selection works in a predator-prey situation by engaging students in making predictions, recording observations, and collecting data.

Objectives

- make predictions about predator and prey success
- identify variations in a species
- record data in a data table
- communicate conclusions

Planning

 1 class period 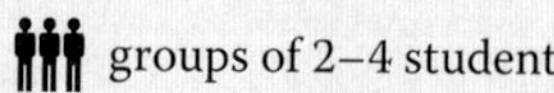

Materials (per group)

- 1 sheet of newspaper
- 1 sheet of white paper
- 50 newspaper disks
- 50 white paper disks
- 1 pair of forceps or tweezers
- clock or watch with a second hand
- pencil and paper
- hole-punch

Advance Preparation

- Collect newspapers; save only black-and-white sheets. Using a hole-punch, punch out enough disks for each group to have 50 newspaper disks and 50 white paper disks.
- Before the activity, draw the following data tables on the board for each group to copy:

Data Table 1: Newspaper Background

Predator	Newspaper Disks Picked	White Disks Picked
1		
2		
3		
4		
total number of disks picked		

Data Table 2: White Background

Predator	Newspaper Disks Picked	White Disks Picked
1		
2		
3		
4		
total number of disks picked		

Engagement Guide

- Challenge students to think about adaptations and variations within a species by asking:
  - *How does this activity simulate species adaptation?* (In each setup, the disks are either visible or camouflaged. This simulates the presence of dark-colored moths and light-colored moths. Those that are visible are easily spotted and picked up, which is similar to being eaten by predators. Those that are camouflaged are not easily picked up, which is similar to being hidden from predators.)
  - *Which organism will survive in its environment?* (the organism that is best-suited for its environment)
  - *Which trait will most likely be passed on to the next generation?* (The trait that helps the organism survive in its environment will most likely be passed on to the next generation, because organisms with those traits are better adapted to that environment and more likely to survive and reproduce. Introduce the term *natural selection* at this time. Organisms that adapt to their environment and pass on their traits to the next generation demonstrate the process of natural selection.)
- Encourage students to communicate their conclusions in creative ways, such as a drawing or demonstrating one of the types of adaptations predators and prey can exhibit.

Going Further

Encourage students to repeat this activity for several generations and graph the data for both backgrounds. Have students present their conclusions to the class.

5B Measuring Variations in a Population

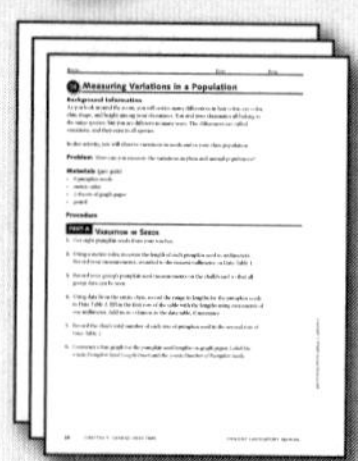

Objectives

- observe variations in populations
- measure seeds and hand spans
- record data
- use data to construct a graph

Skill Set

observing, measuring, recording and analyzing data, inferring, graphing, stating conclusions

Planning

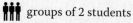

 1 class period  groups of 2 students

Materials

Materials for this activity are listed in the Student Laboratory Manual.

Answers to Observations: Data Tables 1, 2, and 3 and Line Graphs

Draw Data Tables 2 and 3 on the board before the lab begins. For Data Table 2, you may want to set the measurements according to the range of data the students are recording.

Data Table 1: Students' data will vary according to seeds used.

Data Table 2: Class data will vary.

Data Table 3: Class data will vary.

Line Graphs: Both graphs should have a bell-shaped curve.

Answers to Analysis and Conclusions

1. Most pumpkin seeds should fall close to the middle of the range.
2. The fewest pumpkin seeds will be at the extremes of the range.
3. The general shapes of the graphs should be a bell-shaped curve. Most of the lengths are near the average, with fewer lengths at both extremes.
4. Answers will vary but might include the advantage of grasping large tools and weapons, carrying large loads, and fighting off predators with bare hands.
5. Having more seeds is more useful because it increases the likelihood that a seed will land in a suitable place to grow.

Going Further

Have students repeat this activity using other variations. For plant populations, students could measure plant leaves or lima beans. For animal populations, students could measure their heights or cubits (length between the fingertip and elbow).

5C The Genetics of Natural Selection

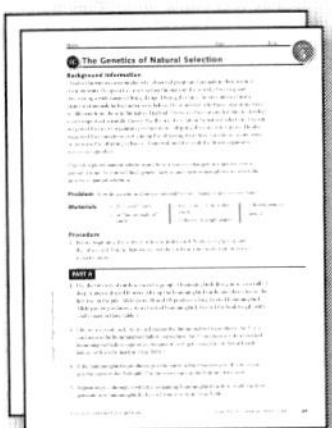

Objectives

- construct a model of natural selection
- observe how selection changes a species
- record observations
- predict how environmental changes will affect natural selection
- use data to create a graph

Skill Set

observing, comparing and contrasting, recording and analyzing data, predicting, graphing, stating conclusions

Planning

1 class period 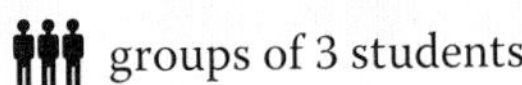 groups of 3 students

Materials

Materials for this activity are listed in the Student Laboratory Manual.

Advance Preparation

- To make the 25 "event" cards for each group, mark 5 cards with an *R*, 1 card with a *F*, 1 card with a *P*, and 18 cards with an *S*.
- To make 50 "hummingbird" cards, mark 25 cards with a *B* and 25 cards with a *b*. Generate a template for each set of cards on the computer, and print out sets for groups.
- Divide the class into groups of three, and assign each student a task. Have one student be in charge of the hummingbird cards, one be in charge of the event cards, and the third be in charge of recording the tally marks in the data tables. Check to make sure students are assigning the correct phenotype to each genotype.

Answers to Observations: Data Table 1 and Data Table 2

Answers will vary according to the genotypes of the hummingbirds and the order in which the hummingbird and event cards are drawn.

Answers to Graphs

Answers will vary according to the data collected, but the first graph should show a decrease in the number of long-beaked hummingbirds that fail to reproduce in each generation and an increase in the number of short-beaked hummingbirds that fail to reproduce. The second graph will show the opposite.

Answers to Analysis and Conclusions

1. There would be an increase in the number of long-beaked hummingbirds.
2. In Part 2, the number of short-beaked hummingbirds increases in each generation because the long-beaked hummingbirds are selected against, whereas in Part 1, the number of long-beaked hummingbirds increases in each generation because the short-beaked hummingbirds are selected against.
3. This model demonstrates the principles of natural selection: more offspring are produced than survive, variations exist among offspring, and offspring with favorable adaptations are the most fit to survive and reproduce in their environment.
4. This model does not show competition among offspring for resources, nor does it show environmental factors such as weather, predation, and disease that are likely to influence an organism's chances of surviving and reproducing.
5. Increasing the number of *S* cards would cause natural selection to be stronger, meaning the number of birds with disadvantageous beaks would decrease more quickly. Decreasing the number of *S* cards would cause natural selection to be weaker, meaning the number of birds with disadvantageous beaks would decrease more slowly.

Going Further

Create a few hypothetical contrasting environments for students, and have them identify different organisms that could demonstrate natural selection. Students could use the same cards to model what might happen to the organisms in their contrasting environments.

Chapter 6 Lessons

Introduce Chapter 6

As a starting activity, use LAB 6A Classifying Screws and Bolts on page 32 of the Laboratory Manual.

ENGAGE Ask students if they recognize what is being shown in the photograph. Help them identify the compact discs. Point out that in stores, types of music are usually organized into separate sections. Within each section, the music is often arranged in alphabetical order by musician. Ask students to describe examples of how they, their friends, or their families organize music, movies, or video games.

Think About Classifying

ENGAGE Ask students to think about other objects they observe or use daily that are organized into groups. Try to elicit responses such as items in a supermarket, books in a library, tools in a hardware store, utensils in a kitchen drawer, or food in a vending machine. Discuss the basis for each grouping and the advantages of organizing objects.

Instruct students to complete each bulleted activity. As a class, discuss student results. Make sure students understand that each system is based on identifying the similarities and differences among the objects being organized.

Chapter 6 Classification of Living Things

KEY CONCEPT The classification of living things is based on similarities and differences among organisms.

Imagine going into a music store to find a CD. As you look around, you discover that the CDs are not arranged in any particular order. The only way to find what you want is to look through the thousands of CDs one by one. It could take you all day!

Your best bet is to go to a store that organizes its CDs in an easy-to-use system. Organizing items into groups is useful and important for many things people do every day. Life scientists organize living things into groups in order to describe and study them.

Think About Classifying

Describe one way in which you organize into groups objects such as books, clothing, or coins. What do you use as the basis for your organizational system? Now describe a way in which you might organize living things. What is the basis for this system?

- Compare your two systems. How are they alike? How are they different?
- Write one or two sentences in your Science Notebook summarizing how things can be organized into groups.

www.scilinks.org
Classification **Code: WGB06**

106

Chapter 6 Planning Guide			
Instructional Periods	**National Standards**	**Lab Manual**	**Workbook**
6.1 1 Period	A.1, A.2, C.1, G.1, G.2; C.2, C.3, G.1, G.2; UCP.1, UCP.3, UCP.4, UCP.5	**Lab 6A—p. 32** Classifying Screws and Bolts **Lab 6B—p. 33** Using a Dichotomous Key to Identify Vertebrates **Lab 6C—p. 36** Using a Classification Key to Identify Chemical Substances	Key Concept Review p. 35 Vocabulary Review p. 36 Graphic Organizer p. 37 Reading Comprehension p. 38 Curriculum Connection p. 39 Science Challenge p. 40
6.2 2 Periods	A.2, C.1; A.2, C.3; UCP.1		
6.3 2 Periods	A.2; A.2; C.1, C.3, F.6; UCP.1, UCP.2		

Middle School Standard; High School Standard; Unifying Concept and Principle

6.1 What Is Classification?

Before You Read

Create a K-W-L-S-H chart in your Science Notebook. Think about the title of this lesson. In the column labeled *K* on the chart, write what you already know about classifying things. In the column labeled *W*, write what you want to learn about how living things are classified.

Learning Goals

- Identify the characteristics by which organisms are organized into groups.
- Describe how a dichotomous key is used.

New Vocabulary

classification
taxonomy
dichotomous key

Do you think that the more than 2.5 million types of organisms already discovered include all of the organisms on Earth? If so, think again. Scientists predict that several million more organisms are yet to be discovered!

Recently, damp caves in Sequoia National Park were found to be home to 27 types of spiders, centipedes, scorpions, and other creatures never seen before. Some of the organisms exist only in one section of a single cave! When scientists discover a new organism, they work to describe it, name it, and relate it to other organisms based on how they are alike and different. In other words, they classify it.

Early Classification

Arranging organisms into groups according to how they are alike is known as **classification**. The branch of biology that involves identifying, classifying, and naming organisms is **taxonomy** (tak SAH nuh mee). Scientists who study taxonomy are called taxonomists.

The science of taxonomy is not new. The Greek philosopher Aristotle (384–322 B.C.) developed the first widely accepted system of classification. Aristotle classified organisms into two basic groups: plants and animals. He further divided each group according to characteristics he could observe. For example, plants could be described as herbs, shrubs, or trees. Animals were classified according to whether they swam in water, flew through the air, or walked on land.

Figure 6.1 Aristotle classified more than 500 organisms as either plants or animals.

6.1 Introduce

ENGAGE Have students describe spiders, centipedes, and scorpions. Tell them that some of the organisms recently discovered in Sequoia National Park are these kinds of animals. Tell students that scientists discover new organisms like these all the time. Ask: *Besides caves, what are some other places where new organisms might be found? What kinds of organisms might scientists find in these places?*

As a class, brainstorm examples of places and organisms and record them on the board. Guide students to think about unexplored or remote areas, such as rain forests and the arctic. Have students compare the types of organisms they think might be found in the different regions.

Before You Read

Have students create a five-column K-W-L-S-H chart in their Science Notebooks. Have students work individually to complete the first two columns of the chart.

Vocabulary terms are listed on the first student page of each lesson. You may wish to preview the terms before introducing each lesson. Strategies for teaching the vocabulary appear on the pages where the terms are introduced.

Teach

EXPLAIN to students that they will learn about the history of classification. Point out that the first accepted classification system was developed by the Greek philosopher Aristotle more than 2,000 years ago when he divided organisms into two basic groups: plants and animals. Ask students to predict how the classification system has changed since the time of Aristotle.

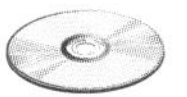

Vocabulary

classification Explain that *classification* refers to the "arrangement of any items into groups based on common characteristics."

taxonomy Explain that this word comes from the Greek terms *taxis*, meaning "arrangement," and *nomos*, meaning "law." Have students discuss how these terms relate to the science of taxonomy.

Background Information

Aristotle was an ancient Greek philosopher who studied a variety of subjects. His ideas were the basis of Western thought for centuries and are still influential today. Aristotle studied both the sciences and the arts. He did major work in the scientific fields of biology, zoology, botany, physics, and chemistry. He was also influential in the areas of political theory, psychology, ethics, history, and logic.

Science Notebook EXTRA

Encourage students to use the vocabulary section they created in their Science Notebooks. Remind them to record prefixes, suffixes, and root words to help them remember the meanings of vocabulary terms.

Teach

EXPLAIN Emphasize that the classification system we use today is based on Linnaeus's system of grouping organisms with similar physical and structural features. Have students describe the three main types of information that today's scientists use to determine how organisms are related.

As You Read

Have students fill in the *L* column of their K-W-L-S-H charts individually.

ANSWER Linnaeus developed the classification system used today.

CONNECTION: Chemistry

Ask students to discuss some of the elements in the table. Point out that chemical elements are directly related to living things. Explain that all living things are made up of chemical elements.

Some elements such as oxygen, carbon, hydrogen, and nitrogen are very common in living things. In fact, they account for more than 99 percent of the atoms in the human body. Some other elements such as iodine, cobalt, and zinc are present in trace, or small, amounts. Still other elements such as lead and arsenic are toxic to living things in large amounts.

The periodic table of the elements has changed since Mendeleev's time. New elements have been added, and the elements are now arranged in order of increasing atomic number instead of mass. The atomic number is the number of protons, or positive charges, in the nucleus of an atom of an element. The horizontal rows of the table are called periods. The vertical columns of the table are called groups or families.

EXTEND Tell students that each group of the periodic table is assigned a number and name. Ask students to recall or research the names and properties of the groups of the table. Have small groups create their own versions of the table using the names they have researched.

As You Read

In the column labeled *L* in your K-W-L-S-H chart, write three or four important things that you have learned about classification.

Identify the scientist who developed the classification system used today.

A New Approach

Aristotle's system of classification lasted for centuries. Over time, however, many organisms were discovered that did not fit into the system. In the late eighteenth century, the Swedish botanist Carolus Linnaeus (luh NAY us) (1707–1778) developed a new method of classification.

Linnaeus's system was based on physical and structural similarities of organisms. Using observations he made, he placed the organisms into groups and subgroups. You will learn more about Linnaeus's levels of classification in the next lesson. You will also discover how he used his system to name organisms.

Linnaeus's system of classifying and naming organisms survives to this day. However, the method of grouping organisms has changed. Modern classification is based on the idea that organisms that share a common ancestor are related and also share a similar evolutionary history.

CONNECTION: Chemistry

Classification is not limited to life science. Scientists in all fields of study benefit from organizing information. Chemists, for example, classify chemical elements. To date, there are more than 110 known chemical elements.

In 1863, when only 63 elements had been discovered, the Russian scientist Dmitri Mendeleev recognized the need to organize them. He compiled a list of the known physical and chemical properties of the elements and wrote the information for each element on a separate card. He arranged and rearranged the cards until he recognized a pattern. The result became known as the periodic table of the elements because the properties of the elements repeated in a periodic, or regular, fashion.

Mendeleev's table was first published in 1869. The organization of the table made it possible to predict the existence and properties of elements that had not yet been discovered.

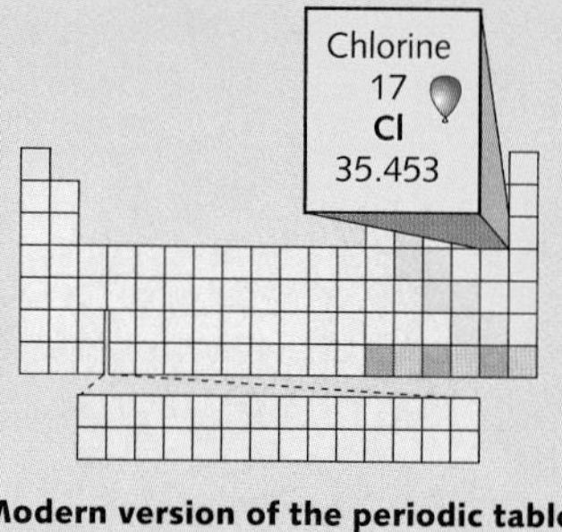

Modern version of the periodic table

Science Notebook EXTRA

Ask students to write a paragraph in their Science Notebooks describing how Mendeleev's periodic table might have impacted chemists of his day. Then, suggest that students write an announcement describing the periodic table as if they were newspaper reporters during Mendeleev's time.

Differentiated Instruction

Kinesthetic Have students work in pairs or groups to collect and sort items, such as buttons, coins, shells, and leaves, according to Aristotle's system. Encourage students to evaluate the usefulness of a two-group system and to suggest possible improvements.

Basis for Classification

When scientists try to determine the evolutionary relationships among organisms, they gather a variety of information. This information includes the similarities between the structures of organisms, the structures of chromosomes, and the DNA sequences.

Structural Similarities If two organisms have similar structures, they likely evolved from a common ancestor. Lynxes and bobcats, for example, are more similar to each other than to members of any other group. This suggests that they share a common ancestor. Taxonomists identify the characteristics of organisms and compare them to those of known organisms. They use this information to make inferences about the evolutionary history of the organisms.

Chromosomes Scientists can study the number and structure of chromosomes to learn about relationships. If the structure of the chromosomes of two organisms is similar, the organisms may have shared a common ancestor. Taxonomists classify cabbage, cauliflower, and kale together because their chromosomes are almost identical in structure.

DNA Organisms that are closely related have similar DNA sequences. Recall that DNA is made up of sequences of nucleotides. In general, the more similar the nucleotide sequences of two organisms are, the more closely related they are. Consider the giant panda and red panda in **Figure 6.3**. Although they are both called pandas, the giant panda's DNA sequences are more similar to a bear's than to a red panda's.

Figure 6.2 Why do you think taxonomists classify the lynx (top) and the bobcat (bottom) in the same group?

Figure 6.3 DNA evidence shows that giant pandas (left) are more closely related to bears than to red pandas (right). Red pandas are related to raccoons.

Did You Know?

The skeletons of dinosaurs indicate that these animals share many characteristics with birds. Current research suggests that dinosaurs, therefore, share a more recent common ancestor with birds rather than with reptiles, as previously thought.

Teach

EXPLAIN Introduce the idea that in order to determine evolutionary relationships among organisms, scientists look for important similarities those organisms possess. The three areas in which such similarities can be observed are structure, chromosomes, and DNA. If necessary, review the definitions of *chromosomes* and *DNA*.

Use the Visual: Figure 6.2

ANSWER The lynx and the bobcat look alike and share similar structures.

Science Notebook EXTRA

Ask students to think about different pairs of organisms that they believe may be related. Have them write the names of three to five pairs in their Science Notebooks and describe why they think the organisms in each pair are related.

Use the Visual: Figure 6.3

EXTEND Ask students to look carefully at the photograph of the red panda in Figure 6.3. Have pairs or small groups of students locate photos of bears and raccoons in reference books or on the Internet. Have students identify observable characteristics of each type of animal and then compare the characteristics with those of the red panda in the figure. Say: *We know that the DNA of a red panda is similar to that of a bear and a raccoon. Look at your photos.* Ask: *Do you think there are any structural similarities between a red panda, a bear, and a raccoon? If so, describe them.*

ELL Strategy

Reinforce Vocabulary Pair advanced English-language learners with beginner or intermediate ELL students who speak the same native language. Have pairs discuss and clarify the lesson's new vocabulary terms in their native language. Then, have the advanced student say the definition of each term aloud in English.

Teach

 Review the dichotomous key for identifying common beans (Figure 6.4) with students. Make sure students understand how to read and interpret the key.

Vocabulary

dichotomous key Point out that the word *key* has more than one meaning. Have students brainstorm meanings and examples of various keys they have used or know about. Then, discuss which definition and example best relate to the term *dichotomous key*.

Explain It!

Students may create a dichotomous key for one of the items suggested (books, utensils, sports equipment) or they may choose to classify different items from home.

Alternatively, you may have students complete this activity in pairs or small groups during class time, using items found at school.

Check that students' explanations and keys are clear, logical, and correct. Students should recognize that a scientist uses a dichotomous key when he or she is trying to identify an organism because the key shows how related organisms are alike and different.

Figure It Out: Figure 6.4

ANSWER **1.** The garbanzo bean is the only round bean. **2.** It is a kidney bean.

Assess

EVALUATE Use the After You Read questions and the Alternative Assessment to help you assess students' understanding of this lesson.

Explain It!

Write a paragraph explaining how a dichotomous key is useful. Then create a dichotomous key to classify items in your home, such as books, utensils, or sports equipment.

Dichotomous Key

Taxonomists often use the information they collect to develop **dichotomous keys** for identifying an unknown organism. The word *dichotomous* means "two parts." A dichotomous key is made up of several pairs of opposing statements. A person trying to identify an organism must choose the one of the two statements that describes the organism.

At the end of each statement is either the name of an organism or a directive to go to another pair of statements. If the person selects the statement with the name of an organism, he or she has identified the unknown organism. No further statements need to be considered. If the person selects the statement with a directive, he or she must move on to another pair of statements.

A person must work through the pairs of statements one at a time in order to identify an unknown organism. A dichotomous key for identifying common beans is shown in **Figure 6.4**.

Figure It Out

1. Which is the only type of bean that is round?
2. Suppose you discover a bean that is reddish-brown, oblong, and has pigments that are spread out evenly. How would you classify it?

Dichotomous Key

1a. The bean is round. 1b. The bean is elliptical or oblong.	**Garbanzo bean** Go to 2
2a. The bean is white. 2b. The bean has dark pigments.	**White northern bean** Go to 3
3a. The pigments are spread out evenly. 3b. The pigments are mottled.	Go to 4 **Pinto bean**
4a. The bean is black. 4b. The bean is reddish-brown.	**Black bean** **Kidney bean**

Figure 6.4 This dichotomous key contains four sets of statements to identify common beans.

After You Read

1. What is classification?
2. What characteristics do taxonomists use to classify an organism?
3. Using the completed K-W-L columns in your chart, describe how a dichotomous key is used to identify an organism. Complete your chart by indicating what you would still like to know about classification in the *S* column and how you can find this information in the *H* column.

After You Read

1. Classification is the process of arranging organisms into groups.
2. Taxonomists use structural similarities, chromosomes, and DNA to classify an organism.
3. The person using the key must choose the correct statement from each pair of statements in the order indicated.

Alternative Assessment

EVALUATE Have students look at their completed K-W-L-S-H charts. Ask them to describe something they wanted to find out about before reading the lesson and then tell what they learned about it after reading. Then, have them write a new question they have about classification. Ask student volunteers to share their new questions with the class.

Differentiated Instruction

Visual Have visual learners match pictures of beans to statements in the dichotomous key (Figure 6.4). Before class, make a set of three cards for each bean described in the key: one card with the bean name, a second card with a written description of the bean, and a third card with a picture of the bean. Have students use the dichotomous key to match the three cards for each bean.

6.2 Levels of Classification

Before You Read

Create a lesson outline. Use the lesson title as the outline title. Label the headings with the Roman numerals *I* through *III*. Use the letters *A*, *B*, *C*, etc., under each heading to record information you want to remember.

Learning Goals

- Describe how scientists classify organisms.
- Identify the seven levels of classification.
- Explain the system used to give organisms scientific names.

New Vocabulary

kingdom
phylum
class
order
family
genus
species
binomial nomenclature

If you were asked to identify yourself as part of a group, which group would you choose? You could choose your family, your class, or your school. Perhaps you would select a club or sports team. There are many groups of varying sizes to which you belong. The same is true of the more than 2.5 million living things that exist today. How are these groups organized? Read on to learn about the levels of classification scientists use to bring order to the study of living things.

What Is It?

Whenever a new organism is discovered, scientists carefully study its characteristics. They determine how many cells make up the organism, how the organism gets its food, and how it reproduces. For many years, scientists used this information to classify newly discovered organisms as either plants or animals.

With advances in technology, scientists learned even more about the great variety of living things. For example, they discovered tiny organisms, such as the slime mold shown in **Figure 6.5**. These organisms, now known as protists, have characteristics of plants as well as of animals. They are classified in their own group.

Figure 6.5 Many microscopic organisms have characteristics of both plants and animals, yet they are different enough to need their own group. What type of organism is the slime mold (center)?

6.2 Introduce

ENGAGE the class by encouraging students to draw upon prior knowledge about classifying items into groups. Ask: *What are some other ways in which you might identify yourself by groups?* Brainstorm examples and make a list of student answers on the board. Help students recognize how larger groups are divided into smaller ones.

EXPLAIN Tell students that scientists also organize items into groups. In this case, the items are living things. Challenge students to suggest some criteria upon which they might organize a large group of living things into smaller groups.

Before You Read

Review outlining with the class. Start the outline on the board if students need help. Check student outlines throughout the lesson.

Teach

EXPLAIN to students that in this lesson, they will learn how and why scientists classify living things. Emphasize the millions of living things that exist today and the need to bring order to that vast diversity. Ask students to think about how technological advances help scientists observe and classify different forms of life.

Use the Visual: Figure 6.5

ANSWER A slime mold is a protist.

EXTEND Ask students to identify the slime mold in Figure 6.5. Then, ask for examples of other organisms that would belong to the protist, plant, and animal groups. Explain that the photo of the slime mold is magnified and color-enhanced.

ELL Strategy

Paraphrase As students read through the lesson, have them write each vocabulary word on the front of an index card, using a separate card for each word. Have students write the definition of each vocabulary word or term in their own words on the back of its index card. For struggling English-language learners, one strategy might be to take notes in their native language and then work in pairs to translate their notes into English. Students can add the words to their Science Notebooks. Another strategy might be to have students illustrate the meaning of each word or term in their Science Notebooks.

Practice Using Vocabulary If time permits, have students play a word game. Ask them to take turns reading their own vocabulary definitions aloud in small groups. Have other members of the group guess the vocabulary word or term being defined.

Teach

EXPLAIN that the system of classification used today consists of seven levels, with each succeeding level becoming more specific and containing fewer types of organisms. Have students refer to Figure 6.7.

Explore It!

Collect a variety of music samples. The local library should have an adequate selection. You need only a one- or two-minute segment.

If possible, play at least 10 samples, including classical music, jazz, rock, and country. Assign a number to each sample. Play each sample at least twice, and remind students to take notes describing what they hear.

Have pairs of students develop classification systems to divide the music samples into groups. Guide students to use more than two or three groups. Allow the class to compare their systems. Emphasize the fact that there is no single correct classification system by asking students to compare their systems to those made by other pairs. Students should note that a classification system must be practical to those who use it.

As You Read

ANSWER Organisms within a species have similar characteristics and can mate and produce offspring of the same type.

Explore It!

There are many different types of music. Your teacher will play several samples of music for your class. Listen closely to each one. Take notes describing the characteristics of each music sample. Work with a partner to develop a method of classifying the music samples into different groups. Create a chart or a diagram showing your results.

As You Read

Look at your outline. Make sure that you have recorded additional information. Share your outline with a partner, and add any missing information.

Explain what organisms within the same species have in common.

A System of Levels

As you just learned, plants, animals, and protists are classified into different groups. Not all of the organisms within each group are identical. For example, dogs, whales, and worms are all considered animals. They are identified as animals because, among other things, they are multicellular (many-celled) and must consume other organisms as food. They have little else in common, however.

For this reason, scientists divide each major group into smaller groups based on how organisms are alike or different. The system of classifying organisms that Linnaeus devised is hierarchical (hi uhr AR kih kul), which means that it has levels. Each successive level is more specific and contains fewer types of organisms. The organisms in each successive level share more characteristics with one another than they do with the organisms in the level above.

As you can see in **Figure 6.7**, the largest and most general group into which an organism can be classified is known as a **kingdom**. Animals, plants, and protists make up three kingdoms of organisms. You will learn more about kingdoms in the following lesson.

Each type of organism within a kingdom is then organized into a smaller and more specific group called a **phylum** (FI lum, plural: phyla).

Members of each phylum are further divided into different **classes**. Classes are more specific than phyla and kingdoms. A class is made up of different **orders**.

An order is separated into **families**. Each family consists of at least one **genus** (JEE nus, plural: genera).

Each genus is then divided into **species**. A species is the smallest and most specific group into which organisms are classified. Organisms within a species have similar characteristics and can mate and produce offspring of the same type.

Figure 6.6 These dogs are members of the same species. No other type of organism, such as house cats or killer whales, can belong to this species.

Background Information

Each of the seven levels of classification is called a taxon. Linnaeus used his system of classification to describe more than 4,400 species of animals and 7,700 species of plants. Since Linnaeus first devised the system, it has been expanded as scientists learn more about organisms. For example, kingdoms have been added, and many organisms are identified by subgroups within levels.

Not all organisms in a species are identical. However, they share more characteristics with each other than with any other type of organism. Dogs of different breeds can mate to produce offspring. This is not true of two different species, such as dogs and cats.

Figure It Out

1. How many different types of organisms would you expect to find at the species level?
2. Which animal or animals disappear at each successive level? Why?

Classification of the Domestic Dog

Kingdom Animalia

Dogs are in the kingdom Animalia. All but one of the animal phyla contain only animals without a backbone. Dogs belong to only phylum that contains animals with backbones.

Phylum Chordata

Dogs are classified in the phylum Chordata. Animals in this phylum have a spinal cord and most have a backbone. Bears, foxes, turtles, wolves, and whales are also in this phylum.

Class Mammalia

Dogs belong to the class Mammalia. Mammals are warm-blooded animals with backbones whose females nourish young with milk. Turtles belong to a different class.

Order Carnivora

Dogs are members of the order Carnivora. The ancestors of these mammals had special teeth for tearing meat. Wolves, foxes, and bears also belong to this order.

Family Canidae

Dogs, as well as wolves and foxes, belong to the family Canidae. Members of this family are generally hunters that can run long distances.

Genus *Canis*

Dogs and wolves both belong to the genus *Canis*. Of all the animals shown in this table, dogs and wolves are the most closely related.

Species *Canis familiaris*

Only domestic dogs make up the species known as *Canis familiaris*. A species is the smallest and most specific classification group.

Figure 6.7 Many types of organisms can belong to the same kingdom. A kingdom is the largest and most general group. Fewer organisms belong in each successive level.

Figure It Out: Figure 6.7

Help students recognize that the diagram is in the shape of an inverted triangle.

ANSWER **1.** There is only one type of organism at the species level. **2.** The jellyfish disappears at the phylum level because it does not have a spinal cord. The turtle disappears at the class level because it is not a mammal. The whale disappears at the order level because it is not a carnivore. The bear disappears at the family level because it does not have the body structure for running long distances. The fox disappears because it does not have the characteristics of genus *Canis*. Only the domestic dog has the characteristics of species *Canis familiaris*.

Vocabulary

kingdom Ask students what comes to mind when they hear the word *kingdom*. Explain that rulers, such as kings, reign over a territory known as a *kingdom*. Point out that in science, a *kingdom* is a large grouping of organisms.

phylum Tell students that the word *phylum* was first used in 1876 to describe a division of the plant or animal kingdom. The word is related to the Greek word *phylē*, which means "tribe" or "clan."

class Explain that the word *class* has many common uses. People might describe a *class* of students, a grade of mail, or a social ranking. Have students contrast these meanings with the scientific meaning of *class* as a group of similar organisms.

order Have students brainstorm common meanings of the word *order*. For example, a person might *order* an item from a store, a general might give an *order* to the troops, or a student might arrange books in *order*. Explain that in taxonomy, an *order* is a group of related families of organisms.

family Explain that the word *family* comes from the Latin *familia*, which means "household." Point out that the people in a household are usually connected in some way, much like the organisms in a scientific family.

genus Tell students that *genus* is a Latin word meaning "race," "stock," or "kind." Ask students to relate this origin to its use in science.

species *Species* is a Latin word meaning "kind" or "sort." Students may be familiar with the term *endangered species*. Tell students that this term, which describes a type of organism that is close to extinction, was first used in 1964.

Differentiated Instruction

Interpersonal, Kinesthetic Make sure students realize that a similar diagram can be made for each of the animals shown at the top of the diagram in Figure 6.7. Have students work in pairs to select one of the animals (other than the domestic dog) and create a diagram showing its levels of classification. You may also create a "living" diagram using students from the class as representative animals.

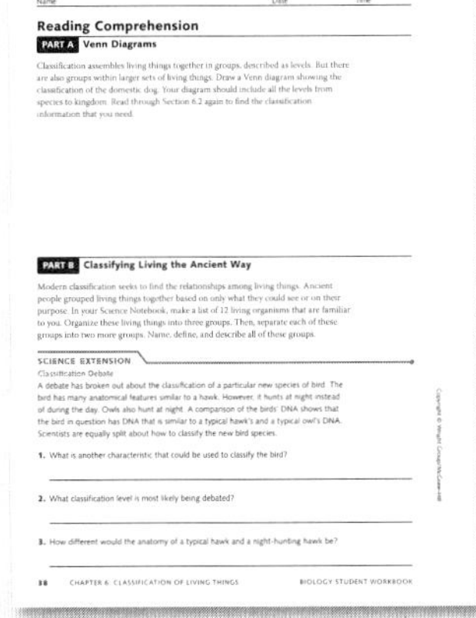

Reading Comprehension

PART A Venn Diagrams

PART B Classifying Living the Ancient Way

SCIENCE EXTENSION

Reading Comprehension Workbook, p. 38

Teach

EXPLAIN Introduce the idea that all living things have a unique scientific name. Ask students to explain why this is important in identifying an organism.

Science Notebook EXTRA

Some common names can be misleading; for example, a prairie dog is not a dog and a jellyfish is not a fish. Challenge students to make a list of common names similar to these examples in their Science Notebooks. Have them explain why each name is misleading. Then, have students add the scientific name of each organism to their list.

Vocabulary

binomial nomenclature Ask students to list other words with the prefix *bi-* and give their meanings.

Use the Visual: Figure 6.8

ANSWER Each has a different species descriptor *(grevyi, hemionus, caballus)*, so each is a separate species of genus *Equus*.

CONNECTION: Art

Student drawings should show some of the major characteristics of dogs and wolves (e.g., fur, four legs, tail). *Canis* should be the first word in the new species name.

Assess

EVALUATE Use the After You Read questions and the Alternative Assessment to help you assess students' understanding of this lesson.

After You Read

1. A hierarchical classification system has different, increasingly smaller levels.
2. The scientific name identifies the genus and the species of the organism.
3. Smaller units of time make up larger units. For example, hours make up days, which make up weeks, which make up months, which make up years. Similarly, seconds make up minutes, which make up hours.

Grevy's Zebra
Equus grevyi

Onager
Equus hemionus

Domestic Horse
Equus caballus

Figure 6.8 All three of these animals are in the same genus. Each one belongs to a different species. How can you tell?

Naming Organisms

When you describe an animal as a cat or a dog, you are using its common name. Common names vary among people in different places. In fact, a single organism may have as many as 50 common names. The panther is an endangered species of wildcat. In Florida, this animal is called the Florida panther. In other parts of the country, it is called a cougar, puma, mountain lion, or catamount.

Linnaeus recognized the need to use a unique name for each type of organism. He gave each one a two-part scientific name made up of the genus name and a species descriptor. He used Greek and Latin words because those languages were understood by most scientists of his day. Linnaeus's system is known as **binomial nomenclature**. The word *binomial* means "two names," and the word *nomenclature* means "naming."

Look at the name of the domestic dog in **Figure 6.7** on page 113, *Canis familiaris*. This name is also the species of the domestic dog. The first part of the name identifies the genus: *Canis*. Remember, a genus is a group of closely related species. The second part of the name, *familiaris*, specifies which species. Since only one type of organism makes up a species, only domestic dogs belong to the species *Canis familiaris*. All breeds of domestic dogs belong to this species and have this scientific name.

Notice that in a scientific name, the genus is capitalized and the species descriptor is not. Also notice that the scientific name is written in italic letters. Sometimes the genus is abbreviated as a letter. For example, the scientific name for humans is *Homo sapiens*. This name can also be written as *H. sapiens*.

CONNECTION: Art

You are a scientist who has discovered a new species of animal. It is closely related to the wolf and the domestic dog. Make a detailed drawing of this new species in your Science Notebook. Describe the animal in detail, and name it using binomial nomenclature.

After You Read

1. Describe a hierarchical classification system.
2. Explain what you can learn from the scientific name of an organism.
3. Use the information in your outline. Think about how the classification of living things is similar to the organization of time using calendars and clocks. In your Science Notebook, write a well-developed paragraph summarizing your thoughts.

Alternative Assessment

EVALUATE Struggling readers can draw pictures or cut out magazine photos of animals with similar characteristics that are likely to be members of the same species.

Background Information

Early attempts at assigning scientific names involved describing the physical characteristics of the organism in great detail. As a result, some names were up to 20 words long! Not only was a name for an organism cumbersome, it could vary because different scientists might have focused on different characteristics.

6.3 Domains and Kingdoms

Before You Read

Read the lesson title, the Learning Goals, and the headings, and look at the photos and table. Predict what you think you will learn in this lesson. Write two or three sentences in your Science Notebook.

As you learned in Lesson 6.2, all organisms are grouped into kingdoms. Although Aristotle used two kingdoms and Linnaeus used three, most modern biologists classify organisms into six kingdoms: Eubacteria, Archaebacteria, Protista, Fungi, Plantae, and Animalia.

Three Domains

Since the time of Linnaeus, biologists have developed a new taxonomic category called the **domain**. The domain is larger than the kingdom. There are three domains. The six kingdoms are grouped into these three domains. The domain Bacteria includes the kingdom Eubacteria. The domain Archaea includes the kingdom Archaebacteria. The domain Eukarya includes protists, fungi, plants, and animals.

Four basic characteristics can be used to compare and contrast the kingdoms. These are cell type, cell structures, number of cells, and method of obtaining nutrition.

Cell Type Recall that there are different types of cells. Cells with a nucleus and organelles bound by membranes are called eukaryotic cells. Organisms with these types of cells are called eukaryotes. In prokaryotes, the cells do not have a membrane-bound nucleus or organelles. In addition, the DNA is not organized into X-shaped chromosomes. These types of cells are prokaryotic.

Cell Structures Many cell structures help the cell function properly. One such structure is a cell wall, which surrounds and protects the cell membrane in some cells. Another structure is the chloroplast, a membrane-bound organelle that contains pigments that capture the energy of sunlight in some eukaryotic cells. Identifying cell structures helps scientists classify organisms.

Number of Cells Some organisms consist of a single cell. In these unicellular organisms, all life functions are carried out by one cell. Multicellular organisms are made up of more than one cell. Cells or groups of cells are usually specialized to perform a specific function.

Learning Goals

- Relate domains and kingdoms.
- Identify and compare the six kingdoms.

New Vocabulary

domain
Eubacteria
Archaebacteria
Protista
Fungi
Plantae
Animalia

Extend It!

Research the development of the six-kingdom system. Find out why some scientists still use a five-kingdom system. Based on your research, predict whether additional kingdoms will be proposed in the future.

As You Read

Refine your predictions using any information you have learned in this lesson. What four characteristics are used to compare kingdoms?

6.3 Introduce

ENGAGE students by asking what the class learned about levels of classification in Lesson 6.2. Say: *In the last lesson, you learned that dogs belong to the kingdom Animalia.* Ask: *What are some other organisms that might belong to that kingdom? What are some organisms that do not belong to the same kingdom as dogs?* Record the responses in a T-chart on the board.

Before You Read

Help students identify what the photos and illustrations show. Have students share their predictions with a partner or with the class.

Teach

EXPLAIN that students will learn how domains and kingdoms are related. Emphasize that a domain is an even larger and more general category than a kingdom.

Vocabulary

domain Tell students that other definitions of the word *domain* include "land or territory belonging to one person or government" and "a sphere of knowledge." Help students relate these meanings to the scientific definition of *domain* as the largest category in the classification system.

Extend It!

Provide students with opportunities to conduct research at a library or on the Internet during class. Encourage students to share the results of their research with the class. Explain that some scientists still use a five-kingdom classification system because not all scientists recognize Eubacteria and Archaebacteria as separate kingdoms. They instead use one kingdom, Monera, for all prokaryotes. Suggest that if trends continue, more kingdoms may be added in the future.

As You Read

ANSWER The four characteristics used to compare kingdoms are cell type, cell structures, number of cells, and nutrition.

Differentiated Instruction

Linguistic Have students choose any two organisms that belong to two different kingdoms. Ask them to write in their Science Notebooks an "autobiographical" paragraph of each organism for the purpose of comparing the organisms. Encourage them to create a diagram of each organism. Students should include the four main characteristics that scientists use for comparing kingdoms.

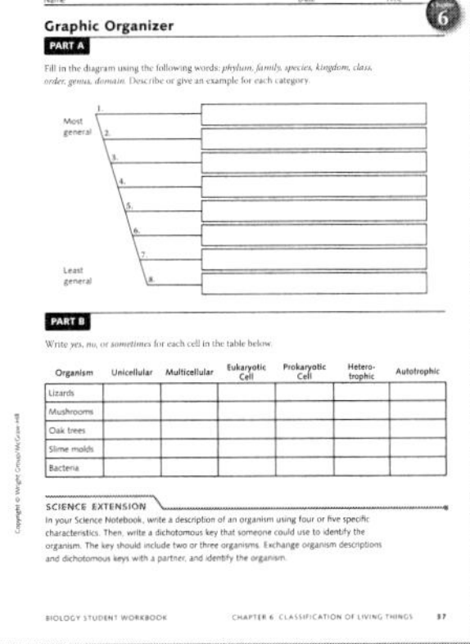

Graphic Organizer
Workbook, p. 37

Teach

EXPLAIN Go over the table of domains and kingdoms in Figure 6.9 with students.

EXPLORE Have students write one example of an organism belonging to each of the six kingdoms. Then, ask them to write the name of each organism's domain.

Vocabulary

Eubacteria Tell students that the prefix *eu-* means "good" or "well." Discuss why some eubacteria, such as the bacteria in yogurt, are good bacteria.

Archaebacteria Point out that the prefix *archae-* means "ancient" or "original." Remind students that archaebacteria exist in harsh conditions like those that would have existed on ancient Earth.

Protista Explain that *protista* comes from the Greek *prōtistos*, which means "first." Tell students that organisms in this kingdom were mistakenly described as being "first animals" by scientists who identified them under the earliest microscopes.

Fungi Ask students to name a common fungus that people eat. Tell them that mushrooms are probably the most well-known kind of fungus. In fact, *fungus* is the Latin word for mushroom, and *mycology*, the study of fungus, comes from the Greek word for mushroom, *mykēs*.

Plantae Point out the word "plant" in *plantae*. Have students describe a common plant. Discuss how their description differs from the scientific definition of the kingdom Plantae.

Animalia Tell students that *animale* is Latin for "living being" and *anima* means "life principle" or "soul." Have students talk about how these meanings relate or do not relate to the scientific definition of the kingdom Animalia.

Figure It Out: Figure 6.9

ANSWER **1.** They are both eukaryotes. A protist may have cell walls of cellulose and have chloroplasts like a plant. Protists may also be multicellular and autotrophic like plants. **2.** The kingdoms Plantae and Animalia do not contain unicellular organisms.

Use the Visual: Figure 6.9

ANSWER The kingdoms are organized into domains.

Figure It Out

1. What are four characteristics that a protist can have in common with a plant?
2. Which kingdoms do not contain unicellular organisms?

Domains and Kingdoms

Domain	Kingdom	Cell Type	Cell Structures	Number of Cells	Nutrition
Bacteria	Eubacteria	prokaryotic	cell walls with peptidoglycan	unicellular	autotrophic or heterotrophic
Archaea	Archaebacteria	prokaryotic	cell walls without peptidoglycan	unicellular	autotrophic or heterotrophic
Eukarya	Protista	eukaryotic	cell walls of cellulose in some; chloroplasts in some	most are unicellular; some are multicellular	autotrophic or heterotrophic
Eukarya	Fungi	eukaryotic	cell walls of chitin	most are multicellular; some are unicellular	heterotrophic
Eukarya	Plantae	eukaryotic	cell walls of cellulose; chloroplasts	multicellular	autotrophic
Eukarya	Animalia	eukaryotic	no cell walls or chloroplasts	multicellular	heterotrophic

Figure 6.9 Organisms can be classified into six different kingdoms. How are the kingdoms organized?

Figure 6.10 Archaebacteria such as *Halococcus* are found in harsh environments, such as these seawater evaporating ponds (top). Eubacteria such as cyanobacteria (bottom) live in freshwater.

Nutrition All organisms need nutrients in order to survive. Autotrophic organisms use inorganic nutrients and make organic nutrients through photosynthesis. Heterotrophic organisms must obtain nutrients by eating other organisms as food.

Domain Bacteria

This domain contains the kingdom **Eubacteria**. Bacteria are unicellular. Their cells are prokaryotic and have a thick cell wall around a cell membrane. Some bacteria are autotrophic, and others are heterotrophic.

Domain Archaea

The members of this domain look much like bacteria. They are unicellular prokaryotes that can be autotrophic or heterotrophic. They belong to the kingdom **Archaebacteria**.

Archaea are found in some of the most extreme environments on Earth. They exist in volcanic hot springs, very salty water, and thick swamps. Some live near hot vents in the ocean. Archaea have even been found in the digestive tracts of cows and termites.

ELL Strategy

Use Visual Information: Tables Provide students with additional support for reading the domains and kingdoms table (Figure 6.9). To help with pronunciation of names, students can listen to audio enunciations on the Student CD-ROM. Go over how to read information down and across the table. Ask: *Where are the three domains located in the table? What are the names of the domains? What are the names of the kingdoms?*

Teacher Alert

Students may need support in recalling the definitions of terms associated with cell type, cell structure, cell number, and method of obtaining nutrition. Spend some time reviewing each category and its associated terms.

Cell type: *prokaryote, eukaryote*

Cell structure: *cell wall, cell membrane, chloroplast*

Cell number: *unicellular, multicellular*

Nutrition: *autotroph, heterotroph*

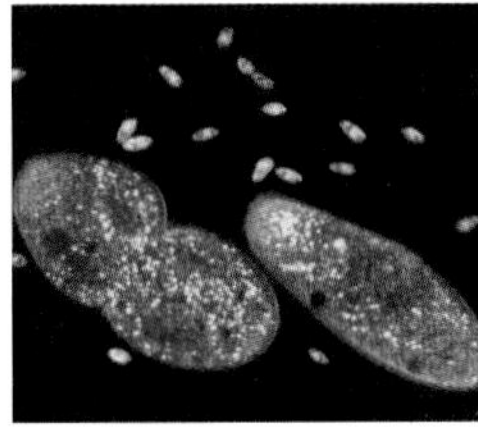

Figure 6.11 Slime molds (left) are fungus-like protists that live in damp forests. Kelps (center) are multicellular plant-like protists. Paramecia (right) are animal-like protists that move through water.

Domain Eukarya

All of the organisms in this domain are eukaryotes. This domain contains four kingdoms.

The kingdom **Protista** shows the greatest variety. Most protists are unicellular, but some are not. Some protists conduct photosynthesis, while others do not. Some protists, such as slime molds, have features in common with fungi. Other protists, such as algae, resemble plants. Still others, such as protozoa, share characteristics with animals.

Members of the kingdom **Fungi** are heterotrophs. Most fungi (singular: fungus) obtain nutrition by feeding on dead or decaying organic matter. Some fungi, such as mushrooms, are multicellular. Others, such as yeasts, are unicellular.

The kingdom **Plantae** contains multicellular organisms that are photosynthetic autotrophs. This means they can use inorganic nutrients to produce organic nutrients that heterotrophs can use as food.

Members of the kingdom **Animalia** are multicellular and heterotrophic. Animals obtain nutrition by eating plants or other animals that have eaten plants. Almost all animals are motile, which means they are able to move from one place to another.

Figure 6.12 The cheetah (left) is one species of animal. Tropical ferns (right) are species of plants. What are some ways in which these organisms are similar? How are they different?

Did You Know?

Fungi were originally classified as plants. Because fungi do not conduct photosynthesis, however, they were later classified into a separate kingdom.

After You Read

1. Which two domains include only organisms that are prokaryotes?
2. Explain to which kingdom you belong.
3. According to your predictions, if the cells of a multicellular organism have cell walls, to which kingdoms could the organism belong?

Teach

EXPLAIN that in this section, students will learn about the domain that includes most living things.

Use the Visual: Figure 6.12

ANSWER The organisms are similar because they are both multicellular and their cells are eukaryotic. They are different because a tropical fern has cells with cell walls and chloroplasts, whereas a cheetah's cells do not contain these structures. Ferns are autotrophic; cheetahs are heterotrophic.

Science Notebook EXTRA

Ask students to think of an organism that they encounter almost every day. Tell them to write in their Science Notebooks a paragraph about the organism. They should identify its domain and kingdom and describe its cell type, cell structures, number of cells, and method of obtaining nutrition.

Assess

EVALUATE Use the After You Read questions and the Alternative Assessment to help you assess students' understanding of this lesson.

After You Read

1. Domain Bacteria and domain Archaea include only prokaryotes.
2. I belong to the kingdom Animalia because I am multicellular, heterotrophic, and motile.
3. A multicellular organism with cells that have cell walls could belong to the kingdoms Protista, Fungi, or Plantae.

Background Information

Fungi Facts

- Fungi may be found on land or in freshwater or saltwater environments.
- Some fungi are microscopic. Others may be quite large. One of the largest fungi measured was a giant puffball with a diameter of more than 150 cm.
- Though only about 50,000 species of fungi have been identified, scientists estimate that there may be anywhere from 100,000 to 250,000 species.

Field Study

Have students become familiar with the different kingdoms in a relevant context by encouraging them to visit a local supermarket to identify products from each kingdom. Have students record their observations in a creative way and share them with the class.

Alternative Assessment

EVALUATE Struggling readers can answer the After You Read questions for the table of domains and kingdoms on page 116 (Figure 6.9). Have them work with a partner and use the table to answer the questions.

Chapter 6 Summary

VOCABULARY REVIEW

Check students' sentences or paragraphs to make sure they understand the meaning of each vocabulary term.

PREPARE FOR CHAPTER TEST

Evaluate students' essays using the following criteria:

1. The topic sentence, or main idea, should restate the Key Concept.
2. The supporting paragraphs should incorporate the answers to the Learning Goal questions students have written and include details, facts, and examples they have recorded in their Science Notebooks.
3. The concluding sentence should sum up the main idea of the chapter and restate the Key Concept.

MASTERING CONCEPTS

True or False

1. True
2. False, dichotomous
3. False, phylum
4. True
5. False, Animalia
6. False, Fungi

Short Answer

7. Taxonomy is important to biologists because it provides a method of identifying and analyzing the millions of organisms found in nature.
8. Carolus Linnaeus developed the system of classification that is still used today. Linnaeus also developed a system of naming organisms based on their classification.
9. In Linnaeus's system, a kingdom is the largest taxonomic group. A kingdom is made up of related phyla, which are in turn made up of similar classes. Each class is made up of similar orders, which are composed of related families. A family contains similar genera that each contain related species.
10. The first word identifies the genus. The second word is a species description. Both names together make up the species name, or scientific name, of the organism.

Chapter 6

Summary

KEY CONCEPTS

6.1 What Is Classification?

- Classification is the practice of using similarities and differences to organize living things into groups.
- Taxonomy is the branch of biology that identifies, classifies, and names living things.
- The Swedish botanist Carolus Linnaeus developed a system of classification in which organisms are placed into groups and subgroups according to their physical and structural similarities.
- A series of opposing statements known as a dichotomous key can be used to identify unknown organisms.

6.2 Levels of Classification

- Scientists classify organisms by comparing their characteristics and grouping organisms with similar characteristics together.
- An organism is classified into a kingdom, phylum, class, order, family, genus, and species.
- A kingdom is a large and general group. A species is the smallest and most specific group.
- The system of assigning a two-part scientific name to an organism is known as binomial nomenclature.
- The scientific name of an organism is its species name, which consists of its genus and a species descriptor.

6.3 Domains and Kingdoms

- The domain is a level of classification into which kingdoms can be grouped.
- The three domains are Bacteria, Archaea, and Eukarya.
- The organisms in the domain Bacteria and the domain Archaea are all prokaryotes.
- All of the organisms in the domain Eukarya are eukaryotes. This domain contains four kingdoms: Protista, Fungi, Plantae, and Animalia.

VOCABULARY REVIEW

Write each term in a complete sentence, or write a paragraph relating several terms.

6.1
classification, p. 107
taxonomy, p. 107
dichotomous key, p. 110

6.2
kingdom, p. 112
phylum, p. 112
class, p. 112
order, p. 112
family, p. 112
genus, p. 112
species, p. 112
binomial nomenclature, p. 114

6.3
domain, p. 115
Eubacteria, p. 116
Archaebacteria, p. 116
Protista, p. 117
Fungi, p. 117
Plantae, p. 117
Animalia, p. 117

PREPARE FOR CHAPTER TEST

To prepare for the chapter test, create a question from each Learning Goal. Use the information in your Science Notebook to answer each question. Then use these answers to write a well-developed essay about the chapter. Use the Key Concept on the first page of this chapter as your topic sentence.

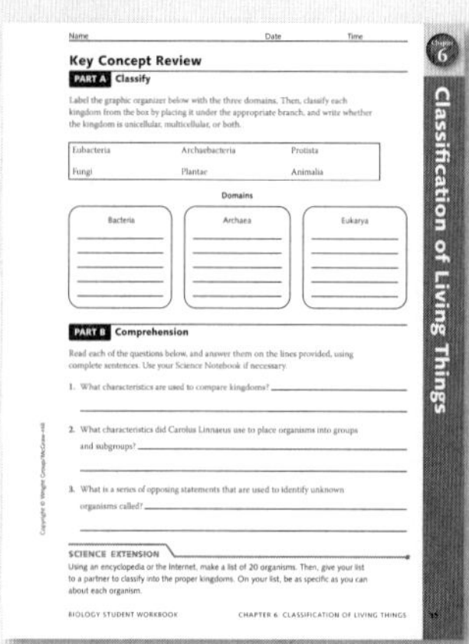
Key Concept Review Workbook, p. 35

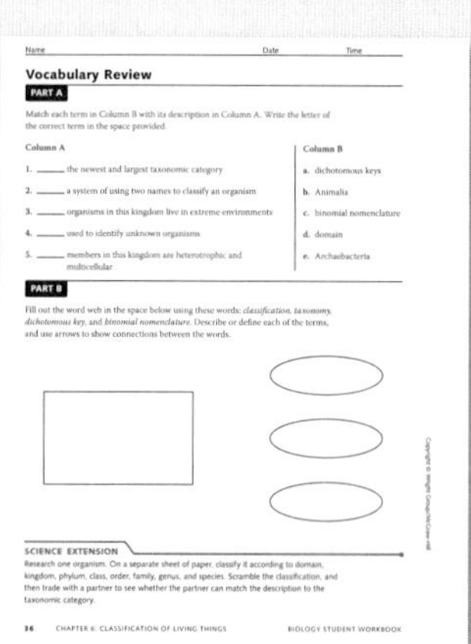
Vocabulary Review Workbook, p. 36

MASTERING CONCEPTS

True or False

If the statement is true, write "true." If it is false, change the underlined word or words to make the statement true.

1. A scientist who works to identify, classify, and name organisms practices taxonomy.
2. New organisms can often be classified by selecting statements from a domain key.
3. A genus is a group of related classes.
4. Binomial nomenclature is a two-word system of naming organisms.
5. A multicellular eukaryotic organism belongs in the kingdom Protista if it is heterotrophic and its cells do not have cell walls.
6. Many members of the kingdom Eubacteria are heterotrophic eukaryotes that feed on dead and decaying organic matter.

Short Answer

Answer each of the following in a sentence or brief paragraph.

7. Explain why taxonomy is important to biologists.
8. Why is Linnaeus often called the Father of Taxonomy?
9. Describe the levels of classification in Linnaeus's system.
10. A bird known as the white ibis has the scientific name *Eudocimus albus.* Identify the information provided by its name.
11. How do members of the domain Eukarya differ from members of the other two domains?
12. Explain why classification systems are updated as scientists learn new information about organisms.

Critical Thinking

Use what you have learned in this chapter to answer each of the following.

13. **Compare and Contrast** How is modern taxonomy different from early taxonomy? How is it similar?
14. **Infer** The structure of the chromosomes of two organisms is very similar. What is probably true about the relationship between the organisms?
15. **Apply Concepts** Why might a classification system be described as organization by elimination?

Standardized Test Question

Choose the letter of the response that correctly answers the question.

	Northern Red Oak	American Chestnut	Southern Red Oak
Kingdom	Plantae	Plantae	Plantae
Phylum	Anthophyta	Anthophyta	Anthophyta
Class	Dicotyledones	Dicotyledones	Dicotyledones
Order	Fagales	Fagales	Fagales
Family	Fagaceae	Fagaceae	Fagaceae
Genus	*Quercus*	*Castanea*	*Quercus*
Species	*Q. rubra*	*C. dentata*	*Q. falcata*

16. According to the table, which trees are most closely related?
    - A. Northern Red Oak and American Chestnut
    - B. Northern Red Oak and Southern Red Oak
    - C. American Chestnut and Southern Red Oak
    - D. all of these

Test-Taking Tip

If "all of these" is one of the choices in a multiple-choice question, be sure that none of the choices is false.

11. Members of Eukarya are eukaryotes, which means they have a membrane-bound nucleus and organelles that the other domains lack.
12. As new discoveries are made and technology is improved, scientists learn more about organisms and sometimes find that organisms have differences that make it impractical to classify them together. For example, organisms now known as Archaea were found to have a chemical composition that is quite different from bacteria.

Critical Thinking

13. Both systems were designed to give living things unique names. Early taxonomists used many observations about organisms in their names and did not have one agreed upon name for each species. Modern taxonomists use a two-word system of latinized names that are standard and agreed upon by all.
14. The organisms are probably closely related and share a common ancestor.
15. As the items are organized into groups and subgroups, only those that are similar stay together. Those that are different are eliminated at each level.

Standardized Test Question

16. B

Reading Links

One Night in the Coral Sea

Through beautiful illustrations and interesting information, this book introduces the reader to the incredible diversity of species in the Great Barrier Reef. It also examines the coral's life cycle.

Collard, Sneed B., III. Illustrated by Robin Brickman. Charlesbridge Publishing. 32 pp. Trade ISBN 1-57091-389-7.

Lizards (Animal Ways)

This introduction to lizards outlines the lizard "family tree," lizard biology, and the different ecological niches of the suborder Sauria. The book also provides information about unusual lizard species.

Greenberg, Dan. Illustrated with prints and photographs. Benchmark Books/Marshall Cavendish. 112 pp. Library ISBN 0-7614-1580-7.

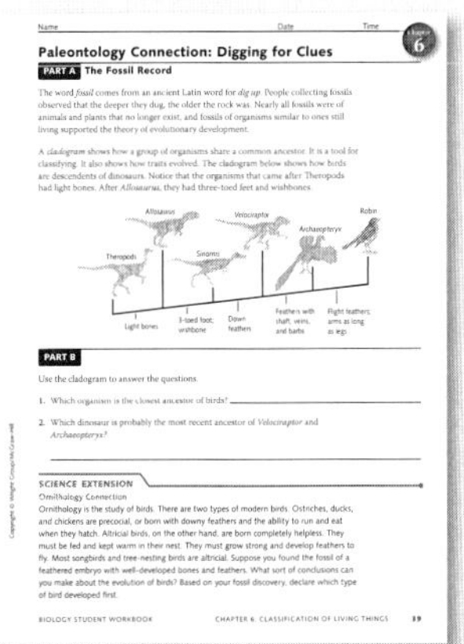

Paleontology Connection: Digging for Clues

PART A The Fossil Record

Curriculum Connection Workbook, p. 39

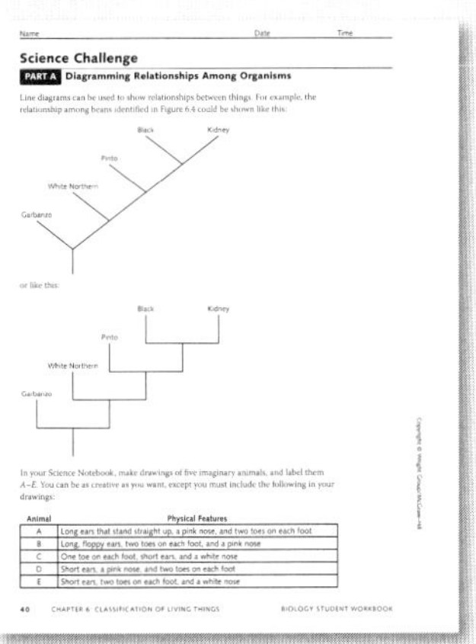

Science Challenge

PART A Diagramming Relationships Among Organisms

Science Challenge Workbook, pp. 40–41

6A Classifying Screws and Bolts

This prechapter introduction activity is designed to determine what students already know about the classification of living things by engaging them in examining, comparing, contrasting, and arranging familiar objects into groups according to similarities.

Objectives

- compare and contrast a variety of screws and bolts
- use observed similarities to divide the objects into groups
- record data in a suitable way
- communicate conclusions

Planning

 1 class period 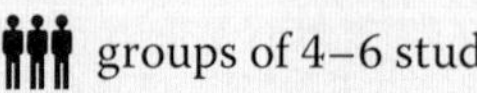

groups of 4–6 students

Materials (per group)

- Ten or more screws and bolts of differing sizes, head types, threading, and usage (You can purchase these items at a hardware store, ask the industrial arts teacher to make a "contribution," or encourage students to bring a variety of them to class.)
- pencil and paper

Advance Preparation

- Choose as many unique screws and bolts as possible. Here are some suggestions: wood screw, machine screw, automotive screw, flat-head screw, round-head screw, pan-head screw, slotted head screw, Phillips head screw, round bolt, square-head bolt, hex-head bolt, eye bolt.
- Place the screws and bolts in a container, making sure there are no two exactly alike in a collection. Remind students that the objects need to be returned at the end of the activity unless you have given them permission to use them in their poster displays.

Engagement Guide

- Challenge students to think about how they can classify a collection of objects such as screws and bolts by asking:
    - *What characteristics will be most helpful in dividing the objects into groups?* (those that show how the objects are alike and different)
    - *Do you think the classification systems of all groups in the class will be the same? Explain your answer.* (Students should recognize that the characteristics used by each group to classify the screws and bolts might not be the same, so the classification systems will differ. Explain to the students that this happens in the scientific world in the same manner.)
- Encourage students to communicate their conclusions in creative ways.

Going Further

- Encourage students to repeat this activity using other objects, such as leaves, seeds, shells, bugs, buttons, trees, or any objects they obtain your permission to use. Have students present their conclusions to the class.
- Ask the students to choose a screw that is the most ancient or old-looking based on its design. Challenge them to create a history ("family tree") of the screws beginning with the "ancient" screw. Have them try to show how the screws have evolved. Ask students questions that will help them think of where to put the screws in relationship to each other. Ask: *How closely related are these two screws? How close together would you put them on the tree?*

6B Using a Dichotomous Key to Identify Vertebrates

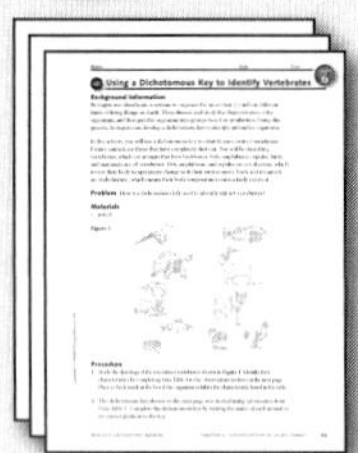

Objectives

- interpret diagrams
- categorize data
- compare and contrast extinct vertebrates
- apply data to a dichotomous key

Skill Set

observing, comparing and contrasting, recording and analyzing data, classifying, stating conclusions

Planning

 1 class period 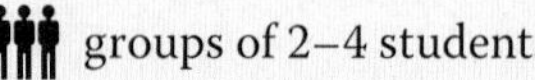

groups of 2–4 students

Materials

Materials for this activity are listed in the Student Laboratory Manual.

Answers to Observations: Data Table

Round Island boa: scales, ecto, lungs; Palestinian painted frog: forelegs, hind legs, smooth skin, ecto, lungs; Oregon bison: forelegs, hind legs, horns, hair, endo, lungs; New Zealand grayling: fins, scales, ecto, gills; domed tortoise: forelegs, hind legs, scales, ecto, lungs; dodo: wings, hind legs, feathers, endo, lungs; Utah Lake sculpin: fins, scales, ecto, gills; Texas red wolf: forelegs, hind legs, hair, endo, lungs; passenger pigeon: wings, feathers, hind legs, endo, lungs; Eastern elk: forelegs, hind legs, horns, hair, endo, lungs

Answers to Observations: Dichotomous Key

3a. passenger pigeon; **3b.** dodo; **4b.** Texas red wolf; **5a.** Eastern elk; **5b.** Oregon bison; **7a.** Utah Lake sculpin; **7b.** New Zealand grayling; **8b.** Palestinian painted frog; **9a.** domed tortoise; **9b.** Round Island boa

Answers to Analysis and Conclusions

1. Amphibians have smooth skin and live part of their lives in water and part on land. Reptiles have scales and live only on land. Fish are ectothermic and all live in water and have gills, fins, and scales; birds are endothermic and most live on land and have wings, feathers, and lungs.
2. Birds: passenger pigeon, dodo; Mammals: Texas red wolf, Eastern elk, Oregon bison
3. reptiles and amphibians
4. Mammals; endothermic, lungs, and have hair.
5. They organize living things into groups based on similarities and can be used to identify unfamiliar living things.

Going Further

- Bring in a selection of leaves, and ask students to identify them using their dichotomous keys or those of their classmates. If collecting leaves is not safe or easy for students to do, you can use shells, buttons, or pasta instead.
- Have students select 10 to 12 leaves of different shapes, sizes, colors, and vein patterns. Have them develop a classification key for their leaves and share it with the class.
- Have students make their own dichotomous key based on the example from the lab. This is easily done if they have at least five objects. This can be done with writing utensils, leaves, buttons, etc.

6C Using a Classification Key to Identify Chemical Substances

Objectives

- use chemical reactions to classify substances
- record observations
- use data to develop a dichotomous key

Skill Set

measuring, observing, comparing and contrasting, recording and analyzing data, classifying, stating conclusions

Planning

1 class period (Additional time may be needed to construct the classification key.)

 groups of 2–4 students

Materials

Materials for this activity are listed in the Student Laboratory Manual.

Lab Tips

- Even when they are wearing safety goggles, students should be cautioned about how carefully and slowly solvents are added to solutes to prevent spills due to chemical reactions.
- As you walk around the classroom, ask students what they see happening in each cup to help them to write better observations.

Advance Preparation

To make the dilute iodine solution, dissolve 10 g of potassium iodide in 500 mL of distilled water and stir until completely dissolved. Add 2 g of iodine crystals to the solution and stir until completely dissolved. Store the solution in a dark bottle. To dilute, prepare a 1:1 dilution with distilled water. For example, add 50 mL of iodine solution to 50 mL of distilled water.

Answers: Classification Key

Classification keys will vary. However, all keys should illustrate use of the test results to group the powders according to similarities until one property (test result) sets each powder apart from the others. The key should be useful in identifying additional powders that are unfamiliar.

Answers to Observations: Data Table 1

Powdered chalk: not soluble in water, foams in vinegar, no reaction with iodine solution; powdered sugar: soluble in water, does not foam in vinegar, no reaction with iodine solution; talcum powder: not soluble in water, does not foam in vinegar, no reaction with iodine solution; baking soda: soluble in water, foams in vinegar, no reaction with iodine solution; baking powder: soluble in water, foams in water, foams in vinegar, no reaction with iodine solution; cornstarch: not soluble in water, does not foam in vinegar, turns blue-black with iodine solution

Answers to Analysis and Conclusions

1. The properties that were helpful were their reactions with other substances to form solutions or new substances.
2. No, neither color nor state would be a useful property because all six powders are white solids.
3. Powdered sugar, baking soda, and baking powder dissolved in water.
4. Baking powder reacted with water. Bubbles were released, so a chemical reaction occurred.
5. Powdered chalk, baking soda, and baking powder reacted with vinegar. Only cornstarch reacted with iodine solution.
6. Answers will vary but should include the idea of selecting various properties based on the test results by which to group the powders. The key is developed by narrowing each group down to a single powder by describing properties that the powder does or does not possess.

Going Further

- Have students use each other's keys to figure out what solid each cup contains. Then have the groups critique each other's keys.
- Have students construct a classification key for items in a supermarket. Have them compare their classification keys with those of their classmates.

Unit 2

Case Study 1: Where Is Linnaeus When We Need Him?

Gather More Information

Encourage students to use the library or the NSTA SciLinks Web site noted at the start of each chapter to learn more about these case study topics and to conduct further research.

Have students use the following keywords to aid their searches:

- Carolus Linnaeus
- classification of living things
- discovery of new species
- binomial nomenclature
- taxonomy
- ZooBank

Research the Big Picture

- Have each student identify and research a species that has been discovered within the last five years. Each student should prepare a fact sheet about his or her species, including the following information: scientific name and classification; where and when it was discovered and by whom; and the significance of the discovery. The fact sheets should also include general species characteristics and, if possible, photographs or illustrations.
- Have students work in pairs to investigate the numbers of new species discovered each year over the last ten years. Of these, have students determine how many are eubacteria, archaebacteria, fungi, protists, plants, and animals. Ask students to determine the best method of presenting their results, and then create graphical data displays.
- As a class, discuss why new species are still being discovered. Ask students whether, based on their findings, they believe the rate of new species discovery will increase or decrease.

SCIENCE JOURNAL

Where Is Linnaeus When We Need Him?

IN THE 1700S, the scientist Carolus Linnaeus created a system to organize the many new species being discovered. His system is still used today. Linnaeus believed that there were fewer than 15,000 species of plants and animals on Earth. If he were alive today, he would be amazed that more than 2.5 million species have been identified!

The Problem: Keeping Track of Millions of New Species Names

Believe it or not, scientists have not yet named all of the living things on Earth. Better technology and increased funding for research have led to an increase in the number of species being discovered each year. However, there is a problem—scientists do not have a central place to record the name of every new species that is discovered. Without a central place to record the names and information about new species, important information may be lost.

Solutions to the Naming Problem

Recently, a group of scientists suggested a solution to the naming problem. They created a Web-based tool called ZooBank. One goal of ZooBank is to create a complete record of the scientific names of animals. This is something that does not yet exist. It will be a long, difficult project. There is also no such record of scientific plant names, fungi names, or protist names. Although scientists agree that a naming system is needed, they disagree about who should control the system. They also disagree about how it should work.

There are many ideas about how to best track and name new species. They include BioCode, uBio, the ALL Species Foundation, Wikispecies, Species 2000, the Electronic Catalogue of Names of Known Organisms, the Taxome Project, and many more. Each approaches the listing and naming of species in a different way. It will be a challenge to develop a system that works for all scientists.

Research and Report

With a partner, research ZooBank and a few of the other projects mentioned in the article. Then come up with your own system to help scientists keep track of new species names and other important species information. Describe how your system works. What are its advantages and disadvantages? Create a poster with your information.

CAREER CONNECTION Genetic Engineer

DID YOU EVER WONDER if there is a way to make food healthier, tastier, and easier to grow? Genetic engineers do this for a living. They create plants that produce more food. They also make fruits and vegetables that ripen faster and stay fresh longer. They are even researching ways to make vegetables that contain vaccines and pigs that lower our cholesterol!

Charles Darwin observed that plants and animals change over time through variation and adaptation. But genetic engineers don't have to wait thousands of years for organisms to change. They can alter the genes of organisms to create new plants and animals with desired traits. This process is called genetic engineering.

Farmers and scientists have used a type of genetic engineering called hybridization since the 1800s. To make a hybrid plant, one type of plant is fertilized using pollen from another type of plant. The new plant that grows

120

Case Study 2: New Newt Species Raises Difficult Questions

Gather More Information

Encourage students to use the library or the NSTA SciLinks Web site noted at the start of each chapter to learn more about these case study topics and to conduct further research.

Have students use the following keywords to aid their searches:

- endangered species protection
- exotic pet
- Laos warty newt
- salamander
- pet trade

Research the Big Picture

- Convene a mock panel to decide the fate of the Laos warty newt in the pet trade. Assign students roles as stakeholders, including pet owners, scientific researchers, conservation officials, pet

New Newt Species Raises Difficult Questions

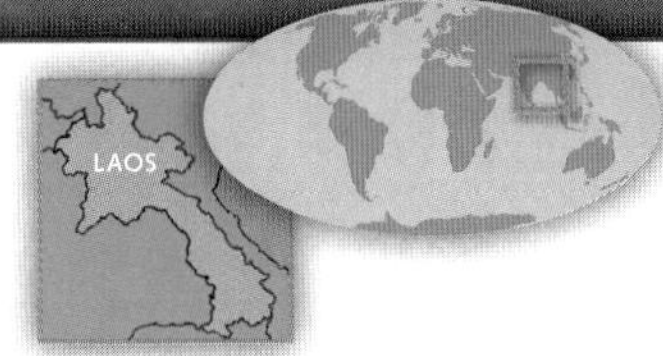

IT IS NOT every day that scientists find a new species that people want as a pet. When they do, it can lead to trouble.

In 1999, a researcher in the Southeast Asian country of Laos made an exciting discovery. Living in certain wet places were strange, colorful new animals that no one had seen before. They were newts, or salamanders, but they looked very different from any other type of newt. Scientists have named them Laos warty newts, but there is still a lot to learn about the species.

This new newt looks like a black lizard and can fit in your hand. Like other newts in its genus, it has stumpy legs, a long tail, a head shaped like a triangle, and warts on its skin. The Laos warty newt has something special, though, that helps it survive. It has bright yellow stripes down its dark back, and the skin of its belly has a pattern almost like a leopard's coat.

The bold colors and patterns are not just for decoration. These warty newts live in bright, shallow streams. They can swim around during the day and at night because they blend in with their habitat. This makes them hard for predators to see.

Now that people know they exist, the Laos warty newts have new predators who hunt them for their colors—people. In 2002, scientists published a paper about the new species, which is known as *Paramesotriton laoensis*. Just a few years later, the bright newts were being sold as pets!

Scientists are worried that the pet trade could be a big problem for the Laos warty newt. If pet dealers take away too many newts or disrupt their habitat, scientists might not be able to study them. Not enough is known yet about these animals to add them to the endangered species list. Scientists need to learn more about the newts before they can be legally protected.

The case of the Laos warty newt raises a difficult question. When scientists discover a species that people might want for a pet, should they publish their findings as they normally would? Or should they keep their discoveries private until the species can be protected? Perhaps governments could create laws to protect new species as soon as they are announced to the world.

The Laos warty newts are so rare and have such an unusual look that they have been sold for as much as $170 each.

from the resulting seed is a hybrid. This means it has some DNA from each type of plant. Most of the corn and apples we eat today come from hybrid plants.

Since the 1950s, genetic engineers have been altering genes using a more exact method. They select a single gene that is the "code" for a desired trait. They then insert that gene into an organism's DNA. This kind of genetic engineering has been used to make rice plants that produce more grain and corn plants that repel damaging caterpillars. It has also been used to grow tomatoes with thick skins that make them easier to store and transport. Genetic engineers today also work with the genes of animals.

In recent years, some people have worried that foods from plants and animals whose genes were altered might not be safe to eat. However, the U.S. Food and Drug Administration (FDA) requires that all of these foods be tested for safety before they are sold.

Because of discoveries about DNA, it is an exciting time to work in a genetic engineering lab. Genetic engineers are creative thinkers who are excited about science. They usually have advanced experience and doctoral degrees. Lab assistants, who usually have a bachelor's degree, help genetic engineers with their research.

121

dealers, and local citizens and businesspeople. Before the discussion, ask each student to imagine his or her stakeholder's position and write a one-paragraph profile. Then, encourage the panel to work together to develop a plan for the warty newt that could also govern other newly discovered exotic pets. Remind students that additional research could be part of the plan.

- Have students work in small groups to research other animals in the international pet trade. Have each group identify a type of exotic animal kept as a pet and report back to the class. Have students find out the conditions of its capture and care, whether the animal is rare or endangered, and how demand for the animal in the pet trade has affected the population of the species in the wild. As part of their oral presentation, groups should judge whether their animal should be kept as a pet and explain their decision.
- As an extension, have students conduct a survey of exotic pet ownership in your school or community. Have students identify the number of families that keep exotic pets, find out how the pets were obtained, and record their experiences.

CONNECTION: Career

Have students summarize the information in the feature in the form of a time line in their Science Notebooks. Discuss why a career as a genetic engineer might be more relevant and important today than ever before. Students might cite new DNA discoveries and also new challenges in feeding a growing world population and in keeping food supplies safe.

Challenge each student to produce one question or problem that might be solved by work in genetic engineering. Then, have each student write a paragraph describing some of the issues he or she would confront in solving it. Conclude by having students share their paragraphs.

Unit 3

Introduce Unit 3

Ask a volunteer to read the unit title aloud. Then, have students look at the photos on this page. Ask: *What do the photos show you about these organisms?* Invite students to share any experiences with viewing these organisms, either with a microscope or with the unaided eye. As students read the unit, ask them to identify the kingdoms and the distinguishing characteristics of these of these organisms in their Science Notebooks.

Unit Projects

For each project below, students can use the Student Presentation Builder on the Student CD-ROM to display their results and their Science Notebooks for their project notes.

Career Have each student research a career that involves working with microorganisms or fungi (e.g., medical lab technician, microbiologist, mycologist) and then write a job description for the career. The job description should include the name of a potential employer, the required education and experience, the types of tasks that will be involved, and an explanation of why an understanding of microorganisms and/or fungi is required. Post finished descriptions on a "job board" in the classroom.

Apply Have students look for fungi over several days and write down every instance they identify (e.g., mushrooms in grocery stores, molds on lawns, lichen on rocks or walls, bread mold, baker's yeast, toadstools). Encourage students to sketch fungi examples in their Science Notebooks and note where they were found. Have students share their findings with the class.

Technology Discuss why technology is necessary to the study of microorganisms. Then, have groups of students identify problems that scientists working in microbiology or fungal research are trying to solve, as well as the technologies they are using. Each group should identify one research problem and describe the task and the technology to the class.

Unit 3

Microorganisms and Fungi

Chapter 7 **Viruses and Bacteria**

What are viruses and bacteria, and how do they affect humans and the environment?

Chapter 8 **Protists and Fungi**

What are the characteristics of these diverse groups of organisms, and what is their role in the world?

Software Summary

Student CD-ROM
—Interactive Student Book
—Vocabulary Review
—Key Concept Review
—Lab Report Template
—ELL Preview and Writing Activities
—Presentation Digital Library
—Graphic Organizing Software
—Spanish Cognate Dictionary

Interactive Labs
Chapter 7C—Preventing the Spread of Infectious Diseases

Viruses and Bacteria

KEY CONCEPT Viruses and bacteria share many common characteristics and impact humans and the environment.

Imagine spending the day at a nature preserve. Some animals and plants would be more familiar to you than others. Now imagine that you have the ability to see microscopic objects. You would surely be surprised by all the viruses and bacteria that inhabit the nature preserve! There are viruses and bacteria in the air, water, and soil. You would even see them on and in your body.

Think About Viruses and Bacteria

You know that viruses and bacteria are often responsible for making people sick. But viruses and bacteria do much more than that!

- In your Science Notebook, make a T-chart. Label one column *Disease* and the other *Cause*. Think about diseases that you have had or that you know about and list them in the first column. In the second column, predict the cause of each disease. Is the disease caused by a virus or by a bacterium?
- Can you think of ways in which viruses and bacteria affect you or the environment positively and negatively? Make a second T-chart with columns labeled *Positive Impact* and *Negative Impact*. Write your ideas in the appropriate columns.

www.scilinks.org
Bacteria **Code: WGB07A**
Viruses **Code: WGB07B**

Chapter 7 Planning Guide			
Instructional Periods	**National Standards**	**Lab Manual**	**Workbook**
7.1 2 periods	A.1, A.2, C.1, C.2, E.1, F.1, G.1; B.6, C.3, C.4, E.1, F.1, F.5, G.1; UCP.5	**Lab 7A—p. 38** Got Bacteria? **Lab 7B—p. 39** Using a Dichotomous Key to Identify Bacteria **Lab 7C—p. 42** Preventing the Spread of Infectious Diseases	Key Concept Review p. 42 Vocabulary Review p. 43 Interpreting Diagrams p. 44 Reading Comprehension p. 45 Curriculum Connection p. 46 Science Challenge p. 47
7.2 2 periods	A.2, B.3, C.1, C.2, C.4, F.1, G.1, G.3; C.1, C.5, F.1, G.1, G.3; UCP.1, UCP.2, UCP.3		

Middle School Standard; High School Standard; Unifying Concept and Principle

Chapter 7 Lessons

Introduce Chapter 7

As a starting activity, use LAB 7A Got Bacteria? on page 38 of the Laboratory Manual.

ENGAGE Ask each student to form a mental picture of a nature preserve, populated with a variety of living things. This could be from the ocean, a rain forest, a savannah, or a desert. Remind students to picture both animals and plants in the scene. Now, ask them to "zoom in" on one of the living things. Ask students to imagine what the living thing looks like up close. Tell them that in this chapter, they will be learning about the tiniest organisms that inhabit Earth: bacteria and viruses.

Think About Viruses and Bacteria

ENGAGE Students' familiarity with viruses and bacteria probably relates to disease. First, find out how much they know about disease-causing organisms by having them work in pairs to create the first T-chart. Create a class T-chart using their responses. You will probably find that there are differing opinions about the causes of diseases. You might want to return to this class chart after you complete the chapter.

Introduce the idea that not all viruses and bacteria have negative effects on other living things and the environment. Ask students if they know about making cheese or yogurt. Encourage them to complete the second T-chart as best they can. Tell them they will have an opportunity to modify their charts at the end of the chapter.

7.1 Introduce

EXPLORE Have students form groups of three or four. Give a meterstick to each group. Have students examine their metersticks and identify the size of a centimeter and millimeter.

Next, tell students to visualize (or possibly try) dividing the millimeter line into 1,000 smaller units. Tell them to think of dividing one of those units into 1,000 smaller units. The resulting units would be the correct size for measuring viruses.

Then, ask students to suggest how this activity explains why the discovery of viruses was so difficult.

Before You Read

Model the biopoem on the board. For the *r* in virus, write *reproduces*. Tell students to complete the poem for the other letters. Check student poems throughout the lesson.

Vocabulary terms are listed on the first student page of each lesson. You may wish to preview the terms before introducing each lesson. Strategies for teaching the vocabulary appear on the pages where the terms are introduced.

Teach

EXPLAIN to students that viruses are different from living things. Ask students to identify the characteristics shared by all living things, and write their responses on the board. (Answers: made up of cells, sense and respond to stimuli, adapt to their environment, reproduce, and use energy to grow and develop) Ask students if viruses possess any of these characteristics.

Use the Visual: Figure 7.1

ANSWER Viruses invade living cells in order to reproduce.

Science Notebook EXTRA

Encourage students to use the vocabulary section they created in their Science Notebooks. Remind them to record prefixes, suffixes, and root words to help remember the meanings of vocabulary terms.

Learning Goals

- Describe a virus.
- Explain how viruses reproduce.
- Identify ways in which viruses affect the world.

New Vocabulary

virus
host
parasite
lytic cycle
lysogenic cycle

7.1 Viruses

Before You Read

In your Science Notebook, write the word *virus* vertically down the left side of the page. Create a "biopoem" using words or phrases that you predict will describe a virus. Use the letters in the word *virus* to begin each of your descriptive words or phrases.

You could probably write a movie script in which the bad guys sneak into an airport, take control of it, and then run it for their own benefit. Fortunately, the hero in your movie would probably find a way to regain control of the airport and save the day. A similar scenario occurs thousands of times a day as viruses invade living cells and hijack their operations.

What Is a Virus?

Sitting on a desk, viruses are no more "alive" than your pencil or textbook. But just like the bad guys in your movie script, when a virus connects with the right type of cell, it sneaks in, takes control, and runs the cell for its own benefit. In the photos of viruses in **Figure 7.1**, each virus has found the right type of cell and has taken control of it. A **virus** is a nonliving particle that invades and uses parts of a cell to reproduce itself and distribute more viruses.

Living or Nonliving? A virus does not exhibit the characteristics of living things because it is not made of cells and it does not have the cell structures that carry out the basic functions of an organism. The only way in which viruses resemble living things is in their ability to reproduce. However, they can only reproduce by using a cell. The living cells used by viruses to reproduce are called **hosts**. Hosts provide a home and energy for a parasite. A **parasite** (PER uh site) is an organism that lives on or in a host and does harm to it. Viruses act like parasites because they harm the host cell, often destroying it.

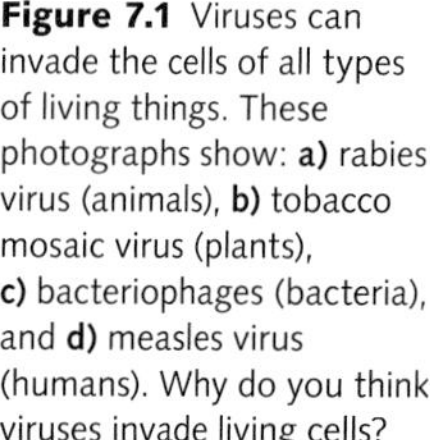

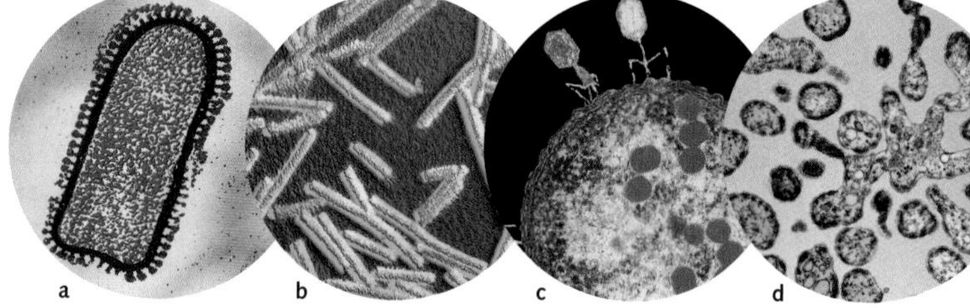

Figure 7.1 Viruses can invade the cells of all types of living things. These photographs show: **a)** rabies virus (animals), **b)** tobacco mosaic virus (plants), **c)** bacteriophages (bacteria), and **d)** measles virus (humans). Why do you think viruses invade living cells?

Vocabulary

virus Tell students that *virus* is derived from the Latin word *vīrus*, meaning "poison."

host Encourage students to think of common uses of *host*. Students might mention a restaurant host, a computer host, or a talk show host.

parasite Explain that the prefix *para-* is Greek and means "alongside of." The root *site* is from the Greek word *sitos*, meaning "food." Ask students to explain why this is an appropriate name for viruses.

ELL Strategy

Think, Pair, Share Ask each student to write a sentence or two describing how the words *virus*, *host*, and *parasite* are related. Have students read their sentences to partners. Ask pairs of students to illustrate and label a virus, host, and parasite and to share their illustrations with the class.

Naming Viruses Because viruses are not living things, they are not classified and named like other organisms. A virus may be named for the disease it causes. The rabies virus infects nerve cells in animals and causes rabies. Some viruses, such as the tobacco mosaic virus, are named for the first host they infect and the type of damage they cause. Others are named for the place where the virus was first found or the scientist who first identified it. The deadly Ebola virus was named for the Ebola River in the Democratic Republic of Congo in Africa, where it was first identified.

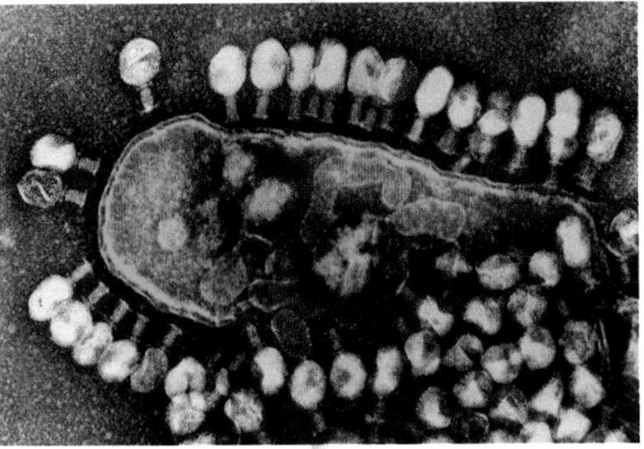

Figure 7.2 This bacterial cell is being attacked by a number of viruses called bacteriophages—viruses that attack only bacteria cells. What is the host for a bacteriophage?

Structure of Viruses Although viruses vary in size and shape, they all share the same basic structure. A virus contains a core of genetic material surrounded by a protective protein coat. The genetic material in a virus contains instructions for making copies of the virus after it invades the host. The genetic material can be the nucleic acid DNA or RNA.

The arrangement of proteins in a virus's protective coat determines the shape of the virus. It also plays a role in determining which type of cell the virus can invade. The arrangement of proteins in the protein coat creates a unique shape that allows the virus to recognize and attach to a matching spot on its host cell. Like puzzle pieces that fit together perfectly, the protein coat of the virus snaps into place on the host cell, and the invasion of the host cell begins.

As You Read

Use what you have learned in this lesson so far to add to or correct the information in your "biopoem."

How do these characteristics compare with your predictions?

Figure 7.3 The protein coat of each of these viruses has a specific shape that determines the type of cell to which the virus can attach. Once attached, the virus can invade the cell with its genetic core.

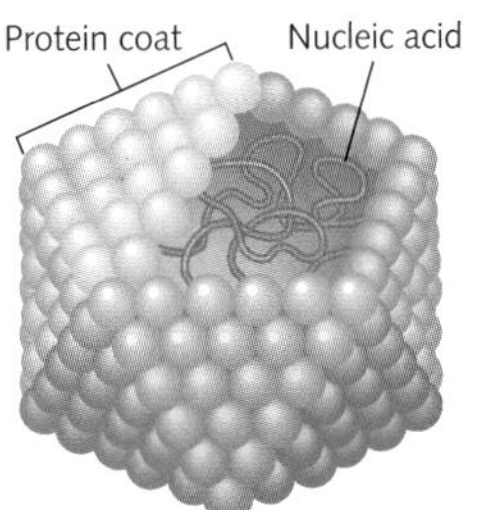

Polyhedral viruses, such as the papilloma virus that causes warts, resemble small crystals.

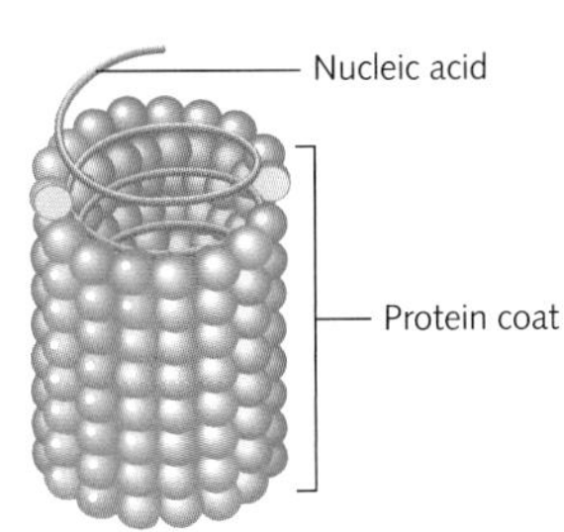

The tobacco mosaic virus has a long, narrow helical shape.

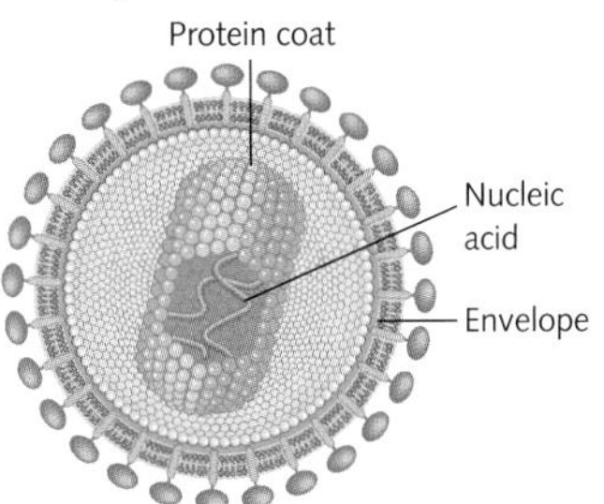

An envelope studded with projections covers some viruses, including the AIDS-causing virus.

Teach

EXPLAIN that students will read about the structure of viruses and the way they are named. A virus can be named for the disease it carries, for where it was found, or for the scientist who identified it. All viruses contain a core of genetic material surrounded by a protein coat. The shapes and sizes of various types of viruses differ.

EXPLORE Provide students with a variety of materials and supplies—construction paper, pipe cleaners, straws, tape, glue, foil, scissors, paper clips, string, rubber bands—to use in designing and building a virus and a host cell. Remind students that their designs for viruses should include a protein coat and a genetic core.

After students have constructed their viruses, use interlocking puzzle pieces to visually demonstrate how the protein coat creates a unique shape that matches its host cell. Then, have students check to see if the host cells they constructed to match the exchanged viruses fit in the same way.

EXTEND Provide students with the following list of viruses. Ask them to hypothesize the origin of each virus name.

Epstein-Barr: named for the scientists who discovered it

Chicken Pox: named for the type of damage

Kissing Disease (mononucleosis): named for the way it may be transmitted

Rhinovirus (common cold): named for the way it is transmitted (*rhino-* means "nose")

Use the Visual: Figure 7.2

ANSWER A bacteriophage is a virus that invades bacteria, so the host is a bacterium.

As You Read

Ask students to return to the word poems they made in their Science Notebooks. Give students a few minutes to review their original poems and to revise them based on what they have read and learned. Ask for volunteers to share any changes they have made to their poems.

Teacher Alert

Students may think that AIDS (acquired immunodeficiency syndrome) is a virus. AIDS is actually a disease of the immune system caused by infection with the retrovirus HIV (human immunodeficiency virus). HIV severely damages the immune system by destroying certain white blood cells; it can be transmitted through blood or certain bodily fluids.

Differentiated Instruction

Musical Encourage students to create a short song or rap to accompany the *virus* poems in their Science Notebooks. They can use background music from existing songs and write their own verses, or musically inclined students can write the music, as well. Digital sound mixing and editing software can be incorporated.

Teach

EXPLAIN to students that they will learn about how viruses reproduce. Tell students that there are two different cycles of infection and reproduction: the lytic cycle and the lysogenic cycle.

Vocabulary

lytic cycle Tell students that the word *lytic* comes from the Greek word *lyein*, which means "to break down." During this cycle, a virus injects its genetic material into a host cell. The genetic material enters the nucleus and is inserted into that cell's DNA. The cell immediately begins to produce the viral protein coats and nucleic acids that make up viruses. Eventually the cell explodes, or "breaks down," releasing more viruses.

lysogenic cycle Explain to students that the lysogenic cycle for virus infection and reproduction is similar to the lytic cycle, but reproduction is delayed in the lysogenic cycle.

Explain It!

Ask students how computer viruses are spread from computer to computer. Answers will vary but may include email, software, and document sharing. Tell students to reflect on how computer viruses are spread and how the virus can affect the computer. Have students compare viruses and computer viruses in their Science Notebooks.

Figure It Out: Figure 7.4

ANSWER **1.** attachment, entry, replication, assembly, and release **2.** The lytic and lysogenic cycles are similar because the host cell is used to produce new virus particles and is destroyed in the process. The cycles differ because the virus has an immediate effect on the host in a lytic cycle, while in the lysogenic cycle, the virus is incorporated into the host cell's genetic material but remains inactive for a period of time.

Did You Know?

The word *reproduce* is commonly used when discussing viruses, but in the strictest sense, viruses do not reproduce. Viruses use the machinery of the host cell to replicate themselves by creating an exact copy of the virus, just as a copy machine is used to replicate a document. Whatever you call it, however, the result is the same: viruses multiply!

Explain It!

Once a computer virus infects a machine, the virus can spread to other disks, programs, and even other computers. In your Science Notebook, explain why the term *virus* is a good description of these computer invaders.

Figure It Out

1. What are the steps in a lytic cycle?
2. Compare and contrast a lytic cycle and a lysogenic cycle.

Reproduction of Viruses

The structure of viruses allows them to succeed in their main mission—reproduction.

Lytic Cycle Once attached to a host cell, a virus injects its nucleic acid into the cell. The nucleic acid takes over the normal operation of the host cell and produces multiple copies of the virus's protein coat and nucleic acid. Once produced, the protein coats and the nucleic acids are assembled into new viruses. As the host cell fills with newly assembled viruses, it bursts, just like a balloon with too much air. The host cell then dies, and the released viruses begin searching for the next host cell. This type of viral reproduction is called a **lytic** (LIT ihk) **cycle**. The steps of a lytic cycle for a bacteriophage are illustrated in **Figure 7.4**.

Lysogenic Cycle Some viruses, such as herpes and HIV, enter the host cell but remain hidden for years. Even though the viral nucleic acid becomes part of the host cell's chromosome, it does not seem to affect the functions of the cell. At some point, however, the viral nucleic acid becomes active. It separates itself from the host cell's genetic material, takes over the functions of the cell to produce new viruses, and destroys the host cell as the new viruses are released. This type of viral reproduction is called a **lysogenic** (li suh JE nihk) **cycle**. The steps of a lysogenic cycle are also shown in **Figure 7.4**.

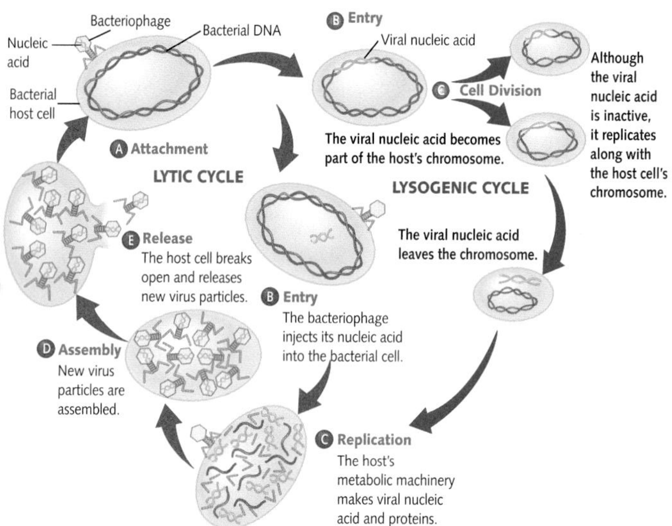

Figure 7.4 In a lytic cycle (red arrows), the virus uses the host cell's organelles to make new viruses. In a lysogenic cycle (blue arrows), the virus "hides" in the host cell's chromosome until it becomes active and uses the host cell's organelles to reproduce.

Background Information

The lytic cycle has five stages:

(1) Attachment: The virus attaches to the cell wall at a receptor site. (2) Entry: Viral enzymes weaken the cell wall, and the DNA of the virus is injected into the host cell. (3) Replication: The viral DNA replaces the DNA of the host cell and takes over, making viral proteins and viral nucleic acid. (4) Assembly: Viral protein coats are assembled with the nucleic acids and fill the cell with new virus particles. (5) Release: Enzymes dissolve the host cell membrane from inside the cell. The cell bursts open, and the newly formed virus particles are released.

The lysogenic cycle is the same as the lytic cycle, with one exception. In the lysogenic cycle, the viral nucleic acid becomes part of the host cell's DNA, and the virus can hide, or be dormant, for years. Stimuli that can activate the virus include radiation and chemicals; however, the virus may become active spontaneously.

Viruses in the World

If you have ever had a cold or the flu or a childhood illness such as measles or chicken pox, you know that viruses can make you sick. But did you know that viruses can also protect you from diseases and save your life? As a young child, you received vaccinations (vak suh NAY shunz) made of dead or weakened viruses to protect you against viruses that try to invade your body.

Scientists are also using the ability of viruses to invade cells as a "delivery service" for genetic information that a person needs to treat or cure a disease. In gene therapy, viruses deliver normal genes that replace missing or faulty genes. Although gene therapy is a relatively new medical treatment, doctors are hopeful that it will be used widely in the future.

Viruses also affect plants and other animals. Your pets are vaccinated against diseases such as rabies and distemper to prevent infection by these deadly viruses. Other viruses that infect plants and animals can have an important economic impact. In the 1990s, cattle in Europe were infected with the virus that causes hoof-and-mouth disease. Thousands of animals had to be destroyed to prevent the spread of the disease. This caused a loss of millions of dollars.

Viruses can also be used to control pests that destroy crops used as food. The advantage of treating crops in this way is that it destroys harmful insects without polluting the environment.

European explorers were able to conquer the Americas with small armies because they unknowingly brought with them a powerful weapon—an invisible army of viruses. Native Americans had never been exposed to these viruses, and the deaths caused by mumps, measles, diphtheria, and smallpox allowed the Europeans to defeat even the mighty Aztec empire.

After You Read

1. Review the words and phrases you used in your "biopoem." Correct any of your predictions now that you know more about viruses. Select a title for your poem that you think best describes viruses. Are all viruses harmful? Explain your answer in a well-developed paragraph.
2. Describe the structure of viruses.
3. Compare the two ways in which viruses reproduce.
4. Is a virus a host or a parasite? Explain your answer.

Figure 7.5 These young people are receiving vaccinations for polio. Vaccines protect and save millions of lives. What vaccines have you received?

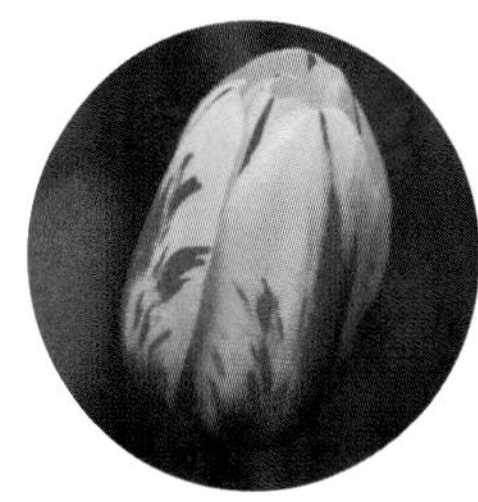

Figure 7.6 The stripes on this tulip were produced by the tulip mosaic virus.

Extend It!

Most schools require students to receive specific vaccinations at specific times before they can enroll or remain in school. Ask your school nurse or other administrator for a list of the vaccinations required by your school. Review the requirements and prepare a chart that shows the vaccination schedule for students in your grade. Why do you think it is important to have this requirement?

Teach

Extend It!

Organize students into groups of three or four. Ask each group to choose one student to participate in an interview group. Have students in each group work together to create a list of questions. Arrange a time for the interview group to talk with the appropriate staff member at your school. These students can then share the information with their original groups to create a vaccination schedule.

CONNECTION: History

Provide students with test tubes of water and pipettes or droppers. Contaminate one student's tube with a drop of yellow food coloring and another student's tube with a drop of blue food coloring. Direct students to use the droppers to exchange water with at least three other people. Then, ask students to examine the color of their water. List the colors on the board, and discuss why there are differences. Discuss the similarities of the activity and the spread of European viruses among Native Americans.

Assess

EVALUATE Use the After You Read questions and the Alternative Assessment to help you assess students' understanding of the lesson.

After You Read

1. Students should be able to justify their titles. Beneficial uses include gene therapy, vaccinations, and crop pest control.
2. a core of genetic material—DNA or RNA—surrounded by a protein coat
3. In a lytic cycle, a virus invades a cell, takes over the host's genetic material, and begins producing new viruses. In a lysogenic cycle, a virus invades a cell and combines its genetic material with the host's, but it does not affect the functioning of the cell for some time.
4. A virus is a parasite because it requires a living cell—the host—to reproduce.

Background Information

Present-day vaccinations for children from birth to five years old include DTaP, hepatitis A, hepatitis B, Hib, influenza, MMR, pneumococcal, polio, and varicella.

Present-day vaccinations recommended for adolescents include hepatitis B; a new tetanus toxoid, reduced diphtheria toxoid, and acellular pertussis vaccine; and meningococcal conjugate vaccine (MCV4).

Alternative Assessment

EVALUATE Struggling readers can draw and label pictures to illustrate the structure of viruses and the lytic and lysogenic cycles.

7.2 Introduce

ENGAGE Tell students that bacteria exist almost everywhere, including the human body. Ask students where they think most bacteria live on or in humans. Record students' hypotheses on the board, and elicit their reasons for choosing those locations.

Then, tell students that there are 128 types of bacteria in the human stomach, as found by researchers at Stanford University in January 2006. Explain that bacteria serve some functions that are necessary for living things to survive; they will learn more as they read and discuss this lesson.

Before You Read

Draw a K-W-L-S-H chart on the board. Tell students that this chart will help them organize their learning throughout the lesson. Ask students to reflect on what they already know about bacteria. Write one or two responses under *K* on the board. Then, ask students to think about what they want to learn about bacteria, and write a few of their questions on the board under *W*. Have students draw their own K-W-L-S-H charts in their Science Notebooks and complete the *K* and *W* columns. Remind students to complete the *L* (learned) column on their charts throughout the lesson.

Teach

EXPLAIN to students that they will gain new understandings of what bacteria are, how they differ from viruses, how they reproduce, and how they impact our world.

Learning Goals

- Describe bacteria.
- Explain how bacteria reproduce.
- Identify how bacteria are important in the world.

New Vocabulary

bacterium
bacillus
coccus
spirillum
flagellum
binary fission
conjugation

7.2 Bacteria

Before You Read

In your Science Notebook, create a K-W-L-S-H chart. Think about the title of this lesson and read the Learning Goals. In the column labeled *K*, write what you already know about bacteria. In the column labeled *W*, write what you want to learn about bacteria.

Bacteria are everywhere. They can live in the saltiest waters on Earth, in hot springs and volcanic vents, in the freezing ice of the arctic, and even on your body. You cannot see or feel them, but bacteria live in your hair, lungs, mouth, stomach, and intestines. They practically cover your skin. They especially like your warm, moist armpits and your sweaty feet.

What Are Bacteria?

Microscopic prokaryotic cells are called **bacteria** (bak TIHR ee uh, singular: bacterium). As discussed in Chapter 3, prokaryotes do not have a membrane-bound nucleus or membrane-bound organelles, and their DNA is not organized into chromosomes.

Living or Nonliving? Even though a bacterium is microscopic and composed of only one cell, it is considered a living thing. Unlike the viruses you studied in Lesson 7.1, bacteria can sense and respond to stimuli, adapt to their environment, reproduce, and use energy to grow and develop. This is similar to the behavior of more complex organisms.

Classifying Bacteria Because bacteria are among the most numerous organisms on Earth, an amazing variety of them exists. Biologists group bacteria into two kingdoms, Archaebacteria and Eubacteria. *Archaebacteria* means "ancient bacteria." Scientists believe that these bacteria resemble Earth's first forms of life. Archaebacteria are often found in very harsh environments. Eubacteria is a much larger group of bacteria, and members of this kingdom are found everywhere that members of Archaebacteria are not. These are the bacteria that are found on and in your body, as well as in the soil, the air, and the water.

Types of Bacteria

There may be thousands of different types of bacteria, but they all have one of the three basic shapes shown in **Figure 7.7**. These basic shapes provide biologists with one way to identify different bacteria.

Did You Know?

Bacteria get their energy in a variety of ways. Some bacteria are heterotrophs and get their food from other organisms. Some bacteria are autotrophs that capture matter and energy from their surroundings using energy from the Sun or chemicals in the environment.

ELL Strategy

Use a Venn Diagram Ask students to create Venn diagrams in their Science Notebooks, using one circle for viruses and the other for bacteria. Tell them to write the characteristics of each organism in the appropriate circle and common characteristics where the circles overlap.

Background Information

The prefix *hetero-* comes from the Greek word *heteros,* which means "different." The prefix *auto-* means "self." The suffix *troph* originates from the Greek word *trephein,* which means "to nourish." When combined, *heterotroph* literally translates to "other nourishment." *Autotroph* is "self nourisher."

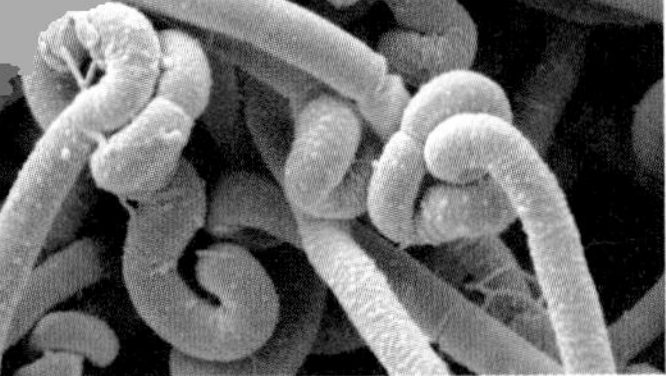

Bacilli

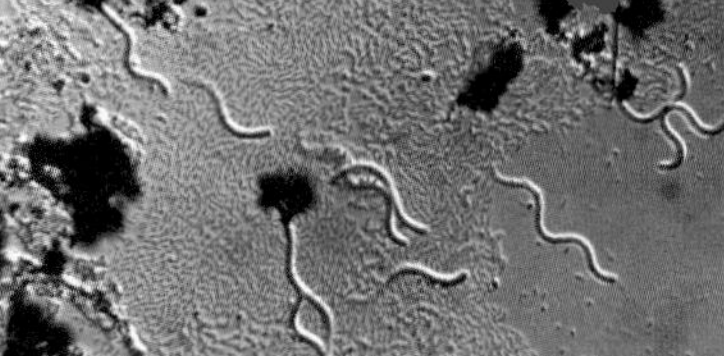

Spirilla

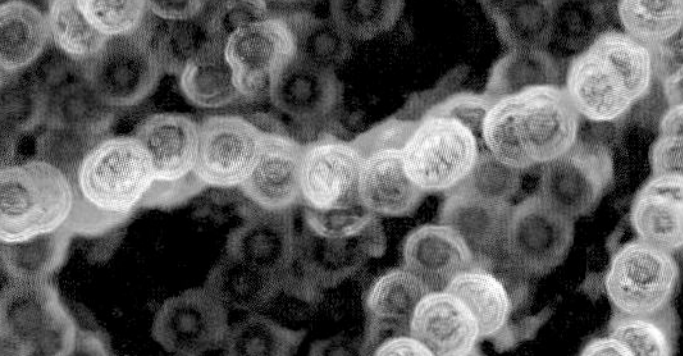

Cocci

Figure 7.7 Bacteria can be identified by their shapes.

Bacteria that are shaped like sticks or rods are called **bacilli** (buh SIH li, singular: bacillus). Bacteria that are shaped like globes or spheres are called **cocci** (KAH ki, singular: coccus). Bacteria that are shaped like corkscrews or spirals are called **spirilla** (spi RIH luh, singular: spirillum).

Structure of Bacteria The cells of bacteria are prokaryotic cells. Because bacteria are cells, they have some of the same structures that were discussed in Chapter 3. As you read this section, locate each structure in **Figure 7.8**.

The outer wall of most bacteria is the cell wall. The cell wall is rigid and tough, and it protects the bacterial cell and determines its shape. Inside the cell wall is the cell membrane. The cell membrane controls what substances enter and leave the bacterial cell. Inside the cell membrane is the jelly-like cytoplasm that contains all the other structures found in a bacterial cell.

DNA, the bacterial cell's genetic material, is the rope-like tangle in the cytoplasm. Because bacteria are prokaryotes, their DNA is not enclosed in a nucleus. However, the DNA still controls the activities of the cells. The production of proteins is carried out by the ribosomes found throughout the cytoplasm.

Another structure found on some bacteria is the flagellum. **Flagella** (fluh JEH luh, singular: flagellum) are whiplike structures that extend outward from the cell membrane into the bacterial cell's environment and move the cell through that environment. Bacteria without flagella must depend on air or water currents or other living organisms to move from one place to another.

As You Read

In the column labeled *L* in your K-W-L-S-H chart, write three or four things you have learned about bacteria.

Are bacteria prokaryotes or eukaryotes? How do you know?

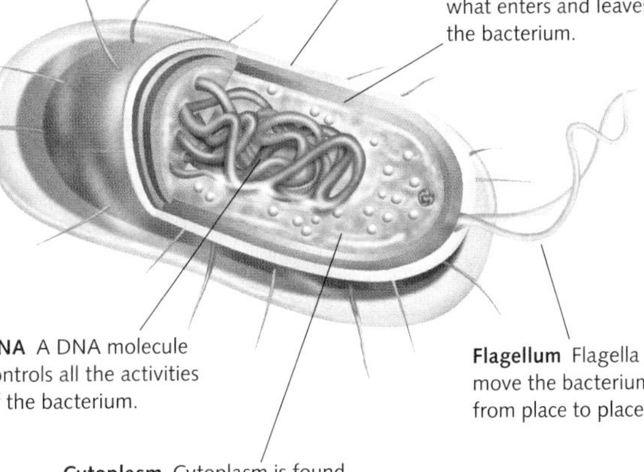
Cell wall A cell wall surrounds and protects the cell and gives the bacterium its shape.
Cell membrane A cell membrane controls what enters and leaves the bacterium.
DNA A DNA molecule controls all the activities of the bacterium.
Flagellum Flagella move the bacterium from place to place.
Cytoplasm Cytoplasm is found inside the cell membrane and contains the bacterium's ribosomes.

Figure 7.8 A typical gram-negative bacterial cell would have the structures shown in this diagram.

Teach

EXPLAIN that bacteria are characterized by their shapes and that there are three basic shapes. Bacterial cell structure is similar to that of other prokaryotes.

Use the Visual: Figure 7.8

EXTEND Have students research gram-negative and gram-positive bacteria. In a class discussion, allow volunteers to share their learnings with the class.

Vocabulary

bacterium Tell students that bacteria are single-celled, microscopic prokaryotic cells. They do not have distinct nuclei or organized cell structures.

bacillus Tell students that *bacillus* is derived from the Latin word *baculum,* which means "rod" or "staff."

coccus Explain to students that *coccus* comes from the Greek word *kokkos,* meaning "seed" or "berry."

spirillum Tell students that *spirillum* is derived from the Latin word *spira,* meaning "a coil."

flagellum Explain that *flagellum* comes from the Latin word *flagrum,* which means "whip."

As You Read

Tell students to return to the K-W-L-S-H charts in their Science Notebooks and to write in the *L* column facts about bacteria. On the board, model the following fact: Bacteria have three basic shapes: rods (bacilli), spheres (cocci), and spirals (spirilla).

ANSWER Bacteria are prokaryotes because their DNA is not enclosed in a nucleus and they are single celled.

Differentiated Instruction

Linguistic Have students examine the derivatives of *bacilli, cocci,* and *spirilla* (include other words from Chapter 7 if time permits) and find words in their native language that are related. They can list the English word, its derivative, and the related word in their Science Notebooks.

Field Study

Have students walk around the school and hypothesize likely locations of bacteria. If possible, have students interview workers at a hospital or a doctor's office to find out what measures are taken to prevent the spread of bacteria.

Teach

EXPLAIN to students that bacteria can reproduce very quickly and that there are two ways in which bacteria reproduce.

Vocabulary

binary fission Tell students that *binary* comes from the Latin word *bini,* which means "two at a time," and that *fission* comes from the Latin word *findere,* which means "to split." Together, they literally translate to "split into two."

conjugation Explain that conjugation is the act of joining together. When bacteria conjugate, they exchange part of their DNA.

CONNECTION: Math

On the board, draw one bacterium whole and another splitting by binary fission. Explain that the first drawing is the bacterium at the beginning of the activity and that the second drawing is the bacterium at the end of 30 minutes. Ask: *How many 30-minute periods are in 4 hours?* (8) Remind students that they must use eight reproductive events when calculating the number of bacteria but that their charts should report the number of bacteria by the hour (two reproductive events per hour). Suggest that students use drawings to help them do the calculations.

ANSWER There would be 256 bacteria.

EXTEND the activity by having students explain why the number of bacteria increases more rapidly as time passes. (Answer: The bacteria are reproducing exponentially.)

Explore It!

Each group of students needs a microscope and prepared slides of different types of bacteria. The slides should include spirilla, bacilli, and cocci bacteria. Have students display their finished charts in the classroom.

Figure It Out: Figure 7.9

ANSWER **1.** through the hollow tube that connects the bacteria **2.** Daughter cells produced by binary fission are genetically identical to each other and the parent. In conjugation, daughter cells are genetically different from each other and the parent.

Did You Know?

Some bacteria survive by producing endospores. Endospores protect the DNA and cytoplasm of bacterial cells by resisting very high and very low temperatures and drought. When able, the bacteria become active and reproduce.

Explore It!

Working in a small group, observe the prepared slides of the different types of bacteria your teacher provides. Design and complete a chart that contains the following information about each bacteria sample: name, diagram, and type.

Figure It Out

1. How do two bacteria transfer genetic information during conjugation?
2. Explain how the offspring produced by the process of binary fission are different from those produced by conjugation.

CONNECTION: Math

Bacteria can reproduce very quickly, especially if conditions are suitable. If a bacterium reproduces by binary fission every 30 minutes, how many bacteria would there be after four hours? Construct a chart to show the number of bacteria present at each hour of the four-hour period. Then create a graph using this information.

Reproduction of Bacteria

When conditions are favorable, bacteria can grow and reproduce at amazing rates. Some bacteria can reproduce every 20 minutes! Bacteria reproduce by both asexual and sexual processes.

Asexual Reproduction When a bacterium has doubled in size, it makes a copy of its single chromosome and divides in half, producing two identical bacterial cells. This type of reproduction is called binary fission. **Binary fission** (BI nuh ree • FIH zhun) is a type of asexual reproduction because it requires only one parent and the daughter cells are identical to the parent cell.

Sexual Reproduction Some bacteria are able to exchange part of their genetic information in a form of sexual reproduction called **conjugation** (kahn juh GAY shun). During conjugation, a hollow tube connects the two bacterial cells, and one bacterium transfers part of its DNA along the tube to the other bacterium. Conjugation is a type of sexual reproduction because two parent cells are involved and the new bacterial cells are genetically different from the parent bacteria. Once the transfer of DNA is complete, the bacteria separate and then reproduce by binary fission.

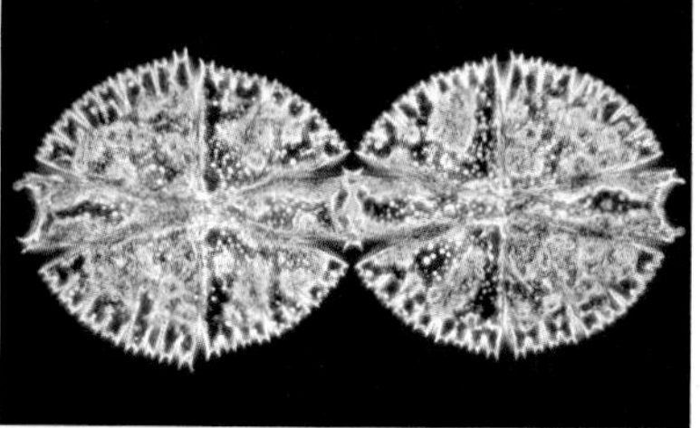

Binary fission

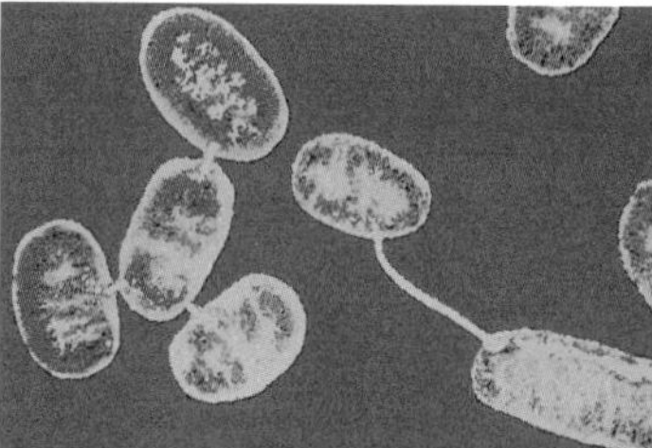

Conjugation

Figure 7.9 Most bacteria reproduce asexually by binary fission. Some bacteria reproduce sexually through conjugation followed by cell division.

Science Notebook EXTRA

Have students summarize the role of bacteria in the world by writing their answers to the following questions in their Science Notebooks: *What do you think would happen to life on Earth if all bacteria were killed? What do you think would happen if all living things except bacteria were killed?*

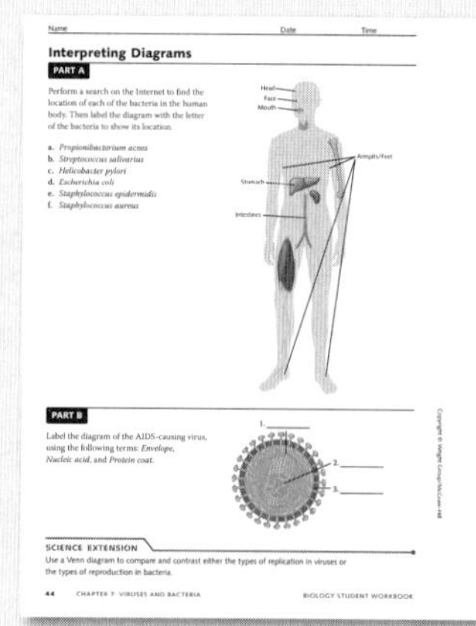

Interpreting Diagrams
Workbook, p. 44

Bacteria in the World

Figure 7.10 Bacteria play many important roles in the world.

Nitrogen-fixing bacteria in the nodules of legumes replenish nitrogen in the soil.

Bacteria can change the harmful chemicals in an oil spill into substances safe for the environment.

Some bacteria are used to produce antibiotics, which kill disease-causing bacteria.

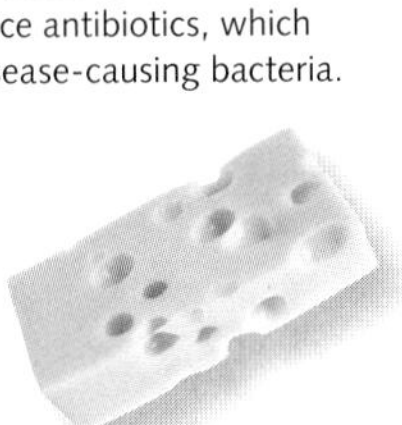

As bacteria carry out normal life processes, they help produce foods such as cheese.

Bacteria break down nutrients in dead plants and animals and return them to the environment.

PEOPLE IN SCIENCE On the Trail of a Killer

On July 21, 1976, the American Legion began its annual convention in Philadelphia. Several weeks later, 34 of those who had attended the convention would be dead from a mysterious form of pneumonia.

On August 2, a team of epidemiologists—scientists who investigate disease—arrived in Philadelphia. They came from the Centers for Disease Control and Prevention (CDC) to track the killer, which had been named Legionnaires' disease. The team pinpointed the location of the outbreak as the Bellevue Stratford Hotel. Then they began testing tissue samples from those who had died, looking for bacteria or viruses.

In January 1977, the "disease detectives" announced that they had found the bacteria that had infected 221 people and killed 34. The bacteria were named *Legionella pneumophila*.

Eight years after the initial outbreak, the CDC team found the source of the bacteria—the hotel air-conditioning system. Today, air conditioners and other systems that hold water are regularly disinfected to prevent Legionnaires' disease.

After You Read

1. Draw a bacterial cell. Label the parts and describe their functions.
2. Compare the two types of bacterial reproduction.
3. Using the completed K-W-L columns in your chart, explain how bacteria are both helpful and harmful to other living things. Then complete the chart by indicating in the *S* column what you would still like to know about bacteria. Write in the *H* column how you would find this information.

Teach

EXPLAIN Discuss Figure 7.10. Ask students to write in their Science Notebooks three ways in which they rely on bacteria.

PEOPLE IN SCIENCE

Explain that the Centers for Disease Control and Prevention (CDC) is one of the 13 major operating components of the Department of Health and Human Services (HHS), the principal agency in the United States government for protecting the health and safety of Americans.

EXTEND Place students in small groups, and tell them to imagine that they were part of the CDC team in 1976 that analyzed the cause of Legionnaires' disease. Tell them to write a list of questions that they would ask survivors of the disease in an effort to locate the source of the disease. Have them explain the reasons for their questions and provide possible follow-up questions, based on victims' responses.

Assess

EVALUATE Use the After You Read questions and the Alternative Assessment to help you assess students' understanding of the lesson.

After You Read

1. cell wall (protects it and determines its shape), cell membrane (controls what enters and leaves the cell), cytoplasm (contains ribosomes and DNA), DNA (controls the bacterium's activities), and ribosomes (produce proteins)
2. Binary fission is asexual reproduction that produces genetically identical daughter cells. Conjugation is a simple form of sexual reproduction in which bacteria exchange genetic material and produce genetically different cells.
3. Helpful bacteria recycle nutrients, rid the environment of harmful substances, and produce food, fuel, or medicines. Harmful bacteria spoil food and cause diseases.

Background Information

Legionnaires' disease affected 211 people at the American Legion convention in 1976, and 34 of those died. Symptoms of the disease include fever, cough, chest pain, and difficulty breathing. Typically, Legionnaires' disease affects people who are already ill—for example, those with lung disease and those who have received organ transplants. The bacterium usually travels through water supplies.

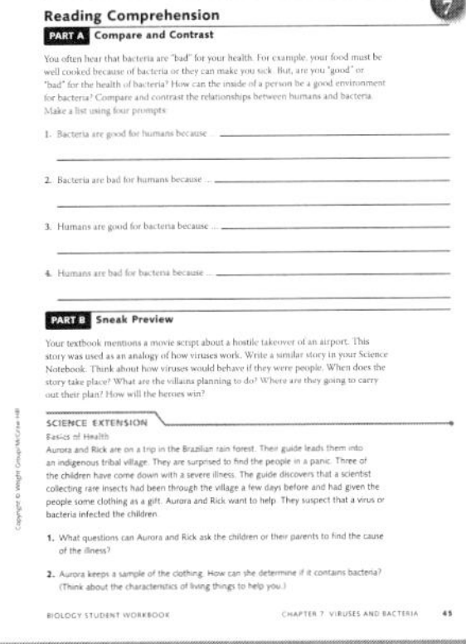

Reading Comprehension

PART A Compare and Contrast

PART B Sneak Preview

SCIENCE EXTENSION

Reading Comprehension Workbook, p. 45

Alternative Assessment

EVALUATE Struggling readers can illustrate cells undergoing conjugation and binary fission or illustrate or find magazine pictures of helpful and harmful bacteria.

Chapter 7 Summary

VOCABULARY REVIEW

Check students' sentences or paragraphs to make sure they understand the meaning of each vocabulary term.

PREPARE FOR CHAPTER TEST

Evaluate students' essays using the following criteria:

1. The topic sentence, or main idea, should restate the Key Concept.
2. The supporting paragraphs should incorporate the answers to the Learning Goal questions students have written and include details, facts, and examples they have recorded in their Science Notebooks.
3. The concluding sentence should sum up the main idea of the chapter and restate the Key Concept.

MASTERING CONCEPTS

True or False

1. False, viruses
2. False, parasites
3. True
4. False, binary fission
5. False, bacterium
6. True

Short Answer

7. Viruses do not have cell structures to perform functions required of living things, and viruses cannot reproduce.
8. In a lytic cycle, the virus takes over the host cell immediately and quickly begins to produce new viruses. In a lysogenic cycle, the virus becomes part of the host cell's genetic material but does not immediately affect the cell. When the virus becomes active, it produces new viruses.
9. Bacteria type is determined by shape.
10. Viruses require living cells to invade; they cannot reproduce on a nonliving nutrient substance.
11. Bacteria are considered prokaryotes because they are single celled and do not have nuclei or membrane-bound organelles in their cytoplasm.

Chapter 7

Summary

KEY CONCEPTS

7.1 Viruses

- A virus is a nonliving particle that invades a cell and uses the cell's parts to reproduce and distribute more viruses.
- Viruses contain a core of genetic material surrounded by a protective protein coat. The genetic material contains the instructions by which viruses make copies of themselves inside the host cell.
- In a lytic cycle, a virus enters the host cell, makes copies of itself, and then destroys the cell to release the new viruses.
- In a lysogenic cycle, a virus stays hidden within the host cell's chromosome until the virus becomes active. Once active, it makes copies of itself and then destroys the cell to release the new viruses.
- Viruses can cause diseases in plants, humans, and animals. However, they can also protect humans from disease. Viruses are used in gene therapy and in crop-pest control.

7.2 Bacteria

- Bacteria are microscopic prokaryotic cells whose genetic material is found in the cytoplasm. Bacterial cells do not have nuclei.
- There are three different shapes of bacteria. Bacilli are rod-shaped bacteria, cocci are sphere-shaped bacteria, and spirilla are spiral-shaped bacteria.
- Bacteria reproduce asexually by binary fission. Two identical daughter cells are produced during binary fission. Some bacteria reproduce sexually by conjugation. Conjugation produces bacteria with new combinations of genetic information.
- Bacteria play many important roles in the world. Bacteria produce food, medicines, and fuel. They help clean up the environment and recycle nutrients for use by other living things.

VOCABULARY REVIEW

Write each term in a complete sentence, or write a paragraph relating several terms.

7.1
virus, p. 124
host, p. 124
parasite, p. 124
lytic cycle, p. 126
lysogenic cycle, p. 126

7.2
bacterium, p. 128
bacillus, p. 129
coccus, p. 129
spirillum, p. 129
flagellum, p. 129
binary fission, p. 130
conjugation, p. 130

PREPARE FOR CHAPTER TEST

To prepare for the chapter test, create a question from each Learning Goal. Use the information in your Science Notebook to answer each question. Then use these answers to write a well-developed essay about the chapter. Use the Key Concept on the first page of this chapter as your topic sentence.

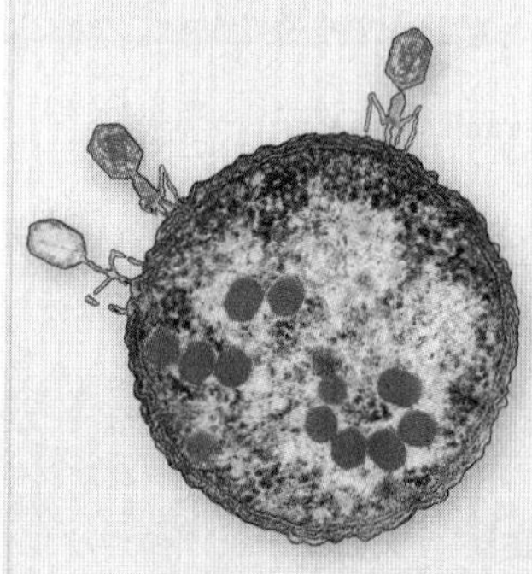

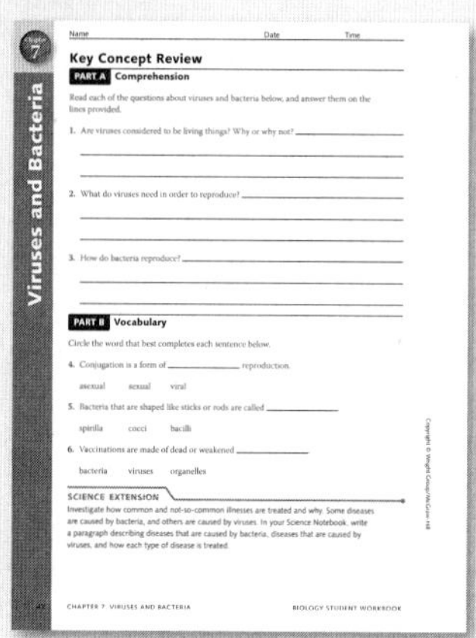
Key Concept Review
PART A Comprehension
PART B Vocabulary
SCIENCE EXTENSION

Key Concept Review
Workbook, p. 42

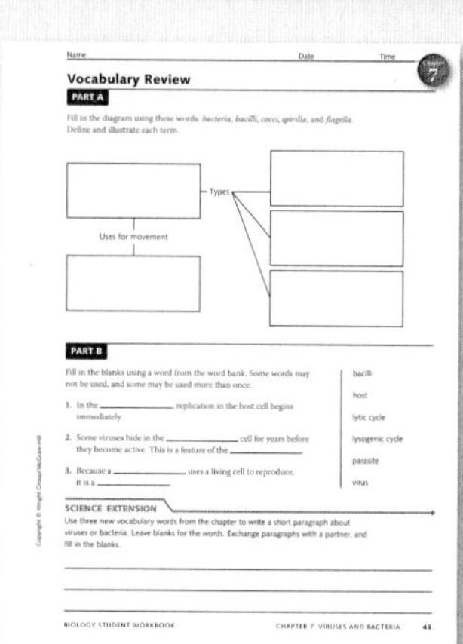
Vocabulary Review
PART A
PART B
SCIENCE EXTENSION

Vocabulary Review
Workbook, p. 43

MASTERING CONCEPTS

True or False

If the statement is true, write "true." If it is false, change the underlined word or words to make the statement true.

1. Particles that are made up of a protein coat and a core of genetic material are <u>bacteria</u>.
2. Viruses are <u>hosts</u> that cause harm to the cells that they invade.
3. In order to reproduce, a <u>virus</u> must invade a host cell.
4. Bacteria reproduce asexually by <u>conjugation</u>.
5. A flagellum is a whiplike structure that helps a <u>virus</u> move.
6. A bacterial cell does not have a <u>nucleus</u>.

Short Answer

Answer each of the following in a sentence or brief paragraph.

7. How are viruses different from living cells?
8. What is the difference between a lytic cycle and a lysogenic cycle?
9. What characteristic of bacteria determines their type?
10. Can viruses be grown in the laboratory using a nonliving nutrient substance? Explain your answer.
11. Why are bacteria considered prokaryotes?

Critical Thinking

Use what you have learned in this chapter to answer each of the following.

12. **Compare and Contrast** Identify ways in which reproduction in viruses is similar to and different from reproduction in bacteria.
13. **Apply** Farmers often rotate their crops with legumes such as soybeans. When the soybeans are mature, farmers plow the soybeans into the ground and then plant another crop, such as cotton. Explain the role that bacteria play in this process.
14. **Make Inferences** Scientists hypothesize that viruses could not have existed before bacteria or other organisms. What do you know about viruses that would support this hypothesis?

Standardized Test Question

Choose the letter of the response that correctly answers the question.

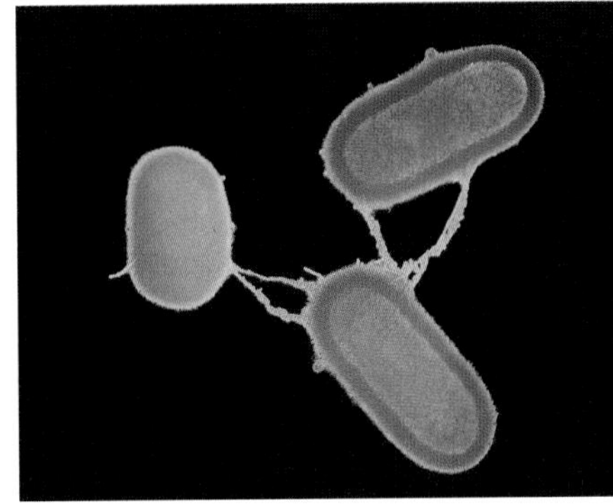

15. Which reproductive process is shown in the photo?
    - A. lytic cycle
    - B. lysogenic cycle
    - C. conjugation
    - D. binary fission

Test-Taking Tip

After you read a multiple-choice question, answer it in your head before reading the choices provided. This way the choices will not confuse or trick you.

Critical Thinking

12. Viruses cannot reproduce without a host cell. New viruses, like bacteria produced by binary fission, are genetically identical to the original cell invader. Bacteria, unlike viruses, can reproduce on their own, and through conjugation, they can produce genetically different offspring.
13. The farmer is using the nitrogen-fixing bacteria on the roots of legumes to fertilize the soil. The bacteria convert nitrogen in the air into a form that plants can use.
14. A virus can only reproduce when it has invaded a living cell.
15. C

Reading Links

Attack of the Superbugs: The Crisis of Drug-Resistant Diseases (Issues in Focus Today)

Particularly since the advent of antibiotics in the mid-twentieth century, the advance of disease-fighting technology has been an uphill battle as viruses and bacteria evolve resistance to drug treatments. This book examines the origins of the problem, responses from the scientific community, and potential solutions through several case studies (including the reemergence of older diseases, such as smallpox and tuberculosis). It also equips young adults with information about avoiding or minimizing infections and the ways in which improper use of substances such as antibiotics can contribute to the problem.

Kowalski, Kathiann M. Enslow Publishers. 128 pp. Illustrated. Library ISBN: 978-0-7660-2400-7.

Invisible Enemies: Stories of Infectious Disease

With its comprehensive and often gripping study of seven deadly diseases that have altered the course of human history, updated to include recent medical and social developments, this book is an excellent resource for students interested in learning more about the history and impact of viruses and bacteria. Each chapter tells the story of a major disease with interesting visual accompaniment, such as cartoons, public health posters, and riveting text that easily avoids being dry or laboratory-bound.

Farrell, Jeanette. 272 pp. Illustrated. Trade ISBN: 978-0-374-33607-3.

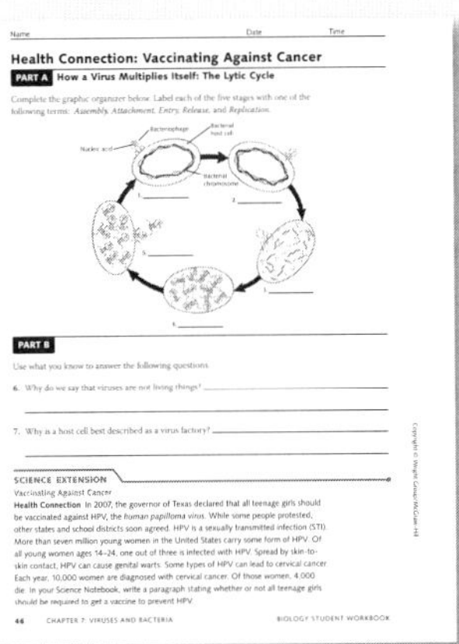

Curriculum Connection Workbook, p. 46

Science Challenge Workbook, p. 47

Chapter 7

Labs

7A Got Bacteria?

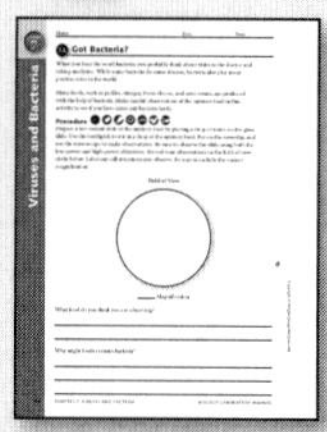

This prechapter introduction activity is designed to introduce students to the uses of bacteria by engaging them in observing, examining, and describing bacteria found in familiar types of foods.

Objectives

- use the proper technique in preparing a wet-mount slide
- demonstrate proper use of a microscope
- make observations
- make predictions

Planning

 30 minutes  groups of 2–4 students

Materials (per group)

- microscope
- toothpick
- unpasteurized yogurt
- dropper
- methylene blue
- water
- small condiment-sized containers for yogurt
- glass slide
- coverslip
- lab aprons
- safety goggles

Lab Tips

- It may be necessary for some students to remove goggles while using the microscope to obtain a clear view of the sample.
- You may want to draw on the board an example of an observation from the microscope slide. Many students do not draw the important elements and sketch things such as a scratch on the lens.

Advance Preparation

- Mix the unpasteurized yogurt with several drops of methylene blue until it is bright blue in color. The bacteria will be stained a dull brown color.
- Place yogurt in small condiment-type containers so that each group will have a sample to observe and use. Replace the yogurt several times throughout the day so that it stays fresh.

Engagement Guide

- Challenge students to think about the positive roles bacteria play in the world by asking:
  - *Where do you find bacteria?* (Students should realize that bacteria are everywhere.)
  - *Do you think bacteria play any positive roles in the world?* (Students may not be able to identify any positive roles played by bacteria beyond use in food at this point in the lesson.)
  - *What food do you think is used in this activity?* (Students' answers will vary. Possible answers include sour cream and yogurt.)
- Encourage students to communicate what they have learned about bacteria in creative ways, such as by making a public service announcement on behalf of the positive roles of bacteria.
- Students may observe rod-shaped or circular-shaped stained bacteria in the yogurt. You may need to remind students that even though a blue stain was used, the bacteria will not necessarily be blue in color.

Going Further

Encourage students to research how bacteria are used in the production of foods such as sour cream, pickles, vinegar, buttermilk, and cheese.

7B Using a Dichotomous Key to Identify Bacteria

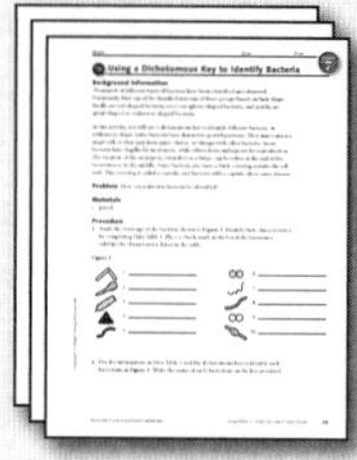

Objectives

- interpret diagrams
- categorize data
- compare and contrast bacteria
- apply data to a dichotomous key

Skill Set

observing, comparing and contrasting, recording and analyzing data, classifying, stating conclusions

Planning

 1 class period 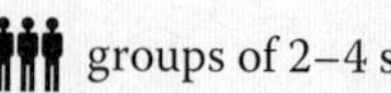

Materials

Materials for this activity are listed in the Student Laboratory Manual.

Answers to Observations: Data Table 1

Bacterium 1: rod, pairs; bacterium 2: rod, single, capsule, endospore at end; bacterium 3: rod, single, flagella present; bacterium 4: round, clumps, capsule; bacterium 5: round, chains; bacterium 6: round, pairs, capsule; bacterium 7: spiral, single; bacterium 8: rod, chains; bacterium 9: round, pairs; bacterium 10: rod, single, capsule, endospore at middle

Answers for Figure 1

1. *Bacillus lactis* **2.** *Clostridium tetani* **3.** *Salmonella typhosa* **4.** *Staphylococcus aureus* **5.** *Streptococcus lactis* **6.** *Diplococcus pneumoniae* **7.** *Treponema palladium* **8.** *Bacillus anthracis* **9.** *Diplococcus meningitidis* **10.** *Bacillus botulinum*

Answers to Analysis and Conclusions

1. the shape of the bacterial cell
2. *Diplo-* means "two" and describes a pattern of growth found in some types of bacteria.
3. Dichotomous keys are useful because they can be used to identify unknown living things.
4. The genus name identifies the shape of the bacteria. It is similar to a person's last name because it applies to a larger group, the person's family (genus). The second name in the scientific name is like your first name. Both together identify a specific member (species) of the genus.

Going Further

Have students apply the skills they used in this lab to observe prepared slides of different bacteria. Students should draw each bacterium they observe and identify its shape and growth pattern. If the slides are labeled with the name of the bacteria, cover these labels so that students must use their observations to identify each bacterium. Provide a list of names of bacteria on the board from which students can select.

7C Preventing the Spread of Infectious Diseases

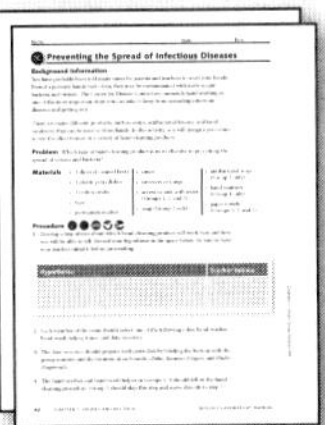

Objectives

- develop and perform an experimental procedure
- design an appropriate data table
- make predictions
- draw conclusions based on observations

Skill Set

hypothesizing, observing, comparing and contrasting, recording and analyzing data, stating conclusions

Planning

1 class period (plus one week for observations during class)

 5 groups of students

Materials

Materials for this activity are listed in the Student Laboratory Manual.

Advance Preparation

- The antibacterial soap should contain an antiseptic such as triclosan, and the hand sanitizer should have either ethyl or isopropyl alcohol. Cans of sliced beets and a can opener will be needed for this lab.
- Have the class discuss the proper method of hand washing. You might want to invite the school nurse to class to discuss the importance of washing hands and the proper technique. Have students agree upon a specific procedure that each group will follow. For example: Hand-wash helper turns on water, and hand-washer rubs hands together using the assigned product for 15 s (making sure to wash palms, fingers, and under fingernails). Hand-wash helper turns off water while hand-washer dries hands with paper towel, touching nothing after washing hands. Groups 3 and 4 should follow directions on the assigned products, being sure to wash for 15 s and include palms, fingers, and under fingernails.
- Be sure to disinfect the tongs, can opener, and top of the can with alcohol in front of the class. You might want to wear gloves while performing this task and then ask students why you are disinfecting these items and wearing gloves.
- As you designate groups (1 = water only, 2 = soap and water, 3 = antibacterial soap and water, 4 = hand sanitizer, 5 = control group/no hand washing) and students review the procedure, remind them to formulate and record their hypotheses in the first step.
- Disposal: The beets should contain normal molds and bacteria and can be disposed of in the trash can. Students should not open the petri dishes once they have been sealed.

Answers to Observations (Procedure Step 9)

Molds and bacteria are most likely to grow on the beet slices. Molds will look fuzzy and will probably be green or white, while bacteria may be several different colors or colorless and can be shiny or dull. As bacteria continue to grow, individual colonies may grow together to produce a mat of bacteria.

Answers to Analysis and Conclusions

1. All beet slices should show evidence of bacterial growth; however, the group that used antibacterial soap should notice less growth than the group that used regular soap, and the group that used hand sanitizer should show the least growth. The control group should show the most growth.
2. Hands should be washed to kill microorganisms that cause diseases. Hands should be washed before eating; throughout the food preparation process; after using the restroom; after blowing one's nose, sneezing, or coughing; after handling animals; and after being in contact with someone who is ill.
3. Bacteria could have come from other sources, such as the air, the tongs or tweezers, the outside of the can of beets, or the can opener.
4. The beet slices provide the nutrients and water for the bacteria and mold growth.
5. Recommendations will vary depending on the observations of the class.

Going Further

Have students predict which areas of the school would produce the greatest growth on beet slices. Students should develop a procedure and test their predictions. Taking swabs of toilet seats, door handles, etc., all work well in a school environment.

Chapter 8 Lessons

Introduce Chapter 8

As a starting activity, use LAB 8A A Whole New World on page 44 of the Laboratory Manual.

ENGAGE students by forming groups of three and having them read the first two paragraphs together. Ask them to imagine that they are walking through the woods, and then have them write everything they would see, hear, and smell. Ask them to repeat the process for the pond described in the text. Share students' observations with the class. Tell them that in this chapter, they will be learning more about algae, a type of protist.

Think About Protists and Fungi

Have a slice of moldy bread in a plastic bag for students to observe. **CAUTION:** Students should not open the bag and touch or breathe in the spores. Before asking students to answer questions in their Science Notebooks, ask students to talk in pairs to form hypotheses about how quickly mold will grow on bread and what factors might increase the rate of growth. As a class, discuss students' hypotheses as well as the role of preservatives in food.

Chapter 8 Protists and Fungi

KEY CONCEPT Protists and fungi are diverse groups of organisms that play many important roles in the world.

Imagine that it is a hot, humid summer day and you are ready for a swim in your favorite pond. The pond, however does not look very inviting—it is covered with bright green scum!

While you might describe the pond scum as disgusting, what you are really looking at are millions of microorganisms that are very important to you. They are responsible for much of the oxygen you breathe. Beneath that pond scum are other microorganisms. You probably used some of them this morning to brush your teeth. Protists and fungi are found everywhere, and you could not live without them.

NSTA SCILINKS
www.scilinks.org
Protists Code: WGB08A
Fungi Code: WGB08B

Think About Protists and Fungi

Have you ever seen bread that did not look quite right? Bread should be soft and spongy, not covered with green, powdery dots that are probably mold.

- What caused the green dots to appear? Why should you throw away the bread and not eat it? What other types of food spoilage are you familiar with?
- Write one or two sentences in your Science Notebook to describe the appearance of bread or other foods that have spoiled.

Chapter 8 Planning Guide

Instructional Periods	National Standards	Lab Manual	Workbook
8.1 2 periods	A.1, C.1; C.1, C.5; UCP.1, UCP.5	**Lab 8A—p. 44** A Whole New World **Lab 8B—p. 45** Food Fit for a Fungus **Lab 8C—p. 47** An Explosion of Algae	Key Concept Review p. 48 Vocabulary Review p. 49 Graphic Organizer p. 50 Reading Comprehension p. 51 Curriculum Connection p. 52 Science Challenge p. 53
8.2 2 periods	A.2, C.1, G.2; B.4,C.1, C.6, F.6, G.2; UCP.1		
8.3 2 periods	A.2, C.1; G.1; C3, D.2, G.1; UCP.1, UCP.2		
8.4 2 periods	A.1, C.1, C.4; C.4, F.1, F.5; UCP.5		
8.5 2 periods	A.2, C.1, C.2, C.5, F.1; C1, C.4, C.6; UCP.3, UCP.5		
8.6 1 period	C.4, C.5; C.4, C.6		

Middle School Standard; High School Standard; Unifying Concept and Principle

8.1 Protists

Learning Goals

- Describe the characteristics of protists.
- Explain on what basis biologists divide protists into groups.

New Vocabulary

protist

Before You Read

Create a concept map by writing the lesson title *Protists* in the middle of a sheet of paper. As you read the lesson, scatter words or phrases that describe these organisms around the title and connect them to the title with lines.

Is there a closet in your home that contains a variety of different things? It might be full because it holds everything that does not fit anywhere else in the house. You can think about the kingdom Protista as the "hold-everything" kingdom of living things because organisms in this kingdom do not fit anywhere else. Even though these organisms are incredibly diverse, they do have some characteristics in common.

What Is a Protist?

A **protist** (PROH tihst) is any organism that is a eukaryote but is not a plant, an animal, or a fungus. Remember that a eukaryote is a living thing made of cells with a membrane-bound nucleus that directs the activities of the cell. Most protists live in moist environments such as salt water, freshwater, or very moist soil.

As You Read

Use the headings and the vocabulary term in this lesson to add descriptive words to your concept map.

What is a eukaryote?

Types of Protists

Because of the diversity among protists, one way that biologists group them is based on how they obtain their food. The three categories of protists are animal-like protists, plant-like protists, and fungus-like protists.

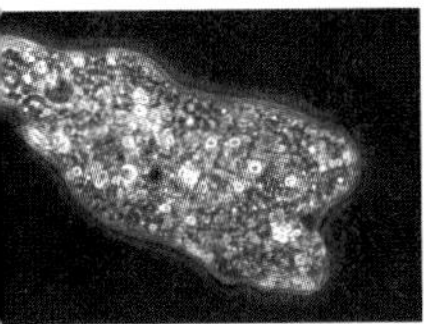

Figure 8.1 Kingdom Protista includes animal-like, plant-like, and fungus-like protists. A microscopic amoeba *(left)* lives in freshwater environments. Giant kelp *(center)* can reach heights of more than 50 m and grows in saltwater kelp forests. A slime mold *(right)* is a fungus-like protist.

Figure It Out

1. Which photograph depicts a plant-like protist?
2. What characteristics might scientists use to identify a protist as an animal-like protist?

After You Read

1. What characteristic do all protists share?
2. Name the three groups of protists.
3. Review your concept map. Which word or phrase best describes all protists?

8.1 Introduce

ENGAGE Provide several items, most of which can be easily categorized (e.g., paper clip, stapler, pencil, pen, eraser) and some which cannot (e.g., refrigerator magnet). Ask students to identify the category to which most items belong and to list those items. Then, ask how they would classify the other items. Explain that protists are similar to the items that are difficult to classify.

Before You Read

Model the concept map on the board by writing *PROTISTS*. Write *Examples*, and then write *Algae*. Connect *Algae* to *Examples*, and connect *Examples* to *PROTISTS*.

Vocabulary terms are listed on the first student page of each lesson. You may wish to preview the terms before introducing each lesson. Strategies for teaching the vocabulary appear on the pages where the terms are introduced.

Teach

EXPLAIN that protists are eukaryotes and are classified by how they obtain food.

Vocabulary

protist Tell students that *protist* is derived from the Greek word *prōtistos*, meaning "the very first."

As You Read

ANSWER A eukaryote is an organism with a nucleus that directs the activities of the cell.

Figure It Out: Figure 8.1

ANSWER **1.** the giant kelp in the center **2.** Most students will predict that animal-like protists move and "eat food."

Assess

EVALUATE Use the After You Read questions and the Alternative Assessment to help you assess students' understanding of this lesson.

ELL Strategy

Ask Questions Have each student use the information in his/her concept map to create three questions pertaining to the lesson. Have students exchange their questions and try to answer the questions they receive. Discuss the questions as a class, and identify those that students had difficulty answering.

After You Read

1. All protists are eukaryotes.
2. animal-like, plant-like, fungus-like
3. the word *eukaryote*

Alternative Assessment

EVALUATE Use concept maps to assess understanding. Maps should include the three groups of protists and the concept that all protists are eukaryotes.

8.2 Introduce

ENGAGE Ask students to brainstorm why protozoans are called animal-like. Write all responses on the board. Then, ask students to name the characteristics of living things. Highlight *ability to move* and *heterotrophs,* and tell students that protozoans share these characteristics with animals.

Before You Read

Model the lesson outline on the board by writing *Animal-Like Protists: Protozoans* as the title. Below the title, write:

I. Protozoans with Pseudopods
  A. have "false feet"
  B. have a contractile vacuole
  C. reproduce asexually

Discuss with students the difference between subheadings and details. Then, have students create their own outlines.

Teach

EXPLAIN to students that in this section, they will be learning about the different types of animal-like protists (protozoans).

Use the Visual: Figure 8.2

ANSWER heterotrophs, such as protozoans

Science Notebook EXTRA

Encourage students to use the vocabulary section they created in their Science Notebooks. Remind them to record prefixes, suffixes, and root words to help them remember the meanings of vocabulary terms.

Learning Goals

- Compare and contrast the different types of animal-like protists.
- Identify the roles played by animal-like protists in the living world.

New Vocabulary

heterotroph
protozoan
pseudopod
contractile vacuole
cilia
spore

Recall Vocabulary

binary fission (p. 130)
conjugation (p. 130)
flagellum (p. 129)
parasite (p. 124)

8.2 Animal-Like Protists: Protozoans

Before You Read

Create a lesson outline. Use the lesson title as the outline title. Label the subheadings with the Roman numerals *I* through *IV*. Use the letters *A, B, C,* etc., under each subheading to record important information.

Animal-like protists get their name because they share two characteristics with animals—they are able to move and they are heterotrophs. **Heterotrophs** (HE tuh roh trohfs) are organisms that cannot convert inorganic materials into organic molecules and must consume other organisms for food. Animal-like protists are called **protozoans** (proh tuh ZOH unz). Unlike an animal, however, a protozoan is unicellular.

Types of Protozoans

Protozoans are usually divided into groups based on how they move. Some protozoans use "false feet," others use structures similar to oars or whips, and still others rely on their hosts.

Protozoans with Pseudopods This group includes protozoans that have "false feet" called pseudopods. **Pseudopods** (SOO duh pahdz) are extensions of the cell membrane that fill with cytoplasm. As the cell membrane bulges outward, the cytoplasm streams into the extension and the rest of the cell follows.

Figure 8.2 shows an amoeba using its pseudopods to capture prey. **Figure 8.3** illustrates how an amoeba encloses the prey in a food vacuole. The amoeba's food vacuole functions like a digestive system. Protozoans, such as amoebas, have a **contractile** (kun TRAK tul) **vacuole** (VAK yuh wohl) that collects extra water that enters the cell and pumps it out.

Most amoebas reproduce by asexual reproduction, which requires only one parent. The offspring are genetically identical to the parent. When the amoeba's cytoplasm divides in half, two identical amoebas are produced.

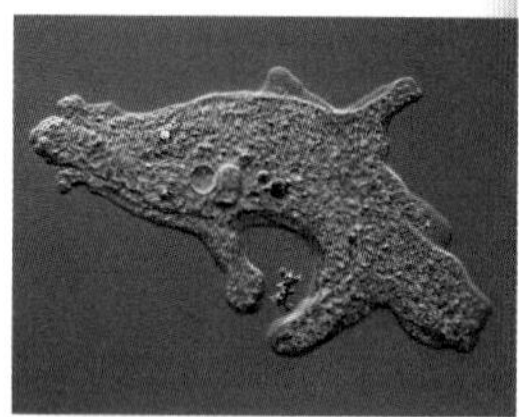

Figure 8.2 *Protozoa* means "first animals." Protozoans are the main hunters in the microscopic world. Notice how this amoeba has moved to capture its food. What type of organisms must consume other organisms for food?

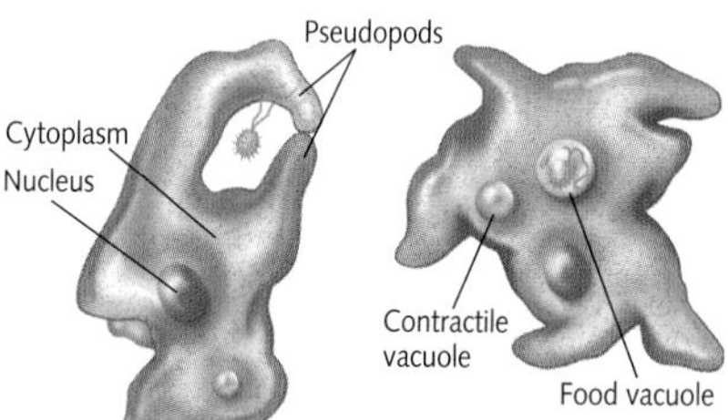
❶ The food becomes trapped by the pseudopods. When the pseudopods meet, they join to form a food vacuole.
Pseudopods
Cytoplasm
Nucleus
Contractile vacuole
Food vacuole
❷ Food is broken down inside the food vacuole by digestive enzymes, and the nutrients then move out into the cytoplasm.

Figure 8.3 These diagrams show the structure of a typical amoeba, such as *Amoeba proteus*.

Vocabulary

heterotroph Tell students that *hetero-* means "other" and that *troph* is from the Greek word *trephein,* meaning "to feed."

protozoan Explain that the prefix *proto-* is derived from the Greek word *prōtos,* which means "first," and that the root *zoo* comes from the Greek word *zôion,* meaning "animal."

pseudopod Tell students that *pseudo* means "false" and *pod* means "foot". Thus, pseudopods are "false feet." Discuss the meanings of *pseudonym* and *pseudoscience.*

contractile vacuole Explain that *contractile* means "capable of contracting" and that a *vacuole* is a tiny cavity.

Differentiated Instruction

Kinesthetic Provide students with a variety of materials, such as yarn, cardboard, markers, and modeling clay. Have students create a model of each type of protozoan, using a specific example for each type. Ask students to label the method of locomotion.

Protozoans with Cilia Another type of animal-like protist is the ciliate, or protozoan with cilia. **Cilia** (SIH lee uh) are tiny hairlike projections that move with wavelike rhythm. The cilia act like tiny oars that propel the protozoan through the water.

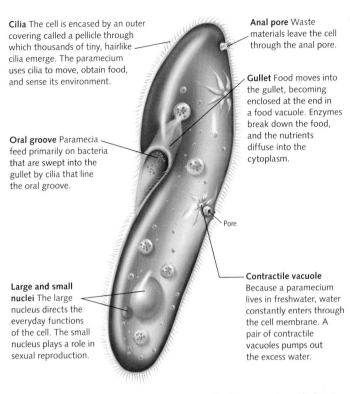

Cilia The cell is encased by an outer covering called a pellicle through which thousands of tiny, hairlike cilia emerge. The paramecium uses cilia to move, obtain food, and sense its environment.

Anal pore Waste materials leave the cell through the anal pore.

Gullet Food moves into the gullet, becoming enclosed at the end in a food vacuole. Enzymes break down the food, and the nutrients diffuse into the cytoplasm.

Oral groove Paramecia feed primarily on bacteria that are swept into the gullet by cilia that line the oral groove.

Pore

Contractile vacuole Because a paramecium lives in freshwater, water constantly enters through the cell membrane. A pair of contractile vacuoles pumps out the excess water.

Large and small nuclei The large nucleus directs the everyday functions of the cell. The small nucleus plays a role in sexual reproduction.

Figure 8.4 A paramecium contains many organelles that carry out specific functions.

Ciliates usually reproduce asexually by binary fission, and the daughter cells are genetically identical. Ciliates can, however, reproduce sexually by conjugation. Two ciliates join together temporarily to exchange genetic material. Once the exchange is complete, they separate and divide by binary fission. Both types of reproduction are shown in **Figure 8.5**.

Protozoans with Flagella Animal-like protists called zooflagellates move using flagella. Zooflagellates also use their flagella to sweep bacteria and other protists into their mouthlike openings. Many species of zooflagellates live inside other organisms.

Some zooflagellates are disease-causing parasites. African sleeping sickness is a serious disease caused by a zooflagellate that spreads to humans when they are bitten by the tsetse fly.

Figure It Out

1. What organelles are used for catching and digesting food?
2. Compare the amoeba in **Figure 8.3** with the paramecium in **Figure 8.4**. How are these organisms similar? How are they different?

As You Read

Review your outline. Then write a brief summary in your Science Notebook about protozoans with cilia and protozoans with flagella.

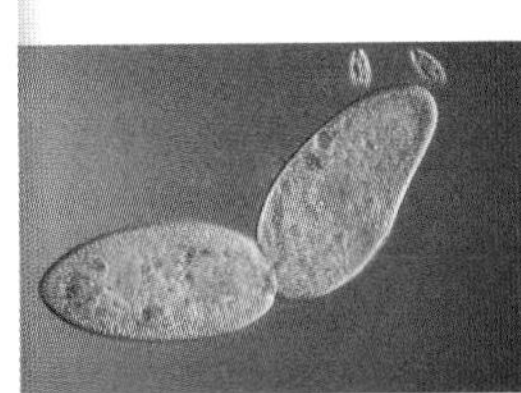

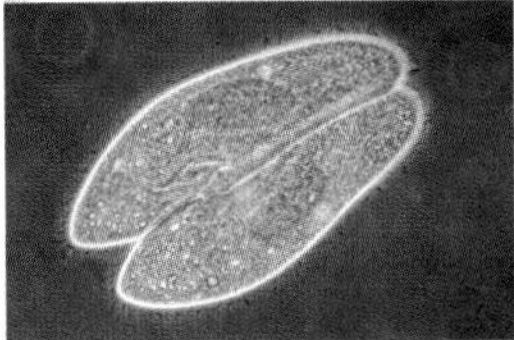

Figure 8.5 Ciliates usually reproduce asexually *(top)*, but when environmental conditions change, they can also reproduce sexually *(bottom)*.

Teach

EXPLAIN to students that in this section, they will learn about two more types of protozoa: those with cilia and those with flagella.

Vocabulary

cilia Tell students that cilia are very small bits of protoplasm that project from some protozoans and aid them in moving, capturing food, and responding to environmental conditions.

Figure It Out: Figure 8.4

ANSWER **1.** The cilia, oral groove, gullet, and food vacuole are used by the paramecium to catch and digest food. **2.** Paramecia and amoebas both have nuclei, cytoplasm, cell membranes, and contractile vacuoles. They are different because paramecia have cilia while amoebas have pseudopods; paramecia ingest food through the oral groove, while amoebas surround food with pseudopods; and paramecia have two nuclei, while amoebas have only one.

As You Read

Give students about five minutes to review their outlines and to add newly learned information. Recommend that they include the mode of locomotion, the method of reproduction, and an example for each. Check students' summaries to make sure they have included this information for both types of protozoa.

ELL Strategy

Use a Venn Diagram To help them differentiate between paramecia and amoebas, have students create Venn diagrams in their Science Notebooks and compare the two organisms.

Background Information

Sleeping sickness is found only in Africa and is fatal if not treated. It attacks the nervous system in vertebrates, including humans. Sleeping sickness is caused by zooflagellates called trypanosomes. The tsetse fly, which lives in bodies of water in Africa, becomes infected with the trypanosomes by biting animals infected with sleeping sickness; the fly then transmits the disease by biting uninfected animals.

Teach

EXPLAIN that in this section, students will learn about the fourth type of protist—those that produce spores—and the influence of all protozoans on other organisms.

Vocabulary

spore Tell students that *spore* originates from the Greek word *spora*, meaning "seed" or "a sowing."

Extend It!

Provide a variety of resources for students, including encyclopedias, medical reference books, and Internet access.

Amoebic dysentery is caused by Entamoeba, a sarcodine that moves using pseudopods. The disease is transmitted when food and water contaminated by feces from infected individuals is ingested. Sanitation and clean food and water supplies can reduce the impact of this disease.

Assess

EVALUATE Use the After You Read questions and the Alternative Assessment to help you assess students' understanding of this lesson.

After You Read

1. eukaryotic, unicellular heterotroph
2. Protozoans with pseudopods: move with pseudopods, often reproduce asexually; Protozoans with cilia: called ciliates, move with cilia, reproduce sexually by conjugation; Protozoans with flagella: called zooflagellates, move with flagella; Protozoans with spores: called sporozoans, depend on their host for movement, all are parasitic
3. Summaries should include the fact that protozoans are important organisms in aquatic food chains, are deadly parasites, and are important in recycling nutrients.

Alternative Assessment

EVALUATE Have students draw an example from each of the four groups of protozoans. Students should name their examples and identify how the protozoans move.

Extend It!

In a small group, research the disease amoebic dysentery. Identify the protozoan that causes the disease, how the protozoan moves, how the disease is transmitted, and its symptoms and treatment. You may want to include additional information, such as where the disease occurs, how many people it affects yearly, and how outbreaks of the disease can be controlled. Report your findings in a short paragraph or a chart in your Science Notebook.

Protozoans That Produce Spores Another type of animal-like protist is a parasite that produces spores. This protozoan depends on its host for movement and a supply of food. Called sporozoans, these organisms produce reproductive cells called **spores**. Spores develop into new organisms when environmental conditions are favorable. Spores pass easily from host to host when food that contains spores is eaten, or when a mammal, bird, or fish is bitten by an insect that carries spores in its body. Sporozoans often have complex life cycles that can require more than one host organism.

Perhaps the best-known sporozoan is *Plasmodium* (plaz MOH dee um), the protist that causes malaria. Malaria spreads when a healthy mosquito bites a person with the disease and becomes infected with *Plasmodium* spores. When the infected mosquito then bites a healthy person, the spores pass into that person's body, infect red blood cells, and cause the cells to rupture. Symptoms of malaria can last for weeks at a time and include high fevers that alternate with severe chills.

Protozoans in the World

Protozoans play many important roles in the world. Parasitic protozoans cause diseases such as malaria and African sleeping sickness. These diseases affect millions of people all over the world and cause many deaths. Two major goals of health organizations are to control the protozoans that cause these diseases and to develop new treatments.

Not all protozoans are parasitic. Termites would starve to death without the protozoan *Trichonympha* in their intestine to digest the wood they eat. Other protozoans are decomposers that recycle nutrients in dead plants and animals. Many protozoans are important links in freshwater and saltwater food chains. Protozoans eat bacteria and other protists and then become a meal for small animals that are, in turn, eaten by larger animals.

After You Read

1. Describe the characteristics of an animal-like protist.
2. Use your outline to produce a chart that identifies the four groups of protozoans, describes how they move, and includes interesting facts about each group.
3. Use the information in your outline to write a well-developed paragraph summarizing the roles protozoans play in the living world.

Background Information

In parts of the world where sanitation is a problem, millions of people are infected by *Entamoeba*. The parasitic amoebas live in the intestines, where they absorb food from the host and attack the lining of the intestines, causing it to bleed. Those infected are weakened by the disease and are susceptible to other diseases.

Teacher Alert

Not all diseases spread by mosquitoes are caused by protists. Eastern equine encephalitis, known as EEE or Triple E, is a mosquito-borne viral disease prevalent in the eastern half of the United States. It affects humans, horses, and some bird species and has a high mortality rate.

West Nile virus is another example of a mosquito-borne viral disease. Birds are often carriers of the virus; infected mosquitoes spread the disease to humans.

8.3 Plant-Like Protists: Algae

Before You Read

Create a table to organize the information presented in this lesson. Use the lesson title as the table title and create columns titled *Structure, Habitat, Nutrition,* and *Important Information.* Each subheading that identifies a type of plant-like protist should have a row in your table.

Learning Goals

- Compare and contrast the different types of plant-like protists.
- Identify the roles played by plant-like protists in the living world.

New Vocabulary

alga
autotroph
pigment
phytoplankton

What Are Algae?

If you have seen brown seaweed washed up on a beach, or green scum floating on top of a pond, you are familiar with plant-like protists. Plant-like protists are autotrophs called **algae** (AL jee, singular: alga). **Autotrophs** (AW tuh trohfs) are organisms that capture energy and matter from their surroundings. Autotrophs are food for many heterotrophs. Algae live in several different environments and come in a variety of shapes, sizes, and colors. Algae have different colors because they contain different **pigments** (PIG munts), or chemicals that produce colors. These pigments allow algae to capture and use energy from the Sun to produce organic molecules through the process of photosynthesis.

Figure 8.6 Algae range in size from microscopic diatoms that look like pieces of jewelry to giant kelp found in underwater forests.

Types of Algae

Algae are divided into several groups based on the pigments they contain.

Dinoflagellates These unicellular algae, whose flagella spin them through the water, look like tiny toy tops. Like euglenoids, they can be both autotrophic and heterotrophic. Although beautiful, some of these algae produce harmful toxins.

A population explosion of toxin-producing dinoflagellates has deadly consequences. When there is an increase in nutrients in the water, the dinoflagellate population can explode, or "bloom," to produce a red tide. Shellfish, such as clams and oysters, that eat large quantities of these algae store toxins in their cells. When these shellfish are eaten by fish or by humans, the toxins are passed through the food chain.

As You Read

Review the table you developed at the beginning of this lesson.

What characteristic do euglenoids, dinoflagellates, and diatoms have in common?

8.3 Introduce

ENGAGE Give each student or pair of students a prism, white paper, and a flashlight. Ask students to shine the light through the prism onto the paper and to draw and label the resulting spectrum. Students should be able to label red, orange, yellow, green, blue, indigo, and violet. Tell students that these colors are similar to pigments. Different algae have different pigments, resulting in different colors.

Before You Read

Have students complete the rows of their tables using the subheadings in the section titled *Types of Algae*. Describe for students the type of information needed in each column:

Structure—unicellular, multicellular, colony
Habitat—where the algae can be found
Nutrition—heterotroph, autotroph, or both
Important Information— distinguishing details

Teach

EXPLAIN that in this section, students will learn about the characteristics of plant-like protists and different types of plant-like protists.

As You Read

Give students about five minutes to review and update their charts. Check student charts to ensure that each type of plant-like protist has its information organized in the same row.

ANSWER All are unicellular, have chlorophyll, and live in water.

Vocabulary

algae Explain that *algae* describes a group of photosynthetic organisms that can be either unicellular or multicellular. Algae contain chlorophyll but do not have tissues and organs.

autotroph Explain that *auto-* means "self" and that *troph* is from a Greek word that means "to feed."

pigments Tell students that the word *pigment* is derived from the Latin root *pingere,* which means "to paint or color."

ELL Strategy

Use a Concept Map In their Science Notebooks, have students return to the *PROTISTS* concept map from Lesson 8.1. Have them add details and examples for plant-like protists.

Graphic Organizer Workbook, p. 50

CHAPTER 8 139

 Teach

EXPLAIN to students that they will learn about another type of plant-like protist, the diatom, and its characteristics.

 **Explain It!**

Have students make Venn diagrams or charts to show the similarities and differences. Remind them to analyze cell structure and method of locomotion.

CONNECTION: Earth Science

Place students in pairs, and tell them that scientists use diatoms to study El Niño cycles. Explain that El Niño is an abnormal climate event that begins with changes that occur in the Pacific Ocean every two to seven years. Ask students to hypothesize about the relationship between diatoms and climate and to write their hypotheses in their Science Notebooks. Ask for a few student pairs to share their hypotheses with the class.

After students read the article, ask them to revise their hypotheses by stating their new understanding of the relationship between diatoms and El Niño. Again, ask a few student pairs to share their statements. As a class, agree upon two or three sentences that best describe the relationship. Have students document the class statements in their Science Notebooks.

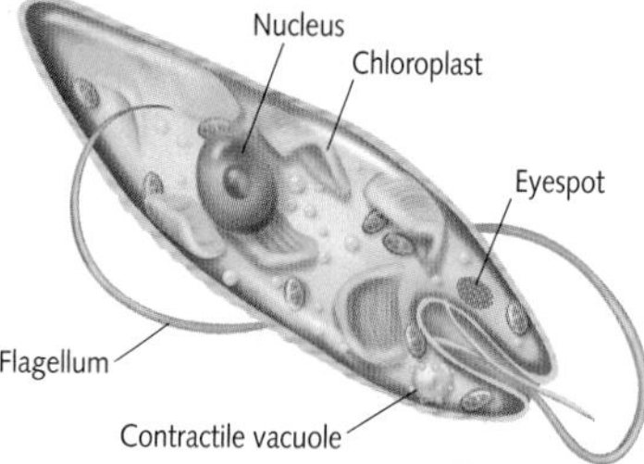

Figure 8.7 The eyespot of *Euglena gracilis* is not really an eye, but it contains pigments that are sensitive to light. The flagella of these organisms help them move toward light or food sources.

 **Explain It!**

Compare the euglena in **Figure 8.7** with the paramecium in **Figure 8.4**. Explain how these organisms are similar and how they are different.

Euglenoids This type of alga is closely related to the protozoans. Although euglenoids are green, unicellular algae usually found in freshwater, they can be heterotrophs. When light is not available for photosynthesis, they can find and capture food from their environment.

Diatoms Another type of plant-like protist is the diatom. These unicellular algae are enclosed in a two-part cell wall made of the element silicon, the main component of glass. Diatoms are often called "golden algae" because they contain pigments that give them a golden yellow color. These algae store the organic molecules they produce as oils, not starches. Because oil is less dense than water, it helps diatoms float in the upper part of the water so that they can absorb light from the Sun.

Figure 8.8 Diatom cell walls are covered with patterns that give each species a unique design.

Did You Know?

Forensic scientists use scientific evidence to solve possible crimes. If a body is recovered from water, diatoms may become key evidence in the case. Diatoms can be collected from a deceased person to determine the time of year in which the death occurred and to identify where the death occurred. Diatoms collected from suspects are used to place them at the crime scene.

CONNECTION: Earth Science

When diatoms die, their hard silicon cases fall to the floor of an ocean or lake and form deposits called diatomaceous earth, or diatomite. These deposits are important tools for studying events in Earth's history.

Diatoms are sensitive to changes in water conditions such as temperature, salinity (the amount of salt in water), and nutrient level. This sensitivity to the environment allows Earth scientists to use the fossilized remains of diatoms to reconstruct events such as ice ages and plate tectonic activity. By studying the diatom populations in coastal waters, Earth scientists can document the changes in water quality produced by the clear-cutting of forests, the damming of rivers and streams, and the use of fertilizers.

Diatomaceous earth, or diatomite, is used in fine china, swimming pool filters, acoustic tile, potting soils, and many household powders for cleaning or polishing. Because diatomite is also highly absorbent and does not react with other chemicals, it is also used in industrial absorbents that clean up oil and chemical spills and in pet litter to absorb odors. It can also be added to soil, where it acts as an insecticide. The sharp edges of the diatoms' silicon cell walls puncture the bodies of insects as they crawl through the soil.

Background Information

Diatoms can be found in bodies of water, such as oceans, lakes, rivers, and streams, and on moist soil. In water, they can live attached to rocks, sand, or plants or can float freely. In oceans, diatoms are one of the organisms that make up plankton. Common baleen whales, humpbacks, minkes, and right whales feed on plankton. Scientists estimate that there may be more than 12,000 species of diatoms distinguished by differences in the shells.

Red, Brown, and Green Algae These three types of algae are the most plant-like. Like plants, most of these algae are multicellular. They also have cell walls, pigments that are identical to those of plants, and reproductive cycles that are very similar to those of plants. The major difference among these three groups of autotrophic algae is the type of photosynthetic pigments they use to absorb light.

Figure It Out

1. What differences do you see among red, brown, and green algae?
2. Which type of algae is thought to be an ancestor of modern plants?

Figure 8.9 Red algae include seaweeds that can grow at depths of 100 m or more. They range in color from red to green to purple to black. They might look like flat sheets, rock formations, or clumps of hair swaying in the water. Red algae provide food for the animals that form coral reefs.

Figure 8.10 Brown algae contain yellowish-brown pigments that give them their brown color.

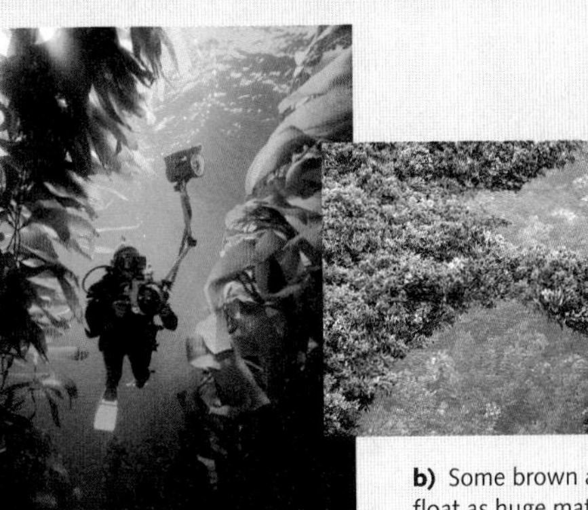

a) This diver is swimming in a forest of giant kelp, which can grow up to 50 m long. Kelp forests are ecosystems that provide many marine organisms with homes and food.

b) Some brown algae float as huge mats of seaweed at or near the ocean's surface, where there is plenty of sunlight. This carpet of brown algae is home to many different animals.

Figure 8.11 Green algae have cell walls made of cellulose, contain chlorophyll *a* and *b* pigments, and store their food as starch. Many scientists hypothesize that green algae and plants may have a common ancestor.

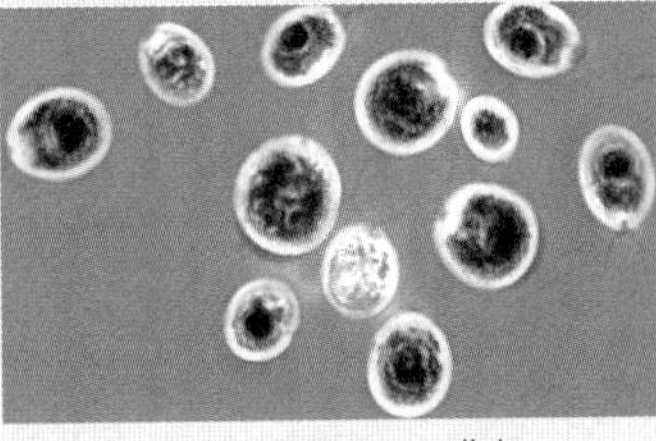

a) *Chlamydomonas* is a unicellular green algae found in freshwater and moist soil.

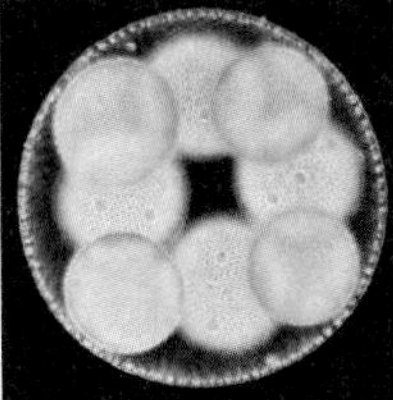

b) Some green algae, such as *Volvox*, live in multicellular colonies.

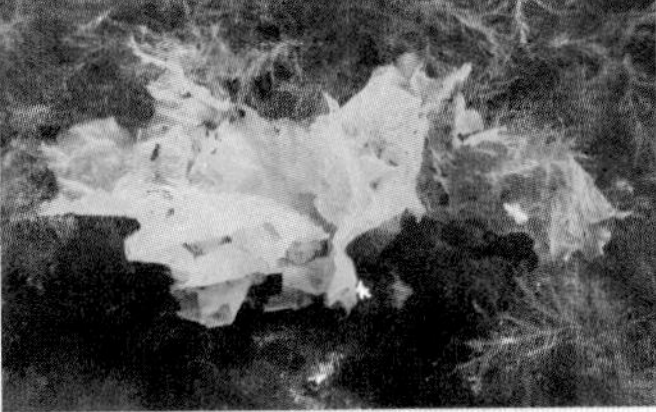

c) *Ulva*, commonly called sea lettuce, are multicellular green algae that live along rocky coasts.

Teach

EXPLAIN to students that red, brown, and green algae are the most closely related to plants. Students will learn about these algae and their characteristics.

Figure It Out: Figures 8.9, 8.10, and 8.11

ANSWER **1.** The main difference among these algae is the color of the pigments they contain. **2.** Green algae are believed to be the ancestor of modern plants.

Science Notebook EXTRA

Discuss with students the idea of a balance in ecosystems and its importance to the organisms living there. Have students imagine what might occur if algae became rampant and overgrown in a lake. What would the consequences be? Have students write a paragraph or draw a picture to illustrate the results of this imbalance.

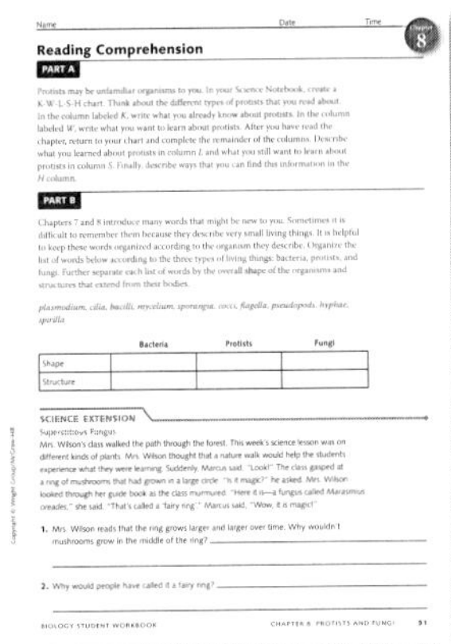
Reading Comprehension

PART A

PART B

SCIENCE EXTENSION

Reading Comprehension Workbook, p. 51

Background Information

Eutrophication occurs when bodies of water are polluted with chemicals, especially ones with nitrogen or phosphorus. These chemicals promote algal blooms that disrupt natural cycles. Algae grow faster than the cycle permits, and the lower layer of an algal bloom does not receive the light needed for photosynthesis. These algae die and decay, using up large amounts of oxygen in the water. Consequently, fish and other organisms can die from a lack of oxygen in the water. Their bodies similarly decay, and oxygen is further depleted in the water. A layer of mud results from all this decay, and the amount of water gradually shrinks.

Eutrophication is a natural process in lakes that is accelerated by human pollution. Detergents that contain phosphate, water from sewage treatment plants, and nitrates from fertilizers and automobile exhaust all contribute to this problem.

Teach

 EXPLAIN to students that they will learn about the effects of algae on other organisms in the world.

Vocabulary

phytoplankton Tell students that the prefix *phyto-* means "plant" and that the root *plankton* comes from the Greek word *planktos*, meaning "wandering." Phytoplankton are photosynthetic, microscopic organisms that float in the ocean.

Explore It!

Have students examine products at home, looking for alginate, carrageenan, or beta-carotene in ingredient lists. Ask students to make charts with two columns (*Product* and *Ingredient*) to organize information in their Science Notebooks. Have students note similarities of products with each ingredient.

Assess

EVALUATE Use the After You Read questions and the Alternative Assessment to help you assess students' understanding of this lesson.

After You Read

1. Plant-like protists are unicellular or multicellular, have eukaryotic cells with cell walls, and are autotrophs that capture energy and matter from their surroundings through photosynthesis.
2. Algae produce food for hetertrophs and oxygen.
3. Paragraphs should reflect the information in students' charts. Dinoflagellates and euglenoids are unicellular algae that can be autotrophic or heterotrophic. Diatoms are unicellular and autotrophic and have shells made of silica. Red, brown, and green algae are similar to plants, and they are autotrophic and often multicellular.

Alternative Assessment

EVALUATE Students can use their charts to write a short paragraph about each type of plant-like protist that contains information about the protist's structure, habitat, nutrition, and other essential details.

Algae in the World

Perhaps the most important role of algae is that of producers. Algae make up a large part of phytoplankton. **Phytoplankton** (FI toh PLANK tun) are photosynthetic organisms that live floating near the surface of the ocean and carry out much of the photosynthesis that occurs on Earth. Phytoplankton are the main producers in many aquatic food chains and food webs. Through the process of photosynthesis, algae produce about half of the oxygen found in Earth's atmosphere!

Algae are also used as a food supply for humans. In some parts of the world, algae are an important source of protein and are actually grown on large farms. In the United States, algae are used in ice cream, pudding, and candy to thicken them and to keep them from separating.

Algae are also used to study microorganisms such as bacteria. Agar, which is made from seaweed, is used to thicken the nutrient mixtures used to grow bacteria so that the bacteria can be studied.

Figure 8.12 The seaweed used to wrap the fish, rice, and vegetables in Japanese sushi is a type of algae.

Algal blooms also occur in freshwater. When nutrients from the land run off into a pond or lake, algae populations explode, or "bloom." The rapid growth of algae makes it impossible for sunlight to reach other algae and plants beneath the surface. These organisms die and sink to the bottom, where bacteria break down their bodies. As the bacteria use the oxygen in the water, fish begin to die. The only organisms that survive these population explosions are the algae themselves. Freshwater blooms of algae are easier to control than red tides are because ponds and lakes have definite boundaries. Wastes from human sources, such as crop fertilizers or pipes that leak sewage, are often responsible for the increased nutrients. If the source of the nutrients can be eliminated, the lake can eventually return to normal.

Explore It!

Go on a scavenger hunt in your home, and identify as many products as you can that contain algae. Record your observations in your Science Notebook.

After You Read

1. Describe the characteristics of plant-like protists.
2. How are algae important to living things on Earth?
3. Use the information in your table to compare dinoflagellates, euglenoids, and diatoms with red, brown, and green algae. Write a well-developed paragraph describing the main differences among these groups of algae.

Background Information

Carrageenan is derived from the cell walls of red algae such as *Rhodophycaea* and is used for its abilities to suspend, emulsify, stabilize, and gel. About 80 percent of its use is in food processing, especially in dairy products. Other industries that use carrageenan include the cosmetics, pharmaceutical, printing, and textile industries.

Alginate is found in the cell walls of brown algae, including rockweeds and kelps, where it is partly responsible for the flexibility of the algae. Brown algae that grow in turbulent conditions usually have higher alginate contents than those that grow in calmer waters and are best suited for extracting alginate. Alginate is useful because of its suspending, emulsifying, and gelling properties. About half of all alginate used is in dairy products. Alginate is also used in textiles, paper, printing supplies, paint, cosmetics, and pharmaceuticals.

8.4 Fungus-Like Protists

Before You Read

Record each heading in this lesson in the form of a question. Write the questions in your Science Notebook. As you read, write answers to the questions.

Learning Goals

- Compare and contrast the different types of fungus-like protists.
- Identify the roles played by fungus-like protists in the living world.

New Vocabulary

plasmodium
hypha

Imagine stepping into your backyard to find a huge, reddish, jelly-like mass on the grass. Many questions would probably come to mind. Is it alive? Is it an animal, a plant, or a new life-form? Is it dangerous? In 1973, a Dallas resident had exactly this experience. Biologists called to the scene were able to assure neighbors that a menacing creature was not about to ooze its way throughout the area, eating everything in its path. The biologists identified the mass as a slime mold. Slime molds, water molds, and mildews are fungus-like protists.

What Are Fungus-Like Protists?

Fungus-like protists resemble fungi. You will learn more about fungi in Lessons 8.5 and 8.6. To understand what fungus-like protists are, you need to know that fungi are organisms that are similar to both animals and plants. Like animals, fungi are heterotrophs that obtain food by consuming organic molecules from the environment. Like plants, fungi have cells that are surrounded by cell walls.

Fungus-like protists are heterotrophs that obtain food by decomposing dead plants and animals and then absorbing the nutrients. These protists have cells with cell walls, and they reproduce by spore formation.

Figure 8.13 Slime molds grow in moist, shaded environments where there are plenty of dead organisms to feed on.

Figure 8.14 Fungus-like protists such as the water mold on this fish are similar to both the plant-like protists and animal-like protists discussed in earlier lessons.

8.4 Introduce

ENGAGE Provide students with a maze worksheet. Ask them to find their way from the entrance to the exit. Time how long it takes most students to solve the maze. Tell them that they have probably heard that rats and other intelligent organisms have been able to find their way through mazes. Then, inform students that a slime mold was also able to find the shortest path through a maze when scientists placed bits of oat at each end. It did take the slime mold eight hours to complete the task—probably a longer amount of time than was required by the students to complete their own mazes.

Before You Read

Read the first Learning Goal as a class. Ask student volunteers to practice forming the goal into a question. Write their responses on the board. Possible answers include: *What are the characteristics of fungus-like protists? How are fungus-like protists different from other protists?*

Have students create questions for the other Learning Goal in their Science Notebooks, allowing space after the questions for notes and answers. Check students' questions throughout the lesson.

Teach

EXPLAIN to students that in this section, they will learn about the characteristics of fungus-like protists and the ways in which types of fungus-like protists are alike and different.

ELL Strategy

Paraphrase Have students paraphrase, or reword, the important information about fungus-like protists—slime molds, water molds, and mildews—by writing the new wording in their Science Notebooks. Then, have pairs of students share their paraphrasing so that they can revise their work based on feedback from their partners.

Teach

EXPLAIN to students that in this section, they will learn about three types of fungus-like protists: slime molds, water molds, and mildews.

EXPLORE Write the words *Plant* and *Animal* on the board. Ask students to identify characteristics of each type of organism, and list student responses on the board under the appropriate heading. Ask a volunteer to put a star next to each characteristic that can be used to describe fungus-like protists.

As You Read

ANSWER Fungus-like protists are heterotrophs that reproduce by spores and whose cells have cell walls.

Vocabulary

plasmodium Explain to students that the root *plasm-* refers to cytoplasm of a specified type; the word part *-ode* means "like." The suffix, *-ium*, denotes a biological structure. When these parts are combined, the literal meaning is "a biological structure like a cytoplasm."

hypha Tell students that *hypha* originates from the Greek word *hyphē*, which means "web." The mass of threadlike filaments, or hyphae, may appear to be similar to a spider's web.

Figure It Out: Figure 8.15

ANSWER **1.** Spores develop into new slime mold cells. **2.** Environmental conditions are no longer favorable when the plasmodium develops spore-producing structures called fruiting bodies.

Use the Visual: Figure 8.16

ANSWER Hyphae secrete digestive enzymes onto the food organism. The food organism's nutrients are then absorbed through the hyphae.

As You Read

According to the questions and answers in your Science Notebook, what are the characteristics of fungus-like protists?

Types of Fungus-Like Protists

Fungus-like protists include organisms known as slime molds, water molds, and mildews.

Slime Molds One of the more interesting types of fungus-like protists is the slime mold. A slime mold is made up of a large number of individual cells that come together to form a jelly-like mass called a **plasmodium** (plaz MOH dee um). The plasmodium of most slime molds is visible to the unaided eye and can be more than a meter in diameter. Slime molds ooze along like giant amoebas and eat decaying plants, bacteria, fungi, and even other slime molds.

As long as there is enough food and moisture in the environment, the cells of a slime mold work together. But when food and moisture become scarce, the slime mold begins the reproductive process shown in **Figure 8.15**. The plasmodium grows stalks topped by spore-producing structures called fruiting bodies. Spores released into the environment are carried by rain or wind to new locations, where they can germinate and produce new cells that allow the slime mold to start a new life cycle.

Figure It Out

1. What do spores released by a slime mold become?
2. At what point in this cycle would you infer that food and water have become scarce in the environment?

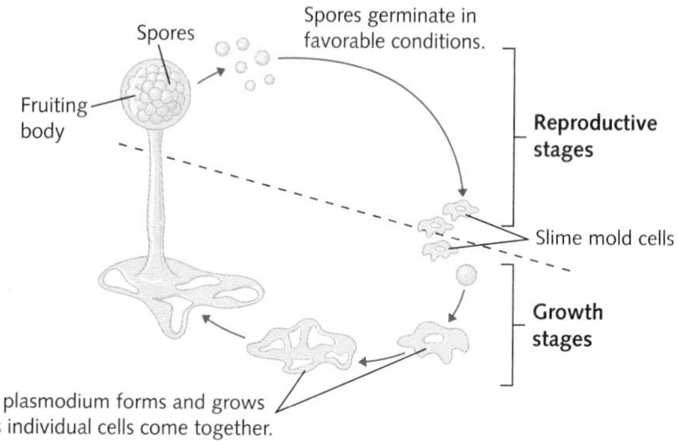

Figure 8.15 Slime molds go through many stages in their life cycles.

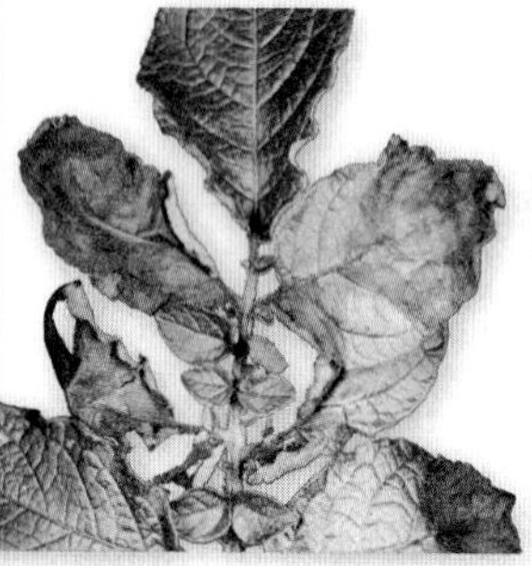

Figure 8.16 Water molds and mildews live in moist environments and cause plant and animal diseases. What function do hyphae of fungus-like protists have?

Water Molds and Mildews These types of fungus-like protists live in wet environments such as freshwater or the upper layers of moist soil. These organisms absorb their food from the surrounding water or soil, or they may invade the body of another organism to feed. The fish in Figure 8.14 on page 143 has been attacked by a water mold. Water molds and mildews that attack fish and plants are disease-causing parasites.

The thin, fuzzy threads growing on the fish in Figure 8.14 are called **hyphae** (HI fee, singular: hypha). Digestive enzymes ooze out of the hyphae onto the fish and break down the nutrients in its body. Once digested, the nutrients are absorbed by the water mold through the hyphae.

Background Information

There are two types of slime molds: cellular and plasmodial. Plasmodial slime molds are the most common type, and they form when amoeba-like cells fuse their cell membranes to produce a multinucleated mass. In cellular slime molds, the individual cells remain separated by cell walls throughout the life cycle. Cellular slime molds come together as a mass when environmental conditions are unfavorable and work together to produce fruiting bodies and spores.

Reproduction in Fungi

Depending on the type of fungus and the environmental conditions, most fungi reproduce both asexually and sexually.

Asexual Reproduction Fungi are able to reproduce asexually by fragmentation, by budding, or by the production of spores. During fragmentation, pieces of hyphae that are separated from the mycelium grow into a new mycelium. Fragmentation often occurs when the ground is disturbed in preparation for planting. Plows and shovels used to prepare the soil cut through the underground mycelia of fungi. Each fragment grows into a new mycelium.

Most fungi use spores to reproduce. A spore is a reproductive cell that can grow into a new organism. Some fungi produce spores in reproductive hyphae that have grown up from the mycelium. The reproductive hyphae that produce spores are called **sporangia** (spuh RAN jee uh, singular: sporangium). Above ground structures such as mushrooms are fruiting bodies that contain many closely packed sporangia. When a fungal spore is transported to a favorable environment, hyphae sprout from the spore and a new fungus begins to grow. If the spore lands in an unfavorable environment, it protects the new fungus until conditions improve or the spore is carried to a new location.

Fungi have developed a number of ways to distribute spores in the environment. Some fungi produce a fluid that smells like rotting meat and attracts flies. As the flies eat the fluid, they also eat the spores and then deposit them as they fly around. Some fungi actually throw their spores away from the mycelium. Many spores are carried by wind and animals.

Sexual Reproduction Fungi can also reproduce sexually, primarily when environmental conditions are unfavorable. During sexual reproduction, the hyphae of two fungi grow together and exchange genetic material. A new spore-producing structure grows from these joined hyphae. Spores produced by this process are genetically different from either parent fungus.

Explore It!

Carefully scrape or shake spores from the cap of a mushroom onto a sheet of white paper. Observe the spores with a hand lens. Place several spores on a microscope slide, and use a microscope to observe the spores. Make drawings of your observations in your Science Notebook.

Figure It Out

1. What is contained in the cloud above the puffballs?
2. Do you think most fungi reproduce sexually or asexually?

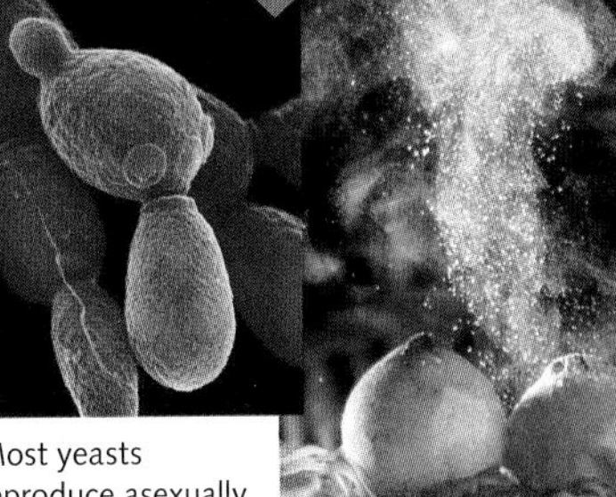

Most yeasts reproduce asexually by budding.

Puffballs are fruiting bodies that can produce up to a trillion spores to guarantee species survival.

Figure 8.19 Fungi reproduce asexually by fragmentation, budding, or the production of spores.

After You Read

1. What characteristics do all fungi have in common?
2. How do fungi reproduce?
3. Review the facts you recorded in your Science Notebook. Which fungi fact is the most interesting to you? Justify your selection.

Background Information

Poisonous mushrooms produce toxins, or harmful chemical compounds. If eaten by humans, most poisonous mushrooms will produce symptoms such as nausea, diarrhea, or headaches. Eating most poisonous mushrooms would not be fatal; however, those that are fatal cause delayed reactions, including abdominal pain, violent vomiting, and weakness. If left untreated, the toxins may cause liver damage, kidney damage, or death.

Amanitas are the deadliest of mushrooms. Some of the specific mushrooms in this group include the destroying angel, the fly agaric, and jack-o'-lantern.

Teach

EXPLAIN to students that they will learn about the different ways in which fungi reproduce.

Figure It Out: Figure 8.19

ANSWER **1.** The cloud above the puffballs contains spores. **2.** All reproduce asexually, and most reproduce sexually.

Explore It!

Be sure to provide students with mushrooms from a grocery store only. Students can also make spore prints of the mushrooms. To make a spore print, cut the cap off the mushroom and place it gill-side down on clean white paper. Cover the cap with a plastic container, and allow it to sit for two days. When the container and the mushroom cap are removed, students should observe lines radiating outward from the center. You may want to provide different groups of students with different types of edible mushrooms and have them compare the spores of each species.

Assess

EVALUATE Use the After You Read questions and the Alternative Assessment to help you assess students' understanding of this lesson.

After You Read

1. All fungi are eukaryotic heterotrophs that use spores to reproduce.
2. Fungi reproduce both asexually and sexually. Asexual reproduction occurs by budding, fragmentation, and spore formation.
3. Answers will vary.

Alternative Assessment

EVALUATE Have students use their lists of facts to create concept maps explaining the different ways that reproduction occurs in fungi.

8.6 Introduce

ENGAGE About 20 to 30 minutes before class, set up an example of active yeast. Fill a clear glass about 1/3 full of warm water (40°C), add 2 teaspoons of sugar, add 1 teaspoon of yeast, and stir to dissolve.

Ask students to hypothesize what the foam is (bubbles of carbon dioxide) and how it might have formed (by yeast). After a few responses, give the following clues one at a time, allowing students to hypothesize after each clue: **1.** A fungus made the foam. **2.** The foam contains bubbles of a gas you exhale. **3.** This fungus is used to make bread products. **4.** This fungus makes the bread rise.

Before You Read

Demonstrate the process of speculating about the definition of a word. Then, ask students to correct their definitions as they read the information in this lesson.

Teach

EXPLAIN that in this lesson, students will learn how the four groups of fungi are classified and find out about the importance of fungi in the world around us.

Vocabulary

mold Explain that *mold* is a woolly or furry growth, often green or white, that appears on food and other animal or vegetable substances when left in a warm, moist place or when they decay.

sac fungus Tell students that *sac fungi* produce spores in special pods, or saclike structures.

club fungus Explain that *club fungi* produce spores in microscopic, clublike structures.

imperfect fungus Tell students that *imperfect fungi* either have no sexual phase or have a sexual phase that has not yet been discovered.

lichen Tell students that a lichen is a symbiotic association between a fungus and a green alga or a bacterium. Review the meaning of *symbiosis*.

Figure It Out: Figure 8.20

ANSWER **1.** molds **2.** shape of spore-producing structures and how it reproduces

As You Read

ANSWER The largest group is the sac fungi. The most well-known are the mushrooms.

8.6 Diversity of Fungi

Learning Goals

- Describe how scientists classify fungi.
- Name and describe the four groups of fungi.
- Identify the roles played by fungi in the living world.

New Vocabulary

mold
sac fungus
club fungus
imperfect fungus
lichen

Before You Read

Select three of the terms from the vocabulary list. Write them in your Science Notebook. Under each, write what you think the term means. As you encounter each term while you read, correct or add to your definition.

Fungi are classified into four groups based on the shape of their spore-producing structures and how they reproduce. **Figure 8.20** shows examples of these four groups.

Types of Fungi

Threadlike fungi, or **molds**, are easily identified as the fuzzy growths on rotten food. Most molds reproduce asexually by producing spores in sporangia. Molds function in nature as decomposers or parasites.

The largest group of fungi are the **sac fungi**. They are called sac fungi because most of them produce spores during sexual reproduction in structures that look like small sacs. When the sacs burst, spores are released into the environment. Some sac fungi are multicellular and are visible as they grow. Other sac fungi, such as yeast, are unicellular and reproduce by budding.

Mushrooms are probably the most well-known fungi. Mushrooms are **club fungi** that produce spores sexually in structures shaped like clubs. The clublike structures are found on the gills of the mushroom.

Fungi that are not known to reproduce sexually are called **imperfect fungi**. The best known of the imperfect fungi is *Penicillium*, which is a mold that grows on fruit and is the source of the antibiotic penicillin.

As You Read

Reread the definitions of the vocabulary terms. Add to or correct your definitions.

Which is the largest group of fungi? Which is the most well-known group?

Figure It Out

1. Which group of fungi would be unwelcome in your refrigerator?
2. What would you need to know in order to classify a fungus you found?

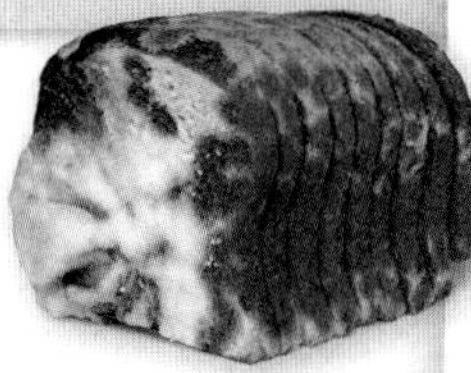

Figure 8.20 The four groups of fungi—*(left to right)* molds, sac fungi, club fungi, and imperfect fungi—exhibit a wide range of shapes, sizes, and colors.

ELL Strategy

Share Information Have students work in small groups to find additional information and photographs of each of the four types of fungi. Then have students share their newly gained knowledge with their peers.

Field Study

Have students walk in a shady, moist, and wooded area and look for different fungi. Provide labeled pictures of fungi likely to grow in your climate. Ask students to sketch the fungi they find, note where each was found, and try to match each fungus with the provided pictures.

Fungi in the World

Fungi are adapted to playing many important roles in Earth's ecosystems.

Recycling Nutrients Fungi are decomposers. Decomposers break down the remains of dead plants and animals and return nutrients to the environment. The most important role played by fungi in Earth's ecosystems is that of decomposer.

Food The smell of fresh-baked bread, the sight of blue streaks in bleu cheese, and the taste of mushrooms in a salad would not be possible without fungi. Fungi are sources of food, and they are used in the production of some foods. Yeast is needed to make bread. Molds are important in the production of some cheeses. The blue streaks in bleu cheese are patches of spores from the mold *Penicillium roqueforti.*

Medicines In 1928, Alexander Fleming observed that mold in a petri dish not only prevented bacterial growth but also killed the bacteria near it. This led to the development of the first antibiotic—penicillin. The mold *Penicillium* provided an effective treatment against bacteria. Many other antibiotics have been developed from other fungi.

Relationships with Other Living Things Fungi have different relationships with other organisms in ecosystems. Fungi in parasitic relationships cause diseases in plants and animals. Corn smut and wheat rust are club fungi that attack crops as they grow. Some fungi destroy crops already harvested and stored, such as wheat, rice, and rye.

Parasitic fungi can also attack humans. The itch and irritation of athlete's foot is produced as the mycelium of the fungus grows into the outer layers of the skin. The red sores that form release the spores of the fungus, which spread easily to other human feet that come in contact with the spores. Fortunately, athlete's foot and other irritations caused by fungi are easily treated with antifungal medications.

Some fungi form mutualistic relationships with other organisms in which both organisms benefit. One example is a lichen. A **lichen** (LI kun) is the partnership between a fungus and an alga. The fungus provides a stable, moist environment for the alga, and the alga provides food for the fungus. This relationship allows lichens to live in places where algae and fungi could not live alone.

Figure 8.21 The mushroom *Amanita muscaria (top)* is extremely poisonous. The mushroom *Amanita caesarea (center)* is edible. The multicolored spots on the rocks *(bottom)* are lichens.

After You Read

1. How do scientists classify fungi?
2. Describe roles that fungi play in the world. Identify the most important.
3. Review the vocabulary terms in your Science Notebook. Use them to develop a concept map to illustrate groups into which fungi are classified.

Extend It!

Research the discovery and history of penicillin. Summarize your research in your Science Notebook.

Teach

EXPLAIN to students that they will be able to better understand how fungi impact other organisms.

Extend It!

Provide resources for student research, including scientific journals, encyclopedias, and Internet access. Guide students through research on the Internet by using keywords and student-appropriate search engines such as the Librarians' Internet Index at **http://lii.org/**.

Assess

EVALUATE Use the After You Read questions and the Alternative Assessment to help you assess students' understanding of this lesson.

After You Read

1. Fungi are put into groups based on the shapes of their spore-producing structures and the ways in which they reproduce.
2. Fungi are important sources of food and are used in the production of foods and medicines. The roles played by fungi in Earth's ecosystems include decomposition of dead organisms and recycling nutrients, but they can also cause disease. The role of fungi as decomposers is the most important.
3. Concept maps will vary, but the four groups of fungi should all be on the same level in a student's concept map. The key word between the title, *Fungi*, and the name of each of the four groups should correctly identify the spore-producing structure for that group.

Differentiated Instruction

Visual Provide students with drawing paper and markers. Have students illustrate the different types of fungi they have read about. Create a bulletin board display titled *Diversity of Fungi*.

Background Information

Before the discovery of penicillin, there had been no treatment for illnesses such as pneumonia and rheumatic fever, and it was not unusual for people to die or suffer chronically from those diseases. Although Fleming discovered penicillin in 1928, it was not until 1941 that penicillin was successfully used to treat a patient. Merck & Co. was able to produce enough penicillin in 1942 to treat 11 cases. In 1944, Pfizer opened the first commercial plant for the large-scale production of penicillin in Brooklyn, New York.

Alternative Assessment

EVALUATE Have students use the definitions in their Science Notebooks to summarize the characteristics of each of the four groups of fungi. Students should also include the spore-forming structure for each.

Chapter 8 Summary

VOCABULARY REVIEW

Check students' sentences or paragraphs to make sure they understand the meaning of each vocabulary term.

PREPARE FOR CHAPTER TEST

Evaluate students' essays using the following criteria:

1. The topic sentence, or main idea, should restate the Key Concept.
2. The supporting paragraphs should incorporate the answers to the Learning Goal questions students have written and include details, facts, and examples they have recorded in their Science Notebooks.
3. The concluding sentence should sum up the main idea of the chapter and restate the Key Concept.

MASTERING CONCEPTS

True or False

1. False, red tide
2. False, algae
3. True
4. False, contractile vacuoles
5. True
6. True
7. False, Sporangia
8. True

Short Answer

9. A paramecium uses its cilia to direct food into the gullet. The end of the gullet is enclosed in a food vacuole, where digestive enzymes break down the complex substances into simple substances that the paramecium can use.
10. Animal-like and fungus-like protists are heterotrophs; plant-like protists are autotrophs.
11. Fungi reproduce sexually when hyphae from two different fungi grow together, exchange genetic material, and produce a new spore-forming structure.
12. The fungus in a lichen benefits because the alga or bacterium provides food; the alga or bacterium in a lichen benefits because the fungus provides a stable environment with a ready supply of water and minerals.

Chapter 8

Summary

KEY CONCEPTS

8.1 Protists

- Protists are eukaryotic organisms that cannot be classified as animals, plants, or fungi.
- Protists are divided into three general groups based on how they obtain nutrition: animal-like protists, plant-like protists, and fungus-like protists.

8.2 Animal-Like Protists: Protozoans

- Protozoans are unicellular heterotrophs that can move.
- Heterotrophs are organisms that must consume other organisms for food.
- Protozoans are divided into four groups based on how they move.
- Amoebas move by extending pseudopods, ciliates use cilia, zooflagellates use flagella, and sporozoans depend on their host organism.
- Some protozoans are parasites, and some are decomposers.

8.3 Plant-Like Protists: Algae

- Algae are unicellular and multicellular autotrophs.
- Algae are a source of food and oxygen for many organisms.

8.4 Fungus-Like Protists

- Fungus-like protists are heterotrophic decomposers.
- Slime molds, water molds, and mildews make up this group of protists.
- Some fungus-like protists cause diseases in plants and animals.

8.5 Fungi

- Fungi are heterotrophs that obtain food by digesting the substances on which they are growing.
- Fungi are made of hyphae, which grow in a tangled mass to form a mycelium.
- Fungi reproduce using spores, which can be produced through both asexual and sexual reproduction.

8.6 Diversity of Fungi

- The four groups of fungi are molds, sac fungi, club fungi, and imperfect fungi.
- Most fungi are decomposers, but some are involved in parasitic or mutualistic relationships.
- A lichen forms when an alga and a fungus form a mutualistic partnership.
- Some fungi are disease-causing parasites that attack both plants and animals.

VOCABULARY REVIEW

Write each term in a complete sentence, or write a paragraph relating several terms.

8.1
protist, p. 135

8.2
heterotroph, p. 136
protozoan, p. 136
pseudopod, p. 136
contractile vacuole, p. 136
cilia, p. 137
spore, p. 138

8.3
alga, p. 139
autotroph, p. 139
pigment, p. 139
phytoplankton, p. 142

8.4
plasmodium, p. 144
hypha, p. 144

8.5
fungus, p. 146
mycelium, p. 146
sporangium, p. 147

8.6
mold, p. 148
sac fungus, p. 148
club fungus, p. 148
imperfect fungus, p. 148
lichen, p. 149

PREPARE FOR CHAPTER TEST

To prepare for the chapter test, create a question from each Learning Goal. Use the information in your Science Notebook to answer each question. Then use these answers to write a well-developed essay about the chapter. Use the Key Concept on the first page of this chapter as your topic sentence.

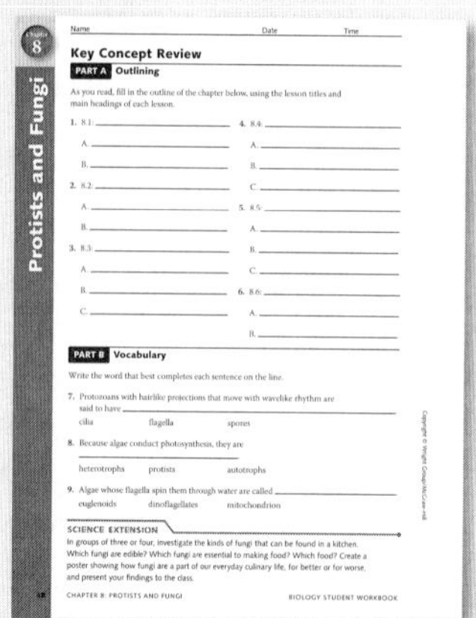

Key Concept Review Workbook, p. 48

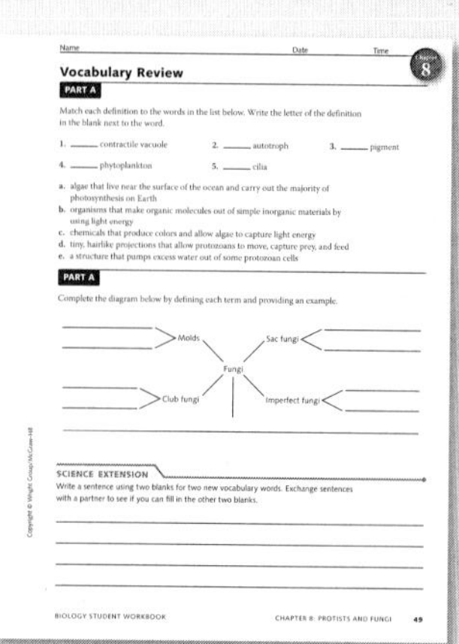

Vocabulary Review Workbook, p. 49

MASTERING CONCEPTS

True or False

If the statement is true, write "true." If it is false, change the underlined word or words to make the statement true.

1. A population explosion of dinoflagellates is called a <u>lichen</u>.
2. Phytoplankton in aquatic food chains are <u>protozoans</u>.
3. All protists are <u>eukaryotes</u>.
4. In protists, <u>flagella</u> eliminate extra water that might cause the cell to burst.
5. Hyphae are threadlike tubes that form the <u>mycelium</u> of fungi.
6. <u>Yeasts</u> are fungi that reproduce by budding rather than by spore formation.
7. <u>Cilia</u> are structures in fungi that produce spores.
8. <u>Fungi</u> can be unicellular or multicellular, but they are all heterotrophs.

Short Answer

Answer each of the following in a sentence or brief paragraph.

9. Describe how a paramecium obtains and digests food.
10. Compare how animal-like, plant-like, and fungus-like protists obtain nutrients. Use the words *autotroph* and *heterotroph* and their definitions in your answer.
11. Describe how sexual reproduction in fungi occurs.
12. Explain why lichens are considered to be a mutualistic relationship.

Critical Thinking

Use what you have learned in this chapter to answer each of the following.

13. **Hypothesize** A neighboring farmer recently fertilized his fields. After a heavy rain, you notice that the surface of a nearby pond is covered with a thick layer of green algae. Develop a hypothesis to explain your observation.
14. **Predict** What would happen to life on Earth if protists suddenly disappeared? Explain your answer.
15. **Apply Concepts** Design a poster for the locker room to educate athletes on how to prevent athlete's foot.

Standardized Test Question

Choose the letter of the response that correctly answers the question.

16. Malaria is most common in tropical regions of the world, such as Africa, Southeast Asia, and Central and South America. Why is malaria **not** common in North America and Europe?
    A. The climate in tropical regions of the world provides a warm, moist environment in which the mosquito host for the malaria parasite can live and reproduce.
    B. The fungus that causes malaria is not found outside tropical regions of the world.
    C. The climate in North America and Europe is not as warm and moist as that in tropical regions of the world.
    D. People in North America and Europe are resistant to the malaria parasite.

Test-Taking Tip

If more than one choice for a multiple-choice question seems correct, ask yourself if each choice completely and directly answers the question. If a choice is only partially true or does not directly answer the question, it is probably not the correct answer.

Critical Thinking

13. Runoff from the rain carried excess nutrients from the fertilizer into the pond. The algae in the pond used the nutrients to reproduce and rapidly increase their population to form the layer of green scum on the pond's surface.
14. Life on Earth would probably disappear. Algae and protozoans provide food for many animals as the base of most aquatic food chains and food webs. Algae are also key organisms in the production of the oxygen found in Earth's waters and atmosphere.
15. Posters should be both informative and creative. Posters should illustrate how important it is to avoid providing the warm, moist environment favored by this fungus.

Standardized Test Question

16. C

Reading Links

Lake and Pond

This colorful, well-organized exploration of lake and pond biomes, full of interesting facts, photos, and diagrams, examines the life-forms that thrive in these habitats. Also included are discussions of diatoms, algae, and other organisms covered in this chapter.

Sayre, April Pulley. Lerner Publishing Group. 64 pp. Illustrated. Library ISBN: 978-0-8050-4089-0.

Guide to Microlife

With excellent photographs, sketches, interesting facts, and a useful six-part appendix, this handbook offers an extensive cataloguing of microorganisms with just enough information for the student or amateur scientist. Information about microfungi and protists makes up two of the book's four sections. Treatment of each individual specimen, most of which are readily found in puddles, woods, and other local habitats, includes specific instructions about collection, slide preparation, and microscope use in addition to information about taxonomy, behavior, environment, and characteristics (often accompanied by project suggestions).

Rainis, G. Kenneth and Russell, J. Bruce. Scholastic Library Publishing. 288 pp. Illustrated. Trade ISBN: 978-0-531-11266-3.

History Connection: Famine in Ireland

Curriculum Connection Workbook, p. 52

Science Challenge — Toxoplasmosis

Science Challenge Workbook, pp. 53–54

CHAPTER 8 151

Chapter 8

Labs

8A A Whole New World

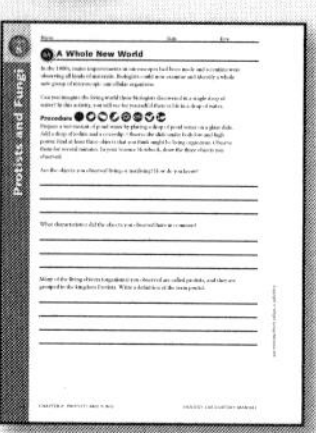

This prechapter introduction activity is designed to allow students to observe a variety of protists and identify similarities within this diverse group of organisms.

Objectives

- demonstrate proper use of a microscope
- prepare a wet-mount slide
- make and record observations
- form an operational definition of the term *protist*

Planning

 1 class period  groups of 2–4 students

Materials (per group)

- mixed protist culture or pond water
- microscope slide
- coverslip
- microscope
- iodine
- droppers

Advance Preparation

- Collect pond water samples or purchase a prepared culture that contains a variety of protists for students to observe. Observe this first to make sure that it contains living organisms.
- **CAUTION:** *Students should use iodine carefully. Iodine is poisonous if ingested and will stain clothing and skin.*
- You may also want to have students prepare and observe a slide of diatomaceous earth. Diatomaceous earth can be purchased at plant nurseries. Prepare a slide by swirling a toothpick dipped in diatomaceous earth in a drop of iodine on a slide and covering with a coverslip. If you collect pond water, it may contain more than just protists. Depending on the time of year it is collected, the water may have larva of insects or midges.

Engagement Guide

- To begin the activity, show students a container of pond water. Add some of the water to a petri dish, and place it on the overhead projector. Ask:
  - *Do you think there are any living organisms in this water? Why?* (Answers will vary. Most students will say yes, but the organisms are too small to be seen without using a microscope.)
  - *What characteristics can you use to determine if the objects you observe are living things?* (Students should recall that living things exhibit the characteristics of life: they are made of cells, respond to their environment, reproduce, and grow and develop.)
  - *What cell parts might be observed if you see living things in the water?* (Students might predict that the cell membrane and nucleus would be visible. Remind students that organisms can be unicellular or multicellular and that cells can be prokaryotic or eukaryotic, meaning they have a nucleus and other organelles.)
- Remind students to base their definitions of *protist* on their observations and their knowledge of cells.

Going Further

Encourage students to use prepared slides of a variety of different protists, such as paramecia, euglenas, amoebas, and multicellular algae, to identify the protists they observed in the pond water.

8B Food Fit for a Fungus

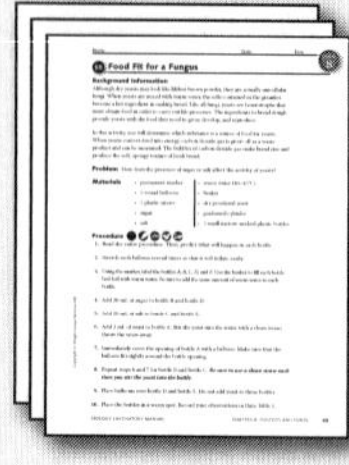

Objectives

- make predictions
- record observations
- recognize cause and effect
- draw conclusions

Skill Set

observing, comparing and contrasting, recording and analyzing data, stating and drawing conclusions

Planning

 1 class period  groups of 4 students

Materials

Materials for this activity are listed in the Student Laboratory Manual.

Lab Tip

It may be a good idea to give the students an average time it will take before they can expect visible results.

Answers to Observations: Data Table 1

Students' predictions will vary. Bottle A: did not inflate; bottle B: inflated; bottle C: did not inflate; bottle D: did not inflate; bottle E: did not inflate

Answers to Analysis and Conclusions

1. The balloon for bottle B inflated because carbon dioxide gas was produced in this bottle; balloons for bottles A, C, and D did not inflate because carbon dioxide gas was not produced in these bottles. The balloons were stretched out so that they would inflate easily.
2. Bottle A was the control because it did not contain either of the substances being tested as a food source for yeast (salt and sugar).
3. Bottle D was included to show that sugar alone does not produce carbon dioxide gas. Bottle E was included to show that salt alone does not produce carbon dioxide gas. Yeast is needed.
4. Sugar is a food source for yeasts. When sugar was converted to energy, carbon dioxide gas was produced and filled the balloon of bottle B. Carbon dioxide gas was not produced in any other bottle.
5. Without sugar, the bread would not rise because the yeast would not have a source of food to convert to energy, and no carbon dioxide gas would be released. Forgetting to add salt would not affect bread rising.

Going Further

Using similar materials, have students design an experiment to test the effect of temperature on the metabolic activity of yeasts.

8C An Explosion of Algae

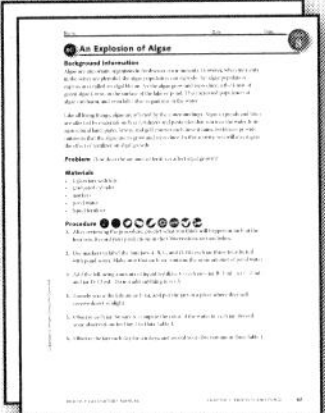

Objectives

- control variables
- make predictions about algal growth
- make observations over an extended period of time
- draw conclusions about fertilizer use

Skill Set

measuring, observing, comparing and contrasting, recording and analyzing data, stating conclusions

Planning

 1 class period (plus daily class time to make and record observations)

 groups of 2–4 students

Materials

Materials for this activity are listed in the Student Laboratory Manual.

Lab Tips

A list of safe liquid fertilizers should be provided.

Advance Preparation

Collect pond water samples several days before the lab, or purchase algae cultures from a biological supply house. Data Table 1 is set up for ten days of observations; however, depending on the amount of algal growth, you may increase or decrease the observation period.

Answers to Observations

Predictions: Students' predictions will vary, but students should predict that there will be less algal growth in jars with less fertilizer.

Data Table 1: The water should be a more intense green color as you move from jar A to D and as the observations progress from Day 1 through Day 10.

Answers to Analysis and Conclusions

1. The differences in the color and cloudiness of the water in the jars are due to the amount of fertilizer.
2. Jar A serves as a control and is used for comparison.
3. Algae use the nutrients in the fertilizer to reproduce very rapidly. As the algae population in the water increases, the water changes to a darker green.
4. Fertilizer increases algal growth. The greatest algal growth occurred when the greatest amount of fertilizer was added to the pond water.
5. Because light required for photosynthesis would not have been present, the color of the pond water in each jar would not have changed.
6. Algal blooms result in the death of other plants and algae because the thick layer of algae at the surface prevents those organisms from obtaining necessary sunlight. As bacteria decompose these dead organisms, they use the oxygen in the water; without oxygen, other fish and animals will also die.

Going Further

Phosphates are ingredients found in many fertilizers and in detergents used to clean clothes. Have students design an experiment that compares the effect of regular detergent and low-phosphate detergent on the growth of algae.

Unit 3

Case Study 1: Pollution-Fighting Microbes

Gather More Information

Encourage students to use the library or the NSTA SciLinks Web site noted at the start of each chapter to learn more about these case study topics and to conduct further research.

Have students use the following keywords to aid their searches:

- bioremediation
- *Geobacter sulfurreducens*
- chemical contamination
- microbial cleanup
- pollution-eating microbe
- pollution-fighting plant

Research the Big Picture

- Bioremediation is being used all over the world. Have students form groups to locate and research sites where bioremediation has been or is currently being used successfully. Have each group prepare a brief report about one site that describes location, pollutant, history of contamination, technology being used, and assessment of the cleanup. Encourage students to use graphic aids and illustrations to present information.

  As a class, discuss whether there are limits to bioremediation as a way to solve waste problems and what those limits might be.

- Organize the class into a task force to fight local sources of waste using microorganisms. Have students identify areas where microbial activity could potentially be enhanced to clean up pollution in their town or region. Areas could include factory sites, polluted surface water or groundwater, and places where runoff might have contaminated soils. Remind students that composting and gardening are simple ways to involve microorganisms in breaking down pollutants. Conclude the activity by writing a plan that makes recommendations.

  You might also wish to investigate whether there are any nearby waste sites currently using bioremediation.

SCIENCE JOURNAL

Pollution-Fighting Microbes

MOST INDUSTRIAL PROCESSES create pollution. Pollution is the presence of harmful or unwanted substances in the environment. Foul-smelling clouds rise from factories. Mines leak waste into soil and streams. Coastal waters become coated with oil as a result of oil spills. Although there are ways to clean up this pollution, they're not simple. Most require a lot of equipment and a lot of time. In cases where pollution reaches deep into soil or groundwater, cleanup may be impossible.

Fortunately, nature has provided a way to clean up pollution. Many microbes actually eat some of the pollutants that dirty our soil and water. Today, scientists are putting these microbes to work in a process called bioremediation. In this process, bacteria and fungi help clean up harmful substances in water and soil by eating and digesting the pollutants. Then they turn substances that were once toxic, or poisonous, into harmless ones, such as carbon dioxide and water.

Scientists have been testing bioremediation for several years. In some cases, the pollution-eating microbes are already in the soil, but there are too few present for them to be useful. Researchers have learned that adding certain chemicals to the soil increases the microbe populations. The more microbes there are, the more pollution gets eaten. For example, the microbe *Geobacter sulfurreducens* can help take uranium out of groundwater. By adding vinegar to the soil, researchers can increase the number of the hungry bacteria living there. As the microbes eat the uranium in the groundwater, they cause reactions that change it from a soluble form to an insoluble form. The metal precipitates out of the groundwater and can be collected and removed. Seaweed does a similar job. Scientists mix small amounts of seaweed into soil contaminated with the pesticide DDT. The seaweed causes the growth of microbes that destroy DDT and clean the soil.

Researchers have evidence that bioremediation works. The goal now is to get the processes to work on larger and larger scales. With help from hungry microbes, cleaning up pollution could one day be an easy task.

Research and Report

You've just read about some of the uses of bacteria and fungi—from cleaning up pollution to baking bread. With a partner, do some detective work of your own. Find another use that people have for bacteria or fungi. Report to the class on the type of bacterium or fungus you have researched and what it is used to do.

CAREER CONNECTION Mycologist

WHAT TYPE OF PERSON becomes a mycologist, you might wonder? Someone who just *loves* fungi. That's right, a mycologist is a scientist who studies fungi—organisms such as yeasts, molds, and mushrooms.

Mycologists do an amazing variety of things. Some are disease detectives. Several years ago, dogwood trees started to die mysteriously. Mycologists were called in to track down the killer. Medical mycologists study fungi that cause human diseases. They also look for ways to use fungi to make medicines. Some fungi are already the source of important drugs. A current hepatitis B vaccine is based on an antigen that yeasts produce. The work of medical mycologists has also led to the development of antibiotics such as penicillin and streptomycin.

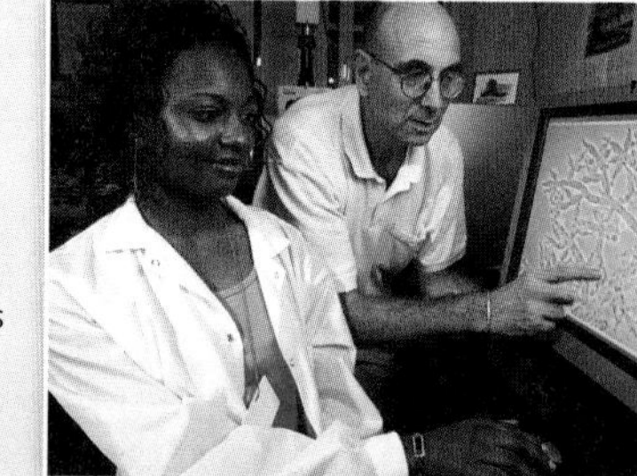

Mycologists work with border and port security officers, too. They guard our borders and ports against unwanted visitors—of the fungal variety.

152

Fungus-Washed Jeans

AS YOU PROBABLY KNOW from experience, jeans are always more comfortable after you've worn them for a while. They feel soft and lived-in. Companies that make jeans figured this out long ago and came up with a process called stonewashing.

Originally, stonewashing was just what it sounds like. Brand-new jeans were thrown into huge washing machines with pumice stones. During the wash cycle, the stones pounded on the jeans, wearing out the cotton fabric. The process made the jeans look worn even before they left the factory.

Stonewashing was a big success. People loved the soft, faded look. However, there were problems with the process, which was hard to control. Sometimes, the jeans became too beaten-up. Seams were torn and the shiny rivets and buttons were often scratched. At other times, the jeans didn't look or feel worn enough. In addition, the stones clanking around inside the washers did plenty of damage.

As an alternative to stonewashing, acid-washing was tried for a while. The acid bath faded the jeans. But this process, too, had its problems. Luckily, at this point jeans manufacturers turned to a fungus for help.

A new process called biostoning became the choice for making worn-looking jeans. In fact, there's a good chance your jeans were treated using this process. In biostoning, an enzyme wears out jeans by eating away at the cotton fibers. The enzyme, called cellulase, was first found in the fungus *Trichoderma reesei*. This enzyme digests cellulose, a major component of the fibers of plants such as cotton. Scientists have isolated the gene that makes the fungus produce cellulase. By putting that gene into bacteria, large amounts of the enzyme can be produced quickly. Cellulase attaches to the surface of the cotton fibers in jeans. Then, it loosens dye particles and starts to break down the cotton fibers.

Of course, the process has to be controlled so that the enzyme does not destroy the jeans. But the benefits of this process are many. It creates less pollution than other methods. It also does less damage to clothing and machinery. Drains do not clog up with pumice grit, and there is no acid-disposal problem. Also, the material on jeans that is not cotton—polyester trim or plastic buttons—is unharmed by the enzyme. It works only on cotton. So the next time you wear your favorite faded jeans, you can thank a fungus!

Foods, plants, and products made from plants enter the United States all the time. Some carry harmful fungal pests. If security officers find something suspicious, they can call on government mycologists to check it out. The mycologists would identify the fungus. Then they would determine if it is harmless, or if the shipment containing it should be destroyed or kept out of the country.

Lots of foods are fungi (like mushrooms) or are made using fungi (like cheese, bread, soy sauce, beer, and wine). So mycologists are at work at mushroom farms, helping farmers grow the best mushroom crops possible. They also work with huge food manufacturing companies that use fungi in their production processes.

People who work as mycologists usually have a background in biology and a doctorate degree in mycology. Mycologists work in a variety of places, including government agencies such as the United States Department of Agriculture, drug companies, and wineries. Mycologists also work at universities, where they teach and do research. Mycologists agree that there is still a lot to learn about fungi and that many new species are yet to be discovered. For mycologists, the learning and discovery process is often the best part of the job.

153

CONNECTION: Career

Remind students that mycologist is one of the jobs they may have researched for the Career Research project at the beginning of this unit.

Explain to students that a mycologist is an example of a career that can lead to many different kinds of jobs. Ask students to list in their Science Notebooks all the different things that mycologists do, as presented in the feature. Have students choose the jobs that interest them most to research further. For example, some students may be intrigued by medical mycology; others may be interested in making cheeses. Then, have each student write a monologue from the perspective of someone with the chosen job. The monologue should describe important aspects of the work in detail. Encourage students to use props and costumes for their presentations.

Case Study 2: Fungus-Washed Jeans

Gather More Information

Encourage students to use the library or the NSTA SciLinks Web site noted at the start of each chapter to learn more about these case study topics and to conduct further research.

Have students use the following keywords to aid their searches:

- acid-washed jeans
- biostoning
- cellulase
- jeans processing
- stonewashing
- *Trichoderma reesei*

Research the Big Picture

- Biostoning of blue jeans is one economic use of fungi; baking with yeast is another. Have students form groups to research other uses of fungi in science and industry. Tell students that they may research historical or modern uses. Challenge groups to find the most surprising or interesting uses and present informative reports to the class. You might wish to award "prizes" in different categories, such as most unusual use, most profitable use, or most useful for society.
- Have students research the processes for "fading" jeans or other denim products sold in local clothing stores. Have pairs of students visit or telephone clothing outlets to find out as much information as they can about how those items are processed. This may involve writing to denim manufacturers or contacting brand representatives online. Ask student pairs to write about their findings to augment what they learned in the article.

Unit 4

Plants

Introduce Unit 4

Have students look at the photos on this page. Ask: *What do you already know about plants? What do you want to know about plants?* Have students discuss their answers with a partner. Then, have students draw in their Science Notebooks a K-W-L-S-H chart in which to record what they know and want to know. Tell students to add to or revise their questions and write what they learn as they read through the unit.

Unit Projects

For each project below, students can use the Student Presentation Builder on the Student CD-ROM to display their results and their Science Notebooks for their project notes.

Career Have each student research a career that is related to plants (e.g., botanist, florist, forester, organic farmer, nursery owner). Ask each student to define the chosen job, describe what it entails, and identify the skills or experience needed to prepare for the job. Have students record this information in their Science Notebooks. Have students share what they learned with the class by holding a mock job fair.

Apply In the classroom or outdoors, make available several types of plants. Have students work in groups to research how to take care of one of the plants and then care for the plant for several weeks. Provide tools such as rulers, magnifying glasses, scales, watering cans, and fertilizer. Place a logbook next to each plant, and have group members record everything that is done to care for the plant (e.g., watering, fertilizing, light exposure). Each group should also keep a journal that includes observations and labeled illustrations of their plant.

Technology Have students work in small groups to identify a plant-related topic (e.g., transport tissues or root, stem, or leaf structures) that would require a microscope to investigate. Have students explain why the use of a microscope is integral to investigating this topic.

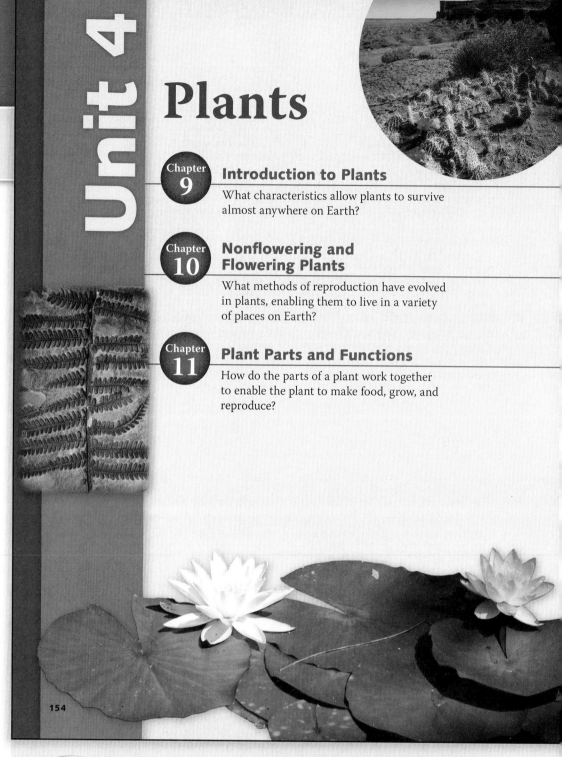

Unit 4

Plants

Software Summary

Student CD-ROM

- Interactive Student Book
- Vocabulary Review
- Key Concept Review
- Lab Report Template
- ELL Preview and Writing Activities
- Presentation Digital Library
- Graphic Organizing Software
- Spanish Cognate Dictionary

Interactive Labs

Chapter 9A—Bubbling Plants

Chapter 11C—Seed Adaptations

Introduction to Plants

KEY CONCEPT Plants are able to capture energy and matter from their surroundings and are found on most of Earth's land.

Most years, Death Valley, California, earns its name. It is a difficult place in which to live. Temperatures there commonly reach 54°C (120°F) during a hot summer day. At night, temperatures can fall below freezing.

In an average year, Death Valley gets only about 5 cm (2 in.) of rain. Yet, Death Valley is full of life. When the heavy spring rains fall, plants quickly grow and bloom in large numbers, delighting those who visit this unusual place. How do plants grow in these and other conditions? Why are plants important to all life on Earth?

Think About Plants

If you have ever planted a garden or taken care of a houseplant, you know something about plants. Where did your plants grow? What did you do to take care of them? How well did they grow?

- Think about what plants need to grow. Do plants need the same things that animals need in order to survive?
- In your Science Notebook, summarize the things that you did to help your plants grow well. What things are essential to a plant's survival?

www.scilinks.org
Plant Characteristics **Code: WGB09**

Chapter 9 Lessons

Introduce Chapter 9

As a starting activity, use LAB 9A Bubbling Plants on page 50 of the Laboratory Manual.

ENGAGE Show students pictures of a variety of plants. Include examples such as trees, cacti, Venus's-flytraps, and mosses. Ask students to brainstorm a list of characteristics that plants share. Lists may include *plants are green, grow in most climates, are alive,* and *are made of cells.* On the board, create a class list, accepting all reasonable answers. Encourage students to explain their thinking for each of the common traits. Explain that in this chapter, students will learn about the characteristics of plants, the ways in which plants have evolved over time, plant chemistry, and how plants grow.

Think About Plants

ENGAGE students by asking them to close their eyes and imagine a garden or a houseplant they have cared for or observed regularly, such as a neighbor's garden. Tell students to picture this garden or plant in different seasons and to note how the climate affected the plant(s). Some students may benefit from making a sketch.

Direct pairs of students to briefly discuss the needs of animals and plants. Then, have students complete the bulleted items in their Science Notebooks.

Chapter 9 Planning Guide			
Instructional Periods	National Standards	Lab Manual	Workbook
9.1 1 periods	A.1, C.1; C.1; UCP.1	**Lab 9A—p. 50** Bubbling Plants	Key Concept Review p. 55
9.2 2 periods	G.1; A.2, C.3, G.1; UCP.2	**Lab 9B—p. 51** Looking at Cells of Plants	Vocabulary Review p. 56 Interpreting Diagrams p. 57 Reading Comprehension p. 58
9.3 2 periods	B.3; B.2, B.3, B.6, C.5, F.6	**Lab 9C—p. 54** Plant Tropisms	Curriculum Connection p. 59 Science Challenge p. 60
9.4 1 period	C.3, F.2; C.6, F.4; UCP.3		

Middle School Standard; High School Standard; Unifying Concept and Principle

9.1 Introduce

ENGAGE Pose the following questions to students: *What is the largest plant? What is the smallest plant?* As a class, discuss their responses.

Before You Read

On the board, model the K-W-L-S-H chart. Discuss what students already know about plants, and write one or two examples in the *K* column. Then, write one or two questions in the *W* column.

Vocabulary terms are listed on the first student page of each lesson. You may wish to preview the terms before introducing each lesson. Strategies for teaching the vocabulary appear on the pages where the terms are introduced.

Teach

EXPLAIN that all plants share four characteristics. Place students in four groups, and direct each group to read the first paragraph of the section labeled *Characteristics of Plants.* Then, ask groups to each discuss one characteristic; their goal is to be able to explain that characteristic to the class.

As You Read

Allow students to update the *L* column in their charts. Check to ensure that students have included that all plants are multicellular, nonmotile, and photosynthetic and their cells have cell walls made of cellulose.

ANSWER cellulose

Science Notebook EXTRA

Encourage students to use the vocabulary section they created in their Science Notebooks. Remind them to record prefixes, suffixes, and root words to help them remember the meanings of vocabulary terms.

Learning Goals

- Identify the characteristics of plants.
- List the four needs of plants, and explain their importance.

New Vocabulary

multicellular
chloroplast
cellulose

9.1 What Is a Plant?

Before You Read

Create a K-W-L-S-H chart in your Science Notebook. Think about the title of this lesson. In the column labeled *K* on the chart, make a list of things you already know about plants. In the column labeled *W*, write what you want to learn about what plants are and how they live.

It would be difficult to define the word *plant* by looking at the plants that grow around you. Plants vary widely in appearance. They can be as small as the soft green mosses that grow only a few centimeters above a forest floor. They can be as tall as giant redwoods that can grow more than 100 m high.

As You Read

In the column labeled *L*, list the four characteristics of plants.

What are a plant's cell walls made of?

Figure 9.1 The places where plants grow, as well as the size to which plants grow, can vary widely.

Characteristics of Plants

Plants, whether large or small, or growing in deserts or forests, have important characteristics that set them apart from other living things.

- All plants are **multicellular**, or made up of more than one cell.
- Almost all plants can make complex organic molecules from simple chemicals in cell structures called **chloroplasts** (KLOR uh plasts).
- Plants have a substance called **cellulose** (SEL yuh lohs) in their cell walls. Cellulose is made up of chains of glucose units.
- Plants cannot move from place to place.

All plants are multicellular. Plants are made up of more than one cell. These cells make up different tissues and organs. The most obvious of these are roots, stems, and leaves. Roots anchor a plant in the ground, and they take in water and dissolved substances for the plant to use. Stems hold plants up. Leaves are the primary sites of photosynthesis.

Almost all plants can make their own organic molecules. Most plant cells have chloroplasts. These structures use light to power the chemical reactions of photosynthesis, the process by which simple inorganic chemicals are used to make complex organic molecules. Any green part of a plant can conduct photosynthesis. Plants that lack chlorophyll take their nutrients from other plants or fungi.

Plants have cell walls. Each plant cell has a cell wall that surrounds its cell membrane. This wall is made of cellulose.

Plants are not motile. Plants are unlike animals in that they are not able to move from one place to another. If conditions are not suitable in the place where they are growing, some plants stop growing and lose their leaves. They can begin growing again when conditions improve. Other plants die during such times.

Vocabulary

multicellular Explain that the prefix *multi-* is derived from the Latin word *multus*, meaning "many." The word *multicellular* means "of many cells."

chloroplast *Chloro-* is derived from the Greek word *chlōros*, meaning "green." The root *plast* originates from the Greek word *plastos*, meaning "molded."

cellulose Explain that the root *cellule* is from the Latin word *cellula*, meaning "a very small room." The suffix *-ose* denotes a kind of carbohydrate.

ELL Strategy

Ask and Answer Questions After the activity described in the Teach section on this page, have group members act as student "teachers" of their characteristic. Each group member should create one or two questions about their content. Assemble new groups, and tell the "teachers" to ask their group members these questions. Have group members share answers and develop a group response.

Needs of Plants

Plants can grow in a variety of different places, including places that most people would find very uncomfortable—Death Valley, for example. In large numbers, plants can form a forest, carpet a lawn, or cover a prairie. To grow, plants need sources of water, minerals, light, and carbon dioxide.

Water The most important need of a plant is a source of water. Almost all plant cells contain water. Plants use water as a raw material for photosynthesis.

Minerals Plants also need a source of certain minerals. For most plants, the soil in which they grow is the source. However, some plants grow on other plants, and their roots never reach the ground. For these plants, fallen leaves and animal wastes provide the needed minerals.

Light Plants also need light for photosynthesis. Different kinds of plants have adaptations that allow them to survive in places with various amounts of light. Some plants grow well in places where the Sun shines directly on them for most of the day. Other plants grow well under the low-light conditions present on the floor of a tropical rain forest.

Carbon Dioxide Carbon dioxide is abundant in the air. Plants use carbon dioxide as a raw material for photosynthesis. They combine carbon dioxide from the air with organic molecules already in their cells to make new organic molecules for growth and energy storage. The process of adding the carbon dioxide is called carbon fixation.

Figure 9.2 Mistletoe *(left)* grows on this tree branch because more sunlight reaches it. *Welwitschia (right)* produces only two leaves during its entire life. These leaves, which become torn and shredded, collect moisture from the air.

Did You Know?

The Venus's-flytrap is a plant that traps insects. It and several other species of insect-eating plants usually live in damp areas where the soil is very acidic. In these places, it is hard for plants to get the minerals from the soil that they need to grow well. The insects they trap provide these nutrients.

Explain It!

In your Science Notebook, write a paragraph that tells what a plant is.

Include a chart that illustrates how a plant differs from an animal.

Figure It Out

1. What does mistletoe, like all other plants, need to survive?
2. In what unique ways do these plants meet their needs?

After You Read

1. What characteristics do plants have?
2. If you know where a plant grows naturally, how will this information help you grow that plant in a pot in your house?
3. Using your chart, describe how knowing the characteristics of plants can help you identify an unknown one. Complete the chart by writing what you would still like to know in the column labeled *S* and how you could find the information in the column labeled *H*.

Teach

EXPLAIN that all plants require four things to remain alive. Create a concept map on the board using *Plants' Needs* as the main idea. Add each of the needs (water, minerals, light, and carbon dioxide) as the class reads the page. Include important information about each of the needs. Encourage students to add this information to the *L* column of their chart.

Figure It Out: Figure 9.2

ANSWER **1.** water, minerals, light, and carbon dioxide **2.** Mistletoe grows on another plant to get the sunlight it needs. *Welwitschia* uses its shredded leaves to collect water from the air.

Explain It!

Have students create outlines for their paragraphs using their Science Notebooks. Then, have students draft their paragraphs and share them with peers for a review.

Encourage students to use a Venn diagram to compare plants and animals. Items that belong in both categories include *are living things, are multicellular, have basic needs, grow,* and *reproduce.*

Assess

EVALUATE Use the After You Read questions and the Alternative Assessment to help you assess students' understanding of the lesson.

After You Read

1. All plants are multicellular, make organic molecules from inorganic materials, have cellulose in cell walls, and are not motile.
2. Plants have adaptations that allow them to survive under certain conditions. Knowing where a plant came from in nature would provide valuable clues as to the kind of care needed in a home.
3. Knowing the characteristics of some major groups of plants can help identify the very broad group of plants into which an unknown plant can be placed. Answers in the *S* column will vary. The *H* column can list Internet or library sources.

Background Information

The *Guinness Book of World Records* states that the smallest flowering plant is an aquatic duckweed (*Wolffia angusta*) with a length of 0.61 mm (0.24 in.) and a width of 0.33 mm (0.013 in.).

Hydroponics is the process of growing plants without soil, using a porous material such as peat, sand, or gravel. Gardeners fertilize the plants by adding nutrients directly in a liquid solution, and plants receive the necessary minerals.

Alternative Assessment

EVALUATE Students should compare their initial thoughts about plants from their writing at the start of this chapter (*Think About Plants* from the Chapter Opener) with the information in their K-W-L-S-H charts. Have students write short paragraphs about what they have learned.

9.2 Introduce

ENGAGE Have students make a T-chart and label one column *Nonvascular Plants* and the other column *Vascular Plants.* Write the following words on the board, and instruct students to write them in the correct column based on what they already know about plants: *moss, liverwort, pine tree, fern, rose bush, redwood tree, daisy.*

Before You Read

Model a concept map on the board with *Plant* as the main topic and *Nonvascular Plant* and *Vascular Plant* as subtopics. Direct students to make similar maps in their Science Notebooks and to include all of the lesson's vocabulary words.

Teach

EXPLAIN that students will learn how plants evolved, or changed, over time.

EXPLORE Have groups of students draw diagrams to represent the evolution of plants from simple to complex. Students should provide examples of plants at each stage, as well as details about the differences between stages. Have students record the group diagram in their Science Notebooks.

Vocabulary

vascular tissue Explain to students that *vascular* is derived from the Latin word *vasculum,* which is a form of *vas* and means "vessel" (a receptacle for liquids). A tissue, in both animals and plants, is a group of similar cells that function together.

nonvascular plant Explain that plants that lack vascular tissue are called nonvascular and do not have the ability to move water throughout the plant. Ask students to suggest meanings of the prefix *non-*.

vascular plant Review the meaning of *vascular tissue* given on this page. Be sure that students understand that vascular plants have vascular tissue.

fern Explain that ferns are flowerless, feathery-leaved plants that reproduce by spores and do not form seeds.

Figure It Out: Figure 9.3

ANSWER **1.** Algae belong to kingdom Protista. **2.** Nonvascular plants are plants that lack vascular tissue, which is the special tissue through which water and other materials move inside a plant.

9.2 Plant Evolution

Learning Goals

- Describe the evolution of plants.
- Compare and contrast nonvascular and vascular plants.

New Vocabulary

vascular tissue
nonvascular plant
vascular plant
fern
monocot
dicot

Before You Read

In your Science Notebook, make a concept map for the word *plant.* Use the following vocabulary terms: *nonvascular plant, vascular plant, fern, monocot,* and *dicot.*

During Earth's early history, green algae lived in the water. Green algae were once considered plants, but they are now grouped with other similar organisms in Kingdom Protista. There is evidence that these organisms are the ancestors of today's plants.

Bryophytes: Liverworts and Mosses

Bryophytes (BRI uh fites) are considered to be among the least complex living plants. Their life cycles are tied to damp places. Liverworts and mosses are bryophytes.

Liverworts and their relatives are small and grow on the surface of wet soil. Mosses are the small plants that form a green carpet on the floor of many forests. Mosses also grow on trees and rock surfaces.

The cells of both liverworts and mosses take in water by osmosis. Liverworts and mosses lack **vascular tissue,** or the special tissue through which water and other materials move inside a plant. Plants that lack vascular tissue are called **nonvascular plants.** Liverworts and mosses also lack true roots, stems, and leaves.

Did You Know?

Scientists estimate that as many as a quarter of a million species of plants exist today. However, because large areas of Earth are still unexplored, this number cannot be stated with absolute certainty. Tragically, many natural areas where plants thrive are being destroyed before they can be explored. The plants that live in these areas might disappear before they can be studied.

Figure It Out

1. To what kingdom do algae belong?
2. What are nonvascular plants?

Figure 9.3 The evolution of modern plants begins with green algae *(left).* Liverworts *(center)* and mosses *(right)* are bryophytes, which are nonvascular plants.

ELL Strategy

Read Aloud Arrange students in pairs or small groups, and then have each group work in a different area of the room. Direct students to take turns reading aloud paragraphs from the lesson. Encourage peers to help one another with pronunciation.

Tracheophytes: Vascular Plants

Tracheophytes (TRAY kee uh fites) are true land plants because they have evolved ways to survive independent of wet environments. They are **vascular plants** because they are able to move water from their surroundings through their bodies in vascular tissues. Tracheophytes include club mosses, horsetails, and ferns, as well as gymnosperms and angiosperms.

Ferns are nonflowering vascular plants. Although they produce a variety of leaf shapes, many ferns have leaves that look a great deal like green feathers. Unlike the vast majority of vascular plants, ferns do not make seeds. The reproductive structures that ferns release are dustlike spores.

Gymnosperms (JIHM nuh spurmz) are vascular plants that produce seeds that are not enclosed within a fruit. Pines, firs, redwoods, and sequoias are all gymnosperms that produce seeds in cones. Angiosperms (AN jee uh spurmz) are the most easily recognizable seed-producing plants. Angiosperms are flowering plants. Roses, corn, bamboo, orchids, daisies, and fruit trees are angiosperms that are familiar to most people. In angiosperms, seeds are enclosed in fruits. The fruit protects the seeds as they develop. Because most fruits are edible and the seeds not easily digested, animals often spread seeds far from the parent plants. Although gymnosperms evolved long before flowering plants, today there are many more species of angiosperms than gymnosperms.

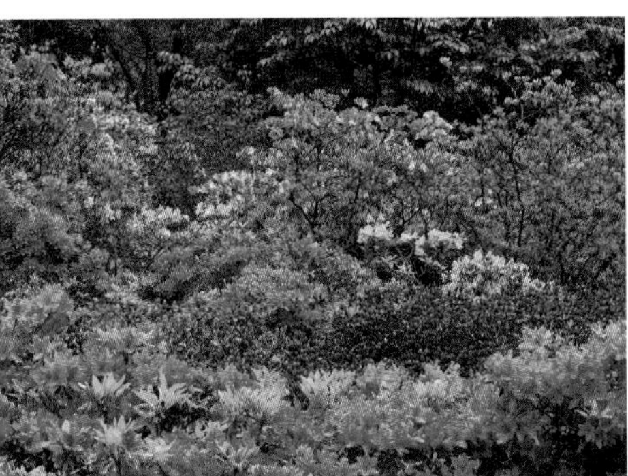

Figure 9.5 Angiosperms, the flowering plants, number more than 235,000 species. How do the angiosperms differ from other vascular plants?

CONNECTION: Earth Science

Fossils are the preserved remains or evidence of ancient living things. Fossils of early plants are usually molds. When a plant died, it was buried by sediment that hardened into rock. When the plant itself decayed, the impression it left in the rock was preserved. The rocks in which molds are found can be dated using radioactive elements to determine the age of the mold and the plant that created it.

Figure 9.4 Ferns are tracheophytes, the next step in the evolution of plants. More than 12,000 species of ferns exist.

As You Read

Use the headings and vocabulary words to add branches to your concept map.

What type of plants are ferns, gymnosperms, and angiosperms?

Figure 9.6 The first plants to evolve with seeds were the gymnosperms. The sugar pine is a gymnosperm.

Teach

EXPLAIN to students that they will learn about different types of vascular plants, how they have evolved, and how they reproduce.

Science Notebook EXTRA

As students read the text, have them sketch and label examples of each vocabulary term in their Science Notebooks.

Use the Visual: Figure 9.5

Unlike the other groups of vascular plants, angiosperms have flowers.

As You Read

Give students a few minutes to review and update their concept maps. Remind them to clearly define the relationships among the vocabulary words in the map. Have each student quickly check the maps of two peers and provide feedback.

ANSWER Ferns, gymnosperms, and angiosperms are all vascular plants. Students' concept maps should have these three terms as branches from the term *vascular plants*.

CONNECTION: Earth Science

If possible, bring in plant fossils. Students can describe characteristics they observe and use their concept maps to identify the group of plants to which each fossil belongs.

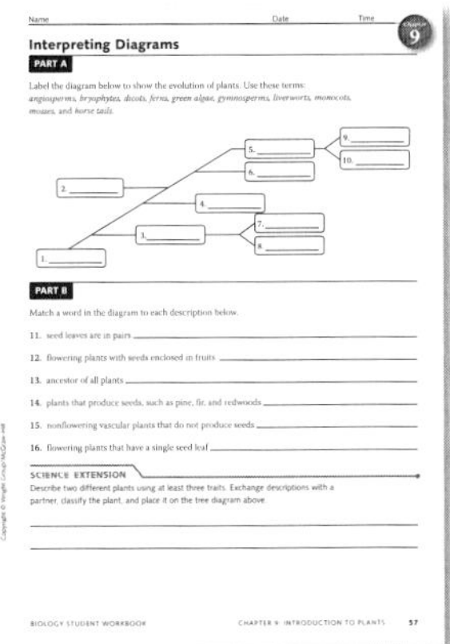

Name Date Time

Chapter 9

Interpreting Diagrams

PART A

Label the diagram below to show the evolution of plants. Use these terms: *angiosperms, bryophytes, dicots, ferns, green algae, gymnosperms, liverworts, monocots, mosses,* and *horse tails.*

1. ______ 2. ______ 3. ______ 4. ______ 5. ______ 6. ______ 7. ______ 8. ______ 9. ______ 10. ______

PART B

Match a word in the diagram to each description below.

11. seed leaves are in pairs ______
12. flowering plants with seeds enclosed in fruits ______
13. ancestor of all plants ______
14. plants that produce seeds, such as pine, fir, and redwoods ______
15. nonflowering vascular plants that do not produce seeds ______
16. flowering plants that have a single seed leaf ______

SCIENCE EXTENSION

Describe two different plants using at least three traits. Exchange descriptions with a partner, classify the plant, and place it on the tree diagram above.

BIOLOGY STUDENT WORKBOOK CHAPTER 9 INTRODUCTION TO PLANTS 57

Interpreting Diagrams Workbook, p. 57

Background Information

Radioactive decay is the process by which the nucleus of a radioactive atom (radioisotope) releases radiation and turns into a stable atom of a different element. The rate of decay is constant for a particular radioisotope; it is not affected by conditions such as temperature or pressure. Each radioisotope has a characteristic rate of decay known as its half-life.

In 1905, Lord Rutherford (Ernest Rutherford, First Baron Rutherford of Nelson) (1871–1937), a nuclear physicist from New Zealand, suggested using radioactivity as a tool to measure geologic time. This practical application of radioactive decay helped show that Earth's actual age was much greater than most scientists at the time believed.

Teach

EXPLAIN that students will continue to learn how plants are identified. Provide small groups of students with a few varieties of both monocots and dicots. Have students examine each plant and identify it as a monocot or dicot, providing the reason(s) for its classification.

Vocabulary

monocot Tell students that the prefix *mono-* means "one." The root *cot* is derived from the Greek word *kotylēdōn*, which means "cup."

dicot Explain to students that the prefix *di-* means "two." A dicot plant has seeds with two cotyledons.

EXPLORE Pair students and have them brainstorm a list of all the herbs they know. Have students identify the use(s) of each herb. Create a class list of herbs from these lists. Then consult Blackwell's "Curious Herbal" to see how many herbs appear both on the class list and in the book.

Explore It!

Have students create three-column charts in their Science Notebooks before observing the plants. Review one or two plants with the whole class, noting in which column the plant would appear. Remind students to look for plants in less obvious places such as in driveway or sidewalk cracks, on their houses or fences, or on other living and nonliving things.

Explore It!

Conduct a plant tour of your home, yard, or neighborhood park, and record your observations, including drawings, in your Science Notebook. Prepare a chart in your Science Notebook with three columns labeled *Ferns, Gymnosperms,* and *Angiosperms.* Based on the characteristics of the plants you observe, write the name of each plant in the correct column.

Monocots and Dicots

Flowering plants are classified into two groups based on the appearance of their seeds. **Monocots** (MAH nuh kahts) have a single seed leaf. If you cut open a corn kernel, which is a seed that may develop into a new plant, you will find one seed leaf. **Dicots** (DI kahts) have two seed leaves. If you cut open a lima bean, you will find a pair of seed leaves—the two halves of the bean.

In addition to corn, other monocots include grasses, bamboo, and orchids. Monocots have parallel veins in their leaves. The flower parts of monocots usually occur in threes or multiples of three.

Dicots have veins in their leaves that look like nets. The flower parts of dicots often appear in multiples of four and five. Roses, maples, and most other broadleaf trees are dicots.

PEOPLE IN SCIENCE: Elizabeth Blackwell 1700–1758

Science does not occur only in the laboratory. Often, people who are not trained in science make important contributions to the body of scientific knowledge.

Herbals are early medical recipe books that describe medical uses for certain plants. Many herbals also include illustrations that help identify the plants described. Many people consider *A Curious Herbal*, done by Elizabeth Blackwell in the first half of the eighteenth century, to be among the most beautiful herbals ever made.

When her husband was imprisoned, Elizabeth, who was a trained artist, decided to produce an herbal to pay off her husband's debts. She moved near a small botanical garden in London and made her drawings from plants that grew there. She sought information about the plants' names and uses from her husband. She made printing plates of her drawings and then hand-colored the plates—all 500 of them. She then sold the plates to bookstores. Elizabeth's herbal is a book that made important contributions to the understanding of plants and their medical uses.

After You Read

1. Use drawings to illustrate how plants have evolved over time. Use arrows to connect your drawings in the correct sequence.
2. Describe the adaptations that allow plants to survive on land.
3. Use your concept map to identify the two main types of plants. In a well-developed paragraph, explain how these two groups are different.

Assess

EVALUATE Use the After You Read questions and the Alternative Assessment to help you assess students' understanding of the lesson.

After You Read

1. Drawings should show green algae, a nonvascular plant, and then a vascular plant.
2. Cell walls and vascular tissues allow plants to survive in the drier conditions found on land.
3. The two main types of plants are nonvascular and vascular. Nonvascular plants do not have vascular tissues, stay small, and live in damp environments. Vascular plants have vascular tissues, grow larger, and live in drier environments.

Alternative Assessment

EVALUATE Have students use their concept maps to write a few sentences explaining the evolution of plants. Then, have students compare angiosperms and gymnosperms.

Field Study

Have students continue the Explore It! activity in an area near the school. Assign a different area to each group of four to six students, and then have the groups compare findings with the rest of the class.

Differentiated Instruction

Visual Have students sketch plants that they find during the Explore It! activity in their Science Notebooks. Encourage students to label the seeds.

9.3 Plant Chemistry

Before You Read

Create working definitions for *photosynthesis* and *cellular respiration.* A working definition is one that develops as you read and think about an idea. Write what you know about these terms before you begin reading. Then add to the definitions as you read and discuss the lesson.

Learning Goals

- Describe the processes of photosynthesis and cellular respiration.
- List functions that are controlled by plant hormones.

New Vocabulary

photosynthesis
cellular respiration
hormone
auxin

Although plants do not appear to be active, important chemical reactions are occurring in their cells. In fact, many scientists agree that the most important manufacturing process on Earth happens in the cells of plants that are exposed to light. This process is photosynthesis.

Plants as Chemical Factories

Photosynthesis (foh toh SIHN thuh sus) is the main process that producers use to make complex organic molecules out of simple inorganic chemicals. Photosynthesis uses the energy of sunlight, which is absorbed by the green pigment chlorophyll (KLOR uh fihl). The process is often summarized by the equation

$$\underset{\text{carbon dioxide}}{12CO_2} + \underset{\text{water}}{12H_2O} \xrightarrow[\text{chlorophyll}]{\text{light energy}} \underset{\text{starch}}{C_{12}H_{22}O_{11}} + \underset{\text{oxygen}}{12O_2}$$

According to this equation, the raw materials of photosynthesis are carbon dioxide and water. The products are starch and oxygen. The process requires the presence of light energy and chlorophyll, which is contained in the chloroplasts. Photosynthesis takes place in any plant parts that contain chlorophyll.

Chloroplasts are able to trap the energy of light and use it for photosynthesis. Visible light, or white light, is made up of different colors. Each color has a different amount of energy associated with it. Plants use the energy present in red and blue light primarily. The light energy is used to split water molecules, which produces oxygen gas, and to form the new bonds that hold together the atoms in organic molecules. Most plants appear green because they do not absorb this color. Instead, green is reflected off the leaves and other parts of the plant.

Figure 9.7 Plant leaves contain a variety of pigments of different colors. The colors are masked by the green color of chlorophyll, but they show up when cold temperatures and shorter days cause the breakdown of chlorophyll.

ELL Strategy

Model Have each student create a model to illustrate the process of photosynthesis. Provide a variety of materials to use, such as plastic foam balls, pipe cleaners, modeling clay, markers, and glue.

Teacher Alert

Photosynthesis also occurs in conifers and evergreen plants and trees. Their needles function similarly to leaves in the process. Evergreens keep most of their leaves during the winter, when photosynthesis continues to occur at a slower rate.

9.3 Introduce

ENGAGE students by reviewing the first two lessons of this chapter, in which they have learned what plants need in order to survive, how plants evolved, and how plants are characterized. Ask students to think about and share with a partner the ways in which plants benefit other organisms on Earth. Give students a few minutes to write their thoughts before sharing. Summarize the activity for students by explaining that plant processes enable other organisms on Earth to survive.

Before You Read

Model thinking aloud using a term and its definition. Because the title for this lesson is *Plant Chemistry*, you could use the word *chemistry* to model. Tell the class: *The word* chemistry *looks like it has the same root as the word* chemical, *so the two words must be related. The suffix* -istry *looks familiar; it also appears in the word* dentistry. *I think it means* "the practice of something." Direct students to take a few minutes to think about their vocabulary words and write about them in their Science Notebooks.

Teach

EXPLAIN that in this lesson, students will be learning about two processes that take place in green plants: an energy-capturing process (photosynthesis) and an energy-releasing process (cellular respiration).

Vocabulary

photosynthesis Tell students that the word part *photo-* is derived from the Greek word *phōs* and means "light." The root *syn* means "together," and *thesis* is "placing." Literally, *photosynthesis* means "placing together with light." Ask students to provide examples of other terms that have the word part *photo-* and to define these terms using the meaning of *photo.* (photograph, photography, phototropism, photocopy, photo finish)

Teach

EXPLAIN to students that they will learn about cellular respiration, the process of releasing energy from chemical bonds.

Figure It Out: Figure 9.8

ANSWER **1.** The raw materials of photosynthesis are carbon dioxide and water. The products are starch and oxygen. **2.** Plants left in the dark would not be able to make their own food because light energy is needed for photosynthesis to occur. The plants would be straggly, spindly, small-leafed, and pale in color. The plants would likely not survive for long.

Vocabulary

cellular respiration Tell students that *respiration* is derived from the Latin word *respirare,* which means "to breathe." Make the point that cellular respiration is not, however, breathing. It is the process by which glucose is broken down in the presence of oxygen to produce water, carbon dioxide, and energy.

hormone Tell students that the word *hormone* is derived from the Greek word *horman,* which means "to stimulate."

auxin Explain that the derivation of *auxin* is Greek: *auxein.* It means "to increase."

As You Read

Give students about five minutes to review and revise the first drafts of their definitions. Remind them to include the raw materials, products, and energy. Have students engage in a quick peer review to ensure their definitions are written accurately.

ANSWER Photosynthesis occurs in chloroplasts because that is where chlorophyll is found in the plant cell. Photosynthesis produces the raw materials needed for cellular respiration.

Figure It Out

1. What are the raw materials of photosynthesis? The products?
2. Hypothesize about what would happen to plants left in the dark.

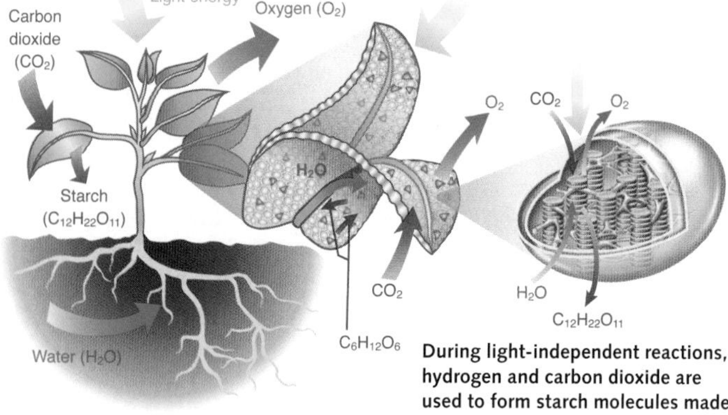

Figure 9.8 Photosynthesis includes two sets of reactions. One set *(blue)* requires the presence of light; the other *(red)* does not.

As You Read

Review your working definitions for *photosynthesis* and *cellular respiration.*

Where in the plant cell does photosynthesis take place? What process produces the raw materials for cellular respiration?

Cellular Respiration

Like all forms of life, plants need energy to grow and survive. Plants get this energy from photosynthesis and by a process called cellular respiration. **Cellular respiration** (res puh RAY shun) is the process that releases potential energy stored in chemical bonds. Cellular respiration occurs in all living cells. In cellular respiration, the energy stored in organic molecules is released when chemical bonds are broken. The process is often summarized by the equation

$$C_6H_{12}O_6 + 6O_2 \rightarrow 6CO_2 + 6H_2O + \text{energy}$$

glucose oxygen carbon dioxide water

According to this equation, the raw materials of cellular respiration are glucose and oxygen. The products are carbon dioxide, water, and energy. The equation for cellular respiration is essentially the opposite of the equation for photosynthesis. This means that the products of one process are the raw materials for the other process.

CONNECTION: Math

The equation for cellular respiration is called a balanced chemical equation because the number of atoms of each element is the same on both sides of the equation. Prove that this is true by calculating the total number of atoms of carbon (C), hydrogen (H), and oxygen (O) on each side of the equation.

Science Notebook EXTRA

Have students compare the processes of photosynthesis and respiration. Give them the options of creating a Venn diagram, a compare-and-contrast chart, or a side-by-side examination of the two equations. Ask students to analyze each process's raw materials and products and to describe the role of energy in each reaction.

CONNECTION: Math

Show students how to write a balanced equation by using the combining of hydrogen and oxygen to produce water ($2H_2 + O_2 \rightarrow 2H_2O$). Count the number of atoms on each side of the equation as you balance it. Students will find that there are 6 carbon atoms, 12 hydrogen atoms, and 18 oxygen atoms on the left side of the equation and 6 carbon atoms, 12 hydrogen atoms, and 18 oxygen atoms on the right side of the equation.

Background Information

The law of conservation of mass, developed by the French scientist Antoine-Laurent Lavoisier, is the rationale for balancing equations. In a chemical reaction, the mass of the products equals the mass of the reactants. Scientists summarize the concept with the statement "Matter can neither be created nor destroyed by ordinary means."

Plant Hormones

Scientists have discovered that plants make substances called hormones. **Hormones** (HOR mohnz) are special chemicals made in one part of an organism that affect growth and development in other parts of the organism. Very small amounts of hormones are usually able to produce significant effects in cells.

Auxins (AWK sunz) are a group of hormones made by plants. Auxins can cause some plant cells to enlarge and can stop the growth of other plant cells. For example, scientists believe that plants bend toward sunlight because of the action of auxins. Auxins build up on the side of a plant's stem that is away from a source of light. These cells on the dark side of the stem grow longer than the cells on the side of the stem that faces the light source. The longer cells cause the stem to bend toward the light source.

Auxins are also produced at the growing tip of a plant stem. They have the ability to keep potential growth buds on the stem from growing. When the tip of a plant is damaged or removed, the supply of these auxins is stopped. When this happens, the tiny growth buds begin to grow all along the stem, producing more stems and a bushier plant. Gardeners often pinch off or cut off the growing tip for this reason.

Figure 9.9 In an effort to trap more light energy for photosynthesis, many plant stems bend toward the light *(left)*. The bending is caused by auxins. Plants that do not get enough light often grow tall and spindly *(right)*. They look like they are "reaching" for the light they need to survive.

Other Chemicals Made by Plants

Plants are also able to make a wide variety of other chemicals. Many of these chemicals are made as defense mechanisms. Tannic acid, for example, is present in the leaves of many plant species. Tannic acid makes the leaves of plants taste bitter. Many insects avoid eating leaves with high levels of tannic acid. Evidence shows that plants can increase the level of tannic acid in their leaves in response to insect attack. For some other organisms, the tannic acid in leaves is a bonus. People drink tea because the tannic acid in tea leaves has a pleasant taste.

The chemical that is the active ingredient in aspirin, acetylsalicylic acid, was originally discovered in the bark of willow trees. Long ago, people noticed that a solution made from willow twigs soaked in water would lower fevers. Scientists fear that other important medicines might be lost if a plant species is destroyed before it can be studied.

Did You Know?

People who supply fruits to markets use ethylene gas to make the fruits ripen faster. Ethylene gas acts like an auxin. When ethylene gas is pumped into a fruit storage area, the ripening process begins and the fruits are then shipped to stores. Many different kinds of fruits can be treated this way so that they ripen as market demand for them increases. You can have ripe fruits year-round, even outside of their natural growing seasons.

After You Read

1. Describe the processes of photosynthesis and cellular respiration.
2. What functions do plant hormones control?
3. Use your working definitions for *photosynthesis* and *cellular respiration* to describe the relationship between these two processes.

Teach

EXPLAIN to students that they will learn about plant hormones and their function within plants.

EXPLORE To demonstrate for students the effect of ethylene, place a ripe banana in a brown paper bag with an unripe piece of fruit, such as a pear. As a control, keep a similar piece of fruit (pear) on a counter, a little distance away from the paper bag. Before beginning the experiment, have students note the condition of each pear and record their observations. After a few days, have students determine which pear ripened more by observing the two pears and comparing each to the preexperiment observations.

Assess

EVALUATE Use the After You Read questions and the Alternative Assessment to help you assess students' understanding of the lesson.

After You Read

1. During photosynthesis, plants use the light energy absorbed by the pigment chlorophyll to split water molecules to produce oxygen and use carbon dioxide molecules to make more organic molecules that store energy. During cellular respiration, energy stored in the chemical bonds of organic molecules is released as organic molecules are broken down in the presence of oxygen. Carbon dioxide and water are also produced.
2. Plant hormones control plant growth and reaction to stimuli (such as sunlight).
3. The two processes are opposites. The products of one reaction provide raw materials for the other reaction.

Background Information

Plants from rain forests are an important source of medicinal products. About 25 percent of medicines contain ingredients from such plants. Derivatives of plants from rain forests have been used to create anesthetics, contraceptives, enzymes, hormones, cough medicines, antibiotics, and antiseptics. Diseases they treat include cancer, malaria, heart disease, bronchitis, hypertension, dysentery, and tuberculosis.

Reading Comprehension Workbook, p. 58

Alternative Assessment

EVALUATE Have students use their definitions for *photosynthesis* and *cellular respiration* to compare and contrast the two processes. Students can also create a diagram that shows plants and the two chemical processes. The diagram should show the relationships between the two processes.

9.4 Introduce

ENGAGE Write a list of plant names on the board (or have photographs of plants available), including annuals, biennials, and perennials, in random order. Ask students to analyze the list, to create three categories of their liking, and to sort the plants into those categories. Allow students to work in pairs. Have a few pairs share their categories and reasons for creating them.

Before You Read

Create the T-chart on the board and label each side. Model the process of adding the first vocabulary word, *annual*, to the chart. Think aloud about where the word should belong. You might talk about common uses of *annual*, such as descriptions of an annual Fourth of July parade and annual business reports. Hypothesize that the word belongs on the side labeled *Plant Life Spans*, since *annual* refers to a period of time. Give students a few minutes to make T-charts in their Science Notebooks, and then have them place all vocabulary words in it.

Teach

EXPLAIN that students will learn about the three different types of plant life spans: annual, biennial, and perennial.

Vocabulary

annual Tell students that *annual* is derived from the Latin word *annus*, meaning "year."

biennial Explain that the prefix *bi-* refers to having, involving, using, or consisting of two things—in this case, years.

perennial Explain to students that the prefix *per-* is derived from Latin and means "through." Literally, *perennial* means "through the years."

tropism Tell students that the root of the word *tropism* is derived from the Greek word *tropos*, meaning "a turn." Ask students to explain why this is an appropriate derivation.

stimulus Explain to students that a stimulus is something, such as a drug, heat, or light, that causes a specific response. Point out that the plural form of the word is *stimuli*. Cells, tissues, organs, and organisms respond to stimuli.

phototropism Tell students that the word part *photo-* is derived from the Greek word *phōs*, meaning "light." The root *tropos* means "a turn," and the suffix *-ism* denotes a quality or state. Literally, *phototropism* means "a state of turning toward light."

thigmotropism Explain that the prefix *thigmo-* is derived from the Greek word *thígma*, meaning "to touch." With students, discuss the literal definition of a word made by combining this prefix with the root *tropism*.

Learning Goals

- Describe three patterns of plant growth.
- Identify ways plants respond to the environment.

New Vocabulary

annual
biennial
perennial
tropism
stimulus
phototropism
thigmotropism

9.4 Patterns of Growth

Before You Read

Read the Learning Goals and vocabulary terms for this lesson. In your Science Notebook, draw a T-chart. Label one side *Plant Life Spans* and the other side *Plant Responses*. Place each vocabulary term on the side of the T-chart where you think it belongs.

Just as flowering plants vary in appearance, so too do they vary in life span, or the time between seed germination and death. Some plants live for only a few days and complete their life cycle; others live for hundreds of years. The life spans of plants are determined by both genetic and environmental factors.

Annuals, Biennials, and Perennials

Plants are grouped according to life span into three general categories: annuals, biennials, and perennials.

Annuals (AN yoo ulz) are plants that complete their life cycle—grow from a seed, mature, produce seeds, and die—in one growing season. Many common garden flowers, such as petunias and zinnias, are annuals. Tomatoes and other plants that are killed by frost are also annuals. These plants are grown each year for the fruits or flowers they produce. Their seeds are able to withstand harsh environmental conditions and will sprout when conditions improve.

Biennials (bi EN ee ulz) are plants that complete their life cycle in two years. Many biennials change their appearance dramatically over the two years that make up a normal cycle. Carrots are a common biennial often grown in gardens. During its first growing year, a carrot plant produces green tops and the orange roots that people eat. In its second growing season, a carrot plant produces flowers and seeds. Biennials die after flowering, but the seeds that they produce help their species survive.

Perennials (puh RE nee ulz) are plants that live longer than one or two years. Although some perennials can flower in the first season of growth, many take several years before they are mature enough to produce flowers. Some perennials can live for many years; others are relatively short-lived.

Perennials have various ways of surviving for long periods of time. The stems of peonies die in the winter, but the thick roots store food supplies for next year's growth. Other perennials, such as trees, grow tough, woody stems.

Figure 9.10 Angiosperms can be classified according to their life spans. A petunia *(top)* is an annual. A pansy *(center)* is a biennial. A peony *(bottom)* is a perennial.

Tropisms

Tropisms (TROH pih zumz) are ways in which plants respond to stimuli in their environment. A **stimulus** (STIHM yuh lus, plural: stimuli) is something that produces an action or response. Bending toward light is known as a **phototropism**. As discussed before, this tropism is the result of auxins producing changes in a plant's cells.

Tropisms are said to be positive or negative depending on a plant's response to a particular stimulus. Growing toward light is considered a positive phototropism. Growing away from the pull of gravity is a negative gravitropism. A plant can show both positive and negative tropisms at the same time. When a seed sprouts, its stem grows toward the light and away from the pull of gravity.

Some plants also exhibit **thigmotropism**, or a tropism in response to touch. A positive thigmotropism is most commonly seen in climbing plants, such as peas, grapes, and clematis.

Figure 9.11 The tendrils on a pea plant hold it tight to the object it is climbing on. The tendrils always coil in the same direction.

After You Read

1. Explain how annuals, biennials, and perennials differ.
2. Describe the stimulus and the plant response in two types of plant tropisms.
3. A homeowner wants to purchase a plant that will grow up a decorative trellis in a flower bed and be attractive for many years. Use a vocabulary word from each side of your T-chart to describe the type of plant that should be purchased.

As You Read

Check your predictions about the placement of the vocabulary terms in your T-chart.

What determines whether a plant is an annual, a biennial, or a perennial?

Figure It Out

1. What type of tropism is this plant exhibiting?
2. How might thigmotropism help a plant survive in the dense growth of a rain forest?

Extend It!

Working with a partner, design an experiment that would answer one of the following questions:

- Can a plant find its way out of a maze?
- Does a plant know which way is up?

Describe your experiment in your Science Notebook.

Teach

EXPLAIN that students will learn ways in which plants respond to the environment.

Figure It Out: Figure 9.11

ANSWER **1.** thigmotropism **2.** by allowing the plant to grow on another plant to reach an area in the forest where it can receive sunlight

As You Read

Give students about five minutes to review and revise their T-charts. Have students discuss the words and their T-charts with a partner to ensure understanding.

ANSWER how long a plant lives and takes to reproduce

Extend It!

Remind students to follow the steps of the scientific method in designing and recording their experiments. You may want to allow students to carry out their experiments.

Assess

EVALUATE Use the After You Read questions and the Alternative Assessment to help you assess students' understanding of the lesson.

After You Read

1. Annuals complete their life cycles in one growing season; biennials complete their life cycles in two growing seasons; and perennials live more than two years.
2. Light is the stimulus in a positive phototropism; plants respond by growing toward light. Thigmotropism is a response to touch; some plants respond to touch by coiling around objects they touch.
3. The homeowner should buy a perennial plant that exhibits thigmotropism.

Alternative Assessment

EVALUATE Have students illustrate or describe in their own words the terms from their T-charts.

ELL Strategy

Practice Using Vocabulary Have students role-play using the roles of nursery owner (or horticulturist) and novice gardener. Direct students to hold conversations about purchasing plants to populate a garden for maximum blooming and appropriate climate conditions.

Background Information

Hydrotropism is the response of a plant in which it bends or grows toward water. Gravitropism is the term for the way a plant grows in response to gravity.

Chapter 9 Summary

VOCABULARY REVIEW

Check students' sentences or paragraphs to make sure they understand the meaning of each vocabulary term.

PREPARE FOR CHAPTER TEST

Evaluate students' essays using the following criteria:

1. The topic sentence, or main idea, should restate the Key Concept.
2. The supporting paragraphs should incorporate the answers to the Learning Goal questions students have written and include details, facts, and examples they have recorded in their Science Notebooks.
3. The concluding sentence should sum up the main idea of the chapter and restate the Key Concept.

MASTERING CONCEPTS

True or False

1. True
2. False, water
3. False, green algae
4. False, vascular plant
5. False, Photosynthesis
6. True
7. False, annuals
8. True

Short Answer

9. Vascular tissue allows a plant to efficiently transport water and other materials to all of its cells and allows the plant to live away from water.
10. Chlorophyll absorbs most colors of light except green, which it reflects. The energy in this light is needed to split water molecules, which releases oxygen gas, and to use carbon dioxide molecules to form new organic molecules.
11. Thigmotropism is a response to touch and causes plant stems to curl around objects they touch. Phototropism is a response to light and causes plant stems to grow toward light.
12. Gymnosperms and angiosperms both produce seeds. Gymnosperms produce seeds in structures called cones; angiosperms produce seeds that are enclosed in fruits.

Chapter 9

Summary

KEY CONCEPTS

9.1 What Is a Plant?

- Plants are multicellular organisms that capture matter and energy from their surroundings.
- Plants have cell walls composed of cellulose.
- Unlike animals, plants cannot move from place to place.
- Plants can be found in many environments, but all plants need sources of water, minerals, light, and carbon dioxide in order to survive.

9.2 Plant Evolution

- The first plants evolved from green algae that developed adaptations enabling them to survive on land.
- Nonvascular plants lack the specialized tissues that allow water and minerals to move inside the plant. These plants must live in damp places where water is readily available. Mosses and liverworts are examples of nonvascular plants.
- Vascular plants such as ferns, gymnosperms, and angiosperms have specialized vascular tissues that allow water and minerals to move inside the plant. With specialized vascular tissues, these plants can live in different types of environments.

9.3 Plant Chemistry

- Photosynthesis uses energy from the Sun to convert simple inorganic chemicals into complex organic molecules and also releases oxygen gas. Photosynthesis occurs in the cells of the green parts of plants.
- Cellular respiration is the process that releases energy stored in the chemical bonds of organic molecules. This process occurs in the cells of all living organisms.
- Plant hormones such as auxins are chemicals that control a plant's growth and development.

9.4 Patterns of Growth

- A plant can be classified according to its life span as an annual (a plant that completes its life cycle in one growing season), a biennial (a plant that requires two years to complete its life cycle), or a perennial (a plant that lives longer than two years).
- Tropisms are a plant's response to stimuli in the environment. Phototropism is a plant's response to light; thigmotropism is a plant's response to touch.

VOCABULARY REVIEW

Write each term in a complete sentence, or write a paragraph relating several terms.

9.1
multicellular, p. 156
chloroplast, p. 156
cellulose, p. 156

9.2
vascular tissue, p. 158
nonvascular plant, p. 158
vascular plant, p. 159
fern, p. 159
monocot, p. 160
dicot, p. 160

9.3
photosynthesis, p. 161
cellular respiration, p. 162
hormone, p. 163
auxin, p. 163

9.4
annual, p. 164
biennial, p. 164
perennial, p. 164
tropism, p. 165
stimulus, p. 165
phototropism, p. 165
thigmotropism, p. 165

PREPARE FOR CHAPTER TEST

To prepare for the chapter test, create a question from each Learning Goal. Use the information in your Science Notebook to answer each question. Then use these answers to write a well-developed essay about the chapter. Use the Key Concept on the first page of this chapter as your topic sentence.

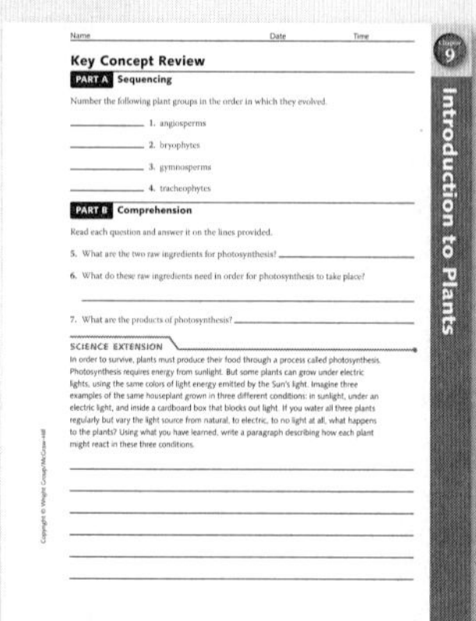

Key Concept Review Workbook, p. 55

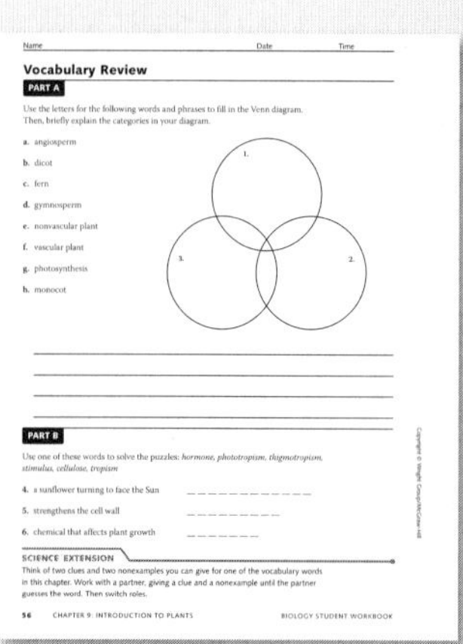

Vocabulary Review Workbook, p. 56

MASTERING CONCEPTS

True or False

If the statement is true, write "true." If it is false, change the underlined word or words to make the statement true.

1. Plants are multicellular organisms that can <u>capture energy from sunlight</u> but are not motile.
2. A source of <u>minerals</u> is the most important need that plants must meet in order to survive.
3. Plants evolved from <u>bacteria</u> that adapted to life on land.
4. A <u>nonvascular plant</u> can live independent of water because it has special tissues that move water and minerals through the plant.
5. <u>Cellular respiration</u> is the process that green plants use to produce oxygen and organic molecules.
6. The products of photosynthesis are essentially the <u>raw materials</u> for respiration.
7. Plants that complete their life cycle in one growing season are <u>biennials</u>.
8. The response of a plant to stimuli in the environment is called a <u>tropism</u>.

Short Answer

Answer each of the following in a sentence or brief paragraph.

9. Why is vascular tissue important to a plant?
10. What role does chlorophyll play in photosynthesis?
11. Describe two tropisms that affect the stems of a plant.
12. Compare and contrast gymnosperms and angiosperms.

Critical Thinking

Use what you have learned in this chapter to answer each of the following.

13. **Infer** As vascular tissues evolved, plants became much larger. Explain the relationship between these two events.
14. **Compare and Contrast** Compare the processes of photosynthesis and cellular respiration.
15. **Apply Concepts** People often grow plants near windows in their houses. Explain why the plants should be turned every week.

Standardized Test Question

Choose the letter of the response that correctly answers the question.

16. Which of the following are basic needs of plants?

I. sunlight
II. water
III. carbon dioxide

A. I only
B. I and II only
C. II and III only
D. I, II, and III

Test-Taking Tip

If you don't understand the directions, you can usually ask the teacher to explain them. When the directions are clear enough for you to understand the question completely, you are less likely to pick the wrong answer.

Critical Thinking

13. Plants without vascular tissues depend on osmosis to move water from cell to cell, which limits their size. To get water to all cells by osmosis, the cells must be in relatively close contact with water in the environment. When vascular tissues evolved, water could be transported efficiently through the plant, enabling it to grow much larger.
14. Photosynthesis and cellular respiration are essentially opposite processes. Photosynthesis removes carbon dioxide from the environment, but respiration returns it to the environment. Photosynthesis releases oxygen into the environment, but cellular respiration uses oxygen. The reactants of one process are the products of the other.
15. Plants on windowsills should be rotated to ensure that the plants grow evenly; otherwise, all the leaves will grow toward the window due to a plant's phototropic response to light.

Standardized Test Question

16. D

Reading Links

Plants (Walch Hands-On Science Series)

This collection of supplemental lab activities provides a variety of hands-on ways to reinforce topics covered in this chapter. The experiments teach important lessons about plant life, from germination to chlorophyll production and grafting, and are supported by detailed teacher resource pages.

Beller, Joel and Carl Raab. J. Weston Walch, Publisher. 96 pp. Trade ISBN: 978-0-8251-3757-0.

Plants on the Trail with Lewis and Clark

By focusing on a study of plants in a specific historical context, this book draws on a wealth of relevant information and a spirit of discovery that render it an engaging resource. Students may not know that Lewis and Clark kept detailed botanical records during their famous exploration, and students will benefit from this highly visual study of those efforts. Readers will emerge with a greater appreciation for both plant taxonomy and this moment in American history.

Patent, Dorothy Hinshaw. Photos by William Munoz. Clarion Books. 112 pp. Trade ISBN: 978-0-618-06776-3.

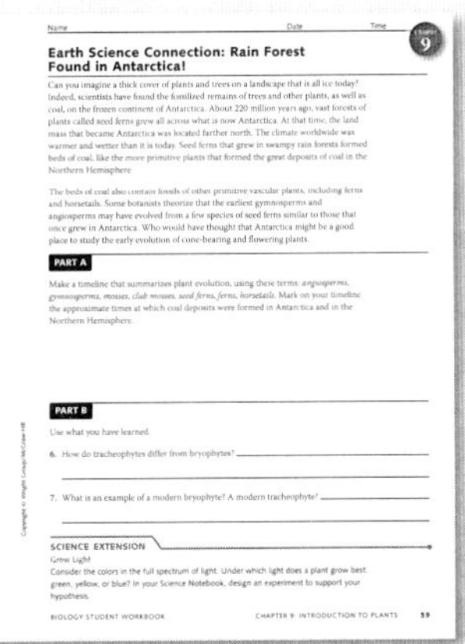
Earth Science Connection: Rain Forest Found in Antarctica!

Curriculum Connection
Workbook, p. 59

Science Challenge

Science Challenge
Workbook, pp. 60–61

Chapter 9

Labs

9A Bubbling Plants

This prechapter introduction activity is designed to determine what students already know about photosynthesis and demonstrate measurement of its rate by engaging students in observing, inferring, analyzing, recording, and communicating data.

Objectives

- observe evidence of photosynthesis in a water plant
- analyze the effects of altering light intensity and carbon dioxide amounts
- record data in a suitable way
- communicate conclusions by graphing

Planning

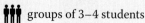

 30–45 minutes 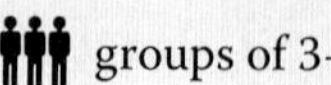 groups of 3–4 students

Materials (per group)

- *Elodea*
- test tube
- beaker or test-tube rack
- distilled water
- sodium bicarbonate (baking soda)
- lamp (40-watt)
- lamp (75-watt)
- scalpel
- clock or timer

Advance Preparation

- *Elodea* (a water plant) can be purchased at an aquarium supply store. It must be kept fresh in water.
- If bubbles fail to appear, have students cut off more of the stem and recrush.
- **CAUTION:** *Students to be careful when using the scalpel. Model for students how to cut the* Elodea *on an angle.*

Engagement Guide

- Challenge students to think about how the number of bubbles counted was evidence that the rate of photosynthesis was affected by an independent variable by asking:
  - *What kind of effect did adding the lamp, which represented an increase in light intensity, have on the rate of photosynthesis?* (The number of bubbles increased, showing an increase in the rate of photosynthesis.)
  - *What other independent variable would the light souce also represent?* (temperature)
  - *When the rate of photosynthesis increases or decreases, what products of photosynthesis would be affected?* (organic molecules, oxygen)
- Encourage students to communicate their conclusions by using their data tables and graphing their results.

Going Further

Encourage students to write out the word equation for photosynthesis and then the chemical equation underneath it. Have students share their equations with the class.

Objectives

9B Looking at Cells of Plants

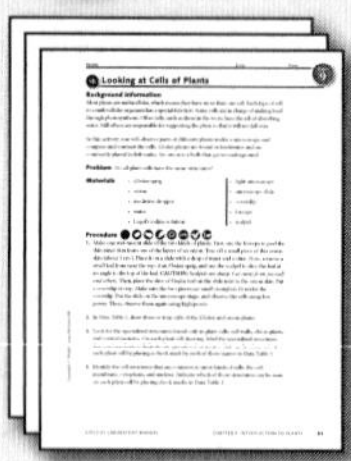

- observe different plants under a microscope
- identify specialized plant cell structures
- compare and contrast cells

Skill Set

observing, comparing and contrasting, recording and analyzing data, stating conclusions

Planning

 1 class period 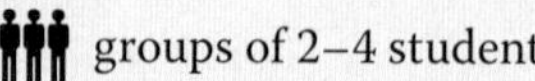 groups of 2–4 students

Materials

Materials for this activity are listed in the Student Laboratory Manual.

Lab Tip

Students may need to remove their goggles to examine the *Elodea* and onion samples with the microscope.

Answers to Observations: Data Table 1

Students' drawings of *Elodea* leaf should show three to four connected cells, with cell wall, chloroplast, and vacuole labeled on at least one of the cells. Onion drawings should show three to four connected onion cells, with cell wall and vacuole labeled on at least one of the cells. The onion cells will not have chloroplasts and will have a larger central vacuole.

Answers to Observations: Data Table 2

Students should place check marks beside all of the cell structures in the *Elodea* Leaf column and should check all parts except the chloroplasts in the Onion column.

Answers to Analysis and Conclusions

1. chloroplasts, for photosynthesis
2. The *Elodea* cells need chlorophyll because their function is to carry out photosynthesis; the onion is a root and does not carry out photosynthesis.
3. All plant cells have cell walls to give strength and support to the plant.
4. Plant cells are connected to each other by the shared cell walls of adjacent cells.
5. Students should predict that the central vacuole stores water.
6. Not all plant cells are the same. Some have different structures, which depend on the function of the cell.

Going Further

Have students make thin cross-section mounts of celery stalks, which are stems, and thin cross-section mounts of carrots, which are roots. Have students look at these under the microscope and compare the cell structures they see. Have students make data charts that show what cell organelles can be seen. The charts can be shared with the class.

9C Plant Tropisms

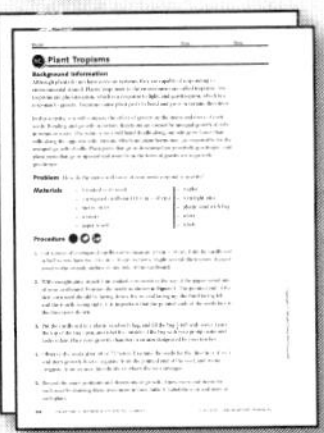

Objectives

- build a growth chamber to observe root and stem growth patterns
- observe and record growth patterns of roots and stems
- determine if root and stem growth are affected by gravity

Skill Set

observing, recording, analyzing, relating, interpreting

Planning

30 minutes (Day 1); 30 minutes 2–3 days later

groups of 3–4 students

Materials

Materials for this activity are listed in the Student Laboratory Manual.

Advance Preparation

Soak corn seeds in water for 24 hours before using them in class. Soaked seeds will allow pins to pass through and will germinate faster. Brace the growth chamber bags against a book or box to keep them from collapsing. Stems might already be green if bags are placed in light. This may aid students in distinguishing the root from the stem. Roots may also exhibit secondary branch roots.

Answers to Observations: Data Table I

No matter what position a corn seed point is facing, each corn seed will have the root growing down and the stem growing up.

Answers to Analysis and Conclusions

1. The direction of root growth in all four seeds is down.
2. The direction of stem growth in all four seeds is up.
3. No, the position does not have an effect on the growth of the root or stem.
4. Roots grow toward gravity and stems grow away from gravity, regardless of the original seed position.
5. Roots are positively geotropic, and stems are negatively geotropic.

Going Further

After observations have been made, have students snip off the root tips (1–2 mm) and turn the seeds 90 degrees on the pin. Have students observe any changes after 24 hours.

Chapter 10 Lessons

Introduce Chapter 10

As a starting activity, use LAB 10A "Moving" Plants on page 56 of the Laboratory Manual.

ENGAGE Have students close their eyes and imagine they are in the rain forest. Describe a rain-forest scene, including animals and plants but emphasizing plant life. Playing music with waterfall, rain, or animal sounds would enhance the imagery. Have students open their eyes and draw what they imagined during the description. Encourage them to add details and to include plants you may not have mentioned.

Think About Ways in Which Plants Reproduce

ENGAGE Encourage students to close their eyes again and think about one of their houseplants or garden plants or another plant that they see frequently. Urge students to remember what the plant has looked like throughout the year. It may also be useful to take a short walk around school grounds and directly observe flowers, plants, and trees. Then, direct students to complete the bulleted items. Remind them to sketch the plants they are describing.

Chapter 10 Nonflowering and Flowering Plants

KEY CONCEPT Plants have evolved with methods of reproduction that enable them to live in a variety of places on Earth.

Tropical rain forests teem with plant life. High above the ground are towering trees and climbing vines. The forest floor is carpeted with lush, green plants of astounding diversity. Yet, a tropical rain forest is only one of the many places on Earth where plants are found.

How are plants able to survive in the various places on Earth? How do they reproduce and ensure the continuation of their species? You will learn the answers to these questions in this chapter.

Think About Ways in Which Plants Reproduce

You may not have been to a rain forest, but you are familiar with many different types of plants. Plants are part of your environment at home and at school. Take a moment to observe the plants in your environment.

- What characteristics can you observe?
- In your Science Notebook, select one plant that you are familiar with and describe its characteristics and how you think it reproduces. Include a diagram to support your description.

NSTA SCILINKS THE WORLD'S A CLICK AWAY
www.scilinks.org
Vascular and Nonvascular Plants
Code: WGB10

168

Chapter 10 Planning Guide

Instructional Periods	National Standards	Lab Manual	Workbook
10.1 2 periods	C.2, C.5; UCP.2, UCP.3	Lab 10A—p. 56 "Moving" Plants Lab 10B—p. 57 Anatomy of a Flower Lab 10C—p. 60 Comparing Adaptations of Plants	Key Concept Review p. 62 Vocabulary Review p. 63 Interpreting Diagrams p. 64 Reading Comprehension p. 65 Curriculum Connection p. 66 Science Challenge p. 67
10.2 2 periods	A.2, B.3, C.2, C.5; B.6, C.1, C.5; UCP.1, UCP.3		
10.3 2 periods	C.1; C.2, C.3, C.4, F.3, UCP.5		
10.4 2 periods	C.1, C.2; A.1, B.4, C.4, F.3, F.6; UCP.5		

Middle School Standard; High School Standard; Unifying Concept and Principle

10.1 Bryophytes: Nonvascular Plants

Before You Read

Use the headings of this lesson to form questions. Write the questions in your Science Notebook. As you read, write answers to the questions.

Learning Goals

- Identify the characteristics of bryophytes.
- Explain how bryophytes reproduce.
- Describe the features of liverworts and mosses.

New Vocabulary

alternation of generations
sexual reproduction
gamete
zygote
sporophyte generation
spore
gametophyte generation
bryophyte
vascular system

From fossil evidence, scientists believe that bryophytes began to live on land about 480 million years ago. The first true land plants, they remain nearly unchanged in appearance to this day. The study of bryophytes, and other early groups of plants, helps in understanding how plants became so successful on land. A basic pattern that occurs in the life cycles of all plants is particularly easy to observe in bryophytes.

The Life Cycle of Plants

All plants have a life cycle, or stages of growth and reproduction, that includes a pattern called alternation of generations. **Alternation of generations** means that plants spend one part of their life cycle as diploid individuals and the other part as haploid individuals. Recall from Chapter 4 that the terms *diploid* and *haploid* refer to the number of sets of chromosomes in cells. Diploid ($2n$) cells have two sets of chromosomes, and haploid (n) cells have one set.

Figure 10.1 summarizes alternation of generations. Cell division that follows meiosis reduces the chromosome number of the cells produced from $2n$ to n. In most organisms, meiosis leads directly to the production of cells used in sexual reproduction. In **sexual reproduction**, two sex cells unite to begin the life of a new individual. In most organisms, the sex cells, or **gametes**, are called eggs and sperm. The female parent produces eggs, and the male parent produces sperm.

Figure It Out

1. Which stage begins with fertilization? With meiosis?
2. What is another name for sex cells?

An egg and a sperm unite in fertilization. Because each gamete has a haploid number of chromosomes, the union produces an offspring with diploid cells. The fertilized egg is called a **zygote** (ZI goht). Offspring of sexual reproduction are genetically different from their parents.

In the plant life cycle, the $2n$ stage is called the **sporophyte** (SPOR uh fite) **generation** because the plant reproduces with spores. A **spore** is a cell that is able to begin growing into a new plant without joining with another cell. The n stage is called the **gametophyte** (guh MEE tuh fite) **generation** because the plant produces gametes.

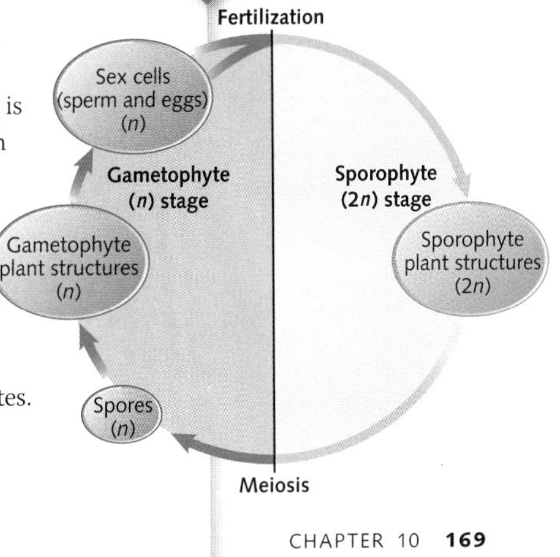

Figure 10.1 Alternation of generations consists of a sporophyte stage and a gametophyte stage.

10.1 Introduce

ENGAGE Have students look at the backs of their hands and notice the veins and arteries. Have partners write as many functions of veins and arteries as possible. On the board, create a class list and categorize like functions. Explain that some plants—vascular plants—have similar systems. Then, ask students to infer the functions of a plant's vascular system. Tell students that this chapter covers vascular and nonvascular plants.

Before You Read

Model turning headings into questions. On the board, write: *What are the characteristics of bryophytes?* Have students write questions for the following two goals, and remind them to leave space between each question in which to write their answers.

Vocabulary terms are listed on the first student page of each lesson. You may wish to preview the terms before introducing each lesson. Strategies for teaching the vocabulary appear on the pages where the terms are introduced.

Teach

EXPLAIN that all plants have a life cycle characterized by alternation of generations.

Figure It Out: Figure 10.1

ANSWER **1.** The sporophyte generation begins with fertilization; the gametophyte generation begins with meiosis. **2.** gametes

Vocabulary

alternation of generations Tell students that the root *alternate* means "every other." *Generate* is derived from the Latin word *genus,* which means "a kind." Alternation of generations means that "one kind is produced every other time." In plants, the "kinds" are the sporophyte and the gametophyte.

sexual reproduction Tell students that *reproduction* has two common meanings, "a copy of something" and "production of offspring." Then, explain that *sexual* means "involving sex cells," or gametes. So, *sexual reproduction* means "producing offspring through the union of gametes."

gamete Explain that *gamete* is from the Greek word *gamein,* meaning "to marry."

zygote Explain that *zygote* is a derivative of *zygon*, a Greek word meaning "yolk."

sporophyte generation Explain that the root word *phyte* comes from the Greek word *phyton*, meaning "plant." *Sporophyte* means "plant with spores."

spore Explain that *spore* is from the Latin word *spora*, meaning "seed." Tell students that a spore is able to grow into a new plant.

gametophyte generation Explain that *gametophyte* means "plant with gametes."

ELL Strategy

Use a Concept Map Have students create a concept map with *Bryophytes* as the main topic. Subtopics can include *Life cycle, Reproduction,* and *Characteristics.* Students can later compare this concept map with the one they create about gymnosperms in Lesson 10.3.

Teach

EXPLAIN that all nonvascular plants are commonly referred to as bryophytes. Liverworts are one major group of nonvascular plants, and the mosses are the other. All nonvascular plants have gametophytes that depend on water to reproduce.

EXPLORE Provide students with small samples of living moss and sphagnum peat moss, and give them microscopes or hand lenses. Or, under supervision, have students gather moss from a wooded or mossy area near their home or school and bring some to school. Have students work with partners to examine each sample and sketch what they see in their Science Notebooks.

As You Read

Give students about ten minutes to review their Learning Goal questions and to respond to each.

ANSWER This plant could not be a bryophyte because bryophytes are small plants that grow close to the ground in damp environments.

Vocabulary

bryophyte Tell students that *bryo-* is derived from the Greek word *bryon* and refers to a moss or liverwort. Remind students that *phyte* also comes from a Greek word, *phyton*, meaning "plant."

vascular system Explain to students that the word *vascular* originates from the Latin word *vasculum*, which came from *vas* and means "vessel." Encourage students to think of common uses of the word *system*. Their responses may include "a set of interrelated parts working together" or "a way of working." A vascular system is the set of vessels running throughout a plant.

Science Notebook EXTRA

Have each student draw a diagram that shows each stage of the life cycle of a liverwort, making sure to label each stage. Have students compare their diagrams to Figures 10.1 and 10.3.

In plants, spores are produced by cell division that involves meiosis, and thus they are haploid (n). The spores develop into haploid gametophytes that produce the haploid gametes.

As You Read

Using your answers to the questions you wrote, predict whether a tall plant found in the desert could be a bryophyte. Explain your answer.

Characteristics of Bryophytes

As you may recall from Chapter 9, **bryophytes** are nonvascular plants. A nonvascular plant stays small because it lacks a **vascular system**, or internal system of tubes that conducts water and nutrients throughout the plant. Such plants get water by taking it in through the parts that grow aboveground. The water enters and moves through these tiny plants by osmosis. Bryophytes, which include liverworts and mosses, are most frequently found growing in clumps in damp, shady places.

Like the earliest land plants, all bryophytes require water for sexual reproduction. Their sperm must swim to and fertilize their eggs. The gametophytes have a closely packed growth habit, which means that the sperm do not have far to swim. Both the sporophyte and gametophyte generations are relatively easy to identify in most bryophytes.

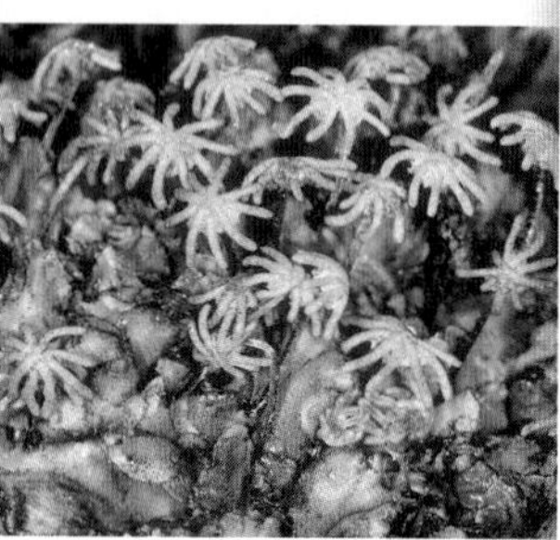

Figure 10.2 This liverwort species has gametophytes that look like flattened leaves from which tiny umbrella-like stalks rise. Most liverwort species, however, do not take this form.

Liverworts

About 8,000 species of liverworts have been identified. The best-known liverwort species has a gametophyte with a flattened, leaf-shaped body from which umbrella-like stalks rise. Shown in **Figure 10.2**, only the gametophyte of this liverwort is easy to see. Gametes are produced in structures found under the "umbrellas." Male and female gametes are produced on separate umbrella-like stalks.

The sporophyte generation grows from fertilized eggs underneath the "umbrellas" of female stalks. The sporophytes have no chlorophyll and get all their nourishment from the gametophytes they grow on. The sporophytes produce spores that are carried away and grow into new gametophytes.

Mosses

Mosses vary greatly in appearance, but many look like small green brushes. Mosses often form in large colonies that carpet the areas in which they grow. Moss gametophytes look like they have stems and leaves, but these structures are not true stems or leaves. The leaflike structures are mostly only one single cell thick.

A moss sporophyte, which grows from the tip of a gametophyte, is a slender stalk that ends in a spore capsule. Like the sporophytes of liverworts, moss sporophytes lack chlorophyll and take nutritents from the gametophytes they grown on.

Differentiated Instruction

Naturalistic Have students research the types of liverworts and mosses that grow in your climate. Challenge students to find samples of as many different types as they can. Students could make posters, labeling their various plants.

Teacher Alert

The saying that moss grows on the north side of trees is true—at least, in the northern hemisphere. Moss actually grows on all sides of trees. In northern latitudes, trees receive more sunlight on their southern side, so more moss will grow on the opposite or shady side. In southern latitudes, the reverse is true. In addition to finding moss on trees, one would also find lichens, algae, and a variety of vascular plants.

Life Cycle of a Bryophyte

Once an egg is fertilized, the zygote develops into a sporophyte that is even smaller than the gametophyte on which it grows. The spores are tiny, almost like dust. When released, spores can be carried great distances by currents of water or wind. Unlike the more familiar seed plants, nonvascular plants are dispersed by spores. **Figure 10.3** shows the life cycle of a moss.

Young sporophytes

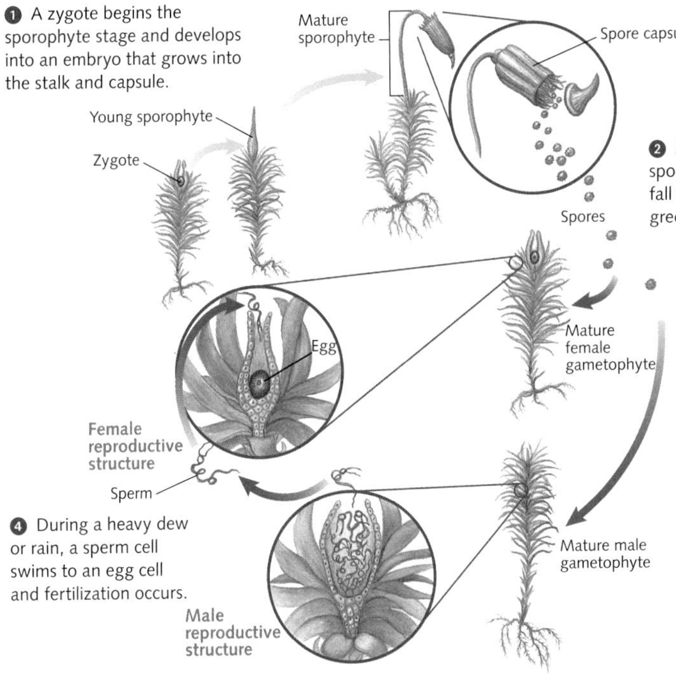

1 A zygote begins the sporophyte stage and develops into an embryo that grows into the stalk and capsule.
Mature sporophyte
Spore capsule
Young sporophyte
Zygote
2 Meiosis occurs in the capsule and spores are produced. When the spores fall to the ground, they grow into the green gametophytes.
Spores
Egg
Mature female gametophyte
3 Sex cells are produced in reproductive structures of male and female moss gametophytes.
Female reproductive structure
Sperm
4 During a heavy dew or rain, a sperm cell swims to an egg cell and fertilization occurs.
Male reproductive structure
Mature male gametophyte

Figure 10.3 Life Cycle of a Moss. According to the diagram, what structures are produced by the gametophyte generation? By the sporophyte generation?

After You Read

1. What characteristics do bryophytes share?
2. Arrange the following words so that when they are connected with arrows, they correctly illustrate a life cycle that includes alternation of generations: *zygote*, *gametophyte*, *sporophyte*, *spores*, and *gametes*.
3. Design a chart that compares liverworts and mosses. Your chart should have three columns—*Characteristics*, *Liverworts*, and *Mosses*—and three rows: *Vascular Tissue Present*, *Where They Grow*, and *Relative Size of Generations*.

Explore It!

Place about 5 cm of sand in the bottom of one plastic cup and 5 cm of peat moss in the bottom of a second plastic cup. Predict in your Science Notebook which material will absorb the most water. Test your prediction by using a dropper to add water to each cup. Record the amount of water absorbed by each. Was your prediction correct? Based on your observations, do you think it would be better to add peat moss or sand to a flower bed to help keep the soil moist?

Teach

EXPLAIN that students will learn about the life cycle of a moss, which is similar to the life cycle of a liverwort. Tell students that all nonvascular plants have gametophytes that depend on water for sexual reproduction.

Use the Visual: Figure 10.3

ANSWER Gametes are produced by the gametophyte generation, while spores are produced by the sporophyte generation.

Explore It!

Put students in pairs or in groups of three. Provide each group with two clear plastic cups, sand, peat moss, a metric ruler, an eyedropper, and water.

Have students write their predictions in their Science Notebooks before beginning the experiment. Explain that they can count the number of drops added to both the sand and the peat moss to judge their water-holding capacities. Drops should be added until water pools on top of each medium.

ANSWER Peat moss will absorb more water than sand, especially if the water is added slowly; therefore, peat moss should be added to the flower bed to absorb water.

Assess

EVALUATE Use the After You Read questions and the Alternative Assessment to help you assess students' understanding of the lesson.

After You Read

1. Bryophytes lack vascular tissues, have a gametophyte that is much larger than their sporophyte, and require water for sperm to swim to eggs.
2. Charts should show words, in a circular arrangement, connected by arrows in the following order: *zygote—sporophyte—spores—gametophyte—gametes—zygote.*
3. Students' charts should show that both liverworts and mosses lack vascular tissue; grow in damp places; and have very small sporophytes and much larger gametophytes.

Background Information

Peat moss is an organic additive to soil that enhances growing conditions for plants. It holds and then releases water as plants need it. Peat moss improves growing conditions in both clay soil and sandy soil through its water-holding and releasing properties. Peat moss works for two to three years, while compost often decomposes in one year.

Alternative Assessment

EVALUATE Have each student write a three- to four-sentence summary for each Learning Goal.

10.2 Introduce

ENGAGE Arrange students in small groups, and provide each group with a stalk of celery, a cup of water, food coloring, and a knife that can cut the celery. Instruct students to darken the water with food coloring and, after cutting about 2 cm from the bottom of the celery, to place the celery in the cup. Caution students to be careful when cutting the celery. Have students observe the celery stalks throughout class and then again the next day. During the next day's class, have students cut the celery at about 2-cm intervals. Ask students to follow the path of colored water through the stalk.

Before You Read

Create the three-column chart on the board. Then, model previewing the section on club mosses and writing facts in the chart, such as *grow on forest floors* and *found in tropical and temperate areas.*

Teach

EXPLAIN to students that celery is an example of a vascular plant. The vascular tissue that carries the colored water up the stalk is xylem. Phloem is another kind of vascular tissue. Remind students of the Engage activity from page 169, and ask them to compare their predictions of the functions of a plant's vascular system with what they observed with the celery.

In this lesson, students will learn about three types of tracheophytes, or vascular plants, and how they reproduce.

Vocabulary

tracheophyte Explain that the word part *tracheo* is derived from the Latin word *trachea*. In air-breathing vertebrates, the trachea is also called the windpipe, and it allows air to move from the throat to the bronchi in the lungs. Similarly, plants have long tubular cells that allow water and nutrients to move throughout the plant. The word *phyte* is derived from the Greek word *phyton*, meaning "plant."

rhizome Tell students that the word *rhizome* is derived from the Greek word *rhiza*, which means "root."

Learning Goals

- Identify the characteristics of club mosses, horsetails, and ferns.
- Recognize stages in the reproductive cycles of club mosses, horsetails, and ferns.

New Vocabulary

tracheophyte
rhizome
sporangium

10.2 Tracheophytes: Vascular Plants

Before You Read

In your Science Notebook, create a chart with three columns. Label the first column *Club Mosses*, the second column *Horsetails*, and the third column *Ferns*. As you read about these three kinds of plants, add information that describes their characteristics.

Hundreds of millions of years ago, when the seas receded and more of Earth's land became exposed, new types of plants evolved. These plants had adaptations that allowed them to survive on dry land. One important adaptation was a system of internal tissues through which water and other nutrients could be carried to all of a plant's parts.

Characteristics of Tracheophytes

Tissues that carry water and nutrients inside an organism's body are called vascular tissues. Most plants that have two types of vascular tissues—xylem and phloem. Plants with xylem and phloem are called vascular plants, or **tracheophytes** (TRAY kee uh fites). Most familiar plants are vascular plants. Because they have vascular tissues, these plants are able to form the organs known as true roots, stems, and leaves.

In mosses and liverworts, the gametophytes, or gamete-producing plants, are much larger than the sporophytes, or spore-producing plants. In tracheophytes, however, the sporophytes are the only generation large enough to be seen without magnification. The gametophytes are either very small or, as in most vascular plants, hidden in specialized organs. Like the bryophytes, the most primitive vascular plants still depend on water for sexual reproduction.

Club mosses, horsetails, and ferns are the most primitive vascular plants. Unlike the more familiar conifers and flowering plants, these plant phyla do not produce seeds. All of these groups of plants make drought-tolerant spores in conelike structures. The spores of these primitive tracheophytes disperse, or spread, new individuals.

Club Mosses

The name "club mosses" can be misleading. These land plants are not related to true mosses. Club mosses are small plants (most are under 30 cm in height) that grow on forest floors and look like small evergreen trees. They thrive in very moist places. **Figure 10.4** shows one species of club moss.

Figure 10.4 This club moss has leafy green stems and yellow conelike structures that produce spores.

ELL Strategy

Ask and Answer Questions Have students work in groups of three to preview the lesson and create questions about its content. At the end of the lesson, ask the same groups to carefully answer their questions. Have groups exchange their questions with another group and answer those they receive. This will provide another way for students to review for the chapter test.

172 NONFLOWERING AND FLOWERING PLANTS

When a spore lands in a suitable place, it grows into a gametophyte. This tiny plant can grow below the soil surface or on top of the soil. The gametophytes have structures that produce eggs and sperm on the same plant. A continuous film of water on the plant or on the ground is required for a sperm to reach and fertilize an egg. The fertilized egg develops into a new sporophyte.

Horsetails

Horsetails are relatively small, curious-looking plants that are easily recognized. Some species of horsetails produce frilly branches that resemble the tail of a horse. This bushy appearance gives horsetails their name. Horsetails have silica in their stems. Silica is an abrasive substance. Native Americans and early settlers used bunches of these plants to scrub pots and other utensils, giving horsetails the common name "scouring rushes." Horsetails are common to areas such as marshes, shallow ponds, and stream banks.

Horsetails grow from special underground stems called **rhizomes** (RI zohmz). Conelike structures form at the tips of horsetail stems. Spores are produced in these structures. When the spores are ripe, they are released and carried by air currents to new areas. If a spore lands in a place where conditions are favorable, it begins to grow into a tiny gametophyte plant. The gametophytes make either eggs or sperm. A fertilized egg grows into a new sporophyte individual.

As You Read

With a partner, select one section of this lesson. Take turns reading paragraphs to each other. After each paragraph reading, have the listening partner verbally summarize the paragraph. Then make sure you and your partner add notes to your charts.

How did the structure of horsetails lead to their use in scrubbing pots?

Figure 10.5 Slender stalks of horsetails grow in colonies. Conelike structures at the tips of the silica-containing stems are the sites of spore production.

Teach

EXPLAIN to students that they will learn about two other types of tracheophytes, horsetails and ferns, and how they reproduce.

As You Read

Give students five to ten minutes to update the *Club Mosses* and *Horsetails* columns of their charts. Check students' charts for accuracy.

ANSWER Horsetails were used as scrubbing brushes because their stems contain an abrasive mineral called silica.

Science Notebook EXTRA

Have students compare the reproductive stages of club mosses, horsetails, and ferns. Students could analyze the stages of the three different types of tracheophytes in three ways: using a comparison chart, sketching and labeling, or writing a list for each plant. Students should then add this information to their three-column charts.

Background Information

Field horsetail is a perennial that is native to North America and Europe. It can grow uncontrollably due to its rhizome systems, which can reach up to two meters in depth. Herbicides can be used to control its growth, but this has a negative impact on the soil for up to one year. Physically pulling the plants is another option, but since the rhizome system is extensive, soil is removed in the process and has to be replaced.

Differentiated Instruction

Visual and Kinesthetic Provide students with large sheets (or a roll) of paper and materials such as glue, sand, felt, tissue paper, and fabric scraps. Ask students to make either life-sized or scaled replicas of horsetail plants, including the rhizomes. Encourage students to hypothesize about ways to control the growth of field horsetails. Students could write or draw their solutions to display next to their life-sized illustrations.

Teach

 to students that ferns are another type of tracheophyte. Fern rhizomes are different from horsetail rhizomes. Horsetail rhizomes grow well below the surface of the soil; fern rhizomes are shallow and can grow above the soil. In both, rhizomes are stems that allow the plant to spread.

Vocabulary

asexual reproduction Tell students that the prefix *a-* means "without." Have students define the term *asexual reproduction* using that meaning and the definition of *sexual reproduction.*

sporangia Tell students the literal definition of *sporangia* is "spore vessels." The word is derived from the Latin word *spora,* meaning "spore," and the Greek word *angeion,* which translates to "vessel."

Use the Visual: Figure 10.7

ANSWER A rhizome is a horizontal underground stem of a vascular plant.

CONNECTION: Math

Have students work in pairs, being sure that each pair includes a student with strong math skills. Provide each pair with grid paper. Remind students to review the range of their data to construct a reasonable scale for the *y*-axis.

Check students' bar graphs to be sure they have used the data correctly and have each prepared a labeled graph with an appropriate key.

Have partners write three to four sentences in their Science Notebooks to analyze their graphs.

Students should recognize that there are more living species of bryophytes than there are of the three groups of tracheophytes for which data are given.

Figure 10.6 Boston ferns are a popular houseplant.

Ferns

In nature, most ferns grow in shady areas. Because they need water for their sperm to swim to eggs during the gametophyte generation, most ferns grow in damp areas. Most fern sporophytes produce leaves called fronds. Almost everyone is familiar with the featherlike fronds. The leaves of other fern species can be very different in shape. Some look like small buttons, and others look a bit like small swords. In addition to differences in frond shapes, fern species also differ in size. Some ferns are very small (about 1 cm in diameter), while others—tropical tree ferns, for example—can grow many meters tall.

Ferns produce fronds from a rhizome. The rhizome is not a root but rather an underground stem with roots. Fern rhizomes can grow for many years and produce new leaves every growing season. The rhizomes can be cut into many pieces, each of which can grow into separate but identical fern plants. Reproduction that does not involve the union of an egg and a sperm, which is common in all plants, is called **asexual reproduction**.

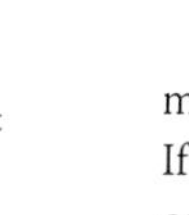

Figure 10.7 Characteristic features of a fern sporophyte include a rhizome, roots, and fronds. What is a rhizome?

Fern fronds grow in a special way: they unroll. This makes it easy to tell a fern from other kinds of plants. If you look at a young frond as it starts to develop, you can see why it is sometimes called a fiddlehead. As shown in **Figure 10.8**, the unrolling frond looks like the carved top of a violin, fiddle, or cello. As it grows, the frond continues to unroll until it reaches its mature shape and size.

Fern sporophytes produce spores in structures called **sporangia** (spuh RAN jee uh, singular: sporangium), which are usually located on the lower surface of a frond. Some species produce sporangia on separate stalks, while others bear their spores on the top of the fronds. Sporangia are often found in clusters called sori, which are located on the undersides of fronds. In some fern species, the sori form lines. In others, they are arranged around the edge of a frond. Some people even mistake these clusters of sporangia for insects and try to rub them off a frond.

Figure 10.8 New fronds are called fiddleheads because their shape resembles the carved top of a violin.

CONNECTION: Math

The approximate numbers of living species of bryophytes and tracheophytes are provided here. *Mosses: 20,000; Liverworts: 6,500; Hornworts: 100; Club Mosses: 1,150; Horsetails: 15; Ferns: 11,000* Use this information to prepare a bar graph. Show bryophytes with bars of one color and tracheophytes with bars of another color. Label each bar correctly and include a key. Note: Hornworts are a type of bryophyte.

What conclusion can you reach by looking at your completed graph?

Background Information

Scientists recently discovered that brake ferns can be used to clean up polluted soil. These plants can absorb arsenic from contaminated soil without any negative consequences to the plant. Arsenic (As) is a naturally occurring element that is used within industry and agriculture; if released into the environment, it can contaminate the water supply. Overexposure to arsenic can increase the risk of lung, skin, bladder, liver, kidney, and prostate cancers.

Life Cycle of a Fern

Fern spores form by cell division that begins with meiosis. When the spores are ripe, the sporangia open. The released spores are light and float on the air. If they land in a suitable damp area, they begin to grow. They produce the gametophyte generation of the fern, which is a small, delicate green heart-shaped plant growing on the surface of damp soil. A fern gametophyte is shown in **Figure 10.9**.

The gametophyte produces sperm and eggs in separate structures. The antheridium (an thuh RIH dee um, plural: antheridia) is the male reproductive structure in which sperm are produced. The archegonium (ar kih GOH nee um, plural: archegonia) is the female reproductive structure in which eggs are produced. Sperm need water in order to swim to the archegonia to fertilize the eggs.

Figure 10.9 The fern gametophyte looks like a small green heart growing on the damp soil surface.

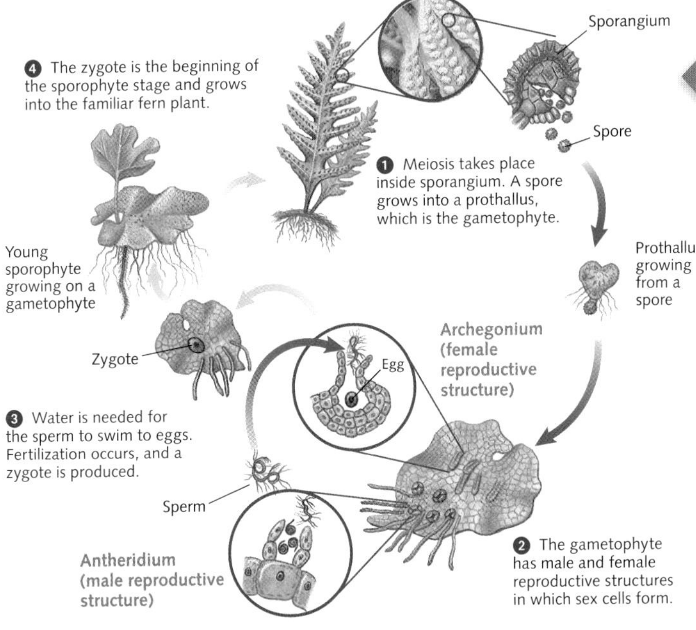

Sporangium
4 The zygote is the beginning of the sporophyte stage and grows into the familiar fern plant.
Spore
1 Meiosis takes place inside sporangium. A spore grows into a prothallus, which is the gametophyte.
Young sporophyte growing on a gametophyte
Prothallus growing from a spore
Archegonium (female reproductive structure)
Egg
Zygote
3 Water is needed for the sperm to swim to eggs. Fertilization occurs, and a zygote is produced.
Sperm
Antheridium (male reproductive structure)
2 The gametophyte has male and female reproductive structures in which sex cells form.

Figure 10.10 Life Cycle of a Fern. Both stages are photosynthetic and can thus live independently.

Figure It Out

1. What is the name of the male reproductive structure? The female reproductive structure?
2. What stage begins with the formation of a zygote?

Extend It!

Ferns were among the plants in Earth's ancient forests. Although they may have died 300 million years ago, these ancient ferns are important sources of energy today. Research how ancient ferns became the coal deposits used for fuel today. Present your research as a sequence chart or a series of drawings to illustrate this process.

After You Read

1. What characteristic do tracheophytes share?
2. Which stage in the life cycle of tracheophytes is most easily recognized?
3. In a well-developed paragraph, explain why club mosses, horsetails, and ferns grow in damp places.

Teach

EXPLAIN that a fern's reproductive process involves gametophytes producing sperm in antheridia and eggs in archegonia. As with all the tracheophytes discussed so far, the sperm require water so that they can swim to fertilize eggs.

Figure It Out: Figure 10.10

ANSWER **1.** The antheridium is the male structure; the archegonium is the female structure. **2.** the sporophyte stage

Extend It!

Provide students with scientific reference books and access to the Internet. Encourage students to research fossil fuels as a way to gain understanding of coal and fern fossils. Students may benefit from "grazing" over a number of resources before beginning their specific research. Providing concept maps or time lines for students to complete may help them organize their thoughts.

Students' sequence charts or illustrations should show that as ferns died, they formed thick layers in Earth's ancient swamps. Over millions of years, the layers at the bottom were compressed by the weight of the upper layers and became the coal deposits that are mined for fuel today.

Assess

EVALUATE Use the After You Read questions and the Alternative Assessment to help you assess students' understanding of the lesson.

After You Read

1. Tracheophytes have vascular tissues, true roots, stems, and leaves, and a sporophyte that is much larger than the gametophyte.
2. the sporophyte stage
3. Club mosses, horsetails, and ferns grow in damp places because they depend on water for sperm to swim to and fertilize eggs.

Background Information

Fossil fuels come in three forms: coal, oil, and natural gas. These fuels were formed during the Carboniferous Period of the Paleozoic Era. Coal is composed of carbon, hydrogen, oxygen, nitrogen, and different amounts of sulfur.

Alternative Assessment

EVALUATE Using their charts, have students compare and contrast the characteristics of two types of the tracheophytes in this lesson. Students could use Venn diagrams or write paragraphs to discuss the similarities and differences.

10.3 Introduce

ENGAGE Ask students to brainstorm a list of plants that produce seeds. It may be helpful to start with examples such as pine trees, pear trees, and tomato plants. Have students work with partners and compare lists, adding any plants that they may have forgotten originally. Make a class list to display in the classroom and to use throughout the lesson.

Before You Read

Model the concept map on the board. After creating the main topic of *Gymnosperms*, write *Is a seed plant* and draw a line to *Gymnosperms*. Encourage students to preview the lesson if they are unable to generate any prior knowledge.

Teach

EXPLAIN to students that all seed-bearing plants are classified as either gymnosperms or angiosperms. Gymnosperm plants produce seeds that are not contained in fruits, and the plants do not flower. Angiosperm plants produce seeds that are encased in fruits and do flower.

Emphasize that both gymnosperms and angiosperms are tracheophytes that have evolved with methods of reproduction that do not require water for sperm to reach and fertilize eggs.

Vocabulary

gymnosperm Explain to students that the word part *gymno-* means "naked." The word *sperm* is derived from the Greek word *sperma*, meaning "seed."

cycad Explain to students that the word *cycad* is derived from the Greek word *kykas*; it is a kind of gymnosperm that resembles a palm tree.

pollen Tell students that in Latin, the word *pollen* means "fine dust." Ask students to explain why this is an appropriate definition.

Learning Goals

- Identify the characteristics of gymnosperms.
- Describe the four phyla of gymnosperms.

New Vocabulary

gymnosperm
cycad
pollen
ginkgo
conifer
ovule
pollination

10.3 Seed Plants: Gymnosperms

Before You Read

In your Science Notebook, create a concept map based on the word *gymnosperms*. Start by writing anything you already know about gymnosperms. Add information as you read the lesson.

Plants that make seeds are the dominant form of plant life on Earth today. Their ancestors are first seen in the fossil record about 350 million years ago. Seed plants, which have microscopic gametophytes, are not dependent on water for their reproduction. The seeds, not spores, disperse seed plants. Seed plants are generally classified into two major groups: gymnosperms and angiosperms.

Characteristics of Gymnosperms

Gymnosperms (JIHM nuh spurmz) are seed plants that do not produce flowers and produce seeds that are not contained in fruits. Nearly all gymnosperms, such as pine trees and redwood trees, produce seeds in cones. The leaves of most gymnosperms are scalelike or needlelike. Many gymnosperms are called evergreens, because some green leaves are always on their branches. There are four phyla of plants that are classified as gymnosperms: cycads, ginkgoes, gnetophytes, and conifers.

Cycads

Cycads (SI kadz) are gymnosperms that resemble small palm trees. Cycad plants are either male or female. A male cycad plant has cones that produce pollen. **Pollen** grains are the small structures of seed plants in which sperm develop. A female cycad plant has conelike structures that produce eggs.

Figure 10.11 Cycad plants produce either male *(top)* or female *(bottom)* cones.

Figure 10.12 The sago palm *(left)* is a cycad, not a palm. The heavily thorned leaves of *Encephalartos horridus (right)* keep animals from eating this cycad.

ELL Strategy

Compare and Contrast Have students use compare-and-contrast charts to differentiate among three groups of gymnosperms: cycads, ginkgoes, and conifers. Students should complete the charts with partners.

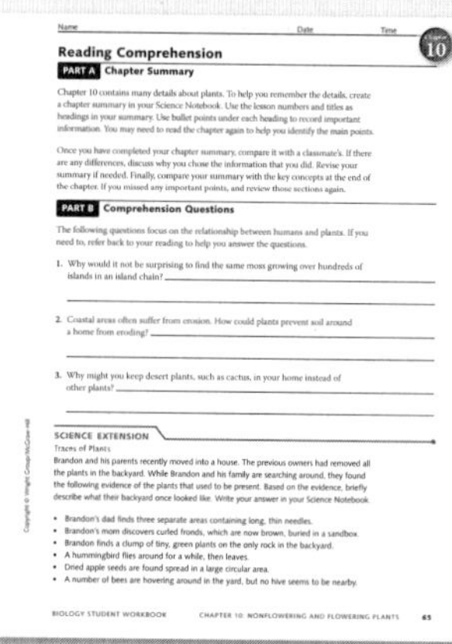

Name ______ Date ______ Time ______

Chapter 10

Reading Comprehension

PART A Chapter Summary

Chapter 10 contains many details about plants. To help you remember the details, create a chapter summary in your Science Notebook. Use the lesson numbers and titles as headings in your summary. Use bullet points under each heading to record important information. You may need to read the chapter again to help you identify the main points.

Once you have completed your chapter summary, compare it with a classmate's. If there are any differences, discuss why you chose the information that you did. Revise your summary if needed. Finally, compare your summary with the key concepts at the end of the chapter. If you missed any important points, and review those sections again.

PART B Comprehension Questions

The following questions focus on the relationship between humans and plants. If you need to, refer back to your reading to help you answer the questions.

1. Why would it not be surprising to find the same moss growing over hundreds of islands in an island chain? ______
2. Coastal areas often suffer from erosion. How could plants prevent soil around a home from eroding? ______
3. Why might you keep desert plants, such as cactus, in your home instead of other plants? ______

SCIENCE EXTENSION

Traces of Plants

Brandon and his parents recently moved into a house. The previous owners had removed all the plants in the backyard. While Brandon and his family are searching around, they found the following evidence of the plants that used to be present. Based on the evidence, briefly describe what their backyard once looked like. Write your answer in your Science Notebook.

- Brandon's dad finds three separate areas containing long, thin needles.
- Brandon's mom discovers curled fronds, which are now brown, buried in a sandbox.
- Brandon finds a clump of tiny, green plants on the only rock in the backyard.
- A hummingbird flies around for a while, then leaves.
- Dried apple seeds are found spread in a large circular area.
- A number of bees are hovering around in the yard, but no hive seems to be nearby.

Copyright © Wright Group/McGraw-Hill

BIOLOGY STUDENT WORKBOOK CHAPTER 10: NONFLOWERING AND FLOWERING PLANTS 65

Reading Comprehension Workbook, p. 65

Ginkgoes

Ginkgoes (GINK ohz) are gymnosperms with broad, flat leaves that are fan-shaped and usually have two lobes. Like many broadleaf trees, ginkgoes drop their leaves as temperatures fall with the onset of cold weather. The ginkgo has often been called a "living fossil." Fossils that look remarkably like the single existing species of ginkgo have been found in rock layers that date back in time about 270 million years.

Ginkgo trees can live for a long time—a tree that might be almost three thousand years old has been identified. The trees are resistant to many insects, and their very deep roots enable them to withstand strong winds. The leaves turn a beautiful yellow-gold color in the fall before they drop. Like cycads, ginkgo trees are either male or female.

Gnetophytes

Gnetophytes (NEE tuh fites) are found in Asia, North America, Africa, and Central and South America. They include desert shrubs and tropical trees and climbing vines that produce seeds in conelike structures. The shrubs known as Mormon tea (*Ephedra*) in American deserts are gnetophytes.

Conifers

California is home to the world's tallest living thing, largest living thing, and oldest living thing. All three of these record holders are **conifers** (KAH nuh furz), or gymnosperms that produce seeds in cones. The world's tallest living thing is a coast redwood tree called Hyperion. It is more than 115 meters tall. The largest living thing is the General Sherman tree, a giant sequoia. Its volume has been estimated to be about 1,487 m^3. The oldest living thing is a bristlecone pine that grows in the White Mountains. According to its rings, it is 4,700 years old!

Figure 10.14 Coast redwood trees *(left)* are the tallest conifers. Bristlecone pines *(right)* are conifers with very long life spans.

Figure 10.13 Ginkgoes are often planted on city streets because they can tolerate the smog and air pollution common in many urban areas.

As You Read

Add information to your concept map.

What are the four groups of gymnosperms?

Did You Know?

Like rustlers in the Old West who stole horses, cattle, and sheep, "cycad rustlers" steal cycads. Because cycads are rare and grow slowly, a mature cycad of a desirable species can be worth many thousands of dollars. Today, it is not uncommon for people to put alarms on mature cycad plants in their gardens and greenhouses!

Teach

EXPLAIN to students that they will learn about two more types of gymnosperms: ginkgoes and conifers. Both of these types of plants are capable of living for a very long time. Ginkgoes have lived as long as 3,000 years, and conifers have remained alive for 4,700 years.

Vocabulary

ginkgo Explain to students that the source of the word *ginkgo* is the Japanese word *ginkyō*. This word was derived from two Chinese words: *yin*, meaning "silver," and *hing*, meaning "apricot."

conifer Explain that in Latin, *conifer* means "cone-bearing."

As You Read

Give students five to ten minutes to update the concept maps in their Science Notebooks. Encourage them to review the lesson title, new vocabulary terms, and section headings as they add to their maps.

ANSWER The four groups of gymnosperms are cycads, ginkgoes, gnetophytes and conifers.

Science Notebook EXTRA

Have students research the largest giant sequoias at **http://www.nps.gov/archive/seki/bigtrees.htm**. Students should study the data about location, height, circumference, and volume provided for the ten largest trees. Ask students to respond to the following questions and record their responses in their Science Notebooks:

Which tree is the oldest? Why do you think that?

What environmental factors contribute to the size of the sequoia?

What, if any, are the relationships among the different measurements?

Background Information

Ginkgo biloba extract (GBE) is a medicinal herb traditionally used to treat circulatory disorders and enhance memory. Scientific research supports its effectiveness for those purposes. Recently, GBE has been shown to improve blood circulation to the brain. Additionally, ginkgo leaves contain flavonoids and terpenoids. These chemicals are thought to be strong antioxidants. Ginkgo is used to treat dementia, eye problems, intermittent claudication (limping), memory impairment, and tinnitus.

Teach

EXPLAIN that conifers are the largest group of gymnosperms. Emphasize that most conifers are evergreens; that is, they remain green throughout the year. Bald cypress is an example of a conifer that is deciduous; that is, it drops all of its leaves once a year. Students will learn how cones are an integral part of the reproduction process.

EXPLORE Have available a variety of cones from different types of conifers for students to touch and observe. After students hypothesize about the origin of each cone, provide the correct answer.

EXTEND Arrange students in small groups, and provide a variety of resources, such as plant reference books, general encyclopedias, and Internet access. Have each group do quick preliminary research on three to four different conifers and then choose one to study in depth. For their group's chosen conifer, students will identify in their Science Notebooks the best planting practices, mature size, appearance, and native location. They should also sketch the plant. Each group should create a summary document to be placed into a class book about conifers.

Have students research the planting zones. They can include a map of the planting zones and identify in which zones their conifer will grow.

Extend It!

Arrange students in small groups, and provide access to resources such as online databases and reference books. Each group should identify a seed bank to research and answer the questions presented. In addition to those questions, ask students to explain why they think seed banks exist.

Figure 10.15 Conifers, the largest group of gymnosperms, form large forests of closely spaced trees, an adaptation for wind pollination.

Extend It!

Scientists are engaged in efforts to save the seeds of many useful and endangered plants in places called seed banks. Conserving seeds in this way will ensure that such plants do not disappear completely from Earth. Use library and Internet resources to find out about seed banks. What organizations manage seed banks? Where are the seed banks located? What kinds of plants are the targets of conservation efforts?

Features of Conifers There are about 550 species of conifers alive today. The vast majority of conifers are trees, but some are smaller shrubs. All conifers are woody plants. Conifers are the most common trees found in the large forests in colder areas of North America, Europe, and Asia. Conifers include pines, spruces, firs, cedars, yews, redwoods, larches, and junipers.

Most conifers are evergreens, which are plants that have green leaves throughout the year. Some conifers have leaves called needles. Pines, firs, and spruces have clusters of long, thin needles. Other conifers, such as yews, have short, flat leaves. Still others, such as junipers, have small, scalelike leaves. Although most conifers are evergreens, a few species shed their leaves during cold winter weather. In fact, all conifers lose some leaves all the time. A walk in a pine forest will show the soft carpet of brown pine needles that have fallen over the years.

Cones are one of the most obvious features of conifers. Cones are the structures in which conifers produce seeds. In most species, male and female cones form on different branches of the same plant. Male cones produce pollen, which contains the sperm. Female cones produce **ovules** (AHV uhz), which are structures of seed plants in which egg cells are produced. The female cones of most conifers are green when they are young and turn brown and woody when they mature. In junipers, mature female cones have fleshy scales and look like small berries. Some conifers do not produce cones. Instead, their seeds are surrounded by a fleshy protective coating. In yews, the coating is a bright red color that often attracts birds.

Reproduction in Conifers In order for seed plants to reproduce, pollination must take place. **Pollination** (pah luh NAY shun) is the transfer of pollen grains to the female structures of a plant. Conifers are wind-pollinated. The male cones release large amounts of pollen. This increases the chances that fertilization will occur. The seeds are held in the female cones until they mature. Then, the scales that make up the cones open, and the seeds are dropped. In some species, this process can take place in as little as four months, while in other species, it can take several years.

Usually, conifer seeds that fall from mature female cones are carried away by wind. Seeds are also spread when cones fall to the ground or when birds eat the seeds and deposit undigested ones in their wastes. The cones of some pines will only release their seeds after fire burns the area in which they live. The fire kills adult trees and clears the ground of its thick layer of dropped needles. The seeds sprout because the death of the larger, older trees permits more sunlight to reach the seeds on the ground, which is now clear of debris.

Vocabulary

ovule Tell students that the suffix *-ule* denotes something diminutive, or smallness. The root, *ova*, is "an egg." *Ovule* can be translated literally to mean "small egg."

pollination Explain to students that the word *pollination* is made up of the root *pollen* and two suffixes, *-ate* and *-ion*. Encourage students to remember the meaning of the word *pollen* (the fine powder produced by plants in which sperm cells develop). Then, tell students that the suffix *-ate* denotes "causing to be" or "to have." The suffix *-ion* signifies a condition or state.

Differentiated Instruction

Visual, Mathematical Have students draw an evergreen garden to scale. Students should choose a small area of the school grounds or nearby park that could be improved with plantings. Students' drawings should include conifers of varying heights and colors that will create visual interest.

To extend the project further, students could write a group letter to the school principal or local town/village official advocating the construction of such a garden.

Life Cycle of a Pine

Pines produce male and female cones on the same tree. First, spores form inside the cones through meiosis. The spores develop into male and female gametophyte structures. The male gametophyte is inside a pollen grain, and the female gametophyte is inside an ovule. Wind carries pollen from the male cones to the female cones, where fertilization takes place. Once eggs are fertilized, a cone's seeds develop on the tops of scales.

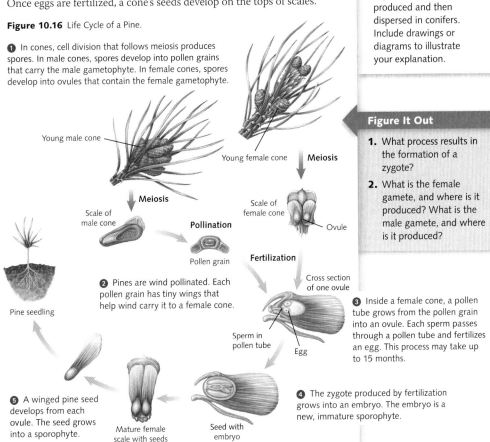

Figure 10.16 Life Cycle of a Pine.

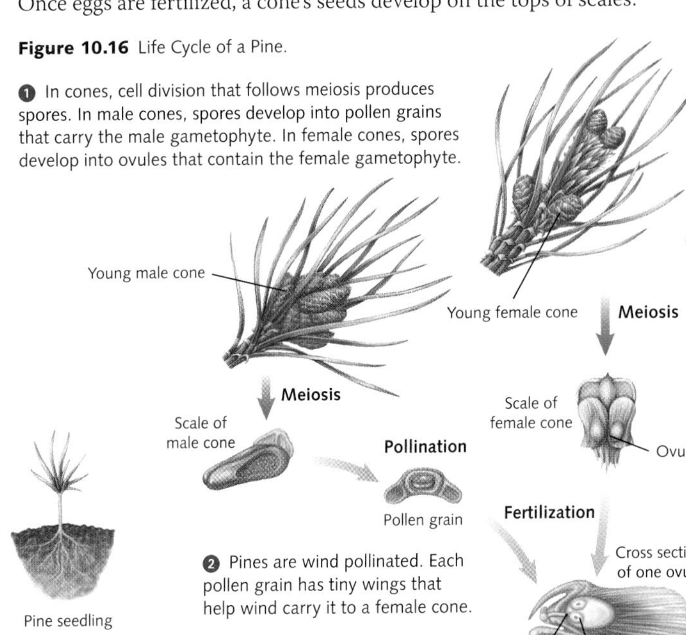

❶ In cones, cell division that follows meiosis produces spores. In male cones, spores develop into pollen grains that carry the male gametophyte. In female cones, spores develop into ovules that contain the female gametophyte.
Young male cone
Young female cone
Meiosis
Meiosis
Scale of male cone
Pollination
Scale of female cone
Ovule
Pollen grain
Fertilization
Cross section of one ovule
❷ Pines are wind pollinated. Each pollen grain has tiny wings that help wind carry it to a female cone.
Pine seedling
❸ Inside a female cone, a pollen tube grows from the pollen grain into an ovule. Each sperm passes through a pollen tube and fertilizes an egg. This process may take up to 15 months.
Sperm in pollen tube
Egg
❹ The zygote produced by fertilization grows into an embryo. The embryo is a new, immature sporophyte.
❺ A winged pine seed develops from each ovule. The seed grows into a sporophyte.
Mature female scale with seeds
Seed with embryo

Explain It!

In your Science Notebook, explain how seeds are produced and then dispersed in conifers. Include drawings or diagrams to illustrate your explanation.

Figure It Out

1. What process results in the formation of a zygote?
2. What is the female gamete, and where is it produced? What is the male gamete, and where is it produced?

After You Read

1. What three characteristics do most gymnosperms share?
2. Compare and contrast male and female cones.
3. Use the Learning Goals on page 176 to reorganize the information in the concept map you made in your Science Notebook.

Teach

EXPLAIN that students will learn about the life cycle of one kind of conifer, the pine.

Figure It Out: Figure 10.16

ANSWER **1.** fertilization **2.** The female gametes, eggs, are produced in female cones. The male gametes, sperm, are produced in male (or pollen) cones.

Explain It!

Wind carries pollen from male cones to female cones. Fertilization occurs in female cones. The seeds produced are held inside the female cones until they mature. Seeds can be dispersed by wind and animals.

Have each student review one other student's work and provide feedback.

Assess

EVALUATE Use the After You Read questions and the Alternative Assessment to help you assess students' understanding of the lesson.

After You Read

1. Gymnosperms are seed plants that do not produce flowers. Their seeds are produced in cones instead of being enclosed in fruit. Most gymnosperms have needlelike leaves, and many are evergreens.
2. Male cones are smaller, produce pollen, and are usually found on the lower branches of a tree. Female cones are larger, produce eggs, and are usually found higher in a tree.
3. Answers will vary, but concepts maps could have two main branches extending from the title *Gymnosperms*. One branch could include characteristics of gymnosperms, and the other branch could show the groups of gymnosperms.

Background Information

Certain pines have edible seeds known as pine nuts, pignoli, and piñon. Nut-producing pines include the stone pine of southern Europe, the Swiss stone pine native to the Swiss Alps region, and the pinion pine from the arid region of the southwest United States. The nut-like seeds are inside the small cones; the seeds are removed by heating the cones, an expensive process.

Alternative Assessment

EVALUATE Have each student use his or her concept map to write a paragraph summarizing the characteristics of gymnosperms.

10.4 Introduce

ENGAGE As a class, briefly review the list of seed-producing plants that students created at the start of Lesson 10.3 (page 176). Have pairs of students classify each plant as a gymnosperm or angiosperm. Ask students to count the number of plants in each category. Then, discuss quantities for each category as a class. Tell students that there are about 1,000 species of gymnosperms and 250,000 species of angiosperms.

Before You Read

Model previewing the lesson with the picture on the first page of the lesson. Read the caption aloud, and predict how the information is related to the title of the lesson. Have students finish previewing the lesson, and give them about ten minutes to write their prediction paragraphs. Have some students read their paragraphs aloud, and record these predictions on the board.

Teach

EXPLAIN to students that flowering plants are able to grow in most environments on Earth. This is one of the reasons that so many species exist. Angiosperms provide fruits, vegetables, and grains for the diets of animals and humans.

Vocabulary

angiosperm Explain that *angiosperm* is composed of *angio-* and *sperm*. The word part *angio-* is derived from the Greek word *angeion* and means "vessel." Remind students that *sperm* means "seed."

sepal Explain that *sepal* is derived from the Greek word *skepē* and means "cover."

petal Tell students that the word *petal* is derived from the Greek word *petalon* and means "leaf." Petals are modified leaves that are often scented and brightly colored.

stamen Explain that *stamen* refers to the male reproductive organ of a plant. It is made up of two parts, the anther and filament.

anther Tell students that *anther* is derived from the Greek word *anthos*, meaning "flower."

filament Explain that *filament* is derived from the Latin word *filum*, meaning "thread."

Learning Goals

- Describe the characteristics of flowering plants.
- Identify the parts of a flower and their functions.
- Explain how pollination and fertilization are related.

New Vocabulary

angiosperm
sepal
petal
stamen
anther
filament
pistil
stigma
style
ovary

10.4 Seed Plants: Angiosperms

Before You Read

Preview the lesson by looking at the pictures, reading the captions, and reviewing the Learning Goals. In your Science Notebook, write a paragraph predicting what you think the lesson is about, based on your preview.

Flowering plants are probably the most familiar group of plants and are the most diverse group of organisms in the plant kingdom. The first fossil evidence of flowering plants dates to about 140 million years ago. Flowering plants are also called angiosperms.

Characteristics of Angiosperms

Angiosperms (AN jee uh spurmz) are flowering plants that produce seeds that develop inside of fruits. They number more than 250,000 different species and grow almost everywhere. Angiosperms thrive in tropical areas that have few gymnosperms, in deserts that have little water, in temperate areas with seasonal supplies of water, and in cold areas where it becomes warm enough for ice and snow to melt. Some angiosperms even grow in water. Angiosperms provide many of the foods people eat, including fruits, vegetables, and grains.

Structure and Function of Flowers

Flowers are the main reproductive organs of flowering plants. Most flowers have four main parts: petals, sepals, stamens, and a pistil. Each flower part plays an important role in a plant's ability to produce more of its kind. These parts and their functions are shown in **Figure 10.18** on page 181.

Figure 10.17 Within the tough green sepals, the delicate petals and reproductive parts of this rose flower are protected.

Petals and Sepals In most plants, flowers are produced on the ends of stems. When a flower is developing, it is covered by green leaflike structures called **sepals** (SEE pulz) that surround the bud and protect the delicate tissues inside. When the flower bud is ready to open, the sepals begin to separate at the top and fold downward. **Petals** are the soft parts of the flower that most people think of as the flower itself. A flower's petals are a form of plant "advertisement," attracting animals that the flower needs to complete its life cycle.

Stamens The **stamens** (STAY munz) are the male reproductive organs of a plant. Each stamen consists of an **anther** (AN thur), which produces pollen grains, and a **filament** (FIL uh mint), which holds the anther above the flower petals. Pollen grains contain the sperm that will fertilize the eggs.

ELL Strategy

Activate Background Knowledge Arrange students in groups of two or three, and ask them to share what they know about flowering plants. Encourage students to give examples of plants from their countries of origin. Provide photos of flowering plants grown locally and access to the Internet. Ask each group to research the local plants and plants from students' native countries and to note any similarities. Have each group share what they learned with other groups.

Field Study

Have students walk around the school property and surrounding neighborhood if possible. Have them observe, sketch, analyze, and identify as many plants as they can, classifying them as bryophytes or tracheophytes and as mosses, ferns, gymnosperms, or angiosperms. Encourage students to identify the process of reproduction for each plant.

Pistil The **pistil** (PIHS tul), which is made up of the stigma, style, and ovary, is the female reproductive organ of a plant. The **stigma** (STIHG muh) is the sticky tip of a pistil that holds on to any pollen grains that land on it. The **style** connects the stigma to the ovary below. The **ovary** (OH vuh ree) holds the ovules, in which the eggs develop and are fertilized. Once fertilization has occurred, the ovules develop into seeds. The ovary swells and becomes the fruit in many species of flowering plants.

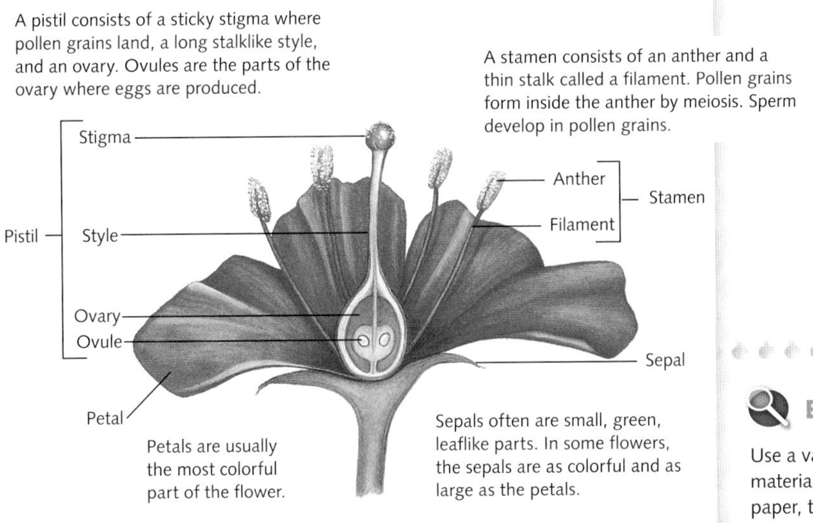

A pistil consists of a sticky stigma where pollen grains land, a long stalklike style, and an ovary. Ovules are the parts of the ovary where eggs are produced.

A stamen consists of an anther and a thin stalk called a filament. Pollen grains form inside the anther by meiosis. Sperm develop in pollen grains.

Pistil — Stigma, Style, Ovary, Ovule

Stamen — Anther, Filament

Sepal

Petal

Petals are usually the most colorful part of the flower.

Sepals often are small, green, leaflike parts. In some flowers, the sepals are as colorful and as large as the petals.

Figure 10.18 Some angiosperms produce flowers with all the major parts shown in this illustration. The stamens and the pistil are reproductive structures. Sepals and petals protect the reproductive structures and attract pollinators.

CONNECTION: History

Cotton has long been an important and useful plant. Cotton was the main crop in the South before the Civil War. Cotton is picked after the bolls, or fruit of the cotton plant, split open. Just-picked cotton has a number of seeds scattered throughout the long, thin fibers that make up the cotton. Before the invention of the cotton gin by Eli Whitney in 1793, these seeds had to be separated from the cotton fibers by hand. This difficult and often painful task took many hours to complete. Whitney's invention automated the seed-removal process and revolutionized the cotton industry in the United States. Cotton production became more profitable.

Once they are "cleaned" of seeds, the cotton fibers are combed, spun into thread, and woven into cloth. Cotton cloth can be dyed a rainbow of colors and used to make articles of clothing and household goods.

Explore It!

Use a variety of materials—construction paper, tissue paper, clay, straws, toothpicks, peas, beans, etc.—to build a model of a flower. Your model should have both male and female reproductive structures in addition to petals and sepals. Be sure to include a key that identifies each part of your flower model.

Teach

EXPLAIN to students that they will learn about the structure of flowers and the function of their parts.

Vocabulary

pistil Explain that *pistil* is from the Latin word *pistillum*, which means "pestle." Tell students that a pestle is a club-shaped tool used to grind solids in a ceramic bowl called a mortar. A pistil, the female reproductive organ of a flowering plant, resembles a pestle and consists of a stigma, style, and ovary.

stigma Tell students that in a flowering plant, the stigma is the sticky surface that receives pollen. It is situated at the tip of the style.

style Tell students that *style* is derived from the Latin word *stilus*, meaning "a writing tool." Explain that many flowers, but not all, have a style with a shape that is similar to that of a writing tool, such as a pen.

ovary Explain that the source of *ovary* is Latin, *ovum*, and means "egg."

Explore It!

This activity can be done individually or in small groups. Students can gather materials for their models at home, or you can provide craft materials for them to use. Materials that work well for this activity include construction paper or tissue paper, drinking straws, coffee stirrers, toothpicks, modeling clay, cornmeal, peas, and beans. Each student model should include some type of key. You may want to have students present their flower models to the class.

CONNECTION: History

Have each student discreetly read his or her clothing labels and identify the materials and location of production for each garment. (This may be assigned as homework.) Each student should create a three-column chart listing the garment, material, and place of production for each clothing item examined. (Let students know that rayon is often created from cotton pulp.)

Arrange students in groups of four, and have each group create a comprehensive chart from its members' data. Ask groups to analyze relationships among the three columns, and discuss findings as a class.

Background Information

China, India, Pakistan, Turkey, the United States, and Brazil lead the world in both cotton production and cotton consumption. China produces and exports the greatest amount of cotton. U.S. production accounts for about 25 to 30 percent of the world trade.

Science Notebook EXTRA

Have each student draw a common flower, such as rose or tulip, and its parts. Encourage students to draw in pencil. Students should use all vocabulary words from this page to label the flower's parts. When students complete this section of the lesson, encourage them to review their drawings and make necessary corrections.

Teach

EXPLAIN to students that they will learn how the process of pollination is different from the process of fertilization. Pollination simply involves pollen grains being transferred to the female part of a plant. Fertilization is a more complex process that follows pollination.

EXTEND In their Science Notebooks, have students diagram both the process of pollination and the process of fertilization. Encourage students to label all parts of the flowers they draw. Have students review one another's work when they have finished.

As You Read

Provide students with about five minutes to review their paragraphs and affirm correct predictions. Have students revise their incorrect predictions and rewrite those sentences. As a class, review the predictions that you had recorded at the beginning of the chapter and correct those, as well.

ANSWER Flowers are the reproductive structures of angiosperms.

Figure It Out: Figure 10.19

ANSWER **1.** Pollination occurs when pollen grains from the anthers land on the sticky stigma of the flower. 2. The male gametophyte is the pollen grain that contains the sperm cells; the female gametophyte is the ovule.

As You Read

Read the paragraph you wrote in your Science Notebook about this lesson. Place a check mark next to predictions that are correct. Correct any predictions you now know are wrong.

What is the reproductive structure of angiosperms?

Life Cycle of an Angiosperm

Many flowering plants have both male and female parts in the same flower. However, other plants, such as begonias, have separate male and female flowers on the same plant. Still other plants, such as hollies, produce male and female flowers on separate plants. In order to get colorful holly berries, both male and female holly plants are needed.

With a few exceptions, pollination must take place before seeds can form. Pollen grains can be carried by wind, water, gravity, or animals. Once a pollen grain lands on the female part of the plant, sperm cells and a pollen tube develop. The sperm cells move down the tube, into the ovary, and to an ovule. Fertilization can then take place between a sperm and an egg. The resulting fertilized egg, or zygote, develops into an embryo. **Figure 10.19** illustrates these processes.

Figure It Out

1. At what point does pollination occur?
2. A plant with flowers is a mature sporophyte. What is the male gametophyte? The female gametophyte?

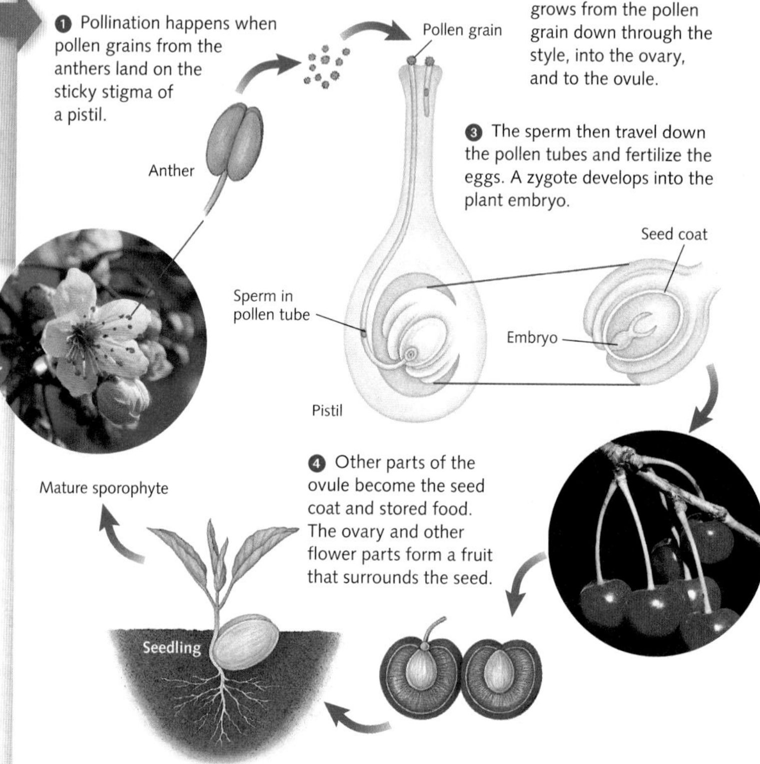

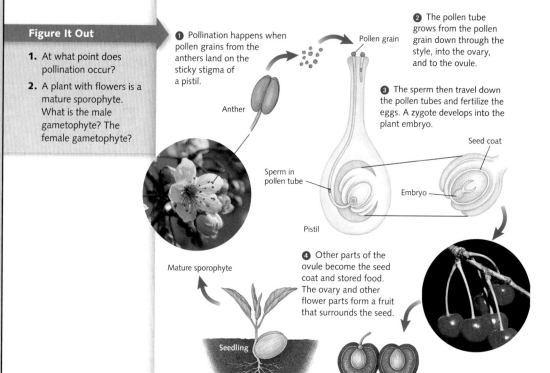

Figure 10.19 Life Cycle of an Angiosperm. This illustration traces the life cycle of a cherry tree.

Background Information

Cross-pollination is the process by which pollen from one plant is delivered to a flower on a different plant. Genetic modification does occur naturally in cross-pollination. Genetic modification is also done artificially by isolating, copying, and introducing a fragment of DNA from one species of plant to another.

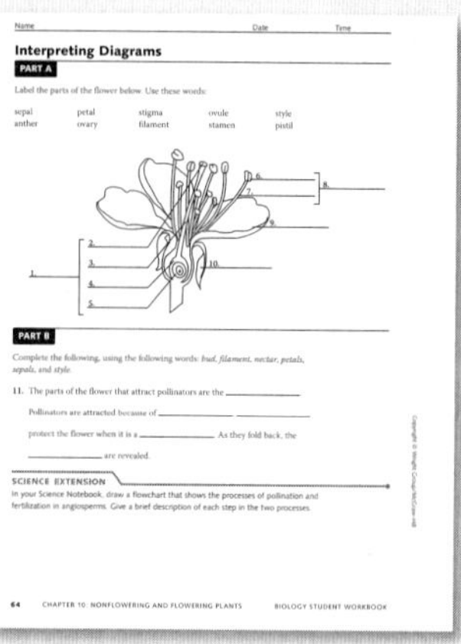

Interpreting Diagrams Workbook, p. 64

Agents of Pollination

Wind, water, gravity, and animals are the main agents of pollination. Pollination can occur when wind carries pollen to a stigma. In many plants, however, it is an animal—often an insect—that brings pollen to a stigma. The animal is called a pollinator.

In their search for food, honeybees commonly transfer pollen as they work, as do many other insects. In the United States, bees are the most common pollinators of food plants. Farmers place hives of honeybees in their fields and orchards. When the bees' work is finished, the hives are moved to other fields and orchards.

Some insects are "deceived" into acting as a pollinator by a flower. For example, certain orchid flowers resemble female insects. The orchid gives off a scent that attracts a male insect. The male insect serves as a pollinator when he attempts to mate. Moving in, the male receives a touch of pollen on his head. Later, when another "female" flower attracts the same insect, the flower gets pollinated. Other flowers give off scents that attract pollinators.

Mice, other small rodents, and bats are also agents of pollination. Some birds eat nectar, a sweet liquid made by some flowers, and transfer pollen from anther to stigma. **Figure 10.20** shows some animal pollinators.

CONNECTION: Physics

While many plants depend on other organisms for pollination, some plants depend on physical forces to help them reproduce. Gravity, the force that pulls two objects toward each other, can also pollinate flowers.

When flowers whose filaments hold the anthers above the stigma release pollen grains, the force of gravity pulls the pollen grains down. As the pollen grains fall, they come into contact with the sticky stigma of the flower. With gravity's help, pollen has been delivered to the female reproductive structure, and fertilization can occur. In large fields of corn, pollen is dispersed by wind, but it is also affected by gravity. When released, corn pollen travels relatively short distances as it falls to Earth at the rate of about 30 cm per second.

After You Read

1. What characteristics do angiosperms share?
2. List the parts of a flower. Identify appropriate parts as male or female structures. Describe the function of each part.
3. How is pollination related to fertilization?
4. Rewrite the prediction paragraph in your Science Notebook to include three things you now know about angiosperms.

Did You Know?

The carrion flower has a unique method of making sure pollination occurs—it stinks! The carrion flower smells like rotting flesh. The smell attracts pollinators such as beetles and flies looking for a meal.

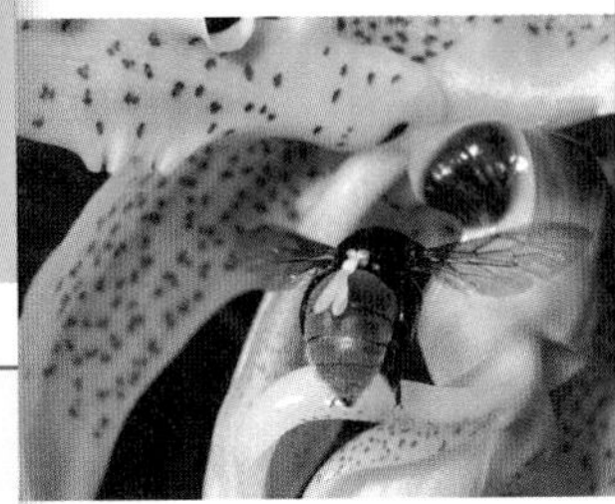

Figure 10.20 A honeybee looking for nectar *(top)*, a bat approaching a cactus flower *(center)*, and a male bee fooled into thinking the orchid flower is a female bee *(bottom)* are all pollinators.

Teach

EXPLAIN that pollination can happen in many ways. Give students a few minutes to review the photographs on the page. Ask them to infer the different methods of pollination, and write their inferences on the board.

CONNECTION: Physics

Have students describe the relationship between gravity and pollination of flowers.

EXTEND Place students in small groups, and provide each group with white flour, dark paper, measuring spoons, and a measuring tape. Tell students that they will engage in a simulation of pollen being released from a flower. Have them experiment with releasing small amounts of flour from different heights and at different angles. Have students identify the role of gravity in this process with reference to where the greatest quantity of flour lands. You could use a small fan to simulate wind and have students determine the wind's effect on pollen distribution.

Assess

EVALUATE Use the After You Read questions and the Alternative Assessment to help you assess students' understanding of the lesson.

After You Read

1. Angiosperms are flowering plants that produce seeds contained in fruits.
2. Petals attract pollinators; sepals surround a flower bud and protect the tissues inside. A stamen is a male part of a flower and includes an anther, which produces pollen grains, and a filament, which holds the anther above the petals. The pistil is the female part of a flower and includes the stigma, which holds pollen grains; the style, which connects the stigma to the ovary; and the ovary, which holds the ovules that contain eggs and develop into seeds.
3. Pollination delivers sperm contained in pollen to the female parts of a flower so that fertilization can occur.
4. Students' answers should identify the main characteristics of angiosperms, the structure and function of flowers, and the processes of pollination and fertilization.

Background Information

The word *gravity* comes from the Latin word *gravitas*. During the time Newton lived, Latin was the language most commonly used by academics and scientists throughout Europe. *Gravitas* means "heaviness" or "weight." Heavy bodies were thought to possess the property of gravity; it was their weight that made them fall.

Alternative Assessment

EVALUATE Have students use their prediction paragraphs to create two-column charts. The first column heading should be *I used to think*; the second heading should be *Now I know*. Have students complete the charts with at least five facts they learned in the lesson.

Chapter 10 Summary

VOCABULARY REVIEW

Check students' sentences or paragraphs to make sure they understand the meaning of each vocabulary term.

PREPARE FOR CHAPTER TEST

Evaluate students' essays using the following criteria:

1. The topic sentence, or main idea, should restate the Key Concept.
2. The supporting paragraphs should incorporate the answers to the Learning Goal questions students have written and include details, facts, and examples they have recorded in their Science Notebooks.
3. The concluding sentence should sum up the main idea of the chapter and restate the Key Concept.

MASTERING CONCEPTS

True or False

1. False, nonvascular
2. True
3. False, rhizomes
4. False, fertilization
5. False, pollination
6. False, gymnosperms
7. True
8. True

Short Answer

9. Plants have complex life cycles in which a sporophyte generation alternates with a gametophyte generation. The sporophyte generation produces spores that develop into a gametophyte. The gametophyte generation produces the eggs and sperm. When an egg is fertilized by a sperm, a zygote is produced. The zygote develops into a new sporophyte.
10. Moss plants remain small because they lack specialized vascular tissues that can transport materials over larger distances and support a larger plant.
11. Petals are brightly colored parts of the flower that attract pollinators. Sepals are leaflike structures that surround the bud and protect the reproductive structures.
12. Wind, water, gravity, and animals are the main agents of pollination.

Chapter 10 Summary

KEY CONCEPTS

10.1 Bryophytes: Nonvascular Plants

- All plants have life cycles that include a pattern called alternation of generations. Alternation of generations means that a plant spends one part of its life in a stage that produces spores and the other part in a stage that produces sex cells.
- Bryophytes lack vascular tissues for moving water and nutrients throughout the plant. They also have easily distinguished spore-producing and gamete-producing plants.
- Bryophytes depend on water for sexual reproduction and are dispersed by spores.
- The union of a sperm and an egg, or fertilization, produces a zygote, or fertilized egg that develops into a new sporophyte.
- Mosses and liverworts are examples of bryophytes.

10.2 Tracheophytes: Vascular Plants

- Tracheophytes, such as club mosses, horsetails, and ferns, use vascular tissues to move water and nutrients in their bodies.
- Tracheophytes have a tiny gamete-producing stage and a relatively large sporophyte. Primitive tracheophytes are dispersed by spores.
- Horsetails and ferns have underground stems called rhizomes.
- The reproductive structures of ferns include sporangia, antheridia, and archegonia.

10.3 Seed Plants: Gymnosperms

- Seed plants are vascular plants that produce seeds for dispersal. They also have a microscopic gametophyte stage.
- Gymnosperms produce seeds that are not protected by fruit, and they have needlelike or scalelike leaves.
- Cycads, ginkgoes, gnetophytes, and conifers are types of gymnosperms.
- Cones are the reproductive structures of gymnosperms. Male cones produce pollen grains, which are small structures in which sperm develop. Female cones produce eggs.
- Pollination is the process of delivering pollen, which contains the male gamete, to the female parts of the flower so that fertilization can occur.

10.4 Seed Plants: Angiosperms

- Angiosperms are flowering plants that produce seeds protected by fruits.
- Flowers are the reproductive structures of angiosperms.

VOCABULARY REVIEW

Write each term in a complete sentence, or write a paragraph relating several terms.

10.1
alternation of generations, p. 169
sexual reproduction, p. 169
gamete, p. 169
zygote, p. 169
sporophyte generation, p. 169
spore, p. 169
gametophyte generation, p. 169
bryophyte, p. 170
vascular system, p. 170

10.2
tracheophyte, p. 172
rhizome, p. 173
asexual reproduction, p. 174
sporangium, p. 174

10.3
gymnosperm, p. 176
cycad, p. 176
pollen, p. 176
ginkgo, p. 177
conifer, p. 177
ovule, p. 178
pollination, p. 178

10.4
angiosperm, p. 180
sepal, p. 180
petal, p. 180
stamen, p. 180
anther, p. 180
filament, p. 180
pistil, p. 181
stigma, p. 181
style, p. 181
ovary, p. 181

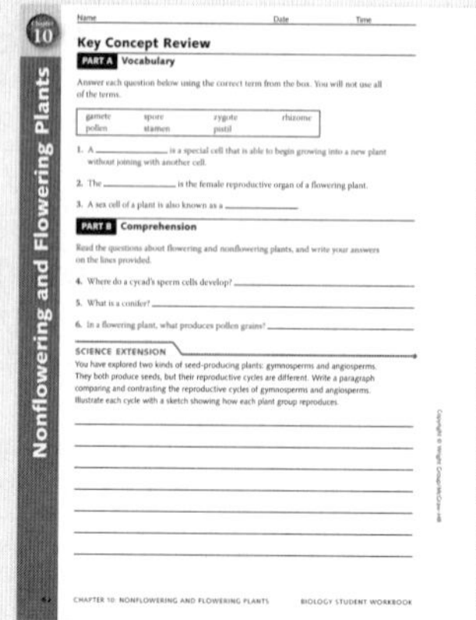

Key Concept Review Workbook, p. 62

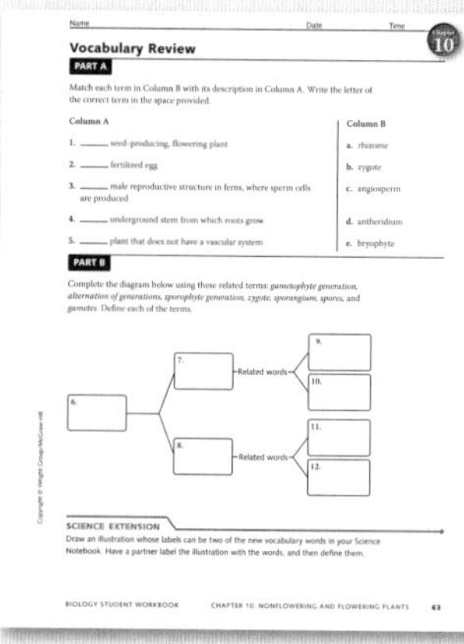

Vocabulary Review Workbook, p. 63

MASTERING CONCEPTS

True or False

If the statement is true, write "true." If it is false, change the underlined word or words to make the statement true.

1. Liverworts and mosses are <u>vascular</u> plants.
2. The male gamete is the <u>sperm</u>, and the female gamete is the <u>egg</u>.
3. Special underground stems from which horsetails grow are called <u>sporangia</u>.
4. The fact that club mosses, horsetails, and ferns live in moist areas aids in <u>pollination</u>.
5. Transfer of pollen grains from the male to the female plant is called <u>fertilization</u>.
6. Cones are the reproductive structures of <u>angiosperms</u>.
7. The seeds of <u>angiosperms</u> are dispersed in fruits.
8. The male part of the flower is the <u>stamen</u>.

Short Answer

Answer each of the following in a sentence or brief paragraph.

9. Describe the life cycle pattern of plants.
10. Why do moss plants remain small?
11. What functions do sepals and petals perform in a flower?
12. What are three ways in which pollination can occur?

Critical Thinking

Use what you have learned in this chapter to answer each of the following.

13. **Infer** A new plant has just been discovered. The plant has small, gray-colored flowers that are hard to see and have no scent. Describe how this new plant might be pollinated.
14. **Compare and Contrast** How are gymnosperms and angiosperms similar? How are they different?
15. **Predict** Pesticides are chemicals designed to kill harmful insects. However, pesticides often kill beneficial insects, as well. What effect would widespread pesticide use have on angiosperms?

Standardized Test Question

Choose the letter of the response that correctly answers the question.

16. Which flower part includes all of the others?
    A. stigma
    B. style
    C. pistil
    D. ovary

Test-Taking Tip

Use scrap paper to write notes. Sometimes making a sketch, such as a diagram or a table, can help you organize your ideas.

PREPARE FOR CHAPTER TEST

To prepare for the chapter test, create a question from each Learning Goal. Use the information in your Science Notebook to answer each question. Then use these answers to write a well-developed essay about the chapter. Use the Key Concept on the first page of this chapter as your topic sentence.

Critical Thinking

13. The new plant is probably pollinated by the wind because its flowers have no scent and are not large and colorful to attract animal pollinators.
14. Angiosperms and gymnosperms are both seed plants; however, gymnosperms produce their seeds in cones, while angiosperms use flowers as their reproductive structures. Unlike angiosperms, most gymnosperms have needlelike leaves and are evergreens.
15. Angiosperms would be negatively affected by widespread pesticide use because insects are important pollinators.

Standardized Test Question

16. C

Reading Links

Essential Atlas of Botany

This is a valuable and information-rich resource for any science teacher's bookshelf, despite its brevity. It is also a good reference and enrichment tool for struggling readers. Its coverage of botanical topics is comprehensive and well organized. Emphasis is on visual explanation, so the book is packed with color photographs and illustrations. The text—originally published in Spanish—is as informative as it is concise, and it aims to help situate the study of plant life in a larger ecological and scientific context.

Parramon Editorial Team. Barron's Educational Series, Inc. Illustrated. 96 pp. Trade ISBN: 978-0-7641-2709-0.

Essential Gardening for Teens

This highly accessible guide presents readers with the basic science behind gardening and enables them to apply these concepts to a hands-on project that they plan and execute independently. The language is simple and the advice encouraging even for the easily frustrated. Students will learn how this chapter's discussion of flowering and nonflowering plants can help them personalize, plant, and care for a garden of their own at home, now or in the future.

Chasek, Ruth. Scholastic Library Publishing (Children's Press). Illustrated. 48 pp. Trade ISBN: 978-0-516-23356-7.

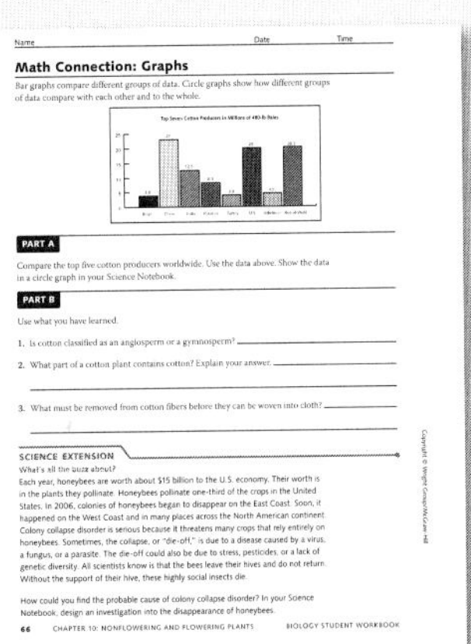
Math Connection: Graphs

PART A

PART B

SCIENCE EXTENSION

Curriculum Connection
Workbook, p. 66

Science Challenge
Workbook, pp. 67–68

CHAPTER 10 185

Chapter 10

Labs

10A "Moving" Plants

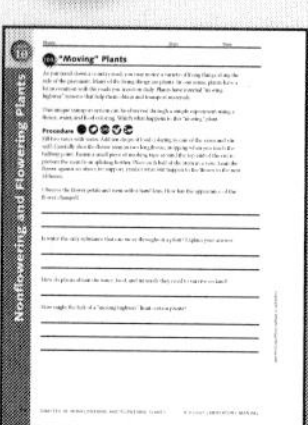

This prechapter introduction activity is designed to determine what students already know about the vascular system in plants by engaging them in predicting, observing, and comparing the results of a substance moving throughout a plant.

Objectives

- predict the movement of materials throughout a plant
- observe the movement of materials throughout a plant
- compare the results of two experimental setups

Planning

 1 class period, with observation time the following day

groups of 2–4 students

Materials (per group)

- 2 clear vases or beakers
- red or blue food coloring
- white or pale-colored carnation
- sharp knife
- water
- masking tape
- hand lens

Advance Preparation

- Purchase carnations at a grocery store or flower shop, and keep them in a bucket of water. A few hours before class, take the flowers out of the water. You may want to slice the stems for students to avoid any injuries. Have students set up their experiment and make predictions and initial observations on one day and final observations the next day.
- This activity can easily be done as a teacher demonstration. Celery stalks that contain leaves will work as a substitute.

Engagement Guide

- Challenge students to think about the function of a vascular system in plants and the differences between nonvascular and vascular plants by asking:
  - *How does one side of the flower differ from the other side?* (Students should notice streaks of food coloring in the petals and stem on the side of the plant whose stem was placed in the colored water. The opposite side should not have any colored streaks in the petals or stem.)
  - *If plants are not able to move about, how do they obtain the food, water, and minerals they need to survive on land?* (Plants either have to absorb the substances through their cells [nonvascular plants] or transport the substances through a system of tubes [vascular plants].)
  - *How do the top parts of a plant receive all the substances necessary for survival?* (Plants must move the substances up the stem to the very top of the plant.)
  - *How do mosses and liverworts differ from carnations?* (Mosses and liverworts live in moist areas and are much shorter in length because they lack stems. The carnation plant is taller, lives in drier conditions, and is able to support itself by a stem.)
- Encourage students to communicate their conclusions in creative ways.

Going Further

Encourage students to repeat this activity using different types of flowers or a stalk of celery. Have students look at celery strands with a hand lens to observe the long, narrow tubes bundled together. Have students present their observations and conclusions to the class.

10B Anatomy of a Flower

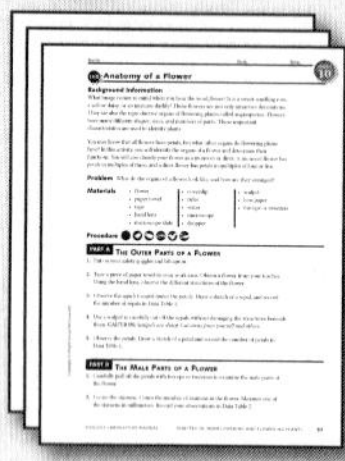

Objectives

- examine and measure the organs of a flower
- compare the male and female parts of a flower
- relate flower parts to their functions
- classify a plant as a monocot or a dicot

Skill Set

observing, measuring, identifying, comparing and contrasting, inferring, recording and analyzing data, stating conclusions

Planning

 1 class period  groups of 2–3 students

Materials

Materials for this activity are listed in the Student Laboratory Manual.

Advance Preparation

Select a flower that is easy to obtain in your area. Collect wildflowers or go to your local flower shop or grocery store. Some suggestions are lilies, gladiolis, tulips, yuccas, and hibiscuses. Be aware of student allergies. **CAUTION:** Some students may be highly allergic to pollen.

Lab Tip

Some students may have to remove their goggles to have a clear view through the microscope.

Answers to Observations

Data Table 1: Answers will vary depending on the flower used. If the flower is a monocot, the petals will be in multiples of three. If the flower is a dicot, the petals will be in multiples of four or five. Students' sketches should look similar to the plant they dissected. You could have students tape the organs to the data table instead of drawing a sketch.

Data Table 2: Answers will vary depending on the flower used. Students should realize that there are numerous stamens and only one pistil. The height of the stamens might be higher or lower than the pistil, depending on the flower used. Students can estimate the number of pollen grains they observe on the slide. The size of the pollen grains will be microscopic. The ovules will most likely be less than 1 mm, depending on the flower used.

Answers to Analysis and Conclusions

1. Answers will depend on the flower used. Sepals protect the flower bud from insect damage and dryness. Petals' color and smell attract insects and birds that aid in pollination.
2. The main function of the flower is to produce seeds. The stamens produce the pollen, which contains the sperm cells. The pistil produces the eggs in the ovary. When a sperm fertilizes an egg as a result of pollination, an ovule becomes a seed.
3. Answers will vary depending on the flower used. The flower is a monocot if the petals are in multiples of three. The flower is a dicot if the petals are in multiples of four or five.
4. Answers will vary depending on the flower used.
5. Answers will vary, but students may suggest that a longer pistil would give the flower an advantage because insects and other animals could see it more easily. Longer stamens would ensure that the pollen is picked up by an insect and transferred to another plant or that it falls on the stigma of the same plant.
6. Colorful flowers attract birds, insects, or other animals in search of nectar. Small, inconspicuous flowers are pollinated by wind.

Going Further

Have each group dissect a different flower and record its results in a class data table similar to Data Table 2. Have each student create a line graph from the class data, showing length in millimeters (y-axis) v. flower type (x-axis). Using two colored lines, they should graph the average lengths of the pistils and stamens for each flower type.

10C Comparing Adaptations of Plants

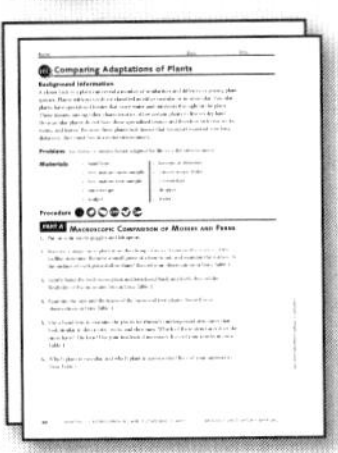

Objectives

- compare and contrast structures of vascular and nonvascular plants
- prepare wet mounts of leaflike structures
- record observations
- conclude which plant is better adapted for a dry environment

Skill Set

measuring, observing, comparing and contrasting, recording and analyzing data, classifying, stating conclusions

Planning

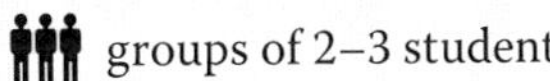
2 class periods groups of 2–3 students

Materials

Materials for this activity are listed in the Student Laboratory Manual.

Advance Preparation

Moss and fern samples are available from biological supply houses. **CAUTION:** For Part B, instruct students to be very careful when pressing the two slides together. The slides could break and cut students' fingers. Have glass-disposal buckets available in case students break slides.

Answers to Observations

Data Table 1: Students should observe that the moss plant was dull. The fern frond was shiny because of the waxy cuticle. This layer of wax helps ferns live on dry land by preventing them from drying out. The fern should be firmer. Students may point out that the fern has vascular tissue that makes the fern firmer. The moss was small and thin. The fern was large and thicker. The moss has rhizoids, and the fern has roots and rhizomes. Through their observations, students should conclude that the moss is nonvascular and the fern is vascular.

Data Table 2: The moss's leaflike structures are one cell thick. The fern frond has a multicell thickness. Students may also find that the ferns have veins and the mosses do not. Students' sketches will vary, but the moss should show a single layer of cells and the fern should show several layers of cells.

Answers to Analysis and Conclusions

1. Mosses have small, thin leaflike structures and have rhizoids instead of roots. Mosses are classified as nonvascular plants because they lack vascular tissue. Ferns have larger, thicker leaflike structures and contain roots and rhizomes. Ferns are classified as vascular plants because they have vascular tissue.
2. Rhizoids are small, colorless, and unicellular or multicellular. They lack vascular tissue. Roots are large and multicellular and have vascular tissue.
3. Since the leaflike structures of mosses are only one cell thick, water and nutrients move through the structures by diffusion. The fern fronds have many layers of cells; water and nutrients are transported through the leaves through vascular tissue.
4. The lack of vascular tissue to carry substances throughout the plant limits the size of these plants. They must grow close to the ground so that the water does not have to travel a long distance to the various parts of the plant.
5. the fern; It has both a waxy cuticle and vascular tissue to help prevent it from drying out. The vascular tissue also provides support for the fern.

Going Further

Have students observe a moss plant with stalks and capsules and a fern plant with spores. Have them use toothpicks to gently crush moss capsules to release the spores. Students should examine the spores under the microscope. Students can use a scalpel to gently scrape sporangia from the underside of a fern frond and examine the spores under the microscope.

Chapter 11 Lessons

Introduce Chapter 11

As a starting activity, use LAB 11A What Plant Parts Do You Eat? on page 63 of the Laboratory Manual.

ENGAGE Have available pictures of five or six different types of plants. If you can bring some plants into the classroom, do that as well. Include a houseplant, a common flowering plant, a broccoli or cauliflower plant, a leafy vegetable plant, a nut-bearing plant, and a fruit-bearing plant. Have students work with partners to sketch each plant in their Science Notebooks, including and labeling the root, stem, and leaf for each (to the best of their abilities). Explain that students will refer back to their sketches throughout the chapter and make any necessary revisions.

Think About the Structure and Function of Plant Parts

Ask students to identify the root, stem, and leaf of a flowering plant or houseplant. Then, ask students to hypothesize about the different functions of these plant parts. Have students complete the first bulleted item in their Science Notebooks.

Recommend to students that they create three-column charts in their Science Notebooks. Columns should be labeled *Roots*, *Stems*, and *Leaves*. In each column, students should write their plant food sources.

Chapter 11 Plant Parts and Functions

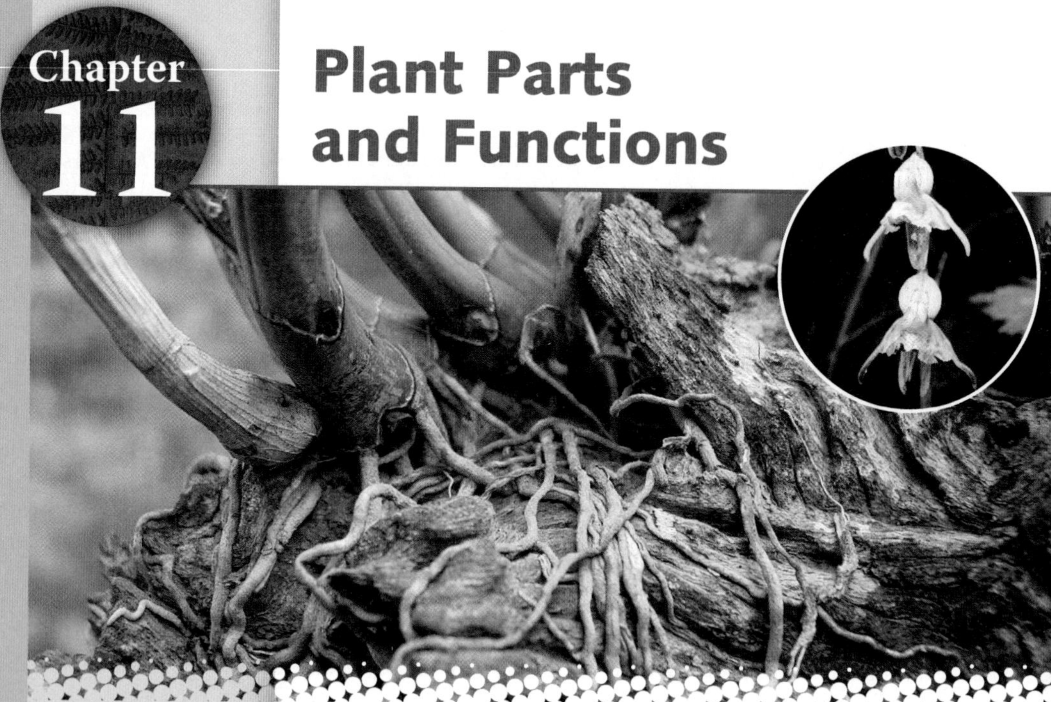

KEY CONCEPT The parts of a plant work together to enable the plant to capture energy and matter, grow, and reproduce.

Most plants have roots, stems, and leaves. However, one species of orchids, native to Florida, is a remarkable exception to the majority of plants. An adult ghost orchid does not appear to have either a stem or leaves. Its roots look like a tangled mess of spaghetti. Chlorophyll in its roots captures energy for the plant. When it blooms, its flowers are dramatic and beautiful, appearing like white ghosts floating in the air.

Think About the Structure and Function of Plant Parts

Some plants have parts that are easily recognizable as roots, stems, and leaves.

- Think about the roots, stems, and leaves of some familiar plants. How do you think these plant parts work together to enable the plants to survive? Record your thoughts in your Science Notebook.
- Plant parts are the source of many of the foods you eat. In your Science Notebook, list some of the plant parts you eat. Organize your list by *Roots*, *Stems*, and *Leaves*. When you have completed the chapter, go back to your list and see if you were correct.

www.scilinks.org
Plant Anatomy **Code: WGB11**

186

Chapter 11 Planning Guide

Instructional Periods	National Standards	Lab Manual	Workbook
11.1 2 periods	C.1 D.1; B.3, C.4, C.5, C6, D.1, F.6; UCP.1, UCP.5	**Lab 11A—p. 63** What Plant Parts Do You Eat? **Lab 11B—p. 64** Investigating Stomata **Lab 11C—p. 67** Seed Investigations	Key Concept Review p. 69 Vocabulary Review p. 70 Interpreting Diagrams p. 71 Reading Comprehension p. 72 Curriculum Connection p. 73 Science Challenge p. 74
11.2 2 periods	A.1, C.1 C.5; B.3, C6; UCP.2, UCP.5		
11.3 2 periods	C.1; C.1, C.6, F.4; UCP.5		
11.4 2 periods	A.2, C.1, C.5; C6; UCP.3, UCP.5		

Middle School Standard; High School Standard; Unifying Concept and Principle

Roots

Before You Read

Create a working definition of the term *root.* A working definition is one that develops as you learn more about a topic. Write what you know about this term before you begin reading. Then, revise your definition as you read and discuss the lesson.

Learning Goals

- Identify the parts of a plant root.
- List four functions of plant roots.

New Vocabulary

root
taproot
fibrous root
vegetative propagation
root cap
apical meristem
epidermis
root hair
cortex
endodermis
xylem
phloem
hydrotropism

All vascular plants have systems. These systems, like all living systems, are made of cells, tissues, and organs that work together to perform specific functions that keep the plants alive. The shoot system of a plant is the aboveground part of the plant. The root system of a plant is generally below the ground. Thus, the roots of most plants are not easily seen. However, the root system is usually about the same size as the shoot system.

Roots are plant organs that have four major functions. Roots anchor and support a plant. Roots absorb water and dissolved minerals from the soil. Roots contain vascular tissues that transport materials to and from the stem. Roots store excess products of photosynthesis in the form of starch.

Types of Roots

Roots come in various shapes and sizes. Roots give a plant the surface area it needs to absorb the water and minerals essential to its survival. The surface area, or total outside layer, of a plant's roots can be as much as 50 times greater than the surface area of its leaves.

Plant roots are adapted to the plant's environment—specifically, to the soil type, temperature, and water. For example, certain desert plants have roots that are more than 20 m long, which enables the plant to obtain water from deep underground. There are two main types of root systems: taproots and fibrous roots.

Taproots Have you ever tried to pull a dandelion out of the ground? If so, you probably found yourself holding a tuft of green leaves and yellow flowers. The top of the dandelion broke off from the root. If you dug up the rest of the dandelion with a shovel and shook off the soil, you would have found the root system. The main root of a dandelion plant looks a bit like a small, pale carrot. It is a taproot.

A **taproot** is a thick, single structure that grows straight into the ground. Smaller, branching roots grow out from its sides. A taproot securely anchors a plant in the soil and serves primarily as a storage organ. It contains starch and sugar made by a plant. Carrots and beets are taproots. Taproots are most commonly found in dicots and gymnosperms. If the top of a dandelion plant breaks off, a new top will grow.

Figure 11.1 The long taproot of a dandelion plant makes it very difficult to remove the dandelion from the soil. How could this plant be removed?

ELL Strategy

Use a Concept Map Have each student create a concept map for the term *roots.* Model creating the map by writing *Roots* as the main topic on the board and then adding four circles around the main topic for each type of root discussed. Then, explain that they will be filling in each circle with types of roots and the characteristics of them. Have students create their own maps in their Science Notebooks. Explain to them that they will add to their maps throughout the lesson. Return to this concept map frequently, reminding the English-language learners of the task, as many students have not had uniform exposure to completion of concept maps.

Furthermore, as each type of root is addressed, students could add circles around that type to describe it.

11.1 Introduce

ENGAGE Have students work with partners to discuss the similarities and differences among plants' roots using the pictures from the Engage activity on page 186 as well as fresh (unbagged) carrots and beets.

Before You Read

Model creating a working definition of the term *root.* Start by recording what you know. For example, you could write: *A root usually grows in the ground.*

Vocabulary terms are listed on the first student page of each lesson. You may wish to preview the terms before introducing the lesson. Strategies for teaching the vocabulary appear on the pages where the terms are introduced.

Teach

EXPLAIN that roots support a plant's structure as well as provide and store nutrients for the plant. Students will learn about the four different types of roots in this lesson.

Science Notebook EXTRA

Encourage students to use the vocabulary section they created in their Science Notebooks. Remind them to record prefixes, suffixes, and root words to help them remember the meanings of vocabulary terms.

Vocabulary

root Ask students to give other meanings of the word *root.* Encourage students to identify any relationships between those meanings and the definition provided in this lesson. (as a noun: "cause," "source," "word from which other words are made"; as a verb: "to search through," "to dig with the snout," "to cheer or support enthusiastically")

taproot Have students suggest why the word part *tap* might be appropriate for of this type of root.

Use the Visual: Figure 11.1

ANSWER Its taproot must be dug up and removed from the soil.

Teach

EXPLAIN that students will learn about two more types of roots and how the structures of these roots adapt to the plants' functions.

Vocabulary

fibrous root Tell students that the suffix *-ous* denotes a particular quality or character. Therefore, a fibrous root is one whose qualities are similar to those of fibers, long and thin.

vegetative propagation Explain that the word *vegetative* refers to vegetation or plants. The word *propagation* means "to reproduce or multiply."

As You Read

Provide five to ten minutes for students to review and edit their working definitions. Check students' definitions for revision and accuracy.

ANSWER A taproot is a thick structure that grows straight into the soil with smaller branching roots extending from its sides. A taproot provides a secure anchor for a plant and stores food in the form of sugars and starches. Fibrous roots are masses of thin, branching roots that grow outward from a central point. Fibrous roots hold the plant in the ground and provide a large surface area for water and mineral absorption.

EXPLORE Have students analyze plant fertilizer and plant-food labels. Ask students to note for which plants the fertilizer is recommended and which minerals are in highest concentration. Have students infer which minerals are most necessary for different plant types.

CONNECTION: Geology

Explain that soils lacking sufficient mineral nutrients that plants need are enriched by adding fertilizers.

EXTEND Arrange students in small groups, and have them research the difference between chemical fertilizer and organic fertilizer. Students can use online resources as well as plant reference books. Have students create comparison charts in their Science Notebooks, noting the advantages and disadvantages of each method.

CONNECTION: Geology

Most plants require soil in order to grow. Soil is mostly a mixture of small particles of rock that was broken down through various natural processes. Soil also contains water, air, and the remains of dead plants and animals. As dead organisms decay, various chemicals are released into the soil.

Soils also have naturally occurring mineral nutrients. Different soils have different amounts of rock particles, air, decaying organisms, and mineral nutrients. Nitrogen is one of the most important mineral nutrient plants need to grow. Other nutrients, sometimes called trace elements, are needed by plants in much smaller amounts.

Naturally occurring bacteria are also considered by some scientists to be an important part of soil. Some kinds of bacteria found in soil convert nitrogen in the air into forms of nitrogen that plants can use to grow. Other kinds of bacteria in soil make forms of nitrogen that plants need by breaking down animal wastes and dead organisms.

As You Read

With a partner, discuss your working definition of the term *root*. In your Science Notebook, add facts to the definition and rewrite it if necessary.

Describe the two main types of root systems.

Fibrous Roots If you pulled out some grass plants instead of a dandelion plant, you would notice a different kind of root system. Grass plants have **fibrous roots**. Fibrous roots consist of a great many thin, branching roots that grow from a central point. Fibrous roots look like tufts of stringy hairs. Fibrous roots store less food than taproots do and are most commonly found in monocots. They serve primarily to hold the plant in the ground and provide a large surface area for water and mineral absorption.

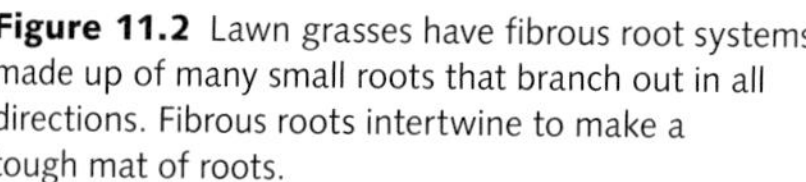

Figure 11.2 Lawn grasses have fibrous root systems made up of many small roots that branch out in all directions. Fibrous roots intertwine to make a tough mat of roots.

Figure 11.3 One kind of adventitious roots are prop roots. These roots help anchor a plant in the ground and keep a tall and top-heavy plant upright.

Adventitious Roots Roots that grow from the stem are called adventitious roots. These roots have different shapes and functions. Corn plants often produce a type of adventitious roots called prop roots, which help support the plants. Plants that grow in wet places often produce roots that grow upward from the mud and, eventually, above the water. Cypress trees produce these roots, which are called "knees." Knees take in the oxygen that cells in a plant's roots need for respiration. Strong buttress roots can be seen on many tall tropical trees. Buttress roots grow from the base of the tree's trunk. These roots help support the tree as it grows.

Background Information

Most fertilizers are labeled with three numbers, representing three quantities: the percent nitrogen, the percent phosphate (P_2O_5), and the percent potash (K_2O). One example would be 10-20-10: this fertilizer has the same amount of nitrogen and potash and twice as much phosphate. The percentages will not add up to 100 because the fertilizer also contains other elements in lesser quantities, as well as filler. Different fertilizer ratios support the growth of different plants.

Some plants, such as the ghost orchid, produce another kind of adventitious roots called aerial roots. Aerial roots are aboveground roots. These roots hold on to the stems of other plants. Some kinds of ivy, including English ivy, produce aerial roots. The roots support the plant as it grows up a tree or on a wall. Aerial roots do not take nutrients from the plant on which they grow. Instead, they get their nutrition from leaves that fall and decompose near them.

One way to reproduce some plants is to cut a piece of the stem and place it in water or in moist soil. In time, adventitious roots will form from cells in the plant's stem. Coleus and begonias are two kinds of plants that can be reproduced in this way. This is one important method of vegetative propagation. **Vegetative propagation** uses parts of plants to make more plants that are genetically identical to the parent plant. An example of vegetative propagation is shown in **Figure 11.5**. Some roots can also be used to produce a new plant. If such roots are cut apart and then planted, new stems will begin to grow. Dividing a plant's roots is another method of vegetative propagation. Gardeners often use this method to increase the numbers of their plants.

Figure 11.4 English ivy plants attach themselves to vertical surfaces, such as tree trunks, by means of hairy-looking aerial roots.

Uses of Roots

People have used roots in a variety of ways for thousands of years. Some roots are used for food, some for spices, and some for substances such as dyes, medicines, and insecticides. Some plants have roots that absorb toxins left in the soil from pollution along with nutrients from the soil. These plants can be used to "clean" contaminated soil.

Beets, carrots, yams, turnips, and radishes are among the many roots that are eaten. The root of the cassava plant is used to make tapioca, an ingredient in puddings and baby food. The root of the marsh mallow plant was the original source of marshmallow candies. Roots such as licorice, sassafras, and horseradish are used as spices.

Figure 11.5 Roots grew from one of these cut stems of a pyracantha plant. Gardeners often add rooting hormones to the stem to encourage more rapid production of roots. The production of plants from plant parts is called vegetative propagation.

CONNECTION: Physics

Roots grow downward with the force of gravity. However, the water taken in by the roots flows upward, defying gravity. How can that be possible?

Two processes are responsible for the water in roots traveling as far as 100 m to the tops of the tallest trees. The first of these processes is the attraction of water molecules to one another, which is called cohesion. The second process is transpiration, which is the giving off of water from the leaves of a plant.

Because the cohesive force between water molecules is so strong, every molecule that evaporates from a leaf pulls on another molecule of water in the leaf. If each leaf of a tree gives off billions of molecules of water, a tremendous force pulling water up is created. Water molecules also stick to, or adhere, to the sides of the narrow tubes that carry water upward.

Differentiated Instruction

Visual, Kinesthetic Have students sketch or make models of the four different types of roots. Provide materials such as markers, yarn, string, and fabric paint. Students should create models for each type of plant, labeling the plant and root.

Teacher Alert

Based on their experience, students may not be familiar with the fact that root systems can be extensive in size. Common large trees have root systems that extend more than 10 m in length. Scientists have determined that the root system of a rye plant measures more than 600,000 m in length.

Teach

EXPLAIN that students will learn about the fourth type of root, as well as common uses of roots.

CONNECTION: Physics

Tell students that water molecules are polar, meaning that they have positive and negative regions. The positive region of one water molecule is attracted to the negative region of another water molecule or any negatively charged surface. The reverse is true, as well.

Cohesion is the attraction of water molecules to each other because they are polar. Adhesion is the attraction of water molecules to nonwater molecules that have regions of positive or negative charge. Cohesion helps to explain the pull created as a result of transpiration. Adhesion helps to support the column of water within xylem tubes.

EXPLORE To illustrate these two terms, provide pairs of students with a small glass beaker, a dropper, water, and a paper towel. Ask students to try the two activities, but do not explain the principle responsible for each action.

1. Fill the beaker to the top with water. Then using the dropper, add water until students can see the water's surface above the top of the beaker. (This illustrates cohesion.)
2. Dip a corner of the paper towel into the water-filled beaker, and watch the action of the water. (This illustrates adhesion.)

EXTEND Ask students to match the activity with the term it demonstrates. Then, have them define *cohesion* and *adhesion* in their own words in their Science Notebooks. Students' definitions should include sketches of water molecules interacting in each activity.

Teach

EXPLAIN that all roots have similar structures and grow in similar ways. Students will learn how cells and tissues work together to support the plant, absorb water and nutrients from the soil, transport materials throughout the stem, and store the excess products of photosynthesis.

Vocabulary

root cap Encourage students to brainstorm common uses of the word *cap*. In all examples, a cap covers the top of something. A root cap covers and protects some of the cells of the root.

apical meristem Tell students that the word *apical* is derived from *apex*, which means "the highest point" or "tip." The word *meristem* is derived from the Greek word *meristos*, meaning "divisible."

epidermis Explain that the prefix *epi-* means "outer" or "attached to." The root *dermis* is from the Greek word *derma* and means "the skin." Plants and animals can have this outermost layer of skin.

root hair Encourage students to brainstorm common uses of the words *root* and *hair*. Root hairs are hairlike structures growing on the plant root.

cortex Explain that the word *cortex* is derived from Latin for "tree bark." *Cortex* refers to an outer layer that is different from the inner layer.

endodermis Tell students that the prefix *endo-* means "internal" or "inside." Have students use the meaning of the root *dermis* they just learned to define the term *endodermis*.

xylem Explain that *xylem* is from the Greek word *xylon*, which means "wood." Xylem is woody tissue that transports water and minerals throughout the plant. It also provides structural support.

phloem Tell students that *phloem* is derived from the Greek word *phloios*, which means "bark." Phloem transports organic molecules throughout the plant.

hydrotropism Explain that the prefix *hydro-* is from the Greek word *hydōr* and means "water." The root *tropism* is derived from the Greek word *tropos*, which means "a turn." The literal meaning of *hydrotropism*, then, is "a turn toward water."

Science Notebook EXTRA

Have students sketch and label a cross section of a root. Students should use all the vocabulary terms in their drawings.

Root Structure and Growth

Plant growth differs from animal growth in an important way. Animals have what is called a closed pattern of growth, while many plants have an open pattern of growth. Animals reach a certain shape and size, and then they stop growing. Many plants continue to grow throughout their lives, producing new cells at their growing tips, which include roots.

Tough cells that make up the root cap cover the end of a root. The tough cells in the root cap are in contact with particles in the soil. The **root cap** protects the more delicate cells that lie just behind the cap. These cells make up the **apical meristem** (AY pih kul • MER uh stem). *Apical* is a word that means "tip" or "end." The cells in a meristem continuously undergo mitosis and cell division. An apical meristem is also located at the tip of each plant stem.

As the cells in the root's apical meristem continue to divide, the newly formed cells enter a zone of elongation. Here the cells become longer, pushing the tip of the root ahead through the soil. The growth in the length of a root is called primary growth.

The **epidermis** (eh puh DUR mus) is the tissue that surrounds the outside of a root. Small **root hairs**, which are extensions of epidermal cells, stick out of the epidermis. Root hairs absorb water, oxygen, and dissolved minerals. They also greatly increase the surface area of the root that contacts the soil. The root **cortex** is found inside the epidermis. The cortex makes up most of the root and is the location where starch made by the plant is stored.

The **endodermis** (en duh DUR mus) is the innermost layer of the cortex. The endodermis surrounds the plant's vascular tissues—xylem and phloem. **Xylem** (ZI lum) is plant tissue that is made up of tube-shaped cells that transport water and dissolved minerals to all parts of a plant. Water and dissolved minerals that enter a root move through the cortex, into xylem cells, and then throughout the plant. **Phloem** (FLOH em) is plant tissue that is similar to xylem in that it is made up of tube-shaped cells. However, phloem transports organic molecules made in a plant's leaves to all parts of the plant. Some of these molecules are stored as starch in the roots.

Figure It Out

1. What two processes account for the growth of the root?
2. What is the relationship between root hairs and xylem and phloem tissues?

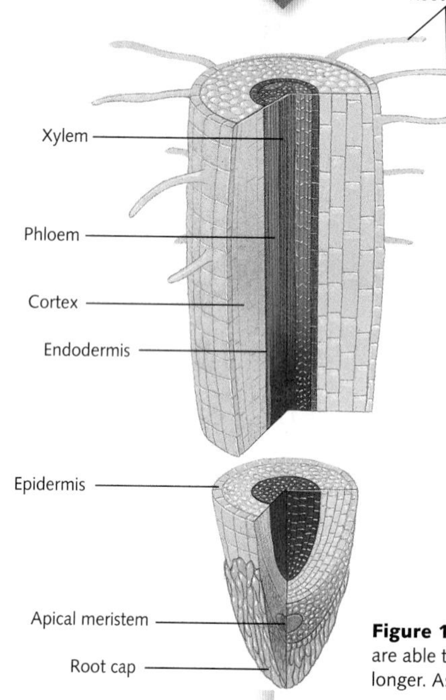

Figure 11.6 Many specialized tissues make up a root. Only cells in the root tip are able to divide. Just behind the area of cell division is an area where cells grow longer. As the number and size of cells increase, the root gets longer and wider.

Figure It Out: Figure 11.6

ANSWER **1.** The processes of mitosis and elongation produce root growth. **2.** Root hairs increase the surface area that comes into contact with the soil in order to absorb the water and minerals transported by xylem and phloem.

Background Information

A number of environmental factors affect roots. In dry soil, roots grow straighter and shorter and form more lateral roots. In compact soils, there are fewer and smaller spaces between soil particles. In order to grow through these spaces, roots become thicker. They also increase their lateral root growth; these lateral roots are usually thinner and can grow through the compact soil more easily.

The arrangement of xylem and phloem differs in the roots of dicots and monocots. Recall that angiosperms, or flowering plants, are classified into two large groups: dicots and monocots. Dicots produce seeds that have two cotyledons, or seed leaves. Monocots produce seeds with a single cotyledon.

The xylem cells in a dicot root are arranged in a star-shaped fashion in the center of the root. Phloem cells are found between the arms of the star. In a monocot root, xylem cells and phloem cells alternate in a ring around the root. **Figure 11.7** shows the arrangement of xylem and phloem tissues in a dicot root and a monocot root.

Roots generally exhibit positive gravitropism and grow downward toward the pull of gravity. Roots have also been said to show positive hydrotropism. **Hydrotropism** is growth toward water. Because it is impossible to separate the growth of a plant's roots as a result of gravity's pull from the growth of a plant's roots in response to water, some scientists believe that hydrotropism may not be an actual tropism.

The growth of plant roots occurs only in damp soil. Roots will not grow in soil that is completely dry. In addition to water, plant roots need oxygen for cellular respiration. Cellular respiration is the process that enables cells to get energy needed for growth.

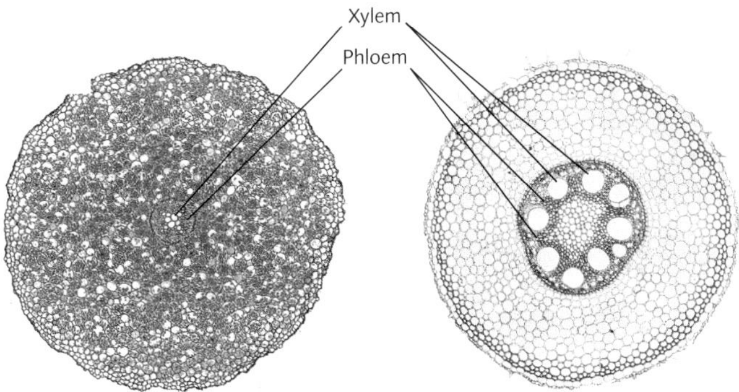

Figure 11.7 You can see the different arrangement of similar structures in these cross sections of a dicot root *(left)* and a monocot root *(right)*. What other types of cells can be seen?

Extend It!

Hydroponics is a method of growing plants without soil. Research the process of hydroponics. Use your research to prepare a list in your Science Notebook of the advantages and disadvantages of growing plants using this process. How does hydroponics affect root growth?

After You Read

1. Review the working definition of *root* in your Science Notebook. Then identify the type of root system that you might eat as part of a meal and the type of root system that you might mow over during the summer.
2. What are the main functions of plant roots?
3. Draw and label the parts of a root. Identify the root you have drawn as a monocot or a dicot. Explain how monocot and dicot roots differ.

Teach

EXPLAIN that although dicots and monocots have the same root structures, the arrangement of the vascular tissues is different.

Use the Visual: Figure 11.7

ANSWER Cells from the epidermis, cortex, and endodermis can also be identified in these cross sections.

Extend It!

Provide students with a variety of resources, including botany books and access to the Internet. Students' research should indicate that one advantage of hydroponics is faster growth because nutrients are always available to the plant and extensive root growth is not necessary. Another advantage is that pesticides and herbicides are not needed to eliminate weeds and pests. The disadvantage of hydroponics is that it is a very expensive process.

Assess

EVALUATE Use the After You Read questions and the Alternative Assessment to help you assess students' understanding of the lesson.

After You Read

1. A taproot such as a carrot or a turnip could be eaten, and grasses with their fibrous root system require mowing.
2. Roots anchor and support plants, absorb water and minerals from the soil, contain vascular tissues that transport materials to and from the stem, and store excess products of photosynthesis.
3. Students' drawings should include the following parts of a root: apical meristem, epidermis, root hair, cortex, endodermis, xylem, and phloem. Students should also label their roots as monocots or dicots. Monocot and dicot roots differ in the arrangement of xylem and phloem cells.

Background Information

Some problems that people encounter while growing plants hydroponically include yellowing bottom leaves or older growth; curling leaf tips; leaf tips curling under or browning; and leaching. Most of these problems can be solved by adjusting the hydroponic solution.

Alternative Assessment

EVALUATE Using his or her working definition of *root*, each student should write a paragraph describing the four root functions and four different types of roots. The paragraph should include one example of a plant for each type of root. Some students may benefit from using the concept map they created.

11.2 Introduce

ENGAGE Have students return to their sketches from the Engage activity on page 186. Pair students and ask them to revise their drawings of the plants' roots using their new knowledge. Then, ask students to infer the functions of plant stems, basing their inferences on their knowledge of roots. Students should list these functions in their Science Notebooks.

Before You Read

Model the process of creating a question from the first Learning Goal. Read the goal aloud. On the board, write *What are the functions of plant stems?* Give students a few minutes to write questions in their Science Notebooks for the other two Learning Goals. Suggest that students leave space between questions to write their answers and that they write the first question near their inferences from the Engage activity.

Teach

EXPLAIN that students will learn about different types of plant stems and their structures and functions. Although plant stems can look different in different plants, their jobs remain essentially the same.

Use the Visual: Figure 11.8

ANSWER Stems provide support and hold a plant's leaves toward the sunlight. They contain vascular tissues that transport water, minerals, and sugars. They conduct photosynthesis. They also store water and/or food.

Learning Goals

- List the functions of plant stems.
- Describe the structure of a plant stem.
- Differentiate among the types of plant stems.

New Vocabulary

stem
herbaceous stem
woody stem
node
internode
axil
pith
cork cambium
vascular cambium

11.2 Stems

Before You Read

Use the headings of this lesson to form questions. Write the questions in your Science Notebook. As you read, write answers to the questions.

Stems are the most visible parts of nearly all plants. **Stems** are part of a plant's shoot system. Most stems grow above the ground. However, the stems of some plants grow underground or along the soil surface. The trunks of trees are likely the largest and most noticeable stems.

Stems have many important functions. Stems support the leaves, cones, fruits, flowers, and even seeds of plants. Stems hold a plant's leaves up toward the sunlight. Stems contain vascular tissues—xylem and phloem—that transport water, dissolved minerals, and organic molecules to and from the roots and leaves. Stems that are green conduct photosynthesis. In some plants, stems store water or products of photosynthesis. This can help the plant survive during times of drought or severe cold.

Types of Stems

Plant stems vary greatly in size and shape. Think about the trunk, branches, and twigs of a tree. All of these structures are stems! As **Figure 11.8** shows, the baobab tree has an enormous trunk and short, stubby branches. The rose plant has thin stems covered with thorns.

There are two classifications of stems: herbaceous stems and woody stems. **Herbaceous** (hur BAY shus) **stems** are green, soft, and flexible stems that usually carry out photosynthesis. Examples of plants with herbaceous stems include basil, petunias, impatiens, carnations, sunflowers, and tomatoes. **Woody stems** are hard, strong, and rigid. Trees, shrubs, and roses have woody stems.

Figure 11.8 Notice the difference between the stems of a baobab tree and those of a rose plant. What are the functions of a stem?

ELL Strategy

Paraphrase Arrange students in groups of two to four. Have each student paraphrase the big ideas of one to two pages of the lesson (depending on group size). Students should then share their big ideas with the other group members. Collectively, the group should summarize the lesson. Students can then write or share the big ideas in their own words to assure they understand the concepts.

Structure of Stems

A stem is divided into nodes and internodes. A **node** is the point at which leaves are attached to a stem. Some plants produce a single leaf at a node, while other plants produce several leaves at a node. An **internode** is the part of the stem between nodes. A plant that does not receive enough light is easily identified by its longer internodes. The leaves on most plants are arranged in ways that expose the leaves to the greatest amount of light possible, as **Figure 11.9** shows. It is unusual to find a plant whose leaves are arranged in such a way that they shade other leaves under normal growing conditions.

The top angle between a leaf and a stem is called the **axil**. The axil often contains a bud that can grow into a new branch. There is also a bud at the tip of the stem. The stem increases in length when this bud grows. Recall from Chapter 9 that hormones are produced at the tip of a stem. These hormones prevent other buds lower down on the stem from growing. If the bud at the tip of a stem is damaged or removed, the hormones are not produced. The other buds, called axillary buds, begin to grow. The plant produces new stems and grows bushier.

The outside layer of a stem is the epidermis. The epidermis is usually waterproof and may also be covered with a thick, protective layer of dead tissue called bark. In some kinds of trees, the bark is very thick. Just inside the epidermis is a layer of cells that fill in the area surrounding the xylem and phloem. These cells contain chlorophyll. When light strikes this layer, these cells can conduct photosynthesis.

Herbaceous Dicot Stems The epidermis of a herbaceous dicot stem is covered by a waterproof layer called the cuticle. In some plants, there are pores in the stem that allow the exchange of gases between the stem and the surrounding air. The vascular tissues are arranged in bundles that form a ring near the outside edge of the stem. The cortex is found between the vascular bundles and the epidermis. Tissue known as **pith** fills the rest of the stem within the ring of vascular bundles. An example of a plant with this kind of stem is the pea plant.

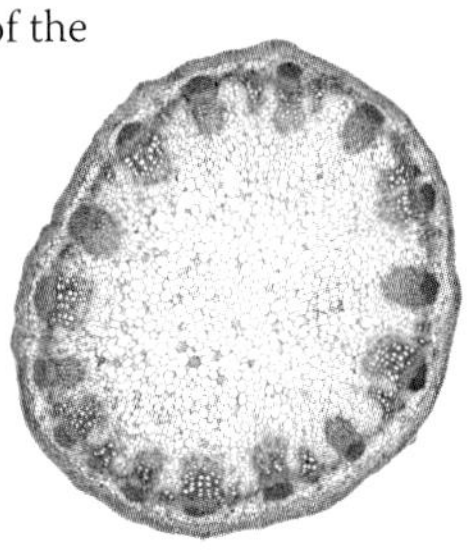

Figure 11.11 In the stem of a young herbaceous dicot, separate bundles of xylem and phloem form a ring.

Figure 11.9 Leaves are spaced along a stem in a regular pattern. Note the tiny bud at each spot where a leaf is attached to the stem.

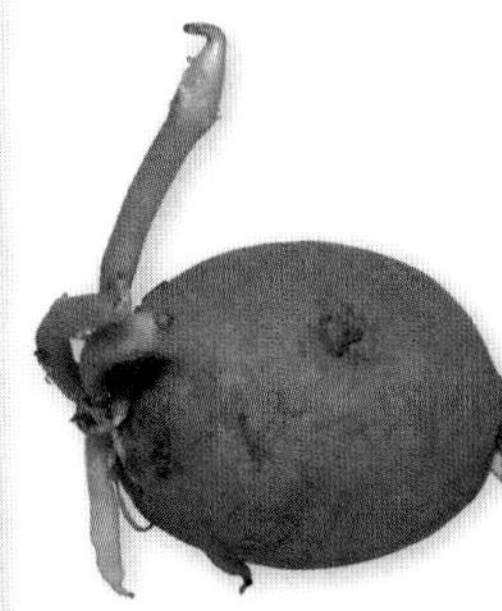

Figure 11.10 A white potato looks like a root, but it is actually a part of an underground stem called a tuber. Tubers store starch. A white potato tuber has buds from which new stems can grow. These buds are commonly called eyes.

Teach

EXPLAIN to students that the external structures of stems include nodes, internodes, axils, and the epidermis. Xylem and phloem are part of the internal structure of stems.

EXPLORE Provide students with hand lenses and common flowers or small branches from bushes or trees (or have students supply their own stem samples). Have students examine the stems and identify nodes, internodes, and axils. With your supervision, have students cut the stems and identify the epidermis layer of each as well as any internal structures, if possible. Have students sketch and label their stems in their Science Notebooks.

Vocabulary

stem Encourage students to think of common uses of the word *stem*. Examples might include a leaf stem, the stem on an apple, or the stem of a watch. When used as a verb, *stem* means "to curb" or "to stop." Explain to students that *stems* are the parts of the plant that grow upward from the roots.

herbaceous stem Highlight the root, *herb*, and explain to students that this word can be generally used to describe a flowering plant. Work with students to list familiar aromatic or culinary herbs.

woody stem Explain to students that the suffix *-y* signifies "full of" or "characterized by." A woody stem is "full of" wood and is stiff and less flexible than a herbaceous stem.

node Tell students that *node* is derived from the Latin word *nodus*, which means "knot." *Node* is also used in human biology to describe a structure of the lymphatic system and in physics to describe a wave characteristic.

internode Explain to students that the prefix *inter-* means "between" or "among." An internode is the part of the stem between nodes.

axil Tell students that *axil* is derived from the Latin word *axilla*, which means "armpit." Ask students why this is an appropriate term for the place where the leaf is attached to the stem.

pith Explain that *pith* also means "the essential part, or core." Ask students to relate this meaning to the word's scientific definition and explain why the term is appropriate for that part of a stem.

Differentiated Instruction

Interpersonal, Naturalistic Have students talk with a horticulturist, expert gardener, or nursery employee about growing and maintaining plants, including flowers, shrubs, and trees. Students should write interview questions in advance. Questions could cover such topics as watering and fertilizing plants, trimming shrubs and trees, choosing appropriate plants for one's climate, and raising plants from seedlings.

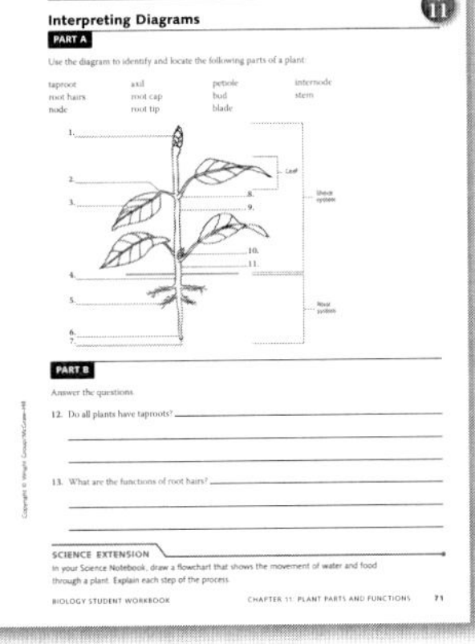

Interpreting Diagrams

PART A

PART B

SCIENCE EXTENSION

Interpreting Diagrams Workbook, p. 71

Teach

EXPLAIN that herbaceous dicot stems and woody dicot stems are different from each other and also vary from monocot stems. Woody dicot stems have two layers of cells that make the stems woody: cork cambium and vascular cambium.

Vocabulary

cork cambium Tell students that the word *cambium* is derived from Latin and means "exchange." Encourage students to think of common uses of the word *cork*. Student responses may include bulletin boards and bottle stoppers.

vascular cambium Have students recall the meaning and usages of the term *vascular*. Then, have them relate the meaning to this term. Explain to students that vascular cambium helps the woody stem grow thicker and more resilient each year.

Figure It Out: Figure 11.12

ANSWER **1.** Xylem makes up most of a woody dicot stem. **2.** Cork cells function primarily as protection for the stem.

As You Read

Students' questions may vary, but sample questions and answers are shown below.

What are the functions of stems?

Stems provide support and hold a plant's leaves toward the sunlight; they contain vascular tissues that transport water, minerals, and sugars; they conduct photosynthesis; and they store water and/or food.

What is the structure of plant stems?

Stems are divided into nodes and internodes, with leaves found along the stem in regular patterns. The outer layer of a stem, the epidermis (or bark), is a waterproof layer that provides protection for the tissues below. The stem contains xylem and phloem, which transport materials throughout the plant.

What are the different types of plant stems?

Plant stems may be herbaceous (soft, green, flexible stems that contain chloroplasts and carry out photosynthesis), woody (hard, strong, rigid stems), or specialized (designed to carry out a specific function, such as nutrient storage or reproduction).

As You Read

Answer the question you wrote in your Science Notebook for each heading. You should be able to answer all three of the questions you wrote. Then, share your answers with a partner and modify them as needed.

Woody Dicot Stems Woody dicot stems have two layers of meristematic cells that produce new cells. The first layer is called the **cork cambium**. The cork cambium produces tough cork cells that will become part of the bark of a tree. The cork cells contain a waxy substance that repels water, making the stems waterproof. The cork cells also protect the tree from physical damage.

The second layer is called the **vascular cambium**. This layer produces secondary xylem and phloem cells. A thin layer of secondary phloem cells is found just beneath the bark. Secondary xylem cells fill the inside of a woody stem. The diameter of a tree trunk increases with the growth of layers of secondary xylem cells. Because the amount of growth produced by the vascular cambium differs from season to season, visible rings of tissue can be seen in a woody stem. These rings can be counted to determine the age of a tree. In some tropical areas, trees grow all year long. The wood in the trunks of these trees does not show obvious rings, and so the trees' ages are not easily determined.

Figure It Out

1. What tissue makes up most of a woody dicot stem?
2. What cells function primarily as protection for the stem?

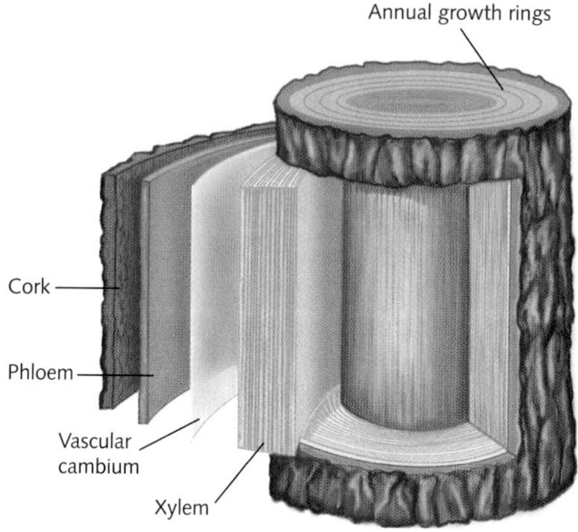

Figure 11.12 The production of secondary vascular tissue increases the size of a woody dicot's stem. Woody stems are composed primarily of dead xylem cells. People put the stems that produce this woody tissue to a variety of uses.

The widths of a tree's annual growth rings provide important information about conditions in the tree's environment. In years when moisture is abundant, the rings are wide. In drier years, the rings are narrower. Careful examination of tree rings allows scientists to reconstruct the weather conditions and climate patterns in an area.

CONNECTION: Meteorology

EXPLORE Give students hand lenses and cross sections of tree trunks (or diagrams that show tree rings). Have students reconstruct the weather conditions represented by their samples. Students should count the rings to determine the ages of the trees and look for areas where the rings are close together, which indicate drought, or farther apart, which indicate abundant moisture.

Background Information

The cork oak (*Quercus suber*) trees grow primarily in countries on the coast of the Mediterranean Sea (including Portugal, Algeria, Spain, Morocco, France, Italy, and Tunisia). The climate in these countries is often harsh, with frequent droughts, brush fires, and wide-ranging temperatures. These conditions contribute to the cork oak's ability to protect itself with a thick layer of cork bark.

Monocot Stems The surface of a monocot stem, such as the stem of a corn plant, is covered by an epidermis. In most monocots, the bundles of xylem and phloem are scattered throughout the stem. However, in some monocots, a ring of scattered bundles of xylem and phloem cells can be observed near the outside edge of the stem. Within a single bundle of vascular tissue, xylem cells can be found facing the center of the stem. Phloem cells can be found facing the outer edge of the stem. There is also an air space in the vascular bundle.

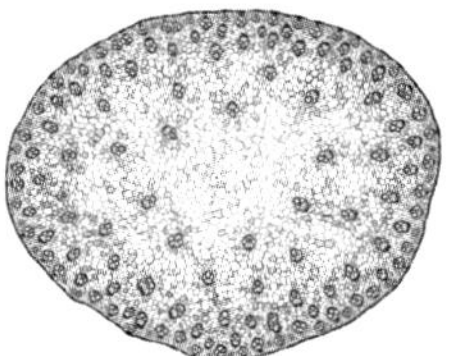

Figure 11.13 The vascular bundles in a monocot stem are scattered throughout the stem.

Specialized Stems

Tubers, bulbs, and rhizomes are types of underground stems. A tuber is a fat stem that stores food. The eye of a tuber is a bud that is capable of developing into a new plant. A white potato is an example of a tuber. An onion is an example of a bulb, which is a short, underground stem with thick, food-storing leaves. When planted, a bulb develops into a new plant. Garlic and scallions are other examples of bulbs that are eaten for food. Tulips, daffodils, crocuses, and hyacinths are examples of decorative plants that form bulbs that are not eaten. Rhizomes are stems that grow horizontally beneath or along the ground. As they grow, they produce buds that develop into new plants. Morning glories, strawberries, irises, and ginger plants produce rhizomes. The corkscrew-shaped tendrils on grape vines are another example of a specialized stem. Such stems enable grape vines to cling to a supporting object as they grow.

Figure 11.14 The thick stem of a cactus, such as this saguaro, is an example of a specialized stem. What do you think is the function of such a stem?

Explore It!

Design an experiment that would demonstrate that some specialized stems store organic nutrients produced by the plant through photosynthesis. In your Science Notebook, list the materials that you will need and the procedure you plan to follow. With approval from your teacher, conduct the experiment. Record your observations in your Science Notebook.

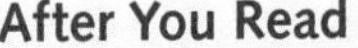

After You Read

1. A plant has a thick stem that is gray in color and very rough. Use answers to your heading questions to identify the function of this plant's stem.
2. What structures are found in all stems?
3. Design a concept map that illustrates the different types of stems.

Teach

EXPLAIN to students that all monocot stems have xylem and phloem cells. Some stems have an outer ring of phloem and an inner ring of xylem, while others have bundles of xylem and phloem dispersed throughout the stem.

Use the Visual: Figure 11.14

ANSWER The stem of a saguaro cactus is specialized to store large amounts of water.

Explore It!

Provide pairs of students with iodine and potatoes and/or onions. Students should record their procedures, observations, and conclusions in their Science Notebooks.

Remind students that iodine turns blue-black in the presence of starch, and caution them that iodine can stain their skin and clothing.

Assess

EVALUATE Use the After You Read questions and the Alternative Assessment to help you assess students' understanding of the lesson.

After You Read

1. The function of this plant's stem is to hold the plant upright, prevent water loss, and protect the plant. It does not carry out photosynthesis.
2. All stems have an epidermis and contain xylem and phloem.
3. Students' concept maps should be titled *Types of Stems* and have three main branches: *Herbaceous, Woody,* and *Specialized.* The *Specialized* branch should be further divided into *Tubers, Bulbs,* and *Rhizomes.*

Alternative Assessment

EVALUATE Have students use their Learning Goal questions to draw and label two different types of stems (of their choice). Drawings should include lateral as well as cross-sectional views of the stems.

Background Information

Growth that increases the diameter of a stem or a root is called secondary growth. The cambia are meristematic tissues that produce secondary xylem and phloem. Primary growth lengthens a stem or a root and occurs in apical meristems.

Bulb and bulblike plants are usually perennials. They typically grow and flower in the warm season and then enter a time of dormancy. During dormancy, they die back to ground level. True bulbs have five parts: basal plate, fleshy scales, tunic, shoot, and lateral buds. True bulbs can be divided into tunicate bulbs and imbricate bulbs. Tunicate bulbs have tunics, or paperlike coverings that protect the scales from drying and from injury (examples include tulips, daffodils, and hyacinths). Imbricate bulbs do not have tunics (examples include lilies).

11.3 Introduce

ENGAGE Provide students with a variety of different leaves. The selection should include simple, compound, dicot, monocot, pinnate, and palmate leaves. Identify the leaves by number. After pairing students, have each pair choose three to four different leaves to observe and analyze. Have students write as many observations about each leaf as possible in their Science Notebooks. For instance, a description of an oak leaf might read *Leaf #1 is symmetrical and green, has small points at the end of the tips, has "veins" running through it, and has nine points.*

Before You Read

Model dividing the page into four quadrants and writing *Leaf Variation* in one of the squares. Using some student observations from the Engage activity on this page, write a sentence about leaf variation. One example is *Leaves can be made up of one part or several parts.*

Teach

EXPLAIN to students that leaves vary from plant to plant, just like roots and stems vary. The structures and functions of leaves are interrelated; that is, the structures support the functions.

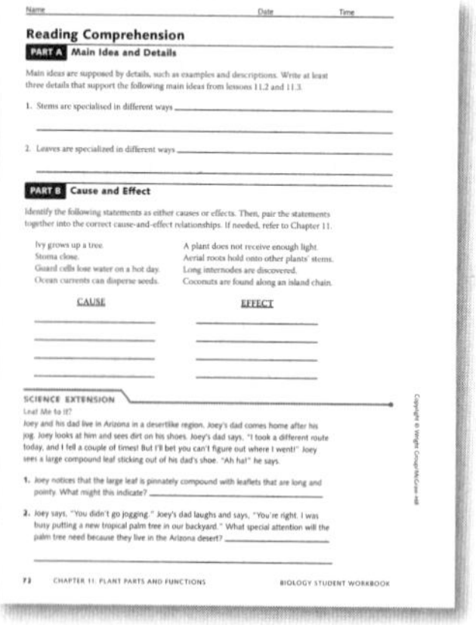

Reading Comprehension
PART A Main Idea and Details
PART B Cause and Effect
SCIENCE EXTENSION

Reading Comprehension Workbook, p. 72

Learning Goals

- List the functions of leaves.
- Describe the structure of leaves.
- Relate the structure of leaves to their environment.

New Vocabulary

leaf
blade
petiole
cuticle
mesophyll
stoma
guard cell
transpiration

11.3 Leaves

Before You Read

Look at the four main headings within this lesson. Divide a page in your Science Notebook into four sections. Write one heading in each section. Then, write a sentence summarizing what you know about each heading.

You have probably seen solar panels on the roofs of buildings. These large, flat surfaces collect the energy of sunlight. A plant's leaves do the same thing. In fact, leaves can be thought of as the world's oldest solar-energy collectors.

Leaves are part of a plant's shoot system. **Leaves** are plant organs whose main functions include capturing the energy of sunlight, making organic molecules through the process of photosynthesis, and exchanging gases with the environment. Most leaves are flat and have a relatively large surface area that receives sunlight. However, leaves come in a great variety of sizes and shapes.

Tulip poplar

Horse chestnut

Locust

Figure 11.15 The leaf of the tulip poplar *(top)* is a simple leaf. The leaves of a horse chestnut *(center)* and a locust *(bottom)* are compound leaves, in which the blade is divided into leaflets. The horse chestnut leaf is palmately compound. The locust leaf is pinnately compound.

Leaf Variation

The flat part of a leaf is called the **blade**. Leaves are classified as either simple or compound. A simple leaf is made up of a single blade. Oak trees and apple trees have simple leaves. A compound leaf has a blade that has split into two or more smaller sections. These small sections are called leaflets. Palms, roses, and clovers have compound leaves. If the leaflets of a compound leaf are attached to each other at a single point, the leaf is palmately compound. This name comes from the fact that the leaf form resembles the way the fingers of a hand are attached to the palm. If the leaflets are attached along an extended stalk, the leaf is pinnately compound. Pinnately compound leaves look something like feathers.

The stalk that joins a leaf blade to a stem is called a **petiole** (PET ee ohl). Most leaves are attached to stems by petioles. A petiole is usually small. Some plants, however, have large petioles. The large petioles of celery and rhubarb are often eaten. Not all leaves are joined to stems by petioles. Some leaves, such as grass blades, are joined directly to the stem. The petiole contains vascular tissues—xylem and phloem—that extend from the stem into the leaf and form veins.

Figure 11.16 The maple *(left)* has leaves attached to its stem by a petiole. The St. John's wort *(right)* is a plant that has leaves attached directly to its stem.

ELL Strategy

Use a Concept Map Have each student create a concept map to classify the leaves from the Engage activity at the start of this lesson. *Leaf Variation* should be the main topic, and subtopics should include *Simple, Complex, Pinnate, Palmate, Monocot,* and *Dicot.* Alternatively, for a more comprehensive concept map, *Leaf* could be the main topic, with *Structures, Functions, Variation,* and *Specialized* as subtopics. Struggling English-language learners could diagram and label the distinctions they see among the leaves they are provided.

The leaves of a dicot, such as a maple tree, have a branching network of veins. The leaves of a monocot, such as an iris, have veins that run parallel to one another. The veins connect with xylem and phloem in the stem. Water enters the leaves through the xylem, and organic molecules are moved out of the leaves through the phloem.

Figure 11.17 The veins in a dicot leaf have a branching pattern. A monocot leaf has parallel veins.

Leaf Structure

The internal structure of a plant leaf can more easily be seen if the cut surface of the leaf is examined under a microscope. The outermost layer of a leaf is the epidermis. A leaf has both an upper and a lower epidermis. The epidermis acts like a clear window to let sunlight pass into the leaf. The upper epidermis is covered with a waxy, waterproof coating called the **cuticle** (KYEW tih kul). The cuticle, which can make real plants look as if they are made of shiny plastic, helps prevent the leaf from losing excess water. The epidermis of some plants has glands and hairs, and sometimes even soft, fuzzy surfaces. **Figure 11.18** shows the structures of a leaf.

Just beneath the epidermis are two layers of cells known collectively as **mesophyll** (MEZ uh fihl). Mesophyll is the photosynthetic tissue of a leaf. Palisade mesophyll lies very close to the upper epidermis, where it receives maximum exposure to sunlight. The cells in this layer are column-shaped and are packed very closely together. They contain many chloroplasts—the structures in plant cells that contain chlorophyll.

Beneath the palisade mesophyll is the spongy mesophyll. The cells in this layer are loosely packed and irregularly shaped. These cells have air spaces that allow carbon dioxide, oxygen, and water vapor to flow freely around the cells. Carbon dioxide enters a leaf through tiny pores in the epidermis and diffuses into the mesophyll cells. Water vapor and oxygen pass out of the mesophyll cells and the leaf through these openings.

As You Read

Add new information to the summaries you wrote in your Science Notebook for *Leaf Variation* and *Leaf Structure*. Be sure to include the vocabulary terms used in each section.

What is the waxy, waterproof coating of a leaf called?

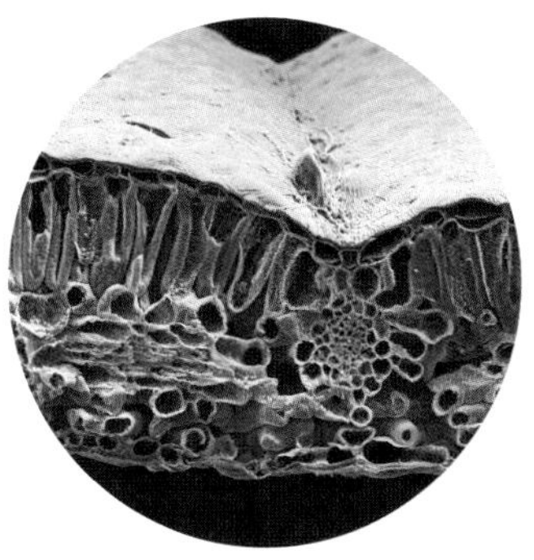

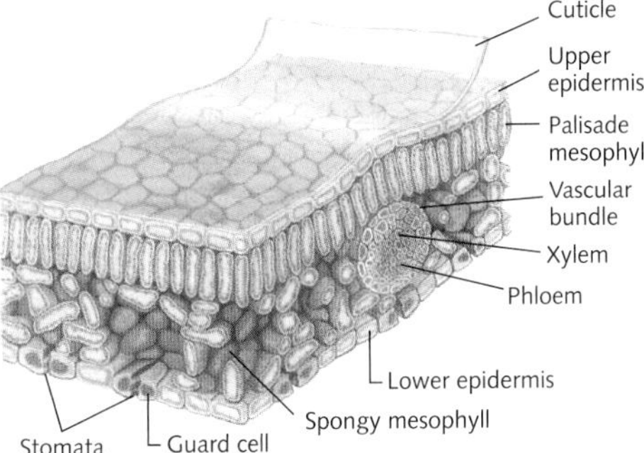

Figure 11.18 The labels in the diagram *(right)* identify the parts of a leaf seen in cross section. Match these labels to the leaf parts shown in the micrograph of a cross section of a leaf *(left)*. In which layers does photosynthesis take place? How are the cells in these layers adapted to their function?

Teach

EXPLAIN that veins in dicot and monocot leaves vary. This variation should help students more easily classify unknown plants. Structures in a leaf control the amounts of water and gas entering and exiting the leaf.

Vocabulary

leaf Introduction of the term *leaves* provides opportunity to discuss with students singular and plural forms of words. Tell students that *leaf* is the singular form and that the plural form is made by dropping the *f* and adding *ves*. Ask students to identify other words that follow this rule (*calf/calves, half/halves, loaf/loaves*).

blade Encourage students to brainstorm common uses of the word *blade*. Their examples may include the blade of a knife, a blade of an ice skate, or the flat part of an oar. Explain that all of these examples are flat; the blade of a leaf is the flat part.

petiole Explain that *petiole* comes from the Latin word *petiolus*, meaning "little foot." The petiole is the part of the leaf that joins the blade to a stem.

cuticle Tell students that the origin of the word *cuticle* is the Latin word *cuticula*, which is the diminutive form of *cutis* ("skin"). The cuticle on a leaf performs a skinlike, or protective, function.

mesophyll Tell students that the root word *phyll* refers to the leaf, and the prefix *meso-* means "in the middle" or "intermediate." Have students use these meanings to define the term *mesophyll* in their own words. Ask students if they know any words with either this prefix (*mesoderm, Mesolithic, Mesozoic*) or this root (*chlorophyll*).

Use the Visual: Figure 11.18

ANSWER **1.** the palisade and spongy mesophyll layers **2.** These cells are adapted for photosynthesis because they are packed with chloroplasts that absorb light energy.

As You Read

Give students five to ten minutes to review and revise their summaries.

Encourage students to use labeled diagrams to illustrate new vocabulary terms such as *leaf, blade,* and *petiole* in the section *Leaf Variation*. Have students briefly share work with a peer to receive feedback about the accuracy of their summaries.

ANSWER The waxy, waterproof coating of a leaf is called the cuticle.

Differentiated Instruction

Linguistic Have students create word maps for each vocabulary term or other unknown word in the lesson. Make sure each student has access to a dictionary and thesaurus, if possible. One vocabulary word should be at the center of each map.

Connected to each word, students should add to their maps:

- the definition
- a synonym
- an antonym
- a connection to the word (this may be a quick sketch)
- a new sentence using the word

Teach

EXPLAIN to students that they will learn about the inner structure of a leaf: those parts that are located in the layers of leaf between the epidermal layers.

Vocabulary

stoma Explain that *stoma* is derived from the Greek word *stoma*, meaning "mouth." The stomata on leaves are little openings similar to mouths.

guard cell Explain to students that the word *guard* originates from the French word *garder*, meaning "to protect." Guard cells help control the amount of water entering and exiting the stomata.

transpiration Explain to students that the word *transpire* is derived from the Latin word *transpirare*, which came from *spirare*, meaning "to breathe." Ask students to explain why this is an appropriate term for the process of transpiration.

Figure It Out: Figure 11.19

ANSWER **1.** As water enters and leaves the guard cells, the water pressure opens and closes the stomata. **2.** Plants need carbon dioxide from the environment as a raw material for photosynthesis. Plants also give off the waste gas oxygen, produced during photosynthesis, through the stomata.

Explore It!

Give students about five minutes to reflect and write about the purpose of covering leaves with a plastic bag. Encourage students to think about the functions of the leaf and how the plastic bag will allow them to observe one of those functions.

Place a clear plastic bag over a cluster of leaves on a potted plant. Carefully seal the bag in place with tape, and have students observe the plastic bag over a two- to three-day period. Students should observe small water droplets on the inside of the bag. Review the definition of *transpiration* with the class, and make sure that students understand that transpiration is responsible for the water droplets inside the plastic bag.

Figure It Out

1. How do guard cells regulate the size of the opening of a stoma?
2. Why is gas exchange important to a plant?

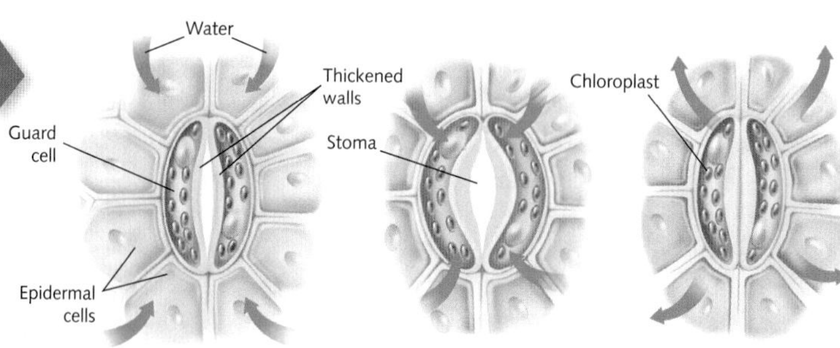

Figure 11.19 One guard cell is located on each side of a stoma. Water movement into and out of the guard cells regulates the size of the opening of each stoma.

1. The guard cells have flexible cell walls.
2. When water enters the guard cells, the pressure causes them to bow out, opening the stoma.
3. As water leaves the guard cells, the pressure is released and the cells come together, closing the stoma.

The tiny pores, or openings, in the lower epidermis of most leaves are called **stomata** (STOH muh tuh, singular: stoma). Stomata control gas exchange between the leaf and the outside environment. The number of stomata in leaves varies greatly. Some plants may have as many as several million stomata on a single leaf. Plants such as water lilies that float on the surface of water have leaves with stomata in the upper epidermis. Other plants have leaves with stomata in both the upper and lower epidermis. Two **guard cells** lie on either side of a stoma. Guard cells are epidermal cells that contain chloroplasts. Guard cells are able to change shape as they absorb and release water. As a result, the guard cells open and close the stoma. **Figure 11.19** illustrates this process. The opening and closing of the guard cells regulates the amount of carbon dioxide, water vapor, and oxygen that enters and leaves the leaf.

Explore It!

In your Science Notebook, predict what will happen if the leaves of a plant are covered with a plastic bag. Help your class design an experiment to test your prediction. As your teacher performs the experiment, record the hypothesis, materials, and procedure in your Science Notebook. After two days, carefully observe the inside of the bag. Record and explain your observations.

The Movement of Nutrients in Plants

The veins in a leaf contain xylem and phloem cells. These cells join with the xylem and phloem in the stems and roots of a plant. Water and mineral nutrients enter a root and move into the xylem. The water and minerals move up the xylem in the plant's stem and enter the leaves. In the leaves, some of the water is used in the process of photosynthesis, which occurs primarily in the palisade mesophyll. Recall that during photosynthesis, water molecules are split in the presence of sunlight and chlorophyll, and oxygen gas is given off.

Most of the water passes out of leaves as water vapor through stomata in a process called **transpiration** (trans puh RAY shun). Because water molecules attract other water molecules, water that leaves the stomata by transpiration actually "pulls" water up from the roots. Organic molecules made in the leaves move around the plant in the phloem. Water drawn into the phloem by osmosis helps push nutrients through the phloem.

Background Information

A number of factors determine how much water plants transpire, including:

- *Temperature*: As temperatures increase, transpiration rates increase as well. Guard cells open in higher temperatures.
- *Relative humidity*: As relative humidity rises, the rate of transpiration decreases. Leaves release more water into drier air.
- *Wind and air movement*: A higher transpiration rate occurs with increased movement of air.
- *Type of plant*: Different varieties of plants transpire water at different rates.
- *Soil moisture*: When soil is dry, plants transpire less water. Soil that is too dry causes premature aging of plants, and leaves can be lost.

Specialized Leaves

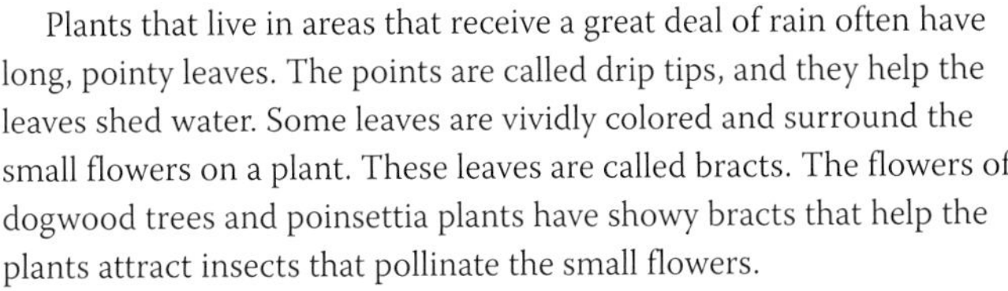

The shapes and sizes of leaves vary depending on the plant's environment. Many species of cactus, for example, lack typical leaves. Their leaves are the spines that protect these plants from being eaten. Other plants that live in dry environments often have thick, fleshy leaves that are covered with a thick cuticle, which helps prevent water loss.

Figure 11.20 The leaves of a cactus plant are its spines. Photosynthesis occurs in the stems of the plant.

Plants that live in areas that receive a great deal of rain often have long, pointy leaves. The points are called drip tips, and they help the leaves shed water. Some leaves are vividly colored and surround the small flowers on a plant. These leaves are called bracts. The flowers of dogwood trees and poinsettia plants have showy bracts that help the plants attract insects that pollinate the small flowers.

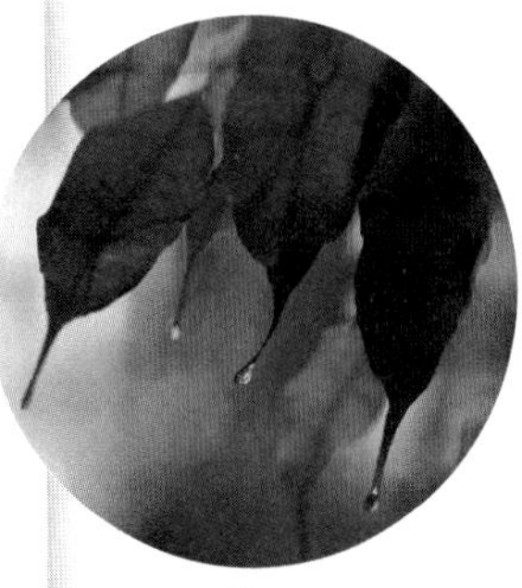

Figure 11.21 Drip tips help the leaves of plants in a rain forest shed water *(top)*. The colorful leaves on this poinsettia plant look like flower petals *(bottom)*. The actual flowers are the small structures in the center.

Tendrils that help some plants hold on to supports as they climb are modified leaves. These tendrils look like small, delicate whips that are able to coil tightly around the structures on which they climb. Tendrils can be seen on garden pea plants.

Perhaps the most incredible leaves are those found on plants that trap insects. The leaves on a Venus's-flytrap snap shut when an insect touches hairs in the trap. Digestive juices then help break down the insect. Pitcher plants have modified leaves that look like pitchers and act as traps for catching insects. Any insect that gets caught inside these plants is decomposed by the plants' digestive juices.

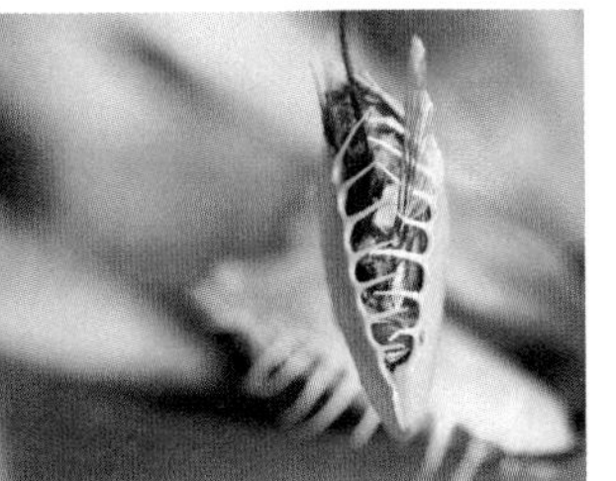

Figure 11.22 The Venus's-flytrap *(left)* snaps shut to trap an insect. Pitcher plants *(right)* make a sweet-tasting liquid in glands on the rims of their traps. This liquid attracts insects.

After You Read

1. Describe three functions of leaves.
2. What structures in a leaf make up its transport system?
3. Select one specialized leaf described in your Science Notebook, and explain how its structure is related to its environment.
4. Use the information recorded in your Science Notebook about movement of water and organic molecules in plants to write a summary paragraph.

Teach

EXPLAIN that students will learn about leaves that grow on plants in extreme climates—places that are very hot or very wet.

Assess

EVALUATE Use the After You Read questions and the Alternative Assessment to help you assess students' understanding of the lesson.

After You Read

1. Primary functions of leaves include capturing the Sun's energy, producing organic molecules through the process of photosynthesis, and exchanging gases with the environment.
2. Petioles and veins contain xylem and phloem that transport water, minerals, and organic molecules in the leaf.
3. Answers will vary depending on the leaf selected.
4. Water is carried throughout the plant in xylem, while organic molecules produced in photosynthetic tissues are transported throughout the plant in phloem. The plant's vascular system consists of connected xylem and phloem tissue that is found from the roots to the topmost leaves.

Alternative Assessment

EVALUATE Have students use the section summaries in their Science Notebooks to classify two or three of the leaves used in the Engage activity at the start of this lesson (page 196). Students should describe the leaves as being simple or complex, pinnate or palmate, and monocot or dicot.

Field Study

Have pairs of students explore the school grounds or a surrounding neighborhood under your supervision. Provide plant reference books to each pair if available. Students should identify four to five different trees or plants by examining their leaves, stems, and roots if visible, and then sketch the characteristic parts of each plant in their Science Notebooks. Students should also identify the plants as dicots or monocots and the type of stem and leaf for each plant.

Teacher Alert

Discuss the various activities that reduce the concentration of oxygen in the air. Oxygen is a waste product of photosynthesis. The destruction of tropical rain forests and the clearing of large areas of coniferous forest reduce the amount of photosynthesis that takes place and thus the amount of oxygen released into the atmosphere.

11.4 Introduce

ENGAGE Have students work in pairs to sketch and label as many different seeds as they can remember. Encourage students to include not just fruits and vegetables but also the seeds of trees and other plants. It may be useful to have students categorize each seed by its plant alongside the sketch. Tell students that they will learn to further classify seeds in this lesson.

Before You Read

Model the T-chart on the board, and then write one fact about seed structure in the appropriate column. One example is *Many seeds have a protective covering*. Give students a few minutes to create the T-charts in their Science Notebooks and to write what they already know in each column.

Teach

EXPLAIN to students that in this lesson, they are going to learn about the structure of seeds as well as how seeds are dispersed, or spread. Tell students that although seeds may look different from one another, the basic structure of the seeds within each of the major groups of seed plants—monocots, dicots, and gymnosperms—is the same.

Vocabulary

seed Tell students that the term *seed* is used in a variety of ways as both a noun and a verb. Ask students to provide examples, such as the kernel of an idea, a ranked tournament competitor (nouns), to sow, to treat clouds in order to produce rain, to rank, and to extract the seeds (verbs). Ask students to suggest a meaning common to these and to the definition of a seed provided in this lesson.

seed coat Explain that *testa*, derived from the Latin word *testa*, meaning "shell," is another name for the seed coat.

embryo Tell students that *embryo* originates from the Greek word *embryon*, which is derived from *bryein*, meaning "to swell." The embryo grows (swells) into a larger plant.

cotyledon Explain to students that *cotyledon* is derived from the Greek word *kotylē*, meaning "cup."

Learning Goals

- Describe the structure of a seed.
- Identify ways that seeds can be dispersed.

New Vocabulary

seed
seed coat
embryo
cotyledon
plumule
epicotyl
hypocotyl
radicle
germination
dormancy

11.4 Seeds

Before You Read

In your Science Notebook, create a T-chart. Label one column *Seed Structure* and the other column *Seed Dispersal*. As your first entry, record what you already know about each topic. Then, in the appropriate column, record important information discussed in this lesson. Try to use the vocabulary terms in your entries.

Seeds can be thought of as a plant's insurance that there will be another generation of its kind. A **seed** is a structure from which a new plant grows. Seeds look quite different from one another. Seeds can be as fine as dust or as large as coconuts. Orchid plants produce seeds that are so small they are hardly recognizable as seeds. Because these seeds are so fine, they cannot contain a great deal of food for a developing plant. In fact, orchid seeds depend on certain species of fungi to provide the food they need to grow. Orchids produce millions and millions of seeds, which helps increase their chances of survival.

Although seeds vary widely in appearance, they all have the same basic structure. A seed consists of a seed coat, an immature plant, and stored food. A seed develops from a fertilized ovule and contains a new plant and all that is necessary for its development.

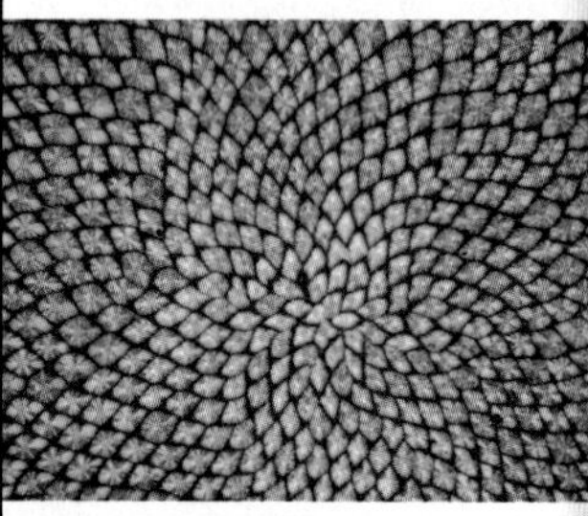

Structure of a Seed

The **seed coat** is a tough protective coat that envelops the entire seed. Seed coats vary in thickness from the thin, brown, papery covering of a peanut to the thick covering of a coconut. A seed coat protects the delicate tissues of the young plant in the seed. It keeps these tissues from losing water and protects them from certain kinds of physical damage. The seed coat generally opens only after the seed has fallen in a moist place and has begun to take in water. The "skins" of peanuts, corn kernels, and lima beans are seed coats.

Enclosed within the seed coat is the embryo. The **embryo** (EM bree oh) is the immature plant that begins to grow when environmental conditions are just right. The embryo develops from a fertilized egg. The embryo eventually gives rise to the leaves, stem, and roots of a new plant.

Figure 11.23 The seeds of a sunflower *(top)* show an intricate spiral arrangement with symmetry. Sunflower seeds are eaten by humans, birds, and other animals. A useful oil can be extracted from sunflower seeds. Vanilla *(bottom)* comes from the seed pods of the vanilla orchid. Each seed pod contains millions of tiny seeds that are used to flavor many kinds of food.

ELL Strategy

Use a Venn Diagram In their Science Notebooks, students should make Venn diagrams comparing dicot and monocot seeds. Students can be provided a drawing of monocot and dicot seeds at the start of this lesson. They can label their diagram as the lesson proceeds. Then, students can do a self-assessment when they reach Figure 11.25.

Figure 11.24 Peanuts are one of the few kinds of seeds that develop underground. Peanuts are sometimes called "ground nuts." After the peanut plant flowers and is fertilized, the stem bends toward the ground and pushes its tip below the soil surface.

In addition to the seed coat and the embryo, a seed contains stored nutrients. In many seeds, the stored nutrients make up a large part of the seed. The seedling plant will use the stored nutrients until it is able to manufacture its own organic molecules through photosynthesis. In some seeds, the stored food surrounds the embryo. In other seeds, the stored food is contained in one or more **cotyledons** (kah tuh LEE duns), or seed leaves. **Figure 11.25** shows examples of seeds with different numbers of cotyledons.

Dicot Seeds The seeds of dicots have two cotyledons. If the seed coat is removed with care, the two cotyledons can be gently separated at the seam where they are joined together. Inside are two tiny leaves called the **plumule** (PLOOM yool). These tiny leaves are usually folded, and they lie on one of the cotyledons. Both cotyledons are attached to the embryo just below the plumule. A short stem is located just above the point at which the cotyledons are attached. This stem is called the **epicotyl** (EH pih kah tul). The epicotyl will become the stem of the mature plant. Another stem, called the **hypocotyl** (HI puh kah tul), is located just below the point of attachment. At the base of the hypocotyl is a region called the **radicle** (RA dih kul). The primary root of the plant begins to grow from the radicle.

Explore It!

Use a hand lens to observe bean seeds that have been soaked in water. Carefully remove the seed coat, and then separate the two halves of each seed. Use the hand lens to identify and observe the parts of the seed. In your Science Notebook, draw and label the parts of the seed you have observed.

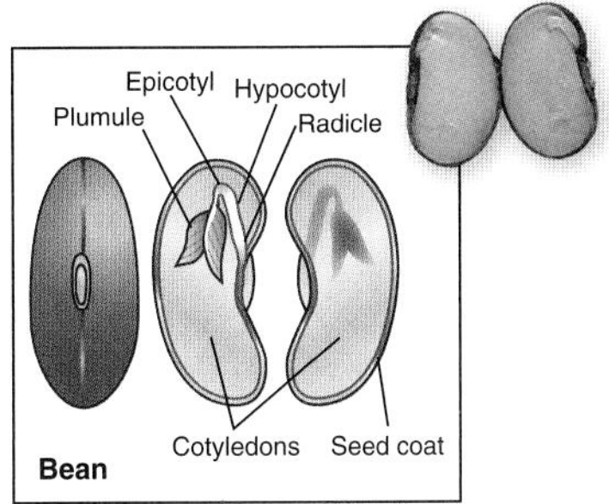

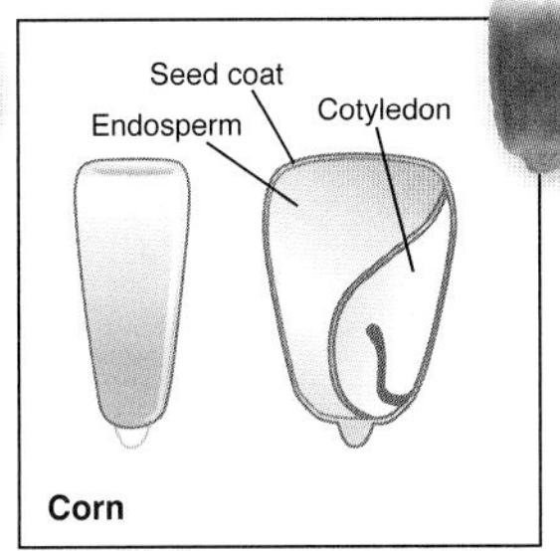

Figure 11.25 A bean is a dicot; corn is a monocot. In bean seeds *(left)*, all of the nutrients are stored in the cotyledons. In seeds such as corn kernels *(right)*, most of the nutrients are stored in a tissue called endosperm.

Figure It Out

1. How are these seeds alike? How are they different?
2. What part of the embryo becomes the plant stem? What part becomes the primary root?

Teach

EXPLAIN to students that all seeds include stored food for the embryo, or the immature plant, that will begin to grow when environmental conditions are just right. The embryo will use this food to fuel its growth after the dormant stage.

Vocabulary

plumule Explain that *plumule* is derived from the Latin word *plumula* and is the diminutive (smaller) form of *pluma*, meaning "feather."

epicotyl Tell students that the prefix *epi-* signifies "outer" or "upon." Remind students of the meaning of *cotyledon*, from which the root *cotyl* originates.

hypocotyl Explain that the prefix *hypo-* means "under." The root *cotyl* comes from *cotyledon*. Have students use the meanings of *epi-*, *hypo-*, and *cotyledon* to distinguish the epicotyl from the hypocotyl.

radicle Point out that *radical*, which can be both a noun and an adjective, has many meanings. Ask students if they are familiar with any meanings from math or chemistry. One of the meanings is "a basic principle or foundation." Ask students how this meaning relates to the meaning of *radicle*.

Explore It!

Prepare a variety of different types of seeds by soaking dried kidney or lima bean seeds for several hours and/or dried pea seeds for 24 hours. You may also want to prepare peanuts by removing the shells and storing them in a moist place for three to four days so that the cotyledons will open. Although the peanuts will not be eaten by students, you will want to confirm that no students participating in the activity are allergic to peanuts. Students will observe the cotyledons, epicotyls, and radicles.

Figure It Out: Figure 11.25

ANSWER **1.** Both seeds have these parts: seed coat, hypocotyl, epicotyl, embryo, and radicle. In both seeds, the primary root emerges as the seed coat cracks. The corn seed is a monocot; it has one seed leaf. The bean seed is a dicot; it has two cotyledons. In corn seeds, the embryo does not depend upon the single cotyledon for food. Instead, food for the embryo is stored as endosperm. Bean seeds do not have endosperms. **2.** The epicotyl becomes the plant stem; the primary root grows from the radicle.

Differentiated Instruction

Kinesthetic, Linguistic Over a period of one or two days, have students collect seeds from a variety of sources. Have students touch each of the seeds while closing their eyes. Encourage students to focus on the sense of touch. Immediately after students have touched each seed, ask them to write as many adjectives as possible describing that seed. Students should include adjectives describing how the seed feels as well as how it looks. Students could then create posters illustrating their results by gluing down each seed and writing these adjectives in a corresponding space. To extend this activity, students could have a set of seeds before them. One student could describe a seed for a partner who must then choose the correct seed from among the group.

Teach

EXPLAIN to students that the seeds of monocot and dicot plants differ by the number of cotyledons in the seed. Remind students that *di-* is a prefix meaning "two," *mono-* is a prefix meaning "one," and *cot* is a shortened reference to *cotyledon.*

As You Read

Give students about five minutes to review and revise the T-charts in their Science Notebooks. Remind them to include vocabulary words when writing the important information from the lesson.

ANSWER A seed is a structure from which a plant grows, and it includes the following structures: seed coat, embryo (the immature plant that will grow and develop), and cotyledon (a structure that helps nourish the embryo).

Vocabulary

germination Tell students that the root *germinate* is derived from the Latin word *germinare,* meaning "to sprout or bud."

dormancy Tell students that the root word *dormant* comes from the Latin verb *dormire,* meaning "to sleep."

Extend It!

Divide the class into small groups, and randomly assign each group a method of seed dispersal. Provide groups with a variety of materials to use in designing their seeds, such as cotton balls, tissue paper, hook-and-loop fasteners, foam packing material, clay, pipe cleaners, and glue. You may want to use group designs to assess students' ability to identify types of seed dispersal.

Background Information

Seedling growth entails one of two different types of growth: epigeous germination or hypogeous germination. Both refer to the placement of the cotyledons during germination. In epigeous germination, the cotyledons are pushed above the soil surface, such as with beans or other legumes. In hypogeous germination, the cotyledons as well as most of the seed remain underground; only the shoot appears above the soil.

As You Read

Review the information you have recorded in the column labeled *Seed Structure.* Define and describe a seed using the following terms: *seed, seed coat, embryo,* and *cotyledon.*

Monocot Seeds The seed of a monocot has one cotyledon. Corn is an example of a monocot. In corn seeds, the embryo does not depend upon the single cotyledon for food. Instead, food for the embryo is stored as endosperm, and the delicate new leaves are protected in a cylinder of tissue. Endosperm is formed during fertilization and is rich in important nutrients. The cotyledon helps transfer nutrients to the embryo.

Gymnosperm Seeds Gymnosperms also have cotyledons in their seeds. Pines produce seeds with eight cotyledons. When a pine seed begins to grow, the cotyledons that resemble smaller versions of pine needles are in a ring around the baby plant's stem, as **Figure 11.26** shows.

Figure 11.26 Pine seeds have eight tiny cotyledons. The pine cotyledons look like the small leaves or needles on adult trees.

Seed Dispersal

Seeds that fall close to the parent plant often have to compete for available nutrients and other resources, such as light and water. Plants have evolved many ways to ensure that seeds are transported from where they are formed. The transportation of seeds is called seed dispersal. Seeds are dispersed by water, wind, humans, and other animals.

Coconuts produce some of the largest seeds in the plant kingdom. These seeds are encased in tough husks made of strong fibers with air spaces in between them. Thus coconut seeds can float in water and are dispersed from one place to another on ocean currents. Other plants that live in or near water produce seeds that can be dispersed by moving water and waves.

Dandelion seeds have small fluffy threads attached to them. The threads help the wind carry the seeds aloft. Other seeds, such as those produced by maple trees, have two winglike structures. These structures act much like propellers to move the seeds from tree to ground.

Animals and humans play a part in seed dispersal. Animals carry fruits to other locations and leave behind the seeds. They also excrete indigestible seeds in their body wastes. Humans and animals can pick up and carry seeds that have sharp barbs on their seed coats. The barbs stick in an animal's fur or on a human's clothing, and the seeds get carried to another place. When the seeds eventually fall off, they can grow where they land. The invention of self-sticking fabric tape is said to have its origin in observations of the tiny hooks that attach tick seeds to the fur of animals.

Extend It!

Your teacher will divide the class into groups of three to four students and assign each group a method of seed dispersal. Work with your group to design a seed that can be dispersed in that way. Use the materials provided by your teacher to construct your group seed. Materials might include cotton balls, tissue paper, hook-and-loop fasteners, foam packing material, clay, pipe cleaners, and glue. Once you have constructed your seed, devise an experiment to determine how successful your design is.

Seed Germination

The process by which the embryo in a seed begins to develop into a new plant is called **germination** (jur muh NAY shun). Germination begins when growing conditions are favorable. Water, oxygen, and favorable temperatures are common requirements of germination. Absorbed water causes the cotyledons to swell, cracking open the seed coat and activating the embryo. **Figure 11.27** illustrates seed germination.

Seeds often undergo a period of inactivity called **dormancy** (DOR mun see) before they begin to grow. During dormancy, the embryo can survive long periods of bitter cold, extreme heat, or drought. The embryo will not begin to grow until dormancy is broken. The embryos in many tree seeds, for example, must go through a period of cold temperatures or through several winters before they will begin to grow. Some seeds need darkness to break dormancy, while others need exposure to light. The seeds of some plants have begun to grow after periods of dormancy lasting as long as 1,000 years! Having some knowledge of the conditions that seeds need to break dormancy is essential to growing plants from seeds.

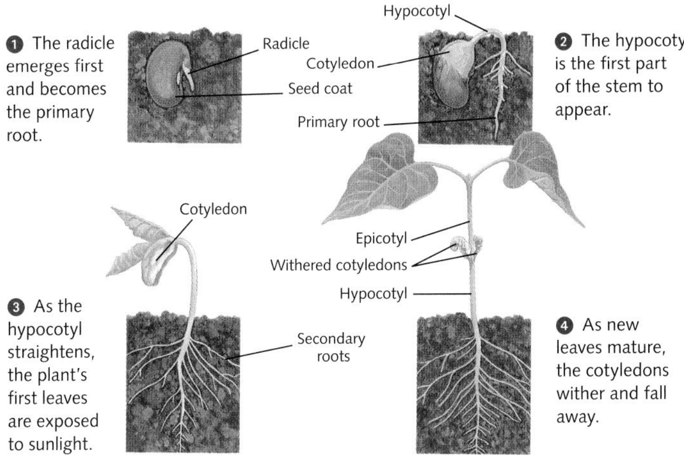

1 The radicle emerges first and becomes the primary root.
Radicle
Cotyledon
Seed coat
Hypocotyl
Primary root
2 The hypocotyl is the first part of the stem to appear.
Cotyledon
Epicotyl
Withered cotyledons
Hypocotyl
Secondary roots
3 As the hypocotyl straightens, the plant's first leaves are exposed to sunlight.
4 As new leaves mature, the cotyledons wither and fall away.

Figure 11.27 The events of seed germination vary in different kinds of plants. This illustration shows how a bean seed germinates to begin the growth of a new plant.

After You Read

1. Use the information in your T-chart to draw and label the parts of a seed.
2. How might each of the following seeds be dispersed to a new location: A seed inside a sweet berry? A lightweight seed that spins? A seed that floats?
3. In a well-developed paragraph, define and describe the process of germination. Accompany your paragraph with a correctly labeled drawing.

Explain It!

The seeds of some plants, such as prairie wildflowers and conifers, will not germinate until dormancy is broken by exposure to fire. Research plant species such as the bishop pine or lupines that depend on exposure to fire to germinate. In your Science Notebook, explain why this method of ending dormancy is an important adaptation for survival.

CONNECTION: Math

Many seeds absorb water before germinating. Determine the amount of water absorbed by ten bean seeds prior to germination using a graduated cylinder and the technique of water displacement. In your Science Notebook, describe the technique of water displacement, and record all of your measurements.

Teach

EXPLAIN to students that seeds are dispersed in a variety of ways. Plant evolution has ensured that seeds are transported to locations away from parent plants.

Explain It!

Provide resources to students such as botany books and access to the Internet. Encourage students to use keywords such as *germination* and *dormancy* in their research. Germination after exposure to fire ensures the survival of the plant species and allows the seedling to develop in an environment with limited competition.

CONNECTION: Math

Provide students with graduated cylinders, water, and ten seeds. Students should first determine the volume of the ten seeds by placing them in the graduated cylinder with a known volume of water. The new volume less the original volume equals the volume of the seeds. After the seeds have soaked for 24 hours, students should repeat the water displacement technique to calculate the volume of the soaked bean seeds. The change in volume is due to the seeds' absorption of water.

Assess

EVALUATE Use the After You Read questions and the Alternative Assessment to help you assess students' understanding of the lesson.

Background Information

Seeds of flowering plants differ in size; some may be as small as grains of sand, while others may be larger, such as chestnuts. Generally, larger seeds are able to store more food for the embryo. This greater amount of food allows more time for the embryo and seedling to grow.

Alternative Assessment

EVALUATE Have students use their T-charts to name and define the structures of a seed. They should also summarize the differences between monocots and dicots. Struggling English-language learners could create two diagrams (one monocot and one dicot), labeling the various parts of each seed and/or means of seed dispersal.

After You Read

1. Students' drawings should include the following parts and labels: seed coat, embryo, and cotyledons.
2. Seeds inside fruits are usually dispersed by animals; lightweight seeds are most often dispersed by the wind; and seeds that float are usually dispersed by water.
3. Students' paragraphs should accurately describe the seed germination process.

Chapter 11 Summary

VOCABULARY REVIEW

Check students' sentences or paragraphs to make sure they understand the meaning of each vocabulary term.

PREPARE FOR CHAPTER TEST

Evaluate students' essays using the following criteria:

1. The topic sentence, or main idea, should restate the Key Concept.
2. The supporting paragraphs should incorporate the answers to the Learning Goal questions students have written and include details, facts, and examples they have recorded in their Science Notebooks.
3. The concluding sentence should sum up the main idea of the chapter and restate the Key Concept.

MASTERING CONCEPTS

True or False

1. True
2. False, Xylem
3. True
4. False, Roots
5. True
6. False, dispersed
7. True
8. False, transpiration

Short Answer

9. Xylem and phloem are vascular tissues that transport material throughout a plant. Xylem transports water; phloem transports organic nutrients.
10. The primary functions of a taproot are to securely anchor the plant in the ground and to store excess organic compounds produced by the plant. The primary function of a fibrous root system is to provide a large area for the absorption of water from the soil.
11. In addition to supporting the plant and transporting materials, a green stem also carries out photosynthesis.
12. The leaves of the cactus protect it from being eaten. The stem of the cactus stores water.

Summary

KEY CONCEPTS

11.1 Roots

- Roots anchor and support a plant, absorb water and minerals from the soil, and contain vascular tissues that transport materials to and from the stem.
- Two major types of root systems are taproots and fibrous roots.
- The epidermis surrounds the vascular tissues—xylem and phloem—that transport water, minerals, and organic molecules throughout the plant.

11.2 Stems

- Stems provide support for a plant, hold leaves up toward the sunlight, and transport material between a plant's leaves and roots.
- Plants can have woody stems that are hard and rigid or herbaceous stems that are more flexible and carry out photosynthesis.
- The arrangement of vascular tissues differs in monocot and dicot stems.
- Some stems are specialized to carry out other functions.

11.3 Leaves

- Leaves are designed to capture the Sun's energy and carry out photosynthesis.
- Leaves are plant organs whose structure is closely related to their function and well adapted to their environment.
- The flat part of a leaf is called the blade. Leaves are classified as either simple or compound depending on the number of blades. A simple leaf is made up of a single blade. A compound leaf consists of several leaflets.

11.4 Seeds

- Seeds contain a protective coating, stored food, and an immature plant that grows and develops when conditions are favorable.
- Seeds can be dispersed to new environments by water, wind, humans, and animals.
- Germination is the process by which the embryo in a seed begins to develop into a new plant. Water, oxygen, and favorable temperatures are common requirements of germination. Germination begins when dormancy ends and growing conditions are favorable.

VOCABULARY REVIEW

Write each term in a complete sentence, or write a paragraph relating several terms.

11.1
root, p. 187
taproot, p. 187
fibrous root, p. 188
vegetative propagation, p. 189
root cap, p. 190
apical meristem, p. 190
epidermis, p. 190
root hair, p. 190
cortex, p. 190
endodermis, p. 190
xylem, p. 190
phloem, p. 190
hydrotropism, p. 191

11.2
stem, p. 192
herbaceous stem, p. 192
woody stem, p. 192
node, p. 193
internode, p. 193
axil, p. 193
pith, p. 193
cork cambium, p. 194
vascular cambium, p. 194

11.3
leaf, p. 196
blade, p. 196
petiole, p. 196
cuticle, p. 197
mesophyll, p. 197
stoma, p. 198
guard cell, p. 198
transpiration, p. 198

11.4
seed, p. 200
seed coat, p. 200
embryo, p. 200
cotyledon, p. 201
plumule, p. 201
epicotyl, p. 201
hypocotyl, p. 201
radicle, p. 201
germination, p. 203
dormancy, p. 203

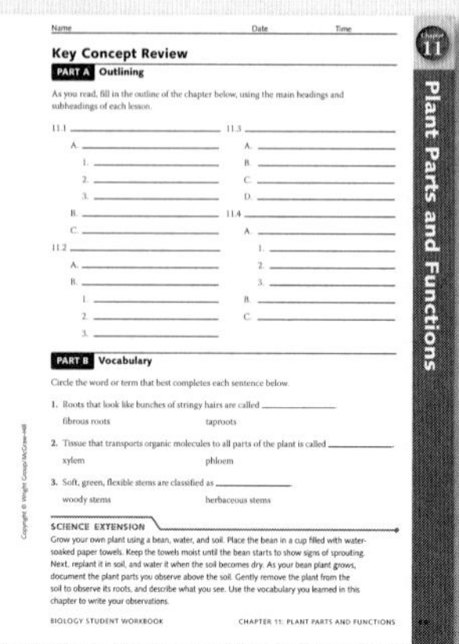
Key Concept Review
Plant Parts and Functions

Key Concept Review
Workbook, p. 69

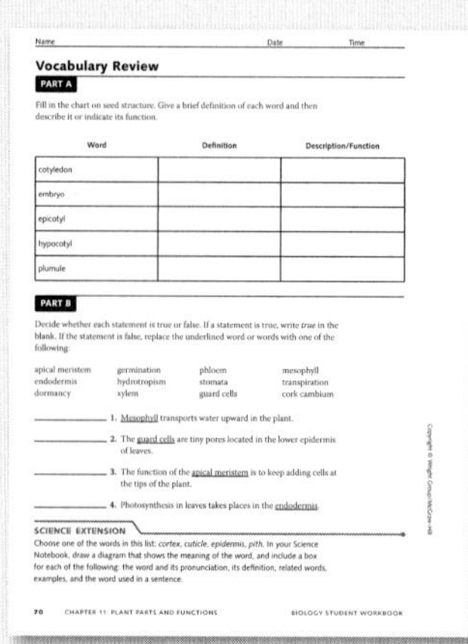
Vocabulary Review

Vocabulary Review
Workbook, p. 70

MASTERING CONCEPTS

True or False

If the statement is true, write "true." If it is false, change the underlined word or words to make the statement true.

1. The epidermis is the protective tissue found in the leaves, stems, and roots of plants.
2. Phloem transports water throughout a plant.
3. Stems support a plant and transport water and nutrients between plant parts.
4. Leaves are responsible for anchoring a plant and absorbing water and minerals from the soil.
5. Leaf stomata control the exchange of gases with the environment.
6. Seeds can be germinated by animals, humans, wind, and water.
7. The arrangement of some plant tissues of monocots and dicots is different.
8. Water vapor is given off by plants in a process called photosynthesis.

Short Answer

Answer each of the following in a sentence or brief paragraph.

9. Name and describe the functions of the two types of vascular tissues found in plants.
10. How do the functions of taproots and fibrous roots differ?
11. A plant's stem is soft, flexible, and green. What are the probable functions of this stem?
12. What functions are the leaves and stem of a cactus specialized to perform?

Critical Thinking

Use what you have learned in this chapter to answer each of the following.

13. **Apply Concepts** During late winter, holes are drilled into some sugar maple trees in order to collect syrup. What type of tissue is being "tapped"?
14. **Analyze** Why are the roots of a plant usually the first part of the plant to appear from a germinating seed?
15. **Infer** Why are seeds a good food source for animals?

Standardized Test Question

Choose the letter of the response that correctly answers the question.

16. Where does most of the photosynthesis occur in a typical plant?
    - A. xylem
    - B. roots
    - C. leaves
    - D. stems

Test-Taking Tip

Remember that qualifying words such as *most* can mean that all the choices could be considered true. Ask yourself which choice best answers the question.

PREPARE FOR CHAPTER TEST

To prepare for the chapter test, create a question from each Learning Goal. Use the information in your Science Notebook to answer each question. Then use these answers to write a well-developed essay about the chapter. Use the Key Concept on the first page of this chapter as your topic sentence.

Critical Thinking

13. Students might infer that the phloem in the stem of the tree is being "tapped" so that the sugars it transports can be harvested. However, the sugar-carrying fluid, or sap, that rises from the roots in spring flows within the outer ring of xylem, or sapwood, in the trunks of maple trees.
14. The root anchors the plant in the soil, and the water and minerals it absorbs from the soil allows the plant to continue to grow and develop.
15. Seeds are an excellent source of food for animals because they contain stored nutrients for the developing plant embryos.

Standardized Test Question

16. C

Reading Links

Seeds: Time Capsules of Life

With its astonishing images (captured through photography and electron microscopy by accomplished visual artist Kesseler), this resource provides a fascinatingly intimate look at seeds. The text, while best for more advanced readers, is the work of an expert affiliated with the Millennium Seed Bank Project and provides information about the organization's international conservation efforts. Learners of all levels will appreciate the book's visuals, which can powerfully reinforce the chapter's study of plant parts.

Kesseler, Rob and Wolfgang Stuppy (with Alexandra Papadakis, Ed.). Firefly Books, Ltd. 264 pp. Illustrated. Trade ISBN: 978-1-55407-221-7.

Peterson First Guide to Trees

This clear and detailed guide is ideal for students who wish to test their knowledge of plants in the field or for use as a classroom reference tool. The easy organization allows users to identify over 200 North American trees by visible characteristics, testing observation skills while accessing valuable information about leaf type, growth, reproduction, habitat, historical uses, and more.

Petrides, George A. (with Roger Tory Peterson, Ed.). Houghton Mifflin. 128 pp. Illustrated by Janet Wehr and Olivia Petrides. Trade ISBN: 978-0-395-91183-9.

Curriculum Connection Workbook, p. 73

Science Challenge Workbook, pp. 74–75

Chapter 11

Labs

11A What Plant Parts Do You Eat?

This prechapter introduction activity is designed to determine what students already know about the value of plant parts as food sources by engaging them in examining, comparing, and classifying food plants as fruits or vegetables.

Objectives

- examine food plants
- determine what part of the plant a food is
- classify food part as a fruit or vegetable
- communicate conclusions

Planning

 1 class period  groups of 2–4 students

Materials (per group)

- assorted fresh fruits and vegetables, cut into pieces
- assorted dried fruits
- pencil and paper

Advance Preparation

- Choose as many fresh fruits and vegetables as possible. Suggestions:
  Fresh fruits: strawberries, oranges, apples, tomatoes, cucumbers, peppers. Dried fruits: raisins, peas, dry beans, peanuts. Fresh vegetables: celery, asparagus (stem), carrots, radishes (root), broccoli spears, cauliflower (flower), spinach, cabbage, lettuce (leaves).
- Draw a data table on the board with the following column titles: *Common Name of Plant; Fruit or Vegetable; Part of the Plant Eaten; Cooked, Raw, or Both; My Favorite.* Have each student make a copy in their Science Notebook to record his or her results.

Engagement Guide

- Challenge students to think about how many of the food plants they were able to classify as a fruit or vegetable and whether they were able to determine the plant part that is eaten by asking:
  - *How were you able to determine if the plant food was a fruit or vegetable?* (Knowing which structure—root, stem, or leaf—the plant food represents helps determine that it is a vegetable, and seeing seeds or remains of a flower part helps determine that it is a fruit.)
  - *Why are some fruits mistaken as vegetables?* (Students should recognize that if a plant food is not sweet, it might be called a vegetable even if it has developed from a flower.)
  - *What are some common fruits that people refer to as vegetables?* (Many students will use tomatoes as an example.)
- Encourage students to communicate their conclusions by making data tables to show their results.

Going Further

Encourage students to list foods they think are fruits and, separately, foods they think are vegetables other than those used in this activity. After they write these lists, have students do research to find out the correct classifications. Students should correct their lists and put a star next to those answers that surprised them. Then, have students compare lists with those of classmates.

11B Investigating Stomata

Objectives

- prepare two wet mounts of green onion epidermis in different environments
- locate and observe stomata of both onion wet mounts
- compare and contrast the stomata of both wet mounts
- determine the effect of the different environments on stomata appearance

Skill Set

observing, comparing and contrasting, recording data, predicting, stating conclusions

Planning

 1 class period 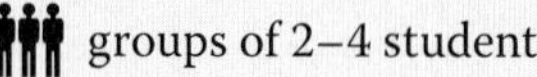 groups of 2–4 students

Materials

Materials for this activity are listed in the Student Laboratory Manual.

Lab Tip

It may be necessary for some students to remove their goggles to see objects clearly when using the microscope.

Advance Preparation

To prepare the 4% salt solution, mix 4 g of NaCl (table salt) in 96 mL of water. Place solution in dropper bottles for easy dispensing. Other plant leaves may be substituted, but green onion (leek) is superior for this activity and is readily available in grocery stores. **CAUTION:** Remind students about carefully using the razor blade or scalpel. Model for students how to use the razor blade to make the proper action on the green onion. Students must make critical observations of cells in order to observe differences in cell appearance.

Answers to Observations: Data Table 1

The drawing of the onion wet mount with water should show that the guard cells have absorbed water, swelling so the stomata are open. An epidermis cell, guard cell, and stoma should be labeled. The onion wet mount with salt should show that the guard cells have lost water and shrunk, closing the stomata. An epidermis cell, guard cell, and stoma should be labeled.

Answers to Analysis and Conclusions

1. thicker
2. The stomata in water are open, and the stomata in the salt solution are closed.
3. Water moves out of the cells, from an area of higher concentration to an area of lower concentration. It helps to have students draw their answer for this to help them see what is happening.
4. As water is lost, the guard cells become smaller, or less plump and less rigid. As water is gained, the guard cells become larger, or plumper and more rigid.
5. A less-rigid cell causes the stomata to close. A more-rigid cell causes the stomata to open.
6. As cells fill with water, pressure builds, causing the thick cell wall to bulge or push open. Cells that lose water cause the cell walls to shrink due to cell collapse.
7. When sugar is formed in guard cells, water moves into these cells from adjoining cells. This causes the guard cells to swell, opening the stomata.

Going Further

Bring in two live plants, such as ivy. Put one plant in the dark and one in the light for several days prior to conducting this activity. Have students form hypotheses about the number of open stomata found in the plant kept in the dark compared to a plant in the light. Have students select a leaf from each plant. With the underside of the leaf facing upward, have them bend and then tear the leaf at an angle to reveal part of the thin, colorless lower epidermis. Have them peel off some epidermis and observe it under the microscope. Then have each student write a conclusion, determine if his or her hypothesis was correct, and share results with the rest of the class.

11C Seed Adaptations

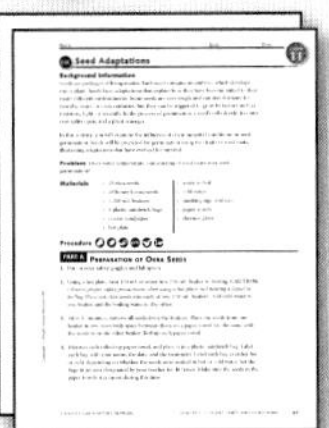

Objectives

- prepare seeds for germination using two different treatments for each type of seed
- count and record the number of seeds that germinate for each treatment
- determine if water temperature and scarring of seed coats alter seed germination
- relate seed coat adaptation to the seeds' responses to different environmental conditions

Skill Set

observing, recording and analyzing data, relating, stating conclusions

Planning

1 class period (additional time will be needed after 48 hours)

 groups of 2–4 students

Materials

Materials for this activity are listed in the Student Laboratory Manual. The number of seeds may be reduced from 20 to 10 if they are in short supply.

Lab Tip

Make sure "cold" water is cold enough. Tap water may not be cold enough to produce the anticipated results.

Advance Preparation

For seeds that will be scarred, use seeds that are fairly large and flat, such as honey locust, black locust, watermelon, or pumpkin seeds. This activity is started on day 1 and concludes 48 hours later. The conclusion may be delayed to 72 or 96 hours if necessary. Student questions refer to class totals, not individual data.

Answers to Observations: Data Table 1

Students' data will vary. However, hot okra should show a higher percentage of germination than cold okra. Scarred locust should show a higher percentage of germination than unscarred locust.

Answers to Observations: Data Table 2

Class data will vary. However, trends in germination should be the same as for individual results.

Answers to Analysis and Conclusions

1. Those soaked in hot water show a higher germination percentage than do those soaked in cold water.
2. The cold temperatures will kill the seedlings.
3. The water temperature is warmer in the spring than in the fall or winter. The weather is warm and the plant is able to grow through an entire season.
4. Those with a scarred seed coat allow water in for germination. Very few of those seeds with unscarred seed coats germinated.
5. The seed coat must first be cracked or scarred (scraped).
6. Wind action may scrape the seeds against the soil. Bacteria may also soften the seed coat. Animals that eat certain fruits scratch the seeds up when they travel through the animal's intestinal tract.

Going Further

Have students design a controlled experiment to test other environmental factors that might affect seed germination. For example, students might soak seeds in different detergent solutions (1%, 10%) and use a control with no detergent. Have students share experiment conclusions by making posters that include their data and a graph. Encourage them to include any researched information about the effects of chemicals on seed germination. Students should present their posters to the class.

Unit 4

Case Study 1: Not-So-Delicious Apples

Gather More Information

Encourage students to use the library or the NSTA SciLinks Web site noted at the start of each chapter to learn more about these case study topics and to conduct further research.

Have students use the following keywords to aid their searches:

- Red Delicious apple
- grafting
- genetic mutation
- sports
- apple grower
- rootstock tree

Research the Big Picture

- Have students work in small groups to develop an idea for a new or improved fruit that can be grown using grafting. Groups should consider new desirable traits and the possibility of breeding out existing desirable traits. Each group should then share its creation in a poster presentation containing a detailed description of the new or improved fruit, possible negative aspects, and illustrations.
- Have students work in pairs to identify pros and cons of the new Red Delicious apple described in the feature and decide whether or not growers developed a better apple. All pairs who think growers ended up making a better apple should come together to discuss why they made this decision. All pairs who think the new apple is not better should do the same. The two groups should then debate the sides of the issue.

Case Study 2: Arctic Bank

Gather More Information

Encourage students to use the library or the NSTA SciLinks Web site noted at the start of each chapter to learn more about these case study topics and to conduct further research.

Have students use the following keywords to aid their searches:

- arctic vault
- extinction
- seed bank
- Norway's Svalbard Islands
- plant species

SCIENCE JOURNAL

Not-So-Delicious Apples

THE FRUIT KNOWN as the Red Delicious apple first appeared in an Iowa field in the 1880s. This round, juicy apple was called the Hawkeye. People loved it and later renamed it the Delicious apple. Although it was very popular, breeders thought they could improve sales of the apple by improving it. The improvements changed the apple's original shape, color, and taste almost completely.

Over the years, breeders crossed Delicious apples with apples that had a less rounded shape and a redder color. They renamed it the "Red" Delicious. Careful breeding made it crispy and firmed its skin so it would not bruise easily. Breeders also changed the apple to make it last longer on the store shelf.

Unfortunately, breeding can go too far. Breeding for one desirable trait can accidentally breed out other desirable traits. For example, apples with genes for a deep red color may also have genes that make them less sweet or less juicy. Breeders may end up with beautiful, red apples that people would rather look at than eat! This is what happened to the Red Delicious. At some point, it became a beautiful, crispy, firm, long-lasting apple that just didn't taste as good as the original.

Once a new variety has been bred, how do growers produce only that variety of apples? The answer lies in a process called grafting. Most apples you buy in stores came from trees propagated by grafting rather than trees grown from seeds.

In grafting, growers cut pieces from the tips of branches of trees that produce a particular variety of fruit. These branch tips will become grafts. Growers then attach the grafts to the ends of the branches of a rootstock chosen for its hardiness. The rootstock's branches and their new branch tips grow together. Year after year, each tree produces the same variety of fruit as the tree from which the grafts came.

Occasionally, however, slight variations may occur as a result of gene mutations. Branches in which these mutations occur are called sports. A sport might form apples with a desirable trait, such as a redder color, more sweetness, or a slightly different shape. Growers can graft branch tips from a sport onto a rootstock to produce apples with the desirable new trait. And, this is how an 1880s Iowa farmer's discovery began its journey to becoming the Red Delicious apple.

Research and Report

There are hundreds of varieties of apples. The Red Delicious is just one of them. With a partner, research one of the apple varieties. Find its origin, its characteristics, how it is used, and how it was developed. Include a drawing of the apple, as well as a map that shows where farmers grow it today.

CAREER CONNECTION ORGANIC FARMER

MANY PEOPLE WANT healthier, safer foods. They want fruits and vegetables free of chemicals. They don't want to eat plants or animals that have been genetically altered. They also want to make sure their food is produced in a way that protects the environment. Organic farmers provide the foods that such people want to buy.

Like other farmers, organic farmers must produce good crops. However, they make sure their crops get nutrients and are protected from diseases and pests in different ways. They do not use chemical fertilizers or chemical poisons to help keep foods safer and reduce pollution.

To grow crops naturally, organic farmers must know how their crops interact with the soil and with other living organisms. Instead of using pesticides, they might attract beneficial insects that eat crop pests. To enrich the soil, they might rotate crops. Organic farmers also use natural fertilizers, such as compost.

Organic farmers love living on the land, and they enjoy providing fresh, healthy food to their own families and to other people.

206

Research the Big Picture

- Have students work in small groups to discuss how scientists may have come to the decision to create a seed bank on the Svalbard Islands. Ask students to use the scientific method to guide their thinking. Have each group share its ideas with the class.
- Tell students that the survival of a species depends on the resources available to that species. Ask students to work in pairs to consider the resources that are necessary for plants to survive. Then, have students think about resources that could become unavailable if a disease attacked one type of food crop or if a natural disaster occurred. Finally, have each group create one such plausible scenario and its consequences to plants and share their ideas with the class.

Arctic Bank

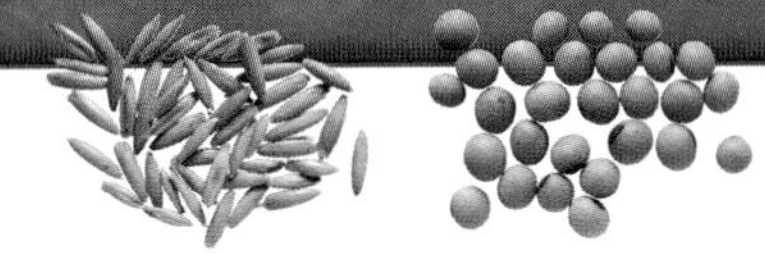

ON A SMALL, windswept island at the edge of the Arctic Ocean, scientists are busily burying something of great importance. They are storing this treasure in a vault deep in a mountainside. The vault has thick, concrete walls. Huge steel doors stand at the entrance. Outside, a sturdy fence surrounds the vault, and polar bears roam the grounds. What is being hidden in the vault? Seeds. Millions of seeds.

Why bury millions of seeds in an arctic vault? The reason is that burying the seeds could prevent the extinction of many plant species. Scientists know that regional wars have already wiped out some unique types of plants. They worry that even greater damage could be done by a global disaster, such as a large-scale war, a natural catastrophe, or a disease that attacks a type of food crop. The result could be the disappearance of many important plants—and the seeds that could grow into new ones.

The seed bank being constructed on Norway's Svalbard Islands is the scientific community's response to this potential disaster. Many of the world's nations will cooperate to stock the seed bank. The bank will serve as insurance against losing crop species and as a means of preserving Earth's plant diversity. It will contain seeds of every food crop grown today—even unique plants that grow in limited areas. So if a type of plant disappears from the world outside the vault, it won't be lost forever.

The Svalbard Islands site is an excellent choice of location. There, the vault is very safe. The seeds are well preserved by constant cold temperatures, always below freezing. If the electricity were to fail, permafrost around the vault would keep the seeds cold.

Although there are other seed banks on Earth, the one on the remote island off Norway will be the largest. When all two million seeds are safely in place, this vault will protect a treasure more valuable than gold—the continuation of plant species.

The Fastest Vine in the South

YOU CAN RIP IT OUT of the ground. You can pour pesticides on it. You can even set fire to it. Yet you still might not kill it. That's the problem with kudzu, a fast-growing vine that is creeping across America.

Kudzu is an invasive species—one that doesn't grow here naturally. Because it's native to Japan, it has no natural enemies in North America. It just grows wild—and fast. This vine can grow up to 30 cm per day!

Wherever kudzu takes root, it smothers everything around it. It grows over other plants, killing them. It twists itself around trees, often uprooting them.

Kudzu was first brought to the United States in 1876. People in the South were soon planting the fast-growing vines to provide decoration and shade on porches. Today, it has spread as far north as Massachusetts and as far west as Texas and Iowa.

To begin to eliminate kudzu, a combination of mowing, pesticides, and burning is needed. Scientists are also considering the use of a beetle native to Asia that attacks kudzu roots. But they will not import the beetle until they know that it will not attack other native species. They are cautious about solving one problem by creating another!

Case Study 3: The Fastest Vine in the South

Gather More Information

Encourage students to use the library or the NSTA SciLinks Web site noted at the start of each chapter to learn more about these case study topics and to conduct further research.

Have students use the following keywords to aid their searches:

- kudzu
- pesticide
- invasive species
- vine
- native Japanese plant species

Research the Big Picture

- Have students work with a partner to speculate about why kudzu has been able to survive and take over so many areas of the United States. Students should think about the plant's possible adaptations over time as it has been transplanted to many different areas and climates.
- Have students hypothesize about what will happen as a result of attempts to eliminate kudzu (a combination of mowing, pesticides, and burning). Students should consider whether these methods will or will not be successful and explain their ideas.
- Have students work in groups to discuss how scientists could ensure that the use of Asian beetles is a safe, successful way to eliminate kudzu in the United States. Students should also discuss what negative consequences could occur if scientists brought Asian beetles into the country to attack kudzu without ensuring success beforehand. Each group should present its ideas to the class.

CONNECTION: Career

Before students read the Career Connection feature, have them refer back to the Career Research project they completed earlier. Have them recall that organic farmer is one of the jobs they may have researched. Remind them that organic farmers grow crops without the use of chemical fertilizers or pesticides.

Ask students to read the feature and take notes on any new information they find and any questions they have.

Have students share their questions and record them on the board. Ask students to brainstorm how they could get answers to their questions (go to an organic market, send a letter to a local organic farmer, interview the produce manager of a local grocery store, invite an organic farmer to address the class, etc.). Have pairs of students make and carry out a plan to obtain the answers.

Unit 5

Animals

Introduce Unit 5

Ask students to brainstorm with a partner what they already know about animals. Then, have students look at the photos and read the questions on this page. As a class, have students share what they noticed in the photos and what they think the answers to the questions might be. Ask students to think of other animal-related questions, and have them write these in their Science Notebooks. Tell them to add to and answer their questions as they read the unit.

Unit Projects

For each project below, students can use the Student Presentation Builder on the Student CD-ROM to display their results and their Science Notebooks for their project notes.

Career Have each student research a career that is related to animals (e.g., animal shelter worker, wildlife rehabilitation worker, animal breeder, guide dog trainer, conservation education specialist). Ask each student to define the job, describe what it entails, and identify the skills or experience needed for the job. Have each student prepare a brochure describing his or her chosen career.

Apply Have students observe animals during out-of-school hours for two weeks. Suggest going to a zoo, an aquarium, or a pet store or watching a birdfeeder or a pet. Have each student create a journal with space for recording the date, time, and visual details for each observation session. Each student should write a summary of what he or she observed and learned.

Technology Assign each student one of the following animal groups to research: invertebrates, arthropods, echinoderms, fishes, amphibians, reptiles, birds, or mammals. Have them decide which type of technology would most effectively enable them to determine where on Earth the animals in the assigned group live.

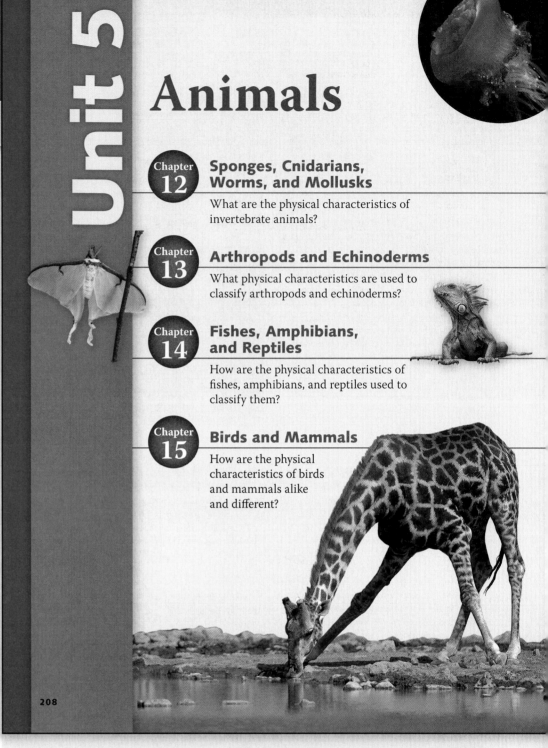

Unit 5

Animals

Software Summary

Student CD-ROM
- —Interactive Student Book
- —Vocabulary Review
- —Key Concept Review
- —Lab Report Template
- —ELL Preview and Writing Activities
- —Presentation Digital Library
- —Graphic Organizing Software
- —Spanish Cognate Dictionary

Interactive Labs
- Chapter 12C—Modeling an Open and Closed Circulatory System
- Chapter 13C—Examining Insect Metamorphosis
- Chapter 14C—Frog Anatomy
- Chapter 15C—Who Did It?

Sponges, Cnidarians, Worms, and Mollusks

Chapter 12

KEY CONCEPT Invertebrate animals can be classified based on their physical characteristics.

You put on your diving gear and jump into the cool, clear ocean water. As you go deeper, you notice an amazing variety of fishes and other animals that you do not recognize.

Sponges, corals, and jellyfish are all types of organisms you might find during your underwater exploration. These unusual animals have special characteristics that allow them to live in Earth's great ocean depths.

Think About Identifying Animals

Animals inhabit Earth's land, air, and water. Each animal has a specific role to play in its environment and special characteristics that help it survive.

- Spend some time observing and thinking about the animals you see on a regular basis. Then, look through books and magazines for pictures of animals that may be less familiar because they live in places not easily observed.
- In your Science Notebook, make a T-chart. Label one column *Land* and the other column *Water*. List at least ten animals that live in each type of environment. At the bottom of each column, identify some characteristics that those animals must have in order to live successfully in that environment.

www.scilinks.org
Animals **Code: WGB12**

209

Chapter 12 Lessons

Chapter 12 Planning Guide			
Instructional Periods	National Standards	Lab Manual	Workbook
12.1 1 period	A.2, C.1, C.2; C.3; UCP.1, UCP.5	**Lab 12A—p. 70** Identifying Symmetry **Lab 12B—p. 71** Observing Earthworm Responses **Lab 12C—p. 74** Modeling an Open and Closed Circulatory System	Key Concept Review p. 76 Vocabulary Review p. 77 Interpreting Diagrams p. 78 Reading Comprehension p. 79 Curriculum Connection p. 80 Science Challenge p. 81
12.2 2 periods	C.1, C.2; C.1, C.3; UCP.2, UCP.5		
12.3 2 periods	A.1, C.1; UCP.3, UCP.5		
12.4 2 periods	C.1, C.2, C.5; C.4, F.6, G.3; UCP.3, UCP.5		
12.5 2 periods	B.2, C.1; C.4; CP.5		

Middle School Standard; High School Standard; Unifying Concept and Principle

Introduce Chapter 12

As a starting activity, use LAB 12A Identifying Symmetry on page 70 of the Laboratory Manual.

ENGAGE Tell students that they are going to take a virtual tour of an ocean. Ask them to close their eyes and imagine the sights under the water. Encourage them to remember what they've seen at aquariums and zoos or in fish tanks. Ask a few students to share what they "see." Afterward, ask students to open their eyes. Show pictures of sponges, corals, and jellyfish to students, and tell them that these are some of the animals that they will be learning about.

Think About Identifying Animals

Encourage a class discussion of the concept that the success or failure of one animal species can affect the survival of other species. Ask students to supply examples of this idea. Then, ask why it is important for humans to do what they can to protect animals in nature. Make sure students consider both land and water animals.

Direct students to complete each bulleted activity. Provide a variety of illustrated books and magazines such as *National Geographic* for students to review. As a class, complete a T-chart for a leopard and an octopus.

12.1 Introduce

ENGAGE Create a T-chart on the board. Label one column *Invertebrate* and the other *Vertebrate*. Then, have students brainstorm a list of animals next to the chart. Ask volunteers to choose animals from the list and write them in the correct columns. Have students record this in their Science Notebooks and correct it as they complete Unit 5.

Before You Read

Have pairs of students discuss their definitions and the three characteristics. Ask them to revise their original writings based on their discussions.

Vocabulary terms are listed on the first student page of each lesson. You may wish to preview the terms before introducing each lesson. Strategies for teaching the vocabulary appear on the pages where the terms are introduced.

Teach

EXPLAIN that students will begin studying the animal kingdom by learning about common characteristics of invertebrates.

Vocabulary

sexual reproduction Explain that sexual reproduction happens when a sperm cell and egg cell combine to create a new individual.

asexual reproduction Tell students that the prefix *a-* means "not" or "without." Asexual reproduction refers to an organism's ability to reproduce by itself.

vertebrate Tell students that a vertebra is one of the bones of the backbone, or spinal column. An animal that has a backbone is called a vertebrate.

invertebrate Explain that the prefix *in-* means "not." An invertebrate is an animal that does not have a backbone.

radial symmetry Tell students that *radial* means "like radii" (*radii* is the plural of *radius*). Explain that *symmetry* describes a figure that is the same or corresponding in shape and size.

bilateral symmetry Explain that the prefix *bi-* means "two," and *lateral* is "of the side." An animal with bilateral symmetry has symmetry on two sides.

asymmetrical Remind students that the prefix *a-* means "not." An asymmetrical shape does not have symmetry.

Learning Goals

- Identify the common characteristics of animals.
- Describe the difference between vertebrates and invertebrates.
- Compare the three types of animal symmetry.

New Vocabulary

sexual reproduction
asexual reproduction
vertebrate
invertebrate
radial symmetry
bilateral symmetry
asymmetrical

12.1 Introduction to Animals

Before You Read

In your Science Notebook, write your own definition of the word *animal*. Make a drawing of an animal, and list three physical characteristics that make it an animal.

Think of some of the living things you see on your way to school each day, such as people, birds, dogs, cats, and insects. What do all of these organisms have in common? You would be correct if you said that they are all different types of animals. The animal kingdom includes an amazing variety of living things, from tiny insects to giant jellyfish to giraffes to people like you.

Characteristics of Animals

All animals have characteristics that separate them from bacteria, fungi, protists, and plants. One of these characteristics is nutrition. Unlike plants, animals depend on other livings things for food. Some animals eat plants, some eat other animals, and some eat both plants and animals.

All animals are multicellular, which means they are made up of many cells. Your own body is made up of between 10 trillion and 100 trillion cells. An animal cell has a nucleus and other organelles, is surrounded by a cell membrane, and lacks a cell wall.

Most animals are motile, which means they are able to move from place to place. Moving around enables animals to escape from enemies and find important things, such as food, water, shelter, and mates.

Animals usually reproduce by sexual reproduction. **Sexual reproduction** occurs when a sperm cell and an egg cell join to form a new organism. Some animals, however, can reproduce asexually. **Asexual reproduction** occurs when an individual produces a new individual identical to itself.

Figure It Out

1. What physical characteristics do all of the animals shown have in common?
2. Identify ways in which these animals are different from one another.

Figure 12.1 From *(left to right)*, the monarch butterfly, sea slug, rhinoceros, and dolphin are all members of the animal kingdom.

Figure It Out: Figure 12.1

ANSWER 1. They are multicellular, motile, and have bilateral symmetry. 2. They have different colors, shapes, sizes, diets, methods of reproduction, and body systems.

ELL Strategy

Use a Concept Map Have students draw a concept map with *Animal* as the main topic and the characteristics of animals as subtopics in their Science Notebooks. Students can include details or examples for each subtopic.

Peer Tutoring English-language learners may not be familiar with the English names for common animals. Pair these students with peer tutors familiar with the names.

Groups of Animals

The animal kingdom can be divided into two large groups: vertebrates and invertebrates. A **vertebrate** (VUR tuh brayt) is an animal that has a backbone. Humans, snakes, horses, tigers, and dogs are all examples of vertebrates. An **invertebrate** (ihn VUR tuh brayt) is an animal that does not have a backbone. Grasshoppers, earthworms, octopuses, and jellyfish are all invertebrates. Invertebrates make up about 95 percent of all animal species.

Animals can also be divided into groups based on their body plan, the way the features of the body are arranged. **Figure 12.2** shows the three basic body plans of animals. Animals with **radial** (RAY dee ul) **symmetry** have bodies that are arranged in a circle around a central point, the way spokes are arranged around the hub of a bicycle wheel. These animals have a top and a bottom, but no front, back, or head. If you were to draw an imaginary line across the top of a jellyfish, you would see that both halves look the same. You could draw the line in any direction and still see two halves that look alike.

Animals with **bilateral** (bi LA tuh rul) **symmetry** have bodies with two similar halves. They can be divided into right and left halves by drawing an imaginary line down the length of the body. Animals with bilateral symmetry have a front side, back side, head end, and tail end. If you draw an imaginary line down the middle of a lizard's body, you will see the same features on both sides of the line.

The simplest animals have no symmetry and are called **asymmetrical**. The prefix *a-* means "without." Sponges are asymmetrical.

CONNECTION: Geography

One of the characteristics common to most animals is their ability to move freely from one place to another. People of all cultures use animals such as horses, camels, elephants, llamas, and donkeys to transport goods. Each culture must use animals that are well adapted to the local climate.

After You Read

1. List three common characteristics of all animals.
2. How is a vertebrate different from an invertebrate? How does this difference explain the fact that the bodies of invertebrates are usually smaller than those of vertebrates?
3. Review the animal drawing in your Science Notebook. Identify the type of symmetry the animal has, and explain how this type of symmetry will help it survive in its environment.

As You Read

Look at the animal you drew in your Science Notebook.

Is your animal a vertebrate or an invertebrate? Explain your answer.

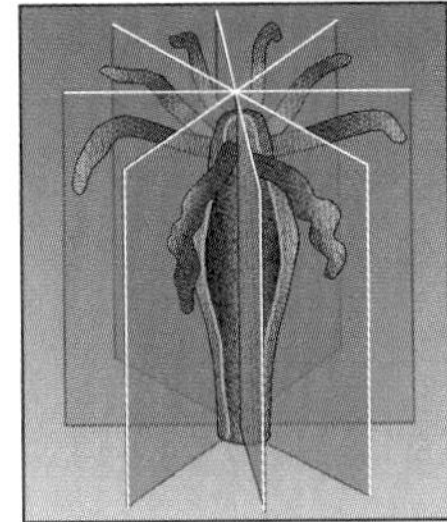

Radial symmetry

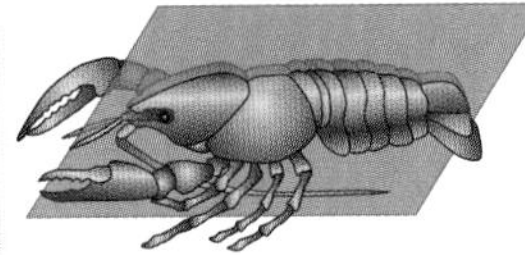

Bilateral symmetry

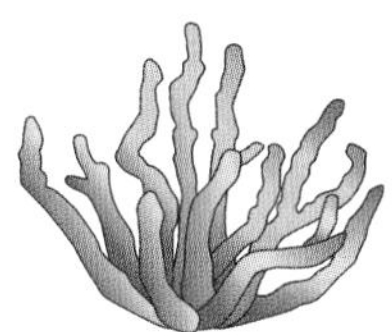

Asymmetry

Figure 12.2 The body plan of an animal helps it survive in its environment. What type of body plan do humans have?

Teach

ENGAGE Show students several geometric shapes, such as hexagons, squares, parallelograms, and scalene triangles. Ask them to classify the shapes as being asymmetrical or having bilateral or radial symmetry.

EXPLAIN that animals are grouped according to whether or not they have a backbone and according to its shape.

As You Read

Give students a few minutes to review the picture of the animal they drew. Have them identify the animal as a vertebrate or an invertebrate and to define its type of symmetry. Ask a few students to share their animals and their classifications.

Use the Visual: Figure 12.2

ANSWER Humans have bilateral symmetry.

CONNECTION: Geography

Give students a world climate map. Ask them to hypothesize about which of the animals in the feature would be best suited to transporting goods in various climates.

Assess

EVALUATE Use the After You Read questions and the Alternative Assessment to help you assess students' understanding of the lesson.

After You Read

1. Animals must eat food, their cells lack cell walls, and they are multicellular.
2. Vertebrates have backbones, and invertebrates do not. Invertebrate bodies are generally smaller because they do not have a backbone to support body weight.
3. Students should correctly explain how a type of symmetry helps the animal survive in its environment.

Alternative Assessment

EVALUATE Have each student draw an animal to illustrate each type of body plan: asymmetrical, radical symmetry, and bilateral symmetry.

Differentiated Instruction

Kinesthetic Make available different animal skeletons or models for students to explore. The examples should include vertebrates and invertebrates, as well as animals with different types of symmetry. Give students time to explore the models, and then ask them to classify the animals and to explain their reasons for the classifications.

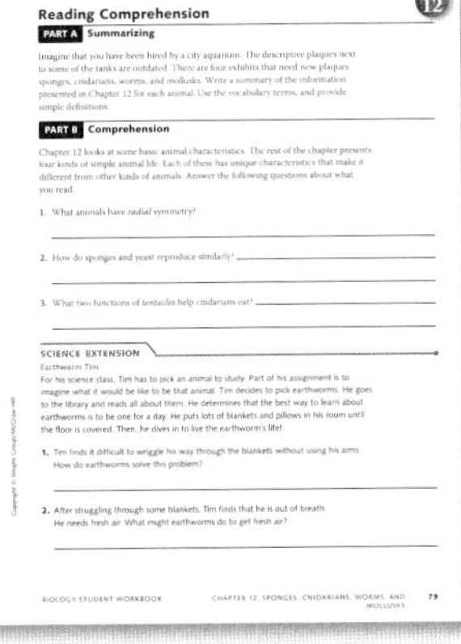

Name Date Time Chapter 12

Reading Comprehension

PART A Summarizing

Imagine that you have been hired by a city aquarium. The descriptive plaques next to some of the tanks are outdated. There are four exhibits that need new plaques: sponges, cnidarians, worms, and mollusks. Write a summary of the information presented in Chapter 12 for each animal. Use the vocabulary terms, and provide simple definitions.

PART B Comprehension

Chapter 12 looks at some basic animal characteristics. The rest of the chapter presents four kinds of simple animal life. Each of these has unique characteristics that make it different from other kinds of animals. Answer the following questions about what you read.

1. What animals have *radial* symmetry?
2. How do sponges and yeast reproduce similarly?
3. What two functions of *tentacles* help cnidarians eat?

SCIENCE EXTENSION

Earthworm Tim

For his science class, Tim has to pick an animal to study. Part of his assignment is to imagine what it would be like to be that animal. Tim decides to pick earthworms. He goes to the library and reads all about them. He determines that the best way to learn about earthworms is to be one for a day. He puts lots of blankets and pillows in his room until the floor is covered. Then, he dives in to live the earthworm's life!

1. Tim finds it difficult to wriggle his way through the blankets without using his arms. How do earthworms solve this problem?
2. After struggling through some blankets, Tim finds that he is out of breath. He needs fresh air. What might earthworms do to get fresh air?

BIOLOGY STUDENT WORKBOOK CHAPTER 12 SPONGES, CNIDARIANS, WORMS, AND MOLLUSKS 79

Reading Comprehension Workbook, p. 79

12.2 Introduce

ENGAGE Place a variety of natural sponges in a closed box with an opening big enough for a student's hand, so that the contents cannot be seen. Tell students that they are going to feel the simplest kind of invertebrates, and ask them to hypothesize what they are. Ask them to write down their hypotheses and to keep them private until everyone has had a chance to guess. Pass the closed box around the room, and allow each student to touch the sponges. At the end of the activity, ask students to share their hypotheses and the reasons behind them. Then, show the sponges to the students.

Before You Read

Draw and label the two circles on the board. Ask students to reflect on how the sponges in the box felt and to name one or two characteristics of sponges. Write the characteristics in the larger circle, and ask students to complete their own circles in their Science Notebooks. Check students' examples throughout the lesson.

Teach

EXPLAIN that in this lesson, students will gain new understandings of sponges, including what characteristics they share.

Vocabulary

filter feeding Encourage students to think about common uses of the word *filter*, and discuss them with the class. Students might mention a coffee filter, oil filter, or filter on a search engine.

spicules Explain that *spicule* is from the Latin word *spiculum*, meaning "sharp point" or "dart."

budding Tell students that a bud is a small swelling or group of cells that will create a new sponge. Since a sponge can do this by itself, it is an example of asexual reproduction.

regeneration Explain that the Latin prefix *re-* means "again," and *generare* is Latin for "to produce." When a sponge regenerates, it produces a part of itself again.

Figure It Out: Figure 12.3

ANSWER **1.** Sponges have pores, live in water, are not able to move as adults, have hollow bodies shaped like sacs, are asymmetrical, and filter feed. **2.** shape, color, and size

12.2 Sponges

Learning Goals

- Identify the common characteristics of sponges.
- Describe the physical appearance of a sponge.
- Explain how sponges reproduce.

New Vocabulary

filter feeding
spicule
budding
regeneration

Before You Read

In your Science Notebook, create a concept map with the word *Sponge* in the center. Draw a circle outside the smaller circle. In the outside circle, write or draw any information that you predict describes the characteristics of a sponge.

Examine a kitchen sponge closely and you will see that it is filled with pores, or little holes. These pores are what give sponges their phylum name Porifera (puh RIH fuh ruh), which means "pore bearer." Your artificial kitchen sponge was most likely made by humans, but natural sponges are animals that live in water.

Characteristics of Sponges

Sponges are the simplest group of invertebrates. They are asymmetrical and are found in a variety of colors, shapes, and sizes. Most species of sponges live in the ocean, but a few species live in freshwater. As adults, sponges are not able to move. Because they show little or no movement, sponges were once classified as plants. Since sponges cannot conduct photosynthesis like plants do, they are now classified as animals.

A sponge has a hollow body shaped like a sac. The inside of the sponge's body contains two layers of cells. Moving water carries algae, tiny animals, and oxygen through the pores into the sponge. The sponge's cells remove the food and oxygen from the water in a process called **filter feeding**. The cells also release waste products into the water. The water and waste products leave the sponge through a larger opening at the top of its body.

Did You Know?

Some sponges can pump 10,000 times their own size in water in one day. A sponge the size of a two-liter soft drink bottle could pump enough water to fill a swimming pool in one day!

Figure It Out

1. Describe physical characteristics that all sponges have in common.
2. Identify ways in which these sponges are different from one another.

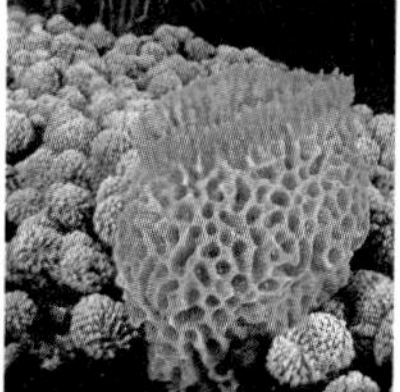

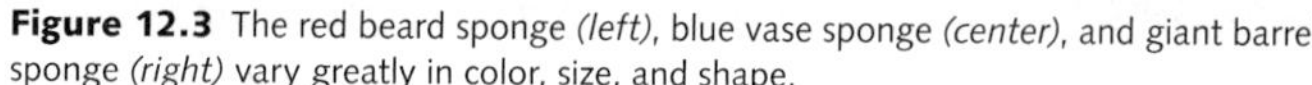

Figure 12.3 The red beard sponge *(left)*, blue vase sponge *(center)*, and giant barrel sponge *(right)* vary greatly in color, size, and shape.

ELL Strategy

Visual Provide both kitchen and natural sponges for students. Have students sketch both in their Science Notebooks and label the structures of the sponges.

Teacher Alert

The use of *ocean* in this text refers to saltwater. However, *sea* could be used interchangeably, as both words refer to saltwater. All the world's oceans and seas are part of one continuous mass of seawater; seas are usually smaller than oceans and are partially enclosed by land.

Structure of a Sponge

A sponge has a skeleton that supports its cells. Many sponges have skeletons made of small, sharp structures called **spicules** (SPIH kyewlz). Spicules are made of either a glasslike or a chalky substance. In other sponges, the skeletons are made of a softer, rubberlike substance. These sponges are the ones used as bath sponges. In still other sponges, the skeletons are made of both spicules and the rubberlike substance. A sponge's spiny skeleton helps protect it from predators. Some sponges release poisonous chemicals as a defense mechanism against predators that try to eat them.

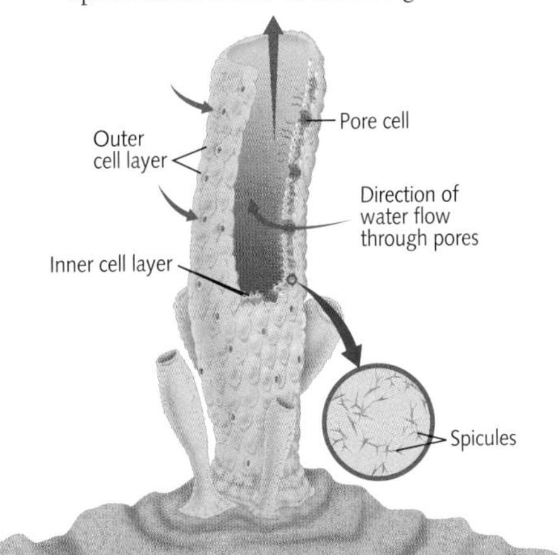

Figure 12.5 A sponge has no tissues, organs, or organ systems. The body of a sponge consists of two layers of cells surrounding a central cavity. The red arrows indicate the flow of water into and out of the sponge.

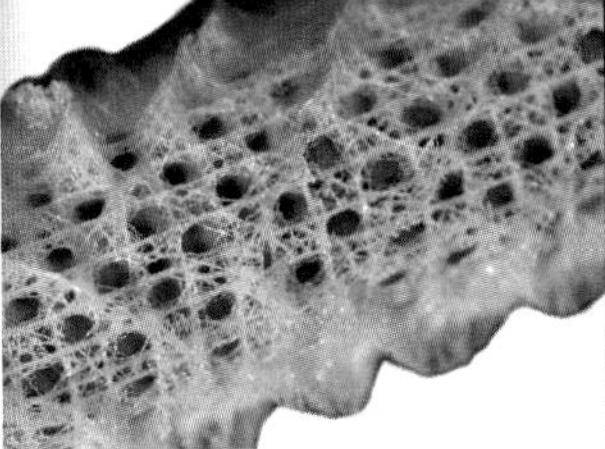

Figure 12.4 The skeleton of the glass sponge is made of thousands of glasslike spicules. What is one function of the spicules?

As You Read

Look at the characteristics of sponges you predicted in your Science Notebook. Add characteristics to your concept map.

What is regeneration?

Reproduction in a Sponge

Sponges reproduce both asexually and sexually. Sponges reproduce asexually by **budding**. In budding, a small bulge grows on the side of a sponge. When this bulge falls off the parent, it grows into a new sponge. The ability of an organism to regrow body parts is called **regeneration** (rih je nuh RAY shun). Regeneration is common among simple animals.

Most sponges produce both sperm cells and egg cells, but at different times of the year. During sexual reproduction, sperm are released by the sponge and carried through the water to the eggs of another sponge. The fertilized egg develops into a swimming larva. The larva attaches itself to a rock or the ocean floor and develops into an adult sponge.

Explore It!

Use a hand lens to observe pieces of artificial and natural sponges. How are the sponges similar? How are they different? Design and conduct an activity that compares how well each type of sponge absorbs water.

After You Read

1. Review the characteristics of sponges you included in the concept map in your Science Notebook. Why are sponges classified as animals?
2. How does a sponge take food and oxygen into its body?
3. How does a sponge reproduce?

Teach

EXPLAIN that students will learn about the structure of sponges and how sponges reproduce.

Use the Visual: Figure 12.4

ANSWER support and protection

As You Read

Explain that sponges contain many pores, are filter feeders, reproduce asexually or sexually, and live in water.

ANSWER Regeneration is the ability of an organism to regrow body parts.

Explore It!

Provide natural sponges, artificial sponges, and hand lenses to students. Students may use a medicine dropper or small graduated cylinder to determine how much water each type of sponge will absorb. The pieces of sponge should be similar in size to make the results accurate. Sponges will need to be squeezed dry or weighed prior to each trial.

Assess

EVALUATE Use the After You Read questions and the Alternative Assessment to help you assess students' understanding of the lesson.

After You Read

1. They are multicellular, have cells with no cell walls, and must have food for nutrition.
2. A sponge takes in food and oxygen as water moves through its pores.
3. A sponge reproduces asexually by budding and sexually through the fertilization of an egg cell by a sperm cell.

Background Information

There are no large-scale commercial farms to grow and harvest sponges. Attempts have been made to artificially cultivate sponges in the Bahamas, the Florida Keys, and the South Pacific with mixed success. Sponge farms require a large investment of time to begin harvesting—about three to four years. The chance of disease and the high cost of labor make sponge farming a risky business.

Alternative Assessment

EVALUATE Have students draw and label a sponge. Tell students that their drawings should include spicules and demonstrate filter feeding, budding, and regeneration. (More than one drawing may be required.)

12.3 Introduce

ENGAGE Ask students to share any experiences they have had with jellyfish. Then, ask them to hypothesize about the origin of the name "jellyfish." Tell them that since jellyfish are not fish, some people call them "jellies" or "sea jellies."

Before You Read

With students, review the images in this lesson. Ask students to observe similarities, differences, and interesting features in the images, and then have them ask a question based on those observations. Direct students to write two more questions about their observations in their Science Notebooks.

Teach

EXPLAIN to students that in this lesson, they will learn about the common characteristics of cnidarians, including two body plans and two types of reproduction.

As You Read

Have students review the questions they wrote at the beginning of this lesson and answer them as they are able.

ANSWER The two types of body plans are the polyp and the medusa.

Vocabulary

tentacles Tell students that tentacles are long, thin, flexible growths that are used by cnidarians to touch, hold, and move.

polyp Explain that *polyp* is derived from the Greek words *polýs*, meaning "many," and *poús* or *podós*, meaning "foot."

medusa Share the Latin origin of *Medūsa*, given because one species has feelers that look like the snake hair of Medusa.

Science Notebook EXTRA

Have students find out what is in a jellyfish sting and what treatment is given to a victim. Have them record the information in their Science Notebooks. Encourage them to include first-aid measures they would use to assist someone who had been stung.

Learning Goals

- Identify the common characteristics of cnidarians.
- Describe the two body plans of cnidarians.
- Explain how cnidarians reproduce.
- Compare the different types of cnidarians.

New Vocabulary

tentacle
polyp
medusa

As You Read

Look at the questions in your Science Notebook. Add information that will help you answer those questions.

What are the two types of body plans cnidarians show?

12.3 Cnidarians

Before You Read

Look at the photographs and diagrams in this lesson. In your Science Notebook, write two questions that this lesson might answer. Your questions should relate to something about cnidarians that you would like to know.

Have you ever had this experience? You and a friend are walking along the beach. You see a jellyfish and start to poke it with your foot. Your friend yells out, "Be careful! Don't touch that jellyfish because it might sting you!" A jellyfish is a type of animal called a cnidarian (ni DARE ee un). Like sponges, cnidarians are invertebrate animals that live in water.

Characteristics of Cnidarians

The phylum name Cnidaria comes from the Greek word for "nettle." A nettle is a plant with stinging cells along its surface. Cnidarians are animals that have stinging cells along their bodies. Being stung by a jellyfish or other cnidarian can be a very painful experience.

Cnidarians are more complex than sponges. A cnidarian's body has a hollow central cavity with an opening called the mouth. Most cnidarians have armlike structures called tentacles that surround the mouth. The **tentacles** (TEN tih kulz) contain stinging cells that help cnidarians capture food. The stinging cells paralyze or kill prey, and the tentacles then help get the prey into the mouth to be digested in the body cavity.

Cnidarian Body Plans

Cnidarians have two basic body plans: the polyp and the medusa. The **polyp** (PAH lup) is shaped like a vase and usually does not move about. A sea anemone is a type of polyp. The **medusa** (mih DEW suh, plural: medusae) is shaped like a bell and is free to swim around. A jellyfish is a type of medusa. Both polyps and medusae have radial symmetry.

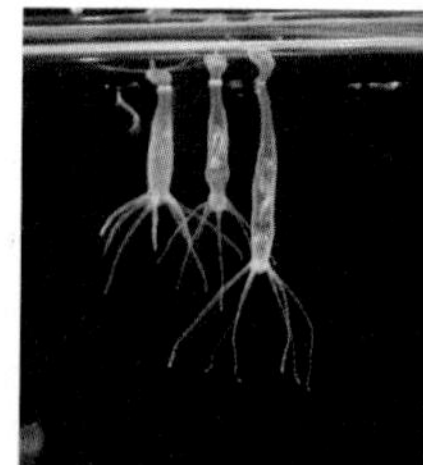

Figure 12.6 A sea anemone *(left)*, jellyfish *(center)*, and the hydras *(right)* are cnidarians.

ELL Strategy

Use a Concept Map Have each student create a concept map in his or her Science Notebook to organize the lesson's information about cnidarians. Have students include the two types of body plans, polyp and medusa, and three main classes of cnidarians, hydras, jellyfish, and sea anemones and corals. Have them add details about where the different classes live.

Background Information

In Greek mythology, Medusa was a female character whose gaze could turn people into stone. In Ovid's version of the Medusa tale, she was originally a beautiful woman who had sexual intercourse with Poseidon in Athena's temple. After Athena found out about the desecration of her temple, she punished Medusa by turning her hair into snakes and making it so that her glance would turn others into stone.

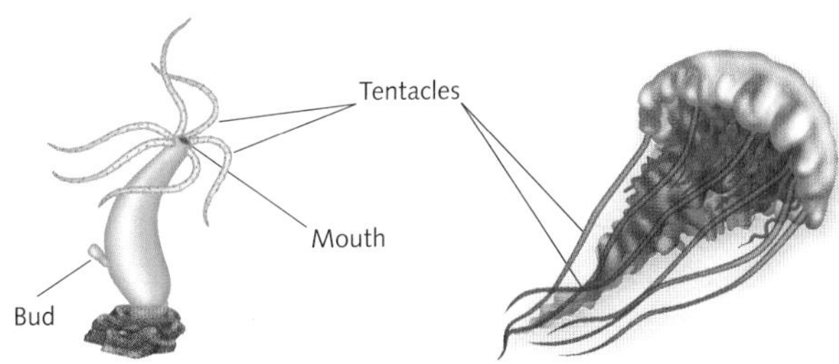

Figure 12.7 Cidarians have two basic body plans: the vase-shaped polyp *(left)* and the bell-shaped medusa *(right)*. The medusa's mouth is centered under the "bell."

Reproduction in a Cnidarian

Cnidarians reproduce both asexually and sexually. Like sponges, cnidarians reproduce asexually by forming buds that fall off the parent and grow into new polyps. **Figure 12.7** shows a bud on the polyp body plan. Cnidarians can also reproduce sexually by producing eggs and sperm. Sperm are released into the water and fertilize eggs. Many cnidarians have a life cycle that includes both a polyp stage and a medusa stage.

Types of Cnidarians

There are three main classes of cnidarians: hydras, jellyfish, and sea anemones and corals. Hydras live in freshwater and spend their entire lives as polyps. Jellyfish spend most of their time as medusae.

Sea anemones and corals are polyps that live attached to rocks on the ocean floor. They are brightly colored and look like flowers. Sea anemones are larger than corals and do not have hard outer skeletons. Corals live in large groups called colonies and have hard outer skeletons. When the coral polyps die, their skeletons remain behind. Over time, the skeletons build up and form large, rocklike structures called reefs. Coral reefs provide homes, protection, and food for many sea animals.

Figure 12.8 The Great Barrier Reef, off the coast of Australia, is the world's largest coral reef. It is 2,000 kilometers long and can be seen from space.

Figure It Out

1. How does a cnidarian obtain its food?
2. Compare the location of the mouth in the polyp and in the medusa.

Extend It!

In a small group, research the Great Barrier Reef in Australia and other coral reefs throughout the world. In your Science Notebook, write a letter to your local newspaper explaining why people should work to protect the world's coral reefs.

After You Read

1. What are the characteristics of cnidarians?
2. How are the two body forms of cnidarians the same? How are they different?
3. How do cnidarians reproduce?
4. Read the questions and answers you wrote in your Science Notebook. What changes would you make now that you have finished this lesson?

Teach

EXPLAIN to students that cnidarians reproduce by both sexual and asexual reproduction. Once students have read about reproduction in cnidarians, have them compare it to reproduction in sponges.

Figure It Out: Figure 12.7

ANSWER **1.** Stinging cells on the tentacles paralyze the prey so it can be drawn into the mouth. **2.** The mouth in the polyp faces up, and the mouth in the medusa faces down.

Extend It!

Provide resources that students can use to research the Great Barrier Reef and other coral reefs. Ask students to note important functions of reefs, and then have them each write a business-style letter to the editor of your local newspaper. Place students in pairs to review and edit their letters.

Assess

EVALUATE Use the After You Read questions and the Alternative Assessment to help you assess students' understanding of the lesson.

After You Read

1. Cnidarians are soft-bodied invertebrates that have tentacles with stinging cells and live in ocean water or freshwater.
2. Both body forms include a hollow central cavity, a mouth, and tentacles with stinging cells. The polyp is vase-shaped and usually does not move. The medusa is bell shaped and is free moving.
3. asexually, by budding, or sexually
4. Answers will vary. Accept all logical responses.

Alternative Assessment

EVALUATE Ask students to write five to seven important facts about cnidarians. Two of the facts should include information about body plans and reproduction.

Background information

Coral reefs are important for many reasons. They provide protection and shelter for many species of fish. Coral reefs are also essential in controlling how much carbon dioxide is present in the ocean water. Without coral, the amount of carbon dioxide in the water would rise and adversely affect all living things on Earth. Coral reefs also protect coasts from strong currents and waves by slowing down the water before it gets to the shore. Because coral is similar to human bone, doctors are now using it to repair serious bone breaks. In order for coral to be used for bone transplants, it is first chemically treated and all organisms are removed from it. It then has the same chemical composition and physical structure as human bone. Bone tissue and blood vessels gradually grow into the coral graft; bone eventually replaces most of the coral.

12.4 Introduce

ENGAGE Ask students to listen as you read the second, third, and fourth paragraphs on the page. As you read, tell students to quickly sketch what they think each type of worm would look like, based on the worms' names. Later, students can compare these drawings to images in the lesson.

Before You Read

Draw the three-column chart on the board, and label each of the columns. As a class, read the first few sentences about flatworms and ask students to name a flatworm's characteristics. Write the information in the appropriate column.

Have students create their own three-column charts in their Science Notebooks. Review student' charts throughout the lesson.

Teach

ENGAGE students in an introduction to flatworms by placing a live planarian in water in a 35-mm deep-well slide that can be used with a slide projector. Have students observe its movement, bilateral symmetry, head area, and flat body. Tell students that planarians have many characteristics common to all species of flatworms. Also tell students that in this lesson, they will learn about three kinds of worms—flatworms, roundworms, and segmented worms—and the ways in which they are similar and different.

Vocabulary

parasite Tell students that a parasite is an organism that lives on or in another organism from which it gets its food. A parasite is usually unable to exist independently.

anus Tell students that the anus is a structure at the end of the digestive system through which wastes leave the body.

Learning Goals

- Describe how worms are different from cnidarians.
- Identify the three main phyla of worms.
- Compare the characteristics of flatworms, roundworms, and segmented worms.

New Vocabulary

parasite
anus

12.4 Worms

Before You Read

In your Science Notebook, create a chart with three columns. Label the first column *Flatworms*, the second column *Roundworms*, and the third column *Segmented Worms*. As you learn about these three kinds of worms, add to your chart information that describes their characteristics.

A flash of lightning wakes you up as a rainstorm moves into the area. The next morning, you notice that the streets and sidewalks are covered with earthworms! The rain has flooded the earthworms' underground homes, forcing them to escape by crawling to the surface.

Earthworms are just one kind of worm in the animal kingdom. There are three main phyla of worms based on shape: flatworms, roundworms, and segmented worms. Worms are soft-bodied invertebrates.

Worms differ from cnidarians in several ways. They have bilateral symmetry with a definite head and tail. Sense organs and nerves are found in the head. They have long, narrow bodies with no arms or legs. They can live in water and on land.

Flatworms

Worms with a flattened shape are called flatworms. They are grouped in the phylum Platyhelminthes (Pla tih hel MIHN theez). The word *Platyhelminthes* comes from two Greek words: *platy*, meaning "flat," and *helminth*, meaning "worm." Flatworms are the simplest of all worms. There are three main classes of flatworms. The planarian is a free-living, freshwater flatworm. Most planarians are only a few centimeters long and are harmless to humans.

Two classes of flatworms are parasites. A **parasite** is an organism that lives inside or on another organism. Parasites take food from this organism. The two classes of parasitic flatworms are the flukes and tapeworms. Flukes live in the body tissues of animals and cause sickness. Tapeworms live in the intestines of humans and other vertebrates. The tapeworms absorb the digested food of the animals in which they live.

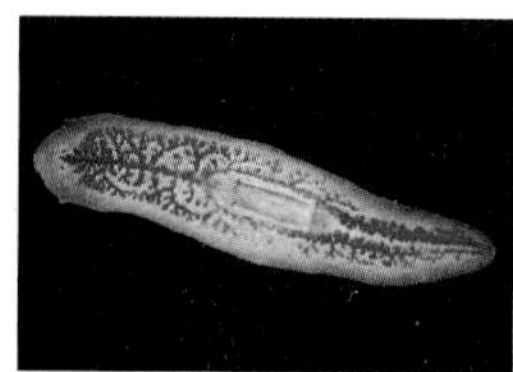

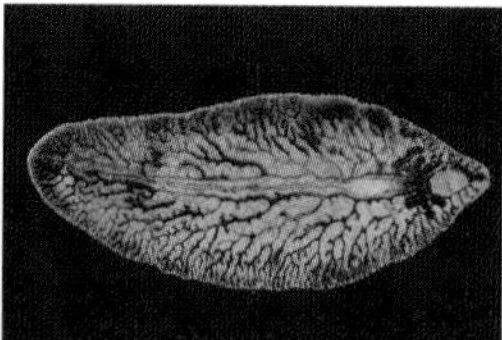

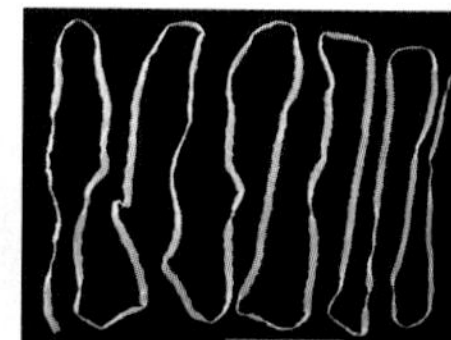

Figure 12.9 The planarian *(left)*, the fluke *(center)*, and the tapeworm *(right)* are all types of flatworms.

ELL Strategy

Illustrate Provide students with colored markers or pens, and ask them to draw and label each type of worm based on its characteristics and the images in the lesson.

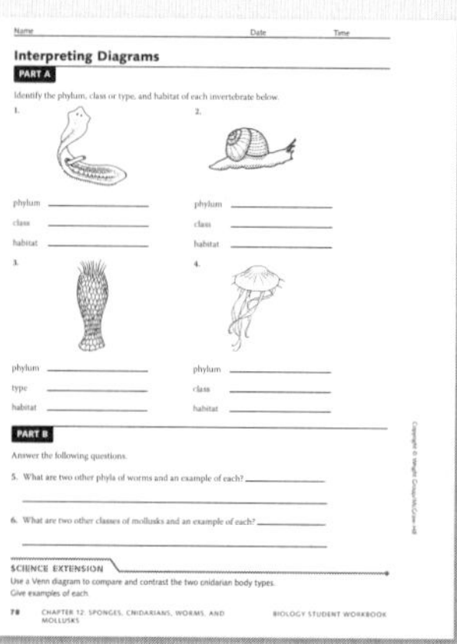

Interpreting Diagrams
Workbook, p. 78

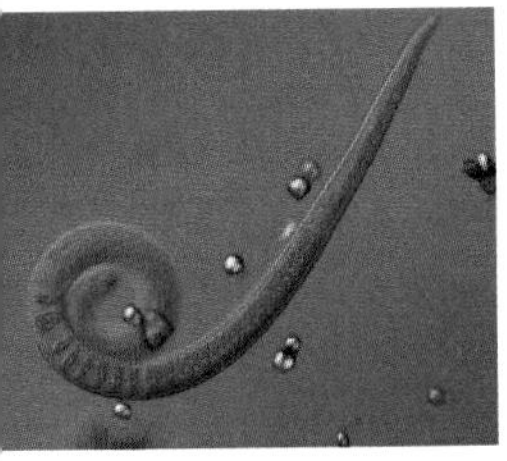

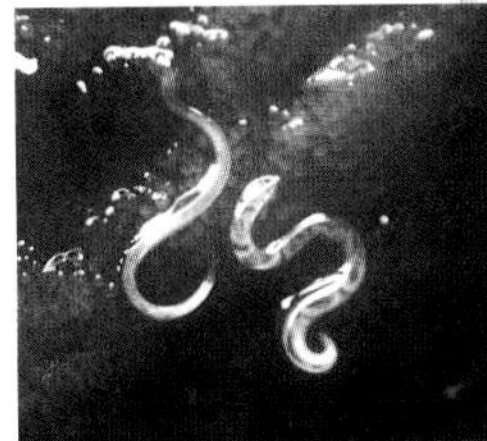

Figure 12.10 The trichina worm *(left)*, the *Ascaris lumbricoides (center)*, and the hookworm *(right)* are all types of parasitic roundworms.

Roundworms

If you have a cat or dog, you may at one time have had to get medicine from a veterinarian to protect your pet from heartworms. Heartworms are a type of parasitic roundworm. Roundworms make up the largest phylum of worms. Many different types of roundworms are parasites. Trichina, *Ascaris*, and hookworm are all types of parasitic roundworms that can infect humans. There are about 50 species of roundworms that are human parasites.

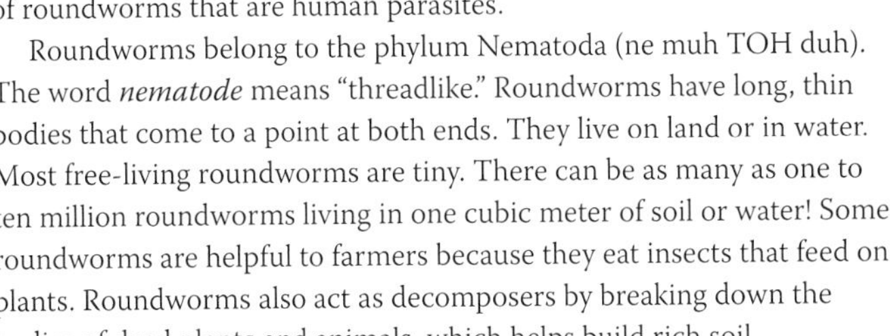

Roundworms belong to the phylum Nematoda (ne muh TOH duh). The word *nematode* means "threadlike." Roundworms have long, thin bodies that come to a point at both ends. They live on land or in water. Most free-living roundworms are tiny. There can be as many as one to ten million roundworms living in one cubic meter of soil or water! Some roundworms are helpful to farmers because they eat insects that feed on plants. Roundworms also act as decomposers by breaking down the bodies of dead plants and animals, which helps build rich soil.

Roundworms have complete, yet simple, digestive systems with two openings—a mouth and an anus. Food enters the body through the mouth and wastes leave the body through the **anus** (AY nus). This makes the digestive system of the roundworm more complex than that of the sponge or cnidarian.

Figure It Out

1. Why is *nematode* a good name for this roundworm?
2. How might the heartworms keep the heart from working properly?

Figure 12.11 This dog heart is infected with heartworms.

As You Read

Use the information you have learned to describe flatworms and roundworms.

What is a parasite?

Explain It!

In your Science Notebook, write a public service announcement for a local television or radio station explaining the importance of preventing heartworm disease in dogs and cats.

CONNECTION: Health

Parasitic roundworms can cause serious disease in humans and other animals. *Trichinella* is a parasitic roundworm that lives in the muscle tissue of pigs and other mammals. People should never eat pork or game animals such as deer and wild hogs unless the meat is well cooked.

Teach

EXPLAIN to students that roundworms are the largest phylum of worms. Ask students to read about roundworms with a comparison with flatworms in mind.

Figure It Out: Figure 12.11

ANSWER **1.** The word *nematode* means "threadlike." Heartworms are long and stringy, like threads. **2.** Heartworms will clog blood vessels in the heart and keep it from pumping blood properly.

As You Read

Give students a few minutes to update the flatworm and roundworm columns in their three-column charts. Ask a few students to share characteristics for both types of worms.

ANSWER A parasite is an organism that lives on or in another organism and takes food from this organism.

Explain It!

Have students listen to public service announcements on a local radio station. Discuss the length, audience, style, and tone of the announcements. In writing their own announcements, students should incorporate the idea that parasitic roundworms can dramatically affect the health of pets. Drugs available from veterinarians can prevent roundworm infections. Have students practice reading their announcements with partners.

Background Information

When humans eat undercooked meat containing *Trichinella spiralis* larvae, these larvae mature into adult worms in the intestine over several weeks. The adult worms then produce larvae that penetrate muscle and other tissue.

Mild cases of trichinosis may produce no symptoms or only mild stomach or muscle aches. More severe cases of trichinosis, when one's body is infested with hundreds of worms, result in additional symptoms and complications. Trichinosis usually is not serious and can be cured with time. To treat symptoms, physicians prescribe antiparasite medication to be used before muscle invasion, pain relievers for muscle aches, and corticosteroids for controlling inflammation.

CONNECTION: Health

Tell students that trichinosis can be prevented by cooking meat (pork, bear, or other wild-animal meat) to an internal temperature of 150°F before eating it. Provide students with meat thermometers, insulated containers such as plastic foam cups, and hot water. Have students practice reading the thermometers until they can accurately determine the temperature.

Teach

EXPLAIN to students that they will now learn about the third phylum of worms, segmented worms. Earthworms and leeches are examples of segmented worms.

CONNECTION: Chemistry

Arrange students in pairs, and ask each student to share with the partner how he or she would respond to finding a leech on his or her leg. Then, ask the pairs to take turns reading aloud the article *Leeches Make a Comeback*. After they read the article, ask them to discuss with their partners how they might respond to the use of leeches as part of a medical treatment. Ask: *Do you feel any differently about finding a leech on your leg? Why?*

EXTEND Have students write in their Science Notebooks about the advantages and disadvantages of using leeches after surgery.

Assess

EVALUATE Use the After You Read questions and the Alternative Assessment to help you assess students' understanding of the lesson.

After You Read

1. The flatworms (Platyhelminthes), roundworms (Nematoda), and segmented worms (Annelida) are the three main phyla of worms.
2. The worms vary in shape, size, food source, and level of complexity.
3. Answers will vary. Accept all logical responses.

Alternative Assessment

EVALUATE Have each student create a chart to compare and contrast the characteristics of the three-worm phyla. Some students may need to refer to their three-column charts for information.

Figure 12.12 Earthworms *(top)* are the most common annelid worms. Hundreds of earthworms can live under the surface of a square meter of soil. Most leeches *(bottom)* live in freshwater.

Segmented Worms

A segmented worm has a body divided into many segments, or sections. The phylum Annelida (an NEL ud uh) contains the segmented worms, the most complex of the worms. The word *annelid* means "little rings" and describes the bodies of these worms. Earthworms and leeches belong to this phylum. Segmented worms can live in soil, freshwater, or the ocean.

Earthworms The earthworm is the most familiar of the segmented worms. The body of an earthworm is divided into at least 100 segments. The earthworm has a slimy outer layer of mucus that helps it glide through the soil. It also has tiny, stiff hairs called bristles on its skin that help it move along the ground.

As earthworms burrow through the soil, they eat dead plants and animal bodies. They digest some of this food, but the rest is passed out through the anus into the soil. This produces fertilizer for the soil. Earthworm tunnels loosen the soil and allow air to move into it. This air helps plants grow.

Leeches Leeches are another type of segmented worm. Some leeches are free-living and eat small invertebrates. Other leeches are parasites that attach to the skin of a vertebrate and feed on its blood.

CONNECTION: Chemistry

Thousands of years ago, parasitic leeches were used by the ancient Egyptians for a medical procedure called bloodletting. It was believed that sick people contained "bad blood" and that leeches could remove it. Over time, doctors realized that illness was caused by many other factors and that leeches might be weakening and hurting patients. But, once again, leeches are popular with doctors.

Leech saliva contains a chemical called hirudin that keeps blood from clotting. Surgeons who reattach body parts such as fingers and toes find that hirudin helps blood flow through the body parts, which aids the healing process after surgery. Leech saliva also contains a chemical that acts like a natural anesthetic to lessen pain. Leeches can also be used to drain blood from a wound.

After You Read

1. What are the three main phyla of worms?
2. How are flatworms, roundworms, and segmented worms different from one another?
3. Look at the chart in your Science Notebook. Add to the chart to describe the characteristics of segmented worms.

Background Information

In 2004, the Food and Drug Administration cleared leeches *(Hirudo medicinalis)* for use as medical devices. By definition, a medical device is an article intended to diagnose, cure, treat, prevent, or mitigate a disease or condition, or to affect a function or structure of the body, that does not achieve its primary effect through a chemical action and is not metabolized. Patients may require two to three leeches at a time. A leech "team" will feed through their disk-shaped suckers for about 40 minutes, and then another team is applied. Each leech costs only about $7, so the treatment is cost-effective.

Field Study

Take students to a nearby grassy area, and remove a layer of grass over a small plot of land (30 cm × 30 cm) or move some rocks in an area of trees and bushes. Have students observe earthworms and add information on behavior and characteristics to the segmented worm columns of their charts.

12.5 Mollusks

Before You Read

In your Science Notebook, divide a page into three columns. Label the first column *Snail*, the second column *Clam*, and the third column *Octopus*. Draw a picture of each animal in the correct column. Predict some characteristics of each, and write them under the appropriate drawing.

Learning Goals

- Identify the common characteristics of mollusks.
- Describe how mollusks are divided into classes.
- Compare the characteristics of gastropods, bivalves, and cephalopods.

New Vocabulary

radula

If you have watched a snail move across the ground, collected shells on the beach, or eaten oysters, clams, or octopus, you are familiar with mollusks. The word *mollusk* comes from the Latin word meaning "soft." Mollusks are animals in the phylum Mollusca (mah LUS kuh).

Characteristics of Mollusks

Mollusks are soft-bodied invertebrates that usually have hard inner or outer shells. Mollusks live on land, in freshwater, and in the ocean. Like worms, mollusks have bilateral symmetry.

Mollusks are divided into three main classes based on whether or not they have a shell, the kind of shell they have, and the kind of foot they have. The foot of a mollusk is the part of its body used for movement. The three main classes of mollusks are the snails and slugs, the two-shelled mollusks, and the tentacled mollusks.

Snails and Slugs

Gastropods (GAS troh pahdz), which include snails and slugs, are mollusks with a single shell or no shell at all. The word *gastropod* means "stomach foot." Most gastropods move by using a foot found on the same side of their body as their stomach.

A snail is a gastropod with a single shell. A snail's head contains two pairs of tentacles. The longer pair of tentacles has eyes at each tip. The shorter pair helps the snail detect smells. A snail's head also contains a mouth and a jaw.

Most snails eat plants. A snail has a structure in its mouth called a radula. The **radula** (RA juh luh) is like a file that helps a snail scrape off small pieces from plants that it can easily swallow. As a snail moves, it leaves a trail of mucus behind. This mucus helps the snail's foot glide over different types of surfaces.

Slugs are gastropods that do not have shells. They protect themselves from predators by hiding under rocks and logs during daylight hours. Some slugs have chemicals in their bodies that are poisonous to predators.

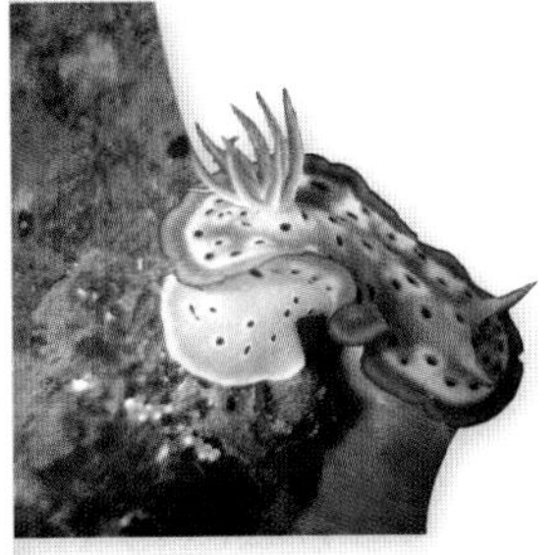

Figure 12.13 A snail *(top)* and a sea slug *(bottom)* are mollusks called gastropods.

12.5 Introduce

ENGAGE Provide students shells from snails and clams. Allow students to touch and feel the shells. Ask: *Where could I have found these shells? What lived in the shells?* Explain to students that animals called mollusks used to inhabit the shells but not all mollusks have shells.

Before You Read

Draw and label the three-column chart on the board. In the second column, sketch a picture of a clam, and then write: *Has two shells that open and close.* Direct students to make their own charts and to predict some additional characteristics for each class of mollusks. Check students' charts throughout the lesson.

Teach

EXPLORE Divide the class into groups of five or six students. Provide each group with a live snail on one half of a petri dish. Have students observe the snails and record their observations in their Science Notebooks. Instruct students to watch the snails through the undersides of the dishes. Then, have students gently touch the antennae of the snails using a pencil eraser and make observations about the snails' behavior.

Supply each group with a lettuce leaf or other plant leaf, and have students place the snails on the leaf and observe them. Finally, have students place the snails on a piece of sandpaper and observe the snails' movement and any indication of a deposit on the paper. At the end of the activity, collect the snails and dispose of them appropriately. Have students wash their hands thoroughly with soap and warm water.

Vocabulary

radula Tell students that the word *radula* is derived from the Latin word *radere*, which means "to scrape."

ELL Strategy

Paraphrase Have students work with partners to paraphrase the important points for each type of mollusk. After they paraphrase, they should add the information to the three-column charts in their Science Notebooks.

Background Information

The root *pod* is derived from the Greek word *podos*, which means "foot." Other examples of the use of *pod* in the English language include *podiatrist*.

Teach

EXPLAIN to students that they will learn about the second type of mollusks, the bivalves (or two-shelled mollusks).

Explore It!

Provide students with hand lenses and oyster, clam, mussel, and scallop shells. Give the class 10 to 15 minutes to examine and compare the shells. Have students take notes about the shells' characteristics, similarities, and differences in the three-column charts in their Science Notebooks. Students should also sketch the shells in their Science Notebooks. They should observe that all of the bivalve shells have similar shapes, textures, and lines or ridges on them. The shells will differ somewhat in size and color.

As You Read

Ask students to review their three-column charts and to update their information for snails and slugs and for two-shelled mollusks.

ANSWER The three main classes of mollusks are the snails and slugs, the two-shelled mollusks, and the tentacled mollusks.

CONNECTION: Physics

Have pairs of students blow up balloons and twist the ends around a paper clip to keep the air from escaping. While one student holds the balloon with the paper clip end facing his or her body, have the other student release the paper clip. Simultaneously, the student holding the balloon should release it. The balloon will be propelled forward, demonstrating the equal and opposite reaction. (As the air is forced out of the balloon in one direction, the balloon is propelled in the other direction with equal force.)

Explore It!

Working with a partner, use a hand lens to examine the shells of an oyster, a clam, a scallop, and a mussel. In your Science Notebook, describe how they are alike and how they are different. Add diagrams of the shells to support your descriptions.

As You Read

Review the characteristics of each mollusk you drew. Make corrections or additions to your list as you learn more about these animals.

What are the three main classes of mollusks?

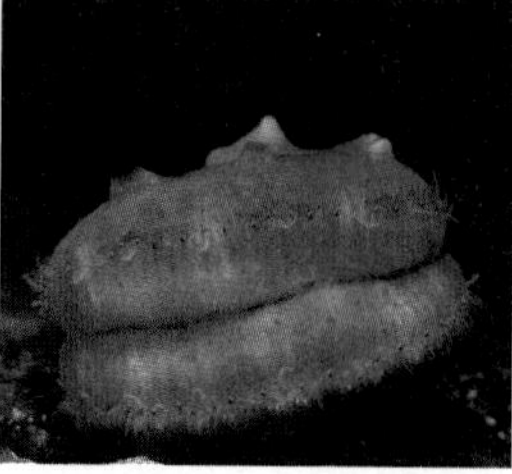

Figure 12.14 The clam *(left)*, the scallop *(center)*, and mussels *(right)* are all types of bivalves. The shells of bivalves are held together by hinges and strong muscles.

Two-Shelled Mollusks

Mollusks that have two shells held together by strong muscles are called bivalves. The word *bivalve* means "two shells." Oysters, clams, scallops, and mussels are bivalves. All bivalves live in the ocean or in freshwater. Unlike a gastropod, a bivalve does not have a radula. Bivalves get their food by filter feeding, like sponges. As water moves into the shell of a bivalve, food particles stick to a mucus layer on its body.

Some bivalves stay in one place throughout their lives, and others move freely. Oysters and mussels attach themselves to rocks under the water. Clams and scallops move freely through the water. They clap their shells together, forcing water out of the shell. The movement of the water pushes them forward. Clams and scallops can also use their feet to bury themselves in sand or mud.

Figure 12.15 A pearl was produced by this oyster. Sometimes, an oyster will contain more than one pearl.

Many people enjoy bivalves as food. Bivalves can be cooked or eaten raw. Some bivalves, such as oysters, are valued for their ability to produce pearls. When a grain of sand gets into an oyster shell, it acts as an irritant. In response, the oyster secretes a substance to coat the sand particle so it will not rub against the oyster's body. Over time, the sand becomes completely covered with many layers of secretions, and a pearl is formed. Pearls are used to make jewelry.

CONNECTION: Physics

Newton's third law of motion states that for every action, there is an equal and opposite reaction. The movement of a clam or a scallop demonstrates Newton's third law of motion. As bivalve shells snap shut, water is forced out in one direction, moving the bivalve in the other direction. Octopuses and squids move in a similar way, using jets of water.

Background Information

Sir Isaac Newton was an English scientist, mathematician, and astronomer who is regarded as one of the greatest scientists and mathematicians in history. One of his most important contributions was his theory of gravitation, which explains how the universe is held together.

Newton's laws of motion:

1. Newton's first law (the law of inertia) states that an object at rest stays at rest and an object in motion stays in motion unless acted upon by an external force.
2. Newton's second law states that the acceleration of an object depends upon two variables, the net force acting upon the object and the mass of the object. It can be stated through the equation $F = ma$, where F = force, m = mass, and a = acceleration.
3. Newton's third law states that for every action, there is an equal and opposite reaction.

Tentacled Mollusks

The most complex of the mollusks are the tentacled mollusks, also called the cephalopods (SEHF uh loh pahdz). The word *cephalopod* means "head-footed." Cephalopods have large, well-developed heads. They also have tentacles that they use to capture food and to move themselves. The octopus, the squid, and the chambered nautilus are different types of cephalopods. A cephalopod may have an outer shell, an inner shell, or no shell at all.

Octopuses and Squids The octopus has no shell. It has eight arms lined with suction cups to help it capture food. The octopus lives mostly on the ocean floor, usually crawling in search of food. The squid has an inner shell that runs along its back and keeps its body stiff. A squid has eight arms of equal size, plus two longer arms called tentacles. Squids are fast swimmers and usually stay in open water.

Both the octopus and the squid can move quickly to hunt or to avoid predators. They can squirt jets of water out of their bodies to move them through the water. This type of movement is called jet propulsion. Octopuses and squids also produce a dark-colored ink that they can release into the water. This ink helps them hide so that they can escape from predators.

Chambered Nautilus The chambered nautilus has a coiled outer shell with many chambers, or rooms. By taking in or giving off gas from these chambers, the nautilus can move to different depths in the ocean. As a nautilus grows, it gains more living space by building new chambers connected to the old ones. It moves to hunt for food, but not as quickly as the octopus or the squid.

Figure 12.17 The chambered nautilus is a type of cephalopod that has an outer shell. How is it similar to the octopus and the squid?

Figure It Out

1. What are some characteristics of the octopus and the squid?
2. Compare movement in octopuses and squids with movement in clams.

Figure 12.16 The octopus *(top)* and squid *(bottom)* are examples of cephalopods.

Did You Know?

An octopus has three hearts. Two of the hearts pump blood through each of the two gills, and the third heart pumps blood through the body.

After You Read

1. Review the characteristics of the mollusks you drew in your Science Notebook. In a well-developed paragraph, describe the three characteristics that are common to all mollusks.
2. How are mollusks divided into classes?
3. How are gastropods, bivalves, and cephalopods different from one another?

Teach

EXPLAIN to students that tentacled mollusks include the octopus, squid, and chambered nautilus.

Figure It Out: Figure 12.16

ANSWER **1.** The octopus and squid are invertebrates with multiple arms. They can swim by jet propulsion and can escape from predators by releasing dark-colored ink from their bodies. **2.** All of them propel themselves through the water by ejecting water from their bodies (jet propulsion).

Use the Visual: Figure 12.17

ANSWER It is a soft-bodied invertebrate that has tentacles for hunting and catching its prey.

Assess

EVALUATE Use the After You Read questions and the Alternative Assessment to help you assess students' understanding of the lesson.

After You Read

1. They are all soft-bodied invertebrates with bilateral symmetry. Most have shells.
2. They are divided into classes based on the presence or absence of a shell, the kind of shell, and the kind of foot.
3. They do or do not have shells, they live on land or in water, and they vary greatly in size. But, the main difference is in the location and shape of the foot used for movement.

Alternative Assessment

EVALUATE Have students draw a gastropod, a bivalve, and a cephalopod. Ask them to classify each as a vertebrate or invertebrate, write its type of symmetry, note whether it has a hard or soft body, and add one additional detail, such as method of moving or obtaining food.

Background Information

Octopuses have an amazing ability to change color, which camouflages the octopus. An octopus's eight tentacles are lined with suckers that can "taste" sweet, sour, or bitter and can feel if something is rough or smooth. An octopus has no hard shell, and a beak is the only hard part of its body. This enables the octopus to squeeze through very narrow slits and between underwater rocks.

Differentiated Instruction

Musical Have groups of students select a familiar tune/song and use it to create their own song about mollusks. The lyrics of their songs should identify the characteristics of mollusks, examples of mollusks, how the various classes of mollusks are the same and different, and other interesting facts about these invertebrates. Encourage student groups to perform their songs for the class.

Chapter 12 Summary

VOCABULARY REVIEW

Check students' sentences or paragraphs to make sure they understand the meaning of each vocabulary term.

PREPARE FOR CHAPTER TEST

Evaluate students' essays using the following criteria:

1. The topic sentence, or main idea, should restate the Key Concept.
2. The supporting paragraphs should incorporate the answers to the Learning Goal questions students have written and include details, facts, and examples they have recorded in their Science Notebooks.
3. The concluding sentence should sum up the main idea of the chapter and restate the Key Concept.

MASTERING CONCEPTS

True or False

1. False, Sexual reproduction
2. False, invertebrates
3. True
4. True
5. False, leech
6. False, gastropod

Short Answer

7. Animals get nutrition by eating food, their cells do not have cell walls, and they are multicellular.
8. Sponges reproduce asexually by budding and sexually through the fertilization of an egg cell by a sperm cell.
9. The polyp is vase shaped, has a mouth on its top surface, and usually does not move. The medusa is bell shaped, has a mouth on its lower surface, and is free moving.
10. A parasite is an organism that lives inside or on another organism. Parasites take food from that organism.
11. Cephalopods use their tentacles to move from one place to another. They also squirt water from inside their bodies. As the water leaves their bodies, they are propelled in the opposite direction.

Summary

KEY CONCEPTS

12.1 Introduction to Animals

- Vertebrates are animals with backbones. Invertebrates are animals without backbones.
- The bodies of animals can show radial symmetry, bilateral symmetry, or asymmetry.

12.2 Sponges

- Sponges belong to the phylum Porifera. Their bodies are covered with pores.
- Sponges remove food and oxygen from water as it enters their pores.
- Sponges can reproduce asexually by budding. Sponges can reproduce sexually by the joining of a sperm cell and an egg cell.

12.3 Cnidarians

- Cnidarians have a hollow body cavity with one opening, called the mouth.
- Cnidarians have stinging cells on their tentacles. They use their tentacles to catch prey.
- Cnidarians have two body plans: the polyp and the medusa.

12.4 Worms

- Flatworms are members of the phylum Platyhelminthes. They have flat bodies and live in freshwater.
- Roundworms are members of the phylum Nematoda. Some nematodes are free-living. Some are parasites that live off other organisms.
- Segmented worms are members of the phylum Annelida. Earthworms and leeches are annelids.

12.5 Mollusks

- Mollusks are members of the phylum Mollusca. They have soft bodies, and many are protected by inner or outer shells.
- Most mollusks have a thick muscular foot or tentacles.

VOCABULARY REVIEW

Write each term in a complete sentence, or write a paragraph relating several terms.

12.1
sexual reproduction, p. 210
asexual reproduction, p. 210
vertebrate, p. 211
invertebrate, p. 211
radial symmetry, p. 211
bilateral symmetry, p. 211
asymmetrical, p. 211

12.2
filter feeding, p. 212
spicule, p. 213
budding, p. 213
regeneration, p. 213

12.3
tentacle, p. 214
polyp, p. 214
medusa, p. 214

12.4
parasite, p. 216
anus, p. 217

12.5
radula, p. 219

PREPARE FOR CHAPTER TEST

To prepare for the chapter test, create a question from each Learning Goal. Use the information in your Science Notebook to answer each question. Then use these answers to write a well-developed essay about the chapter. Use the Key Concept on the first page of this chapter as your topic sentence.

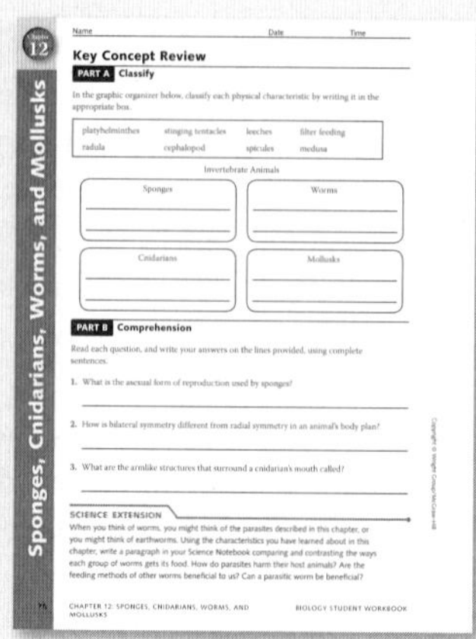

Key Concept Review

PART A Classify

platyhelminthes	stinging tentacles	leeches	filter feeding
radula	cephalopod	spicules	medusa

Invertebrate Animals: Sponges, Worms, Cnidarians, Mollusks

PART B Comprehension

SCIENCE EXTENSION

Sponges, Cnidarians, Worms, and Mollusks

Key Concept Review
Workbook, p. 76

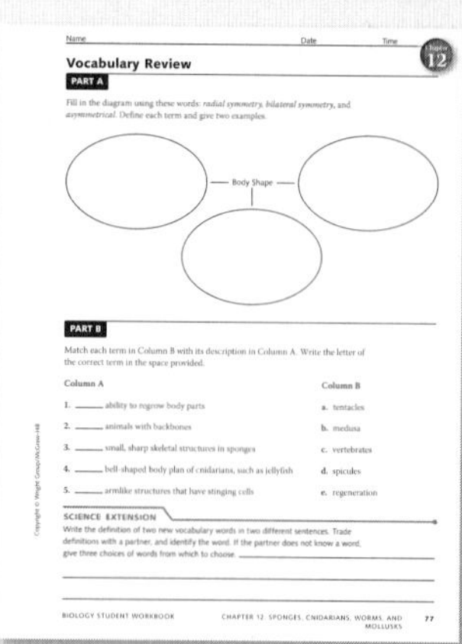

Vocabulary Review

PART A

Body Shape

PART B

Column A	Column B
1. ____ ability to regrow body parts	a. tentacles
2. ____ animals with backbones	b. medusa
3. ____ small, sharp skeletal structures in sponges	c. vertebrates
4. ____ bell shaped body plan of cnidarians, such as jellyfish	d. spicules
5. ____ armlike structures that have stinging cells	e. regeneration

SCIENCE EXTENSION

Vocabulary Review
Workbook, p. 77

MASTERING CONCEPTS

True or False

If the statement is true, write "true." If it is false, change the underlined word or words.

1. Asexual reproduction occurs when a sperm cell and an egg cell join to form a new individual.
2. Animals without backbones are called vertebrates.
3. Sponges remove food and oxygen from water by a process called filter feeding.
4. Cnidarians use tentacles to capture food.
5. An earthworm is a parasitic segmented worm that attaches to the skin of a vertebrate and feeds on its blood.
6. A snail is a type of cephalopod.

Short Answer

Answer each of the following in a sentence or brief paragraph.

7. What are the common characteristics of all animals?
8. Describe how sponges reproduce asexually and sexually.
9. Compare the two body plans of cnidarians.
10. How are parasites harmful to humans and other animals?
11. What methods do cephalopods use to move from one place to another?

Critical Thinking

Use what you have learned in this chapter to answer each of the following.

12. **Compare and Contrast** Identify ways in which sponges are similar to and different from cnidarians.
13. **Apply Concepts** Sponge farmers cut parent sponges into smaller pieces and throw the pieces back into the water. Why do they do this?
14. **Relate** A chemical is used to kill unwanted insects in a flower garden. This chemical also kills the earthworms. How might this affect the plants growing in the garden?

Standardized Test Question

Choose the letter of the response that correctly answers the question.

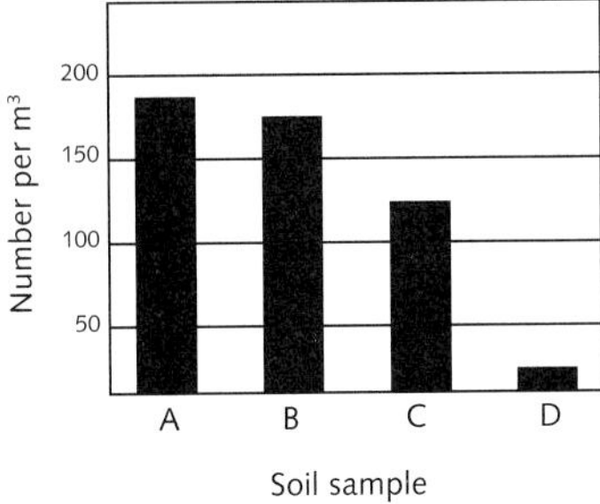

15. The graph shows the number of earthworms per cubic meter in different types of soil. What can you infer about soil sample D?
    - A. It is the perfect temperature for earthworms.
    - B. It contains plenty of food for earthworms.
    - C. It is unhealthy for earthworms.
    - D. It provides earthworms with protection from predators.

Test-Taking Tip

Resist the urge to rush, and don't worry if others finish before you. Use all the time you have. If you are able, clear your mind by closing your eyes and counting to five or taking another type of short break. Extra points are not awarded for being the first person to finish.

Curriculum Connection Workbook, p. 80

Science Challenge Workbook, p. 81

Critical Thinking

12. Sponges and cnidarians live in water, reproduce asexually and sexually, and are simple, soft-bodied invertebrates. Sponges get their food by filter feeding. Cnidarians get their food by using the stinging cells on their tentacles to capture prey and get it into the mouth.
13. Parts of a sponge can regenerate into completely new sponges. So many more new sponges are made by cutting adult sponges into small pieces.
14. The plants will receive less air and fertilizer. This will likely slow their growth.

Standardized Test Question

15. C

Reading Links

The Worm Book: The Complete Guide to Worms in Your Garden

This friendly and informative guide is perfect for independent projects and reports or for general classroom reference. Readers will come away with a greater appreciation for worms, their characteristics, the ecological roles they play, and their relevance to a variety of human activities. For the more ambitious, the book gives instructions for building worm composting bins and provides thorough coverage of the home worm-cultivation process.

Nancarrow, Loren and Janet Hogan Taylor. Ten Speed Press. 160 pp. Illustrated. Trade ISBN: 978-0-89815-994-3.

Grzimek's Student Animal Resource: Corals, Jellyfish, Sponges and Other Simple Animals

An excellent source of supplementary information about specific types of sponges, cnidarians, worms, and mollusks, this book features entries arranged by taxonomy that include details about each animal's characteristics, habitat, diet, reproductive processes, and more (along with links to facilitate further research). The volume is packed with informative, colorful maps and illustrations, and it concludes with a variety of extra resources.

Allen, Catherine Judge, et. al. Thomson Gale. 274 pp. Illustrated. Trade ISBN: 978-0-7876-9412-8.

12A Identifying Symmetry

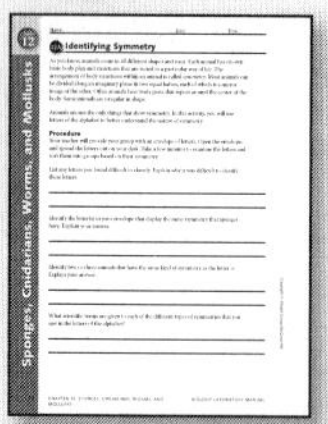

This prechapter introduction activity is designed to determine what students already know about the body plans of animals by engaging them in arranging alphabet letters into groups according to their symmetry.

Objectives

- classify letters based on symmetry
- compare symmetry in letters to symmetry in animals
- communicate conclusions

Planning

 1 class period  groups of 2 students

Materials (per group)

- envelope containing letters of the alphabet
- pencil and paper

Advance Preparation

- The letter envelopes should contain 5 or 6 different letters of the alphabet. The only letter of the alphabet that exhibits radial symmetry is the letter *O*. You might want to include the letter *O* in each envelope so that each student will be able to recognize the three types of symmetry. You can use letter tiles from a board game or write the letters on small pieces of paper.

Engagement Guide

- Challenge students to think about how they can sort letters into groups based on symmetry by asking:
    - *Which letters in the alphabet can be divided into matching right and left halves in only one way?* (Letters *A, H, I, M, T, U, V, W, X,* and *Y* can be divided into matching right and left halves.)
    - *Which letters in the alphabet have a central point that can be cut like a pie in roughly equal parts?* (Students should recognize that the letter *O* is the only letter in the alphabet that has such a central point.)
    - *Which letters are asymmetrical?* (Letters *B, C, D, E, F, G, J, K, L, N, P, Q, R, S,* and *Z* are difficult to classify because they cannot be divided in half and do not have a central point.)
- Encourage students to develop their own definition for each kind of symmetry found in the letters, and have students communicate their conclusions in creative ways.

Going Further

Encourage students to repeat this activity using other objects around the room or imaginary animals they have created. Have students present their conclusions to the class.

12B Observing Earthworm Responses

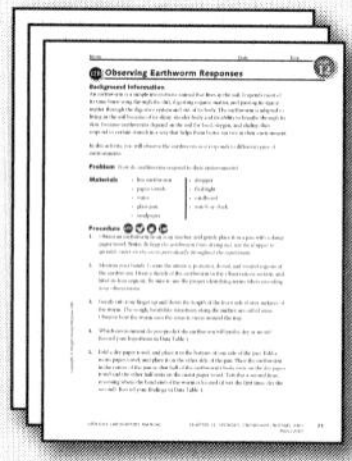

Objectives

- observe earthworm responses to different stimuli
- compare and contrast different environments
- recognize cause and effect
- interpret data

Skill Set

observing, comparing and contrasting, recording and analyzing data, inferring, stating conclusions

Planning

 1 class period  groups of 2–3 students

Materials

Live earthworms can be obtained from biological supply stores, bait shops, or from a garden. Keep the earthworms moist at all times. Any slick surface can be used instead of the glass pan. Remind students to treat the earthworms with care. Make sure students wash their hands after the experiment.

Answers to Observations: Earthworm Drawing

Prior to the lab, review with students the terms *anterior, posterior, dorsal,* and *ventral.* Students' drawings should resemble an earthworm's anatomy. The anterior region of the earthworm will most likely be pointed in comparison with the shape of the posterior region. The dorsal side is the top of the earthworm, and the ventral side is the underside of the earthworm.

Answers to Observations: Data Table 1

Students' answers may vary, but most likely the earthworm will prefer a moist, rough surface and will avoid the light.

Answers to Analysis and Conclusions

1. The anterior end of the earthworm is located closest to the clitellum (a smooth band or bump). The posterior end is not as pointed as the anterior end. Also, the earthworm will tend to move forward, which is another indication of which end is the anterior end.
2. Earthworms travel through the soil by using their setae as anchors and pushing themselves forward or backward using strong stretching and contracting muscles.

3. Students' answers may vary, but most worms prefer a moist, dark environment and rough surfaces.
4. The earthworm prefers the moist environment because its skin must remain moist or the animal will dry out and die. The earthworm prefers the darkness because it is protected from predators. The earthworm prefers the rough surface because it can move more easily and quickly on such a surface. All of these preferred environments increase the earthworm's chances of survival.
5. During the drought, the earthworms were very difficult to find because they were buried deep in the ground where the soil is moist. The sudden increase in moisture caused the worms to come to the surface because the ground was too saturated for them to breathe.

Going Further

Have students design their own experiments to test different stimuli, such as hot and cold temperatures, sugar solutions and salt solutions, and response to gravity.

12C Modeling an Open and Closed Circulatory System

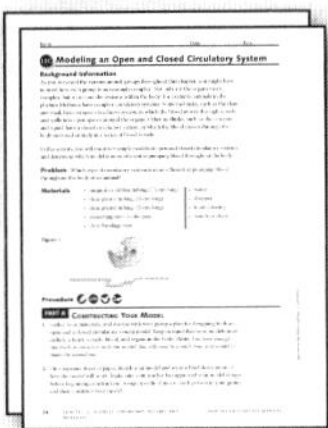

Objectives

- design and construct models
- compare and contrast open and closed models
- experiment to test a hypothesis
- record data
- draw conclusions based on data

Skill Set

modeling, measuring, observing, comparing and contrasting, recording and analyzing data, stating conclusions

Planning

 1–2 class periods 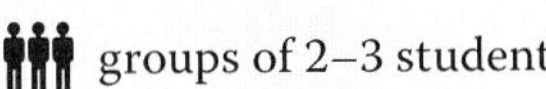 groups of 2–3 students

Materials

Materials for this activity are listed in the Student Laboratory Manual.

Lab Tips

- It may be useful to include clear bandage tape to help secure the tubing and prevent leaks.
- Do not allow students to cut the tubing. Cut the needed pieces before the lab.

Advance Preparation

You can purchase the surgical (rubber) tubing and plastic tubing through any biological supply company or hardware store. Be sure the diameter of both types of tubing is the same so that students can connect all three tubes. You might want to pour a small amount of food coloring into small plastic cups for students before the lab. Cover the lab station with newspaper or a plastic tablecloth, if necessary. To begin the experiment, students might need a few tips on how to construct the model. The two pieces of plastic tubing should represent the vessels, and the surgical tubing should represent the heart because it can be "pumped" easily. Once they construct the open circulatory system, students should be able to easily modify it for the closed circulatory system.

Answers to Procedure A: Constructing a Model

The short plastic tubing should connect to the surgical tubing. The longer plastic tubing should connect to the other end of the rubber tubing, forming a horseshoe shape. To construct the open circulatory system, students should not connect the plastic tubing. To construct the closed circulatory system, all of the tubes should be connected.

Answers to Procedure B: Testing Your Model

To get the water in the tubing, students should submerge the connected tubes in a pan of shallow water. Students should use the dropper to insert the food coloring into the short plastic tubing. To pump the food coloring through the system, students should squeeze the rubber tubing with their hands.

Answers to Observations: Data Table 1

Students' answers will vary. They should have a data table that represents a measurement of the time it took and/or the number of pumps it took for the food coloring to pass through the tubing in each model. In their observations, students should recognize that the closed circulatory system model will be more efficient at pumping blood throughout the body because it pumps the fluid faster.

Answers to Analysis and Conclusions

1. The pan represents the organs in the body. The surgical tubing represents the heart. The plastic tubing represents the vessels, and the colored water represents the blood.
2. The squeezing action on the surgical tubing represents the pumping action of the heart.
3. Students' answers will vary but might include that the open and closed circulatory systems both have a heart, vessels, blood, and organs. Students should recognize that in the open circulatory system, the blood spills out into the open spaces around the organs, and in the closed circulatory system, the blood continues to travel through blood vessels throughout the entire body.
4. The closed circulatory system proved to be more efficient at pumping blood throughout the body because it was faster.
5. The advantage of having a closed circulatory system is that the animal is able to move around more quickly because the blood is pumped faster to provide more oxygen to the different organs in the body.

Going Further

Have each student select an animal they have not studied in this chapter and research its circulatory system. Have students make posters or models to represent the type of circulatory systems the animals display.

Chapter 13 Lessons

Introduce Chapter 13

As a starting activity, use LAB 13A Characteristics of Arthropods and Echinoderms on page 77 of the Laboratory Manual.

ENGAGE Direct students to look at the pictures of the scorpion and sea urchin. Explain to students that the scorpion and the sea urchin are both invertebrates. Review with students the definition of *invertebrate*. The scorpion belongs to the phylum Arthropoda, and the sea urchin belongs to the phylum Echinodermata. Ask students to think about possible similarities and differences between these phyla based on these two invertebrates. Elicit from students any experiences with scorpions and/or sea urchins, such as at zoos, aquariums, and nature centers or along a beach.

Think About Making Observations

ENGAGE Draw a T-chart on the board. Label one column *Insects at Home* and the other column *Insects at School*. Ask each student to share one of the insects from his or her list. Record student responses on the board. Discuss with students the similarities and differences between the insects on the two lists. Circle the insects that appear on both lists.

Chapter 13 Arthropods and Echinoderms

KEY CONCEPT Arthropods and echinoderms can be classified based on their physical characteristics.

Are you afraid of scorpions? Many people are. But did you know that some people keep scorpions as pets? Scorpions are members of the phylum of invertebrates called the arthropods.

Another phylum of invertebrates is the echinoderms. Echinoderms include the beautiful but poisonous Hawaiian sea urchin shown in the photo, as well as sand dollars, sea cucumbers, and sea stars. In this chapter, you will learn about these land and sea invertebrates.

Think About Making Observations

Each time you make an observation about your surroundings, you may think of questions that you would like to have answered. As you find the answers to these questions, you will learn more about the things around you.

- Insects make up the largest class of arthropods. In your Science Notebook, make a list of five insects you have observed around your home or yard and a separate list of five insects you have observed around your school.
- Look at your two lists. What insects did you add to both lists? What insects did you add to only one list? What do your observations suggest?

www.scilinks.org
Invertebrates **Code: WGB13**

224

Chapter 13 Planning Guide

Instructional Periods	National Standards	Lab Manual	Workbook
13.1 2 periods	A.1, C.1, C.3, F.1; C.3, C.6, F.1; UCP.1	**Lab 13A—p. 77** Characteristics of Arthropods and Echinoderms **Lab 13B—p. 78** Examining a Grasshopper **Lab 13C—p. 81** Examining Insect Metamorphosis	Key Concept Review p. 82 Vocabulary Review p. 83 Graphic Organizer p. 84 Reading Comprehension p. 85 Curriculum Connection p. 86 Science Challenge p. 87
13.2 2 periods	C.1, C.3; C.5, G.1, G.3; C.3, C.6, F.1, G.1, G.3; UCP.3, UCP.5		
13.3 2 periods	A.2, C.1, C.5, C.6, B.4, UCP.1, UCP.2, UCP.5		

Middle School Standard; High School Standard; Unifying Concept and Principle

13.1 Arthropods

Before You Read

In your Science Notebook, draw a Venn diagram. Label the circle on the left *Spider.* Label the circle on the right *Crab.* In the left circle, list three physical characteristics of a spider. In the right circle, list three characteristics of a crab. In the overlapping area, list three physical characteristics that a spider and a crab have in common.

If you have ever been bitten by a mosquito or frightened by a spider, you have been bothered by an arthropod. The arthropods (AR thruh pahdz) are the largest phylum of animals on Earth. So far, more than one million species of arthropods have been identified. Insects, spiders, ticks, and crabs are all examples of arthropods.

Arthropods have been on Earth for a long time. Some arthropod fossils are more than 500 million years old. Arthropods called trilobites (TRI luh bites) inhabited Earth's oceans for millions of years, where they lived successfully and in great numbers. Today, none of these early arthropods exist. They are extinct.

Figure 13.1 Trilobites were some of Earth's earliest arthropods.

Characteristics of Arthropods

All arthropods share some of the same structural characteristics. They all have jointed appendages. An **appendage** (uh PEN dihj) is a structure such as a leg, an arm, or an antenna that grows out of an animal's body. The phylum name Arthropoda comes from the Greek words meaning "jointed legs." An appendage with joints allows an animal to be more flexible as it moves or grabs prey. Think about how the joints in your fingers allow you to do many things.

Like segmented worms, arthropods also have segmented bodies. Because of this, some scientists believe that segmented worms and arthropods have a common ancestor.

All arthropods have a hard outer covering called an **exoskeleton**. The exoskeleton acts like a suit of armor to protect the arthropod. The exoskeleton does not grow as the animal grows. It must be shed and replaced with a new, larger exoskeleton. This process is called **molting**.

Learning Goals

- Name three characteristics of all arthropods.
- Describe the characteristics of arachnids and crustaceans.
- Compare the characteristics of centipedes and millipedes.

New Vocabulary

appendage
exoskeleton
molting
antenna

Recall Vocabulary

regeneration (p. 213)
parasite (p. 216)

Figure It Out

1. How is an exoskeleton useful to an arthropod?
2. Infer why an arthropod would be in danger while it is molting.

Figure 13.2 In order to get bigger, arthropods must molt, or shed their exoskeletons.

13.1 Introduce

ENGAGE Tell students that there are many different types of arthropods. Ask: *What are some other arthropods that you can think of?* Record answers on the board. Encourage students to brainstorm as many examples as they can, even if they are not sure that the animals are arthropods.

Tell students that certain characteristics identify arthropods. These include jointed appendages and an exoskeleton that must be shed in order for the arthropod to grow. Impress upon students that Arthropoda is the largest animal phylum on Earth, with more than one million species identified. Write *1,000,000* on the board.

Before You Read

Have students work individually to list three physical characteristics of a spider and a crab. Then pair students, and have them share what they have written and add to their lists.

Vocabulary terms are listed on the first student page of each lesson. You may wish to preview the terms before introducing each lesson. Strategies for teaching the vocabulary appear on the pages where the terms are introduced.

Teach

EXPLAIN that students will identify three characteristics of all arthropods.

Figure It Out: Figure 13.2

ANSWER **1.** It protects the arthropod. **2.** It does not have the protection of its hard exoskeleton.

Vocabulary

appendage Explain that *appendage* comes from the Latin *appendere*, which means "to hang on." An appendage is a structure that "hangs on" to the body, such as a leg or an arm.

exoskeleton Tell students that the prefix *ex-* in *exoskeleton* means "out." An exoskeleton is a skeleton on the outside of the body.

molting Explain that *molting* and *mutate* share the root *mutare*, meaning "to change." When animals molt, they shed their outer covering, grow, and change.

ELL Strategy

Use Visual Information, Compare and Contrast Provide students with pictures of animals that are arthropods and animals that are not. Have students classify these animals into a group of arthropods and a group of non-arthropods. Encourage students to look for similar characteristics when classifying pictures.

Science Notebook EXTRA

Encourage students to use the vocabulary section they created in their Science Notebooks. Remind them to record prefixes, suffixes, and root words to help them remember the meanings of vocabulary terms.

Teach

EXPLAIN Tell students that spiders are one type of animal in the arachnid class, which also includes scorpions, ticks, and mites. All arachnids have eight legs and two body regions, the head-chest section and the abdomen. Explain to students that spiders usually feed on insects, killing their prey by injecting them with poison from their fangs. Many spiders make webs of silk, which they use to catch their prey.

Use the Visual: Figure 13.5

EXTEND Have students research the different ways in which spiders of different kinds make their webs. Ask students to share what they learn with the class in a poster presentation.

ANSWER A spider has four pairs of legs.

Did You Know?

The most dangerous spider in the United States is the female black widow. The venom of a black widow spider is about 15 times stronger than the venom of a rattlesnake. Because the black widow injects little venom with her bite, however, people do not usually die from it.

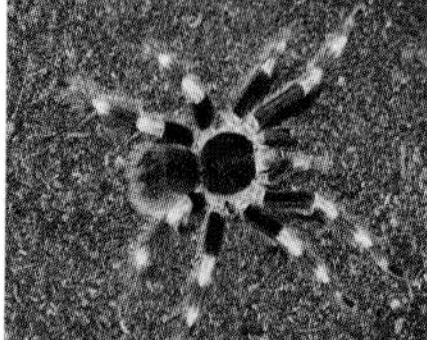

Figure 13.3 The Brazilian white knee tarantula *(left)*, deathstalker scorpion *(center)*, and American dog tick *(right)* are all examples of arachnids.

Arachnids

Spiders, scorpions, ticks, and mites belong to the class Arachnida (uh RAK ni duh). All arachnids have eight legs and two body regions: the head-chest region and the abdomen. The head-chest region contains the arachnid's sense organs, heart, and appendages. The abdomen contains the arachnid's reproductive, respiratory, and digestive organs.

Spiders

Does seeing a spider make you fearful or curious? Of the more than 35,000 species of spiders, only about a dozen are dangerous to humans. In North America, you need to look out for only the two species shown in **Figure 13.4**—the female black widow and the brown recluse.

Spiders usually feed on insects. Some large spiders can feed on small vertebrates such as mice, birds, lizards, and frogs. Spiders catch prey in different ways. Many make webs of a thin, strong, flexible substance called silk. Silk is released from glands in the spider's abdomen. Some spiders jump out and catch their prey by surprise. All spiders kill their prey by using fangs to inject poison into the prey's body.

Figure 13.4 The female black widow spider *(top)* is black with a red, hourglass-shaped mark on the lower side of her abdomen. The brown recluse spider *(bottom)* is brown with a violin-shaped mark on its head.

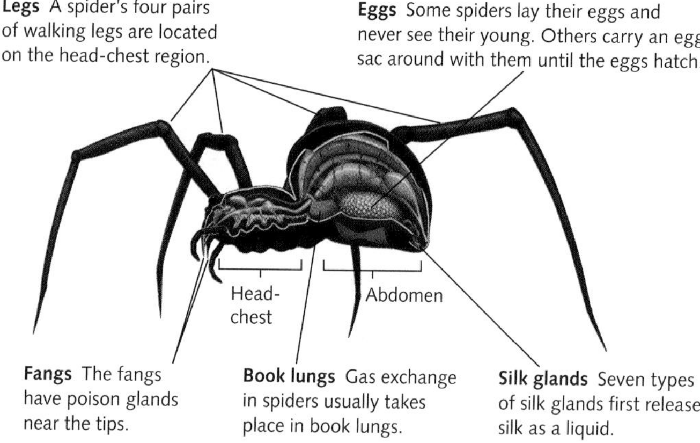
Legs A spider's four pairs of walking legs are located on the head-chest region.
Eggs Some spiders lay their eggs and never see their young. Others carry an egg sac around with them until the eggs hatch.
Head-chest
Abdomen
Fangs The fangs have poison glands near the tips.
Book lungs Gas exchange in spiders usually takes place in book lungs.
Silk glands Seven types of silk glands first release silk as a liquid.

Figure 13.5 The external and internal structures of a spider are shown in this diagram. How many pairs of legs does a spider have?

Differentiated Instruction

Visual, Musical, Linguistic Students are probably familiar with the book and/or animated film *Charlotte's Web* (written by E. B. White). Have students read the book or watch the movie and record facts about spiders in their Science Notebooks as they read or watch.

Background Information

Adult female black widow spiders are about 3.8 cm long with their legs stretched out. Sometimes, the mark on its abdomen is white or yellow. The females are much larger than the males and are much more dangerous. One of the most dangerous types of black widow, the southern black widow, can be found in barns, garages, sheds, and woodpiles throughout the southeastern United States.

Spiders use special organs called book lungs to get their oxygen. They reproduce sexually. The female's eggs are fertilized by the male's sperm. Female spiders wrap their eggs in a silken sac or cocoon, where the eggs remain until they hatch. Internal and external structures of a spider are shown in **Figure 13.5**.

Scorpions, Ticks, and Mites

Scorpions live mainly in hot climates such as deserts, tropical rain forests, or grassy prairies. Scorpions are active at night. During the day, they hide under rocks or logs to stay cool. If you go camping, be careful to check your shoes in the morning. Sometimes scorpions hide inside them to stay warm.

A scorpion has a stinger at the end of its abdomen. It uses the stinger to inject venom into its prey. The sting of a scorpion is painful to humans, but it does not usually cause death.

A tick has a different body shape than that of other arachnids. The head and the abdomen of a tick are joined together. Ticks are parasites that live on animals and plants. Some ticks that attach to humans can cause disease. Lyme disease and Rocky Mountain spotted fever are two human diseases caused by ticks.

If chiggers have ever made you itch, you have experienced a mite. Like ticks, chiggers and other mites are parasites. Ear mites cause the ears of dogs and cats to itch. Dust mites feed on dead skin cells found in house dust and on bedding.

Figure 13.6 Scorpions are the only arthropods that give birth to live young. The young scorpions stay on the mother's back until they molt for the first time. How is this helpful to the young?

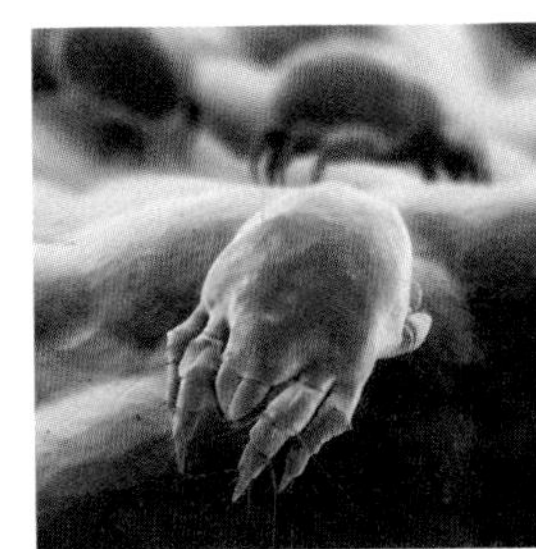

Figure 13.7 The deer tick *(left)* transmits Lyme disease to humans. The dust mite *(right)* feeds on dead skin cells.

CONNECTION: Health

People who have a dust allergy may be allergic to the exoskeletons and droppings of dust mites. Dust mites are found in large quantities in pillows, mattresses, carpeting, and upholstered furniture.

Extend It!

Many people suffer from dust allergies caused by dust mites. Research the topic of allergies to dust mites. Find out what people can do in their homes to help reduce the number of dust mites. Record your findings in your Science Notebook.

Teach

EXPLAIN to students that scorpions, ticks, and mites are also arachnids, like spiders. One way a scorpion is different from a spider is the stinger at the end of its abdomen. A tick has a different body shape: its head-chest and abdomen are joined together. Tell students that mites are like ticks but much smaller.

Use the Visual: Figure 13.6

EXTEND The adult scorpion provides protection for its young.

Extend It!

Provide students with books and Web-site addresses to help with their research. Students should find that dust mites tend to accumulate in mattresses, bed sheets and pillow covers, carpets, and upholstered furniture. Cleaning all of these things on a regular basis will help control the dust mite population.

CONNECTION: Health

Dust mites are less than half a millimeter in size. They generally live in mattresses and bedding, because they feed on the dead skin cells that are abundant there. Explain to students that dust mites are microscopic. Show students the head of a pin, and tell them that about six dust mites could fit there.

Teacher Alert

After seeing enlarged pictures of dust mites, students may become alarmed about sleeping in their beds. It is important to stress to students that dust mites are extremely small and are only bothersome to a small population (10 to 15 percent) of people. It is also possible to control the population of dust mites by washing bedding often and using protective covers on pillows.

Teach

EXPLAIN to students that the majority of crustaceans live in water and that we eat many of them, such as lobsters, crabs, and shrimp. Tell students that all crustaceans have at least five pairs of appendages, with one pair attached to each body segment.

Vocabulary

antenna Tell students that before cable TV, antennae were used on radios and televisions to pick up different stations. Like these electronic devices, crustaceans use their antennae to pick up information about the world around them.

As You Read

Check students' Science Notebooks. Spiders and crabs both have hard outer shells that molt, but they have a different number of body segments and appendages.

ANSWER Crabs belong to the class Crustacea; they are crustaceans.

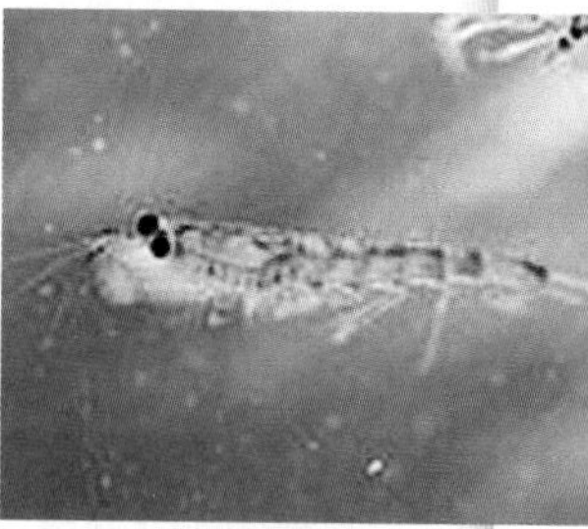

Figure 13.8 The krill *(left)*, lobster *(center)*, and pill bug *(right)* are all examples of crustaceans.

As You Read

Look at your Venn diagram. Make any additions or corrections to the list of characteristics shared by a spider and a crab and characteristics that make them different.

To what class do crabs belong?

Crustaceans

Have you ever eaten shrimp, crabs, lobsters, or crayfish? All of these animals belong to the class of arthropods called Crustacea (krus TAY shee uh). Most crustaceans live in water. Some, such as pill bugs, live in moist soil. Crustaceans are an important food source for many living things. Whales eat tiny crustaceans called krill.

Crustaceans have five or more pairs of appendages. Each body segment of a crustacean has appendages. Lobsters, crabs, and crayfish have claws as their first pair of appendages. These claws help crustaceans catch prey and protect themselves. Crustaceans also have two pairs of antennae. **Antennae** (singular: antenna) are sense organs used for taste, touch, smell, and balance.

Crustaceans obtain their food in many ways. Some eat dead plants and animals. Others eat prey they have captured with their claws. Some crustaceans eat small, plantlike organisms.

Most crustaceans take in oxygen through gills. Gills are organs used to absorb oxygen from water. Most crustacean species exhibit male and female sexes. They reproduce when the female's eggs are fertilized by the male's sperm.

Did You Know?

The stone crab shown in **Figure 13.9** lives in the warm water off the coast of Florida. If one of its claws is removed, the stone crab will regenerate, or regrow, the claw. Because stone crab claws are sold as food, people who fish for them remove one claw and return the animals to the water. The same stone crab can be caught again and have another claw removed in about one year. This helps prevent their extinction from overfishing.

Figure 13.9 Lobsters, crabs, and crayfish have claws. The stone crab *(left)* can regrow its claws if they are removed. While most crustaceans live in the ocean, the crayfish *(right)* lives in freshwater.

Background Information

There are more than 42,000 different species of crustaceans. Most live in salt water, some live in freshwater, and a few live on land. Crustaceans range in size from 3.7 meters (for the largest species, the Japanese spider crab) to one millimeter (for the smallest, the water flea).

The legal size of a stone crab claw in Florida is 7 cm: if a claw is at least that big, it can be harvested. People can take claws from male or female crabs, as long as the crabs are of legal size and females are not pregnant. The claws must be removed correctly so that a membrane will form over the wound and prevent excessive bleeding. Depending on the size of the crab, it can take anywhere from one to three molts (one to three years) for a crab to regenerate a claw of legal size.

Centipedes and Millipedes

Centipedes and millipedes have long, wormlike bodies with many body segments. They also have many legs. Centipedes have one pair of legs on each body segment. Millipedes have two pairs of legs on each body segment.

Although the word *centipede* means "100 legs" in Latin, most centipedes have between 30 and 50 legs. Centipedes have flat bodies. They are carnivores, or animals that feed on the flesh of other animals. Centipedes actively hunt for their food and kill it using poisonous claws attached to the first segment of their bodies. They move quickly and inject their prey with deadly venom. Centipedes eat insects, snails, slugs, and worms.

Although the word *millipede* means "1,000 legs" in Latin, most millipedes have far fewer legs. A millipede has more body segments than a centipede does. Unlike centipedes, millipedes are not carnivores. They eat dead or decaying plant material. Millipedes are slow-moving animals that do not have claws.

If a millipede is attacked, it will roll up into a ball. The animal has stink glands that can give off a poisonous and bad-smelling substance. This helps drive away predators.

Figure 13.10 The giant desert centipede *(top)* is the largest centipede in the United States. It is usually about 18 to 20 centimeters in length and can live for up to five years. A millipede *(bottom)* has two pairs of legs per segment. A millipede's legs move in a wavelike motion as it walks.

CONNECTION: Art

In your Science Notebook, draw diagrams of what you think a centipede and a millipede look like. Make your diagrams resemble the diagram of a spider in Figure 13.5. Label each diagram. Using a marker, indicate characteristics that distinguish one animal from the other.

Did You Know?

Several millipede species live with ants. The millipede lives in an ant nest and helps clean mold and dead plant material from the nest. When the ants move to a new location, the millipede goes with them.

After You Read

1. What are the three common characteristics of all arthropods?
2. What are two ways in which a spider catches its prey?
3. How are antennae important to an arthropod?
4. According to your Venn diagram, in what ways are a spider and a crab alike? In what ways are they different?

Teach

EXPLAIN Remind students that the prefix *milli-* means "one thousand" and that the prefix *centi-* means "one hundred." Explain that while *millipede* means "one thousand legs," most millipedes have fewer legs than that. Similarly, while *centipede* means "one hundred legs," most centipedes have between 30 and 50 legs. Discuss with students how these animals might have gotten their names.

CONNECTION: Art

Provide students with colored markers, pencils, or crayons to help them with their diagrams. Students might also choose to cut out colored paper for their pictures. Check that students have labeled their diagrams correctly.

Assess

EVALUATE Use the After You Read questions and the Alternative Assessment to help you assess students' understanding of this lesson.

After You Read

1. All arthropods have an exoskeleton, segmented bodies, and jointed appendages.
2. A spider can catch its prey in a web or jump out to capture the prey.
3. The antennae act as sense organs for an arthropod. They are used for taste, touch, smell, and balance.
4. Both have an exoskeleton and jointed appendages. A spider has eight legs and injects venom into its prey. A crab has ten legs and uses its claws to catch prey.

ELL Strategy

Compare and Contrast Have each student create a chart with three columns labeled *Arachnids*, *Crustaceans*, and *Centipedes and Millipedes*. Students should list characteristics under each type of arthropod. Provide highlighters, and have students highlight the common characteristics of all three types of arthropods.

Background Information

The relationship between some millipedes and ants is symbiotic. They are two different species of organisms that live together and help each other. The ants provide food and shelter for the millipedes, and the millipedes keep the ants' shelter clean. This type of symbiotic relationship is called mutualism because both species benefit.

Alternative Assessment

EVALUATE Ask students who have difficulty answering the After You Read questions to pick two types of arthropods to compare and contrast. Check students' work. Allow them to refer to their Science Notebooks for information.

13.2 Introduce

ENGAGE Tell students that there are millions of different insects. These insects populate the world and have survived for millions of years. Ask students to list all the different types of insects they can name and write whether or not they have ever seen the insects they list.

Have each student share his or her list with a partner and add any types that are not included. Go around the room and ask each pair to give an example of an insect. Record student answers on the board.

Before You Read

Model a concept map on the board. Use the word *Spider* as an example, and have students suggest five characteristics of spiders that they learned about in the previous lesson. Explain to students that they should create similar maps in their Science Notebooks using the word *Insect*. Emphasize that spiders are not insects; they are arachnids.

Teach

EXPLAIN that in this lesson, students will learn why insects are so successful. They will also examine the body structure of insects and compare the behavior of insects. Finally, students will learn to distinguish between complete and incomplete metamorphosis and will be able to describe the ways in which insects are helpful and harmful to humans.

Learning Goals

- List two reasons why insects are so successful.
- Describe the body structure of insects.
- Distinguish between complete and incomplete metamorphosis.
- Describe how insects are helpful and harmful.

New Vocabulary

thorax
metamorphosis
larva
pupa
nymph
camouflage

Insects

Before You Read

In your Science Notebook, create a concept map for *Insects*. Preview the lesson, and predict some characteristics of insects to include in your map.

You may have noticed that the largest group of arthropods was not discussed in the previous lesson. This group is the insects. Flies, ants, grasshoppers, and butterflies are all insects. There are more species of insects—more than one million—than of all other animals put together.

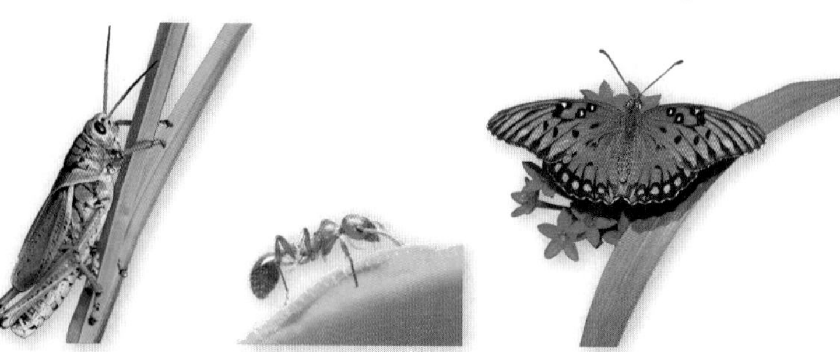

Figure 13.11 The grasshopper *(left)*, ant *(center)*, and butterfly *(right)* belong to the largest group of animals on Earth—the insects.

The Success of Insects

Scientists believe that insects appeared on Earth about 400 million years ago. They developed into an amazing variety of shapes, colors, and sizes. It is estimated that there are 200 million insects for every person on Earth! Insects are found in all of Earth's environments.

Specialized body parts are one reason that insects became such a successful group of animals. Different species of insects, for example, have different kinds of mouth parts. This allows insects to eat many types of food. Many insects are also able to fly. Thus, they can more easily hunt for food, escape from predators, and move to new places to live.

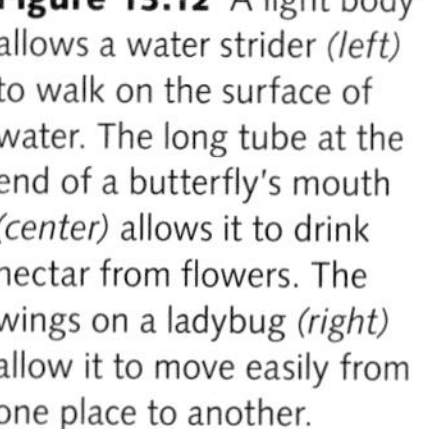

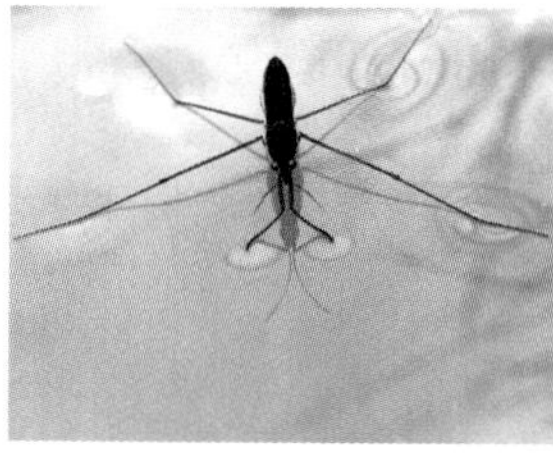

Figure 13.12 A light body allows a water strider *(left)* to walk on the surface of water. The long tube at the end of a butterfly's mouth *(center)* allows it to drink nectar from flowers. The wings on a ladybug *(right)* allow it to move easily from one place to another.

ELL Strategy

Relate to Personal Experience Have students share their own experiences with insects. Ask if any of them are afraid of insects. In groups, have students discuss the different insects they have seen and how they have felt about them. Students who come from other countries may have seen insects that do not live in the United States.

Insect Structure

Insects have three main body sections: a head, a thorax, and an abdomen. The **thorax** is the middle, or chest, section of the insect's body. The head contains the eyes and antennae. Insects have two kinds of eyes: simple and complex. Simple eyes contain only one lens and are used to detect light. Compound eyes contain many lenses. They help the insect detect movement.

The insect's wings and legs are attached to the thorax. Insects have six legs. In jumping insects, such as grasshoppers, one pair of legs is larger than the others. Most insects have one or two pairs of wings.

The abdomen of an insect contains many of its organs. The insect has a system of tubes that carry oxygen through the exoskeleton and into the body. These tubes also remove carbon dioxide from the body.

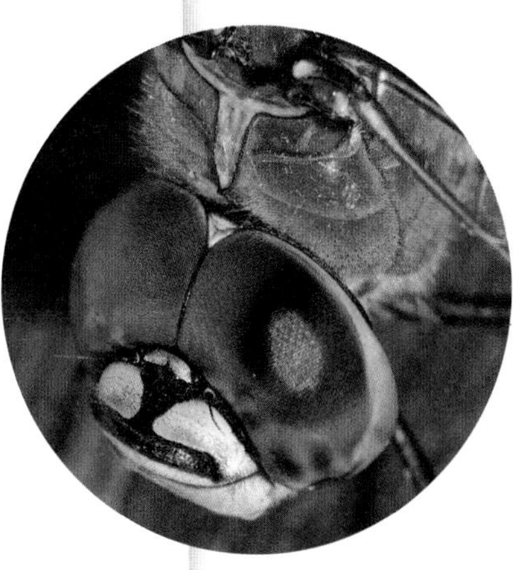

Figure 13.13 The compound eyes of this dragonfly help it detect movement. This allows the dragonfly to catch its prey and avoid predators.

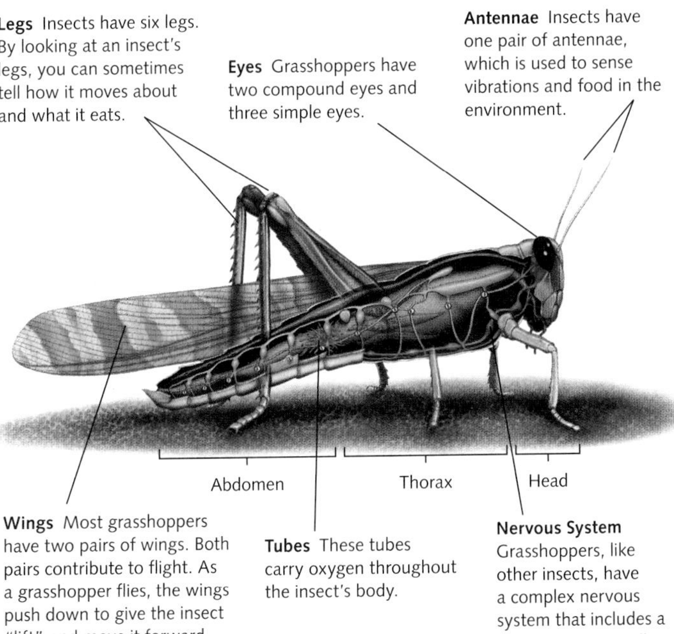

Legs Insects have six legs. By looking at an insect's legs, you can sometimes tell how it moves about and what it eats.
Eyes Grasshoppers have two compound eyes and three simple eyes.
Antennae Insects have one pair of antennae, which is used to sense vibrations and food in the environment.
Abdomen
Thorax
Head
Wings Most grasshoppers have two pairs of wings. Both pairs contribute to flight. As a grasshopper flies, the wings push down to give the insect "lift" and move it forward.
Tubes These tubes carry oxygen throughout the insect's body.
Nervous System Grasshoppers, like other insects, have a complex nervous system that includes a brain and nerve cells.

Figure 13.14 The external and internal structures of a grasshopper are shown in this diagram. How does a grasshopper's number of legs compare with that of a spider?

Did You Know?

The abdomen of an ant contains two stomachs. One stomach holds the food for the ant itself, and the other stomach holds food that can be shared with other ants if another food source is not available.

Explore It!

Use a hand lens to examine the insects given to you by your teacher. How would you describe the exoskeletons? How many legs, wings, body sections, and antennae does each insect have? Record your observations in your Science Notebook.

Teach

EXPLORE Ask students to describe the characteristics of insects that they have seen. Tell students that in order for an arthropod to be classified as an insect, it must have three body sections, two kinds of eyes, and six legs. In addition, many insects have one or two pairs of wings. Ask students to think about the ways in which the characteristics of insects differ from the characteristics of arachnids and echinoderms.

Vocabulary

thorax Explain to students that the word *thorax* comes from the Latin word *thōrax,* which means "chest." Tell students that the word *thorax* refers to the middle or chest section of an insect (and also that section of a human).

Explore It!

Place a variety of insect specimens around the room. Have groups of students move around the room, recording observations of the different insects in their Science Notebooks. Encourage students to notice the similarities and differences among the insects.

Students should find that the exoskeleton is a hard outer covering. The insects that the students observe should have six legs, one or two pairs of wings, three body sections, and two antennae.

Use the Visual: Figure 13.14

EXTEND Grasshoppers have two fewer legs than spiders do.

Field Study

Provide pairs of students nets and lidded jars filled with a small amount of rubbing alcohol. Bring students to a field or wooded area outside the school and have them collect insects. **CAUTION**: Be sure students with insect allergies avoid contact with stinging insects. Bring the insects back to class. Have students observe and try to identify these insects.

Background Information

The part of an ant's stomach that holds food that can be shared with other ants is called the *crop.* It is also known as the *social stomach.* The food in the crop is not digested, so that the ant can spit it up to share with other ants. Periodically, the food from the crop is pumped into the stomach, where it is digested.

Teach

EXPLAIN that all insects reproduce sexually, but they develop in two different ways. Most insects go through complete metamorphosis, but some only go through incomplete metamorphosis. Ask students if they have heard the word *metamorphosis* and if they know what it means.

Vocabulary

metamorphosis Explain to students that the word *metamorphosis* contains the prefix *meta-*, which means "change," and the root *morph*, which means "form." Tell students that when insects go through metamorphosis, they change form.

larva Tell students that the word *larva* is Latin for "ghost." Ask students to think about why the early form of an insect might be thought of as a ghost.

pupa Explain to students that the word *pupa* comes from the Latin word *pupa*, which means "girl" or "doll."

nymph Tell students that the word *nymph* also refers to a Greek and Roman goddess of nature or a graceful young woman. Ask students what an insect in the nymph stage might have in common with a graceful young woman.

camouflage Explain to students that the word *camouflage* comes from the French word *camoufler*, which means "to disguise." Insects that blend in with their surroundings have a disguise.

Explain It!

Encourage students to write about their experiences in the first person. Tell them to imagine what it would be like to be a butterfly in each stage. Students should include all four stages of complete metamorphosis in their writing: egg, larva, pupa, and adult.

Figure It Out: Figure 13.15

ANSWER **1.** A larva is growing very rapidly and needs a large amount of food. **2.** The larva is very active and constantly searching for food. The pupa is inactive while its body goes through many changes.

As You Read

ANSWER complete metamorphosis and incomplete metamorphosis

Explain It!

Imagine that you are a butterfly. In your Science Notebook, describe your experience as you develop from an egg into an adult. Describe each stage of your development. Include diagrams if you wish.

Growth and Development of Insects

All insects reproduce sexually. In most species, the male's sperm fertilize the female's eggs inside her body. As a young insect grows, it undergoes a series of changes called **metamorphosis** (me tuh MOR fuh sihs). There are two types of metamorphosis: complete and incomplete.

Most insects, including flies, beetles, bees, moths, and butterflies, go through complete metamorphosis. There are four stages in complete metamorphosis. The first stage is an egg. The egg hatches into the second stage, a larva (LAR vuh, plural: larvae). The **larva** is the wormlike stage of an insect. A larva spends most of its time eating.

Next, the larva enters the third stage, called the pupa stage. During the **pupa** stage, the larval tissues are broken down and replaced by adult tissues. The pupa stage of a moth is protected by a structure called a cocoon. The last stage is the adult insect that comes out of the cocoon.

Figure It Out

1. Why does a larva eat so much?
2. Compare the activity of an insect in the larva stage with the activity of the insect in its pupa stage.

1 Insects begin life as a fertilized egg. The egg hatches into a larva.
2 Larvae eat huge amounts of food to supply the energy needed for tremendous growth.
3 The insect is not active during the pupa stage. It is being reorganized into a new body form.
4 The adult insect emerges from the pupa.

Figure 13.15 During complete metamorphosis, insects change from an egg to an adult.

As You Read

Use what you have learned in this lesson to make corrections or additions to your concept map.

What are the two types of insect metamorphosis?

Incomplete metamorphosis has three stages. The first stage is an egg. The egg hatches into the second stage, a young insect called a **nymph**. A nymph looks much like the adult insect. The nymph grows into the last stage, the adult. A grasshopper goes through incomplete metamorphosis.

Figure 13.16 During complete metamorphosis, a Monarch butterfly larva *(left)* becomes a pupa *(center)*. A grasshopper nymph *(right)* grows from an egg during incomplete metamorphosis.

Differentiated Instruction

Visual Assign each student a different type of insect. Have students create color posters showing their insects, with labels for each of the parts.

Insect Behavior

Insects have a wide range of behaviors. Some behaviors help insects survive. Most insects live by themselves. They compete with each other for food, water, and mates.

Some insects, such as ants and bees, live and work together in colonies. Each member of an insect colony has a specific job. In an ant colony, the female worker ants build and defend the nest and gather food. They also care for the young ants. The queen ants lay the eggs, and the male ants fertilize the eggs.

Insects have many defenses against predators. Bees and wasps defend themselves with painful stings. Stinkbugs taste or smell bad to predators. Some insects have body colors or shapes that help them blend in with their surroundings. This adaptation is called **camouflage** (KA muh flahj).

CONNECTION: Chemistry

One way insects can communicate with each other is by releasing special chemicals called pheromones. An insect that finds food may drag its abdomen along the ground and release a pheromone as it returns to the colony. Other insects can follow this scent back to the food source.

Figure 13.17 Worker ants *(left)* protect the larvae in the colony. A bee *(center)* uses its stinger for protection. A praying mantis *(right)* uses camouflage to blend in with its surroundings.

PEOPLE IN SCIENCE Karl von Frisch 1886–1982

Karl von Frisch was an Austrian scientist who studied insect behavior. He won the Nobel Prize in Medicine and Physiology in 1973 for his studies of bees. In his early work, von Frisch showed that honeybees can see colors. He also found that bees can distinguish among dozens of similar smells.

Von Frisch also found that honeybees use dances to give other bees information about the distance and direction to a food source. Bees use a round dance to show other bees that a food source is a short distance (up to about 50 meters) away from the hive. Bees use a zigzag or waggle dance to show other bees that food is farther away. Bees will also angle their bodies during this dance to show other bees the direction in which they should travel to find the food.

Teach

EXPLAIN to students that while most insects live by themselves, there are some that live in groups and work together to survive. Ask students if they know of any insects that do this. Tell students that bees and ants are good examples of insects that work together for the good of their entire group.

CONNECTION: Chemistry

Scientists use insect pheromones in place of pesticides to attract insects and prevent them from reproducing while avoiding harm to the environment. One method is to bait a trap with pheromones. Another method that farmers use is called communication disruption. Farmers spray their entire crop with insect pheromones, and this makes it very difficult for the males to find the females and mate.

EXPLORE Divide the class in two. Have half the class put on some kind of perfume or scent. Blindfold the other half of the class and see if the blindfolded students can find the other students using their noses.

PEOPLE IN SCIENCE

Von Frisch also found that at certain times of day, the bees' dances gave incorrect information about where to find food. This error was consistent over time. It wasn't until much later that von Frisch's colleague, Lindauer, together with his student H. Martin, found that this error was due to Earth's magnetic field.

EXTEND Von Frisch found that bees can distinguish among dozens of similar smells. Have students work with a partner and explore their own sense of smell. Place different foods, flowers, and other aromatic objects in different jars. Blindfold students and see how many scents they can identify. Have students record their results in their Science Notebooks.

Background Information

Termites are another group of insects that live in colonies. Although they resemble ants, their midsections are thicker and their antennae are elbowed and resemble a string of beads. A termite colony is made up of many different types of termites.

The worker termites make up the largest group, and they do most of the work of the colony. They find food, clean and maintain their hive, and take care of the young. Members of the soldier caste protect the hive from predators, and members of the reproductive caste lay eggs and reproduce.

Teach

EXPLORE Ask students to share their feelings about insects. Explain to students that while many people are afraid of insects, there are many insects that we couldn't live without. Insects play an important role in our lives. Some insects, such as bees, produce the honey that we eat. Other insects, such as silkworms, produce the silk fabric that we wear.

Assess

EVALUATE Use the After You Read questions and the Alternative Assessment to help you assess students' understanding of this lesson.

After You Read

1. They have a wide variety of mouth structures that allow them to eat many different types of food. Most can fly from one place to another.
2. Both types of metamorphosis represent the growth of an insect through a series of stages. In complete metamorphosis, there are four stages and the young insect does not resemble the adult. In incomplete metamorphosis, there are three stages and the young insect looks like a smaller version of the adult.
3. Insects can sting a predator and release chemicals that make the insects taste or smell bad to predators.
4. Insects produce things that humans use, such as honey, beeswax, and silk. They also eat other insects that destroy crops, and they can be used in medicines. Harmful insects can destroy crops and spread disease.
5. Insects have exoskeletons, segmented bodies, and jointed appendages.

Did You Know?

Silk fabric comes from the cocoons of silkworms. The silkworm originally came from China. Each cocoon is made of a single thread that is about one kilometer long when unraveled. Approximately 3,000 cocoons are needed to make 500 grams of silk. Nearly 32 million kilograms of silk are produced every year.

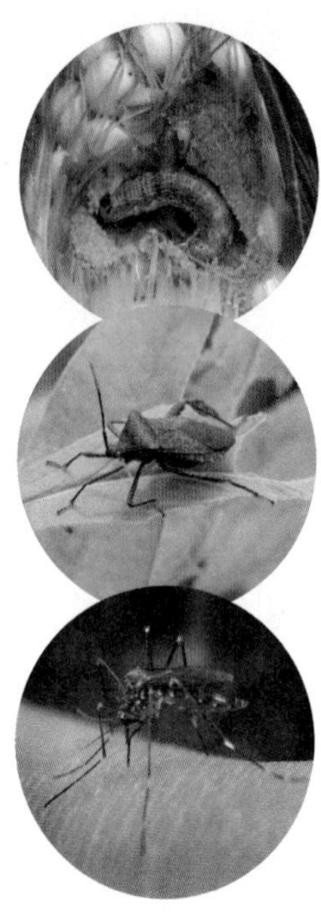

Figure 13.19 The corn earworm *(top)* and the squash bug *(center)* are insects that damage crops. The mosquito *(bottom)* is a parasite that can transmit diseases to humans.

Insects and Humans

What is your reaction when you see an insect? Many people do not like insects. They believe it is better to kill them than to leave them alone. Although some insects are harmful to people, many are helpful.

Bees produce honey and beeswax. They also help plants reproduce by carrying pollen from one plant to another. Honeybees pollinate many commercial crop plants. Without pollination, plants such as apples, peaches, cherries, pumpkins, squash, and tomatoes would not produce the fruits we eat.

Silk comes from the cocoons of silkworms. Silk thread is the strongest natural fiber. It is also elastic, which allows fabric made from it to spring back into shape when stretched.

Insects also eat other insects that can destroy plants. Ladybugs feed on aphids that can destroy many crops, for example. Some insects feed on dead plant and animal material. The dung beetle breaks down cow droppings into substances that make the soil good for planting.

Substances from some insects have been used in medicines for arthritis. Blowfly larvae, for example, are used to treat infections. These larvae feed on dead tissue and secrete a substance that helps the healthy tissue heal.

Some insects are harmful to humans. Species such as grasshoppers and beetles can do major damage to crops. Mosquitoes, flies, and fleas can carry small organisms that cause disease. A mosquito is a parasite that can transmit malaria and West Nile virus to humans.

Figure 13.18 Examples of useful insects include the silkworm *(left)*, dung beetle *(center)*, and blowfly larvae *(right)*.

After You Read

1. What are two reasons why insects are so successful?
2. How are complete metamorphosis and incomplete metamorphosis alike? How are they different?
3. What are two ways that insects protect themselves from predators?
4. How are insects helpful to humans? How are they harmful?
5. Use your concept map to describe three characteristics that all insects have in common.

234 ARTHROPODS AND ECHINODERMS

Alternative Assessment

EVALUATE Ask students who have difficulty with the As You Read questions to list all of the characteristics of insects that they have learned from this chapter. Allow students to refer to their Science Notebooks when making their lists.

ELL Strategy

Prepare Presentations Assign each student an insect to research. Students should use books, encyclopedias, and the Internet to research their insects' habitats, diets, and characteristics and whether the insects are helpful or harmful to humans. English-language learners from other countries may be encouraged to research insects indigenous to their home, especially if they are uncommon in the United States. Have students present their findings to the class.

Background Information

When woven into cloth, silk is extremely warm. It is warmer than cotton, linen, or rayon clothing. China is the largest producer of silk in the world. Silk is also produced in Japan, Brazil, India, South Korea, Thailand, and Uzbekistan.

13.3 Echinoderms

Before You Read

Use the lesson title and headings to create a lesson outline. Label the title with the Roman numeral *I*, and label the headings with the letters *A*, *B*, and *C*. Under each heading, record important information from the lesson.

Learning Goals

- Identify the common characteristics of echinoderms.
- Describe the body structure of a sea star.
- Compare the characteristics of sea stars, sea urchins, sea cucumbers, and sand dollars.

New Vocabulary

endoskeleton
water-vascular system
tube feet

Recall Vocabulary

radial symmetry (p. 211)

If you have walked on the beach, it is likely that you have seen a sea star. A sea star belongs to a phylum of animals called the echinoderms (ih KI nuh durmz). Sea stars, sea urchins, sea cucumbers, and sand dollars are echinoderms. Echinoderms live in Earth's oceans. Examples of echinoderms are shown in **Figure 13.20**.

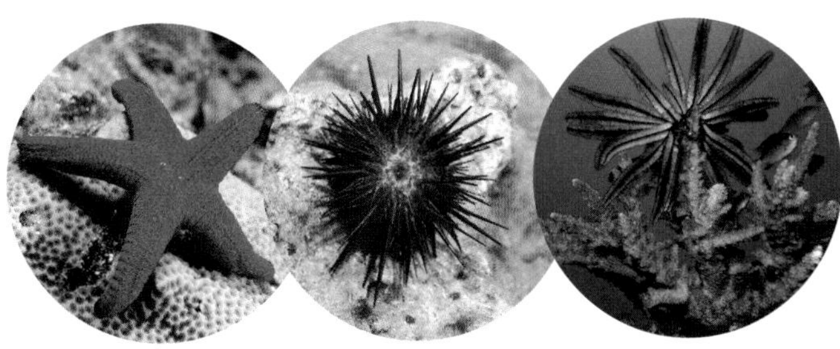

Figure 13.20 A sea star *(left)*, a sea urchin *(center)*, and a feather star *(right)* are all members of the phylum Echinodermata.

Characteristics of Echinoderms

Like humans, echinoderms have an **endoskeleton**, or internal skeleton. The endoskeleton is made of calcium-containing plates from which the spines protrude. The plates and spines are covered with a thin layer of skin for protection. The word *echinoderm* comes from the Greek words meaning "spiny skin."

The adult bodies of echinoderms have radial symmetry. They often consist of five or more arms coming out of a central body. The larval stages of echinoderms have bilateral symmetry. All echinoderms have a **water-vascular system**. This is a system of water-filled tubes that runs through the echinoderm's body. This system functions in obtaining food and oxygen, removing wastes, and helping the echinoderm move.

Thousands of tube feet are connected to the water-vascular system. **Tube feet** act like suction cups. They help the echinoderm move and hold on to captured food.

Figure 13.21 The tube feet of an echinoderm help it gather food and move.

13.3 Introduce

ENGAGE students by telling them that many echinoderms can be found on the beach. Ask: *Have you ever seen a starfish, or a sea star?* If students have seen this invertebrate, ask for a volunteer to draw it on the board. Ask students to describe the characteristics of this animal. Tell students that *starfish* is a name commonly used to refer to a sea star.

Before You Read

Model an outline using Roman numerals on the board. Show students the way the numbers and letters progress in sequence. Begin by writing the lesson title *Echinoderms* next to the Roman numeral *I*. Have students copy this into their Science Notebooks.

Teach

EXPLAIN that in this lesson, students will identify the common characteristics of echinoderms. They will also learn about the body structure of a sea star and compare its characteristics with those of sea urchins, sea cucumbers, and sand dollars.

Vocabulary

endoskeleton Explain to students that the prefix *endo-* comes from the Greek word *endon*, meaning "within." An endoskeleton is a skeleton that is inside of the body. Remind students that an exoskeleton is found outside the body.

water-vascular system Tell students that the word *vascular* comes from the Latin word *vasculum*, which means "vessel." In a water-vascular system, water from the ocean flows through the vessels.

tube feet Explain that *tube* comes from the Latin *tubus*, which means "pipe." Tube feet are shaped like small pipes and act like suction cups to help the echinoderm catch food and move.

Differentiated Instruction

Kinesthetic Provide students with dried specimens of many different echinoderms, such as sea stars, sea urchins, brittle stars, and sand dollars. Have students touch and observe these specimens and record their observations in their Science Notebooks. Encourage students to compare the characteristics of echinoderms with the characteristics of arthropods they have learned about in this chapter.

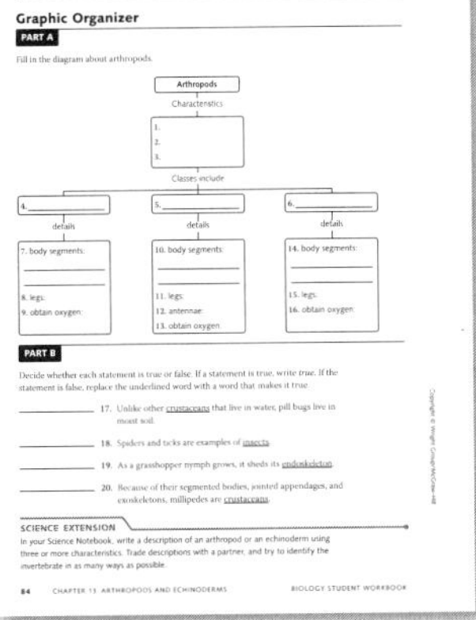

Graphic Organizer

PART A

Arthropods

PART B

SCIENCE EXTENSION

Graphic Organizer
Workbook, p. 84

Teach

EXPLAIN to students that the term *starfish* actually refers to an animal called the sea star. Tell students that a sea star is not a fish at all. It is an echinoderm.

EXPLORE Distribute preserved specimens of sea stars, and have students hypothesize about how a sea star moves, what it eats, how it protects itself, and where it is likely to live. Record student ideas on the board. Tell students that the word *echinoderm* comes from the Greek words meaning "spiny skin." Ask students why this is an appropriate name.

As You Read

ANSWER A sea star uses its arms and tube feet to catch prey such as a clam or an oyster. It grabs a clam with its arms and holds onto the closed shells with its tube feet. The sea star pulls on the shells until the shells open. Then, the sea star pushes its stomach through its mouth and into the opening in the shells. Digestive chemicals break down the clam's body.

Explore It!

Obtain a variety of suction disks from a hardware store. Students should observe that suction disks work best on surfaces that are hard and smooth. An echinoderm's tube feet use suction action to catch prey and move.

Figure It Out: Figure 3.22

ANSWER **1.** The tube feet help the echinoderm feed and move. **2.** A spider has bilateral symmetry, eight legs, two body segments, and an exoskeleton. A sea star has a body with radial symmetry, five arms, hundreds of tube feet, and an endoskeleton. Both are invertebrates.

As You Read

Share your outline with a partner, and make any necessary additions or corrections.

How does a sea star obtain and eat its food?

Figure It Out

1. What is the function of the sea star's tube feet?
2. Compare the physical characteristics of a sea star with those of a spider.

Explore It!

Design and conduct an experiment to show what types of surfaces are best to use with suction cups. In your Science Notebook, describe how an echinoderm's tube feet are similar to suction cups.

Sea Stars

Sea stars are commonly called starfish. Sea stars are not fish, but they do have a star shape. A sea star has five or more arms extending from a central body. The undersides of the arms are covered with tube feet.

Sea stars are hunters that eat mollusks such as clams, oysters, and mussels. A sea star uses its arms and tube feet to catch prey. The sea star grabs an oyster with its arms. It holds on to the closed shell with its tube feet and pulls. When the shell opens, the sea star pushes its stomach through its mouth and into the opening in the shell. Digestive chemicals break down the oyster's body, and the sea star has a tasty meal!

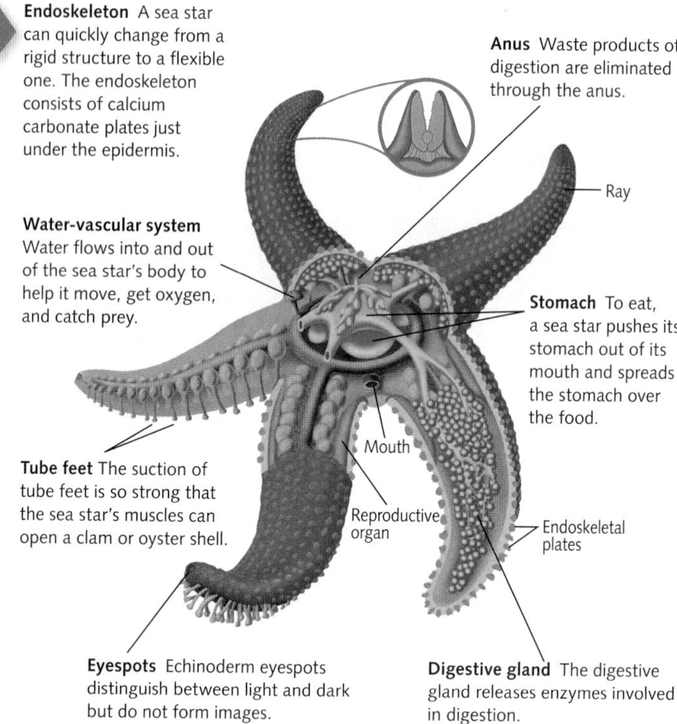
Endoskeleton A sea star can quickly change from a rigid structure to a flexible one. The endoskeleton consists of calcium carbonate plates just under the epidermis.
Anus Waste products of digestion are eliminated through the anus.
Ray
Water-vascular system Water flows into and out of the sea star's body to help it move, get oxygen, and catch prey.
Stomach To eat, a sea star pushes its stomach out of its mouth and spreads the stomach over the food.
Mouth
Tube feet The suction of tube feet is so strong that the sea star's muscles can open a clam or oyster shell.
Reproductive organ
Endoskeletal plates
Eyespots Echinoderm eyespots distinguish between light and dark but do not form images.
Digestive gland The digestive gland releases enzymes involved in digestion.

Figure 13.22 This diagram shows the external and internal structures of a sea star.

Figure 13.23 This sea star is regenerating the rest of its body from one arm.

People who fish for mollusks do not like the sea stars that eat them. Years ago, sea stars found in mollusk beds were chopped into many pieces and thrown back into the ocean. People did not realize that, like other invertebrates, sea stars can regenerate body parts, as **Figure 13.23** shows. Chopping them up only resulted in more sea stars and fewer mollusks!

Background Information

There are approximately 6,000 different types of echinoderms. All echinoderms live in water. This is the only major phylum of animals for which this is true. Echinoderms lay eggs, which become larvae. In the larval stage, echinoderms have bilateral symmetry; as they grow into adults, they develop radial symmetry.

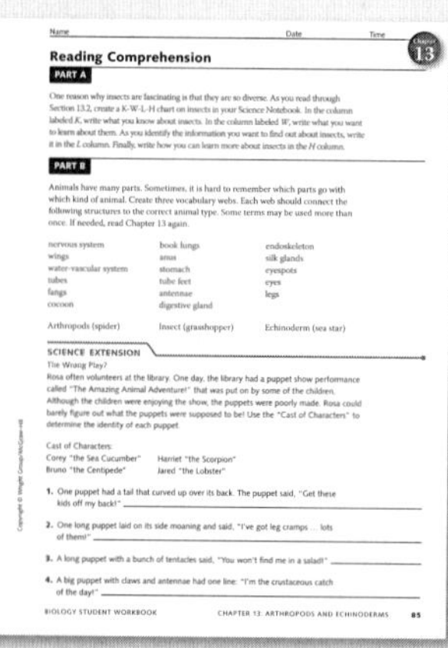

Reading Comprehension Workbook, p. 85

Other Echinoderms

Brittle stars look like sea stars, but their arms are long and whiplike. If you tried to pick up a brittle star, its arms would break off. This is a useful adaptation for getting away from predators. Brittle stars eat dead or decaying plant and animal bodies. Brittle stars move by waving their arms against the ocean bottom.

Sea cucumbers have long, flexible bodies. They look very different from sea stars and brittle stars. Sea cucumbers have rows of tube feet on their underside. This allows them to crawl along the ocean bottom. They are filter feeders that use tentacles to sweep food into the mouth. Feather stars are also filter feeders. These echinoderms have short bodies and many arms that look like feathers.

Long, sharp spines cover and protect the bodies of sea urchins. Some sea urchins have poison in their spines, which can deliver painful stings. Sea urchins have five teeth that scrape off and chew algae for food. Sea urchins use their spines and tube feet to move from one place to another.

Sand dollars have no arms. They look like large coins. Their bodies are flat and covered with very short spines. The spines help them burrow into the sand. Sand dollars usually eat tiny particles of food that float in the water.

Figure 13.25 A sea urchin *(left)* is protected by long spines. Sand dollars *(right)* use their short spines to burrow into the sand.

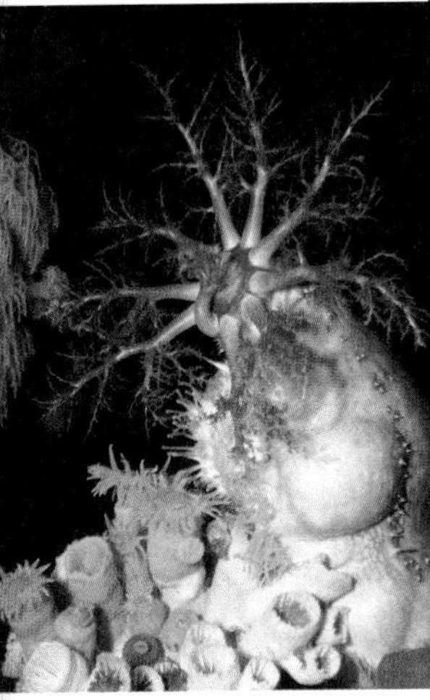

Figure 13.24 A brittle star *(top)* looks like a sea star with longer arms. A sea cucumber *(bottom)* uses its tentacles to gather food.

After You Read

1. What are three common characteristics of echinoderms?
2. Describe the function of an echinoderm's water-vascular system.
3. Explain how sea stars and brittle stars are alike. How are they different?
4. Review the information in your outline. In a well-developed paragraph, describe the adaptations echinoderms have that allow them to catch prey and escape from predators.

Did You Know?

The sea cucumber has an unusual defense system. If attacked by a predator, the sea cucumber will eject its internal organs. The organs are sticky, and they surround the predator while the sea cucumber escapes. The missing organs are quickly regenerated.

Teach

EXPLAIN Tell students that the echinoderm phylum also includes brittle stars, feather stars, sea cucumbers, sea urchins, and sand dollars. Ask them to compare and contrast these different animals. Record their responses on the board.

Science Notebook EXTRA

Write the terms listed below on the board, and have students copy them into their Science Notebooks.

arthropods, arachnid, echinoderms, bee, invertebrates, spider, crustacean, centipede, lobster, insect, sea star

Then, have students organize and summarize the information in this chapter by creating a concept map using the terms. English-language learners could organize the terms, and then create drawings in order to review the content of previous lessons.

Assess

EVALUATE Use the After You Read questions and the Alternative Assessment to help you assess students' understanding of this lesson.

After You Read

1. an endoskeleton, radial symmetry, and a water-vascular system
2. It helps in getting food, bringing in oxygen, and moving.
3. Both have bodies with arms that grow away from a central disk. The arms of brittle stars are longer and more whiplike.
4. Water-vascular systems and tube feet help catch prey and move away from predators. Spines protect the bodies of some.

ELL Strategy

Compare and Contrast Have each student create a chart with a column for each of the echinoderms in this lesson. Students should list the characteristics of each animal in the proper column. Provide students with colored highlighters or markers. Have students color-code the characteristics that all echinoderms have in common. Before filling in their compare-and-contrast charts, struggling English-language learners could draw each echinoderm at the top of the column. They could then explain their drawing to a partner, focusing on explaining and naming each feature of that organism's structure. Finally, they could create their list and highlight the common traits.

Alternative Assessment

EVALUATE Instruct students who are having difficulty answering the After You Read questions to refer to the outlines in their Science Notebooks. Check that outlines include all topics and subtopics from the lesson.

Chapter 13 Summary

VOCABULARY REVIEW

Check students' sentences or paragraphs to make sure that they understand the meaning of each vocabulary term.

PREPARE FOR CHAPTER TEST

Evaluate students' essays using the following criteria:

1. The topic sentence, or main idea, should restate the Key Concept.
2. The supporting paragraphs should incorporate the answers to the Learning Goal questions students have written and include details, facts, and examples they have recorded in their Science Notebooks.
3. The concluding sentence should sum up the main idea of the chapter and restate the Key Concept.

MASTERING CONCEPTS

True or False

1. False, appendage
2. True
3. False, thorax
4. False, larva
5. True
6. False, sea urchins

Short Answer

7. All arthropods have an exoskeleton, segmented bodies, and jointed appendages.
8. As an arthropod grows, it leaves its old exoskeleton and grows a new, larger one.
9. They have a wide variety of mouth parts, allowing them to eat many types of food. Most can fly to catch prey and avoid predators.
10. In complete metamorphosis, there are four stages and the young insect does not resemble the adult. In incomplete metamorphosis, there are three stages and the young insect looks like a smaller version of the adult.
11. The sea star uses its arms and tube feet to pry open the shells of the clam. The sea star squeezes its stomach through its mouth and pours digestive enzymes on the body of the clam. It then sucks the digested clam into its mouth and pulls its stomach back into its body.

Chapter 13

Summary

KEY CONCEPTS

13.1 Arthropods

- All arthropods have jointed appendages, segmented bodies, and a hard exoskeleton.
- Arachnids, including spiders, scorpions, ticks, and mites, have two body regions and eight legs.
- Shrimp, crabs, lobsters, and crayfish are crustaceans. Crustaceans have five or more pairs of appendages and two pairs of antennae. Many crustaceans have claws.
- Centipedes and millipedes have long, wormlike bodies with many segments and many legs. Centipedes are active hunters. Millipedes eat dead or decaying plant material.

13.2 Insects

- Insects have three main body sections: a head, a thorax, and an abdomen. They have six legs.
- As insects grow, they undergo a series of changes called metamorphosis. Complete metamorphosis has four stages: egg, larva, pupa, and adult. Incomplete metamorphosis has three stages: egg, nymph, and adult.
- Some insects live by themselves. Other insects, such as ants and bees, live in colonies.
- Insects can be helpful by making products humans use and by eating other insects that destroy crops. Insects can be harmful by eating crops and by causing disease.

13.3 Echinoderms

- Echinoderms have spiny skin and an endoskeleton.
- Echinoderms use a water-vascular system and tube feet to catch prey and to move.
- Both the sea star and the brittle star have five or more arms extending from a central body. Sea stars eat clams, oysters, and mussels.
- Sea cucumbers have long, flexible bodies. Feather stars have many featherlike arms. Sea urchins are covered with spines. Sand dollars have no arms and look like large coins.

VOCABULARY REVIEW

Write each term in a complete sentence, or write a paragraph relating several terms.

13.1
appendage, p. 225
exoskeleton, p. 225
molting, p. 225
antenna, p. 228

13.2
thorax, p. 231
metamorphosis, p. 232
larva, p. 232
pupa, p. 232
nymph, p. 232
camouflage, p. 233

13.3
endoskeleton, p. 235
water-vascular system, p. 235
tube feet, p. 235

PREPARE FOR CHAPTER TEST

To prepare for the chapter test, create a question from each Learning Goal. Use the information in your Science Notebook to answer each question. Then use these answers to write a well-developed essay about the chapter. Use the Key Concept on the first page of this chapter as your topic sentence.

Key Concept Review
Workbook, p. 82

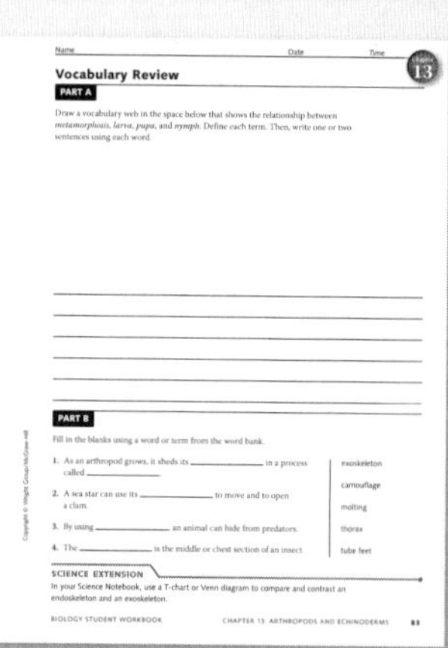

Vocabulary Review
Workbook, p. 83

MASTERING CONCEPTS

True or False

If the statement is true, write "true." If it is false, change the underlined word or words.

1. An exoskeleton is a structure such as a leg or an arm that grows out of an animal's body.
2. Antennae are sense organs used for taste, touch, smell, and balance.
3. The abdomen is the middle, or chest, section of the insect's body.
4. The second stage of complete metamorphosis is called a pupa.
5. A water-vascular system is a system of water-filled tubes running through an echinoderm's body.
6. Spines cover and protect the bodies of sea stars.

Short Answer

Answer each of the following in a sentence or brief paragraph.

7. What are three common characteristics of all arthropods?
8. Describe the process of molting.
9. Explain why insects are so successful.
10. Compare the processes of complete metamorphosis and incomplete metamorphosis.
11. How does a sea star eat a clam?

Critical Thinking

Use what you have learned in this chapter to answer each of the following.

12. **Compare and Contrast** What are three ways in which arthropods and echinoderms differ from each other?
13. **Apply Concepts** Stone crab hunters remove one claw from a crab and return the crab to the water to grow a new claw. Explain why the crab hunters leave the crabs with one good claw.
14. **Classify** Your friend thinks that a spider is an insect. How would you explain why spiders are not classified as insects?

Standardized Test Question

Choose the letter of the response that correctly answers the question.

Effects of a Pesticide on Spiders and Insects

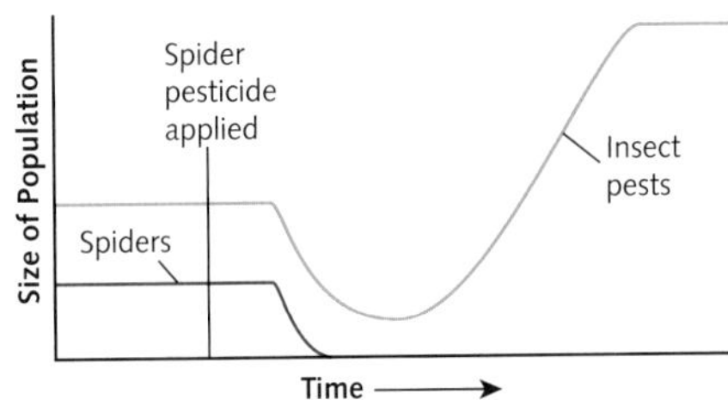

15. A pesticide is a chemical that is used to kill certain arthropods. The graph shows how a spider pesticide affects a spider population and an insect population. Which is most likely the reason for the change in the insect population after a spider pesticide is used?
    - A. The insects eat the pesticide as food.
    - B. The insects eat the spiderwebs as food.
    - C. The pesticide causes the insects to reproduce more quickly.
    - D. The spiders die from the pesticide and do not eat the insects.

Test-Taking Tip

Avoid changing your answer unless you have read the question incorrectly. Usually, your first choice is the correct choice.

Critical Thinking

12. An arthropod has an exoskeleton, and an echinoderm has an endoskeleton. Arthropods have segmented bodies and jointed appendages; echinoderms do not. Arthropods live on land and in water. Echinoderms live only in the ocean.
13. The crab needs one good claw to protect itself from predators and gather food. If left with no claws, it would soon be eaten or starve to death.
14. Insects have only six legs. Since a spider has eight legs, it is not classified as an insect.

Standardized Test Question

15. D

Reading Links

Stinkbugs, Stick Insects, and Stag Beetles: And 18 More of the Strangest Insects on Earth

This guide to the quirkiest aspects of the insect world will surprise students while equipping them with a more thorough understanding of insect characteristics, behavior, and variety. The 21 subjects of close-up examination include giant hissing cockroaches, beetles that spray chemicals as hot as boiling water, and the curious bugs from the title. The book also touches on such topics as mimicry, symbiosis, predation, and pollination, and its appendix includes information about insect zoo locations.

Kneidel, Sally. John Wiley & Sons. 128 pp. Illustrated. Trade ISBN: 978-0-471-35712-4.

The Tarantula Scientist

The career of scientist and spider enthusiast Sam Marshall, who works with Earth's biggest spiders in the rain forests of French Guiana and at the largest comparative spider laboratory in the United States, is the subject of this richly photographed volume. By following Marshall's work as a passionate arachnologist, the book presents students with valuable information about spiders and teaches important lessons about the scientific process. Readers may also find Marshall's triumph over early academic struggles encouraging, and the work of his students is briefly featured.

Montgomery, Sy. Photography by Nic Bishop. Houghton Mifflin. 80 pp. Illustrated. Trade ISBN: 978-0-618-14799-1.

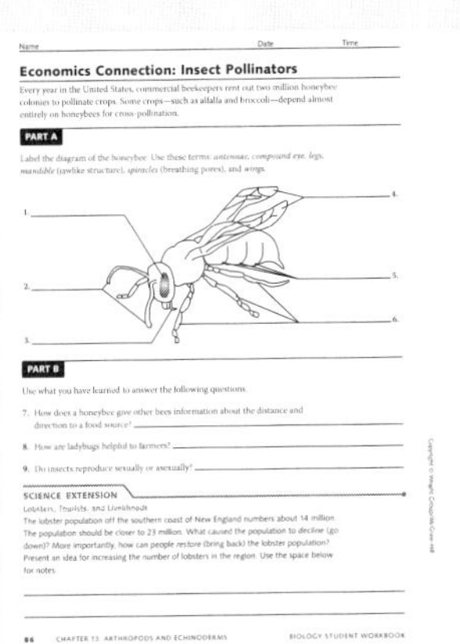

Curriculum Connection Workbook, p. 86

Science Challenge Workbook, p. 87

Chapter 13 Labs

13A Characteristics of Arthropods and Echinoderms

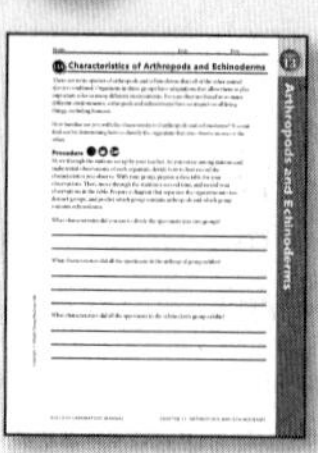

This prechapter introduction activity is designed to determine what students already know about the characteristics of arthropods and echinoderms by engaging them in examining, comparing, contrasting, and classifying arthropods and echinoderms into groups according to similarities.

Objectives

- compare and contrast arthropod and echinoderm specimens
- use observed similarities to divide the specimens into groups
- record data in a suitable way
- communicate conclusions

Planning

1 class period groups of 4–6 students

Materials (per group)

- samples of different arthropods and echinoderms (A nice selection might include a spider or tick; shrimp, crayfish, lobster, and/or crab; centipede; cricket, butterfly, and/or grasshopper; pill bug, sea star and/or sand dollar.)
- pencil and paper

Advance Preparation

- Pictures or preserved specimens can be used if live specimens are unavailable or pose a safety hazard. The local grocery store, seafood market, pet store, or bait shop might be willing to donate samples that can be used. Pictures can be found in science publications. Laminating these will preserve the pictures' life span.
- Set up viewing stations for each specimen so that students can rotate from station to station and observe each organism. Each organism should be contained so that both students and specimens are protected. Remind students not to touch any of the organisms they are observing.
- Plan to allow a short viewing period followed by time for students to discuss and develop data tables in which to record characteristics that might be used to separate the organisms into two groups. Once students have constructed their tables, allow for another round of observations.

Engagement Guide

- After their initial observations, challenge students to think about how they can classify the specimens they have observed by asking:
  - *What characteristics will be most helpful in dividing the specimens into groups?* (Characteristics that show how the specimens are alike and different will be most useful in classifying. Some characteristics that students might notice include presence or absence of wings, antennae, body segments, legs, claws, and body shape or symmetry.)
  - *As you begin your classification of these specimens, is there one characteristic that you think will best allow you to divide the specimens into two distinct groups?* (From their initial observations, students might infer that body shape/symmetry and presence or absence of appendages are major differences between the groups.)
- Encourage students to communicate their conclusions in creative ways.

Going Further

Provide students with several unknown organisms, and have them infer to which group, if either, each organism belongs. Encourage students to use their data tables and then justify their classifications.

13B Examining a Grasshopper

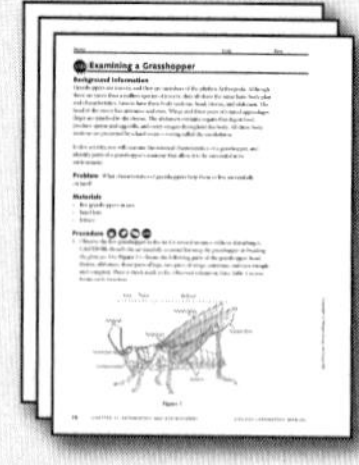

Objectives

- make observations
- identify anatomical structures
- infer the adaptive advantage of anatomical structures

Skill Set

observing, comparing and contrasting, recording data, inferring, stating conclusions

Planning

1 class period

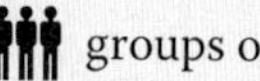

groups of 2–4 students

Materials

Materials for this activity are listed in the Student Laboratory Manual.

Advance Preparation

Grasshoppers can be obtained from biological supply houses or pet stores. Keep them alive in glass jars with holes punched in the lids. Place sticks for perching and lettuce or other green leafy vegetables for food in the jars. Remove the lettuce or other food before the lab to encourage eating when students feed the grasshoppers. If grasshoppers are not available, you can substitute crickets. If students are having difficulty observing some of the structures, you can place additional grasshoppers in the freezer overnight and then allow students to handle and observe these frozen specimens. If you choose to provide frozen samples for students to use, be sure to have students wear goggles and gloves.

Answers to Observations: Data Table 1

Students should place a check mark in the *Observed* column when they identify each listed structure. Head: antennae, eyes, and mouthparts will move as grasshopper feeds; thorax: attachment site for legs and wings; abdomen: divided into segments, moves in and out as a unit during respiration; legs: smaller front legs are used for walking and crawling, while larger hind legs are used for jumping; wings: students may have difficulty observing the two pairs, but you can demonstrate on a frozen specimen that the forewings are tougher and cover and protect the delicate hind wings; antennae: two, tips are covered with small hairs; simple eyes: three small eyes located at the base of each antenna and in the center of the head; compound eyes: larger eyes located on each side of the head; spiracles*: small holes on each side of each abdominal segment; last abdominal segment: students should identify their grasshopper as male or female based on their observation of this segment.

* Students may have trouble locating the spiracles. You might want to circulate and identify the spiracles for each group.

Answers to Analysis and Conclusions

1. The thorax is specialized for movement with the attachment of three pairs of legs and two pairs of wings.
2. Grasshoppers can use their antennae and their eyes to sense movement.
3. Because grasshoppers are similar in color to the grass in their environment, they are able to avoid predators.
4. Students should predict that grasshoppers do not swim because they have both legs and wings for movement. Another observation students might use to support their prediction is the abdominal location of a grasshopper's respiratory organs, spiracles.
5. Answers might include legs for walking and jumping, wings for flying, and respiratory organs—spiracles—that allow gas exchange with the environment. Students might also include the exoskeleton, which provides protection and keeps the grasshopper from drying out in a drier environment.

Going Further

Have students compare and contrast specimens from other classes of arthropods using characteristics listed in Data Table 1.

13C Examining Insect Metamorphosis

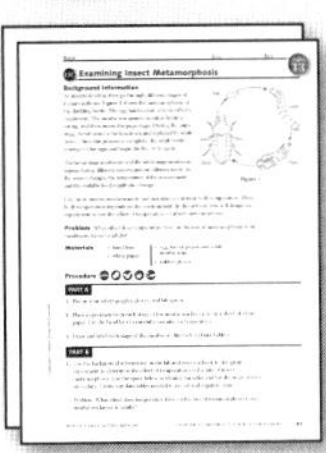

Objectives

- make observations
- design and conduct a controlled experiment
- record and analyze data
- draw conclusions about the effect of temperature on insect metamorphosis

Skill Set

observing, comparing and contrasting, recording and analyzing data, stating conclusions

Planning

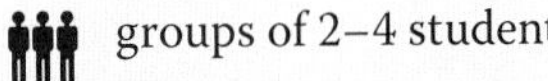

1 class period for Part A; 1 class period for Part B; 15 minutes daily for 10 to 14 days

groups of 2–4 students

Materials

Materials for this activity are listed in the Student Laboratory Manual.

Advance Preparation

Mealworms can be ordered from a biological supply house or purchased from a local pet store. During Part A, you might want to keep each stage of mealworm in a separate container. For Part B, students will need access to a refrigerator and an incubator. A simple incubator can be constructed from a box and a clamp-on utility lamp. Student mealworm cultures should be grown in small, pint-sized containers with loose-fitting lids. You can also cover the containers with fine wire mesh or cheesecloth to prevent adult beetles from escaping. Moistened oatmeal, bran flakes, or cornmeal can be used as culture media. The small cups are useful for moving and observing animals from the culture during the extended observation period. For a mealworm to begin its metamorphosis, it has to be isolated from other mealworms. To keep mealworms from beginning this step, keep them together at each stage.

Answers to Observations: Data Table 1

Check students' drawings for accuracy and for characteristics of arthropods.

Answers to Analysis and Conclusions

1. Larvae have segmented bodies and three pairs of jointed legs.
2. Answers will vary, but students should indicate lower temperatures produced slower metamorphosis and that higher temperatures produced faster metamorphosis.
3. Warmer temperatures speed up the rate of insect metamorphosis.
4. The same stages were observed.
5. The number of adult insects might be greatly reduced because extremely cold temperatures might kill many of the insect larvae and pupa that would normally produce adult insects in the spring.

Going Further

Have students select and test another variable, such as light or moisture, for its effect on mealworm metamorphosis. Have students report their results to the class for further analysis.

Chapter 14 Lessons

Introduce Chapter 14

As a starting activity, use LAB 14A Comparing Vertebrate Characteristics on page 84 of the Laboratory Manual.

ENGAGE Ask students to look at the pictures of the chameleon and blue poison dart frog. Write *reptile* and *amphibian* on the board. Ask if students know which animal is an amphibian and which animal is a reptile. As one or two students answer, ask them to share what they know about reptiles and amphibians, and write those ideas on the board under the appropriate heading. Encourage students to name other animals they think belong in each group. Have students record what you have written on the board in their Science Notebooks.

Think About Classifying Animals

Organize students into pairs, and ask them to brainstorm things that are classified. Examples may include food groups, types of transportation, and geometric shapes. Discuss a few examples and the characteristics used as the basis of classification. Tell students they will learn about how fishes, amphibians, and reptiles are classified.

Model reviewing the headings of the lessons, and write *fishes* on the board. Think aloud about what you already know about fishes. Write these characteristics under *fishes*. Then, name examples of fishes. Direct students to complete each bulleted activity.

Chapter 14 Fishes, Amphibians, and Reptiles

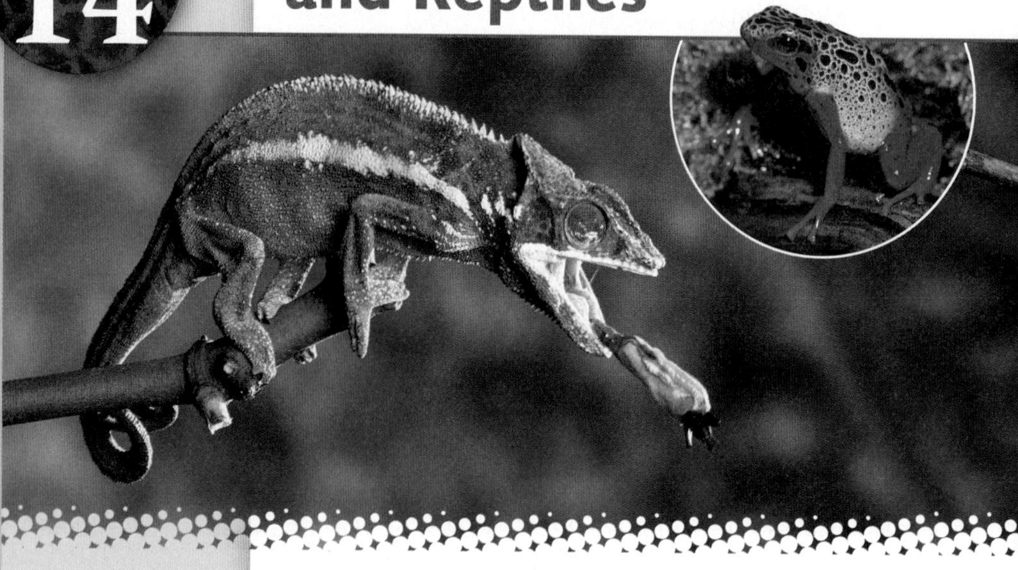

KEY CONCEPT Fishes, amphibians, and reptiles can be classified based on their physical characteristics.

The chameleon lizard sits quietly on a branch, hungry for its next meal. With lightning speed, the chameleon's tongue shoots out of its mouth. The sticky tongue captures a fly and pulls it into the chameleon's mouth.

A chameleon is a type of animal called a reptile. This chapter is about reptiles and two other kinds of animals, the fishes and the amphibians. The blue poison arrow frog is an amphibian. It has a deadly chemical in its skin that people use to make poison arrows. This chemical produces almost instant death in some animals.

Think About Classifying Animals

When things are classified, they are put into groups based on their characteristics. Scientists classify animals into groups.

- Look at the headings of the lessons in this chapter. Think about what you already know about fishes, amphibians, and reptiles.
- In your Science Notebook, describe the characteristics you are familiar with for each of these groups of animals. List some animals that you know belong in each group.

www.scilinks.org
Vertebrates **Code: WGB14**

240

Chapter 14 Planning Guide

Instructional Periods	National Standards	Lab Manual	Workbook
14.1 1 period	A.2, C.1, C.3, C.4; C.3; UCP.1	**Lab 14A—p. 84** Comparing Vertebrate Characteristics **Lab 14B—p. 85** Using a Graph to Identify an Ectotherm **Lab 14C—p. 89** Frog Anatomy	Key Concept Review p. 88 Vocabulary Review p. 89 Graphic Organizer p. 90 Reading Comprehension p. 91 Curriculum Connection p. 92 Science Challenge p. 93
14.2 2 periods	A.1, B.3, C.1; C.5, C.1, C.5, F.6; UCP.5		
14.3 2 periods	C.1; C.2; B.4, C.3, F.4; UCP.2, UCP.3, UCP.5		
14.4 2 periods	C.1; C.2, C.5, C.1, F.6, UCP.1		

Middle School Standard; High School Standard; Unifying Concept and Principle

14.1 What Is a Vertebrate?

Before You Read

Read the lesson title, headings, and Learning Goals. Look at the photos and diagrams. Predict what you think you will learn in this lesson. Write two or three sentences that describe your predictions in your Science Notebook.

Try this: Place your hand on your back at waist level and press gently. Move your hand up and down about five centimeters from that point. You should feel bony protrusions, or "bumps." The bumps are on the bones that make up your spinal column. The bones that go up and down your back are called **vertebrae** (VUR tuh bray, singular: vertebra). These bones are joined together with **cartilage** (KAR tuh lihj), a tissue that is softer than bone. Cartilage is very flexible and strong. This strong column of bone and cartilage is your backbone.

Humans aren't the only animals with backbones. Fishes, frogs, snakes, and birds also have backbones. An animal with a backbone is called a vertebrate. Vertebrates belong to the phylum Chordata (kor DAH tuh). Members of the phylum Chordata are called chordates.

In addition to the vertebrates, two other groups of animals are classified as chordates. Examples of these animals, the tunicates and lancelets, are shown in **Figure 14.1**. Tunicates are also called sea squirts. They live in the ocean attached to objects and are filter feeders. Lancelets, which are also filter feeders, look like small, thin fish that lack fins. They bury themselves in the sand with their heads sticking out to catch prey.

Characteristics of Chordates

All chordates—tunicates, lancelets, and vertebrates—have certain characteristics in common. They all have a hollow nerve cord. The nerve cord is a tube of nerves located near the animal's back. The nerve cord is protected by a notochord. The **notochord** (NOH tuh kord) is a flexible, rodlike structure made up of large, fluid-filled cells and stiff, fibrous tissues that supports the animal's back. In vertebrates, the notochord is replaced by the backbone.

At some point in their lives, all chordates have several pairs of pharyngeal (fuh RIN jee ul) pouches just behind the mouth. In many vertebrates, including humans, the pharyngeal pouches become parts of the ears, the jaws, and the throat. The pharyngeal pouches of fish develop into sets of gills. Fish use their gills to take in oxygen and give off carbon dioxide.

Learning Goals

- Describe the common characteristics of chordates.
- Describe the common characteristics of vertebrates.
- Distinguish between ectothermic and endothermic animals.
- Discuss the origin of the vertebrates.

New Vocabulary

vertebra
cartilage
notochord
ectotherm
endotherm

Recall Vocabulary

vertebrate (p. 211)
endoskeleton (p. 235)
exoskeleton (p. 225)

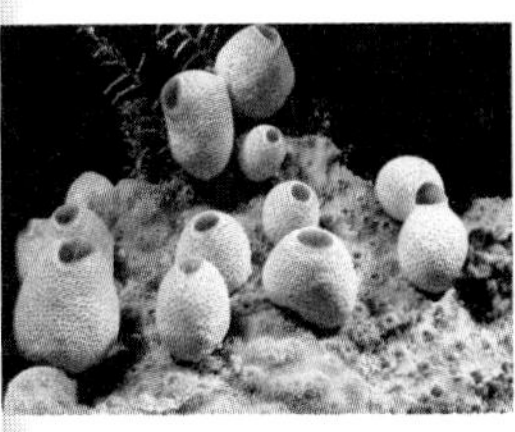

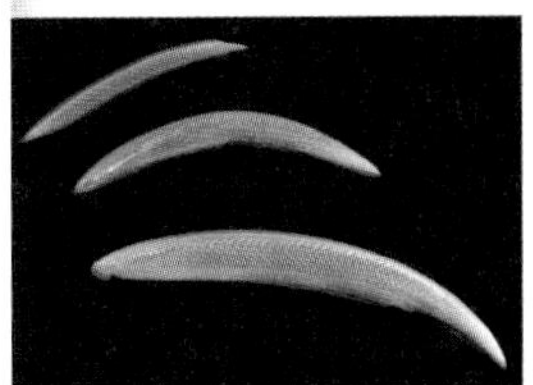

Figure 14.1 Tunicates *(top)* and lancelets *(bottom)* are two types of chordates that are not vertebrates.

ELL Strategy

<u>Use a Concept Map</u> Give each student a large (11 in. × 17 in.) sheet of paper. Have students make concept maps with *Chordates* as the title. Topics should include *Tunicates*, *Lancelets*, and *Vertebrates*. Students should add to the *Vertebrates* section throughout the chapter, using *Fishes*, *Amphibians*, and *Reptiles* as subtopics. If necessary, review how to construct and complete a concept map.

Science Notebook EXTRA

Encourage students to use the vocabulary section they created in their Science Notebooks. Remind them to record prefixes, suffixes, and root words to help them remember the meanings of vocabulary terms.

14.1 Introduce

ENGAGE Tell students that the oldest fossils are microscopic traces of bacteria that probably lived about 3.5 billion years ago. The oldest animal fossils are remains of invertebrates (animals without a backbone) that are about 600 million years old. The oldest fossils of vertebrates (animals with a backbone) are fossil fish about 450 million years old. Have students write each of these numbers. Then, have them create an appropriate time line for this information.

Before You Read

Model reading the lesson title, headings, and the captions for Figures 14.1 and 14.2. Thinking aloud, predict what you think students will learn about animals that are vertebrates. Have students work in pairs to review all the lesson headings and images in the chapter. Then, have them write a few sentences about what they anticipate learning in Chapter 14.

Vocabulary terms are listed on the first student page of each lesson. You may wish to preview the terms before introducing each lesson. Strategies for teaching the vocabulary appear on the pages where the terms are introduced.

Teach

EXPLAIN that in this chapter, students will learn about three kinds of vertebrates—fishes, amphibians, and reptiles—and their characteristics. Remind students that previously, they learned about invertebrates.

Vocabulary

vertebra Explain that *vertebra* is derived from the Latin word *vertere*, meaning "to turn." Ask students how this meaning relates to the definition of the word.

cartilage Tell students that the origin of *cartilage* is the Latin word *cartilaginis*, meaning "gristle." Ask students if they are familiar with gristle in beef or chicken.

notochord Explain that the prefix *noto-* comes from the Greek word *notos*, meaning "back," and that the root *chordē* is a Greek word meaning "string." Have students use those derivations to describe the notochord.

Teach

EXPLAIN that students will learn about the characteristics of vertebrates in this section. Write *endoskeleton* and *exoskeleton* on the board. Ask students to hypothesize about the meanings of the words. If students do not know the meanings, underline and review the prefixes *endo-* ("within") and *exo-* ("outside"). Then, ask students to give examples of organisms with endoskeletons and organisms with exoskeletons.

Figure It Out: Figure 14.2

ANSWER **1.** An endoskeleton provides support and protects the internal organs of a vertebrate. **2.** Both skeletons include a backbone, ribs, and a skull. The frog has large back limbs. The bat has large front limbs.

Vocabulary

ectotherm Tell students that the prefix *ecto-* is from the Greek word *ektos*, meaning "outside." The root *therm* is from the Greek word *thermē*, meaning "heat." These combine in the word *ectotherm*, which means "heat from outside."

endotherm Tell students that the prefix *endo-* is derived from the Greek word *endon*, meaning "within." Have students use what they have learned about the root *therm* to give the meaning of the word *endotherm* as "heat from within."

As You Read

Give students a few minutes to review their sentences and revise their earlier predictions to demonstrate their new knowledge.

ANSWER An endotherm is an animal that maintains a constant body temperature. An ectotherm is an animal whose body temperature changes with the environment.

CONNECTION: Health

EXPLORE Have pairs of students read the Health Connection aloud. Encourage the partners to discuss how their bodies react when they are overheated (they perspire, their skin turns red, and they become thirsty) and when they are cold (they get goose bumps, they shiver, their skin turns blue).

Use the Visual: Figure 14.3

ANSWER an endotherm

Figure It Out

1. What are the functions of an endoskeleton?
2. Compare these two endoskeletons. How are they alike, and how are they different?

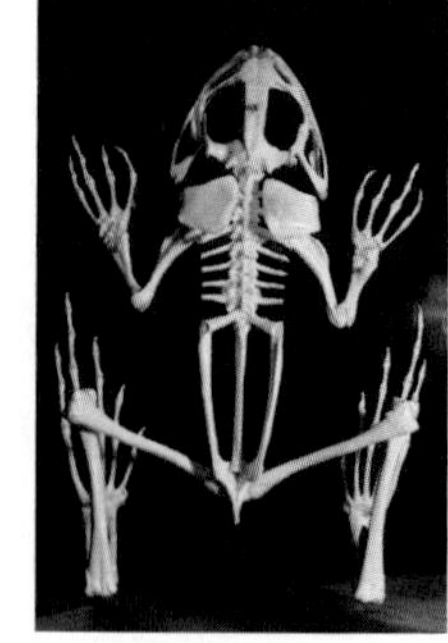

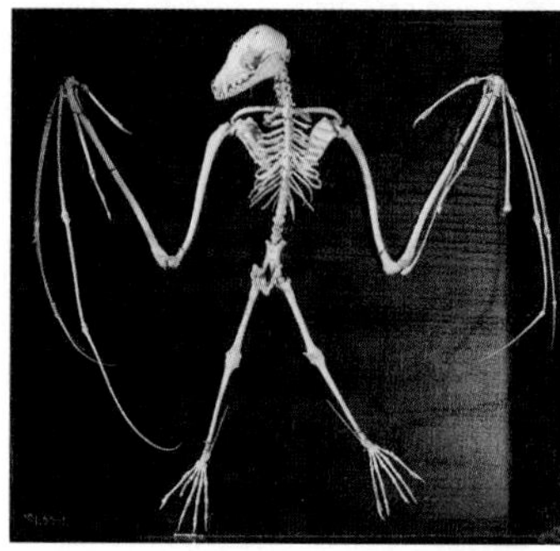

Figure 14.2 The endoskeletons of a frog *(left)* and a bat *(right)* support their bodies.

As You Read

Look at the sentences you wrote in your Science Notebook. Add information to expand or correct your predictions.

What is an endotherm?

What is an ectotherm?

Characteristics of Vertebrates

The backbone of a vertebrate runs down the middle of its back. The vertebrate's backbone is part of its endoskeleton. An endoskeleton is an internal skeleton that supports and protects the body. It also gives the muscles a place to attach. The endoskeleton of vertebrates includes the skull and the ribs. The skull protects the brain, while the ribs protect the heart, lungs, and other internal organs.

As you may recall from Chapter 13, arthropods have an exoskeleton. As an arthropod grows, it must leave its old exoskeleton and produce a new, larger one. By contrast, the endoskeleton of a vertebrate grows as the body of the vertebrate grows. Animals with endoskeletons can grow larger than animals with exoskeletons or no skeletons.

Some vertebrates, such as fishes, amphibians, and reptiles, have body temperatures that change with the environment. This kind of animal is called an **ectotherm** (EK tuh thurm). Look at the lizard in **Figure 14.3**. It will sit in the sunlight on a cool morning to warm itself. When it gets too hot, the lizard will move to a cooler spot in the shade.

Unless you have a fever, your body temperature stays the same most of the time. Birds and mammals are called endotherms. An **endotherm** (EN duh thurm) is an animal that maintains a constant body temperature.

Figure 14.3 This lizard is an ectotherm. Its body temperature will change with the temperature of the environment. The lizard will use the morning sunlight to heat up its body. It will move to the shade if it gets too hot. What is an animal that has a constant body temperature called?

CONNECTION: Health

A device called a thermostat helps control the temperature of your house. A part of your brain called the hypothalamus acts like a thermostat for your body. It keeps your body temperature the same whether the air temperature is hot or cold. The hypothalamus is found in the center of the brain and is about the size of an almond. This region of the brain is part of the endocrine system of the human body.

Background Information

When warm-blooded animals (endotherms) are cold, they increase the production of body heat and decrease the amount of heat lost to the environment. In warmer surroundings, they decrease the production of body heat and increase the amount of heat lost to the environment. This is controlled by the hypothalamus, which receives information from nerves in the skin and other places within the body. Nerves and glands respond to the hypothalamus and regulate the body temperature.

Origin of Vertebrates

Scientists use fossils to determine how long animals have been on Earth. Fossil evidence suggests that vertebrates have been on Earth for more than 500 million years. The first vertebrates developed from small, fishlike chordates that lived in water. Many different kinds of fishes developed from these early vertebrates.

Over time, some new fish species developed and had new characteristics that allowed them to move from water to land. One of these new characteristics was strong fins that could be used to crawl on land. They also had lungs to bring oxygen into their bodies. These animals were the first amphibians. **Figure 14.4** shows that reptiles developed from ancient amphibians. Mammals and birds developed from ancient reptiles.

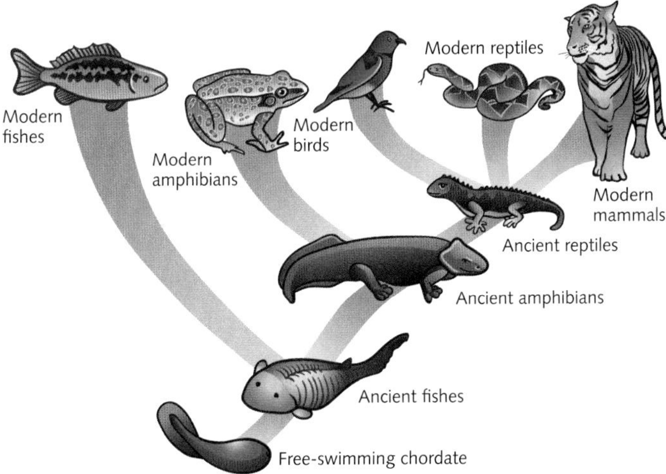

Figure 14.4 This diagram shows the development of the vertebrates. Ancient fish species that lived more than 500 million years ago could be the ancestors of all vertebrates on Earth today.

After You Read

1. Describe three common characteristics of all chordates.
2. What is a vertebrate?
3. How is an ectotherm different from an endotherm?
4. Look at the sentences you have written in your Science Notebook. Use the information to summarize this lesson.

Explore It!

Use beads and string to make a model of a vertebrate backbone. Tie a large knot at one end of a piece of string. Slide the beads onto this string. Tie another large knot at the other end of the string. Gently bend the string of beads at different places and record your observations in your Science Notebook.

Extend It!

Tunicates and lancelets are members of the phylum Chordata. Use the library or the Internet to find out about these animals. Record your findings in your Science Notebook. Include labeled diagrams.

Background Information

Organisms in the phylum Chordata share a number of characteristics in addition to having a notochord at some time during their lives. These characteristics include bilateral symmetry, a segmented body, three germ layers, a well-developed coelom, and a tail extending past the anus at some stage of development; a ventral heart with dorsal and ventral blood vessels and a closed circulatory system; a complete digestive system; and a bony or cartilaginous endoskeleton.

Differentiated Instruction

Kinesthetic Have students make models of fossils demonstrating the evolutionary stages of vertebrates, as illustrated in Figure 14.4. Students should understand that most fossils show only the bony parts of an animal.

Teach

EXPLAIN that vertebrates have evolved from fishlike animals living in the water to mammals living on land.

Explore It!

Provide students with twine or string in 30- to 35-cm lengths in addition to the beads. Demonstrate how to knot one end of the string before adding beads. Students should find that the beads move easily in all directions around the string, and that the beads move closer together at any bend. The backbone of a vertebrate is very flexible.

Extend It!

Encourage students to research specific organisms in the phylum Chordata. Provide Internet access and a variety of reference books for students to use in their research.

Assess

EVALUATE Use the After You Read questions and the Alternative Assessment to help you assess students' understanding of the lesson.

After You Read

1. At some time during development, all chordates have a back (dorsal) nerve cord, a notochord, and pharyngeal pouches.
2. an animal with a backbone
3. The body temperature of an ectotherm varies with the temperature of the environment. The body temperature of an endotherm is constant.
4. Accept all logical answers.

Alternative Assessment

EVALUATE Have students create two-column charts. The first column should contain their predictions from the Before You Read activity at the beginning of the lesson. The second column should contain their corrected predictions and other information learned in the lesson.

14.2 Introduce

ENGAGE Read the first paragraph of this lesson aloud to the class. Then, arrange students in small groups, and have them brainstorm all the names of fishes they have seen in pet stores or aquariums. Then, have students create a second list of fishes they have eaten, have seen on a restaurant menu, or have seen in a fish market or grocery store. Have them compare the lists to see which has more names. Tell students that most of the fish on their lists are bony fish; there are about 20,000 species of bony fishes.

Before You Read

Think aloud about what you already know about fish as a model for students, and write a fact or two on the board. For example: *Fish use fins to swim. Many fish swim in groups called schools.* Working in pairs, have students brainstorm additional facts they know about fish. Have each student choose three facts to write in his/her Science Notebook. Encourage students to choose facts different from their partner's, if they have brainstormed more than three.

Teach

EXPLAIN that students will learn about the characteristics of fishes and the three groups of fishes. In their Science Notebooks, students should quickly sketch a fish. Then, read the *Characteristics of Fishes* paragraph aloud. As you read the text, have students identify and label on their drawings each of the four characteristics.

Vocabulary

scavenger Tell students that the noun *scavenger* is related to the verb *scavenge*, which means "to clean away dirt or refuse." Thus, a scavenger is an animal that feeds on refuse or decaying flesh.

Extend It!

Students should find that the lampreys greatly reduced the fish populations. The Great Lakes states still actively work to control the lamprey populations.

Learning Goals

- Describe the main characteristics of fishes.
- Distinguish among the three groups of fishes.
- Identify the functions of the parts of bony fishes.

New Vocabulary

scavenger
swim bladder

14.2 Fishes

Before You Read

Write three facts that you already know about fish in your Science Notebook. Leave six lines of space below each fact. As you read the lesson, add at least two more facts to each fact you already know.

Have you ever been inside a pet store? Pet stores usually have aquariums, or large water-filled glass containers that hold many species of fish. Fishes come in many colors, shapes, and sizes. There are more than 25,000 species of fishes. Fish are an important source of food for many people.

Figure 14.5 The anemone fish, or clownfish, hides in the tentacles of a sea anemone. The sea anemone's tentacles are poisonous to other fish but not to the anemone fish.

Characteristics of Fishes

Most fishes share four common characteristics. In addition to being ectotherms, fishes have scales, fins, and gills. The scales on a fish protect it from predators. The fins help the fish move through the water. Gills allow the fish to bring oxygen into its body. The gills also remove carbon dioxide from a fish's body.

Fishes can be divided into three main groups. These groups are the jawless fishes, the cartilaginous fishes, and the bony fishes.

Jawless Fishes

The group known as jawless fishes include the lampreys and the hagfishes. Both have soft bodies covered with a slimy skin instead of scales. Lampreys and hagfishes look very different from most fishes. Most lampreys are parasites. A lamprey has sharp teeth that hook onto the body of a fish so that the lamprey can suck out the fish's blood and other body fluids.

A hagfish is a scavenger. A **scavenger** (SKA vun jur) is an animal that feeds on dead or dying animals. The hagfish has tentacles around its mouth. It is almost blind and uses its tentacles to find food.

Extend It!

Lampreys were accidentally introduced into the Great Lakes during the early 1800s. Use the library or the Internet to research the effects of the lampreys. Include a description of the efforts being made to control the lamprey population.

Figure 14.6 The lamprey *(left)* is a parasite that feeds on other fishes. The hagfish *(right)* uses its tentacles to find food.

ELL Strategy

Use a Concept Map Have students add to the concept maps they began in the first lesson. Suggest that students use different colors to add details to the *Fishes* topic.

Compare and Contrast If students are confused or overwhelmed as they attempt to make comprehensive concept maps, have them create simpler compare-and-contrast charts to organize facts about the three groups of fishes.

Background Information

Scientists currently divide fishes into six classes. The lampreys and the hagfish are two separate classes of jawless fishes, also known as agnathans. All cartilaginous fish are in the class Chonrichthyes. Three classes—the lobe-finned fish, the lung fish, and the ray-finned fish—are bony fishes, once classified as class Osteichthyes.

CONNECTION: Earth Science

Because they are made of cartilage, shark skeletons rarely turn into fossils. The cartilage decomposes quickly, and the tissue is not replaced by minerals. Shark teeth are hard and turn into fossils easily. Fossil teeth are often the only evidence of ancient sharks. Some ancient sharks grew quite large—more than 20 meters long—and their fossil teeth measure 10 centimeters or more.

Figure 14.7 The skeleton of the great white shark *(top)* is made of cartilage. The shark jaw *(bottom)* contains many rows of sharp teeth. What is cartilage?

Cartilaginous Fishes

Move the outer part of your ears or nose gently with your fingers. The ears and nose hold their shapes, but they are flexible. This is because they contain cartilage. Cartilaginous (kart uhl AJ uh nuhs) fishes have skeletons made of cartilage instead of bone. This group of fishes includes sharks, rays, and skates.

Although many people think of sharks as fast-swimming, scary predators, this is not the case. Most sharks are actually shy animals that prefer to be left alone. Fewer than ten species of sharks are considered dangerous to humans. More people die each year from bee stings than from shark attacks.

Most sharks are carnivores that spend much of their time hunting prey. They have sharp teeth and powerful jaws. Most sharks have five to 15 rows of teeth in each jaw. As the teeth in the front rows break off, new teeth from the back replace them. Sharks replace their teeth all their lives. A shark may go through 30,000 teeth in its lifetime!

Rays and skates have flat, wide bodies with long, thin tails. Rays and skates travel over the ocean floor in search of food. Most are harmless to humans, but some have poisonous spines on their tails to scare away predators. Some species can stun small fish with an electric shock. Stepping on one of these rays or skates could be a very unpleasant experience!

Figure 14.8 The blue-spotted stingray *(left)* and the skate *(right)* are cartilaginous fishes that search for food on the ocean bottom.

Did You Know?

Sharks do not blink their eyes. They have upper and lower eyelids that do not move or close over their eyes. When biting prey, some sharks protect their eyes with a thin third eyelid.

Teach

EXPLAIN that students will learn about the second type of fishes, cartilaginous fishes.

Tell students that their noses and outer ears are made of cartilage. Ask them to speculate about the advantages of cartilage over bone. (Accept all reasonable responses. Answers may include flexibility, resilience, and the ability to stretch.)

Use the Visual: Figure 14.7

ANSWER Cartilage is strong but flexible tissue that holds its shape.

CONNECTION: Earth Science

A shark's tooth becomes a fossil when it is buried in sediment after falling from a shark's mouth. It takes about 10,000 years for a true fossil to be formed. Most common fossils are from the Cenozoic Era. Scientists have used such fossils to study sharks and shark behavior. Scientists have determined that the size of a shark, its sex, and water temperature influence the location of many sharks.

Science Notebook EXTRA

Have each student choose and research a cartilaginous fish. Students should find information about the fish's anatomy, diet, behavior, and habitat. Instruct students to record their findings in their Science Notebooks. Provide a variety of reference sources. Students can also do research on the Internet, using aquarium Web sites such as that of the Monterey Bay Aquarium (**www.mbayaq.org/**), the Shedd Aquarium (**www.sheddaquarium.org/**), and the National Aquarium in Baltimore (**www.aqua.org/**).

Differentiated Instruction

Visual Have each student draw an example of one fish from each of the three groups of fishes. Students can use images from the text, from reference books, and from the Internet to inform their drawings.

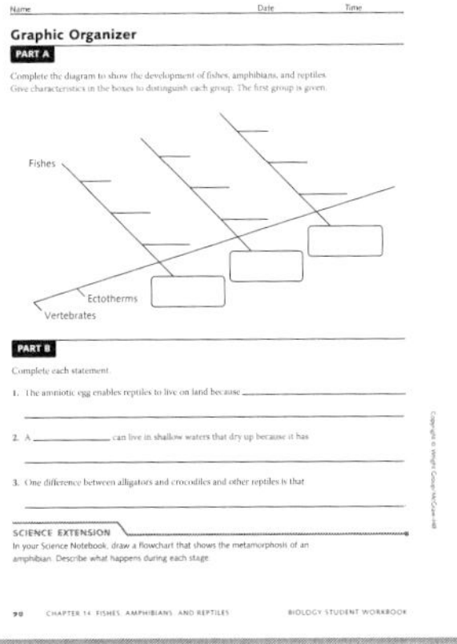

Graphic Organizer

PART A

Fishes

Ectotherms

Vertebrates

PART B

SCIENCE EXTENSION

Graphic Organizer Workbook, p. 90

Teach

EXPLAIN to students that the third group of fishes—bony fishes—are further divided into three classes. These include the lobe-finned fishes, the lungfishes, and the ray-finned fishes. Ray-finned fishes account for more than 95 percent of all fishes and half of all vertebrate species.

As You Read

Give students about five minutes to review the facts in their Science Notebooks. Direct students to revise their original facts and to add additional information about each of the three groups of fishes.

ANSWER The three main groups of fishes are the jawless fishes, the cartilaginous fishes, and the bony fishes.

Reading Comprehension Workbook, p. 91

Bony Fishes

If you have ever eaten a whole trout or catfish, you know why they are called bony fishes. Bony fishes have skeletons made of bone instead of cartilage. About 95 percent of all fish species are bony fishes.

There are three main groups of bony fishes. The first group is the lobe-finned fishes. People thought that lobe-finned fishes had been extinct for millions of years. Then, in 1938, a lobe-finned fish called a coelacanth (SEEL uh kanth) was found in South Africa. Coelacanths have fins that look like paddles.

The second group of bony fishes is the lungfishes. Lungfishes have both lungs and gills. This characteristic allows them to live in shallow waters that dry up in the summer. They cover themselves with mucus to keep moist until water returns.

As You Read

Look at the fish facts you have written in your Science Notebook. Work with a partner to make corrections or additions to this list as you learn more about the different types of fishes.

Describe the three main groups of fishes.

Figure 14.9 Two types of bony fishes are the lobe-finned fishes and the lungfishes. The coelacanth *(left)* is a lobe-finned fish. The African lungfish *(right)* is a lungfish.

Did You Know?

About 50 species of fishes can actually glide through the air to avoid predators! Flying fishes can stay in the air for up to 20 seconds. They can travel at speeds of up to 46 kilometers per hour. Flying fishes have very large flying fins on the sides of their bodies.

The third group of bony fishes is the ray-finned fishes. Ray-finned fishes have fins that are supported by long bones called rays. These fishes are the ones you most commonly see and eat. Catfish, tuna, and trout are ray-finned fishes. So are perch, salmon, and bass. The sea horse is also an example of a ray-finned fish. The sea horse is unusual because it swims upright, moves slowly, has a long snout, and broods its young in the stomach pouches of the males.

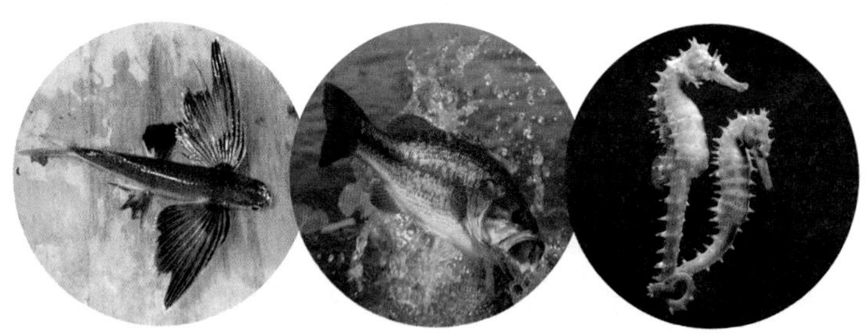

Figure 14.10 The flying fish *(left)*, the largemouth bass *(center)*, and sea horses *(right)* are all examples of ray-finned fishes.

ELL Strategy

Extend Vocabulary Have students use words associated with bony fishes, such as *coelacanth, lungfish, catfish, ray-finned, cod,* and *salmon,* to create their own crossword puzzles. Provide them with grid paper, and model how several word combinations might be arranged. Students should also create a short clue for each word they include. When they are finished, have them exchange puzzles with their peers to solve.

Background Information

Louis Agassiz first described the fossil fish known as *Coelacanthus.* About 125 species of coelacanth have been discovered, ranging in age from 400 to 66 million years old. They were thought to be extinct; no fossils have been found that are less than 66 million years old. However, in 1938, Marjorie Latimer found a living coelacanth in South Africa. More have been discovered in Indonesia.

External Structure A bony fish has a head, body, and tail. The eyes, nostrils, gills, and mouth are found on the head of the fish. A bony fish has different types of fins. These fins help the fish move through the water to hunt for food. They also help the fish avoid predators such as larger fish or people.

The body of a bony fish is covered with scales. The scales are covered with slimy mucus. This mucus keeps the scales moist to help the fish swim better. It also helps the fish slip away from predators.

Internal Structure As **Figure 14.11** shows, a bony fish has an endoskeleton that protects its internal organs. Muscles attach to the fins of the fish to help it move through the water. The gills of the fish help it take oxygen from the water. They also remove carbon dioxide from the fish's body. A bony fish also has a **swim bladder**. The swim bladder acts and looks like a small balloon.

Swim Bladder A swim bladder is an air-filled sac. The fish can add air to the swim bladder to rise. It can release air from the swim bladder to sink.

Scales Scales are covered with slippery mucus. This allows the fish to move through the water with less friction.

Kidney

Urinary bladder

Reproductive organ

Stomach

Intestine

Liver

Heart

Gills Gills are thin, blood-vessel-rich tissues where gases are exchanged.

Fins Fins help the fish move through the water. Different kinds of fishes have different kinds of fins. Fishes that live near coral reefs have small fins. This helps them move through small spaces. A tuna has large fins. This helps it move quickly in open water.

Figure 14.11 The external and internal structures of a bony fish are shown here.

Figure it Out

1. What are some of a bony fish's internal organs?
2. Hypothesize about what could be related to the structure and arrangement of a bony fish's fins.

Rainbow trout

After You Read

1. Explain the three common characteristics of all fishes.
2. How is a cartilaginous fish different from a bony fish?
3. What is a swim bladder?
4. Referring to your Science Notebook, name three facts about fishes.

Teach

EXPLAIN to students that they will learn about the body parts of a bony fish. All bony fishes have three main body regions: head, body, and tail.

EXPLORE Write a list of external body parts on the board. With partners, have students decide in which of the three body regions each part is located. Review the list with the class to make sure that students understand the body part locations.

Vocabulary

swim bladder Tell students that the word *bladder* refers to a membranous sac in animals that holds liquid or contains gas. In bony fishes, the bladder holds air and can be filled with air or emptied to control the buoyancy of the fish in the water.

Figure It Out: Figure 14.11

ANSWER **1.** heart, liver, intestines, stomach, kidney, urinary bladder, reproductive organ, and swim bladder **2.** The structure and arrangement of a bony fish's fins relate to how a fish moves in water.

Assess

EVALUATE Use the After You Read questions and the Alternative Assessment to help you assess students' understanding of the lesson.

Field Study

Have students visit a fish market or restaurant and observe fish being cleaned. Prior to the visit, review with students the internal structures of the fish that they will see. Direct students to notice which part(s) of the fish are prepared to be eaten and which are discarded.

Differentiated Instruction

Visual Have students label the external structures on their fish drawings from the Differentiated Instruction activity on page 245.

After You Read

1. All fishes are ectotherms. They all have scales, fins, and gills.
2. A cartilaginous fish has a skeleton made of cartilage. A bony fish has a skeleton made of bone.
3. A swim bladder is an organ that helps a fish rise or sink in the water. When the swim bladder is filled with air, the fish rises. When the bladder loses air, the fish sinks.
4. Accept all logical answers.

Alternative Assessment

EVALUATE Instruct students to use their concept maps to write a few sentences about the characteristics of fishes. They should also write a few sentences about the structure, including external and internal structures, of bony fishes.

14.3 Introduce

ENGAGE Ask students to name ways in which butterflies and frogs are alike. Record their responses on the board. (Responses will vary and may include the fact that both are alive, have spots, and are colorful.) If students do not already know that both species undergo metamorphosis, sketch on the board a picture of a caterpillar, butterfly, tadpole, and frog (or write the names of each). Explain to students that both butterflies and frogs go through physical changes as they grow from an early form (a larva) into an adult form.

Before You Read

Give students about five minutes to scan this section and to write down each vocabulary term. Students should leave a few lines of space between each term. Direct students to define each vocabulary term as they read about it in the lesson.

Teach

EXPLAIN that in this section, students will learn about the characteristics of amphibians and the process of frog metamorphosis.

Use the Visual: Figure 14.13

EXPLORE Review the process of metamorphosis with students. Emphasize the different physical features in each stage, and discuss the ways in which the changes allow frogs to live on land.

Learning Goals

- Identify the common characteristics of amphibians.
- List the major groups of amphibians.
- Describe metamorphosis in frogs.
- Explain how frogs survive in water and on land.

New Vocabulary

hibernation
estivation
nictitating membrane
tympanum

14.3 Amphibians

Before You Read

In your Science Notebook, write each vocabulary term in this lesson. Leave some space below each term. Using your own words, write a definition for each term as you read about it.

Have you ever caught a frog? If so, you might have found it to be moist and slippery. Frogs have cool, slimy skin. Frogs, toads, and salamanders belong to the class Amphibia (am FIH bee uh). *Amphibia* means "double life." Most amphibians live part of their lives in water and part on land.

There are three main groups of amphibians. They are the frogs and toads, the salamanders and newts, and the caecilians (see SIL yuhns).

Characteristics of Amphibians

All amphibians are ectothermic vertebrates. Many have smooth, moist skin. Their eggs do not have hard outer shells like birds' eggs do. Thus, the eggs must be laid in water or in other moist areas. Amphibians use their lungs, gills, and skin to breathe. Their webbed feet help them move through the water.

Like insects, young amphibians change into adults through the process of metamorphosis. **Figure 14.13** shows the process by which a frog egg becomes an adult frog. In frog metamorphosis, fertilized eggs hatch into tadpoles. Tadpoles look like small fish. They have gills and fins. As the tadpoles grow into adult frogs, they lose their tails. The adult frogs use their lungs and skin to breathe.

Figure 14.12 The leopard frog *(top)*, the golden toad *(center)*, and the spotted salamander *(bottom)* are all types of amphibians.

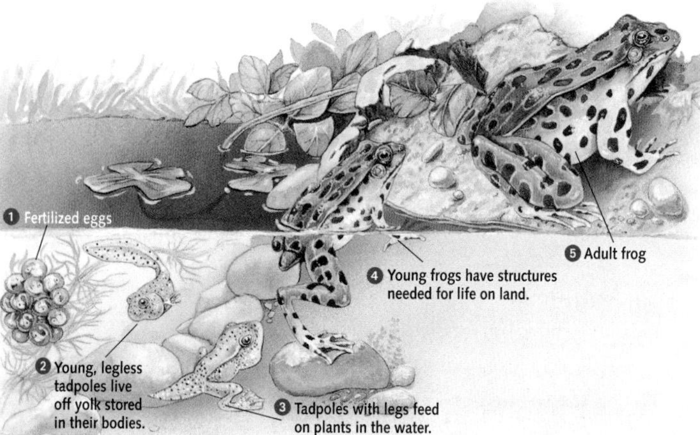
1 Fertilized eggs
2 Young, legless tadpoles live off yolk stored in their bodies.
3 Tadpoles with legs feed on plants in the water.
4 Young frogs have structures needed for life on land.
5 Adult frog

Figure 14.13 A frog begins life in water. As it changes to an adult, it moves to land.

ELL Strategy

Use a Concept Map Have students add information to the *Amphibians* topic of the concept maps they constructed at the beginning of the chapter.

Think, Pair, Share Ask students to list the advantages and disadvantages of being an ectotherm. Have each student write a list and then discuss it with a partner. Ask pairs to make one list with at least five advantages and five disadvantages.

Teacher Alert

Students may be confused about where amphibians live and at what stage they live in water and then on land. Amphibians can live only in freshwater; they cannot survive in salt water. To reproduce, most species lay their eggs in water. Amphibian eggs are porous—oxygen is able to enter and wastes can leave. Their eggs must remain wet so that they do not dry out.

Figure 14.14 The caecilian *(left)*, the barred tiger salamander *(center)*, and the fire-bellied newt *(right)* are amphibians that eat insects, worms, and insect larvae.

Caecilians

Caecilians are amphibians that do not have legs. They look very much like earthworms. Most caecilians are blind, but some have tiny eyes. Some caecilians have bony scales. Most species burrow into the soil to live and find their food. A few species live in freshwater. Since they cannot see, caecilians use tentacles near their noses to find food. Caecilians live in the tropical areas of South America, Africa, and Asia.

Salamanders and Newts

Salamanders and newts are amphibians with legs and tails. Like frogs, they have smooth, moist skin. Found worldwide, most salsmanders and newt spend most of their lives on land. A few species live all their lives in freshwater. Many are poisonous. Most salamanders of North America live under rocks and logs in the woods. Like the caecilians, they eat small invertebrates.

Explain It!

In your Science Notebook, write a letter to the governor of your state. Explain why it is important to protect amphibian habitats in your area. Describe a plan to keep the amphibians from becoming extinct. Form small groups with your classmates, and discuss individual letters. Then, using the most important ideas from each group's letters, create one clearly written letter to send to the governor.

CONNECTION: Environmental Science

How long does it take for a group of animals to become extinct? You might think that the answer is a long time, but this is not always true. Today, many amphibians are in danger of becoming extinct. Some scientists believe that almost one-third of Earth's amphibian species are in danger.

Many amphibian habitats are being destroyed. The destruction of rain forests leaves many amphibians without a place to live. Amphibians are very sensitive to chemical pollution. They have very thin skin, and their eggs do not have hard shells. An amphibian can absorb poison just as easily as it absorbs oxygen. This can kill the amphibian or cause its offspring to be deformed. The frog in the photo has three back legs. This deformity is likely the result of poison absorbed by its parents.

Amphibians are important because they eat many harmful insects. Scientists around the world are now working on a plan to save Earth's amphibians. Protecting amphibian habitats and reducing pollution levels will help save many species of amphibians.

Deformed frog

Teach

EXPLAIN to students that the caecilians and the salamanders and newts are the other two classes of amphibians. Like frogs, caecilians, newts, and salamanders change through metamorphosis.

Science Notebook EXTRA

Using Figures 14.13 and 14.14 and the information on this page for reference, have students conjecture about the larval forms of caecilians, salamanders, and newts. Have students sketch their hypothesized images of the larvae in their Science Notebooks. Then, show students images of actual larvae, and have them correct their drawings, given the new information. Discuss the changes that occur to the larvae as the organisms become adults.

Explain It!

Tell students that a number of human factors are contributing to amphibian extinction, including habitat loss, overuse for food and medicine, and climate change (global warming). Additionally, a fungal disease called chytridiomycosis is killing many frogs.

Brainstorm with students what information would most likely compel the governor to protect amphibian habitats. Then, provide a cause-and-effect organizer to help students organize their thoughts for the letter. After students draft their letters, have them work with their small groups to revise them and to choose the most relevant information to include.

Background Information

All newts are salamanders, but not all salamanders are newts. *Salamander* is the name of the group, or order, of amphibians that have tails as adults.

Newts also undergo metamorphosis; they hatch from eggs in the spring after three to five weeks of incubation. After a few months of living in the water, they develop lungs and can live on land. This form of the newt is known as an eft. Efts can remain in this stage of metamorphosis for up to seven years before becoming adult newts. At that point, they return to the water and can breed.

CONNECTION: Environmental Science

About one-third of the world's amphibian species (1,856 species from a total 5,743 known species) are threatened with extinction. Since 1980, a significant percentage of all amphibian species have lessened in population and 122 species have gone extinct. Loss of habitat is the most serious problem for amphibians.

Teach

EXPLAIN that students will learn about frogs and toads and the differences between these two amphibians. They will also learn about the frog's external structures.

CONNECTION: **Health**

Ask students to share other misconceptions that they have heard about getting sick. For instance, viruses also cause colds, but one may be told to refrain from going outside with a wet head to avoid catching a cold.

Vocabulary

hibernation Tell students that the root of *hiberation, hibernate,* is derived from the Latin word *hibernare,* meaning "to spend the winter."

estivation Explain to students that the root of the word *estivation, estivate,* is derived from the Latin word *aestivare,* which means "to spend the summer."

nictitating membrane Tell students that the origin of the word *nictitating* is the Latin word *nictare,* which means "to wink." A membrane is a thin sheet of tissue that connects, lines, or covers parts or organs in an organism.

tympanum Explain to students that the origin of the word *tympanum* is the Greek word *tympanon,* which is a type of drum. Students may have also heard of tympani drums, which are kettledrums played in the percussion section of an orchestra.

As You Read

Give students a few minutes to complete and revise their vocabulary definitions.

ANSWER Hibernation and estivation are both periods of inactivity. Hibernation occurs during winter, when frogs and toads bury themselves in mud or leaves to escape the cold air. Estivation occurs during summer, when frogs and toads bury themselves to escape the intense heat.

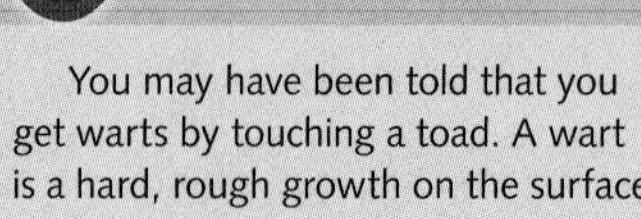

CONNECTION: **Health**

You may have been told that you get warts by touching a toad. A wart is a hard, rough growth on the surface of the skin. Touching the skin of a toad does not cause warts. A wart is caused by a virus.

Figure 14.15 The red-eyed tree frog *(top)* and the American toad *(bottom)* belong to the largest group of amphibians.

Frogs and Toads

Frogs and toads are similar in many ways, but they also have some differences. Frogs spend most of their lives in or near water. Toads spend more time on land. A toad might be found in a backyard or a garden. Frogs have smooth skin, and toads have bumpy skin. Frog eggs are usually found in a ball. Toad eggs are often found in a long chain.

Frogs and toads are ectotherms. Their body temperature changes with the environment. During the winter, they bury themselves in mud or leaves until the temperature gets warmer. This period of winter inactivity is called **hibernation** (hi buhr NAY shun). Other animals, such as bees and snakes, also hibernate in the winter. In the summer months, frogs and toads bury themselves to escape the heat. This period of inactivity during intense heat is called **estivation** (es tuh VAY shun).

External Structure of a Frog Frogs are the most common amphibians. They live near most lakes and ponds. The outside of a frog is adapted to life both in water and on land. A frog's eye has a third eyelid called a **nictitating** (NIK tuh tayt ing) **membrane**. This membrane is clear so the frog can see through it. A nictitating membrane protects each of a frog's eyes and keeps them moist.

Frogs do not have ears. Instead, they have a round structure called a **tympanum** (TIHM puh nuhm) located just behind each eye. These structures are a frog's eardrums. The tympanum allows the frog to hear well in water and on land. Male frogs use sound to attract females. Females call to the males to let them know if they want to mate.

Frogs have two sets of limbs. The hind, or back, legs are strong and muscular. They help the frog jump around on land. Webbed feet help the frog swim. The front legs of a frog are small. They help the frog land after it has jumped.

As You Read

Make corrections or additions to the vocabulary definitions you have written.

How are hibernation and estivation alike? How are they different?

Figure 14.16 The tympanum is the round structure located behind each of a frog's eyes *(left).* A leopard frog *(right)* uses its strong, muscular legs to jump through the air.

Background Information

Warts are caused by viral infections of the skin and mucus membranes. The virus is spread easily from person to person and enters the body through a cut or scratch. The virus is known as the human papillomavirus, or HPV.

Warts most commonly occur in children and young adults, but they can affect older adults, as well. They can be treated by a number of different methods, including salicylic acid, bleomycin injections, and cryotherapy. Often, a wart will disappear on its own.

As **Figure 14.17** shows, a frog has eyes on the top of its head. This helps the frog see above the water when its body is below the surface. In this way, a frog can remain almost completely hidden while it hunts for and then captures insects for a tasty meal! The tongue of a frog is long and sticky. It is attached to the front of the frog's mouth.

Internal Structure of a Frog Frogs have many internal organs you may recognize, including a heart, a liver, and an intestine. Adult frogs use lungs to breathe air. Frogs also exchange gases through their skin. This skin must remain moist. If their skin dries out, most amphibians will die.

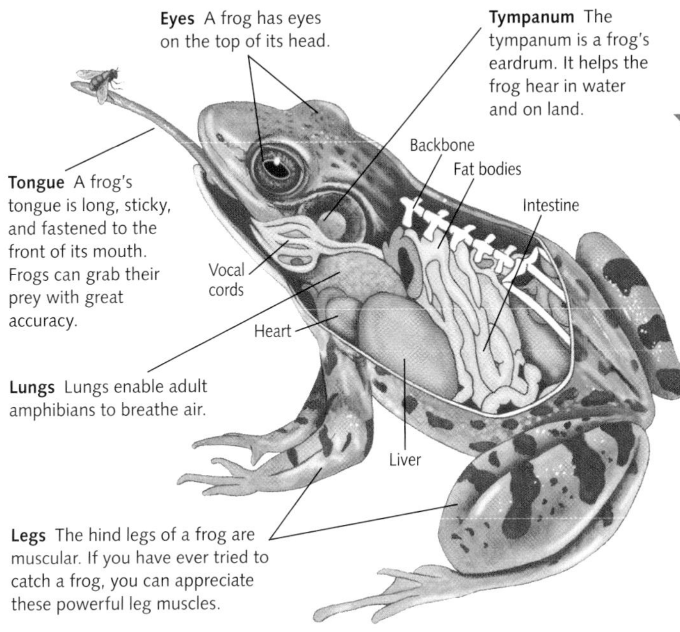
Eyes A frog has eyes on the top of its head.
Tympanum The tympanum is a frog's eardrum. It helps the frog hear in water and on land.
Backbone
Fat bodies
Intestine
Tongue A frog's tongue is long, sticky, and fastened to the front of its mouth. Frogs can grab their prey with great accuracy.
Vocal cords
Heart
Lungs Lungs enable adult amphibians to breathe air.
Liver
Legs The hind legs of a frog are muscular. If you have ever tried to catch a frog, you can appreciate these powerful leg muscles.

Figure 14.17 The external and internal structures of a frog are shown here.

Figure It Out

1. How do the front legs and hind legs of a frog compare? Explain how this relates to their uses.
2. Hypothesize about why having eyes on the tops of their heads is a useful adaptation for frogs.

Did You Know?

The most poisonous amphibian is the golden dart frog, shown below. It is a species found in Colombia, South America. A single frog may contain enough poison to kill 100 human beings—which makes it 20 times more toxic than any other poison dart frog.

Figure 14.18 The golden dart frog is the world's most poisonous amphibian.

After You Read

1. What are three common characteristics of amphibians?
2. Describe what happens during the metamorphosis of a frog.
3. How can frogs survive in water and on land?
4. Using the definitions in your Science Notebook, write a well-developed paragraph that describes what frogs do to survive hot summer and cold winter temperatures.

Background Information

There are about 170 different species of poison dart frogs, and they have a variety of patterns, including spots and stripes. They are usually brightly colored in shades of red, blue, green, and yellow. Poison arrow frogs have about 200 µg (micrograms) of poison in their systems (it takes only 2 µg to kill a human). The poison is excreted in the frog's skin, so humans should not touch the frog.

Teach

EXPLAIN to students that they will learn more about the structures of a frog. Have students examine Figure 14.17 with a partner and read the captions aloud. Students should be able to identify the frog's eyes, tympanum, tongue, and skin.

Figure It Out: Figure 14.17

ANSWER **1.** The front legs are small and help the frog land after it has jumped. The hind legs are strong and muscular. They help the frog jump around on land. **2.** That adaptation allows frogs to stay submerged in the water with only their eyes above the surface. This increases their ability to find and catch prey, as well as to remain hidden from predators.

Assess

EVALUATE Use the After You Read questions and the Alternative Assessment to help you assess students' understanding of the lesson.

After You Read

1. All amphibians are ectothermic vertebrates. Many have smooth, moist skin. Their eggs do not have hard shells. They use lungs, gills, and their skin to breathe.
2. A frog hatches from its egg and develops into a tadpole with a tail and gills. As the tadpole grows into an adult frog, it loses its tail and develops lungs.
3. Frogs have webbed feet to help them move through the water. Tadpoles use their gills to breathe. Frogs have muscular legs that help them jump on land. They use their lungs to breathe.
4. Frogs bury themselves in mud or leaves to escape very hot or cold temperatures. Winter inactivity is called hibernation. Summer inactivity is called estivation.

Alternative Assessment

EVALUATE Have students sketch a frog and label its internal and external structures, including the tympanum, eyes, two sets of legs, and nictitating membrane.

14.4 Introduce

ENGAGE Show students a few pictures of dinosaurs (or list on the board the names of commonly known dinosaurs), and tell students that they are going to be learning about animals closely related to dinosaurs: reptiles. Then, assign students partners, and have them discuss what they already know about reptiles. Encourage them to list the names of animals that they know are reptiles. Write the three main group names on the board, and have students share their lists with the class. As students name reptiles, write their examples on the board under the correct group name.

Before You Read

Review the first Learning Goal, which is to identify the common characteristics of reptiles. Model rewording the goal into a question, such as: *"What are the characteristics of reptiles?"* Have students create questions from all the goals and write these in their Science Notebooks. Remind students to leave four to five lines after each question to answer it as they read the lesson.

Teach

EXPLAIN that in this section, students will learn about the three major groups of reptiles and the characteristics of reptiles.

Vocabulary

amniotic egg Tell students that the amniotic egg was an important evolutionary step for reptiles, since it enabled the egg to survive on land. The fluid-filled amniotic sac (or amnion) protects the developing embryo. Birds and some mammals also lay amniotic eggs.

Use the Visual: Figure 14.20

ANSWER The amnion and the fluid within it protects the embryo and keeps it from drying out.

Learning Goals

- Identify the common characteristics of reptiles.
- List examples from each major group of reptiles.
- Describe how the amniotic egg allows reptiles to live away from water.

New Vocabulary

amniotic egg

14.4 Reptiles

Before You Read

Reword the headings of this lesson so that they form questions. Write the questions in your Science Notebook. As you read, write answers to these questions.

Characteristics of Reptiles

Reptiles are adapted to life on land. They have thick, scaly skin that keeps them from drying out. Since reptiles cannot exchange gases through their skin, they have well-developed lungs. Like the amphibians, reptiles are ectothermic vertebrates. The three main groups of the class Reptilia are the turtles and tortoises, the alligators and crocodiles, and the snakes and lizards.

The Amniotic Egg The eggs of fishes and amphibians do not have hard shells. These eggs dry out easily, so they must be laid in water. A reptile egg, however, has a hard outer shell. Reptile eggs can be laid on dry land. Most reptiles lay their eggs in protected places beneath sand, soil, gravel, or bark. A reptile egg is called an amniotic (am nee AH tihk) egg. An **amniotic egg** surrounds the developing embryo with food and a tough shell and will not dry out on land. A reptile hatches by breaking its shell with a thorny tooth on its snout. This egg tooth drops off shortly after hatching.

Figure 14.19 The thick skin of the marine iguana allows it to successfully live on land.

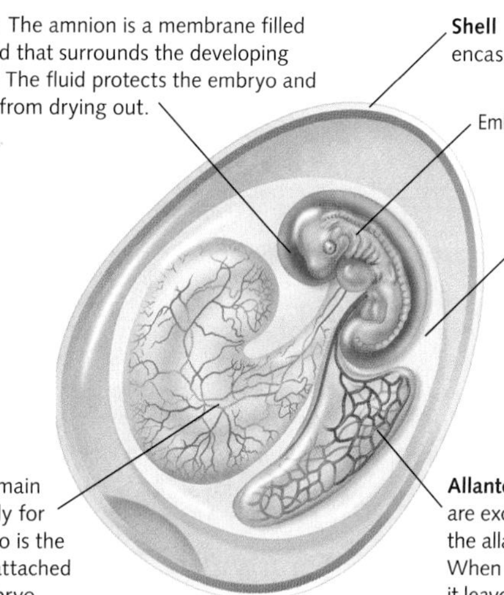
Amnion The amnion is a membrane filled with fluid that surrounds the developing embryo. The fluid protects the embryo and keeps it from drying out.
Shell The reptile egg is encased in a leathery shell.
Embryo
Chorion The chorion (KOR ee ahn) is a membrane that forms around the yolk, allantois, amnion, and embryo. Gas exchange happens in the chorion.
Yolk The main food supply for the embryo is the yolk. It is attached to the embryo.
Allantois The embryo's wastes are excreted into a sac called the allantois (uh LAN tuh wus). When a reptile hatches, it leaves the allantois behind.

Figure 14.20 Reptiles are able to survive exclusively on land because of their amniotic eggs. What is the function of the amnion?

252 FISHES, AMPHIBIANS, AND REPTILES

ELL Strategy

Use a Concept Map Have students add to the concept maps they began in Lesson 14.1. It may be helpful for students to use a different color to add details to the *Reptiles* topic.

Compare-and-Contrast Chart Have each student create a compare-and-contrast chart to analyze the differences and similarities between amphibians and reptiles. Have them include information about feeding, reproduction, habitat, and behavior.

Turtles and Tortoises

There are about 250 species of turtles and tortoises. Turtles live mainly in or near the water. They are found in both freshwater and seawater. Tortoises live mainly on land.

Turtles have flat shells, while tortoises have round, domed shells. The shells of the turtle and the tortoise are connected to their bodies. These reptiles cannot leave their shells. Turtle and tortoise shells are very strong. The shell of a box turtle can hold up to 200 times its own weight! Shells provide protection for turtles and tortoises. Most turtles are able to pull their limbs, tails, and heads into their shells for protection against predators.

Did You Know?

Sea turtles sometimes look like they are crying. It is not because they are sad or upset. They are ridding their bodies of extra salt they absorb from the ocean water where they live.

Figure 14.21 The painted turtle *(left)* and the red-footed tortoise *(right)* are examples of another group of reptiles.

Figure It Out

1. What is the function of a turtle's or a tortoise's shell?
2. Describe how the shells of the painted turtle and the red-footed tortoise are different from each other.

Turtles do not have teeth. They have beaks that are hard like bird beaks. Turtles eat plants and animals. The alligator snapping turtle shown in **Figure 14.22** has a small, wormlike structure on the bottom of its mouth. The turtle sits still with its mouth open on the bottom of a river, a lake, or a pond. When a fish swims up to eat the "worm," the turtle snaps its jaws shut and eats the fish.

The loggerhead turtle might be called the best navigator in the animal kingdom. After it hatches, the young turtle moves to the ocean. As it grows, it travels through thousands of kilometers of ocean water. The turtles will mature and mate. When a female is ready to lay her eggs, she will return to the same beach where she was born. How does she find her way? Scientists think that the loggerhead turtle uses ocean waves and Earth's magnetic field to move in the right direction.

Figure 14.22 The alligator snapping turtle *(left)* lures fish with a wormlike structure in its mouth. The female loggerhead turtle *(right)* will return to her birthplace to lay her eggs.

Teach

EXPLAIN to students that they will learn the differences between turtles and tortoises.

EXPLORE Have student partners read the two paragraphs in the Turtles and Tortoises section aloud. Then, have them work together to create a Venn diagram, labeling one circle *Turtle* and the other circle *Tortoise*. Each student should draw the diagram in his or her Science Notebook. Have students complete these Venn diagrams, using them to illustrate which characteristics are shared and which are unique.

Figure It Out: Figure 14.21

ANSWER **1.** The shells provide protection from predators. **2.** The painted turtle has a flat shell. The red-footed tortoise has a round, domed shell.

Science Notebook EXTRA

Have students research the migration patterns of loggerhead turtles and record what they learn in their Science Notebooks. Encourage students to draw the various turtle paths on a map. Ask students to analyze the paths and explain the reasons for the different routes.

Differentiated Instruction

Logical-Mathematical Have students research a few different species of turtles and find the typical size of an individual from each of those species. Ask students to create a scale for representing the turtle sizes that will allow them to make scale drawings of the turtles on standard paper. Then, have students draw the turtles. Remind students to identify the scale they have devised.

Background Information

The size of turtles can vary from 10 cm for a common bog turtle to 1.2–2.4 m for a leatherback turtle. Similarly, the diet of turtles varies depending on the specific species. Most sea turtles are carnivorous.

More than 250 out of 7,200 reptile species are endangered or are close to being endangered, as are many amphibians. Reasons for the increasing risk include habitat loss, pollution, disease, the pet trade, and harvesting for food.

Teach

EXPLAIN that students will learn about the second group of reptiles, the alligators and crocodiles. Tell students that although they resemble each other, alligators and crocodiles are easily distinguished. Have students sketch and label the different head shapes of the alligator and crocodile in their Science Notebooks. Direct students to include teeth in their sketches.

As You Read

Give students a few minutes to review the questions and answers in their Science Notebooks. Direct them to revise their answers based on their new knowledge. Then, have each student do a brief peer review of a partner's responses to check for accuracy.

ANSWER The three main groups of reptiles are the turtles and tortoises, the alligators and crocodiles, and the snakes and lizards.

CONNECTION: Chemistry

EXPLORE Have students experiment with water to determine the difficulty of maintaining a constant temperature, emulating the conditions of a crocodile nest. Provide students with beakers, warm and cold water, an insulating material such as cotton, and a thermometer. Have students achieve a temperature of either 30°C or one higher than 34°C. Then, have students insulate the water and determine how long they can maintain the same temperature. For students who can sustain the temperature for the class period, challenge them to keep the temperature constant overnight. Discuss their challenges the following day, and relate these to challenges that crocodiles face in their own environment.

EXTEND Have students research captive breeding programs for alligators and crocodiles.

Figure 14.23 Alligators and crocodiles look very similar. The alligator *(left)* shows only its upper teeth when its mouth is closed. The crocodile *(right)* shows both its upper and lower teeth when its mouth is closed.

As You Read

Look at the answers to the questions you have written in your Science Notebook. Make corrections or additions as you learn more about the different types of reptiles.

What are the three main groups of reptiles?

Alligators and Crocodiles

Alligators and crocodiles are the largest living reptiles. They can move quietly through the water to search for food, often with only their eyes visible on the surface. They can spend their days lying in the sunlight along the bank of a river and then floating motionless in the water, looking much like a log.

Do you know how to tell the difference between an alligator and a crocodile? As **Figure 14.23** shows, the alligator has a wide head with a rounded snout. The crocodile has a narrow head with a triangle-shaped snout. When its mouth is shut, only the alligator's upper teeth are visible. You can see both the upper and lower teeth of the crocodile.

Both alligators and crocodiles live in tropical areas. They spend most of their time in the water. Alligators live primarily in North America and Asia. Crocodiles live mostly in North America, Africa, Asia, and Australia.

Unlike most reptiles, alligators and crocodiles care for their young. A female crocodile will stay and guard her nest until her babies hatch from their eggs. The hatching babies call to their mother, and she carries them to the water. The babies then start feeding on crabs, shrimps, and insects.

Figure 14.24 This baby crocodile will be carried by its mother to the water so it can feed.

CONNECTION: Chemistry

For several crocodile species, the temperature inside the nest determines the sex of the young. If the temperature of the nest is 30°C, females will hatch from the eggs. If the temperature is above 34°C, males will hatch from the eggs. If the temperature is between these values, the nest will contain both males and females.

Background Information

Research into TSD (Temperature-Dependent Sex Determination) has provided useful information to captive breeding programs. Captive breeding programs aim to produce either a balanced sex ratio or to produce males because they grow faster and are then farmed. Researchers estimate that less than one percent of hatchlings reach adulthood. Factors responsible for this very low survival rate include predators and the killing and eating of young crocodiles by male crocodiles.

Figure 14.25 The gecko *(left)* is a lizard. The copperhead *(center)* is a snake that injects its prey with venom. The ball python *(right)* is a snake that squeezes its prey to death. To what category of eaters do all snakes and most lizards belong?

Lizards and Snakes

Lizards and snakes are the most common reptiles. They are closely related and share some characteristics. They live mostly in warm areas. They have dry skin covered with scales. As lizards and snakes grow, they shed their old skins. These skins are replaced with new ones.

All snakes and most lizards are carnivores. Large snakes can eat very large prey. The major difference between lizards and snakes is that snakes do not have legs, whereas most lizards have four legs. A snake uses its tongue to find prey and to get information about the world around it. The tip of its tongue senses chemicals. This helps the snake catch prey and avoid predators.

Poisonous snakes have hollow fangs that inject venom into their prey. Some snakes wrap around their prey and squeeze it to death. However, most snakes are neither poisonous nor constrictors. Instead, they get their food by grabbing it with their mouths and swallowing it whole. Their prey includes rodents, amphibians, fish, insects, eggs, and other reptiles. Snakes are afraid of people. People are usually bitten by snakes only when they frighten the reptiles.

Snakes sometimes scare their predators by spitting venom at them. The spitting cobra, for example, can spit its venom over a distance of more than two meters!

After You Read

1. What are three common characteristics of reptiles?
2. Describe the differences between an alligator and a crocodile.
3. How do snakes kill their prey?
4. Use the information in your Science Notebook to describe how the amniotic egg allows a reptile to live away from water.

Did You Know?

A snake's heart can slide within the snake's body. The heart can move up to one and a half times its length. This allows prey to pass through the snake's esophagus and into its stomach.

Figure 14.26 The rattlesnake *(top)* uses its tongue to sense chemicals. Venom of poisonous snakes is collected *(bottom)* for medicinal purposes.

CONNECTION: Medicine

Snake venom can be used to make an antivenin that helps people who are bitten by snakes. Snakes are "milked" to collect the venom from their fangs. Scientists are also researching ways in which snake venom can be used to cure diseases.

Field Study

Take students for a walk in a nearby field, preferably near a river or creek, to look for reptiles and amphibians. Provide pictures or science reference books. Ask students to sketch the animals they find and try to identify their scientific names. After returning to the classroom, make a class list of all animals observed on the walk.

CAUTION: Be sure students know how to identify any poisonous snakes or lizards that live in your area before conducting the activity. Tell students that they are not to capture or touch any reptiles they find.

Teach

EXPLAIN that students will learn about the third and most common type of reptiles, the lizards and snakes.

EXPLORE Have students research and list snakes and lizards that are indigenous to your climate. Provide a variety of reference materials, including access to such Web sites as the U.S. Geological Survey's Nonindigenous Aquatic Species at **nas.er.usgs.gov/queries/**.

Use the Visual: Figure 14.25

ANSWER All snakes and most lizards are carnivores, or meat eaters.

CONNECTION: Medicine

EXTEND Have students research the species of snakes from which venom is "milked." Ask them to then find out how the venom is used. Encourage students to share what they discover with the class.

Assess

EVALUATE Use the After You Read questions and the Alternative Assessment to help you assess students' understanding of the lesson.

After You Read

1. Reptiles have dry, scaly skin, are ectothermic vertebrates, and lay amniotic eggs with leathery shells.
2. An alligator has a wide, round snout; only its upper teeth show when its mouth is closed. A crocodile has a narrow, pointed snout; both upper and lower teeth show when its mouth is closed.
3. by injecting the prey with venom from their fangs, squeezing the prey to death, or grabbing the prey with their mouths and swallowing them whole
4. The amniotic egg has a tough shell that protects the embryo and keeps it moist. It is filled with nutrients for the embryo.

Alternative Assessment

EVALUATE Have students use their questions and answers from Lesson 14.4 to write a summary consisting of sentences that highlight the important facts about reptiles.

Chapter 14 Summary

VOCABULARY REVIEW

Check students' sentences or paragraphs to make sure they understand the meaning of each vocabulary term.

PREPARE FOR CHAPTER TEST

Evaluate students' essays using the following criteria:

1. The topic sentence, or main idea, should restate the Key Concept.
2. The supporting paragraphs should incorporate the answers to the Learning Goal questions students have written and include details, facts, and examples they have recorded in their Science Notebooks.
3. The concluding sentence should sum up the main idea of the chapter and restate the Key Concept.

MASTERING CONCEPTS

True or False

1. True
2. False, vertebrate
3. False, gills
4. True
5. False, hibernation
6. False, alligator

Short Answer

7. A chordate has a nerve cord, a notochord, and pharyngeal pouches at some time in its life.
8. The body temperature of an ectotherm varies with the temperature of its environment. The body temperature of an endotherm remains constant.
9. The frog hatches from an egg and becomes a tadpole. A tadpole has a tail and gills to help it live in the water. The adult frog has large hind legs, loses its tail, and breathes with lungs.
10. A fish has fins to help it move through the water. It also has scales on the outside of its body. The mucus layer on the outside of a fish helps it escape from predators.
11. The turtle's shell is flat. The tortoise's shell is round.

Chapter 14 Summary

KEY CONCEPTS

14.1 What Is a Vertebrate?

- A chordate is an animal with a nerve cord.
- A vertebrate is a chordate with a backbone.
- A vertebrate has an endoskeleton that protects the brain, heart, lungs, and other internal organs.
- An ectotherm is an animal whose body temperature changes with the temperature of the environment. An endotherm has a body temperature that stays the same.

14.2 Fishes

- Fishes are ectotherms. They have scales, fins, and gills.
- The three main groups of fishes are the jawless fishes, the cartilaginous fishes, and the bony fishes.
- The largest group of fishes is the bony fishes. Bony fishes have scales and swim bladders. Swim bladders help bony fish rise and sink in the water.

14.3 Amphibians

- Most amphibians live part of their lives in water and part on land.
- Frogs and toads begin life in the water as tadpoles. They become land-dwelling animals as they undergo metamorphosis.
- The three main groups of amphibians are the caecilians, the salamanders and newts, and the frogs and toads.

14.4 Reptiles

- Reptiles have dry, scaly skin and an amniotic egg. These adaptations allow them to live only on the land.
- The three major groups of reptiles are the turtles and tortoises, the alligators and crocodiles, and the lizards and snakes.

VOCABULARY REVIEW

Write each term in a complete sentence, or write a paragraph relating several terms.

14.1
vertebra, p. 241
cartilage, p. 241
notochord, p. 241
ectotherm, p. 242
endotherm, p. 242

14.2
scavenger, p. 244
swim bladder, p. 247

14.3
hibernation, p. 250
estivation, p. 250
nictitating membrane, p. 250
tympanum, p. 250

14.4
amniotic egg, p. 252

PREPARE FOR CHAPTER TEST

To prepare for the chapter test, create a question from each Learning Goal. Use the information in your Science Notebook to answer each question. Then use these answers to write a well-developed essay about the chapter. Use the Key Concept on the first page of this chapter as your topic sentence.

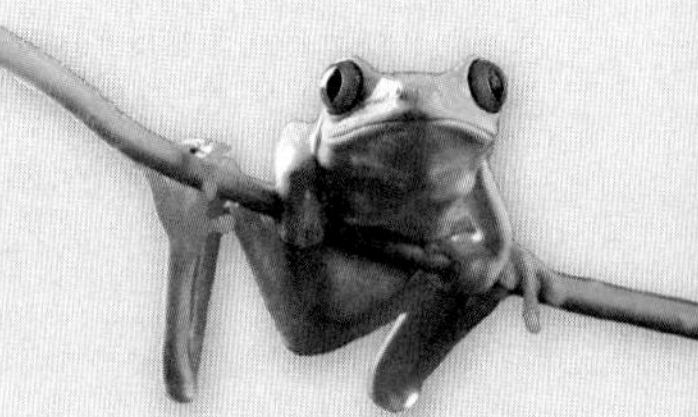

256 FISHES, AMPHIBIANS, AND REPTILES

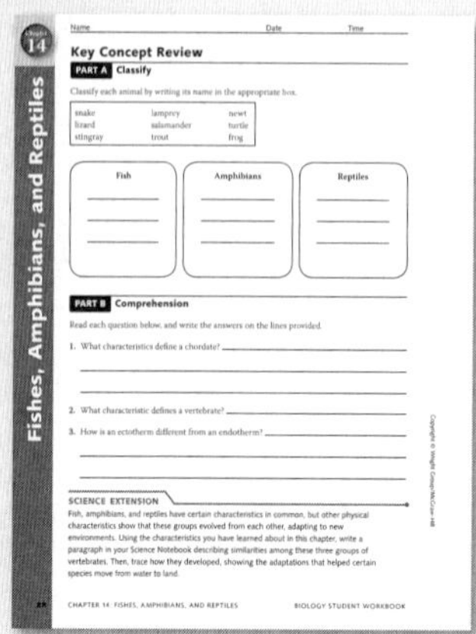

Key Concept Review
Workbook, p. 88

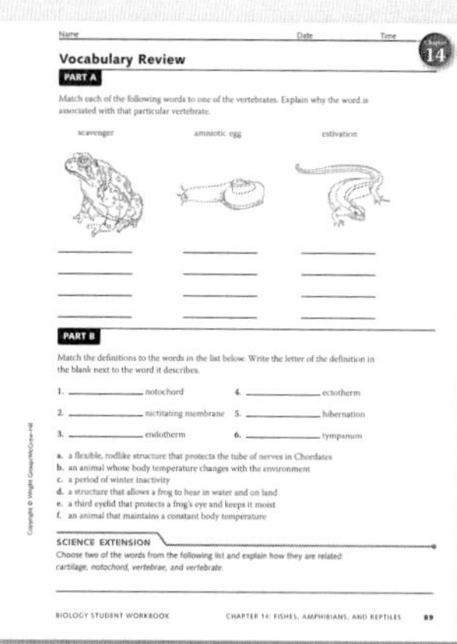

Vocabulary Review
Workbook, p. 89

MASTERING CONCEPTS

True or False

If the statement is true, write "true." If it is false, change the underlined word or words.

1. Vertebrae are bones that go up and down your back.
2. An animal that has a backbone is called a(n) invertebrate.
3. Most fish use lungs to bring oxygen into their bodies.
4. The skeleton of a shark is made of cartilage.
5. Animals that are not active in the winter go through estivation.
6. The head of a(n) crocodile is wide with a rounded snout.

Short Answer

Answer each of the following in a sentence or brief paragraph.

7. What are three common characteristics of all chordates?
8. How is an ectotherm different from an endotherm?
9. Describe what happens to a frog as it goes through metamorphosis.
10. Describe the features of fish that help them survive in nature.
11. How do the shells of the turtle and the tortoise differ from one another?

Critical Thinking

Use what you have learned in this chapter to answer each of the following.

12. **Compare and Contrast** How do caecilians differ from earthworms?
13. **Apply Concepts** The poisonous coral snake has yellow, red, and black bands around its body. The harmless king snake has bands of red, black, and yellow. How is its coloring a useful trait to the king snake?
14. **Make Predictions** What would happen to a frog if it could not move from the land to the water? Explain your answer.

Standardized Test Question

Choose the letter of the response that correctly answers the question.

Body Temperature of a Lizard

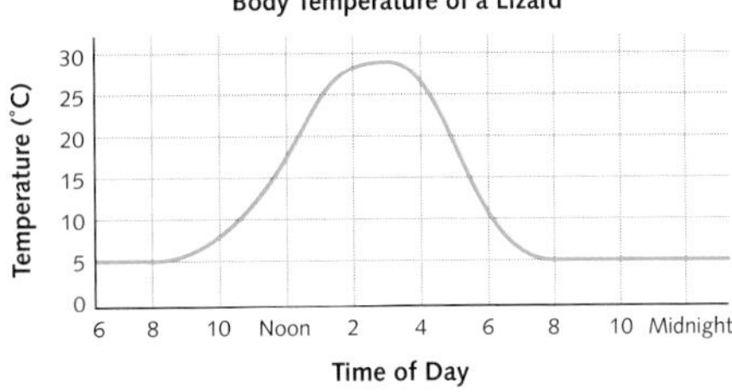

15. The graph shows the body temperature of a desert lizard from 6 A.M. to midnight. Where do you think the lizard was from 8 A.M. to noon?
    - A. sitting on a rock in the sunlight
    - B. sitting in the shade
    - C. burying itself underground
    - D. none of the above

Test-Taking Tip

If "none of the above" is one of the choices in a multiple-choice question, be sure that none of the choices is true.

Critical Thinking

12. Earthworms are soft-bodied invertebrates. Caecilians are vertebrates that have bony scales.
13. Predators might mistake the harmless king snake for the dangerous coral snake and leave it alone. This would allow the king snake to escape from a dangerous situation.
14. The frog would die because it would dry out.

Standardized Test Question

15. A

Reading Links

Amphibians, Reptiles, and Their Conservation

Both an introductory guide and a passionate call for conservation efforts, this treatment of amphibians and reptiles makes for a useful classroom supplement or individual enrichment resource. Its coverage includes detailed attention to the classification, anatomy, behavior, and habitats of these two classes of animals, with an eye to the ways in which human activity can affect their survival.

Crump, Marty. Shoe String Press, Inc. 136 pp. Illustrated with photographs and drawings by the author. Trade ISBN: 978-0-208-02511-1.

Turtles, Tortoises, and Terrapins: Survivors in Armor

Any student curious about turtles will find this comprehensive survey fascinating. Packed with facts, anecdotes, and photographs, the book will help readers understand the history, evolution, anatomy, and life cycle of all groups of turtles, as well as the threats they face today.

Orenstein, Ronald, with Jeanne A. Mortimer and George R. Zug. Firefly Books, Ltd. 304 pp. Illustrated. Trade ISBN: 978-1-55209-605-5.

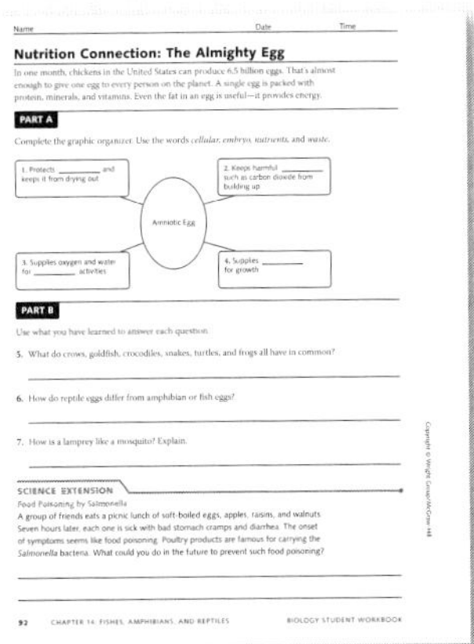

Curriculum Connection
Workbook, p. 92

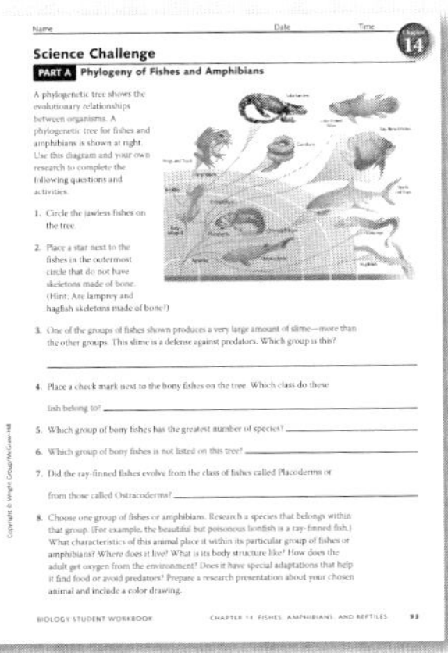

Science Challenge
Workbook, pp. 93–94

Chapter 14

Labs

14A Comparing Vertebrate Characteristics

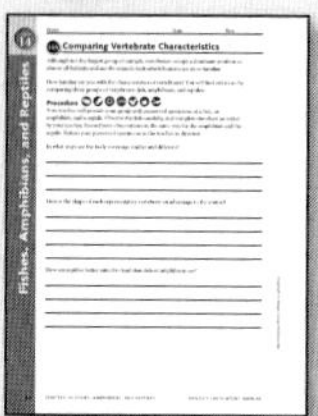

This prechapter introduction activity is designed to determine what students already know about vertebrate characteristics by engaging them in observing and comparing similarities and differences in fish, amphibians, and reptiles.

Objectives

- compare and contrast fish, amphibians, and reptiles
- record observations in a chart
- communicate conclusions

Planning

 30–45 minutes  groups of 3–4 students

Materials (per group)

- preserved fish, frog or toad, and reptile specimens
- pencil and paper

Lab Tip

Specimens obtained should be preserved with chemicals that are nonirritating, nontoxic, and biodegradable. Specimens preserved with formaldehyde should be avoided.

Advance Preparation

- Preserved specimens of fish, frogs or toads, and reptiles (preferably lizards) can be purchased at a biological supply company. Live specimens may be used, such as guppies or goldfish in an aquarium and frogs or toads and lizards or turtles in a terrarium.
- Have students prepare a data table, titled *Vertebrate Information*, with four columns and six rows. The column headings should be *Characteristic, Fish, Amphibian,* and *Reptile.* In each table cell under *Characteristic,* have students write one of the following: *body covering, general shape, respiration, appendages,* and *habitat or environments.*

Engagement Guide

- Challenge students to think about how the vertebrates are alike and how they are different by asking:
  - *What characteristics make these specimens vertebrates?* (They all have backbones and internal skeletons.)
  - *What features help distinguish the specimens from each other?* (Students should recognize that the body coverings are different and that the fish has appendages that differ from those of the amphibian and reptile. They all have different habitats.)
  - *Which animals are more closely related among these three?* (Students should answer that fishes and amphibians are more closely related because they depend more on an aquatic environment. Amphibians can be seen as a transition animal between fish and reptiles.)
- Encourage students to communicate their conclusions in creative ways.

Going Further

Encourage students to make a picture poster of reptiles, amphibians, and fish. For example, reptile pictures would include snakes, lizards, turtles, and crocodiles. Amphibian pictures would include caecilians, salamanders and newts, frogs, and toads. Fish pictures would include the three groups of fishes. Have students display their posters in the classroom.

14B Using a Graph to Identify an Ectotherm

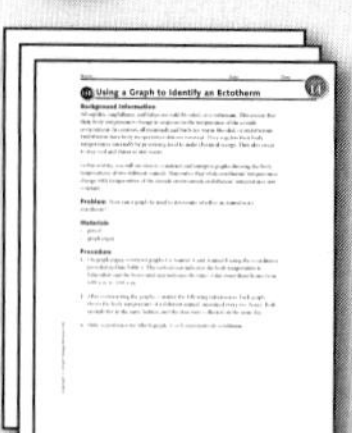

Objectives

- construct graphs of animal body temperatures
- interpret graphs
- compare and contrast ectotherms and endotherms
- predict which graph represents an ectotherm

Skill Set

graphing, interpreting, comparing and contrasting, predicting

Planning

 30–45 minutes  groups of 2–4 students

Materials

Materials for this activity are listed in the Student Laboratory Manual.

Answers to Observations

Graph A represents the body temperature of an ectotherm. Graph B represents the body temperature of an endotherm.

Answers to Analysis and Conclusions

1. Animals A's highest body temperature is near the body temperature of Animal B. The body temperature of Animal A changes, and the body temperature Animal B does not change.
2. The animal could be moving into and out of the sunlight. The animal's body temperature is adjusting to the outside environment.

3. Graph A represents an ectotherm because the changing body temperature indicates that it cannot regulate its body temperature.
4. The ectotherm might be any kind of fish, reptile, or amphibian, such as a perch, trout, lizard, snake, frog, or toad.
5. an endotherm; because shivering and sweating are mechanisms that warm-blooded animals use to regulate their body temperature

Going Further

Encourage students to design and build a class terrarium for amphibians and reptiles. Have students do research in the library or online to determine an appropriate design (including suitable plant and animal specimens) for the terrarium. With your approval, have students build the terrarium and bring in plants and animals to place in it.

14C Frog Anatomy

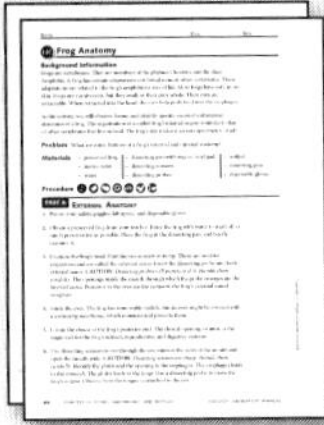

Objectives

- examine a preserved frog's external and internal anatomy
- compare the internal anatomy of a frog to that of a human
- infer the functions of some structures of a frog

Skill Set

examining, measuring, comparing and contrasting, inferring

Planning

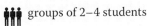

 1 class period  groups of 2–4 students

Materials

Materials for this activity are listed in the Student Laboratory Manual.

Lab Tip

Specimens obtained should be preserved with chemicals that are nonirritating, nontoxic, and biodegradable. Specimens preserved with formaldehyde should be avoided.

Advance Preparation

Preserved frogs can be purchased from a biological supply company. If disposable plastic gloves are not available, advise students to wash their hands periodically with soap and water in order to wash off the preservative. Rolls of plastic bags can also substitute as gloves. You can also advise your students to bring in their own gloves if they wish, and you can store them in the classroom.

Answers to Observations: Figure 1

Drawing of the frog mouth: maxillary teeth, vomerine teeth, internal nares, esophagus, glottis, and tongue should be properly labeled.

Answers to Observations: Data Table 1

Each organ should have a check to indicate the student was able to locate and identify it. If anything was found in the stomach, students should be able to recognize the food because frogs swallow their meals whole. Students' answers will vary for the intestine length and the frog length, but the intestines should be close to the length of the frog.

Answers to Observations: Figure 2

Drawing of frog internal anatomy: fat bodies, gallbladder, esophagus, heart, lungs, liver, stomach, small intestine, large intestine, and cloaca should be properly labeled.

Answers to Analysis and Conclusions

1. The webbed toes help the frog swim in water. The large leg muscles help the frog leap long distances on land and swim in water.
2. Because the small intestine is so long, there is a great amount of surface area to absorb nutrients.
3. When the frog is partially submerged in water, it can breathe through its external nares because they are on top of its head.
4. Answers will vary. Students might suggest that humans require larger lungs for a completely terrestrial life and separate openings for the urinary, digestive, and reproductive systems.
5. Because the tongue is attached to the front of the mouth, it can be extended farther to catch prey, such as flying insects.

Going Further

Have students develop a hypothesis about whether the internal organs of frogs are similar to the internal organs of other amphibians. To test the hypothesis, have students use various resources to learn about the internal organs of frogs and other amphibians and draw or show pictures of their results.

Chapter 15 Lessons

Introduce Chapter 15

As a starting activity, use LAB 15A How Do Birds Fly? on page 92 of the Laboratory Manual.

ENGAGE Have students work with partners to record what they know or can deduce about the fastest, slowest, largest, and smallest birds and mammals. Have two pairs of students discuss their deductions and reasons. With each class, name the animals students have identified from each category, and discuss discrepancies between what students deducted and the facts.

largest bird that cannot fly—ostrich
largest bird that flies—condor
smallest bird—bee hummingbird
fastest flying bird—spine-tailed swift
largest land mammal—African elephant
largest water mammal—blue whale
fastest land mammal—cheetah
slowest land mammal—sloth

Think About Making Inferences

Provide students with photographs of a variety of birds, making sure the legs and feet of the birds are clearly visible.

Have students work in pairs to make inferences about the birds in photographs. Remind them to focus on the clues provided by the structure of the feet and legs. Direct students to write their inferences in their Science Notebooks.

Chapter 15 Birds and Mammals

KEY CONCEPT Birds and mammals can be classified based on their physical characteristics.

The bald eagle is a majestic animal. It glides gracefully through the air. Its blackish-brown body and white head, neck, and tail distinguish it from all other animals. So recognizable is this animal that it is part of the emblem of the United States.

A bald eagle is a type of animal called a bird. This chapter is about birds and another class of animals, mammals. The giraffe is a familiar mammal, easily identified by its long neck, which allows it to eat leaves from tall trees. The lion, another mammal, is the only natural enemy of the adult giraffe.

Think About Making Inferences

When you make an inference, you make a logical conclusion based on something you observe.

- Look at the photographs of birds given to you by your teacher. Concentrate on the feet and legs of each of the birds.
- In your Science Notebook, make inferences about the type of environment each bird may live in based on the structure of its feet and legs.

NSTA SciLINKS THE WORLD'S A CLICK AWAY
www.scilinks.org
Birds **Code: WGB15A**
Mammals **Code: WGB15B**

Chapter 15 Planning Guide

Instructional Periods	National Standards	Lab Manual	Workbook
15.1 2 periods	A.1, B.3, C.1; C.3, C.5, C.6; UCP.3, UCP.5	**Lab 15A—p. 92** How Do Birds Fly? **Lab 15B—p. 93** Behavior and the Environment **Lab 15C—p. 96** Who Did It?	Key Concept Review p. 95 Vocabulary Review p. 96 Graphic Organizer p. 97 Reading Comprehension p. 98 Curriculum Connection p. 99 Science Challenge p. 100
15.2 1 period	C.5; A.1, B.4; UCP.2		
15.3 2 periods	C.1, C.2, C.5, C.3; UCP.1, UCP.2		
15.4 2 periods	C.3, G.1, G.3; A.2, C.6, G.1, G.3		

Middle School Standard; High School Standard; Unifying Concept and Principle

15.1 Birds

Before You Read

In your Science Notebook, draw a three-column chart to organize facts about birds. Label the first column *Characteristics*. Label the second column *Origins*. Label the third column *Types*. Preview the Learning Goals, headings, subheadings, and visuals. In each column, write one or two facts that you already know about each topic.

Learning Goals

- Describe the common characteristics of birds.
- Distinguish among the different types of birds.
- Discuss the origin of birds.

New Vocabulary

feather
contour feather
down feather
preening
sternum

Recall Vocabulary

molting (p. 225)

Like fishes, amphibians, and reptiles, birds are vertebrates. Birds have an important characteristic that sets them apart from these animals.

Characteristics of Birds

Birds are endotherms, or animals that have a constant body temperature. Birds can be active no matter what the temperature is in their environment. Thus, they are found in almost all places on Earth. Like reptiles, birds lay eggs that have hardened shells. Birds share other common characteristics.

Bird Feathers All birds have feathers. A **feather** is made of dead cells that contain the same material found in human fingernails. Feathers come in many colors, shapes, and sizes. Feathers help keep a bird warm. They also help the bird fly, and they cover and protect the bird's skin.

Birds have two main kinds of feathers: contour feathers and down feathers. A **contour feather** is hard and stiff. It gives the bird its shape and protects the bird. A **down feather** is small and fluffy. It is close to the bird's skin and keeps the bird warm. People use down feathers in coats, jackets, blankets, and sleeping bags. Over time, feathers on a bird become worn and damaged. Damaged feathers are replaced through a process called molting. Birds lose only a few of their feathers at a time.

Birds must take care of their feathers. In a process called **preening**, birds apply an oil to their feathers. This oil comes from a gland in the bird's tail. The oil keeps the feathers from drying out and breaking. The oil also makes the feathers waterproof.

Figure 15.1 A bird preens itself *(left)* to protect its feathers. A contour feather *(center)* is strong and stiff. It protects the bird's skin. A down feather *(right)* is small and fluffy. It keeps the bird warm.

15.1 Introduce

ENGAGE Give students a few minutes to write their thoughts about birds—opinions, experiences, observations, and societal views of birds. Have small groups of students discuss their thoughts. Talk as a class about societal views or stereotypes of birds ("bird-brained," "love birds," "early bird," etc.). Tell students that they will be learning factual information about birds.

Before You Read

Model the three-column table on the board, labeling each column as directed. Title the table *Facts About Birds*. Scan the first few Lesson Goals, headings, subheadings, and visuals, thinking aloud as you do. As you read the *Bird Feathers* section, write *Birds have different colored feathers* in the *Characteristics* column. Have students finish scanning the lesson and complete the table in their Science Notebooks as directed.

Vocabulary terms are listed on the first student page of each lesson. You may wish to preview the terms before introducing each lesson. Strategies for teaching the vocabulary appear on the pages where the terms are introduced.

Teach

EXPLAIN that in this lesson, students will learn about birds, including their characteristics, origins, and types. Remind students that birds are vertebrates, and review the definition of the term ("animals with backbones"). Also review the definition of endotherm ("an animal that has a constant body temperature").

Vocabulary

feather Explain that feathers are the light growths that form a bird's soft covering. A feather has a hollow central piece with fine strands on either side.

contour feather Tell students that a contour is an outline. Contour feathers give the bird its shape.

down feather Ask students to identify common meanings of the word *down*. (It usually means "a movement or position toward a lower level.") Explain that down feathers on a bird are those closest to the bird's skin.

preening Explain to students that birds preen by applying oil to feathers with their beaks.

ELL Strategy

Illustrate Have each student draw a bird and identify and label the characteristics of birds. Remind students that most vocabulary words in this section should be included in their drawings.

Science Notebook EXTRA

Encourage students to use the vocabulary section they created in their Science Notebooks. Remind them to record prefixes, suffixes, and root words to help them remember the meanings of vocabulary terms.

Teach

EXPLAIN that students will continue to learn about the characteristics of birds in this lesson.

EXPLORE Provide students with names of birds and the foods they eat. Have students infer and sketch the type of beak each bird has.

pelican—whole fish

hornbill—fruit, various species of invertebrates, and small mammals (all in one gulp)

falcon—small pieces of prey

hummingbird—nectar

woodpecker—bugs in wood

flycatcher—insects

Vocabulary

sternum Tell students that the word *sternum*, derived from the Greek word *sternon*, means "chest." Locate your sternum bone for students, and then have them locate theirs.

Explore It!

Provide students with hand lenses and a variety of bird feathers to examine. Have students first examine the contour feathers and notice their common characteristics. Then, have them do the same for down feathers. Direct students to make Venn diagrams comparing the characteristics of contour and down feathers and to infer how the various structures support the functions these feathers perform.

CONNECTION: Art

Show students a variety of photographs of birds in flight, and tell them to closely examine the wings of the birds. Have students analyze photographs of modern-day hang gliders. Ask students to compare and contrast the birds' wings and the hang gliders. What characteristics are common to both? Which are unique?

Then, have students review da Vinci's sketches of the flying machine, and ask them to suggest revisions to the sketches that might improve the machine's ability to fly.

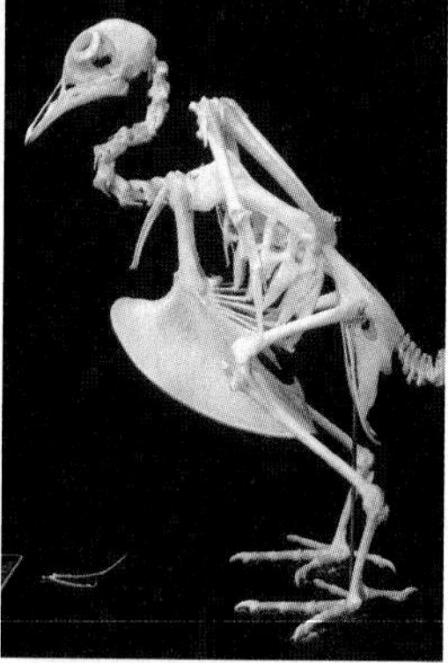

Figure 15.2 The large bone on this bird's skeleton is called the sternum. Muscles attached to the sternum allow a bird to fly.

Explore It!

Use a hand lens to look at a variety of contour and down feathers. In your Science Notebook, draw the different types of feathers. Make a list of the characteristics that the feathers share. Also describe how they are different. How does the structure of these feathers help them perform their functions?

Bird Wings All birds have front limbs that are wings. Most birds are able to fly. Birds that can fly have powerful muscles attached to their breastbones. The breastbone is called the **sternum** (STUR num). Look at **Figure 15.2**. The sternum on this bird skeleton is the large bone above the bird's legs. The muscles attached to the sternum give a bird the power it needs to take off and fly through the air.

Food and Flight

A person who does not eat very much is often said to "eat like a bird." This is not an accurate description, however, because a bird actually eats a large amount of food for its size. This food gives the bird the energy it needs to keep its body temperature constant. It also gives the bird the energy it needs to fly. A hummingbird like the one shown in **Figure 15.3** eats nectar about every ten minutes. It eats about twice its body weight in nectar every day!

Figure 15.3 The tiny hummingbird needs to eat a very large amount of food to give it the energy to fly. The wings of a hummingbird beat about 80 times per second.

A bird has no teeth. It uses its beak to catch its food. Birds eat a wide variety of plants and animals. Birds feed on nectar, seeds, insects, worms, fish, and other birds. Each type of bird has a beak that is well suited to the type of food that bird eats. The hummingbird shown in Figure 15.3 has a long, thin beak. The hummingbird uses that beak to reach deep into a flower and sip its nectar.

CONNECTION: Art

Italian artist Leonardo da Vinci (1452–1519) was fascinated with birds and their ability to fly. He used his knowledge of bird wings to draw designs of various flying machines. Da Vinci's design for a human glider looks very similar to a modern-day hang glider.

Background Information

Leonardo da Vinci was known for his abilities as an architect, anatomist, sculptor, engineer, inventor, geometer, scientist, mathematician, musician, and painter. Some of his most famous works include the *Mona Lisa*, *The Last Supper*, and *Vitruvian Man*. The latter details the proportions of the male human body. As a scientist, da Vinci drew detailed plans for a human-powered flying machine, a bicycle, a helicopter, and a parachute.

Origins of Birds

After their success in the ocean and on land, vertebrates moved to the air. Several hundred million years ago, the air was filled with insects that ancient birds ate for food. The air also kept the ancient birds safe from predators in the ocean or on the land. Fossils show that modern birds may have developed from small, two-legged dinosaurs called theropods. **Figure 15.4** shows the relationship between the theropod and modern bird species that may have developed from it.

The fossil record suggests that the earliest bird was *Archaeopteryx*. *Archaeopteryx* lived about 150 million years ago. It had both reptilelike and birdlike features. It was about the size of a crow, and it had feathers and wings. It was not able to fly, however, and it ran to catch its prey. Scientists believe that *Archaeopteryx* was not a direct ancestor of modern birds and represents a smaller branch of the bird family tree.

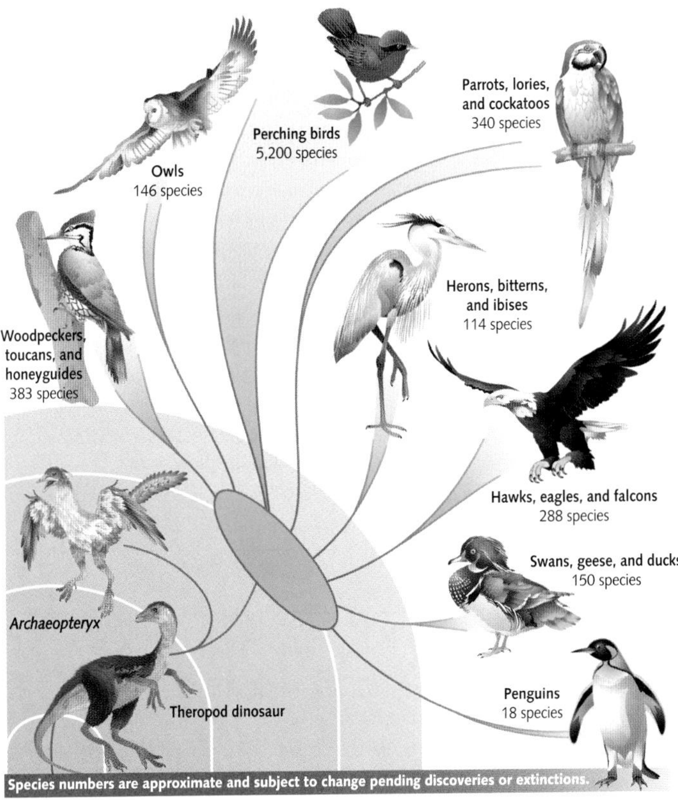

Figure 15.4 Many scientists believe that birds may have developed from an ancient reptile called a theropod. The skeletons of birds and theropods are similar.

As You Read

Review the information in the chart in your Science Notebook. Share your information with a partner. Add any other facts that will help you organize what you learn about birds.

What is molting? Preening?

Extend It!

Find out more about *Archaeopteryx*. How was it similar to a dinosaur? What did *Archaeopteryx* eat? What dinosaurs lived during the same time? Write your findings in your Science Notebook.

CONNECTION: Environmental Science

Birds are important to the environment. They help pollinate plants, and they eat insect pests. You can care for and protect the birds in your neighborhood. Building a birdhouse or setting up a bird feeder can ensure birds will continue to populate the area.

Teach

EXPLAIN to students that they will learn how birds evolved from a vertebrate animal.

Use the Visual: Figure 15.4

EXTEND Have pairs of students compare the sketch of the theropod and a modern bird skeleton. Ask them to note differences and similarities and to infer the reasons for the differences.

As You Read

Give students about five minutes to review and update their tables. Then pair students, and have each partner share his or her facts and provide feedback to the other student.

ANSWER Molting is the process by which birds' damaged feathers are replaced. Preening is the process by which birds apply an oil to their feathers. This oil comes from a gland in the bird's tail. The oil keeps the feathers from drying out and breaking. The oil also makes the feathers waterproof.

Extend It!

Provide resources for student research including encyclopedias, dinosaur reference books, and Internet access.

Student findings might include the following: lived during the Late Jurassic Period, 140 million years ago; mass of about 325 g; wingspan of 0.5 m; feathers similar to those of flying birds, but skeleton closely resembling that of small carnivorous dinosaur; long feathered tail, hollow bones, clawed front toes, shorebird, and eater of fish; brain relatively large for an animal of that time. Other dinosaurs of the time include: the gigantic sauropods, such as *Diplodocus*, *Brachiosaurus*, and *Apatosaurus;* plated stegosaurs; carnosaurs such as *Allosaurus*; small, fast coelurosaurs; and ceratosaurs such as *Dilophosaurus*.

Background Information

Fossils of *Archaeopteryx* have been dated to the Late Jurassic Period (159 million to 144 million years ago). Eight have been found, to date, in the Solnhofen Limestone Formation in Bavaria, Germany.

Teacher Alert

The fossil *Archaeopteryx* is the subject of controversy and debate. In 1985, Hoyle and associates wrote an article in the *British Journal of Photography* stating that the impressions of feathers in stone from *Archaeopteryx* were faked. Additionally, they suggested that the two slabs of the fossil had different textures and do not fit together as they should.

In 1984, another scientist, Thulborn, published an article in the *Zoological Journal of the Linnean Society* claiming that *Archaeopteryx* is not a bird but rather a theropod. Students will probably read this information as they do their research for the Extend It! activity.

CONNECTION: Environmental Science

EXTEND Have students research birds common to your environment, what they eat, and what types of nesting sites the birds need.

Teach

EXPLAIN to students that they will learn about the characteristics of the four main groups of birds: flightless birds, perching birds, birds of prey, and water birds.

Science Notebook EXTRA

Have students use concept maps to organize information about the four main groups of birds. The main topic should be *Types of Birds*, and the four bird groups should be the subtopics. Have students include details about body structure and food sources for each bird group.

Figure It Out: Figure 15.5

ANSWER 1. A bird's wings allow the bird to fly. 2. The ostrich, penguin, and kiwi are all flightless birds. The kiwi has no wings, but the ostrich and penguin have wings.

Assess

EVALUATE Use the After You Read questions and the Alternative Assessment to help you assess students' understanding of the lesson.

After You Read

1. All birds are endothermic vertebrates with feathers, small bodies, and wings. All lay eggs.
2. A contour feather is long and stiff, and it protects the bird's body. A down feather is small and soft and keeps the bird warm.
3. Some scientists think that modern birds developed from a two-legged dinosaur called a theropod.
4. The four major types of birds are flightless birds, perching birds, birds of prey, and water birds.
5. Accept all logical answers.

Alternative Assessment

EVALUATE Have students write a few sentences to summarize the facts for each column of the table in their Science Notebooks.

Figure It Out

1. What is the function of a bird's wings?
2. Describe how the ostrich, the penguin, and the kiwi are alike and how they are different.

Figure 15.5 The ostrich *(left)*, penguin *(center)*, and kiwi *(right)* are all examples of birds that are not able to fly.

Types of Birds

There are about 10,000 known species of birds. Birds are often divided into a few large groups. These groups are based on one or two physical characteristics of the birds. The four main groups of birds are flightless birds, perching birds, birds of prey, and water birds.

Flightless Birds The ostrich, penguin, and kiwi shown in **Figure 15.5** are all examples of birds that are not able to fly. Most flightless birds have small wings. The kiwi has no wings. Many flightless birds are fast runners. This helps them catch their prey and avoid predators. Penguins are excellent swimmers.

Perching Birds Cardinals, woodpeckers, and canaries are types of perching birds. Many of these birds sing songs when they are on their perches. Perching birds can eat insects, worms, or seeds.

Figure 15.6 The cardinal *(top)* is a type of perching bird. The pygmy falcon *(bottom)* is a bird of prey. It uses sharp claws and a strong beak to catch food.

Birds of Prey Hunting birds are also called birds of prey. Hawks, eagles, and owls are all examples of birds of prey. They have sharp claws and strong, curved beaks. Birds of prey fly very fast. The peregrine falcon has reached speeds of up to 290 kilometers per hour while diving for its prey.

Water Birds Water birds swim and dive in lakes and ponds. Many water birds, such as ducks and swans, have webbed feet for swimming. Other water birds, such as the flamingos shown in **Figure 15.7**, have long legs for wading. Some have long beaks they use to pull food from the mud.

Figure 15.7 Flamingos wade through the water in search of food.

After You Read

1. What are three common characteristics of all birds?
2. How is a contour feather different from a down feather?
3. From what animal do some scientists think modern birds developed?
4. Describe the four major types of birds.
5. Using the information you wrote in your Science Notebook, write a well-developed paragraph that summarizes what you have learned about birds.

Background Information

Perching birds are also called songbirds; water birds such as ducks, geese, and swans are sometimes called waterfowl.

Field Study

Provide students with reference books and binoculars, and have them bird-watch in a nearby outdoor area or an indoor place with a likely view of birds. Have students watch two or three birds for five to ten minutes and observe bird behavior, food sources, beak shape and size, and foot structure. Have students write their observations in their Science Notebooks and then infer which species of birds they observed.

15.2 Adaptations for Flight

Before You Read

Look through the lesson, taking note of the Learning Goals, headings, diagram, and photographs. What questions about the information come to mind? Write at least three questions in your Science Notebook that you would like answered by the end of the lesson. Think about information you already know that might help you answer these questions.

Learning Goals

- Describe how a bird's body is adapted for flight.
- Explain how migration is important to the survival of birds.

New Vocabulary

migration

Have you ever wondered how birds fly? A bird's entire body is adapted to enable it to fly. These adaptations either reduce a bird's body weight or make a bird more compact. The body of a bird is small. It does not weigh very much. A bird's small size and light weight enable it to glide through the air.

A Bird's Body

The wings of a bird are wide and thin. They are similar to the wings on an airplane in that they are slightly curved on the top and thicker in the front. As air flows around the wings, it travels faster over the top of the wing than beneath the wing. Where the air travels faster, the pressure is reduced. Thus, the pressure beneath the wings is greater than the pressure above the wings. This difference in air pressure provides the lift needed for flight. Once in flight, the bird's wings allow the bird to use air currents to stay aloft.

The skeleton of a bird is adapted for flight. As Figure 15.9 on page 264 illustrates, the bones of a bird's skeleton are hollow. Hollow bones keep the bird's skeleton light in weight. The crosspieces in the bird's bones keep the bones strong. Some of the bones are connected to other bones. This makes the bird's skeleton stronger and more stable for flight.

Although a bird's skeleton is light in weight, its muscles are large and heavy. The chest muscles make up about 25 percent of the bird's body weight. These muscles are used to move the bird's wings.

Figure 15.8 The adaptations of the great blue heron's body enable it to glide over the water in search of food.

15.2 Introduce

ENGAGE Ask students how they think animals know where to go when they are migrating. Accept all reasonable answers. Then, ask students how they find their way home from school. Pair students and give them a minute or two to close their eyes and picture their routes to school. Then, have each student draw a map of his or her route home, noting landmarks rather than street names. Ask students to keep their maps private.

Have each student orally describe the route while the partner tries to draw it. After each partner has sketched the other's route, have students exchange drawings and compare the original map to the partner's map. Discuss the importance of using landmarks in drawing the routes.

Tell students that some migratory birds use landmarks such as mountains, rivers, and forests in navigating.

Before You Read

Model skimming the section by noting aloud some of the Learning Goals and headings, the diagram, and the photographs. Think aloud about Figure 15.8, and note that the great blue heron is a fairly large bird. Ask: *Do the bodies of all birds have the same adaptations for flight?*

Give students about five minutes to preview the lesson and to write at least three questions in their Science Notebooks.

Teach

EXPLAIN to students that in this lesson, they will learn how a bird's body is adapted for flight and how and why birds migrate.

Have students add information to their bird sketches from Lesson 15.1, page 259 (ELL Strategy). Direct them to identify and label the characteristics of birds that enable birds to fly.

ELL Strategy

Read Aloud Organize students in groups of three, and have them alternate reading aloud paragraphs in Lesson 15.2. One person should read a paragraph and then summarize its important points or main idea. The next student should read the following paragraph and summarize it in the same way. Continue until students read the entire lesson.

CHAPTER 15 263

Teach

EXPLORE Place students in small groups, and direct them to examine photographs of one of the four main groups of birds and analyze the wings for that group. Have each student group create a list of common characteristics of wings for that bird group. Then, ask student groups to share these characteristics with the class. Discuss differences among bird groups, and infer why such differences exist.

Figure It Out: Figure 15.9

ANSWER **1.** Hollow bones make the bird's skeleton lighter and easier to lift for flight. **2.** Flightless birds use their legs to run or their bodies and limbs to swim through the water.

As You Read

Give students about five minutes to review their questions and to write responses to them.

ANSWER The wings of a bird are wide and thin. They are similar to the wings on an airplane in that they are slightly curved on the top and thicker in the front. As air flows around the wings, it travels faster over the top of the wing than it does beneath the wing. Where the air travels faster, the pressure is reduced. Thus, the pressure beneath the wings is greater than the pressure above the wings. This difference in pressure provides the lift needed for flight. Once in flight, the bird's wings allow the bird to use air currents to stay aloft.

Explore It!

Students should find that they tire easily as they flap their arms in the air. Birds have proportionally much larger chest muscles than humans do, and they can move their wings faster and sustain this movement for much longer periods of time than humans can do the same with their arms.

As You Read

Look at the questions you wrote in your Science Notebook. Use information learned so far in this lesson to help you answer this question.

How do a bird's wings enable it to fly?

People have always dreamed of being able to fly. When people hang glide or parasail, they experience a sense of flight. Birds do it naturally! Some of the characteristic structures of birds that enable them to fly are summarized in **Figure 15.9**.

Figure It Out

1. How are hollow bones useful to a bird?
2. Describe how birds that do not fly are able to move from one place to another.

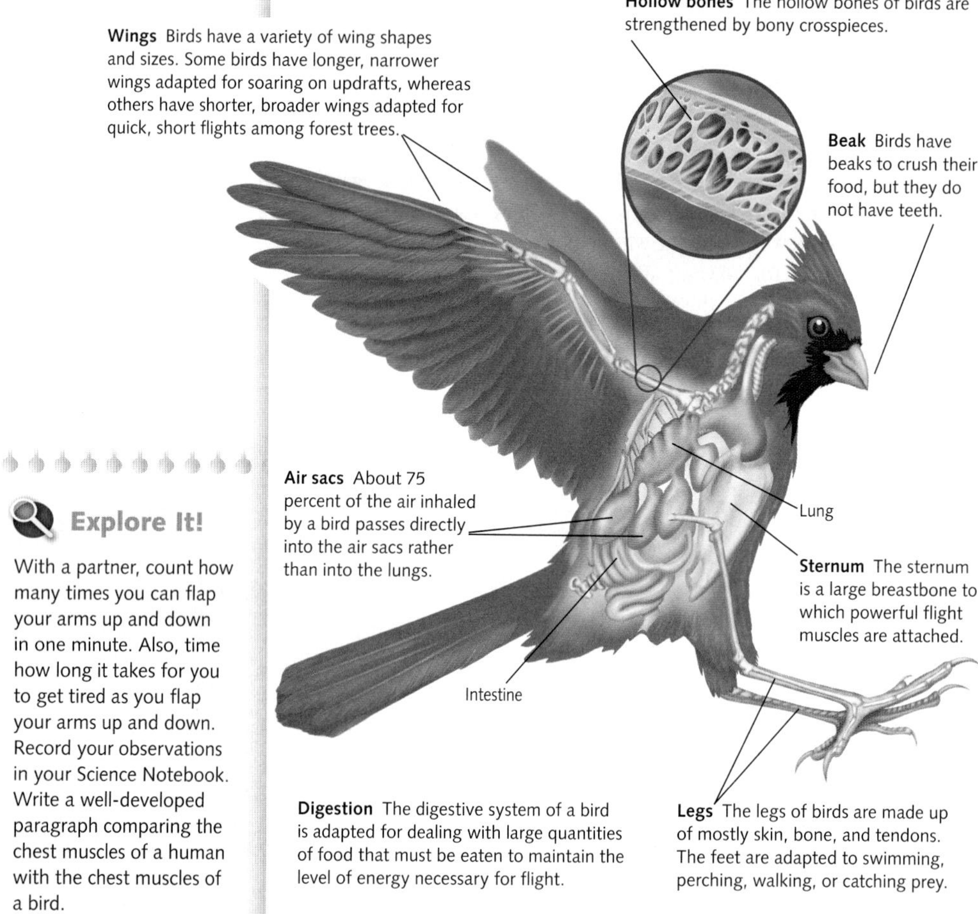

Hollow bones The hollow bones of birds are strengthened by bony crosspieces.
Wings Birds have a variety of wing shapes and sizes. Some birds have longer, narrower wings adapted for soaring on updrafts, whereas others have shorter, broader wings adapted for quick, short flights among forest trees.
Beak Birds have beaks to crush their food, but they do not have teeth.
Air sacs About 75 percent of the air inhaled by a bird passes directly into the air sacs rather than into the lungs.
Lung
Sternum The sternum is a large breastbone to which powerful flight muscles are attached.
Intestine
Digestion The digestive system of a bird is adapted for dealing with large quantities of food that must be eaten to maintain the level of energy necessary for flight.
Legs The legs of birds are made up of mostly skin, bone, and tendons. The feet are adapted to swimming, perching, walking, or catching prey.

Figure 15.9 Many features that enable birds to fly are shown here.

Explore It!

With a partner, count how many times you can flap your arms up and down in one minute. Also, time how long it takes for you to get tired as you flap your arms up and down. Record your observations in your Science Notebook. Write a well-developed paragraph comparing the chest muscles of a human with the chest muscles of a bird.

Differentiated Instruction

Logical and Mathematical Have students estimate how many times they would need to flap their arms for flights of 10, 30, and 60 minutes. Compare these estimates with those for a hummingbird, which flaps its wings about 50 times per second.

Background Information

Wing feathers give a bird wing its shape; wings are shaped differently depending on the needs of the bird. Birds that fly in open air have long, narrow wings. These birds can remain in the air indefinitely, but they may have a more difficult time taking off. Perching birds have short, broad wings and wide feathers to maneuver between branches and to take off frequently.

CONNECTION: Physics

Newton's third law of motion states that for every force applied by an object, there is an equal and opposite force applied on that object. A bird's wing can be used to demonstrate this law. When a bird flaps its wings down, the bird's body moves up, and the bird flies.

Bird Migration

Have you ever looked at the sky during the fall months and seen a flock of birds flying toward a warmer climate? Many birds leave their homes before winter to find a warmer place with more food. How do birds find their way to these winter homes?

Migration is the regular movement of a group of animals from one place to another. Birds are not the only animals that migrate, but more birds travel long distances than any other kind of animal. The arctic tern spends its summer in the arctic circle near the north pole. Each year, as winter approaches, this bird flies 35,000 kilometers to travel to Antarctica!

Most birds migrate to find new sources of food in the winter. When they migrate, many birds travel along certain flying routes. Some birds navigate, or determine the route they will take, by observing the Sun and stars. Others navigate by following coastlines, mountain ranges, or wind currents. Scientists think that some birds have magnetic centers in their brains. These magnetic centers act like compasses to help the birds find their way. However, there are many things that scientists have not yet learned about bird migration.

Figure 15.10 Sandhill cranes move to a warmer climate in the winter. A warmer climate will provide more food for the cranes.

Did You Know?

The golden plover migrates 4,000 kilometers from its North American summer home to its winter home in South America. It arrives in South America with a loss of only 57 grams!

After You Read

1. How is a bird's body adapted for flight?
2. What is migration?
3. How do birds find their way during migration?
4. Look at the questions and answers you have recorded in your Science Notebook. Write a well-developed paragraph explaining two bird behaviors: how they fly and how and why they migrate.

Teach

EXPLAIN to students that they will learn about bird migration in this section.

CONNECTION: Physics

EXTEND Provide supervision for this activity. Have students experience Newton's third law of motion in action, if resources are available, by having each sit or stand on a skateboard as he or she throws a ball hard. The force of throwing the ball will push the student in the opposite direction. Have students describe their experiences in their Science Notebooks, including diagrams to support their descriptions.

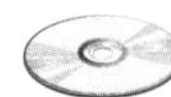

Vocabulary

migration Explain to students that the root of the word *migration*, *migrate*, is derived from the Latin word *migrare*, which means "to move from one place to another." The suffix *-ion* indicates the action or state of the root's meaning. Use this opportunity to discuss parts of speech by identifying *migration* as a noun and *migrate* as a verb. Ask students to provide the noun form of *navigate* (*navigation*).

Assess

EVALUATE Use the After You Read questions and the Alternative Assessment to help you assess students' understanding of the lesson.

After You Read

1. Its body is small. Its wings are long and thin and slightly curved at the top. Its hollow skeleton weighs little. It has large chest muscles attached to the sternum.
2. Migration is the movement of a group of animals from one place to another.
3. Birds migrate by following landmarks such as coastlines, mountain ranges, and wind currents. Some birds have magnetic centers in their brains that act as compasses.
4. Accept all logical answers.

Alternative Assessment

EVALUATE Have each student draw a bird and label its adaptations for flight.

Graphic Organizer
Workbook, p. 97

15.3 Introduce

ENGAGE Have students work independently to write the names of as many mammals as they can. Then, direct students to organize their lists using any sorting characteristics that seem reasonable. Have students share their lists and their reasons for categorization in small groups.

Tell students that they will be learning what characteristics all mammals share, as well as how scientists classify mammals.

Before You Read

Have students review the lesson's new vocabulary terms and write them in their Science Notebooks. Remind students to leave a few lines between words to complete the definitions as they read.

Teach

EXPLORE Have students in small groups make observations about the hair and fur on a variety of mammals by looking at photographs. Direct them to choose mammals that live in different environments, such as in water, in cold climates, and in warm climates. Provide visual reference books, encyclopedias, and Web sites such as the National Wildlife Federation's **www.nwf.org**, for students to use. Ask students to note differences in fur and hair (color, thickness, and length) in the different animals and to infer the reasons for these differences.

Discuss and summarize student inferences in a class discussion.

Learning Goals

- List the common characteristics of all mammals.
- Compare the three main groups of mammals.
- Describe one physical characteristic of each order of placental mammals.

New Vocabulary

monotreme
marsupial
placental mammal
uterus
placenta
gestation
echolocation
carnivore
herbivore
omnivore

15.3 Mammals

Before You Read

Write the vocabulary terms for this lesson in your Science Notebook. As you read the definitions, write a sentence for each term that includes the definition.

Look closely at the surface of your forearm. What do you see? The hairs sticking up through your skin are not a characteristic of any animal group you have studied so far. Mammals are the only group of animals that have hair. People, dogs, and cats are all types of mammals.

Characteristics of Mammals

All mammals are endothermic vertebrates. At some time during their lives, all mammals have hair or fur. For mammals living in cold climates, this hair or fur helps keep them warm. The musk ox, which lives in Alaska and Northern Canada, has fur that is at least ten centimeters long!

All mammals feed their young with milk produced in their mammary glands. The word *mammal* comes from the word *mammary*. Young mammals depend on their mothers for food. Some young mammals stay with their mothers for a long time.

During the time young mammals stay with their mothers, they learn how to survive on their own. Mammals have the most highly developed brains of all of the animal groups. They also have highly developed senses of sight, hearing, taste, and smell. The brains and senses of mammals help them survive in nature.

Figure 15.11 The long, thick fur of the musk ox *(left)* helps it survive in very cold climates. The Bengal tiger *(right)* uses her mammary glands to nurse her young cubs.

ELL Strategy

Use a Concept Map Have each student create a concept map using *Mammals* as the main topic. Subtopics should include *Characteristics* and *Reproduction.* Students will complete the concept maps as they read the lesson.

Reproduction in Mammals

Based on the way they reproduce, mammals can be divided into three groups. These three groups are the egg-laying mammals, the pouched mammals, and the placental mammals. The most familiar mammals in the United States are the placental mammals.

Egg-Laying Mammals Egg-laying mammals, called **monotremes** (MA nuh treems), live in Australia and New Guinea. The eggs have leathery shells. A female incubates her eggs for about ten days. The young nurse by licking milk that oozes from mammary glands onto skin and hair.

The duck-billed platypus and spiny anteater shown in **Figure 15.12** are monotremes. The platypus spends most of its time in the water. It has a broad, flat tail. Its rubbery snout looks like the bill of a duck. The platypus has webbed front feet that help it swim through the water. It also has claws that help it dig through the soil. The spiny anteater has coarse, brown hair. Its back and sides are covered with sharp spines that protect it from predators. The spiny anteater uses its long, sticky tongue to catch insects.

Figure 15.12 The duck-billed platypus *(top)* and spiny anteater *(bottom)* are mammals that lay eggs.

Pouched Mammals Some mammals have a short period of development inside the mother's body. This is followed by a period of development in a pouch outside the mother's body. These pouched mammals are called **marsupials** (mar SUE pee ulz).

Many marsupials are found in Australia and its surrounding islands. The kangaroo and koala are Australian marsupials. The kangaroo has large, powerful back legs that help it jump large distances. The koala is a very slow-moving animal. It sleeps for almost 19 hours a day. Koalas spend about three hours a day eating tree leaves.

The opossum is the only North American marsupial. The female carries and nurses her babies in her pouch until they are about two to three months old. She carries her babies on her back whenever they leave their den for another one to two months.

Did You Know?

The Australian red kangaroo is the largest marsupial in the world. When a baby kangaroo is born, its mass is about one gram. The baby, called a joey, spends about 235 days in its mother's pouch.

Figure 15.13 The kangaroo *(left)* and koala *(center)* are marsupials found in Australia and New Guinea. The opossum *(right)* is the only marsupial found in North America.

Figure It Out

1. What is the function of a kangaroo's pouch?
2. What is similar about the way these animals reproduce?

Teach

EXPLAIN to students that they will learn that mammals are classified into three main groups based on how they reproduce.

Vocabulary

monotreme Tell students that the prefix *mono-* signifies "one" and that the root *treme* is derived from the Greek word *trēm* and means "holed." Monotremes have one hole from which they expel urine and feces; females use it for laying eggs, as well.

marsupial Explain to students that the word *marsupial* is derived from the Latin word *marsupium* and signifies "a pouch."

Figure It Out: Figure 15.13

ANSWER **1.** A kangaroo's pouch is a place where a baby kangaroo completes its development. **2.** They all give birth to live young, and their young all spend some of their developmental time in the mother's pouch.

Background Information

About 25 percent of all human hair is on the head. In total, there are about 90,000 to 140,000 hairs on a human head. Hair grows 0.25 to 0.40 mm per day, and each starts subcutaneously at the follicle, a part of the hair root. At the end of the root is the papilla, which receives nutrients from the blood. The shaft part of the hair grows above the skin, and consists mostly of keratin. The surface of the shaft is covered with tiny plates. For more information about human hair, see Chapter 19.

Teach

EXPLAIN to students that they will learn about the different orders of placental mammals. Have students create lists of the different orders in their Science Notebooks and sketch an example for each, with the defining characteristic clearly identified.

Extend It!

Have students create tables with three columns in their Science Notebooks. The columns should be labeled *Mammal*, *Gestation Period*, and *Number of Offspring*. As students conduct research, have them complete a row for each mammal. It may be helpful to assign individual students or small groups different orders of mammals. A comprehensive class list could then be made, and students might discuss their inferences about what factors contribute to length of gestation period and number of offspring.

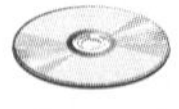

Vocabulary

placental mammal Tell students that the word *mammal* is derived from the Latin word *mamma,* which means "breast." A mammal is any warm-blooded, vertebrate animal characterized by the ability of females to secrete milk from breasts to feed their young. Placental mammals give birth to live young after the young have developed in the mother's uterus.

uterus Explain to students that the uterus is the organ in female mammals in which the young develop after conception and remain until birth.

placenta Tell students that a placenta is a disk-shaped organ attached to the lining of the uterus during pregnancy, and that the embryo obtains nutrients and oxygen through this organ.

gestation Tell students that the root *gestate* is derived from the Latin word *gestare,* which means "to carry." Gestation is the period of time that the mother mammal carries her young in her uterus.

echolocation Explain to students that *echolocation* is a compound word. An echo is a repeated sound caused by sound waves striking a surface and coming back. A location is a site or position of something. An animal sends out a sound and can then determine the location of the object by the manner in which the sound echoes.

Extend It!

Use the library or the Internet to research the gestation period and average number of offspring of different species of mammals. Record your findings in a table in your Science Notebook.

Placental Mammals Most mammals do not lay eggs or have pouches. **Placental mammals** give birth to live young that develop inside the mother's uterus. The **uterus** (YEW tuh rus) is a hollow, muscular organ where the baby develops. A developing mammal gets its food from an organ called the **placenta** (plu SEN tuh). The period of time during which the developing mammal stays in the uterus is called **gestation** (jeh STAY shun). Gestation periods range from 16 days for hamsters to 650 days for elephants.

About 90 percent of all mammals are placental mammals. Scientists classify placental mammals into orders based on their physical characteristics. Some mammals are adapted for walking or running. Others are adapted for swimming. Still others are adapted for flying.

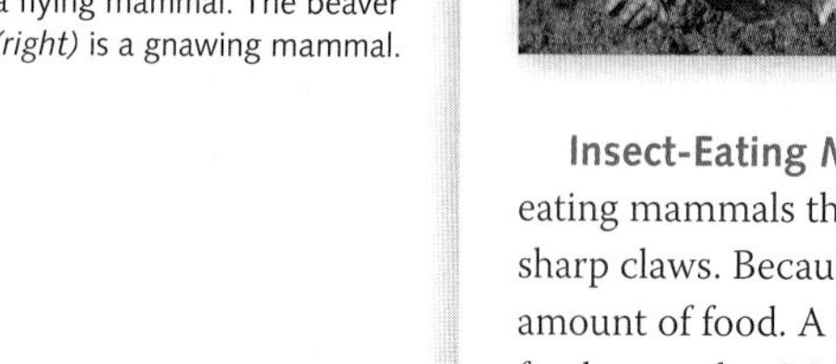

Figure 15.14 The mole *(left)* is an insect-eating mammal. The bat *(center)* is a flying mammal. The beaver *(right)* is a gnawing mammal.

Insect-Eating Mammals Moles and shrews are the only insect-eating mammals that live in North America. They have strong limbs and sharp claws. Because they are active, moles and shrews must eat a large amount of food. A shrew may eat up to 75 percent of its body weight in food every day. Moles feed mainly on worms, and shrews eat insects.

Flying Mammals The bat is the only true flying mammal. A bat's wing is made of thin skin stretched over long finger bones. Bats fly by flapping their wings like birds do. Bats hunt for food at night using echolocation. **Echolocation** is a method some animals use to detect objects. The animal sends out high-pitched sounds that bounce off the object and back to the animal. This helps bats determine how close they are to their prey.

Gnawing Mammals Gnawing mammals that have two pairs of large front teeth are also called rodents. About 40 percent of all mammals are rodents. Mice, rats, squirrels, and beavers are gnawing mammals. The front teeth of a gnawing mammal grow throughout its life. The gnawing mammal chews branches and twigs to wear down its front teeth.

Toothless Mammals Armadillos, sloths, and anteaters are called toothless mammals. They have no front teeth, so they appear to be toothless. Only anteaters have no teeth at all. Armadillos and anteaters use their long, sticky tongues to catch insects. The skin of an armadillo is hard and protects its body like armor. Sloths feed on plants. They have flat teeth that help them grind leaves.

Figure 15.15 The armadillo *(top)* and the anteater *(bottom)* are toothless mammals.

ELL Strategy

Use a Concept Map To continue organizing the information about mammals, have students update the concept maps they made for the ELL Strategy activity on page 266. They should include the different orders of placental mammals, as well as an example of each.

Rodentlike Mammals Rabbits and hares, once classified as rodents, are now placed in a separate order. Rabbits and hares have long teeth for gnawing and long hind legs that help them jump long distances. Rabbits and hares eat plants. Hares are usually bigger than rabbits and have longer ears.

Water-Dwelling Mammals Whales, dolphins, porpoises, and manatees are water-dwelling mammals. Water-dwelling mammals do not have gills like fish. They use their lungs to breathe air, just like people do. A whale takes in air through a hole on the top of its head. Most water-dwelling mammals have teeth and eat fish, which means they are carnivores. A **carnivore** (KAR nuh vor) is an animal that eats other animals. Some whales filter the water to harvest shrimp and other small invertebrates for food. Manatees, shown in **Figure 15.16**, are mainly plant-eaters and can move on land for short periods of time.

Trunk-Nosed Mammals A trunk-nosed mammal has a nose and upper lip that are modified into a trunk. The trunk allows the animal to collect food and water. Only two species of trunk-nosed mammals are alive today. They are the Asian elephant and the African elephant.

Hoofed Mammals Horses, cows, deer, and pigs all have feet with hooves. A hoof is the hard covering on the mammal's toes. Like trunk-nosed mammals, hoofed mammals are herbivores. A **herbivore** (HUR buh vor) is an animal that eats only plants.

Flesh-Eating Mammals Dogs and cats look and act very differently from each other, but they are related. Both dogs and cats are members of the order Carnivora. These mammals have strong jaws and long, sharp teeth for tearing flesh. Lions, tigers, and wolves are also carnivores.

Primates Monkeys, apes, and humans are primates. Except for gorillas, baboons, and humans, most primates live in trees. They have long arms with well-developed hands. Like humans, most primates have hands with four fingers and an opposable thumb. The ability to place the thumb opposite the fingers allows primates to grasp, hold, and use tools. Some primates are herbivores. Others, such as humans, eat plants and animals. Any animal that eats both plants and animals is called an **omnivore** (AHM nih vor).

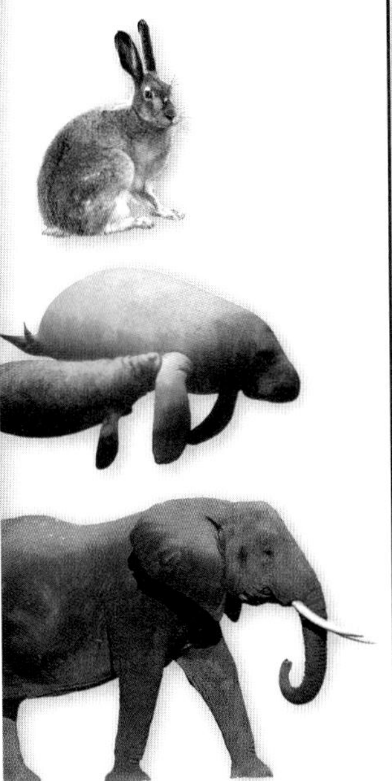

Figure 15.16 The large-eared jackrabbit *(top)* is a rodentlike mammal. The manatee and her calf *(center)* are water-dwelling mammals. The African elephant *(bottom)* is a trunk-nosed mammal.

As You Read

Look at the sentences you wrote for the vocabulary terms. Combine those sentences into a paragraph summarizing the different groups of mammals.

Figure 15.17 The paint horse *(left)* is a hoofed mammal. The cheetah *(center)* is a flesh-eating carnivore. The chimpanzee *(right)* is a primate.

Teach

EXPLORE Have students add to their lists of the different orders of placental mammals in their Science Notebooks, sketching an example for each with the defining characteristic clearly identified.

Vocabulary

carnivore Explain to students that *carni-* is derived from the Latin word *carne*, which means "flesh." The word *vore* is derived from the Latin word *vorare*, which means "to swallow." Literally, *carnivore* means "to swallow flesh."

herbivore Tell students that the word *herb* is from the Latin word *herba*, which means "grass" or "green plants." Review the meaning of *vore*.

omnivore Tell students that *omni-* is derived from the Latin word *omnis*, which means "all" or "every." After reviewing the meaning of *vore*, ask students to hypothesize about the meaning of *omnivore*.

As You Read

Give students a few minutes to review and update the vocabulary definitions in their Science Notebooks.

ANSWER Students' summaries should refer to the three groups of mammals (monotremes, marsupials, and placentals), the characteristics of placental mammals (uterus, placenta, and gestation), and the eating habits (carnivores, herbivores, and omnivores) of various orders of placental mammals.

Science Notebook EXTRA

Have students research manatees and the laws that are already in place protecting them. Have students then write sample letters to officials in Florida suggesting ways to improve manatee preservation efforts. Recommend to students that they build upon existing practices. As a class, compose a letter from individual student samples and send this letter to the appropriate authorities in Florida.

Background Information

Although manatees are also called sea cows, they are closely related to elephants. Manatees and elephants have similar skin, eyes, and feet. A manatee's upper lip functions like an elephant's trunk. Manatees spend most of their days eating (about 45–68 kg of food a day, on average), resting, and swimming. They live in warm water that is at least 21°C and migrate when the water cools. They reproduce only once every two to five years.

Teacher Alert

The term *carnivore* is used in two distinct ways on page 269. In one sense, carnivores are animals that consume other animals. In another sense, carnivores are members of the order Carnivora. This order was named for the fact that these mammals have pointed canine teeth, an adaptation for tearing flesh. Most mammals in the order Carnivora are primarily meat-eaters. However, some, such as raccoons and most bears, are omnivores.

Teach

EXPLAIN that mammals evolved from reptiles and that the extinction of dinosaurs contributed to their evolution.

Use the Visual: Figure 15.18

EXTEND Have students compare the early placental mammal and therapsid. Ask them to identify the characteristics that are similar and those that are different.

Explain It!

Have each student create a compare-and-contrast chart or Venn diagram to compare the two animals' characteristics. Direct students to include physical traits, behavioral traits, and environmental facts. After students organize their information, have them briefly peer-review one another's work. Then, have each student write a brief paragraph comparing the two animals.

Assess

EVALUATE Use the After You Read questions and the Alternative Assessment to help you assess students' understanding of the lesson.

After You Read

1. All mammals are endothermic vertebrates that have hair or fur and feed their young with milk from mammary glands.
2. A pouched mammal spends little time inside its mother's body and most of its developmental time in its mother's pouch. A placental mammal develops completely within the uterus of its mother.
3. A carnivore eats only other animals. A herbivore eats only plants. An omnivore eats both animals and plants.
4. Accept all logical answers. The extinction of the dinosaurs, climate changes, and the appearance of flowering plants helped mammals thrive.

Alternative Assessment

EVALUATE Have each student give an example and name the identifying characteristic of each group of placental mammals described in the lesson.

Explain It!

Think of a mammal that you know a lot about, such as a dog or a cat. Then think of a kind of reptile. In your Science Notebook, draw a picture of each type of animal. Write a description that tells how the two animals you drew are alike and how they are different.

The Origin of Mammals

Many scientists believe that mammals developed from ancient reptiles, just as birds did. The earliest mammals may have lived during the time of the dinosaurs. Fossils show that early mammals may have been about the size of a rat. They looked like rats, too. **Figure 15.18** shows *Eomaia*, the oldest placental mammal fossil discovered. *Eomaia* fossils may be 125 million years old.

Placental mammals may have developed from a reptile called a therapsid (ther AP sid). Therapsids had characteristics of both reptiles and mammals. Figure 15.18 shows an artist's representation of a therapsid.

Figure 15.18 *Eomaia* is the oldest placental mammal fossil discovered. Based on its body structure, scientists believe it may have lived in trees. Therapsids may have been the ancestors of mammals. Therapsids had jaw bones and middle-ear bones like those of reptiles. Like mammals, they had straight legs held close to their bodies.

When dinosaurs became extinct, mammals began to develop quickly. They increased dramatically in number and developed a variety of shapes, sizes, and characteristics. Without the presence of the dinosaurs, and with climate changes and the appearance of flowering plants, mammals had new areas in which to live and new food sources upon which to feed. After a while, mammals were found in almost every habitat on Earth.

CONNECTION: Environmental Science

Manatees are large, water-dwelling mammals that live off the coast of Florida. Manatees are on the threatened species list. Motorboats put manatees in danger. The manatees sometimes collide with boats or get cut by their propellers. Scientists have suggested creating more manatee refuges where boats are not allowed to travel.

After You Read

1. What characteristics do all mammals have in common?
2. How is the development of a pouched mammal different from the development of a placental mammal?
3. How are carnivores, herbivores, and omnivores different from each other?
4. Expand the paragraph you have written in your Science Notebook by identifying and describing the different orders of placental mammals. Then, add a sentence explaining the origin of mammals. What conditions helped the mammals increase in number and diversity?

Background Information

Scientists do not agree about whether fossil therapsids should be classified as mammals or an organism closely related to mammals but not included in the mammal group. Some scientists classify therapsids as mammal-like reptiles, because they lack some of the defining characteristics of mammals. Scientists who include therapsids in the class Mammalia believe that those characteristics are evolutionary and that therapsids are an early form of mammal.

15.4 Animal Behavior

Before You Read

In your Science Notebook, create a lesson outline. Use the lesson title as the outline title. Label the headings with the Roman numerals *I* through *IV*. Use the letters *A*, *B*, and *C* under each heading to record information you want to remember.

Learning Goals

- Differentiate between a stimulus and a response.
- Compare innate behavior and learned behavior.
- Describe the social behaviors that occur in a beehive.

New Vocabulary

behavior
stimulus
response
innate behavior
instinct
learned behavior

Have you ever noticed that when a dog sees a familiar person, the dog wags his or her tail, playfully jumps up, or barks? A cat may rub up against the person's leg and quietly purr. Such actions are considered animal behaviors.

Behavior is the way an animal responds to its environment. A **stimulus** (STIHM yuh lus) is a signal that causes an animal to react in a certain way. The animal's reaction to a stimulus is called a **response**. The sound of a familiar voice is a stimulus that causes a pet to behave the way that it does. There are different types of animal behavior.

Innate Behavior

A behavior that an animal is born with is called an **innate** (ihn AYT) **behavior**. Innate behaviors do not have to be learned. Cats, for example, do not need to be taught how to use a litter box. An **instinct** is a pattern of behaviors that an animal is born with. A newborn kangaroo uses instinct to crawl into its mother's pouch. It then attaches itself to one of her nipples to get milk.

Most birds build their nests without having to be taught. A species of gull, the kittiwake, has a nest on the side of a steep cliff. The baby kittiwakes innately know not to move away from the nest, because they will fall. Spiders are able to spin complicated webs the first time they spin.

Figure 15.19 Kittiwake gulls build their nests on the side of a cliff. The baby birds innately know not to move from the nest.

Learned Behaviors

Some animal behavior is learned. A **learned behavior** is a behavior that develops through experience. Because of their short life spans, arthropods learn very little. Fishes, amphibians, reptiles, birds, and mammals demonstrate learned behaviors. Because of their complex brains, mammals show more learned behaviors than other groups.

Perhaps you remember when you learned to ride a bicycle. You probably fell many times before you learned how to balance on the bike. Practicing helped you learn how to stay balanced. Newborn lion cubs have claws that help them catch prey, but they do not know how to hunt. Their parents must repeatedly show them the correct way to hunt.

Figure 15.20 Lion cubs must be taught how to hunt by their parents.

ELL Strategy

Illustrate Have students work in small groups to create posters that explain the concepts of innate behavior, instinct, and learned behavior. Students should provide a variety of examples for each concept.

innate behavior Tell students that the word *innate* is derived from the Latin word *innatus*, which means "inborn."

instinct Explain that *instinct* is from the Latin word *instinctus*, meaning "prompting."

learned behavior Encourage students to think about nonscientific uses of *learn*, and discuss these uses with the class. Students might mention gaining skills or knowledge in a new sport, hobby, or academic area.

15.4 Introduce

ENGAGE Write the list of behaviors below on the board. Ask students to work with a partner to decide whether each behavior is innate or learned.

crawling (innate)
raising a hand in class (learned)
climbing a ladder (learned)
jumping or moving upon hearing a loud noise (innate)
eating (innate)
sleeping (innate)
getting dressed (learned)

If students require clarification, give a brief explanation of each type of behavior. Emphasize that by thinking deeply about the behaviors, students will come to understand the differences between the two. Discuss students' conjectures and reasoning. Explain that they will learn more about animal behavior in this lesson.

Before You Read

Model creating an outline for the lesson. Talk aloud as you create your outline to explain its organization.

Teach

EXPLAIN Have students draw on prior knowledge to describe familiar stimuli and their corresponding responses. If students confuse the two, have the class discuss and correct the example(s). Relate stimulus and response to cause and effect. Explain that students will learn how stimulus-and-response behavior relationships can be both innate and learned.

Vocabulary

behavior Explain that a behavior is a way of acting.

stimulus Tell students that a stimulus is something that acts as an incentive, inspiration, or provocation. An example is when someone touches something hot and his or her hand moves quickly away from the heat. The heat is the stimulus.

response Explain to students that *response* is from the Latin word *respondēre*, which means "to return like for like." In the example of the hand touching a hot surface, the response is the hand moving.

Teach

EXPLAIN to students that they will learn about social behavior and its impact on animals' survival.

As You Read

Give students five to ten minutes to review and update the lesson outlines in their Science Notebooks. Encourage them to add details to explain each heading more fully.

ANSWER Innate behavior is a behavior that an animal is born with. Learned behavior is a behavior that develops through experience.

Science Notebook EXTRA

After students read the page, have them think about animals that they know or have seen, as well as examples of social behaviors that those animals have exhibited. Have each student work with a partner to make a list in his or her Science Notebook. Have partners share their examples with the class. Accept all reasonable answers.

Figure It Out: Figure 15.21

ANSWER **1.** Animals traveling in a group are less likely to be eaten by predators. **2.** The musk oxen have the offspring in the middle of the circle, thus protecting them from all directions. The fish do not provide this kind of protection for members of their group.

Reading Comprehension Workbook, p. 98

As You Read

Review the lesson outline in your Science Notebook with a partner. Make necessary changes.

What is the difference between innate behavior and learned behavior?

Social Behavior

Many animals live by themselves. Other animals live in groups. Each animal in the group has a special role. The role may be to gather food or to protect group members. It may be to help raise the young animals.

Some fishes swim in schools. Some insects live in large hives. Hoofed mammals, such as sheep or bison, form herds. Living in a group helps many animals survive. The group provides food and protection. A group of musk oxen form a circle when they are threatened by a wolf. They place the young musk oxen in the middle of the circle, where they are protected. A wolf often gives up rather than try to defeat the whole group.

Figure It Out

1. Why is it helpful for animals to form groups?
2. Infer why a group of musk oxen provides more protection for young animals than a group of fish does.

Figure 15.21 The school of fish *(left)* includes many individuals that stay together. The musk oxen *(right)* circle together to protect their young from a wolf.

Figure 15.22 This beehive is home to a queen bee, worker bees, and drones. Each type of bee has a different job in the bee society.

Some animals, including ants, termites, and honeybees, live in groups called societies. In a honeybee society, the queen bee is larger than the other bees. Her main function is to lay eggs. The queen also controls the activities in the hive.

The worker bees are females that do not lay eggs. The worker bees build the hive and maintain it. They also protect the hive from predators. Worker bees make honey from flower nectar. There can be many thousands of worker bees in a honeybee colony.

Drones are male bees that mate with the queen bee. They die soon after they mate. There are several hundred drones in each honeybee colony.

The beehive is made of compartments called cells. Some cells hold bee eggs that hatch into bee larvae. Some cells contain honey made by the worker bees. This honey is used to feed all of the bees in the hive.

In a wolf pack, there is a complicated system of societal importance. There is a top male and a top female in the pack, based on strength. These wolves can come and go from the pack as they please. They are usually the only pair of wolves that produce a litter of pups. All the members of the wolf pack help raise the wolf pups. Wolves also hunt as a pack.

Background Information

Pecking order in chickens is another example of social behavior. This is a well-defined hierarchical pattern of behavior that exists in all flocks of chickens. If roosters and hens live together, a rooster will almost always be "top bird." If hens and roosters are separated, the oldest bird will usually be the top bird. When a new bird is introduced to an existing flock, the natural pecking order will be disrupted. The weakest bird, at the low end of the order, has to survive the pecks of all the birds above her.

PEOPLE IN SCIENCE Konrad Lorenz 1903–1989

Konrad Lorenz was born in Vienna, Austria. As a small boy, he loved animals and collected fishes, dogs, monkeys, insects, ducks, and geese. He was very interested in animal behavior.

Working with geese, Lorenz developed the concept of imprinting, which is a type of learned behavior in which an animal, at a certain critical time of its life, forms an attachment to another object. According to this concept, a baby goose will follow the first thing it sees after it hatches. It recognizes this moving object as its parent.

This behavior works well if the baby goose first sees its mother. If the baby goose first sees a human, it will never learn to recognize members of its own species. To test his ideas, Lorenz arranged for baby geese to see him first after they hatched. The geese followed him around as if he were their own mother.

Communication

If you have ever heard one dog barking at another dog, you have heard animal communication. Communication is the process by which animals share information. Mammals communicate in many ways.

Dogs and wolves mark their territory by placing their scent in an area. This chemical sign tells other animals to stay away. When skunks raise their tails, other animals know that the scent the skunks are about to spray is very strong and offensive. This drives many predators away.

Animals communicate through sound, too. Humpback whales sing songs to communicate to other humpbacks. Many sounds are made by male animals to attract females during mating season. Female crickets are attracted to the chirping of males. Animals also make sounds when they defend themselves. They may growl, hiss, or snarl to make themselves appear more frightening.

Animals can change the shapes of their bodies to communicate, as well. A cat can arch its back and bristle its tail to make itself look larger and stronger. A cobra snake holds its body upright and spreads out the skin below its head to scare away predators. Even an elephant will avoid a cobra when the cobra's body is in this position.

Figure 15.23 The striped skunk *(top)* sprays predators with its strong scent. The humpback whale *(center)* communicates with other humpbacks by singing. The cobra *(bottom)* holds itself upright and spreads out the skin below its head to scare off predators.

After You Read

1. How is an innate behavior different from a learned behavior?
2. What is a stimulus? What is a response?
3. Describe the members of a honeybee colony.
4. What are three ways in which animals communicate with each other?
5. Using the outline you have created in your Science Notebook, write three sentences that describe the behavior of animals.

Teach

EXPLORE Have students observe a conversation between two people without hearing the words being spoken. Alternatively, have students watch a television show for a few minutes with the volume lowered. Ask students to note how the two communicators physically interact. Have students hypothesize about the content and tone of the interaction.

PEOPLE IN SCIENCE

Konrad Lorenz was the son of an orthopedic surgeon. Although Lorenz had a strong interest in animals, his father insisted that he study medicine. After completing medical school, he studied zoology and received a PhD in that field. He then researched animal behavior and developed the concept of imprinting while studying greylag geese. He also found that mallard ducks would imprint on him, but only when he quacked and squatted.

EXTEND Have students read the feature aloud in pairs. Then, have students list the possible challenges and benefits of having a goose imprint on a human rather than on its own mother. Have each student write a paragraph explaining how he or she would help the goose overcome one of the challenges (for example, by teaching the goose how to fly).

Assess

EVALUATE Use the After You Read questions and the Alternative Assessment to help you assess students' understanding of the lesson.

After You Read

1. An innate behavior is a behavior that an animal has at birth. A learned behavior develops through experience.
2. A stimulus is a signal that causes an animal to act in a certain way. A response is an animal's reaction to a stimulus.
3. The queen bee lays eggs. The drones mate with the queen bee. The worker bees maintain and protect the hive and make honey from flower nectar.
4. scent, sound, and body position
5. Accept all logical answers.

Differentiated Instruction

Visual Have students illustrate the concept of imprinting by drawing a series of different stages showing baby geese seeing and following a mother goose, each on a separate sheet of paper. Have students clip or staple the sheets in order. Direct students to flip through the collected sheets and observe the apparent motion.

Alternative Assessment

EVALUATE Have students use their outlines to define and give examples of innate behavior, learned behavior, and stimulus and response.

Chapter 15 Summary

VOCABULARY REVIEW

Check students' sentences or paragraphs to make sure they understand the meaning of each vocabulary term.

PREPARE FOR CHAPTER TEST

Evaluate students' essays using the following criteria:

1. The topic sentence, or main idea, should restate the Key Concept.
2. The supporting paragraphs should incorporate the answers to the Learning Goal questions students have written and include details, facts, and examples they have recorded in their Science Notebooks.
3. The concluding sentence should sum up the main idea of the chapter and restate the Key Concept.

MASTERING CONCEPTS

True or False

1. True
2. False, Migration
3. False, Monotremes
4. False, Herbivores
5. True
6. False, innate behavior

Short Answer

7. All birds are endotherms, vertebrates, lay eggs, and have small bodies with feathers and hollow skeletons. Almost all birds have wings.
8. Birds molt to replace feathers that are old and damaged.
9. Birds of prey have strong grasping claws and strong, hard beaks to grasp their prey. Birds of prey also have very good vision.
10. Mammals are endothermic vertebrates with hair or fur and mammary glands that produce milk for nourishing young.
11. Animals communicate through scent, sound, and by changing body shape.

Chapter 15 Summary

KEY CONCEPTS

15.1 Birds

- Birds are endothermic vertebrates with feathers.
- Birds have contour feathers that protect them. They have down feathers that keep them warm.
- Molting is the process by which birds' damaged feathers are replaced. By preening, birds apply an oil to their feathers.
- Birds that can fly have powerful muscles attached to their sternums, or breastbones.
- The four main types of birds are flightless birds, perching birds, birds of prey, and water birds.

15.2 Adaptations for Flight

- Birds have small, lightweight bodies with hollow bones.
- Bird wings are wide and thin and slightly curved on the top. This allows birds to soar through the air.
- Migration is the movement of animals from one place to another.

15.3 Mammals

- Mammals are endothermic vertebrates with hair or fur. They feed their young from mammary glands.
- Based on the way they reproduce, the three main groups of mammals are the egg-laying mammals, the pouched mammals, and the placental mammals.
- Placental mammals give birth to live young that develop in the mother's uterus. The period of time the young stay in the uterus is called gestation.
- A carnivore is an animal that eats only other animals; a herbivore is an animal that eats only plants; an omnivore is an animal that eats both plants and other animals.

15.4 Animal Behavior

- Behavior is the way an animal responds to its environment. An animal is born with innate behavior. Learned behavior develops through experience.
- A stimulus is a signal that causes an animal to react in a certain way. The animal's reaction to a stimulus is called a response.
- Animals that live in groups show social behaviors. Each animal in a group has a specific role.
- Animals communicate with each other through scent, sound, or body positions.

VOCABULARY REVIEW

Write each term in a complete sentence, or write a paragraph relating several terms.

15.1
feather, p. 259
contour feather, p. 259
down feather, p. 259
preening, p. 259
sternum, p. 260

15.2
migration, p. 265

15.3
monotreme, p. 267
marsupial, p. 267
placental mammal, p. 268
uterus, p. 268
placenta, p. 268
gestation, p. 268
echolocation, p. 268
carnivore, p. 269
herbivore, p. 269
omnivore, p. 269

15.4
behavior, p. 271
stimulus, p. 271
response, p. 271
innate behavior, p. 271
instinct, p. 271
learned behavior, p. 271

PREPARE FOR CHAPTER TEST

To prepare for the chapter test, create a question from each Learning Goal. Use the information in your Science Notebook to answer each question. Then use these answers to write a well-developed essay about the chapter. Use the Key Concept on the first page of this chapter as your topic sentence.

274 BIRDS AND MAMMALS

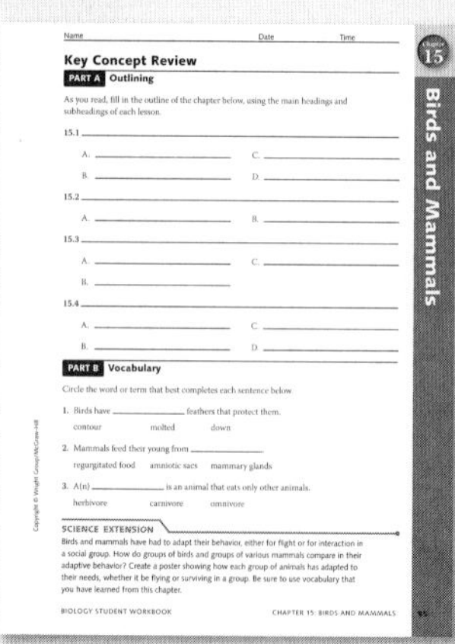
Key Concept Review Workbook, p. 95

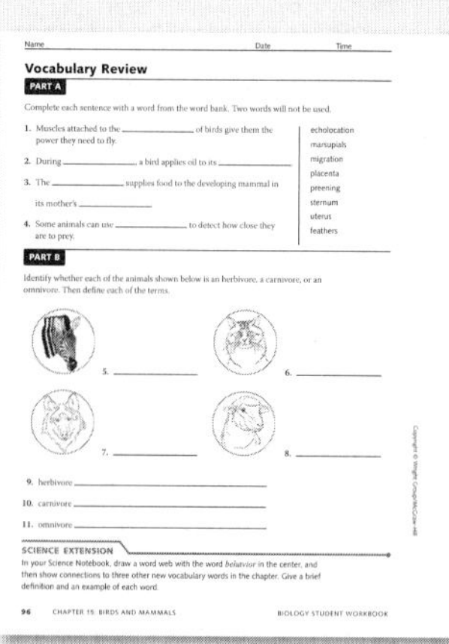
Vocabulary Review Workbook, p. 96

MASTERING CONCEPTS

True or False

If the statement is true, write "true." If it is false, change the underlined word or words to make the statement true.

1. Feathers cover the body of a bird and are made of dead cells.
2. Hibernation is the regular movement of a group of animals from one place to another.
3. Marsupials are mammals that lay eggs.
4. Carnivores are animals that eat only plants.
5. Behavior is the way an animal responds to its environment.
6. A behavior that an animal is born with is called a(n) learned behavior.

Short Answer

Answer each of the following in a sentence or brief paragraph.

7. What are three characteristics common to all birds?
8. Why do birds molt?
9. What adaptations does a bird of prey have for catching its food?
10. What are three characteristics common to all mammals?
11. Describe three forms of animal communication.

Critical Thinking

Use what you have learned in this chapter to answer each of the following.

12. **Hypothesize** Why is preening important to a bird?
13. **Relate Facts** Which group of mammals is most similar to birds? Explain your answer.
14. **Apply Concepts** Why do whales come to the surface of the water many times during the day?

Standardized Test Question

Choose the letter of the response that correctly answers the question.

15. The illustrations show a frog taking a bad-tasting insect into its mouth and then spitting it out. The frog never eats this type of insect again. What type of behavior is the frog showing?
    A. innate behavior
    B. instinctive behavior
    C. learned behavior
    D. social behavior

Test-Taking Tip

Circle key words in a difficult question to help you focus on what the question is asking. If you do not understand a key word, and you are allowed to ask questions during a test, ask the teacher what it means.

Critical Thinking

12. Preening allows a bird to protect its feathers by coating them with oil. This also makes the bird waterproof.
13. Accept all logical answers. Some students may say that bats are the closest to birds because they fly. Other students may say that monotremes are closest to birds because they lay eggs.
14. Whales come to the surface to breathe oxygen into their lungs through their blow holes.

Standardized Test Question

15. C

Reading Links

Feathered Dinosaurs

Drawing on recent fossil evidence and scientific deductions, Sloan argues in favor of the theory that modern birds descended from dinosaurs, with a focus on feathers. Strong visuals, very readable text, and exciting content combine to make this book—which is part of a National Geographic Society series—an excellent supplement to classroom discussion about bird characteristics.

Sloan, Christopher. National Geographic Society. 64 pp. Illustrated. Trade ISBN: 978-0-7922-7219-9.

My Life with the Chimpanzees

Celebrated naturalist Jane Goodall tells about her life's work in a touching manner that will resonate with and be readily comprehended by struggling readers. Her stories about the chimpanzees she lived with incorporate relevant and memorable lessons about the social behavior of animals, the characteristics of mammals, and animal communication.

Goodall, Jane. Simon and Schuster Children's Publishing. 160 pp. Illustrated. Trade ISBN: 978-0-671-56271-7.

Curriculum Connection Workbook, p. 99

Science Challenge Workbook, pp. 100–101

Chapter 15

Labs

15A How Do Birds Fly?

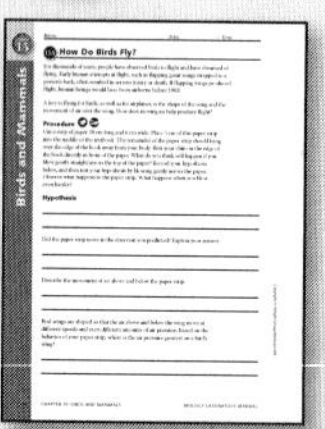

This prechapter introduction activity is designed to introduce students to the physics of flight by engaging them in predicting, experimenting, comparing, and contrasting to determine the importance of wing shape.

Objectives

- make predictions
- make observations
- record data in a suitable way
- communicate conclusions

Planning

 1 class period  groups of 2–4 students

Materials (per group)

- paper
- scissors
- metric ruler
- textbook

Engagement Guide

- Challenge students to think about how the movement of the paper strip relates to the ability of birds to fly by asking:
  - *Why did the paper strip move upward when you blew over it? Why did the extent to which the paper moved upward vary depending on how hard you blew over it?* (When students blow gently across the paper, the paper lifts slightly, but when they blow more strongly, the paper lifts to a horizontal position. Faster-moving air produces less pressure than air that is moving more slowly. Because the air blowing across the top of the paper strip was moving faster than the air beneath the paper strip was moving, it exerted less air pressure than the air beneath the paper, and the paper rose. The upward force produced by the difference in air pressure is called lift.)
  - *How does this phenomenon help birds fly?* (A bird's wing is curved in the front so that air moves faster over the upper surface of the wing. Air pressure is greater below the wing. This difference in air pressure above and below the wing produces lift, which allows the bird to rise into the air.)
- Encourage students to communicate their conclusions in creative ways.

Going Further

Provide students with a variety of construction supplies such as paper clips, rubber bands, glue, string, staples, and tape, and encourage them to apply what they learned about air pressure and lift to design a paper airplane that will generate the greatest amount of lift. Students should conduct test flights and then hold a class competition.

15B Behavior and the Environment

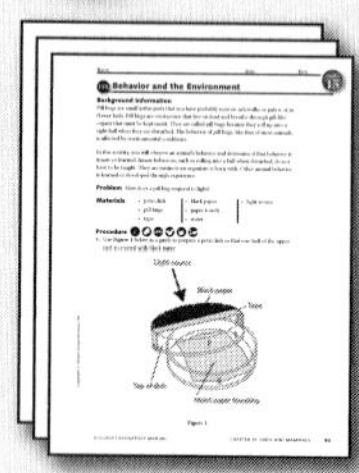

Objectives

- make observations
- record and analyze data
- make and use graphs
- classify a behavior as innate or learned

Skill Set

observing, predicting, recording and analyzing data, classifying, stating conclusions

Planning

 1 class period  groups of 2–4 students

Materials

Materials for this activity are listed in the Student Laboratory Manual.

Advance Preparation

Pill bugs can be purchased from biological supply companies or collected from the school grounds. Plastic or glass petri dishes, small plastic food containers, or cardboard boxes can be used for containers. Have students wash their hands with soap and water after handling lab specimens.

Answers to Observations: Data Table 1

Answers will vary, but pill bugs will move toward the dark side of the petri dish.

Answers to Analysis and Conclusions

1. Pill bugs tend to move toward dark areas. Students' data should show that most pill bugs were found on the covered side of the petri dish.
2. Students' graphs should accurately reflect their data.
3. The observed behavior is innate; pill bugs are born with the instinct to remain in dark areas.
4. Pill bugs breathe through gill-like structures that must remain moist. Dark areas are more likely than light areas to be moist. Pill bugs that move to dark, moist areas are able to keep their gills moist.
5. Natural selection would have favored pill bugs that tended to move into dark, moist areas because they were better able to survive and pass this genetic trait on to their offspring.

Going Further

Allow students to repeat the experiment using other environmental conditions a pill bug might encounter, such as wet and dry or hot and cold. Have students communicate their results and classify the behaviors they observed as innate or learned.

15C Who Did It?

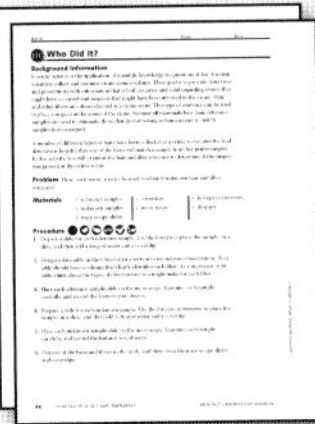

Objectives

- make observations
- record observations
- compare and contrast known and unknown samples
- draw conclusions based on observations collected

Skill Set

observing, comparing and contrasting, recording and analyzing data, classifying, inferring, stating conclusions

Planning

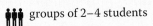

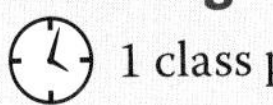
1 class period groups of 2–4 students

Materials

Materials for this activity are listed in the Student Laboratory Manual.

Lab Tip

Students may need to remove their goggles to obtain a better view while using the microscope.

Advance Preparation

- Collect and prepare reference samples as follows: two from humans, two from animals such as a cat or a dog (samples can be removed from clothing or furniture or after grooming), and two fibers from nonanimal sources such as carpets, towels, or clothing. Place each reference fiber in a petri dish labeled with its source. One of the human reference samples should be identified as *Suspect*, the other can be identified as *Homeowner.*
- Collect and prepare unknown samples as follows: two from humans (one sample should be from your suspect), and two that will match either an animal reference or nonanimal reference source. Unknown samples can be placed in petri dishes and labeled *Unknown 1, 2, 3,* and *4.*
- Reference and unknown samples can be placed in a central location and students can retrieve samples as needed.

Answers to Observations: Data Table 1

Students' data tables will vary depending on the types of observations students make, but the tables might include color, texture, shape, and presence or absence of a hair root.

Answers to Analysis and Conclusions

1. Hair will often have a root at one end and a scaly surface, while nonanimal fibers are smooth and look the same at both ends.
2. Probably not; human hair is very similar in structure to hair from other mammals.
3. Yes; one of the unknown hairs matched the suspect's reference sample.
4. No; hair samples do not provide the accuracy and validity of other types of forensic evidence. Students might suggest that they would like to see fingerprint and/or DNA evidence before drawing any conclusions.
5. Students' summaries should be well written and should contain conclusions based on an accurate evaluation of data collected.

Going Further

Explain that teeth are another form of evidence used in forensic science. Provide students with a variety of different mammalian teeth or pictures of different types of mammalian teeth found in the remains of a structure fire. Have students examine the teeth and determine, on the basis of prior knowledge or research results, if any humans were killed in the fire.

Unit 5

Case Study 1: An Endangered Animal Makes a Comeback

Gather More Information

Encourage students to use the library or the NSTA SciLinks Web site noted at the start of each chapter to learn more about these case study topics and to conduct further research.

Have students use the following keywords to aid their searches:

- alligator
- reptile
- extinction
- endangered species
- threatened species
- wetland ecosystem
- American crocodile
- keystone species

Research the Big Picture

- Have students work in small groups to list the reasons that alligators nearly became extinct. Then, have each group research two animals that are currently endangered in the United States and find the reasons that those animals are in that category. Finally, have students compare and contrast the reasons for the near extinction of three animal species. Each group should then present its findings to other groups in a format of its members' choosing.
- Have groups of students identify the steps that scientists likely took before granting alligators protection as an endangered species. Remind students that the scientific method should guide their thinking. Ask: *What other possible conclusions could scientists have reached instead of this decision to protect the species?* Each group should orally present its steps and conclusions to the class.
- Have pairs of students research the process scientists go through to categorize an animal species as endangered. Then, have each pair identify at least ten species that are currently considered endangered. Have each pair share its list of species with the class while a class recorder keeps a master list.

Background Information

Many ecologists see alligators as a keystone species—one that is important to the health of its ecosystem. For example, alligators dig deep holes in the mud. These alligator holes are the only sources of freshwater in some wetland areas during dry periods. They provide a habitat and a source of food and water for many other species.

SCIENCE JOURNAL

An Endangered Animal Makes a Comeback

ALLIGATORS, the largest reptiles in North America, have powerful jaws full of sharp teeth. They can measure more than four meters in length and have a mass of about 450 kg. The most impressive fact about these animals is that they will eat just about anything.

The American alligator is native to freshwater wetlands from the Carolinas to Texas. In the past, as settlers fearful of alligators moved into these areas, they killed the reptiles by the thousands. By the early 1900s, alligators were scarce at the edges of their range, but they still were not in danger of dying out.

The status of alligators changed after World War I, when alligator skins became fashionable for making belts and shoes. The government also contributed to the demise of alligators. As part of major government construction projects, many swamps were drained, thus destroying alligator habitats. By the 1960s, the alligator population was extremely low. The alligator, which had survived on Earth for more than 200 million years, was now in danger of becoming extinct!

Biologists knew that these animals are an important part of wetland ecosystems and that their extinction would have serious effects on the plant and animal life of these ecosystems. In 1967, the U.S. government gave alligators protection as an endangered species, which made hunting them illegal. As a result of this action, the alligator population began to recover. By 1975, there were enough alligators to remove them from the endangered species list.

American alligators, now listed as a threatened species, currently number about three million. After almost disappearing, they have made an amazing comeback.

Research and Report

Choose an animal. Then create a chart that lists its major characteristics. For example, include where it lives, what it eats, and any threats to its survival. Set up the chart in the way that best displays the information. Include a sketch or photocopy of the animal at the top of the chart.

CAREER CONNECTION Animal Shelter Worker

DO YOU LIKE ANIMALS? Do you become concerned when you see an injured or abused animal? Is your first instinct to help? If so, you might enjoy being an animal shelter worker. There is probably at least one animal shelter in or near your community. Animal shelters are places where people take care of lost, homeless, or injured animals.

Animal shelter workers spend their days working hard at a number of tasks. They feed the animals and keep both the animals and their enclosures clean. They watch the animals closely to look for signs of illness. If an animal has a problem, they may assist a veterinarian in treating the animal. Shelter workers also groom the animals—for example, cutting toenails or clipping fur. The shelter workers have fun with the animals, too. They play with the animals and help them get exercise by walking or running with them. Animal shelter workers also deal with the public. They answer questions about the animals and screen people who might want to adopt one.

People who want to become animal shelter workers do not need college degrees. They must be comfortable around animals and have good communication skills. Fortunately, they can learn most of what they need to know on the job. Although this is not a high-paying career, most shelter workers say that helping the animals in their care is the most important reward.

CONNECTION: Career

Have students complete a Career Research project before reading the feature. Ask students who looked into working in an animal shelter to share what they learned about that career.

Have pairs of students read the article aloud and discuss what they learned. Then, have pairs brainstorm other ways to learn about the job of an animal shelter worker. Pairs can share their findings and ideas with the class.

Desert Marvel

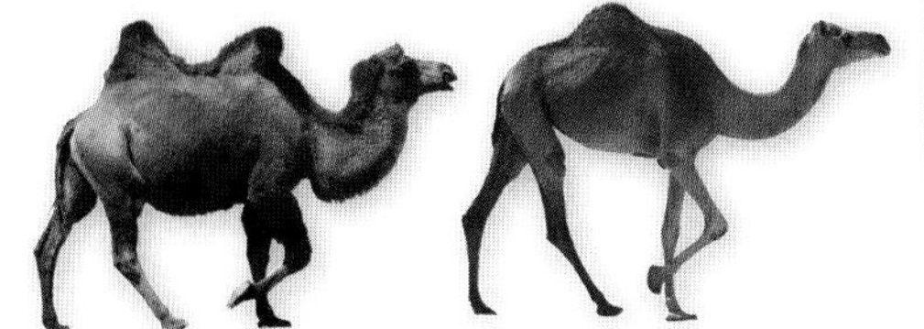

The Arabian camel, or dromedary, has one hump. The smaller Bactrian camel has two.

WHAT ANIMAL comes to mind when you think of survival in the driest places on Earth? Many people think of the camel. From its fine-haired coat that insulates against heat to its ability to go for long periods without food or water, the camel is made for the desert.

Camels do well in deserts because they don't need much water and can conserve what water they have. A camel can go from four to seven days without drinking. If the weather is cool and the camel isn't very active, it can survive for ten months by getting all of its water from eating plants. Although most animals lose lots of water through sweating when the weather is hot, that is not the case for camels. A camel does not sweat until its body temperature rises fairly high, to about 41°C (106°F). This allows the camel to conserve water. But when camels *do* sweat, they can lose more water without suffering than many other animals can. A 20-percent decrease in body weight due to water loss is fatal to most animals. A 12-percent loss would kill a human being. Camels can survive a 40-percent decrease in body weight due to water loss.

A camel's body has other adaptations for desert environments, as well. Thick eyebrows shield its eyes from bright sunlight. A double row of long eyelashes and an inner eyelid help keep sand out of its eyes. A camel can squeeze its nostrils and lips shut against blowing sand. Its feet spread out like pads so it can walk over soft sand without sinking. Pads of tough material on its knees and chest protect a camel from hot sand when it kneels or lies down.

Zoos are the only places camels are found in the United States. But that wasn't always the case. In the mid-1800s, the U.S. government bought several dozen camels for use in transporting goods across the deserts of the Southwest. The camels carried heavier loads than other pack animals. They also lived on desert plants, such as cactuses, that mules and horses would not eat. Although the camels did their job well, most people found them noisy, smelly, and bad-tempered. The experiment ended quickly.

Today, camels are found mostly in the deserts of northern Africa, the Middle East, and Asia. They transport people and goods and work as farm animals. People also make camel hair into cloth. In some places, camels provide milk and meat. These odd-looking animals whose adaptations make them successful at surviving and reproducing in an extreme environment have proved to be a desert lifeline.

Solving the Mystery of the Monarchs

PEOPLE HAVE STUDIED monarch butterflies for more than 100 years. In the 1930s, biologists discovered that these insects migrate each spring and fall. However, scientists had no idea *where* the monarchs went.

Then, in the mid-1970s, hikers stumbled upon the monarchs' winter home in the mountains west of Mexico City. Millions of monarch butterflies covered every square centimeter of the trees in the mountains' forest.

Biologists determined that every yearly cycle of migration involves three or four generations. One group of monarchs leaves the northern United States and southern Canada in late summer. This group reaches Mexico in November and stays through March. As the weather warms, these monarchs head north. They stop in Texas and Louisiana to mate and lay eggs, after which they die. Their offspring continue the journey north. This second generation reaches the area around the midwestern United States. There, adults have more offspring and die. A third generation then crosses the Appalachian Mountains to the East Coast and remains there for the rest of the summer. It is this generation that heads south again to Mexico—to a mountain valley these butterflies have never seen.

Case Study 2: Desert Marvel

Gather More Information

Encourage students to use the library or the NSTA SciLinks Web site noted at the start of each chapter to learn more about these case study topics and to conduct further research.

Have students use the following keywords to aid their searches:

- desert environment
- adaptation
- dromedary camel
- Bactrian camel
- Sahara
- Negev Desert
- Gobi Desert
- Atacama Desert
- Kalahari Desert

Research the Big Picture

- Have students work in pairs to discuss what adaptations have made it possible for the camel to survive in the desert. Each pair should then share its findings with the class.
- Have students work in groups to compare a camel to a similar mammal, such as a horse or a donkey. Ask: *What are the physical and behavioral similarities and differences? In what type of environment does each animal live? Why does each animal live in that particular environment?* Each group should then present its findings to the class in a poster format.

Case Study 3: Solving the Mystery of the Monarchs

Gather More Information

Encourage students to use the library or the NSTA SciLinks Web site noted at the start of each chapter to learn more about these case study topics and to conduct further research.

Have students use the following keywords to aid their searches:

- monarch butterfly
- migration
- Earth's magnetic field
- migration route of monarch butterfly

Research the Big Picture

- Have students work with partners to speculate, then research, how biologists first discovered that monarch butterflies migrated each fall and spring. Have pairs record the information and share it with the class.
- Have students work in groups to calculate the approximate number of kilometers traveled by each generation of the North American monarch butterfly. Groups should report their findings by creating charts or maps that indicate distances and locations.
- Have pairs of students research how the monarch butterfly uses Earth's magnetic field to migrate.

Background Information

The yearly migration is an instinct for the butterflies. Biologists think the monarchs find their way in the same manner that some birds do. They use Earth's magnetic field to navigate across thousands of kilometers. The result is one of the animal world's most amazing stories of migration.

Unit 6

Ecology

Introduce Unit 6

ENGAGE students by asking them to look at the photographs on this page. Explain that the topic of this unit is ecology. Also explain that *eco-* denotes living things in relation to their environment and that *-logy* is a science or study. Ask: *How are the pictures related to ecology?* (They show living things in their environments and different environments.)

Unit Projects

For each project below, students can use the Student Presentation Builder on the Student CD-ROM to display their results and their Science Notebooks for their project notes.

Career

Have each student research an ecology-related career (e.g., ecologist, natural resource manager, meteorologist, park naturalist). Ask them to define the job, describe what it entails, and identify the skills or experience it requires. Each student should present a brief report to share their findings.

Apply

Have small groups observe living things in their environments. Have them make observations regularly, recording the date, what they saw, and how the living things interact with each other and their surroundings. After a month, have groups summarize their data in a written report and present their findings to the class.

Technology

Have students work in groups to determine what kinds of technology are used to track human population growth around the world. Examples include satellite data, census data, surveys, etc. Ask groups to choose a country and research how its population changed over the past 500 years. Have them present their findings and identify the technology that was most helpful.

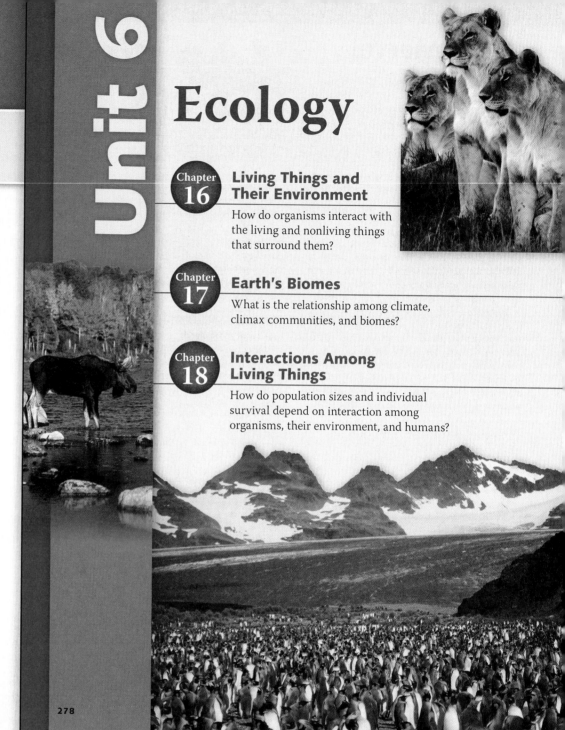

Unit 6

Ecology

278

Software Summary

Student CD-ROM

—Interactive Student Book
—Vocabulary Review
—Key Concept Review
—Lab Report Template
—ELL Preview and Writing Activities
—Presentation Digital Library
—Graphic Organizing Software
—Spanish Cognate Dictionary

Interactive Labs

Chapter 16B – Nothing Is Constant but Change
Chapter 16C – Acids and Seed Germination
Chapter 17B – Suited for Its Surroundings
Chapter 18B – The Fittest Will Survive
Chapter 18C – It's a Small Ocean After All

Living Things and Their Environment

Chapter 16

KEY CONCEPT Each organism interacts with the living and nonliving things around it.

Mars is colder than the arctic, one of the coldest places on Earth. Its coldest places are so frigid that carbon dioxide freezes out of the atmosphere. Mars is also incredibly dry. All of its water is frozen, and it never rains there. The air is so thin that breathing it would make your lungs bleed. You would probably suffocate first, because there is no oxygen in the atmosphere. The Martian environment is harsh, unforgiving, and deadly to humans.

Scientists are planning a manned mission to Mars. If the mission is to succeed, its members must bring along everything people might need to survive. To do that, they must first understand how living things, such as the polar bear, interact with their surroundings on Earth.

Think About Environments

Imagine you are going to Mars and must pack everything you will need.

- In your Science Notebook, list at least six things you need to survive. Think about what your body needs to function and what you could not live without.
- Label items as things you can find on Mars and things you can find on Earth.

SCILINKS
THE WORLD'S A CLICK AWAY
www.scilinks.org
Ecosystems **Code: WGB16**

279

Chapter 16 Lessons

Introduce Chapter 16

As a starting activity, use LAB 16A Parking Lot or Paradise? on page 98 of the Laboratory Manual.

ENGAGE Have students look at the photo and describe the environment shown. Then, challenge students to predict how the environment on Mars might be similar or different. Ask: *How are they alike? How are they different?* Have students think about what it would be like to visit either the arctic or Mars. Explain that in this chapter, they will learn how living things on Earth interact with their environment, which includes other living things and nonliving things.

Think About Environments

Ask students to name things that they do every day. Record the information in a list on the board. Then, ask students to think about visiting Mars. Ask: *How would you do all of these activities on Mars? What would you need to bring with you to live the way you do on Earth?* Write students' ideas on the board. Have students list at least six ideas, either from the board or of their own, in their Science Notebooks. Have them think about ways in which Mars and Earth differ. Ask: *What would you be able to find on Mars?* Have them write *Mars* next to each item they might expect to find on Mars. Ask: *What would you have to bring from Earth?* Have them label each of these items *Earth*.

Chapter 16 Planning Guide

Instructional Periods	National Standards	Lab Manual	Workbook
16.1 1 period	A.1, C.4, F.2; C.4; UCP.1, UCP.2	**Lab 16A—p. 98** Parking Lot or Paradise? **Lab 16B—p. 99** Nothing Is Constant but Change **Lab 16C—p. 102** Acids and Seed Germination	Key Concept Review p. 102 Vocabulary Review p. 103 Interpreting Diagrams p. 104 Reading Comprehension p. 105 Curriculum Connection p. 106 Science Challenge p. 107
16.2 1 period	A.2, B.3; B.6, C.4, C.5		
16.3 2 periods	D.2; B.6, D.2, F.6		
16.4 2 periods	C.4, F.2; C.4, F.2; UCP.3		

Middle School Standard; High School Standard; Unifying Concept and Principle

Introduce

ENGAGE Have students work in small groups to answer the following question: *What do you see and feel around you right now?* Ask students to list everything they can think of and be ready to share with the class. After a few minutes, have one person from each group report to the class. Tell students that what they described is their environment.

Before You Read

Draw the concept map on the board. Ask students what they know about plants, herbivores, and predators. Have students predict how these organisms might live together, or interact. Record the suggestions on the board. Ask students to draw the concept map in their Science Notebooks and write their prediction(s) underneath it.

Vocabulary terms are listed on the first student page of each lesson. You may wish to preview the terms before introducing each lesson. Strategies for teaching the vocabulary appear on the pages where the terms are introduced.

Learning Goals

- Identify the biotic and abiotic parts of an environment.
- List the levels of organization in an environment.
- Understand how organisms divide up resources in a habitat.

New Vocabulary

environment
biotic
abiotic
ecology
population
community
ecosystem
biosphere
habitat
niche

16.1 A Place to Call Home

Before You Read

Create a concept map in your Science Notebook. Start by drawing six circles. Write the word *Plant* in two of the circles, *Herbivore* in another two, and *Predator* in the last two. Predict how these organisms might interact if they lived in the same place. Record your predictions in your Science Notebook.

Look around. Everything you see and feel is a part of your environment. An **environment** (ihn VI run munt) is the place where an organism lives. Your environment includes living things such as plants, animals, people, and even the microbes living inside you. Living things make up the **biotic** (bi AH tihk) parts of the environment. Your environment also includes nonliving things such as your desk chair, the air you breathe, and the sunlight you see each day. Nonliving things make up the **abiotic** (a bi AH tihk) parts of the environment.

Organisms and Their Environments

An organism gets everything it needs to live from its environment. For example, a maple tree gets the energy it needs from sunlight and pulls the water and minerals it needs out of the soil. Living things rely on the abiotic parts of their environment.

Organisms that live in the same environment can affect one another. For example, prairie dogs are rodents that live on the Great Plains in the central part of the United States. They eat grass, and they are always on the lookout for ferrets that want to eat them. If a drought kills the grass, the prairie dogs will starve. The ferrets will also starve unless they can find other animals to eat. All of these organisms are interconnected. Something that affects one part of an environment can affect all of the organisms that live there.

Interactions among organisms and their environments can be very complex. The branch of biology that examines these interactions is called **ecology** (ih KAH luh jee). Scientists who study ecology are called ecologists.

Figure 16.1 Every environment has both living and nonliving parts. How do other living things affect your environment? What about nonliving things?

Figure 16.2 The endangered black-footed ferret depends on prairie dogs for food. If drought or human hunting kills enough prairie dogs, many ferrets will starve.

Teach

EXPLAIN that in this lesson, students will learn how living things interact with their environment.

Use the Visual: Figure 16.1

ANSWER Answers may vary. Plants make oxygen and provide food, while animals compete with humans for food and provide food. Nonliving things that affect humans include the Sun, which provides light and warmth; soil, which provides nutrients for plant growth; air, which contains oxygen; and water, which all living things need.

Science Notebook EXTRA

Encourage students to use the vocabulary section they created in their Science Notebooks. Remind them to record prefixes, suffixes, and root words to help them remember the meanings of vocabulary terms.

Vocabulary

environment Tell students that *environment* comes from the French word *environner*, meaning "about." Ask students how this meaning relates to what they know about environments.

biotic Explain that *biotic* is an adjective that comes from the Greek word *bios*, meaning "life." Ask students to think of other words containing *bio* (biography, biosphere, biology).

ELL Strategy

Discuss Ask students to discuss each section of this lesson with a partner. Pair students who speak the same native language, if possible. Students may choose to speak in English or in their native languages. Encourage students to record explanations of the vocabulary terms in their Science Notebooks.

Levels in Environments

Ecology is an incredibly diverse subject. An ecologist might study a honeybee collecting nectar for its hive, a group of birds competing for food in a field, the interaction of plants and animals in Yellowstone Park, or the way in which sunlight affects the amount of food available at different levels in an ocean. In each case, the ecologist studies relationships between organisms and their environment. For study, ecologists organize these relationships into three levels: populations, communities, and ecosystems.

A **population** of organisms is a group of individuals from the same species living in a specific area at the same time. The cotton-top tamarins shown in **Figure 16.3** represent a population. An ecologist studying a population may look at the ways in which the organisms compete for resources such as food, water, and mates. Or the ecologist might examine how the organisms cooperate to avoid predators or raise young.

A biological **community** is made up of all the interacting populations of species in an environment. An ecologist studying a community may look at the relationships between predators and prey, the ways in which different species compete for the same kinds of food, or the effects of parasites on an infested population.

An **ecosystem** (EE koh sihs tum) is made up of both the community of organisms in an area and their abiotic surroundings. An ecologist studying an ecosystem might look at the mechanisms that move nutrients such as carbon, nitrogen, or phosphorus out of nonliving reservoirs and into living organisms.

All of the ecosystems on Earth are part of the **biosphere** (BI uh sfihr). The biosphere is the part of Earth that contains living things.

Figure 16.3 Members of a population of cotton-top tamarins compete for food but also warn each other about predators. The plants and insects eaten by tamarins are part of the biological community in a South American rain forest. So are the birds and snakes that eat tamarins. The amount of rain and sunlight the forest receives affects which foods are available for tamarins in their ecosystem.

As You Read

Imagine that each of the organisms in your concept map is a unique population of living things. Label each of the six circles with the word *Population*. Then, draw one large circle around all of your population circles.

Which level does the largest circle represent? Explain your answer.

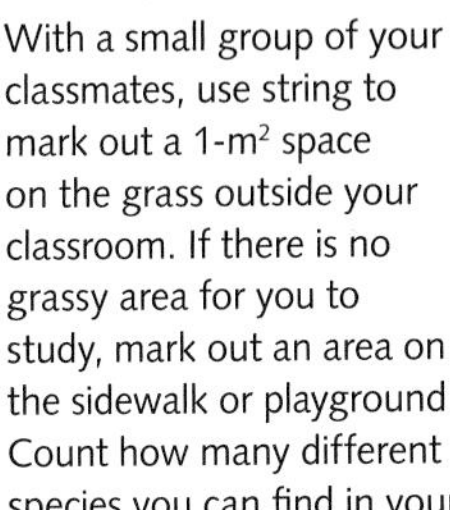

Explore It!

With a small group of your classmates, use string to mark out a 1-m^2 space on the grass outside your classroom. If there is no grassy area for you to study, mark out an area on the sidewalk or playground. Count how many different species you can find in your square of space.

Did You Know?

Earth's atmosphere once contained no oxygen. The first photosynthetic bacteria used carbon dioxide and sunlight to make organic compounds and released oxygen as a waste product. Over time, these bacteria changed the atmosphere!

Teach

EXPLAIN that students will learn about the three levels of environments: populations, communities, and ecosystems.

Vocabulary

abiotic Tell students that the prefix *a-* means "not" or "opposite to." Ask students to explain what *abiotic* means. ("not involving or relating to life")

ecology Explain that *eco* denotes living things in relation to their environment. One meaning of the suffix *-logy* is "a science." Ask students to name other sciences that contain *-logy* (biology, geology, meteorology, psychology).

population Tell students that the common meaning of this word is "all of the people living in a particular area, country, etc." Ask how this meaning differs from the term's meaning in this lesson.

community Explain that in common use, this word means "the people living in a particular place." The word comes from the Latin word *communis*, meaning "common."

ecosystem Remind students that *eco* denotes living things in relation to their environment. Explain that a *system* is a set of interrelated parts that form a whole.

biosphere Remind students that *bio* means "life" and that a *sphere* is a globe or ball. Ask students to put the two meanings together to arrive at a meaning for the term *biosphere*.

As You Read

Give each student a few minutes to label his or her concept map. Ask students to provide examples of populations that could be part of each circle.

ANSWER The largest circle contains all the populations in an environment. Thus, it represents a community.

ELL Strategy

Activate Background Knowledge Before going outside, ask students what they expect to find in 1 m^2 of space. What have they seen in such spaces by their homes or in other places? Write students' answers on the board. After students have finished with the activity, check their observations against the answers on the board.

Background Information

Today, Earth's atmosphere is 78 percent nitrogen, 21 percent oxygen, and 1 percent other gases, including water vapor. This mixture of gases is commonly known as air. The atmosphere protects life on Earth by absorbing ultraviolet solar radiation and reducing temperature extremes between day and night.

Explore It!

Form small groups of three or four students. Provide each group with meter sticks and string or yarn. Explain that students will be going outside to look for living things in 1 m^2 of space. Demonstrate how to measure the space. Explain that students will be looking for all the living things they can find in that space. Have students record their findings in their Science Notebooks.

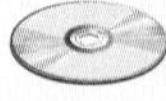

Teach

EXPLAIN that habitats are the environments in which particular species live.

Vocabulary

habitat Tell students that this is a Latin word that means "it inhabits" and is from *habitare*, which means "to dwell."

niche Explain that a common meaning for *niche* is "a position in life in which one feels fulfilled or at ease." It is derived from the Latin word *nidus*, which means "nest."

Figure It Out: Figure 16.5

ANSWER **1.** the bird with the shortest beak
2. If both ate the same food, adults would be competing with juveniles for survival.

CONNECTION: Technology

The U.S. Department of Agriculture's Natural Resources Conservation Service Web site, **www.nrcs.usda.gov**, has many resources for teachers and students, information on USDA-sponsored programs that protect plants and animals, and more about conservation of natural resources.

After You Read

1. Adding nonliving factors such as sunlight, oxygen, and soil would make the concept map represent an ecosystem.
2. If the bobcat population grew larger, the rabbit population would get smaller because of more hunting. If the grass died, the bobcat population would decrease because the rabbit population would get smaller.

Assess

EVALUATE Use the After You Read questions and the Alternative Assessment to help you assess students' understanding of the lesson.

Alternative Assessment

EVALUATE Have students review their concept maps and add missing information. Then, pair students with a partner. Tell each person to explain his or her map to the partner or explain their partner's map to the partner. Urge partners to ask clarifying questions. Finally, have partners work together to create one concept map that includes all the information in the lesson.

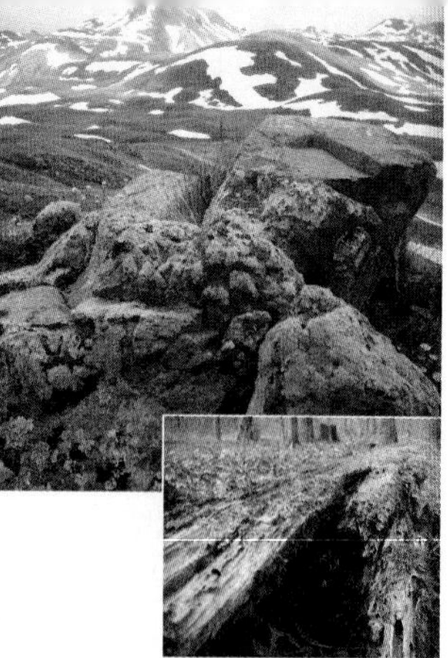

Figure 16.4 The arctic tundra and a rotting log are examples of habitats that vary greatly.

Living in an Ecosystem

If you put a penguin in the Amazonian rain forest or a tropical hummingbird in the Antarctic, neither bird would survive for very long. Each bird is adapted to life in a particular place, or **habitat** (HA buh tat). Habitats can be large, like a forest, or small, like a puddle. Some organisms can even be habitats for others. You are the habitat for bacteria that live on your skin and in your intestines. Even the most barren habitats are home to multiple species that must share a limited amount of resources.

Populations of different species avoid fighting over resources by using them in different ways, as **Figure 16.5** shows. Woodpeckers, nuthatches, and tufted titmice, for example, are birds that share the same habitat. They all hunt insects on trees, but they do not compete for the same insects. Tufted titmice eat insects that live on the surface of bark and leaves. Nuthatches look for insects that live under tree bark. Woodpeckers drill into the tree to find insects hiding deep in the wood. These birds can share a tree because they are adapted for eating different insects in different ways.

Figure It Out

1. Which of these birds is a tufted titmouse?
2. The caterpillar and adult monarch butterfly are eating on different kinds of plants. How is this fact helpful to this species of butterfly?

To avoid competition, woodpeckers *(left)*, tufted timice *(center)*, and nuthatches *(right)* each have a beak adapted for eating different types of insects that live in different parts of trees.

To avoid competition, adult and juvenile butterflies eat different food. A monarch caterpillar *(left)* eats leaves, and an adult butterfly *(right)* sips nectar from flowers.

Figure 16.5 Organisms are adapted to different niches to avoid competition.

Ecologists call the unique strategy a species has for survival its **niche** (NICH). If you think of a species' habitat as its home address, its niche is its occupation. Species hunt, eat, hide, or reproduce in different ways to avoid occupying the same niche as, or competing with, other organisms.

After You Read

1. Review your concept map of a biological community. What elements could you add to make it represent an entire ecosystem?
2. Imagine a community in which rabbits eat grass and bobcats eat rabbits. Predict what would happen to the rabbit population if the bobcat population grew larger. Then, predict what would happen to the bobcat population if a fungus killed the grass. Explain your predictions.

Background Information

Humans change the habitats of animals, for example, deer. As former habitats of deer became homes and roads, the whitetail deer population in the United States has increased from less than 500,000 in the early 1900s to as many as 33 million in 2006. Experts believe that converting land from forest to areas for agriculture and suburban homes has provided year-round food sources for deer.

16.2 Food and Energy in the Environment

Learning Goals

- Describe how organisms move energy and matter through ecosystems.
- Identify the kinds of organisms found at each trophic level of an ecosystem.
- Explain how energy is lost at each step in a food web.

New Vocabulary

producer
autotroph
consumer
heterotroph
herbivore
carnivore
omnivore
decomposer
food chain
trophic level
food web
ecological pyramid
biomass

Before You Read

In your Science Notebook, write the first eight vocabulary terms in this lesson. Leave some space below each term. Then, write a definition for each term in your own words as you read about it in the lesson.

When you eat a hamburger, in a sense you eat sunlight. The lettuce, tomato, onion, pickle, and roll are all made from plants, and plants build their cells with energy from the Sun. The hamburger patty comes from a cow, which uses the solar energy stored in plant cells to build its own tissues. After you eat the hamburger, your body breaks down the meat and vegetables and uses the stored energy.

Energy—along with carbon, nitrogen, and other elements—moves through the environment in food. Plants build sugars with carbon from carbon dioxide in the air, and they build proteins with nitrogen from the soil. Animals build their bodies with elements from other organisms.

Movement of Energy and Matter

Living things that can capture matter and energy from abiotic sources are called **producers**. Producers, such as plants and green algae, use photosynthesis to turn the Sun's energy, water, and carbon dioxide in the air into complex organic compounds. Other producers, such as the bacteria living near deep-sea vents, can capture energy from other materials. Producers are also called **autotrophs** (AW tuh trohfs), or "self-feeders," because they make organic compounds from inorganic compounds and do not need to eat food.

Most organisms have to eat other organisms to obtain the energy they need to survive. Organisms that eat other organisms are called **consumers**, or **heterotrophs** (HE tuh roh trohfs). **Herbivores** (HUR buh vorz) are consumers that eat only autotrophs. **Carnivores** (KAR nuh vorz) are consumers that eat only other heterotrophs. Consumers that eat both autotrophs and heterotrophs are called **omnivores** (AHM nuh vorz).

When an organism dies, small organisms such as fungi, bacteria, and protozoans break down the complex organic molecules in its body for food. These heterotrophs are called **decomposers** (dee kum POH zurz). Decomposers are important parts of every ecosystem. They release the elements stored in dead tissues into the environment, where they can be reused.

Figure 16.6 Energy and matter flow through an environment as organisms eat one another.

ELL Strategy

Venn Diagram Have each student create a Venn diagram in his or her Science Notebook. One circle should be labeled *Herbivores* and the other *Carnivores.* Students can complete the diagrams individually or with a partner.

Field Study

Equip students with clipboards, paper, and pencils. Bring them outside to look for living things. Have them draw and label what they see. In the classroom, each student should determine whether each living thing he or she drew is a producer or a consumer. For consumers, students should also determine whether they are herbivores, carnivores, or omnivores. Provide field guides and Internet access for reference.

16.2 Introduce

ENGAGE Ask students to look at the photograph in Figure 16.9. Ask them to think about what it is showing. What do grass, wheat, lettuce, and tomatoes have in common? What do the arrows mean? Each student should turn to a partner, answer these questions, and then share with the class.

Before You Read

Write the new vocabulary terms from this lesson on the board. Ask students if they recognize any of the words or know any of the word meanings. Tell students to copy the terms in their Science Notebooks, leaving space between each. As they read the lesson, students should draw a picture and write the definition of each word.

Teach

EXPLAIN that in this lesson, students will be learning about relationships between living things, such as those shown in Figure 16.9.

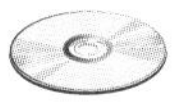

Vocabulary

producer Explain that in common use, a *producer* is "a person, organization, or thing that produces (makes, manufactures, or grows)." Help students relate this common meaning to the definition in the lesson.

autotroph Tell students that *auto* means "self" or "same" and that *troph* comes from the Greek word *trophē*, meaning "food."

consumer Tell students that the common meaning of this word is "someone who buys goods and services for personal use or need." Ask students to relate the common meaning to the definition in the lesson.

heterotroph Tell students that *hetero* means "other" or "different." Ask students to compare this word with *autotroph*.

herbivore Explain that *herbivore* comes from the Latin words *herba*, meaning "grass," and *vorare*, meaning "to swallow."

carnivore Tell students that *carnivore* is from *carnivorus*, which is Latin for "flesh-eating."

omnivore Explain that *omni-* comes from the Latin word *omnis*, meaning "all" or "every." Have students use the meanings of the word parts to define and compare the terms *herbivore, carnivore,* and *omnivore*.

decomposer Tell students that the root of this word is *decompose*, which means "to rot."

Teach

EXPLAIN that students will learn about food chains and food webs. Ask them to predict what they think each is, based on their understanding of the words *chain* and *web*. Encourage students to use examples in their predictions.

Vocabulary

food chain Show students a necklace or another type of chain. Have them describe how it is made (links are connected in a sequence). Tell them that organisms are also connected in this way because of how they obtain nourishment. Give an example of a simple food chain, and ask students how the organisms are interconnected.

trophic level Remind students that *troph* is from the Greek word *trophē*, meaning "food." *Trophic* is the adjective form of *troph*.

food web Tell students that a *web* is "a network of threads that a spider creates to trap insects." Draw a spiderweb on the board. Then, have students look at Figure 16.7. Ask them to explain how the image looks like a spiderweb.

ecological pyramid Tell students that a pyramid is a structure built on a square base, with four sloping sides that come to a point on the top. Draw an example on the board. Have students look at the examples in Figure 16.8 and Figure 16.9 on page 285.

biomass Remind students that *bio* means "life" and that *mass* is the amount of matter in an object.

As You Read

Give students time to complete the definitions and drawings in their Science Notebooks. If anyone needs more support, provide magazines and/or library books about the environment, energy, and food.

ANSWER A food chain shows one pathway of energy flow and matter flow within an ecosystem. A food web has many more parts and shows all the possible feeding relationships, or ways that energy and matter flow, in an ecosystem.

Explain It!

ANSWER If there is not enough grass to feed the lions' prey, the lions will also have a hard time finding enough to eat.

As You Read

Each vocabulary term you have written in your Science Notebook for this lesson describes a type of organism. For each of these terms, list two species that it describes.

What is the difference between a food chain and a food web?

Explain It!

Lions are carnivores that cooperate to hunt large animals such as zebras and wildebeest. In your Science Notebook, explain why lions also depend on the grass in their community.

Food Chains and Webs

Ecologists make models to study how energy and matter flow through an ecosystem. The simplest model of the flow of matter and energy in an ecosystem is called a **food chain**. A food chain can be constructed by writing the names of the organisms in an ecosystem according to the role that each plays and drawing arrows between them. The arrows show that one organism is eaten by the next. One food chain from the desert community in **Figure 16.7** could be shown as:

seeds → kangaroo rats → rattlesnakes

Each step in a food chain is called a **trophic** (TROH fihk) **level**. In this food chain, seeds make up the first trophic level. The next trophic level contains the kangaroo rats that eat the seeds. Organisms that eat plants are called first-order heterotrophs. In this example, the final trophic level contains the rattlesnakes that eat the kangaroo rats. Organisms that eat first-order heterotrophs are called second-order heterotrophs.

A food chain can illustrate and help explain one feeding pathway, but it does not show the complex feeding relationships in a real ecosystem. Biological communities have many species at each trophic level. Organisms may also eat more than one kind of food. These relationships can be drawn as a series of food chains, or they can be connected to form a food web. A **food web** is a model that shows all the possible feeding relationships at each trophic level. The food web in Figure 16.7 summarizes the feeding relationships in a desert community.

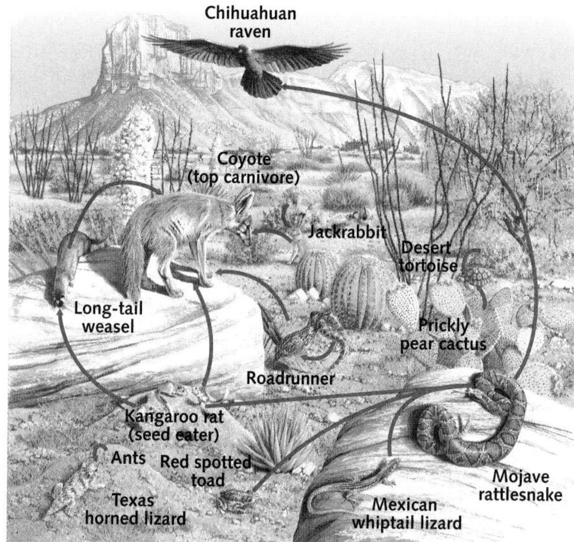

Figure 16.7 Arrows show how energy and matter flow through this desert ecosystem. Every food web starts with producers. Decomposers break down dead tissues at every level.

Background Information

In the year 2000, scientists found that mercury used to extract gold ore during the 1850s California Gold Rush is still found in food chains. The mercury has shown up in the tissues of bass and other fish. This shows that human activities can affect food chains.

Differentiated Instruction

Kinesthetic Have small groups of students create a food chain or food web out of classroom materials such as construction paper, string, and glue. Have students share their projects with each other when they are finished.

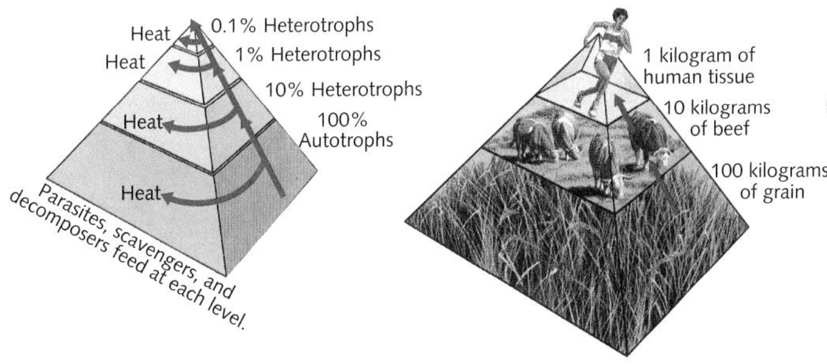

Figure 16.8 An energy pyramid shows that only ten percent of the energy stored in organisms can move to the next level *(left)*. A pyramid of biomass *(right)* shows that each higher level has only ten percent of the mass as the level below it.

Figure It Out

1. How many kilograms of beef must a human eat to make one kilogram of tissue?
2. Use these pyramids to explain why large, fierce animals are rare in ecosystems.

Ecological Pyramids

Food chains and food webs show ecologists "who eats whom" in a community. Another type of model, an **ecological pyramid**, helps ecologists see the relationships among trophic levels. Each layer of an ecological pyramid, as shown in **Figure 16.8**, represents a different trophic level. Autotrophs make up the base of the pyramid, and higher trophic levels are stacked above them.

One type of ecological pyramid shows how energy moves through an ecosystem. Energy is lost as it moves through heterotrophs. Each trophic level contains less energy than the level below it does. This happens because a heterotroph uses most of the energy it gets from food as fuel for life processes. Only about ten percent of the energy a heterotroph takes in is stored in new body tissues. Most of the energy is lost as heat.

Another way to show the stored energy in each trophic level is with a pyramid of biomass, also shown in Figure 16.8. **Biomass** (BI oh mas) is the total mass of living tissue in a trophic level.

An ecological pyramid can also show how many organisms are in each trophic level. Typically, population sizes get smaller in higher trophic levels. There are more autotrophs than herbivores, and there are more herbivores than carnivores. In some cases, however, one organism can feed many smaller organisms. For example, the upside-down pyramid in **Figure 16.9** represents a cow infested with thousands of parasitic roundworms.

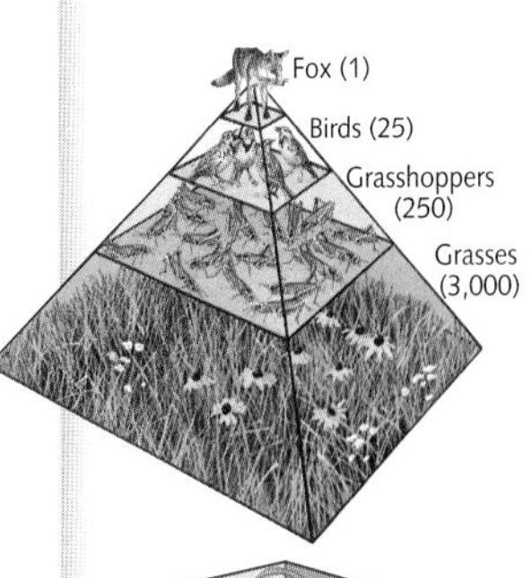

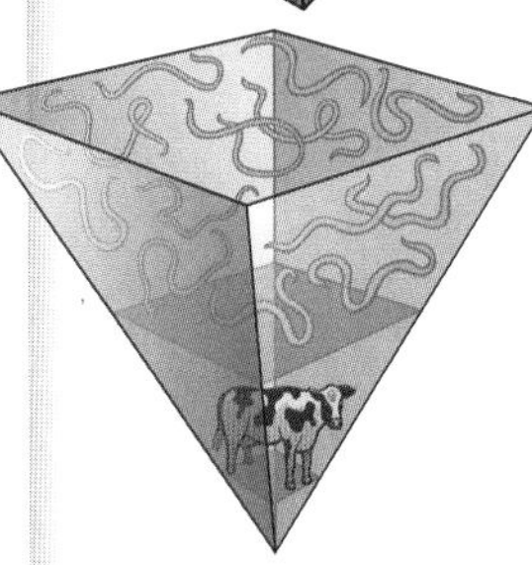

Figure 16.9 A pyramid of numbers *(top)* shows that each level feeds a smaller number of consumers than the level below it. The pyramid can also be inverted *(bottom)*, showing that a large number of parasites feed off of a single organism.

After You Read

1. Explain what would happen if an ecosystem had no decomposers.
2. In your Science Notebook, draw a simple food web of the community in a typical park.
3. Review the list of vocabulary terms you wrote in your Science Notebook. Use the terms to label the species at each trophic level of your food web.

Teach

EXPLAIN that students will learn about another way to show relationships among trophic levels.

Figure It Out: Figure 16.8

ANSWER **1.** The pyramid shows that 10 kg of beef went into 1 kg of muscle. **2.** The pyramids show that energy is lost from the ecosystem at every trophic level. By the time energy reaches the large animals in the top trophic level, most of the energy that was captured from the Sun by autotrophs has been lost. This energy loss means that each higher trophic level can support fewer individuals.

Assess

EVALUATE Use the After You Read questions and the Alternative Assessment to help you assess students' understanding of the lesson.

After You Read

1. Without decomposers, the matter stored in dead tissue would not get recycled. Dead material would pile up in the ecosystem.
2. Sample:

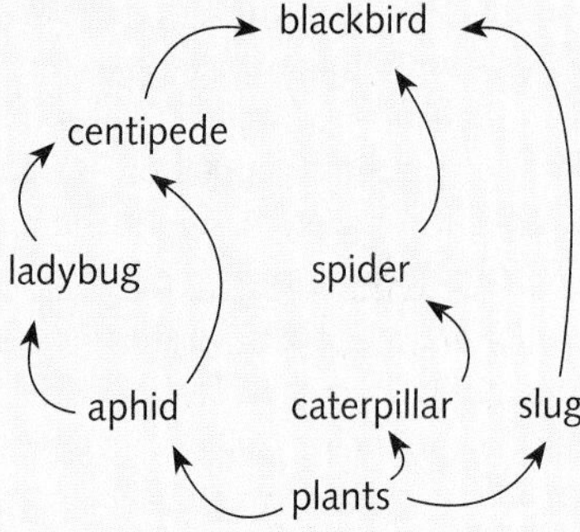

3. Plants should be labeled producers and autotrophs. All animals should be labeled heterotrophs. Aphids, slugs, and caterpillars are herbivores; ladybugs, centipedes, and blackbirds are carnivores.

ELL Strategy

Role Playing Have students work together to create an ecological pyramid with classmates playing the roles of organisms at each level. Assign roles to each class member, and have each student make a label that identifies his or her role. Then, students should form a pyramid by grouping themselves according to their labels.

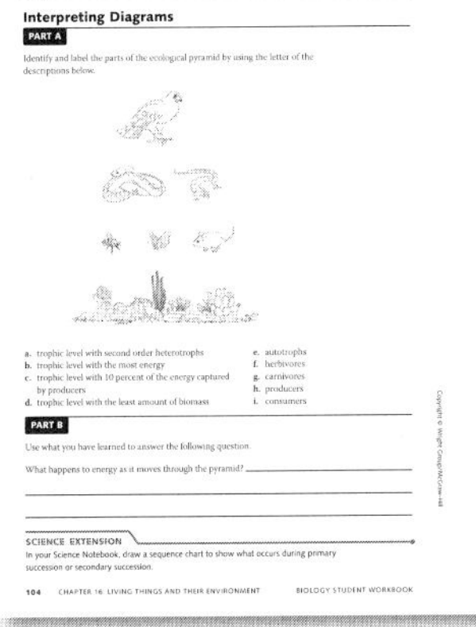

Interpreting Diagrams
Workbook, p. 104

Alternative Assessment

EVALUATE Ask each student to write a paragraph about the relationship between several of the vocabulary terms in this chapter. Examples that students could choose include *producer, autotroph, heterotroph, consumer, herbivore, carnivore, omnivore, trophic level, biological pyramid,* and *biomass.*

Introduce

ENGAGE Ask students what it means to recycle (to use something again). Ask for examples of items that students recycle. Divide the class into small groups, and hand out one recyclable item to each group (e.g., a glass bottle, a plastic soda bottle, a milk carton, or a newspaper). Ask students to discuss what happens to each item when it is recycled.

Before You Read

Discuss the process of predicting and the various parts of the lesson students can use to determine what they will learn. Mention Figure 16.10, and ask students to explain how they might use the diagram in their predictions. Model a response if students appear to be having difficulty.

Teach

EXPLAIN that in this lesson, students will learn about how water is recycled in the environment.

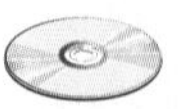

Vocabulary

biogeochemical cycle Ask students to remember what *bio* means, and tell them that *geo* refers to Earth. Explain that *chemical* refers to *chemistry*, which is "the study of the composition, properties, and reactions of substances." Remind students that a *cycle* is "a repeating series of events."

evaporation Explain that this word comes from a Latin word meaning "steam" or "vapor." The suffix *-ation* denotes "an action or process." Ask students to use the meanings of these word parts to define the process of evaporation.

condensation Explain that *condensation* is a noun that refers to a process as well as a product. The change of water vapor to a liquid upon cooling is condensation. The liquid formed is also called condensation.

precipitation Explain that *precipitate* comes from a Latin word that means "to fall." Precipitation is water that falls to the ground as rain, snow, sleet, or hail.

transpiration Explain that *transpire* comes from the Latin word *transpirare*, meaning "to breathe." Ask students to explain why this is an appropriate term for what plants do.

Learning Goals

- Describe how water moves between Earth and the atmosphere.
- Explain how organisms move carbon between Earth and the atmosphere.
- Identify how nitrogen moves between abiotic and biotic reservoirs.

New Vocabulary

biogeochemical cycle
evaporation
condensation
precipitation
transpiration
eutrophication

16.3 Cycles in the Environment

Before You Read

Read the title, headings, and Learning Goals for this lesson, and look at the figures. Predict what you think you will learn in this lesson. Write your prediction in two or three sentences in your Science Notebook.

Have you ever recycled a plastic bottle? After you send the bottle to the recycling center, it is melted down and reused in a new product. The plastic may become part of a backpack, a pair of sneakers, or playground equipment, but it is still the same plastic that made up the original bottle.

This process is similar to the movement of matter through an ecosystem. Water molecules and elements such as nitrogen and carbon constantly move among the ocean, the atmosphere, and terrestrial ecosystems. Energy is lost as it passes through a community, but matter is recycled and reused over and over again. The recycling systems of an ecosystem are called **biogeochemical** (BI oh jee oh KEM ih kul) **cycles**.

Recycling Water

The water cycle starts with evaporation. **Evaporation** (ih va puh RAY shun) is the process by which heat from the Sun turns liquid water on Earth's surface into water vapor. The water vapor moves into the atmosphere, where it cools and turns into liquid droplets that form around dust particles in the air. The process by which water vapor cools and becomes a liquid is called **condensation** (kahn den SAY shun). The liquid droplets produce clouds, and as more water vapor condenses, more water droplets form. When the drops get heavy enough, they fall back to Earth as **precipitation** (prih sih puh TAY shun), which takes the form of rain, snow, sleet, or hail. Some water falls into lakes and oceans. Water that falls on land may flow to the ocean in streams and rivers or soak deep into the ground to form groundwater.

Water also moves through organisms. Plants pull water out of the ground through their roots and lose it by evaporation from their leaves during **transpiration** (trans puh RAY shun). Animals drink water and lose it when they urinate, sweat, and breathe.

Figure 16.10 Water constantly moves between Earth and the atmosphere.

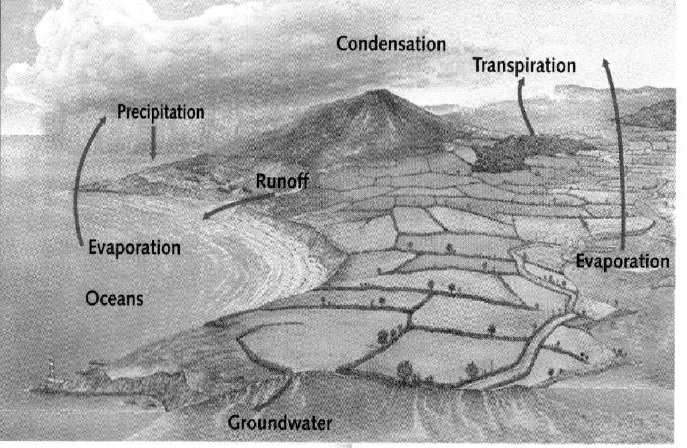

Background Information

According to the United States Environmental Protection Agency (EPA), we recycle about 32 percent of our waste. Fifteen years ago, people in the United States recycled about 16 percent of their waste. When examining individual materials, the numbers are even more impressive. Sixty-seven percent of all major appliances, 50 percent of all paper, 45 percent of all aluminum drink cans, and 34 percent of all plastic drink bottles are recycled today.

Recycling Carbon

Carbon is the main building block of molecules in living things. Every carbon atom in a living thing was, at some point in the past, part of a carbon dioxide molecule in the air.

Autotrophs use carbon dioxide from the air to make the complex organic molecules found in their tissues. Heterotrophs that eat autotrophs break down the autotroph's molecules. Some of the molecules are broken down for energy. The carbon in these molecules then returns to the air as carbon dioxide. Heterotrophs use other molecules to form their tissues. When a heterotroph dies and decays, some of the carbon in its tissues returns to the air as carbon dioxide. The carbon dioxide given off by all living things is reused by autotrophs.

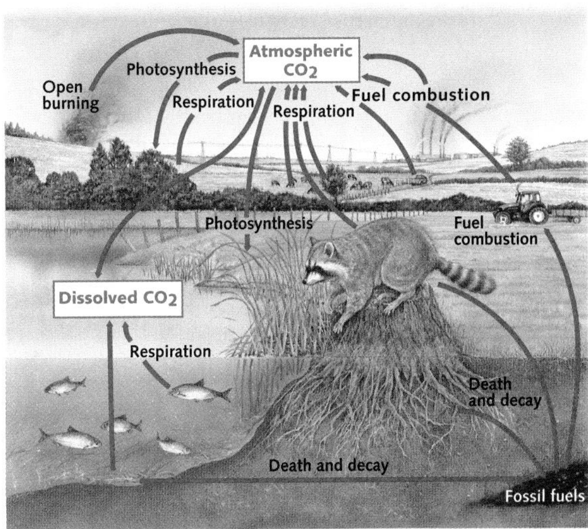

Figure 16.11 Carbon atoms move between the carbon dioxide in the air and the more complex organic molecules inside living things.

As You Read

Compare the water cycle with the carbon cycle. In your Science Notebook, explain one way in which the two cycles are the same and one way in which they are different.

CONNECTION: Atmospheric Science

When organisms use carbon to build tissues, they slow down how fast carbon moves through the carbon cycle. The carbon can be locked in an organism's tissues for its lifetime. These molecules form a carbon reservoir, or a pool of stored carbon.

After an organism dies, its stored carbon will be released if the dead organism is eaten. If the dead organism gets buried, however, the carbon in its tissues enters another carbon reservoir, one that over millions of years forms fossil fuels such as coal and oil.

Burning fossil fuels releases carbon into the atmosphere as carbon dioxide. Carbon dioxide is a greenhouse gas. It traps heat that is radiated from Earth and reflects it back to the planet. The increased amount of carbon dioxide in the atmosphere may be at least partially responsible for global warming.

Extend It!

To model the water cycle, put a pot of water on a stove to boil. When the water boils, hold a glass bowl filled with ice over the steam. Be careful to avoid direct contact with the steam.

Where do beads of water appear? Where do evaporation and condensation occur in this model?

Teach

EXPLAIN to students that in this lesson, they will learn how carbon is recycled in nature.

As You Read

On the board, create a compare-and-contrast chart for the water cycle and the carbon cycle. Each student should create a similar chart in his or her Science Notebook. Solicit one or two responses from students for the water and carbon sections, and record these on the board. Have students copy the information on the board into their Science Notebooks and then add more information on their own. Encourage ELL students to create a Venn diagram to review the concepts.

CONNECTION: Atmospheric Science

Greenhouse-gas emissions in the United States have grown at an annual rate of one percent since 1990. In September 2006, the governor of California signed a bill to reduce the emissions of carbon dioxide by 25 percent by the year 2020. California is the first state to pass such a bill. Encourage students to discuss the importance of reducing these emissions and what they can do to support the effort.

EXTEND Have students research the status of carbon dioxide emissions and bills to reduce those emissions in their home state.

ELL Strategy

Prepare Presentations After the Extend It! activity, have pairs or small groups of students explain how the activity represented the water cycle. Have them prepare a diagram to illustrate their explanations.

Extend It!

This activity allows students to experience the water cycle firsthand. You can do the activity as a demonstration.

EXPLORE You may want students to conduct the activity on their own. Have students work in pairs or small groups. Review the safety rules for working with a heat source and hot materials. When the water is boiling, demonstrate how to carefully hold the glass bowl over the steam.

ANSWER Beads of water will appear on the bottom of the bowl. The water is evaporating from the surface of the boiling water and condensing on the outside of the cold bowl.

Teach

EXPLAIN that students will learn how nitrogen is recycled in the environment.

EXPLORE If possible, purchase a Venus's-flytrap for the classroom. Have students observe its behavior and record what they see in their Science Notebooks. Ask students to compare this plant with "ordinary" plants that they have seen growing.

Vocabulary

eutrophication Explain that the prefix *eu-* is Greek and means "well." Ask students to recall what *troph* means ("food") and what the suffix *-ation* means ("an action or process.") Then, ask them to define *eutrophication* in their own words, based on the meanings of the word parts.

Figure It Out: Figure 16.12

ANSWER **1.** bacterial action and evaporation **2.** Urine cannot be used directly as fertilizer. It contains nitrogen compounds that must be converted by bacteria and fungi into forms that plants can use.

Assess

EVALUATE Use the After You Read questions and the Alternative Assessment to help you assess students' understanding of the lesson.

After You Read

1. Energy from the Sun drives the water cycle. Student answers will vary.
2. Most of the abiotic nitrogen is found in the nitrogen gas in the atmosphere.
3. Answers may vary. Students might suggest growing a control group of plants in pure water, which does not contain nitrogen, and pure carbon dioxide gas. One test group should be grown in pure water and room air, which contains nitrogen gas; another test group should be grown in pure carbon dioxide gas and soil, which would be the only source of nitrogen.

Alternative Assessment

EVALUATE Have students reread the water cycle and carbon cycle sections of their compare-and-contrast charts and add information as needed. Then, have them add and complete a section about the nitrogen cycle.

Recycling Nitrogen

Nitrogen makes up most of the air you breathe. Yet, like most organisms, your body cannot use it to build its nitrogen-rich proteins and nucleotides. Most of the nitrogen in organisms comes from bacteria that convert atmospheric nitrogen into usable forms.

Plants absorb nitrogen compounds made by bacteria and use the nitrogen to build proteins and other molecules. When herbivores eat plants, they reuse the nitrogen in their own tissues. The nitrogen is reused every time one animal eats another. At each step, some nitrogen leaves an animal in urine. Animal wastes return nitrogen compounds to the soil, where plants and bacteria reuse them. Dead and decomposing organisms also leave nitrogen compounds in the soil, and soil bacteria convert these compounds into nitrogen gas, which returns to the air.

Fertilizers with nitrogen make plants grow taller. However, nitrogen also dissolves in water and can be washed away. If extra nitrogen enters aquatic (water) ecosystems, algae grow uncontrollably. Eventually, exploding algae populations use up the oxygen in the water, and other organisms suffocate. This kind of nutrient pollution is called **eutrophication** (YOO troh fih kay shun).

Did You Know?

Venus's-flytraps, pitcher plants, and sundews are plants that live in acidic, nitrogen-poor soils. Instead of getting nitrogen from the soil, they get it by catching insects and digesting them.

Figure It Out

1. Name both ways in which nitrogen returns to the air.
2. Can you use urine as a fertilizer? Explain why or why not.

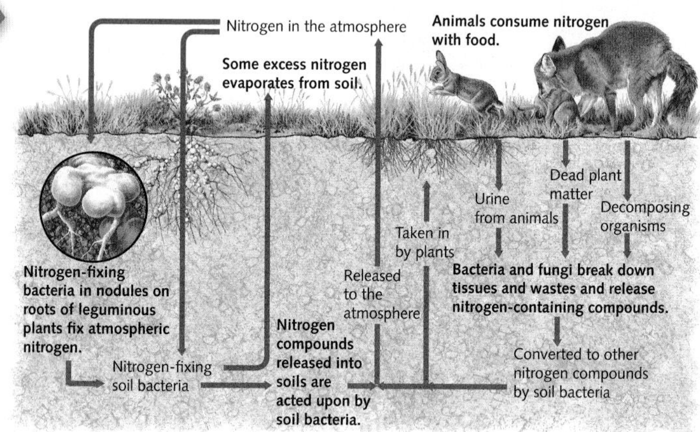

Figure 16.12 Nitrogen moves between the air and living things through life processes and complex reactions inside bacteria. The red arrows represent the movement of nitrogen compounds.

After You Read

1. What drives the water cycle? How does your answer compare with the predictions in your Science Notebook?
2. Where is most of the abiotic nitrogen found?
3. In your Science Notebook, design an experiment to test the idea that plants can only get nitrogen from the soil.

Differentiated Instruction

Kinesthetic Have students in small groups act out the eutrophication example on this page. Provide students with index cards labeled *fertilizer, plants* (lawns or fields), *rain, lake, algae,* and *eutrophication.* Students should show what happens when fertilizer is washed into a body of water.

ELL Strategy

Use Visual Information Have students study the nitrogen cycle in Figure 16.12 and discuss its meaning with a partner. Ask each partner to draw a diagram of what his or her partner is describing. When pairs finish, they should clarify differences between their own drawings and Figure 16.12. Then, have pairs report their understandings to the class, and clarify any misinterpretations.

288 LIVING THINGS AND THEIR ENVIRONMENT

16.4 Changes in the Environment

Before You Read

Draw a T-chart in your Science Notebook. Label one side *Primary Succession* and the other side *Secondary Succession.* In your own words, define the terms *primary* and *secondary.*

Learning Goals

- Understand how living organisms invade and change lifeless areas.
- Compare the processes of primary succession and secondary succession.

New Vocabulary

succession
primary succession
pioneer species
biodiversity
climax community
secondary succession

On May 18, 1980, an earthquake under Mount St. Helens started a tremendous volcanic eruption. The north face of the mountain slid away in a huge avalanche, releasing a blast of superheated, rock-filled gas that ripped up the trees in its path. By the afternoon, slower, hotter flows of gas and rock had destroyed the trees and killed all living organisms in the soil. Mature forests were turned into ash-covered wasteland.

Since then, hardy plants have reappeared in the ash field. The plants attract herbivores that drop seeds from other plants in their dung. More than 28 years after the eruption, the forest is beginning to regrow.

Figure 16.13 Before May 18, 1980, Mount St. Helens was covered with mature forest *(left).* After the eruption, the same spot was a barren ash field *(center).* Now, wildflowers and shrubs have reestablished themselves *(right).*

Ecosystems change over time. Sudden disturbances such as volcanoes, floods, or fires can affect which species will thrive in an environment. Living things also affect their ecosystems. One set of organisms living in an area can change the area's physical conditions in a way that favors the invasion of a new species. Over time, the sets of species that make up a community change. The steady progression of species invasion and replacement in an ecosystem over time is called **succession** (suk SE shun).

Primary Succession

Some places on Earth have no life. In some, land is being built by erupting volcanoes. In others, the soil has been sterilized by volcanoes or scraped away by glaciers. Living things will eventually invade all of these places. Ecologists call that colonization process **primary succession**.

Figure 16.14 Primary succession occurs when living things invade lifeless places. The first organisms to arrive build resources that other species use later.

16.4 Introduce

ENGAGE students by asking them what they know about volcanic eruptions. Ask: *What happens to an area after a volcano erupts? What does the area look like and sound like?* Have available several pre- and post-eruption photographs of various volcanoes. Then, ask what students know about forest fires. Ask: *What does an area look like and sound like after a fire has destroyed it?* Likewise, have available several photographs of forest fire devastation.

Before You Read

Write *Primary* and *Secondary* on the board. Ask students what they know about each word. Ask them if there any smaller words that they recognize within one of the words that could help them understand that word's meaning. When the class has come to agreement, ask students to record the definitions in their Science Notebooks.

Teach

EXPLAIN that in this section, students will learn how living things can invade and survive in a previously lifeless area.

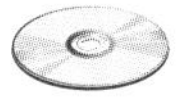

Vocabulary

succession Tell students that the common meaning of this word is "a series of people or things that come or happen one after another."

primary succession Explain that *primary* means "first" or "most important." Have students use the meanings of *primary* and *succession* to develop their own definitions of *primary succession.*

Background Information

Floods are the most common natural hazard in the United States. They can occur in every state. There are several ways in which flooding occurs: heavy rains, overflowing rivers, ocean waves, storm surges, rapid snowmelt, and broken dams or levees. In the summer of 2005, flooding from Hurricane Katrina caused more than $200 billion in damages.

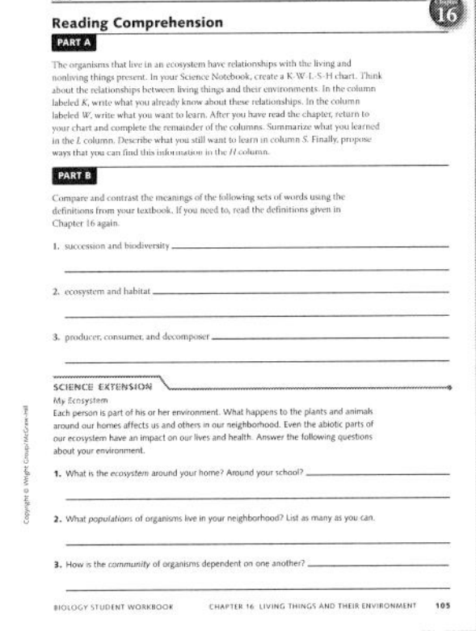

Name ______ Date ______ Time ______ Chapter 16

Reading Comprehension

PART A

The organisms that live in an ecosystem have relationships with the living and nonliving things present. In your Science Notebook, create a K-W-L-S-H chart. Think about the relationships between living things and their environments. In the column labeled *K*, write what you already know about these relationships. In the column labeled *W*, write what you want to learn. After you have read the chapter, return to your chart and complete the remainder of the columns. Summarize what you learned in the *L* column. Describe what you still want to learn in column *S*. Finally, propose ways that you can find this information in the *H* column.

PART B

Compare and contrast the meanings of the following sets of words using the definitions from your textbook. If you need to, read the definitions given in Chapter 16 again.

1. succession and biodiversity ______
2. ecosystem and habitat ______
3. producer, consumer, and decomposer ______

SCIENCE EXTENSION

My Ecosystem

Each person is part of his or her environment. What happens to the plants and animals around our homes affects us and others in our neighborhood. Even the abiotic parts of our ecosystem have an impact on our lives and health. Answer the following questions about your environment.

1. What is the *ecosystem* around your home? Around your school? ______
2. What *populations* of organisms live in your neighborhood? List as many as you can. ______
3. How is the *community* of organisms dependent on one another? ______

Copyright © Wright Group/McGraw-Hill

BIOLOGY STUDENT WORKBOOK CHAPTER 16 LIVING THINGS AND THEIR ENVIRONMENT 105

Reading Comprehension Workbook, p. 105

Teach

EXPLAIN to students that in this section, they will learn what happens in an ecosystem during primary succession.

EXPLORE Provide several examples of lichens growing on rocks and tree branches for students to examine. Students can observe the lichens under a dissecting microscope and look for distinguishing characteristics. Keys that can be used to identify lichens are available on the Internet.

Vocabulary

pioneer species Tell students that a pioneer is an explorer of an unknown area. *Species* is Latin, meaning "kind" or "appearance," and is a derivative of *specere*, which means "to look." Ask students to explain why this term appropriately describes the first organisms to move into a barren environment.

biodiversity Explain that *diverse* means "various" or "assorted." The suffix *-ity* means "a state or quality." Have students recall the meaning of the prefix *bio-* and then use the meanings of all three word parts to define *biodiversity*.

climax community Explain that *climax* means "the high point or culmination of a series of events." The word *community* refers to all the living things in a particular place.

secondary succession Tell students that *secondary*, as used here, refers to the second time something happens. Ask students to compare this meaning with the meaning of the word *recolonization* in the definition.

Figure It Out: Figure 16.16

ANSWER **1.** Plants that grow in water, such as reeds and rushes, are the pioneer species. **2.** Like all plants, willows lose water through transpiration. They keep pulling more water out of the soil with their roots as long as water keeps escaping from the leaves.

As You Read

Discuss with students what they have learned about primary succession. Have volunteers offer facts they have learned, and write these facts on the board. After the discussion, have students record the class list on the board in their Science Notebooks.

ANSWER Biodiversity increases during primary succession.

Did You Know?

A lichen (LI kun) is an association between a fungus and an alga or a bacterium. As a lichen grows, it releases acids that break down the rock underneath it.

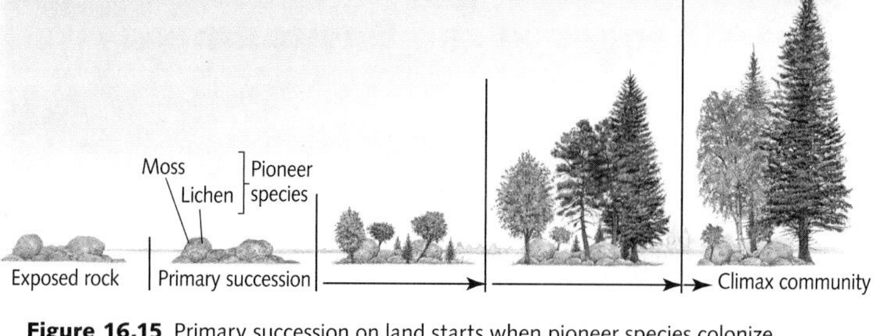

Figure 16.15 Primary succession on land starts when pioneer species colonize exposed rock. As the rock breaks down into soil, species such as ferns and insects move into the area. Later, trees, shrubs, and larger animals replace the smaller species.

As You Read

In the T-chart in your Science Notebook, write at least five bulleted notes to summarize what you have learned about primary succession.

How does biodiversity change during primary succession?

The first organisms to move into a barren environment are called **pioneer species**. Pioneer species, such as mosses and lichens, can thrive in places that supply very few nutrients. When they die, their bodies add organic material to the environment and begin to build up soil. Pioneer species change bare rock into an ecosystem that can support more organisms.

A pioneer community attracts other organisms. Plants attract herbivores, herbivores attract carnivores, and the dead bodies attract decomposers. Over time, the community becomes more complex. As more species move in, the community's **biodiversity**, or variety of life, increases. Eventually, species that are better at competing for nutrients push out the pioneer species. The ecosystem then contains a **climax community**, or a stable community that undergoes little or no change in species. Environmental changes still occur, but the species that make up the community change slowly, if at all.

Figure It Out

1. When succession occurs in shallow lakes, which plants are the pioneer species?
2. Explain how willows can remove large amounts of water from the soil in this environment every day.

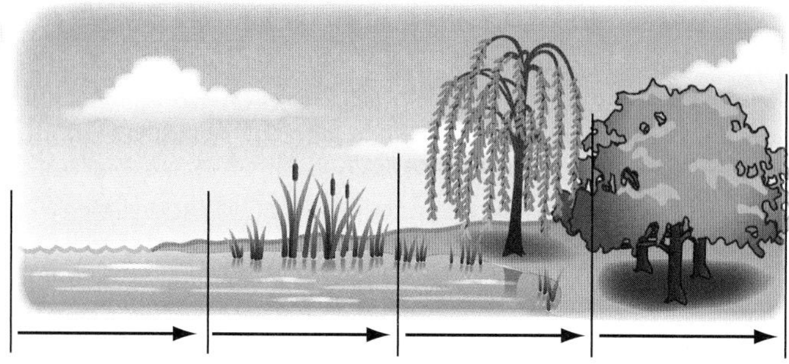

Figure 16.16 Primary succession can also occur in shallow lakes. Plants such as reeds and rushes grow at the edge of a lake and trap soil around their roots, forming new land. Then, plants such as willows grow in the wet soil at the edge of the lake and remove water with their roots. As the ground gets firmer, the willows are replaced by dry-ground climax species such as oaks.

Teacher Alert

Students may have misconceptions about natural disasters from movies they have seen or stories they have heard. To correct these misunderstandings, it might be useful to briefly show and discuss examples of floods, avalanches, volcanic eruptions, and forest fires. Since human lives are often lost as a result of such events, acknowledging this may help students move forward with the lesson.

ELL Strategy

Practice Using Vocabulary Have students write each vocabulary word in this chapter on an index card. Have pairs of students take turns explaining what they know about each word. Encourage students to give definitions of the terms and to use examples and diagrams to expand the definitions.

Secondary Succession

Unexpected events can radically change biological communities. Fire can sweep through a forest, burning everything in its path. Floods can carry away land and everything living on it. People can clear woods to create open fields. An avalanche can destroy every tree in its path. Disease can kill a species of tree in an area, affecting every animal that uses that kind of tree for food. Over time, however, organisms move back into the area.

The recolonization of an area by living things after a disturbance is called **secondary succession**. Secondary succession generally takes less time than primary succession does. This is because the ecosystem already contains soil. The soil stores organic material and nutrients. It also contains seeds from older generations of plants. Weedy pioneer species sprout quickly in the cleared areas. Over time, the community of organisms in the area changes. Pioneer species are replaced with a climax community.

Figure 16.17 Natural events such as fires started by lightning can disturb environments and restart succession. This fireweed is a pioneer in secondary succession.

Figure 16.18 Human activities can also restart succession in an ecosystem. Cutting down a forest obviously disturbs an ecosystem, but so do dams on a river and forest fires caused by carelessness.

Some communities depend on regular disturbances. Without the occasional fire to kill tree seedlings, grasslands like the American prairies would eventually become forests. Recent research in the Grand Canyon has shown that the stream communities there depend on occasional floods to build sandbars. Floods also clean silt out of the streambeds where native fish breed. Climax communities are dynamic places that rebound after they are disturbed.

Extend It!

Obtain photographs of an area that was disturbed at least 30 years ago. Compare the photos with recent photographs of the same area, or visit the area. In your Science Notebook, record how the ecosystem has changed.

CONNECTION: Wildlife

Wolves were reintroduced to Yellowstone National Park in 1995. Through their hunting, wolves cut the elk population in half. With fewer elk, more cottonwood and aspen trees grew. The trees fed beaver and provided homes for birds. By controlling elk numbers, the wolves have made the forest more diverse. As a result, wolves increased the biodiversity of the area.

After You Read

1. In the T-chart in your Science Notebook, summarize what you have learned about secondary succession. What is the most significant difference between primary and secondary succession?
2. Are dandelions a pioneer species? Defend your idea.
3. Does secondary succession begin after an old tree falls in a forest? Explain.

Teach

EXPLAIN that students will learn what happens after natural disaster such as a flood, a fire, or an avalanche occurs.

Extend It!

Provide nature magazines, encyclopedias, library books, and Internet access. Instruct groups to research information about events that happened at least 30 years ago and about what the area is like now.

Science Notebook EXTRA

Ask each student to write a paragraph about the Extend It! activity findings. Then, have each student share his or her writing with a classmate who was in a different group.

CONNECTION: Wildlife

Explain that gray wolves were an endangered species until 2003, when their status was changed to that of a threatened species.

EXTEND Have students find out more information about gray wolves at the U.S. Fish and Wildlife Service's Web site at **http://www.fws.gov/mountain-prairie/species/mammals/wolf/**.

Assess

EVALUATE Use the After You Read questions and the Alternative Assessment to help you assess students' understanding of the lesson.

After You Read

1. Primary succession occurs in places that have no soil. Secondary succession occurs when an established ecosystem is disturbed, but the soil is left intact.
2. Answers will vary. Because dandelions are fast-growing plants that have a lot of offspring, they could be considered a pioneer species in secondary succession.
3. Yes. When a tree falls, conditions in the immediate area are changed.

Differentiated Instruction

Interpersonal Have students interview an adult family member or friend about a personal experience with an event that changed an ecosystem. Questions could include: *What was the event? When did it happen? What do you remember about it? What did the area look like afterward? What does the area look like now?* Have students record their interviews in their Science Notebooks, and ask them to share what they learned.

Alternative Assessment

EVALUATE Discuss with students what they have learned about primary and secondary succession. Have each student reread what he or she wrote about primary and secondary succession in the T-chart in their Science Notebooks. Ask each student to write a paragraph or create an illustration that compares and contrasts the two types.

Chapter 16 Summary

VOCABULARY REVIEW

Check students' sentences or paragraphs to make sure they understand the vocabulary terms.

PREPARE FOR CHAPTER TEST

Evaluate students' essays using the following criteria:

1. The topic sentence, or main idea, should restate the Key Concept.
2. The supporting paragraphs should incorporate the answers to the Learning Goal questions students have written and include details, facts, and examples they have recorded in their Science Notebooks.
3. The concluding sentence should sum up the main idea of the chapter and restate the Key Concept.

MASTERING CONCEPTS

True or False

1. false, habitat
2. false, autotroph
3. true
4. true
5. false, decomposers
6. false, lost

Short Answer

7. Possible answers include earthworms, beetles, mice, squirrels, cats, dogs, and people.
8. Students' answers should show understanding of the basic stages of secondary succession. Seeds of weeds in the forest soil will sprout first, followed by slower-growing plants such as shrubs and then eventually trees.
9. Students should recognize that the pond is undergoing eutrophication. Droppings from the geese have raised nitrogen levels and triggered an algal bloom. The algae are using up the oxygen in the water, killing the fish.
10. Wolves eat rabbits and, thus, are in a higher trophic level. Because energy is lost at each link in a food chain, each trophic level can support fewer larger individuals.
11. Answers will vary. A food chain should include the following: autotroph/producer → herbivore/first-order heterotroph → carnivore/second-order heterotroph.

Chapter 16

Summary

KEY CONCEPTS

16.1 A Place to Call Home

- Environments have biotic (living) and abiotic (nonliving) parts.
- Environments are organized in levels: populations, communities, and ecosystems.
- Organisms live in particular places and have strategies for survival. The place in which an organism lives is its habitat. Its strategy for survival is its niche.

16.2 Food and Energy in the Environment

- As organisms eat one another, they move energy and matter through ecosystems.
- Models such as food chains and food webs show how energy and matter move through ecosystems.
- Ecosystems are organized in trophic levels that are defined by what organisms eat.
- An ecological pyramid shows the relationships that exist among trophic levels.
- Energy is lost at each link of a food web.

16.3 Cycles in the Environment

- Biogeochemical cycles move nutrients and water between abiotic reservoirs and living organisms.
- The water cycle is powered by sunlight.
- Autotrophs remove carbon from the atmosphere and incorporate it into edible tissues.
- Nitrogen-fixing bacteria remove nitrogen from the atmosphere and make it available to living organisms.

16.4 Changes in the Environment

- Ecosystems change over time. The steady change in the species that make up a community is called succession. Over time, succession leads to a climax community.
- Pioneer species can thrive under harsh conditions. They change an ecosystem and make it suitable for other organisms.
- If the climax community is disturbed, succession begins again.

VOCABULARY REVIEW

Write each term in a complete sentence, or write a paragraph relating several terms.

16.1
environment, p. 280
biotic, p. 280
abiotic, p. 280
ecology, p. 280
population, p. 281
community, p. 281
ecosystem, p. 281
biosphere, p. 281
habitat, p. 282
niche, p. 282

16.2
producer, p. 283
autotroph, p. 283
consumer, p. 283
heterotroph, p. 283
herbivore, p. 283
carnivore, p. 283
omnivore, p. 283
decomposer, p. 283
food chain, p. 284
trophic level, p. 284
food web, p. 284
ecological pyramid, p. 285
biomass, p. 285

16.3
biogeochemical cycle, p. 286
evaporation, p. 286
condensation, p. 286
precipitation, p. 286
transpiration, p. 286
eutrophication, p. 288

16.4
succession, p. 289
primary succession, p. 289
pioneer species, p. 290
biodiversity, p. 290
climax community, p. 290
secondary succession, p. 291

292 LIVING THINGS AND THEIR ENVIRONMENT

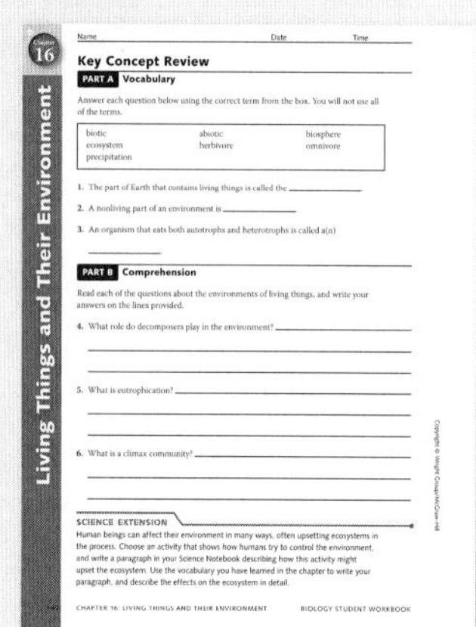
Key Concept Review Workbook, p. 102

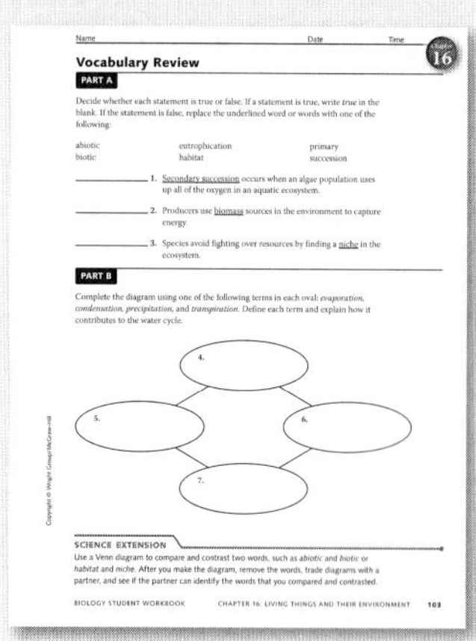
Vocabulary Review Workbook, p. 103

MASTERING CONCEPTS

True or False

If the statement is true, write "true." If it is false, change the underlined word or words to make the statement true.

1. A <u>niche</u> is the place where an organism lives.
2. An organism that does not need to eat food is called a <u>heterotroph</u>.
3. The <u>nitrogen</u> cycle depends on soil bacteria.
4. <u>Secondary succession</u> occurs when a plowed but unplanted field becomes a forest.
5. Without <u>carnivores</u>, ecosystems would be filled with tissues from dead organisms.
6. Energy is <u>gained</u> at each link of a food web.

Short Answer

Answer each of the following in a sentence or brief paragraph.

7. Name three different animal populations that live in your area.
8. A fire destroys 50 square kilometers of mature forest. Summarize how the forest will regrow.
9. One spring, the newspaper reports that a flock of Canada geese has settled at the pond in the town park and is raising goslings. That summer, the newspaper reports that the pond is covered with algae and smells like dead fish. Analyze how these two stories could be related.
10. Discuss why there are more rabbits than wolves living in a forest ecosystem.
11. List a sequence of organisms in a food chain with three trophic levels.

Critical Thinking

Use what you have learned in this chapter to answer each of the following.

12. **Relate** How is photosynthesis related to the carbon cycle?
13. **Give Examples** Humans are omnivores. Give one example of a food humans eat that makes them first-order heterotrophs. Then give another example of a food humans eat that makes them second-order heterotrophs.
14. **Infer** Two closely related species of lice are associated with human beings. Both species drink blood, but head lice are found only in the hair or scalp, and body lice are found only in clothing. Compare the habitat and niche of each species, and infer why they live in these different places.

Standardized Test Question

Choose the letter of the response that correctly answers the question.

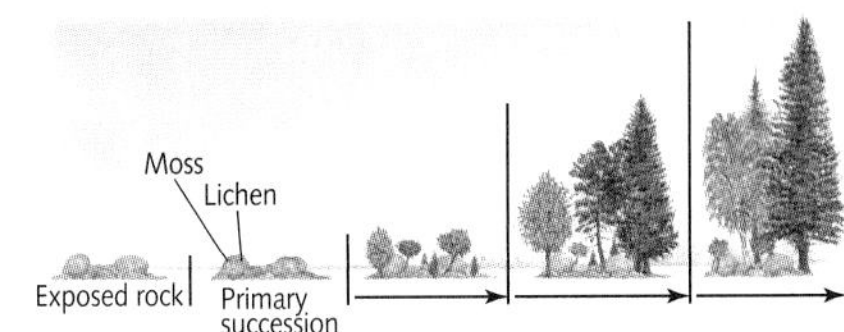

15. The diagram shows the same area over the course of several hundred years. Which term best describes the final picture?
    - A. disturbed ecosystem
    - B. climax community
    - C. abiotic community
    - D. pioneer species

PREPARE FOR CHAPTER TEST

To prepare for the chapter test, create a question from each Learning Goal. Use the information in your Science Notebook to answer each question. Then use these answers to write a well-developed essay about the chapter. Use the Key Concept on the first page of this chapter as your topic sentence.

Test-Taking Tip

If more than one choice for a multiple-choice question seems correct, ask yourself if each choice completely answers the question. If a choice is only partially true, it is probably not the correct answer.

Critical Thinking

12. Photosynthesis removes carbon dioxide from the atmosphere and fixes carbon into organic materials.
13. Humans act as first-order heterotrophs when they eat plants and as second-order heterotrophs when they eat meat.
14. This is a classic example of niche separation. Both species of lice live in the same habitat (the human body) and eat the same thing, but they avoid direct competition by living in different places on the body.

Standardized Test Question

15. B

Reading Links

A Magic Web: The Forest of Barro Colorado Island

With its endless supply of breathtaking full-color visuals, this book is the next best thing to a field trip in a rain forest. The accompanying text, written by a working scientist with decades of firsthand experience studying the tropical forest community of this island off Panama, completes the package. Readers will come away with an understanding of tropical ecology made sharper and more lasting by the context this book so successfully provides.

Leigh, Egbert G. Photographs by Christiane Zeigler. Oxford University Press. 304 pp. Trade ISBN: 978-0-19-514328-7.

Watersheds: A Practical Handbook for Healthy Water

This thoughtful study details the interconnected nature of water systems and underscores the environmental importance of water and nutrient cycles. The book offers a helpful overview of watershed ecology and aquatic habitats, and it discusses the ways in which individuals can help preserve and restore the health of watershed environments. Color illustrations by the author and a simple writing style make this an enjoyable read.

Dobson, Clive and Gregor Gilpin Beck. Illustrated by Clive Dobson. Firefly Books. 160 pp. Trade ISBN: 978-1-55209-330-6.

Curriculum Connection Workbook, p. 106

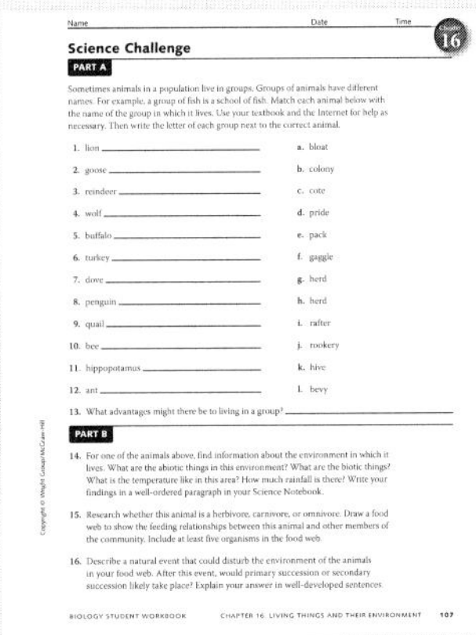

Science Challenge Workbook, p. 107

Chapter 16

Labs

16A Parking Lot or Paradise?

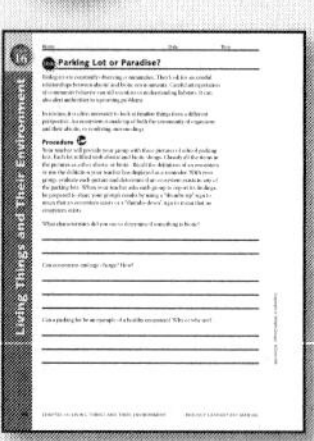

This prechapter introduction activity is designed to determine what students already know about the characteristics of ecosystems by engaging them in classifying, evaluating, and drawing conclusions about familiar areas in the school.

Objectives

- classify abiotic and biotic things
- evaluate known organisms in communities
- draw conclusions about relationships among organisms, nonliving matter, and cycles
- communicate conclusions

Planning

1 class period groups of 4–6 students

Materials (per group)

- 3 pictures of different school parking lots showing cracks in pavement, grass, cars, signs, people, etc.
- 2–3 magnifying glasses or hand lenses
- pencil and paper

Advance Preparation

- In a prominent place in the classroom, display the definition of an ecosystem.
- Choose parking lot pictures that include a variety of abiotic and biotic examples. If time permits, have the class visit the school parking lot and observe some examples firsthand.

Engagement Guide

- Challenge students to think about how they can classify abiotic and biotic things by asking:
  - *What characteristics determine whether an object is living?* (Living things generally exhibit homeostasis, are composed of one or more cells, reproduce, undergo metabolic processes, grow, adapt, and respond to stimuli.)
- Encourage students to recognize relationships within an ecosystem by asking:
  - *What resources are used in an ecosystem?* (Answers include air, water, trees, plants, other animals, and space.)
  - *What characteristics are important for an ecosystem to survive?* Explain your answer. (Students should recognize that many different communities and sufficient abiotic resources are necessary for the ecosystem to survive.)

Going Further

Encourage students to recall any other areas in the school that can be considered an ecosystem and to share their conclusions with the class.

16B Nothing Is Constant but Change

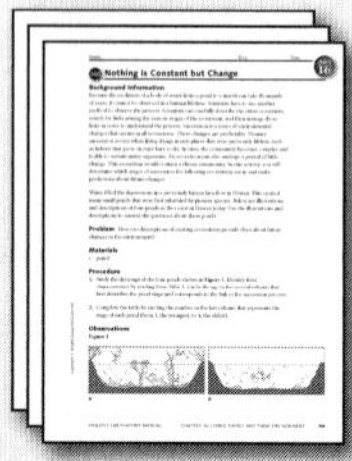

Objectives

- interpret illustrations and descriptions
- identify sequence
- compare and contrast pond stages
- record conclusions

Skill Set

observing, comparing and contrasting, recording and analyzing data, stating conclusions

Planning

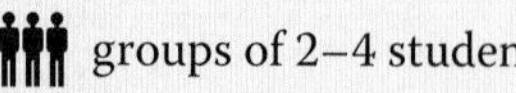

1 class period groups of 2–4 students

Materials

Materials for this activity are listed in the Student Laboratory Manual.

Answers to Observations: Data Table 1

A: Young pond, 2; B: Early pond, 1; C: Mature pond 3; D: Old pond, 4

Answers to Analysis and Conclusions

1. Pond D is the oldest. Pond B is the youngest.
2. Pond B and Pond C; Pond B has ample resources for fish. Pond C would also have the resources to support fish.
3. Pond B is the pond that begins the process of primary succession. There is not a large diversity of organisms. The description mentions the lava field as a base rock; there is no life before the lava.

Going Further

- Bring in pictures of areas around New Orleans after Hurricane Katrina and/or Mount St. Helens after the 1980 eruption. Ask students to determine whether the area is undergoing primary or secondary succession.
- Ask students if there is a limit to the number of times an ecosystem can undergo primary succession or secondary succession.

 Acids and Seed Germination

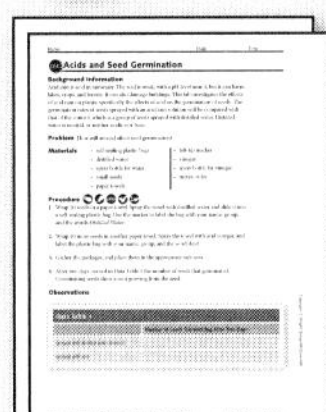

Objectives

- identify cause and effect
- make predictions
- record observations

Skill Set

measuring, observing, comparing and contrasting, recording and analyzing data, classifying, stating conclusions

Planning

 1 class period (Additional time will be needed to observe germinating seeds, record data, and answer questions after two days of seed germination.) Consider doing this lab on Friday and allowing the weekend for germination.

 groups of 2–4 students

Materials

Materials for this activity are listed in the Student Laboratory Manual.

Advance Preparation

Purchase seeds such as radish, turnip, mung bean, or rye grass; aim for 40 seeds per student. Obtain white vinegar (5%). Fill a large container labeled *For Water Spray* with enough seeds for each class. Fill another container labeled *For Acid Spray* with enough seeds for each class. Fill one spray bottle with distilled water for each group. Fill one spray bottle with white vinegar for each group. Gather the other materials, making sure you have enough markers, small cups, toweling, and plastic bags for each group.

Lab Tip

For absolute safety, you may want students to moisten the paper towels by dipping them in the liquids instead of spraying the liquids.

Answers to Observations: Data Table 1

Answers will vary. The number of water-sprayed seeds that germinate will be greater than the number of vinegar-sprayed seeds that germinate.

Answers to Analysis and Conclusions

1. The number of seeds that germinated should be greater in the bag labeled *Distilled Water.* The roots growing from these seeds should be longer than the roots growing from the seeds in the bag labeled *Acid.*
2. The number of sprouted seeds may increase in both bags, but the ratio would still be about the same.
3. Acid rain seems to affect seeds at the very beginning of their growing cycle. If this is accurate, crop and new forest growth would be reduced.
4. Any organism that depends on plants for food could be affected. Examples could include birds, fish, frogs, and humans. There could also be an effect on buildings, statues, roads, and forests.
5. All areas would probably see a decrease in productivity and revenue. This could cause migration of species to other areas, which could cause other problems in the ecosystem.

Going Further

Ask students if the acid rain that is formed in one location stays only in that area. Ask students how people can become informed about the environmental conditions in their city and state.

Chapter 17 Lessons

Introduce Chapter 17

ENGAGE On the board, write and underline the phrase *Summer in [area where students live]*, then write the following words in a column underneath: *weather, plants, animals,* and *land features.* Ask students to close their eyes and picture what summer is like where they live. Ask: *What is the weather like? What plants and animals live in the area? What are the land features (e.g., hills, lakes, mountains)?* Students should share what they visualized with a partner and then with the class. Tell students that they will be looking at these characteristics to learn about the different climates and communities on Earth.

Have students read the Chapter Opener and then discuss with a partner the ways in which summer in the tundra is similar to and different from summer where they live. In their Science Notebooks, they should create a compare and contrast chart to organize this information, using the categories on the board.

Think About Describing a Biome

Provide travel and nature magazines for students to look through if they are having trouble choosing locations. Help students locate their spots on a world map or globe. Encourage students to use their prior knowledge to predict the weather and other natural features of their locations. Students with more limited English fluency may choose to illustrate and label their chosen locations instead of writing about them.

Chapter 17 Earth's Biomes

KEY CONCEPT Around the world, similar communities develop in places with similar climates.

The tundra is a cold, dry, and windy place found in the far north. Short, cool summers and long, cold winters characterize the climate of the tundra. In the summer, the tundra features marshy soil, cool days, and a thick mat of plants that feed caribou, grizzly bears, and many other animals. Tundra also can be found high up on mountains far from the poles. The tundra is one example of a biome. How does the tundra compare with the place where you live?

Think About Describing a Biome

Earth has an amazing variety of landscapes, plant life, and animal life. If you could visit any natural place in the world, where would it be? Would you classify your selected location as a rain forest, coral reef, grassland, or another type of ecosystem?

- Find your travel spot on a world map or a globe. How far is it from the equator?
- In your Science Notebook, describe the plant and animal life, weather, and land or water features of the natural place you would like to visit.

NSTA SCILINKS THE WORLD'S A CLICK AWAY
www.scilinks.org
Biomes **Code: WGB17**

Chapter 17 Planning Guide			
Instructional Periods	**National Standards**	**Lab Manual**	**Workbook**
17.1 2 periods	C.4, C.5, F.2, C.4, D.1; B.6, C.5, UCP.2, UCP.3	**Lab 17A—p. 104** Family Tree or Headstone?	Key Concept Review p. 108 Vocabulary Review p. 109 Graphic Organizer p. 110 Reading Comprehension p. 111 Curriculum Connection p. 112 Science Challenge p. 113
17.2 2 periods	C.4, C.5, F.2, G.2; A.1, C.4, D.1, F.5, F.6, G.2; UCP.1	**Lab 17B—p. 105** Suited for Its Surroundings **Lab 17C—p. 108** Determining the pH of a Solution	
17.3 2 periods	C.4, C.5, F.2; A.2, C.4, D.1, F.3; UCP.1		

Middle School Standard; High School Standard; Unifying Concept and Principle

17.1 The Influence of Climate

Before You Read

Scientists often make observations and then try to trace each observation back to its cause. In your Science Notebook, describe an example of a cause and its effect from your everyday life. Then look for examples of cause and effect as you complete this lesson.

Learning Goals

- Explain how climatic factors determine the distribution of biomes around the world.
- Describe the rain shadow effect.

New Vocabulary

climate
biome
latitude
tropical region
polar region
temperate region
rain shadow effect

Around the world, similar communities develop in places with similar climates. **Climate** is the typical pattern of weather that is observed over a long period of time in an area. A place with water-conserving plants and very little rain is a desert, whether it is in Arizona, China, or Saudi Arabia. Climate is determined by such factors as temperature, precipitation, latitude, altitude, nearness to water, and land features. These factors, in turn, influence the communities that develop. Large areas with similar climax communities are called **biomes** (BI ohmz). A climax community is a stable community that undergoes little or no change in species.

There are two main types of biomes: land biomes and water biomes. The seven major land biomes are shown on the map in **Figure 17.1**.

Figure It Out

1. Which biomes are found in Africa near the Tropic of Cancer?
2. According to the map, which biome is typically found just south of the tundra?

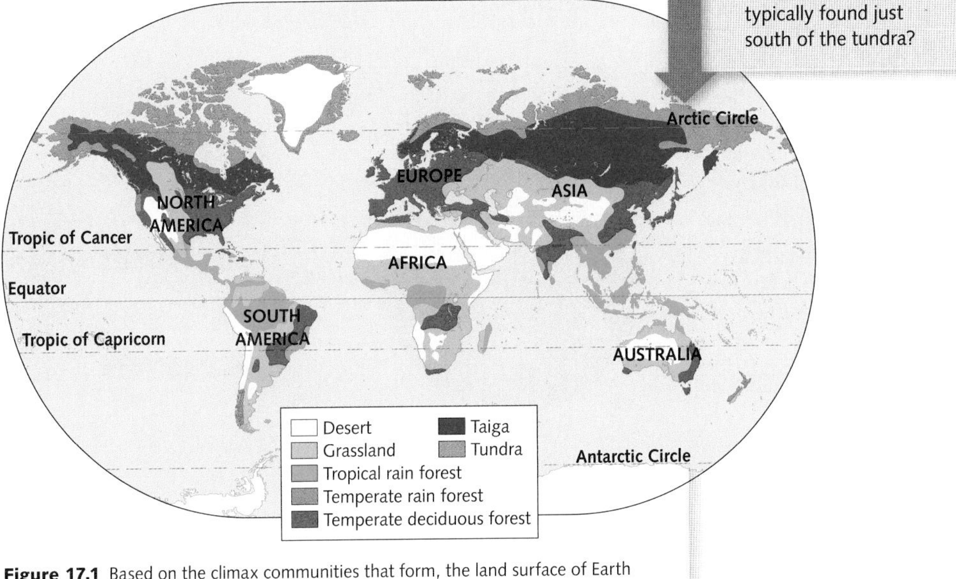

Figure 17.1 Based on the climax communities that form, the land surface of Earth can be divided into seven major biomes.

17.1 Introduce

ENGAGE Ask students if they understand the idea of cause and effect. Accept all reasonable answers and/or examples. Define cause and effect as what makes something happen (cause) and what happens as a result (effect). Provide the following example of cause and effect, and ask students to identify the cause and the effect: *I was tired* (cause), *so I went to bed early* (effect).

Draw a T-chart on the board with the headings *Cause* and *Effect*. Record the above example. Tell students that words such as *because* and *since* help identify a cause, and words such as *so, as a result,* and *therefore* help identify an effect. As partners or in small groups, have students share examples of cause and effect and record them in their Science Notebooks. Ask students to report their ideas to the class.

Before You Read

Check examples of cause and effect that students have recorded in their Science Notebooks, either in sentence form or in T-charts. Discuss with students any errors they may have made in interpreting the relationship.

Vocabulary terms are listed on the first student page of each lesson. You may wish to preview the terms before introducing each lesson. Strategies for teaching the vocabulary appear on the pages where the terms are introduced.

Teach

EXPLAIN that in this lesson, students will learn how climate influences the way plants, animals, and people live.

Figure It Out: Figure 17.1

ANSWER **1.** desert and grasslands **2.** taiga

Science Notebook EXTRA

Encourage students to use the vocabulary section they created in their Science Notebooks. Remind them to record prefixes, suffixes, and root words to help them remember the meanings of vocabulary terms.

ELL Strategy

Think, Pair, Share Ask each student to look at the world map, locate his or her country of origin, and then decide which biome(s) can be found in that part of the world. Encourage students to note the latitude and longitude of their native countries, as well as geographic features and average temperature and rainfall patterns. Have students pair with a partner to discuss their countries and corresponding biomes.

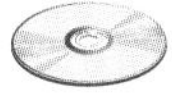

Vocabulary

climate Tell students that *climate* comes from the Greek word *klima*, meaning "having a tendency toward a particular state." Ask students how this definition fits in with their understanding of climate.

biome Unlike many terms with origins that date back thousands of years, this word was created between 1915 and 1920. Explain that *biome* combines the Latin prefix *bio-*, meaning "life," and the Latin suffix *-oma*, meaning "mass."

Teach

ENGAGE Ask students to think about a time when they felt either very hot or very cold. Ask: *Why did you feel that way? Were you dressed properly? What did you do to change the feeling of discomfort?* Write their answers on the board.

EXPLAIN that like humans, plants and other animals have ways of adapting to different temperatures and amounts of precipitation.

CONNECTION: Math

To find his or her height in centimeters, each student must convert his or her height into inches and then multiply by 2.54. For example, 5 ft 3 in. is 63 in.; 63 in. × 2.54 cm = 160.02 cm. To convert centimeters back to inches, divide by 2.54.

To convert degrees Fahrenheit to Celsius, subtract 32 from the temperature, and then multiply by 5 and divide by 9. For example, 45°F − 32 = 13 × 5 = 65 ÷ 9 = 7.2°C. To convert degrees Celsius back to Fahrenheit, use the formula: °F = (°C × 9)/5 + 32.

As You Read

Give students an example of a cause-and-effect relationship involving biomes. For example, because the polar regions are cold most of the year, animals there have developed thicker coats. Have students record examples in their Science Notebooks.

ANSWER As latitude increases, sunlight is less direct and varies greatly with seasons.

Vocabulary

latitude Tell students that latitude is the distance north or south of Earth's equator. On a map or globe, show students the equator and latitude lines.

tropical region Tell students that a region is a large, continuous part of a surface or body. Ask them to think of some examples of regions. Tell them that the word *tropical* means "hot and humid."

polar region The word polar comes from the Latin word *polus*, meaning "pole." Ask students where the poles are on Earth, and explain where the polar regions are.

temperate region Tell students that the word *temperate* means "mild." Have students point to some temperate regions on a globe.

CONNECTION: Math

Scientists use metric units in measurement. A metric unit for length is the centimeter (cm), and a metric unit for temperature is degrees Celsius (°C). The formulas below convert inches (in.) and degrees Fahrenheit (°F) to metric units.

$$\text{cm} = \text{in.} \div 2.54$$

$$°\text{C} = (°\text{F} - 32) \times \frac{5}{9}$$

What is your height in centimeters (cm)? What is the temperature outside in degrees Celsius (°C)?

Temperature and Precipitation

Temperature is a major factor in the development of a community. Some plants have adapted to snow so that it slides off them, and they are able to survive harsh winters. Other plants would be killed by a single frost. The amount of precipitation an area receives also influences the development of a community. Precipitation is water that falls to Earth in the form of rain, snow, sleet, or hail. An oak tree would die quickly from the lack of water in a desert. In a rain forest, a desert cactus would die from too much water. The patterns of temperature and precipitation throughout the year are the most important features of climate.

Latitude and Climate

The **latitude** (LA tuh tewd) of a place describes its distance from the equator. Close to the equator, in the **tropical region**, the Sun's rays strike Earth's surface directly, as shown in **Figure 17.2**. The tropics are hot, with little difference among the seasons. The **polar regions**, near the north and south poles, get less direct sunlight. Polar regions have extremely cold winters and cool summers. During summer at the poles, it is light outside throughout both day and night. But during winter, many days pass without a sunrise. Between the tropical region and the polar regions are **temperate regions**. Temperate regions have four distinct seasons. Conditions in those regions are less extreme than in polar or tropical climates. Look back at Figure 17.1 to see which biomes are found in each region.

As You Read

As you read the lesson, write in your Science Notebook examples of cause-and-effect relationships involving the development of biomes.

How does the amount of sunlight that reaches Earth's surface change as latitude increases?

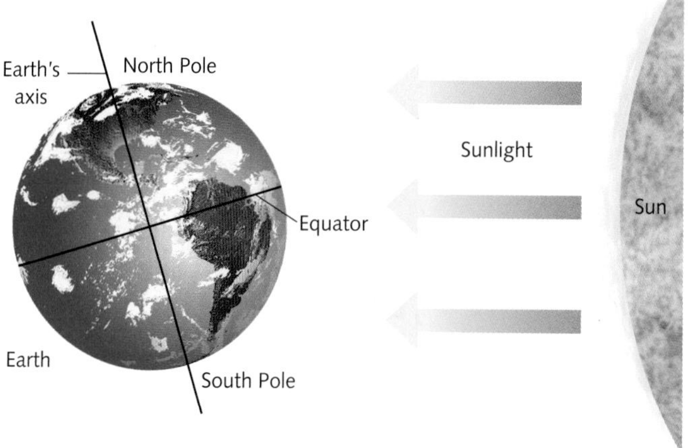

Figure 17.2 Sunlight is more intense near the equator than it is at the north and south poles because the Sun's rays strike the equator more directly. The difference in how the Sun's rays strike various latitudes is due to Earth's curved surface and its tilt on its axis of rotation.

rain shadow effect Tell students that the word *shadow* refers to an area in the shade or an area from which light is blocked. Have students use this meaning to explain why the area beyond a mountain near an ocean is said to be in a rain shadow.

Background Information

The different regions of Earth—tropical, polar, and temperate—have a different climate because of the intensity of the Sun's rays. The tropical region of Earth is the area between the Tropic of Cancer, 23.5 degrees north latitude, and the Tropic of Capricorn, 23.5 degrees south latitude. The polar regions are areas located north and south of 66.5 degrees latitude. The temperate regions are between the tropical and polar regions.

296 EARTH'S BIOMES

Land and Water Features

Altitude is the distance above or below sea level. As you climb up a hill or mountain, your altitude increases. Increasing altitude has the same effect on climate as increasing latitude. The air tends to get colder and drier at higher altitudes. Plants and other organisms that are adapted to these conditions become more common. In fact, a climber may pass through several biomes while going up a single mountain.

Figure 17.3 Climbing a mountain can involve passing through taiga and tundra communities before reaching a cold desert at the top.

Large bodies of water can also affect climate. Land near an ocean tends to have a milder and wetter climate than areas farther inland do. Even large lakes can affect climate. For example, wet air from the Great Lakes causes deep snow to fall on nearby land. This is called lake-effect snow.

A mountain range close to the coast of a continent also affects the climate nearby. Due to the **rain shadow effect**, the area between the ocean and mountains is wet and mild, while the area beyond the mountains is hot and dry. **Figure 17.4** shows how the mountains along the west coast of the United States create a rain shadow.

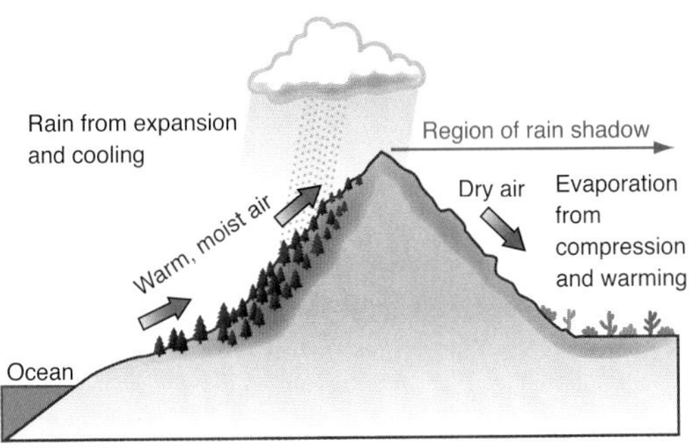

Figure 17.4 Mountains near a coast can create a rain shadow beyond the mountains. Warm, wet ocean air rises over the mountains. As it cools, it releases its moisture as rain. The air that arrives on the other side of the mountains is hot and dry.

After You Read

1. According to the notes in your Science Notebook, what effect does latitude have on climate? Do you think longitude impacts climate? Why or why not? What effect does nearness to a large body of water have on climate?
2. How can the existence of pockets of tundra near the equator be explained?
3. Describe the challenges a polar plant would face if it were moved close to the equator.

Explore It!

Bend two thin slices from a cucumber, and record your observations about their texture. Pour 100 mL of water into each of two shallow bowls. Stir 6 g of table salt into one bowl. Place one cucumber slice in each bowl. Note whether each slice sinks or floats in the water.

After 30 minutes, remove both slices and record your observations about their texture. How are the two slices different? Based on your observations, predict what would happen to a freshwater plant if it were moved to a saltwater environment. Record your answers in your Science Notebook.

Teach

ENGAGE students by asking if anyone has ever gone up a mountain, either by driving, hiking, or skiing. Ask students who have whether they noticed any difference in the way they felt when they were at the top. Give your own example, if necessary.

EXPLAIN that as altitude (the distance above or below sea level) increases, the air becomes less dense. Fewer molecules of air mean less thermal energy; so, the air is colder. Colder air holds less water vapor; so, the air is also drier. Tell students that the presence of oceans, seas, and lakes can also affect climate. The climate near water is often warmer and wetter than that of an area that is not near water.

Explore It!

ANSWER The cucumber slice in freshwater will sink, while the slice in saltwater will float. After soaking, the saltwater slice will be limp and rubbery, while the freshwater slice will be unchanged. The cells of the slice in salt water lose water and internal pressure due to osmosis. A freshwater plant would similarly wilt in salt water.

Assess

EVALUATE Use the After You Read questions and the Alternative Assessment to help you assess students' understanding of the lesson.

After You Read

1. As latitude increases, climate grows cooler and more seasonal, with less direct sunlight. Land near a large body of water tends to have a milder and wetter climate than would an area farther inland.
2. Climate at high altitudes is similar to climate in areas near the north pole.
3. A polar plant would be exposed to stronger sunlight, warmer weather, and possibly more rain.

Background Information

Lake-effect snow occurs when cold air passes over warmer water. Clouds form over the lake, causing snow squalls or showers. The Great Lakes region of the United States often receives lake effect snow. This occurs in the winter when cold, dry arctic air masses blow in from the west or northwest. Areas east or southeast of the Great Lakes receive the most snow; several inches often fall in an hour.

Alternative Assessment

EVALUATE Have students add to the T-charts in their Science Notebooks. On the *Cause* side, students should write *increase in latitude* and then fill in the *Effect* side with ways the climate changes. On the *Cause* side, students should write *close to a large body of water* and then fill in the *Effect* side with the climate. Ask students to draw and label pictures of the three regions found on Earth.

17.2 Introduce

ENGAGE Ask students to think about what they know about Earth: its size, its diversity, its people. Scientists can categorize every land habitat on Earth into one of seven types of communities, or biomes. Ask students to draw upon prior knowledge to explain what a biome is. Then, ask them to think about why scientists divide Earth into these categories the way that they do. Refer students back to the map in Figure 17.1 on page 295 to locate the biomes. Students should share their answers with a partner.

Before You Read

Review the idea that a table is a way to organize information. Draw a table with four columns and seven rows on the board. Label the columns *Biome, Precipitation, Temperature,* and *Important facts*. Write *Tundra* in the first column under *Biome*. Students should create similar tables in their Science Notebooks.

Teach

EXPLAIN that in this lesson, students will learn about the seven land biomes found on Earth. They will record information about each biome in the tables that they created.

Instruct students to read the section on tundra and to study Figure 17.5. When they have finished, do a think-aloud as you complete the first row of the table. Explain the metric conversions by looking at a meter stick for precipitation amount and a metric/English thermometer for temperature.

CONNECTION: Technology

The National Aeronautics and Space Administration (NASA) created a Web site to provide new satellite imagery and scientific information about Earth. The focus is on Earth's climate and environmental changes. The site contains information about seven biomes, including maps, graphs, a biome glossary, and related links. Teacher resources are also included. This Web site can be accessed at **http://eobglossary.gsfc.nasa.gov/Laboratory/Biome/**

Learning Goals

- Describe the characteristics of the seven major land biomes.
- Identify the relationship between specific climatic conditions and the biomes that develop.
- Explain how human activities affect the different biomes.

New Vocabulary

tundra
taiga
temperate rain forest
deciduous forest
grassland
tropical rain forest
desert

Recall Vocabulary

biomass (p. 285)
succession (p. 289)

17.2 Land Biomes

Before You Read

Prepare a table in your Science Notebook with four columns and seven rows. In the first column, record the name of each biome. Use the second and third columns to record precipitation and temperature data. Use the last column to record other important facts you learn about each biome. Preview the lesson and the Learning Goals, and think about where each piece of information will fit into your table.

Tundra

Imagine traveling from the north pole through Canada toward the equator. At the pole, it is so cold and dry that no plants can survive. As you travel south, the temperature gets warmer and low plants emerge. This is the tundra. The **tundra** is a cold, dry, treeless plain. The average daily temperature is –12°C. There is a short summer growing season, but only 15 to 25 cm of precipitation falls each year. Permanently frozen soil, called permafrost, lies beneath the surface and prevents trees from taking root. In the summer, the tundra is filled with flowering plants, lichens, insects, birds, and grazing mammals. During the long, cold winters, most plants and animals become inactive or travel to warmer lands.

Figure 17.5 In summer, the tundra is home to many birds, mammals, and insects. The musk ox is one of the few species that remain active through the long, hard winter.

Taiga

As you proceed south from the tundra, tall trees appear and the summer days grow milder. This is the **taiga** (TI guh), an evergreen forest that covers more area on Earth than any other biome does. Winter is still long and cold, with temperatures falling as low as –50°C, but during the short summer, temperatures can reach 20°C. Precipitation, from 35 to 100 cm per year, falls mainly as snow. Like the tundra, the taiga is full of birds, mammals, and insects throughout the short summer. Animals that stay active in the winter adapt by growing thick coats and living in burrows to keep warm. The coniferous trees have wax-covered needles that conserve water and shed snow.

Figure 17.6 The taiga is dominated by a few species of coniferous trees. Other species may fill in gaps caused by forest fires. Many animals of the taiga migrate south or hibernate during the winter. Others grow warm coats and blend in, like this snowshoe hare.

ELL Strategy

Read Aloud As students read through this lesson, arrange them into groups of three or four, being sure to group similar language speakers together and, if possible, to include a more advanced English speaker in each group. Instruct groups to read aloud to each other, switching roles of reader and listeners within the group after each section of text.

Paraphrase After a student reads each section of text, have members of the group use their own words and language of choice to describe what they read or heard.

Temperate Rain Forest

South of the taiga, several different biomes are possible. Along the rainy Pacific coast lies the largest temperate rain forest in the world. A **temperate rain forest** is a cool, wet, evergreen forest that receives 200 to 400 cm of rain per year. The nearby ocean keeps temperatures, which average 9 to 12°C, mild. Temperate rain forests form between oceans and coastal mountains, where the rain shadow effect causes clouds to drop most of their moisture.

The forest is made up mostly of a few species of hemlock and spruce trees, some of which grow to enormous sizes. Elk, bears, squirrels, and songbirds all thrive in the mild climate. The temperate rain forest has the most biomass of any biome. Biomass is a measure of the density of living and once-living material in an area.

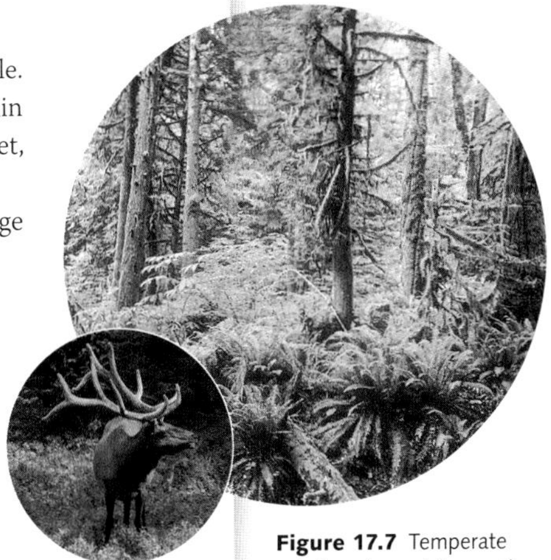

Figure 17.7 Temperate rain forests contain mostly spruce and hemlock trees. These giants can grow for hundreds of years and measure 15 m around at the base. Elk browse the undergrowth and keep the forest floor clear. All but a few small areas of temperate rain forest in North America have been cut down.

Deciduous Forest

Deciduous forests cover much of the eastern United States. **Deciduous** (dih SIH juh wus) **forests** are dominated by hardwood trees that drop their leaves in the cold part of the year. Leaves help trees make food, but they lose water in the winter. Ice can also build up on leafy branches, causing them to break. Deciduous forests receive 70 to 150 cm of precipitation per year. The year is divided into four distinct seasons. Summer temperatures may reach 30°C, while winter temperatures can dip below freezing. Deer, squirrels, turtles, and songbirds can all be found on a walk through a deciduous forest.

The soil of a deciduous forest is rich from the leaves that fall there and decay. European settlers cleared forests for farming and lumber. Some of the forests have since recovered through succession.

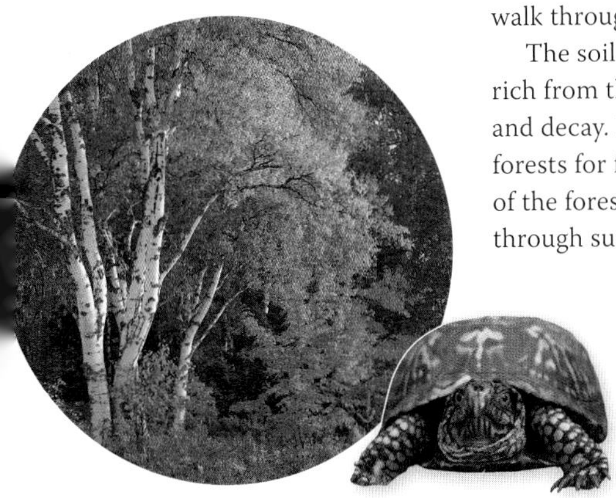

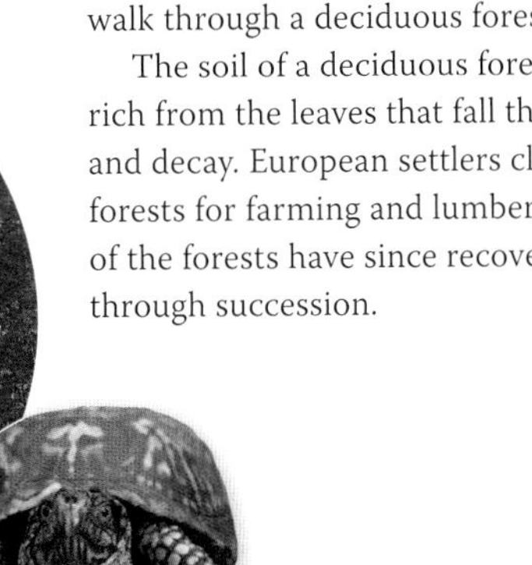

Figure 17.8 Oak, maple, birch, and elm trees are a few of the hardwood species found in a deciduous forest. Animal life includes birds in the treetops and reptiles, such as this box turtle, on the ground.

As You Read

As you read about each land biome, fill in the table in your Science Notebook.

Which biome has long, cold winters and many coniferous trees?

Teach

EXPLAIN to students that in this section, they will learn about the temperate rain forest and the deciduous forest.

Vocabulary

tundra Explain that *tundra* comes from the Finnish word *tunturia*, meaning "treeless plain." The tundra is the coldest of the land biomes.

taiga Tell students that *taiga* is a Russian word and that another name for the taiga is *boreal forest*, which means "northern forest" and is characterized by evergreen coniferous trees. These trees produce needles instead of leaves and cones instead of flowers. They are called evergreens because they have green needles all year long.

temperate rain forest Upon hearing this term, students may think of the tropical rain forest. Explain that *tropical* means "hot and humid." Ask students what *temperate* means ("mild"), and have them describe what they think the temperate rain forest is.

deciduous forest Explain that the word *deciduous* means "to fall off" or "to shed at a specific season or stage of growth." Ask students to think of examples of things that are shed or fall off (antlers, leaves, teeth), and then have them brainstorm what a deciduous forest is.

As You Read

Check each student's Science Notebook to ensure that he or she has been filling in the table correctly. If needed, give students time to complete the first four rows. Remind students to use meter sticks and metric/English thermometers to understand each biome's amount of precipitation and temperatures.

ANSWER The taiga has long, cold winters and evergreen coniferous trees.

Background Information

The coastal or California redwood trees are the tallest trees on Earth. They can grow to a height of 122 m (367 ft). This is the approximate height of a 36-story skyscraper! These trees can measure 7 m (22 ft) wide at the base. The only region in the world where these giants grow is in the temperate rain forest of coastal northern California, where they thrive in moderate to heavy winter rain and summer fog. These redwoods regularly live for more than 600 years, and the longest-living redwood known at this time is more than 2,000 years old.

Name Date Time

Graphic Organizer

PART A

Complete the chart on land biomes.

Biome	Plants	Animals	Temperature
	oak, elm, maple trees	box turtle, deer, squirrel	
desert			
	mostly grasses, few trees		below freezing to 35°C
	coniferous trees	snowshoe hare, bobcat	-50°C to 20°C
		elk, bear, squirrel, songbird	
tropical rain forest			25°C
	low bushes, moss, lichen		-12°C average

PART B

Write the name of the biome on the line next to its description.

_______ 1. found on every continent except Antarctica

_______ 2. covers most of Earth's surface

_______ 3. evergreen forests between oceans and mountains

_______ 4. driest places on Earth

_______ 5. near the equator

SCIENCE EXTENSION

In your Science Notebook, diagram the cause-and-effect relationships between climate, location, plants, and animals in a biome of your choice.

110 CHAPTER 17 EARTH'S BIOMES BIOLOGY STUDENT WORKBOOK

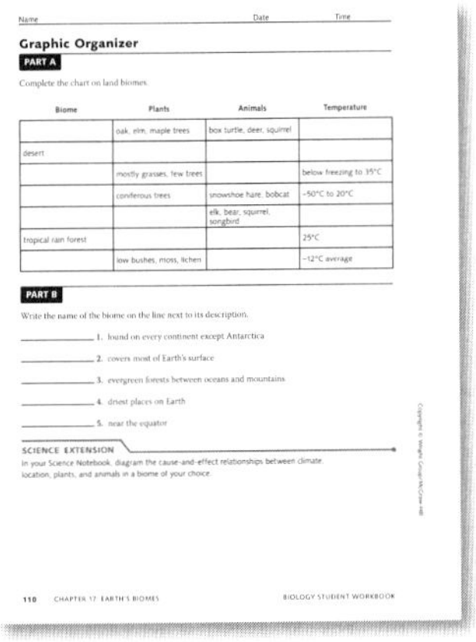

Graphic Organizer Workbook, p. 110

Teach

EXPLAIN that students will learn about the grassland, a biome found on every continent except Antarctica. Have students refer to the world map in Figure 17.1 on page 295 and identify the continents and/or countries where grasslands are located.

Figure It Out: Figure 17.10

ANSWER **1.** There is no rain in June, July, August, or September. **2.** The temperatures are warmer the same during the wet seasons.

CONNECTION: Economics

Elicit students' background knowledge of the term *economist*. If necessary, explain that an economist is a person who studies the economy. Tell students that economics is the science of producing, distributing, and consuming goods and services.

Have students brainstorm natural resources that economists study. If no one mentions land, explain that it is one resource whose value economists estimate.

EXTEND Arrange students into small groups to read the CONNECTION: Economics feature and to discuss the natural areas that students chose to study for the Think About Describing a Biome exercise on page 294. Pair ELL students with English-proficient students, and provide reference materials so that students who have not visited natural areas can learn more about their chosen areas. Encourage students to think about all of the uses and services provided by the areas they selected. These could include oxygen made by plants; water absorption; pest control by birds, bats, and dragonflies; recreation for humans; etc. When students are finished discussing their areas of choice, each student should write a paragraph about the conclusions in his or her Science Notebook.

Figure It Out

1. The climate diagram shows that the Zambian savannah has distinct wet and dry seasons. In which months is there no rainfall at all?
2. What do you notice about temperature during the wet seasons in this area?

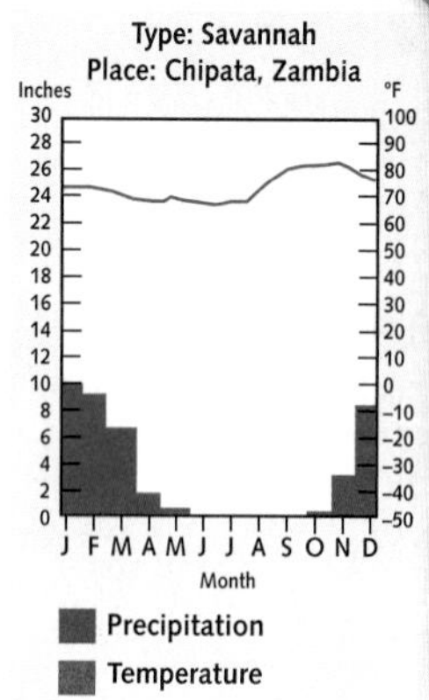

Figure 17.10 A climate diagram shows the average precipitation and temperature range in one area through the year.

Figure 17.9 Grasslands can look like oceans of grass. Many large mammals live there by grazing on the plants that grow from the rich soil. Much of the grasslands in North America have been turned into fields for farming or rangeland for livestock.

Grassland

Grasslands form where there is not enough precipitation to support trees. **Grasslands** are communities in which grasses are the most important plants. In some cases, grasses stretch as far as the eye can see. Trees are found only along the banks of streams and rivers. Grasslands receive 25 to 75 cm of precipitation per year. There is often a long dry season in the summer. The grasslands, or prairies, of North America have cold winters and hot summers. Temperatures range from below freezing to 35°C. Grasslands are found on every continent except Antarctica. In Africa, grasslands are called savannahs; in South America, they are called pampas (PAHM pus); and in Asia, they are called steppes (STEPS).

Many animals live on grasslands, from large grazing mammals such as antelopes to insects such as grasshoppers. Grasses can reach more than 3 m in height. The layers of dead grass that fall on grasslands enrich the soil. Fire is common in grasslands, and both plants and animals are adapted to it. Grasses grow back quickly from their roots after a fire. Animals hide in deep burrows, fly away from harm, or take shelter along a stream.

CONNECTION: Economics

Economists often try to place a value on natural areas. First, the economists calculate the dollar price of the land. Next, they consider the services provided by the land and the enjoyment people get from visiting the land. Wetlands, for example, provide valuable flood control. What value would you place on a park or other natural place you like to visit?

Background Information

The savannahs of Africa are tropical grasslands with individual trees among the grass. High amounts of rain (about 50–120 cm, or 20–50 in.) fall during six to eight months of the year, followed by periods of drought during which fires are common. If this rainfall were distributed throughout the year, the area would be a tropical rain forest instead of grassland.

The pampas of South America and the steppes of Europe are temperate grasslands, which do not contain trees or shrubs. Summers there are hot, winters are cold, and rainfall is moderate. Seasonal droughts also occur in the temperate grasslands. In the United States, the temperate grasslands of the Great Plains are called prairies.

Tropical Rain Forest

Tropical rain forests are lush forests found near the equator, where it is warm and rainy year-round. The forests receive 200 to 600 cm of precipitation per year, and the temperature usually stays close to 25°C. These climate conditions are ideal for many plants, insects, and birds. The greatest competition in the tropical rain forest is for sunlight and nutrients from the soil. Heavy rainfall washes away much of the organic matter on the ground before it has a chance to build up. The poor soil of the tropical rain forest does not make the land good for farming when it is cleared. Nevertheless, over 100,000 square kilometers of tropical rain forest are cleared each year for human use.

Did You Know?

In the 1980s, scientists discovered bacteria living deep underground—some 3 km below the surface. The temperature at that depth is 60°C. Based on the discovery, some scientists think that underground life may outnumber life above ground!

Emergents These giant trees are much higher than the average canopy tree. Birds, such as the macaw, and insects are found here.
Canopy The canopy includes the upper parts of the trees. It's full of life—insects, birds, reptiles, and mammals.
Understory This dark, cool environment is under the canopy leaves but above the ground. Many insects, reptiles, and amphibians live in the understory.
Forest Floor The forest floor is home to many insects, and the largest mammals in the rain forest generally live here.

Figure 17.11 The tropical rain forest contains the most species of any biome. Scientists estimate that 50 to 90 percent of Earth's species live within these rain forests. Each species has a zone in the forest where it lives or spends most of its time.

Teach

ENGAGE Ask students what they remember about tropical regions from the previous lesson. If necessary, remind them that Earth's tropical region is the area between the Tropic of Cancer and the Tropic of Capricorn.

EXPLAIN that in this section, students will learn about the unique structure of the tropical rainforests.

EXTEND To help students understand the temperature that underground bacteria withstand, give students the formula for converting Celsius to Fahrenheit. Ask them to convert 60°C to Fahrenheit: (60°C × 9)/5 + 32 = 140°F. Similarly, to give them a sense of the depth at which some bacteria live, give students the formula for converting kilometers to inches: 3 km × 100,000 = 300,000 cm divided by 2.5 = 120,000 in., or 10,000 ft. Compare this distance to students' heights (approximately 5 ft). It would take 2,000 students standing on each other's shoulders to reach the depth underground that these bacteria live!

Vocabulary

grassland Remind students that a compound word is one word that is made up of two separate words. Ask for an example and its meaning. Then, ask students to identify the two words that make up the word *grassland*. Ask what each word means and then what these words mean when they are combined into one word.

tropical rain forest Ask students to infer what a tropical rain forest is using their knowledge about Earth's tropical regions and temperate rain forests.

Differentiated Instruction

Kinesthetic Have students create a miniature tropical rain forest in the classroom. Each pair of students will need the following materials: one 2-L soda or water bottle with a cap and the top cut off, potting soil, gravel and small rocks, houseplants (such as philodendron), and clear packaging tape. Give students the following steps for making the rain forest: Clean the bottle, and remove its label. Cut the bottle in half. Place about 5 cm of gravel in the bottom half of the bottle. Cover the gravel with 10 cm of potting soil. Place the plants in the soil, and water them. Place the top part of the bottle on the bottom part, and tape the parts together. Place the bottle in a sunny window. Add water in half-cup increments.

In their Science Notebooks, students should record data on the amount of water added, any changes in the plants, and the environment in the bottle.

Teach

 Ask students to look at the photographs in Figure 17.12. Ask them to describe what they think it would be like to live in the environment shown, and why.

EXPLAIN Tell students that in this section, they will learn about deserts, the driest types of places on Earth.

 **Vocabulary**

desert Explain that *desert* has different meanings and pronunciations. As a verb, the second syllable is stressed, and it means "to abandon." As a noun, the first syllable is stressed, and it refers to the next biome that students will learn about. *Desert* contains the prefix *de-*, which means "opposite," and *-sert* from the Latin word *serere*, meaning "to join together." Ask students why they think this biome was named *desert*.

Explain It!

Students may discover that their area does not fall neatly into one of the seven biomes described in the chapter. Provide students with literature from local nature preserves to help them with this activity.

Assess

EVALUATE Use the After You Read questions and the Alternative Assessment to help you assess students' understanding of the lesson.

After You Read

1. Tropical and temperate rain forests both have heavy rain year-round. Tropical rain forests are hotter and wetter and contain an extreme diversity of plants and animals. Temperate rain forests contain only a few species of trees and a moderate number of animal species. Both forests are being clear-cut by humans at a fast rate.
2. Temperate rain forests and deserts are both affected by the rain shadow effect. Mild, wet ocean air travels over coastal land and rises over a mountain range. As the air cools, it drops its moisture as rain, creating a temperate rain forest. After air passes over the mountain, the air drops and warms. This hot, dry air creates a desert.
3. The tundra and desert both get less than 25 cm of precipitation per year.

Figure 17.12 The desert is the driest biome. Desert plants and animals, such as these lizards, are adapted for surviving the lack of water and extreme temperatures.

Desert

A desert forms where there is not enough rainfall to support grasslands. **Deserts** are the driest places on Earth, with less than 25 cm of precipitation per year. In many cases, deserts form because of the rain shadow effect. Moisture from ocean breezes condenses and falls on the sides of mountains. Beyond the mountains, a desert forms. Any rain that does fall on the desert evaporates or runs off the bare soil. Temperatures vary greatly because the dry air does not block the Sun's rays or trap heat overnight. Desert temperatures may rise above 40°C during the day and fall below freezing at night.

Organisms that live in the desert are adapted to temperature extremes and lack of water. Plants such as the cactus store water in their fleshy stems. They have large, shallow root systems that collect rainfall when it occurs. Some cactus species can live for several years off water stored from one rainfall. Other types of plants, including mesquites, have long taproots that reach underground water. Desert plants produce many seeds after a rainfall. These seeds provide food for insects, birds, and small mammals to eat throughout the year. Foxes, coyotes, lizards, and owls are common predators in the desert.

Warm deserts occupy about one-fifth of Earth's land area. Some human activities can increase the size of deserts or make new deserts. Such activities include changing river paths, pumping groundwater, and cutting trees in sensitive areas. Some scientists consider Earth's barren polar regions to be cold deserts. Together, cold deserts and warm deserts occupy about one-third of Earth's land surface.

 **Explain It!**

What is the biome where you live? Find your area on the biome map in Figure 17.1. Use the Internet, books, and other resources to learn what your area was like before its settlement by Europeans. Draw a sketch and write a paragraph to describe a typical natural scene from that time.

After You Read

1. Compare and contrast tropical and temperate rain forests.
2. Which biomes are most affected by the rain shadow effect? Explain how they are affected.
3. Review the table in your Science Notebook. In a well-developed paragraph, discuss which biomes get the least amount of precipitation.

Alternative Assessment

EVALUATE Ask students who have difficulty answering the After You Read questions to answer the following questions using their biome tables:

1. Which biome is hottest?
2. Which biome is coldest?
3. Compare the data of any two biomes. Which is more populated by animals? Which is more populated by humans?

Background Information

There are four types of deserts. Hot and dry deserts are warm year-round and very hot in summer. Rainfall occurs in short bursts. Semiarid deserts have moderately long, dry summers and winters with spotty rainfall. Coastal deserts can be cool or warm, and more rainfall occurs there than in hot and dry and semiarid deserts. Cold deserts have moderate summers and long, cold winters with heavy snow. It rains in spring and fall. Cold deserts get the most precipitation.

17.3 Water Biomes

Before You Read

In your Science Notebook, draw a water depth scale as a vertical line. Label the top of the line *Shallow Water* and the bottom *Deep Water*. Preview the lesson to look for features that change as water becomes deeper. Add any features you find in this lesson to the proper depth on your line.

Learning Goals

- Describe the different water biomes.
- Explain how water biomes are affected by depth and movement.

New Vocabulary

freshwater
wetland
estuary
marine
plankton
coral reef
seashore

Recall Vocabulary

decomposer (p. 283)

About 75 percent of Earth's surface is covered by water. The water may be deep or shallow, fresh or salty, moving or still. Each of these factors affects the kinds of organisms that live in the water and the biome that develops.

The Freshwater Biome

Freshwater is water that contains very little salt. Wetlands, ponds, lakes, streams, and rivers all typically contain freshwater. Only about one percent of the water on Earth is usable freshwater. The rest is salty or is frozen in icebergs and the polar ice caps.

Wetlands Areas where the soil is wet enough for aquatic plants to grow are called **wetlands**. The water in wetlands is very shallow, and the soil may dry out for part of the year. Layers of fallen plants make the soil rich in nutrients. Cattails, water lilies, and cypress trees grow thickly in wetlands. Snails, frogs, birds, and many insects make their homes in wetlands, as well.

Ponds and Lakes Ponds and lakes form where water pools in a low place in the ground. A shallow body of water with plants growing all the way to the middle is called a pond. A larger body of water is called a lake. In the shallow upper layer of a lake, the water is warm and full of nutrients. Sunlight supports the growth of plants. The plants create plenty of oxygen for animals such as fish, frogs, and snails. Sunlight does not penetrate the cold, deeper regions of a lake. There are fewer nutrients in the deep water, and plants cannot grow there. Decomposers consume the oxygen in deep water, preventing most animals from living in the depths. The layers of lake water usually mix in spring and autumn.

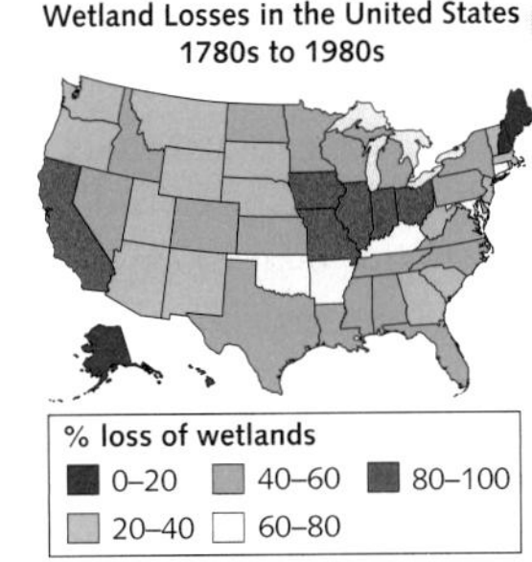

Figure 17.13 Across the United States, wetlands have been drained to gain usable land and to control mosquitoes. Draining wetlands creates good cropland, but it may increase flooding problems downstream.

Figure It Out

1. Which regions of the country have lost the highest percentage of their wetlands?
2. Compare this map with the biome map in Figure 17.1. In which biome are the states with the greatest loss of wetlands located?

17.3 Introduce

ENGAGE Share with students a picture of Earth taken from space. Ask: *Why is Earth called the "blue planet"?* As you listen to and record student answers, have students read the first paragraph on this page.

EXPLAIN Discuss with students the use and value of a pie chart. Encourage them to record information for a chart as they read the lesson. Have them create a pie chart to represent the various forms of Earth's water.

Before You Read

Draw a vertical line on the board, and title it *Water Depth Scale*. Label the top *Shallow Water* and the bottom *Deep Water*. Ask students to draw the same diagram in their Science Notebooks. Explain that as they read the lesson, they will fill in information about temperature, oxygen level, light, and nutrients. Have students predict what they think will happen to these water features as they go from shallow water to deep water.

Teach

EXPLAIN that as with land biomes, Earth has various water biomes. Tell students that in this lesson, they will learn about these freshwater and saltwater biomes.

Vocabulary

freshwater Ask students to identify the two words that make up this compound word.

wetland Ask students what they think this compound word means. Tell them that other words for wetlands are *marsh* and *swamp*.

Figure It Out: Figure 17.13

ANSWER **1.** California and several Midwest states **2.** the deciduous forest biome

Teacher Alert

Freshwater is different from drinking water. Freshwater is nearly or completely free of salt, but it is not necessarily safe for consumption. Water that is safe to drink is called potable water or drinking water.

Background Information

Salt marshes are coastal wetlands that are covered at least once a month by the rising tide. They are sometimes called tidal marshes. Salt marshes are found on the edges of estuaries and in coastal areas between high- and low-tide zones. These areas are rich in marine life. The plants in salt marshes exhibit an interesting array of colors, including gray, brown, and green.

Science Notebook EXTRA

Have each student create a three-column chart titled *Freshwater Biomes* in his or her Science Notebook. Ask students to label the columns *Lakes and Ponds, Estuaries,* and *Rivers and Streams*. Students should complete the chart as they read the lesson. Provide magazines and books as additional resources.

Teach

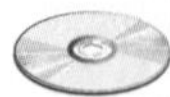

EXPLAIN that students will learn about a third type of freshwater biome, rivers and streams.

Vocabulary

estuary Tell students that *estuary* is derived from the Latin word *aestuarium*, from *aestus*, meaning "boiling" or "tide." Ask students to discuss how *boiling* and *tide* might relate to the word *estuary* and its meaning.

marine Explain that this word is derived from the Latin word *marinus*, from *mare*, meaning "sea." Other words derived from *mare* include *marines*, *mariner*, and *maritime*.

plankton Explain that this word comes from the Greek word *plazesthai*, meaning "to wander" or "to drift." Ask students why these types of sea plants and animals were named *plankton*.

coral reef Explain that *reef* is derived from the old English word *ribb*, meaning "rib." Ask students to look at the photograph of coral reef in Figure 17.15 and hypothesize about why *reef* is an appropriate name.

seashore Explain that a *shore* is "land along the water's edge." *Seashore* refers specifically to land along the sea or ocean.

As You Read

Check each student's Science Notebook to ensure that he or she has included information about temperature, oxygen level, light, and nutrients on the water depth scale.

ANSWER Shallow water contains more oxygen due to the presence of photosynthetic plants and the mixing of surface water and air.

Extend It!

Have students review the concepts of food chains and food webs before beginning the activity.

ANSWER Phytoplankton are suspended aquatic microscopic plants such as green algae; zooplankton are small, generally microscopic animals and fat-rich eggs of animals that float with currents. Plankton are a source of food for many forms of life in the ocean; they form the base of the ocean food chain.

Check students' illustrations for accuracy.

As You Read

Look for information about how temperature, oxygen level, light, and nutrients are affected by water depth. Add pertinent information to your water depth scale.

Does shallow water contain more or less oxygen than deep water does? Explain your answer.

Rivers and Streams Rivers and streams contain moving water. The movement of the water mixes in oxygen from the air. Sunlight reaches the bottom of shallow rivers and streams. Slow-moving rivers have muddy bottoms with plants growing in them. Swift streams have rocky bottoms. The organisms in a fast-moving stream are adapted for clinging to the rocks so they will not be washed downstream. Many fish, insects, and other invertebrates live in rivers and streams. Birds, otters, and alligators visit the streams to eat the creatures living there.

Water gradually travels downhill until it reaches the ocean. The area where the freshwater of a river mixes with the salty water of the sea is called an **estuary** (ES chuh wer ee). Rivers bring many nutrients to the estuary. Estuaries provide rich habitats for grasses, young sea animals, and birds.

Figure 17.14 The freshwater biome includes wetlands *(left)*, ponds and lakes *(center)*, and rivers and streams *(right)*.

Extend It!

Plankton form the base of the ocean food chain. Research plankton and find out the difference between phytoplankton and zooplankton. Record this information in your Science Notebook. Also explain the importance of plankton and support your explanation with an illustration of a marine food chain or food web.

The Marine Biome

The oceans and seas of the world make up the **marine**, or saltwater, biome. The marine biome covers most of Earth's surface. Like freshwater lakes, oceans can be divided into shallow and deep layers. Sunlight penetrates about 200 m into the water, creating a warm layer where plants can grow. The plants produce oxygen, allowing many sea creatures to live. The base of most ocean food chains is made up of **plankton**, tiny algae, bacteria, and animals that float in the water. Even the blue whale, the largest animal on Earth, survives by eating plankton. The deep water of the ocean is cold, dark, and largely lifeless except for areas around undersea volcanoes. Autotrophic bacteria that do not use sunlight as their energy source form the base of the food chains in these areas.

ELL Strategy

Practice Using Vocabulary Ask students to write each of the lesson's vocabulary terms on a separate index card. On the back of each card, students should draw a picture to represent the term. Have pairs of students take turns guessing what each other's pictures represent and then using each word in a sentence out loud.

Field Study

Give students small, lidded jars, and take them to a nearby lake, pond, stream, or river. Have them record observations about the water: size, shape, depth, movement of water, appearance, nearby plant and animal life, etc. Discuss safety cautions for collecting water samples, and have students collect water samples. In the classroom, have students observe and identify organisms in the water. Provide hand lenses and field guides to assist in identification.

Coral reefs form in the shallow, warm water of the tropics. **Coral reefs** are the accumulated skeletons of tiny coral animals. Algae and mollusks that secrete calcium-containing shells help cement colonies of different types of corals together into a reef. The complicated shapes of the reefs provide habitats for many species of invertebrates and fish. Birds and sea mammals depend on the reef animals for food. Coral reefs are sensitive ecosystems that can be damaged easily by ships, pollution, and other human activities.

Seashores are the edge between land and marine biomes. At high tide, the seashore is wet and salty. At low tide, the seashore dries out. The organisms that live on the seashore are adapted to these changing conditions. Near the seashore, forests of giant seaweed called kelp support sea urchins, sea stars, and sea otters.

CONNECTION: Earth Science

The discovery of thriving ecosystems deep in the ocean was a surprise to both Earth scientists and biologists. Sunlight penetrates only about 200 m into the ocean. As a result, scientists expected to find only decomposers in the depths.

The first photographs from thousands of meters below the surface of the ocean were taken in the 1970s. The pictures showed colorful shrimps, worms, and layers of bacteria. Researchers discovered that some bacteria can live off the hydrogen sulfide and other chemicals released by underwater volcanoes. These bacteria form the basis of a new ecosystem never before seen by humans.

Undersea communities are exciting for many reasons. First, they may represent the earliest life on Earth. In addition, scientists have found that some deep-sea creatures contain chemicals that may be useful in medicine and industry. Scientists also recognize that there is more to study and learn about the oceans of the world. Finally, by studying these communities, scientists hope to learn if and how life can survive on planets other than Earth.

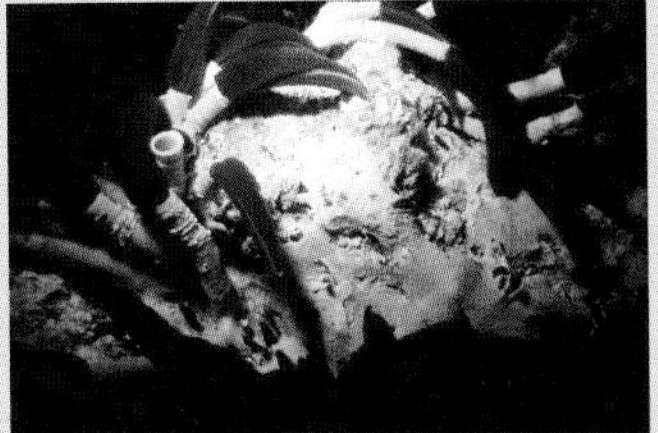

Figure 17.15 Shallow, well-lit ocean water supports many species of fish, including tuna *(top)*. Coral reefs *(center)* provide homes to colorful fish and invertebrates. Plants and animals of the seashore *(bottom)* are adapted to changing water, temperature, and salt levels.

After You Read

1. Compare the amount of freshwater to the amount of salt water on Earth.
2. According to the depth scale in your Science Notebook, where would you expect to find plants growing in water?
3. Create a sample food chain for a freshwater ecosystem.

Teach

EXPLAIN that students will learn about coral reefs and seashores in this section. Ask what they already know about either or both.

CONNECTION: Earth Science

Scientists who research communities near undersea vents travel kilometers beneath the ocean's surface in research vessels to study them. These communities are found in the most extreme environment on Earth, where temperatures are hot enough to melt lead. In 1976, scientists discovered the first of these communities in the middle of the Atlantic Ocean. Since then, scientists have continued to study the communities using more and more advanced technology. A movie was recently made about this topic, called *Volcanoes of the Deep Sea*.

Assess

EVALUATE Use the After You Read questions and the Alternative Assessment to help you assess students' understanding of the lesson.

After You Read

1. There is far more salt water on Earth. About 75 percent of Earth's surface is covered by salt water, and only one percent is covered by liquid freshwater.
2. Plants are found in the shallowest 200 meters, where light can penetrate.
3. Sample answer: aquatic plants → insects → frogs → herons

Alternative Assessment

EVALUATE Have each student use his or her completed water depth scale diagram to write a paragraph about what is found at various water levels.

Background Information

Kelp is large seaweed. It grows in cold, clear, nutrient-rich ocean regions. Colonies of kelp are called kelp forests. The largest kelp grows up to 30 cm per day and to a total length of more than 60 m. Larger kelp forests are found in the Arctic and Antarctic Circles. Fish and invertebrates live in this marine ecosystem.

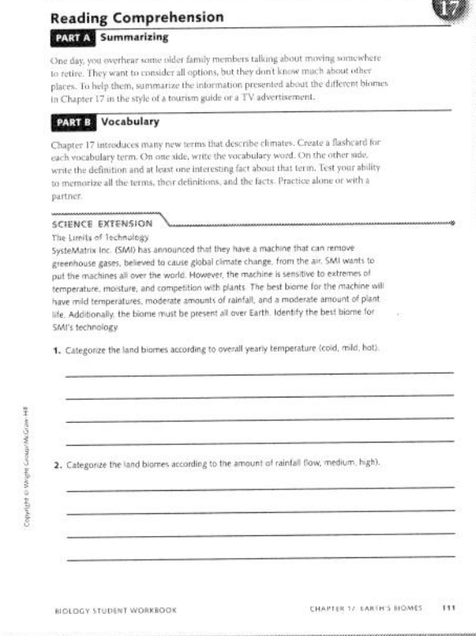

Name Date Time Chapter 17

Reading Comprehension

PART A Summarizing

One day, you overhear some older family members talking about moving somewhere to retire. They want to consider all options, but they don't know much about other places. To help them, summarize the information presented about the different biomes in Chapter 17 in the style of a tourism guide or a TV advertisement.

PART B Vocabulary

Chapter 17 introduces many new terms that describe climates. Create a flashcard for each vocabulary term. On one side, write the vocabulary word. On the other side, write the definition and at least one interesting fact about that term. Test your ability to memorize all the terms, their definitions, and the facts. Practice alone or with a partner.

SCIENCE EXTENSION

The Limits of Technology

SysteMatrix Inc. (SMI) has announced that they have a machine that can remove greenhouse gases, believed to cause global climate change, from the air. SMI wants to put the machines all over the world. However, the machine is sensitive to extremes of temperature, moisture, and competition with plants. The best biome for the machine will have mild temperatures, moderate amounts of rainfall, and a moderate amount of plant life. Additionally, the biome must be present all over Earth. Identify the best biome for SMI's technology.

1. Categorize the land biomes according to overall yearly temperature (cold, mild, hot).

2. Categorize the land biomes according to the amount of rainfall (low, medium, high).

Copyright © Wright Group/McGraw-Hill

BIOLOGY STUDENT WORKBOOK CHAPTER 17 EARTH'S BIOMES 111

Reading Comprehension Workbook, p. 111

Chapter 17 Summary

VOCABULARY REVIEW

Check students' sentences or paragraphs to make sure they understand the meaning of each vocabulary term.

PREPARE FOR CHAPTER TEST

Evaluate students' essays using the following criteria:

1. The topic sentence, or main idea, should restate the Key Concept.
2. The supporting paragraphs should incorporate the answers to the Learning Goal questions students have written and include details, facts, and examples they have recorded in their Science Notebooks.
3. The concluding sentence should sum up the main idea of the chapter and restate the Key Concept.

MASTERING CONCEPTS

True or False

1. True
2. True
3. False, climate
4. False, ponds
5. False, Deciduous forests, grasslands
6. True

Short Answer

7. Permafrost is the main factor that inhibits forests in tundras, as well as a short growing season, low precipitation, and high winds.
8. depth of water; speed of moving water; temperatures at different levels; amount of oxygen in the water; kinds of organisms; and amount of sunlight at different levels
9. A grassland would be too dry for a tree from a tropical rain forest. Also, the tree could not survive the cold winter or fires.
10. One possible marine food chain: plankton → small fish → large fish → shark
11. Tropical regions are hot and moist year round and lack seasons. Temperate regions have four distinct seasons with cold winters and hot summers. Polar regions have long, dark, extremely cold winters and short, cool summers with long periods of daylight.
12. Warm temperatures, abundant moisture, and the many layers of the rain forest provide a range of habitats.
13. tropical and temperate rain forests

Chapter 17

Summary

KEY CONCEPTS

17.1 The Influence of Climate

- Large areas with similar climax communities are called biomes.
- Climate determines which biome develops in an area.
- Major factors influencing climate include temperature, precipitation, latitude, altitude, land features, and water features.
- In the rain shadow effect, the area between the ocean and mountains is wet and mild, while the area beyond the mountains is hot and dry.

17.2 Land Biomes

- Earth's land surface can be divided into seven major biomes: tundra, taiga, temperate rain forest, deciduous forest, grassland, tropical rain forest, and desert.
- Each biome has characteristic plant life and animal life.
- Each biome has characteristic ranges of temperature and precipitation.
- Organisms are adapted to the conditions of their biome.
- Human activities have made major changes in some biomes.

17.3 Water Biomes

- Most of Earth's surface is covered by the freshwater biome and marine biome.
- The freshwater biome includes wetlands, ponds and lakes, and rivers and streams.
- An estuary is the area where the freshwater of a river mixes with the salt water of the sea.
- The marine biome includes oceans and seas, coral reefs, and seashores.
- Depth and movement have important effects on water conditions.

VOCABULARY REVIEW

Write each term in a complete sentence, or write a paragraph relating several terms.

17.1
climate, p. 295
biome, p. 295
latitude, p. 296
tropical region, p. 296
polar region, p. 296
temperate region, p. 296
rain shadow effect, p. 297

17.2
tundra, p. 298
taiga, p. 298
temperate rain forest, p. 299
deciduous forest, p. 299
grassland, p. 300
tropical rain forest, p. 301
desert, p. 302

17.3
freshwater, p. 303
wetland, p. 303
estuary, p. 304
marine, p. 304
plankton, p. 304
coral reef, p. 305
seashore, p. 305

PREPARE FOR CHAPTER TEST

To prepare for the chapter test, create a question from each Learning Goal. Use the information in your Science Notebook to answer each question. Then use these answers to write a well-developed essay about the chapter. Use the Key Concept on the first page of this chapter as your topic sentence.

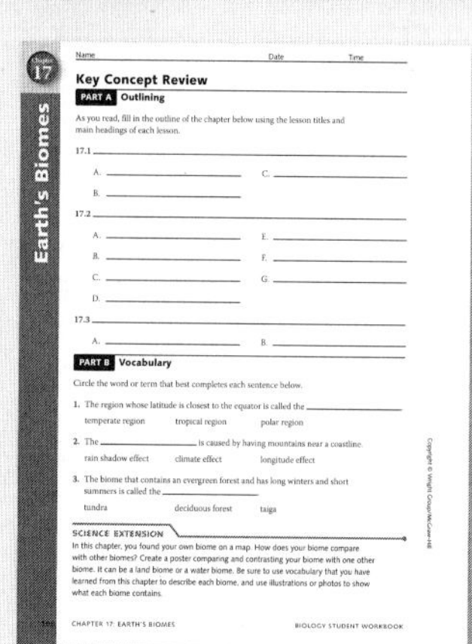

Key Concept Review
Workbook, p. 108

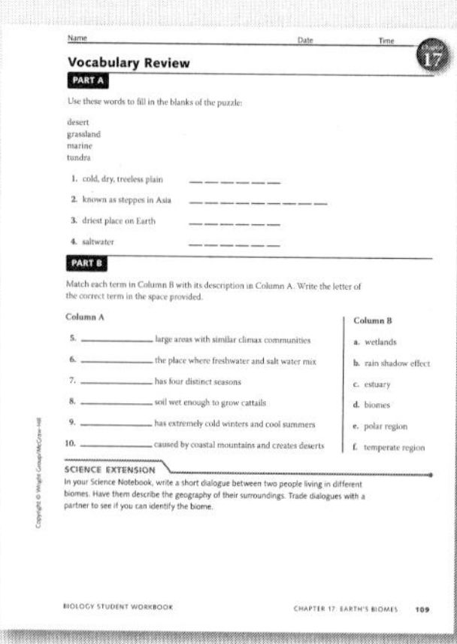

Vocabulary Review
Workbook, p. 109

MASTERING CONCEPTS

True or False

If the statement is true, write "true." If it is false, change the underlined word or words to make the statement true.

1. Deciduous forest trees lose their leaves during winter.
2. Most of the water on Earth is marine water.
3. The weather pattern of an area is called its latitude.
4. Plants grow all the way to the center of lakes.
5. Tropical rain forests and deserts have very rich soil.
6. Freshwater and marine water mix in a(n) estuary.

Short Answer

Answer each of the following in a sentence or brief paragraph.

7. Explain what prevents forests from growing in the tundra.
8. List four differences between a deep lake and a fast-moving stream.
9. Describe the challenges a tree from a tropical rain forest would face in a grassland.
10. Diagram a possible food chain in a marine biome.
11. Describe the seasons in a tropical region, a temperate region, and a polar region.
12. Explain the factors that allow a tropical rain forest to be home to more species than any other biome.
13. Identify the biomes in which the temperature never falls below freezing.

Critical Thinking

Use what you have learned in this chapter to answer each of the following.

14. **Evaluate** Choose one biome that has been largely removed by humans and another that has not been so severely affected. Evaluate why the biomes have been treated differently by humans.
15. **Relate** How do the discoveries of undersea vents and deep underground life relate to the search for life on other planets?
16. **Analyze** Choose an organism that lives near you. Analyze how this organism is adapted to the climate in which you live.

Standardized Test Question

Choose the letter of the response that correctly answers the question.

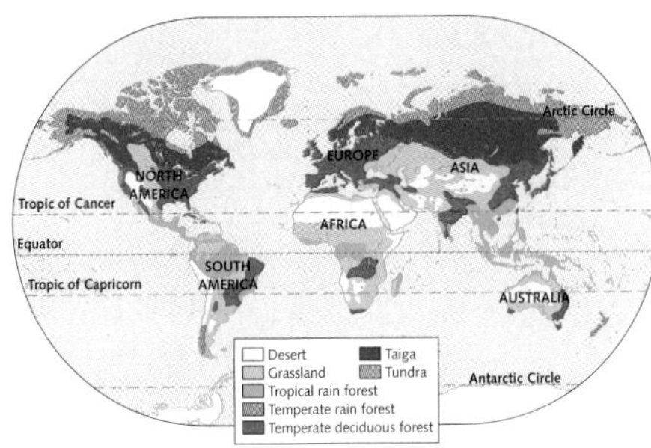

17. According to the map, grasslands are found in ________ regions.
    A. temperate and polar
    B. polar and tropical
    C. polar, temperate, and tropical
    D. temperate and tropical

Test-Taking Tip

If you finish before time is up, check your answers. Make sure you answered each part of every question and did not skip any parts.

Curriculum Connection Workbook, p. 112

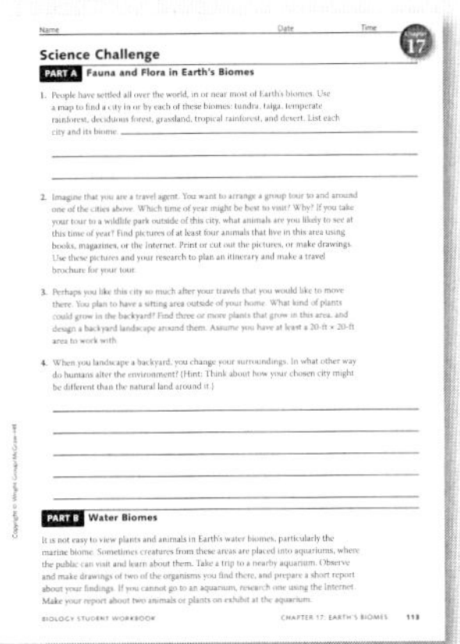

Science Challenge Workbook, p. 113

Critical Thinking

14. Answers will vary. Students may choose several combinations of affected and unaffected biomes. One combination is the wetlands and deserts. Wetlands have been drained because their rich soil makes good cropland. In addition, wetlands harbor mosquitoes that carry diseases. Deserts, on the other hand, have been less affected by human actions because of poor soil, lack of useable timber, and lack of precipitation.
15. Both represent harsh environments similar to those found on some other planets. The organisms found on Earth prove that life can evolve and survive under high pressure, without oxygen or light, and in a bath of chemicals that would kill most creatures. Therefore, life could possibly evolve on other planets.
16. Answers will vary. Students might discuss adaptations to extreme heat or cold, dry weather or floods, wind, fire, or other climatic conditions.

Standardized Test Question

17. D

Reading Links

Biomes of the Future

This exploration of the possible worldwide ecological and climatic effects of global warming, such as the spread of desert regions or the disappearance of coastal areas, offers a timely and important supplement to the study of Earth's existing biomes. The author draws on past evidence of weather and climate change to inform his discussion.

Stein, Paul. Rosen Publishing Group. 64 pp. Illustrated. Library ISBN: 978-0-8239-3410-2.

Life in a Desert

By focusing its study of the desert biome on the Sonoran Desert in North America, this lively and readable book will give students a more thorough understanding of a specific biome in a real context. The volume is filled with interesting maps, figures, and photographs and would serve as a useful resource for independent or group projects.

Patent, Dorothy Hinshaw. Lerner Publishing Group. 72 pp. Illustrations and photography by William Munoz. Library ISBN: 978-0-8225-2140-2.

17A Family Tree or Headstone?

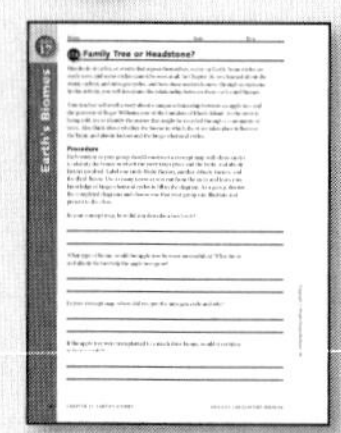

This prechapter introduction activity is designed to determine what students already know about biogeochemical cycles and the global connections among abiotic and biotic factors, biogeochemical cycles, and biomes. These connections are not always easily understood by students. Through a story of familiar organisms and the less familiar jobs they do, complex information about the universal connections among organisms, cycles, and biomes can become more apparent and relevant.

Retelling of "The Gift of the Tree"

Explain to students that Roger Williams, one of the founders of Rhode Island, was a strong supporter of religious freedom and Native-American land rights. In 1652, he was instrumental in passing a law to make slavery illegal in Rhode Island. Roger Williams died in 1864, at the age of 80. He was buried under an apple tree on his property.

Years later, the Rhode Island Historical Society decided to unearth his coffin in order to conduct a proper funeral ceremony for this great historical figure. It is said that when they dug beneath the apple tree he was buried under, they did not find his body! The roots of the apple tree had grown through his coffin. They curved around the area where his head was once located, and grew into his chest cavity and down his spine. The roots then branched where his legs would have been, and turned upward at the location of his feet. It seemed as if his body had been replaced by the roots of an apple tree.

Objectives

- draw conclusions about the effects of cycles
- identify biomes and biotic and abiotic factors
- summarize connections among cycles, biotic and abiotic factors, and biomes

Planning

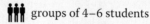

 1 class period 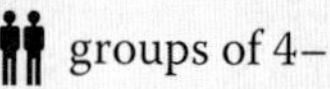 groups of 4–6 students

Materials (per group)

- pencil

Advance Preparation

- Practice retelling the story once before sharing it with students.
- Have copies of the diagrams of the water, carbon, and nitrogen cycles from Chapter 16 (Figures 16.10, 16.11, and 16.12 on pp. 286–288) available for students to reference, or allow students to have their textbooks open to the figures as you retell the story.

Engagement Guide

- Reading or retelling a story aloud to students is a helpful cognitive development tool.
- Proper classroom attitude is important. All students should listen carefully until the story has been told. Use voice inflection to add interest and engage students.
- Pictures of trees or books with trees on the cover could serve as useful visual props for students to view as you retell the story. Try to gather materials that represent a variety of biomes.
- Stimulate student thinking by asking:
  - *In the concept map, how did you describe a tree's role?* (The tree belongs in the *Biotic* circle, because it is a living thing.)
  - *In what type of biome would the apple tree be most successful? Why?* (deciduous forest, because the biotic and abiotic factors—rich soils, rainfall, seasonal weather, pollinators—would best support its survival there)
  - *In your concept map, where did you put the nitrogen cycle? Why?* (in both the *Biotic* and *Abiotic* circles, because it is a biogeochemical cycle and thus has living and nonliving parts)
  - *If the apple tree were transplanted to a much drier biome, would it continue to be successful?* (probably not, as apple trees need fairly temperate weather with regular rainfall)
  - *If the story took place in another biome, what parts of your concept map would change?* (Many parts of the Venn diagram would change, as the biotic and abiotic factors vary greatly from one biome to another.)

Going Further

Pose the following question to students: *Do biomes influence organisms or do organisms influence biomes?* Discuss the answers as a class. Then, have students write stories of their own about a different biome and all the attending biotic and abiotic factors.

17B Suited for Its Surroundings

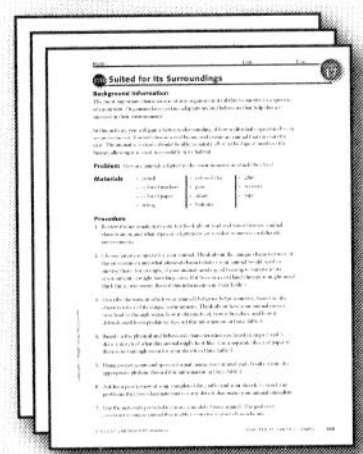

Objectives

- make predictions about effects of environment on living things
- classify characteristics of organisms
- compare and contrast biomes

Skill Set

evaluating, comparing and contrasting, classifying, stating conclusions

Planning

2 class periods  groups of 2–4 students

Materials

Materials for this activity are listed in the Student Laboratory Manual.

Answers to Observations: Data Table 1

The table should be completed before construction of the animal begins. Peer review reduces teaching time and allows students to act as instructors and hear criticism in a nontraditional way.

Answers to Analysis and Conclusions

1. Answers will vary but should include reasonable examples of climate limits and landforms.
2. Answers will vary, but students should list at least three physical conditions and animal characteristics that match the conditions.
3. Answers will vary, but phylum specifications should be met. (Arthropoda: invertebrate, jointed appendages; Chordata: segmented backbone, bilateral symmetry, two pairs of jointed appendages; Echinodermata: endoskeleton, deuterostomes; Mollusca: invertebrate, true body coelom)
4. Answers will vary but should be reasonable for the chosen biome and adaptation for survival.

Going Further

Group and display students' animals by biome. Ask students to individually explain important features of their animals and the reasoning behind their choices. Ask students to put their animals in an evolutionary order. (This could be done by having one student physically arrange animals and then asking for student comments.) Asking students to create a food chain, web, or pyramid using one of the biomes and the new animals that inhabit it is another option.

17C Determining the pH of a Solution

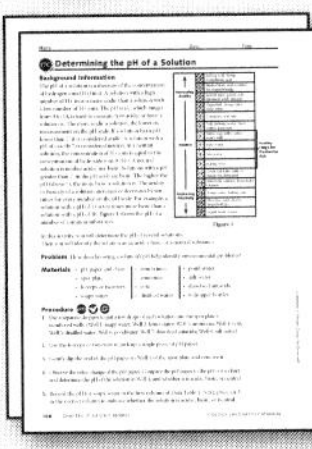

Objectives

- use indicator paper to determine the pH of solutions
- record observations
- use data to infer effects of pH

Skill Set

observing, comparing and contrasting, recording and analyzing data, classifying, stating conclusions

Planning

1 class period groups of 2–4 students

Materials

Materials for this activity are listed in the Student Laboratory Manual.

Lab Tip

Household ammonia can be diluted to one part per hundred in distilled water and still show strong alkalinity with pH paper.

Advance Preparation

Provide pH paper with a pH identification chart. Prepare solutions of soapy water, salt water, and dissolved antacids.

Answers to Observations: Data Table 1

soapy water: 12, basic; lemon juice: 2, acidic; ammonia: 11, basic; cola: 5, acidic; distilled water: 7, neutral; pondwater: 7, neutral; dissolved antacids: 8–10, basic; salt water: 8, basic

Answers to Analysis and Conclusions

1. Lemon juice has the lowest pH; ammonia has the highest.
2. one hundred times more acidic
3. The pH of the pond water is too acidic; that is why the fish are dying. One way to correct the pH would be to add a basic substance to the water.
4. An antacid tablet is basic; it would help neutralize the high acidity of the soda that caused the stomachache.
5. Acid rain is especially dangerous to freshwater animals and plants because it can lower the pH of the medium in which they live from a range that is habitable to one that can be dangerous or life-threatening.

Going Further

Ask students if they know in which part of the United States acid rain occurs in the greatest amount and impacts the greatest area. (Northeast) Brainstorm why this is the case. (Increasing population, industrial development, and prevailing winds from the Midwest contribute to this problem.)

Chapter 18 Lessons

Introduce Chapter 18

As a starting activity, use LAB 18A Connections Within Ecosystems on page 110 of the Laboratory Manual.

ENGAGE Ask why zebras outnumber lions. Then, ask students to think about what happens to these animals in cases of natural disasters, such as droughts and floods. Finally, ask them to hypothesize why scientists are concerned that elephants will die out altogether in the wild.

EXPLAIN Review the concept of ecological pyramids discussed in Chapter 16. Tell students that each lion eats many prey animals each year. Explain that if there were as many lions as zebras, many lions would starve. Explain that when drought strikes, animals might move to wetter locations, dig water holes, rely on water stored in their bodies, or die of thirst. Explain that scientists worry about elephants dying out in the wild due to hunting and habitat loss.

Think About Population Sizes

ENGAGE Consider setting up a bird-feeding station for students to watch. Have students make a six-column table, with the headings *Type of Bird* and *Monday* through *Friday*. Students should observe the feeding station each day at the same time and record the number of each type of bird seen each day. Provide field guides for reference.

Chapter 18 Interactions Among Living Things

KEY CONCEPT Population sizes and individual survival depend on interactions among organisms, their environment, and humans.

The Serengeti Plain in Africa is popular with tourists. Travelers from around the world come to see herds of wildebeest, zebras, and elephants.

The Serengeti is home to many individual animals, but it is striking that some species are much more common than others. Why are there so many zebras but only a few lions? What happens to the animals in times of drought? Why are scientists concerned that elephants will die out in the wild? This chapter is about what determines population sizes and how different species, including humans, interact with one another.

Think About Population Sizes

There are no herds of zebras in your neighborhood, but there is one group of animals that lives and feeds near humans almost everywhere: birds.

- Find a place with wild birds. In your Science Notebook, list the names of the birds you observe, or make a sketch or write a description of each one.
- For each species, note the largest group you see at one time. Why don't you see the same number of each kind of bird? How do you think that living so close to humans affects the birds? Record your thoughts.

NSTA SciLINKS THE WORLD'S A CLICK AWAY
www.scilinks.org
Environment Code: WGB18

Chapter 18 Planning Guide			
Instructional Periods	National Standards	Lab Manual	Workbook
18.1 1 period	A.2, C.4; B.6, C.5; UCP.3	**Lab 18A—p. 110** Connections Within Ecosystems **Lab 18B—p. 111** The Fittest Will Survive **Lab 18C—p. 113** It's a Small Ocean After All	Key Concept Review p. 114 Vocabulary Review p. 115 Graphic Organizer p. 116 Reading Comprehension p. 117 Curriculum Connection p. 119 Science Challenge p. 120
18.2 2 periods	F.1; C.4, F.1; UCP.1		
18.3 2 periods	A.1, C.5, G.1; G.1; UCP.2		
18.4 2 periods	E.2, F.2; F.5; F.2, F.3, F.6		

Middle School Standard; High School Standard; Unifying Concept and Principle

18.1 Population Growth and Size

Before You Read

Make a T-chart in your Science Notebook. Label the columns *Factors that Increase Population* and *Factors that Decrease Population*. Preview the lesson, and predict what you will write in each column.

Have you ever noticed how the number of each kind of tree in one area tends to remain constant, while the number of weeds changes throughout the year? If so, you have made observations about populations of living things. A population is a group of organisms of the same species living in a specific area. The size of a population depends on several **factors**, or elements influencing a result. Population ecologists study the factors that lead a population to grow, shrink, or reach a steady level.

Population Growth

The early English settlers in North America were homesick. They missed the climate, animals, and plants of their homeland. While they could not change the climate, they did send for many of their favorite animal and plant species from England. The dandelion was one plant they introduced to the continent. From a few seeds, the species grew and thrived. Native Americans, westward-traveling pioneers, and the wind took its seeds across the country. Soon, the plant was growing from coast to coast.

The population growth of the dandelion is typical for a new species in an area with many resources. At first, the population grows slowly. Each plant, however, produces many seeds in its lifetime. The population grows faster and faster. The speed at which a population can grow is set by the species' **reproductive cycle**, or rate and timing of reproduction.

Some species, such as whales, sharks, and humans, produce a few large offspring after a long period of growth. Others mature quickly and produce many young. In addition to dandelions, many insects and small rodents follow this pattern. Of the two patterns, organisms that mature early will produce the larger population over a given number of years. This is because after only a short time, there will be many breeding members of the population.

Learning Goals

- Describe population growth without limiting factors.
- Identify the different reproductive styles and their effects on population growth.
- Discuss the limiting factors for a population's growth and size.
- Explain how a population grows to its carrying capacity.
- Understand how natural events can affect populations.

New Vocabulary

factor
reproductive cycle
limiting factor
density
competition
range
carrying capacity

Recall Vocabulary

population (p. 281)
habitat (p. 282)
ecosystem (p. 281)

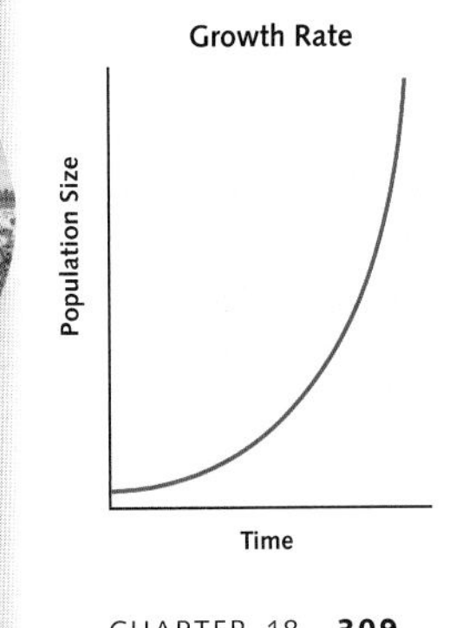

Growth Rate

Population Size

Time

Figure 18.1 Just after it arrived in North America, the dandelion showed uncontrolled population growth. A line graph with a J-shaped curve represents this pattern. What would happen if this rate of growth continued for many years?

Field Study

Take students outside and have them collect population data on a particular plant species. Take students out several times over the course of the school year and have them keep track of the change in population of that species. Ask students to write or sketch their observations in their Science Notebooks.

Vocabulary

factors Tell students that *factor* comes from the Latin word *facere*, meaning "make" or "do." *Factors* are the things that "make" a population grow, shrink, or remain stable.

reproductive cycle Explain that the prefix re- in the root *reproduce* means "again." So, *reproduce* means "to produce again." The word *cycle* means "a recurring series of events."

18.1 Introduce

ENGAGE Tell students that the population of some species grows much faster than the population of other species. Ask: *Can you name some species that produce a lot of offspring? Some species that produce few offspring?* Encourage students to brainstorm as many examples as they can. List student answers on the board. Then, have students compare and contrast the two lists of species.

EXPLAIN Tell students that larger species tend to have fewer offspring than smaller species. Ask students to think about possible scientific explanations for these differences.

Before You Read

Model the T-chart on the board. Record student predictions. As students fill in their T-charts, have them compare the factors that they recorded with their predictions.

Vocabulary terms are listed on the first student page of each lesson. You may wish to preview the terms before introducing each lesson. Strategies for teaching the vocabulary appear on the pages where the terms are introduced.

Teach

EXPLAIN that in this lesson, students will learn how a population grows when there are no limiting factors. They will also learn to identify different reproductive styles and their effects on population growth.

Use the Visual: Figure 18.1

ANSWER After many years, the dandelions would cover much of the planet in a thick blanket, choking out some other kinds of plant life.

EXTEND Have students brainstorm other factors that would affect the distribution of dandelions on Earth. (Possible answers: climate, nutrients in the soil, amount of soil) Help students understand that uncontrolled population growth cannot go on indefinitely.

Teach

ENGAGE Tell students that many factors limit a population's growth. Ask students to think about the limiting factors for the population of their high school. Encourage students to consider the number of teachers, the number and size of the classrooms, and alternatives for students who might be turned away. Write responses on the board.

EXPLAIN that students will gain an understanding of the limiting factors for population growth and size.

Vocabulary

limiting factor Explain that *limit* comes from the Latin word *līmes*, which means "boundary." A limiting factor is a factor that forms a boundary for a population's growth.

density Tell students that *density* is also a term used in chemistry. It means mass per unit of volume. Ask students to compare its use in chemistry with the use in biology. Then, ask students to suggest other ways in which the word could be used. (density of cars on a road, density of weeds in a lawn, etc.)

competition Explain that the prefix *com-* in *competition* means "together." The word *competition* comes from the Latin word *competere*, meaning "to seek together."

range Tell students that a common usage for the word *range* refers to "land for grazing." Remind students of the familiar song "Home on the Range." Explain that the range of a population defines the edges of the areas where that population can be found.

Use the Visual: Figure 18.2

ANSWER Limiting factors could be a body of water, extreme temperature, lack of water, mountains, or lack of prey.

Use the Visual: Figure 18.3

ANSWER Building purple martin houses removes nesting sites as a limiting factor.

As You Read

ANSWER The presence of a lot of waste products would decrease population growth because the wastes can poison organisms directly or spread disease.

Figure 18.2 The orange shading on this map shows the range of the barn owl. What limiting factors could determine the edge of the range in each direction?

As You Read

Complete the T-chart in your Science Notebook. Write each factor that affects population size and growth in the correct column.

Would the presence of a lot of waste products tend to increase or decrease population growth?

Limiting Factors

No population can continue to grow uncontrolled for long. Why not? Imagine a population of houseflies, starting with 100 eggs, half male and half female. If the 50 females each produced 2,000 offspring in 50 days, there would be 100,000 flies in the second generation. Fifty days later, there would be 100,000,000 flies. Within ten generations, the population would have a mass equal to that of planet Earth!

Long before the fly population could reach such a size, individual flies would run short of food and places to lay eggs. They would be subjected to conditions that would limit their rate of growth. Any factor that reduces the growth rate of a population is called a **limiting factor**.

Food, Water, and Nutrients Every organism must take in food or sunlight for energy. In addition, each organism needs water and a supply of vitamins and minerals to build its body. As a population grows in **density** (DEN suh tee), or number of individuals per unit of area, the nutrients available to it may become harder to find.

Living Space and Nesting Sites Some organisms prefer to live closer together than others, but almost all need some personal space or they show signs of stress. Wolverines are an extreme example of spacing, with a population density of one individual per 100 square kilometers. At the other extreme are herbs such as garlic mustard, with millions of individuals per square kilometer.

Plants must have access to light and room for their roots to travel through the soil. Certain animals must have places in which to construct their nests. Many species of birds, for example, have plenty of space in which to live but are limited by the number of available nesting sites, such as holes in large, dead trees.

Wastes and Disease As a population's density increases, its waste products can build up to unhealthy levels. The wastes can poison the organisms directly, or they can spread diseases. Earlier in history, waste and disease were often factors that limited the population growth of humans in cities. Fortunately, humans have developed systems for removing and treating wastes. Without this limiting factor, the populations of cities are able to grow in a healthy way.

Figure 18.3 Building purple martin houses has helped increase the population of this desirable species. What limiting factors are decreased by taking this measure?

Differentiated Instruction

Kinesthetic Mark off one square meter on the floor of the classroom or hallway. To demonstrate population density, have different numbers of students stand inside the square meter. Explain that population density is determined by dividing the number of individuals by the size of the area. Have students calculate the density for each group. Discuss what population densities were comfortable and at what point they became uncomfortable.

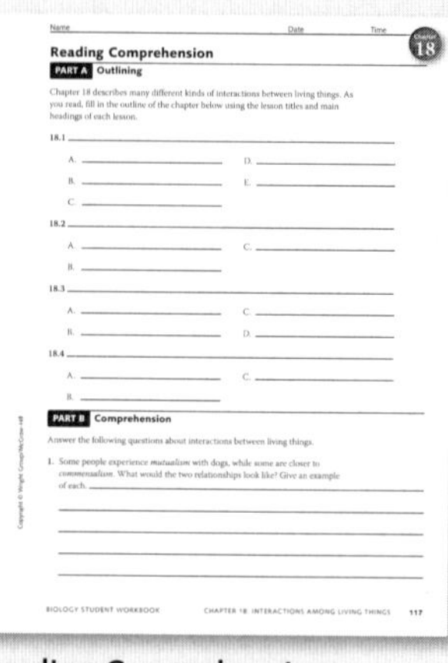

Reading Comprehension
PART A Outlining
PART B Comprehension

Reading Comprehension Workbook, p. 117

Whenever a population's resources are limited, competition will arise. **Competition** is the struggle among living things for the food or space they need in order to survive and produce offspring. There are some places where the limiting factors are so severe that no members of a species can live. The edges of these areas define the **range** of the population, or where it can be found.

Carrying Capacity

The number of organisms of one species that an environment can support for a long time is called the environment's **carrying capacity**. In most cases, populations start small and grow until they are larger than the carrying capacity of their habitat. Limiting factors cause the population to drop below the carrying capacity for a period of time before growing once again. The whole cycle is shown in **Figure 18.4**.

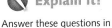

Explain It!

Answer these questions in your Science Notebook.

- What is the population size of your school? Is it growing, stable, or shrinking? Where does it fall on the graph in Figure 18.4?
- In your opinion, is your school at its carrying capacity now? What limited resources affect the population?

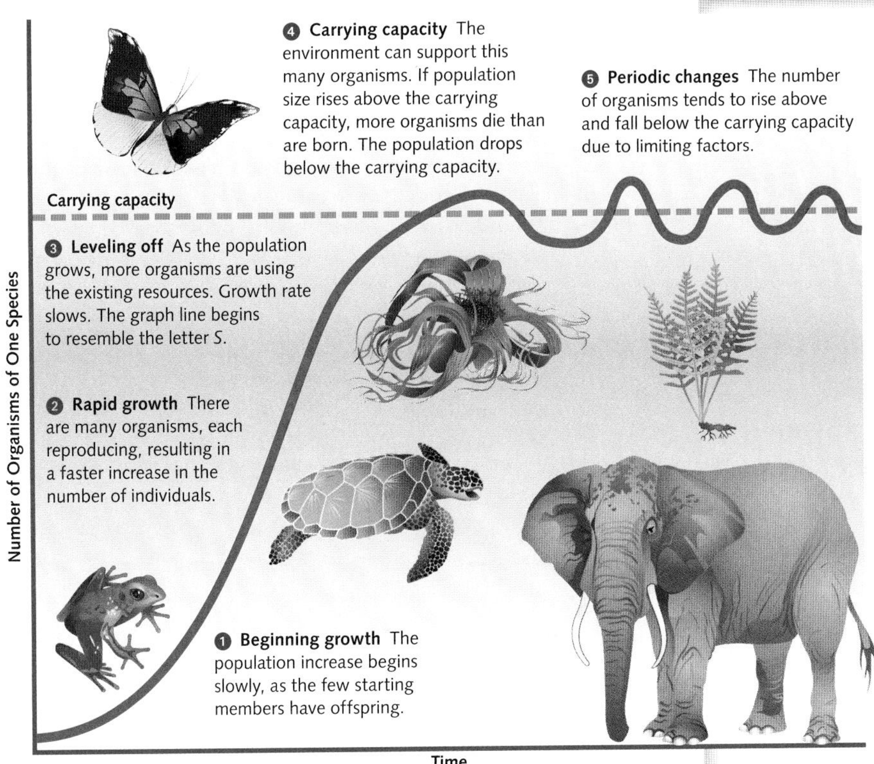

4 Carrying capacity The environment can support this many organisms. If population size rises above the carrying capacity, more organisms die than are born. The population drops below the carrying capacity.
5 Periodic changes The number of organisms tends to rise above and fall below the carrying capacity due to limiting factors.
Carrying capacity
3 Leveling off As the population grows, more organisms are using the existing resources. Growth rate slows. The graph line begins to resemble the letter S.
2 Rapid growth There are many organisms, each reproducing, resulting in a faster increase in the number of individuals.
1 Beginning growth The population increase begins slowly, as the few starting members have offspring.
Number of Organisms of One Species
Time

Figure 18.4 A population in a habitat with few limiting factors grows larger until it reaches the habitat's carrying capacity. Populations grow and change periodically whether they are plant or animal, whether on land or in the ocean.

Teach

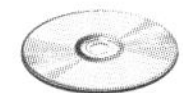
EXPLAIN that in this section, students will learn how a population grows to its carrying capacity. Tell students that many factors determine how many species will survive in an environment. Explain that the population of a species grows larger until it reaches the carrying capacity and then begins to alternately decline and then grow larger. Emphasize that this cycle repeats many times.

Vocabulary

carrying capacity Explain that *carry* comes from the Latin word *carrus*, which means "wagon" or "cart." The word *capacity* comes from the Latin *capāx*, which means "hold." Thus, *carrying capacity* is how much "a wagon can hold," or "the number of species an environment can support."

Explain It!

Discuss with students different ways they could find population data for their school. Divide students into groups, and have each group do research using different sources. Suggest that some students look at Web sites and that others interview school administrators. Have students write their answers to the questions in their Science Notebooks.

ANSWER Answers will vary depending on your school's size and growth. Possible limited resources include classroom space, teachers, books, bathroom stalls, lockers, cafeteria seating, food, chairs, spots on sports teams, buses, parking spaces, etc.

CONNECTION: Population and Government

The U.S. Constitution demands that a census be taken every ten years to determine the number of representatives each state sends to the House of Representatives. In addition to providing data for this use, the census also helps determine how federal funds are distributed, how legislative districts are drawn, and how to render governmental programs successful. All of the data collected in the census can be found on the U.S. Census Bureau's Web site. To learn more, visit **http://www.census.gov/.**

ELL Strategy

Make a Diagram Ask students to research two kinds of organisms—one that produces many offspring rapidly, such as a weedy plant, and one that produces only one or a few offspring at a time, such as horses. Have students use what they learn to draw their own population-growth graphs representing organisms with different reproductive strategies.

Use the Visual: Figure 18.4

EXTEND Ask: *What does the first part of the population-growth curve look like?* (a J-shaped curve) Call students' attention to the shape of the graph line after it rises above the environment's carrying capacity. Explain that biologists call this pattern an S-curve. Have students work with a partner and take turns explaining what causes the graph line to rise and fall in an S-curve pattern. (Normal fluctuation due to limiting factors.)

Teach

ENGAGE Tell students that natural events can have both a positive and a negative effect on population. Ask them to think about some recent natural disasters, such as a hurricane, tornado, or blizzard. For each event, have students think about which species of plants or animals might have been positively affected and which species might have been negatively affected.

EXPLAIN that this section will help students understand how natural events can affect populations.

EXTEND Have students brainstorm possible reasons for the kinds and numbers of birds seen at the bird-feeding station they observed for Think About Population Sizes. (Possible answers: type of food, time of day, size and location of feeder, kinds of plants in the environment)

Figure It Out: Figure 18.5

ANSWER **1.** The population crashed in 1994. The reason is not given in the study; students could think of some possibilities. **2.** Carrying capacity is approximately 225 × 2 (to include females) = 450 grouse.

Assess

EVALUATE Use the After You Read questions and the Alternative Assessment to help you assess students' understanding of the lesson.

After You Read

1. A population grows slowly at first and then faster as the number of breeding individuals increases, forming a pattern called a J-shaped curve.
2. Possible answers include slow reproductive cycle, lack of food or nutrients, crowding, lack of nesting sites, waste products, disease, and competition.
3. Students should find that this year's population = 1,842 + 425 + 83 − 72 − 38 = 2,240.

Alternative Assessment

EVALUATE If students have difficulty answering the After You Read questions, check the T-charts in their Science Notebooks. Ask students to choose a specific population and describe the limiting factors for the growth of that population.

Natural Events

Imagine a stable ecosystem in which most populations are near their carrying capacities. Suddenly, a nearby volcano erupts, or a hurricane floods the area, or a swarm of grasshoppers passes through. In each case, a natural event has changed the rules of the environment for a time, and the populations will respond.

Some natural events destroy almost all of the populations in the area. However, what is a disaster to some populations can be good luck for others. The grasshoppers may eat every blade of grass, allowing clover to sprout and find sunlight. While rabbits may starve without plants to eat, birds, foxes, and mice will feast for a time on insects. Populations may rise or fall dramatically, but in time, most will recover to their earlier levels.

The time it takes a population to return to its carrying capacity depends on the organisms' reproductive style. Aphids, tiny insects that are born pregnant, can repopulate an area in a matter of weeks. Sharks, however, produce only a few young each year, starting when they are several years old. It may take decades for a shark population to recover.

Figure It Out

1. In which year did the population of black grouse drop suddenly?
2. If the population is half male, predict the carrying capacity for grouse in this area.

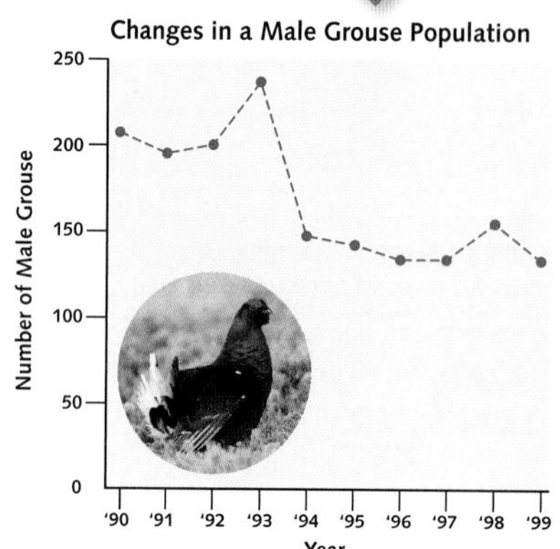

Figure 18.5 This black grouse population dropped significantly in the 1990s.

Population Equation

The number of births and deaths does not always give enough information to calculate the size of a population. Individuals in a population sometimes move to a new community, as well. The size of a population can be calculated using the following equation.

This Year's Population = Last Year's Population + Births + Individuals Moving In − Deaths − Individuals Moving Out

All of the factors you have just read about are limiting factors that affect at least one part of this equation.

After You Read

1. What pattern does a population follow as it grows from a few individuals in a new environment?
2. According to the chart you made in your Science Notebook, what are three factors that tend to decrease a population's growth rate?
3. Last year's population of a species of bird in a certain location was 1,842. During the year, there were 425 births and 72 deaths. A total of 38 individuals moved out of the area, and 83 individuals moved into the area. Calculate this year's population of the bird species.

Background Information

The human population has been growing exponentially, and the rate of growth is rapidly increasing. Developing countries display the highest rate of population growth.

Scientists do not agree about the existence of a carrying capacity for the population of humans on Earth. Some believe that we will outgrow our planet, while others believe that human ingenuity is enough to sustain us and that we will find ways to adapt to any natural limiting factors.

Relationships Among Populations

Before You Read

Create a concept map for the word *Relationships* in your Science Notebook. Use the headings, subheadings, Learning Goals, and vocabulary terms in the lesson to construct your map. Include definitions of the terms, examples of each type of relationship, and other important details.

Learning Goals

- Classify relationships between species.
- Describe the dynamics of symbiosis.
- Explain how the removal of one species from a community can affect the other members of the community, as well as humans.

New Vocabulary

symbiosis
fitness
mutualism
commensalism
parasitism
host
predation

Recall Vocabulary

community (p. 281)

No place on Earth is home to only one species of living organism. Everywhere you look, there are communities made up of many different populations that share the same resources. At first, a forest may appear to be made up mainly of trees. Upon closer examination, you may notice caterpillars eating the tree leaves, fungi growing on the trees, squirrels living in the trees, and bees carrying pollen from one tree to another.

Symbiosis

A close relationship between individuals of two or more species is called **symbiosis** (sihm bee OH sus, plural: symbioses). The word *symbiosis* comes from Greek, in which *syn-* means "together" and *-bios* means "life." The partners in symbiosis typically have effects on each other's lives. They also affect each other's **fitness**, which is the ability of a living thing to survive and reproduce. Symbioses are classified according to which species benefits from the relationship. There are three kinds of symbiosis: mutualism, commensalism, and parasitism.

Mutualism A symbiotic relationship in which both species benefit is called **mutualism** (MYEW chuh wuh lih zum). There are many examples of mutualism involving species from every kingdom of life. The human body is involved in mutualism with the bacteria in the digestive tract. These bacteria get nutrients from food that is eaten, and they get a safe place to live within the body. At the same time, they fight harmful bacteria and produce vitamin K and other chemicals the body cannot make on its own. The proof of mutualism is that both organisms suffer when they are apart from each other.

Most plants form a type of mutualistic relationship with fungi that is called a mycorrhiza (mi koh RI zuh). Fungi have hairlike structures called hyphae (HI fee), which take up water and nutrients. The fungi live off sugars and other food they collect from plant roots. In turn, the fungi use their networks of hyphae to absorb water and minerals that are shared with the plant. Plants that are grown without mycorrhizal fungi are more sensitive to droughts and may not get enough phosphorus from the soil. Mycorrhizal fungi cannot survive away from their plant partners.

Figure 18.6 Relationships between honeybees and flowering plants are mutualism because both species benefit. A bee gets nectar and pollen to eat and also spreads pollen from one flower to another. Separately, the bees would starve and the flowering plants might be unable to make seeds.

Introduce

ENGAGE Tell students that there are many different relationships between people in the school community. Ask: *Can you think of some different relationships that exist in our school community? Can you name some relationships in which one party benefits more than the other? Can you name some relationships in which both parties benefit equally?* Record student answers on the board. Encourage students to brainstorm as many examples as they can.

EXPLAIN Tell students that a relationship between individuals of two or more species is called symbiosis. When that relationship benefits both parties equally, it is known as mutualism.

Before You Read

Model a concept map on the board. Write the word *Relationships* in the center, and ask students to describe what they already know about the relationships between and among species. Record student answers on the board.

Teach

EXPLAIN that in this lesson, students will learn to classify relationships between species. They will also learn to describe the dynamics of symbiosis and explain how the removal of one species from a community can affect the other members of that community, as well as humans.

Vocabulary

symbiosis Have students apply the meaning of the prefix *syn-* to other words they are familiar with that have this prefix (synthesis, synchronize). Remind students that a common form of the prefix is *sym-* (symphony, sympathy). Repeat the exercise using *bio-* (biology, biodegradable, biomass, biosphere).

fitness Explain that this term is also used in relation to adaptation and natural selection. Have students suggest reasons that forming symbiotic partnerships might increase an individual's fitness.

mutualism Tell students that the word *mutualism* comes from the Latin word *mūtuus*, meaning "reciprocal" or "existing on both sides." When both sides benefit from a relationship, the relationship is known as mutualism.

ELL Strategy

Compare and Contrast Have students choose two different examples of symbiosis between species. Ask students to compare and contrast these examples, considering the benefits and disadvantages on each side. Have students determine if the species in each example benefit to the same extent. Students should record their answers in their Science Notebooks.

Teach

EXPLAIN to students that the relationship between organisms is not always beneficial to both organisms. Explain that in some symbiotic relationships, one organism is benefited and the other is unaffected. And in other relationships, one organism feeds off another and survives at the expense of the other organism.

Vocabulary

commensalism Explain to students that the prefix *com-* means "together" and the root *mensa* means "table." The literal meaning of the word *commensalism* is "eating at the same table." Have students explain why this meaning is appropriate.

parasitism Tell students that the word *parasitism* comes from the Greek word *parasitos*, which means "someone who lives at another's expense." Ask students to explain why this is an appropriate description of parasitism.

host Explain that a common usage of the word *host* refers to a person who invites others into his or her house for a meal or a party. Ask students to suggest a difference between the scientific meaning and the common usage. (In a parasitic relationship, the host provides food or shelter for another organism, but that organism comes without an invitation and is damaging to the host.)

predation Explain to students that the word *predation* comes from the Latin word *praedari*, which means "to plunder." A predator "plunders," or steals, the life of its prey.

As You Read

ANSWER An organism fed upon by a parasite is called a host.

Figure 18.7 The remora is a fish that is commensal with sharks. Remoras attach to sharks with a sucker, catching a ride and scraps of food from the sharks' meals. The sharks are neither harmed nor helped.

As You Read

Fill in the concept map in your Science Notebook. For each type of relationship, give a definition, an example, and one or two details. Also indicate which partner benefits from the relationship.

What is the name for an organism fed upon by a parasite?

Did You Know?

Until recently, oxpecker birds and musk oxen were thought to be mutualistic. Oxpeckers remove and eat parasites such as ticks and flies from an ox's skin. When it was discovered that oxpeckers often open old wounds and drink the ox's blood, ecologists realized that oxpeckers are also parasites.

Commensalism A symbiotic relationship in which one organism benefits and the other is not affected is called **commensalism** (kuh MEN suh lih zum). One common type of commensalism occurs between jellyfish and young fish. A young fish benefits from the relationship because it is protected from predators by the jellyfish's stinging tentacles. The jellyfish is neither helped nor hurt by the presence of the fish. **Figure 18.7** shows another example of commensalism.

When two species live closely together, they almost always affect each other's fitness. Over time, most of the examples of commensalism have been reclassified as other types of symbiosis.

Parasitism **Parasitism** (PER uh suh tih zum) is a symbiotic relationship in which one organism, the parasite, feeds off the living body of the other organism. The parasite benefits, while the **host**, or the organism off which the parasite lives, is partially eaten or harmed. The host thus loses fitness. Some parasites, including fleas, mosquitoes, and ticks, live on the outside of the host. Other parasites, such as tapeworms, can live only inside the host's body.

Parasitism is common in nature. All viruses are parasites, as are many bacteria and fungi. Almost every free-living species on Earth is host to at least one parasite. Parasites have evolved in such a way that while they hurt the host, they usually do not kill it. If the host were to die, the parasite would likely also die unless it could quickly find another host.

Many diseases are caused by parasites. Malaria, which infects over 350 million people per year, is caused by a protist called *Plasmodium*. *Plasmodium* uses a mosquito as its first host. When the mosquito bites a person, it injects *Plasmodium*-containing saliva into a vein. The parasite lives and reproduces inside the person, eating red blood cells. When another mosquito bites an infected person, the *Plasmodium* can be passed on to a new host.

Competition

When two species struggle for the same limited resources, they are in competition. Each is hurt by the presence of the other. Plants compete for sunlight, water, and minerals, while animals may compete for food and nesting places. The need to compete successfully for resources is one of the most important causes of evolution by natural selection.

Figure 18.8 Zebra mussels are a species of mollusk from Russia that was accidentally brought to the American Great Lakes on ships. They reproduce very quickly and compete with native mussels for food and places to live. As zebra mussels spread to new waterways, scientists expect native populations to decrease.

Differentiated Instruction

Linguistic, Kinesthetic, Interpersonal Divide students into pairs. Have students write a script of a conversation that might occur between two organisms in each of the different types of symbiotic relationships. Have the members of each group act out their dialogue for the class. Ask the class to guess which type of relationship the dialogue illustrates.

Background Information

Anything that a prey species does or uses to increase its chances of survival against a predator is known as an adaptation. Some adaptations of prey species include camouflage, outrunning predators, looking like a dangerous animal, and having false features such as large eyes to scare off predators. The chemical emissions of skunks and dart frogs and the physical features of turtles and porcupines ward off predators.

Predation

When one creature kills and eats another creature, it is called **predation** (prih DAY shun). Predation involves two individuals—a predator and its prey. The predator benefits by gaining food, while the prey that is eaten can no longer survive and reproduce. Unlike parasitism, which lasts a long time without killing the host, predation is a one-time relationship. Predator and prey species can affect each other's carrying capacity in a community.

Often an ecosystem contains chains or networks of predators and prey. For example, grass is eaten by snails, which are eaten by birds, which are eaten by snakes. If the top predator in a community is removed, all of the other species in the network will be affected, for better or worse. In this example, the removal of snakes will have an effect on the populations of birds, snails, and grass.

Humans have killed off wolves throughout most of the United States. This was done to prevent wolves from eating livestock and to reduce competition between human hunters and wolves. One unexpected result was the great increase in the number and range of coyotes. It turns out that coyotes were competing with wolves for small animal prey. Also, wolves killed and ate many young coyotes. So as the population of wolves decreased, the population of coyotes increased. Elk, rabbit, mouse, and deer populations also grew rapidly after the removal of wolves. These increases led to overgrazing and destruction of crops and plant communities. Without the wolf population, people have to shoot, trap, and poison many of its former prey themselves.

Figure 18.9 Predators come in all sizes. This amoeba, which is a protist, is preying on an algal cell.

Interspecific Relationships

Relationship	Organism 1	Organism 2
mutualism	+	+
commensalism	+ commensal	0 host
parasitism	+ parasite	– host
competition	–	–
predation	+ predator	– prey

Key: + helped – hurt 0 not affected

Figure 18.10 This table shows a summary of the possible relationships between two species.

Figure It Out

1. Which two relationships affect both species in the same way?
2. What does the term *interspecific* mean?

Explore It!

Choose a large animal or plant to be your study subject. Carefully observe all of the interactions your subject has with the plants, animals, and other organisms around it. Record your observations in your Science Notebook. Classify each relationship as mutualism, parasitism, commensalism, competition, or predation.

After You Read

1. Explain what would happen to the population sizes of a parasite and its host if they were separated from each other.
2. According to the concept map in your Science Notebook, what are some benefits an organism could gain from symbiosis?
3. Imagine whitetail deer becoming extinct in the United States. How would this affect ticks, woody plants, mountain lions, and mule deer?

Teach

EXPLAIN to students that predators need their prey to survive. The predator benefits by getting food from its prey. Unlike a parasitic relationship, which can last for a long period of time without killing the host, a predator-prey relationship is short-term and ends with the death of the prey.

Figure It Out: Figure 18.10

ANSWER **1.** In mutualism, both species help each other. Competition involves both species hurting each other. **2.** Interspecific refers to an action that involves two or more species.

Explore It!

For this activity, larger pets or livestock work fine. Outdoor plants are more likely to show parasites, competition, and damage from grazing animals. Students might take a field trip to a local zoo or botanical garden to make their observations.

Assess

EVALUATE Use the After You Read questions and the Alternative Assessment to help you assess students' understanding of the lesson.

After You Read

1. The host population would increase; the parasites would die off.
2. A benefit of symbiosis would be relief from some limiting factor. Possible benefits include protection from predators, vitamins or minerals, food, access to sunlight, a safe place to live, water, or pollination.
3. ticks: population reduction—lack of hosts; woody plants: population increase—fewer eaten; mountain lions: population reduction—less food; mule deer: population increase—less competition

Teacher Alert

Students may believe that predators are "bad" and should be killed to stop them from killing their prey. It is important to stress to students the critical role that predators play in food chains. They are essential to keeping the population of their prey from growing out of control and for eliminating sick and weak individuals, which improves the overall health of the population's individuals.

Alternative Assessment

EVALUATE For students who have difficulty with the As You Read questions, provide a blank concept map. Ask students to fill in the different relationships with examples, and add one or two details for each. Allow students to refer to their Science Notebooks for information.

18.3 Introduce

ENGAGE Explain that predators do not eat all of the individuals in the populations of their prey, partly because their prey adapt over time to avoid being eaten. Ask: *What would happen if the snakes in an environment ate all of the birds in that environment? How have birds adapted to avoid being eaten by snakes?* Encourage students to consider all possible answers.

EXPLAIN to students that if snakes ate all of their prey, it would be hard for them to survive. If they were to run out of one food source, they would have to find another food source. Birds have adapted in many ways to avoid being eaten by snakes. Their coloring helps camouflage them, making them harder to see. They also have the ability to fly away.

Before You Read

Ask students to work in pairs to identify all of the headings in this lesson. Ask pairs to share the headings with the class. Record headings on the board, and have students record them in their Science Notebooks.

Teach

EXPLAIN to students that in this lesson they will learn why it is important that organisms adapt to the other species in their community. They will also learn some of the ways in which organisms can adapt to symbiosis, competition, predation, and natural events.

Figure It Out: Figure 8.11

ANSWER **1.** mutualism **2.** White *Heliconia* flowers would not attract as many hummingbirds. As a result, fewer flowers would be pollinated and fewer seeds would be produced.

Learning Goals

- Explain the importance of organisms adapting to the other species in their community.
- Describe some of the ways in which organisms can adapt to symbiosis, competition, predation, and natural events.

18.3 Adaptations: Challenges and Opportunities

Before You Read

In your Science Notebook, write the headings in this lesson. Leave enough space to write a few lines under each heading. As you read the lesson, look for examples of each type of adaptation.

So far, scientists have found and named more than 2.5 million species. They estimate that another 2 to 50 million species remain undiscovered. Each of these species interacts with many others through symbiosis, predation, and competition. Why don't the most skilled predators simply eat up all of their prey? Why doesn't one species of tree take over all of the forests of the world? The answers lie in the ability of species to adapt, or change in ways that improve their survival and reproductive success. Natural selection favors the individuals that are best adapted to their environment and the other organisms in it.

Figure It Out

1. What relationship exists between the hummingbird and the plants that feed it?
2. Predict what would happen to lobster claw plants with a mutation that caused them to have white flowers.

Figure 18.11 Hummingbirds and the flowers they pollinate are both adapted to their symbiotic relationship. These lobster claw flowers are red, hummingbirds' favorite color. The plant even produces two lengths of flowers that match the beak lengths of male and female birds.

Adaptation to Symbiosis

Two species whose lives are closely connected tend to become adapted to each other. Parasites get better at finding good hosts and feeding on them without causing their deaths. Host species adapt by poisoning parasites or attacking them with their immune systems. Commensal species adapt by seeking partners that will provide the full benefit of the relationship. If small fish are more likely to survive when they are protected by a jellyfish's tentacles, the fish species will likely adapt to recognize and attach themselves to jellyfish.

Mutualism results in some of the most dramatic adaptations. Pollinators, such as birds and insects, and the flowers they pollinate are a good example. Plants produce flowers with the shape, color, smell, and timing that their pollinators prefer. Some flowers even evolved to look much like females of the insect pollinator's species. Mutualism can develop from other relationships, such as the one between predators and prey. Many fruits, for example, contain seeds that are carried by fruit eaters to new places where they can grow.

Sometimes, one partner in symbiosis performs certain life functions for both species. Lichens (LI kunz), for example, are formed by fungi and their bacterial or algal partners. The algae or bacteria produce all of the food for lichens through photosynthesis. The fungi absorb water and minerals and shelter the algae or bacteria. Lichens can grow in habitats that neither species could survive in alone.

316 INTERACTIONS AMONG LIVING THINGS

ELL Strategy

Discuss, Paraphrase Ask students who have difficulty with English to discuss the content of this lesson in their native languages. Then, have students paraphrase the content of the lesson in English, using as many of the lesson's vocabulary terms and their definitions as possible.

Adaptation to Competition

When two species use the same limited resources in the same way, they will compete with each other. The species best adapted to the environment will eventually take over the habitat. The only way for the two species to live together is for each one to have a different adaptation for using the same resource. For example, two species of birds called finches may eat the same kinds of seeds on separate islands. Where the finches are found together, one species has a beak for cracking seeds that is smaller than the other species' beak. This adaptation reduces competition enough for both species to succeed.

Another adaptation to competition involves making the environment unpleasant for competitors. Trees such as black walnuts release from their roots chemicals that prevent the growth of other plants. This reduces competition for sunlight and nutrients. In another case, bluebirds and wild mice are both limited by the number of nest holes in their habitat. Humans have built tens of thousands of nest boxes to increase the population of bluebirds, but many of them have been taken over by mice. Years after a mouse has used a box, the smell will still keep bluebirds away.

Adaptation to Predation

Predators and prey both adapt to their relationships. Prey species adapt by becoming harder to find and less tasty to predators. They may also adopt a reproductive strategy of having many offspring at once. For example, all of the maple trees in a population produce a heavy crop of seeds at the same time every few years. There are too many seeds for predators to eat them all. By the time the predator populations have grown larger, the young trees are too big to be eaten.

Predators also adapt to increase their fitness. They can become better at catching and killing their prey. Behaviors such as speed, teamwork, and quiet movement help lions kill animals larger than themselves. In addition, many predators can survive for a long time without catching any prey. Spiders can wait months between meals, and wolverines store meat under the snow.

Figure 18.12 The katydid on this leaf uses camouflage, or colors and patterns that are hard to see. The fitness of the katydid is greater because a predator is less likely to find it.

As You Read

Record in your Science Notebook examples of adaptations that organisms make to each type of relationship.

What is an adaptation an organism has that reduces competition for food?

Extend It!

Choose one species and research its relationships and adaptations within its community. Record answers to the following questions in your Science Notebook.

- Does your species form any mutualisms or commensalisms?
- What are your species' most important parasites? Is your species ever a parasite?
- What are your organism's predators and prey? Which other species compete for the same resources?
- What adaptations does your species have that relate to the other organisms in its environment? Which other organism affects the fitness of your species the most?

Teach

EXPLAIN to students that animals adapt in order to survive. They adapt to better share the resources in their environment. If two animals share the same kinds of foods, they will adapt to make better use of other foods in their environment so that there will be enough for everyone. If animals do not adapt to their environments, they will die out.

As You Read

Ask students to share their examples with the class. Record their answers on the board.

ANSWER An adaptation would be any trait that that enables an organism to use resources differently, such as sharper teeth or a new way of building a nest, or to make its environment unpleasant for competitors, such as a strong smell or the ability of a seed to germinate and grow faster.

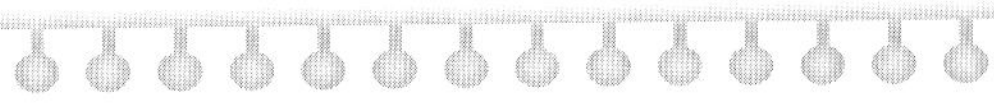

Extend It!

Researching the relationships and adaptations of a particular species will help students better understand the different types of relationships that exist between species. Students can use Internet search engines by trying keywords such as the names of their organisms and terms such as *symbiosis* or *parasite*. If students use books, they may have to read closely to figure out which relationship is being described.

Differentiated Instruction

Visual Have each student choose a plant or an animal that is prey for another animal. Explain that animals that eat plants can be thought of as predators of the plants they eat and that the plants can be thought of as prey. Ask each student to draw a diagram of the food chain that includes his or her plant or animal. Display drawings around the classroom.

Graphic Organizer Workbook, p. 116

Teach

EXPLAIN that what humans consider to be natural disasters, such as fires and floods, are not disasters for all species. These events help some species grow and prosper.

PEOPLE IN SCIENCE

Lynn Margulis received her bachelor's degree from the University of Chicago in 1957. She got a master's degree from the University of Wisconsin in 1960 and a PhD from University of California, Berkeley, in 1963. She taught at Boston University for 22 years and is currently a professor in the Geosciences Department at the University of Massachusetts, Amherst.

EXTEND Have students work in small groups to develop a visual that is clearly labeled and that illustrates the endosymbiotic theory as described here.

Assess

EVALUATE Use the After You Read questions and the Alternative Assessment to help you assess students' understanding of the lesson.

After You Read

1. If a change is an adaptation, individuals that inherit the change will have increased fitness, or be better able to survive and reproduce than the rest of the population.
2. competition for food
3. Possible adaptations include: growing up in the tops of trees to reduce competition for sunlight; producing chemicals that make it taste bad or being poisonous to reduce predation and parasites; growing thorns to reduce predation; producing chemicals that slow the growth of other plants to reduce competition; making seeds that germinate only when a nearby tree has fallen to reduce competition

Alternative Assessment

EVALUATE Provide a list of the headings from this chapter, and ask students to write three to four details under each heading.

PEOPLE IN SCIENCE Lynn Margulis 1938–

In 1966, biologist Lynn Margulis suggested an entirely new way that a prey species can adapt: it can become a working part of the predator! What Margulis meant was that some of the organelles within complex cells started out as simple bacteria that were eaten by other bacteria. The prey bacteria survived inside their hosts and even reproduced themselves. In some cases, the prey bacteria made a useful product, such as sugar, through photosynthesis. Meanwhile, the prey bacteria were protected from other predators and from oxygen, which could poison them. The symbiotic cell had greater fitness than the simpler cells around it.

Margulis's ideas about cell predation turning into mutualism are called the endosymbiotic theory. Margulis predicted that organelles formed in this way would have double membranes and DNA separate from the rest of the cell. In fact, the chloroplasts that carry out photosynthesis and the mitochondria that make energy for cells have both of these predicted characteristics.

Although it took many years for Margulis to convince other scientists, her endosymbiotic theory is today the accepted model for the origin of eukaryotic cells.

Figure 18.13 Most generations of these aphids are wingless. If food becomes scarce, the aphids produce young with wings that can fly to a better habitat. This adaptation helps the population survive in an unpredictable environment.

Adaptation to Natural Events

Natural events can have important effects on populations. Organisms that can adapt to fires, droughts, and floods will gain in fitness. One adaptation developed by some species is forming seeds or eggs that will be ready to take advantage of a natural event. Plant seeds can survive underground for many years until a fire or fallen tree opens a space for the young trees to grow. Jack pine seeds will not germinate, or start to sprout, until a fire has scorched them.

Some species adapt to natural events by leaving the affected area for a time. Other organisms, such as mosquitoes, take advantage of floods to breed rapidly before puddles have time to dry. All of these adaptations save animals and help them reproduce. They also shorten the time it takes for a community to recover from a natural disturbance.

After You Read

1. What evidence indicates that a change in a species is an adaptation?
2. According to the notes in your Science Notebook, what limiting factor is reduced when birds develop different sizes of beaks?
3. Imagine a plant living in the rain forest, where it must compete for sunlight and limited nutrients in the soil. There are many grazing animals at ground level, as well as insect parasites. The forest floods every ten years. What adaptations might increase the plant's fitness in this environment?

318 INTERACTIONS AMONG LIVING THINGS

Teacher Alert

Students often believe that organisms adapt, or develop adaptations, on purpose. It is important to stress that in the evolutionary sense, species—*not individual organisms*—change as a result of genetic recombination and mutations (new genetic variations). Changes that are inherited by certain individuals of a species are sometimes advantageous to the individual in its environment and enable it to leave behind more offspring. The offspring that inherit an advantageous change, or adaptation, will also be better able to survive and leave behind more offspring. Over time, in a population of a species, the number of individuals with an adaptation to an environment will increase. Therefore, stress to students that populations (and species) evolve (adapt to an environment) as the populations of a species consist of more and more individuals with an adaptation.

18.4 People and the Environment

Before You Read

Preview the lesson. Read the headings and the Learning Goals, and look at the pictures. Think about what you expect to learn from this lesson. Write the headings in your Science Notebook, leaving space for a few sentences under each heading.

Learning Goals

- Describe human population growth over the last 1,000 years.
- Explain the ways in which humans affect the environment.
- Identify steps that can be taken to conserve wild populations and habitats.

New Vocabulary

technology
natural resource
renewable resource
nonrenewable resource
sustainable use
habitat destruction
introduced species
pollution
global warming

It's easy to imagine how modern humans can significantly affect the environment. They can use chainsaws to cut down trees, dams to flood valleys, and guns to kill the fiercest animals. In fact, human impact on the environment began many thousands of years ago. At the end of the last ice age, there were llamas, camels, giant sloths, mammoths, and five kinds of wild horses in North America. Today, there are none. All of these species died out soon after the first humans arrived on the continent.

Human Population Growth

All populations are limited by factors that set a carrying capacity, or maximum steady population size. Look at **Figure 18.14**, which shows human population growth over the last 1,000 years. How has the human population continued to increase in size without facing limiting factors? Humans use **technology**, or the ability to control nature, to grow more food, to provide materials, and to treat diseases. So far, humans have not reached their carrying capacity on Earth.

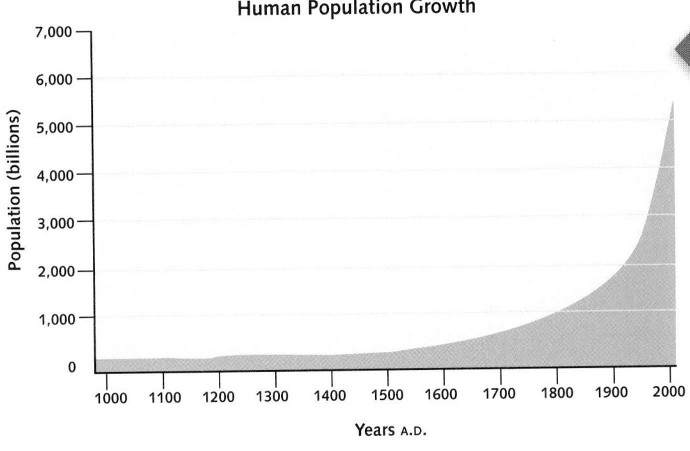

Figure 18.14 The human population has grown faster and faster over the last 1,000 years.

Figure It Out

1. Around what year did the human population reach one billion?
2. What are some factors that could eventually limit the human population?

18.4 Introduce

ENGAGE Tell students that humans, like other species, both adapt to and affect their environment in both positive and negative ways. Ask: *How have humans positively affected the environment in which they live? How have humans negatively affected the environment?* Draw a two-column chart on the board. Label one column *Positive* and the other column *Negative*. Write student responses in the chart. Encourage students to also think about the ways in which humans have attempted to correct the negative effects that they have had on their environment.

Before You Read

Divide students into pairs. Ask each pair of students to choose one of the pictures in the lesson and make predictions about how that picture will relate to what they will learn in the lesson. Students should record their observations and predictions in their Science Notebooks. Ask pairs to share these pictures and ideas with the class.

Teach

EXPLAIN to students that in this lesson, they will learn about human population growth over the last 1,000 years. They will also be able to explain the ways in which humans affect the environment and to identify steps that can be taken to conserve wild populations and habitats.

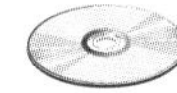

Vocabulary

technology Explain to students that the word *technology* comes from the Greek word *technologia*, which means "systematic treatment." Ask students to think about ways in which a scientist controls nature with a "systematic treatment."

Figure It Out: Figure 18.14

1. approximately 1805 **2.** competition for food and water, disease, violent competition (war), pollution, personal choices about family size

ELL Strategy

Analyze, Prepare Presentations Have pairs of students from different countries investigate and compare population growth in their native countries. Students should look at the factors that are leading to population growth and the ways in which the governments of different countries are addressing population issues. Also have students note possible factors that might cause any differences there are in the population growth rates of the countries they investigate. Groups should present their findings to the class.

Teach

EXPLAIN Tell students that humans require a lot of resources to sustain themselves. If humans do not use resources responsibly, they risk running out of them.

As You Read

Discuss with students the many benefits that humans gain from intact ecosystems, including water filtration, oxygen production, soil retention, pharmaceutical resources, food production, etc.

ANSWER Wild populations must move out, die, or face severely limited resources. Humans risk greater flooding and pollution and loss of food sources, building materials, medicinal plants, and recreation areas.

Vocabulary

natural resource Explain that the prefix *re-* in *resource* means "again" and that the root *source* comes from the Latin word *surgere*, meaning "to rise." Thus, a natural resource is something from nature that can "rise again."

renewable resource Tell students that a resource that is renewable can be replaced or is "new again." Renewable resources can be replaced indefinitely if managed properly.

nonrenewable resource Explain that the prefix non- in *nonrenewable* means "not." Ask students to define this term using the meaning of the prefix *non-*. (Nonrenewable resources cannot be used again.)

sustainable use Tell students that the root of the word *sustainable* comes from the Latin word *tenēre*, which means "to hold." A sustainable use of resources allows us to hold on to those resources over time.

habitat destruction Explain to students that the word *habitat* comes from the Latin word *habitare*, meaning "to dwell." The prefix *de-* in *destruction* means "down," and the Latin root *struere* means "to build." Therefore, habitat destruction is "the tearing down of dwellings or homes."

As You Read

Summarize the key points of each section under the correct heading in your Science Notebook. Be sure to add specific details and facts.

How does habitat destruction affect the well-being of both wild populations and humans?

Human Effects on the Environment

As a result of using technology, humans impact the natural world more than any other species does. Without limits on their behavior, humans can damage the environment in many ways.

Resource Use As the human population grows, it requires more and more resources to keep its members healthy and comfortable. Each new family needs a place to live, food, water, clothing, medicine, and tools. It takes a lot of wood, plastic, grain, cotton, and metal to meet the needs of just the United States!

Natural resources include water, trees, sunlight, coal, animals, wind, and all other useful products of the natural world. Some of these resources are **renewable resources**, or resources that can be used many times if managed properly. Water, trees, air, and sunlight are examples of renewable resources. Other resources, such as coal and crude oil, take millions of years to form. They are **nonrenewable resources** because once they are used, they are gone forever. Responsible planners ensure that they make **sustainable use** of natural resources, taking only as much as can be replaced by nature. Hunting, cutting trees, and pumping water for human use can all be sustainable activities if humans limit themselves to a level that nature can replenish.

Habitat Destruction No matter how carefully people plan, land that is used to grow crops or to build houses is no longer suitable for most of the organisms that once lived there. **Habitat destruction** occurs when a habitat is removed and replaced with some other type of habitat. As a result, the organisms living at the site must move or be destroyed. Examples of habitat destruction include draining wetlands, clearing land for farming, building housing developments, and strip-mining.

Habitat destruction is the most important reason that species are threatened with extinction today. Habitat destruction can hurt humans, too. Scientists believe that the terrible destruction caused by Hurricane Katrina in 2005 resulted from the removal of wetlands that would normally take up much of the regional floodwaters.

Killing of Sensitive Species Throughout history, humans have hunted for several reasons. They obtained food and necessary materials from animals and eliminated competition for crops and prey. Many species were driven to extinction by hunting thousands of years ago. As the human population grew, more and more species of animals were threatened with extinction from too much hunting. Laws were passed to ban the killing of sensitive species and to limit hunting. Nevertheless, poaching, or illegal hunting, continues to threaten many populations.

Some sensitive species of animals and plants play important roles in the ecosystems to which they belong. Whenever one species is removed, countless others are affected.

Did You Know?

Human activities can lead to the loss of even the largest populations. Passenger pigeons were the most numerous birds in the world, flying over North America in flocks estimated from witness accounts at two billion or more up until the mid-1800s. In 1914, the last passenger pigeon died at the Cincinnati Zoo.

Differentiated Instruction

Naturalistic Have each student choose an extinct organism to study. Ask students to look at the factors that led to the extinction of that plant or animal and what might have been done to save it. Students can present their findings to the class.

Background Information

Passenger pigeons were desirable for their meat and their feathers. In the 1850s, large-scale organized trapping and hunting decimated the passenger pigeon population. Because each of these pigeons lays only one egg per year, the pigeons were unable to sustain their population.

Introduced Species Wherever humans go, they take with them animals, plants, and microorganisms. If these species take hold in a new land, they are called **introduced species**. Introduced species, especially diseases, can have serious effects on an ecosystem and on the human population. The smallpox virus, which Spanish explorers brought to North America, killed 25 percent of the Aztecs and 60 to 90 percent of the Inca empire. American chestnut trees, which used to make up a quarter of eastern forests, have been almost completely killed off by an introduced fungus from Asia.

While the introductions of some species are accidental, others are intentional. People sometimes bring in natural enemies of introduced species in order to control them. Unfortunately, only about one in five biological-control efforts is successful. Others, such as the introduction of cane toads to Australia, end up causing even more damage.

Pollution and Atmospheric Change Over the last few centuries, humans have relied heavily on technology to feed and provide for their growing population. All of this machinery and production requires a lot of energy. In just the last 50 years, world use of fossil fuels—coal, oil, and natural gas—has increased by four times.

Two side effects of today's heavy use of fossil fuels are pollution and global warming. **Pollution** is the release of harmful substances into the environment. Sources of pollution include fertilizer in runoff from fields, smoke from power plants, and oil spills. Fertilizers can cause major changes in water ecosystems. Air pollution can result in human sickness and acid rain that kills trees and pond life. Oil spills kill animals by poisoning them.

Global warming is the rise in the average temperature of Earth's air and oceans. During the twentieth century, the planet warmed by about 0.6°C. While this may not sound like a big change, it was enough to speed up melting of polar ice caps and affect weather all over the world. Hurricanes, tornadoes, flooding, and droughts have become more common. Animals such as polar bears that depend on the arctic ice are likely to become extinct. Some species, especially parasites, will be able to expand their ranges as Earth warms, but scientists predict that the total number of species in the world will decrease.

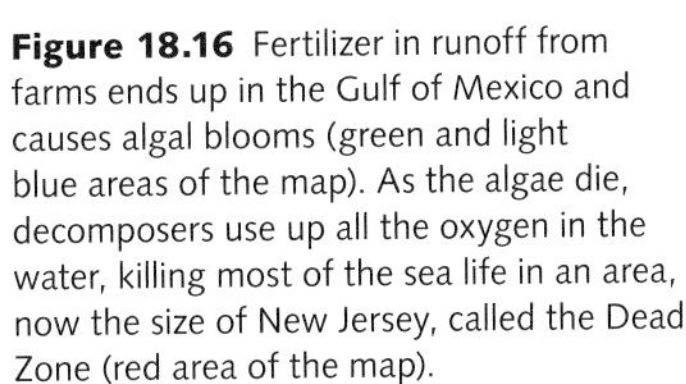

Figure 18.16 Fertilizer in runoff from farms ends up in the Gulf of Mexico and causes algal blooms (green and light blue areas of the map). As the algae die, decomposers use up all the oxygen in the water, killing most of the sea life in an area, now the size of New Jersey, called the Dead Zone (red area of the map).

Did You Know?

Some species have adapted to human cities and now have higher populations than they ever did in the past. Red foxes, crows, and raccoons find plenty of food in human yards and trash. The absence of predators, such as coyotes, in a city environment also helps these commensal species thrive.

Figure 18.15 A common frog is sitting on the head of a South American cane toad in this photo. The very large cane toad was introduced to Australia in the hope that it would destroy sugarcane beetles. Instead, the cane toad eats important pollinators and poisons native animals that try to eat it.

Teach

EXPLAIN to students that deliberate and unintentional changes to an ecosystem by humans through the introduction of a new species result in damage to the ecosystem 80 percent of the time. There are occasions, however, where the introduction of a new species has worked positively to control the uncontrolled growth of another species.

Vocabulary

introduced species Explain that the root of *introduced* is from the Latin *dūcere*, which means "to lead." Ask students to use this meaning to define the term. (When a species is introduced, it is led into the environment.)

pollution Tell students that *pollution* comes from the Latin *polluere*, meaning, "to soil" or "to defile." Have students use the derivation to create their own definitions for this word.

global warming Explain that global warming is the rise in Earth's average temperature. Scientists have noticed that global warming has had many negative effects on the planet's environment. Invite students to discuss what they already know about global warming.

Science Notebook EXTRA

A number of human societies have done so much damage to their environments that the ecosystem collapsed and humans were forced to leave or die out themselves. One example is Easter Island. Another example is the Norse colony in Greenland. Have students research one of these topics and record their findings in their Science Notebooks. Encourage them to identify which categories of human effects on the environment are illustrated by each case.

Background Information

In 2005, a Massachusetts Institute of Technology study found that hurricane wind speed has increased by 50 percent over the last 50 years. The intensity of hurricanes is affected by the temperature of the ocean. For that reason, some scientists believe that global warming is contributing to recent increases in hurricane severity.

Teach

EXPLAIN to students that governments have introduced many laws to protect the environment. Some of these laws have been successful at keeping our air and water clean and protecting wildlife. These laws tend to be controversial, because they force people and companies to make changes that are sometimes costly and difficult.

CONNECTION: **Engineering**

Dr. Lars Angenent, a professor of chemical engineering at Washington University in St. Louis, invented a fuel cell that can generate electricity from wastewater using microorganisms. He has successfully done this on a small scale and is working to improve his system so that it can be used on a larger scale to both clean up and provide energy for communities. Many more scientists are working to find other alternative energy sources.

EXTEND Have students choose a form of alternative energy, such as solar power, wind power, or nuclear power, and find out more about it: what it is, how economical it is, what progress has been made using it to make humans less dependent on nonrenewable sources of energy such as oil. Have students prepare reports on their findings. For more information, see the U.S. Department of Energy's Energy Efficiency and Renewable Energy Home Page at **http://www.eere.energy.gov/.**

CONNECTION: **Government**

The mission of the U.S. Environmental Protection Agency (E.P.A.) is to protect human health and the environment. This agency was established in 1970 and employs 18,000 people across the country. The E.P.A. works on environmental science, research, education, and assessment. To learn more, visit the U.S. Environmental Protection Agency Web site at **http://www.epa.gov/.**

CONNECTION: **Engineering**

Wastewater engineers are working with special microorganisms that produce electricity as they break down pollutants in wastewater. The engineers hope to develop treatment plants that will make all of the energy required to clean water. These new plants could be used in areas that have no wastewater treatment at all.

Figure 18.17 Pollution such as this smog over Los Angeles damaged human health and the environment, leading to the passage of the Clean Air Act.

Choices for Conservation

There are many ways in which humans can change and damage the natural world. There are also steps people can take to preserve it.

Protective Laws and Treaties Governments often make laws to protect species or ecosystems when it is clear that they are in danger of being destroyed by humans. The laws might protect only one or two species, like the Eagle Protection Act of 1940. They might protect whole ecosystems, as in the Wetlands Conservation Act of 1989. In each case, the laws make it illegal to kill or damage the protected species and ecosystems or to develop property in a way that would threaten them.

Some threats are too big for any one country to handle alone. In such cases, many countries will sign a treaty, or international agreement, to prevent further ecological damage. A total ban on the import and export of endangered species products was put in place with the Convention on the International Trade in Endangered Species (CITES). CITES has worked effectively to increase the elephant populations in some countries.

Protective laws are often controversial, meaning that not everyone approves of them. People in the United States value freedom and dislike laws that restrict their actions. Many protective laws are examples of efforts to balance the needs of humans with the needs of the environment.

Antipollution Measures Some environmental laws try to protect the environment as a whole, rather than protect certain species or sensitive habitats. In the nineteenth and early twentieth centuries, there were few laws controlling factory smokestacks and pollution from mines and farms. When it was clear that the health of people and wildlife suffered from the pollution, the Clean Air Act, the Clean Water Act, and related acts were passed. These laws require businesses, farms, and governments to clean up any water or factory waste before it enters the environment.

Preserves Sometimes, the best way to protect a species or a habitat is to set aside land as a nature preserve, or protected area. Preserves may belong to local, state, or national governments, private organizations, or individuals. Nature preserves are managed with the environment in mind, but they usually allow visitors to hike on marked paths. Many preserves have the motto, "Take only pictures; leave only footprints."

Personal Choices You can do a lot to help preserve the natural world. Keep in mind that every purchase you make and every product you use has an impact. Take the catalogs your family gets in the mail as an example. The average American receives more than 60 catalogs in the mail each year. More than nine billion kilograms of catalogs are mailed yearly in the United States. Catalogs are usually made directly from lumber, often from the old-growth forests of Canada. What can you do to help reduce the effects on the environment? You can cancel catalogs you don't read, recycle used catalogs, or call or write to companies urging them to use recycled paper.

ELL Strategy

Relate to Personal Experience Encourage students to think about their own environment and how they affect it on a daily basis. Ask students to list three to four things they do that have a positive effect on their environment and three or four things that have a negative impact. Then, ask students to think about what they could do to reverse and prevent negative effects.

Background Information

The Federal Water Pollution Control Act Amendment, better known as the Clean Water Act, became law in 1972. Since then it has undergone many revisions, but the main purpose of the act is to protect our waters. The act makes it illegal to dump any pollutant into navigable waters without a permit. With the implementation of the Clean Water Act, the amount waste dumped directly into streams and rivers was reduced.

Ordinary citizens can improve human effects on the natural world by insisting that it is the right thing to do. Millions of concerned people boycotted, or refused to buy, tuna caught in fishnets that also drowned dolphins. The result of this campaign is clear: More than 90 percent of the tuna now sold in the world is caught using dolphin-safe nets.

The bald eagle is a large bird of prey with a wingspan of 2 to 2.5 m. It lives near water in every U.S. state except Hawaii, nests in tall trees, and mates for life. Bald eagles hunt for fish and eat dead animals. Without humans, limiting factors for eagle populations include less food in the winter, diseases, and predation on the young by owls and raccoons. **Figure 18.18** summarizes the human threats to bald eagles and what has been done to preserve the species.

Figure It Out

1. In which year did the eagle population rise past 5,000 nesting pairs?
2. When the population reaches its carrying capacity, will it be above or below the level of 1782? Explain your prediction.

Nesting Pairs of Bald Eagles in the Continental United States

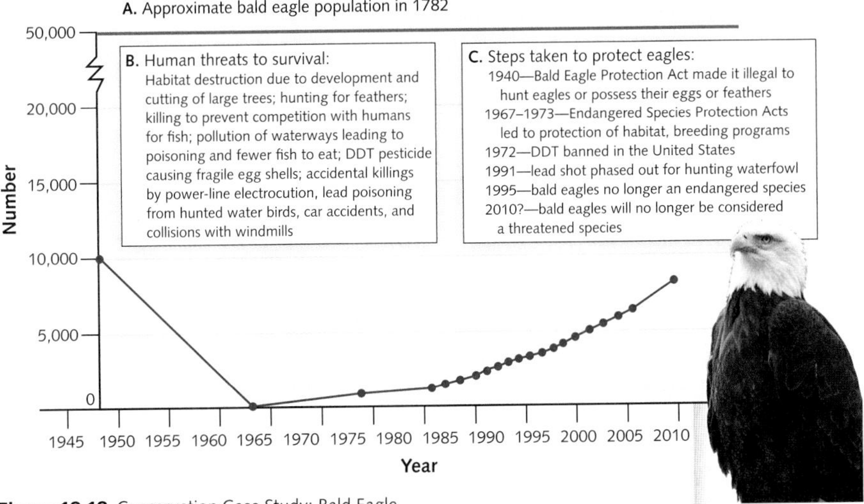

A. Approximate bald eagle population in 1782
B. Human threats to survival:
Habitat destruction due to development and cutting of large trees; hunting for feathers; killing to prevent competition with humans for fish; pollution of waterways leading to poisoning and fewer fish to eat; DDT pesticide causing fragile egg shells; accidental killings by power-line electrocution, lead poisoning from hunted water birds, car accidents, and collisions with windmills
C. Steps taken to protect eagles:
1940—Bald Eagle Protection Act made it illegal to hunt eagles or possess their eggs or feathers
1967–1973—Endangered Species Protection Acts led to protection of habitat, breeding programs
1972—DDT banned in the United States
1991—lead shot phased out for hunting waterfowl
1995—bald eagles no longer an endangered species
2010?—bald eagles will no longer be considered a threatened species
Number
50,000
20,000
15,000
10,000
5,000
0
1945 1950 1955 1960 1965 1970 1975 1980 1985 1990 1995 2000 2005 2010
Year

Figure 18.18 Conservation Case Study: Bald Eagle

After You Read

1. Explain why the human population has not yet reached its carrying capacity.
2. What are five actions people can take to save species and ecosystems?
3. Describe two effects that humans have on the environment that can be repaired and two others that are nearly impossible to undo.

Teach

EXPLAIN that while humans have done a lot to damage their environment, there is a lot they can do to prevent further damage. Discuss with students the different ways in which they can personally work to clean up the environment. Encourage students to think about ways to recycle and conserve energy. Remind students of the saying, "Reduce, reuse, recycle." Ask students what that phrase means to them, and record their responses on the board.

Figure It Out: Figure 18.18

ANSWER **1.** 2001 **2.** The population will be below this level; there is not as much available habitat.

Assess

EVALUATE Use the After You Read questions and the Alternative Assessment to help you assess students' understanding of the lesson.

After You Read

1. Humans have developed technology that raises the carrying capacity of Earth.
2. People can preserve habitats, make laws protecting endangered species, make treaties to prevent trade in endangered species, recycle paper and other materials, clean up polluted water, prevent air pollution, etc.
3. Human effects that can be repaired include wetlands draining, water pollution, over-hunting, and air pollution. Human effects that are impossible, or nearly impossible, to undo include driving a species to extinction, mining ores, producing nuclear wastes, extracting and burning fossil fuels, introducing exotic species, clear-cutting rain forests, and building housing developments.

Differentiated Instruction

Visual Have students research the different ways in which they can help preserve their environment. Tell each student to pick one of these ways and make a poster encouraging people to take an active part in protecting the environment. Students may be encouraged to work in groups on this project. Display student posters around the school.

Alternative Assessment

EVALUATE Provide students who have difficulty answering the After You Read questions with a list of the lesson headings, and have students summarize the main idea from each section of the lesson. Allow students to refer to their Science Notebooks.

Chapter 18 Summary

VOCABULARY REVIEW

Check students' sentences or paragraphs to make sure that they understand the meaning of each vocabulary term.

PREPARE FOR CHAPTER TEST

Evaluate students' essays using the following criteria:

1. The topic sentence, or main idea, should restate the Key Concept.
2. The supporting paragraphs should incorporate the answers to the Learning Goal questions students have written and include details, facts, and examples they have recorded in their Science Notebooks.
3. The concluding sentence should sum up the main idea of the chapter and restate the Key Concept.

MASTERING CONCEPTS

True or False

1. False, mutualism
2. True
3. False, species introduction
4. False, reproductive cycle
5. True
6. False, competition

Short Answer

7. A parasite generally does not kill its host and may live on or in the host's body for an extended period of time. Predators kill and eat their prey, and therefore have a short relationship with the prey.
8. Trees can be limited by the amount of sunlight, the amount of water, and the nutrient levels in the soil. Diseases and animals that eat the trees can also limit tree populations.
9. When a habitat is destroyed, almost all of the organisms in it must move or die.
10. A population's range ends where the limiting factors become too severe for the species to survive.
11. Possible steps include recycling paper and ink cartridges, sharing books or papers, encouraging walking and carpooling, and serving more vegetables.
12. The members of any close relationship are likely to affect each other's fitness.

Chapter 18

Summary

KEY CONCEPTS

18.1 Population Growth and Size

- A population's growth rate is determined by its reproductive style, limiting factors, and natural events.
- Each population has a carrying capacity, or maximum number of individuals that its environment can sustain.

18.2 Relationships Among Populations

- Communities are made up of interacting populations that may help or hurt each other.
- A close relationship between individuals of two or more species is called symbiosis.
- Different species compete with each other for limited resources, causing all to evolve.
- Ecologists design experiments to determine what relationships exist between species, now and in the past.

18.3 Adaptations: Challenges and Opportunities

- Adaptations to relationships with other species increase the fitness of organisms.
- Two species with closely connected lives tend to become adapted to each other.
- Two species that use the same resources can survive in the same area only if they are adapted for using the resources in different ways.

18.4 People and the Environment

- Humans have raised Earth's carrying capacity for the human population through the years by making use of technology.
- Humans can cause enormous changes to the environment by altering habitats, killing other organisms, introducing new species, and releasing pollution.
- There are many steps that governments and people can take to prevent or repair environmental damage.
- Each person's choices about how to use resources affect the environment.

VOCABULARY REVIEW

Write each term in a complete sentence, or write a paragraph relating several terms.

18.1
factor, p. 309
reproductive cycle, p. 309
limiting factor, p. 310
density, p. 310
competition, p. 310
range, p. 310
carrying capacity, p. 311

18.2
symbiosis, p. 313
fitness, p. 313
mutualism, p. 313
commensalism, p. 314
parasitism, p. 314
host, p. 314
predation, p. 315

18.4
technology, p. 319
natural resource, p. 320
renewable resource, p. 320
nonrenewable resource, p. 320
sustainable use, p. 320
habitat destruction, p. 320
introduced species, p. 321
pollution, p. 321
global warming, p. 321

PREPARE FOR CHAPTER TEST

To prepare for the chapter test, create a question from each Learning Goal. Use the information in your Science Notebook to answer each question. Then use these answers to write a well-developed essay about the chapter. Use the Key Concept on the first page of this chapter as your topic sentence.

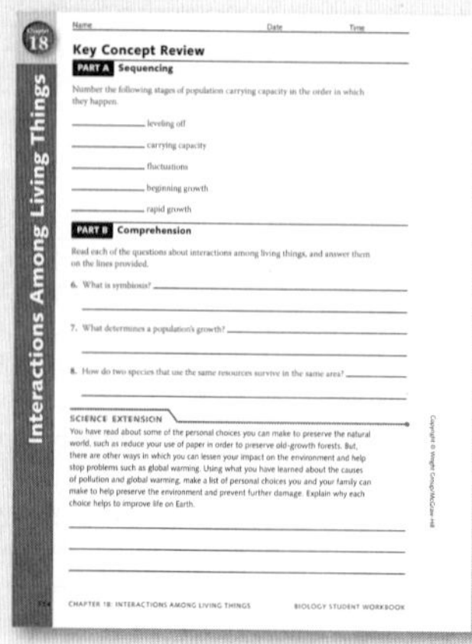

Key Concept Review
Workbook, p. 114

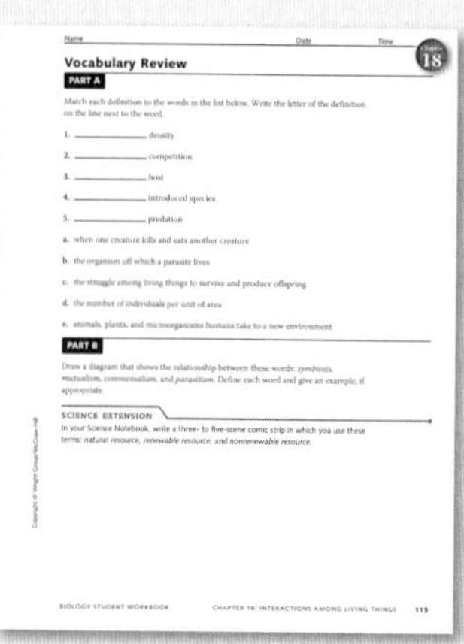

Vocabulary Review
Workbook, p. 115

MASTERING CONCEPTS

True or False

If the statement is true, write "true." If it is false, change the underlined word or words to make the statement true.

1. In parasitism, both species in the relationship benefit.
2. To avoid predation, some species can run fast and have camouflage.
3. Commensalism occurs when people bring plants to a new environment.
4. The rate and timing of a species' reproduction is called its carrying capacity.
5. Humans have not yet reached their carrying capacity due to their use of technology.
6. Two species struggling for the same limited resource is called predation.

Short Answer

Answer each of the following in a sentence or brief paragraph.

7. What are the differences between a parasite and a predator?
8. Describe the limiting factors that affect trees in a forest.
9. Why is habitat destruction the most important reason that species are threatened with extinction?
10. What determines the range of a population?
11. What are some steps that your school could take to make its use of resources more sustainable?
12. Why have most examples of commensalism been reclassified over the years?

Critical Thinking

Use what you have learned in this chapter to answer each of the following.

13. **Analyze** In what ways are snakes adapted to their predatory lifestyle?
14. **Predict** Goats are introduced to an island that previously had no large mammals. Predict the effect on native plants, mice, fleas, and eagles.
15. **Diagram** A fire reduces the populations of two species of mice to very low numbers. One species breeds rapidly at a young age, while the other has only a few offspring at a much later age. Draw a diagram showing how each population grows to its carrying capacity.
16. **Devise a Plan** Pollution, being hunted for meat and oil, and noise in the ocean have nearly caused the blue whale to become extinct. Devise a plan to help the blue whale population recover.

Standardized Test Question

Choose the letter of the response that correctly answers the question.

17. The relationship between this mosquito and the human it is biting is best described as ________________.
   A. predation
   B. commensalism
   C. parasitism
   D. mutualism

Test-Taking Tip

Don't get stuck on a difficult question. Instead, make a small mark next to the question. Remember to go back and answer the question later. Other parts of the test may give you a clue that will help you answer the question.

Critical Thinking

13. Snakes have a mouth that opens wide to eat large prey, venom to subdue prey, fangs that keep prey from escaping, and camouflage to hide from prey.
14. Goats will eat the plants, reducing the plant population. Competition for plants will reduce mouse populations. Fleas will have a new host; their population will increase. Eagles may prey on baby goats, but they will have less prey as the mouse population falls.
15. A sample graph is shown below.
16. Elements of the plan could include passing laws to prevent ocean pollution, making preserves where the whales live, passing laws to limit the noise that boats and machines make in the whale habitat, passing laws to prevent hunting, and signing a treaty to prevent trade in whale meat and oil.

Standardized Test Question

17. C

Reading Links

Saving Birds: Heroes Around the World

This brief treatment of bird conservation efforts increases student awareness of human impact on the environment by telling six success stories with careful attention to social context and relevance. Each of the six rescue projects, in which naturalists saved a species from extinction, is supplemented by resource links for further research and accompanied by remarkable color photos of rarely witnessed habitats and rescue situations.

Salmansohn, Pete and Stephen W. Kress. Tilbury House Publishers. 40 pp. Illustrated. Trade ISBN: 978-0-88448-276-5.

One Kingdom: Our Lives with Animals

This book explores the many facets of the human-animal relationship, from animals' roles as faithful companions to their use as a source of food. Reinforced with black-and-white photographs, the narrative explores the cultural, ethical, and scientific influences on human-animal interactions throughout history. Readers are challenged to approach topics from multiple angles, building an excellent foundation for classroom discussion and debate.

Noyes, Deborah. Houghton Mifflin Company. 144 pp. Illustrated. Trade ISBN: 978-0-618-49914-4.

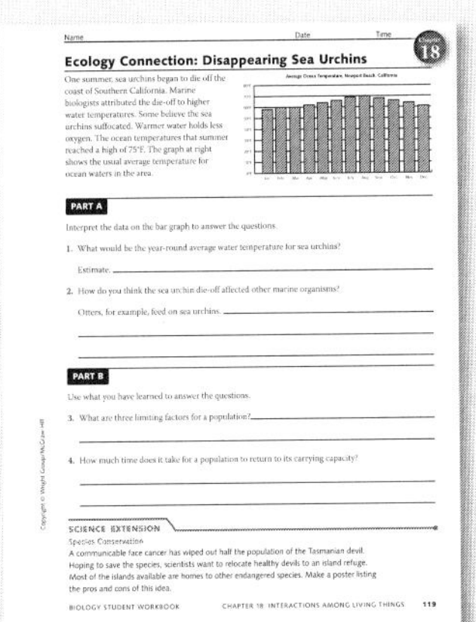

Ecology Connection: Disappearing Sea Urchins

PART A

PART B

SCIENCE EXTENSION

Curriculum Connection
Workbook, p. 119

15.

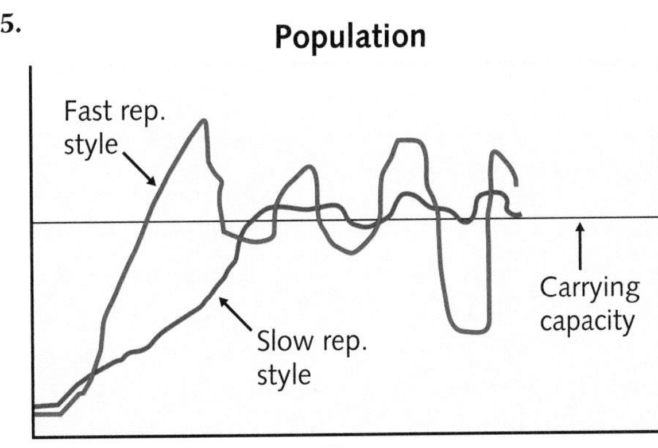

Chapter 18

Labs

18A Connections Within Ecosystems

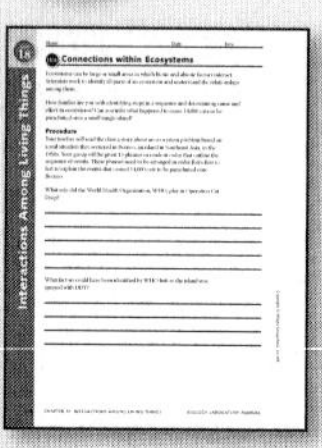

This prechapter introduction activity is designed to determine what students already know about the connections within ecosystems by engaging them in identifying a sequence of steps, making predictions, and identifying cause and effect.

Objectives

- identify the sequence of steps that occurred in Operation Cat Drop
- identify cause and effect for each step
- communicate conclusions

Planning

½ class period groups of 4–6 students

Materials (per group)

- one copy of Sequence Table 1, cut into the 13 steps

Advance Preparation

- Create a sequence chart similar to the one below for each group. Cut out the 13 phrases so that students will be able to move them easily on their desktops. This encourages risk taking and communication within the group. NOTE: *Leaving the phrases attached in one block makes it too difficult for students to obtain the logical sequence.*

Sequence Table 1

Rats brought the plague. (12)	Rats increased. (11)
Cats died. (10)	Caterpillar numbers went up. (3)
WHO sent DDT to Borneo. (1)	Mosquitoes were wiped out. (2)
Caterpillars ate grass roofs. (4)	Cats were parachuted in. (13)
Cats caught lizards containing DDT. (8)	Roaches stored DDT in their bzodies. (5)
Lizards disappeared. (9)	Lizards slowed down. (7)
Lizards ate roaches and absorbed DDT. (6)	

Note that the number in parentheses after each phrase indicates its place in the correct sequence of events.

- Before starting, tell students that the acronym *WHO* stands for the World Health Organization.
- Before starting, tell students that DDT is a pesticide that can be toxic to humans, animals, and the environment.
- Read to students the following background information about Operation Cat Drop:
  - Borneo is a jungle island in the Pacific Ocean. In the 1950s, the island's population suffered from malaria. The World Health Organization had a solution: they sprayed DDT throughout the island to kill the mosquitoes. This caused other problems in the ecosystem, however. Because parasitic wasps that controlled the island's thatch-eating caterpillars were also killed by the DDT, the roofs of houses started to collapse. The DDT also infected insects that were eaten by lizards, which in turn were eaten by cats. The cats died, and the rat population increased. Diseases such as plague and typhus began to appear and spread. To solve this problem, the World Health Organization parachuted in 14,000 live cats onto Borneo.

Engagement Guide

- Ask: *What sequence did your group develop?*
- Encourage students to talk with group members in defense of their sequence.
- Challenge students to think about what steps in the sequence of events might have eliminated the need for the parachuting operation.

Going Further

Encourage students to think of other situations in which an ecosystem's problems worsened because all biotic and abiotic factors were not considered as the remediation efforts were implemented. Then, ask students to think of a situation in which a local community (school) problem was solved correctly. Ask: *What steps were taken that made the solution successful?*

18B The Fittest Will Survive

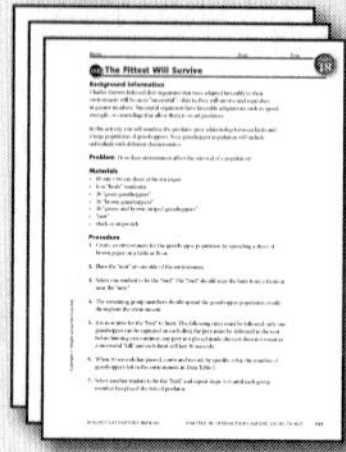

Objectives

- evaluate results from a table
- organize data
- compare and contrast adaptations of organisms

Skill Set

observing, comparing and contrasting, recording and analyzing data, stating conclusions

Planning

 1 class period 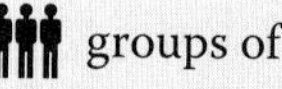 groups of 2–4 students

Materials

Materials for this activity are listed in the Student Laboratory Manual.

Advance Preparation

- The environment can be brown material, such as packaging paper or paper grocery bags. Use the same material to produce the grasshoppers. Use a green marker to produce the green- and brown-striped grasshoppers.
- Any small container can be used for the nest.

Answers to Observations: Data Table 1

Answers for each group will vary, but the general trend will be for a greater number of the green and striped grasshoppers to be picked up before the brown grasshoppers are. It is not unusual for all grasshoppers to be picked up, especially if the class has "active" learners.

Answers to Analysis and Conclusions

1. More green and striped grasshoppers were picked up in the earlier flights than in the last flight.
2. The first bird was the most successful because more prey were available on this flight.
3. The brown grasshoppers were best adapted to the environment because they were the last to be picked up by the bird. These grasshoppers were camouflaged and harder for the birds to see and capture in the environment.
4. Theoretically, in this situation, both animals would have used their adaptations to the environment successfully. The bird would have been able to swoop without regard to dangerous changes in elevation. However, student groups may not have thought of this adaptation since they did not experience it themselves. Students should be able to answer that the brown grasshoppers used their colors to adapt by blending in, but the grasshoppers were more limited in their environment because they had no place to burrow or hide.
5. Based on the data collected, the brown grasshoppers were best adapted to the environment and were more likely to survive and reproduce. This type of adaptation will also help the birds survive, because if there are no grasshoppers, the birds will have to look elsewhere for food.

Going Further

Ask the class what happens if the environment of a population is disrupted. Prompt the class to list abiotic and biotic factors that could disrupt the population (disease, weather, invasion of other organisms). Ask students if there are any national laws to protect organisms. Have students do research to answer this question and, additionally, to find out what happens if all nations do not agree to the laws.

18C It's a Small Ocean After All

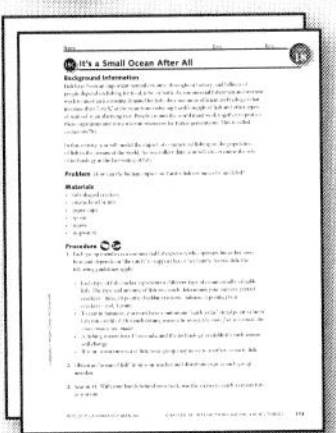

Objectives

- record observations
- evaluate the impact of exploiting resources
- summarize the roles of global citizens

Skill Set

observing, comparing and contrasting, recording and analyzing data, stating conclusions

Planning

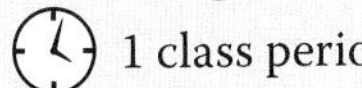 1 class period 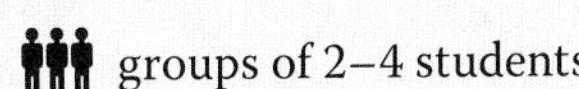 groups of 2–4 students

Materials

Materials for this activity are listed in the Student Laboratory Manual.

Advance Preparation

- Each group needs a large plastic, shallow bowl or tub to represent the ocean, and each student needs a straw and a cup in which to keep his or her "catch." Use different varieties of crackers (cheddar, pretzel, and plain) to represent different types of fish populations. **CAUTION:** *Be careful of student food allergies, and remind students not to eat their "fish."*
- Each group's "ocean" should have 24 fish. You may want to assign a specific ocean to each group and vary the types of crackers so that groups do not have the same fish populations in each ocean.
- Assign one student in each group to have access to the new technology (spoon) in step 7.

Answers to Observations: Data Table 1

Answers will vary. Catch values should increase as technology improves but increase only for students who had access to the spoon during Season #3. Catch values for Season #4 should also show a decrease due to increased competition. Data will vary if one group depletes the fish in its ocean and moves to another ocean for subsequent seasons.

Answers to Analysis and Conclusions

1. Answers will vary but might include the idea that some students were over-fishing in order to improve their "catch value."
2. Answers will vary, but student responses must be supported by their data. Most students will comment that improvements in technology increased catch value but decreased the population of fish remaining in the ocean.
3. Increased competition will result in decreased catch value and decreased population of fish remaining in the ocean. Students should support their answers using data from Season #4.
4. Answers will vary but might include maintaining accurate information about commercially important fish populations, international laws or treaties that establish maximum fishing limits, and guidelines regarding the use of various technologies.

Going Further

Explain to students that fish in the ocean are a common resource that is available to all. Have students identify other common resources and identify problems associated with the use and management of these common resources.

Unit 6

Case Study 1: Going to Extremes

Gather More Information

Encourage students to use the library or the NSTA SciLinks Web site noted at the start of each chapter to learn more about these case study topics and to conduct further research.

Have students use the following keywords to aid their searches:

- extremophile
- extreme environment
- ocean-floor vent
- microorganism

Research the Big Picture

- Have students discuss how scientists are able to safely explore extreme environments such as deep-sea vents. Pose the following questions to students to begin the discussion: *What are some of the challenges and dangers the scientists face? What are the rewards of their exploration? Are the rewards worth the challenges and dangers?*
- Have groups of students research a type of extremophile not detailed in this case study (e.g., organisms that live in very hot, dry deserts, dark caves, or the vents of volcanoes). Have students think about survival in the extreme environment chosen by their group. Questions to think about include: *How is the organism able to survive in the extreme environment? How does the environment support the organism? How has the organism adapted to its environment?*
- When all groups have completed their research, each should present its findings to the class.

SCIENCE JOURNAL

Going to Extremes

MOST LIVING THINGS on Earth exist within strict boundaries—for example, in places that are neither too hot nor too cold, neither too damp nor too dry. But, extremophiles are different. They live comfortably in environments that would kill most other forms of life. They live in boiling springs, bone-dry deserts, dark caves, and even the vents of volcanoes.

Scientists have explored all sorts of extreme environments on Earth in search of these organisms, which are mostly microorganisms. They have found many types. Some thrive in temperatures over 80°C (176°F). Others prefer freezing cold temperatures. There are even those that can withstand environments as acidic as the inside of a car battery.

Amazing ecosystems of extremophiles exist on the ocean floor. They live near seafloor cracks, or vents, in Earth's crust. These vents spew out boiling hot water full of chemicals such as hydrogen sulfide. Until scientists discovered these life-forms, they thought green plants or algae formed the first trophic level of just about every food chain. The extremophile ecosystems on the ocean floor, however, never have access to sunlight. The unusual bacteria at the base of these deep-sea food chains use chemicals that pour out of hot-water vents for the energy they need to make organic compounds. These organisms live in constant darkness, crushing pressure, and scalding temperatures. They include unusual species of fishes, shrimps, crabs, and worms nearly 1 m long.

These extremophiles live in darkness on the seafloor.

Thermophilic (heat-loving) bacteria thrive in this hot spring at Yellowstone National Park.

Extremophiles challenge what we have always thought about life on Earth. Scientists now know that life can exist in environments on Earth that were once thought to be incapable of supporting life. Many scientists think that it is important to look more closely at the hostile environments on other planets. Life could be lurking there, too!

CAREER CONNECTION ARBORNAUT

RAIN FORESTS are the most diverse ecosystems on Earth, but they are very difficult to study. In a rain forest, most of the plant and animal life is high up in the forest canopy. The upper parts of the canopy can reach 30 m (100 ft) above the ground. If you're a biologist who studies rain forests, there is just one thing to do: climb into the trees.

Biologists who do their work at the tops of rain forests are called canopy biologists, or arbornauts. For these scientists, getting to work is an amazing process. They use all sorts of strange contraptions—towers, cranes, rope systems, platforms, and even devices that look like small ski lifts. Once they are up among the branches, they are in danger of falling or being caught in sudden storms. But, the bird's-eye view of the plants and animals of the rain-forest ecosystem makes all of the dangers worthwhile.

How do you become an arbornaut? Most arbornauts go to school for years to earn a doctorate degree in biology. Then, they specialize in studying treetop environments. It also helps to have no fear of heights!

Case Study 2: Disappearing Ice, Disappearing Bears

Gather More Information

Encourage students to use the library or the NSTA SciLinks Web site noted at the start of each chapter to learn more about these case study topics and to conduct further research.

Have students use the following keywords to aid their searches:

- polar bears
- global warming
- carbon dioxide
- greenhouse gas
- atmosphere
- Arctic Ocean

Research the Big Picture

- In small groups, have students list and analyze factors that have affected and are affecting the polar bear population. For their analyses, students should consider such questions as: *What is the nature of the factor? When did the situation become significant? What are possible causes of the factor? Is anything being done to resolve the situation? What are some long-term effects?* As a class, discuss the groups' findings.
- Using the scientific method, have pairs or groups of students discuss solutions to the polar bear problem presented in the case study. Each group should present its work to the class.
- Have small groups of students discuss and record how humans have indirectly

Disappearing Ice, Disappearing Bears

Research and Report

Both the arctic and antarctic are cold and bleak but not lifeless. With a partner, research an arctic or antarctic ecosystem. Present your findings in a report that includes a labeled drawing of a typical arctic food chain.

TROUBLING THINGS are happening in the arctic. Temperatures are rising, having increased an average of 7 to 9°C over the past century. As a result, the thick arctic ice cap is thinning and breaking up. Satellite images show that it has been shrinking at a rate of about 9 percent each decade in recent years.

For most scientists, the cause is clear: global warming. Earth's average temperature is slowly rising, largely due to human actions. Burning huge amounts of fuels such as oil, gas, and coal releases carbon dioxide and other gases into the atmosphere. Carbon dioxide is a natural greenhouse gas—a gas that holds in Earth's heat. As carbon dioxide builds up in the air, the heating effect is increased. In the arctic, the heating effect is magnified.

Polar bears are one species that has been feeling the effects of global warming. Polar bears hunt seals and raise their young on ice floes that drift on arctic waters from late fall through spring. After the ice breaks up in the spring, the bears stay on land and live off their stored fat until the ice returns and they can hunt again. For years, however, the ice has been breaking up earlier and earlier in the spring. This gives the polar bears less time to hunt and build up fat to last them through the summer months. In some cases, female polar bears have become lighter in weight and less successful at reproducing. Polar bear young are also less likely to survive.

Although polar bears are good swimmers, melting ice has another tragic effect: more open water between ice floes and between floes and the land. The bears must swim longer distances between floes to hunt. Exhausted bears are drowning in the open water. If polar bears stay on land to hunt for food, they must compete with more aggressive land animals such as the grizzly bear.

As global warming continues, the worldwide population of 20,000 polar bears could drop by more than 30 percent in the next 45 years. Some scientists predict that continued warming could even bring about an ice-free Arctic Ocean by the end of the century. Unfortunately, that would mean a polar bear-free arctic, as well.

New Marine Species Found

SCIENTISTS EXPLORING the Pacific Ocean off Papua, Indonesia, recently found something quite unusual—a patch of ocean so full of life that it is being called "Earth's richest seascape." The area contains about 1,200 species of fish and 600 species of reef-building coral—about 75 percent of the world's total. They have also discovered some strange marine species, including a shrimp that looks like a praying mantis and a shark that can walk along the seafloor on its fins.

Scientists now face the problem of ensuring that this biodiversity is protected. Local people fish these waters using practices that could damage the ecosystem. Fishing teams often stun the fish first with poisons such as cyanide or blasts of dynamite. Huge fleets of factory fishing ships may soon move into the area. These ships drag along the ocean bottom huge nets that sweep in all marine life and destroy marine ecosystems.

The goal of scientists is to encourage sustainable use of this rich area. That means allowing fishing to occur in ways that will conserve fish populations and protect ecosystems. Ten percent of the area is now protected. There is hope that the government of Indonesia will protect a larger part of these seas.

This shark species walks on the seafloor.

CONNECTION: Career

Before students read the Career Connection feature, have them refer back to the Career Research project they completed earlier. Have them recall that Arbornaut is one of the jobs they may have researched. Ask students to take notes on any new information they learn about the career as they read the feature.

When students are finished reading, ask groups of students to research rain forests located around the world. Assign one or more continents to each group. Record the locations on the board, and then have students help you prepare a map identifying the continents and showing the locations of all the rain forests. Have each student discuss with a partner whether he or she would want a career as an arbornaut living in any of the designated locations, and why. Afterward, have pairs share their discussions with the class.

affected the polar bear population. Then, have students prepare a presentation of the highlights of their discussions.

Background Information

In some parts of North America where sea ice has retreated, more bears are found onshore where it is hard for them to hunt for food. In some of these areas, scientists have seen a decrease in the bear population.

Case Study 3: New Marine Species Found

Gather More Information

Encourage students to use the library or the NSTA SciLinks Web site noted at the start of each chapter to learn more about these case study topics and to conduct further research.

Have students use the following keywords to aid their searches:

- Papua, Indonesia
- marine species
- biodiversity
- sustainable use

Research the Big Picture

- Have students discuss how human influences can affect sustainable use of the world's valuable areas of biodiversity. After students have identified several human influences, have them use reference materials, Internet resources, and photos from magazines and/or newspapers to present their ideas in a visual display.
- Have half of the class analyze the advantages of protecting areas of biodiversity and the other half analyze the disadvantages of protecting areas of biodiversity.
- Upon completion of the analysis, encourage the two groups to orally debate this issue.

Science Challenge Workbook, pp. 120–121

Unit 7

Human Body

Introduce Unit 7

EXPLAIN that this unit includes a discussion of each body system and general health and wellness. Ask: *What human body systems are you familiar with? What do you know about health and wellness? What questions do you have about human body systems and health and wellness?* Have students discuss the questions with a partner and then write the answers in their Science Notebooks. Remind students to add to or revise their questions and answers as they read.

Unit Projects

For each project below, students can use the Student Presentation Builder on the Student CD-ROM to display their results and their Science Notebooks for their project notes.

Career

Have each student research a career related to knowledge of the human body (e.g., lab technician, nurse practitioner, dietician, athletic trainer, doctor, medical researcher). Ask students to define the job, describe what it entails, and identify the skills or experience it requires. Then, have students prepare a short presentation detailing what they learned.

Apply

Ask each student to keep track of everything he or she eats for a week. Then, have students look at the FDA's daily Calorie and fat recommendations and compare them with their own intake. After a week, have each student use this information to create a report that describes healthy changes in lifestyle and dietary habits.

Technology

Have students research a human body system and a medical technology, such as X rays or magnetic resonance imaging (MRI), used to study it.

Unit 7

Human Body

Skin, Skeletal System, and Muscular System

How do the skin, the skeleton, and the body's muscles work together?

Respiratory and Circulatory Systems

What role do the respiratory and circulatory systems play in keeping the body healthy?

Digestive and Excretory Systems

What are the main processes involved in the digestive and excretory systems?

Nervous and Endocrine Systems

How do the nervous and endocrine systems work together?

Reproduction and Development

What are the functions of the organs in the reproductive system?

Disease and the Body's Defenses

How do the body's defense systems help fight disease?

Health and Wellness

What healthful habits should be practiced to care for the human body?

Software Summary

Student CD-ROM
- —Interactive Student Book
- —Vocabulary Review
- —Key Concept Review
- —Lab Report Template
- —ELL Preview and Writing Activities
- —Presentation Digital Library
- —Graphic Organizing Software
- —Spanish Cognate Dictionary

Interactive Labs

Chapter 19C—How Joints, Muscles, and Bones Work Together

Chapter 20B—The Beating Heart

Chapter 21A—A Model of the Digestive System

Chapter 22C—Concentrating on Glands and Hormones

Chapter 23C—Sea Urchin Fertilization

Chapter 24B—How Pathogens Spread

Skin, Skeletal System, and Muscular System

Chapter 19

KEY CONCEPT The skin, skeletal system, and muscular system protect the body, give it shape, and aid in motion.

Imagine a complex machine that can play and do chores. This machine thinks and dreams. It reacts to situations and solves problems. It even feels emotions. This machine is your body! The human body enables you to move, work, and enjoy a sunny day. It enables you to think and wonder. It enables you to feel happiness, sadness, fear, and excitement.

The human body is organized into systems that carry out different functions to keep you alive. Three of these systems consist mainly of the skin, the skeleton, and the muscles.

Think About the Human Body

Most people take for granted all the extraordinary things the human body can do.

- Think about the things your body does every day. What do you think are some functions of your skin, muscles, and bones?
- Make a three-column chart in your Science Notebook, labeling one column *Skin*, one column *Bones*, and one column *Muscles*. Use your chart to list what you think your skin, bones, and muscles do. How do they work to keep you healthy? Review your chart and add to your lists as you read this chapter.

www.scilinks.org
Body Systems **Code: WGB19**

Chapter 19 Planning Guide			
Instructional Periods	National Standards	Lab Manual	Workbook
19.1 3 period	G.1, G.3; C.1, C.2, G.1, G.3; UCP.1, UCP.2	**Lab 19A—p. 116** Muscle Fatigue **Lab 19B—p. 117** Comparing Smooth, Cardiac, and Skeletal Muscle Tissues **Lab 19C—p. 120** How Joints, Muscles, and Bones Work Together	Key Concept Review p. 122 Vocabulary Review p. 123 Interpreting Diagrams p. 124 Reading Comprehension p. 125 Curriculum Connection p. 126 Science Challenge p. 127
19.2 2 period	A.2, C.1, C.3, F.1; F.1; UCP.5		
19.3 2 periods	C.1; B.4, C.1; UCP.5		
19.4 2 periods	A.1, C.1; B.4, C.1; UCP.3, UCP.5		

Middle School Standard; High School Standard; Unifying Concept and Principle

Chapter 19 Lessons

Introduce Chapter 19

As a starting activity, use LAB 19A Muscle Fatigue on page 116 of the Laboratory Manual.

ENGAGE Tell students that you will give them some clues about an object, and you want them to guess what you are describing. The first clue is *a complex machine.* Ask for student guesses, and write them on the board. The second clue is *follows commands from a central location.* Again, gather students' speculations. The third clue is *moves on command and by reflex.* Continue in this manner until students realize that you are describing the human body. Explain that the body is able to perform all these functions because of its organization. Tell students that in this chapter, they will learn about the skin, the skeletal system, and the muscular system.

Think About the Human Body

Model the three-column chart on the board. Ask students to share what they think the functions of the skin, bones, and muscles are. Write some of their ideas in the appropriate columns on the chart. If students have difficulty thinking of ideas, write *Allow body to move* in the *Muscles* column. Have students create their own three-column charts in their Science Notebooks, and give them a few minutes to add their own ideas.

19.1 Introduce

ENGAGE Have students stand in groups of four or five and hold hands. Give each group a plastic toy hoop, and tell students that each member of the group must pass his or her entire body through the hoop without letting go of hands. Have each group time how long it takes to get the hoop around, and give them two or three opportunities to improve their times. Ask students how they had to work together to accomplish the task.

Before You Read

Draw the concept map on the board. As a class, preview the first three headings in Lesson 19.1, *Levels of Organization*, *Cells*, and *Tissues*, and add them to the map. Have students brainstorm how these terms should be connected to the circle entitled *The Human Body*. Then, predict that a smaller circle, entitled *Epithelial Tissue*, will connect to *Tissues*. Give students a few minutes to draw their own maps in their Science Notebooks. Students' predictions should reflect how they think cells, tissues, organs, and organ systems are related. Check students' maps throughout the lesson.

Vocabulary terms are listed on the first student page of each lesson. You may wish to preview the terms before introducing each lesson. Strategies for teaching the vocabulary appear on the pages where the terms are introduced.

Teach

EXPLAIN that in this chapter, students will learn how the human body is organized into cells, tissues, organs, and organ systems.

Learning Goals

- Describe the levels of organization in the human body.
- Review the basic structure of cells.
- Identify the four types of tissue found in the human body.

New Vocabulary

cell
tissue
epithelial tissue
connective tissue
muscle tissue
nervous tissue
organ
organ system

19.1 Human Body Organization

Before You Read

Create a concept map in your Science Notebook by writing *The Human Body* in a circle. Draw several smaller circles around this circle, and connect each small circle to the center circle with a line. Preview the material in this lesson, and predict what you will learn by filling in the smaller circles of your concept map.

It's the top of the ninth inning. The score is six to five in favor of the home team, which will win if it can hold on to its lead. For the visitors, the tying run is at third base, waiting for his chance to even the score. The go-ahead run is on first base. With one out, a new batter comes to the plate. He swings at the first pitch and sends the ball speeding down the first-base line. The first baseman dives for the ball, catches it, and tags the bag for the second out. He hurls the ball to home plate. The catcher tags the runner. It's a double play, and the game is over. The home team has pulled off another win.

Levels of Organization

To win a baseball game, the players on a team must work together. They must be organized, too. Each player has his own role and his own responsibilities. Just as the players of a baseball team work together, the cells of your body work together to keep you alive and healthy. Like baseball players, your cells are organized. Each has a special role.

A baseball team is made up of 30 or fewer members. Your body is made up of about 100 trillion cells! How does your body keep so many individual cells working together?

Figure 19.1 How is your body like a baseball team? Just as the players on a baseball team work together to win a game, the parts of your body work together to keep you alive and healthy.

ELL Strategy

Activate Background Knowledge Pair students and have them brainstorm what they already know about how the human body is organized. Ask each student to create a list, an outline, a labeled drawing, or a concept map in his or her Science Notebook to record this information. Encourage students to use any of the vocabulary terms in the list on page 330 that they know.

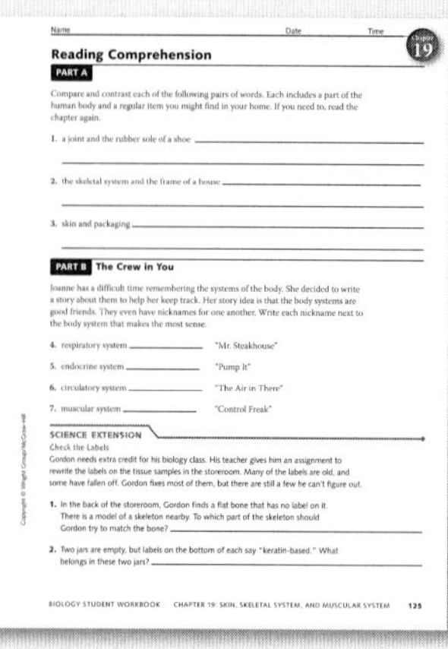

Name Date Time Chapter 19

Reading Comprehension

PART A

Compare and contrast each of the following pairs of words. Each includes a part of the human body and a regular item you might find in your home. If you need to, read the chapter again.

1. a joint and the rubber sole of a shoe
2. the skeletal system and the frame of a house
3. skin and packaging

PART B The Crew in You

Joanne has a difficult time remembering the systems of the body. She decided to write a story about them to help her keep track. Her story idea is that the body systems are good friends. They even have nicknames for one another. Write each nickname next to the body system that makes the most sense.

4. respiratory system ______ "Mr. Steakhouse"
5. endocrine system ______ "Pump It"
6. circulatory system ______ "The Air in There"
7. muscular system ______ "Control Freak"

SCIENCE EXTENSION

Check the Labels

Gordon needs extra credit for his biology class. His teacher gives him an assignment to rewrite the labels on the tissue samples in the storeroom. Many of the labels are old, and some have fallen off. Gordon fixes most of them, but there are still a few he can't figure out.

1. In the back of the storeroom, Gordon finds a flat bone that has no label on it. There is a model of a skeleton nearby. To which part of the skeleton should Gordon try to match the bone?
2. Two jars are empty, but labels on the bottom of each say "keratin-based." What belongs in these two jars?

BIOLOGY STUDENT WORKBOOK CHAPTER 19: SKIN, SKELETAL SYSTEM, AND MUSCULAR SYSTEM 125

Reading Comprehension Workbook, p. 125

Cells

A **cell** is the basic unit of life. All organisms are made up of one or more cells. Cells are too small to be seen with the unaided eye. Cells in the human body are similar to cells in other animals. They are composed of smaller structures that together carry out all the functions of life. **Figure 19.3** shows some of the parts of most human cells.

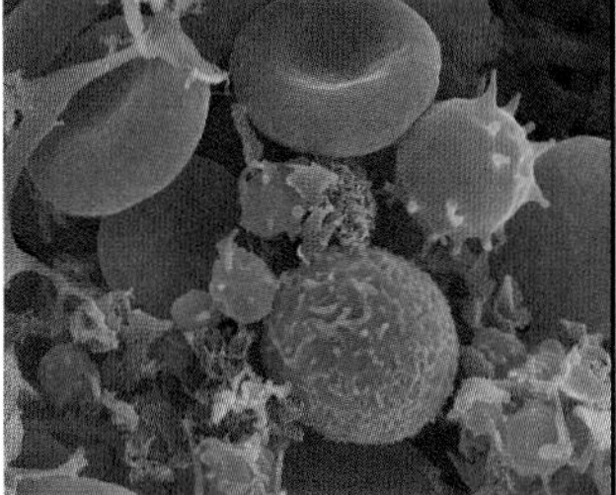

Figure 19.2 All living things are made up of cells. These human cells have been magnified 1,200× with a microscope.

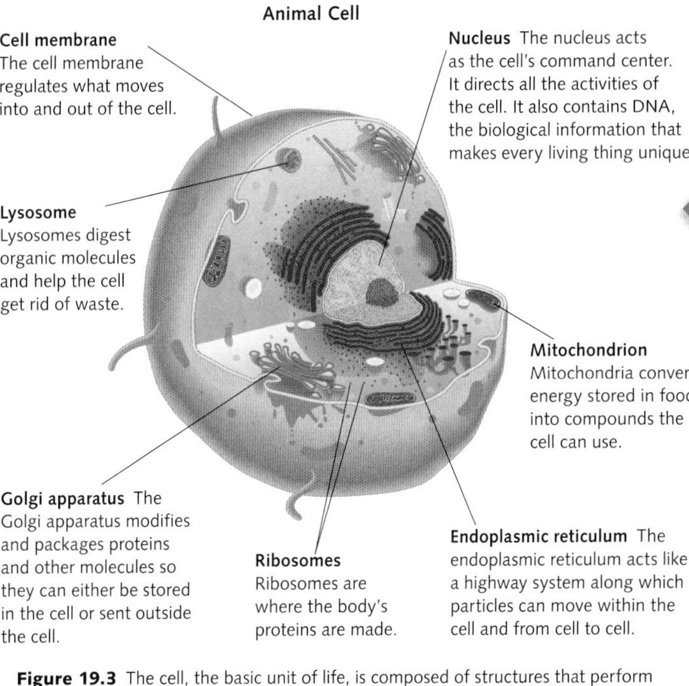

Animal Cell
Cell membrane The cell membrane regulates what moves into and out of the cell.
Nucleus The nucleus acts as the cell's command center. It directs all the activities of the cell. It also contains DNA, the biological information that makes every living thing unique.
Lysosome Lysosomes digest organic molecules and help the cell get rid of waste.
Mitochondrion Mitochondria convert energy stored in food into compounds the cell can use.
Golgi apparatus The Golgi apparatus modifies and packages proteins and other molecules so they can either be stored in the cell or sent outside the cell.
Ribosomes Ribosomes are where the body's proteins are made.
Endoplasmic reticulum The endoplasmic reticulum acts like a highway system along which particles can move within the cell and from cell to cell.

Figure 19.3 The cell, the basic unit of life, is composed of structures that perform specific functions essential to the life of the cell and the organism.

Figure It Out

1. What are the major structures of a human cell?
2. Hypothesize about the number of mitochondria that would be found in a cell that has large energy requirements.

PEOPLE IN SCIENCE Robert Hooke 1635–1703

Robert Hooke is remembered as one of the great scientists of his time. Hooke studied many fields of science, including astronomy, physics, and biology. What Hooke is probably best known for, however, is discovering and naming the cell.

Hooke developed a compound microscope that he used to observe such things as fleas, feathers, and shells. While looking at a thin slice of cork bark, he saw that the bark appeared to be made of many small empty chambers, which he named *cells*. What Hooke saw were the cell walls of dead plant cells. It would be another 200 years before the cell was recognized as the smallest unit of life.

Teach

EXPLAIN to students that they will learn about the organelles in human body cells by reviewing the microscopic structures that are part of an animal cell. If students have done Chapter 2, encourage them to discuss what they recall about the structure and function of the various parts of an animal cell.

EXPLORE Provide students with hand lenses and microscopes along with a variety of items to inspect, such as a bird feather, bark, shells, and prepared slides. Have students examine a few items using both the hand lens and the microscope, and tell them to sketch what they see. As a class, discuss which tools work best for the items

Science Notebook EXTRA

Encourage students to use the vocabulary section they created in their Science Notebooks. Remind them to record prefixes, suffixes, and root words to help them remember the meanings of vocabulary terms.

Vocabulary

cell Remind students that cells are the extremely small, basic units or building blocks of all living matter.

Figure It Out: Figure 19.3

ANSWER **1.** The major structures of a human cell are the nucleus, ribosomes, lysosomes, mitochondria, endoplasmic reticulum, Golgi apparatus, and cell membrane. **2.** Such a cell would probably have many mitochondria.

Background Information

Robert Hooke collaborated or corresponded with a variety of scientists, including Anton van Leeuwenhoek, Robert Boyle, and Isaac Newton. Hooke was an inventor as well as a scientist; he invented the universal joint used in cars, the iris diaphragm in cameras, an early prototype of the respirator, and the anchor escapement and balance spring, which made clocks more accurate. Hooke's other contributions to science include devising an equation describing elasticity that is still used today, identifying Hooke's Law, assisting Robert Boyle in his study of the physics of gases, and improving meteorological instruments such as the barometer, anemometer, and hygrometer.

PEOPLE IN SCIENCE

Have each student write a paragraph in his or her Science Notebook explaining why Robert Hooke should be remembered as one of the "great scientists." Paragraphs should discuss contributions that Hooke made to science, especially the development of the compound microscope.

EXTEND If students are interested in learning more about Robert Hooke or viewing images from Hooke's *Micrographia*, they can visit **http://www.roberthooke.org.uk/**.

Teach

EXPLAIN that students will learn more about the human body's organization by studying the basic types of tissue in the body.

Vocabulary

tissue Tell students that the word *tissue* is derived from a verb meaning "to weave." Discuss why this is an appropriate meaning for a group of similar cells that perform a specific function.

epithelial tissue Explain that the prefix *epi-* means "outer." Have students explain why this is an appropriate term for the layer of tissue that covers all external surfaces of a multicellular animal.

connective tissue Tell students that the word *connective* is an adjective related to the verb *connect* and the noun *connection*. Have students write a sentence using all three forms of the word.

As You Read

Give students several minutes to update their concept maps. Students should include smaller circles with details describing or relating to larger circles.

ANSWER Cells are made up of membranes, cytoplasm, and several internal structures. Tissues are made up of specialized cells that work together to perform a specific function.

Use the Visual: Figure 19.4

ANSWER The four types of human tissue are similar in that they all have cells that contain nuclei. They differ in size, shape, and arrangement of cells.

As You Read

In the outer circles of your concept map, fill in words that describe how the body is organized. Add more circles to the map as you need them. Next to the lines connecting the smaller circles to the large circle, describe the relationships between the connected words. Look to see if some of the smaller circles can be connected to one another.

What are cells made up of? What are tissues made up of?

Tissues

The cells in the human body, as well as in most multicellular organisms, are specialized to perform particular functions. Specialized cells group together to form tissues. A **tissue** is a group of cells that work together to perform a specific function. There are four main types of tissue in the human body.

Epithelial Tissue Gently touch your arms or face. You are touching epithelial tissue! **Epithelial** (eh puh THEE lee ul) **tissue** covers the outside of the body and lines many of the structures inside the body. Your skin is made up of epithelial tissue that you can see and feel. Cells that form this kind of tissue are closely packed. There is little space between them. This gives epithelial tissue its function as a protective barrier for the body. It protects the body from injury, disease, and loss of essential fluids.

Connective Tissue As its name implies, **connective tissue** holds together other tissues in the body. Tendons, ligaments, bones, and even blood are types of connective tissue. Unlike the cells of epithelial tissue, the cells that form connective tissue are loosely packed.

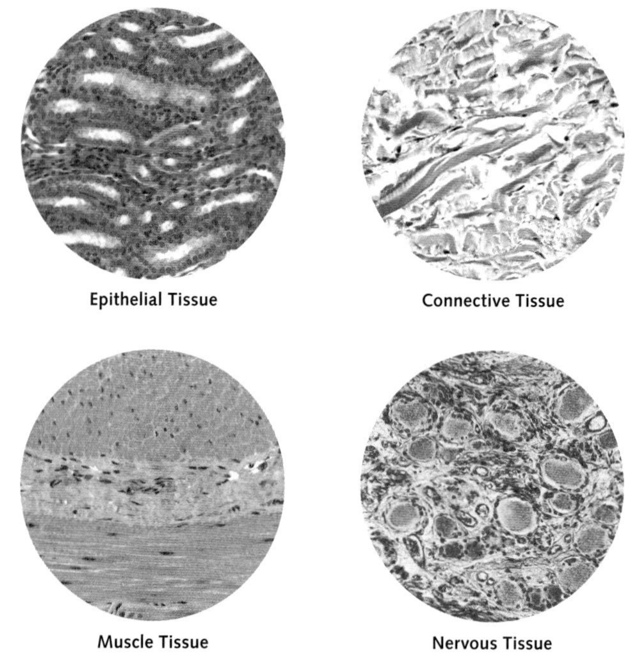

Figure 19.4 Compare the four main types of human tissue. How are they similar in appearance? How do they differ?

Differentiated Instruction

Visual Have students draw an example of each of the four types of tissues in the human body in their Science Notebooks and label the parts shown in each drawing.

Kinesthetic Arrange students in small groups, and ask them to use their bodies to model each of the four types of tissues. Allow five to ten minutes for them to create the models, and then ask each group to share with the class. Have the class decide which model was the best depiction for each type of tissue and explain why.

Muscle Tissue Muscle cells group together to form **muscle tissue**. Muscle tissue surrounds most of the bones in the body. It also combines with other tissues to make up many of the body's internal structures, such as the heart, stomach, and lungs. Muscle tissue gives parts of the body, such as the arms and legs, their ability to move. It allows you to do things such as run, play sports, fold laundry, and reach up for things. Muscle tissue in the heart causes the heart to contract, or tighten, and relax. These motions cause blood to be pumped throughout the body. You will learn more about muscle tissue and what it enables the body to do in Lesson 19.4.

Nervous Tissue Specialized cells called neurons make up **nervous tissue**. Nervous tissue enables the body to sense and respond to things in the environment. You can see, smell, feel, taste, and hear things because of nervous tissue. You can think about and remember things because of nervous tissue. Nervous tissue gathers and transmits information throughout the body.

Organs

Tissues group together to form organs. In Chapter 3, you learned that an **organ** is a group of different types of tissue that work together to perform a specific function. The heart is an organ. So, too, are the stomach, lungs, and eyes. Each of these organs is made up of epithelial tissue, connective tissue, muscle tissue, and nervous tissue working together to perform certain functions. In the stomach, these tissues help the body digest food. In the lungs, they enable the body to take in oxygen and give off carbon dioxide. They work together in the eyes to allow the body to see.

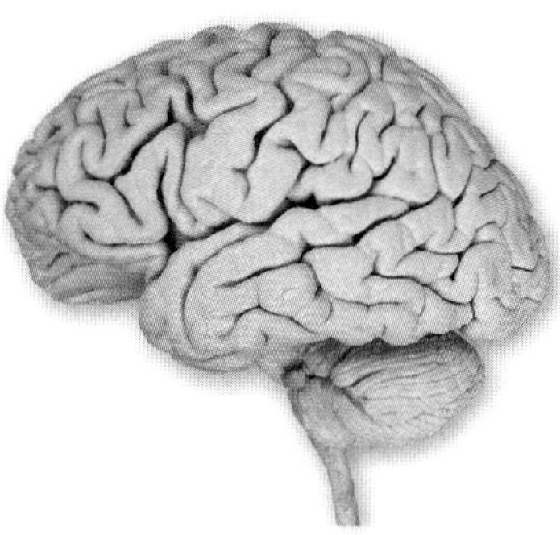

Human Brain

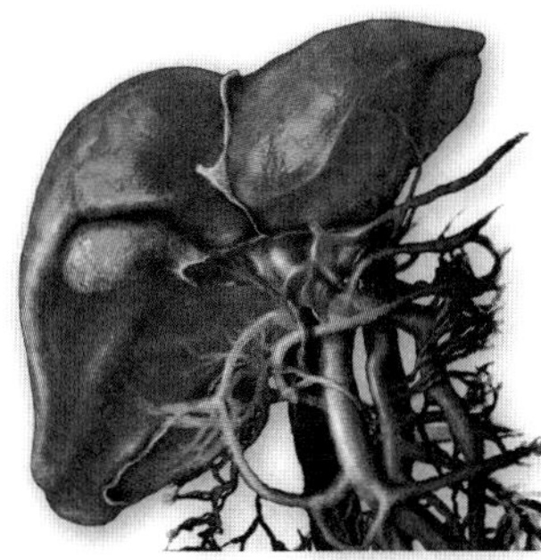

Human Liver

Figure 19.5 The brain and liver are two of the body's vital organs. They are made up of tissues that work together to perform specific functions in the body. What other organs can you name?

Did You Know?

The human heart is not shaped like a Valentine's Day heart. Instead, it is round and somewhat irregular. The heart is about the size of a closed fist. In the average adult, it beats 70 to 80 times per minute to pump blood throughout the body.

Teach

EXPLAIN that students will learn about two more types of tissue, muscle and nervous, and the organization of tissues into organs.

EXPLORE Have each student take his or her own pulse by counting beats against the carotid artery for ten seconds. Remind students to multiply their counts by six to calculate the total number of beats per minute. Tell them that these are their resting pulses. Have small groups of students engage in a variety of different activities, such as climbing stairs, walking slowly, and walking quickly, for about five minutes. Have students take their pulses again immediately following the activity. As a class, discuss the different results and reasons for the variations.

Vocabulary

muscle tissue Tell students that *muscle* is derived from the Latin word *musculus*, which means "a small mouse." Have students speculate about this origin. (Mice twitch like muscles do.)

nervous tissue Explain that nervous tissue is a network of nerves that carry information about sensations and instructions for movement between the brain or spinal cord and other parts of the body. Ask students if they know another meaning for *nervous* (jumpy, uneasy, easily excited, irritated), and help them both distinguish between the meanings and articulate the relationship.

organ Explain that *organ* is derived from the Greek word *organon*, which means "tool."

Use the Visual: Figure 19.5

ANSWER Students' answers might include the stomach, pancreas, kidneys, small intestine, large intestine, nose, ears, brain, and appendix.

ELL Strategy

Compare and Contrast Have each student create a chart comparing and contrasting the four types of tissue. Encourage students to refer to the concept maps they are constructing as a source of information and vocabulary terms to include in their charts.

Teach

EXPLAIN that students will continue to learn about the organization of the human body. They have learned that cells combine to form tissues and that specialized tissues form organs. The next layer of organization is the organ system.

Vocabulary

organ system Tell students that *system* comes from a Greek word that means "to combine." The term *organ system* describes two or more organs that work together (or combine) to perform a function throughout the human body. Ask students to identify other systems that represent combinations. (monetary system, decimal system, transportation system)

Organ Systems

Cells are organized into tissues. Tissues are organized into organs. The parts of your body are further organized into organ systems. An **organ system** is a group of organs that work together to carry out one or more body functions.

Figure 19.6 These major organ systems keep you active and healthy.

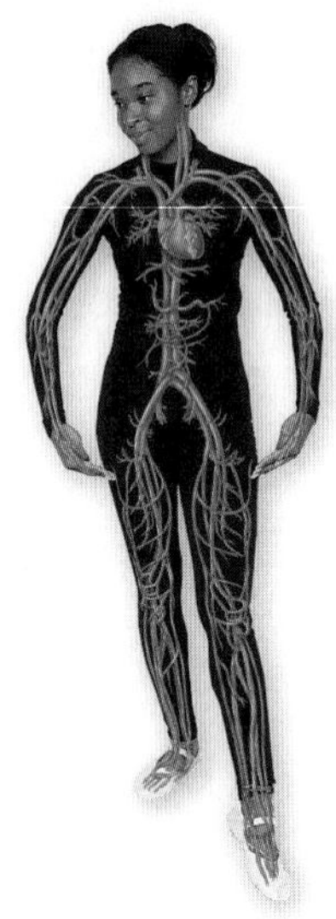

Circulatory system This system pumps blood throughout the body, brings nutrients to the cells, and carries away waste from the cells.

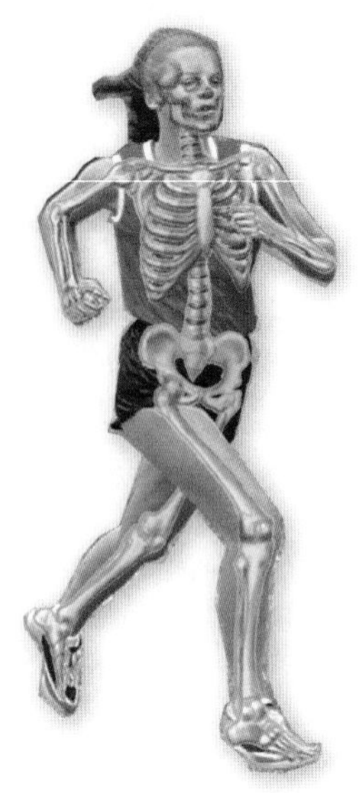

Skeletal system This system supports the body and gives it shape.

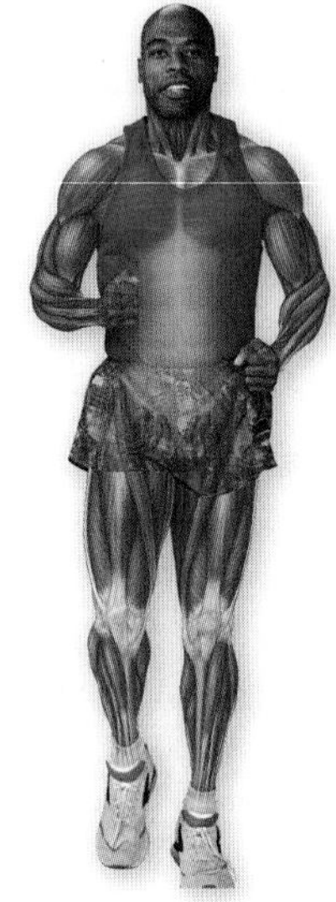

Muscular system This system enables the body to move.

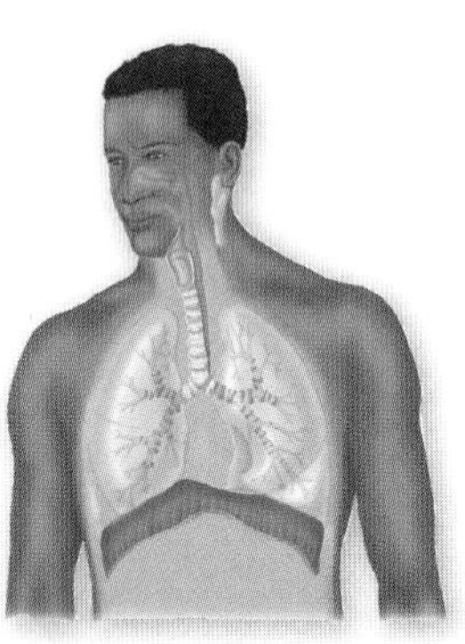

Respiratory system This system is responsible for taking in oxygen from the air and giving off carbon dioxide.

Digestive system This system is responsible for taking in food and breaking it down into usable energy.

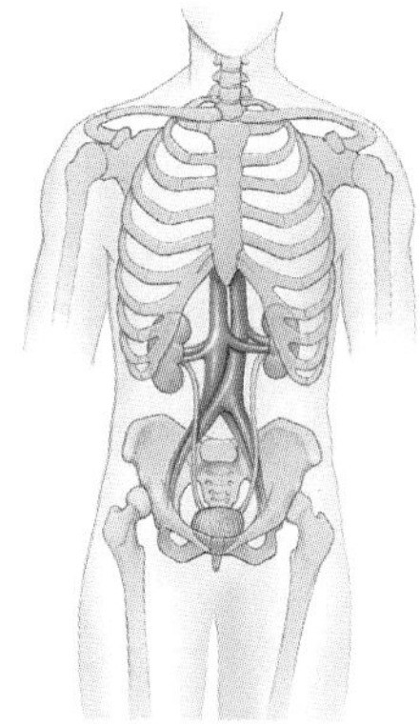

Urinary system This system rids the body of liquid and dissolved wastes and maintains the balance of salts and water in the blood.

Background Information

Following are the human body systems and the major parts of each one.

Circulatory: heart, blood vessels, and blood

Digestive: mouth, tongue, teeth, salivary glands, pharynx, esophagus, stomach, liver, gallbladder, pancreas, intestines, and rectum

Endocrine: pituitary gland, pineal gland, thyroid gland, parathyroid glands, thymus gland, adrenal glands, pancreas, ovaries, and testes

Excretory/Urinary: large intestine, liver, lungs, skin, and kidneys; urinary bladder, ureters, and urethra

Immune: thymus gland, tonsils, spleen, lymph nodes, bone marrow, white blood cells

Integumentary: skin, nails, hair, and sweat glands

Lymphatic: lymph nodes and vessels, tonsils, thymus gland, and spleen

Muscular: muscles, tendons

Nervous: brain, spinal cord, and nerves

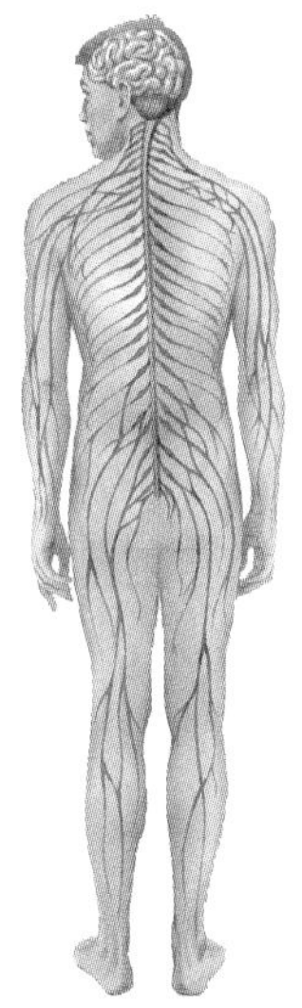

Nervous system This system enables humans to take in and respond to information from the environment.

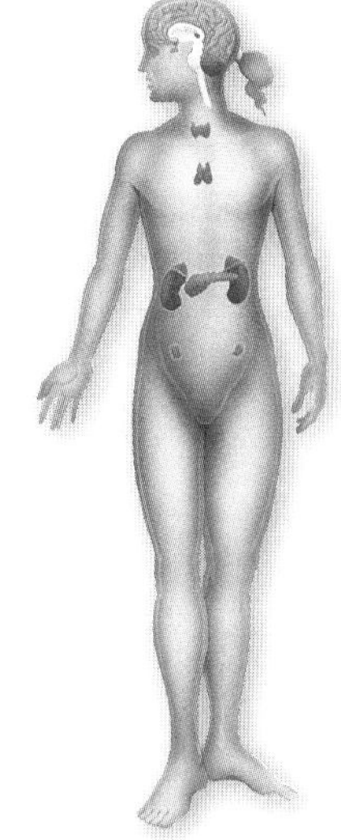

Endocrine system This system helps regulate the body's functions.

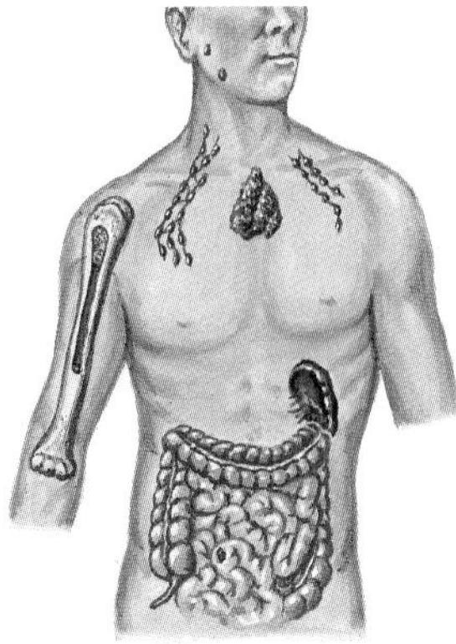

Immune system This system helps the body fight disease.

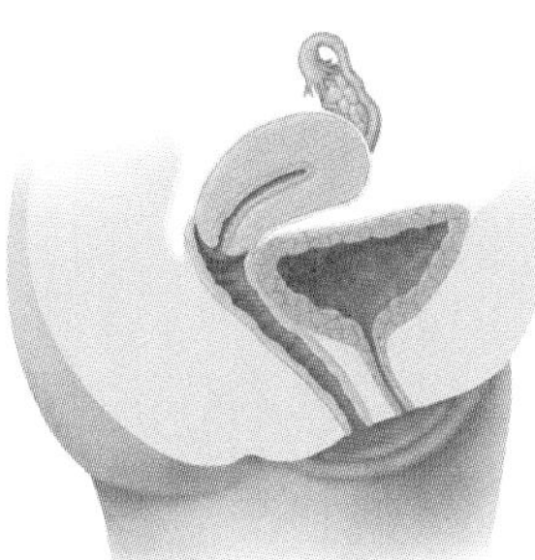

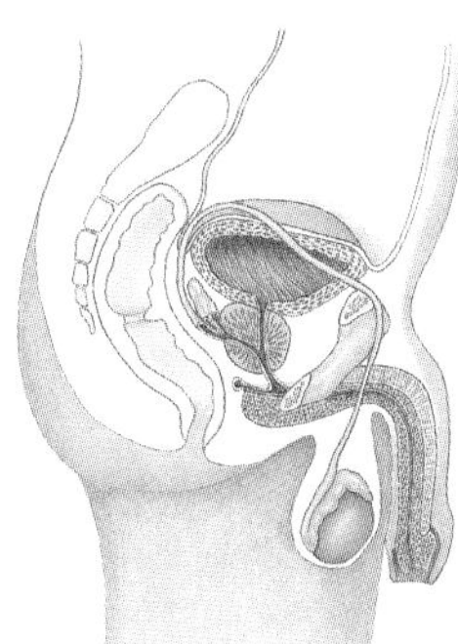

Reproductive system The female *(left)* and male *(right)* systems enable humans to reproduce, or produce offspring.

After You Read

1. Review your concept map. Use it to describe the levels of organization in the human body.
2. Describe the basic structure of a human cell. What does each cell part do?
3. What are the four types of tissue in the human body?
4. What makes up organ systems? In what ways do organ systems help you?

Assess

EVALUATE Use the After You Read questions and the Alternative Assessment to help you assess students' understanding of the lesson.

After You Read

1. The human body is composed of cells that are organized into tissues, organs, and organ systems.
2. A human cell consists of cytoplasm, several organelles, and other specialized structures surrounded by a cell membrane. The nucleus directs all the activities of the cell. Ribosomes make the body's proteins. Mitochondria convert energy from food into compounds the body can use. Lysosomes help break down organic molecules and help get rid of waste. The endoplasmic reticulum helps transport materials throughout the cell and from cell to cell. The cell membrane holds the cell together and controls what enters and exits the cell.
3. The four types of tissue in the human body are epithelial tissue, connective tissue, muscle tissue, and nervous tissue.
4. Organ systems are made up of organs that work together to perform a specific function. Organ systems allow a person to survive. They help with breathing, circulation, coordination, digestion, movement, reproduction, support, defense against pathogens, and the processing of waste.

Alternative Assessment

EVALUATE Have students use their concept maps to create an outline of the levels of organization in the human body.

Reproductive: male: testes, scrotum, penis, vas deferens, and prostate gland; female: ovaries, uterus, vagina, and mammary glands

Respiratory: nasal cavity, pharynx, larynx, trachea, bronchi, and lungs

Skeletal: bones, ligaments, and joints

Teacher Alert

Depending on the resource used, ten to twelve body systems can be identified. Some biologists consider the immune system to be part of the lymphatic system. Others consider the lymphatic system to be a subset of the circulatory system. The important concept to impart to students is that every system depends on other systems to function; a component of one system may also be part of another. No one system can sustain the body.

19.2 Introduce

ENGAGE Provide students with hand lenses, and ask them to observe the skin on different parts of their bodies, such as the palms of their hands, their arms, and their legs. Have them also observe the skin on a peer's eyelid, if students are accepting. Ask them to note differences and similarities in what they see on the different areas of their bodies, and ask them to write hypotheses for the differences.

Before You Read

Model a K-W-L-S-H chart on the board. Think aloud about the title, *Skin*, and look at one or two pictures and headings from the lesson. In the *Know* column, write *Skin – largest organ of the body.* Provide about five minutes for students to write in the *K* and *W* columns. Encourage students to include at least two or three questions they have about skin in the *W* column of their charts.

Teach

EXPLAIN that in this lesson, students will learn about body's largest organ, the skin, and its structure and function.

EXPLORE Explain that people with extreme visual impairment may read text using the Braille alphabet, a series of raised spots. Someone who cannot see can read this text by moving his or her fingers over the raised letters and words. Tell students they are going to make their own alphabet, similar to the Braille alphabet.

Give each student three or four small squares (5 cm x 5 cm) of thick cardboard or cork, as well as sewing pins (those with rounded heads work best). Have students draw a letter on a square and then stick the sharp ends of pins into the cardboard or cork to create a raised version of the letter. Have students create a two- to four-letter word using this method. Then, pair students and have each partner "read" the other's word with his or her fingertips while blindfolded. Once students have "read" one or two words, challenge them to remove some of the pins in the letters before "reading" the word again. Then, have students repeat this action with all the pins removed. Discuss the results and the role of the skin in this activity.

Learning Goals

- Identify the layers of the skin and their functions in the body.
- Describe how nails and hair are part of the body's skin.

New Vocabulary

epidermis
keratin
melanin
dermis
subcutaneous tissue

19.2 Skin

Before You Read

Create a K-W-L-S-H chart in your Science Notebook. Think about the title of this lesson. Then look at the pictures and headings in the lesson. In the column labeled *K*, write what you already know about skin. In the column labeled *W*, write what you would like to learn about skin.

Cool raindrops. Prickly cacti. Smooth snakes. Have you ever wondered what allows you to feel different things? The answer is your skin! Without skin, you could not feel temperature or wind. You could not tell rough objects from smooth ones, or wet objects from dry ones.

The Largest Organ in the Body

Your skin is the largest organ of your body. If you could peel it off and lay it flat, the skin of an average adult would cover an area of about two square meters. That is about the same size as a classroom chalkboard. Skin is more than just a sense organ. It does other important jobs to keep you healthy. It covers your body's organs and protects them from injury. It helps regulate your temperature and keeps you from getting overheated. It helps get rid of harmful wastes and prevents loss of water, blood, and other essential fluids. It even protects your body from disease. The skin has three main layers: the epidermis, the dermis, and the subcutaneous tissue.

Figure 19.7 Skin gives humans their sense of touch. This sense of touch enables people with impaired vision to read and to feel things that they cannot see with their eyes.

Your skin is thinnest on your eyelids.
Your skin is thickest on the palms of your hands and the soles of your feet.

Figure 19.8 Skin covers the body and protects internal organs from injury and disease. Although it is only a few centimeters thick, your skin is the largest organ of your body.

ELL Strategy

Read Aloud Arrange students in groups of three, and have them alternate reading aloud paragraphs in Lesson 19.2. One student should read one paragraph, the next student should read the following paragraph, and so on until the group reads the entire lesson.

Background Information

Why does skin wrinkle when it's wet? Normally, skin is covered with sebum, an oil that makes the skin waterproof. However, soap and oil wash off the sebum, causing the skin to lose its waterproofing. By osmosis, water enters the cells of the skin in the affected area, and the cells expand. The outer layer of skin is connected to the tissue beneath it in certain places. Areas of skin not tied down swell more, so the skin looks wrinkled.

The Epidermis

The **epidermis** (eh puh DUR mus) is the layer that you see. It is the tough, protective outer layer of the skin. It is made up mostly of cells called keratinocytes (KER eh tehn oh sites), which are flat cells stacked like bricks in a wall. These cells produce keratin. **Keratin** is a protein that helps make the skin tough. Keratinocytes protect deeper cells from damage and from drying out. They also help keep out harmful bacteria and other microorganisms.

As keratinocytes mature, they become filled with keratin. They also get pushed upward as new cells are produced in the bottom layer of the epidermis. Because these cells are now far from a food supply, they soon die. In time, they flake off and are replaced. The body produces an entirely new epidermis about every 28 days through this process.

The epidermis also contains melanocytes (meh LAH neh sites) and Langerhans (LAHNG ur hahnz) cells. The melanocytes produce melanin. **Melanin** is a chemical that is responsible for skin color. The more melanin cells produce, the darker the skin is. Melanocytes also absorb sunlight, thereby protecting other cells from the Sun's harmful rays. As melanocytes absorb sunlight, they produce more melanin. This is what causes skin to become tan after exposure to sunlight. The Langerhans cells play an important role in the immune system. They help protect the body from diseases and infections.

Figure 19.9 The chemical melanin produced in the skin is responsible for variations in skin color. It also causes skin to tan upon exposure to sunlight.

Did You Know?

Where does all the dead skin that flakes off your body go? It produces house dust! The dust in your home is made up mostly of dead skin cells.

CONNECTION: Health

Too much sunlight can be harmful to your skin. It can keep the skin from functioning properly and can cause skin cancer. It is important to protect your skin by wearing sunscreen even on cloudy days. Sunscreen contains chemicals that keep your skin from absorbing sunlight. Each brand of sunscreen is rated with an SPF, or sun protection factor. The SPF describes how much sunlight is blocked. Sunscreens with higher SPF values block more sunlight. You should wear a sunscreen with an SPF of at least 30 on bright sunny days.

Teach

EXPLAIN that in this section, students will learn about the outermost layer of the skin, the epidermis.

Vocabulary

epidermis Tell students that the prefix *epi-* means "above," "over," or "upon." The word *dermis* is derived from the Greek word *derma*, meaning "the skin."

keratin Tell students that keratin is the tough fibrous protein produced by the epidermis in vertebrates. It is the main component of hair, nails, feathers, claws, horns, and the outer layer of dead skin cells.

melanin Explain that melanin is the black or dark brown pigment found in differing amounts in the skin, hair, and eyes of humans and animals. Freckles form where melanin-producing cells produce excess amounts of melanin.

CONNECTION: Health

Have students write a letter to a friend convincing him or her to wear sunscreen regularly, especially in the summer. Letters should discuss the benefits of wearing sunscreen and the possible consequences of not wearing it.

Background Information

The Sun Protection Factor (SPF) measures the length of time a product protects skin from the Sun's UVB-containing rays, compared to how long the skin takes to redden without protection. If skin typically reddens in 20 minutes, using an SPF-15 sunscreen theoretically prevents reddening 15 times longer—for about five hours.

Ultraviolet-B (UVB) rays are short-wave solar rays of 290–320 nanometers (billionths of a meter). UVB rays are more potent than UVA rays in producing sunburn and are considered the main cause of basal and squamous cell carcinomas as well as contributors to melanoma.

Ultraviolet-A (UVA) rays are long-wave solar rays of 320–400 nanometers. They cause skin damage, such as wrinkling, through their deep penetration of the skin. These rays combined with UVB rays directly cause melanomas.

Teach

EXPLAIN that in this section, students will learn about the dermis layer of skin, the layer beneath the epidermis.

EXTEND Students who are interested in the use of hair as forensic evidence can test their knowledge by taking the quiz on the FBI's Web site at **http://www.fbi.gov/page2/march05/hair031605.htm**.

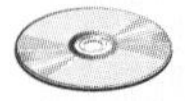

Vocabulary

dermis Remind students that *dermis* is derived from the Greek word *derma*, which means "skin." Have students compare and contrast the words *epidermis* and *dermis*.

subcutaneous tissue Tell students that the prefix *sub-* means "under" or "below." The root *cutane* is derived from the Latin word *cutis*, meaning "skin." Ask students to use these word meanings to define the term.

As You Read

Give students about five minutes to update the *L* columns in their K-W-L-S-H charts. Students should include facts about the layers of skin. Review students' charts for accuracy.

ANSWER The three main layers of skin are the epidermis, the dermis, and the subcutaneous tissue.

Figure It Out: Figure 19.11

ANSWER **1.** Nerve endings, blood vessels, hair follicles, hair shafts, oil glands, and sweat glands are found in the dermis layer of skin. **2.** Sweat glands produce sweat to help the body cool down. When sweat evaporates from the skin, heat is lost. Sweat glands also help release waste from the body. For these reasons, sweat glands must be close to the surface of the body. If sweat glands were deeper in the body, they would not be effective at cooling the body or removing waste.

As You Read

In the column labeled *L* in your K-W-L-S-H chart, write what you have learned about skin.

What are the three main layers of skin?

The Dermis

The **dermis** is the thick layer of skin that lies beneath the epidermis. It is made up mostly of nerve endings, blood vessels, and connective tissue. It also contains fibers, oil glands, sweat glands, and hair follicles.

The nerve endings of the dermis give the body its sense of touch. They collect signals from the environment and send them to the brain, where they are processed. The blood vessels of the dermis help control the body's temperature. They expand, or widen, to allow heat to escape through the skin. They contract, or narrow, to keep heat in. The fibers of the dermis contain chemicals that are responsible for giving your skin its elasticity. These chemicals, known as collagen and elastin, allow skin to stretch and bend without tearing.

Like blood vessels, sweat glands play a role in regulating the body's temperature. Sweat glands produce sweat when the body starts getting too warm. As sweat evaporates from the skin, heat is released and the body is cooled. In addition to keeping the body cool, sweat also plays a role in getting rid of poisonous body wastes. Waste products dissolve in sweat, which is made mostly of water, and are released through the skin.

The dermis's oil glands are located near the hair follicles. The glands produce oil that keeps the skin smooth and waterproof and keeps hair from becoming brittle.

Figure 19.10 When the body becomes warm, sweat glands produce sweat, and blood vessels expand as a way of releasing heat. The expansion of the blood vessels causes lots of red blood cells to flow through the skin. This is what makes your skin look flushed when you are hot.

Figure It Out

1. Which structures are found in the dermis layer of the skin?
2. Explain why you think sweat glands are located in the skin rather than deeper in the body.

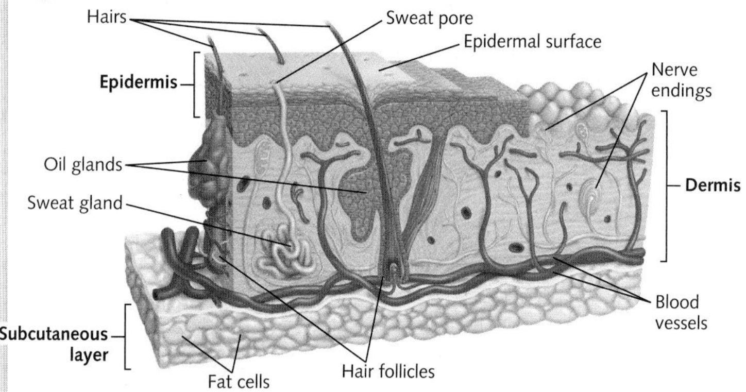

Figure 19.11 The skin is composed of three layers: the epidermis, the dermis, and the subcutaneous tissue.

338 SKIN, SKELETAL SYSTEM, AND MUSCULAR SYSTEM

Background Information

The degree of a burn is related to the layers of skin damaged. A first-degree burn affects only the epidermis, is red in color and painful, can involve swelling, and will heal without scarring.

A second-degree burn, which can be superficial or deep, affects the epidermis and the dermis. Superficial burns affect the outermost layer of the dermis, cause pain, are very sensitive to touch, and involve blisters and redness. Deep burns involve the deepest layers of the dermis, are usually dry and white, cause pain, may take three to four weeks to heal, and may leave a thick scar.

A third-degree burn affects all three layers of skin. The skin turns dark brown or black, appears leathery, and separates from the surrounding tissue. The nerve endings are destroyed by the burn, so these burns usually are not painful. However, these burns are the most serious and can be life-threatening.

The Subcutaneous Tissue

The innermost layer of skin is the **subcutaneous** (sub kyoo TAY nee us) **tissue**. This layer is made up mostly of connective tissue and fat cells. In fact, most of the body's fat cells are in this layer of skin. Fat cells act as insulators for the body. They help conserve heat and thus play an important role in maintaining a healthy body temperature.

Nails and Hair

It might surprise you to learn that nails are modified skin. Nails are made mostly of keratin. They grow from nail roots under the skin at the base and sides of the nails. Nails protect the soft tissue at the tips of your toes and fingers. They help you pick up objects, scratch an itch, and untie knots. They could even get you into the Guinness Book of World Records, as **Figure 19.12** shows.

Figure 19.12 Lee Redmond started letting her fingernails grow in 1979. In this photo, 27 years later, her nails are 84 cm (33 in.) long.

Hair is also part of the skin. Hair covers the entire body except for the palms of the hands, the soles of the feet, and the lips. Hair grows from hair follicles, which are tiny saclike structures in the dermis, and extends out through the epidermis. Like skin color, hair color is determined by melanin. The more melanin cells produce, the darker the hair is.

Like nails, hair is made mostly of keratin. Hair protects the eyes and nose from dust and harmful materials. It also helps keep the body warm. How does it do this? First, humans lose most of their body heat through their heads. A thick head of hair helps keep in some of this heat. Second, muscles attached to the hair shafts contract with cold, fear, or emotion. This causes "goose bumps" to form on the skin and causes hair to stand on end. The lifted hair traps heat and warms the body.

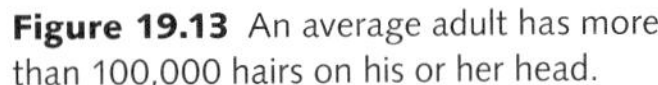

Figure 19.13 An average adult has more than 100,000 hairs on his or her head.

Explore It!

Work with a partner to observe hair and nails under a microscope. Gently pull a strand of hair from your scalp, and place it under the lens of a microscope. Draw what you see. Then, trim the end of one nail. Place the trimming under the lens of the microscope, and draw what you see. How does your nail look compared to your hair?

After You Read

1. Identify and describe the layers that make up skin.
2. What are some ways in which skin helps keep the body healthy?
3. Describe the structure and function of nails and hair.
4. Use your completed K-W-L columns to summarize this lesson in a paragraph in your Science Notebook. Then, write in the *S* column what you would still like to know about skin and how it helps keep you healthy. Complete the chart by writing in the *H* column how you can find this information.

Teach

EXPLAIN that students will learn about the innermost layer of skin, the subcutaneous tissue, as well as hair and nails.

Explore It!

Pair students and provide them with microscopes, nail clippers, and alcohol wipes to clean clippers after use. Have students brush or comb their hair with their fingers to obtain a loose hair. Have students sketch the magnified image of the hair in their Science Notebooks. Have them repeat the process with a nail clipping. Have them share their drawings with one another in small groups.

Assess

EVALUATE Use the After You Read questions and the Alternative Assessment to help you assess students' understanding of the lesson.

After You Read

1. Skin is made up of the epidermis, the dermis, and the subcutaneous tissue. The epidermis is the outermost layer. It contains cells that produce keratin, which keeps the skin tough. It also contains langerhans cells and cells that produce melanin. The dermis contains nerve endings, blood vessels, sweat glands, oil glands, hair shafts, and hair follicles. It helps regulate the body's temperature and gives the body its sense of touch. The subcutaneous tissue is the innermost layer of skin. It is made up mostly of fat cells.
2. Skin keeps the body healthy by protecting internal organs, regulating body temperature, eliminating waste, preventing loss of water and essential fluids, protecting the body from disease, and taking in information from the environment.
3. Nails and hair are modified skin. Both are made up mostly of keratin.
4. Skin is the body's largest organ. It is made up of three layers, the epidermis, dermis, and subcutaneous tissue, that work together to perform a variety of functions to keep the body healthy. Hair and nails are part of the skin. Students' entries in the *S* and *H* columns should be reviewed for accuracy.

Background Information

Hair grows in cycles that begin with a growth phase, anagen, and a resting phase, telogen. A hair stops growing during telogen, when it is called a club hair. The club hair remains in the follicle until the next growth phase.

Human scalp hairs grow less than 1.3 cm per month. The follicles are in anagen for two to six years, then in telogen for about three months. Shorter hairs on the body, including those in the eyebrows and eyelashes, grow for about ten weeks and then rest for nine months.

Alternative Assessment

EVALUATE Have students draw and label a cross-section of skin that includes all three layers. Students should also list some important facts about the function and composition of each layer of skin.

19.3 Introduce

ENGAGE Have pairs of students brainstorm the names (common or scientific) of as many bones as they can remember. Then, as a class, list these names on the board. Count the number of bones on the list. Tell students that the human skeleton contains 206 bones and that they will learn about many of these bones in this lesson.

Before You Read

Model creating an outline on the board, using *The Skeletal System* as the title. The first heading, *Your Bony Body*, should be the first item, Roman numeral *I*, in the outline. The subheadings *Shape and Function* and *Bone Composition* should be listed as the *A* and *B* points under it. Give students about ten minutes in class to create outlines in their Science Notebooks.

Teach

EXPLAIN that in this lesson, students will learn about the role of the skeletal system and how bones are formed and held together at joints.

Use the Visual: Figure 19.14

EXTEND Use the illustration of the axial and appendicular skeletons to familiarize students with the bones of the skeletal system. You will probably need to pronounce some of the names for students. Compare the lists of bones students identified earlier with those illustrated here.

Vocabulary

skeletal system Explain that *skeletal* is derived from the Greek words *skeleton soma*, meaning "dried body." A system is a group of structures that function together.

periosteum Tell students that the prefix *peri-* is derived from the Greek word *peri*, meaning "round" or "around." The root *osteo* is from the Greek word *osteon*, which means "bone."

Learning Goals

- Identify the major functions of the skeletal system.
- Describe the composition of bone.
- Explain how bones meet at joints.

New Vocabulary

skeletal system
periosteum
compact bone
spongy bone
bone marrow
cartilage
joint
ligament

19.3 The Skeletal System

Before You Read

Create a lesson outline in your Science Notebook, using the title, headings, and subheadings of this lesson. Use the outline to summarize what you learn in this lesson.

What do the words *hammer, stirrup,* and *anvil* make you think of? You might say tools, and you would be correct, but think again. They are also the names of bones! In fact, they are the smallest bones in your body. Though they may be tiny—only a few millimeters across—they do a very important job. What do they do? Here is a clue: They are found in your ears. The hammer, stirrup, and anvil help you hear. What else do bones help you do?

Your Bony Body

The 206 bones of the human skeleton make up your **skeletal system**. Together, bones have many functions in the body. They give the body its shape. They support the body and protect delicate internal organs, such as the brain, heart, and lungs. They allow the body to move. They even store minerals and produce blood for the body. Without bones, you would be a disorganized, formless heap of skin and other tissue.

You may think of bones as hard, nonliving material, but they are far from dead matter. Just like the other organs of your body, bones are made up of living tissue. In fact, if bones were not living, you would not grow during childhood, and broken bones would never heal.

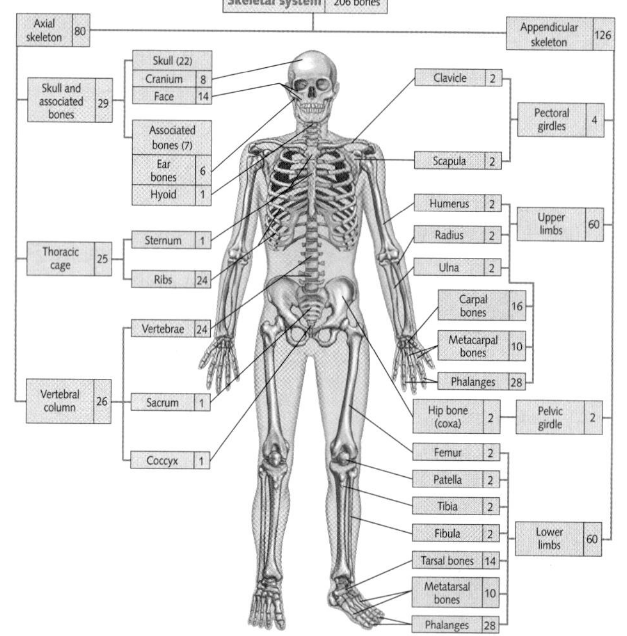

Figure 19.14 The human skeleton is divided into two main parts. The bones labeled on the left support the body and keep you upright. The bones labeled on the right support your limbs—your arms and legs.

ELL Strategy

Activate Background Knowledge Arrange students in small groups, and ask them to discuss what they already know about bones and the skeletal system. They should create a list of facts that they already know about these topics, including the function and composition of bones. Encourage students to begin a diagram of a familiar bone that they can add details to as the lesson progresses.

Background Information

The human skeleton has two main parts: the axial skeleton and the appendicular skeleton. The axial skeleton is composed of three major parts: the skull, the bony thorax (i.e., the ribs and the sternum), and the vertebral column. It includes a total of 80 bones. The appendicular skeleton includes the pectoral girdle, the upper limbs, the pelvic girdle, and the lower limbs. It includes 126 bones.

Shape and Function Bones come in many shapes and sizes. Each one is shaped for a specific function. The short, slender bones in your fingers allow your fingers to move and grasp things. The wide, flat bones in your skull protect your brain. Bones are classified as:

- long bones, such as those found in your legs and arms
- short bones, such as those found in your fingers and toes
- flat bones, such as those found in your skull and pelvis
- irregular bones, such as those found in your backbone and ears

Bone Composition A bone is made up of three layers of connective tissue. The outermost layer of a bone is the **periosteum** (per ee AH stee um). This thin layer of tissue contains blood vessels that bring nutrients and oxygen to the bone. **Compact bone** lies beneath the periosteum. This dense layer of bone consists of blood vessels, nerve cells, and living bone cells called osteocytes. Compact bone is held together by a framework of hard, nonliving minerals such as calcium and phosphorus. **Spongy bone** is found in the ends of long bones and in the middle part of short bones and flat bones. Spongy bone is more porous and lightweight than compact bone, but it is strong and supportive. Cells known as osteoblasts and osteoclasts are found in both compact and spongy bone. Osteoblasts produce bone, while osteoclasts break down bone. Together, these cells are responsible for bone growth and repair.

Two types of **bone marrow**, red and yellow, run through a cavity in the center of many long bones. Red bone marrow produces red blood cells, which transport oxygen throughout the body. It also produces some kinds of white blood cells. White blood cells are part of the immune system. They aid in fighting disease. Yellow bone marrow is made up mostly of fat cells that are a source of stored energy.

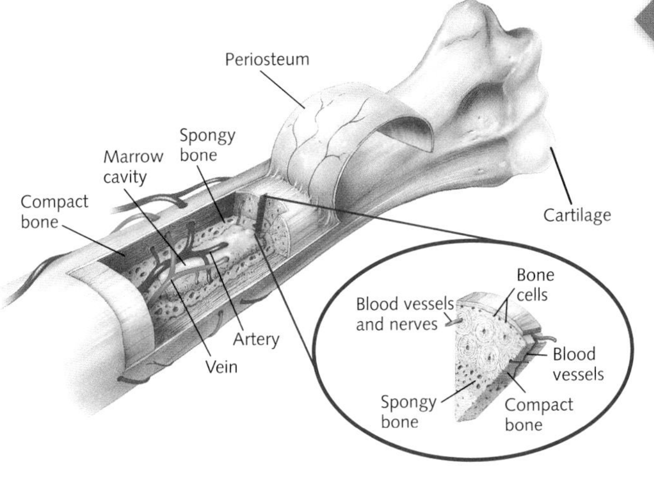

Figure 19.15 The most obvious feature of a long bone is the long shaft, or center, which contains compact bone. Within the shaft are hollow spaces containing marrow.

Extend It!

The most common kinds of bone injuries are broken bones, which heal in time with proper care. Working with a partner or in a small group, do research to find out about other kinds of bone injury and about bone disease. Prepare a presentation, and share your findings with your classmates.

Figure It Out

1. What three layers of tissue make up bone?
2. Describe how bone marrow aids the body.

Teach

EXPLAIN to students that they will learn about the four main shapes of bones and the makeup of different kinds of bones.

Vocabulary

compact bone Explain that *compact* is from the Latin word *compactus*, from *compingere*, which means "to put together closely." The compact layer of bone is dense with blood vessels, nerve cells, and bone cells.

spongy bone Explain that spongy bone contains spicules, which form a latticework with spaces that are filled with embryonic connective tissue or bone marrow.

bone marrow Tell students that bone marrow is soft tissue in bone cavities and that there are two types of marrow. Red marrow produces blood cells, and yellow marrow consists of fat cells.

Extend It!

Encourage each student pair or group to choose a different type of bone disease or injury. Some examples of bone diseases are arthritis, osteoporosis, scoliosis, fibrous dysplasia, and Paget's disease. Students should research the possible causes, symptoms, and treatments for the diseases that they choose. Bone injuries include bruises, simple fractures, complex fractures, and dislocations. Students should research the possible causes, symptoms, and treatments for the injuries that they choose. Provide a variety of resources for use in research, including reference books, medical or scientific journals, and Internet access.

Differentiated Instruction

Musical Have students sing along to the song "Dry Bones." The music and verses for the song can be found online on the National Institute of Environmental Health Sciences (NIEHS) Web site at **http://www.niehs.nih.gov/kids/lyrics/bones.htm.**

Figure It Out: Figure 19.15

ANSWER **1.** Bone is made up of the periosteum, compact bone, and spongy bone. **2.** Bone marrow aids the body by producing blood cells. White blood cells made in bone marrow help the body fight disease. Red blood cells help the body transport oxygen. Yellow bone marrow is made up mostly of fat cells that are a source of stored energy for the body.

Teach

EXPLAIN to students that they will learn about the process of bone formation and about bone joints.

Vocabulary

cartilage Tell students that cartilage is a tough, flexible, semi-opaque material that forms the skeleton of a human embryo and is converted into bone before adulthood. The larynx and trachea are composed of cartilage.

joint Explain that *joint* is derived from the French word *joindre*, meaning "to join."

ligament Tell students that *ligament* is derived from the Latin word *ligare*, meaning "to bind."

EXPLORE Have students work in groups of three, and provide each group with large paper on which to trace an outline of one student's body. Have students draw, label, and identify by type the major bones of the body. Then, have students identify and label two examples of each type of joint.

As You Read

Give students about ten minutes to review and update their outlines with notes from the section. Following their outlines, students should list unanswered questions about the skeletal system. Have students use their questions to quiz their partners, and note any questions that neither partner can answer. Then, make a class list of all unanswered questions.

ANSWER Three types of joints are immovable joints, slightly movable joints, and movable joints.

As You Read

Use your lesson outline to take notes about the skeletal system as you read. Create a list of unanswered questions that you have about this system in the outline, as well.

What are the three types of joints?

Formation of Bones

The formation of bones begins early in a human's life—during the fifth or sixth week of pregnancy. At this early stage, soft, flexible connective tissue called **cartilage** (KAR tuh lihj) begins to form the basis of the skeleton. Within a few weeks of its formation, much of this cartilage is changed into hard bone through a process called ossification. At birth, humans have more than 300 bones. As humans develop, these bones grow longer and fuse together to form the 206 bones of a mature adult. By the time humans reach the age of about 18, their bones are completely ossified and stop growing longer.

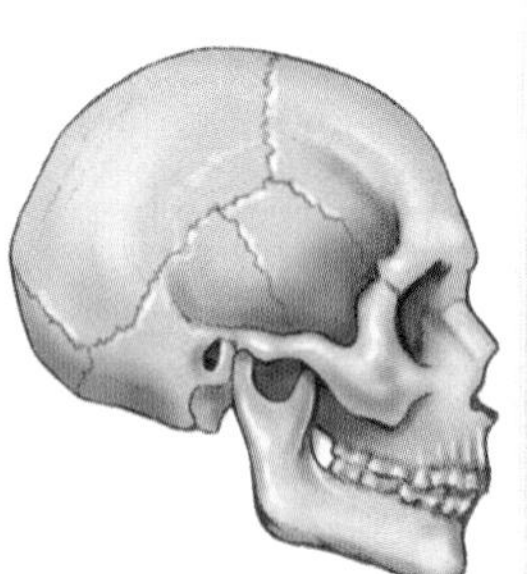

Figure 19.16 The human skull is made up of 29 flat bones that meet at immovable joints.

Joints

The place where two or more bones meet is called a **joint**. Joints are classified as immovable, slightly movable, or movable based on the amount of movement they allow.

Immovable Joints Immovable joints allow no movement. The bones that make up your skull meet at immovable joints. Bones that meet at immovable joints are fused together.

Slightly Movable Joints Slightly movable joints, as their name suggests, allow for a limited amount of movement. Your vertebrae, or backbones, meet at slightly movable joints where adjacent vertebrae are separated by discs that contain cartilage, as shown in **Figure 19.17**.

Movable Joints Movable joints allow movement in one or more directions. A ball-and-socket joint allows for the widest range of movement. The bones of the thigh and pelvis meet at ball-and-socket joints. A gliding joint allows for some movement in all directions. You can spread your fingers wide apart and can move them up and down because of gliding joints. A hinge joint allows for back-and-forth motion in one direction. The knee is a hinge joint. A pivot joint, such as the one found between the forearm and the upper arm, allows one bone to rotate around another. The four main types of movable joints are shown in **Figure 19.18**.

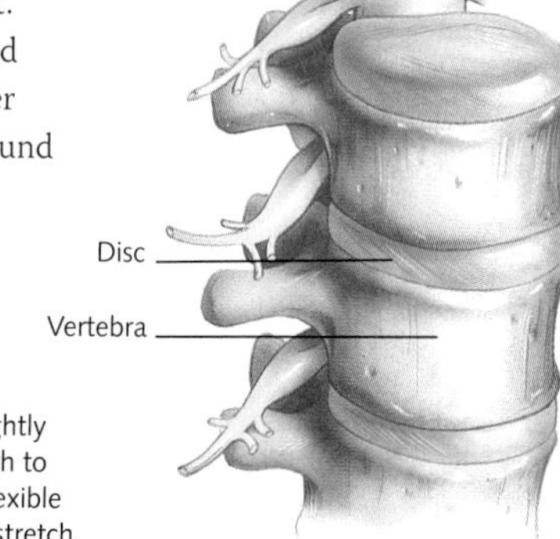

Figure 19.17 The vertebrae meet at slightly movable joints. The joints are rigid enough to keep your body strong and upright but flexible enough to allow you to twist, bend, and stretch.

Did You Know?

Scientists classify animals into two main groups based on whether or not they have backbones. Animals with backbones are called vertebrates. You are a vertebrate. Animals without backbones are called invertebrates. Sponges, snails, and spiders are examples of invertebrates, as are most of Earth's animals.

Background Information

Arthritis is a term used to describe a group of more than 100 medical conditions that affect nearly 70 million adults worldwide—300,000 adults in the United States. Osteoarthritis is the most common form of arthritis, and it predominantly affects people over age 60. Other forms of arthritis can affect infants, young adults, and middle-aged people.

All forms of arthritis affect joints. Symptoms include pain, stiffness, inflammation, and damage to joint cartilage. Eventually, joints are weakened, become unstable, and become visibly deformed.

Some forms of arthritis are systemic and can affect the whole body. These types of arthritis can damage organs and systems, including the heart, lungs, kidneys, blood vessels, and bones.

Bones that meet at movable joints are held together by thick connective tissues called **ligaments** (LIH guh munts). They are also protected from stress by a layer of cartilage that forms on the surface of the bone around the joint. Synovial (suh NOH vee ul) fluid, a watery liquid, further cushions the joint and aids in smooth movement.

Figure It Out

1. What kind of motion does a hinge joint allow?
2. Compare the four types of movable joints. How are they alike? How do they differ?

Ball-and-socket joint Ball-and-socket joints allow movement in all directions. The joints of the hips and shoulders are ball-and-socket joints; they allow you to swing your arms and legs around in many directions.

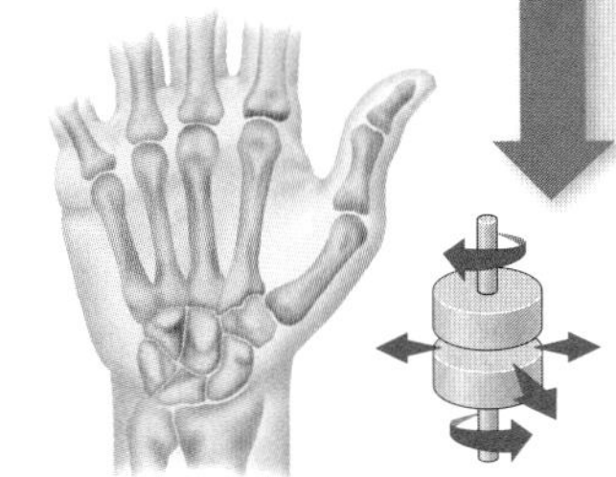

Gliding joint Gliding joints, found in the wrists and ankles, are similar to sliding doors. They allow bones to slide past each other.

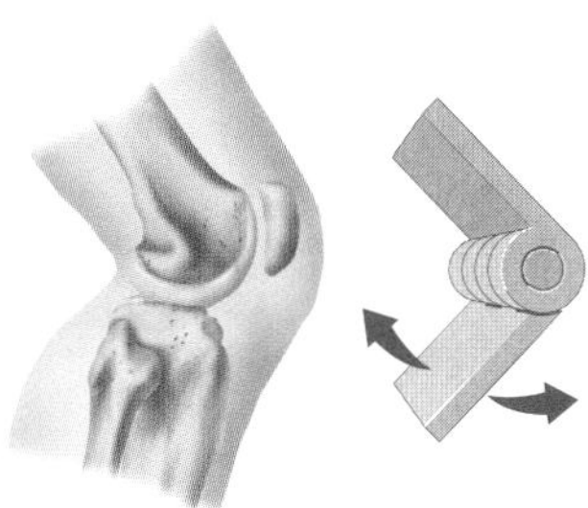

Hinge joint Hinge joints are found in the elbows, knees, fingers, and toes. They allow back-and-forth movement like that of a door hinge.

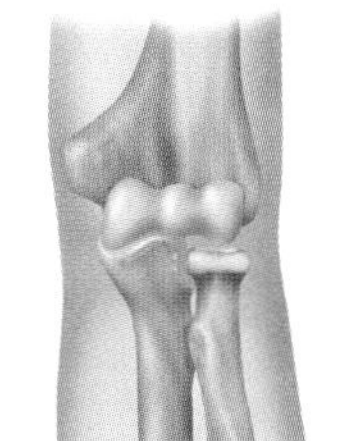

Pivot joint Pivot joints allow bones to twist around each other. One example is in your forearm, between the ulna and the radius. It allows you to twist your forearm around.

Figure 19.18 Joints, or places where two bones meet, are shaped according to how they function in the body.

After You Read

1. What are some of the functions of the skeletal system?
2. Use your lesson outline to describe the composition of bone.
3. What are the three main types of joints?
4. Based on the information in your outline, hypothesize why bones have different shapes.

Differentiated Instruction

Kinesthetic Provide students with brads and paper clips. Have them create the different kinds of movable joints identified in their body outlines.

Field Study

Have students observe different physical education activities or sports. Have students note the key movements for the activity as well as which type of movable joint is being used. As a class, list the movable joints and the activity associated with repetitive use. Use this information to create questions for the interview in the Differentiated Instruction activity on page 346.

Teach

EXPLAIN that students will learn about the four types of movable joints in this section.

Figure It Out: Figure 19.18

ANSWER **1.** back-and-forth motion **2.** They joints are alike in that all allow for some range of motion. They are different in that each allows different amounts and types of motion.

Science Notebook EXTRA

Have students perform the following activity and then write their observations in their Science Notebooks. Students should stand two toilet paper tubes side by side, and then balance a heavy book on their open ends. Encourage students to relate the activity to the strength of hollow bones.

Assess

EVALUATE Use the After You Read questions and the Alternative Assessment to help you assess students' understanding of the lesson.

After You Read

1. gives the body shape, protects delicate internal organs, allows the body to move, stores minerals, and produces blood cells
2. A bone has an outer layer of tissue called the periosteum and inner layers of tissue called compact bone and spongy bone. Compact bone and spongy bone contain many nerves and blood vessels. Many long bones also contain bone marrow.
3. immovable joints, slightly movable joints, and movable joints
4. Answers may vary. Bones have different shapes because they have different functions in the body. Some bones are shaped to protect organs. Others are shaped for movement or support.

Alternative Assessment

EVALUATE Allow students to use their lesson outlines to list and describe the composition of bone and the three types of joints, including the four types of movable joints.

19.4 Introduce

ENGAGE Write the following facts on the board, and have students work with a partner to decide if each fact is true or false.

1. Muscles in the human body account for about 30 percent of body weight. (False; 40–50 percent of the weight)
2. Human jaw muscles can generate a force of 95 kilograms on the molars. (True)
3. The tongue is the busiest muscle in the body. (False; eye muscles are—they move about 100,000 times per day.)
4. To move one of the body's limbs, some muscles pull and some muscles push. (False; all muscles pull.)

After students discuss each item, review the correct fact.

Before You Read

Model previewing the lesson by reading the heading *Your Muscular Body* aloud to the class. Think aloud about questions related to muscles. Examples might include: *Do all people have the same number of muscles? Are the muscles that blink my eye the same as those that move my leg? Are all muscle cells the same?* Encourage students to write at least two or three questions that they have about the muscular system.

Teach

EXPLAIN that in this lesson, students will learn what the muscular system is, what the different types of muscle tissue are, and how muscles move bones in the human body.

Learning Goals

- Identify the major functions of the muscular system.
- Describe three types of muscle tissue.
- Explain how skeletal muscles allow movement of the bones.

New Vocabulary

muscular system
skeletal muscle
smooth muscle
cardiac muscle
tendon

19.4 The Muscular System

Before You Read

Write the title of this lesson in your Science Notebook. Then, look at the pictures and review the headings in the lesson. Record some questions you have about the muscular system.

Weightlifters often impress crowds with their ability to lift and carry tremendous amounts of weight. The strongest women can bench-press more than 225 kg. They can do squats with 338-kg weights.

What would it take for you to have as many muscles as these athletes? Nothing! Your muscles may not be quite as developed or defined, but like these athletes, you were born with the more than 600 muscles that are in your body. Together, your muscles make up your **muscular system**. Big or small, your muscles are responsible for every move you make, from blinking your eyes and breathing to kicking a soccer ball and lifting weights.

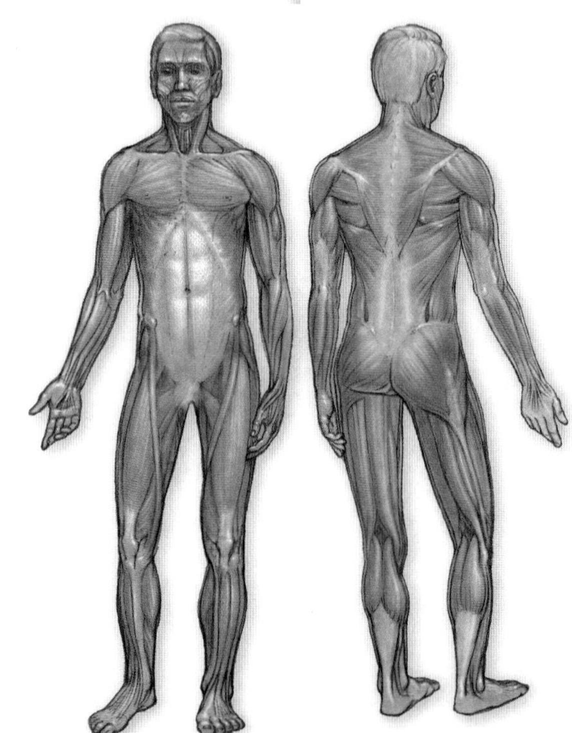

Your Muscular Body

More than 40 percent of the body mass of an average human is muscle. Without this muscle, humans could not move. They could not lift crying babies or pick up groceries. They could not talk, breathe, or eat food. Whether you realize it or not, just about everything your body does to keep you alive involves some kind of movement that is made possible by muscles.

Figure 19.19 shows some of the major muscles of the human body. As you can see, they are found throughout the body. Some, such as those worked on by weightlifters and bodybuilders, are visible beneath the skin. Others are "buried" within the body and help make up vital organs such as the lungs, the heart, and the stomach.

Figure 19.19 The muscles shown here are skeletal muscles, one of the three types of muscles in the human body. Smooth muscles and cardiac muscles make up organs deep within the body and thus cannot be shown in this diagram.

ELL Strategy

Use a Concept Map Have each student make a concept map to organize facts about the muscular system. Their maps should include the three different types of muscle and the structure and location of each, as well as labels identifying whether the muscles are voluntary or involuntary.

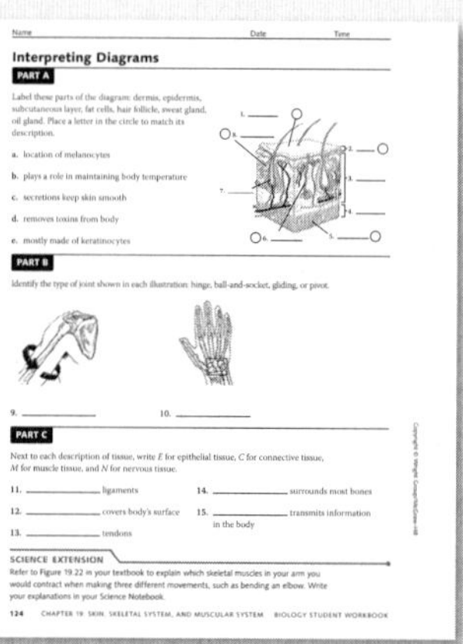

Name Date Time

Interpreting Diagrams

PART A

Label these parts of the diagram: dermis, epidermis, subcutaneous layer, fat cells, hair follicle, sweat gland, oil gland. Place a letter in the circle to match its description.

a. location of melanocytes
b. plays a role in maintaining body temperature
c. secretions keep skin smooth
d. removes toxins from body
e. mostly made of keratinocytes

PART B

Identify the type of joint shown in each illustration: hinge, ball-and-socket, gliding, or pivot.

9. ________ 10. ________

PART C

Next to each description of tissue, write *E* for epithelial tissue, *C* for connective tissue, *M* for muscle tissue, and *N* for nervous tissue.

11. ________ ligaments
12. ________ covers body's surface
13. ________ tendons
14. ________ surrounds most bones
15. ________ transmits information in the body

SCIENCE EXTENSION

Refer to Figure 19.22 in your textbook to explain which skeletal muscles in your arm you would contract when making three different movements, such as bending an elbow. Write your explanations in your Science Notebook.

124 CHAPTER 19 SKIN, SKELETAL SYSTEM, AND MUSCULAR SYSTEM BIOLOGY STUDENT WORKBOOK

Interpreting Diagrams Workbook, p. 124

Three Types of Muscle Tissue

Each muscle in the body is made up of muscle tissue. There are three main types of muscle tissue: skeletal muscle, smooth muscle, and cardiac muscle. Each type is specialized to perform a different function in the body.

Skeletal muscle tissue makes up the skeletal muscles. **Skeletal muscles** are the muscles that attach to bones. The biceps and triceps in the upper arms and the quadriceps in the thighs are examples of skeletal muscles. Skeletal muscle tissue is made up of long, thin cells that each contain more than one nucleus. Skeletal muscle is often called striated muscle because it appears to have alternating light and dark stripes or bands.

Skeletal muscles pull on bones to make the body move. They are responsible for all the body's voluntary movement, such as dancing, playing a piano, and in-line skating. Voluntary movement is movement you can consciously control.

Smooth muscle tissue makes up the muscle found in internal organs such as the stomach, intestines, kidney, and liver. Smooth muscle tissue is not striated. It is made up of spindle-shaped cells that each contain only one nucleus.

Smooth muscle tissue is not usually under voluntary control. Instead, it is responsible for involuntary movement. This is movement you cannot consciously control. The movement of food through the digestive system and the movement of blood through blood vessels are examples of involuntary movements performed by smooth muscle tissue.

Cardiac muscle tissue is the muscle tissue found in the heart. Like smooth muscle tissue, cardiac muscle is not under voluntary control. You do not have to think about your heart beating for it to happen. Like skeletal muscle tissue, cardiac muscle is striated. However, its cells usually contain just one nucleus each. The cells that make up cardiac muscle are smaller than those that make up skeletal muscle.

Figure It Out

1. Compare the three types of muscle tissue. How are they similar? How do they differ?
2. Describe what each type of muscle tissue does in the body.

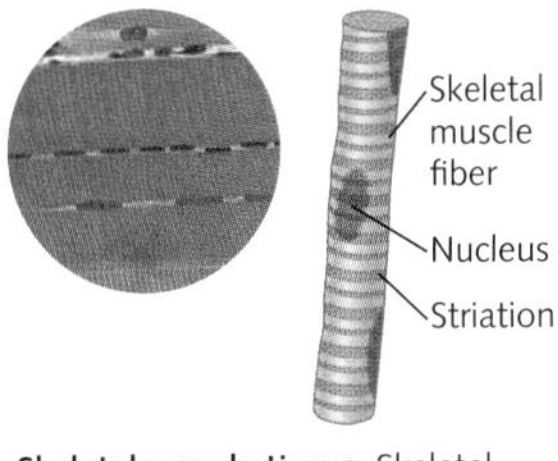

Skeletal muscle tissue Skeletal muscle fibers appear striated, or striped, under a microscope.

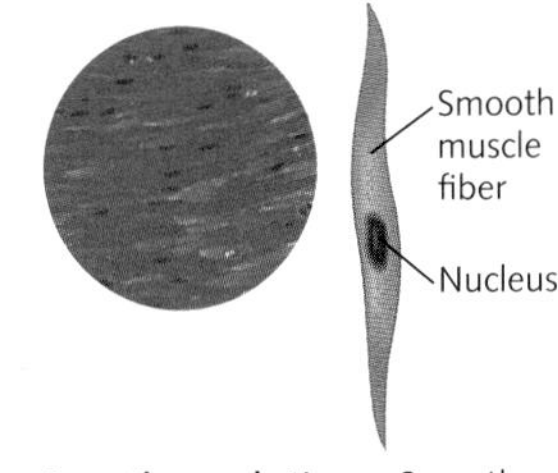

Smooth muscle tissue Smooth muscle fibers appear spindle-shaped when magnified.

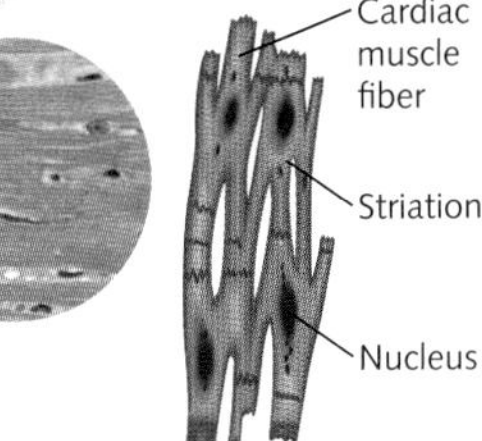

Cardiac muscle tissue Cardiac muscle fibers also appear striated when magnified.

Figure 19.20 The three main types of muscle tissue are skeletal muscle tissue, smooth muscle tissue, and cardiac muscle tissue. Each type of tissue is specialized to perform a different function.

Teach

EXPLAIN to students that they will learn about the three types of muscle tissue: skeletal, smooth, and cardiac.

Vocabulary

muscular system Tell students that the muscular system is composed of muscles that work together to move the body. The muscles move in either a voluntary or involuntary manner. Review the meanings of the words *voluntary* and *involuntary*.

skeletal muscle Tell students that skeletal muscles attach to the skeleton and usually occur in pairs. These are the muscles that students can see and feel.

smooth muscle Explain that smooth muscle is found in the digestive system, the blood vessels, the bladder, the airways, and, in females, the uterus. Smooth muscle is able to stretch and maintain tension for long periods of time.

cardiac muscle Tell students that cardiac muscle is found only in the heart and that it functions with consistency and endurance.

Science Notebook EXTRA

Have students draw each type of muscle tissue in their Science Notebooks. Students could use a different color to represent each type of muscle tissue. They should label each drawing and identify the cell nucleus in each.

Figure It Out: Figure 19.20

ANSWER **1.** Skeletal muscle cells have many nuclei. Skeletal muscle looks like it has stripes. Smooth muscle does not have a fixed pattern of stripes, as skeletal muscle does. Smooth muscle cells have large nuclei. Cardiac muscle cells have nuclei that look similar to those in smooth muscle. Cardiac muscle looks slightly striped, like skeletal muscle. **2.** Skeletal muscle tissue is responsible for voluntary movement. Smooth muscle tissue is responsible for involuntary movement. Cardiac muscle is responsible for movements (beating) of the heart.

Background Information

Skeletal muscle is either slow-twitch (Type 1) or fast-twitch (Type II). Slow-twitch muscle fibers contract slowly and can continue working for a long time. Fast-twitch muscle fibers contract quickly but also tire rapidly. Slow-twitch muscle fibers are good for endurance activities, such as long-distance running or cycling. Fast-twitch muscles are useful for activities that involve sprinting, such as short-distance racing and jumping up to catch a ball. Most muscles are a mixture of both types of muscle. However, eye muscles are made only of fast-twitch muscle fibers. Muscles in the back that are used to maintain posture have mostly slow-twitch muscle fibers.

Teach

EXPLAIN that in this section, students will learn about the composition of skeletal muscle cells.

EXPLORE After students have read this page, arrange them in small groups and have them think about the relationship between the energy that muscles need to move and different physical activities. Ask them to list different activities and sports and then rank the answers according to the amount of energy required by its participants. Ensure that students can identify the size and number of muscles needed as factors of the energy requirement. As a class, create lists of strenuous, moderate, and light activities. Discuss with students the correlation between energy expenditure and Calorie intake.

As You Read

Give students five to ten minutes to review and answer their Science Notebook questions. Review students' work for accuracy.

ANSWER Three types of muscle tissue are skeletal, smooth, and cardiac.

Vocabulary

tendon Tell students that *tendon* is derived from the Latin word *tendo,* meaning "to stretch out."

CONNECTION: History

Tell students that the Achilles tendon is one of the strongest tendons in the body. Have students discuss why its name is suitable.

As You Read

Look for the answers to the questions you have about the muscular system as you read the text. Record the answers in your Science Notebook.

What are the three types of muscle tissue?

Skeletal Muscle Structure

Skeletal muscle cells, often called muscle fibers, consist mainly of two types of protein strands: actin and myosin. Where these two strands overlap, the muscle fiber looks dark. Where the strands do not overlap, the fiber looks light. The alternating light and dark bands give skeletal muscle tissue its striated appearance. These protein strands are responsible for the ability of muscles to contract and relax. The contracting and relaxing of muscles is what causes movement.

At the end of each muscle fiber is a motor nerve. Motor nerves connect the skeletal muscles to the brain. They enable the voluntary control of the skeletal muscles. Blood vessels running through muscle tissue bring oxygen and food to the cells. They give muscle fibers the energy required to contract and relax to make the body move.

Muscle fibers are grouped together into bundles. Small muscles, such as those found in the fingers, can be made up of just a few bundles. Larger muscles, such as those in the legs, have hundreds of bundles.

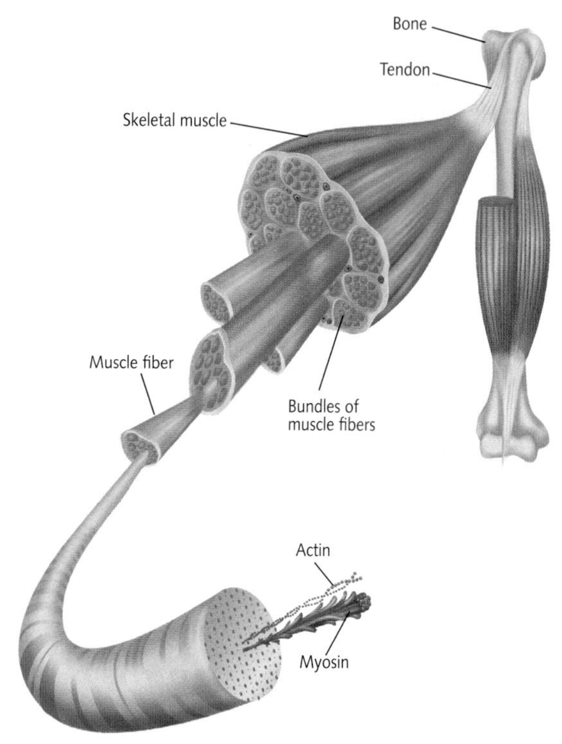

Figure 19.21 Skeletal muscles are bundles of muscle fibers. Each bundle is covered by connective tissue. Each muscle fiber is a single cell that can be as long as 40 cm.

Background Information

Tendons connect the ends of most skeletal muscles to bones. The point of origin is the end of the muscle connected to the bone that does not move when contraction occurs. The insertion point connects the muscle to the bone that does move when the muscle contracts.

In Greek mythology, Achilles was the greatest warrior in the Trojan War. The common version of the myth of Achilles states that his mother, Thetis, tried to make him immortal by dipping him in the river Styx. She held him by his heel and forgot to get it wet, thus leaving this part of his body vulnerable. Achilles was a hero in the Trojan War and is a central character and hero in Homer's *Iliad.*

Muscles and Movement

Skeletal muscles are attached to bones by thick connective tissues called **tendons** (TEN dunz). Touch the back of your ankle. The tough, thick, cordlike structure you feel is your Achilles tendon. It is the largest tendon in the body. It attaches the outermost calf muscle to the heel bone. Hundreds of tendons throughout the body attach the skeletal muscles to the bones. They allow the muscles to pull on the bones and move the body.

Skeletal muscles can only pull on bones. For this reason, most skeletal muscles in the body work in pairs to give the body a range of movement. For example, the biceps and triceps attach to the bones of the forearm and allow the arm to move in a variety of ways. When muscle fibers of the biceps are stimulated by nerves, the actin and myosin in the fibers slide past each other, causing the muscle to shorten, or contract. When the muscle contracts, it pulls on the bone to which it is attached. The forearm lifts up.

When muscle fibers of the triceps are stimulated, the actin and myosin in these fibers slide past each other, causing this muscle to contract. As a result, the forearm stretches out. When one muscle in the pair contracts, the other muscle relaxes. Skeletal muscles throughout the body work in this way to allow the body to move.

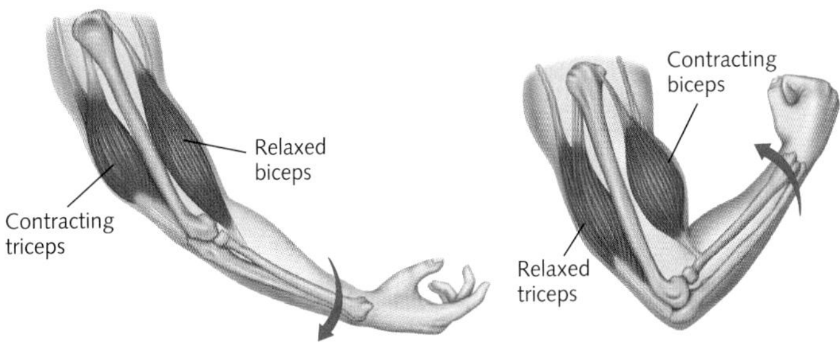

Figure 19.22 If muscles did not work in pairs, movements of the arm such as these would be impossible. What muscle must contract in order for you to bend your elbow?

CONNECTION: Health

The Achilles tendon is named after the Greek hero Achilles. According to legend, Achilles was killed when a poisoned arrow struck this tendon—the only weak spot in his body.

Explain It!

Skeletal muscles, tendons, and joints work together like levers to move bones. Find out about levers. Then, write a paragraph in your Science Notebook explaining how muscles, tendons, and joints are similar to these simple machines. Use diagrams to enhance your explanation.

After You Read

1. What is the main function of the muscular system?
2. Describe the three types of muscle tissue.
3. Explain how muscles help move bones.
4. Use your lesson outline, including the questions you had about the muscular system and the answers you found, to summarize what you learned in this lesson.

Teach

EXPLAIN that in this section, students will learn how skeletal muscles create movement.

EXPLORE Have students do the following activity to understand how muscles work in pairs. Sit on a chair at a table or desk, place the palm of one hand on the underside of the table or desk, and gently push up. With the other hand, feel the front of your upper arm and then the back of your upper arm. Then, place the palm of your hand on the top of the table or desk and gently press down. Again, feel both the front and back of your upper arm. Have students describe what they felt.

Explain It!

ANSWER A lever is a simple machine made of a straight bar and a fulcrum, a fixed point on which the bar pivots. There are first-class, second-class, and third-class levers. In the body, a joint acts as the fulcrum. Muscles provide the force required to lift the load. Some muscle-bone pairs work as first-class levers, while others work as second- or third-class levers.

Use the Visual: Figure 19.22

ANSWER the biceps

Assess

EVALUATE Use the After You Read questions and the Alternative Assessment to help you assess students' understanding of the lesson.

After You Read

1. voluntary and involuntary body movement
2. Skeletal muscle produces voluntary movements, is striated, and is composed of cells having many nuclei. Smooth muscle produces involuntary movement, is not striated, and is composed of cells having one large nucleus. Cardiac muscle, found only in the heart, is striated, but its cells each have one nucleus.
3. Muscles work in pairs. A muscle contracts and pulls on a bone, making it move. Another muscle contracts and pulls on the bone to move it in the opposite direction.
4. Students' paragraphs should show understanding of the lesson's content.

Differentiated Instruction

Interpersonal Have students talk to the school nurse, physical education teacher, or sports coach about injuries most common to student athletes. To inform their questioning, students can use their observations from the Field Study activity on page 343.

Alternative Assessment

EVALUATE Ask each student to use his or her outline to create a four-column chart that lists the three types of muscle tissue, their composition, their functions, and whether they are voluntary or involuntary.

Chapter 19 Summary

VOCABULARY REVIEW

Check students' sentences or paragraphs to make sure they understand the meaning of each vocabulary term.

PREPARE FOR CHAPTER TEST

Evaluate students' essays using the following criteria:

1. The topic sentence, or main idea, should restate the Key Concept.
2. The supporting paragraphs should incorporate the answers to the Learning Goal questions students have written and include details, facts, and examples they have recorded in their Science Notebooks.
3. The concluding sentence should sum up the main idea of the chapter and restate the Key Concept.

MASTERING CONCEPTS

True or False

1. False, cell
2. False, largest
3. True
4. True
5. False, red
6. False, organs

Short Answer

7. The skeletal system is responsible for giving the body shape, protecting internal organs, enabling movement, storing minerals, and producing blood.
8. Hair helps keep the body healthy by protecting organs such as the eyes and by regulating the body's temperature.
9. Muscles are essential because they are responsible for movement in the body. They enable the heart to pump, the lungs to breathe, the jaw to move, etc., allowing the body to meet its needs.
10. Bones are made up of a thin outer layer of tissue called the periosteum, compact bone, spongy bone, and many nerves and blood vessels. Some also contain bone marrow.
11. The epidermis is the outermost layer of the skin. It is thick and tough and therefore protects the body from disease, injury, and dehydration.

Chapter 19 Summary

KEY CONCEPTS

19.1 Human Body Organization

- The body is organized into cells, tissues, organs, and organ systems.
- Cells are the basic building blocks of life. Cells are specialized to perform specific functions in the body.
- Specialized cells group together to form tissues. Four main types of tissue in the human body are epithelial tissue, connective tissue, muscle tissue, and nervous tissue.

19.2 Skin

- Skin covers the body and protects internal organs. It helps regulate the body's temperature and helps prevent disease and loss of essential fluids.
- Skin is made up of three main layers of tissue. The epidermis is the outer layer. The dermis lies beneath the epidermis. The subcutaneous layer is the innermost layer.
- Hair and nails are part of the skin.

19.3 The Skeletal System

- The skeletal system gives the body shape, supports and protects the body, enables movement, stores nutrients, and produces blood.
- Bones are composed of compact and spongy bone and are covered by a layer of tissue known as the periosteum. Bone marrow runs through the center of many long bones.
- A joint is the place where two or more bones meet. Joints are classified as immovable, slightly movable, or movable based on the amount of movement they allow. Ligaments hold bones together at the joints.

19.4 The Muscular System

- The muscular system is responsible for the body's motions.
- The three main types of muscle tissue are skeletal, smooth, and cardiac muscle tissue.
- Skeletal muscles are attached to bones by tendons. When a muscle contracts, it pulls on the bone it is attached to, causing the bone to move.

VOCABULARY REVIEW

Write each term in a complete sentence, or write a paragraph relating several terms.

19.1
cell, p. 331
tissue, p. 332
epithelial tissue, p. 332
connective tissue, p. 332
muscle tissue, p. 333
nervous tissue, p. 333
organ, p. 333
organ system, p. 334

19.2
epidermis, p. 337
keratin, p. 337
melanin, p. 337
dermis, p. 338
subcutaneous tissue, p. 339

19.3
skeletal system, p. 340
periosteum, p. 341
compact bone, p. 341
spongy bone, p. 341
bone marrow, p. 341
cartilage, p. 342
joint, p. 342
ligament, p. 343

19.4
muscular system, p. 344
skeletal muscle, p. 345
smooth muscle, p. 345
cardiac muscle, p. 345
tendon, p. 347

PREPARE FOR CHAPTER TEST

To prepare for the chapter test, create a question from each Learning Goal. Use the information in your Science Notebook to answer each question. Then use these answers to write a well-developed essay about the chapter. Use the Key Concept on the first page of this chapter as your topic sentence.

348 SKIN, SKELETAL SYSTEM, AND MUSCULAR SYSTEM

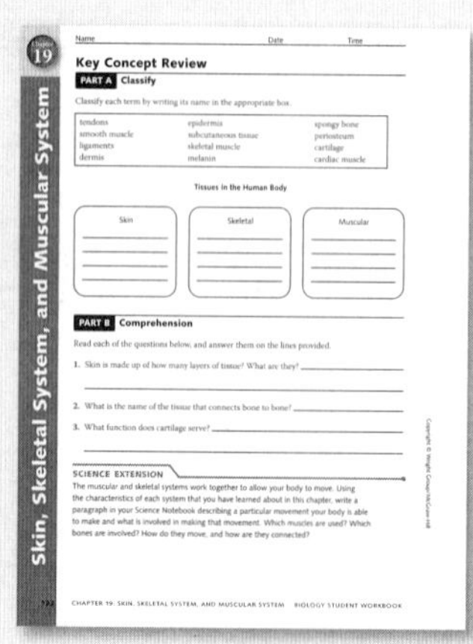
Key Concepts Review
Workbook, p. 122

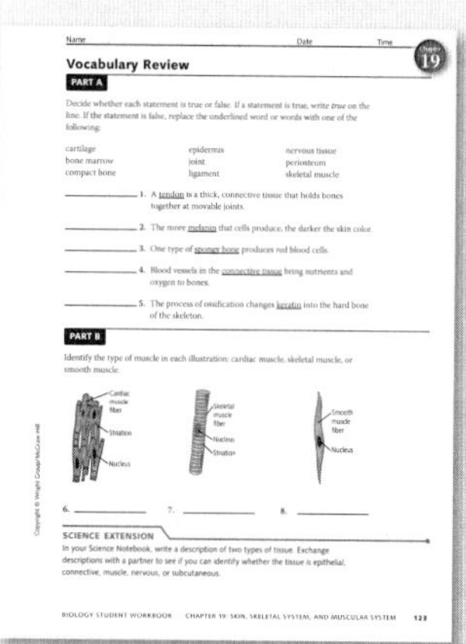
Vocabulary Review
Workbook, p. 123

MASTERING CONCEPTS

True or False

If the statement is true, write "true." If it is false, change the underlined word or words to make the statement true.

1. A tissue is the basic unit of life.
2. Skin is the smallest organ in the human body.
3. Three types of muscle tissue are smooth, skeletal, and cardiac muscle tissue.
4. The skeletal system aids in the production of blood.
5. Many bones contain yellow bone marrow, which produces red and white blood cells.
6. Organ systems are made up of tissues that work together to perform specific functions in the body.

Short Answer

Answer each of the following in a sentence or brief paragraph.

7. What are the basic functions of the skeletal system?
8. In what ways does hair help keep the body healthy?
9. Why are muscles essential to your survival?
10. What are bones made up of?
11. What is the epidermis? Describe its main functions in the body.

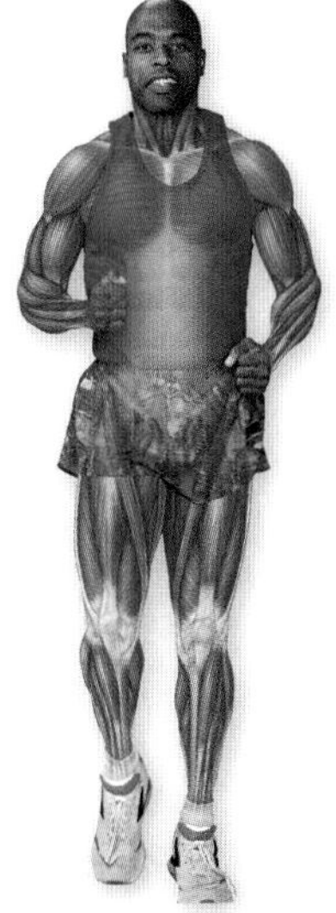

Critical Thinking

Use what you have learned in this chapter to answer each of the following.

12. **Explain** Why do most skeletal muscles work in pairs?
13. **Compare and Contrast** What are the three main types of joints? How are they alike? How do they differ?
14. **Analyze** Why do you think skin is made up of several layers of tissue?

Standardized Test Question

Choose the letter of the response that correctly answers the question.

15. How are skeletal muscles attached to bones?
    - A. by ligaments
    - B. by tendons
    - C. by skin cells
    - D. by smooth muscles

Test-Taking Tip

For multiple-choice questions, use the process of elimination. First eliminate answers you know are incorrect. Then compare your remaining choices to solve the problem or to make an educated guess.

Critical Thinking

12. Skeletal muscles can only pull on bones in one direction. Most skeletal muscles work in pairs to allow for a range of motion.
13. The three main types of joints are immovable joints, slightly movable joints, and movable joints. They are alike in that all occur where two or more bones meet and they are shaped for a specific function. They are different in that they allow for different amounts of motion. Immovable joints allow no motion. Slightly movable joints allow limited motion. Movable joints allow for motion in one or more directions.
14. Skin is made up several layers of tissue because it has many functions and each layer specializes in certain of these functions.

Standardized Test Question

15. B

Reading Links

Written in Bones: How Human Remains Unlock the Secrets of the Dead

Through 38 archaeological case studies, this book shows that bones have stories to tell. By applying modern scientific techniques, experts glean a wealth of information from the careful study of bones, including clues that help them better understand ancient human cultures. The book's compelling forensic mysteries, which include analysis of skeletons found in the Tower of London and the facial reconstruction of a 9,000-year-old man, offer a rich and interesting supplement to a more general classroom study of the human skeletal system.

Bahn, Paul G., ed. Firefly Books, Inc. 192 pp. Illustrated. Trade ISBN: 978-1-55297-659-3.

The Burn Journals

More mature young adult readers will benefit from an intensely personal true story of a fourteen-year-old boy's suicide attempt and subsequent rehabilitation process. With burns covering 85 percent of his body, Brent Runyon underwent months of skin grafts and extensive therapies. His experience and recovery process will offer students a better understanding of burns and their treatment in a memorable and meaningful context.

Runyon, Brent. Knopf Publishing Group. 336 pp. Trade ISBN: 978-1-4000-9642-8.

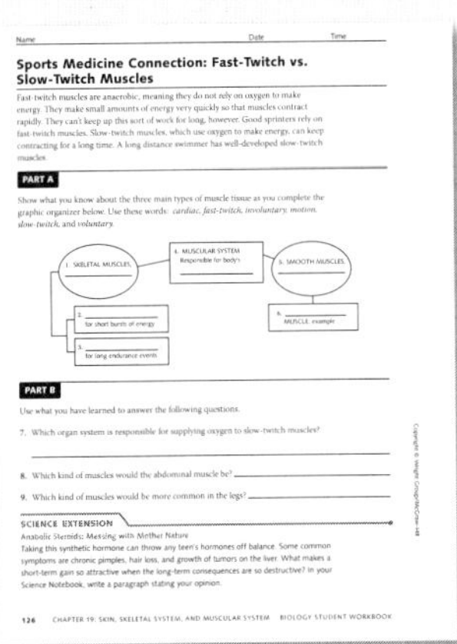

Sports Medicine Connection: Fast-Twitch vs. Slow-Twitch Muscles

Curriculum Connection Workbook, p. 126

Science Challenge

Science Challenge Workbook, p. 127

Chapter 19

Labs

19A Muscle Fatigue

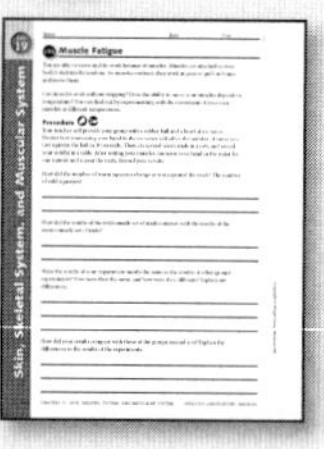

This prechapter introduction activity is designed to determine what students already know about muscles and how they work by making predictions, evaluating, and drawing conclusions about the effect of fatigue and cold on muscles.

Objectives

- predict the effect of cold on muscle endurance
- evaluate how the repeated contraction of a muscle affects performance
- record data in a suitable way
- communicate conclusions

Planning

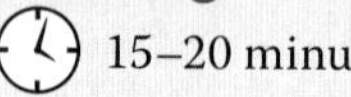
15–20 minutes

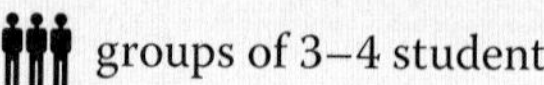
groups of 3–4 students

Materials (per group)

- bowl of ice water deep enough to fully immerse a hand
- a rubber ball, such as a racquetball
- pencil
- ruler
- paper

Lab Tip

Students should be cautioned not to leave their hands in ice water so long that it becomes physically uncomfortable.

Advance Preparation

- Ask students to suggest how they might organize a table to record their results.
- Suggest that students discuss the reasons for their predictions in their groups.
- Remind students that the same person must do the warm and cold trials and that he or she should rest between sets of trials.

Engagement Guide

- Challenge students to think about how they can predict what will happen in the experiment by asking these questions:
  - *What experiences have you had that can help you predict how cold will affect your muscles?* (shoveling snow or doing work or activities on a cold day)
  - *Why do you think the number of times you can squeeze the ball in 30 seconds might change with successive trials?* (Students should recognize that muscles fatigue with repeated use, so the number of squeezes should diminish with each trial.)
- Encourage students to communicate their conclusions in creative ways.

Going Further

Encourage students to repeat this activity using other muscles and actions. Have students present their conclusions to the class.

19B Comparing Smooth, Cardiac, and Skeletal Muscle Tissues

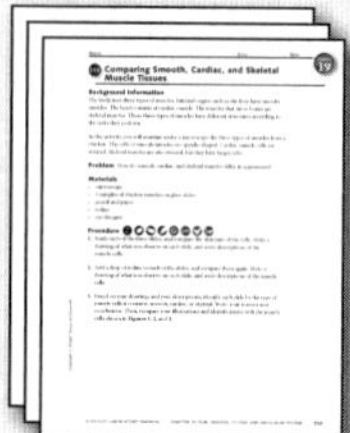

Objectives

- compare and classify muscles by observation
- draw conclusions about the type of muscle based on descriptions
- accurately illustrate the observed cells

Skill Set

observing, comparing and contrasting, recording and analyzing data, illustrating, stating conclusions

Planning

30–35 minutes groups of 3–4 students

Materials

Materials for this activity are listed in the Student Laboratory Manual.

Lab Tip

It may become necessary for students to remove their goggles to obtain a clearer view with the microscope.

Advance Preparation

A set of three slides with thin slices of chicken heart, liver, and breast muscles should be labeled *A*, *B*, and *C*. Make as many such sets as there are student groups, with the same letter corresponding to each muscle type for each set.

Answers to Observations: Slides

Students should observe spindle-shaped smooth muscle cells, striated cardiac muscle cells, and larger striated skeletal muscle cells.

Answers to Analysis and Conclusions

1. Smooth muscles are spindle-shaped, cardiac muscles are striated, and skeletal muscles are also striated but their cells are larger than the cardiac muscle cells.
2. Students should correctly identify each type of muscle with its corresponding letter, as labeled.
3. Muscle cells differ according to their function in the body. A skeletal muscle is used for support and movement of the body. Some skeletal muscles are in constant use, and others are used intermittently. Smooth muscles are used in internal organs and are normally used to move objects such

as food through the digestive system. Cardiac muscle is only found in the heart and works to keep the heart beating.

Going Further

Bring in a selection of cooked beef or chicken muscles, and allow students to examine and compare their consistencies. Skeletal muscle will pull apart easily, but cardiac muscle does not break into long, thin pieces. Students can also examine cartilage, tendons, and ligaments. Make sure that students wear gloves while handling the muscles and wash their hands afterward.

Have students create illustrations and descriptions of the different tissues that they examine, and encourage them to share their descriptions with the class.

19C How Joints, Muscles, and Bones Work Together

Objectives

- identify the tissues of a chicken wing
- describe how tissues work together to allow movement
- illustrate how a chicken wing moves

Skill Set

observing, identifying, recording and analyzing data, classifying, drawing conclusions

Planning

45–60 minutes   groups of 3–4 students

Materials

Materials for this activity are listed in the Student Laboratory Manual.

Lab Tip

It may become necessary for students to remove their goggles to obtain a clearer view with the microscope.

Advance Preparation

Provide one chicken wing per group. The chicken wing should be partially cooked in a microwave, allowing the muscle to remain firmly attached to the bone. Soak the chicken overnight in a solution of 15% distilled vinegar. **CAUTION:** *Some students may be allergic to latex. If so, they should not wear the gloves nor handle the chicken wing. They should be group recorders.*

Answers to Observations: Data Table 1

Muscles: soft tissue, attach to bone in pairs through tendons and pulls bone in movement; tendons: white stiff tissue, attach to bone and to muscles, serve to anchor muscles to bone; bone: hard and stiff, attaches to muscles through tendons and to other bones through ligaments, serves as the lever during movement; cartilage: white and rubbery, attaches to bone, cushions movement of bones at the point where they meet; ligaments: white and elastic, connect two bones at the joint, serve to keep bones aligned properly

Answers to Observations: Drawing

Diagrams will vary. However, all should illustrate the muscles, bones, tendons, cartilage, and ligaments, properly attached.

Answers to Analysis and Conclusions

1. The properties that were helpful were the appearance, the hardness or elasticity, the placement, and how they connected to each other.
2. A muscle attaches to different bones at each end so that it can move the bone like a lever.
3. The muscles pull on the bones to make them move, and the bones act as levers.
4. Cartilage cushions the point of connection and the movement of two bones.
5. Ligaments connect two bones and keep them aligned for movement.
6. Tendons tie the muscle to the bone.
7. Answers will vary, but students should recognize that the components of the chicken wing and human arm are the same in that they both have muscles, tendons, joints, and bones that perform the same kinds of functions in each appendage.

Going Further

Have students perform the same experiment with a chicken leg and thigh. Ask students to compare and contrast the two appendages. Have them predict why the muscles, bones, joints, and tendons are different, based on their functions. Also, have students try to do open hand throws. This is done by making a fist and then throwing your hand open. This maneuver is opposite of the way the muscles in the hand are setup. This will fatigue the hand very quickly. Have students make predictions on how this will affect successive trials.

Chapter 20 Lessons

Introduce Chapter 20

As a starting activity, use LAB 20A What Makes Up Blood? on page 123 of the Laboratory Manual.

ENGAGE Bring in a bicycle air pump or show a picture of one. Either demonstrate or explain how it is used. Ask students to think about the human body and how the heart and lungs work. Ask: *How are these organs like the bicycle pump? What do they do?*

Think About Moving Fluids

Have pairs of students brainstorm other types of pumps that move air or water (e.g., air pumps for car tires and air mattresses, water pumps in wells and aquariums, and sewer pumps). Have volunteers share their ideas with the class. Ask how the examples move air or water. Ask: *Do they push or pull it?* Solicit comments. Ask students to write about three types of pumps and the way in which each type moves air or water. Show one example on the board.

Chapter 20 Respiratory and Circulatory Systems

KEY CONCEPT The respiratory and circulatory systems move essential materials around the body.

If the human body were very, very flat, it would need neither a heart nor lungs. Flatworms live without these organs. However, these worms are never more than a couple of millimeters thick, because all of their cells must be close to the outside environment.

Every human cell gets nutrients and discards wastes by diffusion across its cell membrane. Through diffusion alone, however, an oxygen molecule would take about three years to move between a lung and a foot. Most animals need a faster way to move materials. The heart and lungs are pumps that can quickly move essential materials around the body.

Think About Moving Fluids

Your heart and lungs are pumps. Your lungs move air into and out of your body. Your heart pushes blood around your body.

- In your Science Notebook, make a list of three manufactured systems that use pumps to move air or water.
- Think about these pumps. How do they move fluids? Do they push them or pull them? Write what you think next to each of the pumps on your list.

www.scilinks.org
Respiratory System **Code: WGB20A**
Circulatory System **Code: WGB20B**

350

Chapter 20 Planning Guide

Instructional Periods	National Standards	Lab Manual	Workbook
20.1 3 periods	A.2, C.3, C.5; B.2, C.1; UCP.2, UCP.3	**Lab 20A—p. 123** What Makes Up Blood? **Lab 20B—p. 124** The Beating Heart **Lab 20C—p. 127** A Working Model of the Lung	Key Concept Review p. 128 Vocabulary Review p. 129 Interpreting Diagrams p. 130 Reading Comprehension p. 131 Curriculum Connection p. 132 Science Challenge p. 133
20.2 2 periods	C.1, F.1; F.1, F.6; UCP.1		
20.3 2 periods	C.1, C.3; C.1		
20.4 2 periods	A.1, C.1; B.4, C.1; UCP.5		
20.5 2 periods	C.1, C.2; C.1; UCP.5		
20.6 2 periods	C.1, G.1; G.1		
20.7 1 period	F.1; F.1, F.6		

Middle School Standard; High School Standard; Unifying Concept and Principle

20.1 What Is Respiration?

Before You Read

Make a prediction about what you think respiration is. Write your prediction in your Science Notebook, using descriptive words and examples.

Take a deep breath, and then let it out. Your body is respiring. Now, take a deep breath and hold it. Your body is still respiring. How can that be? The answer is in the distinction between respiration and breathing. **Respiration** (res puh RAY shun) is the process that moves oxygen and carbon dioxide between the atmosphere and the cells inside the body. Respiration is more than just breathing.

Oxygen moves into the body in three stages. The first stage is **ventilation** (ven tuh LAY shun). Ventilation moves air over the tissues of the lungs where gas exchange occurs. In the second stage of respiration, oxygen diffuses into the bloodstream from the outside environment. The third stage of respiration occurs when oxygen diffuses from the blood into the cells. Carbon dioxide leaves the cells using the same pathway in reverse.

Ventilation

Humans ventilate their bodies by breathing. When humans breathe, they pull air into a pair of organs inside the chest called **lungs**. The lungs are surrounded by a cage of bones called the ribs. They are separated from the digestive organs by a thin muscle called the **diaphragm** (DI uh fram).

The lungs fill with air when humans inhale (ihn HAYL). Inhalation occurs when muscles in the diaphragm and between the ribs contract, or shorten. As the muscles shorten, the ribs move upward and outward and the diaphragm moves down. These movements make the space inside the chest cavity larger. As the chest expands, the air pressure inside the space decreases. Air gets sucked into the lungs and expands them like balloons until the pressure inside the chest is the same as the pressure in the outside environment.

Air is pushed out of the lungs when humans exhale (eks HAYL). Exhalation occurs when the muscles around the chest cavity relax. The diaphragm and ribs spring back to their original positions and force the air in the lungs out of the body. Inhalation is an active process that uses energy, but exhalation requires no extra energy. The processes of inhalation and exhalation are illustrated in **Figure 20.1** on page 352.

Learning Goals

- Identify the three stages of respiration.
- Explain how breathing moves air into and out of the lungs.
- Distinguish between respiration and cellular respiration.

New Vocabulary

respiration
ventilation
lung
diaphragm
alveolus
cellular respiration

Did You Know?

Other animals ventilate their bodies in ways that are different from the method used by humans. Fish pump water across their gills to pull oxygen from the water. Frogs pump their throats up and down to force air into their lungs.

ELL Strategy

Paraphrase Have students work in pairs to paraphrase the content of this lesson. Encourage students to use their own words, include examples, and explain all the major principles covered in the lesson.

Teacher Alert

Fluids can be both gases and liquids. Air is a fluid. A fluid is a substance that does not have a rigid shape.

Science Notebook EXTRA

Encourage students to use the vocabulary section they created in their Science Notebooks. Remind them to record prefixes, suffixes, and root words to help them remember the meanings of vocabulary terms.

20.1 Introduce

ENGAGE students by asking them to notice their breathing as they sit at their desks. Then, have them jump up and down several times and notice their breathing again. Ask: *How is your breathing different after exercise? What does exercise require your body to do?* Have students discuss these questions with a partner and then with the class. Tell students that in this chapter, they will learn how the human body takes in oxygen as part of a process called respiration.

Before You Read

After students write their predictions, make a three-column chart labeled *Respiration* on the board. Label the columns *Stage 1, Stage 2,* and *Stage 3,* respectively. Ask students to copy the chart into their Science Notebooks and fill in their charts as they read the lesson.

Vocabulary terms are listed on the first student page of each lesson. You may wish to preview the terms before introducing each lesson. Strategies for teaching the vocabulary appear on the pages where the terms are introduced.

Teach

EXPLAIN that respiration in humans occurs in three stages. In this section, students will learn about the first stage: ventilation.

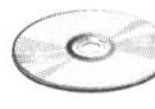

Vocabulary

resipiration Explain that *respiration* is a noun derived from the verb *respire,* which comes from the Latin word *respirare,* meaning "to breathe."

ventilation Tell students that *ventilation* is a noun derived from the verb *ventilate,* the common meaning of which is "to allow air to circulate throughout an area." It comes from the Latin word *ventilare,* which means "to fan," from *ventus,* which means "wind."

lung Tell students that this word is derived from the Anglo-Saxon word *lungen.*

diaphragm Explain that this word comes from the Greek word *diaphragma,* meaning "partition." The prefix *dia-* means "through."

Teach

EXPLAIN that students will continue to learn about respiration in this section.

As You Read

Give students a few minutes to compare their predictions with the lesson's definition of respiration. Then, allow a few minutes for students to review and complete their charts. Check students' work to be sure they understand the steps in the process of respiration. In the first stage, ventilation, air moves over the tissues where gas exchange occurs. In the second stage, oxygen diffuses into the bloodstream from the outside environment. In the third stage, oxygen diffuses from the blood into the cells.

ANSWER Students' answers will vary based on their predictions. However, their lesson definitions of respiration should include the idea that it is the process that moves oxygen and carbon dioxide between the atmosphere and the cells inside the body.

Vocabulary

alveolus Explain that *alveolus* is Latin and means "small cavity." Ask students why this is an appropriate name for the structures of the lungs. Point out that the plural form of the word is *alveoli.*

cellular respiration Explain to students that the word *cellular* is the adjective form of the noun *cell.* Review the definition of *cell,* and then have students combine this definition with the meaning of *respiration.*

As You Read

Compare the prediction in your Science Notebook with the definition of respiration in this lesson. Write a sentence summarizing the similarities and differences between the two.

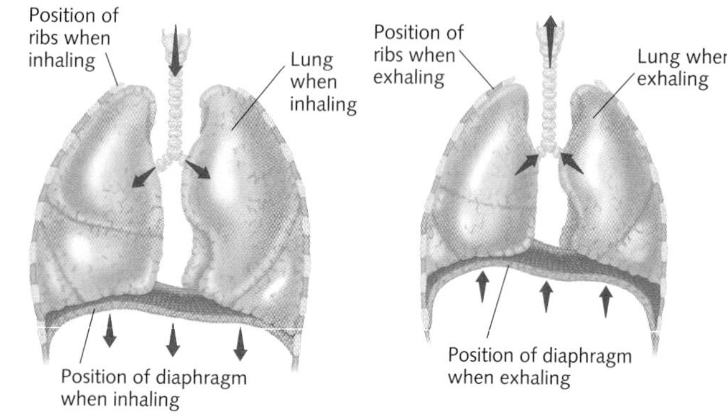

Figure 20.1 When the muscles in the diaphragm and chest contract, the chest cavity gets larger and fills with air *(left).* When the muscles in the diaphragm and chest relax, the chest cavity gets smaller and pushes air out of the lungs *(right).*

Gas Exchange

The oxygen that is inhaled may be inside the lungs, but it is not inside the body. The space inside the lungs is still part of the outside environment. In the second stage of respiration, oxygen enters the body by diffusing across lung tissue and into the bloodstream.

The inside of a lung is divided into many small compartments called **alveoli** (al VEE uh li, singular: alveolus). The alveoli are surrounded by tiny blood vessels called capillaries. Gases move between the alveoli and the capillaries easily, because the walls of both are only one cell thick.

Inside the alveoli, oxygen moves into the bloodstream because there is more oxygen in the air in the alveoli than in the blood. Carbon dioxide leaves the bloodstream because there is more carbon dioxide in the blood than in the air in the alveoli. The blood moves the oxygen to other parts of the body, and the carbon dioxide is exhaled.

The third stage of respiration occurs when the oxygenated blood reaches cells inside the body. Oxygen diffuses out of the blood and across cell membranes to the insides of cells. Carbon dioxide diffuses from the inside of each cell into the blood, where it can be carried to the lungs.

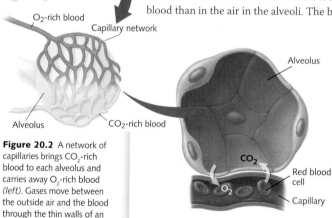

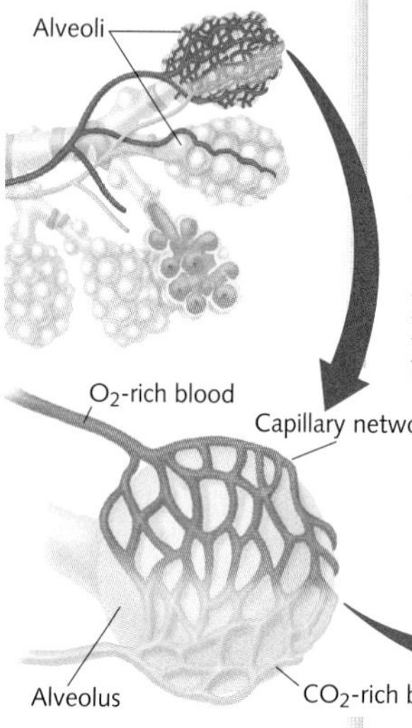

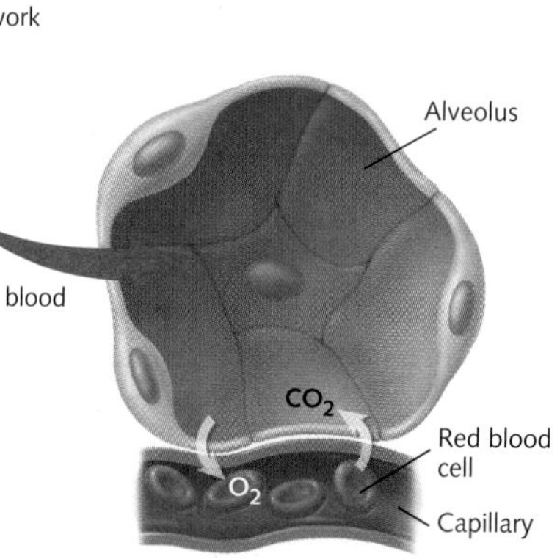

Figure 20.2 A network of capillaries brings CO_2-rich blood to each alveolus and carries away O_2-rich blood *(left).* Gases move between the outside air and the blood through the thin walls of an alveolus and a capillary *(right).*

Differentiated Instruction

Mathematical/Logical Have students devise another experiment to measure lung capacity using balloons or other materials.

Background Information

ATP stands for adenosine triphosphate. It is an energy-storing molecule in cells and is made up of an adenosine molecule and a ribose sugar (an RNA nucleotide) to which a chain of three phosphate groups is attached. ATP is formed from ADP, adenosine diphosphate (two phosphate groups). The breakdown of glucose in cellular respiration provides the energy necessary to attach a third phosphate group to ADP, forming ATP.

Figure It Out

1. When is the oxygen concentration lowest?
2. Explain why the concentration of nitrogen does not change between the time air is inhaled and the time it is exhaled.

Comparison of Gases in Inhaled and Exhaled Air

Gas	Inhaled Air	Exhaled Air
nitrogen	78.00%	78.00%
oxygen	21.00%	16.54%
carbon dioxide	0.03%	4.49%
other gases	0.97%	0.97%

Figure 20.3 Exhaled air is different from inhaled air. Compare the relative percentages of gases in inhaled and exhaled air.

Respiration Inside Cells

Oxygen can move from the blood into the cells because cells contain relatively little oxygen. The cells in the body constantly use oxygen to break down glucose and store its energy in a complex chemical called ATP. The process of breaking down nutrients for energy is called **cellular respiration**.

One waste product of cellular respiration is carbon dioxide. Because cells are constantly breaking down glucose for energy, the concentration of carbon dioxide inside a cell will steadily increase unless the gas is removed. The respiratory system has two functions. It supplies the body with oxygen needed by the cells for cellular respiration, and it also removes waste carbon dioxide from the body.

After You Read

1. Review the two definitions of respiration that you recorded in your Science Notebook. Then, write a well-developed paragraph explaining what organ-level respiration and cellular respiration have in common.
2. Name the three stages of respiration.
3. Sometimes people suffer an injury that punches a hole through the chest wall. After such an injury, these people cannot inhale. Why?
4. Why do you start feeling uncomfortable after you hold your breath for a minute?

Explore It!

How much air is inside your lungs?

- Measure 1 L of water. Pour it into a plastic bread bag, and use a permanent marker to draw a line on the bag at the top of the water level. Write *1 L* at the line. Repeat the process to make marks at the 2-, 3-, and 4-L levels. Pour all the water out of the bag.
- Close the opening of the bag around a straw, and seal it with a rubber band. Flatten the bag so there is no air inside it, and then take a deep breath and exhale into the bag through the straw. When you are finished, pinch the straw to keep the air from escaping.
- Carefully flatten the bag from the top until all the air is pushed to the bottom of the bag. How many liters of air did you exhale? Write the answer in your Science Notebook.

Chemical reactions in cells use ATP molecules as an energy source by taking away their third phosphate group, which forms ADP again. At this point, ADP can again be used to form ATP by bonding with a phosphate group, and the cycle of ATP breakdown and formation continues. This process is important because it means that a cell need not store all of the ATP it needs. As long as glucose, oxygen, and phosphate groups are available, a cell can make all of the ATP it needs.

Alternative Assessment

EVALUATE Have students illustrate their charts by making drawings or diagrams that show how oxygen and carbon dioxide are exchanged during respiration.

Teach

EXPLAIN that in this section, students will learn about how cells use oxygen and produce carbon dioxide in a process called cellular respiration.

Figure It Out: Figure 20.3

ANSWER **1.** in exhaled air. **2.** Nitrogen gas is neither used nor made in respiration.

Explore It!

Provide each student with an empty plastic bread bag, a liquid measuring cup, a rubber band, a permanent marker, and a straw. Demonstrate the procedure as you are reading the instructions, and then instruct students to do the same. Supervise students to ensure that they perform the activity correctly.

ANSWER Answers will vary, as students' volumes will vary.

Assess

EVALUATE Use the After You Read questions and the Alternative Assessment to help you assess students' understanding of the lesson.

After You Read

1. Answers will vary. One similarity is the presence of oxygen and carbon dioxide in the process. Another is that both gases move by diffusion.
2. The three stages of respiration are ventilation, gas exchange between the air and the blood, and gas exchange between the blood and the tissues.
3. Inhalation only works because the lung is inside a sealed chamber. A hole in the chest wall destroys that seal.
4. You feel uncomfortable because you need more oxygen. Oxygen keeps diffusing into the bloodstream as you hold your breath and is being used by your body. After a short time, there is not enough oxygen in the alveoli, and the blood begins to get depleted of this essential gas.

20.2 Introduce

ENGAGE Ask students to think about the two body openings that allow air to enter the body (the nose and mouth). Have students demonstrate breathing through both openings. Have each student talk to a partner about what is different and what is the same about the two types of breathing.

Before You Read

Remind students what a sequence chart is, if necessary. Tell them that they are going to show where and how air travels through the body by creating a sequence chart in their Science Notebooks. On the board, write and underline *How Air Travels in the Human Body.* Underneath, write the word *nose* followed by an arrow pointing down. Have students do the same in their Science Notebooks. Tell students to fill in their charts and include diagrams to accompany the charts as they read this section.

Teach

EXPLAIN that students will learn about the respiratory system, which consists of the lungs and a series of passages. Have pairs of students look at Figure 20.4, and ask students to tell each other about what the diagram shows.

Use the Visual: Figure 20.4

EXTEND Have small groups of students discuss the materials that pass through the trachea and the esophagus. Then, ask them to predict what could happen if food gets past the epiglottis and into the trachea.

ANSWER The person would begin choking.

Learning Goals

- Describe how air moves through the respiratory system.
- Name the structures that make up the human respiratory system.
- Identify the causes and symptoms of colds, bronchitis, pneumonia, and asthma.

New Vocabulary

respiratory system
pharynx
epiglottis
larynx
trachea
bronchus

20.2 The Respiratory System

Before You Read

Create a sequence chart in your Science Notebook that starts with the word *Nose*. As you read, complete the chart with the names of the structures that air travels through after inhalation. Use arrows to indicate the correct sequence.

Each time a person inhales, the air travels through the respiratory system before it gets to the exchange surfaces in the lungs. The **respiratory system** consists of the lungs and a series of passages.

The Pharynx and Larynx

Air can enter the body through two openings: the nose and the mouth. When a person breathes through the nose, the air enters spaces inside the head that warm and moisten the air. Mucus on the walls of these spaces helps clean and filter the air by trapping dust and pollen.

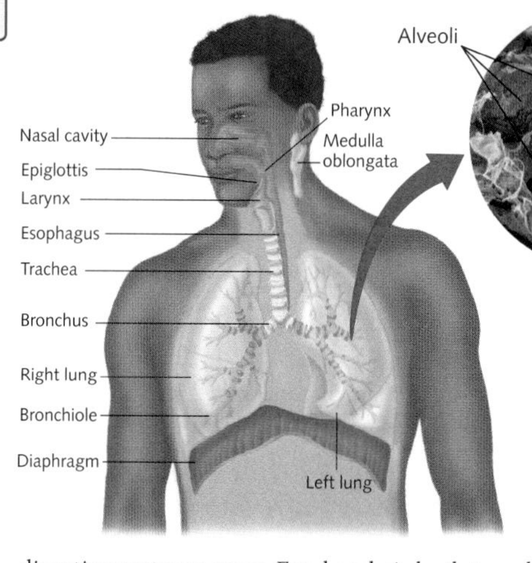

Figure 20.4 Air travels through a series of passageways before it reaches the alveoli of the lungs.

The nose and the mouth are connected in the back of the throat in a region called the **pharynx** (FER ingks). It is the spot where the respiratory and digestive systems cross. Food and air both travel through the pharynx. Food is usually kept out of the respiratory passage by a flap of cartilage at the lower end of the pharynx called the **epiglottis** (eh puh GLAH tus). When a person breathes, the epiglottis stays upright and lets air flow deeper into the lungs. When a person swallows, it folds over the respiratory passageway and deflects food into the esophagus.

After the pharynx, air moves through the **larynx** (LER ingks), which is also called the voice box because it contains the vocal cords. When air is forced through the vocal cords, they vibrate and produce sound.

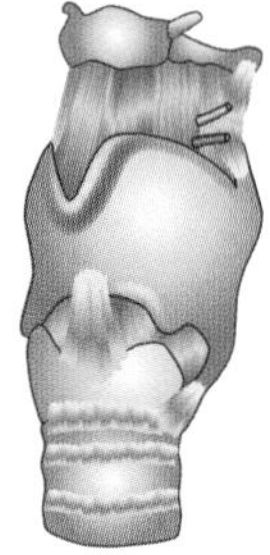

Figure 20.5 The larynx is made of cartilage and muscle and contains folds of tissue called vocal cords.

Vocabulary

respiratory system Explain that like the word *respiration, respiratory* is also a derivative of *respire,* meaning "to breathe." A system is a set of interrelated parts that together form a complex whole.

pharynx Tell students that this word comes directly from the Greek word meaning "throat." Ask students to identify the location of the pharynx.

epiglottis Explain that *epiglottis* contains the Latin word *glottis,* from the Greek word *glotta,* meaning "tongue." The prefix *epi-* is Greek and means "on" or "over." Ask students how these meanings might help them remember what the epiglottis does.

larynx Explain that this noun is the Greek word for the structure that contains the vocal cords and is called the voice box.

ELL Strategy

Think, Pair, Share Ask students to work in pairs to create unlabeled sequence charts with arrows showing the flow of air. Then, have each student exchange his or her chart with a partner. The partners should complete the charts by adding labels.

The Trachea and Bronchi

After passing through the larynx, air enters a large tube that runs down the front of the neck called the **trachea** (TRAY kee uh). It is reinforced with a series of *C*-shaped pieces of cartilage. The cartilage keeps the trachea from collapsing when a person swallows or turns his or her head. The lower end of the trachea splits into two short tubes called the **bronchi** (BRAHN ki, singular: bronchus). The bronchi carry air into the lungs.

Lungs

Humans have two lungs, one on each side of the chest. Each lung is attached to one of the bronchi. As soon as a bronchus enters the lung, it splits into several smaller tubes. The tubes split again and again, carrying air into even narrower and thinner-walled tubes as the air moves deeper into the lung.

Each tube ends in clusters of tiny sacs called alveoli. Recall that each alveolus is only one cell thick and is covered with capillaries. The inner walls of the alveoli are wet, so oxygen and carbon dioxide can diffuse easily between the blood inside the capillaries and the air inside the alveoli. The insides of the alveoli are also coated with a slippery material called surfactant. Surfactant keeps the walls of the alveoli from sticking together and makes it easier for them to expand during inhalation.

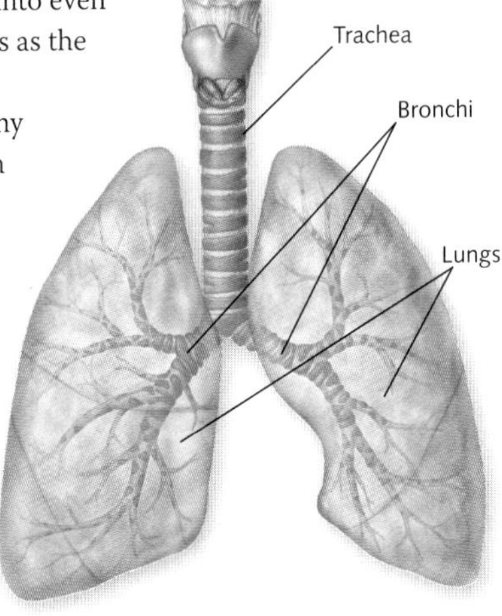

Figure 20.6 The trachea and bronchi contain rings of cartilage that support the air passageway and hold it open. Clusters of alveoli and capillaries make up the lung tissue.

The cells lining the respiratory passages are covered with cilia that constantly sweep mucus out of the lungs. The mucus traps dust and pollen, and the cilia push it into the throat, where it can be coughed up, sneezed out, or swallowed.

Respiratory Disorders

In a healthy person, air moves through the respiratory system easily. Many diseases, however, attack the respiratory system and make it hard to breathe. Some of these diseases can cause discomfort for a few days, but others can be life threatening.

As You Read

On the same sequence chart, use different-colored arrows to draw the path of an exhalation.

Is the path of an exhalation identical to the path of an inhalation?

Explain It!

A choking person can die in minutes if his or her airway is not cleared. Abdominal thrusts, also called the Heimlich maneuver, are one way to get an object out of the trachea in an emergency. One person stands behind the choking person and quickly pulls his or her fist up into the victim's diaphragm. Explain why pushing on the diaphragm can dislodge objects that are stuck in the trachea.

Teach

EXPLAIN that in this section, students will continue to learn about how air passes through the body.

As You Read

Give students a few minutes to add colored arrows to their sequence charts. Check students' Science Notebooks to ensure that they have begun their sequence charts and are correctly adding to them.

ANSWER The path of exhalation is the opposite of the path for inhalation.

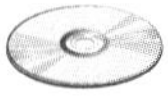

Vocabulary

trachea The common name for the trachea is *windpipe*. It comes from the Greek word *tracheia arteria,* meaning "rough artery."

bronchus Explain that this word comes from the Greek word *bronchos,* meaning "windpipe." Have students explain why the bronchi are thought of as windpipes.

Explain It!

Show students a picture of the Heimlich maneuver to help them understand what an abdominal thrust looks like. For diagrams of the Heimlich maneuver, information on causes and signals of choking, and instructions on performing cardiopulmonary resuscitation (CPR), go to **http://www.nlm.nih.gov/medlineplus/choking.html**.

ANSWER Pushing up on the diaphragm forces a puff of air out of the lungs and through the trachea from below. The air can push the object back out of the trachea.

Background Information

The American Red Cross offers programs in first aid and CPR to school groups and communities. Each program can be tailored to a group's needs. Additionally, the Red Cross offers a Babysitter's Training course for children ages 11 to 14. Participants learn to identify safety problems in the home and yard and to select age-appropriate toys and games for children in their care.

Differentiated Instruction

Kinesthetic Have several student volunteers act as if they were choking and other students show what they would do to help. Remind students to act carefully so that they do not hurt each other.

Teach

EXPLAIN to students that they will learn about several respiratory disorders, some of which are probably familiar to them. Ask what they know about colds, bronchitis, pneumonia, and asthma. Students should share information with a partner.

Figure It Out: Figure 20.8

ANSWER **1.** The graph shows that 14 million new cases of asthma were diagnosed between 1993 and 1994. **2.** The greatest increases in asthma cases occurred in the 5–14, 15–24, and 35–64 age groups.

CONNECTION: Health

During the last 20 years, the number of premature births has increased by more than 30 percent. Infants who are born prematurely (before 37 weeks) often have underdeveloped lungs and difficulty breathing due to a lack of surfactant. This problem is treatable with corticosteroids administered immediately before delivery and by artificial surfactant given to the infant several times after birth. Most babies who lack surfactant require a ventilator, but the artificial surfactant decreases the time that one is needed.

Assess

EVALUATE Use the After You Read questions and the Alternative Assessment to help you assess students' understanding of the lesson.

After You Read

1. The diagram should follow the sequence chart and show the respiratory structures in the correct order.
2. Breathing through the nose warms and moistens the air more than breathing through the mouth does. The nose can also filter more dust and bacteria out of the air.

Alternative Assessment

EVALUATE Check that each student has completed his or her sequence chart and a diagram of the respiratory system. Ask each student to explain his or her diagram or chart to show understanding.

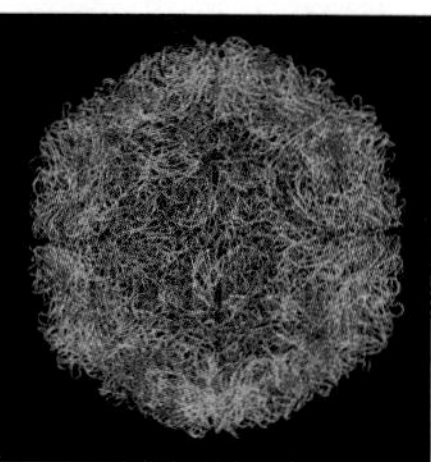

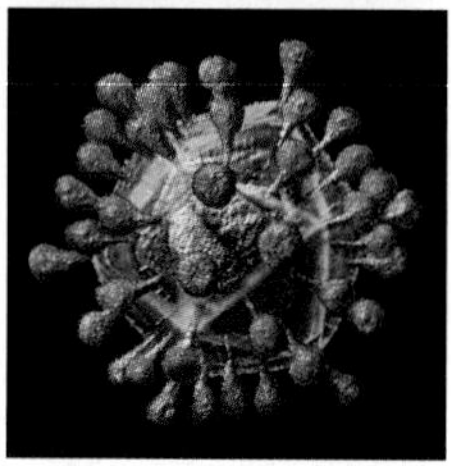

Figure 20.7 Most human colds are caused by rhinoviruses *(top)* or coronaviruses *(bottom)*.

Everybody catches a cold now and then. When this happens, the throat feels scratchy, the person coughs and sneezes, and it gets hard to breathe through the nose. Viruses that attack the cells inside the nose and pharynx cause colds. These viruses cannot be treated with antibiotics. There are also no vaccines to prevent colds because the viruses that cause colds mutate quickly. Each cold a person catches is really a different disease.

The same viruses that cause colds can also cause a condition called bronchitis (brahn KI tus). Infected bronchi swell up and produce extra mucus, causing coughing and shortness of breath. People who smoke get bronchitis more often than nonsmokers do.

An infection inside the lungs is called pneumonia (noo MOH nyuh). The alveoli swell and fill with fluid, making it difficult to breathe. A person with pneumonia usually has a fever and a cough. Pneumonia can be caused by bacteria, viruses, or fungi.

Asthma (AZ muh) is not caused by an infection. It is a condition that contracts the bronchi and makes it hard for a person to exhale. Asthma attacks are often caused by allergies, but they can also be triggered by exercise or stress. A person having an asthma attack may cough or wheeze. Asthma is treated with medicines that are inhaled to relax the bronchi.

Figure It Out

1. How many more people were diagnosed with asthma in 1993–94 than were diagnosed in 1980?
2. In which age groups did asthma cases increase most?

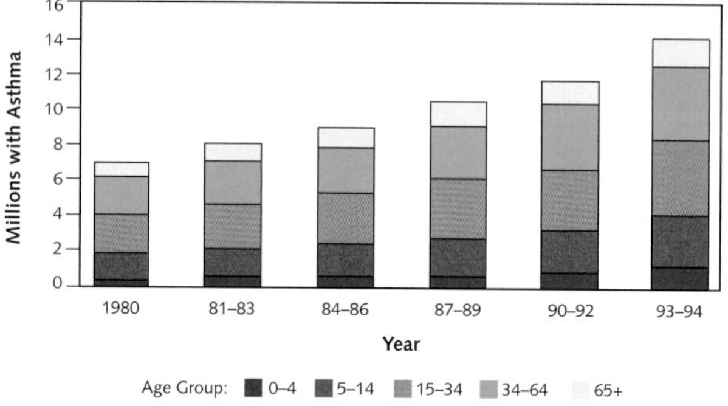

Figure 20.8 During a 15-year study, the number of asthma cases diagnosed in the United States increased.

After You Read

1. Use your sequence chart to draw and label a diagram of the human respiratory system in your Science Notebook. Write the names of the four respiratory conditions you have learned about. Draw an arrow from each name to the part of the respiratory system it affects.
2. Explain one advantage of breathing through the nose instead of through the mouth.

ELL Strategy

Compare and Contrast Ask students to create charts or illustrations that compare and contrast the four types of respiratory disorders that they learned about in this lesson.

Background Information

Asthma is a Greek word that means "labored breathing." Asthma is not an infectious disease. It is a condition whose predisposition is often genetic. Allergens, airborne irritants, respiratory infections, sudden changes in weather, and/or exercise may affect asthmatics.

Many studies have linked asthma, bronchitis, and acute respiratory illnesses to air quality. The incidence of asthma is higher among low-income populations, partly because they are more likely to live near industrial areas. Asthma has also been strongly associated with the presence of cockroaches in homes.

20.3 The Body's Transport System

Before You Read

Read the lesson title, the headings, and the Learning Goals, and look at the figures. Predict what you think you will learn in this lesson. Write your prediction in two or three sentences in your Science Notebook.

How do the cells in a human's toes keep from being oxygen-deprived when they are more than a meter away from the lungs? How does the brain get nutrients when it is just as far from the intestines? And why aren't muscle cells swimming in their own waste? All of the body's cells depend on a transport system to move materials such as oxygen, nutrients, and wastes around the body.

The body's transport system is called the **cardiovascular** (kar dee oh VAS kyuh lur) **system**. It includes the heart, blood, and a series of blood vessels long enough to circle Earth's equator four times. The system has three jobs. It moves a variety of molecules around the body. It also regulates the body's fluids and temperature. Lastly, it helps protect the body from disease and infection.

Transportation

Blood carries many different molecules around the body. Blood moves oxygen and carbon dioxide between the lungs and the cells. It absorbs nutrients, salts, vitamins, and water from the food inside the small intestine and brings them to the cells. The blood carries cell wastes to the kidneys for disposal. Blood absorbs drugs such as alcohol and carries them to the liver. Finally, blood carries hormones to the tissues they affect.

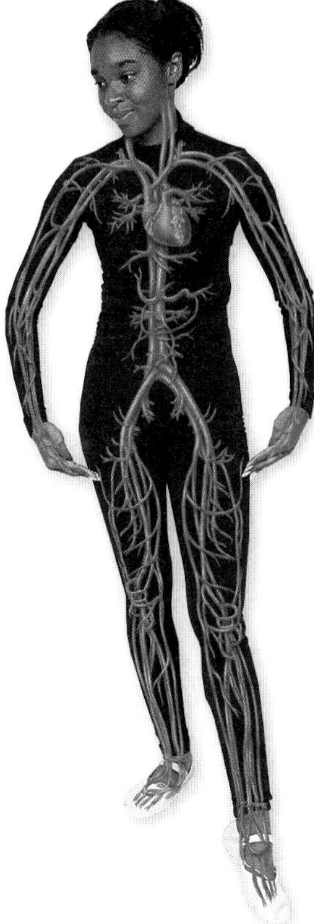

Figure 20.9 The cardiovascular system is also called the circulatory system. It moves many materials around the body, suspended in the blood.

Learning Goals

- Identify the three roles of the cardiovascular system.
- Describe how the cardiovascular system carries out each of these roles.

New Vocabulary

cardiovascular system
cell metabolism

As You Read

Look at the prediction you wrote in your Science Notebook. Compare the role of blood in transporting materials described in this lesson with your prediction. Work with a partner to make necessary corrections to your prediction.

What materials are transported by blood?

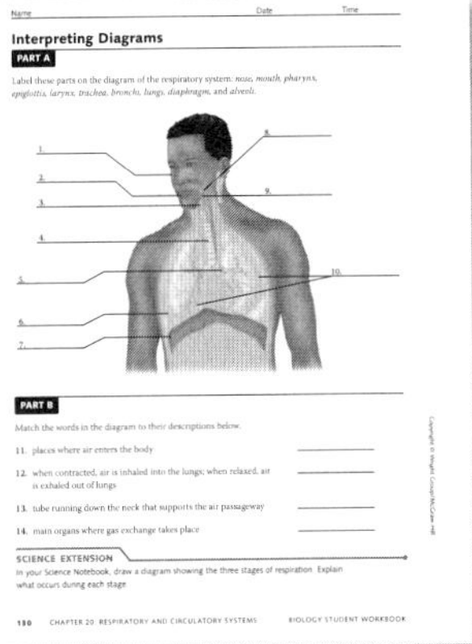

Interpreting Diagrams

PART A

PART B

SCIENCE EXTENSION

Interpreting Diagrams
Workbook, p. 130

ELL Strategy

Read Aloud Have individual students read sections of the lesson aloud to others in a small group.

Paraphrase After each section of text is read aloud, others in the group should explain what they heard.

20.3 Introduce

ENGAGE students by asking them to provide the meanings of the words *transportation, regulation,* and *protection.* Tell them that they will be learning how these words relate to oxygen, nutrients, and wastes in the human body.

Before You Read

Tell students that the cardiovascular system, also called the circulatory system, moves oxygen, nutrients, and wastes around the human body in the blood. Ask students to look at Figure 20.9 and discuss what they see with a partner. Afterward, have each student write an explanation of the figure in his or her Science Notebook.

Teach

EXPLAIN that the cardiovascular system has three jobs: to move molecules around the body, to regulate body fluid and temperature, and to protect tissues from disease and injury. Students will learn about these three jobs in this lesson.

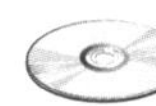

Vocabulary

cardiovascular system Explain that *cardio* is from the Greek word kardia, meaning "heart," and *vascular* is from the Latin word *vasculum*, meaning "small vessel." Ask students to recall what a system is. Then, ask students to use these three meanings to generate a description of the cardiovascular system.

As You Read

Ask students to revise the explanations of Figure 20.9 in their Science Notebook after reading page 357.

ANSWER The blood carries oxygen, carbon dioxide, nutrients, salts, vitamins, water, waste compounds, drugs, and hormones.

Teach

EXPLAIN to students that they will learn how the cardiovascular system regulates, or controls, fluids inside the body and protects the body when it is injured.

Vocabulary

cell metabolism Ask students to recall the meaning of the word *cell* as it pertains to the human body. Then, tell them that the word *metabolism* comes from the Greek word *metabole,* meaning "change." The cell changes that *metabolism* refers to include the processes that build up the cell and those that break it down.

Figure It Out: Figure 20.10

ANSWER **1.** The blood is cooler at point B, where it is farther away from the core of the body. Even though it is in the same blood vessel as it is at point A, heat has been transferred to the adjacent vessel. **2.** Any system where vessels go from the outside of the body into the body's warmer core without a countercurrent vessel will work.

Assess

EVALUATE Use the After You Read questions and the Alternative Assessment to help you assess students' understanding of the lesson.

After You Read

1. The cardiovascular system carries out all three of its roles by moving heat and substances such as water, molecules, ions, platelets, red blood cells, and white blood cells from one part of the body to another.
2. Heat is lost to a cold environment, and blood vessels at the skin's surface constrict to keep warm blood near internal organs.
3. Answers will vary but can include oxygen, nutrients, ions, vitamins, minerals, or hormones. Carbon dioxide is a waste product and is transported away from the cells by the cardiovascular system.

Alternative Assessment

EVALUATE When students have finished the cardiovascular system diagrams in their Science Notebooks, ask each to write a paragraph explaining his or her diagram.

Regulation

The cardiovascular system also regulates the condition of the fluids inside the body. As a result of **cell metabolism** (muh TA buh lih zum), which is the sum of all the chemical reactions that occur in a cell, ions move into the spaces outside the cells, and fluids often follow by osmosis. Blood can move excess ions away from the tissues.

Blood also regulates body temperature by moving heat from one part of the body to another. Human cells work best at a temperature of about 37°C (98.6°F), but the temperature of the tissues is always changing. Blood picks up excess heat from warm parts of the body and moves it to cooler parts of the body.

Figure It Out

1. Is the blood at point A warmer or cooler than the blood at point B?
2. Illustrate one way to arrange blood vessels to cool a warm part of the body.

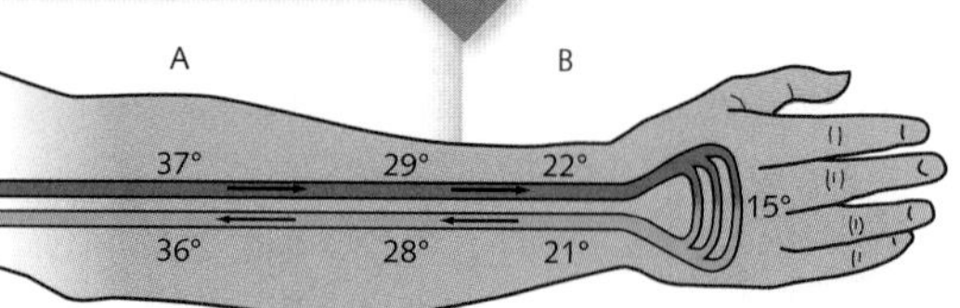

Figure 20.10 Blood vessels carrying blood in opposite directions lie next to one another. Warmer blood flows toward the hand. Cooler blood flows back toward the core of the body. Cooler blood pulls heat away from the warmer blood.

The cardiovascular system can conserve heat when the outside environment is cold, and it can get rid of extra heat when the outside environment is hot. Blood vessels in the skin can squeeze closed to keep warm blood away from the surface of the body and close to internal organs. The same blood vessels can open up and allow blood to reach the skin and give off extra heat into the environment. Countercurrent systems are another way to regulate body temperature. **Figure 20.10** shows an example of how one of these systems works.

Protection

If a person gets a cut, the person bleeds. Harmful organisms may take advantage of the injury and use it to invade the body. Blood can protect against such an invasion. Blood contains cells that attack foreign bacteria and viruses that get into the tissues. It also contains chemicals that make clots, so that there is not too much blood loss from an injury.

After You Read

1. Compare the three roles of the cardiovascular system with the predictions in your Science Notebook. In a well-developed paragraph, explain how the cardiovascular system carries out its three roles.
2. Why do your hands get cold when you are outside on a cold day?
3. Name three things that blood carries to the cells. Why would you not include carbon dioxide in your answer?

Differentiated Instruction

Kinesthetic Divide students into small groups, and have them act out a countercurrent system (one in which blood vessels carrying blood in opposite directions lie next to one another). Ask students to look at Figure 20.10 for reference. Students should take the roles of blood vessels, skin, internal organs, and the outside environment.

Background Information

People who have cold, numb, and pale fingers or toes when the temperature drops slightly or when they are emotionally upset may have Reynaud's Syndrome. This occurs when the arteries that carry blood to the hands or feet constrict, resulting in little blood flow to these areas. Most people with this syndrome are women. In most cases, a slight adjustment in lifestyle is all that is needed to correct Reynaud's Syndrome.

Heart and Blood Vessels

Before You Read

Create a K-W-L-S-H chart in your Science Notebook. Think about the title of this lesson. Then, look at the pictures, headings, and Learning Goals. In the column labeled *K*, write what you already know about the heart and blood vessels. In the column labeled *W*, write what you would like to learn.

Learning Goals

- Describe how blood moves through the heart.
- Compare the structure and function of arteries, capillaries, and veins.
- Explain what determines blood pressure and heart rate.

New Vocabulary

atrium
ventricle
vena cava
aorta
artery
capillary
vein
blood pressure
pulse

The human heart starts beating before birth. It contracts about 70 times every minute, pushing blood through the body with each beat. Over the course of a person's life, the heart will beat about three billion times!

The Heart

The heart is a muscular organ about the size of a fist. It sits inside the rib cage between the lungs. It has four chambers. The two upper chambers are small. Each one is called an **atrium** (AY tree um, plural: atria). The two lower chambers, or **ventricles** (VEN trih kulz), are large.

The heart is a pair of pumps that work together. Oxygen-poor blood from the body enters the right side of the heart. The right atrium and right ventricle pump oxygen-poor blood to the lungs. Waste products are exchanged for oxygen in the lungs. Oxygen-rich blood returns to the left side of the heart from the lungs. The left atrium and left ventricle pump oxygen-rich blood to the rest of the body.

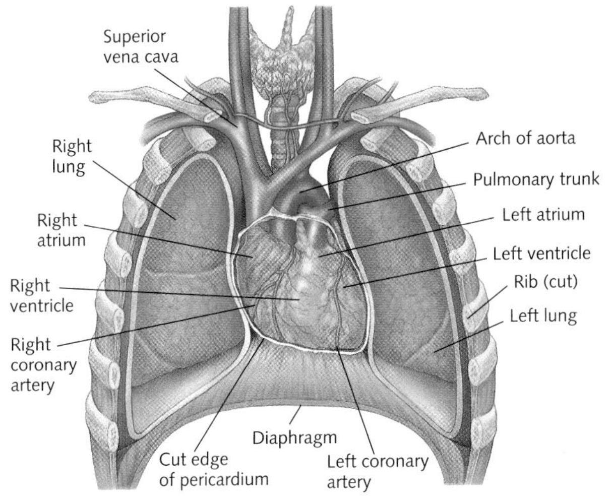

Figure 20.11 Heart contractions move, or "pump," the blood around the body.

Did You Know?

Ventricles cannot expand on their own after they contract in a heartbeat. The blood that is forced into the ventricles when the atria contract pushes the ventricle muscle into position for the next heartbeat.

Differentiated Instruction

Musical Have pairs of students use the Internet or other resources to research songs that include *heart* in the title. Record the titles, and compile a class list of songs. Ask students to hypothesize why there are so many songs that include *heart*. At the completion of the lesson, have students return to the list of song titles and identify as many popular misconceptions about the heart as possible.

Encourage ELL students to research songs in their native language that have *heart* in the title.

20.4 Introduce

ENGAGE students by having them look through the lesson's headings and figures. Ask students to talk with a partner about what they predict they will learn in the lesson.

Before You Read

Ask students what they know about the heart and blood vessels. Write students' answers on the board. Then, draw a sample K-W-L-S-H chart on the board, and ask students to draw the same chart in their Science Notebooks. Remind students what each section of the chart represents. Students should complete the *K* section of their charts first for the heart and then for the blood vessels. Encourage students to use the information on the board.

Teach

EXPLAIN to students that they will learn about the heart's important role in the circulatory system of the human body.

EXPLORE To demonstrate ventricle expansion and contraction, have groups of students fill a balloon with water (to show an expanded ventricle) and then let the water out (to show it contracting). Ask students to explain what the water and the balloon represent.

Vocabulary

atrium Tell students that *atrium* is a Latin word that refers to a central courtyard or entrance hall of a house. Ask students to explain how this meaning might relate to the upper chamber of the heart.

ventricle Tell students that *ventricle* comes from the Latin word *ventriculus,* meaning "abdomen." Again, ask students to explain how they think this meaning might relate to the lower chamber of the heart.

Teach

EXPLAIN that in this section, students will learn about blood vessels that carry blood away from the heart.

EXPLORE Students can repeat William Harvey's demonstration showing that blood can flow in only one direction. Give each pair of students a 30-cm strip of cloth. Have one partner tie the strip around the other partner's upper arm, with your supervision. Demonstrate how to snugly tie the strip around the upper arm. Have students note what happens to the arm below the strip of cloth (the veins fill up). Tell one partner to gently push on a vein to direct the blood first toward the hand and then toward the shoulder. Have students discuss what happens. (The vein will collapse as the finger pushes toward the hand and refill from the direction of the hand when the finger is removed.)

Vocabulary

vena cava Explain that this term is Latin and means "hollow vein." Ask students to explain the relationship between this meaning and the definition of *venae cavae.*

aorta Tell students that this word comes from the Greek language. Ask students if they can devise a way of remembering that the aorta is the largest artery that carries blood away from the heart (for example, *a* in *aorta, a* in *artery, a* in *away*).

artery Explain that this word comes from the Greek word *arteria,* meaning "windpipe." Ask students what the other Greek word for windpipe is (*bronchos,* from which *bronchus* is derived).

capillary Tell students that *capillary* comes from the French word *capillarité,* which is from the Latin *capillaris,* meaning "hair." Ask students why this meaning might be a good definition for the term.

vein Tell students that this word comes from the French word *veine,* which is from the Latin *vena,* meaning "vein."

blood pressure Explain that *blood* is a fluid tissue that circulates in the arteries, veins, and capillaries of the body as a result of muscular contractions of the heart. Tell students that *pressure* means "force per unit area." Ask students to define the term by combining the two word meanings.

Movement of Blood

The heart pushes blood with rhythmic contractions that always follow the same pattern. Both atria contract first, followed by both ventricles. When the atria contract, they force blood into the ventricles. When the ventricles contract, they force blood out of the heart. The two-beat pattern makes the "lub-dub" sound of your heartbeat.

Blood can move in only one direction through the heart. Oxygen-poor blood from the body enters the right atrium through two large veins called the **venae cavae** (vee nee KAY vee, singular: vena cava). When the right atrium contracts, blood is pushed into the right ventricle. When the right ventricle contracts, the blood is pushed into blood vessels inside the lungs. After the blood picks up oxygen in the lungs, it returns to the heart and enters the left atrium. Contraction of the left atrium pushes blood into the left ventricle. When the left ventricle contracts, blood is pushed into a large artery called the **aorta** (ay OR tuh). From there, it goes to the rest of the body. One-way valves separate each atrium and ventricle to keep blood from sloshing backward when the heart beats.

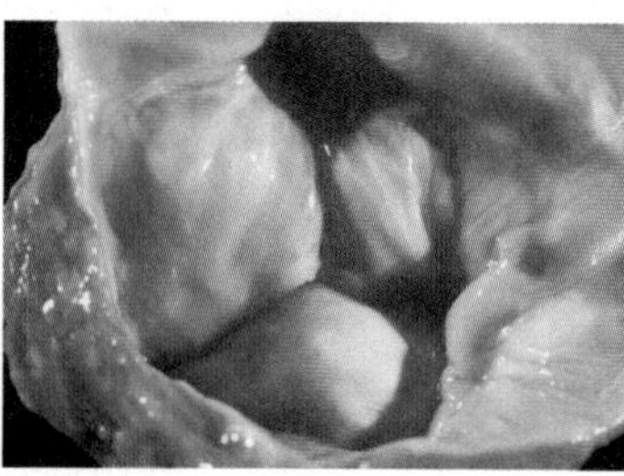

Figure 20.12 One-way valves like this one keep the blood from moving backward when the heart beats.

Blood Vessels

There are three kinds of blood vessels inside the body. After blood leaves the heart, it flows through each type of vessel in order: first through arteries, then into capillaries, and finally into veins. Blood moves fastest in the largest arteries and slowest in the capillaries.

Arteries (AR tuh reez) carry blood away from the heart. They have thick walls containing layers of stiff connective tissue and smooth muscle. Artery walls are elastic. Every time the heart beats, blood is pushed against the artery walls and makes them expand. The arteries store some of this energy and release it slowly between heartbeats. This makes the blood flow smoothly.

As blood moves away from the heart, the arteries get smaller and narrower. They also split again and again, forming a branching network inside the body. When each artery divides into two or three smaller arteries, the total diameter of the new vessels is actually larger than the diameter of the original vessel. The blood slows down, allowing it to deliver nutrients or pick up wastes as it moves through the arteries and into the capillaries.

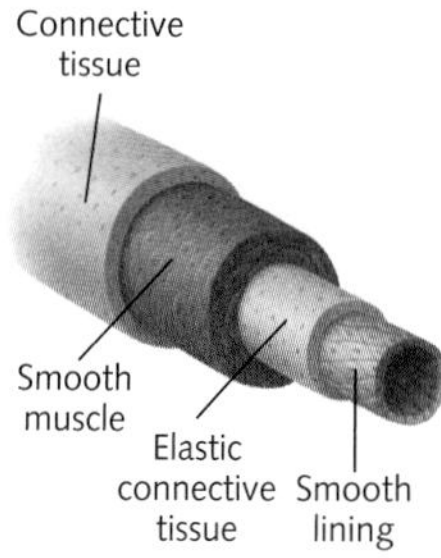

Figure 20.13 Arteries have thick walls that can store energy when blood pushes against them.

Background Information

The normal resting heartbeat of a healthy adult is between 60 and 100 beats per minute. An 8- to 10-year-old healthy child's resting heartbeat is between 70 and 110 beats per minute. A newborn baby's resting heartbeat is between 130 and 160 beats per minute.

Capillaries (KAP uh ler eez) are microscopic vessels that connect arteries and veins. They spread through every part of the body. Each capillary is only one cell thick, as **Figure 20.15** shows. Blood moves slowly through the capillaries, so there is more time for nutrients and oxygen to diffuse through the thin walls into the surrounding cells. Blood also picks up wastes from the cells when it is in the capillaries.

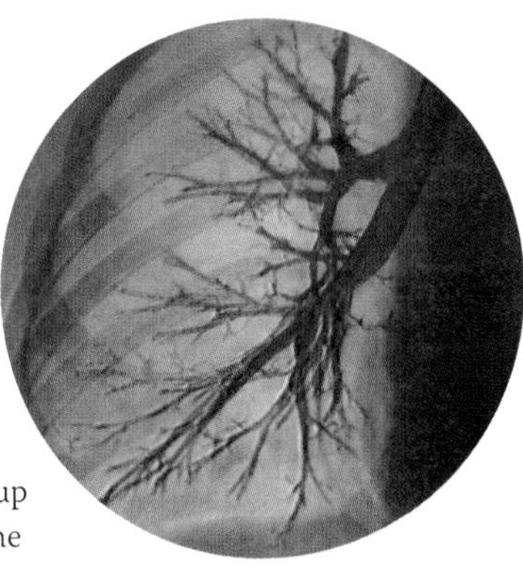

Figure 20.14 As blood moves away from the heart, it travels through smaller and smaller vessels.

Veins (VAYNZ) carry blood back to the heart from the capillaries. Veins have thin walls made of layers of connective tissue and smooth muscle. Veins also contain a series of one-way valves that keep blood flowing toward the heart. When blood flows forward, it pushes the valves open. But if it flows backward, the blood presses against the valves and closes them.

Heartbeats are not strong enough to push the blood inside the veins back to the heart. Instead, contractions of skeletal muscles squeeze the veins and move the blood inside them past the valves.

As You Read

In the column labeled *L* in the chart you made in your Science Notebook, write three or four things you have learned about the heart and blood vessels.

Through which vessels do nutrients and gases move out of the blood and into the tissues?

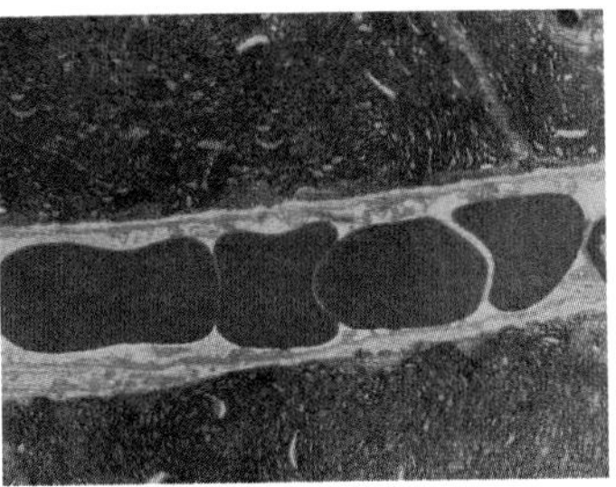

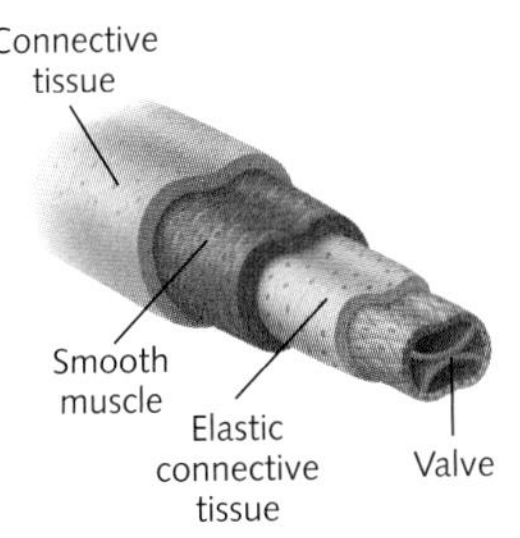

Figure 20.15 A capillary *(left)* is so narrow that red blood cells must squeeze through it in single file. Veins *(right)* contain one-way valves that keep blood from moving backward through the cardiovascular system.

Blood Pressure and Heart Rate

When the heart beats, the muscular contractions push oxygen-rich blood through the aorta and to the rest of the body. As blood is forced out of the heart, it pushes against the walls of the arteries and stretches them. When the heart relaxes between beats, the pressure on the artery walls drops. The force that the blood exerts on the artery walls is called **blood pressure**.

Teach

EXPLAIN that students will continue learning about blood vessels and learn about blood pressure in this section. Ask what they already know about blood pressure. Explain that the scientific definition of pressure is "force per unit area." Tell students to keep this definition in mind as they read.

As You Read

Have students discuss what they have learned about the heart and blood vessels in small groups before recording the information in charts in their Science Notebooks.

ANSWER Nutrients and gases move out of the blood and into the tissues through the capillaries.

Science Notebook EXTRA

Have students draw or sketch pictures to illustrate this lesson's vocabulary words in their Science Notebooks.

ELL Strategy

Practice Using Vocabulary Ask students to write each vocabulary term on the front of an index card and a sentence with a blank for the term on the back of the card. When finished, each student should take turns quizzing a partner about the term that goes in the blank. Then, have students write in their Science Notebooks the definition for each term.

 Teach

EXPLAIN that students will continue to learn about blood pressure in this section.

 Vocabulary

pulse Explain that *pulse* comes from the Latin *pulsus,* meaning "a beating."

Figure It Out: Figure 20.16

ANSWER **1.** systolic pressure: 120 mm Hg; diastolic pressure: 80 mm Hg. **2.** 100 mm Hg

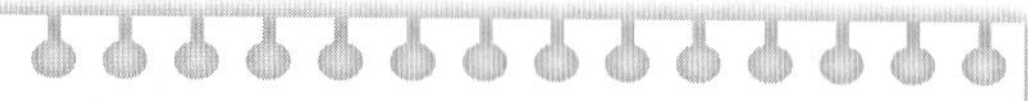

Explore It!

Demonstrate how to take a pulse on a student's wrist. Have students practice taking a pulse for a few minutes before they begin the activity. On the board, draw a T-chart with the titles *Resting* and *Exercise*. Have students copy the chart in their Science Notebooks. Students will fill in these two columns with their own pulse readings.

ANSWER Students should discover that the heart beats faster during exercise, so heart rate increases.

Assess

EVALUATE Use the After You Read questions and the Alternative Assessment to help you assess students' understanding of the lesson.

After You Read

1. Blood moves from the right atrium to the right ventricle to the lungs and then back to the left atrium. From the left atrium, the blood moves into the left ventricle and then into the aorta.
2. Both are hollow tubes. Arteries are thick-walled and able to bounce back when the pressurized blood extends them. Veins are thin-walled and have valves to help move blood back to the heart.
3. Student should correctly summarize the basic functions of the heart, arteries, capillaries, and veins.

Alternative Assessment

EVALUATE Ask students to use their K-W-L charts to draw a diagram that represents the heart and blood vessels' functions.

Figure It Out

1. According to this chart, what are the systolic and diastolic pressures in the aorta?
2. Calculate the drop in blood pressure when the blood reaches the capillaries.

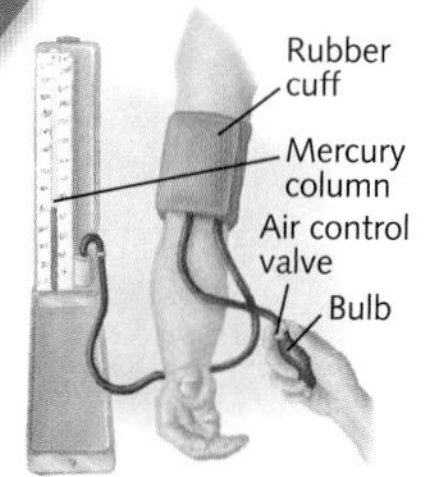

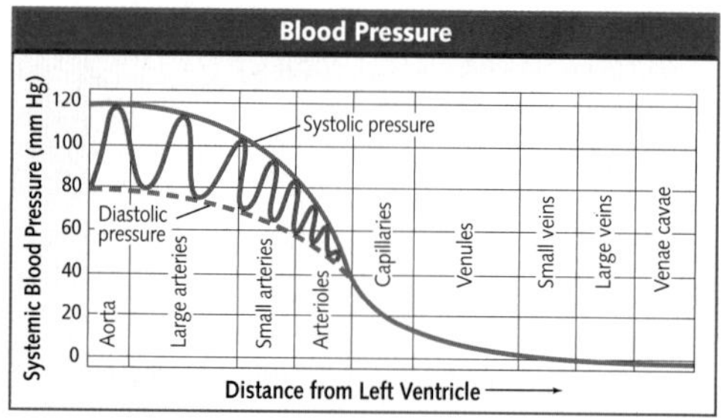

Figure 20.16 Blood pressure rises and falls with each heartbeat. It gets weaker as the blood moves away from the heart.

Blood moves through the arteries in waves. Blood pressure increases when the ventricles contract and push blood out of the heart. Blood pressure drops when the ventricles relax and refill. You can feel these waves of changing pressure by putting your fingers on your throat or your wrist. These waves create your **pulse**. The pressure waves are the reason blood pressure is measured with two numbers, such as 120 over 80. The first number is the systolic (sihs TAH lihk) pressure. It is the pressure on the arteries when the ventricles contract. The second number is the diastolic (di uh STAH lihk) pressure. It is the pressure on the arteries when the ventricles relax.

Measuring the pulse tells you how quickly the heart is beating. The heart rate is set by a bundle of cells on top of the right atrium called the pacemaker. The pacemaker sends a regular electrical impulse over both atria and makes them contract together. The impulse also makes a second set of cells at the base of the right atrium fire off its own electrical impulse. This impulse makes the ventricles contract. The faster the pacemaker fires, the faster the heart beats. Heart rate increases when a person exercises or is frightened or excited. It slows down when a person is at rest or calm.

Explore It!

How does your heart rate change when you exercise?

- Draw a T-chart in your Science Notebook. Title one column *Resting* and the other *Exercising*. Sit at your desk. Have a partner take your pulse for one minute. The number of beats counted in one minute is your heart rate. Write the result in the *Resting* column.
- Jog in place for one minute. Immediately have your partner take your pulse for one minute. Write the result in the *Exercising* column of your chart.
- Find your resting and exercising pulses three or four more times. Then, calculate your average resting and exercising pulses.

After You Read

1. Describe the path of blood through the heart.
2. Compare and contrast the structure of the arteries and the structure of the veins.
3. Use the completed *K, W,* and *L* columns of the chart in your Science Notebook to describe the functions of the heart and blood vessels. Complete your chart by indicating in the *S* column what you would still like to learn about the heart and blood vessels and noting in the *H* column how you can find this information.

Background Information

An artificial pacemaker is a battery-operated medical device that helps regulate the heart rate. An individual may need an artificial pacemaker because his or her natural pacemaker is not operating correctly, causing the heart to beat too fast, too slow, or irregularly. There may also be a blockage of the electrical pathways. Artificial pacemakers are either external and temporary or internal and permanent.

ELL Strategy

Relate to Personal Experience Ask students if they have had their blood pressure taken during a doctor's office visit. Explain what the cuff looks like or how it expands with air if students need prompting. Be aware that people from some cultures may not be comfortable with sharing information about health.

20.5 Blood

Before You Read

Create a three-column chart in your Science Notebook. Label the first column *Red Blood Cells*, the second column *White Blood Cells*, and the third column *Platelets*. As you read about these three parts of blood, add information to your chart that describes their characteristics.

Learning Goals

- Identify the functions of red blood cells, white blood cells, platelets, and plasma.
- Explain the function of the lymphatic system.
- Identify and describe blood types.

New Vocabulary

hemoglobin
antibody
platelet
plasma
lymphatic system
lymph
antigen

Blood is a liquid tissue that contains several different kinds of cells. Each kind has its own job in the body.

Red Blood Cells

Most of the cells in your blood are red blood cells. Red blood cells carry oxygen. A red blood cell has no nucleus, and each side of the cell is pushed inward to form a disc. This shape makes red blood cells thin and flexible and gives them a cell membrane with a large surface area for oxygen to diffuse across.

The inside of each red blood cell is packed with molecules of a protein called **hemoglobin** (HEE muh gloh bun). Each hemoglobin molecule can bind to four oxygen atoms, increasing the total amount of oxygen the blood can carry. When blood is in the lungs, the hemoglobin fills up with oxygen. When the blood gets to tissues with a lower oxygen concentration, the hemoglobin releases oxygen, which then diffuses into the cells.

Hemoglobin can also help move carbon dioxide. Most carbon dioxide combines with water in the blood plasma to form bicarbonate. Some carbon dioxide, however, binds to hemoglobin molecules, which carry it to the lungs.

Did You Know?

Red blood cells, white blood cells, and platelets are all made by stem cells in the bone marrow. Red blood cells live 120 days in the bloodstream before they are destroyed by the spleen, liver, and lymph nodes. Platelets live only ten days before they are destroyed.

White Blood Cells

There are several different types of white blood cells, and these cells make up about one percent of the blood. Each type has a specific role to play in the immune system. They work together to protect the body against disease. Some types engulf and destroy foreign organisms, such as bacteria. Some cause swelling around a wound. Others reduce swelling or produce **antibodies** (AN tih bah deez), which are proteins that detect and bind to foreign proteins.

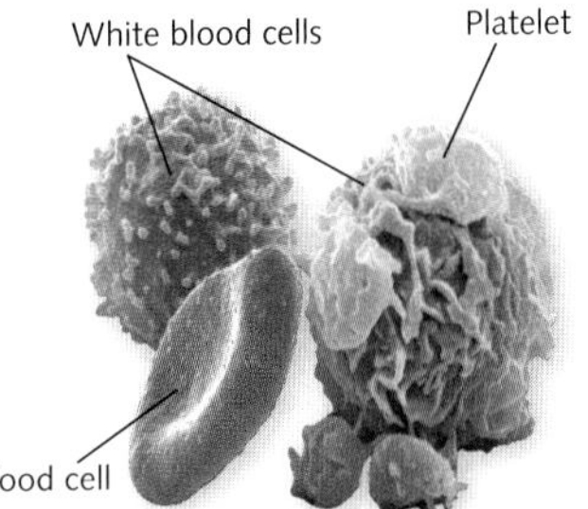

Figure 20.17 White blood cells are much larger than red blood cells. Platelets are smaller than both red and white blood cells and have no nuclei.

20.5 Introduce

ENGAGE Ask students to review the lesson headings and figures to get an overview of the lesson. Have students share their observations with the class.

Before You Read

Write *Red Blood Cells, White Blood Cells,* and *Platelets* in a row across the board. Ask students to talk to someone nearby about what they already know about these three terms. Students should then share their discussions with the class. As needed, explain the terms. Create a three-column chart below the three headings. Tell students that they will learn about these terms in this lesson and that they will be completing the chart in their Science Notebooks as they read.

Teach

EXPLAIN Tell students that they will learn about two kinds of blood cells in this section.

Vocabulary

hemoglobin Explain that *hemo-* denotes "blood" and comes from the Greek *haima* and that *globin* is any of a group of soluble proteins that are present in the iron-containing pigments of animal cells. Ask students if they know any other words that begin with the prefix *hemo-* (hemophilia, hemorrhage, hemorrhoid) and their meanings.

antibody Explain that the prefix *anti-* is a Greek word meaning "against" and that the meaning of *body,* as used here, is "foreign substance or object." Tell students these word-part meanings should help them remember the definition of the term.

ELL Strategy

Paraphrase As students are going through this lesson, have them stop occasionally and review the material with a partner. They should be able to explain the content in their own words.

Background Information

White blood cells, also known as leukocytes, live in the body for several days to several weeks. They are the body's infection-fighting cells. They fight infection by surrounding and devouring bacteria or by producing antibodies that overpower a germ. The body produces more white blood cells in reaction to a persistent infection. White blood cells also work to fight off allergies, tumors, and stress.

Teach

EXPLAIN to students that they will learn about white blood cells, platelets, plasma, and the lymphatic system in this section.

As You Read

Give each student a few minutes to complete and/or review his or her chart. When students are finished, ask them what they have learned about plasma in this section. Ask them to reread the section on the lymphatic system and then talk about how plasma becomes lymph.

ANSWER Plasma is the liquid part of blood. It becomes lymph when it moves through the capillary walls into the tissues and the blood's cellular parts are filtered out of it.

Vocabulary

platelet Tell students that the common meaning of *plate* is "a shallow dish" and the suffix *-let* signifies "small" or "young." Have students look at Figure 20.17 and explain why this meaning is appropriate.

plasma Explain that this word comes from Latin and means "something molded." Tell students that *plasma* is also used to describe the fourth state in which matter can exist.

lymphatic system Explain that *lymphatic* is an adjective derived from the noun *lymph,* which comes from the Latin word *lympha,* meaning "water." Ask students to remember what a system is.

lymph Explain that the archaic meaning of *lymph* was "a spring or stream of pure, clear water." Ask students to explain this derivation in relationship to the definition of *lymph*. Remind students that plasma is mostly water.

antigen Have students recall what *anti-* means. Tell them that *-gen* comes from the Greek word *-genes,* meaning "born."

CONNECTION: Chemistry

Anemia results from the number one American dietary deficiency. Of special concern are toddlers and teens, whose bodies grow too quickly to keep enough iron in their systems. Fifteen to 35 percent of teen athletes are anemic, and twice as many overweight teens as healthy-weight teens are affected. Signs include paleness, excessive tiredness, and lack of concentration.

As You Read

The chart you made in your Science Notebook describes the cellular parts of blood. Under your chart, define plasma, and explain how plasma becomes lymph.

Platelets

When a person gets a small cut, he or she bleeds for a little while, but the blood eventually clots. Clotting is controlled by **platelets** (PLAYT luts) in the blood. Platelets are small fragments of cells that stick to damaged tissues. They also stick to one another, forming a plug that seals the wound and stops the bleeding. They then release chemicals that help build a linked network of a protein called fibrin, forming a leathery clot called a scab that covers the wound until it heals.

Plasma

The blood cells and platelets are suspended in the liquid part of the blood, which is called the **plasma** (PLAZ muh). Plasma makes up more than half of the blood's volume. It is mostly water, but it also contains dissolved proteins, minerals, vitamins, and small organic molecules such as amino acids, fatty acids, and glucose. Blood carries waste products such as carbon dioxide and urea dissolved in the plasma.

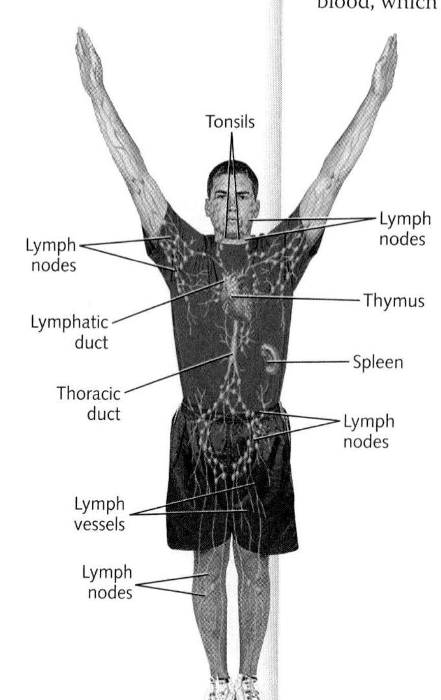

Figure 20.18 The lymphatic system drains fluid from the tissues and moves it back to the cardiovascular system. Like veins, lymphatic vessels have valves to keep the fluid inside them from flowing backward.

The Lymphatic System

As blood moves through the capillaries, some fluid from the plasma leaks out of the vessels and gets into the spaces between the cells. This fluid bathes the cells and keeps them moist. If too much fluid stays in the tissue, however, it can cause swelling. Excess fluid normally leaves the tissue through small vessels in the **lymphatic** (lihm FA tihk) **system**.

The fluid that enters the lymphatic capillaries is called **lymph** (LIHMF). The lymphatic capillaries join to form a network of small, thin-walled tubes that eventually drain into veins near the heart. On the way, lymph passes through filtering tissues called lymph nodes, which are found in many parts of the body, including the tonsils. White blood cells produced by the thymus and the spleen enter the fluid in the lymph nodes to trap bacteria and other foreign particles.

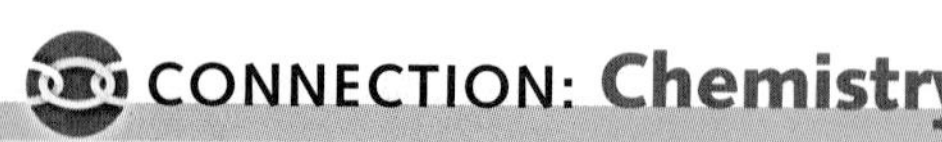

CONNECTION: Chemistry

Each hemoglobin molecule contains four iron (Fe) atoms. When iron binds to oxygen (O), it turns red. This means that blood changes color when it is carrying oxygen. Oxygenated blood in the arteries is bright red. Deoxygenated blood in the veins is a darker red.

364 RESPIRATORY AND CIRCULATORY SYSTEMS

Differentiated Instruction

Interpersonal, Logical/Mathematical
Have students interview several adults at school or at home about their blood types. Students should keep a record of the information. When all data are compiled, develop a class graph.

Field Study

Bring students to a local blood donation center. Set up a tour and interview with the person in charge.

Background Information

The American Red Cross publishes its blood donation eligibility requirements on its Web site, **www.redcross.org/** services. Students who are 17 years old and healthy (16 years old in some states) are eligible to donate. For all of the donor guidelines, information about what to expect when donating blood, and information about the use of donated blood, see the Web site.

Blood Types

For nearly three hundred years, doctors tried to move blood from healthy people into their sick patients. But in most cases, the transfusion of blood would make the patient even sicker. About a hundred years ago, scientists discovered that many people have proteins on the surfaces of their red blood cells that can react with another person's immune system. These proteins are called **antigens** (AN tih junz).

Three important blood antigens are called A, B, and Rh. The combination of proteins on a person's red blood cells determines the person's blood type. Blood types are inherited traits.

Blood type is expressed as a letter and a plus or minus sign. The letters A and B indicate which antigens are on the surfaces of red blood cells. If a red blood cell has A antigens, the person has type A blood. If it has B antigens, the person has type B blood. If it has both antigens, the person is type AB. If it has no antigens, the person is type O. People can also have an antigen called Rh on the surfaces of their red blood cells. People who have the Rh antigen have Rh positive (+) blood. People who lack the Rh antigen have Rh negative (–) blood. If a person has B^+ blood, the person has both the B and Rh antigens on the red blood cells.

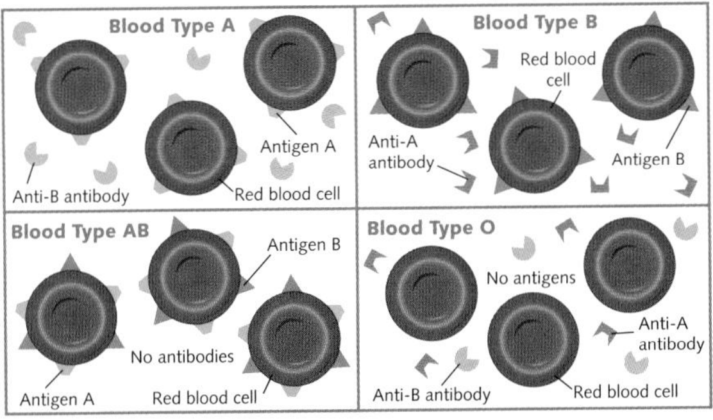

Figure 20.19 Doctors prefer to give patients blood that matches their own blood type, but in an emergency, people can receive any blood that does not contain antibodies that would attack their red blood cells. For example, this chart shows that a person with type A blood could receive type O blood.

Extend It!

Are some blood types more common than others? Find out the percentage of the human population that has each blood type by doing research in the library and on the Internet. Summarize your findings in a pie chart. If the members of your class can find out their blood types, collect this information and determine the percentage of each type. Do the class percentages match your research findings?

Figure It Out

1. What kind of antibody does a person with type B blood have in his or her plasma?
2. Predict which types of blood a type AB person could receive if there were no AB blood at the hospital.

After You Read

1. On one side of the chart you made in your Science Notebook, write the words *Antigen* and *Antibody*. Draw an arrow from each word to the part of the blood where that protein is found.
2. People who suffer from hemophilia do not have normal platelets. Predict how the disease affects their bodies.
3. Define what gives a person type O blood.

Teach

EXPLAIN that students will learn about proteins in the blood called antigens that determine a person's blood type. In their Science Notebooks, have students write all of the blood types and define each one.

Figure It Out: Figure 20.19

ANSWER **1.** A type B person has anti-A antibodies. **2.** A type AB person has no antibodies in his or her plasma, so that person could receive type A, B, or O blood.

Extend It!

Tell students that they will be doing research in small groups to determine the percentage of the human population that has each blood type. Show them a sample pie chart, and explain that each group will be creating a similar chart to demonstrate its findings. In the classroom, provide several books and encyclopedias on the circulatory system for students to use. If possible, provide Internet access as well.

Background Information

Hemophilia is an inherited disease that impairs the clotting ability of the blood. The disease is passed on by mothers, but it usually affects male children only. If the mother is a carrier and gives birth to a son, he has about a 50 percent chance of having the disease. A male cannot pass the disease to sons, but all daughters will be carriers. There are effective treatments for hemophilia, but there is no cure at this time.

Assess

EVALUATE Use the After You Read questions and the Alternative Assessment to help you assess students' understanding of the lesson.

After You Read

1. Antigens are found on the surface of red blood cells. Antibodies are found in the plasma.
2. People with hemophilia cannot form blood clots when they are cut. They do not stop bleeding.
3. People with type O blood have no antigens on their red blood cells.

Alternative Assessment

EVALUATE Discuss with students their understanding of antigens and antibodies. In their Science Notebooks, have students illustrate and label the location of each type of protein.

20.6 Introduce

ENGAGE students by asking what it means for something to circulate. Ask: *What are some things that circulate?* Have them preview the lesson by looking over the subheadings and figures. Then, ask them what they think the human circulatory system is, based on their meaning of the word *circulate* and their lesson preview.

Before You Read

Discuss with students what each of these components is. On the board, write the heading *Circulatory System* with *heart, lungs,* and *tissues* in large circles under the heading. Ask students to do the same in their Science Notebooks, and then have them write their understanding of each term inside the circle containing the word.

Teach

EXPLAIN that in this section, students will learn how blood moves through the lungs.

EXTEND Provide students with books about the heart for reference. Have each student sketch the pulmonary artery and pulmonary vein and indicate the direction of blood flow in each kind of blood vessel.

Vocabulary

circulation Tell students that the word *circulation* comes from the verb *circulate,* meaning "to move" or "to cause to move around freely." Remind them that the suffix *-ation* means "an action or process."

pulmonary circulation Tell students that *pulmonary* comes from the Latin word *pulmo,* meaning "lung."

systemic circulation Tell students that *systemic* is an adjective derived from the word *system.* Ask them to remember what a system is and to combine it with *circulation.*

Learning Goals

- Identify the circulation systems in the human body.

New Vocabulary

circulation
pulmonary circulation
systemic circulation
coronary circulation

Did You Know?

The pulmonary artery carries oxygen-poor blood, and the pulmonary vein carries oxygen-rich blood. This may seem confusing because you have learned that arteries carry oxygen-rich blood and veins carry oxygen-poor blood. These two vessels are not named for the kind of blood they carry. They are named for the direction in which they carry it. The pulmonary arteries carry blood away from the heart, as do all other arteries. The pulmonary veins return blood to the heart, as do all other veins.

20.6 Circulation in the Body

Before You Read

Create a concept map in your Science Notebook using the words *Heart, Lungs,* and *Tissues.* Preview the lesson, and write one sentence describing how you think these three words are related.

Library books circulate. Money, rented DVDs, fresh air, and blood circulate, as well. In each case, **circulation** (sur kyuh LAY shun) means that something moves from one place to another and back again. Circulation moves blood around the body. Humans have two distinct circulations in their bodies. Blood circulates through the lungs before it circulates through the rest of the body.

Pulmonary Circulation

The **pulmonary** (PUL muh ner ee) **circulation** moves blood through the lungs. The right atrium of the heart contracts, forcing the blood into the right ventricle. The right ventricle pushes oxygen-poor blood through the pulmonary arteries and into the lungs. The pulmonary arteries are the only arteries that carry blood that is high in carbon dioxide. The pulmonary arteries divide into capillaries that surround the alveoli. As blood moves through the capillaries, it picks up oxygen and releases carbon dioxide. Then, the oxygen-rich blood moves into pulmonary veins and returns to the left atrium of the heart. The pulmonary veins are the only veins that carry oxygen-rich blood.

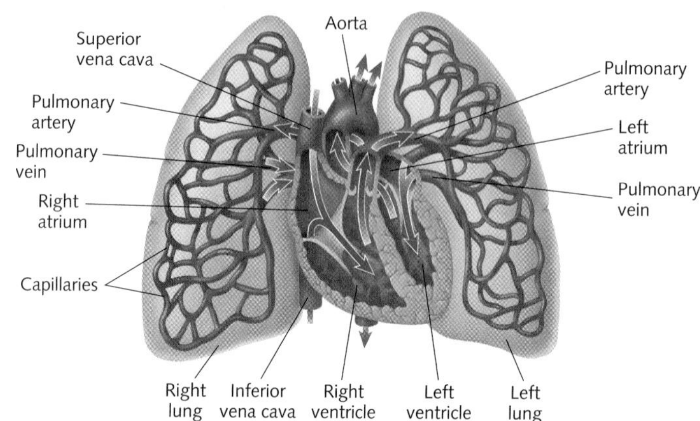

Figure 20.20 The pulmonary circulation moves blood through the lungs, where it picks up oxygen.

Differentiated Instruction

Visual Show students a movie or video clips from the Internet of the circulatory system working in a living human being.

Systemic Circulation

The left side of the heart pumps oxygen-rich blood through the rest of the body. This circuit is called the **systemic** (sihs TE mihk) **circulation**. The left atrium contracts and forces the blood into the left ventricle. The left ventricle contracts, forcing the oxygen-rich blood out of the heart through the aorta. Arteries branch off the aorta and send blood to capillaries in all of the organs and body tissues except for the lungs. The blood exchanges nutrients and oxygen for carbon dioxide and wastes. It then moves into the veins and travels back to the right atrium of the heart through the superior and inferior venae cavae.

As You Read

On your concept map, draw arrows that show the path blood takes in the pulmonary and systemic circulations. Label each circulation on the concept map. Compare your chart with the chart of a partner, and make necessary corrections or additions.

Which of the two circulations is larger?

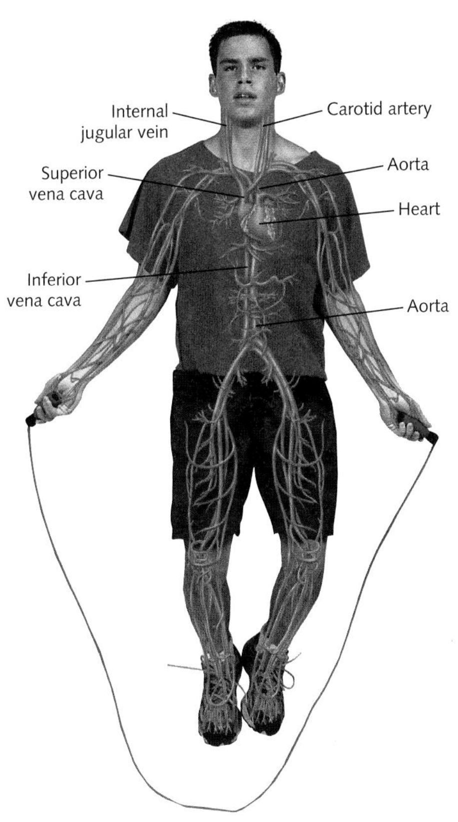

Figure 20.21 The systemic circulation carries blood to the tissues and back to the heart.

Figure It Out

1. What connects the arteries and the veins?
2. Predict which parts of the circuit will have the highest and the lowest blood pressure.

Teach

EXPLAIN to students that in this section, they will learn about the largest circulation system in the human body: systemic circulation.

Figure It Out: Figure 20.21

ANSWER **1.** Capillaries connect the arteries and the veins. **2.** The blood pressure is highest in the aorta and lowest in the venae cavae.

As You Read

Have students review their definitions and modify them based on their reading. Then, ask students to discuss with each other the path blood takes in the pulmonary and systemic circulations. Have each student represent each path in his or her concept map.

The concept map should now have two pairs of arrows. One, labeled *Pulmonary,* should point from the heart to the lungs and back to the heart. The other, labeled *Systemic,* should point from the heart to the tissues and back to the heart.

ANSWER The systemic circulation arrow is larger.

ELL Strategy

Think, Pair, Share After each student has worked on his or her concept map, have students share their maps and ideas with partners.

Teach

EXPLAIN that students will learn about an important doctor, William Harvey, who lived from 1578 to 1657. He was the first person to discover the way in which blood circulates in the human body. Students will also learn about coronary circulation.

Vocabulary

coronary circulation Tell students that *coronary* comes from the Latin word *coronarius,* meaning "pertaining to a crown." Generally, however, the word relates to the heart.

PEOPLE IN SCIENCE

After they read about William Harvey individually, students should discuss the content of the feature in small groups.

EXTEND Have students write in their Science Notebooks thoughts about the first, second, or third paragraph. You might also want to make reference materials available to students and have them find out more about William Harvey and about the discovery of capillaries.

Assess

EVALUATE Use the After You Read questions and the Alternative Assessment to help you assess students' understanding of the lesson.

After You Read

1. Pulmonary circulation takes deoxygenated blood to the lungs and returns oxygenated blood to the heart. Systemic circulation takes oxygenated blood to the body and returns deoxygenated blood to the heart. Coronary circulation delivers oxygenated blood to the heart muscle and returns deoxygenated blood to the heart.
2. Blood pressure in the aorta is higher than blood pressure in the pulmonary artery.
3. Students should show the coronary circulation with an arrow branching off the systemic circulation near the heart and an arrow immediately returning to the heart.

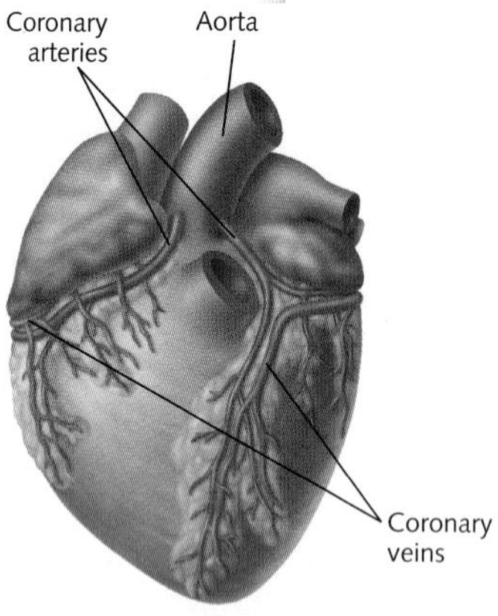

Figure 20.22 The coronary circulation ensures that the heart gets oxygenated blood first.

Coronary Circulation

A special branch of the systemic circulation called the **coronary** (KOR uh ner ee) **circulation** makes sure that the heart gets enough oxygen. The coronary arteries branch off from the aorta immediately after it leaves the left ventricle, bringing oxygenated blood to the heart muscle. One artery brings blood to the right atrium and ventricle. Another brings blood to the left atrium and ventricle. The coronary veins drain directly into the right atrium of the heart.

PEOPLE IN SCIENCE William Harvey 1578–1657

Before 1628, doctors believed that there were two kinds of blood. Venous blood, they thought, was made in the liver and spread through the body in the veins. Arterial blood was made in the heart from air and a tiny amount of venous blood. William Harvey, an Englishman, changed those ideas. Harvey studied in Italy with the most famous physicians in the world. When he graduated, Harvey returned to England and soon became the king's doctor.

One of Harvey's teachers had found a series of valves inside the veins. Harvey wondered about the purpose of these valves. He studied the heart and blood vessels in animals by dissecting them and by doing experiments. Harvey's dissections indicated that all of the blood had to go through the lungs to get from one side of the heart to the other. He pushed blood through the veins and found that the valves only opened in one direction. He could push blood toward the heart, but not away from it.

All of his experiments led Harvey to conclude that blood had to circulate inside the body. He could not explain how blood got from the arteries into the veins, but he predicted that tiny vessels connected the two. Shortly after his death, capillaries were discovered.

After You Read

1. Describe the three circulations that make up the circulatory system.
2. Predict whether the blood pressure inside the pulmonary artery is larger or smaller than the pressure inside the aorta.
3. Add the coronary circulation to your concept map. Is it a specialized circuit of the pulmonary circulation or the systemic circulation?

Alternative Assessment

EVALUATE Give students a few minutes to add the coronary circulation to their concept maps and refine the definitions. Have each student write a paragraph explaining his or her concept map underneath the map.

Background Information

Harvey was able to carry out research to support his heart and circulatory system theories because King Charles I provided him with animals to study. He later became King Charles' personal physician. Harvey was considered quite controversial during his lifetime because of his radical views; however, he was still recognized as a medical leader of his time.

20.7 Cardiovascular Diseases

Before You Read

Draw a T-chart in your Science Notebook. On one side, write a list of the headings in this lesson. Leave several blank lines under each topic. As you read, write the symptoms for each cardiovascular disease on the other side of the chart, across from its name.

Learning Goals

- Identify the symptoms of the major cardiovascular diseases.
- Evaluate the role of diet, exercise, and smoking in the development of cardiovascular disease.

New Vocabulary

hypertension
atherosclerosis
stroke

Do you know what is the number-one killer in the United States? Perhaps you think it is car accidents or sports accidents. Maybe you think it is diabetes or cancer. If so, you would be wrong. The number-one killer is cardiovascular disease. About 40 percent of all deaths in the United States each year are caused by heart disease and stroke.

Some of these deaths could have been prevented. Cardiovascular diseases develop more often in people who eat fatty foods, smoke, and avoid exercise. If a person eats a diet low in cholesterol and saturated fat, exercises regularly, and doesn't smoke, he or she can reduce the chance of developing a cardiovascular disease.

Causes of Death in the United States in 2003

Rank	Cause	Number of Deaths
1	heart disease	685,089
2	cancer	556,902
3	stroke	157,689
4	lower respiratory disease	126,382
5	accidents	109,277
6	diabetes	74,219

Figure 20.23 Two of the top six causes of death in the United States in 2003 were cardiovascular diseases.

Figure It Out

1. How many people died of heart disease in 2003?
2. Cardiovascular diseases include both heart disease and stroke. Calculate the total number of people who died of these diseases in 2003.

Hypertension

Hypertension (hi pur TEN chun) is high blood pressure. It occurs when the heart has to pump harder than normal to push blood through the systemic circulation. Normally, systolic blood pressure is around 120 and diastolic pressure is around 80. A person with hypertension will have systolic pressure higher than 140 and diastolic pressure higher than 90.

20.7 Introduce

ENGAGE Ask students to guess what the most common cause of death in the United States was in 2003. After students have given their answers, ask them to look at the table in Figure 20.23 to see whether they were correct.

Before You Read

Explain to students what *cardiovascular disease* means. Ask them to write the term in their Science Notebooks. Write *hypertension, atherosclerosis, heart attack,* and *stroke* on the board. Tell students that these are all cardiovascular diseases that they will learn about in this lesson.

Teach

EXPLAIN to students that in this section, they will learn about hypertension, or high blood pressure. Ask if anyone is familiar with it.

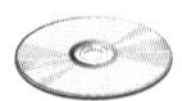

Vocabulary

hypertension Explain that the prefix *hyper-* is a Greek word meaning "over" and that *tension* is an act of stretching. Ask students what the two words should mean when combined.

Figure It Out: Figure 20.23

ANSWER **1.** 685,089 **2.** Students should add the totals for heart disease and stroke to find that 842,778 people died of cardiovascular diseases in 2003.

ELL Strategy

Read Aloud and Discuss Assign students to small groups containing students with the same native language, if possible. Students should take turns reading aloud each section of the lesson and discussing their understanding of it in English or in their native language.

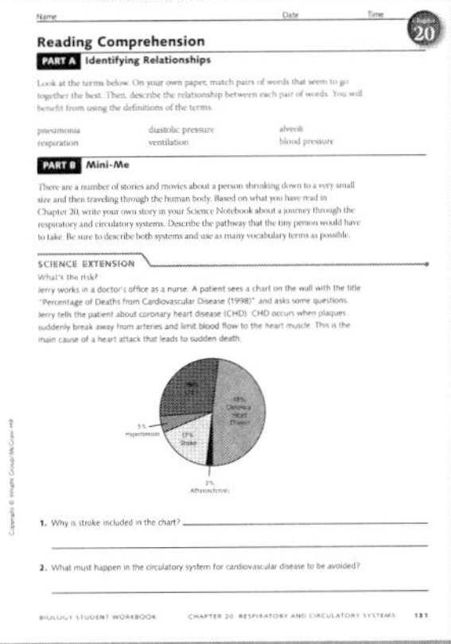

Reading Comprehension Workbook, p. 131

Teach

EXPLAIN to students that they will continue learning about cardiovascular diseases in this section.

As You Read

Give students time to complete the symptoms of hypertension and atherosclerosis in their Science Notebooks. Have each student compare his or her chart with another student's and discuss any differences.

ANSWER Atherosclerosis is sometimes called "hardening of the arteries."

Vocabulary

atherosclerosis Tell students that *athero* comes from the Greek words *athere,* meaning "gruel" (a thin porridge), and *skleros,* meaning "hard." The term refers to an abnormal hardening or thickening of an artery.

stroke Tell students that a common meaning of *stroke* is "any act or way of striking." A second common meaning is "an act of striking a ball," such as in golf. In biology, a stroke occurs when an artery in the brain is blocked or bursts, cutting off the blood supply to part of the brain. Have students discuss why this term was applied to the effects of an artery in the brain being block or bursting.

Use the Visual: Figure 20.24

ANSWER An atherosclerotic artery cannot carry as much blood as a healthy artery can.

EXTEND Have students compare the numbers of red blood cells that can pass through these arteries with that of the artery shown in Figure 20.25. Ask: *What is the role of red blood cells?* (carrying oxygen to the body cells) *How does atherosclerosis affect the body?* (It reduces the amount of oxygen and other nutrients going to the cells.) *What is another effect?* (The blood is less able to carry away wastes made by cells.)

A person with hypertension may have no symptoms. He or she may feel fine. However, consistently high blood pressure can damage other parts of the body. It is one of the major risk factors for cardiovascular disease.

As You Read

Review the symptoms of the cardiovascular diseases you have read about so far.

What is another name for atherosclerosis?

Atherosclerosis

Atherosclerosis (a thuh roh skluh ROH sus) is a common cause of cardiovascular disease. It occurs when deposits made of fats and cholesterol build up on the inner walls of large arteries. The deposits are called plaques (PLAKS). Large plaques make the space inside an artery smaller, so less blood can pass through. This means that the heart has to work harder to pump blood through the arteries. Atherosclerosis can cause hypertension.

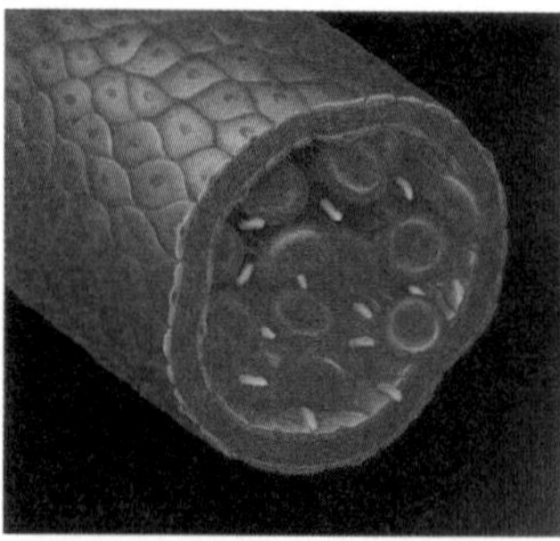

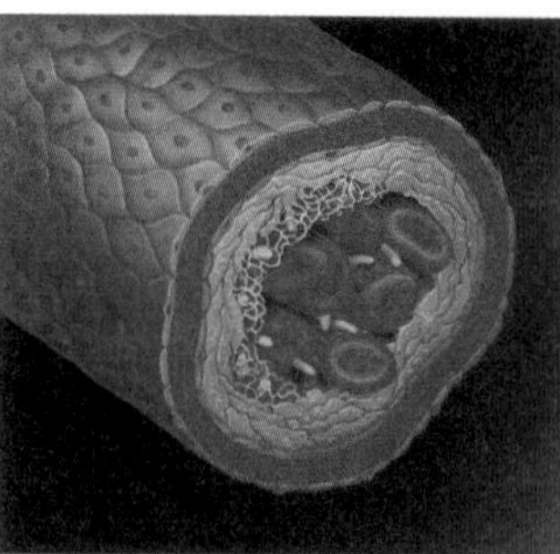

Figure 20.24 Compare the healthy artery on the left and the atherosclerotic artery on the right. Can you see how plaques have made the atherosclerotic artery narrower? Can it carry as much blood as the healthy artery?

If the plaques grow large enough, they can completely block an artery. Blood cannot flow through blocked arteries, and the tissues downstream from the blockage can starve and die. Large plaques also damage the artery walls, making them stiff. Atherosclerosis is sometimes called hardening of the arteries. When the arteries harden, they lose their ability to push the blood. This also makes the heart work harder to pump blood through the arteries.

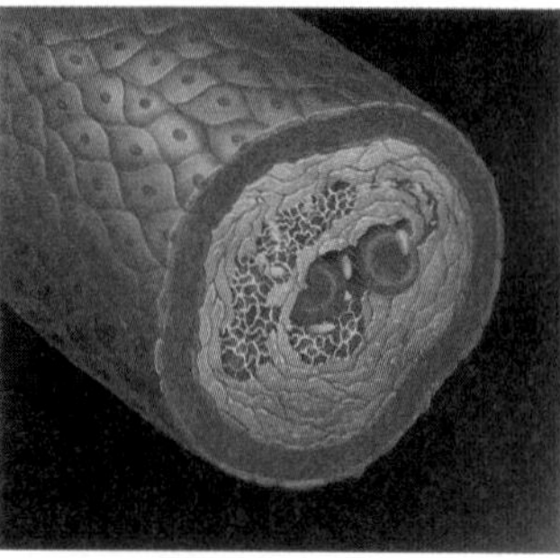

Figure 20.25 This artery is almost completely blocked by plaques. Only a little blood can squeeze through it. If the plaques get any thicker, the artery will be blocked and the tissues it supplies will die.

Differentiated Instruction

Logical-Mathematical Ask students to calculate the per-person annual cost of cardiovascular diseases for Americans. First, students must research how many people live in the United States (approximately 300,000,000). Then, they should divide $403 billion by that number to get the answer.

Platelets can stick to the plaques and form clots. Blood clots or pieces of fatty plaque sometimes break off the artery walls and float in the bloodstream. If they get stuck in blood vessels in the heart or the brain, they can cause a heart attack or a stroke.

Heart Attack

A heart attack starts when a coronary artery gets clogged by a fatty plaque, cutting off the blood supply to one part of the heart muscle. When the muscle cells do not get enough oxygen, they begin to die. The damage can make the heart beat irregularly or even stop. Even if a person survives a heart attack, the damaged heart muscle may be weaker than before. The main symptom of a heart attack is chest pain that often spreads to an arm or a shoulder. Other symptoms include shortness of breath, dizziness, and nausea. A heart attack is a medical emergency.

Stroke

A **stroke** occurs when an artery in the brain is blocked or bursts, cutting off the blood supply to part of the brain. When the nerve cells do not get enough oxygen, they die. A stroke can cause mild damage that the victim eventually recovers from, or it can cause serious disabilities or death. The effects of the stroke depend on which part of the brain was affected. Stroke victims can suffer a wide variety of symptoms, including a sudden severe headache, paralysis, blindness or blurred vision, loss of speech or balance, or amnesia. A stroke is also a medical emergency.

CONNECTION: Economics

Cardiovascular diseases are not just deadly—they are also expensive. The total cost of health care for people with these diseases and their lost time at work is approximately 403 billion dollars each year.

After You Read

1. What causes a heart attack?
2. Could a stroke be caused by an atherosclerotic blockage in the brain? Write one or two sentences to defend your answer.
3. Review the information you have recorded in the T-chart in your Science Notebook. In a well-developed paragraph, predict how people who recover from heart attacks and strokes might change their daily lives in order to avoid having a second heart attack or stroke.

Teach

EXPLAIN to students that they will now learn about two more cardiovascular diseases, heart attack and stroke.

CONNECTION: Economics

Smoking is a contributor to cardiovascular disease. Over $157 billion is spent each year in the United States on lost productivity and cardiovascular medical expenses related to first- and second-hand cigarette smoke.

EXTEND Ask students to compare the health-care cost of smoking with the overall cost of cardiovascular-related health care. ($157 billion v. $403 billion)

Assess

EVALUATE Use the After You Read questions and the Alternative Assessment to help you assess students' understanding of the lesson.

After You Read

1. When oxygenated blood cannot reach the heart tissue, the muscle dies and causes a heart attack.
2. Atherosclerotic plaque inside a blood vessel in the brain could block the blood supply to the tissues and cause a stroke.
3. The same lifestyle changes that help prevent cardiovascular disease also help control the disease. Changing diet, starting to exercise, and quitting smoking can help prevent a second heart attack or stroke.

Alternative Assessment

EVALUATE After students have completed their charts, ask them to review the diseases and write a paragraph comparing and contrasting the diseases. Students should answer the following questions: *What are the similarities among the four? What are the differences?*

Background Information

High blood pressure and high cholesterol are the two major independent risk factors for cardiovascular disease. Even slightly lowering these levels yields positive results. By reducing blood pressure by 12 to 13 points, a person can reduce his or her chances of a heart attack by 21 percent and stroke by 37 percent. By reducing total blood cholesterol by 10 percent, a person may reduce the chances of heart disease by as much as 30 percent.

Chapter 20 Summary

VOCABULARY REVIEW

Check students' sentences or paragraphs to make sure they understand the meaning of each vocabulary term.

PREPARE FOR CHAPTER TEST

Evaluate students' essays using the following criteria:

1. The topic sentence, or main idea, should restate the Key Concept.
2. The supporting paragraphs should incorporate the answers to the Learning Goal questions students have written and include details, facts, and examples they have recorded in their Science Notebooks.
3. The concluding sentence should sum up the main idea of the chapter and restate the Key Concept.

MASTERING CONCEPTS

True or False

1. False, exhale
2. False, coronary circulation
3. True
4. True
5. False, epiglottis
6. True

Short Answer

7. It moves through the pharynx, trachea, and a bronchus and into an alveolus, where it diffuses into a pulmonary capillary and attaches to a hemoglobin molecule in a red blood cell. Next, it travels in the pulmonary vein to the left side of the heart and then goes out through the aorta, into a systemic artery, and to a capillary in a thigh muscle.
8. Arteries carry pressurized, oxygenated blood to the tissues. Exchange occurs in the capillaries. Veins carry depressurized, deoxygenated blood back to the heart.
9. Person 1's heart is working harder. More forceful beats causes higher blood pressure; faster heart rate indicates more beats.
10. Lymph is collected from spaces between cells in body tissues by lymph capillaries. It is then filtered in lymph nodes and returned to the circulatory as lymph vessels empty into veins near the heart.

Chapter 20 Summary

KEY CONCEPTS

20.1 What Is Respiration?

- Breathing moves air to the respiratory exchange surface inside the lungs.
- Oxygen and carbon dioxide move into and out of the bloodstream by diffusion.
- Cells use oxygen to carry out cellular respiration.

20.2 The Respiratory System

- The human respiratory system is a series of passages that channel air to the lungs.
- Gases are exchanged across the walls of the alveoli.

20.3 The Body's Transport System

- The cardiovascular system transports materials, regulates fluid balance and body temperature, and helps prevent infection and blood loss after an injury.

20.4 Heart and Blood Vessels

- The heart pumps blood to the lungs and the rest of the body.
- Arteries carry blood away from the heart, and veins carry blood to the heart. Capillaries connect arteries and veins.
- Blood pressure is the result of the heart pushing blood against the artery walls.

20.5 Blood

- Blood is made up of red blood cells, white blood cells, and platelets suspended in plasma.
- Plasma that enters the tissues is called lymph, and it returns to the blood vessels through the lymphatic system.
- Human blood types are the result of antigens on the surface of the red blood cells.

20.6 Circulation in the Body

- The pulmonary circulation moves blood through the lungs. The systemic circulation moves blood through other tissues.
- The coronary circulation branches off from the systemic circulation to ensure that the heart gets oxygenated blood.

20.7 Cardiovascular Diseases

- Cardiovascular diseases are the leading cause of death in the United States.
- High blood pressure and atherosclerosis can cause heart attacks and strokes.

VOCABULARY REVIEW

Write each term in a complete sentence, or write a paragraph relating several terms.

20.1
respiration, p. 351
ventilation, p. 351
lung, p. 351
diaphragm, p. 351
alveolus, p. 352
cellular respiration, p. 353

20.2
respiratory system, p. 354
pharynx, p. 354
epiglottis, p. 354
larynx, p. 354
trachea, p. 355
bronchus, p. 355

20.3
cardiovascular system, p. 357
cell metabolism, p. 358

20.4
atrium, p. 359
ventricle, p. 359
vena cava, p. 360
aorta, p. 360
artery, p. 360
capillary, p. 361
vein, p. 361
blood pressure, p. 361
pulse, p. 362

20.5
hemoglobin, p. 363
antibody, p. 363
platelet, p. 364
plasma, p. 364
lymphatic system, p. 364
lymph, p. 364
antigen, p. 365

20.6
circulation, p. 366
pulmonary circulation, p. 366
systemic circulation, p. 367
coronary circulation, p. 368

20.7
hypertension, p. 369
atherosclerosis, p. 370
stroke, p. 371

372 RESPIRATORY AND CIRCULATORY SYSTEMS

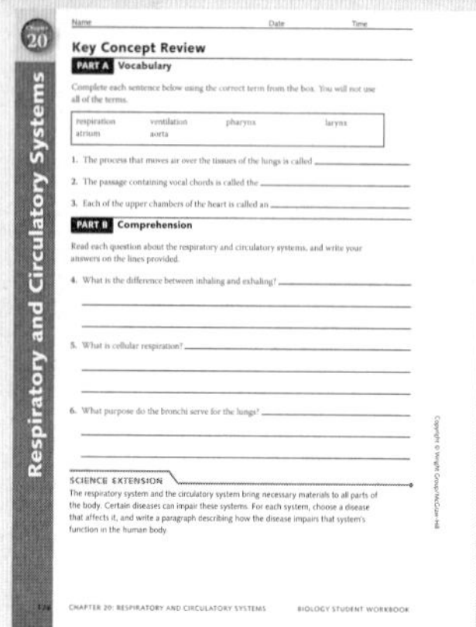
Key Concept Review
Workbook, p. 128

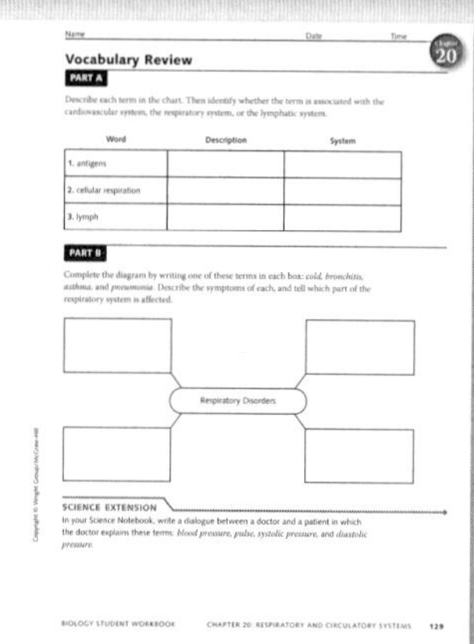
Vocabulary Review
Workbook, p. 129

MASTERING CONCEPTS

True or False

If the statement is true, write "true." If it is false, change the underlined word or words to make the statement true.

1. Air is pushed out of your lungs when you inhale.
2. The pulmonary circulation supplies oxygenated blood to the heart.
3. Red blood cells carry oxygen.
4. The cardiovascular system can move heat around the body.
5. The trachea keeps food out of the lungs.
6. The cells in the heart that set the heart rate are called the pacemaker.

Short Answer

Answer each of the following in a sentence or brief paragraph.

7. Trace the path of an oxygen molecule as it moves from the air near the nose to the muscle cells in the thigh.
8. Describe the functions of the three main groups of blood vessels.
9. Person 1 has a blood pressure of 140 over 80 and a heart rate of 100 beats per minute. Person 2 has a blood pressure of 90 over 60 and a heart rate of 80 beats per minute. Explain which heart is working harder.
10. Describe the path of lymph as it moves from the tissues back to the bloodstream.
11. Draw a graph illustrating how the oxygen concentration in the blood changes as the blood moves around the body. Choose the axes of the graph to reflect the variables being considered.

PREPARE FOR CHAPTER TEST

To prepare for the chapter test, create a question from each Learning Goal. Use the information in your Science Notebook to answer each question. Then use these answers to write a well-developed essay about the chapter. Use the Key Concept on the first page of this chapter as your topic sentence.

Critical Thinking

Use what you have learned in this chapter to answer each of the following.

12. **Infer** "Blue babies" are born with a hole between the right and left atria. Infer what happens to the blood in people with this condition.
13. **Relate** Inhaled air is about 21 percent oxygen and 0.03 percent carbon dioxide. Exhaled air is about 17 percent oxygen and 4.5 percent carbon dioxide. Relate this change in gas composition to the process of cellular respiration.
14. **Predict** People who suffer from anemia do not make as many red blood cells as people normally do. Predict what some of their symptoms are likely to be.

Standardized Test Question

Choose the letter of the response that correctly answers the question.

15. An atherosclerotic plaque can block an artery and prevent blood from getting to the tissues the artery normally supplies. What waste products will build up in those tissues?
    A. oxygen and nitrogen
    B. oxygen and glucose
    C. carbon dioxide and glucose
    D. carbon dioxide and nitrogen

Test-Taking Tip

Use scrap paper to write notes. Sometimes making a sketch, such as a diagram or a table, can help you organize your ideas.

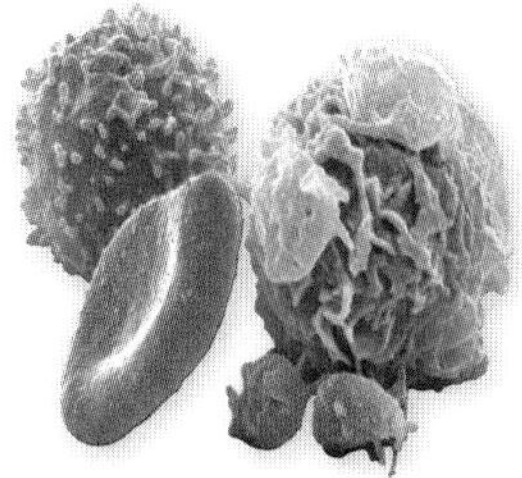

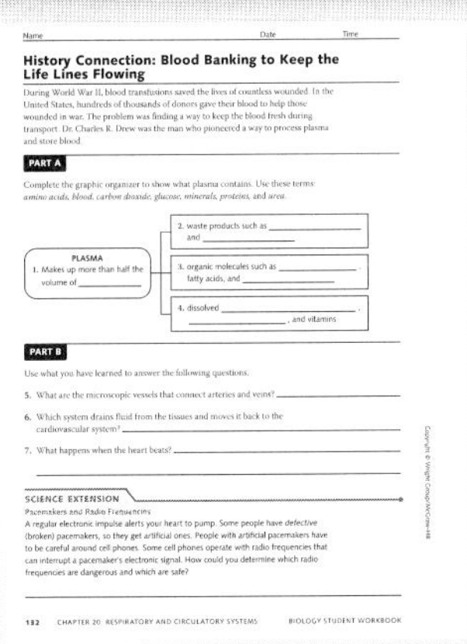

History Connection: Blood Banking to Keep the Life Lines Flowing

PART A

PART B

SCIENCE EXTENSION

Curriculum Connection Workbook, p. 132

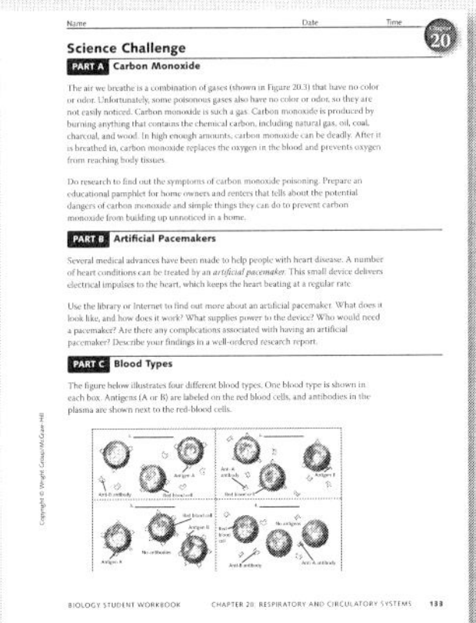

Science Challenge

PART A Carbon Monoxide

PART B Artificial Pacemakers

PART C Blood Types

Science Challenge Workbook, pp. 133–134

11. Graphs may vary. The graph line should rise and fall to represent the different concentrations of oxygen in different parts of the circulatory system.

Critical Thinking

12. Some deoxygenated blood from the right atrium moves directly to the left atrium without going through the lungs. So, their blood has less oxygen than the blood of a person with a normal heart.
13. Cellular respiration uses oxygen and produces carbon dioxide as a waste.
14. They cannot carry as much oxygen to their cells, cannot make as much ATP as normal, and would lack energy (be tired).

Standardized Test Question

15. D

Reading Links

Dr. Charles Drew: Blood Bank Innovator

Through this biography, readers will learn about the personal and professional life of an African American doctor whose pioneering work with blood plasma led to significant medical contributions. Working at a time when most black doctors did not treat white patients, Charles Drew developed blood transfusion and storage innovations that have had a lasting impact on modern medicine while also furthering the civil rights cause and teaching black doctors. Includes suggestions for further reading and internet research.

Schraff, Anne. Enslow Publishers, Inc. 128 pp. Illustrated. Library ISBN: 978-0-7660-2117-4.

Breathe Easy: Young People's Guide to Asthma

This recently expanded edition speaks frankly to teens about controlling asthma and understanding the condition. With its inclusion of information about personal triggers and warning signs, medications, non-medical treatments such as relaxation exercises, and strategies for coping with attacks, this comprehensive guide will be of use to students suffering from asthma and those who would like to learn what it is like to live with it. Includes parent guide, checklists, tips, and additional resources.

Weiss, Jonathan H. American Psychological Association (Magination Press). 80 pp. Illustrated by Michael Chesworth. Trade ISBN: 978-1-55798-956-7.

20A What Makes Up Blood?

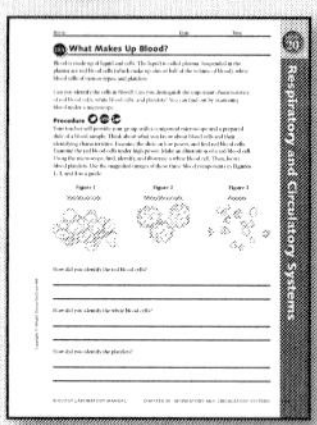

This prechapter introduction activity is designed to determine what students already know about the components of blood by engaging them in the examination of blood cells, the identification of the components of blood, and the comparison and illustration of those components.

Objectives

- identify red blood cells by their shape and color
- identify white blood cells by their color and nuclei
- identify platelets by their size
- illustrate red and white blood cells

Planning

 15–20 minutes  groups of 3–4 students

Materials (per group)

- microscope
- prepared slide of a blood smear
- colored pencils and paper

Lab Tip

Students may need to remove their goggles to obtain a better view while using the microscope.

Advance Preparation

- Ask students to discuss in their groups the distinguishing characteristics of red blood cells, white blood cells, and platelets.
- Suggest that on a prepared slide of blood, red blood cells should be stained red, white blood cells should be stained purple and have visible nuclei, and platelets should be dark and small.

Engagement Guide

- Challenge students to think about how they can identify the various cells in blood by asking:
  - *What kind of cells will be most plentiful?* (red blood cells)
  - *What kind of cells will be largest?* (white blood cells)
  - *What kind of cells will be smallest?* (platelets)
- Encourage students to illustrate what they observe in creative ways.

Going Further

Encourage students to repeat this activity, this time looking for different types of white blood cells. Have students try to distinguish among the types of white blood cells and illustrate them. You can provide photos of various white blood cells and ask students to match the cells that they find to the photos.

20B The Beating Heart

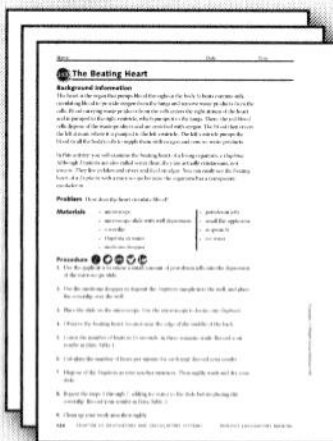

Objectives

- observe the beating heart of a *Daphnia*
- measure the heart rate of a *Daphnia*
- calculate heartbeats per minute
- predict the effect of temperature on heart rate

Skill Set

observing, measuring, calculating, predicting, comparing, stating conclusions

Planning

 30–35 minutes  groups of 3–4 students

Materials

Materials for this activity are listed in the Student Laboratory Manual.

Lab Tips

- Since the living conditions of the *Daphnia* are being manipulated, students should be cautioned about handling specimens in a humane manner.
- Students may need to remove their goggles to obtain a better view while using the microscope.

Advance Preparation

Provide small samples of *Daphnia*, petroleum jelly, and ice water for each group. Advise students that they should be careful not to provide too much light to the slide, or the transparent *Daphnia* might be difficult to see clearly. Ask students to guess whether the heart rate of the *Daphnia* will be faster or slower than that of humans, and have them explain their answers. Ask students to predict the effect of cold temperatures on the heart rate.

Answers to Observations: Data Tables

Students should measure a heart rate of 230–300 beats per minute at room temperature. The heart rate should decrease significantly at the colder temperature.

Answers to Analysis and Conclusions

1. The average heart rate should be 230–300 beats per minute—much faster than the human heart rate, which is 72–76 beats per minute.
2. Students' predictions will vary. Students should observe that the heart rate slowed in cold water because the lower temperature lowers the metabolism of the *Daphnia*.
3. The rapid beating of the heart muscle pumps blood throughout the body of the *Daphnia*.

Going Further

Have students test the effect of dilute solutions of common chemicals that people ingest, such as coffee, alcohol, nicotine, and over-the-counter medicines, on the heart rate of *Daphnia* by following a similar procedure. Have students predict the effect of each chemical and explain their predictions. Be sure that students use a previously untested *Daphnia* for each trial. Ask students to compare and classify the effects of each chemical on the *Daphnia*.

20C A Working Model of the Lung

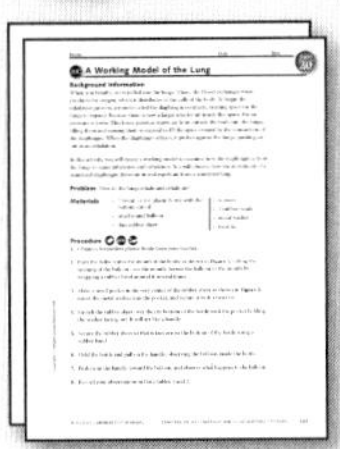

Objectives

- create a model of a working lung
- simulate the process of inhalation and exhalation
- describe how the diaphragm and the lungs work together in breathing

Skill Set

modeling, observing, analyzing data, classifying, drawing conclusions.

Planning

 45–60 minutes 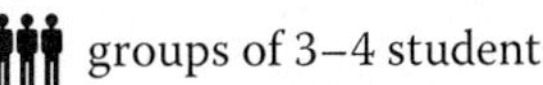 groups of 3–4 students

Materials

Materials for this activity are listed in the Student Laboratory Manual.

Advance Preparation

If thin rubber sheets are not available, you can make them from large balloons or latex gloves. Make sure the plastic bottles are stiff enough to resist the pressure of a rubber sheet stretched across their cut bottoms without bending. To avoid student injuries in the cutting of the plastic bottles, prepare the bottles for the groups ahead of time. Cut the bottom off the plastic bottle at a place that allows the bottle to remain rigid.

Answers to Observations: Data Table 1

In this model, the plastic bottle represents the chest cavity, the balloon represents the lungs, and the rubber sheet represents the diaphragm.

Answers to Observations: Data Table 2

When the rubber sheet is pulled out, the volume of air in the plastic bottle increases, decreasing the air pressure, and the balloon expands, simulating inhalation. When the rubber sheet is pushed in, the volume of air in the plastic bottle decreases, increasing the air pressure, and the balloon collapses, simulating exhalation.

Answers to Analysis and Conclusions

1. Pulling on the rubber sheet created a larger space in the bottle (as contraction of the diaphragm does in the chest cavity), reducing the air pressure and drawing air into the balloon (as do the lungs when they fill with air during inhalation).
2. Pushing on the rubber sheet created a smaller space in the bottle (as relaxation of the diaphragm does in the chest cavity), increasing the air pressure and pushing air out of the balloon (as do the lungs when they push out air during exhalation).
3. As the space in the chest cavity increases, the air pressure decreases. As the space in the chest cavity decreases, the air pressure increases.
4. The difference in the air pressure inside the chest cavity compared to the outside air is what makes breathing possible. The air moves into the area of lower pressure; thus it moves into the lungs when the cavity is larger during inhalation, and it moves out of the lungs when the cavity size decreases during exhalation.
5. The model simulates how changes in air pressure within a space that surrounds a flexible balloon or lung can cause the balloon to draw in or push out air, as the lungs do in breathing.

Going Further

Have students perform the same experiment with a more elaborate model. Ask them to design a model of the lung that includes a trachea and bronchi. Students might include materials such as a bell jar, glass Y-tubes, and multiple balloons to represent left and right lungs. Additionally, ask students to design a device that shows the change in air pressure in their model during breathing. This can be accomplished with a J-tube inserted in the jar, open to the outside air, and filled at the bottom of the *J* with a colored liquid. The liquid will move in the tube as the pressure differences change inside and outside the jar.

Chapter 21 Lessons

Introduce Chapter 21

As a starting activity, use LAB 21A A Model of the Digestive System on page 130 of the Laboratory Manual.

ENGAGE Have students list in their Science Notebooks five to ten of the foods they eat most often. Model the process by creating a list with three to four of the foods you often eat. In your list, be specific about the foods. For example, write *peach yogurt* rather than *yogurt* and *apple* rather than *fruit*. Encourage students to be as specific as possible with their own lists. Inform students that they will revisit these lists later in the chapter. If time permits, have each student share his or her list with a peer.

Think About Feeding

EXPLAIN Think aloud about ways that meals can be eaten without chewing. Say: *Babies aren't able to chew, and they only drink milk. That's one example of eating a meal without chewing.*

Tell students to complete the bulleted activities. Then, make a class list of students' responses, including the animal and human connections.

Chapter 21 Digestive and Excretory Systems

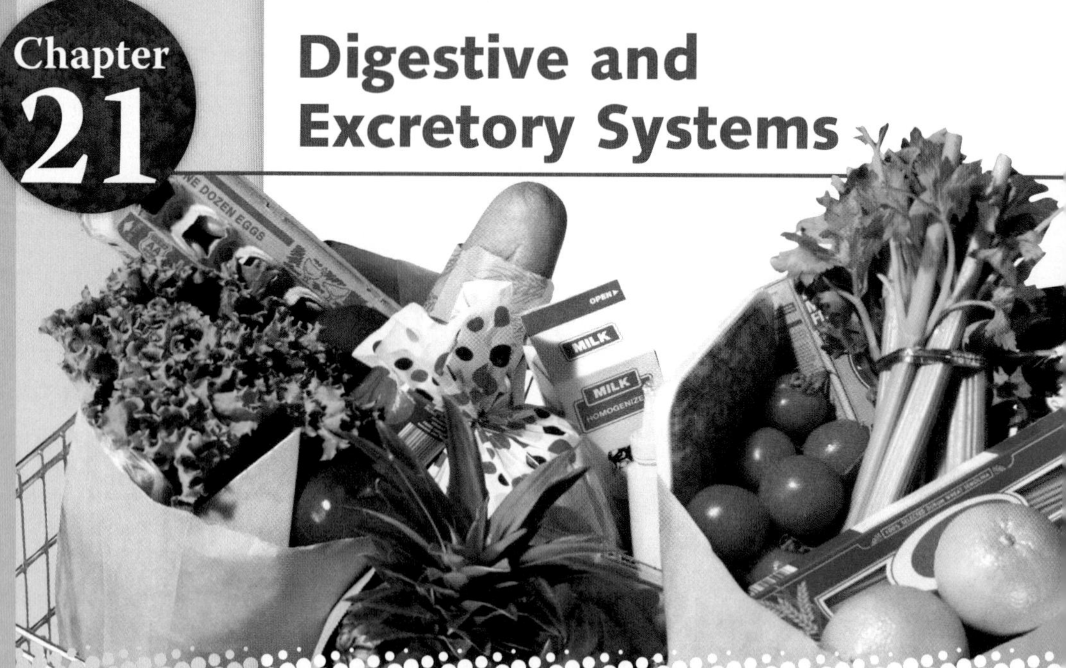

KEY CONCEPT The digestive system processes food, and the excretory system processes wastes.

Animals have lives that revolve around eating. Every animal needs to eat enough food to fuel its body, repair damaged tissues, and store some energy. When it comes to eating, humans are generalists. Humans eat grains, roots, fruits, fungi, milk, eggs, and meat. In some parts of the world, humans eat insects. No matter what people eat, everything put in a person's mouth takes the same trip. Every bit of food you eat, whether it's sushi, popcorn, or tacos, gets digested into nutrients and then is absorbed and used by your body or eventually excreted.

Think About Feeding

Like other mammals, humans chew their food. However, many animals can't chew. Lizards and alligators bite off chunks of food and swallow them whole. Snakes unhinge their jaws to swallow animals that are larger than their heads.

- In your Science Notebook, make a list of three ways a meal can be eaten without chewing.
- Think about these ways of eating. Can you think of animals that eat this way? Can you eat this way? Write what you think next to each method.

NSTA SciLINKS THE WORLD'S A CLICK AWAY
www.scilinks.org
Digestive System **Code: WGB21A**
Excretory System **Code: WGB21B**

374

Chapter 21 Planning Guide

Instructional Periods	National Standards	Lab Manual	Workbook
21.1 1 period	F.1, G2; A.2, C.5, F.1, F.6, G.2; UCP.1	**Lab 21A—p. 130** A Model of the Digestive System	Key Concept Review p. 135
21.2 3 periods	C.1; B.6, C.1, C.5; UCP.2, UCP.3, UCP.5	**Lab 21B—p. 131** Where Digestion Starts	Vocabulary Review p. 136
21.3 2 periods	A.1, C.1, C.3; C.1, C.4; UCP.5	**Lab 21C—p. 133** Testing Food for Nutrients	Interpreting Diagrams p. 137
21.4 2 periods	C.1; C.3; B.2, B.3, C.1; UCP.5		Reading Comprehension p. 138
21.5 2 periods	C.1, F.5; C.1		Curriculum Connection p. 139 Science Challenge p. 140

Middle School Standard; High School Standard; Unifying Concept and Principle

21.1 Nutrition

Before You Read

Read the lesson title, the headings, and the Learning Goals, and look at the photos and tables. Predict what you think you will learn in this lesson. Write your predictions as two or three sentences in your Science Notebook.

Learning Goals

- Identify the six nutrients the human body needs.
- Explain how to plan a balanced diet.
- Understand how to read a food label.

New Vocabulary

nutrition
nutrient
malnutrition
carbohydrate
protein
essential amino acid
fat
vitamin
mineral
Calorie

The human body is like a factory. A factory needs a steady supply of raw materials, whether it makes cars, computers, or boxed cereal. It uses some of the materials to build a product. It burns other materials for the energy to run its machines. The body uses food the same way. Food provides the energy for metabolism and the raw materials for building and repairing body parts. The process of getting the food needed to survive is called **nutrition** (new TRIH shun).

Nutrients

The raw materials the body gets from food are called **nutrients** (NEW tree unts). There are six kinds of nutrients: carbohydrates, proteins, fats, vitamins, minerals, and water. The body needs some of each of these nutrients every day in order to stay healthy. If a nutrient is missing from the diet, the body will not be able to complete some of its metabolic jobs. Over time, that missing nutrient will make a person sick. The person will suffer from malnutrition. **Malnutrition** (mal new TRIH shun) occurs when a person cannot get enough to eat or when the food eaten does not provide a balanced diet. A balanced diet contains all of the nutrients the body needs.

Carbohydrates The main sources of energy for the body are carbohydrates. **Carbohydrates** (kar boh HI drayts) are molecules made up of atoms of carbon, hydrogen, and oxygen. There are three types of carbohydrates: sugar, starch, and fiber.

Sugars are simple carbohydrates. Single sugars and short sugar chains make foods such as fruit and honey sweet. Long chains of sugars are called starch. Starches are found in cereals, bread, pasta, and vegetables such as potatoes and rice. Starch is a complex carbohydrate.

Fiber, such as cellulose, comes from the cell walls of plant cells. Fiber is a complex carbohydrate that is found in peas, beans, fruits, vegetables, and whole-grain breads and cereals. The body breaks down sugars and starches to provide energy. Fiber cannot be digested, but it is essential for the smooth running of the digestive system.

Figure 21.1 Starches are complex carbohydrates found in foods such as rice *(top)* and potatoes *(bottom)*.

Background Information

Simple sugars, or monosaccharides, have the chemical formula $C_6H_{12}O_6$. Disaccharides, or double sugars, have the chemical formula $C_{12}H_{22}O_{11}$. In both sugars, the ratio of hydrogen atoms to oxygen atoms is 2 to 1, which is the ratio of these atoms in water—thus the name carbo*hydrate.*

nutrient Ask students to explain the relationship between *nutrient* and *nutrition.*

malnutrition Explain that the prefix *mal-* is from the Latin word *male,* which means “badly.” Literally, *malnutrition* means “to nourish badly.”

carbohydrate Tell students that *carbo-* means “from carbon.” The second part of the compound word, *hydr-*, is from the Greek word *hydor* and means “water.” The suffix *-ate* means cause “to be” or “to have.”

21.1 Introduce

ENGAGE Pair students, and ask them to explain the idea of healthful eating. Give groups options such as creating a concept map, writing a few sentences, and listing or drawing foods in their Science Notebooks. After students have completed these explanations, discuss their ideas and create a class definition of healthy eating.

Before You Read

Model aloud the process of reviewing the lesson title and two or three subheadings and predicting what you think the class will learn about nutrition in humans. Encourage students to review all photos and tables and to be specific about their own predictions.

Vocabulary terms are listed on the first student page of each lesson. You may wish to preview the terms before introducing each lesson. Strategies for teaching the vocabulary appear on the pages where the terms are introduced.

Teach

EXPLAIN that in this lesson, students will learn about nutrition and the types of foods that are necessary for good nutrition. Review the idea that the human body is continually growing and repairing and replacing cells and tissues. Tell students that good nutrition enables the body to function more efficiently.

Science Notebook EXTRA

Encourage students to use the vocabulary section they created in their Science Notebooks. Remind them to record prefixes, suffixes, and root words to help them remember the meanings of vocabulary terms.

Vocabulary

nutrition Explain that the suffix *-tion* signifies an action or condition. The root *nutrient* comes from the Latin word *nutrire,* which means “to nourish.”

Teach

EXPLAIN to students that they will learn about two more types of nutrients: proteins and fats. Both of these nutrients can be found in animal foods. Plant foods can be healthier choices for people, but vegetarians must plan their diets carefully to be sure that they consume all necessary nutrients.

Vocabulary

protein Explain that *protein* comes from the Greek word *proteios,* meaning "primary."

essential amino acid Ask students to brainstorm common uses of the word *essential*. Responses may include "key," "important," and "necessary." Tell students that the nine essential amino acids are ones that the human body cannot make.

fat Tell students that *fat* can be a noun and an adjective. Ask students to provide examples of both usages. Emphasize that the usage here is as a noun.

vitamin Tell students that *vitamin* is a compound word derived from the Latin word *vita,* meaning "life," and *amine,* which describes a type of organic compound.

As You Read

Give students a few minutes to review and revise their predictions and add information to what they have learned. Then, ask pairs of students to review one another's notes and provide helpful feedback to partners.

ANSWER carbohydrates

CONNECTION: Social Studies

Have student groups find recipes for dishes from either countries in warm climates (e.g., Thailand, the Philippines, Malaysia, and India) or countries in cooler climates (e.g., Finland, Norway, and Sweden). ELLs could research popular dishes of their countries.

Ask students to list spices used in the recipes. Create a class list of spices from each climate, and have students compare the two lists. Ask them to hypothesize about which spices have antibacterial properties. Guard against cultural assumptions about food health safety.

Figure 21.2 Proteins are found in animal and plant foods. Animal foods such as meat, eggs, and milk contain all of the essential amino acids. Plant foods such as beans and rice are missing some essential amino acids.

Proteins A **protein** (PROH teen) is a long chain of amino acids. A protein is made up of atoms of carbon, hydrogen, oxygen, nitrogen, and sometimes sulfur. Muscles, hair, skin, fingernails, and other tissues are all built out of proteins. Each one of the thousands of proteins used in the cells contains a different combination of 20 amino acids. Nine of those amino acids are called **essential amino acids** because people cannot make them from other molecules. The essential amino acids must be eaten every day.

Foods such as meat, fish, milk, and eggs contain all 20 amino acids and are called complete proteins. Plants that are rich in protein often lack some amino acids. Because the body does not store amino acids, vegetarians—people who eat only vegetables, fruits, grains, and nuts—must carefully combine their plant foods to make sure that they get all the amino acids they need every day.

Fats A **fat**, also called a lipid, is a glycerol molecule attached to a series of fatty acid chains. There are two families of fat molecules based on their chemical structure. Saturated fats usually come from animals. They are found in foods such as butter, meat, cheese, eggs, and oily fish. Unsaturated fats usually come from plants. They are liquid at room temperature and are also called oils. Fats and other lipids are an important part of cell membranes, nerve insulation, and molecules known as hormones. They are also an important source of energy. Most of the energy the body stores is stored as fat.

As You Read

Compare the predictions in your Science Notebook with what you have learned so far about nutrition. Write a list of what you learned that is new to you. Share your list with a partner or a small group of classmates.

What nutrient is the main source of energy for the body?

Figure 21.3 There are two types of fats. Saturated fats *(left)* are solid at room temperature. Unsaturated fats *(right)* are liquid at room temperature.

CONNECTION: Social Studies

Highly spiced foods are often eaten in warm climates where meat turns bad more quickly. Scientists have shown that many of the spices have antibacterial properties and protect people from food poisoning.

Background Information

The best all-purpose bacteria killers include garlic, onion, allspice, and oregano. Thyme, cinnamon, tarragon, and cumin were found to kill about 80 percent of bacteria. The next best killers of bacteria include capsicums (chili peppers and other hot peppers). White and black pepper, ginger, anise seed, celery seed, and lemon and lime juices kill about 25 percent of bacteria.

ELL Strategy

Use a Concept Map Have students create a concept map using *Nutrients* as the main idea and the six major kinds of nutrients in the lesson as subtopics. Encourage them to list as many examples of the different kinds of nutrients as possible. Students can add information about each nutrient as they go through the lesson. They may also benefit from sketching examples of foods for each of the nutrients.

Vitamins Complex organic molecules that help the body build new tissues and important molecules are called **vitamins** (VI tuh munz). Vitamins also help regulate body functions and fight disease. Only a few hundredths of a gram of each vitamin is needed every day. The body cannot make vitamins, so they must come from food.

Vitamin C and the B vitamins are soluble in water and cannot be stored in the body. Foods containing these vitamins must be eaten every day. The other vitamins are soluble in fat. They are stored in fatty tissues, and they can be toxic in large quantities. The vitamins needed to keep the body functioning properly are shown in **Figure 21.4**.

Did You Know?

Arctic explorers learned that vitamin A is toxic in large quantities when they ate polar bear liver. Large amounts of vitamin A in the liver made the explorers vomit. They also became dizzy and uncoordinated.

Essential Vitamins

Vitamin	Source	Function	Result of Deficiency
A	orange and dark green vegetables, eggs, dairy	used to form visual pigments	xerophthalmia (progressive blindness)
B_1	grains, meat, legumes, nuts	carbohydrate metabolism	beriberi (neurological symptoms)
B_2	milk, eggs, green leafy vegetables, grains	coenzyme for many metabolic reactions	dermatitis, sensitivity to light
B_3	grains, meat, legumes, nuts	important part of nicotinamide coenzymes	pellagra; dermatitis and neurological symptoms
B_6	meat, fruit, grains, legumes, vegetables	amino acid metabolism	skin lesions, irritability, anemia, convulsions
B_{12}	meat, eggs, dairy	used to maintain nerve cells; fatty acid and amino acid metabolism	anemia, neuropathy
pantothenic acid	liver, eggs, many other foods	used for energy metabolism	sleep disturbances, indigestion
biotin	peanuts, tomatoes, eggs, many other foods	aids fat and glycogen formation, amino acid metabolism	lack of coordination, dermatitis, fatigue
folate	vegetables, legumes	important part of DNA synthesis, red blood cell formation	anemia, digestive disorders, neural tube defects in developing embryo
C	citrus fruit, green vegetables, potatoes	used in synthesis of collagen	scurvy (bleeding gums, loss of teeth, listlessness)
D	fatty fish, eggs, fortified milk	used in skeletal formation; assists calcium absorption	rickets (unmineralized bones)
E	green vegetables, nuts, grains, oils, eggs	prevents damage to cell membranes	hemolytic anemia
K	bacteria in digestive tract, leafy green vegetables	intestinal flora; formation of clotting factors	bleeding disorders

Figure 21.4 According to the table, which vitamin is needed for blood clotting? For proper vision?

Differentiated Instruction

Visual Have students draw pictures or find photos in magazines of the 20 foods most commonly eaten by their classmates. Then, have students write the vitamins and minerals supplied by those foods. Suggest that students create a classroom display of the information they have gathered.

Verbal Alternatively, have students complete the same task for the lunch foods sold in the school cafeteria over a week. Students can interview school nutritionists about the guidelines they use to plan school meals. Encourage ELLs to inquire about the food categories they are learning about. Student should then analyze the lunch options for vitamins and minerals and note which ones are missing.

Teach

EXPLAIN to students that a wide variety of vitamins play essential roles in the human body. Humans must get vitamins from food because their bodies cannot manufacture them.

Science Notebook EXTRA

Have students review their lists of commonly eaten foods from the Engage activity at the start of this lesson (page 375). Have them note in their Science Notebooks which foods are sources of any of the vitamins in Figure 21.4. It may be useful for some students to create a two-column chart with their common foods in the first column and the vitamins in the second. Remind students that some foods are sources of more than one vitamin; for instance, a salad probably contains vitamins A, B_2, B_6, folate, C, E, and K. Then, suggest that students analyze their tables for vitamins not included.

EXTEND Have students conduct research to determine whether taking a multi-vitamin is necessary for most healthy people.

Students can find out the RDIs (Reference Daily Intakes, which are a set of dietary references based on the Recommended Dietary Allowances for essential vitamins and minerals; the name *RDI* replaces the term *U.S. RDA*) by visiting **http://www.fda.gov/FDAC/special/foodlabel/dvs.html**. The site also provides the Daily Reference Values (DRVs) for the energy-producing nutrients (fat, carbohydrate, protein, and fiber).

Students can use this information to become more knowledgeable about whether their diets provide the recommended amounts of vitamins and minerals. Then, have them develop a plan for ensuring that their diets provide all the necessary vitamins and minerals.

Use the Visual: Figure 21.4

ANSWER vitamin K; vitamin A

Teach

EXPLAIN to students that minerals strengthen bones, allow the body to move through muscle contractions and nerve conduction, and maintain appropriate amounts of fluids in the body.

EXPLORE Have students investigate the water supply in your community to find out how much fluoride is in the water. Many communities provide annual reports about the water contents. Students could conduct their research online or in person. Information about the importance of water fluoridation can be found at the American Dental Association's Web site at **http://www.ada.org/public/topics/fluoride/index.asp**.

EXTEND If the fluoride supply is less than that recommended by the ADA, have students create posters with suggestions about how peers can improve their fluoride intake.

Vocabulary

mineral Explain that *mineral* is derived from the Latin word *mineralis,* which denotes a relation to mines. Many minerals are found in the earth, usually combined with another element in what geologists call ores.

Calorie Explain that *Calorie* originates from the Latin word *calor,* meaning "heat." Point out that in this usage, the term has a capital C. Scientifically, a calorie is defined as the amount of heat needed to raise the temperature of one gram of water one degree Celsius; a Calorie is the amount of heat needed to raise the temperature of one kilogram of water one degree Celsius.

Use the Visual: Figure 21.5

ANSWER iron; potassium

Minerals Inorganic elements that the body needs for most of its metabolic functions are called **minerals** (MIH nuh rulz). Minerals make bones stiff, enable nerves to send impulses and muscles to contract, and keep body fluids in balance. Some minerals are incorporated into proteins. The minerals needed to keep the body functioning properly are summarized in **Figure 21.5**.

Essential Minerals

Mineral	Source	Function	Result of Deficiency
calcium	milk, eggs, green vegetables, fish	mineralization of bone	rickets, osteoporosis
phosphorus	cheese, oats, liver	mineralization of bone	osteoporosis, abnormal metabolism
sodium	most foods	fluid balance; muscle contraction; nerve conduction	weakness, cramps, diarrhea, dehydration
potassium	most foods	major cellular action	muscular and neurological disorders
chloride	most foods	fluid balance; formation of hydrochloric acid in stomach	rarely occurs
iodine	seafood, iodized salt	required for synthesis of thyroid hormones	goiter (enlarged thyroid gland)
iron	red meat, liver, eggs, legumes, dried fruit	part of hemoglobin	anemia, indigestion
magnesium	green vegetables, grains, nuts, legumes	part of carbohydrate metabolism	muscular and neurological disorders, arrhythmic heartbeat
manganese	most foods	involved in many cellular processes	possible reproductive disorders
copper	meat, water	formation of hemoglobin; part of some enzymes	anemia
chromium	meat, fats, oils	regulation of blood glucose	inability to use glucose
cobalt	meat, milk, eggs	part of vitamin B_{12}	anemia
zinc	meat, grains, vegetables	part of some enzymes; involved in CO_2 transport	baldness
fluoride	fluoridated water, seafood	prevents tooth decay	dental cavities

Figure 21.5 According to the table, which mineral is found primarily in liver, red meat, and dried fruit? Which mineral is important for normal muscle and nerve functioning?

Background Information

Drinking the right amount of water each day is essential to good health. However, drinking an excessive amount of water can lead to death in a condition known as hyponatremia, or water intoxication. Although rare, this happens most commonly in infants under the age of six months and in athletes.

In infants, water intoxication can occur following the consumption of several bottles of water a day or from drinking infant formula that has been diluted too much. Athletes who have lost sodium through sweat and who then drink too much water can also suffer from water intoxication. They should drink a sports drink containing electrolytes to avoid the condition.

Water Humans can live for weeks without food, but they can live only a few days without water. Water is found inside and around the cells, and it is the largest component of blood. It takes part in most of the reactions of the body, and it is constantly recycled inside the cells. However, water is lost as a result of urination, sweating, and breathing. If the water is not replaced, the body becomes dehydrated.

A Balanced Diet

When you eat meals that contain all of the nutrients your body needs, you are eating a balanced diet. Most foods contain more than one nutrient. How can you be sure to eat enough of all the required nutrients?

Nutritionists are still studying what goes into a healthful diet. They have learned that people should eat more grains, fruits, and vegetables each day than meat and dairy products. Small amounts of oils and fats are healthful.

The energy stored in food is measured in **Calories** (KAL uh reez). One Calorie in heat raises the temperature of one kilogram of water by one degree Celsius. A young woman needs to eat about 1,800 to 2,000 Calories each day to maintain her weight. A young man needs to eat about 2,200 to 2,500 Calories. If a person eats more Calories than his or her metabolism burns, the body will store the extra energy as fat. Exercise burns more Calories than sedentary activities burn.

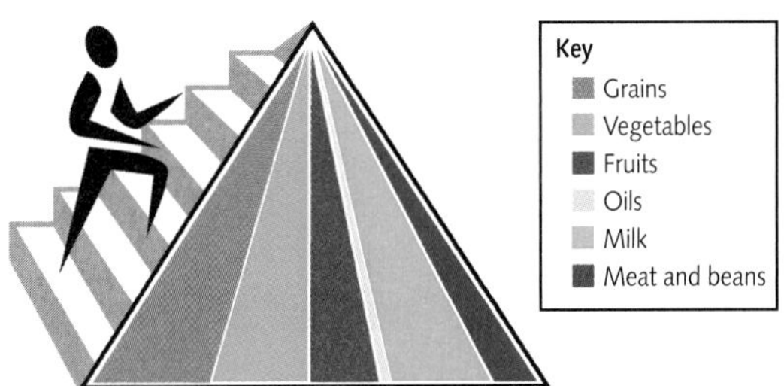

Figure 21.6 The USDA's Food Guide Pyramid is a visual guide that shows how much of each kind of food is found in a healthful, balanced diet.

Extend It!

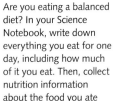

Are you eating a balanced diet? In your Science Notebook, write down everything you eat for one day, including how much of it you eat. Then, collect nutrition information about the food you ate from food labels and nutrition books.

Create a table in your Science Notebook with the following columns: *Food, Calories, Carbohydrates, Protein, Fat, Vitamins*, and *Minerals*. Record the information for each food you ate. Calculate the amount of Calories, carbohydrates, protein, fat, vitamins, and minerals you got from your food that day.

Figure It Out

1. Which foods make up more than half of the pyramid?
2. Which foods should be consumed in the smallest amounts?

After You Read

1. Make a T-chart in your Science Notebook. On one side, list the six nutrients the body needs to function properly. On the other side, list at least two foods that contain each nutrient. Compare this chart with the predictions you recorded in your Science Notebook.
2. What is the difference between a mineral and a vitamin?
3. Why is water an important nutrient?

Teach

EXPLAIN to students that they can achieve a balanced diet by eating foods that are rich in nutrients. Review the class definition of healthful eating from the start of the lesson (page 375). With their newly gained knowledge, students should discuss the definition and refine it to make it more accurate or complete.

Figure It Out: Figure 21.6

ANSWER **1.** grains, vegetables, and fruits
2. oils and meat and beans

Extend It!

Model keeping a food diary by writing a list of your breakfast foods with approximate serving size(s). Demonstrate to students how to read a food label using a milk container or cereal box, and enter the information into the table.

Assess

EVALUATE Use the After You Read questions and the Alternative Assessment to help you assess students' understanding of the lesson.

After You Read

1. Answers will vary; students should provide appropriate sample foods for carbohydrates, proteins, fats, minerals, vitamins, and water.
2. A vitamin is an organic molecule that helps the body build new tissues and important molecules such as hormones. Vitamins also help regulate body functions and fight disease. A mineral is an inorganic element that the body needs for one or more of its metabolic functions.
3. Water is found inside and around the cells and is the largest component of blood. It takes part in most of the metabolic reactions of the body.

Background Information

The USDA's MyPyramid system replaces the Food Pyramid and provides guidance about nutrition, exercise, and fitness. The MyPyramid resources recommend more healthful choices within food groups, as well as serving size and number of servings. Students can receive a personalized MyPyramid Plan by going to **http://www.mypyramid.gov/** and submitting basic information about age, gender, and amount of activity.

Alternative Assessment

EVALUATE Have students use their predictions to write a short paragraph about the importance of good nutrition. Students should discuss the six nutrients—carbohydrates, fats, proteins, vitamins, minerals, and water—and their effects on the body.

21.2 Introduce

ENGAGE Have students brainstorm the parts of the digestive system they are familiar with. List their responses on the board. As students read and discuss this lesson, have them add to the list those parts they did not mention, as well as the function of each recorded part. When you have completed the lesson, have students copy the information from the board into their Science Notebooks.

Before You Read

Model the process of creating the concept map about digestion. Write *Mouth* on the board, and then draw an arrow and write *Esophagus*. Write *Tongue* and *Saliva* so that they connect to *Mouth*. Have students begin their concept maps in a similar manner, and encourage them to allow space to complete the digestive system on the map.

Some students may benefit from sketching some of the digestive system structures on their maps. Have ELLs create diagrams to label, as they follow along with the discussion. Then, vocabulary words can be added to the diagrams to assure more practice with those terms.

Teach

EXPLAIN to students that in this lesson, they will learn about the process of digestion and how organs break down food both physically and chemically.

Use the Visual: Figure 21.7

EXTEND Have students analyze the diagram of the digestive system and write in their Science Notebooks what they already know about each of the organs labeled.

Learning Goals

- Identify the structures that make up the human digestive system.
- Describe how enzymes aid digestion.
- Identify where each kind of mechanical and chemical digestion occurs.

New Vocabulary

ingestion
digestion
enzyme
salivary gland
tongue
taste bud
bolus
esophagus
peristalsis
stomach
chyme
duodenum
liver
pancreas

21.2 The Process of Digestion

Before You Read

Create a concept map for digestion in your Science Notebook. Start with the word *Mouth*. As you read, complete the concept map using the names of the structures that food travels through after it is ingested.

The food you eat has to be broken down into smaller molecules before your body can use it. This process occurs in a series of organs called the digestive tract. Other organs of the digestive system assist by moving food around or by producing chemicals used in digestion.

The digestive tract is a tube with a mouth at one end and an anus at the other end. Food enters the digestive tract at the mouth in a process called **ingestion** (in JES chun). Food moves through a series of organs that break it down into small particles that can pass through cell membranes, a process called **digestion** (di JES chun). The body absorbs the digested food, and any leftover indigestible remains are pushed out of the body.

The organs of the digestive tract break up food in two ways. In mechanical digestion, food is physically chopped up into smaller bits. In chemical digestion, food particles are immersed in chemicals that break the bonds of large molecules. Large molecules are broken into smaller molecules. Mechanical digestion increases the surface area of the food particles and makes chemical digestion more effective. Food can be subjected to both kinds of digestion at the same time.

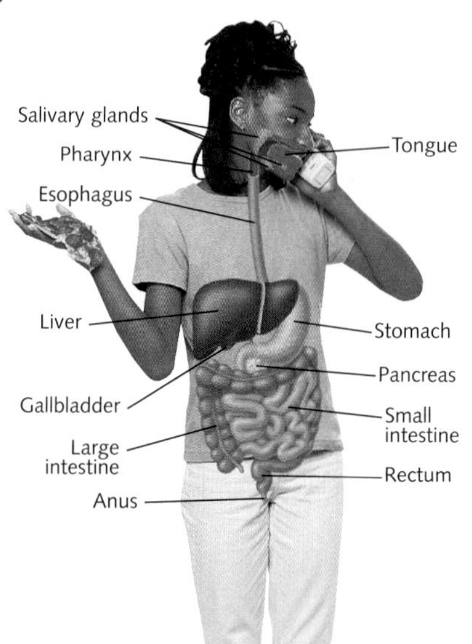

Figure 21.7 The digestive system is made up of many organs that work together in the breakdown of food into nutrients.

ELL Strategy

Activate Background Knowledge Ask students to list in their Science Notebooks the facts they already know about the process of digestion. Then, ask pairs of students to discuss their lists; the discussion may prompt facts that they had forgotten. Have students add to the information in their Science Notebooks as they are reminded.

Enzymes

Enzymes (EN zimez) are proteins that speed up chemical reactions. They make chemical digestion happen. The body could not absorb as much food as it needs without enzymes.

There are many different kinds of enzymes. Each works in only one chemical reaction. Chemical reactions do not change the enzyme. One enzyme molecule can be used over and over again.

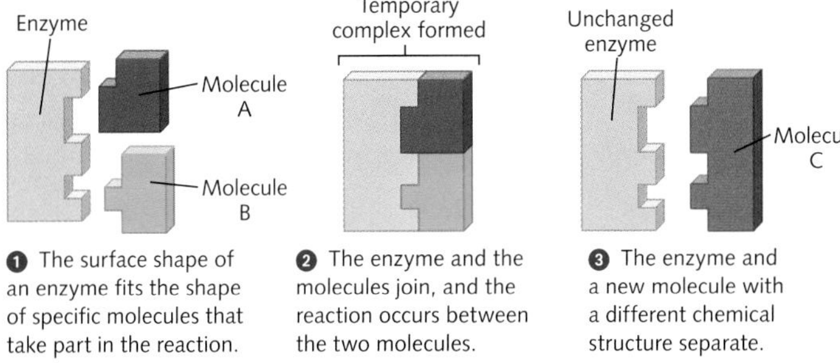

❶ The surface shape of an enzyme fits the shape of specific molecules that take part in the reaction.

❷ The enzyme and the molecules join, and the reaction occurs between the two molecules.

❸ The enzyme and a new molecule with a different chemical structure separate.

Figure 21.8 The surface of each enzyme has a shape that specific molecules fit into like keys in a lock. The reaction between these molecules occurs while they are on the enzyme. The enzyme is not changed.

The Digestive Organs

The organs of the digestive system break down food mechanically and chemically.

Mouth Mechanical and chemical digestion both start in the mouth. Teeth chop up food into smaller bits, creating new surfaces where enzymes can act. The first digestive enzymes to act are found in saliva (suh LI vuh), a fluid that is secreted into the mouth from the **salivary** (SA luh ver ee) **glands**. Saliva contains water to soften food and the enzyme amylase, which breaks starch into shorter sugars.

The **tongue** pushes food around the mouth and mixes it with saliva. The tongue is a muscular organ that can move in many different directions. The top of the tongue is covered with **taste buds**, small bumps that contain sensory receptors. The receptors tell the brain whether food is sweet, sour, salty, savory, or bitter.

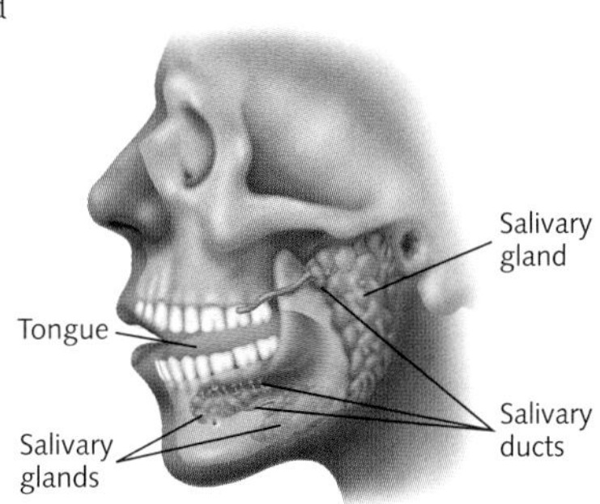

Figure 21.9 Humans have three pairs of salivary glands. Each one has a duct that opens on the inside of the mouth.

Explore It!

You can test whether your mouth digests carbohydrates with crackers and a stopwatch.

Take one plain cracker, and put it in your mouth. Don't chew it. Start a stopwatch at the same time. Hold the cracker in your mouth until it starts tasting sweet. Write the time in your Science Notebook.

Take a sip of water to clear your mouth, and repeat this test with a second cracker. This time, start to chew the cracker when you start the stopwatch. When does this cracker start tasting sweet?

Differentiated Instruction

Kinesthetic Arrange students in groups of three to four, and assign each group an organ from the digestive system. Each group should then act out the role of the organ for the class while the other groups try to guess the organ. Also have students describe the action of each organ being acted out.

Teach

EXPLAIN to students that the process of digestion begins once food or drink enters the mouth. Saliva begins the chemical process and aids the tongue with the physical process.

Vocabulary

ingestion Tell students that *ingestion* is from the Latin word *ingerere,* which means "to carry something in."

digestion Explain to students that *digest* originates from the Latin word *digerere,* which means "to dissolve."

enzyme Tell students that *enzyme* has its derivation in a Greek word meaning "leaven." That word is defined as "lighten or modify." Ask students which definition of *leaven* best matches their understanding of the word *enzyme.*

salivary gland Tell students that *salivary* is an adjective derived from the noun *saliva.* Explain that saliva is a clear alkaline liquid that moistens and softens food and begins the process of digestion. Ask students to identify the connection between the two words. Explain that glands are usually small organs or structures that secrete liquid. The salivary glands secrete saliva.

tongue Explain that the tongue is a muscle used in eating and speaking.

taste bud Tell students that the word *taste* came from the Latin verb meaning "to touch." Encourage students to brainstorm common uses of the word *bud.* Their responses may include a flower bud, a bud on a plant's stem, and something that is not yet developed. Students may also observe their taste buds in a mirror.

Explore It!

Pair students, and provide each group with plain saltine crackers, small cups of water, and a stopwatch. Encourage students to be thoughtful about the activity and to pay active attention to their sense of taste. Have students take turns eating the crackers and watching the time. Partners should agree on a hand signal to start and end the timing.

Teach

EXPLAIN that food moves from the mouth through the esophagus to the stomach. In the stomach, further digestion occurs.

Vocabulary

bolus Tell students that *bolus* is derived from the Greek word *bolos,* which means "a lump."

esophagus Tell students that the prefix *eso-* is derived from *ois-,* which means "to carry." The root *phage* originates from the Greek word *phagos,* which means "food."

peristalsis Explain that *peristalsis* is derived from a Greek word that means to "contract around."

stomach Tell students that *stomach* originated from the Greek word *stoma,* which means "mouth." Remind students that they encountered the word *stoma* when they learned about the structure of a leaf.

chyme Explain that *chyme* comes from the Greek word *chymos,* which means "juice."

duodenum Explain that *duodenum* is from the Latin word *duodecim,* "twelve," due to the idea that the length of this part of the small intestine was twelve fingers' breadth.

liver Explain that the liver is essential in the digestive process and also plays an important role in creating blood proteins and in metabolizing carbohydrates, fats, and proteins.

pancreas Explain that the prefix *pan-* means "all." The root, *creas,* is derived from the Greek word *kreas,* which means "flesh."

Figure It Out: Figure 21.10

ANSWER **1.** When circular muscles contract, the esophagus gets narrower. **2.** If peristalsis reverses itself, food moves *up* the esophagus from the stomach. This phenomenon is known as vomiting.

CONNECTION: Health

Explain that the main cause of ulcers was discovered in 1994. Previously, stress and spicy foods were thought to be the causes. Have students research the bacterium *Heliobacter pylori,* now known to cause ulcers. Have them summarize their findings in a paragraph in their Science Notebooks.

Esophagus Chewing eventually turns food into a soft mass that is pushed into the back of the throat by the tongue. Swallowing pushes a small amount of the processed food called a **bolus** (BOH lus) through the pharynx. As the bolus moves through the pharynx, an involuntary reflex pulls a flap of cartilage called the epiglottis over the opening to the trachea. This reflex keeps food out of the airway and pushes the bolus into the esophagus.

The **esophagus** (ih SAH fuh gus) is a 25-cm-long tube that connects the pharynx with the stomach. It is lined with cells that secrete mucus to keep the bolus wet as it moves through the tube. The esophagus is also lined with smooth muscles. The muscles take turns contracting, creating a wavelike motion called **peristalsis** (per uh STAHL sus) that pushes food toward the stomach.

Figure It Out

1. What happens to the esophagus when the circular muscles contract?
2. Describe what could happen if peristalsis reversed itself in the stomach and esophagus. What might this phenomenon be called?

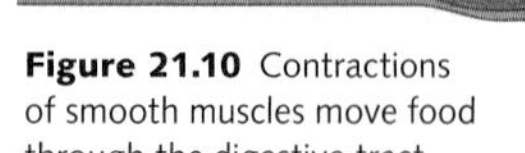

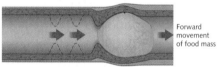

Figure 21.10 Contractions of smooth muscles move food through the digestive tract.

Stomach As food leaves the esophagus, it enters a large, muscular bag called the **stomach**. The stomach has three jobs. It chemically digests food by secreting strong acid and the enzyme pepsin, which breaks down protein chains. It mechanically breaks the boluses of food and saliva into smaller particles and mixes them with stomach enzymes to make a semiliquid mixture called **chyme** (KIME). The stomach also stores food, slowly releasing it into the small intestine between meals.

Some cells in the stomach wall secrete mucus, which forms a protective layer that covers the stomach wall and neutralizes any acid that comes near it. If the layer is damaged, acids can burn into the stomach tissue and cause an ulcer.

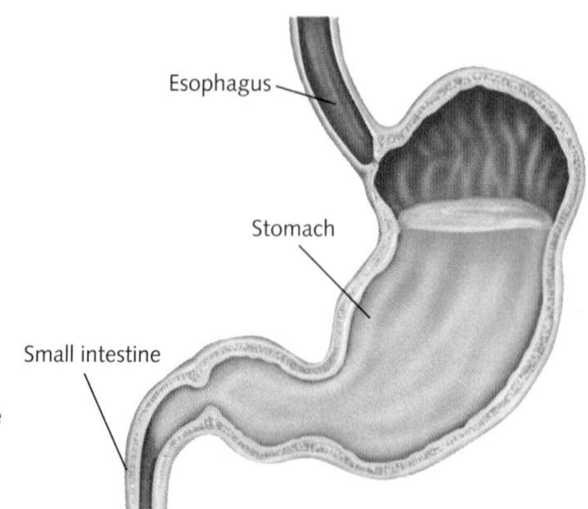

Figure 21.11 The stomach secretes hydrochloric acid, which softens the connective tissue in meat and activates the enzyme that breaks up proteins.

Background Information

At least eighty percent of stomach ulcers are caused by an acid-resistant bacterium called *Helicobacter pylori.* The bacterium grows on the stomach wall and destroys the mucus that protects the stomach tissue. Often, *H. pylori* causes no problems. But, sometimes, it attacks the mucous layer and inflames and erodes the tissue, producing an ulcer. By itself, the bacterium is not enough to cause ulcers. Other factors thought to be involved include smoking, alcohol use, and different strains of the bacterium. *H. pylori* can be passed from person to person through close contact.

The usual symptom of an ulcer is a gnawing or burning pain in the abdomen between the breastbone and belly button, often when the stomach is empty. The pain may be relieved by eating foods or taking antacids. Treatment to cure an ulcer includes one to two weeks of antibiotics, a medicine that reduces acid in the stomach, and lifestyle changes.

382 DIGESTIVE AND EXCRETORY SYSTEMS

Small Intestine The last stages of digestion occur in the small intestine. The small intestine is the longest part of the digestive tract. It is a muscular, 6-m-long tube that is coiled up inside the abdomen. It is called the "small" intestine because it is narrow—only about 2.5 cm wide.

The first section of the small intestine is called the **duodenum** (doo AH dun um). Most digestion happens here. Chyme enters the duodenum from the stomach. The chyme is still very acidic, so the lining of the duodenum secretes mucus for protection. Cells in the wall of the duodenum secrete enzymes that break up the carbohydrates and proteins in the chyme. The liver and pancreas add other enzymes and digestive chemicals to the chyme. Peristaltic contractions of the smooth muscle in the wall of the small intestine mix the chyme with these chemicals and push it down the digestive tract.

The Liver and Pancreas The liver and pancreas are important parts of the digestive system even though food does not move through them. They both make chemicals that aid digestion. The chemicals are sent to the small intestine through small tubes called ducts.

The **liver** is a large organ tucked underneath the diaphragm. It has many functions. Its job in digestion is to make bile, which breaks down fat. The bile made by the liver is stored in a small organ called the gallbladder. When it contracts, the gallbladder squirts bile into the small intestine.

The **pancreas** (PAN kree us) is a leaf-shaped organ that lies on top of the duodenum. It makes both digestive enzymes and hormones. The enzymes that the pancreas makes digest proteins, carbohydrates, fats, and DNA and RNA chains. The pancreas also makes large amounts of an alkaline fluid that reduces the harmful effect that the acid in the chyme would have on the small intestine.

As You Read

On the concept map in your Science Notebook, write *M* next to each organ that digests food mechanically. Write *C* next to each organ that chemically digests food. Compare your concept map with a partner's. Make adjustments or additions as needed.

What enzyme in saliva begins the digestive process? What enzyme in the stomach breaks down protein chains?

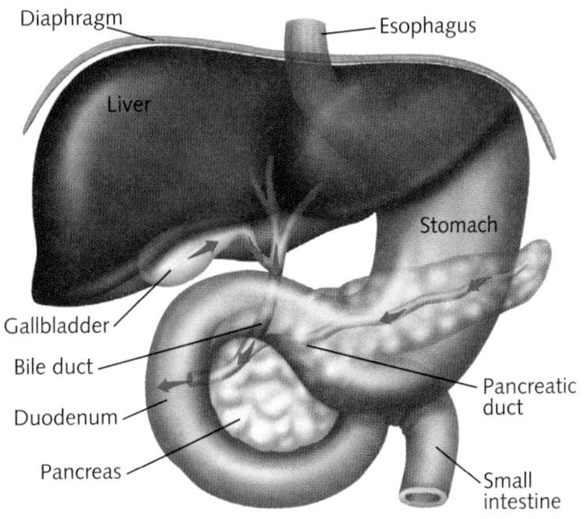

Figure 21.12 The liver and pancreas make digestive chemicals and send them into the small intestine.

After You Read

1. Think of a way to include the liver and pancreas on the concept map in your Science Notebook. Where do they release digestive chemicals?
2. What happens to amylase after it helps break starch into sugars?
3. Which organ makes bile? What does bile do?
4. How is the stomach protected from the strong acid it produces?

Teach

EXPLAIN that digestion continues in the small intestine and that the liver and pancreas both make digestive chemicals that enter the small intestine.

As You Read

Give students a few minutes to update their maps. Students should write both *M* and *C* next to the mouth, stomach, and small intestine and *C* next to the salivary glands, the liver, and the pancreas.

ANSWER Amylase in saliva begins the digestive process. Pepsin in the stomach breaks down protein chains.

Assess

EVALUATE Use the After You Read questions and the Alternative Assessment to help you assess students' understanding of the lesson.

After You Read

1. The concept maps should place the liver and pancreas near the small intestine, with dotted lines pointing to the small intestine. Both release digestive chemicals into the small intestine.
2. Nothing happens. Amylase is an enzyme, and enzymes are not changed by the reactions they mediate.
3. The liver makes bile. Bile helps break down fat.
4. Some cells in the stomach wall secrete mucus. The mucus forms a protective layer that covers the stomach wall and neutralizes any acid that comes near it.

Background Information

The pancreas secretes the hormones insulin, glucagon, and somatostatin. The first two regulate the level of glucose in the blood; the latter prevents the release of the first two.

The liver conducts more than 500 vital functions for the body, some of which include producing proteins for blood plasma, processing hemoglobin for use of its iron, converting excess glucose into glycogen for storage, clearing the blood of drugs and other poisonous substances, regulating blood clotting, regulating blood levels of hemoglobin, and converting poisonous ammonia to urea.

Alternative Assessment

EVALUATE Have students use their concept maps to describe three or four different structures involved in digestion. Students should write a few sentences for each structure describing where it is in the digestive process and how it functions.

21.3 Introduce

ENGAGE Pair students, and provide each group with two graduated cylinders, water, and a variety of absorbent materials, such as white paper, brown (industrial) paper towels, regular paper towels, and sponges. Each student pair should create an experiment to determine which material is the most absorbent. After students have finished their experiments, ask them to infer the characteristic(s) that made some materials more absorbent than others. Tell them that these same characteristics are at work in the human body as it absorbs nutrients from food.

Before You Read

Have students continue to add to their concept maps. Remind them to add sketches when it is helpful to their understanding. Check students' maps for accuracy.

Teach

EXPLAIN to students that the next part of the digestive process, absorption of food, begins in the small intestine. This process allows the nutrients in food to fuel the human body.

Vocabulary

absorption Tell students that the prefix *ab-* means "away." The root *sorp* is derived from the Latin word *sorbēre,* meaning "to suck."

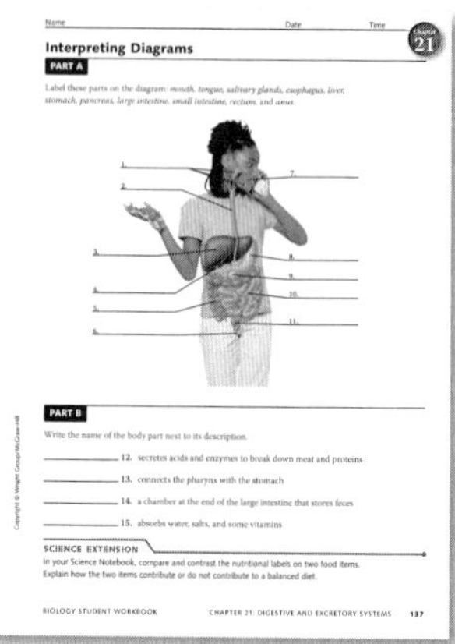

Interpreting Diagrams Workbook, p. 137

Learning Goals

- Describe how the area for absorption is increased in the small intestine.
- Identify what the large intestine absorbs.
- Explain how nutrients enter the bloodstream.

New Vocabulary

absorption
villus

21.3 Absorption of Food

Before You Read

Continue the concept map you started in Lesson 21.2. Add information about the last part of the digestive tract in the appropriate place.

Before the food inside the intestines can be used to provide energy and build new tissues, it has to be moved through the intestinal wall and into the bloodstream. This process is called **absorption** (ab SORP shun).

Food molecules do not just "leak" into the bloodstream. The cells that line the inside of the intestines are similar to the cells in the skin. They are bound together by tiny proteins that form a tight seal. Nothing can squeeze between those cells, so every molecule that enters the bloodstream has to move through the cells. Some molecules move by diffusion, and others are moved by active transport. Each molecule must pass through a cell membrane before it gets into the blood. This step is a filtering process that controls which molecules get in and which ones stay out.

The Small Intestine

Chyme moves through the small intestine in just a few hours. This is the only time the nutrients in food can be absorbed. The small intestine has many adaptations that give it a larger surface for absorbing nutrients.

The small intestine is long—typically three times longer than the body, as **Figure 21.13** shows. A long small intestine means that chyme moves past many absorption surfaces before it enters the large intestine.

Figure 21.13 If the small intestine were stretched out, it would be three times longer than the body. Its enormous length creates a large absorptive area for food to pass through.

ELL Strategy

Model Using anatomy reference books and this text, have students work together to draw a life-sized model of the digestive system. They should include and label all organs and list the functions next to each organ. Students could use colors to indicate whether the organ serves to digest food chemically or mechanically and to show where absorption occurs. Alternatively, pairs could create models without labels. Students can then exchange models with another pair who will label the diagram. Finally, the pairs should compare the final product to assess the completeness and accuracy of the drawings.

384 DIGESTIVE AND EXCRETORY SYSTEMS

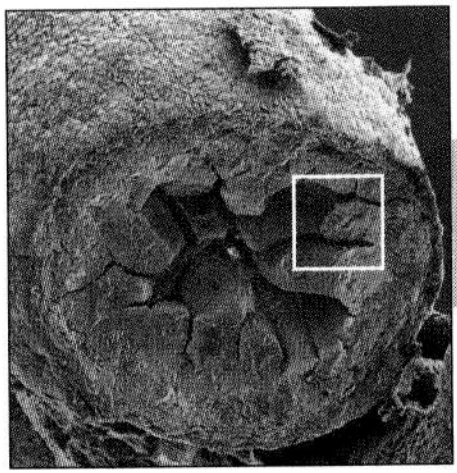
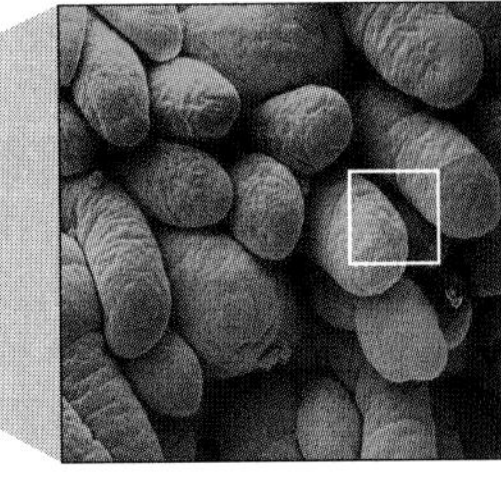
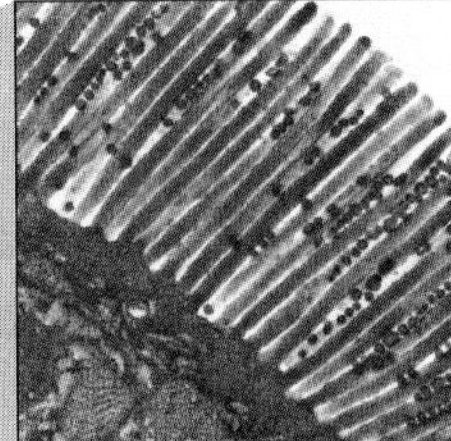

Figure 21.14 The inner surface of the small intestine is very large because it is folded on three levels. Tissue folds into the inside of the small intestine *(left)*. Villi cover the surface of the folds *(center)*. Each cell on the villi has microvilli on its surface *(right)*.

The inner surface of the small intestine is not smooth and flat. It has folds and millions of fingerlike projections called **villi** (VIH li, singular: villus) on each of those folds. Each villus contains a small artery and vein connected by capillaries and a small lymph vessel. Each villus is also covered with a layer of tightly bound cells. Each of these cells has a brush of tiny folds called microvilli on its surface. The folding inner surface and the presence of villi and microvilli, shown in **Figure 21.14**, greatly increase the surface area of the small intestine.

As You Read

Review the concept map in your Science Notebook. Predict what would happen to a person's weight if half of the villi in his or her small intestine disappeared. Write a sentence describing your prediction.

How Absorption Works

Nutrients are absorbed through the cells that line the surface of the villi. Sugars, short proteins, some vitamins and minerals, and simple fatty acids move through the cell membranes of the villi. Some nutrients move passively by diffusion, and others move by active transport. All of the nutrients move through the intestinal cells and are absorbed by capillaries on the other side.

Other nutrients take a different path into the bloodstream. Fats and fat-soluble vitamins are both absorbed by lymphatic vessels in the villi. These nutrients move through the lymphatic system and enter the blood near the heart. After the nutrients enter the blood, they are carried to all the other cells in the body.

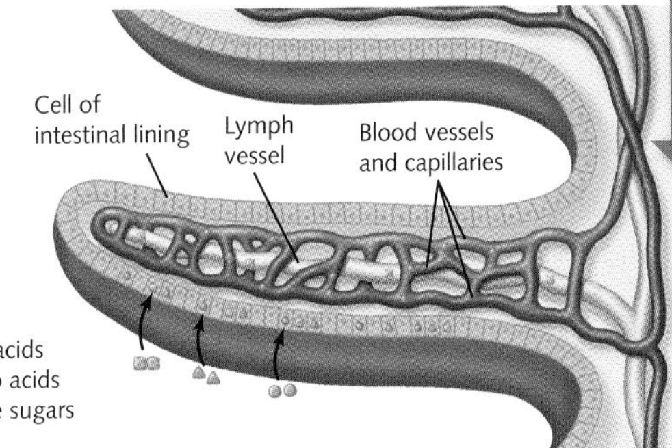

Figure 21.15 The cells of the villi transport nutrients from the inside of the intestine to blood and lymph vessels. From there, they enter the bloodstream.

Figure It Out

1. Which molecules are moving into the blood and lymph vessels in the villi?
2. Reflect on what could happen if a tumor blocked off the arteries that bring blood to the intestines.

Teach

EXPLAIN to students that the unique surface of the small intestine enables it to absorb nutrients efficiently. Remind students of the characteristics of the sponge from the activity at the start of this lesson and how it absorbed more water than the other materials did.

Vocabulary

villus Explain to students that *villus* is derived from the Latin word meaning "shaggy hair." Have students use Figure 21.14 to explain why this is an appropriate name for the fingerlike projections.

Use the Visual: Figure 21.14

EXPLAIN Call students' attention to the three photos in the figure. Be sure that they understand that the second photo is a magnified view of the inner surface of the small intestine, shown in the first photo. Then, point out that the third photo is a highly magnified view of the surface of one of the villi, the fingerlike structures seen in the center photo.

EXPLORE Suggest that students go to the MEDtropolis Web site at **http://www.medtropolis.com/VBody.asp**, where they can take a virtual tour of the digestive system that includes text and audio explanations. Students can also participate in the Organize Your Organs activity, in which they place digestive organs in the correct place on the human body.

As You Read

Give students a few minutes to update their concept maps with their newly gained knowledge.

ANSWER Cutting the absorptive ability of the small intestine in half should make a person lose weight.

Figure It Out: Figure 21.15

ANSWER **1.** The diagram shows sugars and amino acids moving into the intestinal cells. **2.** The intestinal tissue would be starved for oxygen, but the rest of the body would be starved for nutrients.

Differentiated Instruction

Kinesthetic Provide students with a variety of decorative materials such as felt, thread, yarn, fabric paint, glue, fake feathers, tissue paper, etc. Have students work in groups to create models of the inner surface of the small intestine, including the folds, villi, and microvilli. Display and discuss the model created by each group.

Teach

EXPLAIN that during absorption, food molecules are broken down to release the nutrients that are used by the body. Glucose is used to produce energy, amino acids are made into proteins, nucleic acids are used to make new DNA and RNA, and unused energy is stored as fat.

CONNECTION: Zoology

Have students work in small groups to research some common human worm infections, such as *Ascaris, Hymenolepsis nana, Trichuriasis*, and *Enterobiasis*. Students can use encyclopedias and/or online references such as the CDC Web site at **http://www.dpd.cdc.gov/dpdx/HTML/Frames/body_intest_listing.htm**.

Students should include in their research how the worm is transmitted, how it is treated, and what geographic area is most commonly infected. Student groups should present their information to the class.

EXTEND Have each student write a speech in his or her Science Notebook explaining in everyday language how to avoid most tapeworm infections. Students could role-play a scientist educating a class of younger children about the importance of good hygiene practices, especially thorough hand-washing.

Nutrients in the Body

Cells break down some of the food molecules to release the chemical energy stored in their bonds. Molecules that are used for energy are first converted to glucose. Glucose, a simple sugar, is the main energy source for the body. Cells break down glucose bit by bit during a process called cellular respiration. The first part of the process occurs in the cytoplasm, but it does not release much energy. The rest of the process, which releases large quantities of energy, occurs inside organelles called mitochondria. The energy released by cellular respiration is stored in molecules of a chemical called adenosine triphosphate, or ATP.

Cells use some nutrients as the building blocks for larger and more complex molecules. Amino acids are strung into proteins, building functional molecules such as enzymes as well as those that make up tendons, muscles, and skin. Nucleic acids are used to make new strands of DNA and RNA. Unused energy is stored in fats.

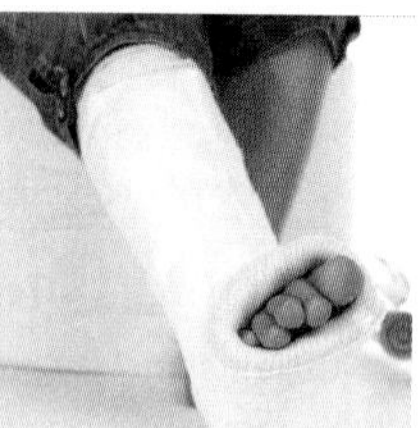

Figure 21.16 Nutrients in food are used by the body for energy and tissue repair.

CONNECTION: Zoology

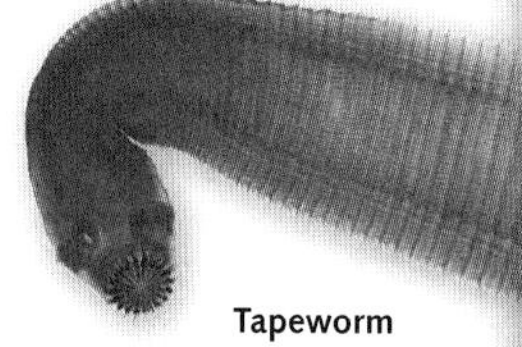

Tapeworm

It may surprise you to learn that there are many organisms that live inside the intestines and absorb the food the body has digested. To these organisms, the body is a habitat!

Some organisms provide something in return for the habitat the body supplies. For example, the bacteria that live inside the intestine are symbiotes. The body provides food and shelter, and the bacteria eat the material that the body cannot digest and secrete vitamins that the body can use.

Other organisms give nothing in return. Parasites such as roundworms and flatworms can live inside the digestive system and absorb food, sometimes causing sickness.

Flatworms from the genus *Taenia* are the source of most human tapeworm infections. They also infect pigs and cows, so eating undercooked meat can be a means of transmitting the tapeworm. When a larval tapeworm gets inside a person, it attaches to the intestinal wall with its spiky head and starts to grow. Adult worms can grow to 7 m long. They have no digestive or circulatory systems, so they simply absorb nutrients directly from the chyme.

Background Information

Tapeworms are flatworms that spend the adult phase of life as a parasite in the intestine of a primary host, a vertebrate animal. Many tapeworms spend a different phase of their life in tissues of intermediate hosts; these may be vertebrates or arthropods. Adult tapeworms living in human intestines often do not cause much harm, but the larvae can cause serious diseases that may lead to death, if left untreated.

Field Study

With permission from the staff, have students tour the kitchen area of the school cafeteria in small groups. Ask staff members to share with students some of the procedures they follow to ensure that food is prepared safely. Topics addressed could include hand-washing, wearing gloves, water temperature for washing dishes, food-washing, and the cleaning of food preparation areas.

The Large Intestine

The large intestine is wider than the small intestine and much shorter—it is only 1.5 m long. It surrounds the small intestine, starting at the lower right portion of the abdomen and running up, across, and down the left side of the abdominal cavity.

By the time the chyme reaches the large intestine, most of the nutrients have been removed from it. It now contains indigestible materials, such as cellulose, and a lot of water. The large intestine reabsorbs most of the water—between 400 and 1,000 mL. This process allows the body to reuse the water and keeps it from getting dehydrated.

Some of the bacteria that live inside the large intestine can digest cellulose. The bacteria give off gas as a waste product of metabolism. They also secrete vitamin K and two B vitamins, thiamine (B_1) and niacin (B_3), that are absorbed by the large intestine.

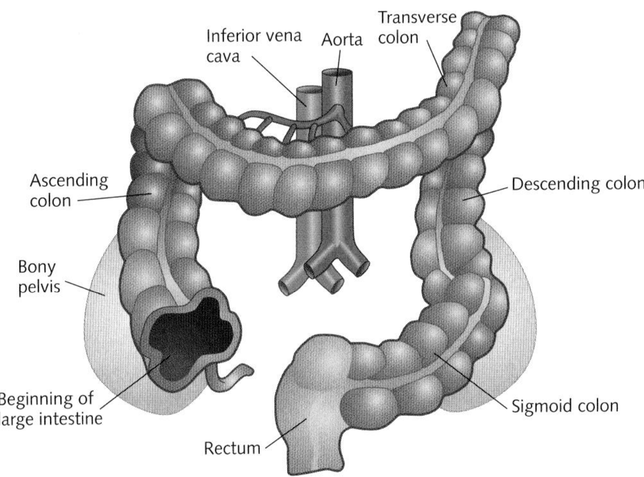

Figure 21.18 The large intestine absorbs water, salts, and some vitamins.

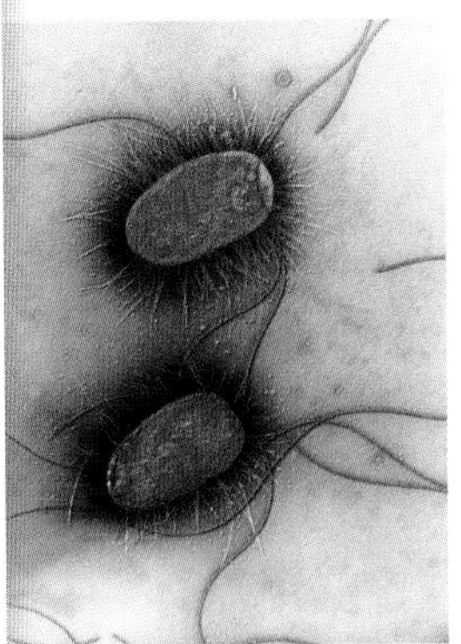

Figure 21.17 Bacteria such as these *E. coli* cells live symbiotically inside the large intestine. Humans give them food and shelter. They give humans vitamins K, B_1, and B_3.

After You Read

1. On the concept map in your Science Notebook, draw a box around the organs that digest food. In a different color, draw another box around the organs that absorb food. Where do the boxes overlap? Write a well-developed paragraph describing the structures and functions of the digestive system.
2. Name two things the large intestine absorbs.
3. Why do the intestinal cells act as filters when they absorb nutrients?

Teach

EXPLAIN to students that absorption is nearly finished when the digested food enters the large intestine. Bacteria living in the large intestine are able to digest cellulose and make vitamin K, niacin, and thiamine.

Science Notebook EXTRA

Have students research foods that contain cellulose, also known as insoluble fiber, and the associated health benefits. Instruct students to record their findings in their Science Notebooks. Explain that foods with soluble fiber are also important to include in one's diet. If time permits, have students research and report on those, as well.

Assess

EVALUATE Use the After You Read questions and the Alternative Assessment to help you assess students' understanding of the lesson.

After You Read

1. The boxes will overlap on the small intestine. Students' paragraphs should accurately summarize the discussion of the digestive system in this lesson.
2. The large intestine absorbs water, vitamins, and salts.
3. The intestinal cells, like all cells, are surrounded by a selectively permeable membrane, which only allows certain kinds of molecules to pass through it. The cell membranes ensure that the rest of the substances in digested food stay inside the small intestine.

Background Information

Foods that are high in insoluble fiber help prevent constipation, manage diabetes, and control weight. Nuts, whole-grain breads and cereals, fruits and vegetables with skins, popcorn, brown rice, and wheat bran are all good sources of insoluble fiber.

The benefits of soluble fiber include lowered bad cholesterol, assistance with the digestive process, and diabetes management. Foods high in soluble fiber include apples, barley, beans, beets, carrots, cranberries, grapefruit, concord grapes, oats, oranges, peaches, pears, prunes, rye, and sesame seeds.

Alternative Assessment

EVALUATE Have each student use his or her concept map to write a paragraph from the viewpoint of a cracker entering a person's mouth. Students should explain the journey the cracker takes through the digestive process.

21.4 Introduce

ENGAGE Arrange students in small groups, and have them list all the ways in which they manage leftover food in their households. Lists may include reheating the foods to eat at a later time, using leftover food in a new dish, throwing the food away, composting the food, or feeding the food to a pet.

EXPLAIN to students that some of these processes are similar to the processes that the human body undergoes as it digests and eliminates food. Some food is utilized in the body (similar to reheating foods or making a new dish), while some is eliminated in different ways (similar to turning leftovers into trash, compost, or pet food).

Before You Read

Model the process by rewording the first Learning Goal into a question. Encourage students to allow space between questions to write their answers.

Teach

EXPLAIN to students that the end result of digestion, if food is not absorbed, is excretion, or the removal of wastes. Wastes are excreted as liquids, solids, or gases.

Use the Visual: Figure 21.19

ANSWER Cellulose is a carbohydrate made of a long chain of glucose molecules. Cellulose makes up the cell walls of plants. It cannot be digested by the human body.

Learning Goals

- Define excretion.
- Identify the solid, liquid, and gaseous wastes the human body excretes.

New Vocabulary

excretion
feces
urine
sweat
urea

21.4 What Is Excretion?

Before You Read

Reword the headings of this lesson so that they form questions. Write the questions in your Science Notebook. Write answers to the questions as you read.

Every factory makes wastes. The human body is no exception. Some wastes can be recycled and reused in other processes. Many wastes, however, are useless to the body. These molecules become poisonous if they build up in the tissues.

Fortunately, the body has systems that remove wastes from the tissues and dump them outside of the body. The process of waste removal is called **excretion** (ihk SKREE shun). Waste is excreted as solids, liquids, and gases.

Solid Wastes

Not everything a person eats can be digested. The solid materials left over after the digestion and absorption of food are called **feces** (FEE seez). Human feces contain water, dead bacteria, bile, salts, and indigestible material such as cellulose.

Most plant tissue is made of cellulose fibers, shown in **Figure 21.19**. Although people can chop up cellulose with their teeth, they do not make enzymes that can digest it. Cellulose passes through the human digestive system unchanged. When the material that holds cellulose fibers together gets digested, the fibers separate into individual strands. These strands absorb water, making feces softer and easier to excrete. This is the reason fiber is an important part of a balanced diet.

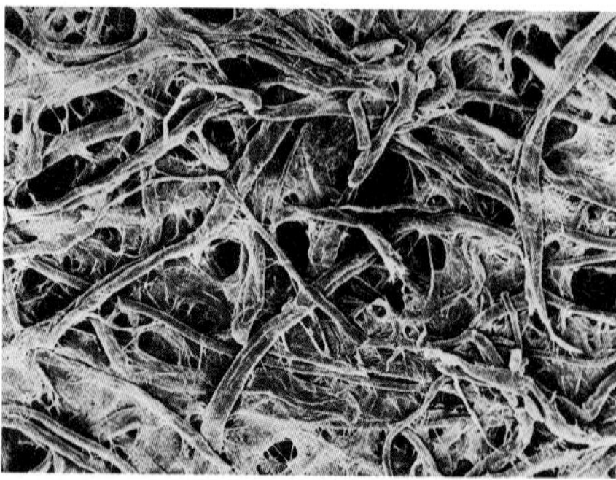

Figure 21.19 Humans cannot digest the cellulose in plant tissues. What is cellulose?

ELL Strategy

Review with students the meaning of the word *waste*. Have students offer examples of waste material (the examples need not be related to digestion). Then, discuss the meanings of the words *solid*, *liquid*, and *gas*. Students may have forgotten what these words mean. Have each student create a three-column chart in his or her Science Notebook, using these three words as the column titles. As they read, encourage students to put the waste they are learning about, and the organs that produce the wastes, in the correct column.

Liquid Wastes

Liquid wastes are excreted in **urine** (YOOR un) and in **sweat**. Both of these wastes are more than 90 percent water. Waste nitrogen and salts are suspended in the water. The exact amount of water in the urine depends on how hydrated the body is. A person excretes more water when he or she is well hydrated than when he or she is dehydrated.

Amino acids are absorbed from food, but the body has no way to store them from day to day. If they are not used immediately in building a new protein, they are broken down for energy. This process releases waste nitrogen as ammonia. Ammonia is toxic, so the body converts it to a less harmful chemical called **urea** (you REE uh). The kidneys filter urea out of the blood for excretion.

Urine also contains salts that the body no longer needs and pigments that make the urine look yellow. Some of the pigments come from the breakdown of old red blood cells. The kidneys filter these molecules out of the blood. Urine is sterile, or free of microorganisms, in the upper part of the urinary tract. As urine flows through the tubes that take it out of the body, the urine cleanses the tubes of microorganisms that could produce infection.

Sweat is excreted from glands in the skin. It cools the body as it evaporates. These glands make sweat by filtering the fluid surrounding the cells. Like urine, sweat contains small molecules such as salts, but it does not contain larger molecules such as proteins. The salts and a small amount of urea are left behind on the skin as the water in the sweat evaporates.

Figure 21.21 Liquid wastes are also excreted when a person sweats.

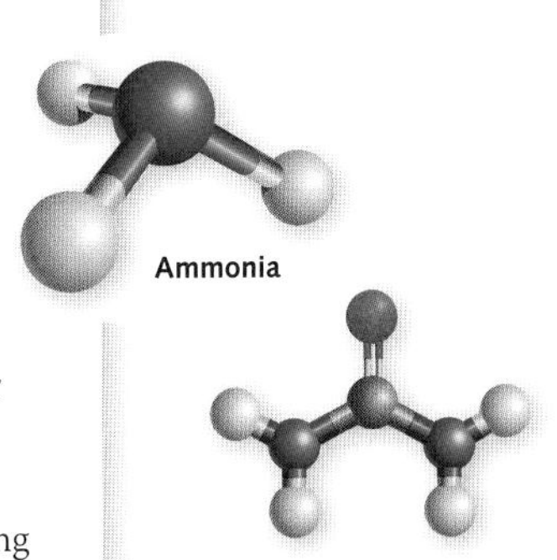

Figure 21.20 Amino acid breakdown releases ammonia, which the body converts into less toxic forms such as urea.

As You Read

Use the answers to the questions you wrote in your Science Notebook to write a few sentences that explain the following statement: Solid wastes contain materials that cannot be chemically processed. Liquid wastes contain the end result of chemical processing.

Teach

EXPLAIN to students that sweat and urine are byproducts of digestion and other metabolic process. Both liquids contain mostly water and some other molecules. The primary purpose of sweat is to cool the body, and urine is excreted to rid the body of urea.

Vocabulary

excretion Explain that *excretion* is derived from the Latin word *excernere,* which means "to sift out."

feces Tell students that *feces* comes from a fifteenth century word meaning "sediment" or "dregs."

urine Explain that urine is the liquid waste filtered from the blood by the kidneys. Tell students that urination is the act of eliminating urine from the body. Students are probably familiar with this word.

sweat Tell students that sweat is produced by the sweat glands and excreted through the pores of the skin.

urea Explain to students that *urea* originates from the Greek word *ouron,* meaning "urine."

As You Read

Have students review and answer their Learning Goal questions. Check students' responses for accuracy.

ANSWER Solid wastes are materials that the human body cannot digest and thus cannot absorb. These materials pass through the digestive system, but they are not chemically processed because body enzymes cannot break them down. They are excreted as feces along with water, dead bacteria, bile, and salts. Liquid wastes contain water and the products of digestion that the body cannot use. These products are formed as a result of the chemical breakdown of foods.

Differentiated Instruction

Logical and Mathematical Have students calculate how much water they should drink on a weekly basis, given that they should drink about eight cups (eight ounces) of water a day. For every continual hour of exercise in which they engage, they should drink an extra two to three cups of water.

Background Information

People perspire in varying amounts all day long. In a cooler environment, a small amount of perspiration, known as insensible perspiration, evaporates almost immediately. When a person is in a warmer environment or is exercising, more perspiration, known as sensible perspiration, is produced, and the person may notice that he or she is sweating. The hypothalamus receives messages from heat receptors in the skin and from blood and maintains body temperature by sending nerve impulses that tell sweat glands to produce sweat.

Teach

EXPLAIN to students that carbon dioxide gas is a product of cellular respiration and is excreted during exhalation.

Figure It Out: Figure 21.22

ANSWER **1.** Oxygen goes into the body during inhalation. **2.** Exercise makes the muscles burn more glucose for energy, dumping large amounts of CO_2 into the bloodstream. Breathing faster (panting) increases the rate at which CO_2 is excreted.

Explain It!

A window or a mirror fogs up when you breathe on it because you also excrete some water vapor when you exhale. The water vapor condenses (changes from a gas to a liquid) on the cooler surface of a window or a mirror.

Assess

EVALUATE Use the After You Read questions and the Alternative Assessment to help you assess students' understanding of the lesson.

After You Read

1. Two liquid wastes are urine and sweat.
2. Excretion is the process of removing wastes from the body. Ingestion is the process of putting food (nutrients) into the body.
3. Gaseous waste is the result of chemical processes. Carbon dioxide is the end product of cellular respiration.

Alternative Assessment

EVALUATE Have students use the Learning Goal questions from their Science Notebooks to compare and contrast the form in which waste is excreted: gas, liquid, and solid. Students should compare the components of the wastes and the processes by which they are excreted.

Gaseous Wastes

Cellular respiration takes glucose and turns it into energy, water, and carbon dioxide. The body can reuse the water in many of its cellular processes. The carbon dioxide, however, is a waste gas. It is carried to the lungs by the blood and is excreted during exhalation.

Figure It Out

1. This person is releasing carbon dioxide during exhalation. What goes into the body during inhalation?
2. Hypothesize why a person breathes faster after exercising than when resting.

Figure 21.22 Carbon dioxide gas is excreted when a person exhales.

Explain It!

Think about the way a mirror or a windowpane fogs up when you breathe on it. In your Science Notebook, write a sentence explaining why this happens.

Carbon dioxide is carried by the blood in three ways. A little bit of the gas dissolves in the plasma. Some of the gas binds to hemoglobin and gets carried in the red blood cells. But most of the carbon dioxide reacts with water to form bicarbonate, which gets carried by the cytoplasm of red blood cells and plasma. Because the blood can carry carbon dioxide in three different ways, it can move more of the gas out of the body.

After You Read

1. Name the two liquid wastes the human body makes.
2. Define excretion. Explain how it differs from ingestion.
3. Review the information you have recorded in your Science Notebook. Explain whether or not gaseous waste is the result of chemical processes.

Background Information

Cellular respiration can occur with and without oxygen. Glycolysis occurs in the absence of oxygen; it is the process by which glucose is broken down into pyruvic acid, thereby releasing energy in the form of adenosine triphosphate (ATP). ATP supplies energy to all cells. Glycolysis produces only a small amount of ATP.

When oxygen is present during cellular respiration, pyruvic acid begins the Krebs cycle, which is a series of chemical reactions. Energy is cycled through a series of different reactions, known as the electron transport chain. The end products are carbon dioxide, water, and ATP. Large amounts of ATP are produced by this process.

21.5 Organs of Excretion

Before You Read

Preview the lesson by reading the headings. In your Science Notebook, create a three-column chart. Label the first column *Organ*, the second column *Waste Produced*, and the third column *Origin of Waste*. Fill in the chart as you read the lesson.

Learning Goals

- Name the organs of excretion.
- Identify where urea is made.
- Understand how the kidney produces urine.

New Vocabulary

rectum
anus
nephron
glomerulus
reabsorption
ureter
bladder
urethra
sweat gland

Many organs in the human body are involved in excretion. Solid wastes are processed and expelled by the large intestine. Carbon dioxide diffuses into the lungs as gas to be exhaled. The liver is an important site for filtering the blood and converting poisons into less toxic materials. The kidneys filter the blood to remove liquid wastes from the body.

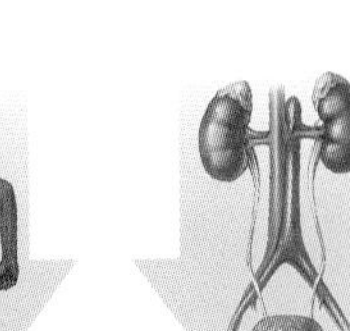

Figure 21.23 The excretory system is made up of several different body systems.

Large Intestine

The large intestine reabsorbs water and salts from chyme. It is also the organ where indigestible material from food is compacted into feces. Chyme is pushed through the large intestine by peristaltic contractions of the smooth muscle in its wall. As the chyme moves up, across, and down the body, water is pulled out of it and indigestible material such as cellulose is left behind.

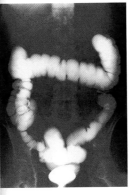

Figure 21.24 This X-ray image of the large intestine shows the path of the organ around the abdomen and down to the rectum.

21.5 Introduce

ENGAGE Write the following words on the board: *paper, electricity, fabric,* and *fertilizer.* Ask students to guess which of these items cannot be a product of animal manure, and ask them to explain their responses. After students have shared their ideas, give them the origin of each item.

Paper – Kangaroo feces contain pulp that can be made into paper.

Electricity – Cow manure releases methane gas that can be used to produce electricity.

Fabric – not a product of animal manure

Fertilizer – A variety of barnyard animals' manure can be used directly as fertilizer.

EXPLAIN that human waste is different and cannot be recycled. Tell students that in this lesson, they will be learning more about what organs produce waste.

Before You Read

Draw the three-column chart on the board, and then model the process of previewing the first heading. In the first row of the chart, write *Large Intestine*. Have students finish previewing the lesson and complete the *Organ* column in their own charts.

Teach

EXPLAIN to students that in this lesson, they will learn about the organs of the excretory system, starting with the large intestine.

ELL Strategy

Model Have students work in small groups to draw and label the organs in the excretory system. Students should use the vocabulary terms from this lesson to identify the characteristic parts of each organ.

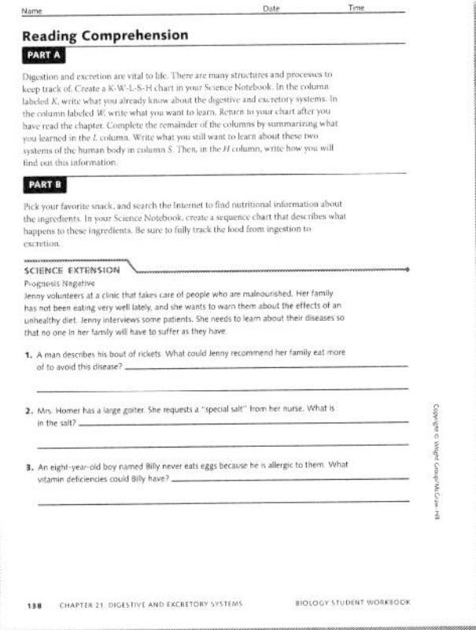

Reading Comprehension Workbook, p. 138

Teach

EXPLAIN to students that in this section, they will learn about the lungs and the liver. The lungs are part of both the respiratory and excretory systems. Similarly, the liver is part of the excretory and digestive systems.

EXPLORE To demonstrate how bile breaks down fat, have students mix detergent, oil, and water. Pair students, and provide each pair with two clear 250-mL containers, dishwashing detergent, a small container of vegetable oil, water, and two stirring sticks.

Direct students to pour about 120 mL of water into each cup and then add enough oil (to both cups) to create a complete layer on top of the water. Tell students to observe the oil immediately and then again in three minutes. Have them record both of their observations in their Science Notebooks.

Have students then add about seven drops of detergent to one of the cups. They should stir both cups with the sticks for about 15 seconds. Have them observe both cups regularly over the next five minutes and then again in about an hour. Remind them to record all observations in their Science Notebooks.

Students should note that in the cup that contains the detergent, the oil has broken into small pieces. Discuss with the class the similarities between detergent and bile.

As You Read

Give students about five minutes to update their charts. Review students' charts for accuracy, or have them peer-review one another's work.

ANSWER The liver changes toxic ammonia into urea and breaks down toxins such as alcohol and drugs, enabling the body to safely dispose of these wastes. A nephron looks like a long tube with a cup at one end. The cups of the nephrons are found in the outer rim of the kidney, called the cortex. Each tube, or tubule, extends into the center of the kidney. The cup of a nephron surrounds a ball of capillaries called the glomerulus.

Indigestible material collects near the end of the large intestine and gets compressed into solid feces. Solid feces are next pushed into the **rectum** (REK tum), a chamber at the end of the large intestine that stores feces until they can be excreted. When the rectum fills, a person gets the urge to defecate, or push the solid wastes out of the body. Feces leave the body through the opening at the far end of the large intestine, called the **anus** (AY nus).

Lungs

The lungs excrete gaseous wastes. Carbon dioxide is a waste product of cellular respiration. It diffuses into the blood and is pumped into the alveoli of the lungs by the heart. The air inside the alveoli contains far less carbon dioxide than does the deoxygenated blood coming from the heart. Because molecules diffuse from areas where they are concentrated to areas where they are less concentrated, carbon dioxide leaves the blood and diffuses across the alveoli and into the air. Air that is rich in carbon dioxide is exhaled, releasing the gaseous waste outside the body.

Liver

The liver is the largest internal organ. It is a huge gland with four lobes, each of which is built out of many small, roughly hexagonal units called lobules. Lobules contain liver cells surrounded by blood vessels, lymphatic vessels, and bile ducts.

Liver cells have many functions. They make bile that dissolves fats in the digestive system. They break down hemoglobin from old red blood cells. They store glucose, iron, and some vitamins. They make cholesterol and many proteins that help blood clot. They also play an important part in removing toxins from the blood.

Liver cells break down toxins such as alcohol, turning them into less poisonous molecules that the kidneys can remove from the blood for excretion. The most important molecule they change is ammonia, which they combine with carbon dioxide to make urea. Urea is much less toxic than ammonia.

As You Read

Under each heading in the chart in your Science Notebook, write what you have learned so far about the organs of the excretory system. Share your chart with a partner. Add to or edit the information in your chart as needed.

How does the liver aid in excretion? Describe the structure of a nephron.

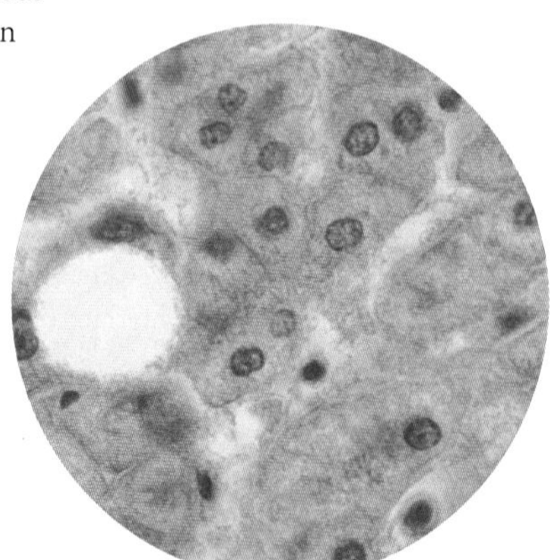

Figure 21.25 Liver cells are the chemical factories of your body.

Teacher Alert

Some people do not consider elimination of undigested food, a process called egestion, to be excretion. However, many sources do not distinguish the two.

Background Information

Bile is mostly composed of cholesterol, bile acids, and bilirubin (a breakdown product of red blood cells). Bile also contains very small amounts of copper and other metals.

Kidneys

The kidneys filter the blood, remove urea and other metabolic wastes, and make urine for excretion. The human body has two kidneys, one on each side of the spine. They sit against the back in the upper part of the abdomen, partly covered by the ribs. Blood enters each kidney through a large artery that branches off the aorta. Inside the kidney, the artery divides into many networks of capillaries that surround the functional units of the kidney, the **nephrons** (NE frahnz).

Each kidney has about one million nephrons. Each nephron looks like a long coiled tube with a cup at one end. The cups of the nephrons are found in the outer rim of the kidney. Each tiny tube, or tubule, extends into the center of the kidney.

The cup of the nephron surrounds a ball of capillaries called the **glomerulus** (gluh MER uh lus). When pressurized blood enters the glomerulus, fluid is forced through the walls of the capillaries and into the nephron. Small molecules such as urea, salt ions, amino acids, and glucose are pushed into the nephron with the fluid. Large proteins and blood cells, however, are too big to fit through the capillary walls. They remain inside the capillaries.

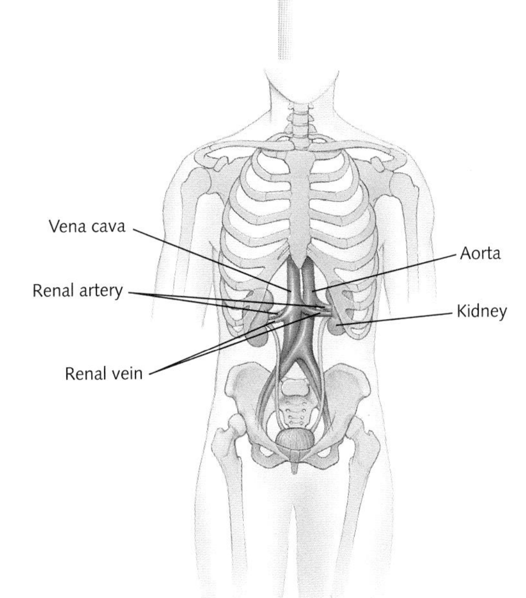

Figure 21.26 The kidneys are located just above the waist, behind the stomach.

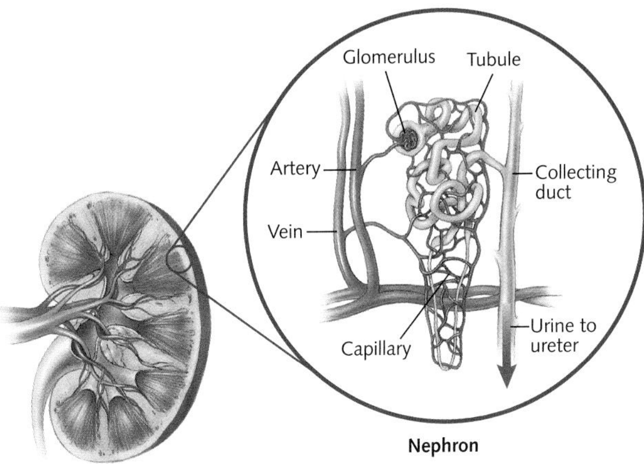

Figure 21.27 This kidney has been split in half so its internal structure can be seen *(left)*. Each nephron *(right)* has a cup and a long tubule.

Did You Know?

Mammals that live in deserts have longer nephrons than mammals living elsewhere do. The long loops help them conserve water by concentrating their urine.

Teach

EXPLAIN to students that the kidneys play an essential role in filtering the blood. Although they are fairly small (about 12 cm long and about 5 cm thick), they process all of the blood in a person's body about every five minutes.

Vocabulary

rectum Tell students that *rectum* is from the Latin word *rectus,* meaning "straight."

anus Tell students that *anus* is a Latin word that means "ring."

nephron Tell students that nephrons help the kidneys reabsorb water and nutrients and that they filter waste products from the blood to form urine.

glomerulus Explain to students that *glomerulus* is the diminutive form of the Latin word *glomus,* which means "ball."

Background Information

Kidney dialysis is the treatment used when end-stage kidney failure develops (when 85 to 90 percent of kidney function is lost). Dialysis removes waste, salt, and extra water from the blood; maintains the chemical balance of potassium, sodium, and bicarbonate; and helps control blood pressure. In some situations, acute kidney failure may get better after treatment, and dialysis is only needed for a short time. In chronic or end-stage kidney failure, kidneys will not get better and dialysis is needed for the rest of the person's life (or a kidney transplant may be possible).

Teach

EXPLAIN that after nephrons filter waste from the blood, they return glucose to the circulatory system. Urea and other wastes in the nephrons pass through the ureters to the bladder and exit the body by the urethra.

Vocabulary

reabsorption Explain that the prefix *re-* denotes "again." To reabsorb is take something in again.

ureter Tell students that *ureter* is derived from the Greek word *ourein,* meaning "to urinate." The ureter carries urine from the kidney to the bladder.

bladder Explain that *bladder* is from *blædre,* an Anglo-Saxon word meaning "a blister."

urethra Review the other two derivatives of the Greek word *ourein: urine* and *ureter.* Show the differences in the endings of the words. Explain that the urethra is the tube through which urine exits the body.

Figure It Out: Figure 21.28

ANSWER **1.** urine **2.** the skin

Science Notebook EXTRA

Have students measure the amount of water lost by each source listed in Figure 21.28. Then, they can pour the water into similarly-sized glass containers for visual comparison. Students should record their observations.

CONNECTION: Medicine

Published reports from the United Network for Organ Sharing show that between 1988 and 2006, there were around 175,700 kidney donors, 87,000 liver donors, 42,260 heart donors, 26,800 pancreas donors, and 14,500 lung donors.

EXTEND Have students do research to find out more about the first kidney transplant and the progress scientists and doctors have made in the field of organ transplantation. Students can research the history of the first kidney transplant at the WGBH Web site, http://www.pbs.org/wgbh/aso/databank/entries/dm54ki.html, and at the NPR site, http://www.npr.org/templates/story/story.php?storyId=4233669. Recent transplant data is found at the Web site of the United Network for Organ Sharing at http://www.unos.org/.

Figure It Out

1. What is the single largest source of water loss in the body?
2. Predict which system will lose more water if a person exercises outdoors on a hot day.

Major Routes for Water Loss

Source	Amount (mL)
urine	1,500
skin	500
lungs	300
feces	150
Total	**2,450**

Figure 21.28 This table shows where the body loses water each day.

The filtered fluid in the nephron now contains wastes, but it also contains molecules that the body needs. The kidney must put these molecules back into the circulatory system. The process in which this occurs is called **reabsorption**. It occurs in the nephron tubule. During reabsorption, amino acids and glucose are returned to the blood.

The nephrons also reabsorb water. Because all of the blood in the body is filtered through the kidneys every five minutes, the kidneys make about 170 L of filtered fluid each day. Most of the water is reabsorbed by the nephrons to form urine. The human body excretes about one liter of urine each day.

The end of each nephron is connected to a collecting duct that brings urine to the **ureters** (YOO ruh turz). Each kidney has a ureter, a long, thin tube that directs urine to the bladder. The **bladder** is a muscular bag that can stretch like a balloon as it fills with urine. It can hold about half a liter of urine. When the bladder fills, it stretches and sends signals to the brain that stimulate the urge to urinate. When a person urinates, urine leaves the body through a short tube called the **urethra** (yoo REE thruh).

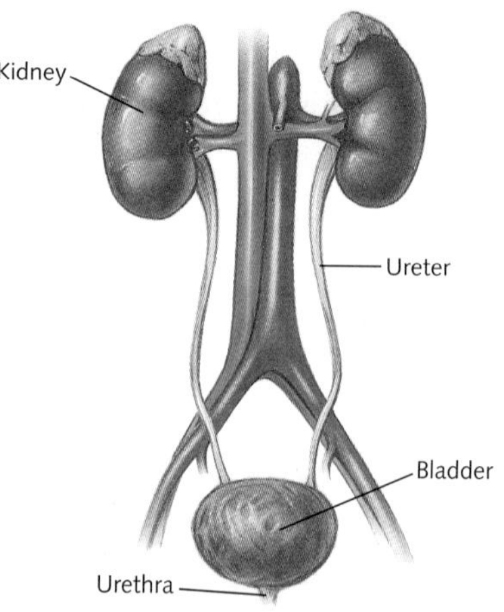

Figure 21.29 The ureters connect the kidneys to the bladder. The urethra connects the bladder to the outside of the body.

CONNECTION: Medicine

The first human organ transplant was performed in 1954. The organ transplanted was a kidney, and the operation was performed at Peter Bent Brigham Hospital in Boston, Massachusetts. Today, organ transplants take place often and are performed in most countries of the world.

394 DIGESTIVE AND EXCRETORY SYSTEMS

Background Information

The first organ transplant involved a man named Ronald Herrick giving his twin brother, Richard Herrick, one of his kidneys. The recipient lived eight more years, and the surgeon who performed the operation, Dr. Joseph Murray, won a Nobel Prize.

One issue that both the patients and doctors involved in the transplant had to face was the ethical implications of performing surgery on a healthy man and removing one of his kidneys. Dr. Murray also experimented on a cadaver to ensure that a transplanted kidney would fit in a new body prior to performing the first transplant.

Skin

The skin is the complex organ that covers your body. In Chapter 19, you learned that the skin is the largest organ of the body. It covers and protects the body's organs and functions as a sense organ and as the body's insulator. It keeps moisture in and disease-causing pathogens out. Besides all of this, the skin is an important organ of excretion.

The skin contains two kinds of **sweat glands**. Both kinds are coiled tubes inside the dermis that open onto the surface of the skin. They make different kinds of sweat. Most sweat glands make watery sweat containing water, salts, and a little urea. This sweat cools the body when it is too hot. Sweat glands found at the base of hairs in the armpits and groin release sweat that also contains some fatty acids and proteins. Bacteria break down the proteins and fatty acids, creating body odors.

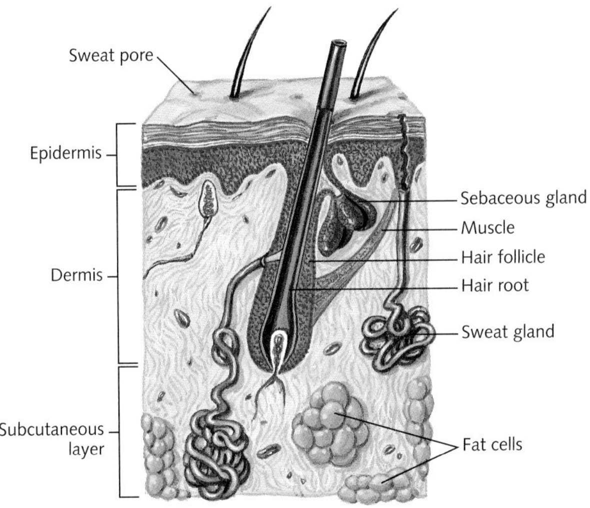

Figure 21.30 A typical sweat gland looks like a knotted ball with a tube leading to the surface of the skin.

After You Read

1. Where is ammonia converted to urea?
2. Name the two main functions of a nephron.
3. Explain why a blocked ureter is a serious medical problem.
4. Refer to the chart of the excretory organs you made in your Science Notebook. Draw a sketch of the human body showing the location of each organ. Label each organ, and identify the waste it is associated with.

Teach

EXPLAIN Tell students that the last organ involved in excretion that they will learn about is actually the largest organ of the human body: the skin. Tell students that although the skin is the largest organ, it excretes less water than the kidneys do.

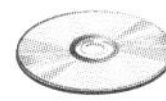

Vocabulary

sweat gland Review with students that the origin of the word *gland* is Latin, *glans,* which means "acorn." Glands are small (acorn-like) organs that produce chemical substances in the human body. Sweat glands produce sweat.

Assess

EVALUATE Use the After You Read questions and the Alternative Assessment to help you assess students' understanding of the lesson.

After You Read

1. Ammonia is converted to urea in the liver.
2. Filtration and reabsorption are a nephron's two main functions.
3. A blocked ureter prevents urine from leaving the kidney. A buildup of waste urea is poisonous.
4. Sketches should include correct locations of the large intestine, lungs, liver, kidneys, and skin. Along with labels, students should identify the wastes associated with each organ (feces for the large intestine, carbon dioxide for the lungs, urea for the liver, urine for the kidneys, and sweat for the skin).

Alternative Assessment

EVALUATE Have students use their charts to write a paragraph that compares and contrasts the liver and the kidneys.

Differentiated Instruction

Logical and Mathematical Have students calculate how many times per hour, and each day, the kidneys filter blood. Knowing that the kidneys make about 170 L of filtered fluid each day, ask students to estimate how much fluid is filtered every hour.

Chapter 21 Summary

VOCABULARY REVIEW

Check students' sentences or paragraphs to make sure they understand the meaning of each vocabulary term.

PREPARE FOR CHAPTER TEST

Evaluate students' essays using the following criteria:

1. The topic sentence, or main idea, should restate the Key Concept.
2. The supporting paragraphs should incorporate the answers to the Learning Goal questions students have written and include details, facts, and examples they have recorded in their Science Notebooks.
3. The concluding sentence should sum up the main idea of the chapter and restate the Key Concept.

MASTERING CONCEPTS

True or False

1. True
2. False, mouth
3. False, cannot
4. False, reabsorption
5. False, days
6. True

Short Answer

7. In the mouth, starch is digested into sugars. It travels through the esophagus and stomach and into the small intestine, where digestive enzymes free the glucose molecules. Glucose is absorbed through the small intestine wall and enters the blood at the capillaries. The blood carries it to a muscle, where it diffuses into a muscle cell.
8. Mechanical digestion increases the surface area of the food particles so that enzymes can attach to them.
9. The functional unit of the lungs is the alveolus. In the liver, it is the lobule; in the kidney, it is the nephron.
10. Humans cannot digest cellulose, but cellulose in the large intestine absorbs water and keeps feces easy to pass.
11. 1 hour, 12 minutes (Dividing the number of Calories in a serving of the snack, 576, by 460 Calories per hour gives 1.2 hours. Two-tenths of an hour is 12 minutes.)

Chapter 21 **Summary**

KEY CONCEPTS

21.1 Nutrition

- The basic nutrients are carbohydrates, proteins, fats, vitamins, minerals, and water.
- A balanced diet contains the correct amount of every nutrient.
- People need to eat more of some nutrients than others.

21.2 The Process of Digestion

- The human digestive tract is made up of a series of organs that starts at the mouth and ends at the anus.
- The digestive system breaks up food mechanically and chemically.
- Enzymes are specialized proteins that speed up chemical reactions.

21.3 Absorption of Food

- Most nutrients are absorbed through the wall of the small intestine.
- The large intestine absorbs water, salts, and some vitamins.

21.4 What Is Excretion?

- Excretion is the process of removing wastes from the body.
- Wastes can be excreted as solids, liquids, or gases.

21.5 Organs of Excretion

- The large intestine excretes solid residues of digestion.
- The lungs excrete carbon dioxide gas.
- The liver transforms nitrogenous wastes into urea.
- Most urea is excreted by the kidneys, but some is released in sweat.

VOCABULARY REVIEW

Write each term in a complete sentence, or write a paragraph relating several terms.

21.1
nutrition, p. 375
nutrient, p. 375
malnutrition, p. 375
carbohydrate, p. 375
protein, p. 376
essential amino acid, p. 376
fat, p. 376
vitamin, p. 377
mineral, p. 378
Calorie, p. 379

21.2
ingestion, p. 380
digestion, p. 380
enzyme, p. 381
salivary gland, p. 381
tongue, p. 381
taste bud, p. 381
bolus, p. 382
esophagus, p. 382
peristalsis, p. 382
stomach, p. 382
chyme, p. 382
duodenum, p. 383
liver, p. 383
pancreas, p. 383

21.3
absorption, p. 384
villus, p. 385

21.4
excretion, p. 388
feces, p. 388
urine, p. 389
sweat, p. 389
urea, p. 389

21.5
rectum, p. 392
anus, p. 392
nephron, p. 393
glomerulus, p. 393
reabsorption, p. 394
ureter, p. 394
bladder, p. 394
urethra, p. 394
sweat gland, p. 395

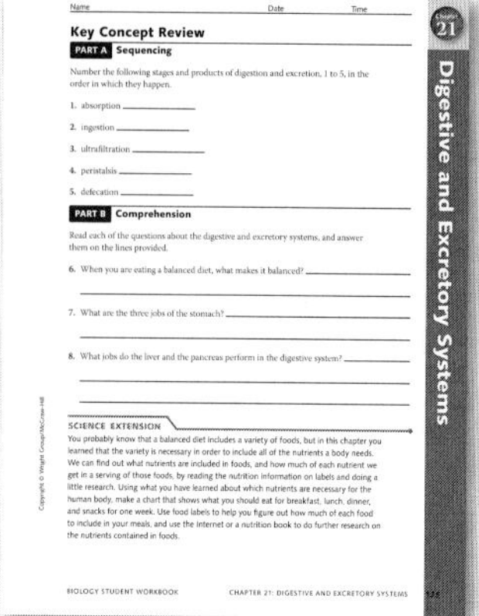

Name ____ Date ____ Time ____

Key Concept Review

PART A Sequencing

Number the following stages and products of digestion and excretion, 1 to 5, in the order in which they happen.

1. absorption ____
2. ingestion ____
3. ultrafiltration ____
4. peristalsis ____
5. defecation ____

PART B Comprehension

Read each of the questions about the digestive and excretory systems, and answer them on the lines provided.

6. When you are eating a balanced diet, what makes it balanced? ____
7. What are the three jobs of the stomach? ____
8. What jobs do the liver and the pancreas perform in the digestive system? ____

SCIENCE EXTENSION

You probably know that a balanced diet includes a variety of foods, but in this chapter you learned that the variety is necessary in order to include all of the nutrients a body needs. We can find out what nutrients are included in foods, and how much of each nutrient we get in a serving of those foods, by reading the nutrition information on labels and doing a little research. Using what you have learned about which nutrients are necessary for the human body, make a chart that shows what you should eat for breakfast, lunch, dinner, and snacks for one week. Use food labels to help you figure out how much of each food to include in your meals, and use the Internet or a nutrition book to do further research on the nutrients contained in foods.

Digestive and Excretory Systems

BIOLOGY STUDENT WORKBOOK   CHAPTER 21: DIGESTIVE AND EXCRETORY SYSTEMS

Key Concept Review
Workbook, p. 135

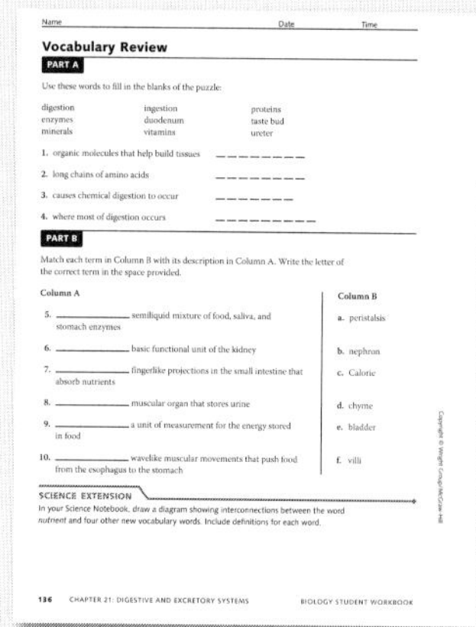

Name ____ Date ____ Time ____

Vocabulary Review

PART A

Use these words to fill in the blanks of the puzzle:

digestion	ingestion	proteins
enzymes	duodenum	taste bud
minerals	vitamins	ureter

1. organic molecules that help build tissues _ _ _ _ _ _ _ _
2. long chains of amino acids _ _ _ _ _ _ _ _
3. causes chemical digestion to occur _ _ _ _ _ _ _
4. where most of digestion occurs _ _ _ _ _ _ _ _

PART B

Match each term in Column B with its description in Column A. Write the letter of the correct term in the space provided.

Column A	Column B
5. ____ semiliquid mixture of food, saliva, and stomach enzymes	a. peristalsis
6. ____ basic functional unit of the kidney	b. nephron
7. ____ fingerlike projections in the small intestine that absorb nutrients	c. Calorie
8. ____ muscular organ that stores urine	d. chyme
9. ____ a unit of measurement for the energy stored in food	e. bladder
10. ____ wavelike muscular movements that push food from the esophagus to the stomach	f. villi

SCIENCE EXTENSION

In your Science Notebook, draw a diagram showing interconnections between the word *nutrient* and four other new vocabulary words. Include definitions for each word.

136 CHAPTER 21: DIGESTIVE AND EXCRETORY SYSTEMS   BIOLOGY STUDENT WORKBOOK

Vocabulary Review
Workbook, p. 136

MASTERING CONCEPTS

True or False

If the statement is true, write "true." If it is false, change the underlined word or words to make the statement true.

1. Saturated fats are solid at room temperature.
2. Carbohydrate digestion starts in the stomach.
3. Humans can digest cellulose.
4. The process in which the nephrons return molecules to the bloodstream is called filtration.
5. A human can live for a few weeks without water.
6. The inner surface of the small intestine has many folds.

Short Answer

Answer each of the following in a sentence or brief paragraph.

7. A glucose molecule is ingested as part of a dinner roll. Trace its path through the digestive system to a muscle cell.
8. Explain how mechanical digestion aids chemical digestion.
9. Name the functional units of the lungs, the liver, and the kidneys.
10. Discuss why people need to eat cellulose.
11. If an hour-long walk burns 480 Calories, how long will it take to burn off one serving of a snack that contains 576 Calories?

PREPARE FOR CHAPTER TEST

To prepare for the chapter test, create a question from each Learning Goal. Use the information in your Science Notebook to answer each question. Then use these answers to write a well-developed essay about the chapter. Use the Key Concept on the first page of this chapter as your topic sentence.

Critical Thinking

Use what you have learned in this chapter to answer each of the following.

12. **Infer** During the eighteenth century, sailing ships would set out for long voyages with plenty of meat and bread for everyone to eat. But, after several months, sailors would begin to get malnourished. They typically had no fresh vegetables or fruit on board. Infer the cause of their malnutrition.
13. **Relate** You are studying a new species of mammal from a tropical rain forest. When you dissect its kidneys, you find that it has very short nephrons. Relate its kidney anatomy to its habitat.
14. **Predict** Some adults do not make the enzyme lactase, which digests milk sugar, or lactose. The bacteria in the large intestine can digest lactose. Predict what might happen if a lactase-deficient person ate a large bowl of ice cream.

Standardized Test Question

Choose the letter of the response that correctly answers the question.

15. Which of the following nutrients is the most important source of energy for the body?
    A. proteins
    B. carbohydrates
    C. vitamins
    D. none of the above

Test-Taking Tip

If "none of the above" is one of the choices in a multiple-choice question, be sure that none of the choices is true.

Critical Thinking

12. The sailors' diets did not include the vitamins found in fruits and vegetables.
13. The animal lives in a tropical environment with lots of available freshwater. It does not need to conserve water by concentrating its urine.
14. The person would not be able to digest the lactose, but the bacteria would. The bacteria would produce lots of carbon dioxide gas as a result of the digestion, causing intestinal bloating and discomfort.

Standardized Test Question

15. B

Reading Links

Guts: Our Digestive System

A good choice for struggling readers, this book closely examines the digestive system through friendly, fact-packed prose and excellent visuals (including X rays, computer-generated and microscopic images, and dissection close-ups). Accomplished science writer Simon treats this subject in an entertaining way that will appeal to students at a range of age and reading levels. The accessible depth of coverage renders this a useful tool for reinforcing classroom study of the digestive process, as students will find it easy and interesting to use independently.

Simon, Seymour. Harper Collins Publishers. 32 pp. Illustrated. Library ISBN: 978-0-06-054652-6.

101 Questions About Food and Digestion (That Have Been Eating at You Until Now)

In a highly approachable question-and-answer format, this book addresses twenty main areas of inquiry related to the human digestive system—including topics such as diet and nutrition, eating behaviors, diseases and treatments, food safety, and global hunger concerns. Included within the well-researched answers are interesting feature articles, diagrams, charts, and photographs. For students seeking specific information, this book will serve as a useful resource; for the more generally curious, it will make for entertaining and informative browsing.

Brynie, Faith Hickman. Illustrated by Sharon Lane Holm. Lerner Publishing Group. 176 pp. Library ISBN: 978-0-7613-2309-9.

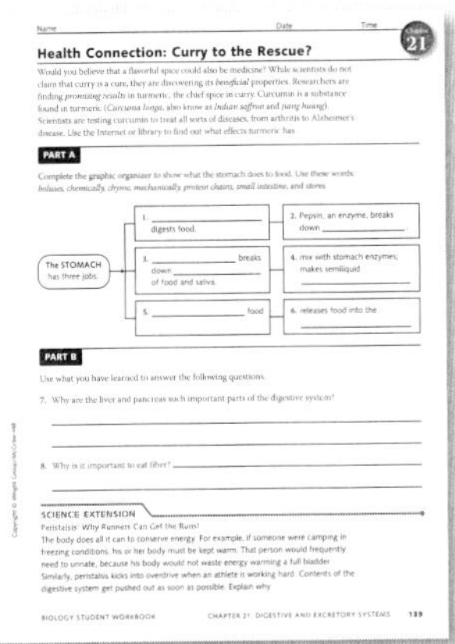
Health Connection: Curry to the Rescue?

Curriculum Connection
Workbook, p. 139

Science Challenge
Workbook, pp. 140–141

CHAPTER 21 397

Chapter 21

Labs

21A A Model of the Digestive System

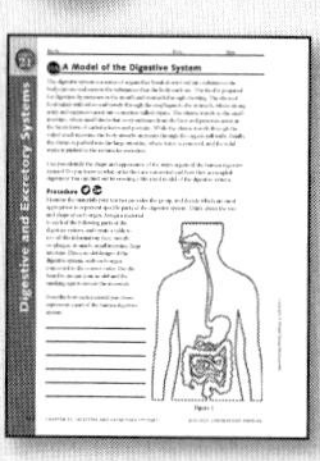

This prechapter activity is designed to determine what students already know about the human digestive system by having them create a simple model and identify the various organs and their functions.

Objectives

- identify the main organs of the digestive system
- identify the shape and appearance of digestive organs
- describe the sequence of digestive organs in the human body and how they work together to digest food
- create a life-sized model of the digestive system

Planning

 25–30 minutes groups of 3–4 students

Materials (per group)

- paper plate
- colored pens or markers
- scissors
- 1-L plastic bottle
- 2-L plastic bottle
- masking tape
- 1.5-cm-wide × 25-cm-long rubber tubing
- 2.5-cm-wide × 6-m-long rubber tubing
- 6-cm-wide × 2-m-long rubber tubing
- foam core or poster board larger than human torso

Advance Preparation

- Ask students to discuss in their groups the parts of the digestive system. Have them identify the function of each part as they currently know it and the sequence of organ involvement in the process of digestion.
- If necessary, review with students the type of data table appropriate for this activity. Ideally, it should have two columns (*Part of the Body* and *Material Representing Body Part*) and seven rows (one for the column titles and one for each part listed).

Engagement Guide

- Challenge students to think about how they can represent the esophagus, small intestine, and large intestine by asking:
  - *What is the size and shape of the esophagus?* (It is a tube 1 ½ to 2 cm wide and about 25 cm long.)
  - *What is the size and shape of the small intestine?* (It is a coiled tube 2 ½ cm wide and about 6 m long.)
  - *What is the size and shape of the large intestine?* (It is a coiled tube 6 cm wide and about 2 meters long.) Many students will not know the size of these organs, which means that you will have to help them to get to these measurements.
- Encourage students to create a face for their human digestive model using markers or pens.
- Students should describe the following in their own words: The paper plate represents the face; the 1-L plastic bottle represents the cavity of the mouth; the 25-cm tube attached to the 1-L bottle represents the esophagus, the other end of which is attached to the 2-L plastic bottle representing the stomach; the 6-m tube coils in loops down from the 2-L bottle like the small intestine, and the end connects to the 2 m-long larger tube, which is looped around the coil of the small intestine and represents the large intestine, ending at the bottom of the model as the rectum.

Going Further

Have student groups compare their models. Ask students to tell what works well in their model and make suggestions for how to improve it to make it more closely model the digestive system. Additionally, encourage students to add materials to this model to represent other organs and parts of the body, such as the liver, pancreas, teeth, heart, lungs, and diaphragm.

21B Where Digestion Starts

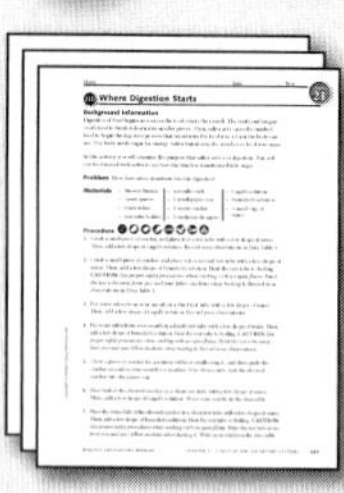

Objectives

- identify the presence of starch in a cracker
- observe the effect of saliva on food
- predict what happens to the starch in a chewed cracker
- identify the transformation of starch into sugar
- analyze the effect of saliva on food

Skill Set

predicting, observing, measuring, calculating, comparing, stating conclusions

Planning

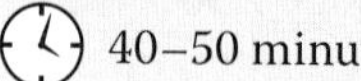 40–50 minutes 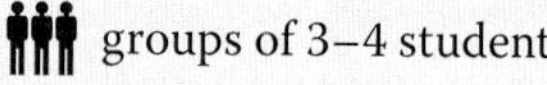 groups of 3–4 students

Materials

Materials for this activity are listed in the Student Laboratory Manual.

Lab Tip

When heating contents over an open flame, it is best to use test tubes made of borosilicate glass.

Advance Preparation

- **CAUTION:** Remind students to be careful when using the Bunsen burner. Explain that the chemicals used in this experiment are to be handled carefully and should never be tasted. Students should immediately wash any body part that comes in contact with chemicals.
- Explain that the Lugol's solution will turn dark blue in the presence of starch. The Benedict's solution will turn orange when heated if sugar is present.

- Make sure that the water crackers used for the experiment have no added sugar. Explain that a cracker contains starch.
- Instruct students as to the correct disposal of their materials. Provide containers at your desk into which students can empty the cooled contents of their test tubes. Then, put all wastes into a plastic bag, seal it, and dispose of it appropriately.

Answers to Observations: Data Table 1

- cracker and Lugol's solution: turns deep blue, starch; cracker and Benedict's solution: remains blue, no sugar; saliva and Lugol's solution: remains light brown, no starch; saliva and Benedict's solution: remains blue, no sugar; chewed cracker and Lugol's solution: remains light brown, no starch; chewed cracker and Benedict's solution: turns orange, sugar

Answers to Analysis and Conclusions

1. Starch is present in the cracker, but sugar is not. The purpose is to verify the presence of starch for the saliva to digest and the lack of sugar before digestion.
2. No starch or sugar is present in the saliva. The purpose is to verify that saliva would not add any sugar or starch to the chewed cracker.
3. Sugar is present in the cracker, but starch is not. The purpose is to verify that the saliva has transformed the starch into sugar.
4. Predictions will vary. Students should conclude that the starch in the cracker was converted into sugar through digestion, and the experiment verifies that. Students should realize that saliva started the process of digesting the cracker.
5. Summaries will vary but should include all aspects of the lab.

Going Further

Have students test different foods that contain starch but do not contain sugar. Suggest that they test the foods with different lengths of time exposed to saliva to determine the time required to digest the food. The students can graph their results for different food types.

21C Testing Food for Nutrients

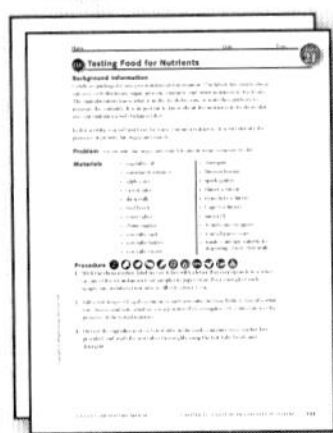

Objectives

- demonstrate the use of indicator tests on foods
- identify the presence of protein, fat, sugar, and starch in common foods
- analyze unknown foods to determine the food category to which they belong
- predict the type of food from unknown samples based on test results

Skill Set

observing, analyzing data, classifying, drawing conclusions

Planning

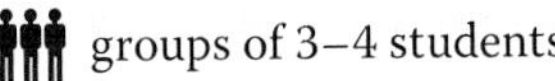

45–60 minutes groups of 3–4 students

Materials

Materials for this activity are listed in the Student Laboratory Manual.

Advance Preparation

- For each group, put each of the six foods to be tested—vegetable oil, cornstarch solution, apple juice, carrot juice, skim milk, and beef broth—in paper cups, and label them A through F. Add enough to each cup to fill the bottom centimeter of test tubes.
- **CAUTION:** Remind students to be careful when using the Bunsen burner. Explain that the chemicals used in this experiment are to be handled carefully and should never be tasted. Students should immediately wash any body part that comes into contact with the chemicals.
- Explain that Lugol's solution turns dark blue in the presence of starch. Benedict's solution turns orange when heated if sugar is present. Biuret solution turns light purple if protein is present. Sudan III solution turns fats red.
- Bring students' attention to the need to dispose of their test chemicals in the trash container you have provided. You may want to have several large containers at your desk into which students can empty the cooled contents of their test tubes. You can then put all the wastes into a plastic bag, seal it, and dispose of it in the appropriate waste receptacle.

Answers to Observations: Data Table 1

The test results for the foods should be similar to the following (results may vary depending on the qualities of the food products):

Unknown Food	Starch	Protein	Fat	Sugar
A: vegetable oil	N–	P+	P+	N–
B: cornstarch solution	P+	N–	N–	N–
C: apple juice	P+	N–	N–	P+
D: carrot juice	P+	N–	N–	P+
E: skim milk	P+	P+	N–	P+
F: beef broth	N–	P+	P+	N–

Answers to Analysis and Conclusions

1. Starch is found in B, C, D, and E.
2. Protein is found in A, E, and F.
3. Fat is found in the A and F.
4. Sugar is found in C, D, and E.
5. Students should be able to predict the foods by their appearance.

Going Further

- Have students repeat the experiment with other foods. You can introduce other tests, such as using silver nitrate solution to test for chloride or indophenol solution to test for vitamin C.
- Have students research what a balanced diet consists of and if they are following that diet. This can be researched online or at the health department. Have students look at the nutritional information on the common items they eat.

Chapter 22 Lessons

Introduce Chapter 22

As a starting activity, use LAB 22A How Quickly Do You React? on page 136 of the Laboratory Manual.

ENGAGE Arrange students into small groups, and ask them to think of a way to communicate without words. After all of the groups have come up with an idea, have each group demonstrate its method to the rest of the class. After the groups have performed, tell the class that just as we can communicate our thoughts in different ways, the human body has systems that communicate with all parts of the body to ensure its smooth and effective functioning.

Think About Communication Systems

ENGAGE Ask pairs of students to brainstorm functions and activities in the body that require control and coordination. Then, have students complete the tasks in both of the bulleted points.

Alternately, ELL students could choose one simple task, such as moving a textbook from one desk to another. Working in pairs, they could write the exact steps that must occur in order to complete the task. Then, two pairs could exchange their directions and evaluate whether the task could be completed with the directions they have.

EXTEND Have partners discuss possible problems that could occur if the body did not have communication systems or if these systems did not work properly.

Chapter 22 Nervous and Endocrine Systems

KEY CONCEPT The nervous and endocrine systems—the body's two communication systems—work together to control and coordinate all the body's other systems.

Think of all the different ways you communicate with people every day. You chat with friends. You write answers to homework questions. You call, email, text message, or send letters to friends and family members. Even your body language is a form of communication. Communication is an essential part of your everyday life.

Just as communication with other people is important, communication within the body is essential to staying alive and healthy. The nervous and endocrine systems are the body's two communication systems. Together, they help control and coordinate all the body's systems.

www.scilinks.org
Nervous System **Code: WGB22A**
Endocrine System **Code: WGB22B**

Think About Communication Systems

Think about all the activities the body does every day.

- Make a list in your Science Notebook of activities that require control and coordination. Can you think of any that do not? Write these as well.
- Choose two of the activities, and name all the body parts that must work together to complete them. Explain how these parts must be coordinated.

398

Chapter 22 Planning Guide

Instructional Periods	National Standards	Lab Manual	Workbook
22.1 3 periods	C.3; A.1, C.1, C.5; UCP.1, UCP.5	**Lab 22A—p. 136** How Quickly Do You React? **Lab 22B—p. 138** How Sight and Smell Affect Taste **Lab 22C—p. 141** Concentrating on Glands and Hormones	Key Concept Review p. 142 Vocabulary Review p. 144 Interpeting Diagrams p. 145 Reading Comprehension p. 146 Curriculum Connection p. 147 Science Challenge p. 148
22.2 2 periods	C.1; E.1; UCP.2, UCP.5		
22.3 2 periods	A.2, C.1, C.3; C.6; UCP.1		
22.4 2 periods	C.1, C.2, C.3, C.3; F.5; C.1; UCP.3		

Middle School Standard; High School Standard; Unifying Concept and Principle

The Nervous System

Before You Read

In your Science Notebook, create a concept map for the nervous system. Write *The Nervous System* in a large central circle, and draw several smaller circles around it. Then, look at the Learning Goals, headings, and pictures in this lesson. What do you predict you will write in the smaller circles of your concept map?

Learning Goals

- Describe the functions of the nervous system.
- Identify the structure and main classes of neurons.
- Explain how nerve impulses are sent through the body.
- Compare the functions of the central and peripheral nervous systems.

New Vocabulary

stimulus
neuron
dendrite
axon
synapse
central nervous system
peripheral nervous system

Recall Vocabulary

tissue (p. 332)
cell (p. 331)

As you read this book, countless things are happening inside your body. Blood is being circulated through arteries and capillaries to deliver oxygen and food to cells. The intestines and liver are working to break down food and process waste. The skin is taking in information about the temperature of the environment. Other information about the environment is being collected by the ears, which are also helping the body keep its balance. Stomach, back, and neck muscles are working to hold the body upright. How can the body do so many things at the same time? What controls and coordinates all of the different functions of the body systems?

Functions of the Nervous System

The nervous system is the body's command system. Like a computer's CPU, the body's nervous system processes and stores information. It communicates information throughout the body and controls the body's response to stimuli (STIHM yuh lye, singular: stimulus). A **stimulus** is any change that happens inside the body or in the external environment.

During a soccer game, for example, the nervous system enables the body to take in and process information about the environment and the players on the field. It coordinates the action of the body's skeletal muscles, which allow the body to move around obstacles and toward the goal. It enables the body to communicate with other players. It even increases the heart and breathing rates so that the body has enough blood flow and oxygen to participate in the game. The nervous system regulates all the tasks that the body performs.

The nervous system does much more than this, however. Unlike a computer's CPU, the body's nervous system allows people to have feelings. It controls a person's mood and shapes a person's personality. It is responsible for emotions and dreams. It helps make us who we are. It helps make us uniquely human.

Working along with the nervous system is the endocrine system. The endocrine system is discussed in Lesson 22.4.

Figure 22.1 The nervous system coordinates the internal changes that enable a soccer player to perform individually and with other players.

22.1 Introduce

ENGAGE Ask students to think about the other body systems that they have studied this year and the facts they already know about body systems more generally. Give students a few minutes to discuss their ideas with a partner. Finally, ask them to discuss their understanding of the nervous system's functions and parts. Partners should then share their discussions with the class.

Before You Read

On the board, draw a concept map with *Nervous System* in the center. Ask students to do the same in their Science Notebooks. Think aloud about what you predict you will learn in this lesson by reviewing the subheadings and figures. Then, instruct students to do the same as they review the lesson with a partner.

Vocabulary terms are listed on the first student page of each lesson. You may wish to preview the terms before introducing each lesson. Strategies for teaching the vocabulary appear on the pages where the terms are introduced.

Teach

EXPLAIN to students that in this lesson, they will learn about the functions and structure of the nervous system.

Science Notebook EXTRA

Encourage students to use the vocabulary section they created in their Science Notebooks. Remind them to record prefixes, suffixes, and root words to help them remember the meanings of vocabulary terms.

ELL Strategy

Read Aloud and Paraphrase Have students form groups of three and take turns reading the lesson aloud. After each person has finished reading a section, the others in the group should paraphrase what was read.

Review Vocabulary As part of the Before You Read activity, ask students to include information about the five senses and their receptors—eyes, ears, nose, tongue, and skin. Review these structures with students before beginning the lesson.

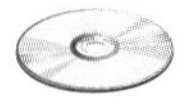

Vocabulary

stimulus Tell students that the word *stimulus* has its origin in a Latin word that means "goad." Explain that *goad* means "something that urges." Write the words *stimulate, stimulant,* and *stimulation* on the board along with *stimulus,* and discuss what the words mean and have in common.

Teach

EXPLAIN that in this section, students will learn about the components and organization of the nervous system.

Use the Visual: Figure 22.2

EXPLAIN Have students work with a partner to describe the basic structure of a neuron and predict how the structures will function.

As You Read

Demonstrate filling in one of the outer circles of the concept map on the board with a word or phrase that is descriptive of the nervous system. Think aloud about why you wrote the word or phrase. Ask students for a few more examples of other descriptive words and phrases, and record them in the map. Have students do the same in their Science Notebooks.

ANSWER The nervous system functions as the body's communication system. It connects and coordinates the body's muscles and internal organs. It allows the body to take in information from the outside world, respond to stimuli, think, and feel.

Vocabulary

neuron Tell students that *neuron* is a Greek word meaning "nerve."

dendrite Explain that the combining form of this word, *dendr* or *dendro*, comes from the Greek word *dendron* and means "tree." Have students look at Figure 22.2 and explain why this meaning might be helpful in remembering which structure is a dendrite.

axon Explain that *axon* is a Greek word meaning "axis." Ask students what Earth's axis is, or solicit other examples of an axis.

synapse Tell students that this word is from the Greek word *synapsis*, meaning "contact" or "junction." Have students use this meaning to create a definition of *synapse*.

As You Read

In the outer circles of your concept map, fill in words that describe the nervous system. Add details by connecting and filling in more circles around the outer circles. Work with a partner to be certain that you include all the important information.

What are some functions of the nervous system?

Organization of the Nervous System

The main organs of the nervous system are the brain, spinal cord, and sensory organs. The eyes, ears, nose, tongue, and skin are the sensory organs. They provide people with the ability to see, hear, smell, taste, and touch, respectively.

Nervous tissue, one of the four main types of tissues that make up organs, is the tissue of the nervous system. It is made up of cells called **neurons** (NOOR ahnz). As shown in **Figure 22.2**, a neuron has a cell body that contains a nucleus. Unlike other cells, however, a neuron has structures that branch out from the cell body. These structures are the **dendrites** (DEN drites) and one long **axon** (AK sahn). A dendrite takes in information from the environment or from other cells in the body. The axon mainly transmits information to other cells.

Neurons are arranged in the body so that the dendrites of one cell connect with the axon of one or more other neurons. Most of the neurons do not actually touch one another. Instead, they are separated by a small fluid-filled space called a **synapse** (SIH naps).

There are three main classes of neurons. Each class has a different function in the body. Sensory neurons carry information from the body or the environment to the spinal cord and brain. Motor neurons carry information from the brain and spinal cord to the muscles or glands. Interneurons are relay neurons. They transmit information to and from sensory and motor neurons.

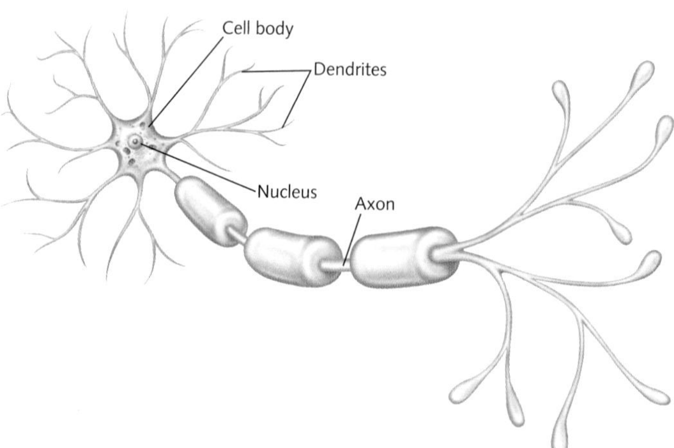

Figure 22.2 Neurons can vary in size, shape, number of dendrites, and location in the body. However, all neurons have the same basic structures, and they all function in essentially the same way.

Background Information

Alzheimer's disease is a progressive, degenerative brain disorder that attacks the brain's neurons and gradually destroys a person's memory, language skills, and ability to learn and make judgments. It also causes behavioral changes. Neurons in the brain stop communicating with other nerve cells and eventually die. Lesions of two types develop in the brain: sticky plaques and insoluble twisted protein fibers. Scientists do not know whether the lesions cause the disease or are a result of it.

Sending Signals

Neurons are responsible for every sight you see, every odor you smell, and every flavor you taste. They are responsible for your hearing and your thoughts. Each of these experiences is complex and very different from the others. However, all information is communicated and processed by neurons in a similar way.

Neurons communicate by changing information from a stimulus into electrical and chemical impulses. Suppose something touches the skin. This stimulus triggers an electrical impulse in the dendrites of a sensory neuron. The electrical impulse travels through the cell body and down the cell's axon. When it reaches the end of the axon, it causes the axon to release chemical messengers called neurotransmitters. The chemicals move away from the axon and across the synapse. Then, they bind to the dendrites of a neighboring neuron. This triggers an electrical impulse in that neuron. The whole process begins again. Neurons are adapted in such a way that all nerve impulses travel in only one direction.

Information travels through one or more neurons in this way until it reaches the brain. The brain processes the information. Then, it sends electrical and chemical impulses back through the body. These impulses let the body know how to respond to the stimulus. All this happens in less than one second!

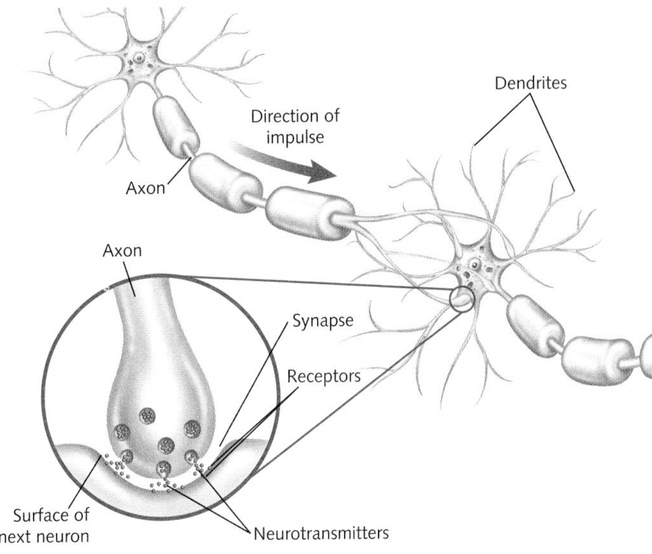

Figure 22.3 To communicate information throughout the body, an impulse moves from the axon of one cell to the dendrites of a neighboring cell.

Did You Know?

You might ask, "If all neurons transmit information in the same way, then what makes a touch different from a sound?" The answer is the path through which the information travels. The dendrites and axon of each neuron form specific connections with other cells. This means that groups of neurons form distinct pathways, or networks, inside the body. Each network is responsible for transmitting a specific type of information. Neurons in the skin form networks that transmit information about temperature and pressure, for example. Neurons in the eye form networks that transmit information about sights.

Teach

EXPLAIN that students will learn that neurons are responsible for outside communication to the brain. Have students look at Figure 22.3 to see how neurons transfer information.

Science Notebook EXTRA

Have students recreate the diagram in Figure 22.3 in their Science Notebooks, correctly labeling the parts. Then, have students add to their diagram to show how an impulse moves from one neuron to another.

Differentiated Instruction

Linguistic After students study the diagram in Figure 22.3, ask them to explain how cells communicate.

Background Information

The brain contains various types of neurons—about 100 billion in all. The neurons, or nerve cells, measure 1 cm to as much as 1 m in length, and they vary in diameter from 0.004 to 0.1 mm. They can transmit signals to and from the brain at up to 320 km/hour.

Teach

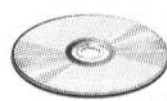 that students will learn about the two divisions of the nervous system.

Vocabulary

central nervous system Explain that *central* is an adjective that means "at the center."

peripheral nervous system Explain that *peripheral* means the opposite of *central.*

Figure It Out: Figure 22.4

ANSWER 1. the central nervous system
2. the peripheral nervous system

Extend It!

Provide students with a variety of reference books and/or Internet access to help in their research. Divide students into small groups. Provide one sheet of poster board for each group to record findings in the format of its choice.

Assess

EVALUATE Use the After You Read questions and the Alternative Assessment to help you assess students' understanding of the lesson.

After You Read

1. It serves as a command system, connects and coordinates internal organs and muscles, and allows the body to receive and respond to stimuli.
2. has a cell body with a nucleus and other internal structures; has dendrites and an axon that branch away from the cell body
3. A sensory neuron first sends an electrical impulse through its cell body and its axon. Then, it releases chemical messengers that travel across the synapse to a neighboring cell. That triggers an electrical impulse in the neighboring cell, and the process repeats until the impulse reaches the brain.
4. the central and peripheral nervous systems; in the functions and organs they serve

Alternative Assessment

EVALUATE Have students write paragraphs comparing and contrasting the central and peripheral nervous systems.

Two Systems in One

The nervous system has two divisions: the central nervous system and the peripheral nervous system. The **central nervous system** (CNS) is made up of the brain and spinal cord. It forms the largest part of the nervous system. It is responsible for such things as communication, memory, and thought.

The **peripheral** (puh RIH frul) **nervous system** (PNS) connects the brain and spinal cord with the rest of the body. It is made up of 12 pairs of cranial nerves and 31 pairs of spinal nerves. Cranial nerves are nerves in the brain. Spinal nerves are nerves that branch off the spinal cord.

The PNS can be further divided into the somatic and autonomic nervous systems. The somatic nervous system controls voluntary actions, which are actions the body consciously controls. Jogging, lifting a book, and opening a door are examples of voluntary actions. The autonomic nervous system controls involuntary actions, which are actions the body does not consciously control. Digestion, breathing, and heart rate are examples of involuntary actions.

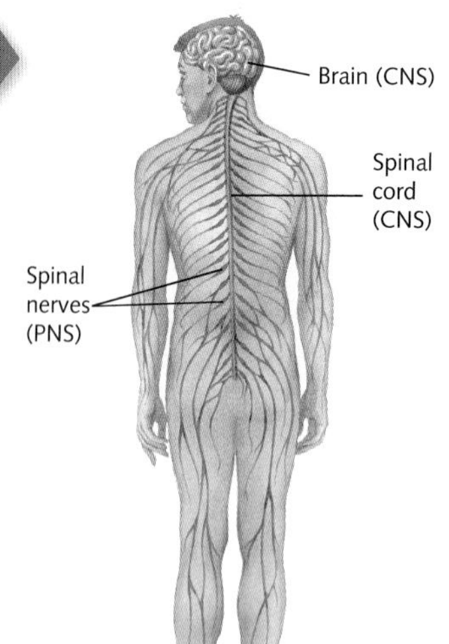

Figure 22.4 The brain and spinal cord make up the central nervous system. The spinal nerves are part of the peripheral nervous system. The CNS and PNS work together to control and coordinate all the actions of the body.

Figure It Out

1. Which division of the nervous system is the largest?
2. Which division of the nervous system does the spinal nerves belong to?

Extend It!

The autonomic nervous system helps keep the body's functions in balance. It is often divided into two smaller classes called the sympathetic nervous system and the parasympathetic nervous system. Working with a group, choose one of these to research. Make a poster to show what the system does. Then, present your findings to the class.

After You Read

1. How does the nervous system help keep the body healthy and active?
2. How are neurons similar to other cells in the body? How do they differ?
3. Sequence and describe the process through which neurons send information to the brain.
4. Review the concept map in your Science Notebook. Work with a partner to answer the following questions. What are two divisions of the nervous system? How do these divisions differ? Record your answers in your Science Notebook.

Background Information

The sympathetic nervous system is in control of what is commonly called "fight or flight" responses. Blood pressure increases, the heart beats faster, and digestion slows. When this occurs, adrenaline is released.

The parasympathetic nervous system is in control of what is sometimes called the body's "rest and digest" responses. The body works to save energy as blood pressure decreases, the heart beats slower, and digestion begins.

The sympathetic nervous system reacts to responses that require immediate action, while the parasympathetic system responses do not.

22.2 The Brain and Spinal Cord

Before You Read

Create a K-W-L-S-H chart in your Science Notebook. Think about the title of this lesson. Then look at the pictures and headings in the lesson. In the column labeled *K*, write what you already know about the brain and spinal cord. In the column labeled *W*, write what you would like to learn.

Learning Goals

- Describe the structures and functions of the brain and spinal cord.
- Explain what a reflex is and how reflexes are transmitted through the body.

New Vocabulary

cerebrum
cerebellum
brain stem
vertebra
reflex
reflex arc

You're in the video store trying to decide what movie you'd like to watch tonight. Are you in the mood for an action movie? No, you've already seen the popular ones at least twice, and none of the others look interesting. Perhaps you'll try a comedy or romance instead. You end up picking a drama and leaving the store.

What happened in this seemingly simple scenario? You thought about something you would like to do in the future. You read and recognized the titles of films. You thought about your mood and how you were feeling. You remembered things you had seen in the past. You reasoned and made choices. In only a short time, you did a number of tasks that no other living or nonliving thing can do. For all this, you can thank the human brain.

The Brain

Humans are among the most complex beings on Earth. This is due in large part to the structure and function of the human brain. The human brain is responsible for reason and intelligence. It enables people to analyze situations, communicate, create, feel, and learn.

The mass of the human brain is only about 1.4 kg. That is about 2 percent of an average adult's body mass. The brain uses between 20 and 25 percent of the body's energy, however. It contains more than 100 billion neurons. Each of these neurons connects with up to 10,000 other neurons to transmit information throughout the body.

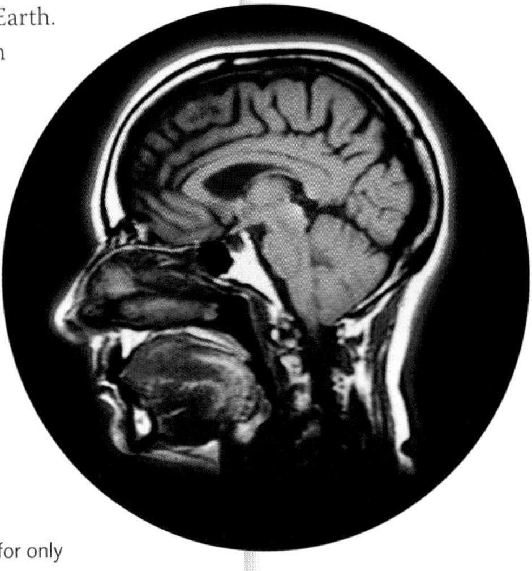

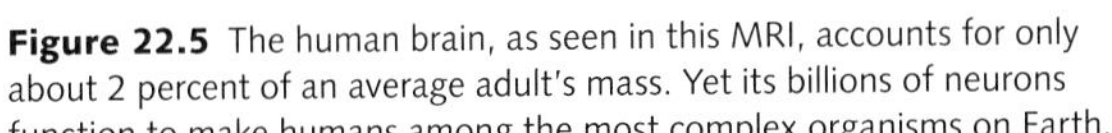

Figure 22.5 The human brain, as seen in this MRI, accounts for only about 2 percent of an average adult's mass. Yet its billions of neurons function to make humans among the most complex organisms on Earth.

22.2 Introduce

ENGAGE Have students talk to a partner about all the actions they think the human brain is responsible for. Have them create a graphic organizer (of their choice) to record their responses. Suggest that students categorize the actions according to any of the following: voluntary v. involuntary, physical v. mental, physical v. emotional, essential to survival v. not essential to survival. When they are finished, students should share their ideas with the class.

Before You Read

On the board, write and underline the headings *The Brain* and *The Spinal Cord.* Underneath, make a K-W-L-S-H chart. Then, ask students what each heading stands for. Have students brainstorm already-known information about the brain and spinal cord. Record answers in the *K* column of the class chart. Have students make the same chart in their Science Notebooks and record their prior knowledge in the appropriate column. Regroup as a class, and ask students what they want to know about the brain and spinal cord. Record this information on the board, and have students do the same in their Science Notebooks. Encourage students to include at least two or three questions they have about the brain and spinal cord in the *W* column of their charts.

Teach

EXPLAIN Ask students to look at the photograph in Figure 22.5. Tell students that they will begin to learn about the extremely complex human brain.

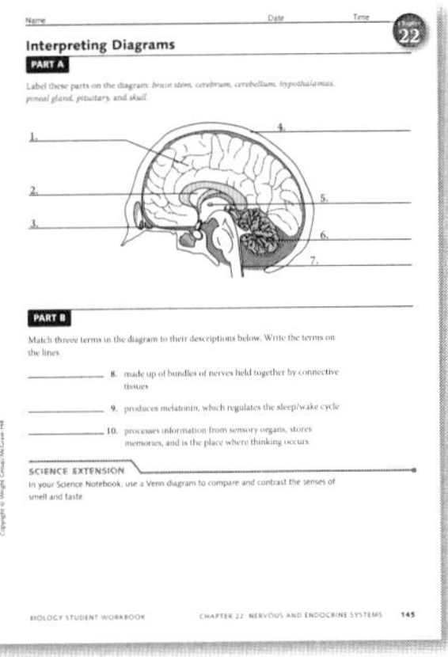

Interpreting Diagrams

PART A

PART B

SCIENCE EXTENSION

Interpreting Diagrams
Workbook, p. 145

Background Information

The human brain makes up a considerably larger percentage of body weight than does the brain of any other animal. For example, the human brain makes up 2 percent of a human's overall body weight, while a beagle's or a rat's brain makes up 0.5 percent and a bottle-nosed dolphin's brain makes up 0.2 percent.

To view over 100 photographs of various structures of the brain and three-dimensional magnetic resonance images (MRIs), visit a portion of Harvard University's Web site entitled *The Whole Brain Atlas* at **http://www.med.harvard.edu/AANLIB/home.html.**

Teach

EXPLAIN that students will learn about the three major parts of the brain. Ask students to look at the brain diagram in Figure 22.6 and identify the three major areas.

EXPLAIN that the brain is divided into two hemispheres, or halves. Ask students to identify the two halves. Tell them that the right hemisphere controls the left side of the body, while the left hemisphere controls the right side of the body.

Vocabulary

cerebrum Tell students that *cerebrum* comes directly from the Latin word meaning "brain." Explain that the combining form of the word, *cerebr* or *cerebro*, is used to make other brain-related words such as *cerebral*, *cerebrate*, and *cerebellum*. Ask students if they have heard of the disability called *cerebral palsy* and if they know what it is.

cerebellum Tell students that *cerebellum* comes from the Latin word that is the diminutive of *cerebrum*. Ask students to use the descriptions of cerebrum and cerebellum to explain why this meaning is appropriate.

brain stem Ask students what a stem is. (The common meaning is "the central part of a plant that grows upward from the root.") Ask why *stem* is an appropriate name for this part of the brain.

Use the Visual: Figure 22.6

ANSWER the cerebellum

CONNECTION: Computer Science

Honda has been working on humanoid robots since 1986 and is currently on its eleventh version. The latest version, called New ASIMO, is able to walk along with a person, greet people, follow them, move in the direction they indicate, and even recognize their faces and address them by name. It can even run at 6 km/hr and can relay information that it finds on the Internet.

EXTEND Have each student write a paragraph arguing whether or not artificial intelligence could one day be as sophisticated as the human brain. Encourage student volunteers to present their thoughts to the class.

Structure and Function The brain is divided into three major parts. These are the cerebrum (suh REE brum), the cerebellum (ser uh BEL um), and the brain stem. The **cerebrum** is the largest part of the brain. It is where memories are stored. It is also where thinking occurs. The cerebrum processes information from the sensory organs. It allows for communication and learning.

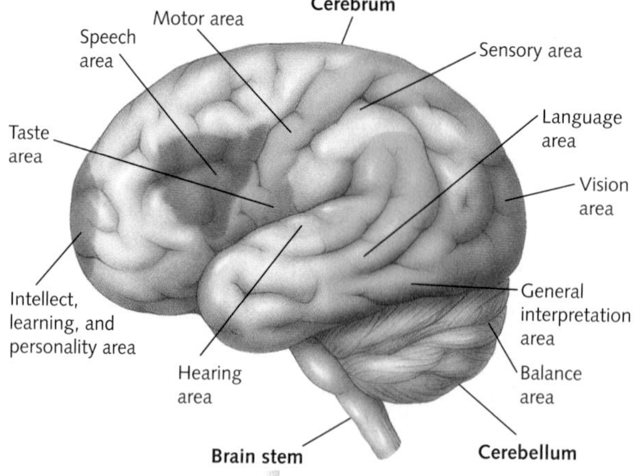

Figure 22.6 The three major parts of the human brain are the cerebrum, cerebellum, and brain stem. Different areas of the cerebrum are thought to be responsible for different activities. What part of the brain is responsible for balance?

The **cerebellum** is located below and toward the back of the cerebrum. It is responsible for coordinating voluntary actions. It regulates skeletal muscles and maintains muscle tone. It also helps the body maintain balance.

The **brain stem** connects the brain to the spinal cord. It is a thick, cylindrical structure that extends from the cerebrum. The brain stem is made up of three smaller structures—the midbrain, pons, and medulla. The midbrain and pons help connect different parts of the brain. The medulla helps control involuntary actions.

The skull, a thin layer of bone, surrounds the brain. The skull helps protect the brain from injury. A layer of protective fluid fills the space between the brain and the skull. This fluid acts as a shock absorber and helps deliver nutrients to the brain.

CONNECTION: Computer Science

Artificial intelligence is a branch of science that aims to build intelligent machines—machines that can think and reason as humans do. Such machines would, in a sense, mimic the processes of the human brain.

Scientists began searching for ways to build intelligent machines in the 1940s. At that time, computers were becoming more sophisticated; they were able to do more complicated tasks with ease. They were also getting smaller. Scientists were learning more about the brain and nervous system. Mathematicians were learning to solve mathematical problems that are related to human reasoning. With continuing advances in these three fields, the science of artificial intelligence experienced great progress.

Scientists have made many advances toward artificial intelligence. Today, computers can mimic many thought processes. They can play a game of chess, for example, and can solve algebraic equations. Yet, they have not advanced to the level of human intelligence. For now, those kinds of computers are still a fictional invention.

Differentiated Instruction

Visual-Spatial Allow students to play games on the Internet, such as chess or Scrabble, as a demonstration of Artificial Intelligence.

Background Information

Each hemisphere of the brain is dominant for certain behaviors. The left hemisphere controls most functions of language, math, and logic; the right hemisphere controls most functions of spatial abilities, face recognition, visual imagery, and music. The corpus callosum divides the two areas and shares information between them, allowing the two sides to work together.

The Spinal Cord

The spinal cord helps connect the brain with the rest of the body. As shown in **Figure 22.7**, the spinal cord is made up of bundles of neurons held together by connective tissue. Sensory neurons and interneurons connect inside these bundles to carry information to the brain. Motor neurons and interneurons connect to carry information away from the brain. Blood vessels within the connective tissue bring food and oxygen to the cells.

The spinal cord is surrounded by strong, flexible bones that together form the spine, or backbone. The spine is divided into 33 irregularly shaped bones called **vertebrae** (singular: vertebra). The vertebrae protect the spinal cord from injury. A layer of protective fluid surrounds the spinal cord within the spine. The extra protection for the spinal cord is crucial.

If the spinal cord is severed or damaged, paralysis can occur. Paralysis is a condition in which a person cannot move parts of his or her body. Paralysis can "freeze" the whole body from the neck down, or it might affect just the legs and pelvis. Paralysis is caused when damage to the spinal cord stops the brain from being able to communicate with parts of the body. The brain can form a signal, but the signal cannot reach its destination.

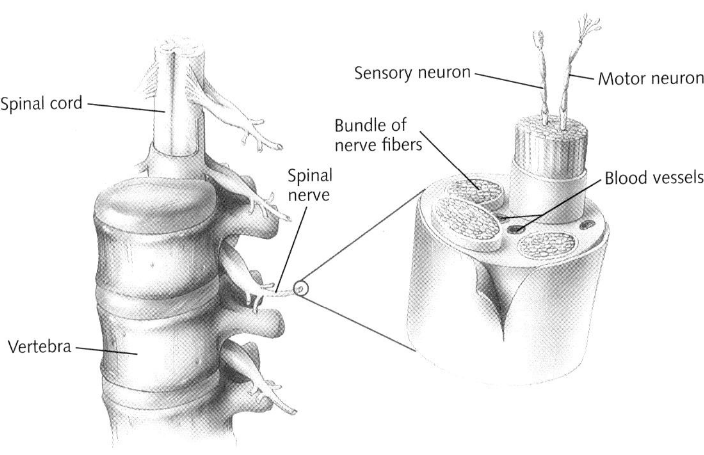

Figure 22.7 A column of vertebrae protects the spinal cord. The spinal cord, which provides the connection between the brain and the rest of the body, is about the width of an adult thumb and about 43 cm long. It is very flexible.

As You Read

In the column labeled *L* in your K-W-L-S-H chart, write what you have learned about the brain.

Why is the spinal cord an important organ?

Did You Know?

Once the spinal cord has been severed, it is unlikely that the connection between the brain and other parts of the body will be reestablished. Scientists hope that technology will one day enable them to re-form connections between the brain and spinal cord.

Teach

EXPLAIN to students that in this section, they will learn about the spinal cord and paralysis. Tell them that paralysis is a condition in which a person cannot move parts of his or her body, and explain that it results from damage to the spinal cord.

As You Read

Have students stop and think about what they have learned so far in this chapter about the brain and spinal cord. Ask them to think specifically about physical characteristics and functions. After discussing this for a few minutes in pairs, students should share answers with the class. Record students' answers on the board as they share information.

ANSWER The spinal cord is an important organ because it connects the brain to the rest of the body and it controls reflexes.

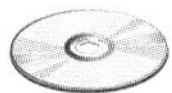

Vocabulary

vertebra Tell students that *vertebra* comes from the Latin word *vertere*, which means "to turn." Ask them to refer to Figure 22.1 and explain why *vertebrae* (plural) are appropriately named.

ELL Strategy

Practice Using Vocabulary Supply students with index cards on which to write definitions of lesson vocabulary terms. Urge students to use illustrations with their definitions. Then, instruct students to find partners and use the completed cards to test their knowledge.

Background Information

Many medical conditions can cause paralysis. Among them is amyotrophic lateral sclerosis (ALS, or Lou Gehrig's disease), a progressive neuromotor disease. Motor neurons control and communicate between the nervous system and the voluntary muscles of the body. A person with ALS loses motor cells (the cells degenerate and die), which causes the muscles under their control to weaken and deteriorate, leading to paralysis. Usually fatal within five years of diagnosis, ALS typically begins during middle age. Men are one-and-a-half times more likely than women to develop ALS.

Teach

 that in this section, students will learn about reflexes. Explain that reflexes are controlled by the spinal cord.

 Vocabulary

reflex Tell students that *reflex* comes from the Latin word *reflexus*, meaning "bent back." Ask students how this meaning is appropriate for the action of a reflex.

reflex arc Tell students that an *arc* is a "continuous section of a circle or curve."

Figure It Out: Figure 22.8

ANSWER **1.** because they are processed in the spinal cord rather than in the brain **2.** by enabling it to quickly respond to stimuli that may be harmful

Explain It!

Have students act out safe reflexes. Possible choices include hitting the knee with a soft mallet and shining bright light into the eye to decrease the size of the pupil.

Assess

EVALUATE Use the After You Read questions and the Alternative Assessment to help you assess students' understanding of the lesson.

After You Read

1. The cerebrum processes sensory input, controls voluntary actions, and is where memories are stored and thought occurs. The cerebellum helps coordinate voluntary actions. The brain stem connects the brain to the spinal cord, connects parts of the brain, and helps control involuntary actions.
2. Reflexes occur when an impulse travels through a sensory neuron and then a motor neuron in a loop called a reflex arc. They are involuntary, automatic, and involve the spinal cord rather than the brain.
3. Students' answers will vary.

Alternative Assessment

EVALUATE Using information in this lesson or other resources, have students draw and label the parts of the brain and spinal cord.

Explain It!

Reflexes enable the body to respond to stimuli more quickly than it does through conscious control. Why do you think it is beneficial for the body to have different methods for responding to stimuli? Write your answer in a well-developed paragraph in your Science Notebook.

Reflexes

Have you ever touched something hot and pulled your hand away quickly without thinking about it? Such an action is an example of a reflex. A **reflex** is an automatic, involuntary response to a stimulus.

During a reflex, an impulse is sent through a simple network called a **reflex arc**. Most reflex arcs are made up of just three neurons: a sensory neuron, an interneuron, and a motor neuron. **Figure 22.8** shows how an impulse flows through a reflex arc. First, a stimulus triggers an impulse in a sensory neuron. The impulse is sent from the sensory neuron to an interneuron in the spinal cord. The interneuron sends the impulse directly to a motor neuron. Then, the motor neuron causes the muscles to move.

Reflexes are controlled in the spinal cord rather than in the brain. That is why people are not aware of them until after they have happened. Reflexes allow the body to quickly respond to stimuli that may be harmful. After the response has happened, the brain processes the information so the body knows what to do next.

Figure It Out

1. Why are reflexes automatic responses rather than conscious responses?
2. How does the withdrawal reflex help keep the body healthy?

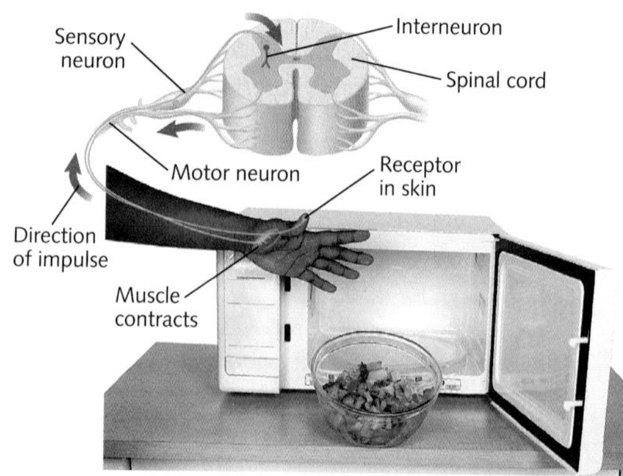

Figure 22.8 Reflex responses are controlled by the spinal cord. The reflex response shown here is known as the withdrawal reflex.

After You Read

1. What are three parts of the brain? What role does each one play in the body?
2. Explain how reflexes occur. How do they differ from other impulses?
3. Review the K-W-L-S-H chart in your Science Notebook. Then, summarize what you learned about the brain and spinal cord. What new questions do you have? How could you find the answers to these questions? Record your questions and ideas in the *S* and *H* columns of your chart.

Background Information

Brain and spinal cord injuries can cause paralysis. Spinal cord injury (SCI) is damage to the spinal cord that results in a loss of function (such as mobility or feeling). Frequent causes of damage are trauma and developmental defects such as spina bifida.

Teacher Alert

Explain to students that a person can "break" his or her back or neck but not sustain a spinal cord injury if only the bones around the spinal cord (the vertebrae) are damaged and the spinal cord is not affected. In these situations, the individual may not experience paralysis after the bones are stabilized. Students who have knowledge of or experience with this condition may need to be informed.

22.3 The Senses

Before You Read

Create a lesson outline in your Science Notebook. Use the title and headings of this lesson to organize the outline. What do you think you will learn about in this lesson? Use the outline and the pictures to help answer this question.

Smell, sight, hearing, taste, and touch are the body's senses. The senses connect people with the outside world. They enrich people's everyday lives and experiences. They help make people aware of the things around them. Without the senses, people would not be able to communicate with one another or to recognize the beauty that surrounds them.

Making Sense of Things

Each of the five senses allows people to experience a different aspect of their surroundings. The senses give the brain information. The brain turns this information into a perception.

The body's sensory organs are the eyes, ears, nose, tongue, and skin. These organs have special cells called **sensory receptors**. These cells are sensitive to specific types of energy, summarized in **Figure 22.10**. The sensory receptors change the energy given off by a stimulus into electrical impulses that can be sent to the brain. The brain then processes these impulses into a sight, a sound, a taste, a smell, or a touch.

The Senses and Energy

Sense	Sensory Organ	Energy Detected
sight	eyes	light energy
hearing	ears	mechanical energy
smell	nose	chemical energy
taste	tongue	chemical energy
touch	skin	mechanical energy, chemical energy, and thermal energy

Figure 22.10 The sensory receptors within a sensory organ allow the organ to respond to specific forms of energy. This table shows the five senses and the forms of energy responsible for each sense.

Learning Goals

- Identify the five sense organs.
- Explain what a sensory receptor is and which stimuli humans are sensitive to.
- Describe how the sensory organs allow the body to see, hear, smell, taste, and touch.

New Vocabulary

sensory receptor
cone
rod
retina
cochlea
cilia

Recall Vocabulary

taste bud (p. 381)

Figure 22.9 How are these teenagers using their senses? What sights, sounds, and smells do you think they are noticing? Describe each example using as many descriptive words as you can.

22.3 Introduce

ENGAGE Ask students to name and explain the five senses and to describe how they might relate to the brain. Then, have students create a list of some of the many ways in which they use their senses every day.

Before You Read

Remind students how to make and use an outline. Have pairs of students review the chapter together and write an outline in their Science Notebooks. Students' outlines should reflect the understanding that they will learn about the five senses and how the body's organs work to allow people to see, hear, smell, taste, and touch.

Teach

EXPLAIN to students that without sensory receptors, people could not take in information from their surroundings. Without the brain, a person could not turn this information into a recognizable experience.

Vocabulary

sensory receptor Tell students that *sensory* refers to the senses and that a *receptor* is a part of the nervous system adapted for receiving stimuli.

Use the Visual: Figure 22.9

ANSWER Students' answers will vary but should include an example of how each sense is being used by the people in the photo. Ask for student volunteers to read their answers, and emphasize the power of using descriptive words.

Use the Visual: Figure 22.10

EXTEND This table offers a valuable opportunity to discuss energy and to integrate biology and physical science. Ask students to define each type of energy and provide examples. Then, have students relate the type of energy to the way they think each sense works.

ELL Strategy

Activate Background Knowledge Have students talk in small groups about their experiences with the five senses. Each group should record a list for each sense.

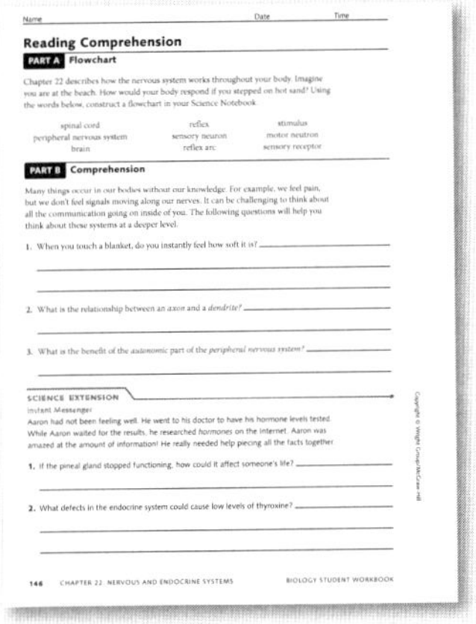

reading Comprehension Workbook, p. 146

Teach

EXPLAIN to students that in this section, they will learn about sight.

Vocabulary

cone Ask students for examples of cones (ice cream, pine) and what shape the word describes. Tell students that the cones of the retina have this basic shape.

rod Ask students what a rod looks like. (a long, thin stick) Give examples of items that are rod-shaped: a pole, a cane, a bar, etc. Tell students that the rods of the retina have this basic shape.

retina Tell students that *retina* likely comes from the Latin word *rete*, meaning "net."

cochlea Explain that this Latin word means "snail" or "snail shell." Ask students to relate this meaning to the description of this part of the ear in the lesson.

cilia Tell students that *cilia* comes from the Latin word *cilium*, meaning "eyelash." Ask students to recall other uses of the word that they have read in this textbook. Students should recall the hair-like structures on a paramecium and those lining the human respiratory and digestive systems.

Explore It!

Provide each student or pair of students with a small mirror, a flashlight, and colored filters that cover the flashlight.

ANSWER Students should notice that in very dim light, the eye is less able to distinguish colors and details. When the light is changed from dim to very bright, students should notice that their pupils become much smaller, a reflex. However, their eyes are better able to distinguish colors and details.

EXTEND Review light and the visible spectrum with students. Discuss reflection, absorption, and why we see color. Help students recognize that perception of color is partly dependent on the color of the light illuminating the object. For example, an object that appears red in white light will look black in blue light. It may be fun for students to compare people's ability to distinguish colors with other animals' abilities.

Use the Visual: Figure 22.11

ANSWER Electrical impulses travel from the eye to the brain along the optic nerve.

Explore It!

Try this simple activity and record your observations in your Science Notebook.

Darken the room so that the light is very dim. Notice the objects around you. Can you see all their colors and details?

In the dim light, use a mirror to observe the size of your pupils. Are they small or large? Turn on all the lights so that the room is very bright and quickly look at your pupils in the mirror again. How have they changed? Why might this have happened?

Sight

Sight allows people to see the things around them. It allows people to detect light energy from the environment and turn it into images. Sight is among the most studied senses and is probably the best understood. The eyes are the sensory organs of sight.

The eye contains two types of sensory receptors that are sensitive to light energy. These receptors are often called photoreceptors, the prefix *photo–* meaning "light." The receptor cells are called **cones** and **rods** for their distinctive shapes. Cones are mainly responsible for day vision, or seeing in bright light. Cones are sensitive to red, blue, and green light. Together, these three types of cones let people see all the colors around them. Rods are responsible for night vision, or seeing in dim light. Rods are not sensitive to different colors of light. This is why images appear in black and white in dim light.

Cone cells and rod cells are located on the **retina**, a thin layer of tissue on the back of the eyeball. Both types of cells change light energy that enters the eye into electrical impulses. These electrical impulses can be sent through the nervous system to the brain. **Figure 22.11** shows how light travels through the eye.

1 Light reflects off the pear and enters the eye through the cornea. The cornea is a tough, clear layer of cells that helps focus light.

2 Light then passes through the pupil, a small opening that looks like a black circle. Tiny muscles in the iris, the colored part of the eye, control the pupil's size. In bright light, the pupil partially closes to let in less light. In dim light, the pupil enlarges to let in more light.

3 Next, light travels through the lens. The lens is made up of clear, muscular material. It changes shape to help focus light on the retina.

4 Once light reaches the retina, the rods and cones change the light into electrical impulses. The image that forms on the retina is upside-down.

5 The electrical impulses are sent to the brain through neurons in the optic nerve. The brain then processes the impulses into the image that is seen.

Lens
Retina
Iris
Cornea
Pupil
Optic nerve

Figure 22.11 The parts of the eye work together with the brain to enable people to see. How are electrical impulses sent from the eye to the brain?

Background Information

Color blindness is a hereditary condition that occurs in 8 to 12 percent of males and in less than one percent of females of European descent. Red/green color blindness is the most common deficiency, but blue/yellow also exists in about one percent of those with the condition. Color blindness occurs when the amount of pigment in the cones is reduced or when one color or more is missing. There is no treatment for the condition.

The visible spectrum is the portion of the electromagnetic spectrum that is visible to (can be detected by) the human eye. Electromagnetic radiation in this range of wavelengths is called visible light, or just light. Visible light is made up of the wavelengths that correspond to the colors red, orange, yellow, green, blue, indigo, and violet (ROY G BIV).

408 NERVOUS AND ENDOCRINE SYSTEMS

Hearing

Hearing involves the detection of sound waves. A sound wave is a vibration. Vibrations are mechanical energy produced when an object moves back and forth quickly. The ears are the sensory organs of hearing.

The ear contains sensory receptors that are sensitive to mechanical energy. These receptor cells are found in the **cochlea**. They contain tiny hairs called **cilia** that change vibrations entering the ear into electrical impulses. These electrical impulses are sent to the brain, where they are processed into sound. **Figure 22.13** shows how mechanical energy travels through the ear.

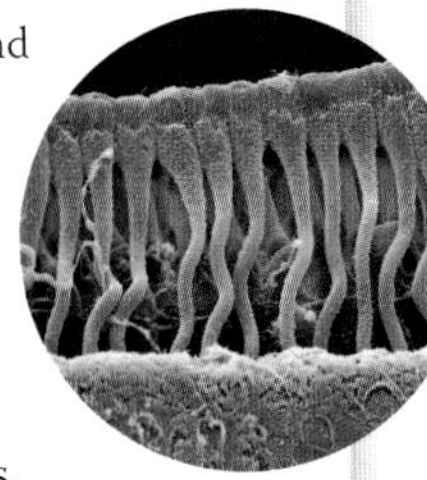

Figure 22.12 Tiny cilia are responsible for detecting sound. They are shown here magnified by about 400x.

Balance

The ears also sense the body's balance. Structures in the inner ear called the semicircular canals contain tiny hair cells and jellylike fluid. Inside this fluid are tiny grains called ear stones. As the body moves, the ear stones roll back and forth, bending the tiny hair cells. The hair cells respond by sending nerve impulses to the brain. If the brain interprets the impulses to mean the body is losing its balance, it will send signals to the muscles to either contract or relax to restore balance.

❶ Vibrations enter the outer ear and travel toward the eardrum.

❷ The vibrations cause the eardrum to vibrate, which in turn causes three tiny bones—the hammer, anvil, and stirrup—to vibrate.

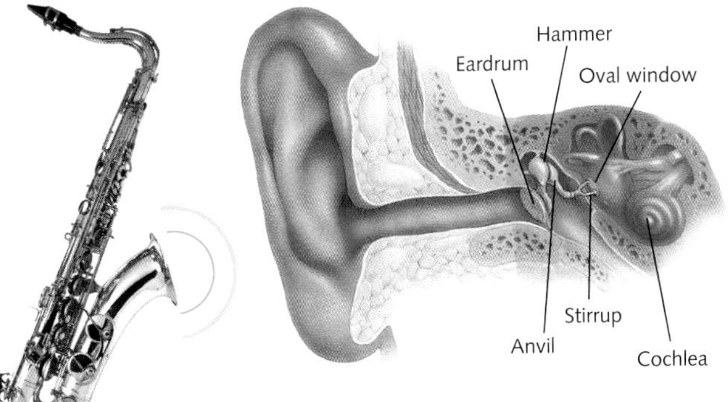

❸ The vibrating stirrup pushes and pulls on the oval window. This causes fluid inside the cochlea to vibrate and move.

❹ The moving fluid causes cilia to sway back and forth and create an electrical impulse that is sent to the brain. The brain processes the impulse into a sound.

Figure 22.13 The parts of the ear work together with the brain to enable people to hear and to sense balance.

As You Read

Use your lesson outline to take notes about the senses as you read. Compare your outline with that of a partner. Add or correct any necessary information. Write any questions you have.

What kind of stimuli is the ear sensitive to? Why can't people see with their ears?

Figure It Out

1. Where are sensory receptors located in the ear?
2. Describe the sequence of events that must happen in order for you to hear a sound.

Teach

EXPLAIN to students that they will learn about the sense of hearing and the ears. Tell students that in addition to being the sensory organs of hearing, the ears also control the body's balance. Discuss with students what balance is, and have them provide examples of activities that might disrupt their balance.

Figure It Out: Figure 22.13

ANSWER **1.** in the cochlea **2.** A sound wave is first collected in the outer ear. It travels toward the eardrum and causes the eardrum to vibrate. This causes the hammer, anvil, and stirrup to vibrate. The stirrup pushes and pulls on the oval window, causing fluid in the cochlea to vibrate. The vibrating fluid causes cilia to sway back and forth. The cilia change the mechanical energy of a vibration into an electrical impulse, which is sent along the cochlear nerve to the brain.

As You Read

Give students a few minutes to work on their outlines. Remind them to include major categories, vocabulary words, and information about the ways in which each sensory organ works.

ANSWER The ears are sensitive to mechanical energy. People cannot see with their ears because the ears do not have receptor cells that are sensitive to light.

CONNECTION: Music

Play various types of music in the classroom. As students listen, tell them what each type is (e.g., jazz, classical, rock) and ask them to notice their emotional responses to each one. Ask students to record in their Science Notebooks each type of music and their emotional responses to it. Have students do the same at home using music of their choice.

Point out to students that the same notes played in two different tempos and rhythms can cause very different experiences or feelings. Help students understand rhythm and tempo by demonstrating this in class.

Differentiated Instruction

Kinesthetic Briefly review with students the concepts of pitch, volume, and sound waves. Have students make simple instruments to demonstrate how sound works. Ideas could include using straws or a box and rubber bands to investigate pitch and volume, using a slinky to mimic a sound wave, and using a tuning fork in water to observe sound waves.

Field Study

Bring students to an outdoor location close to the school. Each student should have a clipboard and pencil. Ask students to become aware of their surroundings by focusing on the senses (all except taste). They should record everything they notice by category: sight, sound, smell, and touch. When they are back in the classroom, have students review notes in small groups to compare similarities and differences.

CHAPTER 22 409

Teach

EXPLAIN to students that they will learn about the remaining senses: taste and touch.

Science Notebook EXTRA

Tell students that there are common expressions that make reference to the sense of touch. Write the following expressions on the board, and have students explain each one as best they can, based on what they have learned about the sense of touch: *a person who is a soft touch, rubbing someone the wrong way, a thick-skinned person, and a touchy person.*

Assess

EVALUATE Use the After You Read questions and the Alternative Assessment to help you assess students' understanding of the lesson.

After You Read

1. The body's five sensory organs are the eyes, ears, nose, tongue, and skin.
2. The eyes are organs that are sensitive to light energy. Light travels through the cornea, pupil, and lens to the retina. Rod and cone cells on the retina change this light into electrical impulses that are sent to the brain.
3. Both smell and taste are chemical senses. Receptor cells in the nose control the sense of smell, while receptor cells on the tongue control the sense of taste. Humans are sensitive to thousands of different smells but to only five tastes.
4. Students' answers will vary. Answers should reflect that different senses allow people to take in information from different kinds of stimuli in the environment.

Alternative Assessment

EVALUATE Have students complete their outlines and then compare them with a partner's and make any necessary changes. Underneath the outline, have each student write a paragraph summarizing the lesson using the outline as a guide.

Smell

Humans can detect thousands of smells, including the sweet scent of perfume, the unpleasant odor of a skunk, and the delicious aroma of a freshly baked pie. The nose is the sensory organ of smell. Chemicals enter the nose when people inhale. They bind to sensory receptors and trigger an electrical impulse. When the impulse reaches the brain, it is processed and interpreted as a smell.

Taste

Like the sense of smell, the sense of taste is a chemical sense. The tongue is the sensory organ of taste. The sense of taste is probably the least understood of the senses. What scientists do know is that people experience taste when chemicals enter the mouth and bind to sensory receptors. Most sensory receptors for taste are found on the tongue, bundled together in structures called taste buds. Humans are sensitive to five tastes—sweet, salty, bitter, sour, and umami, which is a taste sensation described as meaty or savory. Scientists believe that each receptor cell is sensitive to only one of the five tastes.

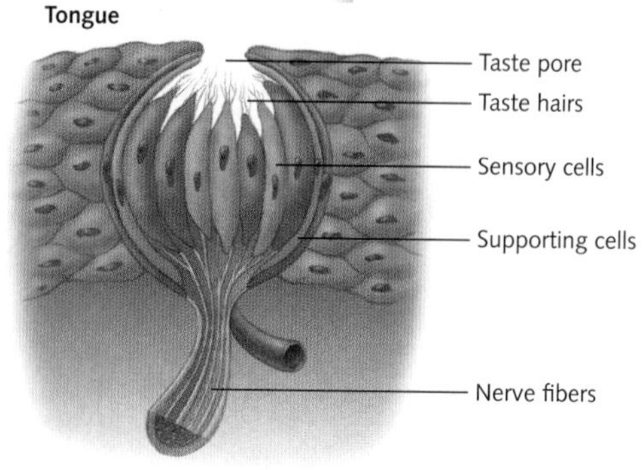

Tongue
Taste pore
Taste hairs
Sensory cells
Supporting cells
Nerve fibers

Figure 22.14 Each taste bud contains many receptor cells. The cells have taste hairs projecting from them. As food dissolves in the saliva in the mouth, the mixture stimulates the taste hairs. An impulse is sent to the brain and interpreted as a specific taste.

Touch

The sense of touch enables people to feel things such as pressure, temperature, and pain. The skin is the body's sensory organ of touch. Some sensory receptors in the skin are sensitive to chemicals. Other sensory receptors are sensitive to heat. Still other sensory receptors are sensitive to mechanical energy.

After You Read

1. What are the body's five sensory organs?
2. Describe the process by which people see. Why are the eyes, not the nose or tongue, the organs of sight?
3. Compare the sense of smell with the sense of taste. How are these senses alike? How do they differ?
4. Use the lesson outline in your Science Notebook to explain why you think the body has different senses.

ELL Strategy

Activate Background Knowledge Ask students if they have expressions similar to those described in the Science Notebook EXTRA activity. Have students translate their expressions into English and share their translations with the class.

Background Information

Smell is the strongest of the human senses. People are able to distinguish over 10,000 different odor molecules. Smell is believed to be thousands of times more sensitive than taste, accounting for 80 to 90 percent of flavor. People are able to recognize each other by scent. For example, a baby knows its mother by smell. People who lack a sense of smell are called anosmias.

22.4 The Endocrine System

Before You Read

Create a Venn diagram in your Science Notebook. Write *The Endocrine System* above one of the circles and *The Nervous System* above the other. Then, read the headings and subheadings in this lesson and look at the pictures. What are some ways in which the two systems might be alike? What are some ways in which they might differ?

Learning Goals

- Describe the functions of the endocrine system, and compare these with the functions of the nervous system.
- Identify the body's endocrine glands, and explain what each one does in the body.
- Explain the role of hormones and their control by feedback systems.

New Vocabulary

hormone
gland
negative feedback system

Suppose it were time for your school to have a fire drill. The goal of the fire drill is to make sure that every student and teacher gets out of the building quickly and safely. How should the principal let each class know that a drill is taking place? She could walk from classroom to classroom to tell the teachers and students individually, but that could take a long time. A faster and easier way might be for her to use the public address and alarm systems. These systems would inform all the students and teachers at the same time that a drill was occurring. Everyone would get out of the building quickly.

The endocrine system is a little like the public address and alarm systems in your school. It allows the body to send a mass message to many cells at once.

A Messenger System

Like the nervous system, the endocrine system is a messenger system. It works with the nervous system to help control many of the body's internal functions. The two systems are very different, however. Whereas the nervous system makes specific connections in the body, much like the principal traveling from classroom to classroom, the endocrine system sends mass messages throughout the body. It does this by releasing chemicals called **hormones** (HOR mohnz) directly into the bloodstream. Because hormones are released into the bloodstream, they can travel throughout the entire body. Chemicals released by neurons of the nervous system, you will recall, are directed to one cell or a small group of cells. They do not travel throughout the body.

The speed at which hormones travel in the bloodstream is slow compared with the speed of nerve impulses. Thus, the endocrine system tends to regulate body processes that happen slowly over a long period of time. These processes include cell growth and development, metabolism, sexual function, and reproduction. The endocrine system is also involved in regulating the body's response to danger or stress.

22.4 Introduce

ENGAGE Have students return to page 398 to reread the opening paragraphs of the chapter. Ask them to talk in small groups about the ways in which the nervous system regulates communication in the body. Then, have them scan this lesson and speculate as to how the endocrine system also functions as a communication system.

Before You Read

Draw a Venn diagram on the board with *The Endocrine System* above one circle and *The Nervous System* above the other. Have students do the same in their Science Notebooks. Ask them to list ways in which the two might be similar or different. Write one or two correct suggestions in the diagram on the board. Instruct students to work on their diagrams as they read through the lesson.

Teach

EXPLAIN to students that in this section, they will begin to learn about the endocrine system and how it compares to the nervous system.

Vocabulary

hormone Explain that *hormone* comes from the Greek word *horman*, meaning "to stimulate."

Differentiated Instruction

Linguistic Have students research the name origins of the glands of the human body that are discussed in this chapter. Students may also choose to research the derivatives of the words (e.g., *adrenal gland, adrenal cortex, and adrenaline*).

Teach

EXPLAIN to students that they will learn about the structure and function of the endocrine system in this section.

EXPLORE The online medical library of the National Library of Medicine and the National Institutes of Health, accessible at **http://www.nlm.nih.gov**, contains information about diseases, conditions, and wellness, as well as current health news. There is also a medical encyclopedia and dictionary. Have students choose a topic to research and write about their findings in their Science Notebooks.

Vocabulary

gland Tell students that *gland* comes from the Latin word *glans*, meaning "acorn." Ask students to name other glands that they have learned about (salivary glands and sweat glands).

Use the Visual: Figure 22.15

ANSWER hormones

Structure and Function

The main organs of the endocrine system are glands. A **gland** is an organ that produces and releases a substance. In the case of the endocrine system, this substance is a hormone. Some glands release substances directly to the organ that uses them through tubelike structures called ducts. Endocrine glands release hormones into the bloodstream. Because endocrine glands do not have ducts, they are often called ductless glands.

Figure 22.15 shows the major glands of the endocrine system. Endocrine glands are scattered throughout the body. In general, they are not directly connected with one another.

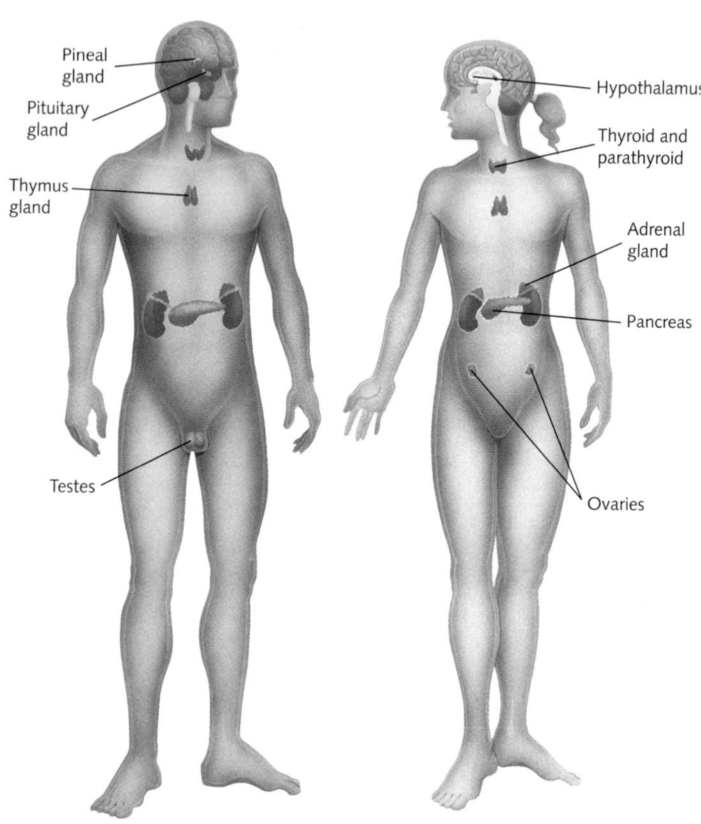

Figure 22.15 The endocrine system consists of many different glands and organs that are involved in regulating and coordinating various body functions. What is the name of the chemicals produced by endocrine glands?

Background Information

Glands that release substances through a duct are called exocrine glands. *Exo-* means "outside" or "external." Some of these substances, such as tears or sweat, are released outside of the body. *Endo-* means "inside" or "internal."

The pituitary gland secretes human growth hormone. For about 20 years, a synthetic growth hormone that promotes bone and muscle growth has been prescribed to adolescents who do not produce the hormone naturally. Some athletes and aging adults use the drug to increase muscle mass and stay young. The known side effects are few, but the long-term effects of the drug have yet to be fully determined.

Hypothalamus The hypothalamus, an area in the brain, connects the nervous system with the endocrine system. Its major function is to control the pituitary gland.

Pituitary Gland The pituitary gland is directly connected to the hypothalamus. It secretes nine different hormones. Some of these hormones directly regulate body processes. Others indirectly regulate body processes by controlling other glands. A few of the pituitary's many hormones and functions are shown in **Figure 22.17**.

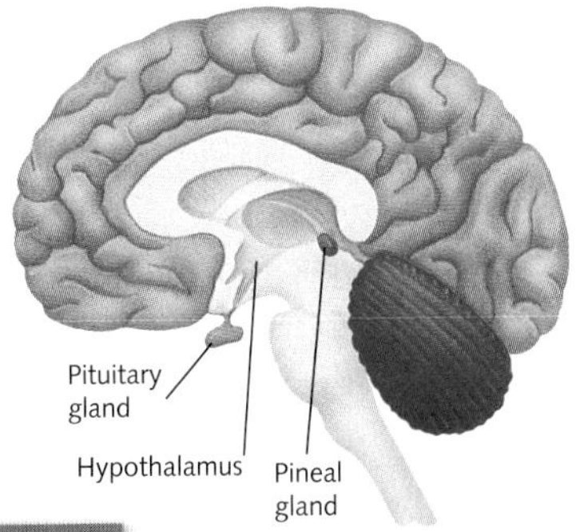

Pituitary gland

Hypothalamus

Pineal gland

Figure 22.16 The hypothalamus, pituitary gland, and pineal gland are located in the brain. What is the primary function of each of these structures?

Figure It Out

1. Which hormones regulate body processes indirectly?
2. How would you describe the functions of the pituitary gland?

Pituitary Hormones

Hormone	Function in the Body
growth hormone	triggers the body to produce proteins; regulates growth in cells
follicle-stimulating hormone	triggers the body to produce sperm and mature egg cells
prolactin	triggers the production of milk in females after giving birth
thyroid-stimulating hormone	triggers the thyroid gland to produce and release a hormone called thyroxine

Figure 22.17 For a gland the size of a bean, the pituitary has many functions.

Pineal Gland The pineal gland is about the size of a bean and is buried deep within the brain. It produces and releases a hormone called melatonin. Melatonin is involved in regulating the body's rhythms, such as the sleep-wake cycle.

Thyroid Gland The two-lobed thyroid gland, located at the base of the neck, releases a hormone called thyroxine. Thyroxine regulates the process through which cells break down chemicals and get energy.

Parathyroid Glands Located on the back surface of the thyroid gland are four parathyroid glands. These tiny glands help regulate the amount of calcium that is in the body. Calcium is important for proper functioning of neurons. It is also important for bone development and muscle control.

As You Read

Use the Venn diagram in your Science Notebook to record important information about the endocrine system.

What are the main organs of the endocrine system? What chemicals do they release?

Teach

EXPLAIN to students that they will learn about the major glands of the endocrine system. Have students look back at the diagram of the endocrine system in Figure 22.15 on page 412. Ask them to follow along as you read aloud the labels indicating the glands.

Use the Visual: Figure 22.16

ANSWER The hypothalamus is a part of the brain that controls the pituitary gland, which produces hormones that directly and indirectly regulate body processes. The pineal gland produces the hormone melatonin, which is involved in regulating the body's rhythms, such as the sleep/wake cycle.

Figure It Out: Figure 22.17

ANSWER **1.** Thyroid-stimulating hormone regulates body processes indirectly.
2. The pituitary gland has a broad range of functions in the body. It works both directly and indirectly to control body processes. Because it controls the functioning of other endocrine glands, it plays a central role in the endocrine system.

As You Read

Give students time to fill in their Venn diagrams. Ask volunteers to share the information they have found about similarities and differences between the two systems.

ANSWER The main organs of the endocrine system are glands, including the pituitary, thyroid, parathyroid, thymus, adrenal, ovaries, and testes. Organs such as the brain and pancreas also contain groups of cells that act as endocrine glands. Endocrine glands release chemicals called hormones.

ELL Strategy

Practice Using Vocabulary Have one group of students make cards describing the function, but not the name, of each of the following glands: pituitary, thymus, adrenals, pancreas, and ovaries and testes. Have another group create cards on which each gland's name is partially spelled. For example, a card might read *pi_it_ry*. Have the groups work together to complete the names of the glands and match each gland to its function.

Background Information

Hypothyroidism occurs when the thyroid gland is under-active, meaning it does not produce enough hormone. Symptoms include fatigue and sluggishness and may also include constipation, pale dry skin, greater sensitivity to cold, weight gain, muscle aches, and muscle weakness. Women, especially those over 50, are more likely than men to have hypothyroidism.

Teach

EXPLAIN to students that in this section, they will continue to learn about the glands of the endocrine system.

Use the Visual: Figure 22.18

ANSWER Insulin and glucagon work together to control the amount of sugar in the blood.

Vocabulary

negative feedback system Tell students that *negative* relates to saying no or denying. Feedback is the process by which part of the output of a system is returned to the input in order to regulate or modify later output.

Science Notebook EXTRA

Have students create charts of the endocrine system glands listed on pages 413 and 414. Students should include the name of each gland, its location in the body, the hormone(s) it secretes, and the function of each hormone. When students have finished, arrange them in groups of three to create group charts. The group charts can be used to create a class chart for display.

CONNECTION: Health

Have students use the Internet or resource books to conduct research into Type 1 or Type 2 diabetes. Specifically, have students find information to answer one or more of the following questions: *What are the problems caused by diabetes? How can the problems be prevented? What foods are helpful in controlling diabetes? What exercise is helpful in controlling diabetes?*

Figure 22.18 Tiny clusters of endocrine tissue called the islets of Langerhans are scattered throughout the pancreas. The millions of cells that make up the islets produce the hormones insulin and glucagon. What is the function of these hormones?

Figure 22.19 Located just behind the sternum in the upper chest, the thymus gland produces infection-fighting cells that are part of the body's immune response.

Pancreas The pancreas, an organ of the digestive system, is also an endocrine gland. The pancreas releases hormones called insulin and glucagon. These hormones work together to control the amount of sugar that is in the blood.

Thymus Gland The thymus is located in the upper chest. It produces hormones that aid in the body's ability to fight disease. In particular, it helps the body form T cells, which are found in the blood and fight infection.

Adrenal Glands The adrenal glands are located above the kidneys. The adrenal glands release a hormone that is commonly called adrenaline. Adrenaline is responsible for the rush you feel when you are particularly nervous or excited. It helps the body cope with stressful situations. The adrenal glands also release more than 24 other hormones that help regulate other processes in the body.

Reproductive Glands The testes in males and the ovaries in females are the body's reproductive glands. The reproductive glands produce hormones that control secondary sex characteristics, such as pubic hair, a male's deep voice, and a female's breasts. The hormone testosterone plays a role in the production of sperm cells in males. The hormones estrogen and progesterone aid in the development of ova, or egg cells, in females. These hormones also help regulate a female's menstrual cycle.

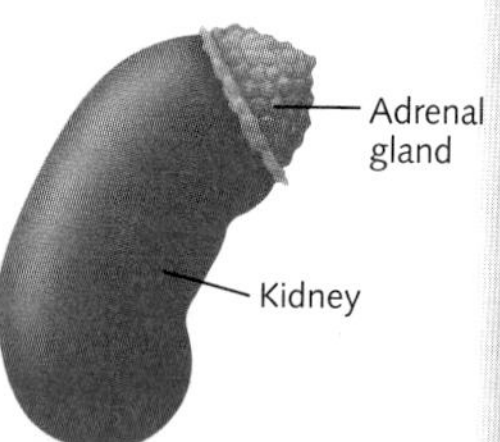

Figure 22.20 One adrenal gland sits atop each kidney. The two adrenal glands are complex glands that produce a variety of hormones, some of which help stabilize the levels of sugar in the blood.

Controlling the Endocrine System

The endocrine system sends messages throughout the body. It does this by releasing hormones that travel through the bloodstream to target cells. A target cell is a cell that has receptors for a particular hormone. Once the hormone reaches a target cell, it triggers the cell to carry out a specific task. How are the actions of hormones controlled in the body? What causes a gland to start or stop releasing a particular hormone?

The body uses feedback systems to help control the production and release of hormones. Regulation of the endocrine system is most often controlled through a type of internal feedback system called a **negative feedback system**. In such a system, the hormones or the products of their effects are fed back to stop the original signal. Thus, if homeostasis is disrupted, the endocrine system can act to restore it.

Background Information

Adrenaline, also known as epinephrine, is one hormone secreted by the adrenal glands. It raises blood pressure, causes the heart to beat faster, and increases sweat production. When the body is under stress or in danger, epinephrine acts as a neurotransmitter. Epinephrine is often administered to a person who is having a life-threatening allergic reaction to an insect bite or food, for example. It relaxes the muscles in the airways, allowing the person to breathe easier, and constricts the blood vessels, raising the blood pressure.

Figure 22.21 shows an example of how negative feedback controls a function of the endocrine system. First, low blood sugar signals the hypothalamus to stimulate the pituitary gland. The pituitary gland then releases human growth hormone. The growth hormone (hGH) travels through the bloodstream to target cells in the liver. It triggers the liver to release glucose into the bloodstream. Increased blood sugar signals back to the hypothalamus to stop stimulating the pituitary gland. The pituitary gland stops releasing growth hormone, and the liver stops releasing glucose. When the blood sugar level drops again, the process will repeat itself.

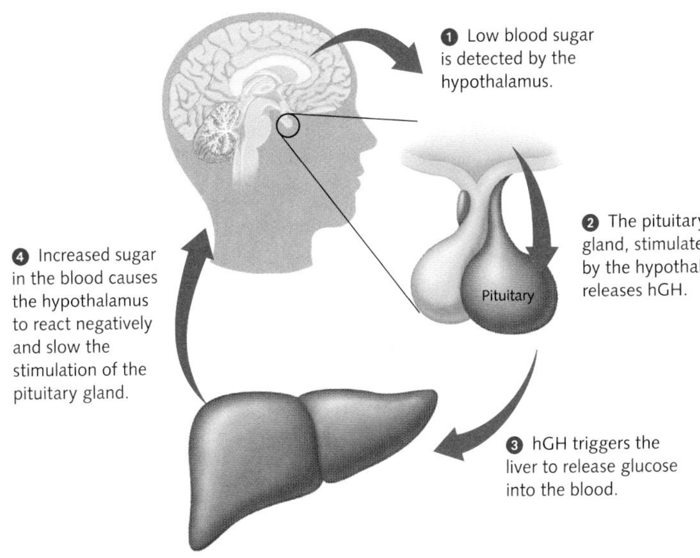

1 Low blood sugar is detected by the hypothalamus.
2 The pituitary gland, stimulated by the hypothalamus, releases hGH.
Pituitary
3 hGH triggers the liver to release glucose into the blood.
4 Increased sugar in the blood causes the hypothalamus to react negatively and slow the stimulation of the pituitary gland.

Figure 22.21 The endocrine system is a control system, but it too must be controlled. The body does this through a negative feedback system.

After You Read

1. What are the main functions of the endocrine system?
2. List three glands of the endocrine system, and describe what each one does in the body.
3. Explain how the endocrine system is controlled.
4. Complete the Venn diagram in your Science Notebook by filling in ways in which the endocrine and nervous systems are alike and different. Use your Venn diagram to write a well-developed paragraph that compares and contrasts the two body systems.

Did You Know?

For many years, the pituitary gland was nicknamed the "master gland" because it was thought that all other glands were controlled by hormones produced in the pituitary gland. However, the pituitary is not the master gland. Almost all of its secretions are triggered by hormones or nerve impulses from the hypothalamus, which can be thought of as the "master of the pituitary gland."

Explain It!

The operation of a thermostat in your home or school is an example of a negative feedback system. Explain how a thermostat works. Use a diagram similar to the one in Figure 22.21 to illustrate your explanation. Record your work in your Science Notebook.

Teach

EXPLAIN Ask students to recall the meaning of *homeostasis* (the state of internal balance that is maintained by continually responding to external and internal stimuli). Tell students that negative feedback is one method of maintaining homeostasis.

Explain It!

Ask students what a thermostat is, and show one in the classroom or school, if possible. Ask if anyone knows what a thermostat does. Explain if necessary. (A thermostat controls a heating/cooling system in order to maintain the temperature within certain desired limits. If the temperature in a room goes above or below the temperature at which the thermostat is set, the thermostat turns the heating/cooling system on or off until the desired temperature is reached.) Draw a diagram on the board showing how a thermostat works. Ask students to do the same in their Science Notebooks and then write a paragraph or two explaining what they drew.

Assess

EVALUATE Use the After You Read questions and the Alternative Assessment to help you assess students' understanding of the lesson.

After You Read

1. regulation of metabolism, growth, and reproduction
2. Answers will vary but should reflect the information provided in the lesson.
3. A negative feedback system triggers the release of hormones when their levels drop and stops their release when levels rise.
4. Students' answers will vary. Students should recognize that both systems are communication systems, but that they function in different ways to control different processes. The two systems involve different organs and different types of messengers.

Background Information

The release of thyroxine is controlled by negative-feedback. The pituitary gland senses the thyroxine level in the blood. When the level drops too low, it releases thyroid-stimulating hormone (TSH), which causes the thyroid gland to produce more thyroxine, restoring the thyroxine level in the blood. When the thyroxine level rises, the pituitary gland stops releasing TSH, causing the thyroid gland to stop producing thyroxine.

Alternative Assessment

EVALUATE Allow students to discuss in small groups how the endocrine and nervous systems differ. Then, they can add this information to their Venn diagrams. Instruct each student to use the information in his or her diagram to write a paragraph comparing and contrasting the two systems.

Chapter 22 Summary

VOCABULARY REVIEW

Check students' sentences or paragraphs to make sure they understand the meaning of each vocabulary term.

PREPARE FOR CHAPTER TEST

Evaluate students' essays using the following criteria:

1. The topic sentence, or main idea, should restate the Key Concept.
2. The supporting paragraphs should incorporate the answers to the Learning Goal questions students have written and include details, facts, and examples they have recorded in their Science Notebooks.
3. The concluding sentence should sum up the main idea of the chapter and restate the Key Concept.

MASTERING CONCEPTS

True or False

1. True
2. False, eyes
3. False, chemicals
4. True
5. True
6. True

Short Answer

7. A reflex is an automatic, involuntary response of the nervous system that starts in a sensory receptor, travels through a sensory neuron to the spinal cord, and then travels back to muscle or organ through a motor neuron.
8. Receptor cells called rods and cones allow the eyes to sense light.
9. The cerebellum coordinates the body's voluntary actions. It regulates skeletal muscles and helps maintain muscle tone and balance.
10. Hormones are chemical messengers of the endocrine system. Hormones travel through the bloodstream to target cells and trigger the cells to carry out certain functions.
11. The nervous system can be divided into the central nervous system and the peripheral nervous system.

Chapter 22

Summary

KEY CONCEPTS

22.1 The Nervous System

- The nervous system helps control all the other body systems.
- Neurons are the cells of the nervous system. They have three main segments: a cell body, dendrites, and an axon.
- Information is sent through the nervous system in the form of electrical and chemical impulses.
- The nervous system can be divided into two smaller systems. The central nervous system (CNS) is made up of the brain and spinal cord. The peripheral nervous system (PNS) is made up of all the other nerves in the body.

22.2 The Brain and Spinal Cord

- The brain is divided into three parts: the cerebrum, cerebellum, and brain stem. The brain controls all of the body's voluntary actions, as well as many of the body's involuntary actions. It is the site of thought, reason, and emotion.
- The spinal cord connects the brain with the body's other organs. It is made up of bundles of nerves held together by connective tissue, and it is surrounded by bone and fluid.
- A reflex is an automatic, involuntary response to a stimulus. Reflexes involve short networks called reflex arcs. They are controlled in the spinal cord rather than in the brain.

22.3 The Senses

- The eyes, ears, nose, tongue, and skin are the organs responsible for the senses.
- Sensory receptors are able to change energy from a stimulus into an electrical impulse.
- When stimulated, the eyes, ears, nose, tongue, and skin produce electrical impulses that can be sent to the brain.
- The ears also sense the body's balance.

22.4 The Endocrine System

- The endocrine system helps control body processes such as growth, metabolism, and reproduction.
- The endocrine system is made up of glands and tissues that release hormones into the bloodstream.
- Hormones travel through the bloodstream to target cells. Their production and release is controlled by a negative feedback system.

VOCABULARY REVIEW

Write each term in a complete sentence, or write a paragraph relating several terms.

22.1
stimulus, p. 399
neuron, p. 400
dendrite, p. 400
axon, p. 400
synapse, p. 400
central nervous system, p. 402
peripheral nervous system, p. 402

22.2
cerebrum, p. 404
cerebellum, p. 404
brain stem, p. 404
vertebra, p. 405
reflex, p. 406
reflex arc, p. 406

22.3
sensory receptor, p. 407
cone, p. 408
rod, p. 408
retina, p. 408
cochlea, p. 409
cilia, p. 409

22.4
hormone, p. 411
gland, p. 412
negative feedback system, p. 414

PREPARE FOR CHAPTER TEST

To prepare for the chapter test, create a question from each Learning Goal. Use the information in your Science Notebook to answer each question. Then use these answers to write a well-developed essay about the chapter. Use the Key Concept on the first page of this chapter as your topic sentence.

416 NERVOUS AND ENDOCRINE SYSTEMS

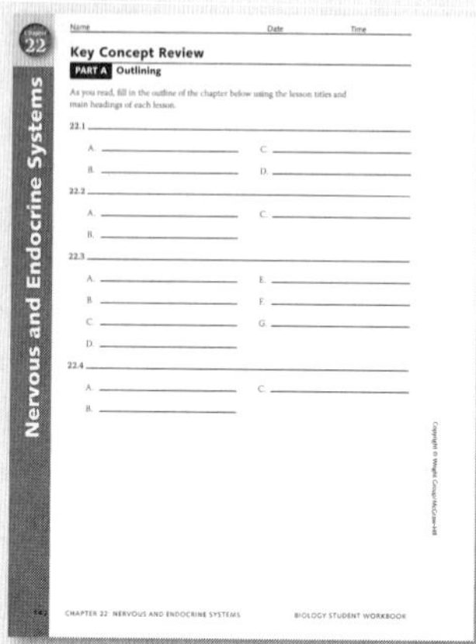

Key Concept Review Workbook, p. 142

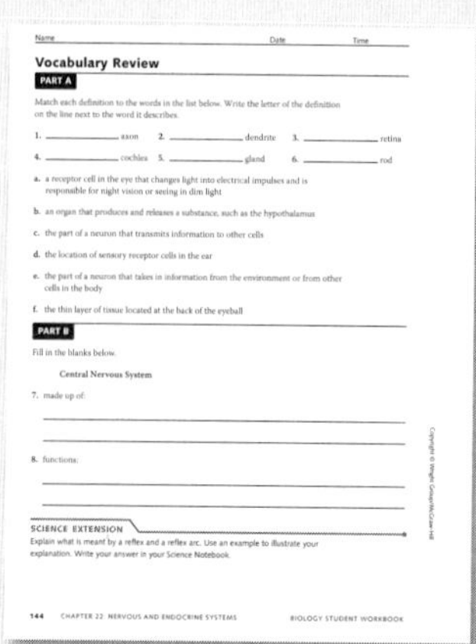

Vocabulary Review Workbook, p. 144

MASTERING CONCEPTS

True or False

If the statement is true, write "true." If it is false, change the underlined word or words to make the statement true.

1. The endocrine system helps control growth.
2. The ears are sensitive to light.
3. Receptors inside the nose are sensitive to mechanical energy.
4. The nervous system is responsible for people's ability to think and reason.
5. The spinal cord connects the brain with the rest of the body.
6. The endocrine system is made up of organs called glands.

Short Answer

Answer each of the following in a sentence or brief paragraph.

7. What is a reflex?
8. What kinds of cells allow the eyes to sense light?
9. What are the main functions of the cerebellum?
10. What do hormones do? How do they work in the body?
11. What are two divisions of the nervous system?

Critical Thinking

Use what you have learned in this chapter to answer each of the following.

12. **Compare and Contrast** How are reflexes similar to voluntary actions controlled by the nervous system? How do they differ?
13. **Explain** Why is it important to care for your ears and other sensory organs?
14. **Classify** What are three types of neurons? How do they differ?
15. **Infer** Why might the body have two different communication systems?

Standardized Test Question

Choose the letter of the response that correctly answers the question.

16. All of the following structures are essential to the process of hearing *except* the ________.
    - A. semicircular canal
    - B. cochlea
    - C. eardrum
    - D. cilia

Test-Taking Tip

Be careful of words such as *except*. This word means that all the answers are correct *except* for one.

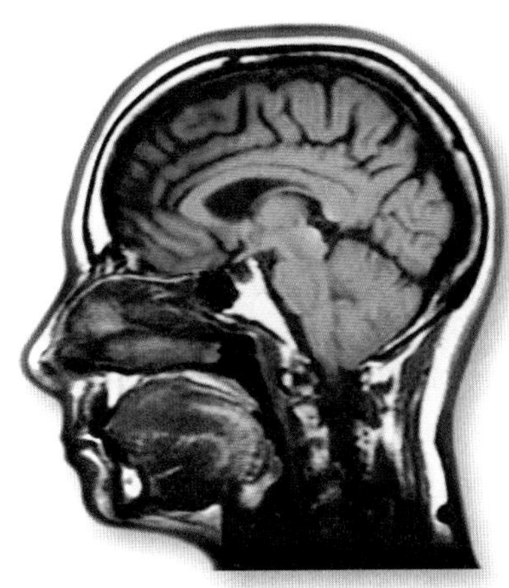

Critical Thinking

12. Similar to voluntary actions, reflexes involve transmission of information from a stimulus via nerve impulses in neurons. They differ by involving simple reflex arcs processed in the spinal cord instead of the brain.
13. The sensory organs act as connections to the outside world. If sensory organs do not function properly, people will not be able to take in information from their surroundings.
14. Sensory neurons carry impulses toward the CNS, interneurons relay impulses, and motor neurons carry impulses to muscles.
15. Answers will vary. Students should recognize that the body needs to be able to respond quickly and specifically to certain stimuli, but that slower mass signals are a more efficient for regular body maintenance.

Standardized Test Question

16. A

Reading Links

The Great Brain Book: An Inside Look at the Inside of Your Head

This reviewer favorite is sure to liven up the study of the body's communication systems. For confident readers, Newquist's text is rich with anecdotes, interesting details, and historical background, but students of all levels will benefit from the book's extensive and engaging use of diagrams, illustrations, and photos. The book includes a short list of online resources.

Newquist, H.P. Illustrated by Keith Klasnot. Scholastic, Inc. 160 pp. Trade ISBN: 978-0-439-45895-5.

No-Sweat Science: Optical Illusion Experiments

For an entertaining, interactive twist on the scientific inquiry process, students of all levels can spend time with the visual puzzles contained in this collection. The experiments illustrate various aspects of visual perception and information processing. The activities are an inexpensive way to engage students in a classroom or to get individuals excited about "bringing science home" to impress friends and family.

DiSpezio, Michael A. Illustrated by Jack Gallagher. Sterling Publishing Co., Inc. Trade ISBN: 978-1-4027-2336-0.

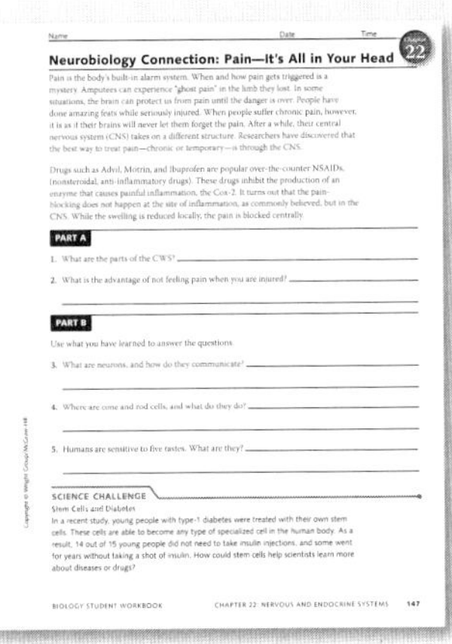

Neurobiology Connection: Pain—It's All in Your Head

Curriculum Connection
Workbook, p. 147

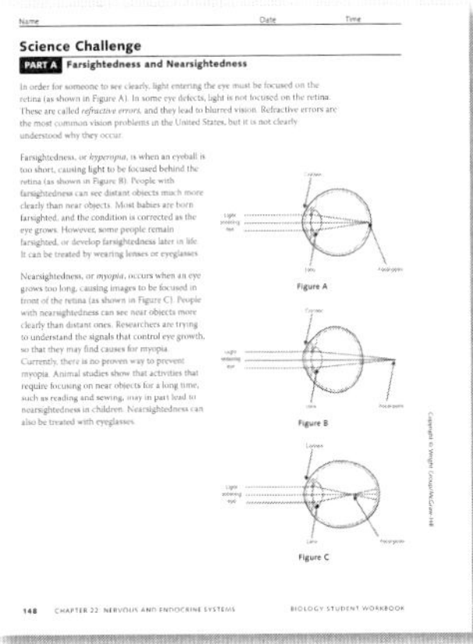

Science Challenge

PART A Farsightedness and Nearsightedness

Science Challenge
Workbook, pp. 148–150

Chapter 22

Labs

22A How Quickly Do You React?

This prechapter introduction activity is designed to determine what students already know about the body's control and communication system by allowing students to measure, compare, and evaluate sensory response time.

Objectives

- measure eye-to-hand reaction time
- compare and contrast reaction to visual and auditory stimulation
- evaluate data from successive trials
- communicate conclusions

Planning

 20–30 minutes  groups of 2 students

Materials (per group)

- meterstick
- masking tape
- string
- metal washer

Advance Preparation

- Explain to students that they must subtract the starting point of the washer from the point where it ends up to find the distance the washer traveled.
- Give students the formula **reaction time = $\sqrt{2}$ × distance washer falls in cm/980 cm/s^2** (the square root of 2 times the distance the washer falls in centimeters, divided by 980 centimeters per second squared).

Engagement Guide

- Challenge students to think about the factors that affect reaction time by asking:
  - *How do you think performing several trials affects reaction time?* (Reaction time should get better, or require less time, with practice.)
  - *What is different about reacting to sight instead of sound?* (Students might conclude that reaction time to something observed is slightly shorter than reaction time to something heard. However, students should recognize that there might be a slight difference in time between when the student says "now" and when the string is actually released.)

Going Further

Encourage students to repeat this activity with the introduction of other factors that could affect reaction time, such as distraction or fatigue. Have students present their conclusions to the class.

22B How Sight and Smell Affect Taste

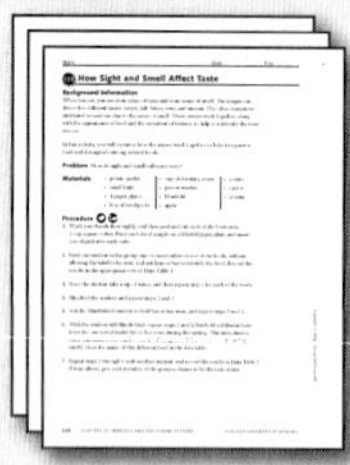

Objectives

- compare and contrast the sensations of various foods
- evaluate the properties of foods based on the senses
- identify foods based on the combination of sensations they cause

Skill Set

observing, comparing and contrasting, classifying, stating conclusions

Planning

 1 class period  groups of 3–4 students

Materials

Materials for this activity are listed in the Student Laboratory Manual.

Lab Tip

Food samples should also be rinsed before and after being peeled.

Answers to Observations: Data Tables 1 and 2

Results will vary, but students should discover that smell is a very important contributor to the correct identification of food.

Answers to Analysis and Conclusions

1. Having all the senses unblocked was best for identifying the foods. Students should find that smelling a different food was the worst for correct food identification.
2. Responses will vary, but students should recognize that no matter how skilled a student is at guessing the food, smell is still an important factor.
3. Responses will vary, but students should recognize that smell is the most important factor, and this should be supported by the results recorded when the student smelled a different food from the one tasted.
4. Responses will vary, but students should recognize that smell was more important than taste.
5. Responses will vary, but students should understand that taste depends on a combination of senses.

Going Further

Bring in a selection of different foods, and have students repeat the experiment. Students might try different methods of confusing the senses—for example, showing the taste-tester one food while he or she tastes another, or putting nonfood smells under the nose during tasting.

22C Concentrating on Glands and Hormones

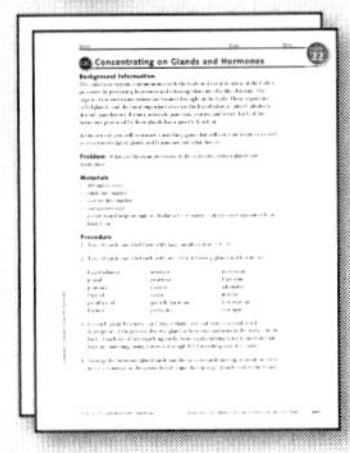

Objectives

- describe the processes performed by each gland and hormone in the endocrine system
- test memory and knowledge by matching the gland or hormone to the correct associated process

Skill Set

observing, comparing and contrasting, remembering, classifying, defining

Planning

1 class period groups of 3–4 students

Materials

Materials for this activity are listed in the Student Laboratory Manual.

Advance Preparation

Explain how the matching game works. Each group of students will create all the cards for the game. The board has a matrix of 36 cards, numbered 1 to 36. These cards are taped by the top edges so they can be swung up to reveal 36 more cards underneath. Of the cards underneath, 18 have the name of a gland or hormone written on them. The other 18 have a short description of the process performed by one of the glands or hormones. Each process card matches one gland or hormone card. For example, a process card match for the card with *thyroid* might say *regulates body metabolism.* These two cards would both have an *A* written on the back to confirm they are a match. Other gland/hormone and process matches would be coded *B* through *R* for all 18 matches. When student groups have completed their matrices, select one group to be the matrix presenter, and have the other two groups play the game as competing teams. The game can be played two more times, using the sets created by the other two groups.

Answers to Analysis and Conclusions

1. Answers will vary, but students should recognize that they needed to distinguish between the descriptions of a process performed by a gland and the process performed by a hormone produced by that gland.
2. Answers will vary, but students should recognize that it was important to remember whether a card was a gland/hormone card or a process card so that one of each type could be chosen for a match.
3. Answers will vary, but students should recognize that this exercise in relating glands/hormones to processes is a good way to learn to distinguish among the various parts of the endocrine system.

Going Further

Have students construct a game to test other knowledge, such as parts of the nervous system.

Chapter 23 Lessons

Introduce Chapter 23

As a starting activity, use LAB 23A How Gender Is Determined on page 143 of the Laboratory Manual.

ENGAGE Give small groups of students photographs of two or three families. The photographs should be cut apart so that each person is alone. Some families should have members who look very similar, while others should contain members who do not resemble each other as much (possibly with adopted members). Have each group work to put together members of the same families. Ask: *What strategies did you use to put the families together? What was easy about the task? What was a challenge?*

Think About Life Cycles

ENGAGE Ask students to think of the stages in a butterfly's or a frog's life and share them with the class. Explain that a stage is a distinct, successive period. Tell students that humans also pass through life stages, and ask what these stages might be.

Instruct students to complete each bulleted activity. Then, discuss their results as a class. Give students a few minutes to make adjustments to the list of human life stages in their Science Notebooks.

Chapter 23 Reproduction and Development

KEY CONCEPT The reproductive system is responsible for making new individuals.

One of the defining characteristics of living things is their ability to make new living things. Most animals—including humans—reproduce sexually. In sexual reproduction, a male and a female from the same species mix their genes to make a new, genetically unique individual.

Mixing genes has its advantages. By having offspring that are not exact copies of each other, the parents reduce the chance that all of their babies can be wiped out by a passing bacterium or parasite. To mix their genomes, however, animals need to make special cells that can fuse together. Each sex has a specialized system to produce those cells.

Think About Life Cycles

Every animal has a life cycle—a series of stages that it passes through from the beginning of its life until it has offspring of its own.

- In your Science Notebook, list all the human life stages you can think of.
- How many stages have you passed through already? Draw an arrow marking where you are now. Add arrows with labels for your parent(s) or guardian(s) and for any aunts, uncles, and grandparents.

NSTA SciLinks THE WORLD'S A CLICK AWAY
www.scilinks.org
Reproductive System **Code: WGB23**

418

Chapter 23 Planning Guide			
Instructional Periods	**National Standards**	**Lab Manual**	**Workbook**
23.1 3 periods	C.1, C.2, C.3, G.1, G.2; A.1, C.1, C.2, G.1, G.2; UCP.3, UCP.5	**Lab 23A—p. 143** How Gender is Determined **Lab 23B—p. 144** Model of a Placenta **Lab 23C—p. 146** Sea Urchin Fertilization	Key Concept Review p. 151 Vocabulary Review p. 152 Interpreting Diagrams p. 153 Reading Comprehension p. 154 Curriculum Connection p. 156 Science Challenge p. 157
23.2 2 periods	C.1, C.2; C.5; UCP.2, UCP.3		
23.3 1 period	A.2;; A.2, C.5; UCP.2, UCP.3		

Middle School Standard; High School Standard; Unifying Concept and Principle

23.1 The Reproductive System

Before You Read

Draw a T-chart in your Science Notebook. Label one side *Male* and the other side *Female*. As you read this lesson, write the characteristics of males and females in the correct columns.

Learning Goals

- Describe the formation of a zygote.
- Name the organs in the male and female reproductive systems.
- List the events in the menstrual cycle.

New Vocabulary

gamete
sperm
ovum
fertilization
zygote
testis
testosterone
epididymis
scrotum
vas deferens
semen
ovary
oviduct
uterus
cervix
vagina
menstruation
estrogen
ovulation
progesterone

Reproductive systems are essential to the survival of the species but not to individual survival. Men and women are different, and their reproductive systems contain different organs. The physical differences between men and women reflect their different roles in reproduction.

Gametes Make Zygotes

A man and a woman each contribute one **gamete** (GA meet), or sex cell, to make a baby. Male gametes are called **sperm**. Each of these small cells has a head and a long tail. A portion of the tail just behind the head is packed with mitochondria that produce energy a sperm uses to swim toward an egg. The head contains the nucleus of the cell and enzymes that help the sperm enter the egg. Female gametes are called **ova** (OH vuh, singular: ovum), or eggs. Ova are large cells that are filled with nutrients and other materials to help new life grow. **Figure 23.1** shows an ovum and several sperm.

Gametes are haploid cells. They contain only one set of chromosomes. When a haploid sperm fuses with a haploid egg, a cell with the diploid number of chromosomes results. The diploid number is the number of chromosomes an adult has. Thus, the chromosome number remains the same from one generation to the next.

Fertilization (fur tuh luh ZAY shun) occurs when a sperm cell fuses with an ovum to form a new cell called a **zygote** (ZI goht). The zygote combines the chromosomes from the sperm and the egg in its nucleus, making a new diploid cell. The zygote will develop into a new human being.

A human zygote contains 46 chromosomes. Half of them come from the sperm, and the other half are from the ovum. One pair of the chromosomes controls whether the zygote becomes a boy or a girl. If the zygote contains two large sex chromosomes, which are also called X chromosomes, the zygote becomes a girl. If the zygote contains one X chromosome and a small chromosome called the Y chromosome, the zygote becomes a boy. The Y chromosome carries fewer and different genes than the X chromosome does. This means that males have only one copy of the genes on the X chromosome. Recessive genetic traits on the X chromosome are always expressed in males. These traits, such as hemophilia and color blindness, are called sex-linked traits.

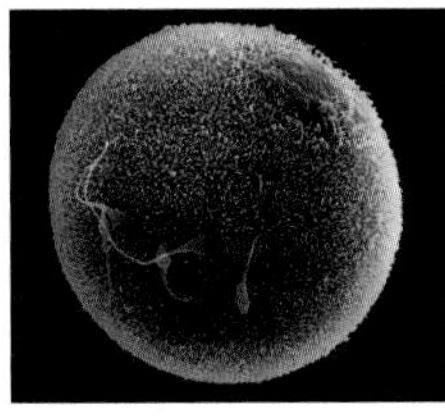

Figure 23.1 Males and females make different kinds of gametes. Five tiny sperm can be seen on the surface of this much larger ovum.

23.1 Introduce

ENGAGE Ask students what they already know about human reproduction. Discuss the importance of reproduction in the continuation of the species.

Before You Read

Tell students that their T-charts should include body systems, sex cells (gametes), and male and female reproductive system organs, structures, and hormones.

Vocabulary terms are listed on the first student page of each lesson. You may wish to preview the terms before introducing each lesson. Strategies for teaching the vocabulary appear on the pages where the terms are introduced.

Teach

EXPLAIN Tell students that in this lesson, they will be learning about the differences between the male and female reproductive systems, the sex cells each system produces, and the role of each in producing offspring.

Science Notebook EXTRA

Encourage students to use the vocabulary section they created in their Science Notebooks. Remind them to record prefixes, suffixes, and root words to help them remember the meanings of vocabulary terms.

ELL Strategy

Practice Using Vocabulary Have students work in pairs to list vocabulary terms by category and indicate any relationships between the terms in each category. Encourage students to draw diagrams illustrating the nouns. After categorizing, each pair of students should explain its grouping choices to another pair.

Teacher Alert

Be sensitive about families with adopted members. Acknowledge that some family members are not blood relatives. Whenever students are required to consider family, suggest that they think about the extended family.

Vocabulary

gamete Explain that *gamete* comes from the Greek word *gamein,* meaning "to marry."

sperm Explain that this word comes from the Greek *sperma,* meaning "seed."

ovum Tell students that this word comes from the Latin word *ovum,* meaning "egg."

fertilization Explain that another meaning of this word is "the process of supplying soil with extra nutrients to improve plant growth."

zygote Have students define *zygote* in their own words, using the three preceding vocabulary terms. Encourage them to use the terms *diploid* and *haploid* in their definitions.

Teach

 **EXPLAIN** to students that they will learn about the important work of scientist Patricia Jacobs, who studied human chromosomes. They will also learn about the structure of the male reproductive system.

Vocabulary

testis Explain that *testis* is Latin and means "witness (of virility)." The word *virility* comes from the Latin word meaning "man."

testosterone This word includes *testis* + *sterol* + *-one*. Sterols are fat-soluble organic compounds, and *-one* signifies a type of organic compound.

epididymis Explain that this is a Greek word that contains the prefix *epi-*, meaning "upon," and the root *didymos*, meaning "a twin" or "double." In Greek, *didymoi*, which is the plural of *didymos*, refers to the testes.

scrotum Explain that *scrotum* is a Latin word similar to *scrautum*, meaning "quiver." A quiver is a case that holds arrows.

vas deferens Tell students that this word comes from Latin and means "carrying down."

semen Tell students that this is a Latin word meaning "seed." Ask what other word in this chapter also has this meaning. (sperm)

PEOPLE IN SCIENCE

Show students a karyotype and explain what it is. Have them read about Patricia Jacobs with a partner and discuss what they learn.

EXTEND Have students find examples of karyotype charts on the Internet or in library books. Ask students to determine the gender of the person represented by looking at each chart. Students may also research the karyotypes of people with various diseases.

Explore It!

Examples of karyotypes can be found in many resources, including library books and the Internet. Sheets of randomly mixed photos of human chromosomes from cells of different sexes and individuals with certain chromosomal disorders can be ordered from biological supply houses. You can use such materials to make sets of chromosomes for karyotyping by laminating the sheets and cutting apart the chromosomes.

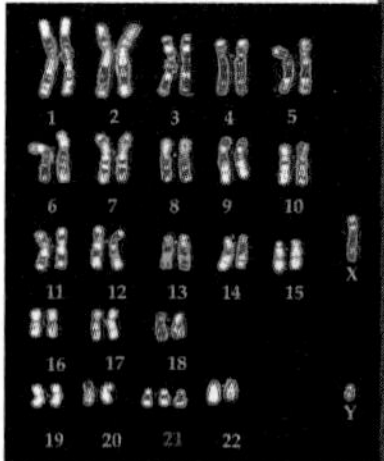

PEOPLE IN SCIENCE Patricia Jacobs 1934 –

Sometimes, chromosomes do not separate correctly during meiosis. Sometimes, they form gametes that contain either too many or too few chromosomes. Patricia Jacobs has spent her career studying disorders that develop when these gametes become part of a zygote.

Jacobs was born in London in 1934. During the 1950s, she began to study human chromosomes by observing cells from different people. She organized the chromosomes into a karyotype (KER ee uh tipe), which shows the chromosomes arranged in order from largest to smallest. In a karyotype, the chromosomes are given numbers based on their size and are paired by matching their patterns of light and dark bands.

By comparing karyotypes from different people, Jacobs found that some people had an abnormal number of chromosomes. In 1959, she discovered that people with Down syndrome had an extra copy of chromosome 21.

Explore It!

Get a set of paper human chromosomes from your teacher. Use their sizes, colors, and patterns of light and dark bands to match up the pairs of like chromosomes and arrange them in rows and from largest to smallest. You just made a karyotype.

Male Reproductive System

Males make sperm in a pair of organs called the **testes** (TES teez, singular: testis). The testes also make the male sex hormone **testosterone** (tes TAHS tuh rohn).

Males constantly make new sperm cells. A grown man can make about 300 million sperm every day. The new sperm cells are collected in the **epididymis** (eh puh DIH duh mus). The epididymis stores sperm cells while they mature and develop the ability to swim. Each testi and its epididymis is suspended in a pouch of skin, called the **scrotum** (SKROH tum), that hangs between the thighs. The testes are found outside the main body cavity because sperm can only mature at temperatures that are cooler than the normal human body temperature.

A **vas deferens** (VAS • DEF uh runz) moves sperm out of each testis and into the urethra. As sperm move toward the urethra, a series of glands add fluids that help the sperm move toward an ovum. The sperm combine with these fluids to form **semen** (SEE mun), which leaves the man's body.

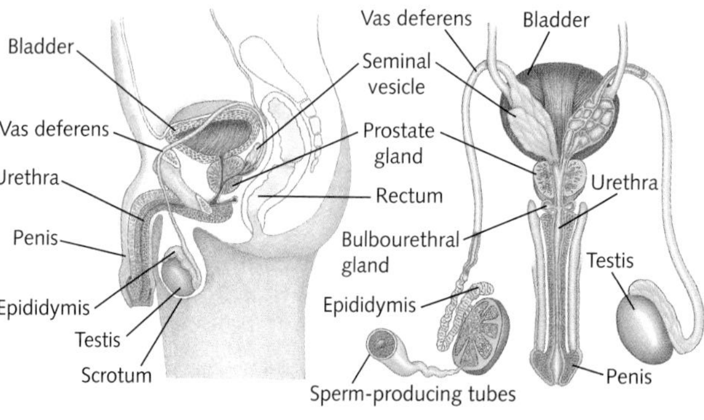

Figure 23.2 Men have both external and internal reproductive organs.

Differentiated Instruction

Visual Have students draw and label the parts of the male and female reproductive systems in their Science Notebooks. Encourage them to include notes about the parts to help them better remember structure and function.

Background Information

It is normal for only 75 percent of a healthy man's sperm to be alive at any given time.

Teacher Alert

Some students may wonder if the bands visible on the chromosomes in a karyotype are genes. They are not. The banding patterns are helpful in matching the homologous pairs of chromosomes. The mapping of genes on chromosomes is a much different processes. A research program called the Human Genome Project has mapped all the genes on human chromosomes. To find educational resources, visit **http://www.genome.gov**.

Semen leaves a man's body through the urethra after it travels through a specialized reproductive organ called the penis. The penis places sperm inside the female reproductive tract.

Female Reproductive System

Women make ova in a pair of organs called the **ovaries** (OH va reez, singular: ovary). Unlike men, women do not continually make new ova. A newborn girl's ovaries already contain all of the cells that will mature into eggs over her lifetime.

A tube called the **oviduct** (OH vuh duct), or fallopian tube, is wrapped around one end of the ovary. When an ovum is released from the ovary, cilia inside the oviduct sweep the egg into the tube and push it toward the uterus. Fertilization usually occurs inside the oviduct.

The **uterus** (YEW tuh rus) is a pear-shaped organ located between the ovaries and oviducts. It has a thick lining in which fertilized eggs implant and develop. Its muscular walls are capable of stretching as the embryo grows and producing strong contractions to push the baby out at birth.

The lower end of the uterus has an opening called the **cervix** (SUR vihks). The cervix opens into a stretchy muscular tube, called the **vagina** (vuh JI nuh), that opens to the outside of the body. The vagina is also called the birth canal.

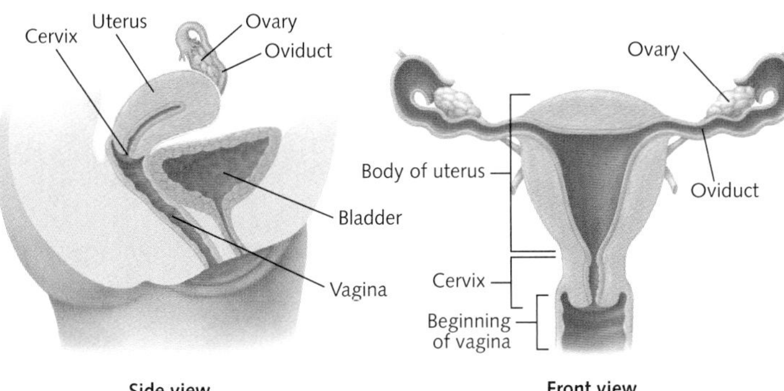

Figure 23.3 Unlike some male reproductive organs, all female reproductive organs are internal.

The Menstrual Cycle

Every month, sexually mature women shed their uterine lining and release a new egg from an ovary. These events repeat over and over again, month after month. The cycle lasts about 28 days on average. The cycle is only broken when an egg gets fertilized and starts to develop into an embryo.

As You Read

Your T-chart shows the differences between male and female reproductive systems. Write a few sentences in your Science Notebook describing similarities between the two systems.

CONNECTION: History

The person who discovered the oviduct, or fallopian tube, was Gabriele Falloppio (1523–1562), an Italian anatomist. Although his family was noble, Falloppio had to struggle to obtain an education. He received his medical degree in 1548. Falloppio studied the male and female reproductive organs, and he described the tube that connects the ovary to the uterus in females. That tube—the fallopian tube—was named after him.

Teach

EXPLAIN that in this section, students will begin learning about the female reproductive system. Encourage them to think about the differences between the two systems as they read.

As You Read

Give students a few minutes to complete and review their T-charts. Have each student discuss the information he or she included with a partner to check for accuracy.

ANSWER There are a number of general similarities between male and female reproductive systems: both have specialized organs that make gametes, both have long thin tubes that transport the gametes, and both are controlled by hormones.

Vocabulary

ovary Explain that *ovary* comes from the Latin word *ovum*, meaning "egg." Ask what other word that students learned in this chapter has this meaning. (ovum)

oviduct Explain that a duct is a tube in the body that carries some object or substance. The prefix *ovi-* relates to "ovum," or "egg." Have students combine these word meanings to define *oviduct*.

uterus Explain that *uterus* comes from a Greek word that means "belly." Tell them that the uterus is sometimes referred to as the "womb."

cervix Tell students that *cervix* is Latin and means "neck."

vagina Explain that *vagina* is Latin and means "sheath," which is a case or covering.

CONNECTION: History

Gabriele Falloppio was one of the most important anatomists and physicians of his time. As an anatomist, he spent much time studying the head, but he also studied male and female reproductive organs as well as bones and muscles. His work is especially remarkable because he died at age 39.

EXTEND Ask students to draw the ovaries, oviducts, and uterus in their Science Notebooks. Have them indicate where an egg originates, its direction of travel, and where fertilization and implantation occur.

Background Information

In a pregnant woman, the uterus grows from its normal pear size to the size of a small melon after three months of pregnancy and to the size of a basketball by the end of six months. Between eight and nine months, the uterus is large enough to hold a baby with a mass of between 2.75 and 4.25 kilograms. As the baby grows, the uterus expands upward. At the beginning of pregnancy, the uterus is in the pelvic area. It continues to ascend until it is right under the ribcage.

Teach

EXPLAIN to students that in this section, they will learn about a woman's menstrual cycle. Ask them to look at the figures on this page to preview the section.

Vocabulary

menstruation Tell students that this word is the noun form of the verb *menstruate,* which comes from the Latin word *menstruare,* from *mensis,* meaning "month." Ask students to identify the relationship between the vocabulary word and its derivative.

estrogen Explain that this word comes from *oestrus,* which is a brief, regularly occurring time of sexual receptivity that occurs in most female mammals, said to be "in heat," but not in humans.

ovulation Tell students that this is a noun derived from the verb *ovulate.* Ask students what the relationship is to the word *ova.*

progesterone Tell students that this word comes from *progestin* + *sterol.* Ask what other word from this lesson contains *sterol* and what that word means.

Figure It Out: Figure 23.4

ANSWER **1.** day 14 **2.** 12 x 37 = 444 eggs

Assess

EVALUATE Use the After You Read questions and the Alternative Assessment to help you assess students' understanding of the lesson.

After You Read

1. Answers will vary; similarities: both make gametes, both are influenced by hormones; differences: sperm mature externally and eggs internally.
2. A zygote is formed.
3. The corpus luteum secretes hormones that build up the uterine lining. The uterine lining is shed after the unfertilized egg dies, so the corpus luteum must degenerate.

Alternative Assessment

EVALUATE Ask each student to write a paragraph in his or her Science Notebook explaining the menstrual cycle. Students should refer to the text as well as Figures 23.4 and 23.5.

Figure It Out

1. According to this chart, on which day does a woman ovulate?
2. If a woman begins to ovulate at age 13 and continues to release one egg each month until she is 50, how many eggs will she release during her reproductive lifetime?

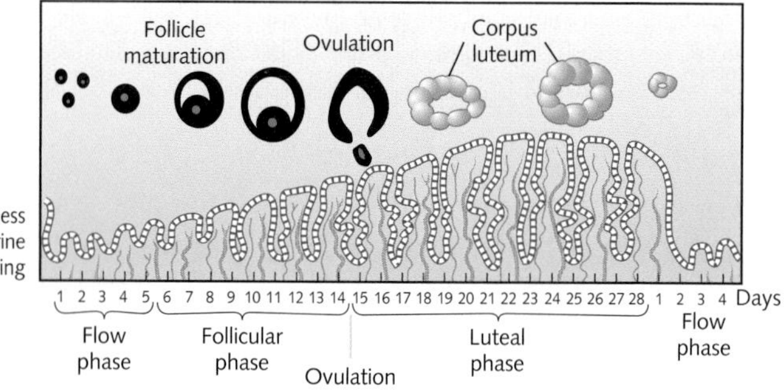

Figure 23.4 The menstrual cycle is caused by a regular pattern of hormones that prepare the uterus for a pregnancy each month.

The female reproductive cycle is called the menstrual cycle, and the process of shedding the uterine lining is called **menstruation** (men stroo AY shun).

For one week after menstruation, a woman's pituitary gland releases hormones that make an egg develop in one of her ovaries. The two ovaries usually take turns releasing eggs. An egg matures inside a case called a follicle (FAH lih kul). The follicle secretes the female sex hormone **estrogen** (ES truh jun), which makes the uterus grow a new lining. On day 14 of the cycle, pituitary hormones make the follicle rupture, releasing the mature egg into the oviduct. The release of the mature egg is called **ovulation** (ahv yuh LAY shun).

After ovulation, cilia in the oviduct push the ovum toward the uterus. The empty follicle becomes a structure called the corpus luteum (KOR pus • LEW tee um). It continues to release estrogen and also begins to release a second hormone called **progesterone** (proh JES tuh rohn). These hormones make the uterine lining grow even thicker so it can support a fertilized egg. If the egg is not fertilized, it dies and disintegrates. The woman will shed the uterine lining at the start of the next menstrual cycle.

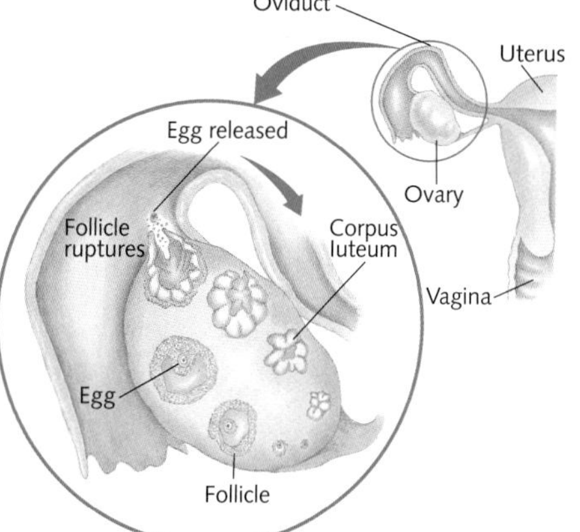

Figure 23.5 Each month, an egg matures inside a follicle. When the follicle ruptures, the egg is released into the oviduct.

After You Read

1. Under the T-chart in your Science Notebook, compare and contrast the testes and ovaries using a Venn diagram. Then, write a paragraph that summarizes the similarities and differences in the two organs.
2. What is formed when an ovum and a sperm cell fuse?
3. Predict what will happen to the corpus luteum if an egg is not fertilized.

Background Information

Higher levels of hormones are present in women during and immediately after pregnancy and are the cause of a variety of symptoms. Mood swings, irritability, weepiness, and irrationality are often displayed, especially during the first trimester of pregnancy and after giving birth. Hormones are also the reason for morning sickness, the nausea and vomiting that strikes most women in the first trimester. Hormones are also at least partially responsible for food cravings and food aversions, which the majority of pregnant women experience.

422 REPRODUCTION AND DEVELOPMENT

Development Before Birth

Before You Read

Create a concept map in your Science Notebook for the content of this lesson. Start by writing the word *Zygote* and circling it. Draw four circles vertically beneath this circle. Draw an arrow from each circle to the one below it. Write the word *Newborn* in the bottom circle. As you read, fill in the remaining circles with the names of the stages that the offspring moves through during pregnancy.

Learning Goals

- Describe the stages of human development.
- List the events that occur during childbirth.
- Understand what causes identical and fraternal twins.

New Vocabulary

blastocyst
pregnant
placenta
umbilical cord
embryo
development
amniotic sac
fetus
labor
fraternal twins
identical twins

Two hundred million sperm will try to penetrate an ovum. Only one will succeed. None of the other sperm will be allowed to enter. The zygote that forms when a sperm and an egg fuse will divide, change, and grow for nine months. In the end, the zygote becomes a baby that is ready to be born.

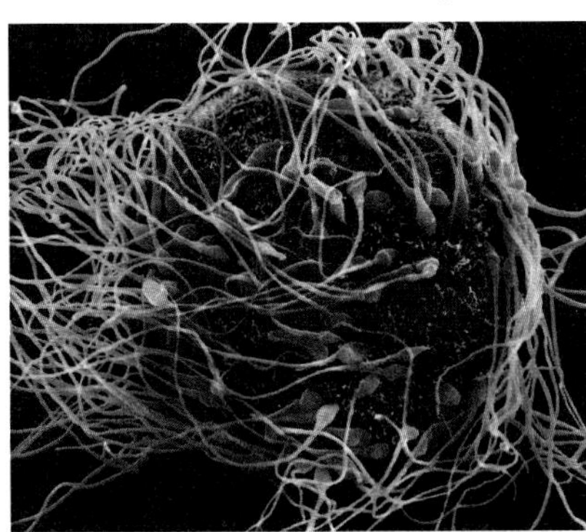

Figure 23.6 Many sperm reach the egg, but only one will fertilize it.

Fertilization

When a sperm cell enters an ovum, it triggers a series of events that prevent any other sperm from entering the egg. The haploid nuclei of the egg and sperm fuse together to form a new diploid zygote.

Fertilization usually occurs in the oviduct. The zygote starts to divide as it is pushed toward the uterus. One cell becomes two, two cells become four, and so forth, until a hollow ball of cells called a **blastocyst** (BLAS toh sist) is formed. When the blastocyst reaches the uterus, it burrows into the uterine lining. The woman is now **pregnant**, or carrying a developing offspring.

Some of the cells in the blastocyst will continue to develop into a new individual. The rest of the cells form an exchange organ called the **placenta** (plu SEN tuh). The placenta exchanges nutrients, oxygen, and wastes between the mother and her offspring. The main part of the placenta grows into the uterine lining and makes contact with the mother's circulatory system. The embryo is attached to the placenta by a stalk of tissue that eventually becomes the **umbilical** (um BIH lih kul) **cord**.

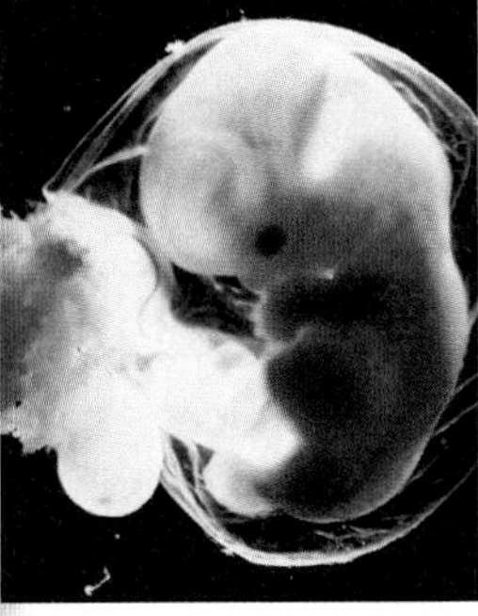

Figure 23.7 After several weeks of pregnancy, a developing human floats inside the amniotic sac. Part of the placenta is visible on the left side of the photo.

ELL Strategy

Ask and Answer Questions Divide students into groups of three to ask and answer questions about this lesson. Each student should write at least two questions and read them aloud for the other members of the group to answer.

Field Study

Arrange for students to visit a nearby science museum's human development exhibit.

Background Information

The placenta contains a barrier that acts as a filter to block potentially harmful substances from reaching the fetus. However, alcohol and some chemicals in cigarettes are not filtered out. Chemicals in cigarette smoke, for example, lessen a baby's oxygen supply. Slower fetal growth and weight gain, preterm labor, and other complications can result from smoking during pregnancy.

Introduce

ENGAGE Ask students what they know about pregnancy and birth. Ask: *Do you know anyone who is or was recently pregnant?* After a brief discussion, have students look at the figures in this lesson. Have small groups of students discuss what they see. Ask: *What surprises you about the process of development? What do you notice? When does the embryo start to resemble a person?* After a few minutes, have students share their discussions with the class.

Before You Read

Draw a concept map on the board with the word *Zygote* in the first circle and the word *Newborn* in the last. Ask students to remember what a zygote is, and ask them what a newborn baby is. Tell them that these two stages of human development are the beginning and the end of pregnancy. Tell students that in this lesson, they will learn about these stages and the ones in between. Instruct students to fill in the remaining circles as they learn about them in the lesson.

Teach

EXPLAIN that in this section, students will learn about the processes by which an egg is fertilized and begins to develop into a new living thing.

Vocabulary

blastocyst Explain that a blastocyst is an embryo that consists of 30 to 150 cells.

pregnant Tell students that this word comes from the Latin *pare-*, meaning "before," paired with *(g)nascent*, "to be born."

placenta Encourage students to recall what they learned about placental mammals and to relate it to the placenta that develops in human females during pregnancy.

umbilical cord Explain that *umbilical* is from *umbilicus*, a Latin word meaning "navel." Ask students to identify the relationship between the umbilical cord and the navel.

Teach

EXPLAIN to students that in this section, they will continue to learn about human development in the uterus.

Vocabulary

embryo Explain that *embryo* is a Greek word that means "to swell." Challenge students to recall the embryo of a seed plant—its parts and what it becomes. Then, have them relate a plant embryo to a human embryo.

development Explain that this word is the noun form of the verb *develop,* from the French verb *developer,* meaning "to unroll."

amniotic sac Have students recall the introduction and meaning of the term *amniotic egg* in Chapter 14. Encourage them to look for similarities between *amniotic egg* and *amniotic sac.*

fetus Tell students that this Latin word means "offspring."

labor Ask students to give the common meaning of the word *labor* ("hard work, especially the physical type, for which a person is paid").

As You Read

Write the words *Oviduct* and *Uterus* on the board. Ask students what they learned about these terms. Instruct them to draw boxes around the stages of development that take place in each of these two parts of the reproductive system.

Students should have the following labels in their circles: *Zygote, Blastocyst, Embryo, Fetus,* and *Newborn.* A box labeled *Oviduct* should surround the circles containing *Zygote* and *Blastocyst.* A box labeled *Uterus* should surround the circles containing *Embryo* and *Fetus.*

ANSWER a fetus

Figure It Out: Figure 23.8

ANSWER **1.** no **2.** Descriptions will vary, but students should indicate that the head is increasing in size, changing shape, and developing recognizable features such as eyes, ears, and a mouth.

Pregnancy

After it implants itself in the uterus, the offspring is called an **embryo** (EM bree oh). For the next few weeks, the embryo grows and changes. It gets larger, and the cells inside its body move and change in a process called **development**. **Figure 23.8** shows how a human embryo changes early in development.

When it first enters the uterus, the embryo is a ball of cells that all look the same. After one week, it is 2 mm long with a distinctive head region and an internal tube that will become the digestive system. After two weeks, it has doubled in size and has grown a simple tube-shaped heart. After a month, it is about 10 mm long and has begun to develop four limb buds that will become its arms and legs. The embryo is now surrounded by tissues that make a fluid-filled bag called the **amniotic** (am nee AH tihk) **sac**. The amniotic sac cushions the embryo as it grows.

Eight weeks after fertilization, the embryo becomes a **fetus** (FEE tus). Although it has developed all of its organ systems, it is still only 4 cm long. It cannot live outside of its mother. Over the next seven months, the fetus grows larger. Its brain and other organs mature. It starts making its own blood cells. Fat develops underneath its skin, making the fetus look less wrinkled. It grows hair, fingernails, and toenails.

The fetus also starts to move. It practices sucking and swallowing, breathing, and moving its arms and legs. After about the fourth month of pregnancy, the mother can feel the fetus move. By the ninth month, the fetus has changed position so that it is head-down against the cervix. It has enough fat to help it stay warm. Its lungs are ready to expand and breathe air. It is about 50 cm long and has a mass of about 3 kg. It is ready to be born.

As You Read

On the concept map in your Science Notebook, draw a box around the stages of development that take place inside the oviduct. Label the box *Oviduct*. Draw another box around the stages of development that take place inside the uterus. Label this box *Uterus*.

What is an embryo called eight weeks after fertilization?

Figure It Out

1. Does the three-week-old embryo have arms or legs?
2. Describe how the appearance of the head region changes from week 5 to week 9.

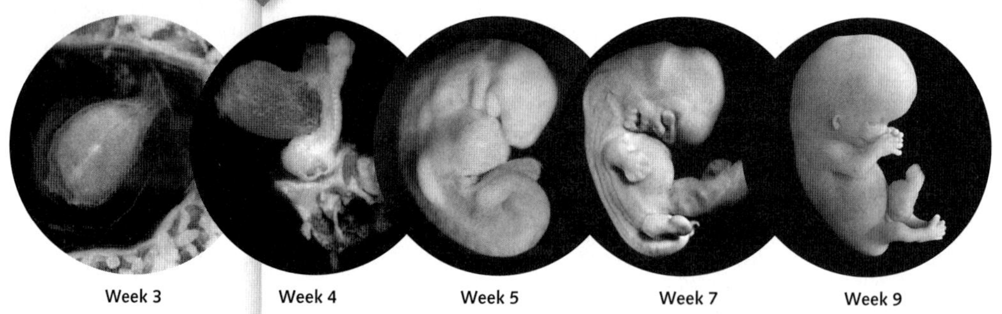

Figure 23.8 Human embryos change dramatically during early development.

Differentiated Instruction

Logical and Mathematical Ask students to convert the metric measurements given in this lesson to U.S. standard measurements.

Background Information

Alcohol is broken down in a fetus's body much more slowly than it is in the mother's. Any alcohol consumption during pregnancy increases the risk of miscarriage, low birth weight, and stillbirth. Excessive or binge drinking could cause Fetal Alcohol Syndrome, a combination of mental and physical birth defects that persist throughout life.

Birth

Birth is the process that pushes a fetus out of the uterus and into the outside world. A protein from the fetus's lungs crosses the placenta and enters the mother. When the mother's body detects the protein, her brain releases a hormone that makes her body push out the fetus. The fetus only makes the protein when it is ready to breathe on its own.

The process of giving birth is called **labor**. Labor begins after the woman releases a hormone called oxytocin (ahk sih TOH sun). The hormone makes the muscles in the uterus contract regularly. The contractions pull open the cervix. The amniotic sac usually ruptures during labor, and the amniotic fluid flows out through the vagina, or birth canal.

When the cervix is fully open, the uterine contractions become very forceful. They push the baby through the birth canal and the cervix and the vagina until it is out of the mother's body. After the baby is born, the placenta separates from the uterine wall and is pushed out through the birth canal. The uterus keeps contracting to close off blood vessels and to prevent bleeding.

After birth, the baby is still attached to the placenta by its umbilical cord. Doctors clamp and cut the umbilical cord near the baby's belly. After a few days, the stump of cord dries up and falls off, leaving a scar called the navel (NAY vul)—commonly known as the belly button.

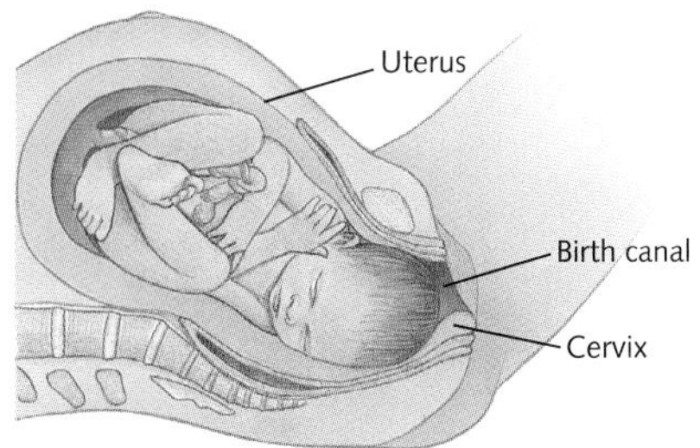

1 Dilation Labor contractions open the cervix.

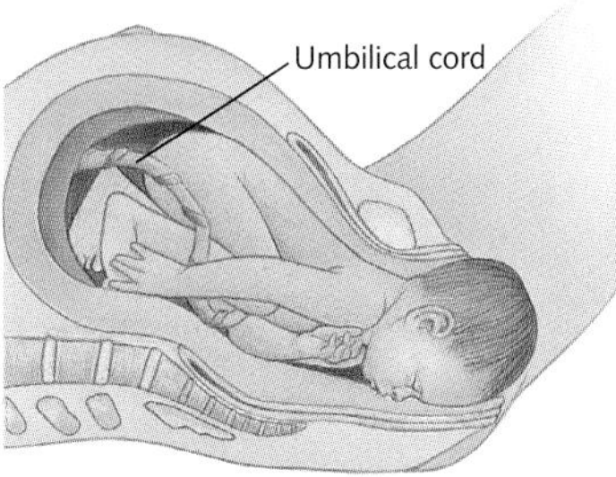

2 Expulsion The baby rotates as it moves through the birth canal, making expulsion easier.

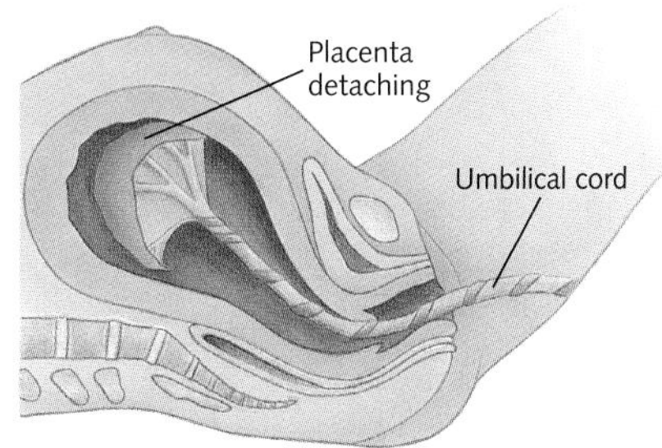

3 Placental stage During the placental stage, the placenta and umbilical cord are expelled.

Figure 23.9 Labor has three stages. **1)** During the first stage, uterine contractions open the cervix. **2)** During the second stage, the baby is pushed out through the birth canal. **3)** During the third stage, the placenta is pushed out through the birth canal.

 CONNECTION: **Physics**

When a newborn baby takes its first breath, its lungs inflate for the first time. The pressure change in the lungs immediately reroutes blood through the heart. In the fetus, most blood bypasses the lungs. In the newborn baby, most blood moves through the lungs.

Teach

EXPLAIN to students that in this section, they will learn about the process of giving birth, also called labor.

Use the Visual: Figure 23.9

EXTEND If a baby's feet or hips are in position to pass through the birth canal before the head, the baby is said to be in a breech position. Have students research the causes and challenges of a breech delivery. Provide students with access to reference materials such as books and Internet access. Have students discuss their findings in small groups.

 CONNECTION: **Physics**

Surfactant, a substance produced from 34 to 37 weeks of pregnancy, allows the lungs to expand upon birth. A baby born prematurely may not have enough surfactant for the lungs to expand, possibly causing respiratory distress syndrome (RDS). RDS is an acute lung disease that is fatal if not treated. A fetal lung maturity test conducted before birth is able to identify whether the baby will have RDS after birth. A ventilator is used on infants with premature lungs. As a preventive measure, an expectant mother can be given a steroid hormone to help the fetus's lungs develop before birth.

Differentiated Instruction

Visual Have students draw a series of illustrations that depict the different stages of development.

Background Information

Although some women go into premature labor for no known reason, there are many possible medical reasons. These include a weak cervix; a ruptured amniotic sac (the reason for this is unknown); urinary tract infections; chronic diseases including high blood pressure, diabetes, kidney diseases, and lupus; an abnormally shaped uterus; a previous preterm labor; substance abuse; malnutrition; and excess amniotic fluid.

Reading Comprehension Workbook, p. 154

Teach

EXPLAIN that in this section, students will learn about multiple births.

Vocabulary

fraternal twins Explain that *fraternal* is from the Latin word *frater,* meaning "brother."

identical twins Ask students to think about the word *identical,* which means "exactly the same." Have students compare and contrast fraternal twins and identical twins based on the word meanings of *fraternal* and *identical.*

Explain It!

Remind students that hemoglobin is a protein in red blood cells that carries oxygen from the lungs to tissues that need it. During pregnancy, a mother and baby share blood. Explain that by the time blood reaches the baby, the blood has less oxygen in it. Next, discuss what an adaptation is and ask students for examples. Explain that a fetus's ability to grab more oxygen than an adult is an adaptation.

ANSWER A fetus can only get oxygen from its mother's hemoglobin, so it has to be able to attract oxygen more strongly.

Assess

EVALUATE Use the After You Read questions and the Alternative Assessment to help you assess students' understanding of the lesson.

After You Read

1. The unboxed arrow represents birth.
2. A blastocyst is a hollow ball of cells that develops from the zygote. The embryo and placenta develop from the blastocyst.
3. Identical twins are genetically identical because they are derived from one zygote that splits during development. Fraternal twins are not genetically identical because they develop from two different zygotes.

Alternative Assessment

EVALUATE Have students complete their concept maps. Then, have each student write a few paragraphs that explain the concept map and include a description of each stage of development.

Explain It!

A growing fetus has the ability to make hemoglobin that is better able to bind to oxygen than the hemoglobin of an adult is. Explain how this is a good adaptation for living inside its mother.

Multiple Births

Only one baby usually develops during a pregnancy, because a woman usually releases one egg at a time. But sometimes, a woman can have more than one baby from a single pregnancy.

If a woman releases two eggs at the same time, they can both get fertilized and implant in the uterus. They will develop into **fraternal** (fruh TUR nul) **twins**. Fraternal twins come from different eggs and sperm cells. They can, but do not always, look alike—as with any other pair of siblings. They can be two girls, two boys, or a boy and a girl.

Sometimes, a single zygote will split in two early in its development. The two zygotes grow into **identical twins**. Identical twins have the exact same genes. They look exactly the same. They are either two girls or two boys.

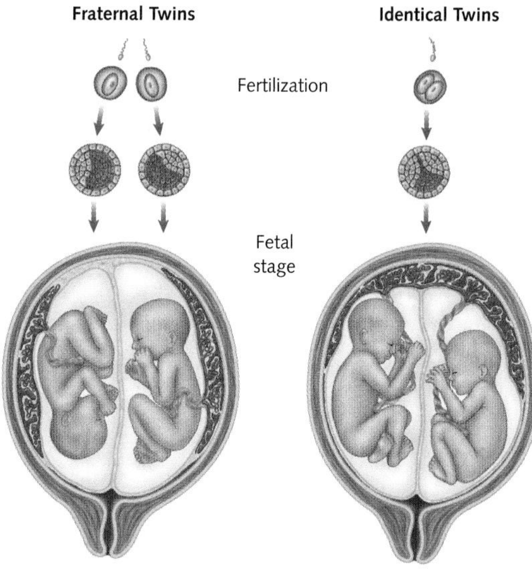

Figure 23.10 Fraternal twins and identical twins develop differently.

After You Read

1. Review the concept map you created in your Science Notebook. You should have one arrow in your concept map that is not in a box. What physical process does that arrow represent? Write it in your Science Notebook.
2. What is a blastocyst? What two things develop from it?
3. Explain the difference between identical twins and fraternal twins.

Background Information

Preeclampsia, also called toxemia or pregnancy-induced hypertension, occurs in five to eight percent of all pregnancies. It is defined as high blood pressure and excess protein in the urine, and it occurs after the twentieth week of pregnancy. Women who are most at risk include those who are over 40 or less than 18 years of age and those who have a family or personal history of the disorder, have chronic high blood pressure, diabetes, a kidney disorder, are expecting multiple births, or are overweight. The only cure for preeclampsia is delivery of the baby.

23.3 Human Life Stages

Before You Read

Look at the five main headings in this lesson. Make a chart in your Science Notebook with five columns. Write one heading in each column. Then, write a sentence summarizing what you know about each one.

People continue to grow and change after birth. Over time, a helpless newborn baby learns to walk and talk, becoming an active toddler. The toddler grows into a child, the child grows into a teenager, and the teenager eventually becomes an adult.

Infancy

A newborn baby cannot do very much. It cannot hold up its own head, roll over, or smile. It can only see about as far as its mother's face from her breast. It spends most of its time asleep. But for the next 18 months, it will go through some dramatic changes. This period of great physical and mental change is called **infancy**.

Infants grow quickly. Most newborn babies are about 50 cm long and have a mass of between 3 and 4 kg. Within the first six months of their lives, they will double their weight. By the end of their first year, they will have tripled their birth weight and will have grown about 50 percent in height. Imagine what you would look like if you grew that much in the next year!

Infant brains also develop and change quickly. Babies learn to coordinate their nervous system with their muscles, rapidly learning to roll over, sit up, grab toys, and crawl. Most infants learn the complex balancing act of walking by the time they are 18 months old. Their ability to think and reason also grows during infancy. Most children speak their first words by the end of this period.

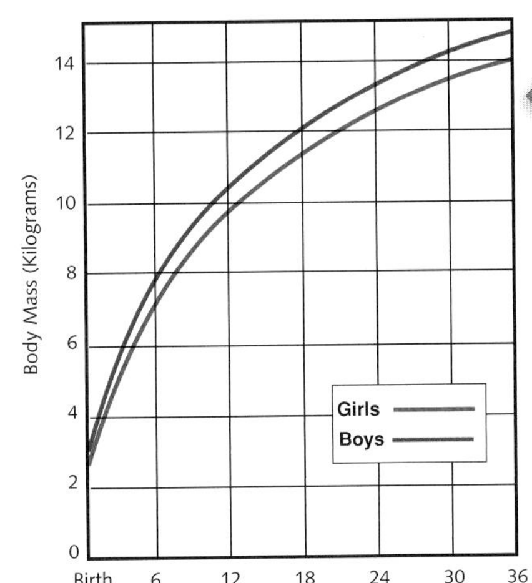

Learning Goals

- Name the human life stages.
- Describe the physical changes that occur at puberty.
- Identify some of the physical changes of old age.

New Vocabulary

infancy
puberty
fertile
secondary sex characteristic
menopause

Figure It Out

1. What is the body mass of an average three-month-old girl?
2. How do the masses of the average three-month-old boy and the average three-month-old girl compare?

Figure 23.11 This graph illustrates the rapid growth of infants during their first year of life.

23.3 Introduce

ENGAGE Ask students to think about human life. What stages do humans go through after they are born? Give magazines to small groups of students. Have them find and cut out pictures of people at various life stages. When they are finished, students should put the photographs in chronological order and name each stage.

Before You Read

Write the headings of this lesson on the board. Ask students to do the same in their Science Notebooks. Review these headings with the class, asking students to tell what they know about each one.

Teach

EXPLAIN to students that in this section, they will learn about the first life stage, infancy.

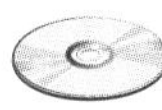

Vocabulary

infancy Explain that this word comes from the French word *enfant*, from Latin *infans*, meaning "a child" or "someone who cannot speak."

Figure It Out: Figure 23.11

ANSWER **1.** about 5.5 kg **2.** The average three-month-old boy is about 6 kg, 0.5 kg more than a girl the same age.

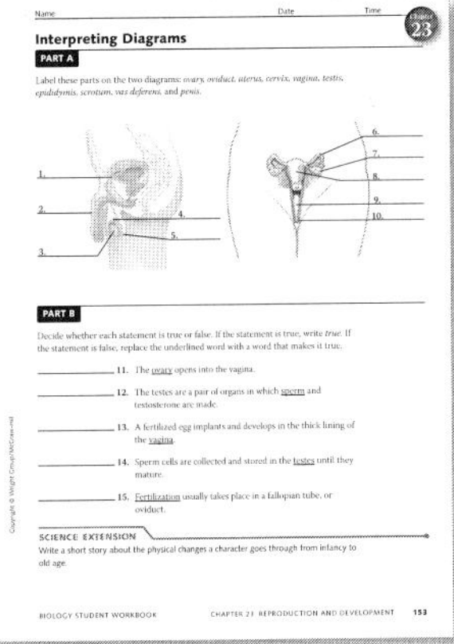

Interpreting Diagrams Workbook, p. 153

Differentiated Instruction

Visual Ask students to use the Internet or reference books to research photographs and descriptions of infants from birth to 18 months.

ELL Strategy

Analyze and Discuss Have students work with a partner to analyze and discuss the graph in Figure 23.11. Ask: *What do you notice about the rate of growth for boys versus girls? What surprises you? What did you already know?* Then, working in pairs, students can choose a weight and have another pair determine the age that coincides with that weight (both for boys and for girls).

Teach

 to students that they will next learn about the life stages of childhood and adolescence. Ask what they already know about each one.

Vocabulary

puberty Explain that this word comes from the Latin word *pubertas,* meaning "the age of maturity," from *puber,* meaning "youth."

fertile Tell students that *fertile* is from the Latin word *fertilis,* from *ferre,* meaning "bear." Have them explain the relationship between *fertile* and its word origin.

secondary sex characteristic Explain that *secondary* means "being of lesser importance than the primary." *Sex* refers to either of two classes, male and female, into which animals and plants are divided according to their role in reproduction. A characteristic is a distinctive quality or feature. Have students use these word meanings to develop a definition for this term.

As You Read

Discuss with students what physical changes are. Have students brainstorm examples of physical changes that occur during the various stages.

ANSWER Infancy is the time of fastest brain and muscular growth.

CONNECTION: Social Studies

In United States, the Catholic Church usually confers confirmation between the "age of discretion" and age 16. The Mexican Quinceanera, meaning "fifteen", is a celebration of a girl's passage from childhood into womanhood. Bar Mitzvah translates from Aramaic to English as "son of the commandment." *Bat mitzvah* means "daughter of the commandment." The term refers to a Jewish child who is coming of age (13 for boys and 12 for girls).

Science Notebook EXTRA

Ask students to do research on one coming-of-age rite and write about it in their Science Notebooks.

As You Read

Record important information about the physical changes in each life stage in your chart. In your Science Notebook, write your hypothesis about the following question.

Why do the most dramatic changes occur during infancy?

CONNECTION: Social Studies

Many cultures mark the onset of puberty with special events that show the child is becoming an adult. There are many different coming-of-age rites. They can be religious, such as Roman Catholic confirmation and Jewish bar or bat mitzvah, or cultural, such as the Latino *quinceañera.*

Childhood

The period between 18 months of age and the onset of sexual maturity at around age 12 to 13 is called childhood. Growth is not as rapid as in infancy, but a child still grows quickly and steadily.

Children continue to develop physically and mentally. Their control over their bodies improves, and they learn to speak in complex sentences. Formal education begins later in childhood.

Adolescence

Adolescence begins with **puberty** (PYEW bur tee) and lasts through the teen years. During puberty, a child's body changes into an adult body. These physical changes start when the brain begins to release hormones that make the testes or ovaries release sex hormones. These hormones mature the organs of the reproductive system and make the person **fertile**, or capable of having children. They also induce the development of adult physical characteristics, or **secondary sex characteristics**. Boys begin to look like men, and girls start to look like women.

In boys, puberty begins when the testes start releasing testosterone. The penis and testes grow larger, and the testes begin to make sperm. The larynx grows, deepening the voice, and the boy grows facial and body hair. The muscles in the shoulders and chest get bigger than those in women. In girls, puberty begins when the ovaries start releasing estrogen. The menstrual cycle begins as the eggs in the ovaries start to mature regularly. The hips grow wider, and breasts develop. Boys and girls both grow underarm and pubic hair and go through a rapid growth spurt to reach their adult height. Girls finish growing around age 16, and boys finish around age 18. Puberty in both boys and girls can be a time of intense emotional shifts as the sex hormones are released into their bodies. Many of the changes associated with puberty occur rapidly and simultaneously, making this a difficult time for adolescents.

Figure 23.12 A child's body grows faster than its head.

Background Information

Emotional changes also come with puberty. This life stage is marked by a desire for independence from parents. Most teenagers move from closeness with family into important relationships with peers and possibly other adults. They strive to create their own identities. Acceptance by others, especially peers, becomes important.

Adulthood

Figure 23.13 Humans spend most of their lives as adults.

Adulthood starts at the end of adolescence and continues through middle and old age. Adults stop growing taller and remain approximately the same size for the remainder of their lives. Most people work and raise families during this life stage.

Aging begins to change the adult body after age 45. The body's metabolism slows down and physical strength declines, sometimes leading to weight gain. The bones begin to become more brittle. The skin becomes less elastic and begins to get wrinkled. Hair loses its pigment and becomes gray. In women, the ovaries lose the ability to make estrogen and the menstrual cycle stops. This change in the reproductive system is called **menopause** (MEN uh pawz). Menopausal women stop ovulating and lose the ability to have children. The lack of estrogen also signals other changes, such as greater risk of heart attack and increased loss of bone density. Menopause means women must adjust their lifestyles to accommodate these changes and stay healthy.

Older Adulthood

Figure 23.14 Aging slowly changes most of the tissues in the body.

After adults pass the age of 60, their cells do not divide and the tissues do not repair themselves as well as they did in youth. This makes it harder for the body to respond to external stresses caused by injury or disease. Skin wrinkles deepen, eyesight and hearing diminish, and reflexes slow down. Nerves and muscles work more slowly, leading to slower response times for physical tasks such as driving. The lenses in the eyes get harder, making it more difficult to focus on things that are nearby. However, older adults can still continue to learn new things, and many remain physically active.

After You Read

1. Name the human life stages.
2. Using the information you have recorded in your Science Notebook, create a Venn diagram to compare and contrast the physical changes boys and girls go through during puberty.
3. What are some physical characteristics of adulthood and older adulthood?
4. What is menopause?

Extend It!

With a partner, spend an hour with a person in each of the five human life stages. Using the chart in your Science Notebook, write each person's age and what you observe about him or her during that hour.

Teach

EXPLAIN that students will learn about adulthood in this last section of the chapter.

Vocabulary

menopause Tell students that this word comes from the French word *ménopause*, from the Greek *men*, meaning "month," paired with *pauses*, meaning "cessation."

Extend It!

If students do not know people in each of the life stages, suggest that they contact a daycare provider to observe infants and young children, an elementary school to observe children, and a nursing home to visit the elderly.

Assess

EVALUATE Use the After You Read questions and the Alternative Assessment to help you assess students' understanding of the lesson.

After You Read

1. infancy, childhood, adolescence, adulthood, and older adulthood
2. Students' diagrams should indicate the following: *for boys*—testes start releasing testosterone; penis and testes grow larger; testes begin to make sperm; larynx grows, deepening the voice; facial and body hair grow; shoulders and chest muscles get bigger; and growth finishes around age 18; *for girls*—ovaries start releasing estrogen, menstrual cycle begins as the eggs in the ovaries start to mature regularly, hips grow wider, breasts develop, and growth finishes around age 16; *similarities*—growth of underarm and pubic hair; a rapid growth spurt; skin and scent changes; and mental changes reflecting sexual maturity.
3. Adults stop growing taller and stay about the same size for the rest of their lives. In older adulthood, people's cells do not divide and repair themselves as well as they did in youth, nerves and muscles work more slowly, and the lens in the eye gets harder.
4. Menopause is the time of a woman's life when estrogen production by the ovaries has stopped and ovulation and menstruation have stopped.

Background Information

Researchers are looking at the role of exercise in keeping nerves and the brain healthy and functioning properly. Research has found that when people exercise, they get oxygen-rich blood into the brain, keeping it working properly. There is also evidence that eating healthfully and keeping the brain active (e.g., socializing, doing crossword puzzles, and reading) aid in the maintenance of good brain health.

Alternative Assessment

EVALUATE Ask students to think about one family member or friend. In their Science Notebooks, students should write about what human life stage the person is in and give examples of the physical characteristics that demonstrate this stage. Encourage them to include photographs, if possible.

Chapter 23 Summary

VOCABULARY REVIEW

Check students' sentences or paragraphs to make sure they understand the meaning of each vocabulary term.

PREPARE FOR CHAPTER TEST

Evaluate students' essays using the following criteria:

1. The topic sentence, or main idea, should restate the Key Concept.
2. The supporting paragraphs should incorporate the answers to the Learning Goal questions students have written and include details, facts, and examples they have recorded in their Science Notebooks.
3. The concluding sentence should sum up the main idea of the chapter and restate the Key Concept.

MASTERING CONCEPTS

True or False

1. False, Sperm
2. True
3. False, Fraternal
4. True
5. False, puberty
6. False, Menstruation

Short Answer

7. From the testis, a sperm cell travels through the epididymis, vas deferens, and urethra (through the penis) before it leaves the man's body
8. As people age, the ability to repair tissues is reduced and their skin becomes less elastic and can no longer snap back into shape.
9. The fetus's lungs make a protein that causes the mother to release the hormones that start labor.
10. Answers may vary. Obvious answers include smiling, crawling, walking, holding objects, eating solid food, and speaking.
11. Each gamete contains a haploid nucleus. When two haploid nuclei fuse, the result is a cell with the correct number of chromosomes. If more than one sperm cell were allowed to enter an ovum, the result would be a cell with too many chromosomes.

Chapter 23 Summary

KEY CONCEPTS

23.1 The Reproductive System

- Men and women have different reproductive anatomies.
- Sperm are the male gametes, and ova, or eggs, are the female gametes.
- A new individual results when a sperm and an egg cell fuse. The resulting zygote has the diploid number of chromosomes.
- Males have a pair of sperm-producing organs called the testes.
- Females have a pair of egg-producing organs called the ovaries.
- Female reproduction is characterized by a cycle of hormonal changes.

23.2 Development Before Birth

- A zygote becomes an embryo and then a fetus before being born.
- A woman is pregnant once the developing embryo has become attached to the wall inside her uterus.
- During a woman's pregnancy, the developing embryo becomes a fetus. Nurients and wastes are exchanged between mother and baby within the placenta.
- Childbirth has three stages: cervical dilation, birth of the child, and expulsion of the placenta.
- Twins can result from two zygotes or a single zygote that splits in two.

23.3 Human Life Stages

- Infancy and childhood are periods of rapid growth and mental development.
- People become sexually mature during puberty.
- Aging is linked to the degeneration of cells.

VOCABULARY REVIEW

Write each term in a complete sentence, or write a paragraph relating several terms.

23.1
gamete, p. 419
sperm, p. 419
ovum, p. 419
fertilization, p. 419
zygote, p. 419
testis, p. 420
testosterone, p. 420
epididymis, p. 420
scrotum, p. 420
vas deferens, p. 420
semen, p. 420
ovary, p. 421
oviduct, p. 421
uterus, p. 421
cervix, p. 421
vagina, p. 421
menstruation, p. 422
estrogen, p. 422
ovulation, p. 422
progesterone, p. 422

23.2
blastocyst, p. 423
pregnant, p. 423
placenta, p. 423
umbilical cord, p. 423
embryo, p. 424
development, p. 424
amniotic sac, p. 424
fetus, p. 424
labor, p. 425
fraternal twins, p. 426
identical twins, p. 426

23.3
infancy, p. 427
puberty, p. 428
fertile, p. 428
secondary sex characteristic, p. 428
menopause, p. 429

430 REPRODUCTION AND DEVELOPMENT

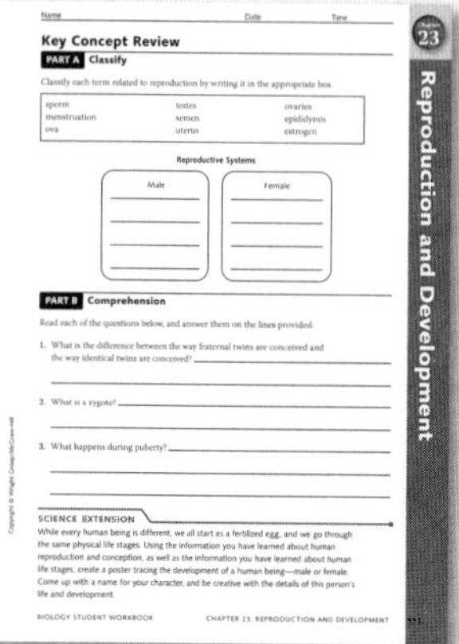
Key Concept Review
Workbook, p. 151

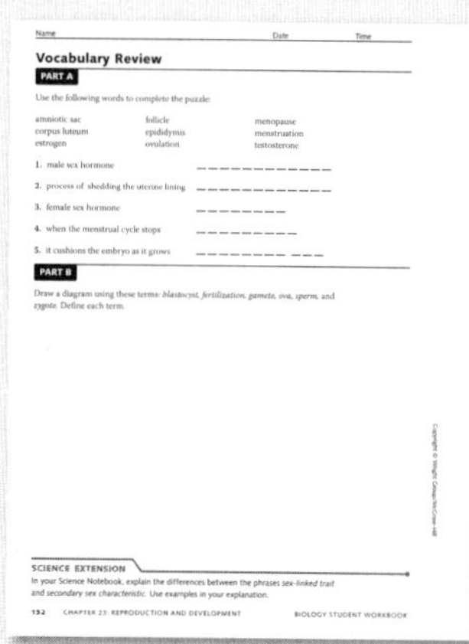
Vocabulary Review
Workbook, p. 152

MASTERING CONCEPTS

True or False

If the statement is true, write "true." If it is false, change the underlined word or words to make the statement true.

1. Ova are male gametes.
2. The fetus gets nutrients and oxygen from its mother through the placenta.
3. Identical twins develop from two different zygotes.
4. People triple their weight during the life stage called infancy.
5. People become sexually mature after they go through menopause.
6. Ovulation is the shedding of the uterine lining.

Short Answer

Answer each of the following in a sentence or brief paragraph.

7. Trace the path a sperm cell takes from a testis to the outside of the man's body.
8. Explain why skin gets wrinkled with age.
9. Describe how labor begins.
10. Name three things an infant learns to do before it is 18 months old.
11. Why does an ovum let only one sperm cell enter?

Critical Thinking

Use what you have learned in this chapter to answer each of the following.

12. **Relate** The tail of a sperm cell contains many mitochondria. Relate this arrangement to the function of the mitochondria.
13. **Infer** Imagine that a follicle did not develop into a corpus luteum after ovulation. If the egg gets fertilized, will it be able to implant in the uterus?
14. **Predict** Some XY individuals do not have testosterone receptors on their cells. These people produce testosterone, but their bodies cannot detect it. Predict how these individuals will appear at birth.

Standardized Test Question

Choose the letter of the response that correctly answers the question.

15. Which of the following terms is associated with pregnancy?
    - A. umbilical cord
    - B. blastocyst
    - C. placenta
    - D. all of the above

Test-Taking Tip

If "all of the above" is one of the choices in a multiple-choice question, be sure that none of the choices is false.

PREPARE FOR CHAPTER TEST

To prepare for the chapter test, create a question from each Learning Goal. Use the information in your Science Notebook to answer each question. Then use these answers to write a well-developed essay about the chapter. Use the Key Concept on the first page of this chapter as your topic sentence.

Critical Thinking

12. Sperm cells use a lot of energy while swimming toward an ovum. Mitochondria make ATP for a cell, and they are concentrated in the region where the sperm use the most energy for swimming.
13. The corpus luteum secretes hormones that prepare the uterus for implantation. If a corpus luteum does not form, no hormones would be produced, the uterus would not be prepared, and a zygote would not be able to implant.
14. Such individuals will appear more like females at birth because testosterone would not be able to affect the cells that make products that create the secondary male sex characteristics.

Standardized Test Question

15. D

Reading Links

Birth Defects (Diseases and Disorders Series)

For curious readers or students seeking specific information about birth defects and their repercussions, this book is a solid learning tool. A variety of diseases and disorders are discussed in everyday language, with attention to diagnosis, treatment, history, and current research. Includes photos and captions, diagrams, notes, bibliography, and details about related resources.

Sheen, Barbara. Gale Group (Lucent Books). 112 pp. Illustrated. Library ISBN: 978-1-59018-406-6.

Tuck Everlasting

This timeless and moving novel, written at a level and in a manner ideal for keeping struggling readers engaged, raises tough questions about life stages and aging that teens might not otherwise think to pose or tackle. When the protagonist encounters the Tuck family, she discovers their secret—access to a natural spring of eternal youth—and its implications. The modern classic is a memorable read, particularly in conjunction with a study of the human life cycle.

Babbitt, Natalie. Thorndike Press. 152 pp. Trade ISBN: 978-0-7862-6322-6.

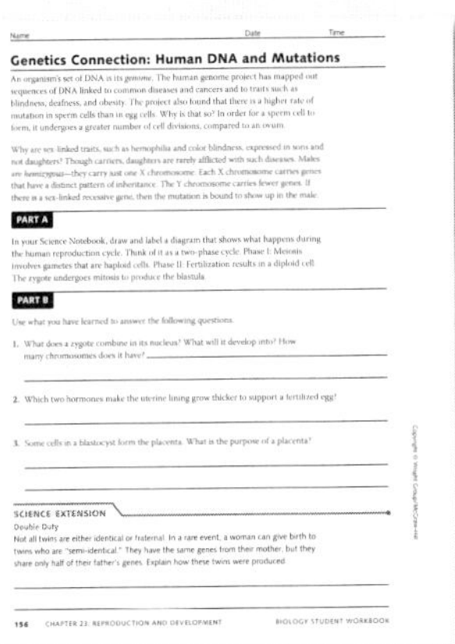

Curriculum Connection Workbook, p. 156

Science Challenge Workbook, pp. 157–158

23A How Gender Is Determined

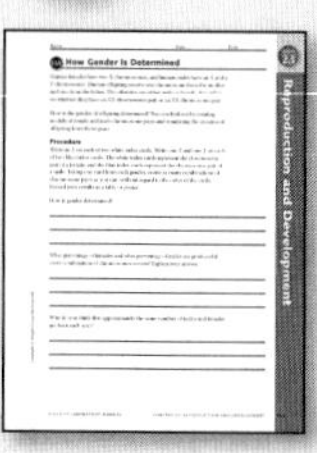

This prechapter introduction activity is designed to determine what students already know about how X and Y chromosomes determine gender by allowing them to create models of chromosome pairs and combine these to simulate the generation of feasible offspring.

Objectives

- identify and model the chromosome pairing of human females and males
- compare and contrast the chromosome pairs of females and males
- analyze the way chromosomes from females and males can be paired during reproduction
- communicate conclusions

Planning

 20–30 minutes 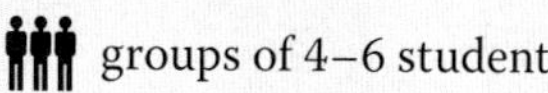 groups of 4–6 students

Materials (per group)

- 4 white index cards
- 4 blue index cards
- marker

Advance Preparation

Remind students that for two sets of pairs, there are four possible combinations:

- the first female chromosome and the first male chromosome
- the first female chromosome and the second male chromosome
- the second female chromosome and the first male chromosome
- the second female chromosome and the second male chromosome

Engagement Guide

- Challenge students to think about how they can form chromosome pairs by asking:
    - *What chromosomes can a male contribute to determine gender?* (The male can contribute either an X or a Y chromosome.)
    - *What chromosomes can a female contribute to determine gender?* (The female can contribute only X chromosomes.)
- Encourage students to communicate their conclusions in creative ways.
- Students' responses to questions should indicate an understanding that the chromosomes of the male determine gender. They should understand that if every combination of chromosomes occurs, 50 percent of the offspring will be male, and 50 percent will be female. This occurs because the male has both an X and a Y and always contributes one to the pair for the offspring. The probability of a male or a female child being born is the same, so other than the effects of environmental factors on male sperm, about the same number of males and females should be born each year.

Going Further

To reinforce the concept of probability and possible combinations, have students create an imaginary organism whose offspring gender is determined by four chromosomes, two from each parent. Have students repeat the activity with the appropriate number of cards, record their results, and report the results to the class. Encourage students to create visuals for communicating their conclusions.

23B Model of a Placenta

Objectives

- observe the diffusion of a substance through a membrane
- compare and contrast the functioning of a placenta and diffusion through a membrane
- analyze the implications of the exchange of substances between mother and fetus

Skill Set

observing, comparing and contrasting, classifying, stating conclusions

Planning

 1 class period  groups of 2–4 students

Materials

Materials for this activity are listed in the Student Laboratory Manual.

Advance Preparation

Create an isotonic solution by mixing 1 part corn syrup with 2 parts water. Make enough to fill the beaker for each group to a height of 6 cm. Dissolve the shells of the eggs by immersing them in a solution of 1 part distilled vinegar (5% acetic acid) and 1 part water. Keep them in a refrigerator for several days until the shells dissolve. Advise students to work very carefully with the eggs, because without the shell they can break easily.

Answers to Observations: Data Table 1

Responses will vary, but students should note that the egg absorbed the color from the solution and became progressively deeper in color the longer it was in the solution.

Answers to Analysis and Conclusions

1. The egg absorbed the color dye from the solution and became increasingly darker with additional immersion time.
2. Students should recognize that if substances can move past the membrane into the egg, they can also move in the other direction. Students should recognize that this would be like CO_2 moving from the fetus through the placenta to the mother.
3. The alcohol would probably pass through the placenta and affect the fetus.
4. The model is like the functioning of the placenta because it demonstrates how substances can be transported through a membrane, but it is unlike the functioning of the placenta in that it is a very simplified demonstration of a very complex process and illustrates movement in only one direction.

Going Further

Allow students to experiment with different types of permeable membranes to discover how some allow more and some allow less of a substance to penetrate them over time.

23C Sea Urchin Fertilization

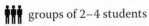

Objectives

- identify the eggs and sperm of sea urchins
- observe the fertilization of sea urchin eggs
- observe the development of sea urchin zygotes

Skill Set

observing, comparing and contrasting, recording and analyzing data, classifying, stating conclusions

Planning

 1 class period groups of 2–4 students

Materials

Materials for this activity are listed in the Student Laboratory Manual.

Lab Tips

- There should likely be an advance discussion about this investigation, since students will be manipulating the reproductive process of another living organism.
- Students may need to remove goggles to obtain a better view while using the microscope.
- It may be helpful to include a coverslip when using the well microscope slides.

Advance Preparation

- To encourage sea urchins to release eggs or sperm, use a syringe to inject 1 to 2 mL of a 0.5 M potassium chloride solution into the soft tissue surrounding the mouth, pushing the needle in about 1 cm. Place the sea urchins, mouth-side down, across the top of a petri dish full of seawater. In a few minutes, the sea urchin will emit either sperm or eggs from its gonopores (surrounding the anus). Semen is white, and eggs are yellow. The eggs should be viable for at least 6 hours. Distribute small amounts of the eggs and sperm to petri dishes of seawater for each group. The diluted sperm will be viable for only a half-hour, so you should dilute and distribute them only as needed.
- Provide each group with a petri dish of sea urchin sperm and sea urchin eggs.
- Have containers available on your desk for students to use to discard unused seawater samples.

Answers to Observations: Data Table 1

Only a small percentage of the sperm will appear to be swimming with tails whipping. The eggs are round in shape. Once fertilized, the eggs release a membrane that forms a wall around them to keep out other sperm. As the egg prepares to divide, radiating lines will appear from the nucleus.

Answers to Analysis and Conclusions

1. Answers will vary. Students should find that only a small percentage of the sperm are moving when they are by themselves but that more are moving when eggs are present. Students may predict that this is because eggs release a chemical (a peptide) that alerts the sperm to their presence.
2. The eggs release a membrane after they are fertilized to prevent other sperm from entering.
3. After the protective membrane forms, lines appear to radiate from the nucleus as the zygote begins to divide.
4. Answers will vary, but students should find that most of the eggs are fertilized after a half-hour.
5. Answers will vary, but students should recognize that sperm are very successful at penetrating the eggs.

Going Further

Have students mix sea urchin sperm and eggs in a beaker of seawater and store the beaker in a dark, cool place. Students can examine the larvae as they develop. Do not crowd the larvae, and feed them with algae (*Rhodomonas*) for best results.

Chapter 24 Lessons

Introduce Chapter 24

As a starting activity, use LAB 24A Live Bacteria on page 149 of the Laboratory Manual.

ENGAGE Write the following in two lists on the board: 100 trillion (human body), 20,000/mL (milk), 100,000/g (deli meat), 50,000/g (frozen food), 1,000,000/g (ground beef), 1,000,000/mL (tap water). Numbers (of bacteria) go in one list, and the names in parentheses (correct responses) go in the other list. Scramble the order of one list. Explain that each number is how many bacteria are in one of the things in the other list. Then, ask pairs of students to match each item in the second list to the correct number and to provide reasons for their matches. Ranking the numbers from greatest to least might help students make matches. When they finish, discuss correct answers and why some things have more bacteria than others. Point out that the number of bacteria in the human body (100 trillion) is ten times the number of human body cells (10 trillion)!

Think About Disease

Give students a few minutes to remember the specific symptoms of their last illness, and then have them record their responses in their Science Notebooks. Students may need additional prompting for the second bulleted activity. Ask: *How do you think you caught the illness? Do you remember any friends or family members being ill before you were?* Encourage students to be as specific as possible for both items.

Chapter 24 Disease and the Body's Defenses

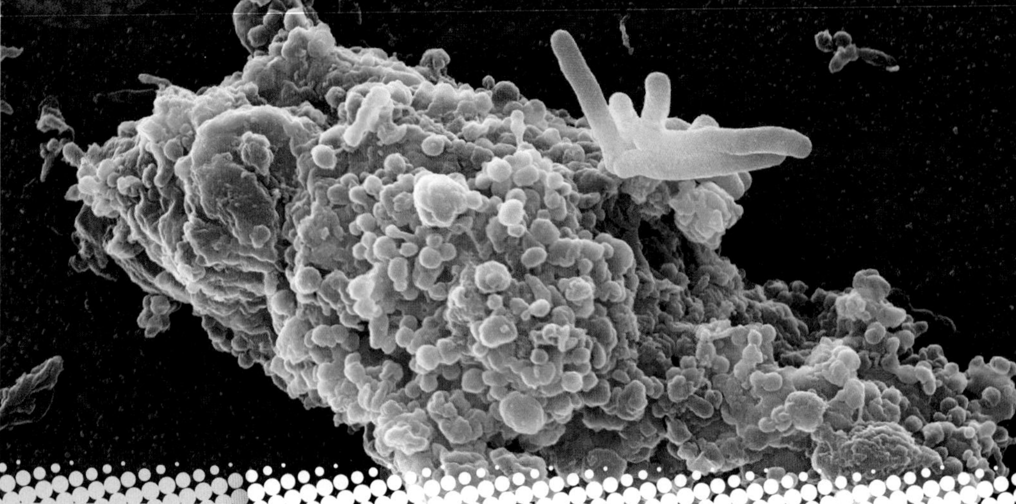

KEY CONCEPT The body's failure to defend against pathogens results in infectious disease.

Microorganisms are everywhere. Tens of thousands of bacteria are inhaled every time a person takes a breath. The large intestine is home to 100 trillion bacteria, many of which would cause diseases if they were able to enter body cells. How does the body keep microorganisms out of its cells and tissues? How does the body distinguish between harmless and disease-causing organisms? The human body has several amazing defenses.

Think About Disease

Although you cannot directly see or feel the microorganisms that make you sick, you do exhibit symptoms.

- Think about a cold or other illness you have had in the past and the symptoms you exhibited. How did you feel? How long did you have the symptoms? What made you get better?
- Where do you think you might have picked up the microorganisms that made you sick? What could you do in the future to prevent the spread of illness? Record your responses in your Science Notebook.

www.scilinks.org
Immune System **Code: WGB24**

432

Chapter 24 Planning Guide			
Instructional Periods	National Standards	Lab Manual	Workbook
24.1 3 periods	E.1, F.1, F.4, F.5, G.3; C.3, F.1, F.6, G.3; UCP.5	**Lab 24A—p. 149** Live Bacteria **Lab 24B—p. 150** How Pathogens Spread **Lab 24C—p. 152** Effectiveness of Disinfectants in Killing Bacteria	Key Concept Review p. 159 Vocabulary Review p. 160 Graphic Organizer p. 161 Reading Comprehension p. 162 Curriculum Connection p. 163 Science Challenge p. 164
24.2 2 periods	A.1, C.1, F.4; F.1; UCP.1, UCP.3, UCP.5		
24.3 2 periods	A.2, C.1, C.3, F.1; F.1; UCP.2, UCP.5		

Middle School Standard; High School Standard; Unifying Concept and Principle

24.1 Disease

Before You Read

Create an outline for this lesson in your Science Notebook. Label the lesson title with the Roman numeral *I* and the headings with the letters *A*, *B*, *C*, and *D*. Record the information you want to remember under each heading using proper outline format.

Learning Goals

- Distinguish between noninfectious diseases and infectious diseases.
- Describe how pathogens are transmitted.
- Compare and contrast how bacteria and viruses cause disease.
- Explain how the germ theory and antibiotics contributed to modern medicine.

New Vocabulary

disease
noninfectious disease
pathogen
infectious disease
symptom
vector
epidemic
antibiotic

Having a disease can make a person feel awful. Sore throat, headache, and itching are all symptoms of disease. Sick people also show signs such as a fever or white spots in the throat.

What Is Disease?

A **disease** is any condition that disrupts the normal functioning of the body. You have already learned about some diseases specific to certain body systems. For example, asthma is a disease of the respiratory system, and stroke is a disease of the circulatory system. These diseases are called **noninfectious** (non ihn FEK shus) **diseases** because they are not caused by an invasion of the body.

Many other diseases are caused by microorganisms, viruses, and parasitic worms. These disease-causing agents are called **pathogens** (PA thuh junz). Pathogens invade the body and use the host's resources for food and reproduction. Once pathogens get inside the body, they produce an infection. Diseases that are caused by pathogens are called **infectious diseases**.

A person may have an infection for a long time without realizing it. Tuberculosis and HIV infections often go unnoticed for years. In other cases, an infected person may quickly start to feel **symptoms** (SIHM tumz), or changed sensations resulting from the infection. Tiredness, aching, chills, and pain are all examples of symptoms. Diseases can also cause signs, such as rashes, that are visible to other people. Each disease has a characteristic pattern of symptoms and signs. Doctors ask about symptoms and check for signs of infection when they treat an illness. Sometimes, they will test a patient's body fluids to identify the pathogen causing the infection. Once they do that, doctors can recommend an effective treatment.

Figure 24.1 Most people know when they are sick. A headache, exhaustion, or general discomfort tell them that something is wrong. A fever and chills are symptoms of certain diseases.

24.1 Introduce

ENGAGE Write *disease* on the board, and give students a few minutes to define it. Use volunteers' definitions to create a working definition for the class. Then, ask students to list the names of diseases they know, and create a class list from their responses. Throughout the lesson, refer to these diseases and have students categorize them as noninfectious or infectious, identify their symptoms, and identify their cause.

Before You Read

Model creating the outline on the board. Review the first few headings aloud with students. Then, have students create their outlines in their Science Notebooks, using your model. Remind them to leave space between headings to add information.

Vocabulary terms are listed on the first student page of each lesson. You may wish to preview the terms before introducing each lesson. Strategies for teaching the vocabulary appear on the pages where the terms are introduced.

Teach

EXPLAIN that in this lesson, students will learn what causes diseases, how they affect the body, how they are passed from person to person, and how they are treated.

Science Notebook EXTRA

Encourage students to use the vocabulary section they created in their Science Notebooks. Remind them to record prefixes, suffixes, and root words to help them remember the meanings of vocabulary terms.

ELL Strategy

Paraphrase Pair students and assign each pair one or two paragraphs to paraphrase. If possible, assign all content-rich paragraphs from the lesson, as well as paragraph that contain vocabulary terms. Encourage students to define important vocabulary in context in their paraphrases. After each pair has paraphrased the paragraph, have the students share their new paragraph with the class.

pathogen Explain that *pathogen* comes from the Greek word *pathos*, meaning "suffering" or "disease," and that the suffix *gen-* means "something that produces."

infectious disease Have students define this term in their own words using the absence of *non-* from the term. Ask students to provide a synonym for the term. (contagious disease)

symptom Encourage students to think about common (nonscientific) uses of the word *symptom*, and discuss these as a class.

Vocabulary

disease Explain that the prefix *dis-* means "away from" and that the root *ease* means "comfort."

noninfectious disease Explain that *non-* means "not" and that *infectious* is the adjective form of the verb *infect*, from a Latin word that means "to make" or "to do." A common synonym is *noncontagious*.

Teach

ENGAGE Ask students if they can think of ways that pathogens can be transmitted to people. Have students recall their responses to the Think About activity on page 432. Ask students if they are familiar with the term *epidemic* and to give examples of epidemics they know about.

Vocabulary

vector Explain that *vector* comes from a Latin word that means "to carry." Tell students that *carrier* is a synonym for *vector.*

epidemic Tell students that *epidemic* is from the Greek prefix *epi-*, "among," and root *demos,* which means "the people."

As You Read

Have students add information to the outlines in their Science Notebooks. Have each student exchange his or her outline with a partner and provide feedback on the accuracy and completeness of the partner's outline.

ANSWER through meat, saliva, body wastes, and parasites

Explore It!

Ask the "infected" student not to alert his or her peers. At the end of class, disclose the original "infected" person and ask students to try to determine how they were infected. Have students reflect on the exploration by writing about preventing the spread of disease.

ANSWER by touching, sneezing, coughing, being eaten as food, etc.

CONNECTION: Social Studies

Several epidemics have decimated human populations and led to great historical changes. Some examples include smallpox in North America and the influenza pandemic of 1918. Have students imagine what would happen if an epidemic were to kill a large part of the population of the United States.

As You Read

Fill in the outline in your Science Notebook. Share your outline with a partner. Add information or make corrections as necessary.

How can an animal transmit a disease to a human?

Transmission of Pathogens

Pathogens are unable to move to a new host on their own. They must be carried from one host to another. Often, people transmit pathogens to one another. One person with a cold might sneeze, spreading virus-filled saliva through the air and onto nearby surfaces. Another person could breathe in the virus or pick it up from an object, such as a doorknob, on which the virus landed. Contaminated food can transmit pathogens such as *E. coli.* Human wastes in unclean water can transmit pathogens, as well.

Many pathogens are transmitted by vectors. **Vectors** are animals that spread pathogens through their saliva, parasites, body wastes, and meat. Some of the infectious diseases that require a vector include malaria, rabies, and bubonic plague, also known as the Black Death. Bubonic plague is transmitted from infected rats to humans by fleas. This disease killed more than half the population of Europe during an epidemic in the fourteenth century. An **epidemic** (eh puh DEH mihk) is the spread of a disease to many people.

Explore It!

Try this experiment to see how easily pathogens can spread. At the beginning of a class or lab period, your teacher will put two small drops of peppermint extract on the palm of one student's hand. This student is the "infected" person. Go through the class or lab period as usual, exchanging papers, sharing lab equipment, sharing pencils or pens, etc. At the end of the class period, smell your hands. Check with your classmates to determine how many students picked up the peppermint smell from the "infected" student. In your Science Notebook, list some ways to prevent disease from spreading through your school.

Figure 24.2 Chickens are important vectors for bird flu. Infected chickens can transmit the flu to humans. Many millions of infected chickens have been destroyed. Scientists hope that these measures will prevent a human epidemic of bird flu.

CONNECTION: Social Studies

Several federal agencies work to prevent the spread of diseases.

- The Centers for Disease Control and Prevention (CDC) help doctors identify unusual diseases and work to prevent disease epidemics.
- The Food and Drug Administration (FDA) makes sure that foods, food additives, medicines, and medical devices are safe for consumers.
- The National Institutes of Health (NIH) conduct and pay for medical research.

Background Information

As of November 2006, the total number of humans affected by Avian Influenza A (N5N1), as reported to the World Health Organization, was 258. Deaths resulting from those cases numbered 154. Of primary concern to scientists is the ability of influenza viruses to change. Since little or no immunity to avian flu currently exists in humans, a world outbreak of disease is possible.

An endemic disease is a disease that is constantly present in the population. The common cold is an endemic disease. A pandemic is an outbreak of a disease that affects an exceptionally large part of the population over a wide geographic area.

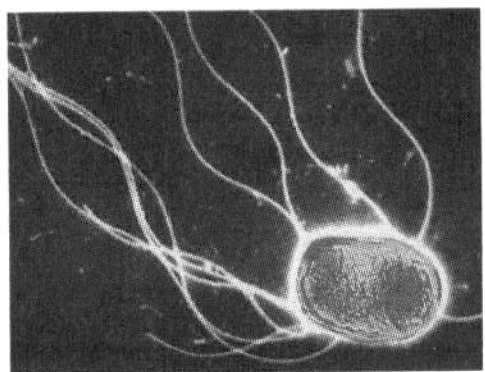

Bacterium
Salmonella

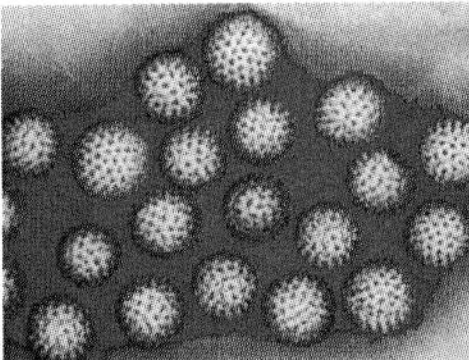

Virus
Rotavirus

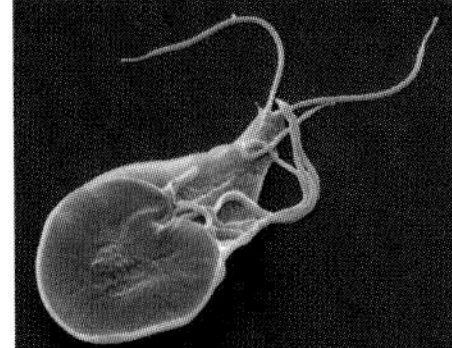

Protozoan
Giardia lamblia

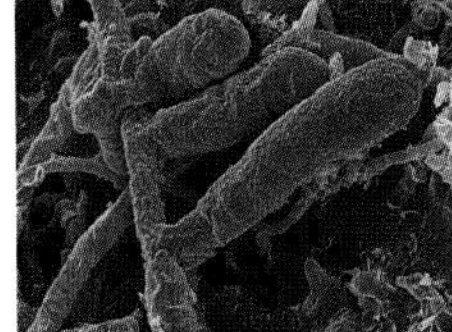

Fungus
Epidermophyton

Figure 24.3 Many types of pathogens can cause human diseases. *Salmonella* is a food-borne bacterium that causes diarrhea. Viral infections caused by rotavirus kill 600,000 children in developing countries each year. *Giardia* is a protozoan transmitted by drinking unclean water. Fungal infection by *Epidermophyton* causes the itchy, peeling skin of athlete's foot.

Pathogens and Disease

Bacteria and viruses cause many serious diseases. Fungi also cause some mild diseases. Protozoans and parasitic worms are common pathogens in other parts of the world. Each type of pathogen invades the body in a different way and causes specific diseases. Most infectious diseases in the United States are caused by bacteria and viruses. **Figure 24.4** lists some of the diseases caused by bacteria, viruses, protozoans, and fungi.

Bacteria Bacteria are single-celled organisms found in every imaginable place on Earth. Only a small fraction of the thousands of species of bacteria cause human diseases. However, these pathogenic bacteria lead to about five million deaths each year. The main danger from bacteria comes from the toxins, or poisons, they produce. Bacterial toxins can cause fever, diarrhea, and cell death.

Viruses Viruses are not living organisms. They consist of genetic material enclosed in a protein shell. Viruses can reproduce only with the help of a host cell, which they destroy in the process. The destruction of host cells is what causes the symptoms of viral diseases. The single deadliest infectious disease, AIDS, is caused by a virus called HIV.

Pathogens that Cause Infectious Diseases

Type of Pathogen	Diseases Caused
bacterium	food poisoning, strep throat, sinus infection, tooth decay, tuberculosis, plague, anthrax
virus	cold, influenza, viral hepatitis, viral pneumonia, AIDS, SARS, Ebola, chicken pox, measles, rabies, smallpox, diarrhea
protozoan (protist)	malaria, traveler's diarrhea, amebic dysentery
fungus	athlete's foot, ringworm
animal (worm)	tapeworm, trichinosis, hookworm

Figure 24.4 Each infectious disease is caused by a different pathogen.

Figure It Out

1. Which type of pathogen causes ringworm?
2. Which kingdoms of life do not cause infectious diseases in humans?

Teach

EXPLORE After students complete their outlines by including information from this page, have them work in small groups to list the characteristics of bacteria and viruses in their Science Notebooks. Then, ask each student to make a Venn diagram comparing bacteria and viruses.

Science Notebook EXTRA

Have students review Figure 24.4 and compare the diseases named with the class list of diseases from the Engage activity on page 433. Have students revise the class list as needed and copy it into their Science Notebooks. Ask students to note the pathogens for their list of diseases. Have students reflect on the accuracy of their initial responses based on the information in the figure.

Figure It Out: Figure 24.4

ANSWER **1.** fungus **2.** Archaebacteria and Plantae

EXTEND Have students choose one of the diseases named in the table and research the scientific name of the causal agent, symptoms of the disease, how it is treated, and where the disease has the greatest impact on a human population. Have students summarize their findings in a written report or poster presentation.

Field Study

Have students walk around the school and observe the school nurse, cafeteria workers, and custodians as they engage in their daily activities. Ask students to note which tasks are related to avoiding the spread of bacteria and viruses.

Differentiated Instruction

Interpersonal After students engage in the field study, have them work in small groups to create a list of questions to ask one school staff member about his or her role in preventing bacterial and viral diseases. Review and revise the lists as a class; then, have student groups conduct brief interviews with a specific staff member. Have each student group share the interview responses they gathered in a short report or presentation to inform the class.

Teach

EXPLORE Students may be surprised to learn that the knowledge and treatment of infectious diseases is a relatively young science, so make a point of discussing the contents of the first two paragraphs. You may want to do a read-aloud. Ask students if they are familiar with some of this history. Also ask students what they know about antibiotics and whether they have ever used them to fight disease.

Vocabulary

antibiotic Explain that this word contains the prefix *anti-*, which means "opposed to" or "against," and the root *biotic*, which means "relating to life or living organisms." The literal meaning of *antibiotic* is "against life." Ask students to relate this literal meaning to the definition of the term.

Use the Visual: Figure 24.5

ANSWER Possible answers include differences in facilities, clothing, sanitation, lighting, instruments, and kinds of people present.

Assess

EVALUATE Use the After You Read questions and the Alternative Assessment to help you assess students' understanding of the lesson.

After You Read

1. Hand washing, the cleaning of surgical instruments, and clean clothes became more common. Scientists also started to look for ways to combat the pathogens causing diseases.
2. No. Bacteria release toxins that poison cells. Viruses destroy the cells they invade.
3. by person-to-person contact, by vectors, or by contaminated food, water, or air

Alternative Assessment

EVALUATE Have each student use his or her lesson outline to write a paragraph summarizing the lesson content. Suggest that students use the lesson Learning Goals to direct their writing. Main ideas discussed should include what a disease is, how diseases are transmitted, how bacteria and viruses cause diseases, and how the germ theory impacted medicine.

Figure 24.5 These photos show how surgery was performed before *(right)* and after *(left)* the acceptance of the germ theory. How many differences can you find between the two scenes?

Did You Know?

New diseases are emerging all the time. Sometimes, animal pathogens evolve to infect humans. Other times, once-harmless microorganisms mutate to become pathogenic. Recently discovered diseases include AIDS, West Nile virus, SARS, and bird flu. Many scientists are deeply concerned that bird flu could cross over to humans and cause a worldwide epidemic.

Medicine and Disease

Pathogens were discovered in the mid-nineteenth century. Before that time, physicians and common people alike had no idea what caused infectious diseases. Most people believed that sickness came from wrongful actions, clouds of diseased air, or even glances from diseased people. Diseases were treated by bleeding victims or feeding them poisonous mixtures of chemicals. Many patients were more hurt than helped by doctors' treatments.

Louis Pasteur and other scientists discovered that pathogens, commonly called germs, cause many diseases. This idea is called the germ theory. Pasteur had a difficult time convincing doctors that washing hands and using clean surgical instruments could save lives. Medicine became much more effective after the germ theory was accepted. Doctors were able to slow the spread of infectious diseases.

Antibiotics Chemicals that kill bacteria are called **antibiotics** (an ti bi AH tihks). Sir Alexander Fleming first discovered antibiotics in 1928 when spores from the airborne mold *Penicillium notatum* accidentally fell on a sample of bacteria he was growing in his lab. All around the mold, the bacteria died. Fleming was able to purify the substance the mold secreted—penicillin—and use it to treat patients with bacterial diseases. The use of antibiotics has saved millions of lives.

Antibiotics have their limits in fighting disease, however. First, antibiotics are only useful against bacteria. Viruses and other pathogens are not affected. Second, bacteria can develop resistance to commonly used antibiotics. Bacteria evolve quickly through mutation and natural selection. Scientists are concerned that a "superbug" bacterium will evolve that is resistant to all known antibiotics. This is why it is important to use antibiotics only when needed and to finish all of the medicine prescribed by a doctor.

After You Read

1. Describe how medicine changed after the acceptance of the germ theory.
2. Do bacteria and viruses make you sick in the same way? Explain your answer.
3. According to your lesson outline, what are three ways in which pathogens can be transmitted? Answer this question in a well-developed paragraph in your Science Notebook.

Background Information

Prior to the development of the germ theory, people believed in spontaneous generation—the idea that living things grew from nonliving things. A number of scientists contributed to the germ theory, including Anton van Leeuwenhoek, Ignaz Semmelweis, Joseph Lister, Robert Koch, Dmitri Iwanowski, and Alexander Fleming.

436 DISEASE AND THE BODY'S DEFENSES

24.2 The Nonspecific Defense System

Learning Goals

- Identify the role and actions of the nonspecific defense system.
- Explain the purpose and effects of inflammation.

New Vocabulary

nonspecific defense system
inflammation
phagocyte
natural killer cell

Before You Read

Some processes take place in a specific order. Think about a process that is routine to you. In your Science Notebook, describe the order of events involved in the process. Preview the lesson, and note the order of events as a pathogen invades the body.

All of the surfaces of the body are coated with bacteria. Bacteria also live and thrive inside the body. For the most part, the bacteria on the skin and in the gut are harmless. They compete with pathogenic bacteria and prevent infections. The symbiotic bacteria in the intestines help digest food and manufacture vitamins. As long as these microorganisms do not enter body tissues, they cause no harm. Problems begin when symbiotic bacteria or more dangerous bacteria enter body tissues.

The Role of the Nonspecific Defense System

Microorganisms can become pathogens once inside body tissues. Pathogens disrupt normal body functions and release toxins. It is the job of the **nonspecific defense system** to keep foreign cells out of body tissues and destroy them if they do get inside. The skin and mucous membranes keep most pathogens away from body tissues. White blood cells fight pathogens that succeed in invading the body.

Babies are born with a functioning nonspecific defense system. That is why it is often called the innate, natural, or inborn defense system. This system attacks all cells and large molecules that it recognizes as foreign to the body. Pathogens, pollen, splinters, and transplanted tissues are all treated the same way.

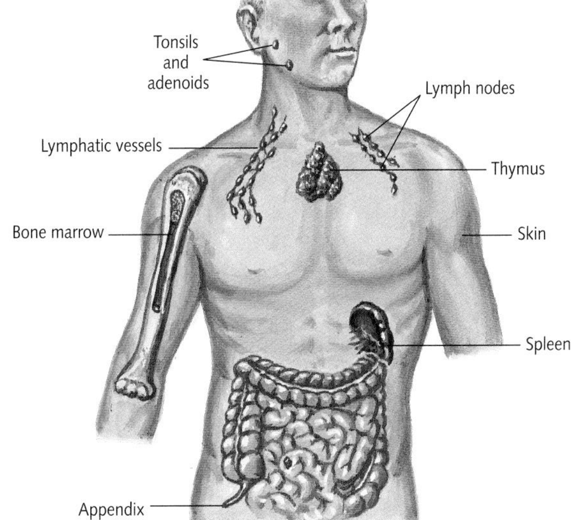

Figure 24.6 Many different parts of the body function in the nonspecific defense system.

24.2 Introduce

ENGAGE Have pairs of students play all or part of a game of checkers or tic-tac-toe. Tell students that they may only make offensive moves to try to win and may not engage in any defensive moves (those that block their opponents). Then, have pairs play the game again. This time, tell them to use as much defense as possible. Finally, have students discuss their experiences. Encourage them to think about how the pace and outcomes of the games differed.

EXPLAIN that the games served as a metaphor for diseases and the body's nonspecific defense system. The defensive moves (the components of the nonspecific defense system) work to stop the offense (the disease).

Before You Read

Model a routine process such as brushing your teeth. Go through the steps out loud (getting your toothbrush, adding toothpaste, and then brushing top, bottom, both sides, the front of all teeth, and the tongue), noting each step on the board. Next, have students reflect on a process in which they engage routinely, and have them write the order of events in their Science Notebooks. Then, have students review the lesson and take notes on the events that occur when a pathogen invades the body.

Teach

EXPLAIN Remind students that they will continue to learn how the human body protects itself. The body has external structures that serve as the first general lines of defense. Once a disease has entered the body, more specific processes occur in the body's defense mechanism.

Vocabulary

nonspecific defense system Encourage students to think about common uses of each word in *nonspecific defense system*, and discuss these as a class. When all the words are combined, the term means "a general way of protecting the body" and refers to the actions of the skin, mucous membranes, eyes, blood, and bone marrow.

ELL Strategy

Use a Concept Map Have students create a concept map to organize the information for this lesson. The main topic should be *Nonspecific Defense System*. The subtopics of the map should include *Skin, Eyes, Mucous Membranes, Blood,* and *Bone Marrow*. Encourage students to add details as they read the lesson.

Teacher Alert

Point out that the spelling of the membranes that line body cavities exposed to the outside world is *mucous*, whereas the sticky liquid that these membranes produce, which traps germs and other foreign particles before they can invade cells membranes, is spelled *mucus*.

Teach

EXPLAIN Tell students that in this section of the lesson, they will learn about the first two parts of the body's nonspecific defense system—the skin and the mucous membranes.

Use the Visual: Figure 24.7

Students have likely heard the admonition to cover their mouths many times. Invite students to comment on the wisdom of this advice, based on what this photo shows.

EXTEND Some students could keep a tally of how many of their fellow students and teachers do and do not cover their mouths when sneezing throughout the day. Students could design posters to encourage all to cover their mouths.

As You Read

Give students about five minutes to review and revise the notes in their Science Notebooks. Pair students, and have them provide their partners with feedback on the accuracy of their order of events.

ANSWER The outer layers of skin are dead cells. The environment is too dry and acidic for most pathogens. Oils and sweat on the skin contain chemicals that inhibit bacterial growth. Finally, symbiotic bacteria on the skin compete with potential pathogens.

CONNECTION: Language

Have students research and list all the ways that people in different cultures respond when a person sneezes. ELL students can share the response from their native language and country.

As You Read

Record the order of events as pathogens invade the body through the skin. Share your event order with a partner. Then, create a sequence chart of events.

Why can't pathogens directly invade the outer skin cells?

CONNECTION: Language

What do you say when a person near you sneezes? Many people say "Bless you!" This custom dates back at least 2,000 years. German speakers say "*Gesundheit*" (geh ZOONT hite), and Spanish speakers say "*Salud*" (saw LEWD). Both of these words mean "Good health!" In some countries, it is considered more polite to ignore the sneeze altogether.

Keeping Pathogens Out

There is a saying that "the best offense is a good defense." That is certainly true when it comes to fighting disease. The energy required to keep pathogens out of the body is much less than the energy it takes to defeat an active infection. The nonspecific defense system of the body consists of the skin, mucous membranes, inflammation, and white blood cells.

Skin The skin is designed to keep bodily fluids in and foreign material out. The outer layers of skin are made of dead cells that pathogens cannot invade. The skin is a dry, acidic environment that is unsuitable for most microorganisms. Sweat and oils produced by glands in the skin contain proteins that disrupt bacterial cell walls. The symbiotic bacteria that normally live on the skin are adapted to these hostile conditions. The symbiotic bacteria compete with dangerous microorganisms and produce chemicals that kill them.

Mucous Membranes Skin is not the only part of the body that comes in contact with pathogens. Pathogens can also enter the body through the eyes, respiratory tract, digestive tract, and any other part that comes in contact with the air. Body cavities that are exposed to the outside world are lined with mucous membranes. The mucus, or sticky liquid, that these membranes produce traps germs and other foreign particles before they can invade cells. In the nose and throat, tiny hairs called cilia sweep mucus to the throat, where it can be swallowed. Once in the stomach, most pathogens are destroyed by stomach acid. Other ways in which the body expels pathogens include tears, sneezing, coughing, urination, and defecation.

The body would quickly be overwhelmed by invading pathogens without the skin and mucous membranes. Any gap in these defenses allows microorganisms into body tissues. At that point, the next level of bodily defenses is activated.

Figure 24.7 Sneezing is one way that the body expels pathogens. Sneezing can spread pathogens from one person to another.

Differentiated Instruction

Kinesthetic Have students work in small groups to make a model of one of the nonspecific defense system components. Provide a variety of materials, such as tissue paper, tape, yarn, cardboard, balloons, and plastic containers. Have each group write a short explanation of the function of the component to include with the model.

ELL Strategy

In a new CDC initiative to prevent the spread of pathogens, public health officials are now asking parents and teachers to train children to sneeze or cough into their elbows. Encourage students to go to the CDC Web site at **http://www.cdc.gov/flu/protect/covercough.htm** to download information about the "Cover your cough" program. Have students translate the information into their first language.

Inflammation: The Body's First Response

Cells respond immediately to an injury or invasion by pathogens. Cells in the damaged area release chemicals that cause inflammation. **Inflammation** (ihn fluh MAY shun) is redness, heat, swelling, and pain at the site of an injury or infection. Chemicals released by cells near the injury or infection cause blood vessels to expand. The blood vessels become leaky, allowing fluids and cells to pass from them into the injured tissues.

Figure 24.8 Inflammation is the body's first response to injury or infection. An insect sting can cause the skin to swell, become red, and feel warm to the touch. Inflammation may be painful, but it speeds the body's repairs.

Inflammation starts a series of body defenses. Blood platelets flow through gaps in the blood vessels. The platelets seal out microorganisms from an injury or infection. A fever may develop, speeding body repairs and slowing pathogen reproduction. Various types of defensive cells are also attracted to the inflammation. All of these defensive cells are types of white blood cells.

Too much inflammation can cause damage to the body. The chemicals involved in inflammation have powerful effects on cells and their DNA. Constantly inflamed tissues cannot function properly. Their cells may change and become cancerous. Scientists suspect that inflammation is also important in the development of heart disease, arthritis, and other diseases.

Figure It Out

1. What temperature range is ideal for the body's defense response?
2. Is it a good idea to take a fever reducer as soon as the body temperature rises above 37°C?

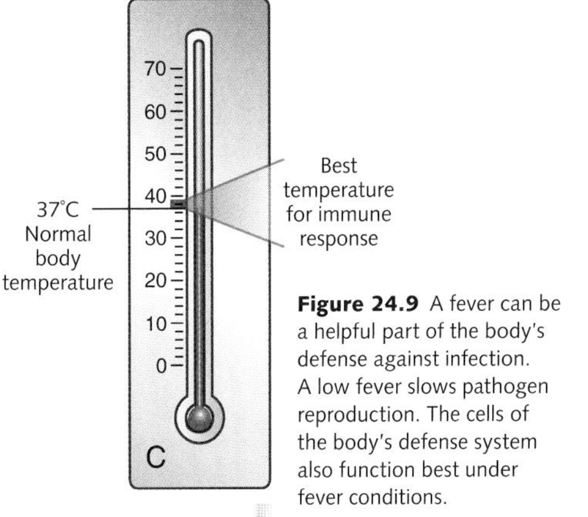

Figure 24.9 A fever can be a helpful part of the body's defense against infection. A low fever slows pathogen reproduction. The cells of the body's defense system also function best under fever conditions.

Teach

EXPLAIN that in this section, students will learn what causes inflammation in the body and how the body responds to it. As you discuss inflammation, remind students of the essential question of this chapter: How does the human body defend itself?

EXTEND Have students work in pairs to create a flow chart in their Science Notebooks to illustrate the body's defense response to inflammation. The chart should begin with platelets entering the injured site and end with the results of uncontrolled inflammation.

Vocabulary

inflammation Tell students that the root *inflame* comes from the Latin word *inflammare*, which means "to kindle" or "to begin to burn." The suffix *-tion* means "the condition or state." The literal meaning of *inflammation* is "the condition of burning." Ask students to relate this literal meaning to the definition of the term.

Figure It Out: Figure 24.9

ANSWER **1.** 37°–39°C **2.** No. A low fever slows pathogen growth and helps the body's defenses.

CONNECTION: Technology

Federal agencies have Web sites that provide information to consumers. Have each student work with a partner to review one of the sites and share an overview of the contents with the class. The overview will help clarify the role and actual work of each agency. Give students the following list of government Web sites:

CDC: **http://www.cdc.gov/**

FDA: **http://www.fda.gov/**

NIH: **http://www.nih.gov/**

Background Information

The white blood cells that respond to an injury site are called leukocytes. These cells release chemokines and cytokines to organize the body's response. To control inappropriate or uncontrolled inflammation, doctors prescribe anti-inflammatory drugs such as aspirin, ibuprofen, and corticosteroids. Scientists are also working to create new drugs to block cytokines and chemokines.

The literal meaning of *arthritis* is "joint inflammation." The root *arth* is from the Greek word *arthron*, meaning "joint." The prefix *-itis* means "inflammation." Typically, the body heals most inflamed areas, and the inflammation recedes. In many forms of arthritis, however, the inflammation does not diminish. Rather, the inflammation damages healthy tissue and causes more inflammation. The cycle continues, and the inflamed tissues may never heal properly.

Teach

 **EXPLAIN** Tell students that in this section of the lesson, they will learn about three more parts of the body's nonspecific defense system—phagocytes, natural killer cells, and interferons.

 **Vocabulary**

phagocyte Explain that the prefix *phago-* is from the Greek word *phagein*, meaning "to eat." The suffix *-cyto* means "a cell." Phagocytes are cells that "eat" pathogens.

natural killer cell Have students think about common uses of each of the word in *natural killer cell*, and discuss these uses as a class. Natural killer cells are the body's first defense against cancer and virus-infected cells.

Extend It!

Have students work with a partner to research and synthesize their findings. In addition to addresses of reputable Web sites, provide students with medical reference texts such as *The Merck Manual of Medical Information* to use as they research phagocytes.

Assess

EVALUATE Use the After You Read questions and the Alternative Assessment to help you assess students' understanding of the lesson.

After You Read

1. They are coated in sticky mucus that traps pathogens and have cilia that sweep trapped pathogens toward the throat, where they are swallowed and destroyed in the stomach by stomach acid or coughed or sneezed out of the body with mucus.
2. inflammation
3. They are able to recognize infected cells by the antigens on an invader's surface.

Alternative Assessment

EVALUATE Using their notes, students should draw charts that demonstrate the chain of events that results when the body's nonspecific defense system responds to a pathogen.

Extend It!

Phagocytes include monocytes, which develop into macrophages, as well as neutrophils and eosinophils. Macrophages are found in body tissues. The other cells circulate in the blood. Use library and Internet resources to find out more about these phagocytes. What do they do? What do they look like? What part of the immune response are they involved in? Record your findings in your Science Notebook, and then prepare a presentation for the class. Include diagrams in your presentation.

Fighting Invaders Inside Body Tissues

Defensive cells respond quickly to the alarm signal of inflammation. Some of the defenders are **phagocytes** (FA guh sites), white blood cells that recognize and eat pathogens. The phagocytes can identify pathogens by their pattern of antigens, or proteins on their surfaces. Most phagocytes die after consuming pathogens. The dead cells build up as a pocket of pus at the infection site. The body absorbs this pus within a few days.

Just as pathogens have an identifiable pattern of antigens on their surface, so too does an infected cell. The infected cell shows the antigens of an invader on its surface. Another type of defender called a **natural killer cell** recognizes these antigens and attacks the infected cell. The natural killer cell releases chemicals that destroy the infected cell's outer membrane.

Viruses activate a different kind of defense. A cell infected by a virus releases chemicals called interferons (ihn tuhr FIH rahns). The interferons stimulate nearby cells to resist viral attacks. Natural killer cells recognize viral antigens on the infected cells and destroy the cells. A third type of defensive cell attacks larger parasites, such as hookworms. These cells attach to the parasite's body and release chemicals that damage its tissues.

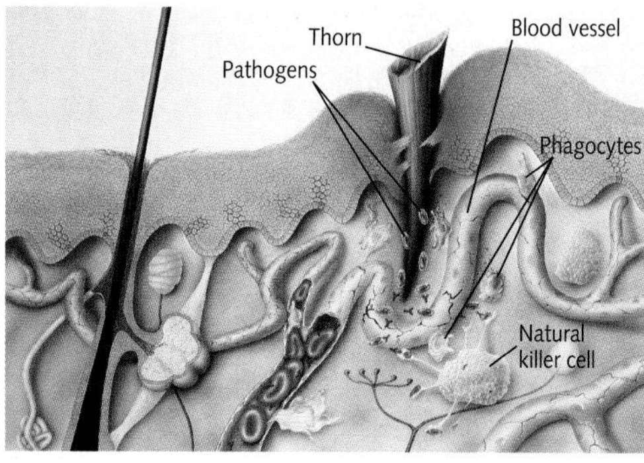

Figure 24.10 The body's nonspecific defenses respond to an injury within seconds.

After You Read

1. Explain what features make mucous membranes difficult for pathogens to invade.
2. According to the sequence chart in your Science Notebook, what is the body's first response to an infection?
3. Describe how defensive cells distinguish between healthy body cells and infected cells.

Background Information

During the period after entering tissues where infection is occurring, monocytes enlarge as they produce granules within their cytoplasm. These granules, now called macrophages, contain enzymes that help digest bacteria and other foreign cells. Macrophages remain in the tissues and ingest bacteria, foreign cells, and damaged and dead cells. This process is called phagocytosis. The cells become known as phagocytes.

Both neutrophils and eosinophils ingest bacteria and foreign cells and contain granules filled with enzymes to digest the eaten bacteria and cells. Neutrophils circulate in the bloodstream and enter tissues when signaled. Eosinophils also immobilize and kill parasites and function in allergic reactions.

24.3 The Immune System

Before You Read

Preview the lesson, and look for examples of immune functions and disorders. In your Science Notebook, record your examples by using the lesson headings and subheadings as organizing titles. Share your examples with a partner. Add any necessary information to your list.

Learning Goals

- Describe the four major features of the immune system.
- Explain immunity and the ways the body can acquire it.
- Describe the different types of immune disorders.

New Vocabulary

immune system
incubation period
memory cell
immunity
active immunity
passive immunity
vaccine
artificial immunity
allergic reaction
autoimmune disorder
cancer

The nonspecific defense system works all the time to prevent pathogens from invading body tissues. Despite these efforts, however, pathogens are sometimes successful at creating an infection. At that point, the body uses its system of defense against specific pathogens: the **immune system**.

Features of the Immune System

The immune system has several unique features. First, the immune system responds to specific pathogens. The antigens displayed on the outsides of pathogens and other foreign substances alert the immune system to the presence of a threat to the body. White blood cells called B cells and T cells that target the specific invader are produced. B cells produce proteins, called antibodies, that attach to the antigens on the pathogen. These antibodies interfere with the functions of the pathogen and mark it for destruction. Killer T cells seek out infected cells and pathogens marked by antibodies and destroy them.

A second feature of the immune system is its ability to respond to millions of different threats. The B cells that respond to each invader are present in the bone marrow of a newborn baby. The immune cells are inactive until each one is awakened by the presence of a specific antigen in the body.

Third, the immune system is capable of distinguishing between body cells and cells from other organisms. Immune cells respond to pathogens, cancerous cells, transplanted tissues, and insect venoms. Finally, the immune system is able to remember pathogens and develop immunity.

Features of the Immune Response	
specific	responds only to the pathogen involved
adaptive	responds to millions of different pathogens
self-recognizing	can distinguish between body cells and foreign or cancerous cells
able to remember	creates memory cells that respond quickly to a second invasion by a pathogen

Figure 24.11 The immune response is very different from the nonspecific body defenses.

24.3 Introduce

ENGAGE Quickly review with students the effects of bacteria, viruses, and other pathogens. Explain that some of the effects are lessened and even eradicated when the body's immune system "fights off" the disease. Ask students to imagine what a superhero's immune system would be able to do. Have them quickly sketch or list the qualities of the superhero, and then ask some students to share their ideas with the class. Throughout the lesson, review these qualities to see how they compare with the actual abilities of the immune system.

Before You Read

Model reviewing the lesson and looking for immune functions and disorders. Direct students to preview the rest of the lesson, and tell them to write lesson headings, subheadings, and examples in their Science Notebooks.

Teach

EXPLAIN Encourage students to review what they have learned about how the body protects itself. Tell them the immune system has the specific role of defending the body from pathogens. Explain that students will learn about the four ways in which the system accomplishes that.

Vocabulary

immune system Explain that the immune system is composed of specialized cells, tissues, and organs that work together to defend the body against attacks by specific invaders such as certain bacteria and viruses.

ELL Strategy

Read Aloud This lesson is filled with medical terms that students will encounter for the rest of their lives. Provide time during class for them to work in small groups and practice reading paragraphs of the text aloud. Circulate among the students and provide feedback on pronunciation.

Have students work in groups of three. After one student reads aloud, a second student should summarize what was said. The third student can check off any vocabulary words recognized during the reading. This student, acting as a "vocabulary checker," could quiz the others on the definition of the word. Or, the second student could ask the reader to read the sentence where the word occurs, based on the definition the "vocabulary checker" provides.

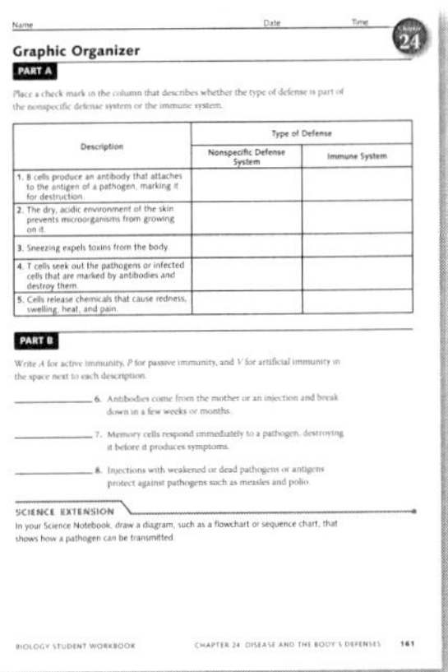

Graphic Organizer
Workbook, p. 161

Teach

EXPLAIN Tell students that in this section of the lesson, they will learn about the two different types of immunity (active and passive). Ask students to volunteer what they know about immunity. They will likely have some familiarity with the concept as a result of having had certain illnesses or of having received vaccines (acquired immunity).

Explain It!

Encourage students to review the notes in their Science Notebooks and to outline or visually organize their responses before writing them.

ANSWER A person unable to produce B cells or T cells would not have *active immunity* because he or she would lack *memory cells* and would not produce *antibodies* in response to a pathogen's *antigens* or be able to destroy infected cells or the pathogens before their *incubation period* ends. The *nonspecific defense system* might protect against some *pathogens*, but once pathogens entered body tissues, an *infection* would develop.

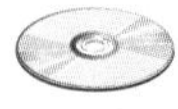

Vocabulary

incubation period *Incubate* is from the Latin word *incubare*, meaning "to lie on."

memory cell Encourage students to think about common (nonscientific) uses of the word *memory*, and discuss them with the class. Explain that memory cells act more quickly the second time a pathogen invades because they "remember" the pathogen.

immunity Explain that *immunity* comes from the Latin word *immunis*, meaning "free from."

active immunity Explain that *active* means "doing something," such as responding to an antigen by making antibodies.

passive immunity Explain that *passive* is the antonym, or opposite, of *active*. Passive immunity results from receiving antibodies made by another organism or individual.

Figure It Out: Figure 24.12

ANSWER **1.** 15 or 16 **2.** Memory cells recognize the virus and trigger production of antibodies that quickly destroy the virus before the end of its incubation period.

Explain It!

People who suffer from certain hereditary diseases cannot produce B cells or T cells. In your Science Notebook, explain what effects this condition would have on a person's immunity and general health. Include the following terms in your explanation: *antigen, nonspecific defense system, antibodies, memory cells, active immunity, infection, pathogens,* and *incubation period.*

Immunity

Pathogens in the body must race to reproduce themselves before the immune system is ready to attack them. Each disease has an **incubation period** of several days to years before the first symptoms appear. For example, chicken pox has an incubation period of 14 to 16 days. The first time the body is exposed to chicken pox, it takes the immune system a week or two to start producing B cells and T cells. During that time, the population of the chicken pox virus multiplies rapidly. A patient may get very sick before the immune response can start to defeat the disease.

Some of the immune cells developed against the chicken pox virus become memory cells. The **memory cells** remain in the body after infection and respond immediately if the pathogen invades a second time. Memory cells allow the body to fight off a second chicken pox infection before the incubation period ends. **Immunity** means that a person does not suffer symptoms of disease when he or she is exposed to a pathogen. The type of immunity that memory cells provide is called **active immunity**. In active immunity, the body makes its own antibodies in response to an antigen.

Passive Immunity Babies are born without any memory cells in their immune systems. However, they do have antibodies given to them by their mother's body during pregnancy and nursing. The transfer of antibodies from another's body is called **passive immunity**. Passive immunity sometimes involves injecting antibodies into a person's body. This is often done to combat snake venom and the rabies virus. Passive immunity lasts only for a few weeks or months, until the antibodies break down in the body.

Did You Know?

Venomous snakebites can be deadly. In order to save snakebite victims, doctors give them antivenin. The antivenin consists of antibodies produced by a horse or other large animal that has been exposed to snake venom. The antivenin gives the victim passive immunity to snakebites that lasts for a few weeks.

Figure It Out

1. After how many days is the first immune response strongest?
2. Why doesn't a person feel any symptoms of a viral disease after being exposed to it for the second time?

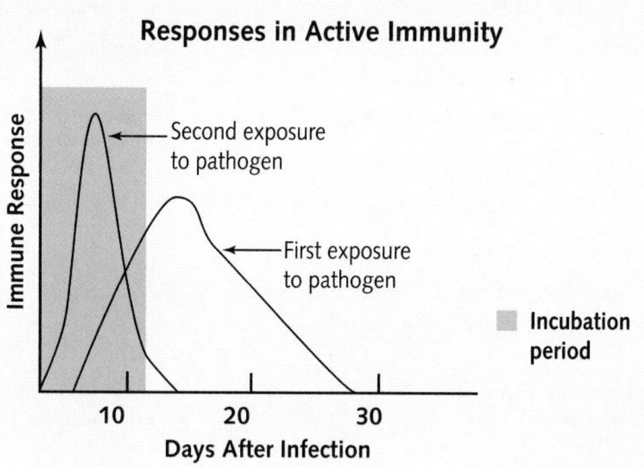

Figure 24.12 After a viral infection, memory cells for the virus remain in the body. The immune system responds much faster to a second exposure to the same virus.

Background Information

After a person is exposed to a disease, an incubation period is followed by a contagious period. During this time, a sick person can pass the disease to others. For major illnesses such as hepatitis, children should stay at home or in a hospital until the contagious period has passed. For minor illnesses, recommendations are that children stay at home until they feel better and have been without fever for at least 12 hours.

Differentiated Instruction

Mathematical Have students calculate how many other people might be infected if they were infected with a contagious disease with an incubation period of 12 days. Remind students to include in their counts all persons with whom they have direct contact.

Vaccines and Artificial Immunity The development of vaccines against pathogens was a great step forward in medicine. **Vaccines** (vak SEENZ) contain weakened, dead, or incomplete portions of pathogens or antigens. When injected into the body, the pathogens or antigens cause an immune response without causing serious disease. Vaccines produce immunity because they cause the body to react as if it were naturally infected. Thus, the immune system produces a response to the pathogen's antigens and creates memory cells against it. Immunity produced by a vaccine is called **artificial immunity**. Vaccines against polio, smallpox, and measles have saved millions of lives around the world. Newly developed vaccines against chicken pox and the virus that causes cervical cancer hold great promise for the coming decades.

As You Read

Compare the examples of immune functions and disorders you recorded at the beginning of the lesson with what you know now. Make corrections or additions to your entries.

What is one example of a way in which a person can gain passive immunity to a disease?

Causes of Disease Before and After Vaccine Availability in the U.S.

Disease	Average Number of Cases per Year Before Vaccine Available	Cases in 1998 After Vaccine Available
measles	503,282	89
diphtheria	175,885	1
tetanus	1,314	34
mumps	1,152,209	606
rubella	47,745	345
pertussis (whooping cough)	147,271	6,279

Figure 24.13 There were many more serious childhood illnesses in the United States before vaccines became available. Which disease was almost completely eradicated by 1998 as a result of a vaccine?

CONNECTION: Medicine

Polio, measles, mumps, and tetanus are dangerous childhood diseases that have something in common: they are now rare in the United States. Widespread use of vaccines has reduced the number of deaths caused by infectious diseases to low levels. Children who live in developing countries are not so lucky. One-quarter of the children born each year in these countries are not vaccinated. Three million of them will die of diseases that could be prevented using $30 worth of vaccines per child. Unfortunately, many developing nations spend as little as $3 per citizen on health care each year.

Many international organizations are striving to raise vaccination rates around the world. The GAVI Alliance (formerly known as the Global Alliance for Vaccines and Immunisation) is a worldwide group that helps developing nations set up and run vaccination programs. Americans have pledged billions of dollars to GAVI in an effort to someday make measles, rotavirus, and hepatitis as rare in Africa as they are now in the United States.

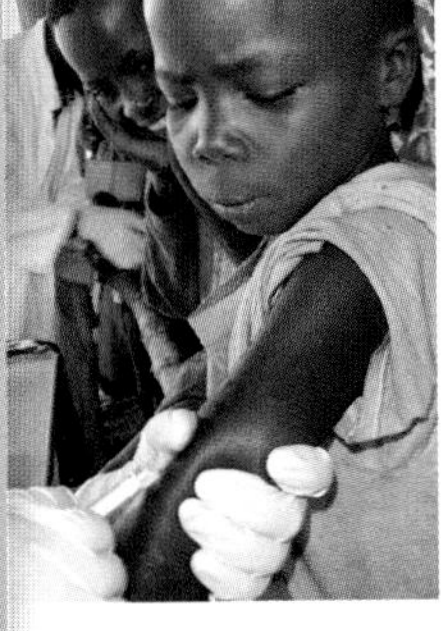

Teach

EXPLAIN that vaccines represent another type of immunity—acquired immunity—because they cause the body to react as if it were naturally infected, triggering a response to the pathogen's antigens and creating memory cells against it.

Vocabulary

vaccine Tell students that *vaccine* is derived from the Latin word *vacca*, meaning "cow." Explain that one of the first scientists to study vaccines used cowpox to test them.

artificial immunity Tell students that *artificial* is derived from the Latin word *artificialis*, which means "of or belonging to art." *Artificial* came to mean "made by humans," or the opposite of *natural*.

Use the Visual: Figure 24.13

ANSWER diphtheria

As You Read

Give students five to ten minutes to review and revise their notes for the lesson in their Science Notebooks. Encourage them to add examples to make the concepts of immunity more concrete.

ANSWER Passive immunity can come from a mother during pregnancy and breastfeeding. Antibodies can also be injected to combat snake venom and the rabies virus.

CONNECTION: Medicine

ENGAGE Arrange students in small groups, and have each group research an underdeveloped country and its rate of immunization for childhood diseases. Students can find information about immunization rates on the World Health Organization's Web site at **http://www.who.int.immunization_monitoring/diseases/en/**.

Have students record their findings in their Science Notebooks and then use the information to make a class presentation. On a poster or in another form of presentation, have groups compare these rates to those in the United States. Students could use this information to encourage family and community members to support organizations such as UNICEF and GAVI.

Background Information

Reasons for the high rate of infectious disease in poor countries include:

- Air and water pathogens are more common.
- The people have an incomplete diet, weakening their immune systems.
- The people eat wild animals (bush meat, which is a vector for diseases) to obtain protein. Many scientists believe that HIV first crossed over to humans from primate bush meat infected with simian immunodeficiency virus (SIV).
- Poor people in the United States tend to engage in risky behaviors and lack access to health care.

The World Health Organization (WHO) and GAVI (Global Alliance for Vaccines and Immunisation) work jointly to provide vaccines to underdeveloped countries. The WHO is the United Nation's agency for health. GAVI focuses on vaccinations, while WHO works to provide health care for everyone, prevent chronic disease, and enhance global health and security.

Teach

ENGAGE Ask students what they know about allergies. If any students have allergies and wish to share their information with the class, encourage them to do so. Common allergies include allergies to food, dust, pollen, animal hair, and penicillin. Ask students if they have heard of the diseases multiple sclerosis, AIDS, or lupus. Tell them that these diseases are autoimmune diseases and that they, as do allergies, represent immune system disorders.

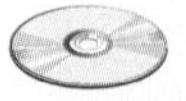

Vocabulary

allergic reaction Tell students that *allergic* is the adjective form of the noun *allergy* and means "of or caused by an allergy." Explain that an allergy is a hypersensitivity to a substance in the environment. Also tell students that another word with the same root as *allergy* is *allergen*, which ends in a suffix that denotes a cause, *-gen*. An *allergen* is "something that causes an allergy."

autoimmune disorder Explain that the prefix *auto-* means "self" and a *disorder* is "a disease or illness." Literally, an *autoimmune disorder* is "an illness caused by an immune response that targets one's own body cells."

cancer Tell students that cancer is a disease in which dangerous cells grow quickly and can produce malignant tumors.

Extend It!

As students learn more about one disease, they will be able to connect their knowledge to the concepts presented in this lesson and chapter. Encourage students to choose a disease with which they have some experience or prior knowledge.

Provide students with access to the Internet and medical reference books. If students require scaffolding, create a visual organizer that lists the main questions for them to complete. Suggest that during their presentations, students use visuals such as posters, pictures, and medical items.

Extend It!

Research a disease and the efforts that are being made to combat it. Record your findings in your Science Notebook. Then, prepare a class presentation that answers the following questions:

- What causes the disease? Is the disease preventable?
- How does the body normally defend against this disease?
- What are the symptoms and signs of the disease?
- What medical treatments are available? What new treatments might be available in the near future?

Immune System Disorders

The immune system has a very difficult job to do. It must recognize and respond to millions of potential pathogens. At the same time, the immune system must not attack the healthy cells of its own body. At times, this delicate balance falls apart.

Allergic Reaction Sometimes, the immune system mistakes harmless molecules for pathogens. An **allergic reaction** is an immune response to a food, medication, or other chemical. Minor symptoms of an allergy include itching, sneezing, runny nose, and coughing. More serious allergies can lead to rashes, asthma, and low blood pressure. About 700 people in the United States die each year from allergic reactions to antibiotics, foods, and insect stings.

The percentage of Americans with allergies and asthma is increasing. There is evidence that the rise in allergies is due to our cleaner homes. The immune system is designed to seek out and destroy pathogens. A century ago, the immune system was kept busy fighting parasites and infectious diseases. Now, with our much cleaner homes, the immune system may target and attack previously harmless molecules.

Autoimmune Disorders When the immune system attacks the cells of its own body, **autoimmune disorders** result. The disease multiple sclerosis (MS) is caused by an immune attack on the tissues of the nervous system. Type 1, or juvenile onset, diabetes results when the insulin-producing cells of the pancreas are mistaken for pathogens. In some forms of arthritis, the cartilage in the joints is the target. Autoimmune diseases are not curable, although medications can slow their progress and ease symptoms.

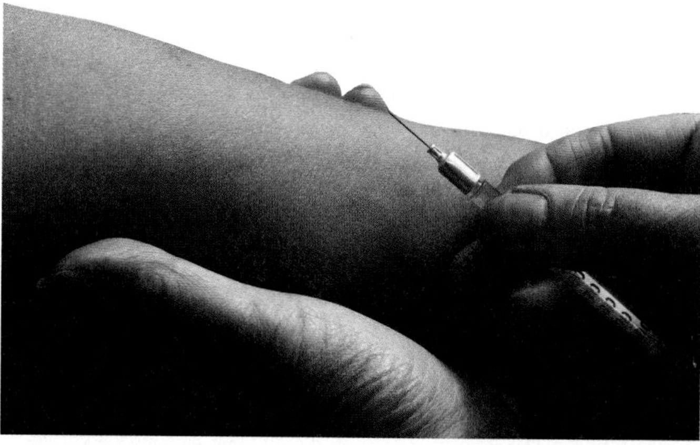

Figure 24.14 One in five people in the United States suffers from allergies. A skin-prick test is one way to find out which allergens are causing allergic symptoms.

Differentiated Instruction

Visual Have students draw diagrams to illustrate the concept of an allergy. Tell them their drawings should include the substance(s) causing the allergic reaction and both the minor and the more serious symptoms of the allergy.

Reading Comprehension Workbook, p. 162

444 DISEASE AND THE BODY'S DEFENSES

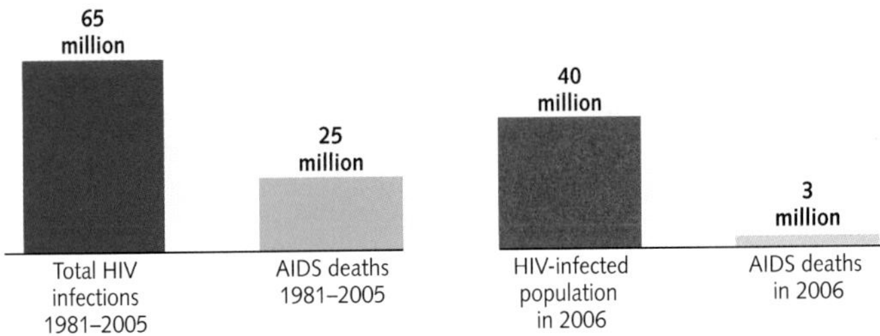

Figure 24.15 The AIDS epidemic is already one of the worst in human history. Although there is currently no cure for the disease, antiretroviral treatment can prolong life.

AIDS The human immunodeficiency virus (HIV) causes disease by invading the cells of the immune system. HIV disables T cells and prevents the body from defending itself. Untreated HIV infection leads to acquired immunodeficiency syndrome (AIDS). Pathogens invade AIDS patients and cancers develop. AIDS patients generally die within a few years without treatment. Good health care can prolong the lives of patients infected with HIV for many years.

HIV can only be passed from one person to another directly through bodily fluids. The most common means of transmission are unprotected sexual relations and the sharing of needles by drug users. Thousands of scientists and health professionals around the world are working to develop a vaccine against HIV, improve treatments, and prevent HIV infections.

Cancer Cells that grow and divide uncontrollably lead to **cancer**. Cancer results from a series of mutations in the cells' DNA. One of the jobs of the immune system is to detect cancerous cells and destroy them. Cancerous cells produce tumors if they are allowed to multiply. These tumors can grow and spread to any part of the body. Untreated cancer disrupts body functions. Cancer is the second leading cause of death in the United States today.

Fortunately, cancer treatment is improving rapidly. Tumors can be surgically removed or treated with poisonous chemicals or radiation. As scientists learn more about how cancerous cells develop, they can help people avoid cancer. Some of the best ways to prevent certain kinds of cancer are to stay away from tobacco products and to use sunscreen when exposed to sunlight.

After You Read

1. How do killer T cells recognize their targets?
2. Give an example from your Science Notebook of a disease that can be prevented by vaccination.
3. Explain why so much time and money is being spent on research to combat AIDS.

Teach

ENGAGE It is likely that students are familiar with the diseases AIDS and cancer. Ask: *What do you know about these diseases? Why are these diseases considered to be disorders of the immune system?* You might want to introduce the terms *benign* and *malignant* in reference to cancer, especially to calm fears that all tumors are cancerous. Emphasize that good habits, such as not smoking and using sunscreen, can help a person reduce the chances of developing lung cancer and skin cancer.

Use the Visual: Figure 24.15

EXTEND Have small groups of students discuss and analyze the bar graph. Ask: *Approximately what portion of the all the people infected with HIV died of AIDS before 2006?* (two-fifths, or 40 percent) *Approximately what portion of all the people infected with HIV in 2006 died of AIDS?* (less than one-tenth, or 10 percent) *What could account for this change?* (better treatments and education)

Assess

EVALUATE Use the After You Read questions and the Alternative Assessment to help you assess students' understanding of the lesson.

After You Read

1. "Killer" T cells have sites on their cell membranes that are specific to one kind of antigen. They attack any other cell that displays this antigen.
2. Possible answers include any example given in Figure 24.13. Students may also be familiar with other diseases that are preventable with a vaccine, such as chickenpox and smallpox.
3. AIDS has caused one of the worst epidemics in human history, and it still cannot be cured.

Background Information

The politics of AIDS funding and research is very complicated. AIDS is one of the best-funded diseases because it is a new, scary, terminal illness that affects wealthy and poor alike in every nation. The prevalence of HIV infection in the United States in 2006 was 0.6 percent. HIV is a very difficult virus to defeat, with many different stereotypes associated with the infection. Despite scientists' best efforts, they have not been able to develop a cure or an effective vaccine against HIV.

Alternative Assessment

EVALUATE Have students use the notes in their Science Notebooks to identify and list five facts they have learned about the immune system. They should include a fact about immunity, vaccines, and immune system disorders.

Chapter 24 Summary

VOCABULARY REVIEW

Check students' sentences or paragraphs to make sure they understand the meaning of each vocabulary term.

PREPARE FOR CHAPTER TEST

Evaluate students' essays using the following criteria:

1. The topic sentence, or main idea, should restate the Key Concept.
2. The supporting paragraphs should incorporate the answers to the Learning Goal questions students have written and include details, facts, and examples they have recorded in their Science Notebooks.
3. The concluding sentence should sum up the main idea of the chapter and restate the Key Concept.

MASTERING CONCEPTS

True or False

1. False, allergy
2. False, nonspecific defense system
3. True
4. False, passive immunity
5. False, virus
6. True

Short Answer

7. look for symptoms and signs of a disease; look for pathogens
8. All are white blood cells that kill other cells. Phagocytes and natural killer cells are nonspecific defenses. Memory cells are part of the immune system.
9. Antibiotics kill only living things. Neither cancer nor AIDS is caused by a living thing.
10. by sneezing or coughing on food and drinks or by preparing food improperly
11. They line body cavities in contact with outside air, and they help prevent infection by removing pathogens.
12. Memory cells provide immunity by attacking a pathogen that enters the body a second time before it finishes incubation.
13. Bacteria on the skin and in the intestines compete with or kill pathogenic bacteria. Symbiotic bacteria help with digestion and making vitamins.

Chapter 24 Summary

KEY CONCEPTS

24.1 Disease

- Infectious diseases are caused by pathogens that invade the body.
- Pathogens can be transmitted from human to human; through air, water, and food; and by vectors.
- Each pathogen has different effects on the body and causes a different disease.
- The germ theory and antibiotics have greatly improved medicine and human health.

24.2 The Nonspecific Defense System

- The body's nonspecific defense system works to destroy pathogens and keep them out of the body.
- The body's nonspecific defense system includes the skin, mucous membranes, inflammation, and several types of white blood cells.
- Inflammation is the body's first defense against pathogens that get inside the body.
- Phagocytes are white blood cells that recognize and attack pathogens inside body tissues.
- Phagocytes can identify pathogens by the pattern of antigens on the pathogens' surfaces.
- Natural killer cells recognize and destroy infected body cells that show the antigens of their invaders on their surfaces. The killer cells also recognize viral antigens on infected cells and destroy these cells.

24.3 The Immune System

- The immune system recognizes and responds to each specific pathogen.
- Memory cells provide immunity to a second attack by a pathogen.
- Active immunity develops as a result of having a disease and building up antibodies to it. Passive immunity develops when antibodies are transferred from another person's body or from an animal that is already immune to the disease.
- Vaccines, which contain weakened, dead, or incomplete portions of pathogens or antigens, provide artificial immunity to infectious diseases.
- Immune disorders can result in allergies, autoimmune diseases, AIDS, and cancer.

VOCABULARY REVIEW

Write each term in a complete sentence, or write a paragraph relating several terms.

24.1
disease, p. 433
noninfectious disease, p. 433
pathogen, p. 433
infectious disease, p. 433
symptom, p. 433
vector, p. 434
epidemic, p. 434
antibiotic, p. 436

24.2
nonspecific defense system, p. 437
inflammation, p. 439
phagocyte, p. 440
natural killer cell, p. 440

24.3
immune system, p. 441
incubation period, p. 442
memory cell, p. 442
immunity, p. 442
active immunity, p. 442
passive immunity, p. 442
vaccine, p. 443
artificial immunity, p. 443
allergic reaction, p. 444
autoimmune disorder, p. 444
cancer, p. 445

PREPARE FOR CHAPTER TEST

To prepare for the chapter test, create a question from each Learning Goal. Use the information in your Science Notebook to answer each question. Then use these answers to write a well-developed essay about the chapter. Use the Key Concept on the first page of this chapter as your topic sentence.

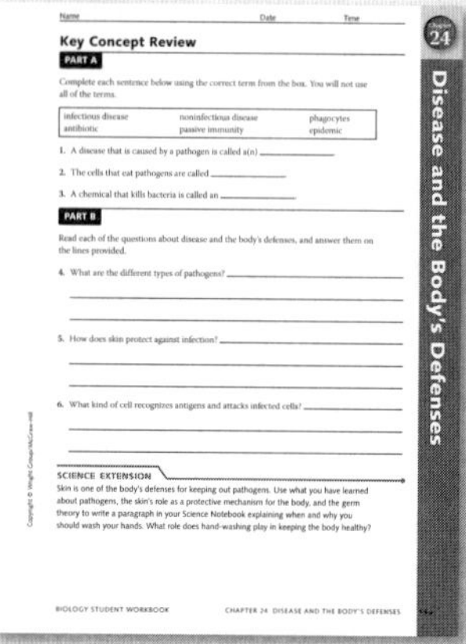
Key Concept Review
Workbook, p. 159

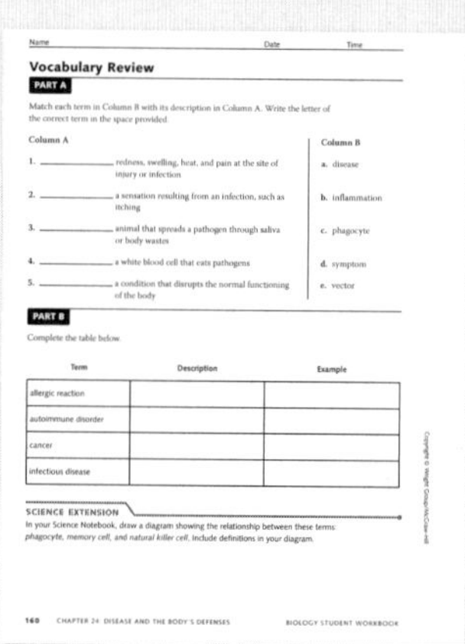
Vocabulary Review
Workbook, p. 160

MASTERING CONCEPTS

True or False

If the statement is true, write "true." If it is false, change the underlined word or words to make the statement true.

1. An immune response to a food or other chemical is a(n) autoimmune disorder.
2. The immune system in a newborn baby is ready to fight any foreign molecules it detects in the body.
3. A(n) epidemic is the spread of a disease to many victims.
4. Artificial immunity lasts only a few weeks or months.
5. The common cold is caused by a(n) bacterium.
6. Immune cells and phagocytes recognize pathogens by the pattern of antigens they display on their surface.

Short Answer

Answer each of the following in a sentence or brief paragraph.

7. What clues do doctors use to determine which pathogen is making a patient sick?
8. Compare and contrast natural killer cells, phagocytes, and memory cells.
9. Explain why cancer and AIDS cannot be treated with antibiotics.
10. Describe how a restaurant employee could start an epidemic.
11. Explain where mucous membranes are found in the body, and describe their role in preventing infection.
12. Explain the relationship among an incubation period, immunity, and memory cells.
13. How can bacteria help the body?

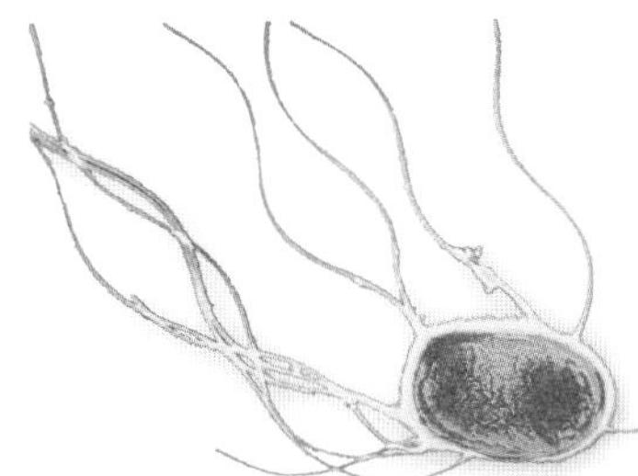

Critical Thinking

Use what you have learned in this chapter to answer each of the following.

14. **Predict** Which of these people would benefit from a measles vaccination: a healthy child, a person with measles, a person with AIDS, or a person who had measles a year ago? Explain your answer.
15. **Infer** What disease-fighting advantages might a breast-fed baby have over a formula-fed baby?
16. **Generalize** What are the major reasons why people in poor countries suffer from more infectious diseases than people in wealthy countries?

Standardized Test Question

Choose the letter of the response that correctly answers the question.

Percentage of Deaths Due to Major Disease

Disease	Year			
	1950	1980	1990	2000
heart disease	37.1	38.3	33.5	29.6
cancer	14.6	20.9	23.5	23.0
stroke	10.8	8.6	6.7	7.0
diabetes	1.7	1.8	2.2	2.9

17. According to the table, which disease showed a steady increase in percentage of deaths from 1950 to 2000?
   A. heart disease
   B. cancer
   C. stroke
   D. diabetes

Test-Taking Tip

After you read a multiple-choice question, answer it in your head before reading the choices provided. This way the choices will not confuse you or trick you.

Critical Thinking

14. the healthy child; The child with measles has antibodies and memory cells against the disease. The person with AIDS is unable to mount an immune response to the vaccination and thus gain immunity. The person who had measles a year ago already has immunity to the disease.
15. It receives antibodies from its mother in the milk, giving it passive immunity to diseases its mother is immune to.
16. They are less likely to get vaccinations, have little money to treat the diseases, and often lack clean water supplies.

Standardized Test Question

17. D

Reading Links

An American Plague: The True and Terrifying Story of the Yellow Fever Epidemic of 1793

The winner of numerous awards (including the Newbery Honor Medal), this book tells a powerful true story in a dramatic, highly engaging narrative style. In the process, its well-researched text and illustrations—including personal accounts and archival photographs—inform readers about medicine in the eighteenth century with attention to social context and the current relevance of past epidemics. The book includes a map, bibliography, index, and an informative afterward with source notes.

Murphy, Jim. Clarion Books (Houghton Mifflin).
176 pp. Illustrated.
Trade ISBN: 978-0-395-77608-7.

Outbreak: Disease Detectives at Work

This close examination of infectious disease epidemics and the scientists who work to control their spread, which includes a new chapter on bioterrorism in its revised edition, is timely and absorbing. Students will learn about past outbreaks, current threats, and challenges that epidemiologists must face in a scientific field of critical importance to people around the world.

Friedlander, Mark P., Jr. Lerner Publishing Group.
120 pp. Illustrated.
Library ISBN: 978-0-8225-0948-6.

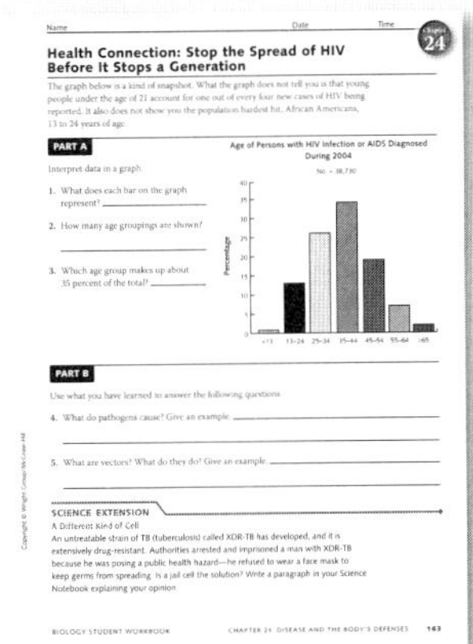

Curriculum Connection
Workbook, p. 163

Science Challenge
Workbook, pp. 164–165

24A Live Bacteria

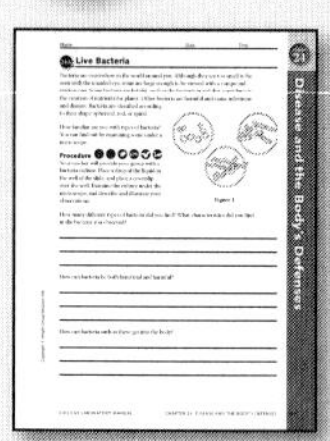

This prechapter introduction activity is designed to determine what students already know about bacteria by engaging them in examining, comparing, and illustrating common bacteria viewed under a microscope.

Objectives

- examine bacteria under a microscope
- compare and contrast a variety of bacteria
- draw bacteria observed under a microscope
- classify bacteria as spherical, rod-shaped, or spiral-shaped

Planning

 20–30 minutes  groups of 4–6 students

Materials (per group)

- bacteria culture in a small paper cup
- medicine dropper
- microscope
- slide with depression well
- coverslip
- colored pencils and paper

Lab Tip

Students may have to remove goggles to obtain a clear view when observing with the microscope.

Advance Preparation

Put dry lima beans in a jar with water two to three days in advance, and place the jar in a warm environment to incubate. The water will become cloudy as bacteria multiply. Remove the cloudy solution, and place some in paper cups for each group. Many types of bacteria may be in the culture from the air, from the soil, and from contact with the skin. Large motile bacteria should be the easiest for students to find.

Engagement Guide

- Challenge students to think about the bacteria they may find by asking:
  - *What characteristics should you look for to classify the type of bacteria?* (The shape of the bacteria should be spherical, rod, or spiral.)
  - *Bacteria that move are called motile bacteria. In what way do you think some bacteria may move?* (Students should predict that some bacteria move by beating flagella.)
- Encourage students to illustrate what they observe in creative ways.
- Students should find more than one type of bacteria. Answers about characteristics will vary depending on the bacteria. Students should find some bacteria that move (movement in one place is most likely just Brownian motion).
- Students do not have enough information about the bacteria to predict if they are helpful or harmful.
- Students should demonstrate an understanding that bacteria such as these can enter the body through cuts and scrapes, as well as the mouth, nose, and pores.

Going Further

Students can look for other types of bacteria in the world around them. Have students dip sterile swabs in distilled water and wipe a commonly used counter surface, door handle, toilet seat, or sink handle. Then, have students wipe the swabs on the agar in a petri dish and put the covered dish in an incubator. Have students mark off different sections of the petri dish with numbers to represent each of the areas swabs were taken from. Students can then examine the colonies that develop under a microscope.

24B How Pathogens Spread

Objectives

- observe the decomposition of an apple caused by decay pathogens
- observe how pathogens can be transferred from one apple to another
- compare and contrast control and experimental results
- draw conclusions about how the spread of decay is like the spread of infections

Skill Set

observing, comparing and contrasting, recording and analyzing data, classifying, stating conclusions

Planning

 15–20 minutes, plus 5 minutes on 3 consecutive days

groups of 2–4 students

Materials

Materials for this activity are listed in the Student Laboratory Manual.

Advance Preparation

In advance of the activity, cut an apple into thick slices and place the slices in a warm, dark place until they begin to decay. When the activity is to begin, pour a few centimeters of hydrogen peroxide into paper cups for each group.

Answers to Observations: Data Table 1

Results will vary, but all the cuts will have oxidized and students should observe that the most decay occurs on cut *C*, where the apple was cut with the contaminated knife. If students sterilized cut *D* well, there should be no decay or less decay. The control *A* and the control *B* with hydrogen peroxide sterilization should also have no decay or less decay.

Answers to Analysis and Conclusions

1. Cut *C* should have developed the most decay because it was cut with a contaminated knife and no antiseptic was applied to the cut.
2. The hydrogen peroxide reduced or eliminated the decay. It served as an antiseptic.
3. The knife had to be sterilized so that each trial cut was made under the same conditions and to avoid the introduction of a contaminated knife as a variable.
4. The transfer of microorganisms from one apple to another is similar to the way pathogens can be spread in humans. Open cuts are a weak point where pathogens can enter the body. Any breaks in the skin should be treated with antiseptic to reduce the chance of infection.

Going Further

Students can repeat the experiment using other foods to see how the spread of microorganisms affects them. Students can try breaking the skin of foods, placing them in the same container with a rotten version (without touching), and comparing them with a control container that doesn't include a rotten food to see whether mold or decay can spread through the air.

 24C Effectiveness of Disinfectants in Killing Bacteria

Objectives

- observe the growth of bacteria on a carrot medium
- test the effects of various disinfectants on bacteria
- compare and contrast the effectiveness of disinfectants

Skill Set

observing, comparing and contrasting, recording and analyzing data, classifying, stating conclusions

Planning

35–45 minutes, plus 10 minutes on 2 consecutive days

groups of 2–4 students

Materials

Materials for this activity are listed in the Student Laboratory Manual.

Advance Preparation

Put samples of the seven disinfectants and distilled water into labeled paper cups for groups to use. For this activity, you will need an incubator large enough to hold all of the test tubes for all of the groups.

Answers to Observations: Data Table

Results will vary, but students should observe that the disinfectants retard the growth of bacteria. There will be differences in how far down the carrot toward the liquid the bacteria culture is able to grow.

Answers to Analysis and Conclusions

1. Answers will vary, but students should note that bacteria cultures formed on the carrot sticks, and some carrot sticks had more thriving cultures than others.
2. Answers will vary, but the strongest disinfectants should retard the bacteria culture for a longer distance up the carrot stick.
3. The test tube with distilled water may have bacteria growth in the water.
4. Random chance in the strain of bacteria, which parts of the carrot stick were affected, and variations in how much the particular carrot stick might wick up the liquid can all affect the results of the activity.
5. Although it doesn't account for or control all variables, the activity shows that some disinfectants are more effective at killing germs because they retarded the growth of bacteria nearest to the liquid.
6. Some of the disinfectants are for cleaning surfaces, some are for use on skin, some can be ingested, and some are toxic. A disinfectant should be chosen for an application not only based on how strong it is but also based on how safe it is for that particular use.

Going Further

Have students design a more controlled experiment under sterile conditions using a prepared, known bacteria culture. Students might choose to grow the bacteria on an agar medium or in nutrient broth. Squares of filter paper soaked with disinfectants can be placed on the growth medium to examine how effective the disinfectants are in retarding and killing bacteria cultures.

Chapter 25 Lessons

Introduce Chapter 25

As a starting activity, use LAB 25A Pulse Rate and Exercise on page 155 of the Laboratory Manual.

ENGAGE students by asking them to describe decisions that people make that affect their health and wellness. Point out that people are constantly making decisions throughout the day and that decisions can have consequences that are positive, negative, or both. Explain to students that some decisions lead to other decisions. Have students provide examples of this, identifying the initial decision and the subsequent decision.

Think About Health and Wellness

ENGAGE Ask each student to make a chart in his or her Science Notebook and to label one column *Positive* and the other *Negative*. Tell students to list their actions in the appropriate column. Point out that some actions might fit into more than one column, and that sometimes you can't predict if an action or decision will have a positive or negative outcome. Ask students to share with the class some of the things they have done that they wish they had done differently.

Chapter 25 Health and Wellness

KEY CONCEPT Body systems can be cared for by practicing healthful habits and avoiding harmful substances.

Although you may not realize it, you make decisions almost every minute of each day that affect your body and overall health. You decide whether or not to eat breakfast. You decide whether or not to shower and brush your teeth. You decide when to cross the street, how loud to play the music you listen to, who to socialize with, and what to do after school. Each of these decisions affects your health in some way. Making decisions that are healthful starts with being aware of the choices you make and how those choices affect your body.

Think About Health and Wellness

Think about the things you do that affect your health and how you feel physically and emotionally.

- Make a list in your Science Notebook of such types of actions.
- Classify the actions on your list as having a positive effect or a negative effect on your health. Choose one or two actions that have a negative effect. How could you change these actions so that they have a positive effect? What could you do differently? Record your thoughts in your Science Notebook.

NSTA SCILINKS THE WORLD'S A CLICK AWAY
www.scilinks.org
Nutrition **Code: WGB25**

448

Chapter 25 Planning Guide

Instructional Periods	National Standards	Lab Manual	Workbook
25.1 2 periods	A.1, C.3, F.1, G.1; F.1, F.3, F.6, G.1; UCP.1, UCP.2	**Lab 25A—p. 155** Pulse Rate and Exercise **Lab 25B—p. 156** Vitamin C in Juice **Lab 25C—p. 158** Calories in Food	Key Concept Review p. 166 Vocabulary Review p. 167 Graphic Organizer p. 168 Reading Comprehension p. 169 Curriculum Connection p. 171 Science Challenge p. 172
25.2 2 periods	A.2, F.1; F.1, F.5, F.6		
25.3 2 periods	F.1; F.1, F.5; UCP.3		

Middle School Standard; High School Standard; Unifying Concept and Principle

25.1 Healthful Living

Before You Read

Create a concept map in your Science Notebook for the term *Healthful Habits*. Then, look at the pictures, headings, and Learning Goals in this lesson. What do you predict you will include in your concept map?

Learning Goals

- Describe how healthful habits are important to one's health.
- Identify five healthful habits a person can practice.
- Explain ways in which healthful habits can be incorporated into daily life.

New Vocabulary

aerobic exercise
stress
hygiene
first aid

Recall Vocabulary

nutrition (p. 375)
nutrient (p. 375)

The organs and systems of the body constantly work together to keep you alive and well. For example, the skin protects the internal organs and helps prevent disease. The circulatory and respiratory systems supply oxygen to the body's cells. The digestive system breaks down food into energy the body can use. Muscles get you out of bed in the morning and to school. Your brain takes in and remembers information and helps you do well on the next science exam. Your immune system fights off disease and infections. Each body organ and system carries out functions you depend on to stay healthy.

Healthful Habits

Most people demand a lot from their bodies. Like all relationships, however, your relationship with your body is one that involves giving and taking. You must practice healthful habits so that your body can do all the things you need and expect from it. If you don't take care of your body, it can't take care of you.

Healthful habits include eating a well-balanced diet, getting exercise and rest, managing stress, practicing good hygiene, and keeping safe. Healthful habits should be a part of your daily life.

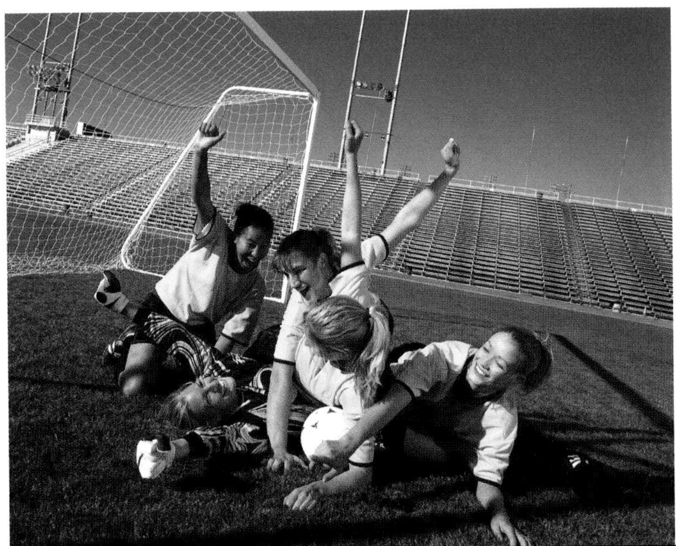

Figure 25.1 Practicing healthful habits, such as getting plenty of exercise, can help you look and feel your best.

25.1 Introduce

ENGAGE Tell students that there are many ways that they can take care of their bodies. Ask: *What are some things you do to take care of your body?* Record student answers on the board. Encourage students to brainstorm as many examples as they can.

Remind students of all of the ways they use their bodies every day—for learning, moving, reading, writing, thinking, and talking. Tell students that taking care of their bodies helps ensure that they will be able to continue doing all these things throughout their lives.

Before You Read

Model the concept map on the board. Fill in one or two circles with the whole class. Students' predictions should reflect an understanding that they will write about nutrition, exercise, rest, hygiene, posture, and safety in their concept maps.

Vocabulary terms are listed on the first student page of each lesson. You may wish to preview the terms before introducing each lesson. Strategies for teaching the vocabulary appear on the pages where the terms are introduced.

Teach

EXPLAIN to students that in this lesson, they will learn how healthful habits are important to one's health. They will also learn five healthful habits that they can practice and incorporate into their daily lives.

ELL Strategy

Activate Background Knowledge Divide students into small groups. To engage students, have the groups discuss what its members already know about healthful habits. Encourage students to first conduct the discussion in their first language. Ask group members to share their lists and where they learned this information with the class.

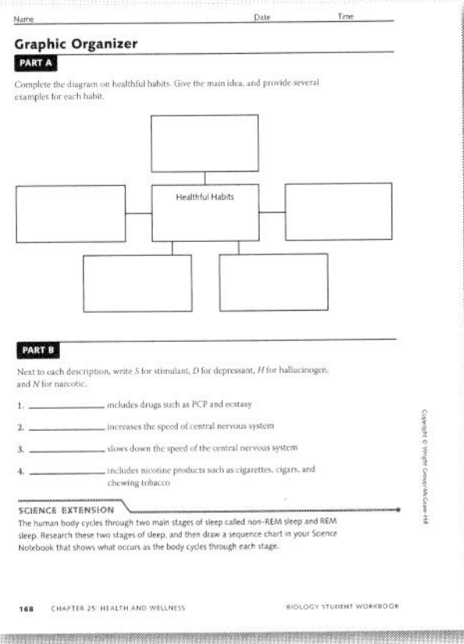

Name Date Time

Graphic Organizer

PART A

Complete the diagram on healthful habits. Give the main idea, and provide several examples for each habit.

Healthful Habits

PART B

Next to each description, write *S* for stimulant, *D* for depressant, *H* for hallucinogen, and *N* for narcotic.

1. ________ includes drugs such as PCP and ecstasy
2. ________ increases the speed of central nervous system
3. ________ slows down the speed of the central nervous system
4. ________ includes nicotine products such as cigarettes, cigars, and chewing tobacco

SCIENCE EXTENSION

The human body cycles through two main stages of sleep called non-REM sleep and REM sleep. Research these two stages of sleep, and then draw a sequence chart in your Science Notebook that shows what occurs as the body cycles through each stage.

Copyright © Wright Group/McGraw-Hill

168 CHAPTER 25: HEALTH AND WELLNESS BIOLOGY STUDENT WORKBOOK

Graphic Organizer Workbook, p. 168

Teach

EXPLAIN Tell students that food is an essential requirement for life and that without food, our bodies cannot function. Ask students to think about other essential requirements for life. Have students prioritize their lists of requirements.

Figure It Out: Figure 25.2

ANSWER **1.** carbohydrates **2.** red meat, chicken, fish, cheese, beans

EXTEND Have students use the table to explain why a vegetarian diet is more healthful than a diet of only meat. (There are examples of foods from plants in every category of essential nutrients, but this is not so for meat.)

Explore It!

Encourage students to share and compare their food labels. Ask: *Which foods have high levels of sodium? What is the recommended amount of sodium per day? Which foods have the highest carbohydrate content? By looking at your labels, can you generalize what kinds of foods are rich in carbohydrates? Which foods have the highest fat content? Can you generalize from looking at your labels what kinds of foods are rich fats?* As students work together to develop their menus, remind them to be aware of portion sizes.

Science Notebook EXTRA

Students may be interested in finding out what the vitamins necessary for good health are. Have them create a three-column table in their Science Notebooks with the following headings: *Vitamin, Role,* and *Source.* Then, have them research the topic of vitamins and fill in their tables with the appropriate information. Start their research off by telling them to find out about Vitamin A; Vitamins B_1, B_2, and B_{12}; folic acid; Vitamin C; and Vitamin D.

Nutrition

Eating healthful foods ensures that you are getting good nutrition. Nutrition is the process of getting the food needed to survive.

The human body needs more than 40 nutrients for good health. As shown in **Figure 25.2**, these nutrients can be grouped into six main categories: carbohydrates, proteins, fats, vitamins, minerals, and water.

Figure It Out

1. Which nutrient is the body's main source of energy?
2. What foods are the major source of proteins?

Essential Nutrients

Nutrient	Function	Food Sources
carbohydrates	provide the body with its main source of energy	bread, rice, pasta, cereals, grains
proteins	help the body build, repair, and maintain tissue	red meat, chicken, fish, cheese, beans
fats	provide the body with energy; help the body use certain vitamins	oils, nuts, meats, dairy products
vitamins	aid the body in the production of certain chemicals and cells; help the body process carbohydrates, proteins, and fats	vegetables, fruits, eggs, cereals, meats
minerals	help the body grow and develop; control chemical reactions in the body; keep bones strong	meats, grains, dairy products, fruits, vegetables
water	makes up more than 50 percent of the body's cells; helps the body digest food and eliminate waste; helps regulate the body's temperature; cushions joints	water, fruits, vegetables

Figure 25.2 There are six groups of nutrients the body needs for good health.

Explore It!

Food labels indicate the types and amounts of nutrients that are found in foods. Collect food labels from a variety of foods. Try to include foods you think are healthful as well as foods you consider to be unhealthful. Compare the nutritional information for each food. Using *MyPyramid* and the information on your food labels, work with the class to develop a well-balanced menu for one day.

Eating a balanced diet ensures the body receives all the nutrients it needs. *MyPyramid* from the United States Department of Agriculture (USDA) can help you make the right food choices.

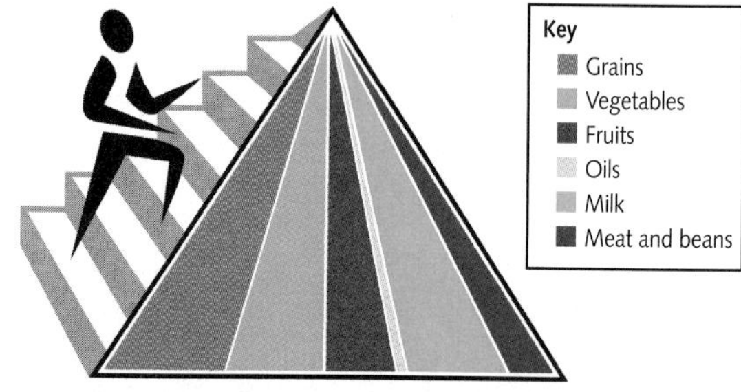

Figure 25.3 The USDA released *MyPyramid* on April 19, 2005. It is a modification of the original U.S. Food Guide Pyramid. The new pyramid stresses activity along with a proper mix of food groups in one's diet.

ELL Strategy

Compare and Contrast Provide students with a copy of the original USDA Food Guide Pyramid. Have each student create a Venn diagram in his or her Science Notebook to compare and contrast the two pyramids. Ask students to think about why the USDA chose to make the changes that it made. Have students write their ideas in their Science Notebooks and share them with the class.

Exercise and Rest

Keeping the body healthy requires more than just good nutrition. It requires plenty of exercise and plenty of rest.

Exercise Exercise strengthens bones and muscles. It reduces the risk of disease and keeps the heart and lungs working efficiently. It keeps joints from becoming stiff and improves flexibility. It can also improve mental health and make a person feel better.

Exercising four to six times per week for about 30 to 60 minutes each time is a good goal for most healthy young adults. A healthful exercise routine can include a combination of aerobic exercise and weight training. **Aerobic** (er ROH bihk) **exercise** is any exercise that increases the heart and breathing rates. Running, swimming, speed walking, and dancing are some examples of aerobic exercise. Weight training helps strengthen bones and muscles. Lifting weights is a weight-training exercise.

As You Read

Add to your concept map words describing healthful habits you can incorporate into your life.

Why are nutrition and exercise important to your health?

Figure 25.4 There are many ways to incorporate exercise into one's daily life. Walking or biking instead of driving and taking the stairs instead of the elevator are just a few things people can do to stay active and fit.

Rest Rest is as important to the body as exercise is. Resting gives the body a chance to recover from the day and to get ready for a new day. Without sleep, people can feel tired, cranky, and irritable. Some people can have trouble thinking clearly and following directions. The immune system and growth can be affected, too. The body is more likely to get sick when it does not get enough rest. Most teens need about nine or more hours of sleep each night. It is important to schedule time for rest so that the body can look, feel, and function at its best.

Teach

EXPLAIN to students that exercise is essential for a healthy body and mind. Ask students to share the different ways in which they exercise. Encourage them to think about the sports they play, the places they walk or bike to, the chores and jobs they do, etc. Explain that in this section, students will learn about the importance of exercise and rest.

Science Notebook EXTRA

Encourage students to use the vocabulary section they created in their Science Notebooks. Remind them to record prefixes, suffixes, and root words to help them remember the meanings of vocabulary terms.

Vocabulary

aerobic exercise Explain that *aerobic* comes from the Greek words *ăéros*, which means "air," and *bios*, which means "life." Thus, the word *aerobic* means "air for life." Then, tell students that *exercise* comes from the Latin word *exercere*, which means "to keep busy." Discuss with students the ways in which exercising can keep you busy. Point out that *exercise* can be a noun or a verb. Have students write a sentence in which they use the word in both forms. Tell students that aerobic exercise is any activity that increases your breathing and heart rates.

As You Read

ANSWER Good nutrition is important for ensuring that the body gets all the nutrients it needs for growth and repair. Exercise is important for strengthening muscle and bone. Exercise also reduces the risk of disease and keeps respiratory and circulatory systems working efficiently.

Differentiated Instruction

Kinesthetic Provide pairs of students with a stopwatch or other means of tracking time. Have each student take his or her resting heart rate and record it in his or her Science Notebook. Then, have each student take turns jumping up and down for a minute at a time and recording his or her heart rate after each minute. Students should graph their heart rates when they are done.

Field Study

Take students outside to observe how their classmates or other people in the area exercise. Have them record what they consider to be exercise in their Science Notebooks. Remind them that exercise is the active use of the body or the movement of muscles in the body. Back in the classroom, record the various exercises observed. Encourage students to create a poster that summarizes their findings.

Teach

EXPLAIN to students that everyone experiences stress. Ask students to describe what they feel like when they are stressed. Have them share the strategies they use to help them cope with this stress.

Vocabulary

stress Tell students that the word *stress* comes from the Latin word *stringere*, which means "to draw tight." Ask students if they have ever felt like they were "drawn tight" when they were stressed. Discuss what that might feel like.

hygiene Explain that the word *hygiene* comes from a Greek word meaning "healthy." Remind students that practicing good hygiene is an important part of staying healthy.

first aid Explain that the word *aid* comes from the Latin word *adjuvare*, which means "to help." Thus, first aid is help that comes first. A first-aid kit is intended to provide immediate help until a medical professional can be consulted.

Use the Visual: Figure 25.5

ANSWER Good hygiene keeps the body clean and prevents a person from catching and spreading disease.

Extend It!

Before they begin their research, ask students to write their opinions of antibacterial soap in their Science Notebooks. Take a poll of the class to find out how many students use this type of soap and how many think it is effective. Students might use the FDA Web site or medical journals to find out what research has been done on the subject. Antibacterial soap is so common in households today that students should understand its effectiveness and drawbacks.

Managing Stress

Most people are familiar with the term *stress*. In science, **stress** is defined as the body's response to the demands of everyday life. Distress is negative stress. People experience distress when they perceive a situation as difficult, dangerous, or painful and they do not have the resources to cope. Eustress is positive stress. A moderate amount of stress can help people improve their performances and achieve their goals. Research shows that some stress is actually necessary for life.

When stress is not managed, it can lead to anxiety, withdrawal, sleeplessness, fatigue, aggression, depression, and physical illness. Here are some things you can do to manage stress.

- Identify your own sources of stress, and make choices that help control the amount of stress you experience.
- Exercise, eat healthful foods, and get plenty of rest.
- Avoid caffeine. It can increase feelings of anxiety.
- Talk with friends, parents, or other respected adults about how you are feeling.
- Try a hobby that you enjoy.
- Manage your time wisely.
- Break large tasks into smaller, more manageable chunks.

Extend It!

Many soaps and detergents are currently marketed as "antibacterial." They are described as being an effective way to protect people from common illnesses. Some researchers, however, argue that the antibacterial agents contained in these soaps and detergents may actually kill off normal bacteria, creating an environment for mutated bacteria that are resistant to antibiotics.

Conduct research to learn more about antibacterial soaps. Are they better than regular soaps? Could they do more harm than good in the long term? Record your findings in your Science Notebook.

Hygiene and Posture

Most healthy people look healthy. That healthy look has a lot to do with good hygiene and good posture. **Hygiene** (HI jeen) describes the things people do to keep clean and to prevent disease. Here are some things you can do to have good hygiene.

Figure 25.5 Keeping neat and clean is part of good hygiene. Why is good hygiene important to good health?

- Bathe or shower daily and after exercise.
- Wash your hair with shampoo at least two times per week.
- Brush your teeth after meals and before you go to bed each night. Floss to remove plaque and food that can get stuck between teeth.
- Keep fingernails and toenails trimmed and clean.
- Have regular physical and dental checkups.

452 HEALTH AND WELLNESS

Background Information

A randomized, double-blind trial of 238 households found no significant difference between the rates of infectious disease in households that used antibacterial soap and those that did not. In fact, many scientists believe that antibacterial soap can be harmful because it gets rid of both harmful and beneficial bacteria and could contribute to the evolution of resistant strains of harmful bacteria.

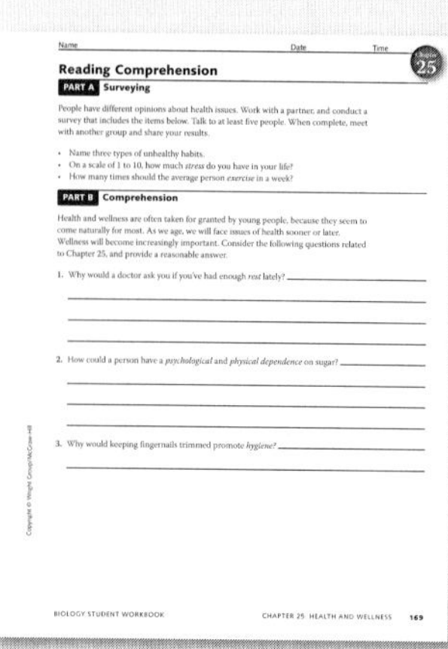

Name Date Time

Chapter 25

Reading Comprehension

PART A Surveying

People have different opinions about health issues. Work with a partner, and conduct a survey that includes the items below. Talk to at least five people. When complete, meet with another group and share your results.

- Name three types of unhealthy habits.
- On a scale of 1 to 10, how much *stress* do you have in your life?
- How many times should the average person *exercise* in a week?

PART B Comprehension

Health and wellness are often taken for granted by young people, because they seem to come naturally for most. As we age, we will face issues of health sooner or later. Wellness will become increasingly important. Consider the following questions related to Chapter 25, and provide a reasonable answer.

1. Why would a doctor ask you if you've had enough *rest* lately? ______
2. How could a person have a *psychological* and *physical dependence* on sugar? ______
3. Why would keeping fingernails trimmed promote *hygiene*? ______

Copyright © Wright Group/McGraw-Hill

BIOLOGY STUDENT WORKBOOK CHAPTER 25 HEALTH AND WELLNESS 169

Reading Comprehension Workbook, p. 169

Posture is also important to health. Standing, sitting, and walking erect allow your backbone to protect your spinal cord and enable the organs of the respiratory system to work more effectively.

Figure 25.6 Practice good posture by consciously standing straight with your shoulders down and your stomach held in.

Safety and First Aid

More than 100,000 people in the United States lose their lives each year in accidents. Accidents can happen anywhere. When accidents do happen, first aid can help minimize the damage. **First aid** is the immediate care given to a person who is injured or sick. First aid skills can be learned by taking a course offered at a hospital or other health care organization, such as the American Red Cross.

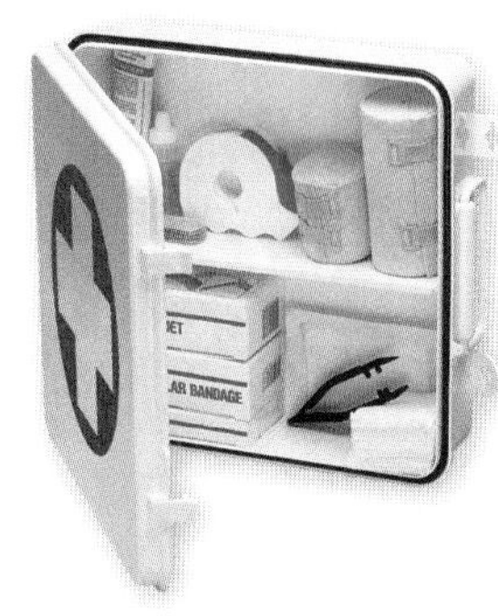

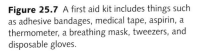

Figure 25.7 A first aid kit includes things such as adhesive bandages, medical tape, aspirin, a thermometer, a breathing mask, tweezers, and disposable gloves.

PEOPLE IN SCIENCE Clara Barton 1821–1912

Clara Barton, known as the "angel of the battlefield," was the founder of the American Red Cross. Clara began what would become her life's work and passion during the American Civil War. Despite dangerous conditions, she aided the sick and injured on the battlefield. Off the battlefield, she gathered supplies and comforted returning soldiers.

After the war, Clara worked to find and identify missing soldiers. She also worked tirelessly to educate the public about the Red Cross, which had been established in Switzerland in 1869. She gave speeches and handed out brochures. In 1881, she began the American Red Cross and acted as its first president for 23 years. The American Red Cross helps people prevent, prepare for, and respond to emergencies.

After You Read

1. Review your concept map. In a well-developed paragraph, describe some healthful habits people can practice to achieve and maintain good health.
2. Explain why healthful habits are important to have. What could happen to a person's body if he or she does not practice healthful habits?
3. What are some ways in which you can make healthful habits a part of your daily life?

Teach

EXPLORE Have students stand up and practice standing with good posture. Then, have students stand with poor posture. Ask students to describe the different feelings of good and bad posture. Discuss the reasons why someone might not have good posture.

PEOPLE IN SCIENCE

Divide students into small groups, and assign each group a natural disaster in which the Red Cross played a role. Have students research the ways in which the Red Cross helped people in these emergencies. Students should record their research in their Science Notebooks. ELLs could research the various organizations in their home countries similar to the Red Cross. They could compare the goals and responses to disaster of the two organizations. Ask groups to present their findings to the class.

Assess

EVALUATE Use the After You Read questions and the Alternative Assessment to help you assess students' understanding of the lesson.

After You Read

1. Possible answers include getting good nutrition, getting exercise and rest, having good hygiene and good posture, keeping safe, managing stress, and learning how to supply first aid.
2. Healthful habits are important because they keep the body systems functioning. Without them, a person will not look or feel his or her best, may have trouble focusing and meeting goals, might not have enough energy to do simple tasks, may be more likely to get and spread disease, and may develop respiratory problems or bone diseases such as osteoporosis later in life.
3. Students' answers will vary. Possible answer: Eat a well-balanced diet of nutrient-rich foods, get exercise by walking to and from school, practice safety measures, and learn first aid to be prepared for accidents.

Teacher Alert

Discussing with students the potential hazards that exist in their environment may raise their anxiety levels. Try to present this issue with an emphasis on the ways students can protect themselves from hazards rather than on the hazards themselves.

Alternative Assessment

EVALUATE Encourage students who have difficulty answering the After You Read questions to fill in blank concept maps with *Healthful Habits* at the center. Allow students to refer to their Science Notebooks.

25.2 Introduce

ENGAGE Tell students that a drug is any substance other than food that, when taken into the body, alters one or more chemical processes in the body. Ask: *Can you name some drugs that are helpful to people? Can you name some drugs that are harmful to people?*

EXPLAIN that when used properly, many drugs help people control pain, recover from disease, and feel better. However, if a drug is overused, it can become harmful and cause addiction or even death.

Before You Read

Model the K-W-L-S-H chart on the board. Ask students to share some of the things they know and want to know with the class. Record their responses on the board. Have students copy the chart into their Science Notebooks. Tell students that they will fill in the *S* and *H* columns of the chart later in the lesson.

Teach

EXPLAIN Tell students that in this lesson, they will learn what a drug is, about drug abuse and its dangers, and how to recognize classes of commonly abused drugs.

Vocabulary

drug Tell students that a drug that is used to help the body is called a medicine and that a drug that harms the body is called a poison.

drug abuse Explain that *abuse* comes from the Latin word *abuti*, which means "misuse." Drug abuse is the misuse of a drug.

tolerance Tell students that an unscientific definition of *tolerance* is "openness to people whose beliefs are different from one's own." Discuss with students how this definition relates to the scientific definition of getting used to a drug and needing higher doses to achieve the same effect.

physical dependence Explain that *physical* means "of the body." Physical dependence causes the body not to function well without the drug.

psychological dependence Explain that *psychological* means "of the mind." In psychological dependence, the mind thinks the body needs a particular drug.

Learning Goals

- Identify what a drug is.
- Understand what drug abuse is and the dangers of drug abuse.
- Recognize classes of commonly abused drugs.

New Vocabulary

drug
drug abuse
tolerance
physical dependence
psychological dependence

25.2 Drugs and Drug Abuse

Before You Read

Create a K-W-L-S-H chart in your Science Notebook. Think about the title of this lesson. Then, look at the pictures, headings, and Learning Goals in the lesson. In the column labeled *K*, write what you already know about drugs. In the column labeled *W*, write what you would like to learn.

Aspirin, cough syrup, and asthma medication probably don't come to mind when you hear the term *drugs*. However, they are all examples of drugs used as medicines.

What Is a Drug?

A **drug** is any substance other than food that, when taken into the body, alters one or more chemical processes in the body. Drugs change the way the body or mind works. All medicines are drugs, from the medicines prescribed by a doctor to the medicines people buy over the counter to treat a cold or flu. Medicines are drugs that are used to fight disease or to treat, prevent, or relieve symptoms of disease.

Caffeine, alcohol, and nicotine are drugs that can be harmful to one's health. Caffeine is a chemical found in coffee, tea, chocolate, cola, and other foods and beverages. It causes the body's heart rate to increase. Alcohol is a chemical found in beer, wine, and liquors such as vodka. Nicotine is found in cigarettes, cigars, and chewing tobacco.

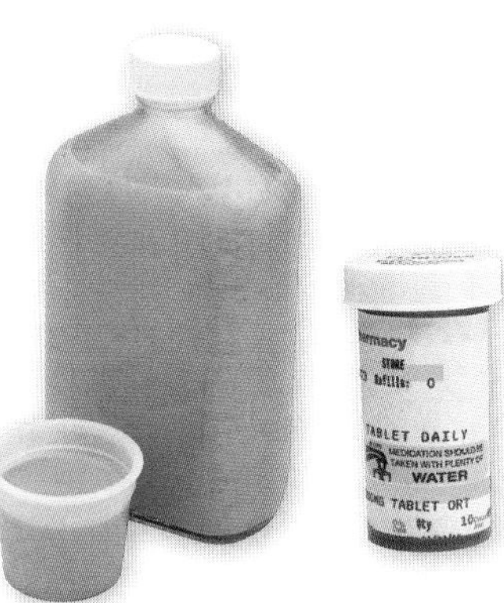

Figure 25.8 An over-the-counter (OTC) drug *(left)* is a drug people can buy without a doctor's prescription. OTC drugs include aspirin, ibuprofen, some types of cold remedies, and some types of cough syrup. A prescription drug *(right)* is a drug that requires a doctor's permission to take.

Did You Know?

The world's oldest-known prescriptions are inscribed on a clay tablet that dates back to about 2000 B.C.

Drug Abuse

Medicines can keep you healthy, but they can also harm your health when they are abused. **Drug abuse** is the intentional misuse of a legally purchased drug or the use of an illegal drug. Drug abuse can be life threatening. It can harm internal organs and can cause your body systems to fail.

ELL Strategy

Compare and Contrast Have students compare and contrast over-the-counter (OTC) drugs and prescription drugs by creating a Venn diagram with those two headings and the third heading *All Drugs*. Students should fill in the area under each heading with the correct information. Then, have students cut out pictures from old magazines and/or newspapers that show examples of each type of drug. Provide materials for affixing the pictures to the appropriate places in their Venn diagrams.

Background Information

The oldest-known prescription was discovered in Nippur in the Middle East. It identified three different "recipes," one for poultices, one for internal remedies, and one for more complex concoctions.

Drug abuse can lead to drug dependence. Drug dependence, or drug addiction, is the continued need for the effects of a drug even when the effects are harmful. Drug dependence can be caused by tolerance, physical dependence, and/or psychological dependence. **Tolerance** is what happens when the body gets used to a drug and needs higher and higher doses of the drug to produce the original effects. **Physical dependence** is a condition in which the user relies on a drug and requires the effects of the drug in order to feel well. **Psychological** (si kuh LAH jih kul) **dependence** is a condition in which the user has an overwhelming, emotional desire to continue using a drug.

Withdrawal symptoms are a sign of physical dependence. These symptoms occur when a drug is no longer in the body.

As You Read

In the column labeled *L* in your K-W-L-S-H chart, write what you have learned about drugs.

Are medicines drugs? Explain your answer.

Types of Drugs and Their Effects

Drug Type	Effects on the Body	Examples
stimulants	• increased activity of the central nervous system • increased heart rate, breathing rate, and blood pressure	caffeine, cocaine, amphetamines
depressants	• decreased activity of the central nervous system • relaxed muscles and sleepiness	alcohol, barbiturates, tranquilizers
narcotics	• decreased pain (when used as painkillers) • increased activity of the central nervous system	morphine, codeine, heroin
hallucinogens	• interference with the senses and perception • hallucinations in which people see or hear things that are not real	LSD, PCP, ecstasy
marijuana	• mood changes • decreased short-term memory	

Figure 25.9 The drugs in this table, classified into groups based on their effects on the body, are commonly abused.

Figure It Out

1. What types of drugs speed up the activity of the central nervous system?
2. Explain why a dependence on hallucinogens is harmful to one's health.

After You Read

1. What is a drug? What is drug abuse?
2. What are some drugs that are commonly abused?
3. Use your completed K-W-L columns to summarize this lesson in a well-developed paragraph in your Science Notebook. Then, write in the *S* column what you would still like to know and in the *H* column how you can find this information.

Teach

EXPLAIN to students that when drugs are abused, they can cause great harm to the body. Tell students that drug abuse affects not only the drug abuser but often those around that person, as well.

As You Read

ANSWER Medicines are drugs because they affect how the mind or body works.

Figure It Out: Figure 25.9

ANSWER **1.** stimulants and narcotics
2. Hallucinogens are harmful to one's health because they can cause people to see things that are not real. They interfere with a person's senses, which may reduce that person's awareness of dangers, and with a person's relationships, work, or school life.

CONNECTION: Health

Many drugs and vitamins labeled "all-natural" contain additives that have no effect or could have a negative effect on the body. Divide students into small groups. Provide each group with a different label from an "all-natural" drug. Have groups research the many ingredients the drug contains and present their findings to the class.

Assess

EVALUATE Use the After You Read questions and the Alternative Assessment to help you assess students' understanding of the lesson.

After You Read

1. Something is a drug if it affects how the mind or body works. Drug abuse is the intentional misuse of a legal drug or the use of an illegal drug.
2. Commonly abused drugs include stimulants, depressants, narcotics, hallucinogens, and marijuana.
3. Answers will vary. Students should cite Web sites for government health agencies and medical reference books as sources of information.

Differentiated Instruction

Mathematical Have students research the rates of drug abuse in the local area or another area of interest to them. They should determine how these rates have changed over the last ten years and then create graphs that illustrate the changes over time. Students may want to treat their findings by age group, if they are especially interested in rates for their own age group. A good Web site at which to start their research is **http://www.nida.nih.gov/NIDAHome.html**.

Alternative Assessment

EVALUATE Ask students who have difficulty answering the After You Read questions to add to their K-W-L-S-H charts and compare their charts with a partner's. Partners should explain the things that they have learned to each other. Students may then add more information to their charts, if appropriate.

25.3 Introduce

ENGAGE students by telling them that while alcohol and tobacco are both legal for use by adults, both substances can cause serious health problems. Ask: *If tobacco is known to cause cancer, and alcohol is known to be addictive, why do you think they continue to be legal drugs?* Discuss the issue of individual rights versus state or federal rights.

EXPLAIN that many people who believe tobacco should be legal also believe that each individual should have the right to put himself or herself at risk and that the government should not interfere with this decision. Tobacco and alcohol companies also have a strong interest in keeping cigarettes and alcohol legal.

Before You Read

Model the Venn diagram on the board. Ask for students' predictions, and record their answers. Students' predictions should reflect what they already know about alcohol and tobacco (e.g., *Alike*: Both are dangerous to health and well-being. They can be abused. Age restrictions govern their purchase. *Different*: Alcohol is a liquid. Tobacco is a solid that gets smoked or chewed.).

Teach

EXPLAIN that in this lesson, students will identify alcohol and tobacco as harmful substances that are commonly abused. They will also learn about the effects of alcohol and tobacco on the body.

Vocabulary

alcohol Explain that alcohols are chemicals and that some are poisonous.

blood alcohol concentration Explain that this is a measure of the amount of alcohol mixed with a certain amount of blood.

Explain It!

Provide some examples of public service announcements. Discuss the qualities that make these effective and the qualities that make them less effective. Have students share their finished PSAs with the class.

Learning Goals

- Describe alcohol's effects on the body.
- Identify harmful substances found in tobacco, and explain their effects on the body.

New Vocabulary

alcohol
blood alcohol concentration
tobacco
nicotine
tar

25.3 Alcohol and Tobacco

Before You Read

Make a Venn diagram to compare and contrast alcohol and tobacco. Predict what you will write in the Venn diagram.

Count out eight seconds. During those eight seconds, somewhere in the world, someone died from tobacco use. Tobacco is responsible for more than 500,000 deaths in the United States every year. That is about one out of every five American deaths. More than 100,000 other American deaths are caused by alcohol use. Nearly 40 percent of all traffic fatalities are alcohol related. Alcohol and tobacco are the most abused substances in the world. They are also the deadliest.

Alcohol

Alcohol is the oldest-known drug. **Alcohol** is a depressant that slows down the central nervous system and can cause both physical dependence and psychological dependence. While present in the body, it can alter people's emotions, perceptions, judgment, and coordination. It can affect people's vision, hearing, and speech. It can even cause people to lose consciousness.

Alcohol enters the bloodstream when a person drinks alcoholic beverages such as beer, wine, or liquor. It travels through the body and begins blocking messages from reaching the brain. In time, it travels to the liver. There, it is broken down into the waste products carbon dioxide and water. Before it is broken down, however, it builds up in the bloodstream. The higher the concentration of alcohol in a person's blood, the more the person's nervous system is affected. In higher concentrations, alcohol can kill brain cells.

Blood alcohol concentration (BAC) describes the amount of alcohol in a person's blood. In most states, a BAC between 0.08 and 0.10 percent is high enough for a person to be considered intoxicated. When a person is intoxicated, he or she is physically or mentally impaired. How much and how quickly a person drinks, how much a person weighs, and how much a person has eaten are some factors that affect a person's BAC. In general, the more a person drinks, the higher his or her BAC becomes and the more intoxicated he or she becomes.

Alcohol can have long-term effects on the body, such as immune system suppression, liver damage, high blood pressure, heart failure, and infertility. These effects are usually caused when a person abuses alcohol over a prolonged period of time.

Explain It!

Write a public service announcement in your Science Notebook warning people about the dangers of alcohol or tobacco use. Include pictures from magazines, or draw your own pictures. Remember that an effective announcement makes an impact on its readers.

Did You Know?

Alcohol contains many Calories, but it has little nutritional value. Its Calories are considered "empty," or wasted.

456 HEALTH AND WELLNESS

Differentiated Instruction

Visual, Musical Have students design posters or write advertising jingles that discourage the use of alcohol and tobacco. Encourage students to think creatively and try to use their persuasive skills to convince others of their point of view.

Background Information

The Centers for Disease Control (CDC) is a government organization. The National Center for Chronic Disease Prevention and Health Promotion (NCCDPHP) is one of the centers within the CDC. The Office on Smoking and Health, a division of the NCCDPHP, has a Web site that offers information about tobacco. Students can visit this Web site at **http://www.cdc.gov/tobacco/index.htm**.

Tobacco

Tobacco is a broad-leafed plant whose leaves can be dried and then smoked in cigarettes or cigars. Its leaves can also be chewed. Smokeless tobacco is tobacco that is chewed.

Tobacco contains a drug called nicotine. **Nicotine** (NIH kuh teen) is a highly addictive stimulant. When tobacco is smoked, chewed, or sniffed, nicotine enters the bloodstream. Within seconds, it enters the brain and alters the way the brain works. It speeds up the activity of the central nervous system and increases blood pressure, heart rate, and breathing rate. It causes glucose to be released into the bloodstream, making the body feel more alert. It causes chemicals that are responsible for feelings of pleasure to be released in the brain. Within 40 minutes of entering the body, nicotine's effects are reduced by half. As the effects wear off, the body has an overwhelming desire for more nicotine. After continued use, the body builds up a tolerance for nicotine. Nicotine use can quickly lead to both physical and psychological dependence.

When tobacco is burned, a thick, sticky fluid called **tar** is produced. Tar can stick in the bronchioles of the lungs. As it builds up in the lungs, it decreases the lungs' ability to pass oxygen into the blood. Tar causes lung cancer, emphysema, and bronchial diseases.

Tobacco smoke also contains at least 4,000 other chemicals. One of these chemicals is carbon monoxide, a substance that can cause heart disease. Finally, tobacco smoke harms the cilia lining the organs of the respiratory system.

Figure 25.10 Compare the lung of a nonsmoker *(left)* with the lung of a smoker *(right)*. Smoking can also cause mouth cancer.

As You Read

Use your Venn diagram to record important information about alcohol and tobacco.

What is alcohol? What are its effects on the body?

Figure It Out

1. How are a smoker's lungs different from a nonsmoker's lungs?
2. Infer the effects of smoking on a person's respiratory system.

After You Read

1. What is alcohol?
2. What substance in tobacco leaves is a drug? What does this drug do to the body?
3. Why are alcohol consumption and tobacco use harmful to one's health?
4. Use your completed Venn diagram to write in your Science Notebook a well-developed paragraph that compares and contrasts alcohol and tobacco.

Teach

EXPLAIN that the effect of drugs differ from person to person.

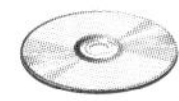 Vocabulary

tobacco Explain that *tobacco* comes from the Spanish word *tobaco* (a roll of tobacco leaves).

nicotine Explain that nicotine was named for Jean Nicot who brought tobacco to France in the 1500s.

tar Tell students that the tar in cigarettes is not the same as the tar used to make roads.

Figure It Out: Figure 25.10

ANSWER **1.** They are smaller, discolored, and unhealthy looking. **2.** It keeps the lungs from taking in oxygen and passing it to the blood.

As You Read

ANSWER Alcohol is a depressant that alters people's emotions, perceptions, judgment, and coordination; affects vision, hearing, and speech; causes people to feel disoriented, confused, or nauseous; and can even causes loss of consciousness or death.

Science Notebook EXTRA

Have students calculate the annual cost of smoking two packs per day if each pack costs $5.00. Then, have them calculate the cost if the person smokes for 50 years.

Assess

EVALUATE Use the After You Read questions and the Alternative Assessment to help you assess students' understanding of the lesson.

After You Read

1. Alcohol is a depressant and the oldest-known drug used by humans.
2. nicotine; It increases heart and breathing rates and causes the release of chemicals related to pleasure in the brain.
3. Both are addictive and cause damage to body organs and personal relationships. Chemicals in tobacco smoke cause cancer, lung disease, and heart disease.
4. Students' essays should show understanding of the concepts in the lesson.

ELL Strategy

Relate to Personal Experience Divide students into small groups. Have them share their opinions about tobacco and alcohol use in their country of origin. Encourage students who have lived in other countries to describe the ways that different countries regulate these drugs. Also have them address the high use of tobacco and marketing of tobacco overseas.

Alternative Assessment

EVALUATE Ask students to fill in a blank Venn diagram comparing tobacco and alcohol. Have each student write a paragraph summarizing the similarities and differences between these two drugs.

Chapter 25 Summary

VOCABULARY REVIEW

Check students' sentences or paragraphs to make sure that they understand the meaning of each vocabulary term.

PREPARE FOR CHAPTER TEST

Evaluate students' essays using the following criteria:

1. The topic sentence, or main idea, should restate the Key Concept.
2. The supporting paragraphs should incorporate the answers to the Learning Goal questions students have written and include details, facts, and examples they have recorded in their Science Notebooks.
3. The concluding sentence should sum up the main idea of the chapter and restate the Key Concept.

MASTERING CONCEPTS

True or False

1. True
2. False; aerobic
3. False; nutrition
4. True
5. False; stimulant
6. True

Short Answer

7. Possible answer: A person can manage stress by exercising and eating healthful foods, avoiding caffeine and alcohol, talking to a trusted adult, keeping a diary, and/or taking care of others.
8. Good posture is standing, sitting, and walking erect. A person who has good posture holds his or her head and neck up, keeps his or her shoulders down, and keeps his or her stomach strong and tucked in.
9. As a person's BAC increases, he or she becomes more intoxicated. His or her nervous system becomes more affected and slows down.
10. A person is considered intoxicated if he or she has a BAC of between 0.08 and 0.1 percent.
11. An over-the-counter drug is a medicine you can buy without a prescription. Some examples include aspirin, cold remedies, and cough syrup.

Chapter 25

Summary

KEY CONCEPTS

25.1 Healthful Living

- Practicing healthful habits is an important part of maintaining one's body systems and overall health.
- Good nutrition, plenty of exercise and rest, stress management, good hygiene, and safety are the goals of practicing healthful habits.

25.2 Drugs and Drug Abuse

- A drug is a substance other than food that affects how the body and mind work.
- Drug abuse is the intentional misuse of a legal drug or the use of an illegal drug.
- Drug abuse can lead to drug dependence. Drug dependence can be caused by tolerance, physical dependence, and/or psychological dependence.
- Some commonly abused drugs include stimulants, depressants, narcotics, hallucinogens, and marijuana.

25.3 Alcohol and Tobacco

- Alcohol and tobacco are harmful substances that are commonly abused.
- Alcohol is a depressant—it slows down the activities of the nervous system. It has both short-term and long-term effects on one's health.
- Blood alcohol concentration (BAC) describes the amount of alcohol present in a person's blood. A BAC between 0.08 and 0.10 percent is high enough in most states for a person to be considered intoxicated.
- Nicotine is a drug found in tobacco. It is a highly addictive stimulant. Tobacco smoke also contains tar, carbon monoxide, and many other chemicals. Tar can cause cancer and lung disease; carbon monoxide can cause heart disease.

VOCABULARY REVIEW

Write each term in a complete sentence, or write a paragraph relating several terms.

25.1
aerobic exercise, p. 451
stress, p. 452
hygiene, p. 452
first aid, p. 453

25.2
drug, p. 454
drug abuse, p. 454
tolerance, p. 455
physical dependence, p. 455
psychological dependence, p. 455

25.3
alcohol, p. 456
blood alcohol concentration, p. 456
tobacco, p. 457
nicotine, p. 457
tar, p. 457

PREPARE FOR CHAPTER TEST

To prepare for the chapter test, create a question from each Learning Goal. Use the information in your Science Notebook to answer each question. Then use these answers to write a well-developed essay about the chapter. Use the Key Concept on the first page of this chapter as your topic sentence.

458 HEALTH AND WELLNESS

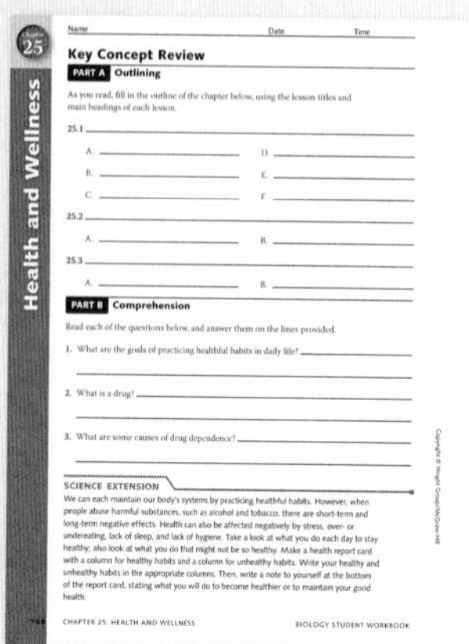
Key Concept Review
Workbook, p. 166

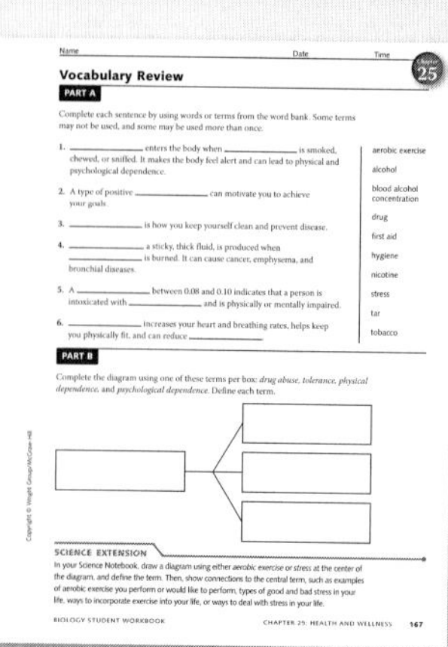
Vocabulary Review
Workbook, p. 167

MASTERING CONCEPTS

True or False

If the statement is true, write "true." If it is false, change the underlined word or words to make the statement true.

1. <u>All</u> medicines are drugs.
2. Running is a <u>weight-training</u> exercise.
3. Eating a well-balanced diet helps you be sure that you get the right <u>first aid</u>.
4. Alcohol is the <u>oldest</u> drug known to humans.
5. Nicotine is a <u>depressant</u>.
6. Caffeine is a <u>drug</u> found in coffee and tea.

Short Answer

Answer each of the following in a sentence or brief paragraph.

7. What are some healthful ways that a person can manage stress?
8. What is good posture?
9. What happens as a person's blood alcohol concentration increases?
10. At what BAC is a person considered intoxicated?
11. What is an over-the-counter drug? What are some examples?

Critical Thinking

Use what you have learned in this chapter to answer each of the following.

12. **Compare and Contrast** How are stimulants and depressants alike? How do they differ?
13. **Explain** Why is rest important to the body?
14. **Infer** How might drug abuse affect one's relationships?
15. **Evaluate** Should people avoid taking all types of drugs? Explain your answer.

Standardized Test Question

Choose the letter of the response that correctly answers the question.

16. Nicotine is a drug found in which of the following?
    - A. caffeine
    - B. tobacco
    - C. alcohol
    - D. tar

Test-Taking Tip

If you don't know an answer and you won't be penalized for guessing, make an educated guess. Use context clues if you don't understand the question.

Critical Thinking

12. Stimulants and depressants are both addictive drugs that affect the nervous system. While stimulants speed up the activity of the nervous system, depressants slow it down.
13. Rest is important to the body because it helps the body recover from the day that has passed and helps the body prepare for the day ahead.
14. Answers will vary. Possible answer: Because drugs affect how the mind works, the behavior of a person who abuses drugs might differ from his or her normal behavior. If a person is always preoccupied by the need for a drug and its effects, that person is probably not available as a friend. As a result, friendships can fall apart.
15. No; some drugs are necessary to treat, prevent, or relieve symptoms of disease.

Standardized Test Question

16. B

Reading Links

Smoking 101: An Overview for Teens

This frank and accessible book examines the implications of nicotine addiction while engaging the teen audience it targets. In addition to learning about the health risks associated with tobacco use, readers will come to better understand the advertising efforts and political relevance of the tobacco industry.

Hyde, Margaret O. and John F. Setaro.
Lerner Publishing Group. 128 pp. Illustrated.
Library ISBN: 978-0-7613-2835-3.

The Teen's Vegetarian Cookbook

Vegetarians and non-vegetarians alike will enjoy these great-tasting, easy-to-prepare recipes while learning about nutrition, self-sufficiency, and healthful lifestyles. Along with over 120 recipes, including responsible meals, snacks, and desserts, the cookbook includes supplementary material from teenage vegetarians.

Krizmanic, Judy. Illustrated by Matthew Wawiorka. Penguin Group. 192 pp.
Trade ISBN: 978-0-14-038506-9.

Curriculum Connection
Workbook, p. 171

Science Challenge
Workbook, p. 172

CHAPTER 25 **459**

Chapter 25

Labs

25A Pulse Rate and Exercise

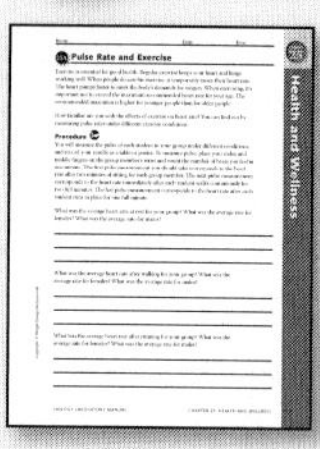

This prechapter introduction activity is designed to determine what students already know about how physical activity affects heart rate by engaging them in measuring how heart rate changes after exercise.

Objectives

- measure heart rate by taking a pulse
- compare and contrast heart rate under various exercise conditions
- calculate maximum heart rates
- evaluate the safety of heart rates compared to recommended maximums

Planning

 1 class period  groups of 2–4 students

Materials (per group)

- stopwatch
- pencil and paper

Engagement Guide

- **CAUTION:** It is essential that you determine the ability of all students to participate in this activity before beginning. If there are students who cannot or do not wish to run in place for one minute, allow them to participate in the activity by playing the role of group recorder.
- Challenge students to think about how they can measure pulse rate by asking:
  - *Do you have to count the number of beats in a full minute to determine heart rate? How else can you do it?* (Some students will recognize that they can count the beats for 15 seconds and multiply by 4, or count for 30 seconds and multiply by 2.)
  - *Why is it important to check pulse immediately after physical activity rather than waiting?* (Students should recognize that the heart rate will slow as the person rests, so the pulse must be taken immediately after exercise to be accurate.)
- Challenge students to think about how they will report group data by asking:
  - *How is an average calculated?* (by adding up all the individual measurements and dividing that number by the number of measurements)
- Encourage students to communicate their conclusions in creative ways.
- The average heart rate at rest should be 60 to 90 beats per minute (the rate depends on age and gender). The average heart rate after moderate exercise should be 50 to 70 percent of the maximum heart rate for the student's age. The average heart rate after strenuous exercise should be 65 to 85 percent of the maximum heart rate for the student's age. Maximum heart rate is 220 minus the age.

Going Further

Have students compare their heart rates after running with the maximum recommended heart rate for their age. Have students approximate the maximum rate by subtracting their age from 220. Strenuous exercise should fall within 65 to 85 percent of the maximum rate. Athletes may have a lower rate. Ask students if they think they should get more exercise if their heart rate exceeds 85 percent of the maximum.

25B Vitamin C in Juice

Objectives

- compare and contrast the effect of juices on vitamin C indicator
- measure the quantity of juices required to change the color of the indicator
- analyze data and reach conclusions about the vitamin content of juices

Skill Set

measuring, observing, comparing and contrasting, recording and analyzing data, classifying, stating conclusions

Planning

 25–35 minutes 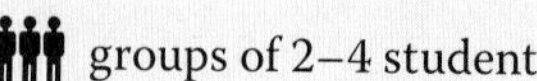 groups of 2–4 students

Materials

Materials for this activity are listed in the Student Laboratory Manual.

Advance Preparation

- To make the vitamin C indicator solution, dissolve 1 g of cornstarch in 100 mL of distilled water. Bring the solution to a boil, and then let it cool. Dilute 8 mL of the starch solution in 1 L of water, and add 1 mL of tincture of iodine. Test the deep-blue indicator by adding drops of orange juice to a 15-mL sample. Dilute the stock solution with distilled water until about 15 drops of orange juice are required to turn the solution clear.
- Provide at least 60 mL of solution to each group in a large paper cup. Provide at least 15 mL of each juice in small paper cups to each group.

Answers to Observations: Data Table 1

Answers will vary depending on the amount of vitamin C in each juice and the dilution of the indicator. However, all of the juices should be high in vitamin C.

Answers to Analysis and Conclusions

1. Answers will vary depending on the amount of vitamin C in each juice. The juice to which the fewest drops were added to turn the indicator clear is the highest in vitamin C.
2. Answers will vary depending on the amount of vitamin C in each juice.
3. Students should conclude that all of the juices are high in vitamin C.

Going Further

Have students try the activity with other juices or with pureed samples of vegetables. Discuss how the concentration of any pureed food will influence the results.

25C Calories in Food

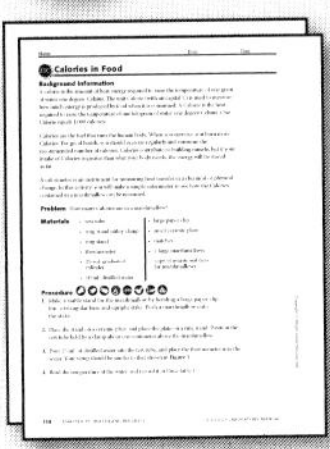

Objectives

- construct a calorimeter
- measure the change in water temperature caused by burning a marshmallow
- calculate the approximate number of Calories in a marshmallow

Skill Set

observing, measuring, recording and analyzing data, stating conclusions

Planning

1 class period groups of 3–4 students

Materials

Materials for this activity are listed in the Student Laboratory Manual.

Advance Preparation

- Explain to students that 1 g of water equals 1 mL, so the 25 mL of water they will heat in their calorimeter will be equal to 25 g. This is important when they do the calculation to determine Calories.
- Show students how to bend a large paper clip into a stable stand for the marshmallow by bending one loop into a flat triangle for a base and straightening the paper clip into an upright stake.
- Make a copy of the nutritional information for the marshmallows for each group.

Answers to Observations: Data Table 1

Answers will vary depending on results. Students should get results that are significantly lower than the Calorie rating on the food label for the marshmallows. This is because the homemade calorimeter can transfer only a small percentage of the heat to the water. A great deal of heat is lost to the air and materials.

Answers to Analysis and Conclusions

1. The two trials should return similar results because there was no change in procedure; however, small differences in the efficiency of heat transfer will cause the results to vary.
2. Because the formula is based on the mass of water in grams, the answer is in calories. To convert calories to Calories, it is necessary to divide by 1,000 (1 Calorie = 1,000 calories).
3. Some marshmallow and ash should remain, and they will contain some Calories.
4. Students should recognize that heat transfer was inefficient in their homemade calorimeters and that much of the heat was lost to the air and the apparatus.
5. Answers will vary.
6. Answers will vary.

Going Further

Students can try the experiment again with other burnable foods. They can compare their results to contrast the number of Calories in different foods. Students might compare regular and low-fat versions of the same food and note the difference in Calories.

Unit 7

Case Study 1: Technology Leads the Way

Gather More Information

Encourage students to use the library or the NSTA SciLinks Web site noted at the start of each chapter to learn more about these case study topics and to conduct further research.

Have students use the following keywords to aid their searches:

- scaffold
- artificial transplant
- bladder
- dairy allergy
- nutritional value
- prosthetic
- bionic
- electrode
- retina
- rod and cell cone

Research the Big Picture

- Have students form small groups based on one of the technologies described in this section. Each group's research of the topic should include specific examples of the technology, when it was created, and how and why it benefits humans. Each group should develop a visual display of what its members learned and share this with the other groups.
- Have students work in pairs to identify the body system(s) to which each technology example relates. Students should also identify the specific part(s) and function(s) of the system to which each example is connected. When students have completed their research, have pairs share their findings in a class discussion.

Background Information

Researchers have designed an artificial arm that can "read" nerve impulses from muscles, signaling the arm to move at the elbow or wrist and the hand to open and close and pick up objects. New prosthetic legs have feet with coiled springs in the heels that aid in walking by giving a boost or bounce as each step is taken. Future types of prosthetics will be almost bionic.

SCIENCE UPDATE

Technology Leads the Way

MEDICAL TECHNOLOGY promises to help many people live healthier lives. Here are just a few new technologies being developed.

Laboratory-Grown Organs

After 16 years of research and development, scientists are now growing artificial bladders in the laboratory. Bladders are simpler to make than many other organs because they have no blood vessels. People who need new bladders donate cells from their damaged organs. Scientists put these cells into "scaffolds," organ-shaped foundations that the cells can grow on. The scaffolds are then transplanted into patients. Bladder cells grow into new tissue over time, and the scaffolds dissolve. Eventually, completely new bladders form.

Researchers can now grow artificial bladders. They hope to make hearts and kidneys one day, too.

Vegetarian Ice Cream

Most people love to eat ice cream. People with dairy allergies cannot eat ice cream. A solution to these two problems just might be an all-vegetable ice cream made from turnips and flower seeds. A special protein made in the laboratory is added to give the product a creamy texture. It even melts like real ice cream and has lots of vitamins but no cholesterol.

New Prosthetics

About half of the two million Americans who have lost arms or legs use prosthetics, or artificial limbs. New technology has made prosthetics more natural and useful. Researchers are working on artificial limbs that will be attached directly into existing bone with rods. Artificial nerves made of glass capsules containing electrodes will be attached to real nerve endings. Nerve impulses will be able to travel between the artificial limb and microchips embedded in the brain. All it will take to move an artificial arm or leg will be thinking about it!

Transplanted Rods and Cones

Today, most loss of sight is permanent. However, that may not be the case in the future if experiments on mice have application in humans. Recently, scientists transplanted rod and cone cells from the retinas of sighted mice into the eyes of blind mice. The cells lined themselves up correctly, connected to other nerve cells, and transmitted signals to the brain, restoring some eyesight. It will be many years before this procedure can be done in humans, but its success in mice could mean a brighter future for many people.

CAREER CONNECTION LAB TECHNICIAN

YOU DON'T SEE lab technicians when you visit the doctor, but doctors could not do their jobs without them. The doctor might take blood or urine samples. He or she might swab an infection or take a tissue sample. These samples all go to lab technicians.

Lab technicians prepare microscope slides, examine blood and other body fluids, and test for certain drugs. They analyze tissue samples to detect bacteria, fungi, or other disease-causing organisms. They also examine tissue samples to look for abnormal cells, such as those that are cancerous. Doctors depend on the information they get from lab technicians to diagnose and treat disease.

Most lab technicians work in hospitals or private labs. They need good problem-solving skills, computer expertise, and lots of patience. Many lab technicians have a two-year associate's degree from a community college or a certificate from a hospital program or a vocational school. Some technicians learn their skills on the job.

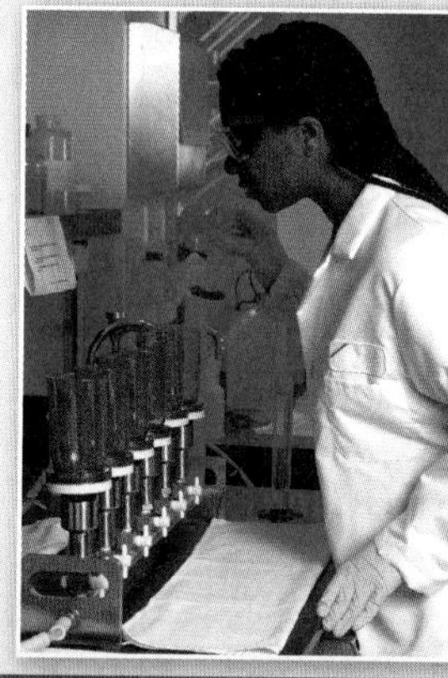

460

Case Study 2: New Ways to Fight Disease

Gather More Information

Encourage students to use the library or the NSTA SciLinks Web site noted at the start of each chapter to learn more about these case study topics and to conduct further research.

Have students use the following keywords to aid their searches:

- *Listeria*
- virus
- blood purifier
- contaminated blood
- chemotherapy
- cancer treatment
- nanoshell

New Ways to Fight Disease

DISEASE-CAUSING AGENTS BEWARE! You are also the targets of new medical technologies.

Portable Blood Purifier

Once blood is contaminated with a deadly virus, it's not easy to get rid of the infection. But a portable, pen-sized gadget may soon do the job. This device is a blood purifier, and it hooks into two arteries in a person's arm. Contaminated blood flows from one artery into a tube and filter in the device. The holes in the filter are so tiny that red blood cells cannot pass through, but tiny viruses can. Antibodies that coat the filter stick to the viruses and keep them from passing back into the blood. Clean, filtered, virus-free blood returns to the person's body.

Disease-Fighting Viruses

Listeria is a deadly bacterium that can lurk in processed foods, such as sandwich meat. One of every three people who eats food contaminated with this bacterium will die, so eliminating the threat is important. Today, scientists are enlisting an unusual helper: viruses that get rid of the bacteria. Some viruses destroy bacteria. Scientists have identified harmless, bacteria-destroying viruses. The viruses can be sprayed on the meat at meatpacking plants, and the meat will stay safe for months.

Nanoshells

Chemotherapy is a cancer treatment that involves the use of strong toxins to kill cancer cells. Many people get sick during treatment because the poisons also kill healthy cells. Now, there is a new way to kill cancer cells while leaving healthy cells untouched. It involves the nanoshell—a carbon polymer sphere that is 1,000 times smaller than the period at the end of this sentence. Nanoshells filled with cancer drugs are injected into the body. Like guided missiles, they seek out and destroy cancer cells by attaching to proteins on the cells of malignant tumors. They burrow into the tumors and release their drugs, destroying them from the inside but not making a patient ill. It will take several more years to do further tests, but scientists are hopeful that these tiny spheres can become a giant weapon against cancer.

Time Line of Progress

Before 1900	1590	The microscope is invented.
	1796	The first vaccine (smallpox) is developed.
	1816	The first stethoscope is developed.
	1818	The first successful blood transfusion takes place.
	1849	The first American woman earns a medical degree.
	1870s	Germs are identified as the cause of disease.
	1895	X rays are discovered.
	1896	Aspirin is developed.
	1897	Penicillin is discovered.
Since 1900	1937	The first blood bank is created.
	1952	The first heart pacemaker is developed.
	1953	Scientists first describe the structure of DNA.
	1954	The first kidney transplant takes place.
	1967	The first human heart transplant takes place.
	1978	The first "test tube baby" is born.
	1980	Smallpox is wiped out worldwide.
	1982	The first artificial heart transplant takes place.
	1983	The virus that causes AIDS is identified.
	1996	The first mammal (sheep) is cloned.

Research and Report

What type of medical breakthrough would you like to see happen in the future? Is there a disease you hope will be cured? Are there new things you hope doctors will be able to do? Identify this future advancement, and write a brief news story that announces it. Base part of your story on information you have learned in this unit. Share what you write with the class.

461

Research the Big Picture

- Have students work with a partner to answer the following questions about each example: *What caused the illness? What body defense(s) did not work properly or was not strong enough to combat the disease? What have scientists done to combat the disease?* When everyone has finished, discuss the answers as a class.
- Have students work in small groups to identify and research another disease in humans to discover its causes, the body's reaction and defense, and possible treatments. Have each group create a PowerPoint presentation of its findings that includes text, photographs, charts, and/or graphs.

Case Study 3: Timeline of Progress

Gather More Information

Encourage students to use the library or the NSTA SciLinks Web site noted at the start of each chapter to learn more about these case study topics and to conduct further research.

Have students use the following keywords to aid their searches:

- microscope
- vaccine
- smallpox
- stethoscope
- blood transfusion
- Elizabeth Blackwell
- penicillin
- blood bank
- pacemaker
- organ transplant
- test tube baby
- AIDS
- cloning

Research the Big Picture

Have students work in pairs to research one of the events on the timeline and then prepare a poster presentation or a short oral report for the class. Give pairs the option of one of the following:

- Find out why the event is significant to medical history. Include information about any social, economic, and/or political events happening at the time.
- Find out what the person or people associated with the event went through to succeed. Answer the following questions: *What obstacles were faced? What critical thinking skills and/or scientific problem solving skills were needed?*

CONNECTION: Career

Remind students that *lab* stands for *laboratory*, and a technician is a specialist in the technical skills of a job.

Ask students to take turns reading paragraphs from the feature aloud. As a class, discuss what being a lab technician might be like. Ask: *What would be the most interesting and desirable parts of the job? What would not be interesting or desirable? What questions do you have about the career?* After the discussion, each student should write a paragraph explaining why he or she would or would not like this career.

Appendix A

LAB SAFETY

Safety Symbols

These safety symbols are used in laboratory and field investigations in this book to indicate possible hazards. Learn the meaning of each symbol and refer to this page often. *Remember to wash your hands thoroughly after completing laboratory procedures.*

Safety Symbols	Hazard	Examples	Precaution	Remedy
Disposal	Special disposal procedures need to be followed.	certain chemicals, living organisms	Do not dispose of these materials in the sink or trash can.	Dispose of wastes as directed by your teacher.
Biological	Organisms or other biological materials that might be harmful to humans	bacteria, fungi, blood, unpreserved tissues, plant materials	Avoid skin contact with these materials. Wear mask or gloves.	Notify your teacher if you suspect contact with material. Wash hands thoroughly.
Extreme Temperature	Objects that can burn skin by being too cold or too hot	boiling liquids, hot plates, dry ice, liquid nitrogen	Use proper protection when handling.	Go to your teacher for first aid.
Sharp Object	Use of tools or glassware that can easily puncture or slice skin	razor blades, pins, scalpels, pointed tools, dissecting probes, broken glass	Practice common-sense behavior and follow guidelines for use of the tool.	Go to your teacher for first aid.
Fume	Possible danger to respiratory tract from fumes	ammonia, acetone, nail polish remover, heated sulfur, moth balls	Make sure there is good ventilation. Never smell fumes directly. Wear a mask.	Leave foul area and notify your teacher immediately.
Electrical	Possible danger from electrical shock or burn	improper grounding, liquid spills, short circuits, exposed wires	Double-check setup with teacher. Check condition of wires and apparatus.	Do not attempt to fix electrical problems. Notify your teacher immediately.
Irritant	Substances that can irritate the skin or mucous membranes of the respiratory tract	pollen, moth balls, steel wool, fiberglass, potassium permanganate	Wear dust mask and gloves. Practice extra care when handling these materials.	Go to your teacher for first aid.
Chemical	Chemicals that can react with and destroy tissue and other materials	bleaches such as hydrogen peroxide; acids such as sulfuric acid, hydrochloric acid; bases such as ammonia, sodium hydroxide	Wear goggles, gloves, and an apron.	Immediately flush the affected area with water and notify your teacher.
Toxic	Substance may be poisonous if touched, inhaled, or swallowed.	mercury, many metal compounds, iodine, poinsettia plant parts	Follow your teacher's instructions.	Always wash hands thoroughly after use. Go to your teacher for first aid.
Open Flame	Open flame may ignite flammable chemicals, loose clothing, or hair.	alcohol, kerosene, potassium permanganate, hair, clothing	Tie back hair. Avoid wearing loose clothing. Avoid open flames when using flammable chemicals. Be aware of locations of fire safety equipment.	Notify your teacher immediately. Use fire safety equipment if applicable.

Eye Safety	Clothing Protection	Animal Safety	Radioactivity
Proper eye care should be worn at all times by anyone performing or observing science activities.	This symbol appears when substances could stain or burn clothing.	This symbol appears when safety of animals and students must be ensured.	This symbol appears when radioactive materials are used.

Safe Laboratory Practices

Your personal safety in the laboratory is your responsibility. Following standard safety procedures will ensure your safety and that of your classmates. Before performing any experiment, read the entire procedure so you are familiar with the steps you will be following. Make note of any CAUTION statements and safety symbols displayed. Familiarize yourself with the safety guidelines and rules given here. Doing all these things will ensure a safe and successful laboratory experience.

Preventing Accidents

- Always wear chemical splash safety goggles (not glasses) in the laboratory. Goggles should fit snugly against the face to prevent any liquid from entering the eyes. Put on your goggles before beginning the lab and wear them throughout the entire activity, cleanup, and hand washing. Only remove goggles with your teacher's permission.
- Wear protective aprons and the proper type of gloves as instructed by your teacher.
- Keep your hands away from your face and mouth while working in the laboratory.
- Do NOT wear sandals or other open-toed shoes in the lab.
- Remove jewelry on hands and wrists before doing lab work. Loose jewelry, such as chains and long necklaces, should be removed to prevent them from getting caught in equipment.
- Do NOT wear clothing that is loose enough to catch on anything. If clothing is loose, tape or tie it down.
- Tie back long hair to keep it away from flames and equipment.
- Do NOT use hair spray, mousse, or other flammable hair products just before or during laboratory work where an open flame is used. These products ignite easily.
- Eating, drinking, chewing gum, applying makeup, and smoking are prohibited in the laboratory.
- Students are expected to behave properly in the laboratory. Practical jokes and fooling around can lead to accidents and injury.
- Students should notify their teacher about allergies or other health conditions that they have which can affect their participation in a lab.

Making Wise Choices

- When obtaining consumable laboratory materials, carefully dispense only the amount you will use. If you dispense more than you will use, check with your teacher to determine if another student can use the excess.
- If you have consumable materials left over after completing an investigation, check with your teacher to determine the best choice for either recycling or disposing of the materials.

Working in the Laboratory and the Field

- Study all procedures before you begin a laboratory or field investigation. Ask questions if you do not understand any part of the procedure.
- Do NOT begin any activity until directed to do so by your teacher.
- Work ONLY on procedures assigned by your teacher. NEVER work alone in the laboratory.
- Do NOT handle equipment without permission. Use all lab equipment for its intended use only.
- Collect and carry all equipment and materials to your work area before beginning the lab.
- Remain in your own work area unless given permission by your teacher to leave it. Keep your work area uncluttered.
- Learn and follow procedures for using specific laboratory equipment such as balances, microscopes, hot plates, and burners. Do not hesitate to ask for instructions about how to use any lab equipment.
- When heating or rinsing a container such as a test tube or flask, point it away from yourself and others.
- Do NOT taste, touch, or smell any chemical or substance unless instructed to do so by your teacher.
- If instructed to smell a substance in a container, hold the container a short distance away and fan vapors towards your nose.
- Do NOT substitute other chemicals/substances for those in the materials list unless instructed to do so by your teacher.
- Do NOT take any materials or chemicals outside of the laboratory.
- Stay out of storage areas unless you are instructed to be there and are supervised by your teacher.

Laboratory Cleanup

- Turn off all burners, gas valves, and water faucets before leaving the laboratory. Disconnect electrical devices.
- Clean all equipment as instructed by your teacher and return everything to the proper storage places.
- Dispose of all materials properly. Place disposable items in containers specifically marked for that type of item. Do not pour liquids down a drain unless your teacher instructs you to do so.
- Clean up your work and sink area.
- **Wash your hands thoroughly with soap and warm water after each activity and BEFORE removing your goggles.**

Emergencies

- **Inform the teacher immediately of *any* mishap, such as fire, bodily injuries or burns, electrical shock, glassware breakage, and chemical or other spills.**
- In most instances, your teacher will clean up spills. Do NOT attempt to clean up spills unless you are given permission and instructions on how to do so.
- Know the location of the fire extinguisher, safety shower, eyewash, fire blanket, and first-aid kit. After receiving instruction, you can use the safety shower, eyewash, and fire blanket in an emergency without your teacher's permission. However, the fire extinguisher and first-aid kit should only be used by your teacher or, in an extreme emergency, with your teacher's permission.
- If chemicals come into contact with your eyes or skin, notify your teacher immediately, then flush your skin or eyes with large quantities of water.
- If someone is injured or becomes ill, only a professional medical provider or someone certified in first aid should perform first-aid procedures.

Appendix B

METRIC SYSTEM AND SI UNITS

The International System of Measurement, or SI, is accepted as the standard for measurement throughout most of the world. The SI is a modernized version of the metric system, which is a system of measurement based on units of ten. In the United States, both the metric system and the standard system are used.

The SI system contains seven base units. All other units of measurement can be derived from these base units by multiplying or dividing the units by a factor of ten or by combining units.

- When you change from a smaller unit to a larger unit, you divide.
- When you change from a larger unit to a smaller unit, you multiply.

Prefixes are added to the base unit to identify the new unit created by multiplying or dividing by a factor of ten.

SI Base Units

Measurement	Unit	Symbol
length	meter	m
mass	kilogram	kg
time	second	s
electric current	ampere	A
temperature	Kelvin	K
amount of substance	mole	mol
intensity of light	candela	cd

Frequently Used Non-SI Base Units

Measurement	Unit	Symbol
volume	liter, cubic centimeter	L, cm^3
density	grams/cubic centimeter, grams/liter	g/cm^3, g/L

Common SI Prefixes

Prefix	Symbol	Equivalents
mega-	M	1,000,000
kilo-	k	1000
hecto-	h	100
deka-	da	10
deci-	d	0.1 or 1/10
centi-	c	0.01 or 1/100
milli-	m	0.001 or 1/1000
micro-	μ	0.000001 or 1/1,000,000
nano	n	0.000000001 or 1/100.000,000,000
pico-	p	0.000000000001 or 1/100.000,000,000,000

THE MICROSCOPE

Microscope Care and Use

1. Always carry the microscope by holding the arm of the microscope with one hand and supporting the base with the other hand.
2. Place the microscope on a flat surface. The arm should be positioned toward you.
3. Look through the eyepieces. Adjust the diaphragm so that light comes through the opening in the stage.
4. Place a slide on the stage so that the specimen is in the field of view. Hold it firmly in place by using the stage clips.
5. Always focus first with the coarse adjustment and the low-power objective lens. Once the object is in focus on low power, the high-power objective can be used. Use ONLY the fine adjustment to focus the high-power lens.
6. Store the microscope covered.

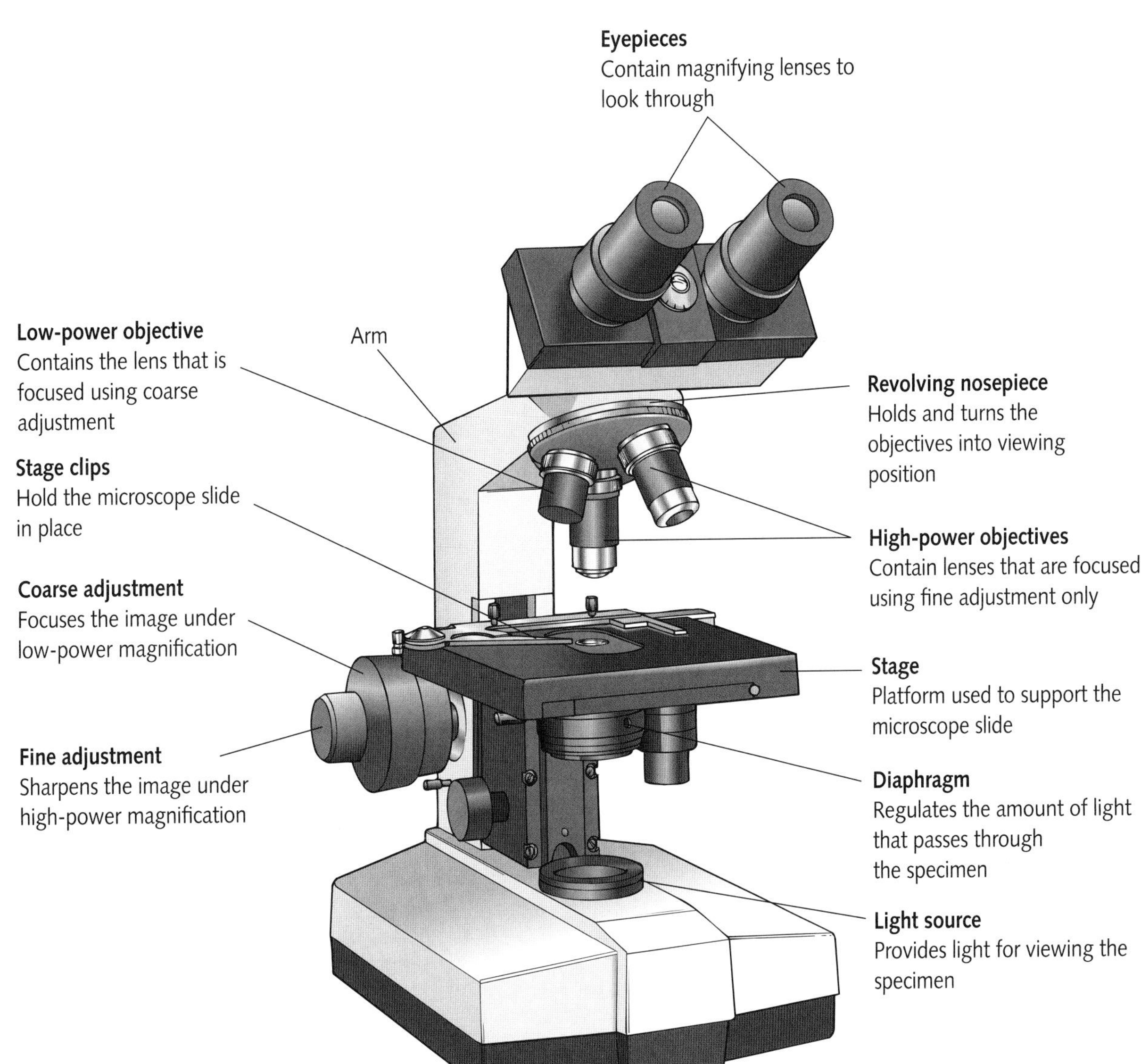
Eyepieces
Contain magnifying lenses to look through
Low-power objective
Contains the lens that is focused using coarse adjustment
Arm
Stage clips
Hold the microscope slide in place
Coarse adjustment
Focuses the image under low-power magnification
Fine adjustment
Sharpens the image under high-power magnification
Revolving nosepiece
Holds and turns the objectives into viewing position
High-power objectives
Contain lenses that are focused using fine adjustment only
Stage
Platform used to support the microscope slide
Diaphragm
Regulates the amount of light that passes through the specimen
Light source
Provides light for viewing the specimen

THE PERIODIC TABLE OF ELEMENTS

PERIODIC TABLE OF THE ELEMENTS

Columns of elements are called groups. Elements in the same group have similar chemical properties.

Element
Atomic number
Symbol
Atomic mass

Hydrogen
1
H
1.008

State of matter

The first three symbols tell you the state of matter of the element at room temperature. The fourth symbol identifies elements that are not present in significant amounts on Earth. Useful amounts are made synthetically.

Gas
Liquid
Solid
Synthetic

The color of an element's block tells you if the element is a metal, nonmetal, or metalloid.

Metal
Metalloid
Nonmetal

Rows of elements are called periods. Atomic number increases across a period.

The arrow shows where these elements would fit into the periodic table. They are moved to the bottom of the table to save space.

The number in parentheses is the mass number of the longest-lived isotope for that element.

* The names and symbols for elements 111–114 are temporary. Final names will be selected when the elements' discoveries are verified.
** Elements 116 and 118 were thought to have been created. The claim was retracted because the experimental results could not be repeated.

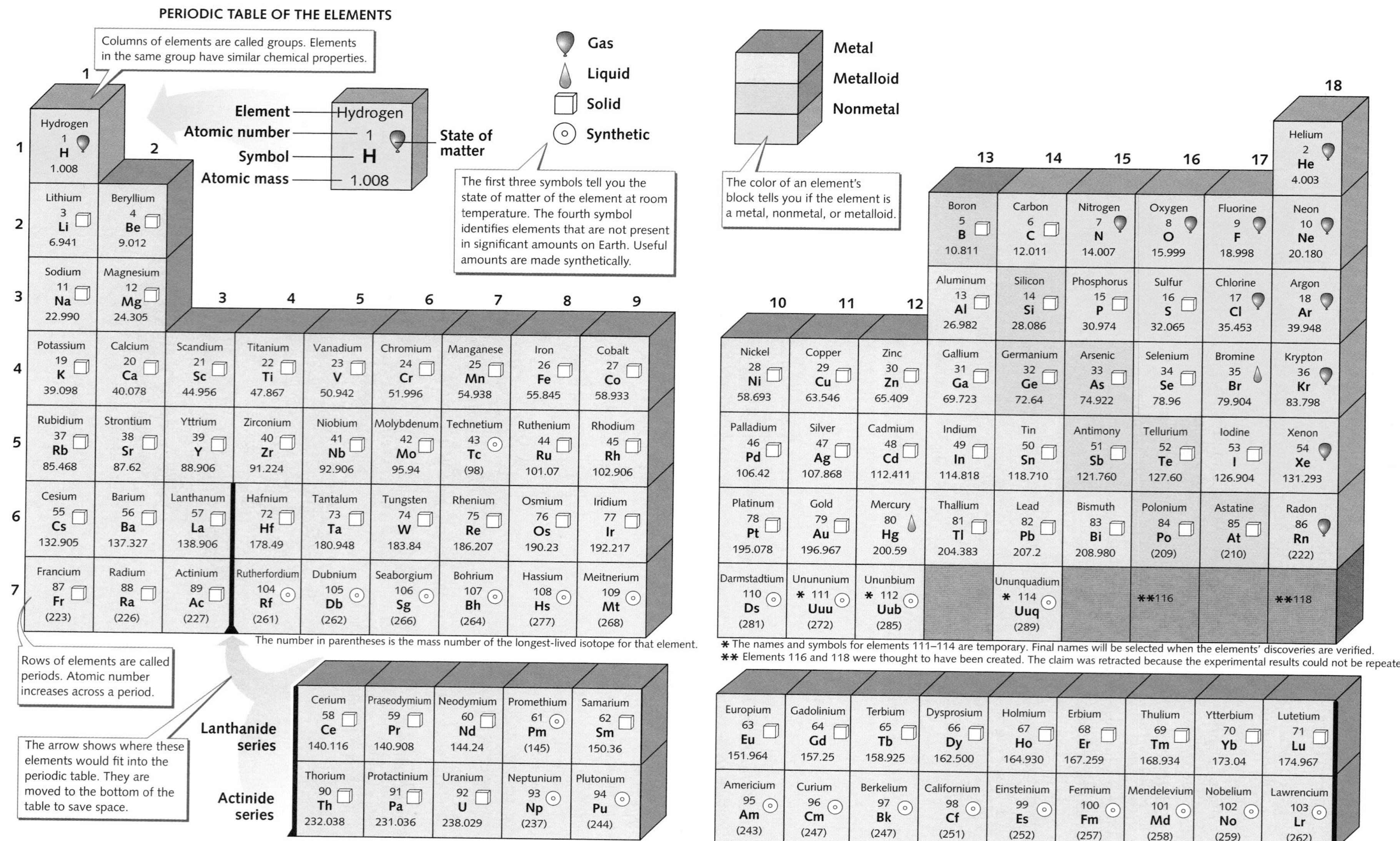

A

Glossary/Index

B

D

Deciduous forest a forest dominated by hardwood trees that drop their leaves in the cold part of the year, **299**

Decomposer a small organism that breaks down the complex molecules in a dead organism's body, **283**, 284

Dehydrated the condition caused by a body not receiving enough water, **379**

Dendrite a neuron that takes in information from the environment or from other cells in the body, **400**

Density, (1) the amount of mass in a given object, **16** (2) the number of individuals per unit of area, **310**

Dependent variable the variable that is observed to find out if it changes as a result of the independent variable, **8**

Derived unit a unit that consists of more than one base unit, **15**

Dermis the thick layer of skin that lies beneath the epidermis, **338**

Desert an environment that is among the driest places on Earth, 295, **302**

Development the process of an embryo's cells moving and changing, **424**

Diaphragm a thick muscle that separates the lungs and the digestive organs, **351**, 352

Dichotomous key pairs of opposing statements that help to identify an organism, **110**

Dicot a flowering plant with two seed leaves, **160**, 191

Diffusion the movement of particles from an area of higher concentration to an area of lower concentration, **45**, 350

Digestion a process in which food moves through a series of organs that break it down into small particles that can pass through cell membranes, **380**–383

Disease any condition that disrupts the normal functioning of the body, 432, **433**–436

DNA (deoxyribonucleic acid) a nucleic acid that stores genetic information used to form all of a cell's proteins, **31**

DNA replication the process of copying DNA during cell division, **72**

E

Food web **a model that shows all the possible feeding relationships at each trophic level, 284**

Fossil **the preserved remains of an organism that was once living, 88**

Fossil record **the organization by scientists of fossils according to type of organism and when it lived, 90**–91

Fraternal twins **siblings that developed from two different eggs at the same time, 426**

Freshwater **water that contains very little salt biome, 303**–304

Fungi **(1) the kingdom that includes heterotrophs that obtain nutrition by feeding on dead or decaying organic matter, 117 (2) heterotrophic eukaryotes that use spores to reproduce, 146,** 117, 134, 146–149

G

Gamete **a sex cell, 57, 169, 419**

Gametophyte generation **the stage of a life cycle that produces sex cells, 169**

Gene **a heritable trait, 60**

Genetic diversity **the variation in genes among members of the same species, 87**

Genetic engineering **a variety of techniques that directly change the hereditary material of an organism, 76**

Genetics **the field of biology devoted to studying heredity,** 6, **57.** *See also* Chromosomes; Heredity

Genotype **a combination of alleles, 61,** 62

Genus **a group that helps make up a family, 112**

Geologic time scale **a record of living organisms' history, divided into geologic eras, periods, and epochs, 91**

Germination **the process by which a seed embryo develops into a new plant, 203**

Gestation **the period of time during which a developing mammal stays in the uterus, 268**

Ginkgo **a gymnosperm with leaves that closely resemble the leaves on more familiar trees, 177**

Gland **an organ that produces and releases a substance, 412.** *See also* specific types

H

Homologous structures structures that have the same evolutionary origins, **93**

Homozygous containing two of the same alleles for a trait, **61**

Hormone a special chemical made in one part of an organism that affects growth and development in other parts of the organism, **163**, **411**

Host the organism off which a parasite lives, 76, **124**, **314**, 318

Hybrid the offspring of parents that have different forms of a trait, **58**

Hybridization a process in which breeders mate or cross organisms with different traits, **75**, 120–121

Hydrotropism growth toward water, **191**

Hygiene the things people do to keep clean and to prevent disease, 449, **452**

Hypertension high blood pressure, **369**–370

Hyphae thin, fuzzy threads that grow on a fish and secrete digestive enzymes that break down nutrients in its body, **144**, 146

Hypocotyl a stem below the cotyledons, **201**, 203

Hypothesis a proposed explanation for an observation, **8**

I

Identical twins siblings that developed from a split zygote and have the same genes, **426**

Immune system the body's system of defense against specific pathogens, 335, **441**–445

Immunity a person does not suffer symptoms of disease when he or she is exposed to a pathogen, **442**–443

Imperfect fungi fungi that are not known to reproduce sexually, **148**

Inbreeding mating or crossing organisms with similar traits, **75**

Incomplete dominance a blend of both parents' traits, **62**

Incubation period a period of time in which a pathogen reproduces itself rapidly before an immune response starts, **442**

Independent variable a variable that is changed, **8**

Infancy the period of great physical and mental change during the first 18 months of life, **427**

Infectious disease a disease caused by pathogens, **433**

Glossary/Index

N

O

Ovary, **(1) a flower structure that holds the egg cells and ovules once the eggs are fertilized, 181 (2) the female organ that produces eggs, 181,** 412, 414, **421**

Over-the-counter (OTC) drug, 454

Oviduct **a tube wrapped around the end of the ovary, 421**

Ovulation **the release of a mature egg, 422**

Ovule **the plant part that contains the embryo sac and will develop into a seed, 178**

Ovum (ova) **a female sex cell,** 414, **419**

fertilization of, 423
Owls, 261, 262
adaptation by, 86
range of, 310
Oxygen
in air, 28
in cellular respiration, 162, 191
in human body, 351, 352
in proteins, 31
Oxygenated blood, 364
Oxytocin, 425
Oysters, 220

P

P_1 generation of plants, 59
Paint horse, 269
Painted turtle, 253

Paleontologist **a scientist who uses fossils to study forms of life that existed in prehistoric times, 88,** 100

Pampas, 300

Pancreas **an organ that makes digestive enzymes and hormones, 383,** 412, 414

Papilloma virus, 125
Papua, Indonesia, sealife in oceans near, 327
Paralysis, 405
Paramecia, 117

Parasite **an organism that lives inside or on another organism, 124, 216,** 217

defensive cell attacks on, 440
in digestive system, 386
fishes as, 244
fungi as, 146
leeches as, 218
mites as, 227
mosquito as, 234
protozoans as, 137, 138
ticks as, 227
Parasitic fungi, 149

Parasitism **a symbiotic relationship in which one organism, the parasite, feeds off the living body of the other organism, 314**

Parasympathetic nervous system, 402
Parathyroid glands, 412, 413
Parent plants, in cross-pollination, 59
Parrots, 261
Passenger pigeons, extinction of, 320

Passive immunity **the transfer of antibodies from another's body, 442**

Passive transport **the movement of materials into or out of the cell without the cell's use of energy, 45**

Pasteur, Louis, 436
spontaneous generation and, 38

Pathogen **a disease-causing organism, 433**

defenses against, 438
disease and, 435
fever and, 439
immune system response to, 441
nonspecific defense system and, 437
transmission of, 434
Pathogenic bacterium, 435
Pathways, neuron, 401
Pea plants, 193
homologous chromosomes in, 66
leaves of, 199
Mendel's study of traits in, 57, 58, 59, 60
Peanuts, 201
Pearls, 220
Penguins, 261, 262
Penicillin, 148, 149, 436
Penicillium, 148
roqueforti, 149
Penis, 421
People, environment and, 319–323

Percent **a unit describing one part of one hundred, 64**

Perching birds, 261, 262

Perennial **a plant that lives longer than one or two years, 164**

Period changes, in population, 311
Periods, eras divided into, 91

Periosteum **the outermost layer of bone, 341**

Peripheral nervous system **a division of the nervous system that connects the brain and spinal cord with the rest of the body, 402**

Peristalsis **the wave-like motion created by the esophageal muscles that pushes food to the stomach, 382**–383

Permeable membranes, 46
Perspiration, 26
Pertussis, 443
Pests, virus controls of, 127

Petal **the soft, fleshy part of a flower that attracts animals, 180**

Petiole **the stalk that joins a leaf blade to a stem, 196**

Pets
heartworms in, 217
vaccination against viruses, 127

Phagocyte **a white blood cell that recognizes and eats pathogens, 440**

Pharyngeal pouches, 241

Pharynx **the region where the nose and the mouth are connected, 354**

Phenotype **a trait an organism displays, 61–62**

Phloem **plant tissue that is made up of tube-shaped cells and transports sugars to all parts of the plant,** 172, **190,** 191

in leaf petiole, 196
Phloem cells, under bark, 194

Photosynthesis **the process by which plants, some bacteria, and most algae change the energy of sunlight into energy that can be stored in food,** 25, 161

air for, 28
algae and, 141
equation for, 48, 161
in leaf, 197, 198
light for, 162, 163

Phototropism **a plant response in which the plant bends toward the Sun, 165**

Phylum **a group that is smaller and more specific than a kingdom, 112**

dogs in, 113

Q

R

RNA (ribonucleic acid) **a nucleic acid that carries information from DNA to the ribosomes and then carries out the process by which proteins are made,** 31, **73**

Rod **a receptor cell in the eye that is sensitive to light energy, 408**

Root **a plant organ that absorbs water, dissolves minerals, transports materials to and from the stem, and stores glucose,** 174, **187**–191

Root cap **tough cells that cover the end of the root and protect the more delicate cells underneath, 190**

Root hair **extensions of epidermal cells that absorb water, oxygen, and absorbed minerals, 190**

S

Sac fungi **the largest group of fungi that produce saclike structures during sexual reproduction, 148**

Safety symbol **a sign or character that warns of possible dangers during scientific experiments, 10**

Salivary gland **the gland that secretes saliva into the mouth, 381**

Scavenger **an animal that feeds on dead or dying animals, 244**

Science **an organized method of using evidence to propose explanations for events in the natural world, 4**

Scientific method **the process through which scientists attempt to answer questions about the natural world, 7**

Scrotum **a pouch of skin that holds the testes and epididymis, 420**

Seashore **the edge between land and marine biomes, 305**

Secondary sex characteristic **an adult physical characteristic, 428**

Secondary succession **the recolonization of an area by living things after a disturbance, 291**

Seed **a structure from which a plant grows, 200**–203

Seed coat **tough coat that protects the seed, 200**

Selective breeding **a process in which people choose plants and animals with preferred traits and allow them to reproduce, 74**–75

Selectively permeable membrane **a membrane across which some particles can pass while others cannot, 46**

Semen **sperm combined with fluids, 420**

Sensory receptor **cells in the sensory organs that are sensitive to specific types of energy, 407**

Sepal **a green leaflike structure that surrounds a bud on a developing flower, 180**

Sex chromosome a chromosome that determines an individual's gender, **69**

Sex-linked trait a trait carried by a gene on a sex chromosome, **70,** 419

Sexual reproduction the type of reproduction that requires the formation of sex cells, **169, 210.** *See also* Meiosis; specific organisms

Skeletal muscle a muscle that attaches to a bone, 344, **345,** 347

Skeletal system the 206 bones of the human skeleton, 334, **340**

Smooth muscle tissue that makes up the muscle found in internal organs, 344, **345**

Solution a mixture of two or more substances, **44**

Solvent a substance in which other substances dissolve, or break apart, **26**

Species, (1) a group of organisms that have similar physical characteristics and can reproduce offspring capable of producing their own offspring, **23** (2) the smallest and most specific group into which organisms are classified, **112**

Sperm a male sex cell, 169, 170, 171, **419,** 420

Spicule a sharp, small structure that helps make up some sponges' bones, **213**

Spirilla bacteria that are shaped like corkscrews or spirals, **129**

Spongy bone a strong structure of bony tissue that makes up the inside of a bone, **341**

Spontaneous generation the belief that living things come from nonliving matter, **36**–38

Sporangia, (1) special reproductive hyphae that have grown up and away from the mycelium, **147** (2) structures located at the bottom of a frond in which fern spores are produced, **174**

Spore production
  in fungus-like protists, 143
  in plasmodium, 144

Spore a reproductive cell produced by sporozoans that develops into new organisms when environmental conditions are favorable, **138, 169,** 171

  distribution by fungi, 147
  fern, 175
  in meiosis, 170
  Plasmodium, 138
Sporophyte, 170, 171
  of ferns, 174

Sporophyte generation the stage of a life cycle that produces spores, **169**

Spruce trees, 178, 299
Squash bug, 234
Squids, 220, 221

Stamen the male reproductive organ of a plant, composed of the anthers and filaments, **180**

Starches, 30, 375
  in photosynthesis, 162
  in tubers, 193
Starfish. *See* Sea star
Steam engine, invention of, 38

Stem part of a plant's shoot system that supports its leaves, cones, fruit, and flowers, **192**–195

  herbaceous, 192
  monocot, 195
  specialized, 195
  structure of, 193–195
  types of, 192
  woody, 192, 194
Steppes, 300

Sternum a bird's breastbone, **260**

Stigma a structure on top of the flower's pistil that holds onto any pollen grains that land on it, **181**

Stimulants, 455

Stimulus, (1) a condition or event in your surroundings, **23, 399** (2) a signal that causes an animal to react in a certain way, **23, 165, 271, 399**

  plant responses to environmental, 165
Stinging cells, in cnidarians, 214
Stingray, 245
Stinkbugs, 233
Stirrup, in ear, 410

Stomach a large, muscular bag that digests, breaks down, and stores food, **382**

  human, 382
  of sea star, 236

Stomata tiny pores that control gas exchange between the leaf and the environment, **198**

Stonecrab, 228
Stonewashed jeans, fungus and, 153
Streams, 303
Strepsirrhines, 96

Stress the body's response to the demands of everyday life, **452**

  management of, 449, 452
Striated muscle, 345

Stroke a condition that occurs when an artery in the brain is blocked, cutting off the blood supply to part of the brain, **371**

  deaths from, 369
Structure
  cell, 115
  of flowers, 180–181
  of fungi, 146
  similarities as basis for classification, 109
Structures (body), 92–94
  analogous, 93
  homologous, 93
  vestigial, 93–94
  students of, 6

Style a flower structure that connects the stigma to the ovary, **181**

Subcutaneous tissue the innermost layer of skin, **339**

Succession the steady progression of species invasion and replacement in an ecosystem over time, **289**

  primary, 290
  secondary, 290
Sucrose (table sugar), 29
Suffixes, *-ology,* 6
Sugars
  simple, 29
  as simple carbohydrates, 375
Sulfur, in proteins, 31
Sun, for telling time, 17
Sunflower seeds, 200
Sunlight
  in lakes, 303
  latitude and, 296
  in oceans, 304
  in photosynthesis, 25, 161
"Superbug" bacterium, 436
Surface area, 53
Surfactant, 355
Surgery, 436

Survival of the fittest organisms that are more fit to survive live to reproduce, **102**

Sushi, 142

Sustainable use taking only as much as can be replaced by nature, **320**

  of oceans, 327
Svalbard Islands, 207
Swallowtail butterflies, variation in, 87
Swans, 261, 262

Sweat a substance that excretes liquid wastes, **389**

Sweat gland a coiled tube inside the dermis that opens onto the surface of the skin, 338, **395**

Swim bladder a structure in a bony fish that acts like a small balloon, **247**

Symbiosis a close relationship between individuals of two or more species, **313**

  adaptation to, 316
  commensalism as, 314
Symbiotes, in digestion, 386
Symmetry, in animals, 211
Sympathetic nervous system, 402

Symptom a changed sensation resulting from an infection, **433**

Credits

Art Credits

McGraw-Hill, Garry Nichols, and Howard Friedman

Photo Credits

Cover © Art Wolfe/Getty Images; **2** (t) ©Kennan Ward/Corbis, (m) ©Tom Brakefield/Corbis, ©hybrid medical animation/Photo Researchers, (b) ©Stephen Dalton/Photo Researchers; **3** ©kristian; **4** ©Vasilev Ivan Mihaylovich; **5** (t) ©Michael Nichols/National Geographic Image Collection, (b, l-r) ©Yo Nayaya/Getty Images, ©David Sutherland/Getty Images, ©StockTrek/Getty Images and ©Chee-Onn Leong; **7** ©Tammy Wolfe; **9** Wikipedia; **12** ©ABN Stock Images/Alamy; **13** ©Eugene Buchko; **14** ©Christine Balderas; **18** ©ABN Stock Images/Alamy; **20** ©Ronald Sherwood; **21** ©S. Greg Panosian, (t) ©Digital Vision/PunchStock, (m) ©Mark Grenier, (b) ©Ivan; **22** (tl) ©Purestock/Getty Images, (tr) ©Emilia Stasiak, (bl) ©Gschmeissner/Photo Researchers, (br) ©Frank Leung; **23** (t) ©Charles D. Winters/Photo Researchers, (b) ©Elena Sherengovskaya; **24** ©Mark D. Phillips/Photo Researchers; **25** (t) ©iStockphoto.com/Grafissimo, (b) ©Anita Elder; **26** (t) ©Jose Manuel Gelpi Diaz, (i) ©Tomasz Pietryszek, (b) ©Stockbyte/Getty Images; **27** ©Ted Kinsman/Photo Researchers; **28** (l) ©U.S. Fish and Wildlife Services, (r) ©Andrew Syred/Photo Researchers; **30** (t, l-r) ©Jovan Nikolic, ©Sebastian Kaulitzki, ©Frank Boellmann, (b) ©Diane Diederich, ©iStockphoto.com/EddWestmacott, and ©Darryl Brooks; **31** ©Johan Swanepoel; **32** ©Tomasz Pietryszek; **34** ©Roy Morsch/zefa/Corbis; **35** (t) ©Omikron/Photo Researchers, (b) ©The Granger Collection, New York; **36** (t) ©Roman Krochuk, (b, l-r) ©Rachel Dewis, ©webartworks.de/Fotolia, ©Maria Veras; **42** (t) ©Keith R. Porter/Photo Researchers, (bl) ©Biophoto Associates/Photo Researchers, (br) ©LSHTM/Photo Researchers; **43** ©Dr. Jeremy Burgess /Photo Researchers, **44** ©Bloomimage/Corbis; **48** ©Elena Elisseeva; **49** ©Eric Wong; **50** ©Wing Tang; **51** (l-r) ©Alfred Pasieka/Photo Researchers, ©Sebastian Kaulitzki, ©Eye of Science/Photo Researchers; **56** ©Frans Lanting/Corbis; **57** ©Image 100/Corbis; **58** ©James King-Holmes/Photo Researchers; **62** ©Liga Gabrane; **66** (l) ©Digital Food Shots, (r) ©Kevin Snair; **70** ©David Nicholls/Photo Researchers; **72** ©Science Source; **74** ©Tom Bean/Corbis; **75** (t) ©John S. Sfondilias; (b) ©Derek Dammann; **77** ©Seoul National University/Handout/Reuters/Corbis; **80** (t) ©Jean Krejca, Ph.D, (b) ©Kim Karpeles/Alamy; **81** (t) ©iStock International, (b) ©Michael Abbey/Photo Researchers; **82** (t) ©Falk Kienas, (b) ©Susan McKenzie; **83** ©Royalty-Free/Corbis; **84** ©Manoj Shah/Getty Images; **85** (t) ©PunchStock, (l-r) ©Claudia Adams/Alamy, ©Gary Buss/Getty Images, ©Joel Sartore/Getty Images; **86** (tl) ©PunchStock, (m) ©Johan Swanepoel/Shutterstock, Inc., (bl) ©Nik Niklz, (br) ©Lane Erickson; **87** (r) ©Matt Meadows, (b) ©J. McPhail; **88** (t, l-r) ©Marlene DeGrood, ©Ismael Montero Verdu, ©www.handini.com/iStock; **89** ©Richard T. Nowitz/Photo Researchers; **93** (t) ©Mark William Penny, (b) ©Creatas/PunchStock; **95** (l) © Christian Riedel, (r) ©Steven Tilston; **97** ©John Reader/Photo Researchers; **98** (t) ©Des Bartlett/Photo Researchers, (b) ©Marion Kaplan/Alamy; **99** (l) ©The Field Museum, (r) ©Volker Steger/Nordstar-"4 Million Years of Man"/Photo Researchers; **101** (t) ©Marius Hainal, (m) ©Nancy Nehring, (b) ©Science Source; **105** ©Falk Kienas; **106** ©Blasius Erlinger/Getty Images; **107** (l-r) ©Tom Brakefield/Getty Images, ©Bettmann/Corbis, ©GK Hart/Vikki Hart/Getty Images; **109** (tr) ©Marina Cano Trueba, (m) ©Getty Images, (bl) ©Digital Vision/PunchStock, (br) ©Lynsey Allan; **110** ©Alex Balako; **111** (l-r) ©PhotoLink/Getty Images, ©Dr. Dennis Kunkel/Getty Images, (r) ©PhotoLink/Getty Images; **112** (l-r) ©Getty Images, ©Erik Lam, ©Getty Images; **113** (1) ©Getty Images, (2) ©Getty Images, (3) ©Corbis, (4) ©PhotoLink/Getty Images, (5) ©Hakan Karlsson, (6) ©Andrew Manley, (7) ©Stanislav Khrapov; **114** (t-b) ©Getty Images, ©Nancy Nehring, ©Pat Powers and Cherryl Schafer/Getty Images; **116** (t) ©Ines Gesell, (b) ©Michael Abbey/Science Photo Library; **117** (t, l-r) ©Sanamyan/Alamy, ©Paul Whitted, ©John Walsh/Photo Researchers, (bl) ©Corbis Royalty Free, (br) ©PhotoLink/Getty Images; **119** ©Getty Images; **120** (t) ©Pierre Perrin/Corbis Sygma, (b) KCNA/epa/Corbis; **121** Bryan L. Stuart; **122** (l) ©Stefan Glebowski, (r) ©Lee D. Simon/Photo Researchers; **123** ©Joseph Van Os, (i) ©Eye of Science/Photo Researchers; **124** (l-r) ©Chris Bjornberg/Photo Researchers, ©Omikron/Photo Researchers, ©Lee. D. Simon/Photo Researchers, ©Hans Gelderblom/Getty Images; **125** ©Lee D. Simon/Photo Researchers; **127** (t) ©Keystone/Getty Images, (m) ©Geogre/Wikipedia; **129** (t, l-r) ©Scimat/Photo Researchers, ©Eric V. Grave/Photo Researchers, ©James Cavallini/Photo Researchers; **130** (l) ©M. I. Walker/Photo Researchers, (r) ©Dr. Linda Stannard, Uct/Photo Researchers; **131** (l-r) ©Ben Osborne/Getty Images, ©Natalia Klenova, ©Nadezda Firsova, ©Scimat/Photo Researchers, ©Aleksander Bolbot; **132** ©Lee D. Simon/Photo Researchers; **133** ©Dr. L. Caro/Photo Researchers; **134** ©Jamie Steffens; **135** (l-r) ©M. I. Walker/Photo Researchers, ©Jeff Rotman/Photo Researchers, ©Daniel Puleo/Wikipedia; **136** ©Wilm van Egmond/Getty Images; **137** (tr) ©Michael Abbey/Photo Researchers, (br) ©Michael Abbey/Science Photo Library; **139** (t) ©Paul Whitted, (b) ©Dee Breger/Photo Researchers; **140** ©PHOTOTAKE Inc./Alamy; **141** (t, l-r) ©2005 GettyImages, ©Visual&Written SL/Alamy, ©Steven P. Lynch, (b, l-r) ©M. I. Walker/Photo Researchers, ©John Walsh/Photo Researchers, ©Andrew J. Martinez/Photo Researchers; **142** ©Jackson Vereen/Cole Group/Getty Images; **143** (t) ©Eric Guinther/Wikipedia, (b) ©Bill Banaszewski/Visuals Unlimited; **144** ©Nigel Cattlin/Holt Studios International/Science Photo Library; **145** ©Courtesy of the General Research Division, the New York Public Library, Astor, Lenox and Tilden Foundations; **146** (t) ©Steve McWilliam, (b) ©Photolink/Getty Images; **147** (l) ©SPL/Photo Researchers, (r) ©Michael & Patricia Fogden/Corbis; **148** (l-r) ©David Toase/Getty Images, ©Bryan Eastham, ©Aleksandra, ©Emily Keegin/fStop/Getty Images; **149** (t-b) ©Tomas Bogner, ©fotosav (Victor & Katya), ©Digital Vision/Getty Images; **151** ©Tomas Bogner; **152** ©Stephen Ausmus/www.ars.usda.gov; **153** ©Rubberball Productions; **154** (t-b) ©Ron Nichols, USDA Natural Resources Conservation Service, ©Jeff Foott/Getty Images, ©Leo; **155** (l) ©Sarah Scott, (r) ©Ei Katsumata/Alamy; **156** (t) ©Comstock/Jupiter Images, (b) ©Royalty-Free/Corbis; **157** (l) ©Maria & Bruno Petriglia/Photo Researchers, (r) ©Louie Schoeman; **158** (l-r) ©Steven P. Lynch, ©Dr. Jeremy Burgess/Photo Researchers, (r) ©Royalty-Free/Corbis; **159** (t-b) ©Dubrovskiy Sergey Vladimirovic, ©Bruce Heinemann/Getty Images, ©Bob Gibbons/Photo Researchers; **160** ©Stapleton Collection/Corbis; **161** ©Heather Barr; **163** (l) ©Maryann Frazier/Photo Researchers, (r) ©Nigel Cattlin/Photo Researchers; **164** (t-b) ©Ivaschenko Roman, ©Kate Tilmouth, ©Zastavkin; **165** ©Maxine Adcock/Photo Researchers; **166** ©Leo; **168** ©Aaron Beernaert; **170** ©Steven P. Lynch; **171** ©Bruce Coleman Inc./Alamy; **172** ©Michael P. Gadomski/Photo Researchers; **173** ©amana images/Getty Images (i)©John W. Bova/Photo Researchers; **174** (t) ©Dennis Purse/Photo Researchers, (b) ©iStockphoto.com/chepatchet; **175** ©Biophoto Associates/Photo Researchers; **176** (t) ©Reg Morrison/Auscape/Minden Pictures, (m) ©Frank Lane Picture Agency/Corbis, (bl)Lisa McDonald, (br) ©Wayne Atkinson c/o p.taihaku@googlemail.com; **177** (t) ©Joseph Malcolm Smith/Photo Researchers, (i) ©Charlotte Erpenbeck/Shutterstock, (bl) ©Michael Grube, (br) ©Rod Planck/Photo Researchers; **178** ©Charlie Ott/Photo Researchers; **180** ©InsideOutPix/Corbis; **182** (l) ©Hannamariah, (r) ©PhotoLink/Getty Images; **183** (t-b) ©Dr. Jeremy Burgess/Photo Researchers, ©Dr. Merlin D. Tuttle/Photo Researchers, ©Michael_Patricia Fogden/Minden Pictures; **184** ©Charlotte Erpenbeck/Shutterstock; **186** ©Adeline Lim, (i) ©Craig Churchill/Alamy; **187** (l) ©John Kaprielian/Photo Researchers, (r) ©suravid; **188** (t) ©Frances Twitty, (b) ©E. R. Degginger/Photo Researchers; **189** (t) ©paradoks_blizanaca, (b) ©Nigel Cattlin/Photo Researchers; **191** (l) ©The McGraw-Hill Companies/Al Telser, Photographer, (r) ©Biophoto Associates/Photo Researchers; **192** (l) ©Muriel Lasure, (r) ©zastavkin; **193** (tl) ©BSIP/Photo Researchers, (tr) ©Alan L. Detrick/Photo Researchers, (m) ©Norman Tomalin/Alamy, (b) ©The McGraw-Hill Companies/Al Telser, photographer; **195** (t) ©Steven P. Lynch, (b) Brand X Pictures/PunchStock; **196** (l, b-t) ©Mark A. Schneider/Photo Researchers, ©Andrzej Tokarski, ©Melba Photo Agency/PunchStock, (tr) ©Sheila Terry/Photo Researchers, (br) ©Ilya D. Gridnev; **197** (tl) ©Royalty-Free/Corbis, (tr) ©Stockdisc/PunchStock, (bl) ©Science Source/Photo Researchers; **199** (r, t-b) ©Brand X Pictures/PunchStock, ©Jacques Jangoux/Alamy, ©Comstock/PunchStock, (bl) ©iStockphoto.com/Vickie Sichau, (br) ©chai kian shin; **200** (t) ©Dr. Jeremy Burgess/Photo Researchers, (b) ©blickwinkel/Alamy; **201** (t) ©The McGraw-Hill Companies/Ken Cavanagh, (b) ©Siede Preis/Getty Images; **202** ©Jean D'Alembert/Wikipedia; **205** ©Brand X Pictures/PunchStock; **206** (t) ©Royalty-Free/Corbis, (b) ©Scott Bauer; **207** (t) ©Martin Rogers/Getty Images, (b) ©Danny E. Hooks; **208** (t) ©Comstock Images/PictureQuest, (l) ©Travis Klein, (r) ©Creatas/PunchStock, (b) ©Jeremy Woodhouse/Getty Images; **209** (l-r) ©Comstock Images/PictureQuest, ©Medioimages/PunchStock, ©Chee-

Onn Leong; **210** (l-r) ©Creatas/PunchStock, ©Diane R. Nelson, ©PhotoAlto/PunchStock, ©BrandXPictures/PunchStock; **212** (l-r) ©Mary Hollinger/NOAA Photo Library, ©Andrew J. Martinez/Photo Researchers, ©ImageState/PunchStock; **213** ©Kenneth M. Highfill/Photo Researchers; **214** (l-r) ©Robert Simon, ©Eugene Buchko, ©Sinclair Stammers/ Photo Researchers; **215** ©Royalty-Free/Corbis; **216** (l-r) ©Michael Abbey/Photo Researchers, ©Volker Steger/Photo Researchers, ©Science Source; **217** (l-r) ©Dr. Daniel Snyder/Getty Images, ©CNRI/Photo Researchers, ©Science Source, (m) ©Joel Mills/Wikipedia; **218** (t) ©www.j-photo.co.uk/ iStockphoto, (b) ©Chris Schuster/Wikipedia; **219** (t) ©Digital Vision/Getty Images, (b) ©Daniel Gustavsson; **220** (t, l-r) ©Ihoko Saito/Toshiyuki Tajima/Getty Images, ©Royalty-Free/Corbis, ©Joy M. Prescott, (b) ©Anyka; **221** (t) ©Rena Schild/iStockphoto, (m) ©Nicola Keegan, (b) ©Michael Aw/Photodisc/GettyImages; **222** ©Michael Aw/Photodisc/GettyImages; **224** (t) ©Digital Vision Ltd., (m) ©David Fleetham/Alamy; **225** (t) ©Siede Preis/Getty Images, (b) ©Design Pics Inc./Alamy; **226** (t, l-r) ©Naude, ©Goodshoot/Alamy, ©Courtesy of the Center for Disease Control, (m) ©Centers for Disease Control, (b) ©S. Camazine/K. Visscher/Photo Researchers; **227** (t) ©Mark Smith/Photo Researchers, (bl) ©Courtesy of the Center for Disease Control, (br) ©Sebastian Kaulitzki; **228** (t, l-r) ©Roger Tidman/Corbis, ©Image100/PunchStock, ©Stuart Elflett, (bl) ©Susan D. Gerhart/FWC, (br) ©Ievgeniia Tikhonova; **229** (t) ©Jupiterimages/Photos.com, (b) ©Jason Poston; **230** (t, l-r) ©CoverStock, ©coko, ©Creatas/PunchStock, (b, l-r) ©Pali A/Fotolia, ©Perennou Nuridsany/Photo Researchers, ©John Foxx/Getty Images; **231** ©Firoooz/Wikipedia; **232** (b, l-r) ©Ken Cavanagh, Photographer, ©Creatas/PunchStock, ©Michael Pettigrew; **233** (l-r) ©WildPictures/Alamy, ©Scott Camazine/Photo Researchers, ©Andre Nantel, (b) ©Associated Press; **234** (l-r) ©iStockphoto.com/BMPix, ©Joy Stein, ©Thomas Mounsey, (t-b) Alan & Linda Detrick/Photo Researchers, ©Bruce MacQueen, ©Courtesy of the Center for Disease Control; **235** (l-r) ©ImageState/PunchStock, ©Knstudios-Fotolia, ©Diane R. Nelson, (b) ©Nature Picture Library/ Alamy; **236** ©F. Stuart Westmorland/Photo Researchers; **237** (t) ©Diane R. Nelson, (m) ©David Wrobel/Getty Images, (bl) ©Lynsey Allan, (br) ©Dann Blackwood & Page Valentine, USGS; **238** ©Centers for Disease Control; **240** (l) ©ITStock/PunchStock, (r) ©Digital Vision Ltd.; **241** (t) ©Ian Cartwright/Getty Images, (b) ©Norbert Wu/Getty Images; **242** (tl) ©PhotoLink/Getty Images, (tr) ©University of Edinburgh, (b) ©Nicholas Rjabow/Fotolia.com; **244** (l) ©Digital Vision/Getty Images, (bl) ©Jacana/Photo Researchers, (br) Tom McHugh/Photo Researchers; **245** (tr) ©Royalty-Free/Corbis, (m) ©Nicola Vernizzi, (bl) ©Georgette Douwma/Getty Images, (br) ©Wernher Krutein/Photovault; **246** (l) ©Tom McHugh/Photo Researchers, (r) ©Tom McHugh/Photo Researchers, (b, l-r) ©Shannon Rankin, NMFS, SWFSC, ©Wally Eberhart/Getty Images (br) ©kristian; **247** (t) ©Darryl Torckler/Getty Images; **248** (t-b) ©Gilles DeCruyenaere, ©Charles H. Smith/USFWS, ©Carsten Reisinger/ Shutterstock, Inc.; **249** (t, l-r) ©Michael & Patricia Fogden/Corbis, ©Suzanne L. Collins/Photo Researchers, ©Brand X Pictures/PunchStock; (b) ©Mark Smith/Photo Researchers; **250** (l, t-b) ©Sebastian Duda, ©Patrick Coin/Wikipedia, ©Darren Green/PhotoSpin, (br) ©Stephen Dalton/Photo Researchers; **251** ©Papilio/Alamy; **252** ©Vova Pomortzeff; **253** (l) ©Arnold John Labrentz, (r) ©Dave Pape/Wikipedia, (bl) ©L.A. Dawson/Wikipedia, (br) ©BrandXPictures/PunchStock; **254** (tl, tr) ©Rodney Cammauf/Ntl. Park Service, (m) ©Anup Shah/Getty Images; **255** (t, l-r) ©Frank & Joyce Burek/Getty Images, ©Danny Reed, (r, t-b) ©Cody Campbell/Wikipedia, ©John Bell, ©Volker Steger/Photo Researchers; **256** ©Sebastian Duda; **258** (l-r) ©Comstock/PunchStock, ©Frank Leung, ©Anup Shah/Photodisc/Getty Images; **259** (l-r) ©Kristine Slipson, ©Brand X Pictures/PunchStock, ©Patrick Blake/Alamy; **260** (t) ©E. R. Degginger/Photo Researchers, (m) ©Creatas/PunchStock; **262** (l-r) ©kristian, ©Digital Vision/PunchStock, ©Tom McHugh/Photo Researchers, (t-b) ©Jeremy Woodhouse/Getty Images, ©Image/Source/PunchStock, ©Krissy VanAlstyne; **263** ©FloridaStock; **265** ©John Gourlay; **266** (l) ©PhotoLink/Getty Images, (r) ©Tom Brakefield/Getty Images; **267** (tr) ©Tom McHugh/Photo Researchers, (br) ©Phil Morley, (l-r) ©Royalty-Free/Corbis, ©Royalty-Free/Corbis, ©Neil Webster; **268** (l-r) ©David Tipling/Getty Images, ©Geostock/Getty Images, ©Simon Phipps, (tl) ©Photodisc Collection/Getty Images, (bl) ©Worldwide Picture Library/Alamy; **269** (t-b) ©Norma G. Chambers, ©U.S. Fish & Wildlife Service/ Galen Rathbun, ©Creatas/PunchStock, (b, l-r) ©Tracie Jibbens/Fotolia, ©Creatas/PunchStock, ©Digital Vision/PunchStock; **271** (t) ©Jerome Whitingham, (b) ©Gerald Hinde/Getty Images; **272** (l) ©Georgette Douwma/Getty Images, (r) ©Royalty-Free/Corbis, (b) ©Robert C. Hermes/Photo Researchers; **273** (t-b) ©Time & Life Pictures/Getty Images, ©Geoff Kuchera, ©Digital Vision, ©Digital Vision/Getty Images; **275** ©FloridaStock; **276** (t) ©Creatas/PunchStock, (b) ©Paul A. Souders/ Corbis; **277** (t) ©david kerkhoff and ©Paul Cowan, (b) ©George Lepp/Getty Images; **278** (t-b) ©Alan and Sandy Carey/Getty Images, ©Jeremy Woodhouse/Getty Images, ©imageshop/PunchStock; **279** ©PhotoAlto/PunchStock; **280** (l-r) ©Serg64, ©Brand X Pictures/PunchStock, ©Digital Vision/PunchStock, ©Dmitry Kosterev, ©The Garden Picture Library/Alamy, (b) ©BLM Colorado; **282** (t) ©David Muench/Corbis, (i) ©Dewitt, (m) ©Creatas/PunchStock, (i) ©Aron Brand; **289** (l-r) ©USFS Mount St. Helens National Volcanic Monument, (r) ©Westend61/Alamy; **291** (t) ©Ron Nielbrugge/www.wildnatureimages.com, (l-r) ©Comstock Images/Alamy, ©Courtesy USDA/NRCS, photo by Lynn Betts, ©Associated Press; **292** ©Alan and Sandy Carey/Getty Images; **294** ©Photodisc/Getty Images; **297** ©Robert Glusic/ Getty Images; **298** (l) ©vera bogaerts, (i) ©U.S. Fish & Wildlife Service/Jo Keller, (r) ©Pavel Filatov/Alamy, (i) ©PhotoLink/Getty Images; **299** (tr) ©Steven P. Lynch, (i) ©Comstock/PhotoStock, (bl) ©Digital Vision/Getty Images, (i) ©Jamie Wilson; **300** ©NorthGeorgiaMedia; **302** (t) ©EcoPrint, (i) ©Fotolia; **304** (l-r) ©Vermont NRCS, ©Tony Campbell, ©Dynamic Graphics Group/Creatas/Alamy; **305** (t-b) ©Ken Usami/Getty Images, ©Asther Lau Choon Siew, ©Medioimages/PunchStock, (m) ©OAR/National Undersea Research Program (NURP), College of William and Mary; **306** ©Jamie Wilson; **308** ©Paul Springett/Alamy; **309** ©Andrei Nedrassov; **310** (t) ©Daniel Hebert, (b) ©PhotoStockFile/Alamy; **313** ©pdphoto.org; **314** (t) ©Ian Scott, (b) ©blickwinkel/Alamy; **315** ©Biophoto Associates/Photo Researchers; **316** ©Kevin Schafer/Getty Images; **317** ©Jennifer Foeller; **318** (t) ©Javier Pedreira/Wikipedia, (b) ©Herbert A "Joe" Pase III/Texas Forest Service; **321** (t) ©Digital Zoo/ Getty Images, (b) ©Courtesy of the NASA Mississippi Dead Zone; **322** ©Kent Knudson/PhotoLink/Getty Images; **323** ©Comstock/JupiterImages; **324** ©pdphoto.org; **325** ©Courtesty of the Center for Disease Control; **326** (tl) ©Science Source, (tr) ©Royalty-Free/Corbis, (b) ©blickwinkel/Alamy; **327** (t) ©Geostock/Getty Images, (b) ©Norbert Wu/Getty Images; **328** ©Don Smetzer/Alamy; **329** ©Wally McNamee/Corbis; **330** ©Michael Ventura/PhotoEdit; **331** (t) ©Visuals Unlimited/Corbis, (b) ©Dr. Cecil H. Fox/Photo Researchers; **332** (tl, tr, bl) ©The McGraw-Hill Companies/Al Telser, photographer, (br) ©Astrid & Hanns-Frieder Michler/Photo Researchers; **333** (l) ©The McGraw-Hill Companies/Photo and dissection by Christine Eckel, (r) ©Anatomical Travelogue/Photo Researchers; **334** (l-r) ©Aaron Haupt, ©John Serro/Visuals Unlimited, ©Digital Stock, and ©Geoff Butler; **336** (l) ©Comstock/PunchStock, (r) ©Rubberball Productions/Getty Images; **337** ©BananaStock/PictureQuest; **338** ©BrandXPictures/PunchStock; **339** (t) ©Tom Smart/Deseret Morning News, (b) ©NU; **344** ©Scott Bodell/Getty Images; **345** (l-r) ©Innerspace Imaging/Photo Researchers, ©SPL/Photo Researchers, ©Innerspace Imaging/Photo Researchers; **349** ©Digital Stock; **350** ©BrandXPictures/PunchStock, (i) ©Diane R. Nelson; **355** ©Articulate Graphics/Custom Medical Stock Photo; **356** (t) ©Alfred Pasieka/Photo Researchers, (b) ©Russel Kightley/Photo Researchers; **357** Aaron Haupt; **360** ©SPL/Photo Researchers; **361** (t) ©CNRI/Photo Researchers, (b) ©David M. Phillips/Photo Researchers; **363** ©Steve Gschmeissner/Science Photo Library; **368** ©English School/Getty Images; **373** ©Steve Gschmeissner/Science Photo Library; **374** ©BrandXPictures/PunchStock, **375** (t) ©Nina Shannon, (b) ©Copyright 1997 IMS Communications Ltd/Capstone Design; **376** (t-b) ©Burke Triolo Productions/Getty Images, ©Pixtal/Superstock, ©Copyright 1997 IMS Communications Ltd/Capstone Design, ©John A. Rizzo/Getty Images, (bl) ©Vincent Giordano, (br) ©C Squared Studios/Getty Images; **379** ©USDA.gov; **380** ©Geoff Butler; **385** (l, r) ©Steve Gschmeissner/Photo Researchers, (m) ©Royalty-Free/Corbis; **386** (l) ©Kevin Dodge/Corbis, (r) ©Kameel4u, (bl) ©Biophoto Associates/Photo Researchers; **387** ©Eye of Science/Photo Researchers; **388** ©Dr. Jeremy Burgess/Science Photo Library; **389** ©Royalty-Free/Corbis; **390** ©Jim Jurica; **391** ©Edward Kinsman/Photo Researchers; **392** ©Visuals Unlimited/Corbis; **396** ©Burke Triolo Productions/Getty Images; **398** ©Michael Newman/Photo Edit; **399** ©Shawn Pecor; **403** ©Jim Wehtje/Getty Images; **407** ©Purestock/PunchStock; **409** (t) ©SPL/Photo Reserachers, (b) ©BrandXPictures/PunchStock; **417** ©Jim Wehtje/Getty Images; **418** (l, r) ©BrandXPictures/PunchStock; **419** ©David M. Phillips/Photo Researchers; **420** ©Phanie/Photo Researchers; **423** (t) ©David M. Phillips/Photo Researchers, (b) ©Claude Edelmann/Photo Researchers; **424** ©National Museum of Health and Medicine; **428** ©KS Studios; **429** (t, b) ©Ryan McVay/Getty Images; **430** ©KS Studios; **432** ©SPL/Photo Reserachers; **433** ©Christine Glade; **434** ©Patrick Dugan; **435** (l-r) ©Dr. Linda Stannard, UCT/Photo Researchers, ©EM Unit, University of Southampton/Photo Researchers, ©Oliver Meckes/Nicole Ottawa/Photo Researchers, ©David Scharf/Photo Researchers; **436** (t) ©Rafal Jurkowski, (b) ©2003 Getty Images; **438** ©Custom Medical Stock Photo; **439** ©David Chapman/Alamy; **440** ©Michael Gilles/Photo Researchers; **443** ©Jean Pierre Aim Harerimana/Reuters/ Corbis; **444** ©PhotoLink/Getty Images; **447** © Dr. Linda Stannard, UCT/Photo Researchers; **448** ©Michael Newman/Photo Edit; **449** ©Creatas/PictureQuest; **450** ©usda.gov; **451** (l) ©Adam Gault/Getty Images, (r) ©Royalty-Free/Corbis; **452** ©Royalty-Free/Corbis; **453** (l) ©Comstock/alamy, (r) ©Bubbles Photolibrary/Alamy, (b) ©Royalty-Free/Corbis; **454** (l) ©Photodisc Collection/Getty Images, (r) ©Comstock/Alamy; **457** ©Arthur Glauberman/Photo Researchers; **459** ©usda.gov; **460** (t) ©Sam Ogden/Photo Researchers, (b) ©BrandXPictures/PunchStock; **461** ©Moredun Animal Health Ltd/Photo Researchers

The editor has made every effort to trace the ownership of all copyrighted material and to secure the necessary permissions. Should there be a question regarding the use of any material, regret is hereby expressed for such error. Upon notification of any such oversight, proper acknowledgement will be made in future editions.

(t) top, (b) bottom, (l) left, (r) right, (m) middle, (i) inset

Lab Materials List

This table of lab equipment and materials can help you prepare for your physical science classes for the years. Quantities listed for the labs are per year and based on a class size of 30 students.

Need class supply on hand: balance scales, beakers, Bunsen burners, cardboard, clock or timer, clear vases, compound light microscopes, construction paper, containers, cotton swabs, coverslips, cups, detergent, disinfectant, disposable gloves, dissecting supplies, glass jars, glass pans, glass slides, glass stirring rods, glue, goggles, graduated cylinders, hard lenses, index cards, knives, lab aprons, labels, magnifying lenses, markers (felt and china), masking tape, measuring cups, medicine droppers, metric rulers/metersticks, microscope slides, microwave, overhead projector, paper clips, paper towels, pencils, petri dishes, plastic utensils, refrigerator, rubber bands, scalpels, scissors, soap, staplers, stopwatches/timers, straight pins, straws, string, tape, test tube brushes, test tube holders, test tube racks, test tubes, thermometers, tongs, toothpicks, triple-beam balance, water, weighing paper, white paper

Material	Labs	Amount Per Class*
Adult mealworms	13C	8 sets
Alcohol	24C	200 mL
Ammonia	17B	200 mL
Antibacterial soap	7C	1 container
Apple juice	21C	500 mL
Apples	22B, 24B	16
Arthropods and echinoderms	13A	8 sets
Assorted dried fruits	11A	40
Assorted fresh fruits and vegetables	2C, 11A	1 can orange slices or 25 grapes (2C), 40 (11A)
Assorted pictures or samples of living and nonliving objects	2A	10
Bacteria cultures	24A	50 mL
Bactine or similar antiseptic	24C	200 mL
Baking powder	6C	24 g
Baking soda	6C, 17C	34g
Balloons (round)	8B, 20C	70
Banana	4A	1
Beef broth	21C	500 mL
Benedict's solution	21B, 21C	200 mL
Biuret solution	21C	100 mL
Black paper squares	18B	240
Blindfolds	22B	8
Brown paper rectangles	2B	40
Buttons	17C	75
Canned beet slices	7C	15
Can opener	7C	1
Carnations (white)	10A	8
Carrots	22B	8
Carrot juice	21C, 25B	1.75 L
Ceramic plates (small)	25C	8
Chicken muscles on glass slides	19B	24 samples
Chicken wings	19C	8
Clay (colored)	17B	2 lbs
Clear plastic tubing	12C	8 (7.5 cm), 8 (15 cm)
Clear sugar syrup	3C	5 L
Clear vases or beakers	10A	16
Coffee, caffeinated and decaffeinated	1C	240 mL ea.
Coffee filters	4A	10
Coffee maker	1C	1
Cola	17C	50 mL
Cold alcohol	4A	150 mL
Copies of Sequence Table 1 (TE, Lab 18A)	18A	8
Corn syrup	3C, 23B	3 L
Cornstarch	3A, 6C, 25B	72g
Corrugated cardboard, 20 x 10 pieces	9C	8
Cutting boards	19C	8
Daphnia in water	20B	8 samples
Dissecting scissors	14C	8 pairs
Distilled water	3C, 9A, 17C, 24C, 25B, 25C	10.1 L
Dry powdered yeast	8B	16mL
Earthworms (live)	12B	10
Eggs (shells dissolved)	23B	8
Elodea	3B, 9A, 9B	1 plant
Envelopes containing letters of the alphabet	12A	15
Extraction buffer	4A	750 mL
Fibers from non-animal source	15C	16
Fish specimen, preserved	14A	8
Fish-shaped crackers	18C	8 packages
Flashlights	12B	15
Flowers	10B	35
Foam cores	21B	8
Food coloring	1A, 10A, 12C, 23B	1 bottle each of four colors
Food samples	2B	5 different foods
Forceps (or tweezers)	3B, 5A, 9B, 10B, 10C, 15C, 17C, 24C	10 pairs
Fresh apple or potato slices	13C	4 apples or potatoes, thinly sliced to yield 20 slices each
Fresh eggs in shells	3C	8
Fresh pineapple	1	2C
Frog or toad specimens, preserved	14A	8
Frogs, preserved	14C	8
Gelatin	2C	8 packages
Glass-disposal buckets	10C	10
Grapefruit juice	25B	550 mL
Graph paper	5B, 5C, 14B	80 pieces
Grasshoppers (live)	13B	8
Green onion leaf (leek)	11B	15
Hand sanitizer	7C	1 container
Honey locust seeds	11C	160
Hot plate	11C	
Household cement (clear, multi-purpose)	2A	1 tube
Hydrogen peroxide	24B, 24C	90 mL
Incubator (for test tubes)	24C	1
Iodine	2B, 8A, 19B	90 mL
Isotonic solution	23B	6.5 L
Jicamas	22B	8
Lamps (40-watt)	9A	8
Large carrots	24C	8
Large marshmallows	25C	16
Larval mealworms	13C	8 sets
Lemon juice	17C	50 mL
Lens paper	10B	10 sheets
Lettuce	13B	1 head
Lima beans	24A	1 package
Liquid detergent	1A, 4A	1 bottle
Liquid fertilizer	8C	168 mL
Live, mature fern samples	10C	10
Live, mature moss samples	10C	10
Lugol's solution	3A, 3B, 9B, 21B, 21C	1.055 L
Lysol (or similar cleaner)	24C	70 mL
Matches	25C	1 box

Suppliers

Carolina Biological Supply Company, Burlington, NC 27215
www.carolina.com

Delta Education, Nashua, NH, 03061
www.deltaeducation.com

Edmund Scientific Co., Barrington, NJ 08007
www.scientificsonline.com

Flinn Scientific, Inc., Batavia, IL, 60510
www.flinnsci.com

Frey Scientific, Mansfield, OH, 44903
www.freyscientific.com

Learning Things, Inc., St. Petersburg, FL, 33711
www.learningthings.us

National Science Resources Center, Washington, DC, 20024
www.nsrconline.org

Parco Scientific Co., Vienna, OH, 44473
www.parcoscientific.com

Science Kit, Inc., Tonawanda, NY, 14150
http://sciencekit.com

Ward's Natural Science Establishment, Inc., Rochester, NY, 14603
www.wardsci.com

Material	Labs	Amount Per Class*
Mealworm eggs	13C	8 sets
Mealworm larvae	13C	8 sets
Meat tenderizer	4A	1 container
Metal washers	20C, 22A	15
Methylene blue	7A	1 container
Microscope slides with depression wells	20B, 23C, 24A	40
Mixed protist culture or pond water	8A	7 samples
Mixing bowls	2C	8
Mouthwash	24C	70 mL
Narrow-necked plastic bottles (small)	8B	40
Newspaper	5A, 18B	16 sheets
Nutrition label for each juice	25B	8 copies
Nutritional data for marshmallows	25C	8 copies
Oatmeal	13C	1 18-oz container
Okra seeds	11C	160
Old pictures of town	16B	15
Onions	9B	8
Orange juice	25B	600 mL
Paper cups	2B, 21A, 21B, 21C, 22B, 24B, 24C, 25B	96 (small), 71 (large)
Peanuts (unshelled)	1B	300
Petroleum jelly	20B	1 container
pH paper and chart	17C	300 pieces
Pictures of different school parking lots showing cracks in pavement, grass, cars, signs, people, etc	16A	24
Pill bugs	15B	48
Pineapple, canned	2C	1 large can
Pins	17B	100
Pinto beans	5B	150
Pipettes, 2-mL	24C	8
Plastic bottles	20C, 21A	38 (1L), 8 (2L)
Plastic cups	1C, 6C	88
Plastic sandwich bags	3A, 9C, 11C, 16C	54
Plastic straws	8B, 18C	70
Plastic wrap	2C	1 package
Plastic/paper bowls	18C, 19A	10
Pond water	8C, 17C	100 mL
Poster boards	21A, 22C	3
Potassium chloride solution (0.5 M)	23C	1–2 mL
Potato peelers	22B	8
Potatoes	22B	8
Powdered chalk	6C	24 g
Powdered sugar	6C	24 g
Prepared slides of "colored threads"	3B	30
Prepared slides of "letter e"	3B	30
Prepared slides of blood smears	20A	8
Pupal mealworms	13C	8 sets
Rabbit cards	5C	200
Reptile specimens, preserved	14A	8
Ring stand utility clamps	25C	8
Ring stands	25C	8
Rotten apple slices	24B	8
Rubber balls	19A	8
Rubber sheets, thin	20C	30
Rubber tubing	12C, 21A	200 cm (1.5 cm), 48 m (2.5 cm), 16m (6 cm), 8 pieces (15-cm long)
Salt	8B, 11B, 17B	464 mL
Salt water	17C	50 mL
Samples from an animal	15C	16
Samples from human	15C	16
Sandpaper	11B, 12B	23 pieces
Screws and bolts of differing sizes, head types, threading, and usage	6A	80 or more
Seawater infused with sea urchin eggs	23C	10mL
Seawater infused with sea urchin sperm	23C	10 mL
Seawater	23C	30 mL
Seeds (small)	16C	320
Skim milk	21C	500 mL
Small, flat applicators	20B	8
Soaked corn seeds	9C	32
Sodium bicarbonate (baking soda)	9A	1 box
Spark igniters	21B, 21C	8
Spot plates	17C	8
Spotted paper squares	18B	240
Spray bottles	16C	16
Sudan III solution	21C	40 mL
Sugar	8B	320 mL
Syringe	23C	1
Talcum powder	6C	24 g
Thermal gloves	11C	8
Tincture of iodine	25B	1mL
Tomato juice	25B	55 mL
Trash containers (suitable for disposing of test chemicals)	21C	3
Twist ties	3A, 20C	38
Unknown samples	15C	as follows: 16 from humans (8 samples should be from your suspect), and 16 that will match either an animal reference or non-animal reference source
Unpasteurized yogurt	7A	1 container
Vegetable oil	21C	1 bottle
Vegetable peelers	24C	8
Vinegar	6C, 19C, 23C, 24C	4 L
Vitamin C indicator	25B	480 mL
Water crackers	21B	8
Wax pencils	2B, 3C	8
White vinegar	3C, 16C	7.25 L
Whole milk	1A	1 L
Window cleaner	24C	200 mL

Chapter 1 Answer Key

Key Concept Review, p. 1

Part A: Life Science box: insects, plants, amoeba, animals, human body; Earth and Space Science box: air, land, solar system, water, weather; Physical Science box: light, sound, electricity, magnetism, motion

Part B: 1. The system of measurement used by scientists is the International System of Units, or SI.
2. An independent variable is the variable that is changed in an experiment. A dependent variable is the variable that is observed to find out if it changes.
3. The control group is the group in an experiment in which all variables are kept the same.
4. A hypothesis is a guess based on observations, previous knowledge, and research.

Science Extension The independent variables in this experiment are the nonwater liquids. The dependent variable is the plants' survival.

Vocabulary Review, p. 2

Part A: All answers are sample answers.
Volume: amount of space an object takes up; Density: amount of mass in a given volume; Mass: amount of matter in an object; Measurement: a quantity, dimension, or amount; Meniscus: the curve in the top surface of a liquid; Derived unit: a unit that consists of more than one base unit; International System of Units (SI): system of measurement used in most countries and in most sciences

Part B: Science; scientific method; observation; hypothesis; controlled experiment; variable; independent variable; dependent variable; data; experiment; hypothesis; theory

Science Extension Answers will vary but should reflect the content of the chapter.

Interpreting Diagrams, p. 3

Part A: 1. eyepieces; **2.** revolving nosepiece; **3.** high-power objectives; **4.** stage; **5.** diaphragm; **6.** light source; **7.** fine adjustment; **8.** coarse adjustment; **9.** low-power objective; **10.** arm

Part B: 11. eyepieces; **12.** revolving nosepiece; **13.** high-power objectives; **14.** coarse adjustment; **15.** stage; **16.** fine adjustment; **17.** diaphragm; **18.** light source; **19.** low-power objective

Science Extension Answers will vary but should reflect understanding of microscopes and the different branches of the life sciences.

Reading Comprehension, p. 4

Part A: Outlining 1. Observations; **2.** begins; **3.** testing; **4.** previous knowledge; **5.** Experiment; **6.** independent; **7.** Collecting; **8.** organize; **9.** hypothesis; **10.** repeat; **11.** theory

Part B: Comprehension

12. Sample answer: something that gives proof or a reason to believe
13. kilogram
14. It means the person focuses in one area of study. That person would have very specific knowledge important to that field or that area of study.
15. because they are always asking questions

Science Extension 1. the vials with the smoke-free fruit flies; **2.** The cigarette smoke; it's the variable that gets changed. **3.** That smoking is dangerous for the smoker as well as the smoker's offspring.

Curriculum Connection, p. 5

Part A: 1. Water has a density of 1.0; density = 1 gram/1 cm^3 = 1 gram/cm^3; **2.** 30.0 cm^3

Part B: 3. 1.83 m; **4.** 90.8 kg; **5.** 41.86 km; **6.** 10°C

Science Extension Ice floats because it is less dense than water. If students need a hint, talk about buoyancy and density. Accept all reasonable responses.

Science Challenge, p. 7

Part A: 1a. Hans and Zacharias Janssen, Robert Hooke, and Anton van Leeuwenhoek developed the first microscopes in the seventeenth century.
1b. Dissecting microscope: ~20 to 40×; Compound microscope: up to 1,000×; Electron microscope: *scanning* electron microscope—1,000× to 10,000×; *transmission* electron microscope—10,000 to 100,000×
1c. There are 1,000,000 micrometers in a meter.
1d. compound microscopes and electron microscopes

Part B: 2a. German Scientist Wilhelm Conrad Roentgen first documented X rays in 1895.
2b. X rays can also be used to view soft tissue. X rays are used to detect foreign objects; for example, coins, rings, or other metal that children and pets may have swallowed.
2c. Professionals taking X-ray photographs often leave the room X rays are taken in, wear protective garments with lead to shield them from X rays, and wear equipment that can monitor their exposure to X rays.

Part C: 3. X-ray computed tomography (CT) scans and positron-emission tomography (PET) scans can be used to visualize tissues. These scans can help identify tissue abnormalities, study metabolism, and diagnose disease. Another type of scans/technique students might come across is an ultrasound, which uses the reflection of sound wave vibrations to produce an image, most commonly of a fetus in the womb.

Part D: 4a. Student answers will vary.
4b. Student answers will vary. Generally, choose information that comes from trustworthy sources, such as government and university-managed sites and databases. Untrustworthy information might come from people or organizations hoping to make money or with other agendas.

Science Extension
Botany: microscopes, computers; Zoology: microscopes, computers; Genetics: microscopes, computers; Anatomy: microscopes, X rays, MRI, computers; Taxonomy: computers; Ecology: microscopes, computers; Microbiology: microscopes, computers; Medicine: microscopes, X rays, MRI, computers

Chapter 2 Answer Key

Key Concept Review, p. 9

Part A: Outlining

2.1: Characteristics of Living Things
- A. Living Things Are Made Up of Cells
- B. Living Things Respond to Their Environment
- C. Living Things Can Adapt
- D. Living Things Reproduce
- E. Living Things Grow and Develop

2.2: The Needs of Living Things
- A. Energy
- B. Water
- C. Temperature
- D. Air

2.3: Chemistry of Living Things
- A. Carbohydrates
- B. Lipids
- C. Proteins
- D. Nucleic Acids

Part B: Vocabulary 1. energy; **2.** autotrophs; **3.** nucleic acids
Science Extension
Student answers will vary.
Vocabulary Review, p. 10
Part A: 1. true; **2.** nucleic acid; **3.** Lipids; **4.** stimulus; **5.** true
Part B:
6. An ectotherm, such as a frog, takes on the temperature of its environment.
7. A stimulus is an event or condition that causes a response.
8. An organism is a living thing, such as a bat, an ant, or a human.
9. *Organic* refers to molecules with carbon, hydrogen, and oxygen atoms.
10. Nucleic acids store genetic material, two of which are DNA and RNA.
Science Extension
Answers will vary but should reflect an understanding of stimulus and response in organisms.
Interpreting Diagrams, p. 11
Part A: 1. rock, nonliving; **2.** water, nonliving; **3.** Sun: nonliving; **4.** tree, living; **5.** snake, living; **6.** soil, nonliving; **7.** frog, living; **8.** grasshopper, living; **9.** beetle, living; **10.** grass, living; **11.** bird, living; **12.** deer, living
Part B: Sample answers:
Organism: tree—Autotroph, Example: algae; **Organism:** grasshopper—Heterotroph, Ectotherm, Example: turtle; **Organism:** bird—Heterotroph, Endotherm, Example: monkey;
Organism: snake—Heterotroph, Ectotherm, Example: crocodile;
Organism: grass—Autotroph, Example: wheat
Science Extension
Diagrams will vary but should reflect the content of the chapter.
Reading Comprehension, p. 12
Part A: Answers will vary.
Part B: 1. Clarie's cell membranes might be compromised, her "insulation" might decrease, and the energy stored in the lipids from her regular diet would be lost.
2. Without proteins, chemical reactions and transport cannot occur in an organism, so the beetle will die.
3. If the amount of carbon dioxide in the air is lowered, the trees in the forest may not be able to undergo photosynthesis. This could cause the plants to become malnourished or even starve.
Science Extension
1. The most straightforward experiment is to poke it, hit the ground near it, to yell at it, shine a light on it, etc. to see if it responds. They should try a number of different things if it doesn't appear to respond right away. If that doesn't work, they should watch it from a distance in case it is not moving because it is responding to their presence.
2. Living things respond to their environments.
Curriculum Connection, p. 13
Part A: 1. lipids; **2.** nucleic acids; **3.** carbohydrates; **4.** proteins
Part B: 5. carbohydrates, fats, proteins, minerals, vitamins, and water;
6. Carbohydrates provide energy to the cells. **7.** glucose, fructose, or galactose; but not sucrose
Science Extension It does not matter if vitamin C is made from rose hips or from laboratory synthesis. Just like "a rose (hip) is a rose (hip)," $C_6H_8O_6$ is $C_6H_8O_6$.
Science Challenge, p. 14
Part A: 1. The living things are: the bird, insects, snake, frog, grass, shrubs, and trees. They meet all of the criteria for life—made of cells, respond to environment, can adapt, reproduce, grow and develop, and also use energy. Water, rocks, and the Sun are nonliving things. They do not meet all the criteria for life.
2. You could not tell if the objects were alive from a photo. A photo is one moment in time, which would not show if the criteria for life (i.e., response to the environment, development, energy use) are met.
Part B: 3. Answers will vary. Examples of various adaptations include webbed feet for swimming birds, different shapes of bird beaks ideal for cracking nuts or picking up fish/insects, and panda "thumbs" used for grasping bamboo. All land animals must be provided with their normal diet of food, water (unless they get water from a food source), space, clean air, and appropriate temperature.
Science Extension Answers will vary. Examples: amino acid supplements (such as lysine) are organic; mineral supplements such as calcium and iron are inorganic.

Chapter 3 Answer Key

Key Concept Review, p. 15
Part A: 1. 3, 1859; **2.** 2, 1745; **3.** 1, 1678
Part B: 4. mitochondria; **5.** Golgi apparatus; **6.** vacuole
Science Extension Answers will vary but should reflect the interconnectedness of two processes.
Vocabulary Review, p. 16
Part A: 4, 1, 2, 3
Part B: Sample answers are given.
chloroplast: where photosynthesis takes place—traps sunlight, converts to energy, stores as food; Plant
cytoplasm: part of cell outside the nucleus—contains organelles, chemicals, cytoskeleton; Both
endoplasmic reticulum: system of membranes and sacs, along which molecules move between parts of cells; Both
Golgi apparatus: a stack of membranes that modifies and packages proteins and other molecules; Both
lysosome: organelle filled with enzymes to digest organic molecules and old organelles; Animal
mitochondria: convert energy stored in food into compounds that the cell can use; Both
ribosome: the place where proteins are assembled according to instructions in DNA; Both
Science Extension Answers will vary but should reflect the content of the chapter.
Graphic Organizer, p. 17
Part A: Sample answers given. **1.** Living matter arises from nonliving matter; **2.** mice come from moldy grain; **3.** mud produces frogs; **4.** maggots come from rotting meat; **5.** experiment with chicken broth shows that microorganisms arise from nonliving matter; **6.** seals flask of chicken broth and removes air to show that microorganisms are in the air and do not arise from nonliving matter; **7.** Redi shows that maggots come from eggs that flies laid on meat; **8.** proves spontaneous generation does not exist; uses a flask with an S-shaped neck to prove that no microorganisms grow in the broth when air is removed and that they do grow in the broth when air is allowed to enter the flask.; **9.** Developed by Virchow: 1. All living things are made up of cells. 2. Cells are the basic units of structure in living things. 3. New cells are produced from existing cells.
Part B: 10. binary fission, prokaryotic cell; **11.** cell cycle, eukaryotic cell
Science Extension Answers will vary but should reflect an understanding of cells and their functions.
Reading Comprehension, p. 18
Part A: Ordering
1. food and oxygen → cell membrane → mitochondria → energy
2. large particles→ cell membrane→ cytoplasm → energy
3. food→ cell membrane → mitochondria→energy and alcohol
Part B: 4. ribosome; **5.** endoplasmic reticulum; **6.** vacuole
Science Extension
If the cell needs to move material against a concentration gradient, it will require energy. Without energy, only passive transport is possible.
Curriculum Connection, p. 19
Part A: 1. sunlight; **2.** carbon dioxide; **3.** water; **4.** glucose; **5.** carbohydrates
Part B: 6. carbon; **7.** oxygen; **8.** Fermentation, energy
Science Extension Answers will vary: Plants use photosynthesis to convert the Sun's light into chemical energy. Energy (sunlight) can change into matter

(organic compounds) and matter can change into energy during cellular respiration or fermentation. Some students may point out the balance of atoms before and after photosynthesis, to show that the Sun's energy becomes the cell's energy.

Science Challenge, p. 20

Part A: 1a. sunlight, carbon dioxide, and water; **1b.** Plants store the energy from sunlight when they use it to make sugar (glucose and other carbohydrates). Animals take these sugars in when they eat plants. Inside the cells of an animal's body, glucose is broken down to release energy by the process of cellular respiration

2. Check students' diagrams.

3. Check students' diagrams.

4. Since it is moving against its concentration gradient, it is moved via active transport.

5. Adipocytes store lipids for future energy use, muscle cells change shape to allow for body movement, sperm cells are used for reproduction and must travel to egg cells within a woman's body, and skin cells provide a protective layer of the body. Muscle and sperm cells need the most energy (for contraction and for movement), and are therefore likely to have the most mitochondria.

Part B: In hemodialysis, a patient's blood is pumped through a series of tubing and then back into his or her body. The tubing is in a salt solution with salt concentrations similar to those found in normal blood. The tubing is selectively permeable—it lets small molecules (waste products in the blood) move across. Because these waste materials are found in a higher concentration in the patient's blood than in the salt solution outside of the tubing, the wastes move down their concentration gradient, diffusing out of the blood through the tubing into the salt solution. (There is no source of energy to move substances across the tubing; active transport does not take place. All transport is passive.) A salt solution is used rather than pure water. If the tubing was placed in water alone, the water would move into the blood via osmosis.

Chapter 4 Answer Key

Key Concept Review, p. 22

Part A: 1. Each trait had a dominant allele and a recessive allele. **2.** A parent passes on at random only one allele for each trait to each offspring. **3.** The trait that an organism displays is called its phenotype.

Part B: There is a 75% chance that their child will be color blind.

Science Extension Students' answers will vary.

Vocabulary Review, p. 23

Part A: 1. Fertilization **2.** Pollination **3.** law of segregation **4.** inbreeding

Part B:

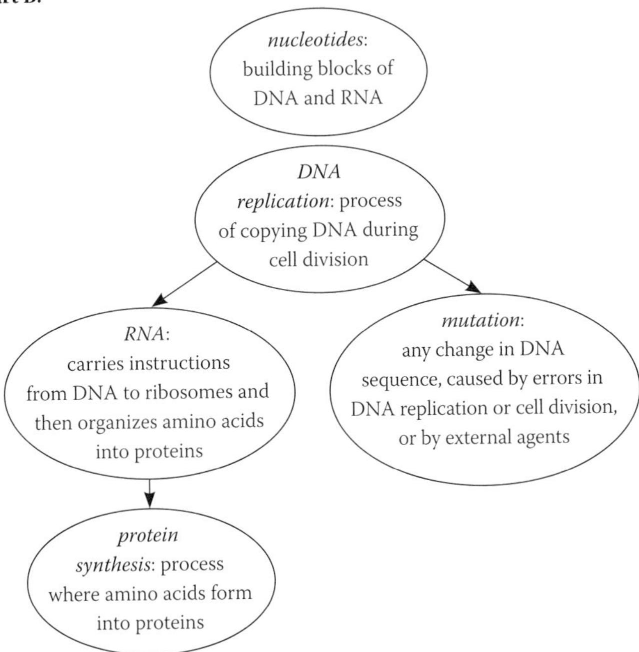

Science Extension Diagrams will vary.

Interpreting Diagrams, p. 24

Part A: Sample answers given for diagram labels. **1.** Alleles for a homozygous, dominant parent; genotype: *RR*; phenotype: red tomato **2.** Alleles for a homozygous, recessive parent; genotype: *rr*; phenotype: yellow tomato **3.** Offspring; heterozygous alleles; genotypes: *Rr*; phenotypes: red tomatoes since each offspring has a dominant allele.

4.

	R	*r*
R	*RR*	*Rr*
r	*Rr*	*rr*

Part B: 5. 0% **6.** *rr* **7.** *rr* and *rr*, *rr* and *Rr*, *or Rr* and *Rr*

Science Extension Diagrams will vary but should reflect understanding of heredity and how it can be changed.

Reading Comprehension, p. 25

Part A: 1. Using a Punnett square, the student can show that if the gene for white color is recessive and both the father and the mother are carriers of the recessive white gene, then 25% of the offspring will have both recessive genes and will be white. There is still a chance that they could have a white puppy even though they are practicing selective breeding. **2.** The student should explain that colorblindness is carried on the X chromosome. The girl could have received the trait from either her mother or father. However, a boy can only receive the trait from his mother. If no one else in their family has colorblindness, then most likely the girl and boy are related through their mother, who is a carrier. **Part B:** Sample answers: **3.** Organisms that are heterozygous have two different alleles for a certain trait; organisms that are homozygous have two of the same alleles for a certain trait. **4.** Mitosis is a form of cellular reproduction in which a non-gamete cell's nucleus divides. Meiosis is a form of cellular reproduction in which a gamete cell divides and produces two new cells with half the number of chromosomes as a body cell. **5.** DNA, or deoxyribonucleic acid, stores genetic information. RNA, or ribonucleic acid, translates the information stored by DNA and uses it to direct the production of proteins.

Science Extension

1. Since both parents are carriers and the trait is recessive, there will be a 25% chance that another child will receive both recessive genes and therefore have sickle-cell anemia.

2. There is a 25% chance that a child will receive both recessive genes. The percentage shows a probability only.

Curriculum Connection, p.26

Part A:

Normal Father: XY

Carrier Mother: X<u>X</u>

	X	Y
X	XX normal (female)	XY normal (male)
<u>X</u>	X<u>X</u> carrier (female)	<u>X</u>Y affected (male)

Part B: 1. She is a carrier. Affected males transmit, or pass on, the trait to all daughters. **2.** No. A son cannot inherit the X-linked recessive allele from his father. A son only inherits his father's Y chromosome.
Science Extension Answers will vary. Encourage students to share their writings. Remind them to use sound science.
Science Challenge, p. 27
Part A: 1.

	TP	*Tp*	*tP*	*tp*
TP	*TTPP*	*TTPp*	*TtPP*	*TtPp*
Tp	*TTPp*	*TTpp*	*TTPp*	*Ttpp*
tP	*TtPP*	*TtPp*	*ttPP*	*TtPp*
tp	*TtPp*	*Ttpp*	*ttPp*	*ttpp*

In the offspring generation, 9/16 of the plants are likely to be tall and purple, 3/16 are likely to be tall and white, 3/16 are likely to be short and purple, and 1/16 are likely to be short and white.
Part B: 2. TTGACGAGATCG **3.** TACATACGGAGGAACTTA **4.** methionine-tyrosine-alanine-serine-leucine-asparagine

Chapter 5 Answer Key

Key Concept Review, p. 29
Part A:
2; Neandertal
4; *Australopithecus africanus*
1; *Homo habilis*
3; Australopithecus afarensis
Part B: 5. They are very fast. **6.** Saguaro cactus **7.** Zebra; no two zebras have the same pattern of stripes.
Science Extension Answers will vary. Encourage students to share their writings.
Vocabulary Review, p. 30
Part A:
adaptation: traits that help an organism survive and reproduce; white rabbit fur in snowy environment
genetic diversity: type of variation in which individuals, except identical twins, have different gene sets; eye and hair color
mutation: variation produced when error occurs in DNA replication; can be helpful, harmful, or neutral; white tiger—harmful since white does not camouflage tiger
predator: organism that kills and eats another organism for food; hawk has keen eyesight to see prey
prey: organism that is eaten for food; skunk produces strong odor to keep predators away
Part B: 1. anthropologist **2.** true **3.** vestigial **4.** radioactive **5.** true
Science Extension Descriptions and answers will vary.
Graphic Organizer, p. 31
Part A: Sample answers given. **1.** Fossils **2.** Body structures **3.** Embryos **4.** Genetic material **5.** Fossil records, such as bones or teeth, show that an organism has changed over millions of years. **6.** homologous **7.** vestigial **8.** Embryos that have the same features, such as an eagle and a rhinoceros, evolved from a common ancestor. **9.** Comparisons of the sequence in amino acids in the DNA code show how closely organisms are related. **10.** Structures such as the forelimbs of birds, whales, and crocodiles have the same arrangement or function. **11.** Body parts, such as wisdom teeth, are no longer useful, but they would have been useful to an ancestor.
Part B: Sample answers given. **12.** Analogous structures have the same function but not the same structure; they do not show a common ancestor. Homologous structures are similar and may have the same function, indicating a common ancestor. **13.** Though fossils show similar bone structure to modern humans, DNA evidence shows they became extinct and did not evolve into *Homo sapiens*.
Science Extension Flow charts will vary but should reflect understanding of fossil formation.
Reading Comprehension, p. 32
Part A:
Concept webs will vary but should include the following information:
homologous structures
Definition: body parts that have the same arrangement and/or function and have the same evolutionary origin; characteristics: similar arrangement, similar function, same origin; example: the forelimb of a cat and the human arm
analogous structures
Definition: body parts that have similar functions but do not have a common evolutionary ancestor; characteristics: similar function, different origin; example: tail fin of a fish and a whale
vestigial structures
Definition: body parts that no longer serve their original purpose; characteristics: no function; example: human appendix
Part B: 1. Variation is the array of traits present within a species, while evolution is a change in the whole species over time. **2.** Relative dating involves determining the age from the layer of rock the fossil is located in. Radioactive dating involves measuring the rate of decay of radioactive elements present in the fossil. **3.** the internal organs, the fur, the skin, and anything else that is not bone **4.** A paleontologist studies the history of other living things besides humans.
Science Extension 1. The fire would have destroyed some of the oak trees, reducing the amount of food available to the mice. The mice population would have decreased if they couldn't adapt. If there are fewer mice, the hawk would have less food. **2.** Students' answers may vary. Sample answer: The mice could adapt to only come out of their holes at night.
Curriculum Connection, p. 33
Part B: 1. bipedal **2.** *Australopithecus afarensis* **3.** *Homo erectus* and *Homo neanderthalensis*
Science Extension
Students' answers will vary but should reflect an understanding of natural selection.
Science Challenge, p. 34
Part A: 1. Answers will vary. Examples of adaptations that students may find include flat teeth for grinding food in plant-eating dinosaurs or other animals and prey adaptations or protective coverings, which tend to fossilize better than soft tissues. **2.** Answers will vary. Many living organisms are evolutionarily related to fossil organisms. These relationships among organisms are determined by comparing anatomy (or in modern times by molecular analysis). **3.** Because the teeth of both types of meat-eaters should look similar, it would be very difficult to determine if an animal was a hunter or scavenger based on teeth alone. Comparing the extinct animal's body shape to other known hunters/scavengers using fossilized bones may provide more clues to its behavior. **4.** Prey adaptations of camouflage, mimicry, and warning colors will likely not show up in fossils. This is because the tissues that would show colors, such as skin and hair, tend to decay rather than become fossils. The predator adaptations of excellent vision and hearing and special senses (such as heat sensors) will also not likely be seen in the fossil record.
Part B: 5. Sample answer: This skeleton was found near the area where "Lucy" was found (the Hadar region of Ethiopia). It was discovered in 2000, in sandstone. The bones have been removed with care, using a dentist drill to prevent damaging them (not all are yet completely uncovered from sandstone). The date of the specimen was determined using *relative dating.* The material it was found in comes from the Hadar Formation, which spans the age of 3.31 to 3.35 million years ago.

This was a very significant discovery because it is the most complete fossil of *A. afarensis* and the most complete skeleton of an ancient child. The child's skull, teeth, shoulder blades, ribs and spinal column, foot and (parts of) leg bones, partial arm bones, finger bones, and hyoid bone (a bone found in the neck) have been recovered. ("Lucy's" skull was never recovered in its entirety—just some skull fragments and the jaw bone were recovered). It is estimated that the child was three years old when she died. The skull was compared with other skull parts from *A. afarensis* and *A. africanus* fossils. It more closely resembles *A. afarensis* and was assigned to that species.

Analysis of the skeleton indicates that the child could climb trees (shoulder blades are similar to young gorillas) and that she could walk on two legs. Comparing this skeleton to adult *A. afarensis* fossils will provide insight into how *A. afarensis* grew and developed. Since this skeleton is so complete, comparing it to other primates can also give information on primate evolution.

6. "Lucy" is 3.2 million years old, several thousand years younger than the child skeleton found near Dikika (3.3 million years old).

Chapter 6 Answer Key

Key Concept Review, p. 35

Part A:

Domains

Bacteria	Archaea	Eukarya
Eubacteria, unicellular	Archaebacteria, unicellular	Protista, both Fungi, both Plantae, multicellular Animalia, multicellular

Part B: 1. cell type, cell structures, number of cells, and method of obtaining nutrition **2.** physical and structural similarities **3.** a dichotomous key

Science Extension Answers will vary. Check students' responses.

Vocabulary Review, p. 36

Part A: 1. d **2.** c **3.** e **4.** a **5.** b

Part B: Word webs will vary but should show connections between the words and should include a definition or description.

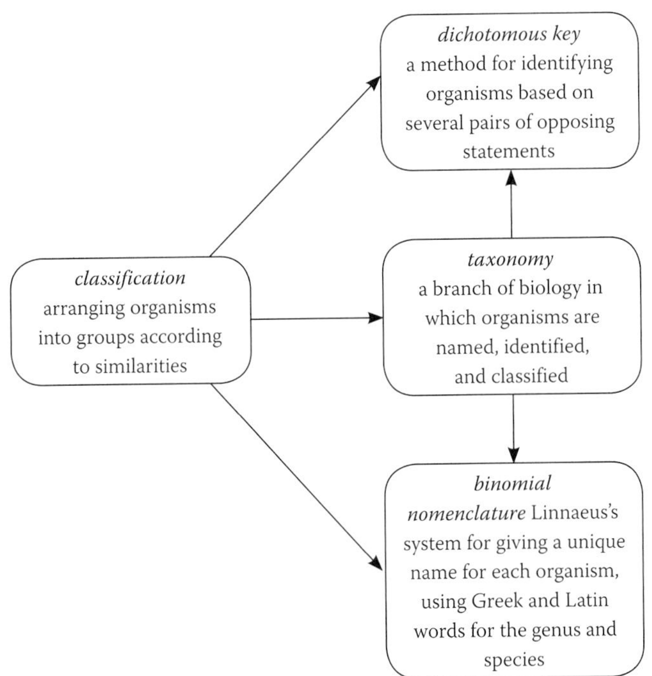

Science Extension

Answers will vary but should reflect understanding of the content of the chapter.

Graphic Organizer, p. 37

Part A: 1. Domain: Bacteria, Archaea, Eukarya **2.** Kingdom: Eubacteria, Archaebacteria, Protista, Fungi, Plantae, Animalia **3.** Phylum: Example: Chordata, which includes animals with a skeletal cord or column, such as bears, birds, humans, and dogs. **4.** Class: Example: Reptilia, which includes cold-blooded animals that have scales. **5.** Order: Example: mammals that eat meat are in the order Carnivora and those that eat insects are in the order Insectivora. **6.** Family: Example: cat family, Felidae, which includes animals that have whiskers and sharp claws, such as lions and cougars. **7.** Genus: Example: the genus *Felis*, includes all small cats, such as the housecat and wildcats **8.** Species: Example: *Felis domestica* includes all housecats

Part B: Lizard: no, yes, yes, no, yes, no; Mushrooms: no, yes, yes, no, yes, no; Oak tree: no, yes, yes, no, no, yes; Slime mold: yes, no, yes, no, yes, no; Bacteria: yes, no, no, yes, sometimes, sometimes

Science Extension

Dichotomous keys will vary but should reflect understanding of the chapter content.

Reading Comprehension, p. 38

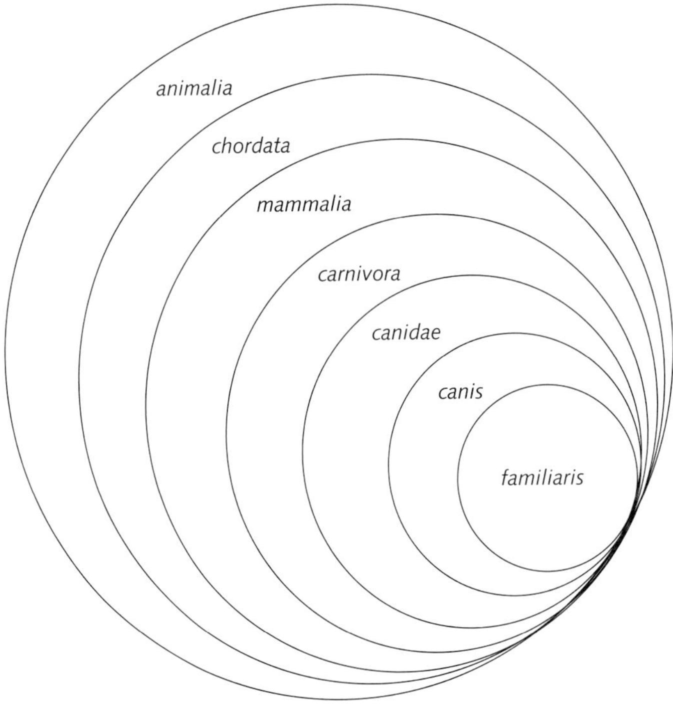

Part B: Student answers will vary.

Science Extension 1. whether it has a similar number or structure of chromosomes to a hawk or to an owl **2.** the level of *genus* **3.** Their eyes would be different. Their wings, feathers, and tails might be different because their flight during hunting would be different.

Curriculum Connection, p. 39

Part B: 1. Archaeopteryx **2.** Sinornis

Science Extension Answers will vary. Encourage students to share their writings.

Science Challenge, p. 40

Part A: 1. C **2.** A and B **3.** This is one example of what a student line diagram might look like:

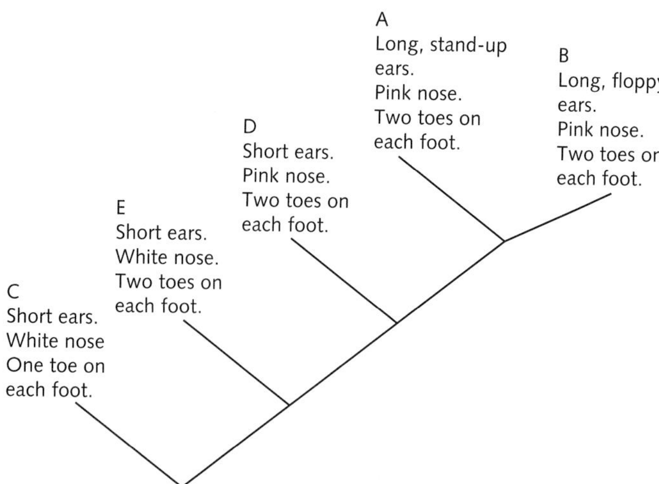

4. Student answers will vary.
Part B: 5. The cladogram and the original branch diagram won't look similar. Based on the characteristics shown in the table (ear type, nose type, number of toes on each foot), animals *A* and *B* seem most similar. However, with the DNA information, it appears that animal *A* may be more closely related to animal *D* than to animal *B*.

Chapter 7 Answer Key

Key Concept Review, p. 42
Part A: 1. They are not considered to be living things, because other than reproduction, they do not exhibit the characteristics of living things.
2. host cells **3.** They reproduce through binary fission or conjugation.
Part B: 4. sexual **5.** bacilli **6.** viruses
Science Extension Answers will vary; check students' paragraphs.
Vocabulary Review, p. 43
Part A: (top left box) Bacteria—Prokaryotic cells because they do not have membrane-bound nuclei or organelles; (bottom left box) Flagella—Whiplike structures extending from cell membrane that some bacteria use for movement; Types (one type per box from top to bottom): Cocci—Bacteria shaped like globes or spheres; Spirilla—Bacteria shaped like corkscrews or spirals; Bacilli—Bacteria shaped liked rods. Illustrations will vary, but should reflect understanding of the basic structure and shape of bacteria.
Part B: 1. lytic cycle **2.** host, lysogenic cycle **3.** virus, parasite
Science Extension Paragraphs will vary but should reflect chapter content.
Interpreting Diagrams, p. 44
Part A: a., e., f.: head, face, skin **b.**: mouth **c.**: stomach **d.**: intestines **a.**: armpits, feet
Part B: 1. Protein coat **2.** Nucleic acid **3.** Envelope
Science Extension Diagrams will vary but should reflect understanding of the chapter content.
Reading Comprehension, p. 45
Part A: Answers may include the following: **1.** They help make some of the food that we eat; they keep the environment clean. **2.** They can make humans sick; they can kill animals and plants that humans eat. **3.** There is plenty of food in the digestive track; they create warm environments with plenty of water and nutrients. **4.** Their immune systems kill bacteria; they clean their living areas to kill off bacteria living there.
Part B: Answers will vary.
Science Extension 1. They could ask if the children ate the food or touched the clothing that the scientist left. They could also find out if the children had any contact with the scientist. **2.** Since viruses are not alive, there is no way to tell if a virus is present. Since bacteria are alive, then she could try to grow the bacteria by providing them nutrition and keeping them in a warm place.

Curriculum Connection, p. 46
Part A:

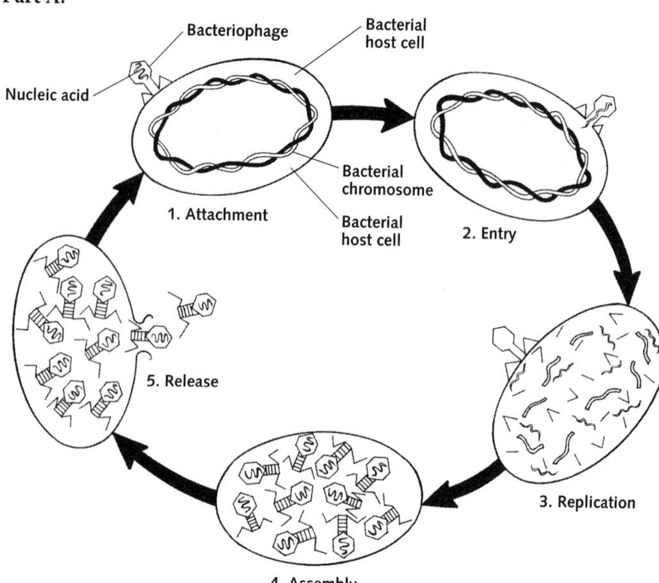

Part B: 6. Unlike organisms, viruses are not made of cells and they lack the cell structure that carries out the basic functions of organisms. Viruses cannot reproduce without taking over a cell. **7.** Once a host cell is taken over by the virus, all its energy and resources go to replicating and reproducing that virus.
Science Extension Answers will vary. Encourage students to share their writings.
Science Challenge, p. 47
Part A: Student answers will vary. Examples include: AIDS (caused by HIV) is spread by exchange of bodily fluids and is not transmissible from animals to humans; the common cold (caused by rhinoviruses, coronaviruses, and others), can be spread through direct or indirect contact; and encephalitis (caused by West Nile virus) is transferred between animals and people by mosquitoes.
Part B: 1. Common answers may be strep throat (*streptococcal* bacteria), staph infections (*Staphylococcus aureus*), bacterial meningitis (*Streptococcus pneumoniae, Haemophilus influenzae, Neisseria meningitidis, Listeria monocytogenes*), tuberculosis (*Mycobacterium tuberculosis*), and pneumonia (*Staphylococcus aureus* and *streptococcal* bacteria) **2.** The immune system protects people from bacterial infections (as well as viral illnesses and other illnesses). People who have weakened immune systems, such as the elderly or those with certain diseases, such as AIDS, are in more danger of bacterial infection than the average person. Additionally, washing food, eating cooked and preserved food, washing hands, and cleaning cuts and scrapes prevent bacterial infections. **3.** Student responses will vary. Students can get ideas from Figure 7.13 in the student book.

Chapter 8 Answer Key

Key Concept Review, p. 48
Part A: 1. 8.1: Protists A. What Is a Protist? B. Types of Protists
2. 8.2: Animal-Like Protists: Protozoans A. Types of Protozoans B. Protozoans in the World
3. 8.3: Plant-Like Protists: Algae A. What Are Algae? B. Types of Algae C. Algae in the World
4. 8.4: Fungus-Like Protists A. What Are Fungus-Like Protists? B. Types of Fungus-Like Protists C. Fungus-Like Protists in the World
5. 8.5: Fungi A. What Are Fungi? B. Structure of Fungi C. Reproduction in Fungi
6. 8.6: Diversity of Fungi A. Types of Fungi B. Fungi in the World
Part B: 7. cilia **8.** autotrophs **9.** dinoflagellates
Science Extension Answers will vary.
Vocabulary Review, p. 49
Part A: 1. e **2.** b **3.** c **4.** a **5.** d

Part B: Sample answers: Molds—threadlike, reproduce asexually, function as decomposers or parasites; bread mold, *Rhizopus*; Club fungi—produce spores sexually in structures shaped like clubs; mushroom; Fungi—All fungi are eukaryotes, hetertrophs, and reproduce by producing spores; Sac fungi—produce spores in structures that look like sacks; can be unicellular or multicellular; Imperfect fungi—not known to produce sexually; *Penicillium*
Science Extension Answers will vary.
Graphic Organizer, p. 50
Part A: 1. Euglena **2.** Amoeba, Euglena, Giardia, Mold **3.** Amoeba, Euglena, Giardia, Mold **4.** Mold **5.** Euglena, Giardia **6.** Amoeba **7.** Mold **8.** Amoeba, Euglena, Giardia, Mold **9.** Mold **10.** Amoeba, Giardia
Part B: 11. algae or autotrophs **12.** hyphae **13.** true **14.** amoeba **15.** asexually
Science Extension Drawings will vary but should reflect understanding of the chapter content.
Reading Comprehension, p. 51
Part A: Answers will vary.
Part B: Bacteria: Shape—bacilli, cocci, spirilla Structure—flagella; **Protist:** Shape—plasmodium Structure—cilia, pseudopod; **Fungi:** Shape—hyphae Structure: sporangia, mycelium
Science Extension 1. Because the fungus removes all the nutrients from the soil as it grows outward, mushrooms only grow on the outer ring. **2.** Without knowing that fungi are living things that need nutrients, people would have thought they were mystical, especially because they grow in rings. The best explanation they could come up with involved mystical creatures of lore, because fairies were considered mischievous beings that lived in the forest.
Curriculum Connection, p. 52
Part A: 1. soil **2.** parasite **3.** hyphae **4.** funguslike
Part B: 5. Protozoans are animal-like; algae, plantlike; molds or mildews, funguslike: Groupings are based on how they obtain their food **6.** They decompose organic material. **7.** when fungi and algae form a symbotic relationship
Science Extension Answers will vary. Encourage students to work in small groups and to share their investigations.
Science Challenge, p. 53
Part A: 1. Toxoplasmosis is caused by infection with a protist called *Toxoplasma gondii. Toxoplasma* is a protozoan or animal-like protist (more specifically, a sporozoan). Protozoans can move, and are heterotrophs. **2.** *Toxoplasma gondii* is carried primarily by cats. A person could contract toxoplasmosis after handling cat feces (i.e., when emptying litterboxes or working in a garden). It can also be contracted from contaminated raw meat or contaminated drinking water. In the United States, several million people are believed to harbor *Toxoplasma*, but most do not get sick because the immune system keeps it from causing illness. However, *Toxoplasma* causes sickness in people with compromised immune systems. **3.** Toxoplasmosis can cause influenza-like symptoms, including swollen lymph glands. Severe cases can cause organ damage, including eye and brain damage. *Toxoplasma* infection can be especially dangerous for infants. Pregnant women are advised to avoid activities in which they could come into contact with *Toxoplasma*. Antimicrobial medications are available for treating toxoplasmosis.
Part B: 4. This is a symbiotic relationship, an example of mutualism. Both organisms (fungus and tree) are benefited by the relationship. **5.** Student answers will vary: *Tuber melanosporum,* French black truffle or Perigord truffle, is native to France; *Tuber magnatum,* Italian white truffle, is native to central Italy; *Tuber aestivum,* summer truffle, is native to France, Italy, and Spain **6.** Different truffles are found in different seasons. Historically, people in France and Italy have used female pigs to root out truffles. In modern times, dogs are used to sniff out truffles. One advantage of using dogs is that they do not like to eat the truffles themselves (unlike pigs). People can also find truffles without using these animals. To do so, they must look under particular trees that will form symbioses with truffles (oaks and several others, but maples do not interact with truffles). They can remove leaf litter from under trees to look for and dig up truffles. People can use weather clues to hunt for truffles, looking for them a little more than a week after wet weather, in warm and moist soil. **7.** Fungus can be poisonous to humans. While truffles aren't known to be poisonous, someone could mistake a poisonous fungus for a truffle. Truffle hunters should make sure that what they think is a truffle actually isn't another fungus. **8.** Student answers and prices will vary.

Chapter 9 Answer Key

Key Concept Review, p. 55
Part A: 1. 2; **2.** 1; **3.** 3; **4.** 4
Part B: 5. water and carbon dioxide **6.** sunlight and chlorophyll **7.** glucose and oxygen
Science Extension Student answers will vary.
Vocabulary Review, p. 56
Part A: 1. c, f, **2.** d, e, f **3.** a, b, d, e, f, g, h The three main categories are: angiosperm, which is a flowering plant; gymnosperm, which is a plant with seeds; and fern, which is a plant that does not have seeds. Ferns, angiosperms, and gymnosperms overlap because they are all vascular plants; angiosperms and gymnosperms overlap because they have seeds; angiosperm, biennial, annual, monocot, perennial, and dicot are in the same category because they all refer to flowering plants with seeds.
Part B: 4. phototropism **5.** cellulose **6.** hormone
Science Extension Words, clues, and nonexamples will vary but should reflect understanding of the content of the chapter.
Interpreting Diagrams, p. 57
Part A: 1. monocots **2.** dicots **3.** angiosperms **4.** gymnosperms **5.** tracheophytes (vasular plants) **6.** liverworts **7.** mosses **8.** bryophytes (nonvascular plants) **9.** green algae **10.** ferns
Part B: 11. dicots **12.** angiosperms **13.** green algae **14.** gymnosperms **15.** ferns **16.** monocots
Science Extension Answers will vary but should reflect understanding of the chapter content.
Reading Comprehension, p. 58
Part A: 1. Auxins **2.** growth and development **3.** tannic acid **4.** Water **5.** Cellulose; **6.** build cell walls
Part B Answers will vary.
Science Extension She can have a bean sprout growing normally and one that is tilted at a 90 degree angle. Both will grow away from gravity demonstrating negative tropism.
Curriculum Connection, p. 59
Part A: Student timelines should list plant evolution in the following order: coal deposits in North America, seed ferns, coal deposits in Antarctica, mosses, club mosses, horsetails, ferns, gymnosperms, angiosperms
Part B: 6. A bryophyte is a nonvascular plant that needs a damp or wet environment to survive. Tracheophytes are vascular plants capable of drawing up water and thus adapted to land environments. **7.** Bryophyte: mosses; Tracheophyte: ferns
Science Extension Designs will vary. Green light does not work. Encourage student discussion.
Science Challenge, p. 60
Part A: 1. No **2.** These plants have no true roots, leaves, stems, or flowers. These plants grow very low to the ground in damp areas. Spores are used in reproduction. **3.** No **4.** These plants have no true roots, leaves, stems, or flowers. These plants often grow in damp areas. Spores are used in reproduction. **5.** No **6.** These small plants may look like miniature pines. They have conelike structures that makes spores. They do not produce seeds. **7.** Yes **8.** These plants have hollow stems and scale-like leaves. They reproduce using spores. There is only one genus in this division. **9.** Yes **10.** Gnetophyta **11.** Fern **12.** These plants have true roots, stems, and leaves. They produce seeds in cones. These plants may look like small palm trees. **13.** Yes **14.** Ginkgo **15.** Yes **16.** Conifers **17.** These plants have true roots, stems, leaves and flowers. They produce seeds that are enclosed inside a fruit. **18.** Yes
Part B: 20. vascular plants are found in anthophyta, coniferophyta, cycadophyta, filicinophyta, lycophyta, ginkgophyta, gnetophyta, psilophyta,

and sphenophyta. Another name for vascular plants is *tracheophytes*, which is used in the textbook. **21.** anthophyta, coniferophyta, cycadophyta, gingkophyta, and gnetophyta **22.** Coniferophyta, cycadophyta, gingkophyta, and gnetophyta can all be considered gymnosperms because they produce seeds that are not enclosed in fruit. Anthophyta are angiosperms. **23.** anthophyta, the flowering plants **24.** Ferns have roots and leaves, whisk ferns do not. **25.** No. Hornworts do not have vascular tissue and are very similar to liverworts, which do not have true stems, roots, or leaves. **26.** Lycophyta, psilophyta, and sphenophyta all contain vascular plants that reproduce using spores, as ferns do.
27. Student answers will vary. The green (chlorophyll) containing parts of the plant carry out photosynthesis (generally this will be the leaves).

Chapter 10 Answer Key

Key Concept Review, p. 62
Part A: 1. spore **2.** pistil **3.** gamete
Part B: 4. A cycad's sperm cells develop in pollen grains. **5.** A conifer is a plant that produces its seeds in cones. **6.** anthers
Science Extension Student answers will vary.
Vocabulary Review, p. 63
Part A: 1. c **2.** b **3.** d **4.** a **5.** e
Part B: 6. alternation of generations: the life cycle pattern in a plant, where one part of the cycle produces spores and the other part produces sex cells **7.** gametophyte generation: part of the life cycle that produces sex cells **8.** sporophyte generation: part of the life cycle that produces spores **9.** sexual reproduction: involves the formation of sex cells **10.** gametes: sex cells; male is sperm, female is egg **11.** asexual reproduction: genetically identical offspring are produced **12.** spore: a type of cell that can grow into another plant without joining another cell
Science Extension Illustrations will vary but should reflect understanding of the content of the chapter.
Interpreting Diagrams, p. 64
Part A: 1. pistil **2.** stigma **3.** style **4.** ovary **5.** ovule **6.** stamen **7.** anther **8.** filament **9.** petal **10.** sepal
Part B: 11. petals; the shape, color, or odors of the petals; sepals; bud; petals
Science Extension Flowcharts will vary but should reflect understanding of the chapter content.
Reading Comprehension, p. 65
Part A: Student answers will vary.
Part B: 1. Mosses are bryophytes that release spores that are carried by the wind. These spores can be dispersed over large distances. **2.** Student answers will vary. Possible answer: Moss spores could be sprayed over an area and grown. When the moss dies, it would promote further moss growth, which would hold the soil in place. **3.** Many other plants require lots of water, especially plants like ferns. Since air conditioning and heating keep the air dry, desert plants would thrive in this desertlike environment.
Science Extension There were probably three or more pine trees and one apple tree that grew in the yard. There were probably ferns that grew near the sandbox. Mosses probably grew in the area on the rocks and trees. There were probably lots of flowers growing nearby, since the bees and hummingbird are around.
Curriculum Connection, p. 66
Part A

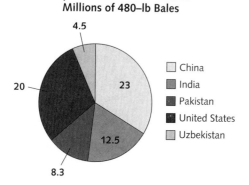

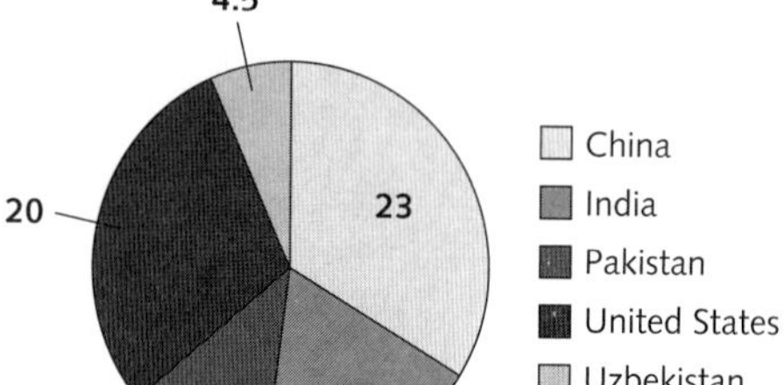

Part B: 1. angiosperm **2.** conifers, cycads, ginkgoes, and gnetophytes **3.** fertilized egg; either a sporophyte or bryophyte
Science Extension Investigations will vary. Encourage students to work in small groups to develop a research proposal.
Science Challenge, p. 67
Part A: The Wollemi pine (*Wollemia nobilis*) was found west of Sydney, Australia, in 1994. It was found by David Noble, a National Parks Officer. The plant is named after both Noble and the park in which he found it, Wollemi National Park. The fossil record shows that the trees once existed in Australia, New Zealand, and the Antarctic. Currently, the few wild Wollemi pines left are only in Australia. The oldest may be several hundred years old.

The Wollemi pine is a tree. The leaves look like needles and are dark green. The closest relatives to the Wollemi pine include kauri Pine, Norfolk Island pine, and hoop pine. The first Wollemi pine specimens were kept in cages. This was to protect them from harm and from people who may have wanted to steal the rare plant.

The Wollemi pine is now being cultivated, and plants will be available for purchase. Research into propagating the Wollemi pine has been extensive, both to conserve the species and to protect original specimens from plant collectors. Few seeds are produced and are difficult to collect, so most of the plants that will go to nurseries are grown from cuttings (via asexual reproduction). The plants grow well in pots. Young plants favor acidic soil and protection from direct sunlight.

The Wollemi pine is a gymnosperm, a conifer. Adult trees will have pollen-producing male cones and egg-producing female cones. After the egg is fertilized, a seed will develop. If conditions are right when a seed is dropped, it will germinate and develop into a new plant.
Part B: Student answers will vary. Clues from the area the plant was found in include the temperature and amount of moisture the plant can tolerate, as well as lighting conditions it may grow in (full sun or shade). The environment may also provide clues about how the plant reproduces sexually. Depending on the type of plant, it may require animals or wind for pollination (seed plants) or water for sex cells to meet (as for some bryophytes). Experiments to determine what the plant needs to grow and reproduce could include attempting to grow the plant from various cuttings (leaf, stem, root), in different soil types, different light levels, various temperatures, and various moisture levels. Similar experiments can be done for plants grown from seeds, or sporophytes from spores. Fertilizers or soil additives can also be tested for their ability to improve growth or general plant health.

Chapter 11 Answer Key

Key Concept Review, p. 69
Part A: 11.1 Roots A. Types of Roots 1. Taproots 2. Fibrous Roots 3. Adventitious Roots B. Uses of Roots C. Root Structure and Growth; 11.2 Stems A. Types of Stems B. Structure of Stems 1. Herbaceous Dicot Stems 2. Woody Dicot Stems 3. Monocot Stems C. Specialized Stems; 11.3 Leaves A. Leaf Variation B. Leaf Structure C. The Movement of Nutrients in Plants D. Specialized Leaves; 11.4 Seeds A. Structure of a Seed 1. Dicot Seeds 2. Monocot Seeds 3. Gymnosperm Seeds B. Seed Dispersal C. Seed Germination
Part B: 1. fibrous roots **2.** phloem **3.** herbaceous stems
Science Extension Answers will vary. **NOTE:** *This activity can be done with a partner.*
Vocabulary Review, p. 70
Part A: Sample answers: cotyledon: a seed leaf, the place where food is stored in a seed; embryo: immature plant that begins to grow when environmental conditions are favorable, develops from a fertilized egg and grows into leaves, stems, and roots; epicotyl: in dicot seeds, the short stem above the place where cotyledons attach to embryo; hypocotyl: in dioct seeds, stem below the place where cotyledons attach to embryo, becomes base of the stem, first part of seeding stem to appear; plumule: two tiny leaves inside cotyledons, develop into first leaves of plant

Part B: 1. phloem **2.** stomata **3.** true **4.** mesophyll
Science Extension Diagrams will vary.
Interpreting Diagrams, p. 71
Part A: 1. bud **2.** axil **3.** blade **4.** taproot **5.** root hairs **6.** root tip **7.** root cap **8.** petiole **9.** internode **10.** axil **11.** node
Part B: Sample answers: **12.** No; Taproots are found in gymnosperms and dicots, such as carrots. Fibrous roots are thin, branching roots growing from a central point and are found mostly in monocots, such as corn. Some plants have adventitious roots growing from the stem and some have aerial roots growing above ground. **13.** Root hairs absorb water, oxygen, and minerals; they also increase the surface area of the root that contacts the soil.
Science Extension
Answers will vary but should reflect an understanding of chapter content.
Reading Comprehension, p. 72
Part A: Student answers should reflect chapter content.
Part B: Cause: Aerial roots hold onto other plants' stems. **Effect:** Ivy grows up a tree. **Cause:** A plant does not receive enough light. **Effect:** Long internodes are discovered. **Cause:** Guard cells lose water on a hot day. **Effect:** Stoma close. **Cause:** Ocean currents can disperse seeds. **Effect:** Coconuts are found along an island chain.
Science Extension 1. The leaf is from a region with a lot of rain. The leaf is probably not native to where they live (Arizona). **2.** plenty of water
Curriculam Connection, p. 73
Part A: 1. endodermis; **2.** xylem; **3.** epidermis; **4.** cortex; **5.** phloem
Part B: 6. Sugar that the plant made is stored as starch. **7.** sugar made by the plant **8.** Stomata are tiny pores in the lower epidermis of most leafs. They control gas exchange between the leaf and the outside environment.
Science Extension Answers will vary.
Science Challenge, p. 74
Part A: 1. Example: apple; plant part: fruit; Example: pine nuts; plant part: seeds. Additional sample answers: Student answers will vary. Common examples are:
apples, bananas, pears, peaches, avocado, oranges, tomato—fruit; potatoes, yams, carrots—roots; onions—bulb; pomegranate, nuts—seeds; celery—stalks/stem; lettuce, cabbage, herbs such as mint and basil—leaves; broccoli—stems and flowers
2. Student answers will vary. Generally, parts of the plant that store food, such as fleshy roots, will be sweeter than seeds/stems/leaves. Fruits are often sweet, as the plant may rely on animals to eat the fruit to then disperse seeds.
Part B: Maple syrup is made from the sap of maple trees, which grow in North America. Sap is the fluid found inside the tree. It is collected by drilling a hole into the trunk of the tree. Maple syrup is condensed sap; it is made by boiling the sap to remove water. Cane sugar comes from *sugar cane*, a type of grass (hybrids of species in the genus *Saccharum*). Sugar cane grows in tropical areas. After the cane is harvested, it is crushed to release the internal liquids (cane juice). Cane juice contains 10–20 percent sucrose. Brown sugar is isolated from cane juice and further refined to white sugar. Molasses is a by-product of the process. Lentils are the seeds of lentil plants. They can be dried and stored for long periods of time. Lentils are legumes grown in dry areas. Flour is made from cereals, or grains. Cereals are grasses. Examples include wheat and rye. The seeds of the grasses are crushed or milled to produce flour. Coffee beans are the seeds of coffee plants. The seeds are removed from fruit and roasted. The roasted seeds are ground into a powder. Coffee is made by passing water over the ground seeds. Cocoa (and chocolate) comes from the seeds of cacao (cocoa trees). These trees grow in equatorial regions. The seeds are removed from fruit and usually roasted. The hard outer portion is removed and the seeds are milled. From the resulting material (cocoa liquor), cocoa butter (fat) is removed. The remains are ground to make cocoa powder. (Chocolate is made from cocoa liquor, cocoa butter, and other ingredients, such as sugar.)

Part C: Answers will vary. Examples of edible flowers include violets, tulips, roses, sage, and dandelions. Rose petals may be used in jam. Dandelion leaves are often eaten in salads.

Chapter 12 Answer Key

Key Concept Review, p. 76
Part A: Sponges: filter feeding, spicules; Cnidarians: stinging tentacles, medusa; Worms: platyhelminthes, leeches; Mollusks: radula, cephalopod
Part B: 1. Budding is an asexual form of reproduction used by sponges. **2.** An animal with bilateral symmetry has a body that has two similar halves. An animal with radial symmetry has a body arranged circularly around a center point. **3.** Tentacles are the armlike structures that surround a cnidarian's mouth
Science Extension Answers will vary.
Vocabulary Review, p. 77
Part A: bilateral symmetry—bodies with similar right and left halves, front and back side, and head and tail end; tapeworm, mussel; radial symmetry—bodies organized in a circle around a central point, with top and bottom, but no front or head; sea anemone, jelly fish; asymmetrical—bodies of simple animals that do not have symmetry; red beard sponge, blue vase sponge
Part B: 1. e **2.** c **3.** d **4.** b **5.** a
Science Extension Words will vary but should reflect new vocabulary in the chapter.
Interpreting Diagrams, p. 78
Part A: 1. platyhelminthes; tapeworms; intestines of vertebrates **2.** mollusca; gastropods; land, freshwater, ocean **3.** porifera; barrel sponge; ocean or freshwater **4.** cnidaria; jelly fish; freshwater, ocean
Part B: 5. nematoda or round worms, such as hookworms, and annelida or segmented worms, such as earthworm **6.** gastropods; bivalves, or cephalopods, shells, bivalves, filter feeding, cephalopods; a well-developed head, tentacles
Science Extension Student diagrams will vary.
Reading Comprehension, p. 79
Part A: Answers will vary.
Part B: 1. plants with circular bodies arranged around a central point **2.** Both involve budding in which a small portion of their bodies falls off and becomes a new organism. **3.** They contain stinging cells that paralyze prey and the tentacles draw food into their mouths.
Science Extension 1. Earthworms have tiny hairs, called bristles, that help push them along. **2.** move closer to the surface or move to looser soil
Curriculam Connection, p. 80
Part A: Diagrams will vary.
Part B: 1. No. Both have tentacles, but an octopus is classified as a mollusk, *cephalopod.* **2.** Both are soft-bodied invertebrates with bilateral symmetry. **3.** It is a structure in a snail's mouth that works like a file. The snail uses the radula to scrape off small pieces from plants that it can easily swallow.
Science Extension Answers will vary. Encourage students to discuss and share their research plans.
Science Challenge, p. 81
Part A: Student presentations will vary. Some materials that are used to create artificial reefs include sunken ships and barges, oil rigs, airplanes and army tanks, steel, concrete, and limestone boulders. Artificial reefs may be built to support at-risk marine life by providing new habitat areas. They also create new areas for recreational fishers and scuba divers (and might protect older, popular reefs from too much human intrusion). However, there is concern that artificial reefs may not actually widely increase the number of animals in an area; they may just attract and group more animals together. In that case, artificial reef sites may be detrimental to certain fish species, particularly because they attract fishers. The exact types of marine life at an artificial reef will depend on the reef location.

Part B: 1. Krakens are many-tentacled large sea creatures that resemble squid. **2.** Giant squids (genus *Architeuthis*) are distributed throughout the world's oceans. These squids have estimated average lengths of ten meters, and estimated average weights of 200 kilograms. Most information gathered about giant squids has been from carcasses, though a live specimen was caught by Japanese scientists in 2006. Giant squids and colossal squids have the largest eyes in the animal kingdom. All squids have two eyes, beaklike mouths, eight arms, and two feeding tentacles. (Student drawings should include the eyes, head, mantle, fins, arms, and tentacles). Colossal squids (*Mesonychoteuthis hamiltoni*) are thought to live in the oceans of the Southern Hemisphere. They are the world's largest invertebrates. These squids have estimated average lengths of 12 meters, and the biggest intact specimen known weighed almost 454.5 kilograms. Since so few have been sighted, their actual average length and weight, as well as life span, are not known. These squids have rotating hooks on their tentacles.
Part C: Student answers will vary. Sample answers: 1a. Flattened Shape, Go to 2; 1b. Rounded Shape, Go to 4; 2a. Free-living, Planarian; 2b. Parasite, Go to 3; 3a. Lives in body tissues, Fluke; 3b. Lives in intestines, Tapeworms; 4a. Has body segments, Go to 5; 4b. No body segments, Go to 6; 5a. Lives in soil, Earthworm; 5b. Lives in freshwater, Leech; 6a. Free-living, Vinegar eel; 6b. Parasite, Hookworm

Chapter 13 Answer Key

Key Concept Review, p. 82
Part A: 1. egg; insect lays fertilized eggs that hatch **2.** larva; hatches from egg into wormlike stage and is always eating **3.** pupa; larva tissues replaced by adult tissues in a cocoon **4.** adult; adult insect emerges from pupa
Part B: 5. They all have jointed appendages, segmented bodies, and a hard exoskeleton. **6.** Millipedes eat dead or decaying plant material. **7.** *Crustacea*
Science Extension Student answers will vary.
Vocabulary Review, p. 83
Part A: Vocabulary webs and sentences will vary.
Part B: 1. exoskeleton; molting **2.** tube feet **3.** camouflage **4.** thorax
Science Extension Charts and diagrams will vary but should reflect chapter content.
Graphic Organizer, p. 84
Part A: 1. exoskeleton **2.** jointed appendages **3.** segmented bodies **4.** arachnids **5.** insects **6.** crustaceans **7.** 2—head-chest, abdomen **8.** 8 **9.** book lungs **10.** 3—head, thorax, abdomen **11.** 6 **12.** 1 pair **13.** tubes **14.** 5 or more, with one pair of appendages per segment **15.** 2 pair **16.** gills
Part B: 17. true **18.** arachnids **19.** exoskeleton **20.** arthropods
Science Extension Descriptions will vary but should reflect chapter content.
Reading Comprehension, p. 85
Part A: Answers will vary.
Part B: Arthropods (spider): legs, cocoon, silk glands, book lungs, fangs
Insect (grasshopper): wings, legs, eyes, antennae, tubes, nervous system
Echinoderm (sea star): endoskeleton, water-vascular system, tube feet, eyespots, digestive gland, stomach, anus
Science Extension 1. Harriett "the Scorpion" **2.** Bruno "the Centipede" **3.** Corey "the Sea Cucumber" **4.** Jared "the Lobster"
Curriculum Connection, p. 86
Part A: 1. compound eye **2.** antennae **3.** mandible **4.** wings **5.** spiracles **6.** legs
Part B: 7. It dances. **8.** They eat the aphids that destroy crops. **9.** All insects reproduce sexually.
Science Extension Answers will vary. Encourage students to do some online research. Probable causes include marine pathogens, pesticide poisoning, and over-fishing. Solutions might include setting up hatcheries and protective no-catch zones and changing the design of lobster traps.

Science Challenge, p. 87
Part A: Example:

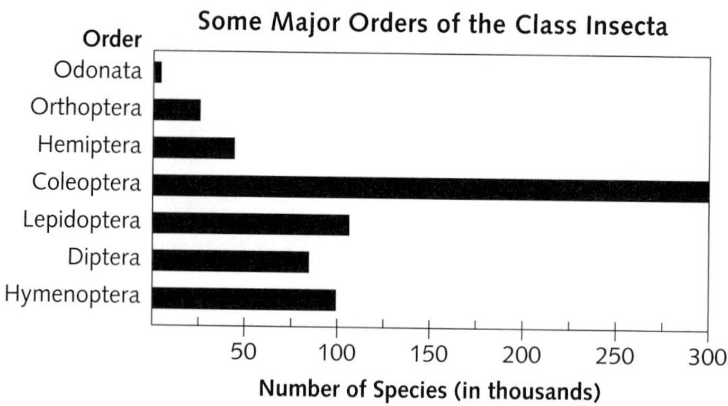

Students could also show circle graphs/pie charts or bar graphs with species number on the *y*-axis.
Part B: 1. Student answers will vary, as there are several hundred potential species of edible insects. Students should recognize that caterpillars eaten represent one life stage of an insect that goes through complete metamorphosis—generally the adult forms of these species are not eaten. Examples of edible insects that form colonies include bees, wasps, and termites. **2.** Answers will vary. **3.** Sea urchins are also used as food. The sexual organs (gonads) of the sea urchins are considered by many to be delicacies. They are called sea urchin roe and are usually eaten raw in sushi (Uni). (Note that the term *roe* usually refers to eggs but is used to describe both male and female gonads in sea urchins.) High demand for sea urchin roe could decrease the number of sea urchins in the ocean, if they are over-fished.

Chapter 14 Answer Key

Key Concept, p. 88
Part A: Fish: lamprey, trout, stingray; Amphibians: salamander, frog, newt; Reptiles: snake, turtle, lizard
Part B: 1. A chordate has a nerve cord and a notochord. **2.** A vertebrate has a backbone. **3.** An ectotherm changes body temperature according to the temperature of its environment, while an endotherm's body temperature stays the same.
Science Extension Student answers will vary but should reflect chapter content.
Vocabulary Review, p. 89
Part A: Toad: estivation—a period of inactivity when toads bury themselves to escape the intense heat; Hagfish: scavenger—a scavenger, such as a hagfish, feeds on dead and dying animals; Lizard: amniotic egg—a type of egg that reptiles lay, which has a hard shell and nutrients that keep embryo moist and fed
Part B: 1. a **2.** e **3.** f **4.** b **5.** c **6.** d
Science Extension Answers will vary.
Graphic Organizer, p. 90
Part A: Fishes—bony; cartilaginous; jawless; scales, fins, throats with fill slits: Amphibians—frogs and toads; salamanders and newts; Caecilians; smooth, moist skin; live in water and on land: Reptiles—snakes and lizards; alligators and crocodiles; turtles and tortoises; thick, scaly skin; amniotic egg
Part B: 1. the egg has a hard shell that protects the embryo and keeps it from drying out **2.** lungfish; lungs and gills with which to breathe **3.** alligators and crocodiles care for their young
Science Extension Flowcharts will vary but should show the main stages of metamorphosis, including descriptions.
Reading Comprehension, p. 91
Part A
Food is scarce; flickers tongue to smell for prey; snake
A fish swims up; snaps beak shut around food; turtle
Winter arrives; hibernates in the mud; frog
Predators swim nearby; hides in a sea anemone; clownfish

Part B: Student answers will vary.
Science Extension 1. Lungfish have lungs and can breathe outside of water. They will be okay for now. 2. Since lampreys are parasites of fish, the lampreys need to be in a special tank far from the other fish.
Curriculum Connection, p. 92
Part A: 1. embryo **2.** waste **3.** cellular **4.** nutrients
Part B: 5. They all lay eggs to reproduce. **6.** The reptile egg is an amniotic egg. Like a bird's, its egg has a hard outer shell, so the reptile does not need to lay its eggs in water and can thus nest on dry land. **7.** Both are parasites. It latches onto its prey and sucks out the other fish's blood and body fluids.
Science Extension Answers will vary. Encourage students to discuss their ideas and online research.
Science Challenge, p. 93
Part A: 1. Lampreys and hagfishes should be circled. **2.** Sharks and rays, lampreys, and hagfishes should be starred. **3.** Hagfish (Note: Other fishes produce slime, but not in amounts as great as the hagfish.) **4.** Placoderms, Early tetrapod, Condrichthyes, and Ostracoderms should be checked. They belong to class Osteichthyes. **5.** There are more ray-finned fishes than lobe-finned fishes. **6.** The group not listed is lungfishes. **7.** Placoderms **8.** Student answers will vary.
Part B: Student answers will vary. Some of the pros they may find in owning these animals are the educational value of having a pet and the ability to have *some* species in a smaller area than is needed for larger pets, such as cats and dogs. In general, however, there are several cons to keeping reptiles and amphibians as pets. They may be difficult to care for because they need specially designed living areas, ways to keep warm or cool, and unique diets that can be difficult to acquire. Amphibians are particularly sensitive to their environments. Some species of snakes and adult lizards may be dangerous and also grow larger than an uninformed pet owner may have anticipated. Any species that is endangered should not be kept as a pet, as the pet trade will reduce their numbers in the wild.

Chapter 15 Answer Key

Key Concept Review, p. 95
Part A: 15.1 Birds A. Characteristics of Birds B. Food and Flight C. Origins of Birds D. Types of Birds; 15.2 Adaptations for Flight A. A Bird's Body B. Bird Migration; 15.3 Mammals A. Characteristics of Mammals B. Reproduction of Mammals C. The Origin of Mammals; 15.4 Animal Behavior A. Innate Behavior B. Learned Behaviors C. Social Behavior D. Communication
Part B: 1. contour **2.** mammary glands **3.** carnivore
Science Extension Posters will vary.
Vocabulary Review, p. 96
Part A: 1. sternum **2.** preening, feathers **3.** placenta, uterus **4.** echolocation
Part B: 5. herbivore **6.** carnivore **7.** carnivore **8.** herbivore **9.** an animal that eats only plants; includes all hoofed mammals **10.** an animal that eats other animals **11.** an animal that eats both plants and animals
Science Extension Word webs will vary.
Graphic Organizer, p. 97
Part A: 1. Placental **2.** Marsupial **3.** Placental **4.** Monotreme, Marsupial, Placental **5.** Monotreme
Part B: 6. A **8.** A **9.** A
Part C: 11. sharp claws and strong, curved beak, fast flyer; hawk **12.** Water bird; swim and dive in lakes and ponds, some have webbed feet **13.** Flightless; penguin **14.** eat insects, worms, or seeds, many sing songs on perches; finch
Science Extension Scenarios will vary but should reflect the chapter content on animal behaviors.
Reading Comprehension, p. 98
Part A: Answers will vary.
Part B: 1. The hummingbird will search out nectar since it needs to eat every ten minutes. **2.** They will migrate to a warmer area where there is more food. **3.** They must outrun the cheetah since they cannot fly.
Science Extension 1. learned **2.** social **3.** innate

Curriculum Connection, p. 99
Part A: 1. flight **2.** skeletons **3.** feathers **4.** laying eggs **5.** vertebrates **6.** reptiles **7.** Bats **8.** Monotremes **9.** Dense **10.** hair, fur **11.** pouch, placenta
Part B: 12. birds of prey, flightless birds, perching birds, and water birds; perching birds **13.** Birds migrate to find food and warmer climates in the winter; no **14.** mammals
Science Extension Answers will vary. Encourage students to discuss their views.
Science Challenge, p. 100
Part A: 1. Mammals from the Mezozoic era were small and rodentlike. No others have been discovered that glide or fly. (The oldest fossils of bats are 70 million years younger than the gliding animal fossil.) **2.** Bats are true flying mammals. They do not use gliding flight, but have powered flight, similar to birds. (These mammals evolved independently of flying dinosaurs and birds.) They must move their wings to produce thrust. They have specially adapted wings composed of skin stretched over finger bones. Bats can maneuver much better than gliding animals. Gliding mammals include both placental mammals (such as flying squirrels) and pouched animals (such as yellow-bellied gliders, feather-tail gliders, and sugar gliders). Some are similar in size to the fossil animal, though they vary in size. Most also eat insects, though many gliding mammals also eat nuts, meat, berries, and other vegetable matter. Gliding animals also have a skin membrane that stretches between their forelimbs and hindlimbs, like the fossil animal. Other animals that can glide include the colugo, or "flying lemur" (which is not actually a lemur), flying fish, the flying dragon lizard (*Draco volans*), and a type of tree frog (*Rhacophorus*).
Part B: 3. b **4.** d **5.** e **6.** a **7.** c **8.** Birds that mimic the sounds or songs of other birds include starlings, scrub jays, blue jays, mockingbirds, catbirds, and brown thrashers. Birds that mimic sounds of their surroundings in captivity include parrots, mynahs, crows, and magpies. Lyrebirds found in Australia can mimic almost any sound. **9.** Birds of prey hunt other birds and small animals. Cities have a large food supply for these birds—rats and pigeons. Skyscrapers and tall building also provide nesting areas. **10.** Student answers will vary.

Chapter 16 Answer Key

Key Concept Review, p. 102
Part A: 1. biosphere **2.** abiotic **3.** omnivore
Part B: 4. They digest the molecules in the bodies of dead organisms and release the elements stored in dead tissue into the environment to be reused. **5.** Eutrophication is the pollution of an environment by an overabundance of a nutrient, such as nitrogen. **6.** A climax community is a stable community that undergoes little or no change in species even if the environment changes.
Science Extension Answers will vary.
Vocabulary Review, p. 103
Part A: 1. Eutrophication **2.** abiotic **3.** true
Part B: evaporation—process in which heat from Sun turns water in lakes and oceans into water vapor that moves into atmosphere; transpiration—process in which plant leaves give off water vapor that evaporates; condensation—process in which water vapor cools, turns into droplets, and forms clouds; precipitation—process in which water droplets get heavy enough to fall back to Earth as rain, sleet, snow, or hail
Science Extension Venn diagrams will vary.
Interpreting Diagrams, p. 104
Part A: Pyramid should be labeled as follows: bottom tier: b, e, h; second tier: c, f, i; third tier: a, g, i; top tier: a, d, g, i
Part B: Energy is lost from one trophic level to the next because organisms use most of the energy for metabolic processes. About 10 percent of the energy from one trophic level passes to the next level.
Science Extension Sequence charts will vary but should reflect content of chapter.
Reading Comprehension, p. 105
Part A: Answers will vary.
Part B: Answers will vary.
Science Extension Answers will vary.

Curriculum Connection, p. 106
Part A: Diagrams will vary but should show an accurate representation of the nitrogen cycle.
Part B: 1. Answers will vary. Accept reasonable responses. **2.** Answers will vary. Accept reasonable responses, such as, mouse/rat catcher. **3.** Ectothermic predators do not need to eat as much to survive; their metabolism is slower and more energy-efficient. Endothermic predators need more food because most of their energy is released in body heat.
Science Extension Answers will vary. Encourage students to research the issue together.
Science Challenge, p. 107
Part A: 1. d **2.** f **3.** g **4.** e **5.** g or h **6.** i **7.** c **8.** j **9.** l **10.** k **11.** a **12.** b **13.** It allows individuals to share resources, better protect themselves from predators, and in some cases look after their young.
Part B: 14. Student answers will vary, depending on the animal and exact species chosen. Example: African lions are found on savannahs and woodlands in Africa. Savannahs are dry grasslands. They get 20 to 60 inches of rainfall a year, usually in a period of weeks. This is sometimes followed by periods of drought. Temperatures are between 80°F and 100°F. Abiotic things found in this environment include water, rocks, sunlight, and air. Biotic things are all living things, including grasses, trees, and other animals. Some other animals found in the African savannah are wildebeest, rhinoceroses, giraffes, elephants, zebras, and vultures. **15.** Lions, wolves, and penguins (which eat fish) are carnivores; reindeer, buffalo, doves, bees, and hippopotamuses are herbivores; geese, turkeys, quail, and ants are omnivores (the birds will at least occasionally eat insects, and ants eat other invertebrates, fruits, and other sweet substances from vegetation). Student food webs will vary. In general, the carnivores are at the highest trophic level; the herbivores and omnivores are at the second/middle trophic level if students also include their predator in the web. **16.** Natural disasters such as droughts, floods, tornadoes, hurricanes, or other storms may occur. These disasters would not remove soil or even all plant life, and secondary succession would occur after such a disturbance. Human-made changes, such as draining of ponds and removal of trees, will likely remove wildlife for as long as people use the area—succession would not necessarily occur. Only after a serious event, such as a volcanic eruption, would primary succession occur (reindeer may be found near volcanoes in Russia, for example).

Chapter 17 Answer Key

Key Concept Review, p. 108
Part A: 17.1 The Influence of Climate A. Temperature and Precipitation B. Latitude and Climate C. Land and Water Features; 17.2 Land Biomes A. Tundra B. Taiga C. Temperate Rain Forest D. Deciduous Forest E. Grassland F. Tropical Rain Forest G. Desert; 17.3 Water Biomes A. The Freshwater Biome B. The Marine Biome
Part B: 1. tropical region **2.** rain shadow effect **3.** taiga
Science Extension Answers will vary.
Vocabulary Review, p. 109
Part A: 1. tundra **2.** grassland **3.** desert **4.** marine
Part B: 5. d **6.** c **7.** f **8.** a **9.** e **10.** b
Science Extension Dialogues will vary.
Graphic Organizer, p. 110
Part A: deciduous forest; below freezing to 20°C
cactus; fox, lizard, owl; below freezing to above 40°C
grassland; antelope, buffalo taiga
temperate rain forest; hemlock and spruce trees; 9°C to 12°C
giant trees; most species of any biome; snakes, macaws monkeys
tundra; musk ox, insects
Part B: 1. grassland **2.** marine **3.** temperate rain forest **4.** deserts **5.** tropical rain forest
Science Extension Diagrams will vary but should reflect understanding of the chapter content.
Reading Comprehension, p. 111
Part A: Answers will vary.
Part B: Be sure students include all vocabulary terms. Suggest that students use a different color pen or marker for each lesson.
Science Extension 1. cold—tundra, taiga; mild—deciduous rain forest, temperate rain forest, tropical rain forest, grassland; hot—desert 2. low rainfall—desert, tundra, taiga; medium rainfall—deciduous forest, grassland; high rainfall—temperate rain forest, tropical rain forest
Curriculum Connection, p. 112
Part A: Student diagrams will vary but should include what they have learned about the ocean's layers.
Part B: 1. Answers will vary. **2.** Answers will vary. **3.** lack of water and severe temperatures
Science Extension Answers will vary. The Labrador Current would essentially stall once all the ice melted, and Europe could experience an ice age.
Science Challenge, p. 113
Part A: 1. Student answers will vary and do not have to be limited to the United States. Examples include: Barrow, Alaska, and Tromso, Norway—tundra; Winnipeg, Canada—taiga; Vancouver, Canada—near a temperate rainforest; Columbus, Ohio, and Springfield, Massachusetts, and other eastern American cities—deciduous forest; Fargo, North Dakota—grassland; San Jose, Costa Rica—tropical rainforest; Alice Springs, Australia—desert. **2.** Student answers will differ depending on city/area chosen. Summer months may be better to travel to tundra, taiga, and temperate forests as more animals will be present, and flowers may be in bloom. On the other hand, summer months in regions near the equator or deserts may be too hot for comfort. Students may also make travel decisions based on rainy seasons. Native plants and animals will vary by region. **3.** Reponses will vary with area. As an example, someone landscaping a backyard near a desert might want to use full-sun, low-water requiring flowering plants/succulents. Plant names should be specific, and students should try to look for native plants in the area. They may also want plants that attract wildlife. **4.** People change the environment as they use natural resources. They may cut down trees, divert or block waterways, and add toxins to the environment from industrial and household waste. Humans may also bring non-native, invasive species of plants and animals to new areas. On a large scale, global warming is changing world temperatures and weather patterns and could be particularly devastating to the tundra and polar regions.
Part B: Student responses will vary.

Chapter 18 Answer Key

Key Concept Review, p. 114
Part A: 3. leveling off **4.** carrying capacity **5.** fluctuations **1.** beginning growth **2.** rapid growth
Part B: 6. Symbiosis is a close dependent relationship between individuals of two or more species. **7.** A population's growth is determined by its reproductive style, limiting factors, and natural events. **8.** They must adapt to use the resources in different ways.
Science Extension Student answers will vary.
Vocabulary Review, p. 115
Part A: 1. d **2.** c **3.** b **4.** e **5.** a
Part B

Symbiosis: close relationship between individuals of two or more species, with each affecting the other's lives

Mutualism: a symbiotic relationship in which both species benefit, such as a honey bee and flower; the bee gets nectar and the pollen of the flower is spread

Commensalism: a symbiotic relationship in which one organism benefits and the other is not affected, such as a jellyfish and young fish; the jellyfish sting predators and protect fish; the fish have no effect on the jellyfish

Parasitism: a symbiotic relationship in which one organism feeds off the body of the other organism, such as a tick that attaches to an animal or human and feeds off its blood

Science Extension Comic strips will vary.
Graphic Organizer, p. 116
Part A: 1. Predation **2.** Symbiosis **3.** Competition **4.** Predation
Part B: Sample answers given. **5.** Predator and prey adaptations involve the predator becoming better at capturing the prey and the prey becoming better at avoiding capture. Competition adaptations involve two species finding different niches in the same habitat or one species taking over the habitat by driving out or destroying the other species. **6.** Parasites find hosts they can feed on without killing them and hosts adapt by releasing toxins or immune cells that will destroy the parasites.
Science Extension Leaflets will vary but should reflect chapter content on conservation.
Reading Comprehension, p. 117
Part A: 18.1 Population Growth and Size A. Population Growth B. Limiting Factors C. Carrying Capacity D. Natural Events E. Population Equation; 18.2 Relationships Among Populations A. Symbiosis B. Competition C. Predation; 18.3 Adaptations: Challenges and Opportunities A. Adaptation to Symbiosis B. Adaptation to Competition C. Adaptation to Predation D. Adaptation to Natural Events; 18.4 People and the Environment A. Human Population Growth B. Human Effects on the Environment C. Choices for Conservation
Part B: 1. Mutualistic owners would need their dogs as much as their dogs need them. This may be for companionship or for a person who is blind with a seeing-eye dog. Commensalism between an owner and a pet would involve the owner being completely independent and indifferent about the pets. Dog breeders might have a relationship like this so that they can easily sell their dogs. **2.** There is concern about asteroids hitting the planet, global warming bringing another ice age, and viruses that spread across Earth. Furthermore, human events such as nuclear warfare and terrorism could also limit populations. **3.** improved flying ability, improved vision, spending less energy when not hunting, become better at catching mice, becoming quieter, hunting together
Science Extension 1. This is an antipollution measure. It reduces the amount of electricity, which reduces the amount of fuel used. **2.** This is a personal choice. It reduces the amount of trees cut down.
Curriculum Connection, p. 119
Part A: 1. Answers will vary; it's about 65°F. **2.** Answers will vary: Increased competition for limited resources could lead to decline in otter population as well.
Part B: 3. Answers include waste, disease, competition, lack of resources, starvation, high density, and loss of habitat. **4.** It depends on the organisms' reproductive style.
Science Extension Posters will vary.
Science Challenge, p. 120
Part A: 1. mutualism, both, neither, neither **2.** commensalism, barnacle (it is taken to new food sources), neither, whale **3.** parasitism, dwarf mistletoe, spruce, neither **4.** commensalism, remora, neither, shark
Part B: Student responses should recognize that invasive species, plants or animals, can harm native species through competition for resources or predation. As an example for a plant, English ivy introduced into the U.S. Pacific Northwest grows quickly and takes away space, sunlight, and nutrients from other plants. It displaces other plants that provide homes for native animal species. As an example for animals, goldfish introduced to lakes and streams eat oxygen-producing plants, which destroys habitat for young native fish and can increase water temperatures. Their feeding habits also harm plant growth. (Note: Teachers may remind students that though there are many stray cats around, house cats are not native species. Stray cats can prey on native bird and rodent populations and spread disease. Most animals kept as pets are not native species.)
Part C: Student answers will vary but must reflect chapter content.

Chapter 19 Answer Key

Key Concept Review, p. 122
Part A: Skin: epidermis, melanin, dermis, subcutaneous tissue; Skeletal: periosteum, cancellous bone, cartilage, ligaments; Muscular: skeletal muscle, smooth muscle, cardiac muscle, tendons
Part B: 1. Skin is made up of three layers of tissue: the epidermis, the dermis, and the subcutaneous layer. **2.** ligaments **3.** Cartilage protects the bones from stress.
Science Extension Answers will vary.
Vocabulary Review, p. 123
Part A: 1. ligament **2.** true **3.** bone marrow **4.** periosteum **5.** cartilage
Part B: 6. skeletal muscle **7.** smooth muscle **8.** cardiac muscle
Science Extension Descriptions and words will vary.
Interpreting Diagrams, p. 124
Part A: 1. a **2.** c, oil gland **3.** hair follicle **4.** d, sweat gland **5.** b, fat cells **6.** subcutaneous layer **7.** dermis **8.** e, epidermis
Part B: 9. ball-and-socket **10.** gliding
Part C: 11. C **12.** E **13.** C **14.** M **15.** N
Science Extension Answers will vary.
Reading Comprehension, p. 125
Part A: 1. Both insulate from impact. Most rubber soles can compress to some degree, while joints come in three different types, according to their ability to move. A shoe sole softens the impact between the foot and the ground, while joints protect bones from bones. **2.** Both provide support for the structure and connect by joints. The skeleton allows for large degrees of motion, while a house frame is not intended to move very much, if at all. **3.** Both create a protective layer on the outside. Skin allows certain things, such as water, to pass through it; packaging is typically meant to keep everything out. Skin is vital to human health, whereas the absence of packaging usually doesn't mean destruction of the package.
Part B: 4. "The Air in There" **5.** "Control Freak" **6.** "Pump It" **7.** "Mr. Steakhouse"
Science Extension 1. the skull or torso **2.** hair and nails
Curriculum Connection, p. 126
Part A: 1. voluntary **2.** fast-twitch **3.** slow-twitch **4.** motion **5.** cardiac **6.** involuntary
Part B: 7. the nervous system **8.** Osteoblasts produce bone, while osteoclasts break down bone. **9.** a ball-and-socket joint
Science Extension Answers will vary. Encourage students to share their opinions.
Science Challenge, p. 127
Part A: The early warning signs of skin cancer in a mole include asymmetry (the two halves of a mole are different), irregular or uneven borders, having a number of colors/shades, and large size. Change in a mole's appearance over time is also a warning sign, and having a large number of moles can be a risk factor for melanoma. To reduce their skin cancer risk, people should wear sunscreen or other sun protection, frequently check moles, and schedule regular exams with a doctor if they have a family history of skin cancer.
Part B: Student answers will vary. As an example, the irregular jaw bone or *mandible* forms joints with the irregular bones in the skull known as the *temporal bones.* The movable joints are each a combination of a hinge joint and a sliding joint.
Part C: 1. Juan likely has a higher proportion of fast-twitch fibers; Marco probably has a higher proportion of slow-twitch muscles. **2.** Student answers will vary. Juan would probably be best at activities that require quick bursts of energy or sprints, including baseball and football (for receivers), as well as short-distance racing (running, skiing, skating) and jumping (long jump). Marco would likely do well at activities that require endurance, such as long-distance races (running, skiing, skating, and swimming). Arguments could also be made that different positions or parts of team sports require more endurance than others (e.g., basketball requires a lot of endurance, but someone who has quick bursts of movement may be able to make many baskets).

Chapter 20 Answer Key

Key Concept Review, p. 128
Part A: 1. ventilation **2.** larynx **3.** atrium
Part B: 4. When humans inhale, they pull air into their lungs; when they exhale, they expel air from their lungs. **5.** It is the process of breaking down nutrients for energy. **6.** The bronchi carry air into the lungs.

Science Extension Answers will vary.
Vocabulary Review, p. 129
Part A: 1. proteins on the surfaces of red blood cells—A, B, and Rh are the most important; cardiovascular **2.** the process in which cells use oxygen to break down glucose and store its energy; respiratory **3.** excess tissue fluid that enters lymphatic capillaries; lymphatic
Part B

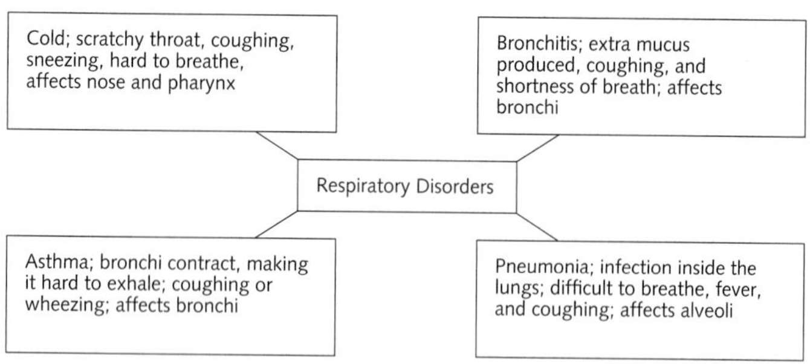

Cold; scratchy throat, coughing, sneezing, hard to breathe, affects nose and pharynx
Bronchitis; extra mucus produced, coughing, and shortness of breath; affects bronchi
Respiratory Disorders
Asthma; bronchi contract, making it hard to exhale; coughing or wheezing; affects bronchi
Pneumonia; infection inside the lungs; difficult to breathe, fever, and coughing; affects alveoli

Science Extension Dialogues will vary.
Interpreting Diagrams, p. 130
Part A: 1. nose **2.** mouth **3.** larynx **4.** trachea **5.** bronchi **6.** lungs **7.** diaphragm **8.** pharynx **9.** epiglottis **10.** alveoli
Part B 11. nose, mouth **12.** diaphragm **13.** trachea **14.** lungs
Science Extension Diagrams will vary but should reflect understanding of chapter content.
Reading Comprehension, p. 131
Part A: respiration and ventilation—Respiration is the process of transporting oxygen and carbon dioxide between the air and the inside of the body. Ventilation is the first stage when air moves over the lung tissue. The tissue absorbs oxygen and releases carbon dioxide; alveoli and pneumonia—Pneumonia is an infection in the lungs that causes the alveoli, or compartments in the lung, to swell and fill with fluid; blood pressure and diastolic pressure—Blood pressure is the force the body exerts on the walls of the artery. Diastolic pressure is the pressure on the arteries when the ventricles relax.
Part B: Answers will vary.
Science Extension 1. deposits of fats and cholesterol **2.** The heart should not be overworked and arteries need to be clear of plaques.
Curriculum Connection, p. 132
Part A: 1. blood **2.** carbon dioxide, urea **3.** amino acids, glucose **4.** proteins, minerals
Part B: 5. capillaries **6.** the lymphatic system **7.** The muscular contraction pushes oxygen-rich blood through the aorta and to the rest of the body.
Science Extension Answers will vary. Encourage students to research in small groups and share their findings.
Science Challenge, p. 133
Part A: Student pamphlets should include: The symptoms of carbon monoxide poisoning can include dizziness, drowsiness, trouble breathing, confusion, weakness, low blood pressure, and loss of consciousness. Carbon monoxide is particularly dangerous because the hemoglobin in red blood cells binds to carbon monoxide more tightly than it binds to oxygen. Most carbon monoxide poisoning cases occur in areas where the weather is cold for at least part of the year, because furnaces are heavily used and windows are closed. Additional household equipment that burns gas or other fuel can also generate carbon monoxide. To prevent carbon monoxide poisoning, people should keep this type of equipment, furnaces, and fireplaces in good working order. Charcoal grills should never be used indoors. In areas where there is a risk for carbon monoxide, simple carbon monoxide detectors that look similar to smoke detectors can be installed.
Part B: Artificial pacemakers are small, battery-powered devices. They may be placed in a permanent position under someone's skin. Electrodes from the pacemaker are guided through a vein into the heart. The electrodes contact the wall of the right ventricle and deliver shocks to this area. This causes the ventricles to contract and then relax, as they would from normal stimulation. The electrical impulses may be delivered continuously or on demand, when the heart's own pacemaker impulse does not arrive on time. Patients whose hearts beat too slowly (bradycardia) or too rapidly (tachycardia) can be helped by pacemakers. (Severe heart failure may be treated with pacemakers that stimulate both ventricles—biventricular pacemakers.) Equipment that has strong magnets (such as MRIs and other hospital scanning devices) may interfere with pacemakers and should be avoided. Pacemaker batteries should also be checked periodically by a doctor.
Part C: 1. blood type A **2.** blood type B **3.** blood type AB **4.** blood type O **5.** No Rh antigen is shown. All are Rh. **6.** They have no antibodies in their blood that would react with donated blood cells **7.** They have no antigens on their red blood cells that would react with antibodies in a recipient's blood.

Chapter 21 Answer Key

Key Concept Review, p. 135
Part A: 3: absorption; 1: ingestion; 4: ultrafiltration; 2: peristalsis; 5: defecation
Part B: 6. A diet is balanced when it contains all the nutrients a human body needs. **7.** The stomach chemically digests food; it squeezes and churns food to mechanically break down the food particles; and it stores food. **8.** The liver and pancreas produce chemicals such as bile, enzymes, and hormones to aid in digestion.
Science Extension Charts will vary.
Vocabulary Review, p. 136
Part A: 1. vitamins **2.** proteins **3.** enzyme **4.** duodenum
Part B: 5. d **6.** b **7.** f **8.** e **9.** c **10.** a
Science Extension Diagrams will vary.
Interpreting Diagrams, p. 137
Part A: 1. salivary glands **2.** esophagus **3.** liver **4.** gall bladder **5.** large intestine **6.** anus **7.** tongue **8.** stomach **9.** pancreas **10.** small intestine **11.** rectum
Part B: 12. stomach **13.** esophagus **14.** rectum **15.** large intestine
Science Extension Answers will vary but should reflect understanding of chapter content.
Reading Comprehension, p. 138
Part A: Answers will vary.
Part B: Answers will vary.
Science Extension 1. eggs, fortified milk 2. iodine 3. vitamins B2, B12, D, E, pantothenic acid, and biotin
Curriculum Connection, p. 139
Part A: 1. chemically **2.** protein chains **3.** mechanically; boluses **4.** chyme **5.** stores **6.** small intestine
Part B: 7. They both make chemicals that aid digestion. **8.** Fiber is essential for the smooth running of the digestive system.
Science Extension Accept all reasonable answers: The body is under stress to absorb nutrients and recycle water; the entire muscular system is working faster, including peristalsis.
Science Challenge, p. 140
Part A: Student answers will vary. A pro to warning labels is that they would provide consumer education. However, consumers may ignore them or feel that they are having their personal decisions judged. Food companies may feel such labels are negative publicity.
Part B: Students should describe a journey through the digestive system in correct order: mouth, esophagus, stomach, small intestine (where bile and pancreatic juices enter), large intestine. They can be creative in their stories. A story should note that carbohydrates are chemically broken down in the mouth and small intestine. Proteins are chemically broken down in the stomach and small intestine, and fats are chemically broken down in the

small intestine. Nutrients are absorbed in the small intestine, and water and some vitamins are absorbed in the large intestine. Digested carbohydrates, fats, and proteins can all be used for energy; amino acids will be used to make new proteins; and lipids will be used to make cell membranes and some hormones.

Part C: 1. Most commonly, kidney stones contain calcium salts (calcium oxalate or calcium phosphate). Less often, stones may be struvite stones, caused by urinary tract infection and composed of magnesium salts. Infrequently, stones are made of uric acid crystals; and rarely, they are composed of the amino acid cystine. Small stones may have no symptoms until they are passed through the urinary tract, which will cause pain. Kidney stones can be diagnosed with X rays, sonograms, or other scans. Surgery is a previously favored treatment to remove large stones. However, nonsurgical treatments are now available. External shockwaves may be passed through the body to break up large stones. The smaller particles can be passed in the urine. (This is *extracorporeal shock-wave lithotripsy.*)

2. Extracorporeal shock-wave lithotripsy could be used to break up gallstones so they pass with bile from the gallbladder.

3. The gallbladder is a storage chamber. It does not make bile itself; bile is made in the liver. Removing the storage chamber will not halt bile production. Bile moves directly from the liver to the small intestine when the gallbladder is gone.

Chapter 22 Answer Key

Key Concept Review, p. 142

Part A: 22.1 The Nervous System A. Functions of the Nervous System B. Organization of the Nervous System C. Sending Signals D. Two Systems in One; 22.2 The Brain and Spinal Cord A. The Brain B. The Spinal Cord C. Reflexes; 22.3 The Senses A. Making Sense of Things B. Sight C. Hearing D. Balance E. Smell F. Taste G. Touch; 22.4 The Endocrine System A. A Messenger System B. Structure and Function C. Controlling the Endocrine System

Part B: 1. neurons **2.** central nervous system **3.** electrical

Science Extension Answers will vary.

Vocabulary Review, p. 144

Part A: 1. c **2.** e **3.** f **4.** d **5.** b **6.** a

Part B: 7. brain and spinal cord **8.** responsible for memory, thought, and communication

Science Extension Answers will vary.

Interpreting Diagrams, p. 145

Part A: 1. cerebrum **2.** hypothalamus **3.** pituitary glands **4.** skull **5.** pineal gland **6.** cerebellum **7.** brain stem

Part B: 1. spinal cord **2.** pineal gland **3.** cerebrum

Science Extension Diagrams will vary but should reflect understanding of chapter content.

Reading Comprehension, p. 146

Part A:

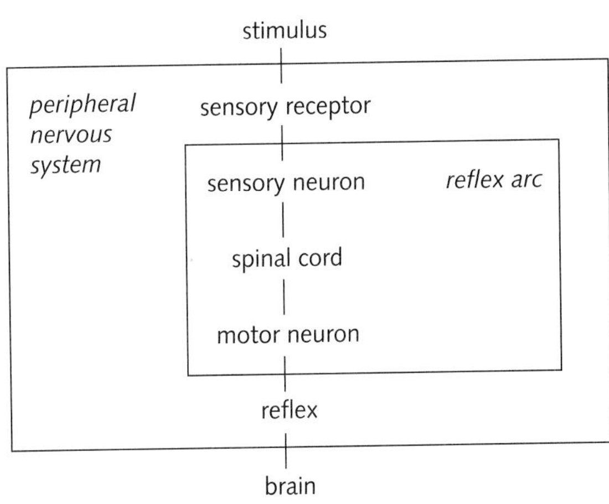

Part B: 1. No, because the sensory receptors in your finger send an electrical message through your nervous system to your brain. Your brain interprets this message as "softness" and sends a signal back to your fingers that it is okay to touch this object. **2.** A dendrite of one neuron communicates to the axon of another neuron. They are separated by a synapse. **3.** Functions such as digestion, breathing, and heart rate are automatic and do not require conscious effort. This ensures that we don't forget to do these vital functions and die.

Science Extension 1. Melatonin wouldn't be released and the sleep-wake cycle might become disrupted, which would cause problems sleeping or staying awake. **2.** The thyroid gland may not be functioning correctly. The pituitary gland could have problems and not release enough thyroid-stimulating hormone. Finally, the hypothalamus, which controls the pituitary gland, could be malfunctioning too.

Curriculum Connection, p. 147

Part A: 1. brain and spinal cord **2.** If you cannot feel pain, you can get yourself out of danger without being distracted or debilitated.

Part B: 3. Neurons are specialized cells that make up the tissue of the nervous system; they communicate by changing information from a stimulus into electrical and chemical impulses. **4.** They are sensory receptors in the back of the eye; they change light energy into electrical impulses that can be sent through the nervous system to the brain. **5.** sweet, salty, bitter, sour, and umami, or meaty or savory

Science Extension Answers will vary. Encourage students to discuss the issue.

Science Challenge, p. 148

Part A: 1. Nearsightedness is much more common than farsightedness. Nearsightedness commonly develops in adolescence. **2.** Reading, working on computers, and playing video games are activities that require focusing on very close objects. Focusing on nearby objects for long periods of time is thought to be a risk factor for developing nearsightedness. Taking breaks will allow the eyes to focus on other more distant objects and give them a rest. **3a.** farsighted **3b.** nearsighted **3c.** nearsighted **4.** In astigmatism, the cornea or lens is oddly shaped. The cornea and lens are responsible for bending light and focusing it on the retina. If they are not smooth, light entering the eye is not focused (it never comes to a focal point). Similar to nearsightedness and farsightedness, this causes blurred vision. However, vision is blurred at all distances—it is no easier to see near objects than far objects, or vice versa. Astigmatism can be treated with corrective lenses.

Part B: 5. sensory neurons, the neurons that carry information to the brain **6a.** local **6b.** local **6c.** general **6d.** general **7.** adrenaline

Chapter 23 Answer Key

Key Concept Review, p. 151

Part A: Male: sperm, testes, semen, epididymis; Female: ovaries, estrogen, menstruation, ova, uterus

Part B: 1. Fraternal twins come from different eggs and sperm cells, when a woman releases two eggs at a time. Identical twins come from a single zygote that has split into two zygotes early in development. **2.** A zygote is an egg that has been fertilized by a sperm. **3.** A child's body develops into an adult's body. Other answers may be acceptable, involving the hormones released in the body and specifics about puberty.

Science Extension Student answers will vary.

Vocabulary Review, p. 152

Part A: 1. testosterone **2.** menstruation **3.** estrogen **4.** menopause **5.** amniotic sac

Part B: Sample Diagram:

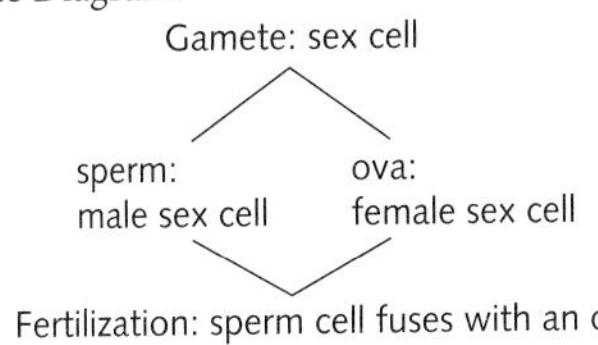

zygote: fertilized egg that will develop into human being

blastocyst: the fertilized egg that has subdivided until it forms a hollow ball of cells

Science Extension Answers will vary but should reflect chapter content.
Interpreting Diagrams, p. 153
Part A: 1. vas deferens **2.** penis **3.** testes **4.** epididymis **5.** scrotum **6.** oviduct **7.** ovary **8.** uterus **9.** cervix **10.** vagina
Part B: 11. cervix **12.** true **13.** uterus **14.** epididymis **15.** true
Science Extension Stories will vary but should reflect understanding of chapter content.
Reading Comprehension, p. 154
Part A: Answers will vary.
Part B: Answers will vary.
Science Extension 1. On the 14th day after menstruation, the ovary releases a mature egg into the oviduct. This egg will travel to the uterus where it can be fertilized by sperm. **2.** Midway through the pregnancy, the fetus is able to move around. It practices all kinds of motions that it will need, such as sucking, swallowing, and breathing. **3.** Fraternal twins can occur when an ovary releases two eggs at a time and they both are fertilized and implanted in the uterus. These twins will not be identical—they could be two boys, two girls, or a boy and a girl.
Curriculum Connection, p. 156
Part A: Diagrams will vary but should reflect understanding of chapter content.
Part B: 1. It combines chromosomes from sperm and ovum; a human being; 46 chromosomes **2.** estrogen and progesterone **3.** It's an exchange organ that moves or exchanges nutrients, oxygen, and wastes between the mother and the fetus.
Science Extension Semi-identical twins result when two sperm cells fertilize one ovum. That doubly fertilized egg then divides, forming two embryos.
Science Challenge, p. 157
Part A
1. There is an extra copy of chromosome 21. This person has Down syndrome.
2. There is an extra X chromosome (two Xs and one Y chromosome). This person is a male, because he has a Y chromosome.
3. This person is female, because she lacks a Y chromosome.
4. It would have an extra copy of chromosome 13 (total—3 copies).
5. Student answers will vary. The most common trisomy disorders are Trisomy 21 (Down syndrome), Trisomy 18 (Edward syndrome) and Trisomy 13 (Patau syndrome). All cause mental retardation and varying degrees of body system abnormalities, depending on the syndrome. Persons with Down syndrome can have full adult lives, while other trisomies most often cause death in early infancy. Syndromes caused by altered numbers of sex chromosomes include Klinefelter syndrome, Jacobs syndrome (XYY), Triple X syndrome (XXX), and Turner syndrome. Persons with these syndromes do not have mental disabilities. They may have alterations in stature (tall for XYY and XXX, short for Turner syndrome) and physical abnormalities of the reproductive system. Other chromosomal abnormalities are also possible, such as chromosomal deletions or rearrangements (e.g., Cri-du-chat syndrome is caused by a deletion of part of chromosome 5).
Part B: In amniocentesis, amniotic fluid is withdrawn from the amniotic sac via a needle. This fluid contains a small amount of fetal cells. The fetal cells are used to produce a karyotype that is examined for chromosomal abnormalities. Amniocentesis can provide genetic information after 14 weeks. Early amniocentesis runs a slight risk of miscarriage, and there may be complications from the needle passing through the abdomen. Women older than 35, women who have had previous pregnancies with chromosomal defects, and women who have had other abnormal test results may consider this test.

In chorionic villus sampling (CVS), tissue is removed from the chorion, the fetal part of the placenta, via a catheter inserted through the cervix or a needle through the abdominal wall. A karyotype is then performed on the collected cells. CVS can provide genetic information about a fetus younger than 14 weeks (8 to 10 weeks). Risks for this procedure are similar to amniocentesis risks, and this test is considered for the same reasons as amniocentesis.

Ultrasonography uses sound waves to create an image of a fetus. This procedure is noninvasive and gives information about the general structure of the fetus. Major structural abnormalities are visible on an ultrasound. Prenatal screening is up to the mother's discretion, and some people may decline tests based on religious or other personal beliefs.

Chapter 24 Answer Key

Key Concept Review, p. 159
Part A: 1. infectious disease **2.** phagocytes **3.** antibiotic
Part B: 4. bacterium, virus, protozoan, fungus, and animal **5.** The outer layer of skin is made of dead cells that pathogens cannot invade, and skin is a dry, acidic environment that is unsuitable for most microorganisms. **6.** the natural killer cell
Science Extension Answers will vary. Check students' work.
Vocabulary Review, p. 160
Part A: 1. b **2.** d **3.** e **4.** c **5.** a
Part B: Sample examples given. allergic reaction: an immune response to food, medicine, or some type of chemical; sneezing when trees bloom in spring
autoimmune disorder: the immune system attacks cells in its own body; juvenile diabetes
cancer: mutation in cells that causes them to grow and divide uncontrollably; leukemia
infectious disease: disease caused by a pathogen that invades the body and uses it for food and reproduction; Ebola
Science Extension Diagrams will vary.
Graphic Organizer, p. 161
Part A: 1. Immune System **2.** Nonspecific Defense System **3.** Nonspecific Defense System **4.** Immune System **5.** Nonspecific Defense System
Part B: 6. P **7.** A **8.** V
Science Extension Diagrams will vary.
Reading Comprehension, p. 162
Part A: Answers will vary.
Part B: Answers will vary.
Science Extension 1. Are all diseases caused by pathogens? No, there are both infectious and noninfectious diseases. Only infectious diseases are caused by microorganisms, viruses, or parasitic worms. **2.** Will a medication work against all pathogens? No. Antibiotics are medications prescribed to kill bacteria. If a person is not infected with the pathogen that the specific antibiotic kills, then it would be useless. Also, the bacteria could become resistant to the antibiotic.
3. What is the incubation period of pathogens? Each pathogen is different. Some only take a few days while others take a few years. Two weeks is a reasonable incubation period, so the illness could have come from your cousin.
Curriculum Connection, p. 163
Part A: 1. the number of people in an age group **2.** 7 **3.** the 35- to 44-year-old age group
Part B: 4. Pathogens cause infectious diseases, such as TB (tuberculosis), AIDS, rabies, the common cold, and malaria. **5.** Vectors are organisms that spread pathogens through their saliva, parasites, body wastes, and meat. Some examples are mosquitoes, birds/chickens, rats, flies, and fleas.
Science Extension Answers will vary.
Science Challenge, p. 164
Part A: 1. Answers will vary. **2.** Answers will vary. Depending on the part of the world, travelers could have vaccinations against viral illnesses (hepatitis A and B, rabies, encephalitis, yellow fever) or bacterial illnesses (typhoid fever). The disease may be spread through human contact (hepatitis), animal to human contact (rabies), via insects (encephalitis), or through food (typhoid fever). Students should recognize that antibiotics cannot be used to treat viral illnesses, though there may be antiviral medications available. For mosquito-born illnesses, insect repellent is an additional way to protect oneself. Watching what one eats and drinks and practicing good hygiene can also help prevent illness when traveling. **3.** The vaccine triggers the immune system to make antibodies against the disease pathogen. Time is needed for the immune system to make sufficient antibodies and memory cells for protection.
4. A doctor needs to know if his or her patient is allergic to any medications

before giving treatments. Allergic reactions can be quite serious and even result in death. Medical information will also provide clues to whether a traveler may be sick from a pathogen or if the illness is due to another reason or pre-existing condition.
Part B: Letters will vary. In general, students should be encouraged to practice good hygiene, such as washing their hands frequently. They can also be told to cover their mouths with their shoulders or elbows when they sneeze. (Covering their mouths with their hands can spread illness, as hands touch desks and doorknobs.) Parents can be requested to keep sick children home (elementary school), and students can be asked to stay home if they are sick (high school and college students). A school may also recommend additional vaccinations, such as vaccinations against influenza. For its part, a school can clean surface areas daily and keep dining areas disinfected.

Chapter 25 Answer Key

Key Concept Review, p. 166
Part A: 25.1 Healthful Living A. Healthful Habits B. Nutrition C. Exercise and Rest D. Managing Stress E. Hygiene and Posture F. Safety and First Aid; 25.2 Drugs and Drug Abuse A. What Is a Drug? B. Drug Abuse; 25.3 Alcohol and Tobacco A. Alcohol B. Tobacco
Part B: 1. Good nutrition, plenty of exercise and rest, stress management, good hygiene, and safety are the goals of practicing healthful habits. **2.** A drug is a nonfood substance that affects how the mind and body work. **3.** Tolerance to a drug, physical dependence, and psychological dependence can all cause a person to become dependent upon a drug.
Science Extension Answers will vary.
Vocabulary Review, p. 167
Part A: 1. Nictotine; tobacco **2.** stress **3.** Hygiene **4.** Tar; tobacco **5.** blood alcohol concentration; alcohol **6.** Aerobic exercise; stress
Part B: Left box: drug abuse: The intentional misuse of a legal or illegal drug, which can lead to a life threatening situation or drug dependence
tolerance: a type of drug dependence in which the body needs higher and higher doses to produce the original effects of the drug
physical dependence: a type of drug dependence in which the user requires the effects of the drug to feel well and will have withdrawal symptoms when the drug is not in the body
psychological dependence: a type of drug dependence in which the user has an overwhelming desire to continue using a drug, even if it causes harm
Science Extension Diagrams will vary.
Graphic Organizer, p. 168
Part A: Sample healthful habits are given.
Exercise and Rest: Exercise 4 to 6 times per week for about 30 to 60 minutes each time, including aerobic exercise that increases the heart rate and breathing rate, such as running and walking, and weight training. Try to get about 9 hours of sleep each night.
Well-Balanced Diet: Get a proper mix of food, including protein, carbohydrates, vitamins, minerals, fats, and water. Follow recommendations in the USDA Mypyramid for grains, milk, oils, fruit, vegetables, and meat and beans.
Manage Stress: To avoid negative stress, practice good nutrition, exercise, and get enough sleep. Talk to friends and trusted people if something is bothering you, break tasks into smaller chunks, manage your time, and try fun hobbies.
Practice Safety: Learn first aid and have a kit ready in case of accidents, keep walkways clear, don't ride in cars with people who have been drinking, wear seat belts, don't use electrical appliances when wet, and don't overload electrical sockets.
Good Hygiene: Bathe or shower regularly and after exercise, shampoo your hair at least twice a week, practice good posture, brush teeth after every meal and before bed, floss everyday, and keep fingernails and toenails clean and trimmed.
Part B: 1. H **2.** S, N **3.** D **4.** S
Science Extension Charts will vary.
Reading Comprehension, p. 169
Part A: Answers will vary.
Part B: 1. If you are not getting enough rest, you put yourself at risk to become ill. If you are currently sick, you will have difficulty getting better without rest. **2.** If the person is using anything, including sugar, as a drug, he or she could become dependent. Physical dependence will occur if that person doesn't feel well without that "daily dose" of sugar. A psychological dependence will occur if he or she cannot stop eating excessive amounts of sugar and has become emotionally attached to high-sugar foods. **3.** Bacteria and fungus can grow underneath fingernails.
Science Extension 1. Eggs have hardly any carbohydrates, so they are not very nutritious in carbohydrates. **2.** Eggs provide a good amount of protein. Eggs can help restore tissues in our bodies. **3.** Eggs contain fat but not in large amounts. These fats can provide the body energy. However, they do have lots of cholesterol, which can be unhealthy. **4.** Eggs are not the perfect food in the sense that you could only eat eggs and get all your nutrients. But, eggs are actually pretty good at supplying protein, fat, and vitamins. So they are a "good food"—but not perfect.
Curriculum Connection, p. 171
Part A: 1. After 2 drinks in 2 hours he is still sober; after 4 hours, he is drunk. **2.** The heavier you are, the more alcohol your body can handle.
Part B: 3. energy and nutrients from food **4.** Answers include: the activity relieves anxiety; you feel better; it helps you relax and focus. **5.** Yes, a drug is any substance other than food that alters one or more chemical processes in the body. Alcohol, like any drug, changes the way the body or mind works.
Science Extension Answers will vary.
Science Challenge, p. 172
Part A: Program descriptions and presentations will vary. In general, the activities should be fun and safe for everyone. The students may be very creative in their activity plans and could teach certain sports, or they might simply make up group games involving walking, running, and jumping. They may also plan field trips or invite speakers such as dental hygienists or nurses. To keep kids safe, students may also require that at least some of the adults and high school students who work with their programs be trained in first aid and CPR.
Part B: Student responses will vary.
Part C: Student responses will vary.